MANAGEMENT ACCOUNTING

The Cornerstone for Business Decisions

Maryanne M. Mowen · *Oklahoma State University*

Don R. Hansen · *Oklahoma State University*

THOMSON

SOUTH-WESTERN

Australia · Canada · Mexico · Singapore · Spain · United Kingdom · United States

THOMSON

SOUTH-WESTERN

Management Accounting: The Cornerstone for Business Decisions
Maryanne M. Mowen and Don R. Hansen

VP/Editorial Director:
Jack W. Calhoun

Publisher:
Rob Dewey

Aquisitions Editor:
Keith Chasse

Developmental Editor:
Aaron Arnsparger

Marketing Manager:
Chip Kislack

Sr. Production Editor:
Kara ZumBahlen

Manager of Technology, Editorial:
Vicky True

Technology Project Editor:
Sally Nieman

Web Coordinator:
Kelly Reid

Sr. Manufacturing Coordinator:
Doug Wilke

Production House:
LEAP Publishing Services, Inc.

Compositor:
GGS Information Services, Inc.

Printer:
R. R. Donnelley, Willard, OH

Art Director:
Chris A. Miller

Cover and Internal Designer:
Bethany Casey

Cover Image:
Getty Images

Photography Manager:
Deanna Ettinger

Photo Researcher:
Terri Miller

ASIA (including India)
Thomson Learning
5 Shenton Way
#01-01 UIC Building
Singapore 068808

CANADA
Thomson Nelson
1120 Birchmount Road
Toronto, Ontario
Canada M1K 5G4

AUSTRALIA/NEW ZEALAND
Thomson Learning Australia
102 Dodds Street
Southbank, Victoria 3006
Australia

UK/EUROPE/MIDDLE
EAST/AFRICA
Thomson Learning
High Holborn House
50-51 Bedford Road
London WC1R 4LR
United Kingdom

LATIN AMERICA
Thomson Learning
Seneca, 53
Colonia Polanco
11560 Mexico
D.F.Mexico

SPAIN (includes Portugal)
Thomson Paraninfo
Calle Magallanes, 25
28015 Madrid, Spain

CONTENTS

CHAPTER 5

JOB-ORDER COSTING 154

CHAPTER 6

PROCESS COSTING 200

CHAPTER 10

FLEXIBLE BUDGETS AND OVERHEAD ANALYSIS 398

CHAPTER 11

PERFORMANCE EVALUATION, VARIABLE COSTING, AND DECENTRALIZATION 436

CHAPTER 15

STATEMENT OF CASH FLOWS 620

CHAPTER 16

FINANCIAL STATEMENT ANALYSIS 654

cor•ner•stone \-stōn\ *n* a basic element: FOUNDATION

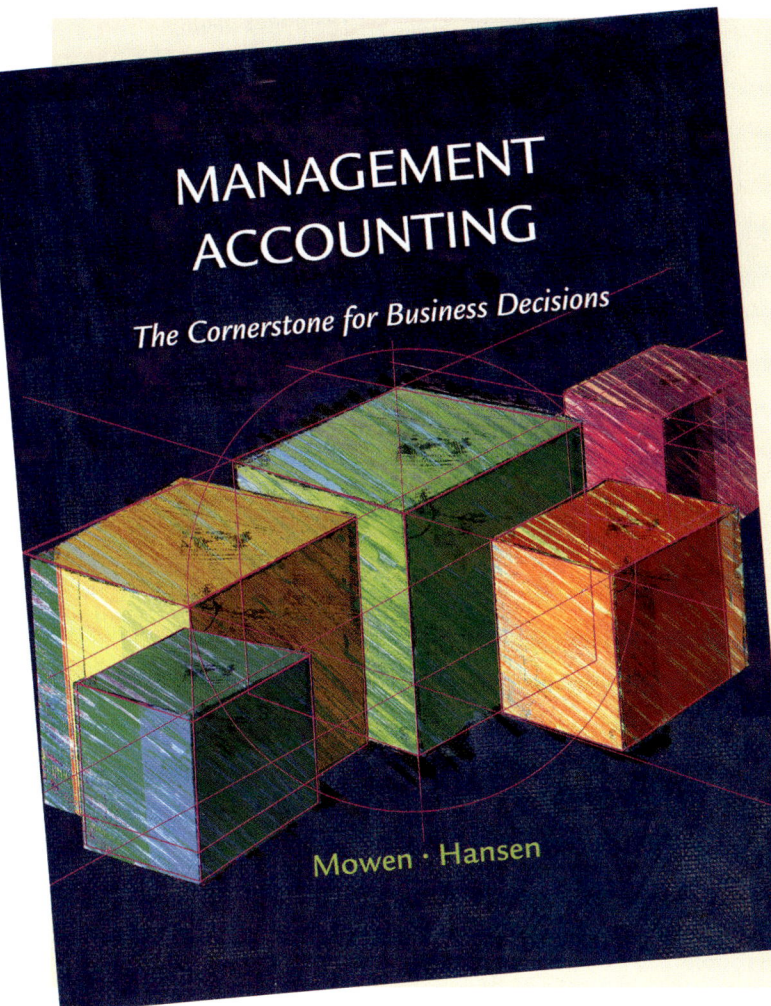

Introducing the new cornerstone in *management accounting*

Management accounting is one of the most important courses in the business curriculum. From manufacturing to service, and every industry in between, management accounting information is used to help managers identify important issues, solve problems, and evaluate performance.

Management Accounting: The Cornerstone for Business Decisions was crafted to help today's students use accounting information to understand the *real issues* at hand in *real companies*. Traditional coverage blends with innovative pedagogy—**Cornerstones**—to illustrate how concepts play out in managerial decision making. The text's step-by-step format, combined with its engaging and consistent use of **Cornerstones**, makes it easy for any student to tackle managerial accounting problems.

Explore this preview and discover why **Management Accounting: The Cornerstone for Business Decisions** has been hailed by students and instructors as a text that gives students a better understanding of managerial accounting concepts and calculations. You'll also find a wealth of powerful teaching and learning tools that make it easy to put management accounting concepts and theories into action.

THOMSON
SOUTH-WESTERN

A tour of management accounting's new cornerstone begins on the next page

Table of Contents

For a detailed table of contents, see pages iii-viii.

PREFACE

"The strengths of the chapters are organization, readable style, and clear analysis of the subject matter. The scenarios at the beginning of the chapters are very helpful and help bring real-world perspective to the subject matter."

Marvin Williams, University of Houston, Downtown

CHAPTER 9

From price and usage to materials and direct labor, this chapter covers every major key variance topic. An appendix to this chapter covers both Target and Kaizen costing—enhancing the authors' discussion of traditional standard costs by showing costing tools currently used by today's managers.

CHAPTER 11

Variable and absorption costing are covered in Chapter 11 as part of a larger discussion about performance evaluation in the firm. This section provides a concise treatment of the subject that clearly demonstrates the different impacts of variable and absorption costing on both income and inventory. The result is a manageable treatment of the subject that provides just the right level of detail.

In addition, Chapter 11 refers readers to an appendix where the authors cover the ways in which the Balanced Scorecard concept helps organizations translate their mission into operational objectives and performance measures. This placement allows instructors to tailor their course to the needs and interest of their students.

CHAPTERS 15 AND 16

Two financial accounting chapters conclude the text, presented in a way that gives instructors the flexibility to cover these topics at any point in their course. The Cornerstones pedagogy continues through these chapters, making it easier for students to reference key concepts related to cash flows and financial statement analysis.

Cornerstones—
the foundation for successful learning

Carefully crafted from the ground up and extensively class tested, this text's *Cornerstones* help students easily set up and solve fundamental managerial accounting calculations.

Cornerstone 4-2

HOW TO Solve for the Break-Even Point in Units

► *Cornerstones* are divided into three sections: *Information, Required,* and *Calculation.* At each step along the way students can see the concepts and theories at work behind the numbers.

Cornerstone 4-2

HOW TO Solve for the Break-Even Point in Units

Information: Whittier Company plans to sell 1,000 mowers at $400 each in the coming year. Product costs include:

Direct materials per mower	$ 180
Direct labor per mower	100
Variable overhead per mower	25
Total fixed factory overhead	15,000

Variable selling expense is a commission of $20 per mower; fixed selling and administrative expense totals $30,000.

Required:
1. Calculate the total variable cost per unit.
2. Calculate the total fixed expense for the year.
3. Calculate the number of mowers that Whittier Company must sell to break even.
4. Check your answer by preparing a contribution margin income statement based on the break-even point.

Calculation:
1. Variable cost per unit = $180 + $100 + $25 + $20 = $325
2. Total fixed expense = $15,000 + $30,000 = $45,000
3. Break-even number of mowers = $45,000/($400 − $325) = 600
4. Contribution margin income statement based on 600 mowers.

Sales ($400 × 600 mowers)	$240,000
Total variable expense ($325 × 600)	195,000
Total contribution margin	$ 45,000
Total fixed expense	45,000
Operating income	$ 0

Indeed, selling 600 units does yield a zero profit.

APPLICATIONS IN BUSINESS

CVP analysis can be a valuable tool to identify the extent and magnitude of the economic trouble a company is facing and to help pinpoint the necessary solution. For example, SAAB was on the brink of collapse in 1990 when GM bought a 50-percent share in the company. Within five years, SAAB had cut costs dramatically and lowered its break-even point from 130,000 cars to 80,000 cars. By 2002, SAAB turned a modest profit. GM learned many lessons from this experience. In the late 1990s, GM restructured all of its operations to eliminate many fixed costs and decrease variable costs, thereby lowering the break-even point. Why would the company do that when 1997 profits were at record levels? As auto analyst Stephen Girsky pointed out to GM executives, "Volume distorts everything." When volume decreases, profits turn down in a hurry. GM needs to aggressively contain costs to compete with rivals like Toyota and DaimlerChrysler.

Source: James Bennet, "Eurocars: On the Road Again," *New York Times* (August 20, 1995): Sec. 3, pp. 1, 10. Paul A. Eisenstein, "Saab Making Big Plans: New 9-3 is Key to Expansion—and Profitability," *The Car Connection* (July 7, 2002), http://www.thecarconnection.com/index.asp?article=5108. Gregory White, "For GM, Hard Line on Strike Has Become a Matter of Necessity," *The Wall Street Journal* (June 12, 1998): A1 and A4.

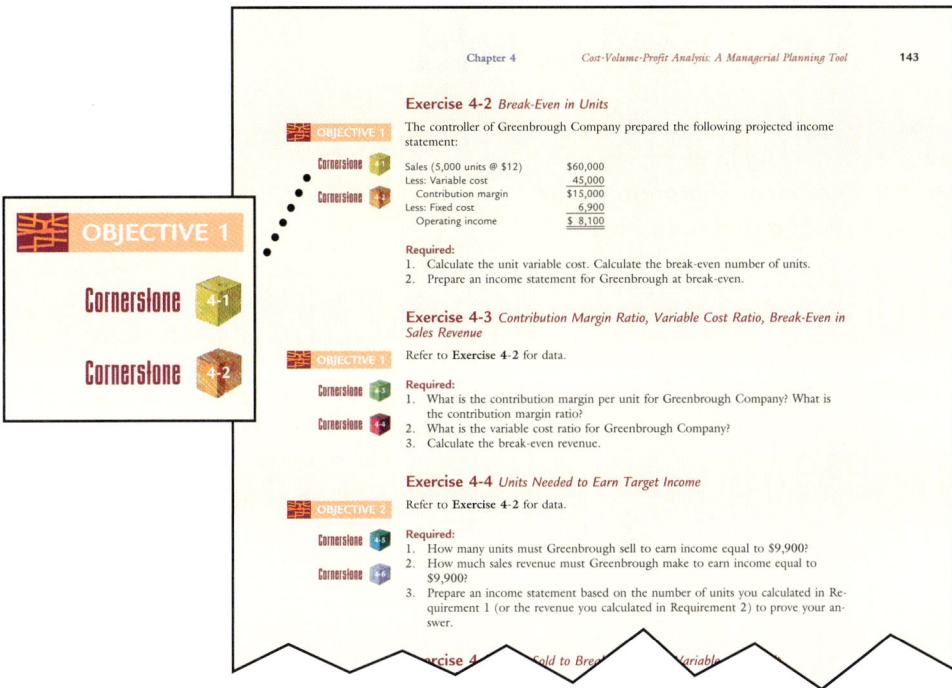

Exercise 4-2 *Break-Even in Units*

OBJECTIVE 1

Cornerstone **4-1**

Cornerstone **4-2**

The controller of Greenbrough Company prepared the following projected income statement:

Sales (5,000 units @ $12)	$60,000
Less: Variable cost	45,000
Contribution margin	$15,000
Less: Fixed cost	6,900
Operating income	$ 8,100

Required:
1. Calculate the unit variable cost. Calculate the break-even number of units.
2. Prepare an income statement for Greenbrough at break-even.

Exercise 4-3 *Contribution Margin Ratio, Variable Cost Ratio, Break-Even in Sales Revenue*

OBJECTIVE 1

Cornerstone **4-3**

Cornerstone **4-4**

Refer to **Exercise 4-2** for data.

Required:
1. What is the contribution margin per unit for Greenbrough Company? What is the contribution margin ratio?
2. What is the variable cost ratio for Greenbrough Company?
3. Calculate the break-even revenue.

Exercise 4-4 *Units Needed to Earn Target Income*

OBJECTIVE 2

Cornerstone **4-5**

Cornerstone **4-6**

Refer to **Exercise 4-2** for data.

Required:
1. How many units must Greenbrough sell to earn income equal to $9,900?
2. How much sales revenue must Greenbrough make to earn income equal to $9,900?
3. Prepare an income statement based on the number of units you calculated in Requirement 1 (or the revenue you calculated in Requirement 2) to prove your answer.

OBJECTIVE 1

Cornerstone **4-1**

Cornerstone **4-2**

End-of-chapter *Exercises* are linked to one or more specific *Cornerstone* features, giving students a chance to try a problem on their own that is similar to the in-chapter example.

"The Cornerstone *sections are OUTSTANDING. I think students would find this very helpful. This is truly an advantage of the text."*

Kelly Richmond, University of North Carolina, Greensboro

"Here's the Real Kicker"—
Real management accounting in the real world

The importance of management accounting in planning, decision making, and day-to-day operations is brought to the forefront through a running example of a real company.

> The authors teamed up with a real company, Stillwater Designs, the maker of Kicker car stereos, and interviewed their top management for relevant and revealing stories about their firm and their use of accounting information. This information is incorporated into each chapter with **Here's the Real Kicker** sections. The first Kicker scenario gives a comprehensive overview of the company, which is a highly successful maker of high-quality car audio systems.

---

4   Chapter 1   *Introduction to Management Accounting*

In writing this textbook, we wanted to show our readers the importance and relevance of management accounting in planning, decision making, and day-to-day operations of companies and not-for-profit organizations. We teamed up with a real company, Kicker, and interviewed their top management for stories about their firm and their use of accounting information. You will see boxes in each chapter called "Here's the Real Kicker," which detail how the company has used management accounting information in its operations. In addition, each chapter includes an exercise or problem based on an actual Kicker experience. Without further ado, let's get better acquainted with Kicker.

HERE'S THE REAL KICKER

A division of Stillwater Designs and Audio, Inc., Kicker makes car stereo systems. Their signature logo, "Livin' Loud," gives you a hint as to the capabilities of the system. As the company Web site says, "Livin' Loud has always been the KICKER way—staying one step ahead of the pack—driven to create components that consistently raise the world's expectations for car stereo performance."

Twenty-five years ago, car stereos were underpowered tinny affairs. They could power a radio or an 8-track tape deck. But the in-home listening experience coveted by audio buffs eluded the automobile market. In 1980, Stillwater Designs virtually invented the high-performance car audio enclosure market when company founder and president Steve Irby developed the Original Kicker®. It was the first full-range speaker enclosure designed specifically for automotive use.

Stillwater Designs began in 1973 as a two-person operation, custom designing and building professional sound and musical instrument speaker systems for churches, auditoriums, and entertainers. Building upon the success of the Original Kicker, the company concentrated on the car audio market, applying the same research and design skills that made its first product so successful to the development of a complete line of high-performance components for car audio. What was once a company with two employees in a single-car garage is now a corporation with more than 200 employees in facilities totaling more than 500,000 square feet. Its world headquarters is in Stillwater, Oklahoma.

The Kicker brand includes a variety of high-performance car stereo products, including subwoofers, midrange and midbass drivers, tweeters, crossovers, matched component systems, speakers, and power amplifiers. Kicker is proud to have won the prestigious AudioVideo International Auto Sound Grand Prix Award, sponsored annually by *AudioVideo International* magazine. Winners are selected by retailers based on fidelity of sound reproduction, design engineering, reliability, craftsmanship and product integrity, and cost/performance ratio. In 2003, seven Kicker products earned Grand Prix awards. Awards emphasizing the performance of the company include the Governor's Award for Excellence in Exporting (2000) and the 1996 Oklahoma City International Trade Association designation as its International Business of the Year.

While Stillwater Designs originally handled research and design, manufacturing, and sales, it now concentrates primarily on R&D and sales. The bulk of manufacturing has been outsourced (performed by outside firms on a contract basis), although the company still builds some product and plans to build even more as it moves into its new facility for factory-installed audio systems. Engineering and audio research is Kicker President and CEO Steve Irby's first love, and he still heads its design team. The day-to-day involvement of top management, coupled with an energetic workforce of talented individuals in all areas of the company's operations and an innate ability to create truly musical components, has been the reason for the company's remarkable success.

THE MEANING OF MANAGEMENT ACCOUNTING

What do we mean by management accounting? Quite simply, **management accounting** is the provision of accounting information for a company's internal users. It is the firm's internal accounting system and is designed to support the information needs of

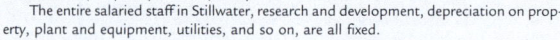

OBJECTIVE 1
Explain the meaning of management accounting.

HERE'S THE REAL KICKER

Kicker separates cost into fixed and variable components by using judgment. Because the bulk of manufacturing is outsourced, the cost of the speakers starts with the purchase price from the manufacturer. This is a strictly variable cost. Also variable are the cost of duty (ranging from 9–30 percent—electronics are at the high end) and freight, as all units are shipped to Stillwater, Oklahoma, for distribution to customers. In-house labor may be needed at Kicker's Stillwater facilities, and that cost has both fixed (salaried workers) and variable (temporary workers) components.

The entire salaried staff in Stillwater, research and development, depreciation on property, plant and equipment, utilities, and so on, are all fixed.

These fixed and variable costs are used in cost-volume-profit analysis (done monthly) and in management decision making. For example, the monthly cost-volume-profit figures can be used to monitor the effect of changing volume on profit and spotlight increases in fixed and variable costs. If costs are going up, management finds out about the problem early and can make adjustments.

> Subsequent **Here's the Real Kicker** sections delve into specific facets of the company's operations. These sections directly tie in to what's being discussed in each chapter, from job-order costing and process costing to profit planning and capital investment decisions.

"Excellent use of examples to convey each of the topics. [The authors] provide context that makes it easier to teach and learn."

Dwight Sneathen, Jr., Mississippi State University

*"The definitions of planning and control are by far
the best I have seen. Nice and simple."*

Janice Pitera, Broome Community College

---

112   Chapter 4   *Cost-Volume-Profit Analysis: A Managerial Planning Tool*

BREAK-EVEN POINT IN UNITS AND IN SALES DOLLARS

Cost-volume-profit analysis (CVP analysis) is a powerful tool for planning and decision making. Managers become very interested in CVP analysis during times of economic trouble. You may have heard or read of various companies trying to break even. CVP analysis can help managers pinpoint problems and fix on the necessary solution.

CVP analysis can address many other issues as well, such as the number of units that must be sold to break even, the impact of a given reduction in fixed costs on the break-even point, and the impact of an increase in price on profit. Additionally, CVP analysis allows managers to do sensitivity analysis by examining the impact of various price or cost levels on profit.

Since CVP analysis shows how revenues, expenses, and profits behave as volume changes, it is natural to begin by finding the firm's break-even point in units sold. The **break-even point** is the point where total revenue equals total cost, the point of zero profit.

OBJECTIVE 1
Determine the break-even point in number of units and in total sales dollars.

Kicker separates cost into fixed and variable components by using judgment. Because the bulk of manufacturing is outsourced, the cost of the speakers starts with the purchase price from the manufacturer. This is a strictly variable cost. Also variable are the cost of duty (ranging from 9–30 percent—electronics are at the high end) and freight, as all units are shipped to Stillwater, Oklahoma, for distribution to customers. In-house labor may be needed at Kicker's Stillwater facilities, and that cost has both fixed (salaried workers) and variable (temporary workers) components.

The entire salaried staff in Stillwater, research and development, depreciation on property, plant and equipment, utilities, and so on, are all fixed.

These fixed and variable costs are used in cost-volume-profit analysis (done monthly) and in management decision making. For example, the monthly cost-volume-profit figures can be used to monitor the effect of changing volume on profit and spotlight increases in fixed and variable costs. If costs are going up, management finds out about the problem early and can make adjustments.

*HERE'S
THE REAL
KICKER*

Using Operating Inco

Remember from Chapter 2 tha
For the income statement, ex
manufacturing (or service pro
trative function. For CVP ana
into fixed and variable compo
costs refer to all costs of the c
able costs are all costs that in
direct labor, variable overhead
fixed cost includes fixed overh
come statement format that is
components is called the **cont**
the format for the contributio

The contribution margin
contribution margin. **Contrib**
expense. It is the amount left
can be used to contribute to
margin can be calculated in to

Let's use Whittier Compa
ample. Whittier's controller ha
ing year:

Each chapter also includes an exercise or problem based on an actual Kicker experience. Found at the end of the chapter, these activities reinforce the key concepts of the chapter and tie in to the chapter *Objectives*. The combination of these Kicker scenarios and problems allows students to reach a new understanding of the importance of management accounting in the workplace.

Chapter 4   *Cost-Volume-Profit Analysis: A Managerial Planning Tool*   153

ees retain their employment? Should the impact on employees be factored into decisions? In fact, is it unethical not to consider the impact of decisions on employees?

OBJECTIVES 1, 5

Problem 4-16

Suppose that Kicker had the following sales and cost experience (in thousands of dollars) for May of the current year and for May of the prior year:

	May, Current Year	May, Prior Year
Total sales	$43,560	$41,700
Less:		
Purchase price paid	(17,000)	(16,000)
Additional labor and supplies	(1,400)	(1,200)
Commissions	(1,250)	(1,100)
Contribution margin	$23,910	$23,400
Less:		
Fixed warehouse cost	(680)	(500)
Fixed administrative cost	(4,300)	(4,300)
Fixed selling cost	(5,600)	(5,000)
Research and development	(9,750)	(4,000)
Operating income	$ 3,580	$ 9,600

In August of the prior year, Kicker started an intensive quality program designed to enable it to build original equipment manufacture (OEM) speaker systems for a major automobile company. The program was housed in research and development. In the beginning of the current year, Kicker's accounting department exercised tighter control over sales commissions, ensuring that no dubious (e.g., double) payments were made. The increased sales in the current year required additional warehouse space that Kicker rented in town.

Required:
1. Calculate the contribution margin ratio for May of both years.
2. Calculate the break-even point in sales dollars for both years.
3. Calculate the margin of safety in sales dollars for both years.
4. Analyze the differences shown by your calculations in Requirements 1, 2, and 3.

A strong foundation structures each chapter

From chapter beginning to chapter end, *Cornerstone*'s approach includes straight-forward learning tools that give students a consistent and organized framework for understanding and applying management accounting theories.

Each chapter begins with an engaging *Scenario* that presents a dialogue between two or more fictional business people. Their situation provides a realistic introduction to the material that will be covered in the chapter. In this example, the owner of a health-supplements company wonders if *all* of her products are profitable. She contacts a business accountant for help in costing out the various products she produces.

Scenario Revisited sections are found at the end of every chapter. These sections provide the solution to the dilemma faced in the chapter-opening scenario, effectively tying the chapter together as one cohesive concept.

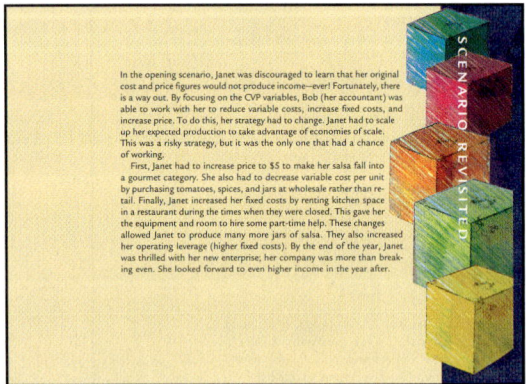

SCENARIO

For years, Janet McFarland's friends and family raved about her homemade jellies and salsas. Janet traditionally canned several gallons of salsa, ladled it into decorative pint jars, wrapped them, and sent them as gifts. Her friends said, "You ought to sell this stuff—you'd make a fortune!" So, Janet decided to give it a try.

First, she decided to concentrate on one product, a green cactus salsa that had gotten rave reviews. She scouted sources of jars, lids, and labels. In addition, Janet got in touch with her local agricultural extension office and learned a considerable amount about laws regulating food sales. One source of surprise was that she was required to obtain an expert confirmation of the ingredients in her salsa. Usually, Janet added a little of this and a little of that until it tasted right. She found out that this casual approach would not work. Foods were required to be labeled with the name of each ingredient in order of amount. Suddenly, it mattered whether ancho or poblano chilis were used and in what proportion. Janet needed a standardized recipe. She located a professional food chemist to analyze the recipe and certify the proportion of ingredients.

Janet traveled to a number of grocery stores and gift shops in the area. Several were willing to stock her product on consignment, placing a few jars by the cash register; others guaranteed shelf space but required a shelf charge for it. She figured that traveling to the stores, checking on sales and stock, and visiting prospective customers would take about one day a week.

Before starting production, Janet consulted with her family accountant, Bob Ryan.

Janet: Bob, I'm really excited about this opportunity; it all seems to be falling into place.

Bob: I'm happy for you, too, Janet. But first, let's do some planning. I need to take a look at the costs and selling price you anticipate.

Janet: I think I can charge $3.50 per jar. It's a new product, and I want to build a market for it. The costs I've come up with are on this sheet. They aren't as high as they could be since I'm going to start slowly and cook small batches at a time in our kitchen.

Bob: (After a couple of minutes of figuring) Janet, do you realize that at a price of $3.50 and with the variable costs that you described, you'll lose money! You can't do that.

Janet: What if I sell more jars? Will that help?

Bob: No, since the price is less than the variable cost, selling more jars will just make it worse. Let's go back to the drawing board and see if there's a way to decrease those variable costs. If that isn't possible, you will need to see if there is a market for your product at a higher price. Otherwise, you would be better off never getting involved with this business.

111

SCENARIO REVISITED

In the opening scenario, Janet was discouraged to learn that her original cost and price figures would not produce income—ever! Fortunately, there is a way out. By focusing on the CVP variables, Bob (her accountant) was able to work with her to reduce variable costs, increase fixed costs, and increase price. To do this, her strategy had to change. Janet had to scale up her expected production to take advantage of economies of scale. This was a risky strategy, but it was the only one that had a chance of working.

First, Janet had to increase price to $5 to make her salsa fall into a gourmet category. She also had to decrease variable cost per unit by purchasing tomatoes, spices, and jars at wholesale rather than retail. Finally, Janet increased her fixed costs by renting kitchen space in a restaurant during the times when they were closed. This gave her the equipment and room to hire some part-time help. These changes allowed Janet to produce many more jars of salsa. They also increased her operating leverage (higher fixed costs). By the end of the year, Janet was thrilled with her new enterprise; her company was more than breaking even. She looked forward to even higher income in the year after.

"I think the opening and closing scenarios are excellent. [They show] the student the purpose of studying the information covered in the chapter."

Cathy Lumbattis, Southern Illinois University, Carbondale

"Each of the opening scenarios was highly effective. Each introduced a common and interesting management problem that required information input from the management accounting system. They were skillfully written so as to motivate student interest but not to be so unstructured as to preclude solution."

David Marcinko, University of Albany, SUNY

Key objectives are clearly stated and highlighted throughout each chapter. Chapter openers begin with a set of objectives.

CHAPTER 4

COST-VOLUME-PROFIT ANALYSIS: A MANAGERIAL PLANNING TOOL

© PHOTODISC/GETTY IMAGES

After studying Chapter 4, you should be able to:

1. Determine the break-even point in number of units and in total sales dollars.
2. Determine the number of units that must be sold, and the amount of revenue required, to earn a targeted profit.
3. Prepare a profit-volume graph and a cost-volume-profit graph and explain the meaning of each.
4. Apply cost-volume-profit analysis in a multiple-product setting.
5. Explain the impact of risk, uncertainty, and changing

These are then highlighted within the body of the chapter with colorful margin notes. *A Summary of Learning Objectives* concludes each chapter, reinforcing these important points.

SUMMARY OF LEARNING OBJECTIVES

In a single-product setting, the break-even point can be computed in units by dividing the total fixed costs by the contribution margin per unit. In essence, sufficient units must be sold to just cover all fixed and variable costs of the firm.

Break-even revenue is computed by dividing the total fixed costs by the contribution margin ratio. Targeted profit is added to fixed costs in determining the amount of revenue needed to yield the targeted profit.

Multiple-product analysis requires that an assumption be made concerning the expected sales mix. Given a particular sales mix, a multiple-product problem can be converted into a single-product analysis. However, it should be remembered that the answers change as the sales mix changes. If the sales mix changes in a multiple-product firm, then the break-even point will also change. In general, increases in the sales of high contribution margin products will decrease the break-even point, while increases in the sales of low contribution margin products will increase the break-even point.

CVP is based on several assumptions that must be considered in applying it to business problems. The analysis assumes linear revenue and cost functions, no finished goods ending inventories, and a constant sales mix. CVP analysis also assumes that selling prices and fixed and variable costs are known with certainty. These assumptions form the basis for simple graphical analysis using the profit-volume graph and the cost-volume-profit graph.

End-of-chapter *Exercises* and *Problems* also tie in to the objectives and are clearly marked.

Chapter 4   *Cost-Volume-Profit Analysis: A Managerial Planning Tool*   145

Cornerstone **Required:**
1. What is Rezler's expected margin of safety?
2. What is Rezler's margin of safety if sales revenue is $280,000?

Exercise 4-11 *Multiple-Product Break-Even*

OBJECTIVE 4
Cornerstone

Switzer Company produces and sells yoga-training products: how-to videotapes and a basic equipment set (blocks, strap, and small pillows). Last year, Switzer sold 10,000 videos and 5,000 equipment sets. Information on the two products is as follows:

	Videotape	Equipment Set
Price	$12	$15
Variable cost per unit	4	6

Total fixed costs are $70,000.

Required:
1. What is the sales mix of videotapes and equipment sets?
2. Compute the break-even quantity of each product.

Exercise 4-12 *Contribution Margin Ratio, Break-Even Sales Revenue, and Margin of Safety for Multiple-Product Firm*

OBJECTIVES 4 5

Refer to **Exercise 4-11** for data.

Cornerstone
Cornerstone

Required:
1. Prepare an income statement for Switzer for last year. What is the overall contribution margin ratio? The overall break-even sales revenue?
2. Compute the margin of safety for last year.

Exercise 4-13 *Multiple-Product Break-Even, Break-Even Sales Revenue*

OBJECTIVES 4 5
Spreadsheet

Refer to **Exercise 4-11**. Suppose that in the coming year, Switzer plans to produce an extra thick yoga mat for sale to health clubs. The company estimates that 20,000 mats can be sold at a price of $18 and variable cost per unit of $13. Fixed cost must be increased by $48,350 (making total fixed cost of $118,350). Assume that anticipated sales of the other products, as well as their prices and variable costs, remain the same.

"I did like the variety of assignment materials, particularly the multiple-choice questions at the end of each chapter, the concept questions and answers in each chapter, and the ethics question in each chapter. The brief exercises will work well in my classes. These are very good for review of the material."

Susan Minke, Indiana University, Purdue University at Fort Wayne

Well developed pedagogy serves as a powerful touchstone for learning

Mowen and Hansen's text implements a number of unique pedagogical features to show students how concepts play out in managerial decision making.

Applications in Business boxes illustrate how real companies have encountered and dealt with situations that required the use and understanding of accounting information. Each brief but interesting section serves as another reminder that the concepts being addressed do really apply to everyday operations. Contemporary topics treated throughout the text and in the Applications in Business boxes include quality and environmental costing, productivity analysis, the Balanced Scorecard, the theory of constraints, Just In Time (JIT) inventory applications, and more.

---

134   Chapter 4   *Cost-Volume-Profit Analysis: A Managerial Planning Tool*

APPLICATIONS IN BUSINESS

A good margin of safety can provide a comfortable cushion for a company in a volatile industry. The restaurant business is considered to be relatively risky. About 27 percent of restaurants fail within one year; about 60 percent fail within five years. "One mistake here or there can cost you your whole profit," according to the founder of a restaurant consulting firm. Typically, the margin of safety is razor thin. Savvy restaurateurs learn to increase it by cutting back on costs. For example, the owners of Don- ley's Old West Steakhouse and Buffet in Union, Illinois, saved unused kale from the salad bar at the end of each day to decorate the buffet the next day. They also made the desserts in-house rather than buying them from a bakery, a move that saved $500 per week. As a result, both fixed and variable costs decreased, and the margin of safety increased. This cushions Donley's in the event of economic downturns or increases in other costs such as beef.

Source: Stephanie N. Mehta, "Restaurant Novices Learn to Turn Popularity into Profit," *The Wall Street Journal* (August 9, 1996): B1 and B2.

APPLICATIONS IN BUSINESS

CVP analysis can be a valuable tool to identify the extent and magnitude of the economic trouble a company is facing and to help pinpoint the necessary solution. For example, SAAB was on the brink of collapse in 1990 when GM bought a 50-percent share in the company. Within five years, SAAB had cut costs dramatically and lowered its break-even point from 130,000 cars to 80,000 cars. By 2002, SAAB turned a modest profit. GM learned many lessons from this experience. In the late 1990s, GM restructured all of its operations to eliminate many fixed costs and decrease variable costs, thereby lowering the break-even point. Why would the company do that when 1997 profits were at record levels? As auto analyst Stephen Girsky pointed out to GM executives, "Volume distorts everything." When volume decreases, profits turn down in a hurry. GM needs to aggressively contain costs to compete with rivals like Toyota and DaimlerChrysler.

Source: James Bennet, "Eurocars: On the Road Again," *New York Times* (August 20, 1995): Sec. 3, pp. 1, 10. Paul A. Eisenstein, "Saab Making Big Plans: New 9-3 is Key to Expansion—and Profitability," *The Car Connection* (July 7, 2002), http://www.thecarconnection.com/index.asp?article=5108. Gregory White, "For GM, Hard Line on Strike Has Become a Matter of Necessity," *The Wall Street Journal* (June 12, 1998): A1 and A4.

"As you would expect from these authors, the material in the chapter is solid and the concepts are presented in a straightforward manner."

Jim Groff, University of Texas, San Antonio

"Its approach is wonderful. I thought it was great that the exhibits were labeled clearly and the process was easy to follow and understand. The supporting examples, exhibits and illustrations complement the text and make it easy to follow."

Richard Filler, Franklin University

Concept Q & A

Suppose that Macy's department store sells two brands of suits: designer suits with a contribution margin of $600 each and regular suits with a contribution margin of $500 each. At break-even, the store must sell a total of 100 suits a month. Last month, the store sold 100 suits in total but incurred an operating loss. There was no change in fixed cost, variable cost, or price. What happened?

Answer:

In all probability, the sales mix shifted toward the low contribution margin suits. That is, relatively more of the low contribution margin suits (the regulars) were sold than the high contribution margin suits. Suppose that the break-even point for regular suits was 80 and the break-even point for designer suits was 20. If the mix shifted to 90 regular and 10 designer, it is easy to see that less total contribution margin (and, hence, operating income) would be realized.

◀ *Analytical Q&A* and *Concept Q&A* sections are spread throughout each chapter, giving readers an opportunity to assess their understanding of the topic being discussed. All *Q&As* provide an ideal way for students to stop and review at key points throughout the text.

Because many people are visual learners, Mowen and Hansen incorporate a wealth of colorful and clarifying graphics throughout the text. From flowcharts and graphs to screen captures and more, each *Exhibit* serves as powerful reinforcement of the concepts being discussed.

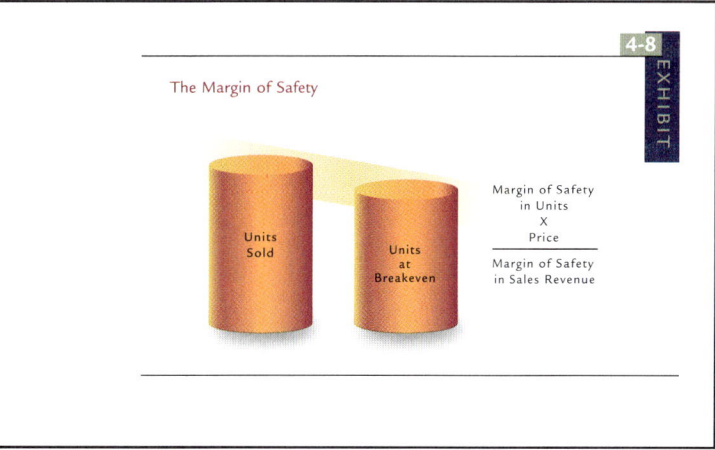

The Margin of Safety

4-8 EXHIBIT

Units Sold

Units at Breakeven

Margin of Safety in Units
X
Price

Margin of Safety in Sales Revenue

PREFACE

With each chapter ending, new understanding begins

Beginning with *Key Terms,* the chapter-ending review materials then move on to *Discussion Questions* and *Multiple-Choice Exercises.* These questions and exercises prompt students to do a quick self-assessment before working the more in-depth *Exercises* and *Problems.*

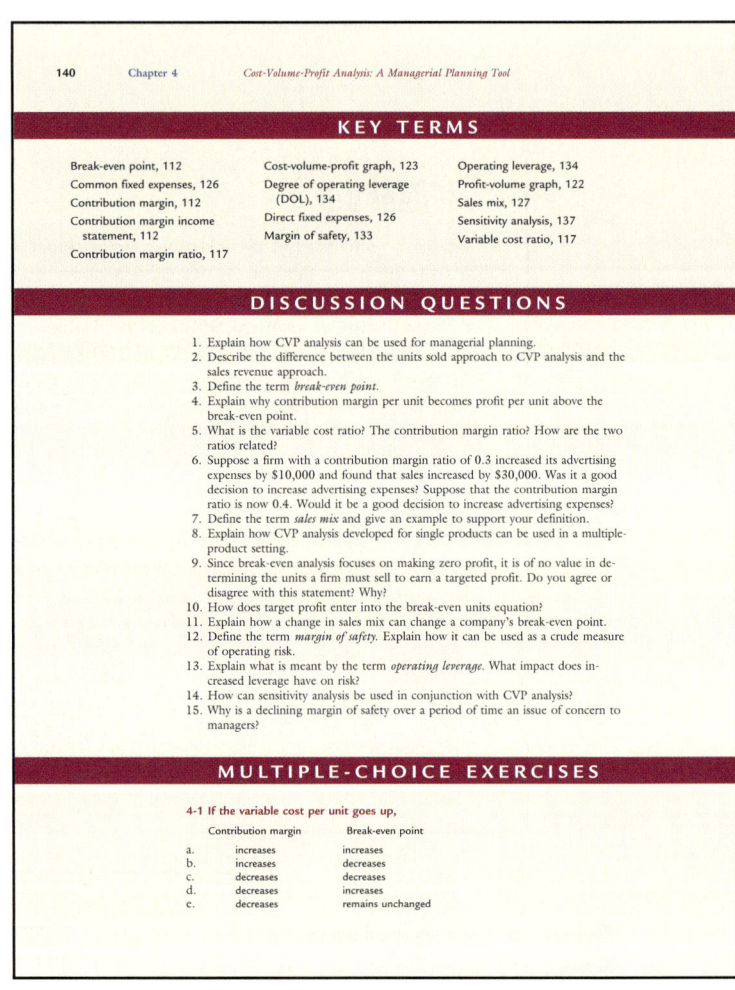

KEY TERMS

Break-even point, 112
Common fixed expenses, 126
Contribution margin, 112
Contribution margin income statement, 112
Contribution margin ratio, 117

Cost-volume-profit graph, 123
Degree of operating leverage (DOL), 134
Direct fixed expenses, 126
Margin of safety, 133

Operating leverage, 134
Profit-volume graph, 122
Sales mix, 127
Sensitivity analysis, 137
Variable cost ratio, 117

DISCUSSION QUESTIONS

1. Explain how CVP analysis can be used for managerial planning.
2. Describe the difference between the units sold approach to CVP analysis and the sales revenue approach.
3. Define the term *break-even point.*
4. Explain why contribution margin per unit becomes profit per unit above the break-even point.
5. What is the variable cost ratio? The contribution margin ratio? How are the two ratios related?
6. Suppose a firm with a contribution margin ratio of 0.3 increased its advertising expenses by $10,000 and found that sales increased by $30,000. Was it a good decision to increase advertising expenses? Suppose that the contribution margin ratio is now 0.4. Would it be a good decision to increase advertising expenses?
7. Define the term *sales mix* and give an example to support your definition.
8. Explain how CVP analysis developed for single products can be used in a multiple-product setting.
9. Since break-even analysis focuses on making zero profit, it is of no value in determining the units a firm must sell to earn a targeted profit. Do you agree or disagree with this statement? Why?
10. How does target profit enter into the break-even units equation?
11. Explain how a change in sales mix can change a company's break-even point.
12. Define the term *margin of safety.* Explain how it can be used as a crude measure of operating risk.
13. Explain what is meant by the term *operating leverage.* What impact does increased leverage have on risk?
14. How can sensitivity analysis be used in conjunction with CVP analysis?
15. Why is a declining margin of safety over a period of time an issue of concern to managers?

MULTIPLE-CHOICE EXERCISES

4-1 If the variable cost per unit goes up,

	Contribution margin	Break-even point
a.	increases	increases
b.	increases	decreases
c.	decreases	decreases
d.	decreases	increases
e.	decreases	remains unchanged

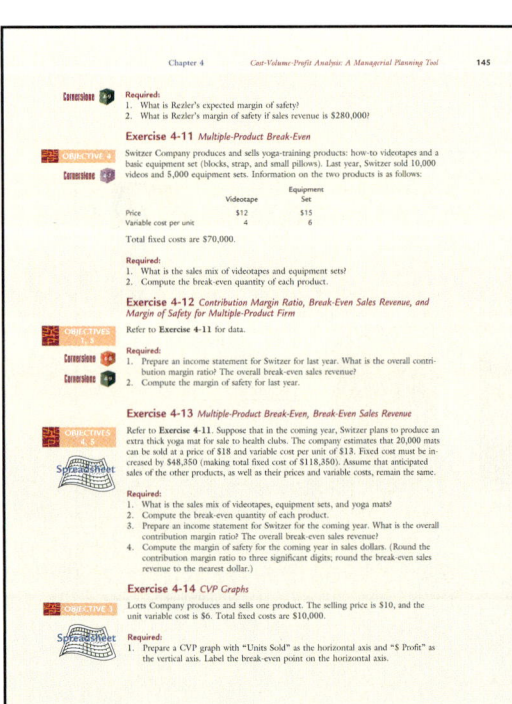

Cornerstone

Required:
1. What is Rezler's expected margin of safety?
2. What is Rezler's margin of safety if sales revenue is $280,000?

Exercise 4-11 *Multiple-Product Break-Even*

OBJECTIVE 4
Cornerstone

Switzer Company produces and sells yoga-training products: how-to videotapes and a basic equipment set (blocks, strap, and small pillows). Last year, Switzer sold 10,000 videos and 5,000 equipment sets. Information on the two products is as follows:

	Videotape	Equipment Set
Price	$12	$15
Variable cost per unit	4	6

Total fixed costs are $70,000.

Required:
1. What is the sales mix of videotapes and equipment sets?
2. Compute the break-even quantity of each product.

Exercise 4-12 *Contribution Margin Ratio, Break-Even Sales Revenue, and Margin of Safety for Multiple-Product Firm*

OBJECTIVES 1 3
Cornerstone
Cornerstone

Refer to **Exercise 4-11** for data.

Required:
1. Prepare an income statement for Switzer for last year. What is the overall contribution margin ratio? The overall break-even sales revenue?
2. Compute the margin of safety for last year.

Exercise 4-13 *Multiple-Product Break-Even, Break-Even Sales Revenue*

OBJECTIVES 4 5
Spreadsheet

Refer to **Exercise 4-11.** Suppose that in the coming year, Switzer plans to produce an extra thick yoga mat for sale to health clubs. The company estimates that 20,000 mats can be sold at a price of $18 and variable cost per unit of $13. Fixed cost must be increased by $48,350 (making total fixed cost of $118,350). Assume that anticipated sales of the other products, as well as their prices and variable costs, remain the same.

Required:
1. What is the sales mix of videotapes, equipment sets, and yoga mats?
2. Compute the break-even quantity of each product.
3. Prepare an income statement for Switzer for the coming year. What is the overall contribution margin ratio? The overall break-even sales revenue?
4. Compute the margin of safety for the coming year in sales dollars. (Round the contribution margin ratio to three significant digits; round the break-even sales revenue to the nearest dollar.)

Exercise 4-14 *CVP Graphs*

OBJECTIVE 3
Spreadsheet

Lotts Company produces and sells one product. The selling price is $10, and the unit variable cost is $6. Total fixed costs are $10,000.

Required:
1. Prepare a CVP graph with "Units Sold" as the horizontal axis and "$ Profit" as the vertical axis. Label the break-even point on the horizontal axis.

Exercises, with an average of 17 in each chapter, are linked to a specific *Objective*—and many are linked to a *Cornerstone,* giving students a chance to try a problem on their own that is similar to the in-chapter example. Students can easily reference back to the associated *Cornerstone* if extra help is needed.

5. Suppose that Candyland, Inc., raises the price to $6.20 per box but anticipated sales drop to 31,500 boxes. What will the new break-even point in units be? Should Candyland raise the price? Explain.

Problem 4-14 *Break-Even Sales, Operating Leverage, Change in Income*

 OBJECTIVE 5

Income statements for two different companies in the same industry are as follows:

	Company A	Company B
Sales	$500,000	$500,000
Less: Variable costs	400,000	200,000
Contribution margin	$100,000	$300,000
Less: Fixed costs	50,000	250,000
Operating income	$ 50,000	$ 50,000

Required:

1. Compute the degree of operating leverage for each company.
2. Compute the break-even point for each company. Explain why the break-even point for Company B is higher.
3. Suppose that both companies experience a 50-percent increase in revenues. Compute the percentage change in profits for each company. Explain why the percentage increase in Company B's profits is so much larger than that of Company A.

Problem 4-15 *Ethics and a CVP Application*

OBJECTIVE 3

Danna Lumus, the marketing manager for a division that produces a variety of paper products, was considering the divisional manager's request for a sales forecast for a new line of paper napkins. The divisional manager was gathering data so that he could choose between two different production processes. The first process would have a variable cost of $10 per case produced and fixed costs of $100,000. The second process would have a variable cost of $6 per case and fixed costs of $200,000. The selling price would be $30 per case. Danna had just completed a marketing analysis that projected annual sales of 30,000 cases.

Danna was reluctant to report the 30,000 forecast to the divisional manager. She knew that the first process was labor-intensive, whereas the second was largely automated with little labor and no requirement for an additional production supervisor. If the first process were chosen, Jerry Johnson, a good friend, would be appointed as the line supervisor. If the second process were chosen, Jerry and an entire line of laborers would be laid off. After some consideration, Danna revised the projected sales downward to 22,000 cases.

She believed that the revision downward was justified. Since it would lead the divisional manager to choose the manual system, it showed a sensitivity to the needs of current employees—a sensitivity that she was afraid her divisional manager did not possess. He was too focused on quantitative factors in his decision making and usually ignored the qualitative aspects.

Required:

1. Compute the break-even point for each process.
2. Compute the sales volume for which the two processes are equally profitable. Identify the range of sales for which the manual process is more profitable than the automated process. Identify the range of sales for which the automated process is more profitable than the manual process. Why did the divisional manager want the sales forecast?
3. Discuss Danna's decision to alter the sales forecast. Do you agree with it? Did she act ethically? Was her decision justified since it helped a number of employ-

▶ *Problems* are also linked to a specific learning objective but are more in-depth than the *Exercises*, often requiring multiple answers. Chapters feature an average of 15 *Problems*. Associated *Cornerstones* are identified in the Instructor's Manual, allowing instructors the option of providing this information to their students.

▶ Additional end-of-chapter "building on a Cornerstone" problems are identified with a special icon. These problems challenge students' analytical skills by taking them beyond the basics and building upon proficiencies learned from a particular *Cornerstone*. These *Cornerstone* problems usually entail expanded exploration, such as group work, analytical reasoning, Internet research, decision making, and/or the use of written communication skills.

▶ Kicker company logos identify *Problems* that incorporate the ideas presented in that chapter's *Here's the Real Kicker* scenario. Spreadsheet icons identify *Problems* and *Exercises* that require the preparation of a cost report with the aid of the *Student Spreadsheet Templates*.

Chapter 4   *Cost-Volume-Profit Analysis: A Managerial Planning Tool*

PROBLEMS

(Note: Whenever you see a [icon] next to a requirement, it signals a "building on a cornerstone" requirement. Assigning this requirement will usually entail additional work, such as a group project, analytical reasoning, Internet research, decision making, and the use of written communication skills.)

Problem 4-1 *Break-Even Units, Contribution Margin Ratio, Margin of Safety*

OBJECTIVES

Cutlass Company's projected profit for the coming year is as follows:

	Total	Per Unit
Sales	$200,000	$20
Less: Variable expenses	120,000	12
Contribution margin	$ 80,000	$ 8
Less: Fixed expenses	64,000	
Operating income	$ 16,000	

Required:

1. Compute the break-even point in units.
2. How many units must be sold to earn a profit of $30,000?
3. Compute the contribution margin ratio. Using that ratio, compute the additional profit that Cutlass would earn if sales were $25,000 more than expected.
4. For the projected level of sales, compute the margin of safety in units.

Problem 4-2 *Break-Even Units, Operating Income, Margin of Safety*

OBJECTIVES

Dory Manufacturing Company produces T-shirts screen-printed with the logos of various sports teams. Each shirt is priced at $10 and has a unit variable cost of $5. Total fixed costs are $96,000.

Required:

1. Compute the break-even point in units.
2. Suppose that Dory could reduce its fixed costs by $13,500 by reducing the amount of setup and engineering time needed. How many units must be sold to break even in this case?
3. How does the reduction in fixed costs affect the break-even point? Operating income? The margin of safety?

Problem 4-3 *Contribution Margin, Break-Even Units, Break-Even Sales, Margin of Safety, Degree of Operating Leverage*

OBJECTIVES

Sohrwide Company produces a variety of chemicals. One division makes reagents for laboratories. The division's projected income statement for the coming year is:

Sales (128,000 units @ $50)	$6,400,000
Less: Variable expenses	4,480,000
Contribution margin	$1,920,000
Less: Fixed expenses	1,000,000
Operating income	$ 920,000

Required:

1. Compute the contribution margin per unit and calculate the break-even point in units (round to the nearest unit). Calculate the contribution margin ratio and the break-even sales revenue.

(continued)

Personal Trainer 3.0

Specially designed to enhance *Management Accounting: The Cornerstone for Business Decisions*, Personal Trainer 3.0 is an ideal teaching and learning companion! Interactive and powerful, Personal Trainer 3.0 features all of the end-of-chapter problems and exercises. This makes it easy for students to complete their assigned homework online—or even to sharpen their skills on unassigned homework.

With Microsoft Excel spreadsheets and full-featured gradebook functionality, **Personal Trainer 3.0** provides an unprecedented real-time, guided, self-correcting, learning reinforcement system outside of the classroom—making it ideal for either a distance learning or traditional course. For instructors, this powerful technology program eases the time-consuming task of grading homework.

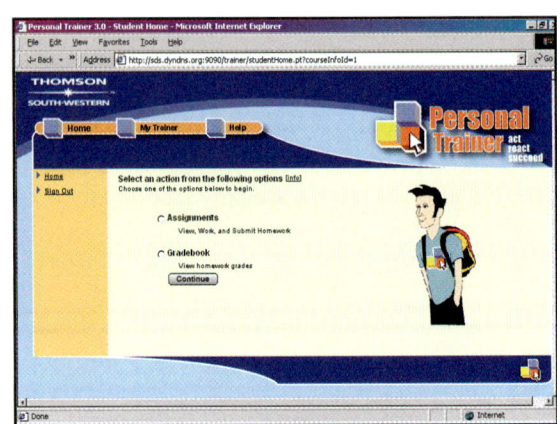

Highlights of Personal Trainer 3.0

Enhanced Questions

Personal Trainer 3.0 includes all exercises and problems from the text. Students can get help entering their answers in the proper format and run a spell check on their answers. On selected questions, students can call up additional, similar questions for extra practice.

Enhanced Instructor Capabilities

The flexible gradebook can display and download any combination of student work, chapters, or activities. Capture grades on demand or set a particular time for grades to be automatically captured. Tag questions as "required" or "excluded," so students only access the questions instructors want them to complete.

Enhanced Hints

Students can receive up to three hints per activity. These hints can be Microsoft® PowerPoint® slides, video clips, images from the text, or references to specific *Cornerstones* within the text. And instructors have the option of adding a hint of their own!

Enhanced Look and Feel

Fast, reliable, dependable, and even easy to use, **Personal Trainer 3.0** features an inviting graphic design.

Personal Trainer is included in **WebTutor™ Advantage** (see page xxiv), or it can be purchased separately online. Visit **http://personaltrainer.swlearning.com** for more information and a comprehensive tour of **Personal Trainer 3.0**, or contact your sales representative to order.

Personal Trainer 3.0: 0-324-18984-2

The Cornerstone Book Companion Website
http://mowen.swlearning.com

FREE! An interactive learning experience begins here—an easy-to-use portal to extensive learning resources that complement this text, helping students succeed in and *beyond* the accounting course. Features include:

- **Interactive Quizzes** with feedback
- **PowerPoint Presentation Slides** for easy review of chapter coverage
- **Excel spreadsheet templates** to help solve selected problems in the text
- **Quick reviews** of chapter *Learning Objectives* and *Cornerstones*

The Cornerstone Book Companion Website is also accessible from the South-Western Accounting Website (http://accounting.swlearning.com), which features content, relevant news, and links to all that we publish for your accounting course.

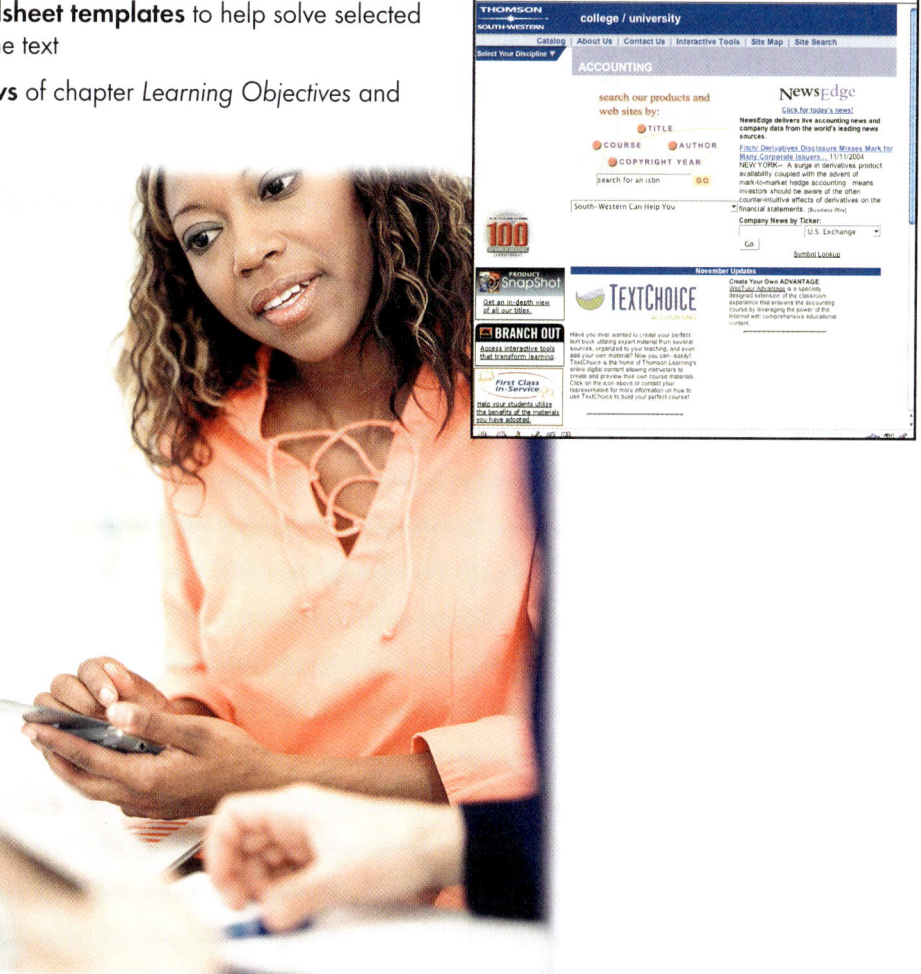

WebTutor™ Advantage
with Personal Trainer 3.0
on WebCT and Blackboard

WebTUTOR™ Advantage

WebTutor Advantage provides you with the most robust and pedagogically advanced content for either the WebCT or Blackboard course management platform. Now instructors can enliven their course with interactive reinforcement for students as well as powerful instructor tools. With the newest version, once the students' content comprehension is assessed, they are then referred to specific content features in **WebTutor Advantage** or in the text to address key areas in which they need additional help.

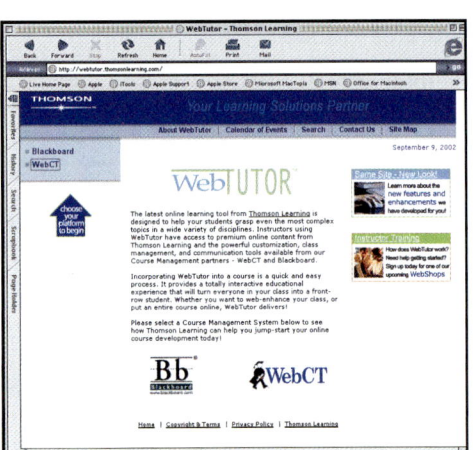

Elements of **WebTutor Advantage** include:

Personal Trainer 3.0
See page xxii of this Preview for details!

Chapter Review
These study outlines provide a framework for the concepts covered within the chapter, and include samples of each individual *Cornerstone* for additional review of the more difficult topics and calculations.

Business in Focus Video Clips
Brief video clips demonstrate how real businesses deal with concepts covered within the chapter.

Animated Cornerstones
Developed specifically for this text, these animated slides provided step-by-step walkthroughs of each individual *Cornerstone* calculation with voice-over narration. Students can master each calculation necessary to complete the homework with this visual reinforcement tool.

Interactive Quizzes
These quizzes test students on the core material within the chapter, providing helpful feedback as they study the more difficult concepts.

Quiz Bowl
A fun, Jeopardy-style game that quizzes students on the more difficult concepts within the chapter.

WebTutor™ Advantage on Blackboard: 0-324-18982-6
WebTutor™ Advantage on WebCT: 0-324-18983-4

Xtra!

Helping students learn and master critical accounting concepts!

Available to be packaged at no cost with this text, **Xtra!** gives students FREE access to the following online learning tools:

Chapter Review

These brief sections review more difficult concepts from each chapter.

Topical Quizzes

Quizzes measure a student's "test readiness" on the concepts in the chapter.

Interactive Quizzes

Additional quizzes help students review chapter concepts and prepare for exams. Feedback on their answers gives page references so they know where to look up the questions they've missed.

Crossword Puzzles

These puzzles are a fun way for students to review their understanding of key terms and concepts.

To order, contact your sales representative.

The Business & Company Resource Center
An easy way to give students access to a dynamic database of business information and resources

The **Business & Company Resource Center (BCRC)** provides online access to a wide variety of global business information including current articles and business journals, detailed company and industry information, investment reports, stock quotes, and much more.

BCRC saves valuable time and provides students a safe resource in which to hone their research skills and develop their analytical abilities. Other benefits of the **BCRC** include:

- **Conveniently accessible** from anywhere with an Internet connection, allowing students to access information at school, at home, or on the go.

- **A powerful and time-saving research tool** for students—whether they are completing a case analysis, preparing for a presentation, creating a business plan, or writing a reaction paper.

- **Instructors can use the** *BCRC* **like an online coursepack**, assigning readings and research-based assignments or projects without the inconvenience of library reserves, permissions, and printed materials.

- **Filters out the 'junk' information often found when searching the Internet**, providing only the high quality, safe, and reliable news and information sources.

- **Easily assign homework, share articles, create journal lists**, and save searches using **BCRC** *Infomarks*.

Instructors can combine the **BCRC** with their favorite **Harvard Business School Publishing** cases to provide students a case analysis research tool at no additional cost. See the next page for information about the **Harvard Business Case Studies**.

Contact your local Thomson South-Western representative to learn how to include Business & Company Resource Center *with your text.*

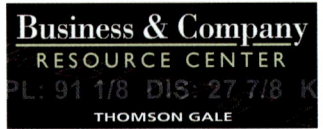

Harvard Business Case Studies
The leader in business education publishing partners with the leader in business cases

As part of Thomson South-Western's commitment to giving customers the greatest choice of teaching and learning solutions possible, we are proud to be an official distributor of Harvard Business School Publishing case collections and article reprints.

The combination of preeminent cases and articles from Harvard Business School Publishing with the unparalleled scope and depth of customizable content from Thomson Business & Professional Publishing provides instructors and students with a wide array learning materials. You can draw from multiple resources and disciplines to match the unique needs of your course.

Convenience for Instructors

Instructors can work with one source instead of multiple vendors, allowing the local Thomson representative to manage the prompt delivery of teaching resources and students materials.

Convenience for Students

Pricing for cases is very affordable—and when packaged with the textbook, students receive a significant discount on the text and coursepak.

Convenient Ordering

Once you have identified the cases and articles you want to use, simply use an ordering form provided by your Thomson representative to indicate your selections and packaging preferences. Once you return your form, you will be contacted within 48 hours by a Thomson Custom representative to confirm your order and walk you through the rest of the process.

Combine Harvard Business School cases and articles with the BCRC and take your coursepak to the next level. Contact your sales representative for details.

PREFACE

InfoTrac® College Edition
The online library—always open!

InfoTrac College Edition is automatically packaged FREE with every new copy of this text! This world-class, online university library offers the full text of nearly 10 million articles from almost 5,000 scholarly and popular publications—updated daily and going back more than 20 years. Publications include:

Accountant

Accounting Today

Atlantic Business

Atlantic Economic Journal

Bottomline

Business Week

Corporate Business Taxation Monthly

Corporate Cashflow Magazine

Corporate Money

Economic & Financial Review

Economic Outlook USA

Economic Progress Report

Forbes

Fortune

Harvard Business Review

Inside Business

Journal of Business

Journal of Management

Journal of Management Accounting Research

Journal of Supply Chain Management

Management Accounting (British)

Management Accounting (USA)

Management Accounting Quarterly

Mid-Atlantic Journal of Business

Newsweek

The New York Times

Operations Management

Profit-Building Strategies for Business Owners

Project Finance

Purchasing

Quarterly Journal of Business and Economics

USA Today

InfoTrac College Edition is delivered online, making it easy for professors to extend their courses and upgrade student use of Internet resources, providing a continuously changing, dynamic value to customers through daily updating. **InfoTrac College Edition** users can quickly research topics and ideas. The outstanding indexing of its database allows users to employ simple keyword searches to quickly and efficiently search across hundreds of sources, 24 hours a day, 7 days a week.

Plus—this online research and learning center now includes **InfoWrite**. This complete writing tool assists students through difficult areas of research writing, such as choosing a topic, composing introductions and conclusions, and crediting sources. Check out **InfoWrite** and see why **InfoTrac College Edition** is more than just a research database!

Learn more about **InfoTrac College Edition** and see a complete list of publications available at **http://www.infotrac-college.com**.

Thomson Custom Publishing
Making *it* happen

At **Thomson Custom Publishing, our mission is to make the educational experience unique and personal for all learners by helping instructors develop custom educational materials that best suit their individual needs. We offer a range of services to fit any classroom.**

Derivative Solutions

Build a book or collection of course material using content from previously published Thomson textbooks, including books from the South-Western, Wadsworth, Brooks/Cole, Course Technology, Delmar, and Heinle & Heinle publishing groups. Include your own content to customize your materials even more.

Database Publishing

Use our online database of content to develop your custom learning materials. Select readings, chapters, or excerpts from more than 40 subject areas, developed specifically for your use.

Gallery of Covers

Visit our gallery of covers to select a professional cover design to complement your book.

Instructor Resources

Our Instructor Resource site provides access to the valuable teaching tools available to complement your Thomson Custom products.

Original Works

Instructors can publish their own original learning materials with the help of our Custom Publishing editors. Textbooks, supplements, study guides, essay collections . . . the possibilities are endless!

Technology Services

Thomson Custom Publishing can provide tailored learning materials in a variety of delivery methods.

TextChoice

TextChoice provides the fastest, easiest way for instructors to create their own learning materials. Instructors can select content from hundreds of our best-selling titles, choose material from one of our databases, and add their own material.

Teaching resources for streamlined teaching and enriched learning

Instructor's Resource CD-ROM

0-324-18979-6

Includes the Solutions Manual, Instructor's Manual, *ExamView* computerized testing software, instructor PowerPoint slides, and Instructor Spreadsheet Solutions on one convenient CD-ROM.

Instructor's Manual

0-324-18973-7

This manual simplifies class preparation by providing lecture outlines, teaching suggestions and strategies, topical overviews, and more.

Solutions Manual

0-324-18974-5

Prepared by the authors, this manual contains independently verified solutions to all end-of-chapter multiple-choice questions, exercises and problems in the text.

Test Bank

0-324-18975-3

Also available in *ExamView* computerized testing format, this Test Bank includes up to 150 questions per chapter, which contains a mix of true/false, multiple-choice (conceptual and problem) questions, problems, and several essay questions.

ExamView® Computerized Testing

0-324-18976-1

ExamView

This easy-to-use assessment and tutorial system allows instructors to create, deliver, and customize tests and study guides (both print and online) in minutes. **ExamView** offers both a *Quick Test Wizard* and an *Online Test Wizard* that guide you step-by-step through the process of creating tests—you can even see the test you are creating on the screen exactly as it will print or display online. You can build tests of up to 250 questions using up to 12 question types. Using **ExamView's** complete word-processing capabilities, you can enter an unlimited number of new questions or edit existing questions.

Microsoft® PowerPoint® Presentation Slides

0-324-18978-8

Available in both instructor and student versions, these slides are available to use in class or print out as overheads.

Solutions Transparencies

0-324-18977-X

Acetate transparencies of solutions for selected end-of-chapter exercises and problems.

Study Guide

0-324-18981-8

The student workbook contains various elements of chapter review, from study outlines to chapter quizzes and practice tests. A great tool for both exam prep and concept reinforcement.

About the Authors

Dr. Maryanne M. Mowen is Associate Professor of Accounting at Oklahoma State University. She received her Ph.D. from Arizona State University in 1979. Dr. Mowen brings an interdisciplinary perspective to teaching and writing in cost and management accounting, with degrees in history and economics. In addition, she does research in areas of behavioral decision making, activity-based costing, and the impact of the Sarbanes-Oxley Act. She has published articles in journals such as *Decision Science, The Journal of Economics and Psychology,* and *The Journal of Management Accounting Research.* Dr. Mowen's interests outside the classroom include reading, traveling, and working crossword puzzles.

Dr. Don R. Hansen is the Head of the School of Accounting and Kerr McGee Chair at Oklahoma State University. He received his Ph.D. from the University of Arizona in 1977. He has an undergraduate degree in mathematics from Brigham Young University. His research interests include activity-based costing and mathematical modeling. He has published articles in both accounting and engineering journals including *The Accounting Review, The Journal of Management Accounting Research, Accounting Horizons,* and *IIE Transactions.* He has served on the editorial board of *The Accounting Review.* His outside interests include family, church activities, reading, movies, watching sports, and studying Spanish.

Reviewers of *Management Accounting: The Cornerstone for Business Decisions*

Carl Allocca, Stony Brook University

Dan Bayak, Lehigh University

Karen Bird, University of Michigan

Steve Bucheit, Texas Tech University

Charles Caldwell, Tennessee Technological University

Sandy Devona, Northern Illinois University

Roger Doost, Clemson University

Richard Filler, Franklin University

Jim Groff, U of Texas–San Antonio

Nancy Lamberton, University of Hartford

Cathy Lumbattis, Southern Illinois University–Carbondale

David Marcinko, University of Albany–SUNY

Peter Margaritis, Franklin University

Paul Mihalek, University of Hartford

Susan Minke, Indiana University–Purdue University at Fort Wayne

J. Lowell Mooney, Georgia Southern University

Marilyn Okleshen, Minnesota State University–Mankato

Gail Pastoria, Robert Morris University

Janice Pitera, Broome Community College

Kelly Richmond, UNC–Greensboro

P.N. Saksena, Indiana University–South Bend

Howard Smith, Southwest Texas State University

Dwight Sneathen, Jr., Mississippi State University

Ron Strittmater, North Hennepin Community College

Marvin Williams, University of Houston–Downtown

Jeff Yost, College of Charleston

MANAGEMENT ACCOUNTING

The Cornerstone for Business Decisions

INTRODUCTION TO MANAGEMENT ACCOUNTING

DIGITAL VISION/GETTY IMAGES

After studying Chapter 1, you should be able to:

1. Explain the meaning of management accounting.
2. Explain the differences between management accounting and financial accounting.
3. Identify and explain the current focus of management accounting.
4. Describe the role of management accountants in an organization.
5. Explain the importance of ethical behavior for managers and management accountants.
6. Identify three forms of certification available to management accountants.

Consider the following comments made by various managers at Kicker, an audio design and manufacturing firm.

A. Head of the Warranty Department:

"From time to time, a dealer returns a defective unit to us. We can rebuild that unit by replacing the defective component (typically a burnt voice coil) with a new one. We test it thoroughly and sell it as used. My question is—how do you value the rebuilt unit?" (product costing)

B. Vice President of Sales and Marketing:

"We put on tent sales where merchandise is sold at fire sale prices. Some of our venues (cities where the tent sales are held) work well; we take in $100,000 of revenue. Others don't. One venue provided just $15,000 in sales. In considering the cost of putting on the tent sale as well as any benefit to our customers, we're not sure that was worth it." (tactical decision making)

C. Director of Research and Development, Quality Testing:

"We study warranty returns and meet weekly to track trends. Reliability is a big issue; the car environment is harsh for a speaker. We had some amplifier returns that we couldn't understand. After extensive testing, we found that one track of Eminem's 'The Slim Shady' has an explosion with full gain and full bass boost that shuts down the amplifier. We put in protective circuitry to solve the problem. Now, playing this track is part of our routine testing procedures." (continuous improvement and quality control)

D. Vice President of Operations:

"We bring all units to Stillwater for shipment to dealers worldwide. Shipping does 25 percent of the month's business on the last day of the month. We have to be flexible to handle it, so we need lots of warehouse space. There was an empty 500,000-square-foot factory building close by. While looking into leasing it, I found it was for sale. We had planned to build a new warehouse on our property, but after considering all the pros and cons, we decided to buy that factory building. We're now in the process of renovating and restructuring it to serve as our warehouse and new world headquarters." (capital investment decision)

In writing this textbook, we wanted to show our readers the importance and relevance of management accounting in planning, decision making, and day-to-day operations of companies and not-for-profit organizations. We teamed up with a real company, Kicker, and interviewed their top management extensively for stories about their firm and their use of accounting information. You will see boxes in each chapter called "Here's the Real Kicker," which detail how the company has used management accounting information in its operations. In addition, each chapter includes an exercise or problem based on an actual Kicker experience. Without further ado, let's get better acquainted with Kicker.

HERE'S THE REAL KICKER

A division of Stillwater Designs and Audio, Inc., Kicker makes car stereo systems. Their signature logo, "Livin' Loud," gives you a hint as to the capabilities of the system. As the company Web site says, "Livin' Loud has always been the KICKER way—staying one step ahead of the pack—driven to create components that consistently raise the world's expectations for car stereo performance."

Twenty-five years ago, car stereos were underpowered tinny affairs. They could power a radio or an 8-track tape deck. But the in-home listening experience coveted by audio buffs eluded the automobile market. In 1980, Stillwater Designs virtually invented the high-performance car audio enclosure market when company founder and president Steve Irby developed the Original Kicker®. It was the first full-range speaker enclosure designed specifically for automotive use.

Stillwater Designs began in 1973 as a two-person operation, custom designing and building professional sound and musical instrument speaker systems for churches, auditoriums, and entertainers. Building upon the success of the Original Kicker, the company concentrated on the car audio market, applying the same research and design skills that made its first product so successful to the development of a complete line of high-performance components for car audio. What was once a company with two employees in a single-car garage is now a corporation with more than 200 employees in facilities totaling more than 500,000 square feet. Its world headquarters is in Stillwater, Oklahoma.

The Kicker brand includes a variety of high-performance car stereo products, including subwoofers, midrange and midbass drivers, tweeters, crossovers, matched component systems, speakers, and power amplifiers. Kicker is proud to have won the prestigious AudioVideo International Auto Sound Grand Prix Award, sponsored annually by *AudioVideo International* magazine. Winners are selected by retailers based on fidelity of sound reproduction, design engineering, reliability, craftsmanship and product integrity, and cost/performance ratio. In 2003, seven Kicker products earned Grand Prix awards. Awards emphasizing the performance of the company include the Governor's Award for Excellence in Exporting (2000) and the 1996 Oklahoma City International Trade Association designation as its International Business of the Year.

While Stillwater Designs originally handled research and design, manufacturing, and sales, it now concentrates primarily on R&D and sales. The bulk of manufacturing has been outsourced (performed by outside firms on a contract basis), although the company still builds some product and plans to build even more as it moves into its new facility for factory-installed audio systems. Engineering and audio research is Kicker President and CEO Steve Irby's first love, and he still heads its design team. The day-to-day involvement of top management, coupled with an energetic workforce of talented individuals in all areas of the company's operations and an innate ability to create truly musical components, has been the reason for the company's remarkable success.

THE MEANING OF MANAGEMENT ACCOUNTING

OBJECTIVE 1

Explain the meaning of management accounting.

What do we mean by management accounting? Quite simply, **management accounting** is the provision of accounting information for a company's internal users. It is the firm's internal accounting system and is designed to support the information needs of

information for external users. It must conform to certain rules and conventions that are defined by various agencies, such as the Securities and Exchange Commission (SEC) and the Financial Accounting Standards Board (FASB). The overall objective is the preparation of external reports (financial statements) for investors, creditors, government agencies, and other outside users. This information is used for such things as investment decisions, stewardship evaluation, monitoring activity, and regulatory measures.

The management accounting system produces information for internal users, such as managers, executives, and workers. Thus, management accounting could be properly called *internal accounting*, and financial accounting could be called *external accounting*. Specifically, management accounting identifies, collects, measures, classifies, and reports information that is useful to internal users in planning, controlling, and decision making.

When comparing management accounting to financial accounting, several differences can be identified. Some of the more important differences follow and are summarized in Exhibit 1-2.

- *Targeted users.* As mentioned, management accounting focuses on providing information for internal users, while financial accounting focuses on providing information for external users.
- *Restrictions on inputs and processes.* Management accounting is not subject to the requirements of generally accepted accounting principles. The SEC and the FASB set the accounting procedures that must be followed for financial reporting. The inputs and processes of financial accounting are well defined and, in fact, restricted. Only certain kinds of economic events qualify as inputs, and processes must follow generally accepted methods. Unlike financial accounting, management accounting has no official body that prescribes the format, content, and rules for selecting inputs and processes and preparing financial reports. Managers are free to choose whatever information they want—provided it can be justified on a cost-benefit basis.
- *Type of information.* The restrictions imposed by financial accounting tend to produce objective and verifiable financial information. For management accounting, information may be financial or nonfinancial and may be much more subjective in nature.
- *Time orientation.* Financial accounting has a historical orientation. It records and reports events that have already happened. Although management accounting also

1-2

EXHIBIT

Comparison of Management and Financial Accounting

Management Accounting	Financial Accounting
1. Internally focused.	1. Externally focused.
2. No mandatory rules.	2. Must follow externally imposed rules.
3. Financial and nonfinancial information; subjective information possible.	3. Objective financial information.
4. Emphasis on the future.	4. Historical orientation.
5. Internal evaluation and decisions based on very detailed information.	5. Information about the firm as a whole.
6. Broad, multidisciplinary.	6. More self-contained.

records and reports events that have already occurred, it strongly emphasizes providing information about future events. Management, for example, may want to know what it will cost to produce a product next year. Knowing what it will cost helps in planning material purchases and making pricing decisions, among other things. This future orientation is needed to support the managerial functions of planning and decision making.

- *Degree of aggregation.* Management accounting provides measures and internal reports used to evaluate the performance of entities, product lines, departments, and managers. Essentially, very detailed information is needed and provided. Financial accounting, on the other hand, focuses on overall firm performance, providing a more aggregated viewpoint.
- *Breadth.* Management accounting is much broader than financial accounting. It includes aspects of managerial economics, industrial engineering, and management science, as well as numerous other areas.

The accounting system should be designed to provide both financial and management accounting information. The key point here is flexibility—the accounting system should be able to supply different information for different purposes.

CURRENT FOCUS OF MANAGEMENT ACCOUNTING

The world has changed significantly over the past 50 years. Huge improvements have been made in technology, transportation, and communication. These developments have led to the need for better information. Management accountants have responded by broadening their focus to include the gathering of information on all types of costs and of the value of the product or service to customers. Consequently, activity-based management accounting systems have been developed and implemented in many organizations. Additionally, the focus of management accounting systems has been broadened to enable managers to better serve the needs of customers and manage the firm's value chain. Furthermore, to secure and maintain a competitive advantage, managers must emphasize time, quality, and efficiency, and accounting information must be produced to support these three fundamental organizational goals.

> **OBJECTIVE 3**
>
> Identify and explain the current focus of management accounting.

New Methods of Costing Products and Services

Companies today need focused, accurate information on the cost of the products and services they produce. Years ago, a company might produce a few products that were roughly similar to one another. Only the cost of materials and labor might differ from one product to another. Figuring out the cost of each unit was relatively easy. Now, however, with the increase in technology and automation, it is more difficult to generate the costing information needed by management to make a wide variety of decisions. As Peter Drucker, internationally respected management guru, points out:

> *Traditional cost accounting in manufacturing does not record the cost of nonproducing such as the cost of faulty quality, or of a machine being out of order, or of needed parts not being on hand. Yet these unrecorded and uncontrolled costs in some plants run as high as the costs that traditional accounting does record. By contrast, a new method of cost accounting developed in the last 10 years—called "activity-based" accounting—records all costs. And it relates them, as traditional accounting cannot, to value-added.*[2]

Activity-based costing is a more detailed approach to determining the cost of goods and services. Activity-based costing improves costing accuracy by emphasizing the cost of the many activities or tasks that must be done to produce a product. The under-

---

[2]Peter F. Drucker, "We Need to Measure, Not Count," *The Wall Street Journal* (April 13, 1993): A14.

pinnings of activity-based costing are widely used today both in manufacturing and service firms. Process-value analysis focuses on the way in which companies create value for customers. The objective is to find ways to perform necessary activities more efficiently and to eliminate those that do not create customer value.

Customer Orientation

Customer value is a key focus because firms can establish a competitive advantage by creating better customer value for the same or lower cost than competitors or creating equivalent value for lower cost than that of competitors. Customer value is the difference between what a customer receives and what the customer gives up when buying a product or service. When we talk about customer value, we consider the complete range of tangible and intangible benefits that a customer receives from a purchased product. Thus, what a customer receives includes basic and special product features, service, quality, instructions for use, reputation, brand name, and any other factors deemed important by customers. What a customer gives up includes the cost of purchasing the product, the time and effort spent acquiring and learning to use the product, and the costs of using, maintaining, and disposing of the product.

Strategic Positioning

A company that increases customer value may create a sustainable competitive advantage. Good cost information can help the company to identify strategies that can achieve a competitive advantage. Generally, firms choose one of two general strategies: (1) cost leadership and (2) superior products through differentiation. The objective of the cost leadership strategy is to provide the same or better value to customers at a *lower* cost than competitors. Thus, a low-cost strategy has the objective of increasing customer value by reducing sacrifice. For example, reducing the cost of making a product by improving a process would allow the firm to reduce the product's selling price, thus reducing customer sacrifice. A differentiation strategy, on the other hand, strives to increase customer value by increasing realization. Providing something to customers not provided by competitors creates a competitive advantage. For example, a local computer store could offer to set up the new purchase, a feature not offered by mail-order firms. Cost information is important to see whether or not the additional service adds more to revenue than it does to cost.

The Value Chain

A focus on customer value means that managers need information about both realization and sacrifice. Collecting information about customer sacrifice means gathering information outside the firm. But there are even deeper implications. Successful pursuit of cost leadership and/or differentiation strategies requires an understanding of a firm's value chain. The **value chain** is the set of activities required to design, develop, produce, market, and deliver products and services to customers. Exhibit 1-3 illustrates the value chain. Emphasizing customer value forces managers to determine which activities in the value chain are important to customers. A management accounting system should track information about a wide variety of activities that span the value chain. Consider, for example, the delivery segment. Timely delivery of a product or service is part of the total product and is, thus, of value to the customer. Customer value can be increased by increasing the speed of delivery and response. Federal Express exploited this part of the value chain and successfully developed a service that was not being offered by the U.S. Postal Service. Today, many customers believe that delivery delayed is delivery denied. This seems to indicate that a good management accounting system ought to develop and measure indicators of customer satisfaction.

It is important to note that companies have internal customers as well. For example, the procurement process acquires and delivers parts and materials to producing

The Value Chain

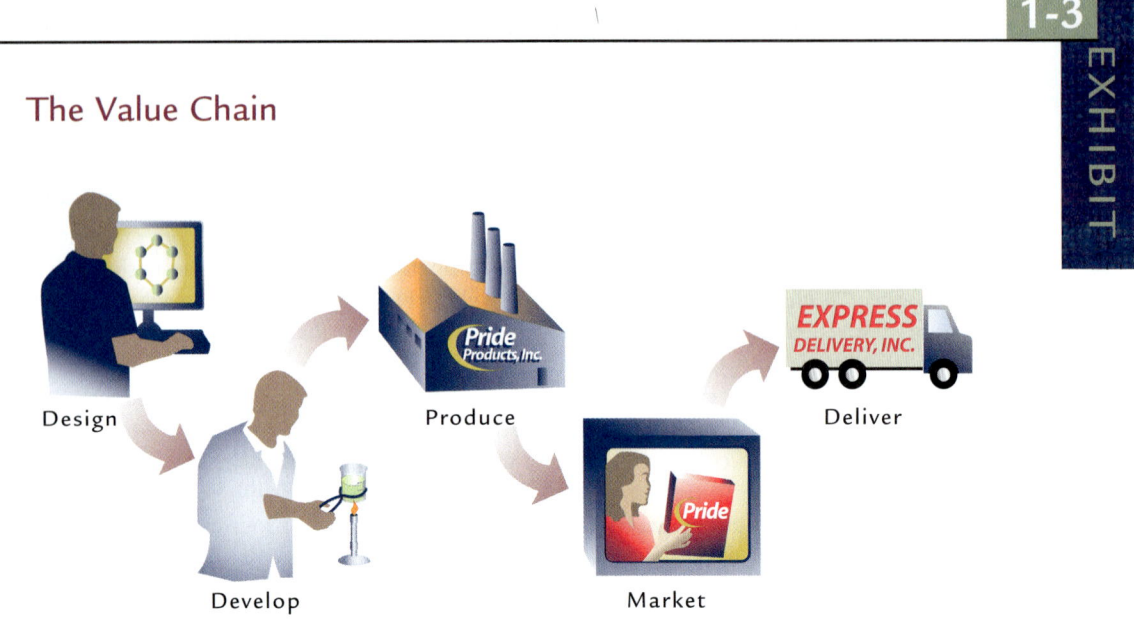

Design   Develop   Produce   Market   Deliver

departments. Providing high-quality parts on a timely basis to managers of producing departments is just as vital for procurement as it is for the company as a whole to provide high-quality goods to external customers. The emphasis on managing the internal value chain and servicing internal customers has revealed the importance of a cross-functional perspective.

Cross-Functional Perspective

Managing the value chain means that a management accountant must understand many functions of the business, from manufacturing to marketing to distribution to customer service. This need is magnified when the company is involved in international trade. We see this, for example, in the varying definitions of product cost. Management accounting has moved beyond the traditional manufacturing cost definition of product cost to more inclusive definitions. These contemporary approaches to product costing may include initial design and engineering costs, as well as manufacturing costs, and the costs of distribution, sales, and service. An individual well schooled in the various definitions of product cost, who understands the shifting definitions of cost from the short-run to the long-run, can be invaluable in determining what information is relevant in decision making. For example, strategic decisions may require a product cost definition that assigns the costs of all value-chain activities, whereas a short-run decision that is concerned with whether a special order should be accepted or rejected may require a product cost that assigns only marginal or incremental costs.

Why try to relate management accounting to marketing, management, engineering, finance, and other business functions? When a value-chain approach is taken and customer value is emphasized, we see that these disciplines are interrelated; a decision affecting one affects the others. For example, salespeople may offer deep discounts at the end of the year to meet their sales targets. Customers, of course, buy more product. The company's factories may have to work double shifts, with a great deal of overtime pay, to meet this sudden increase in demand. A cross-functional perspective lets us see the big picture—to see that the increased revenue came at the expense of much higher product costs. This broader vision allows managers to increase quality, reduce the time required to service customers (both internal and external), and improve efficiency.

Total Quality Management

Continuous improvement means searching for ways to increase the overall efficiency and productivity of activities by reducing waste, increasing quality, and reducing costs. Thus, information is needed to help identify opportunities for improvement and to evaluate the progress made in implementing actions designed to create improvement.

Information about the costs of products, customers, processes, and other objects of interest to management can be the basis for identifying problems and alternative solutions. Similar observations can be made about information pertaining to planning, control, and evaluation. For example, before Apple introduced the ipod mini, its managers seriously considered both the types of functions desired by customers, as well as the price that could be charged. While Apple knew that customers would love to have an ipod for less than $100, it also knew that (given current technology) including a hard drive capable of accomplishing most of the ipod's functions would be impossible at that price. Cost data, then, was an important piece of information for management decision making.

Continuous improvement is fundamental for establishing excellence. Providing products with little waste that actually perform according to specifications are the twin objectives of world-class firms. A philosophy of **total quality management**, in which manufacturers strive to create an environment that will enable workers to manufacture perfect (zero-defect) products, has replaced the "acceptable quality" attitudes of the past. This emphasis on quality has also created a demand for a management accounting system that provides financial and nonfinancial information about quality.

Service industries are also dedicated to improving quality. Service firms present special problems because quality may differ from employee to employee. As a result, service firms are emphasizing consistency through the development of systems to support employee efforts. For example, USAA, a financial services company specializing in insurance for current and former military officers, invested heavily in information technology in the mid-1980s. Incoming documents (for example, policy applications, checks, and appraisals) are scanned electronically and stored on optical disks. When a customer calls USAA to see if a policy application for a new house has been received, a service representative can check the customer's file on the computer and answer the question immediately. This is in contrast to the old system, which required USAA representatives to search a warehouse or others' desks for the relevant files—a process that could take up to two weeks.

Quality cost measurement and reporting are key features of a management accounting system for both manufacturing and service industries. In both cases, the management accounting system should be able to provide information about quality.

Time as a Competitive Element

Time is a crucial element in all phases of the value chain.[3] World-class firms reduce time to market by compressing design, implementation, and production cycles. These firms

---

[3]An excellent analysis of time as a competitive element is contained in A. Faye Borthick and Harold P. Roth, "Accounting for Time: Reengineering Business Processes to Improve Responsiveness," *Journal of Cost Management* (Fall 1993): 4–14.

deliver products or services quickly by eliminating non-value-added time, which is time of no value to the customer (for example, the time a product spends on the loading dock). Interestingly, decreasing non-value-added time appears to go hand in hand with increasing quality. The USAA example given in the previous section demonstrates the improvement in service quality that resulted from the insightful management of time. The overall objective, of course, is to increase customer responsiveness.

What about the relationship between time and product life cycles? The rate of technological innovation has increased for many industries, and the life of a particular product can be quite short. Managers must be able to respond quickly and decisively to changing market conditions. Information to allow them to accomplish this must be available. For example, Hewlett-Packard has found that it is better to be 50 percent over budget in new product development than to be six months late. This correlation between cost and time is the kind of information that should be available from a management accounting information system.

Efficiency

While quality and time are important, improving these dimensions without corresponding improvements in profit performance may be futile, if not fatal. Improving efficiency is also a vital concern. Both financial and nonfinancial measures of efficiency are needed. Cost is a critical measure of efficiency. Trends in costs over time and measures of productivity changes can provide important measures of the efficacy of continuous improvement decisions. For these efficiency measures to be of value, costs must be properly defined, measured, and assigned; furthermore, production of output must be related to the inputs required, and the overall financial effect of productivity changes should be calculated.

THE ROLE OF THE MANAGEMENT ACCOUNTANT

> **OBJECTIVE 4**
>
> Describe the role of management accountants in an organization.

Today's business press writes about world-class firms. These are firms at the cutting edge of customer support. They know their market and their product. They strive to continually improve product design, manufacture, and delivery. These companies can compete with the best of the best in a global environment. Management accountants must also be world-class. They must be intelligent, well prepared, and up to date with new developments. They also must be familiar with the customs and practices of countries in which their firms operate.

The role of management accountants in an organization is one of support. They assist those individuals who are responsible for carrying out an organization's basic objectives. Positions that have direct responsibility for the basic objectives of an organization are referred to as **line positions**. Positions that are supportive in nature and have only indirect responsibility for an organization's basic objectives are called **staff positions**.

For example, assume that the basic mission of an organization is to produce and sell laser printers. The vice presidents of manufacturing and marketing, the factory manager, and the assemblers are all line positions. The vice presidents of finance and human resources, the cost accountant, and the purchasing manager are all staff positions.

Kicker's organization chart is shown in Exhibit 1-4. Because one of the basic objectives of the organization is to design, produce, and sell audio equipment, the president, general manager, and vice presidents for sales and marketing and operations hold line positions. Although management accountants, such as controllers and cost accounting managers, may wield considerable influence in the organization, they have no authority over the managers in the production area. The managers in line positions are the ones who set policy and make the decisions that impact the company. However, by supplying and interpreting accounting information, management accountants can have significant input into policies and decisions.

Kicker, Inc., Organizational Chart

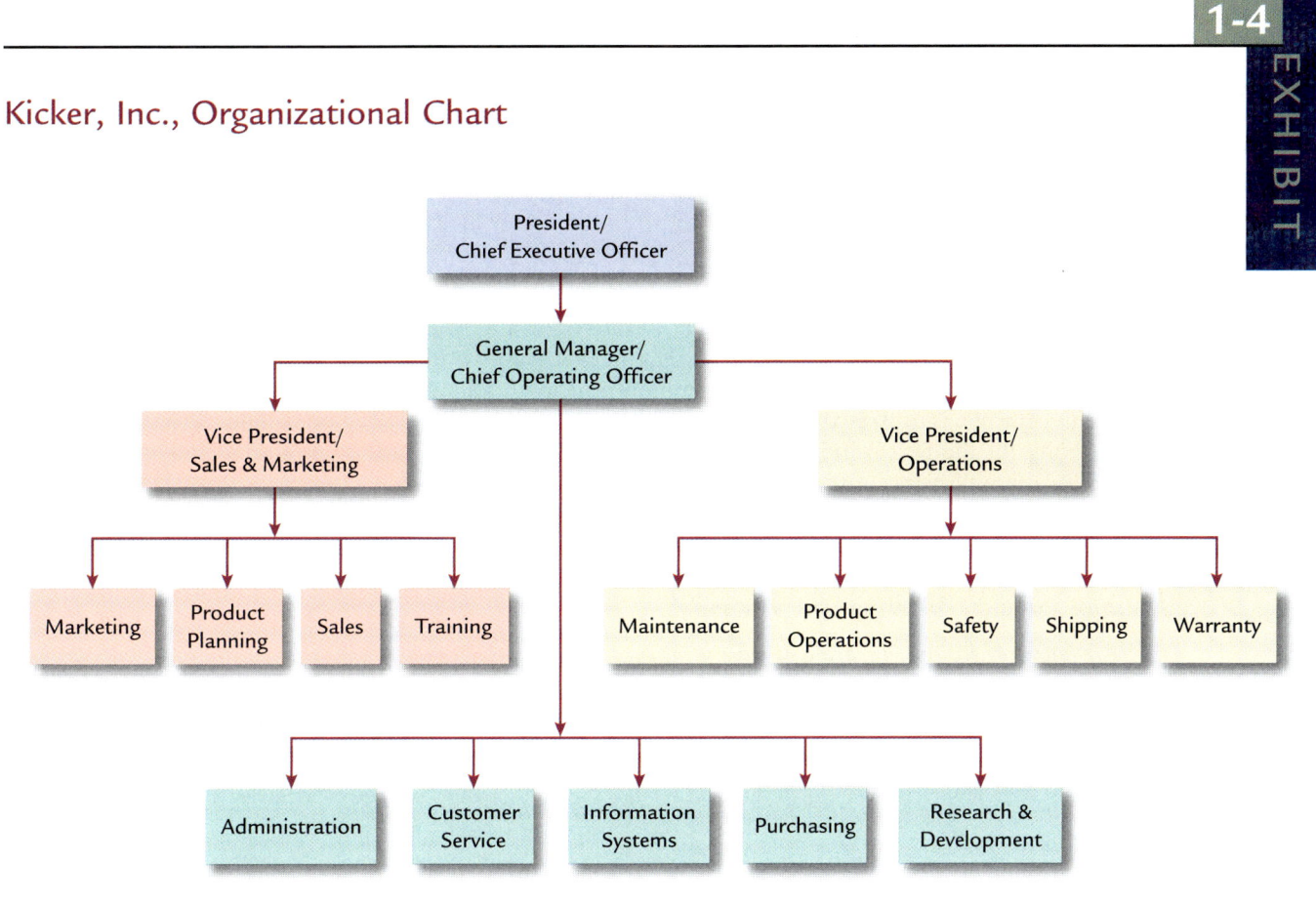

The **controller**, the chief accounting officer, for Kicker is located in the administration department. She supervises all accounting functions and reports directly to the general manager and chief operating officer (COO).

Because of the critical role that management accounting plays in the operation of an organization, the controller is often viewed as a member of the top management team and is encouraged to participate in planning, controlling, and decision-making activities. As the chief accounting officer, the controller has responsibility for both internal and external accounting requirements. In larger firms, this charge may include direct responsibility for internal auditing, cost accounting, financial accounting (including SEC reports and financial statements), systems accounting (including analysis, design, and internal controls), and taxes. The duties and organization of the controller's office vary from firm to firm. For example, in some firms, the internal audit department may report directly to the financial vice president; similarly, the systems department may report directly to the financial vice president or some other vice president.

In larger companies, the controller is separate from the treasury department. The **treasurer** is responsible for the finance function. Specifically, the treasurer raises capital and manages cash and investments. The treasurer may also be in charge of credit and collection and insurance.

OBJECTIVE 5

Explain the importance of ethical behavior for managers and management accountants.

MANAGEMENT ACCOUNTING AND ETHICAL CONDUCT

Virtually all management accounting practices were developed to assist managers in maximizing profits. Traditionally, the economic performance of the firm has been the overriding concern. Yet, managers and management accountants should not become so focused on profits that they develop a belief that the only goal of a business is maximizing its net worth. The objective of profit maximization should be constrained by the requirement that profits be achieved through legal and ethical means. While this has always been an implicit assumption of management accounting, the assumption should be made explicit. To help achieve this objective, many of the problems in this text force explicit consideration of ethical issues.

Ethical Behavior

Ethical behavior involves choosing actions that are right, proper, and just. Our behavior can be right or wrong; it can be proper or improper; and the decisions we make can be fair or unfair. Though people often differ in their views of the meaning of the ethical terms cited, there seems to be a common principle underlying all ethical systems. This principle is expressed by the belief that each member of a group bears some responsibility for the well-being of other members. Willingness to sacrifice one's self-interest for the well-being of the group is the heart of ethical action.

This notion of sacrificing one's self-interest for the well-being of others produces some core values—values that describe what is meant by right and wrong in more concrete terms. James W. Brackner, writing for the "Ethics Column" in *Management Accounting*, made the following observation:

> For moral or ethical education to have meaning, there must be agreement on the values that are considered "right." Ten of these values are identified and described by Michael Josephson in "Teaching Ethical Decision Making and Principled Reasoning." The study of history, philosophy, and religion reveals a strong consensus as to certain universal and timeless values essential to the ethical life.
>
> These ten core values yield a series of principles that delineate right and wrong in general terms. Therefore, they provide a guide to behavior. . .[4]

The 10 core values referred to in the quotation follow:

1. Honesty
2. Integrity
3. Promise keeping
4. Fidelity
5. Fairness
6. Caring for others
7. Respect for others
8. Responsible citizenship
9. Pursuit of excellence
10. Accountability

Although it may seem contradictory, sacrificing one's self-interest for the collective good may not only be right and bring a sense of individual worth but may also make good business sense. Companies with a strong code of ethics can create strong customer and employee loyalty. While liars and cheats may win on occasion, their victories are often short term. Companies in business for the long term find that it pays to treat all of their constituents honestly and loyally.

Company Codes of Ethical Conduct

Organizations commonly establish standards of conduct for their managers and employees. One needs only to hear the name "Enron" to be reminded of the importance

---

[4]James W. Brackner, "Consensus Values Should Be Taught," *Management Accounting* (August 1992): 19. For a more complete discussion of the 10 core values, see also Michael Josephson, *Teaching Ethical Decision Making and Principled Reasoning, Ethics Easier Said Than Done* (Los Angeles, CA: The Josephson Institute, Winter 1988): 29–30.

of ethical conduct. A quick review of various corporate codes of conduct shows some common ground. For example, ChevronTexaco's list of corporate values[5] includes integrity, trust, diversity, high performance, responsibility, and growth. Boeing's Code of Conduct[6] states that it will "conduct its business fairly, impartially, in an ethical and proper manner, and in full compliance with all applicable laws and regulations." All employees must sign the code, and the company "requires that they understand the code, and ask questions, seek guidance, report suspected violations, and express concerns regarding compliance with this policy and the related procedures."

Important parts of corporate codes of conduct are integrity, performance of duties, and compliance with the rule of law. They also uniformly prohibit the acceptance of kickbacks and improper gifts, insider trading, and misappropriation of corporate information and assets. Some, for example, Motorola,[7] outline employee responsibilities to each other, customers, suppliers, business partners, shareholders, governments, communities, and competitors.

Professional associations also establish ethical standards. Both the American Institute of Certified Public Accountants (AICPA) and the Institute of Management Accountants (IMA) have established ethical standards for accountants. Professional accountants are bound by these codes of conduct.[8] Both the AICPA and the IMA stress the importance of competence, confidentiality, integrity, and objectivity.

Can ethics be taught? Philosophers and ethicists from Socrates to those studying business ethics today agree that they can be taught, and even more importantly, learned. Students know that they have been taught in the ways of ethical conduct from preschool on. When they encounter new situations, ethical behavior must be defined and reinforced. For example, when you came to college, you were no doubt advised of the importance of doing your own work (not cheating) and of properly citing sources used in your papers and presentations. Clearly, individual rules were not intrinsically a part of you—they were taught. Similarly, business people must be advised of the finer points of business ethics and of the behavior appropriate to the job. For example, the head chef of a restaurant may be given some choice steaks as a gift for doing business with a meat supplier. Is this OK? The novice may think that it is—but this is wrong! It is the acceptance of a gift meant to render the chef less objective in his/her choice of supplier. The chef could be fired for such behavior. In fact, many corporate codes of conduct explicitly outlaw such behavior. Each chapter of this text includes an ethical problem designed to increase student awareness of the types of conduct considered unethical in business.

CERTIFICATION

OBJECTIVE 6

Identify three forms of certification available to management accountants.

Numerous forms of certification are available to management accountants. We'll briefly describe three of the major types: a Certificate in Management Accounting, a Certificate in Public Accounting, and a Certificate in Internal Auditing. Each certification offers particular advantages to a management accountant. In each case, an applicant must meet specific educational and experience requirements and pass a qualifying examination to become certified. Thus, all three certifications offer evidence that the holder has achieved a minimum level of professional competence.

---

[5]Taken from the ChevronTexaco Web site on May 12, 2004, **http://www.chevrontexaco.com/about/chevtex_ way/values.asp**.
[6]Taken from the Boeing Web site on May 12, 2004, **http://www.boeing.com/companyoffices/aboutus/ethics/**.
[7]Taken from the Motorola Web site on May 14, 2004, **http://www.motorola.com/content/0,,75-107,00.html**.
[8]The AICPA Code of Professional Conduct can be found on the following Web site: **http://www.aicpa.org/ about/code/**. The "Standards of Ethical Conduct for Management Accountants" is found in *Statement on Management Accounting No. 1C* (Montvale, NJ: Institute of Management Accountants, 1983). It is also found on the Web site **http://www.imanet.org/ima/sec.asp?TRACKID=&CID=191&DID=323**.

Furthermore, all three certifications require the holders to engage in continuing professional education in order to maintain certification. Because certification reveals a commitment to professional competency, most organizations encourage their management accountants to become certified.

The CMA

In 1974, the Institute of Management Accountants (IMA) sponsored a new certification called the Certificate in Management Accounting. This certificate was designed to meet the specific needs of management accountants. A **Certified Management Accountant (CMA)** has passed a rigorous qualifying examination, met an experience requirement, and participates in continuing education.

One of the key requirements for obtaining the CMA is passing a qualifying examination. Four areas are emphasized: (1) economics, finance, and management; (2) financial accounting and reporting; (3) management reporting, analysis, and behavioral issues; and (4) decision analysis and information systems. The parts to the examination reflect the needs of management accounting and underscore the earlier observation that management accounting has more of an interdisciplinary flavor than other areas of accounting.

One of the main purposes of the CMA was to establish management accounting as a recognized, professional discipline, separate from the profession of public accounting. Since its inception, the CMA program has been very successful. Many firms now sponsor and pay for classes that prepare their management accountants for the qualifying examination, as well as provide other financial incentives to encourage acquisition of the CMA.

COMSTOCK IMAGES

The CPA

The Certificate in Public Accounting is the oldest and most well-known certification in accounting. The purpose of the Certificate in Public Accounting is to provide minimal professional qualification for external auditors. The responsibility of external auditors is to provide assurance concerning the reliability of a firm's financial statements. Only **Certified Public Accountants (CPAs)** are permitted (by law) to serve as external auditors. CPAs must pass a national examination and be licensed by the state in which they practice. Although the Certificate in Public Accounting does not have a management accounting orientation, many management accountants also hold this certificate.

The CIA

The other certification available to internal accountants is the Certificate in Internal Auditing. The forces that led to the creation of this certification in 1974 are similar to those that resulted in the CMA. Internal auditing differs from external auditing and management accounting, and many internal auditors felt a need for a specialized certification. The **Certified Internal Auditor (CIA)** has passed a comprehensive examination designed to ensure technical competence and has two years' experience.

The opening scenario presented four sets of comments made by Kicker managers. Each set of comments can be addressed by one of the three broad objectives of management accounting.

In Scenario A, the head of the warranty department wanted to know the value of a rebuilt unit. This requires the use of product costing, the first broad objective of management accounting. Chapter 2 will explain product costing in more detail. Why did the warranty department head want to know the cost of the rebuilt units? A number of reasons are possible. One is that the department is held accountable for the rebuilds. The cost of the rebuilt units can be compared to the sales revenue gained by selling those units. The difference is the profit made.

In Scenario B, the vice president of sales and marketing needed to decide whether or not to continue holding tent sales in certain cities. He needed to know both the cost of putting on the tent sales and the revenue generated. If cost was less than or even roughly equal to revenue, he would decide against the tent sale in that city.

In Scenario C, the director of research and development uses accounting data to track the number of returned amplifiers—and the reason(s) for the return. In this way, he can see trends in quality and spot a product with poor product quality early on in its life cycle.

In Scenario D, the vice president of operations used various types of cost information to decide between buying and renovating an existing building for warehouse space and building an entirely new building on Kicker's back lot. This is a capital investment decision and will be handled in more detail in Chapter 13.

SUMMARY OF LEARNING OBJECTIVES

Managers, workers, and executives use management accounting information to identify problems, solve problems, and evaluate performance. Essentially, management accounting information helps managers carry out their roles of planning, controlling, and decision making. Planning is the detailed formulation of action to achieve a particular end. Controlling is the monitoring of a plan's implementation. Decision making is choosing among competing alternatives.

Management accounting differs from financial accounting in several ways. Management accounting information is intended for internal users, whereas financial accounting information is directed toward external users. Management accounting is not bound by the externally imposed rules of financial reporting. Furthermore, it tends to be more subjective and uses both financial and nonfinancial measures, whereas financial accounting provides audited, objective financial information. Finally, management accounting provides more detail than financial accounting, and it tends to be broader and multidisciplinary.

Management accounting must provide information that allows managers to focus on customer value, total quality management, and time-based competition. This implies that information about value-chain activities and customer sacrifice (such as postpurchase costs) must be collected and made available. Activity-based management is a major innovative response to the demand for more accurate and relevant management accounting information. Additionally, managers must decide on the strategic position of the firm. One of two positions is usually emphasized—either cost leadership or product differentiation. Which position is chosen can affect the nature of the management accounting information system.

Management accountants are responsible for identifying, collecting, measuring, analyzing, preparing, interpreting, and communicating information used by management to achieve the basic objectives of the organization. Management accountants need to be sensitive to the information needs of managers. Management accountants serve as staff members of the organization and are responsible for providing information; they are usually intimately involved in the management process as valued members of the management team.

Management accounting aids managers in their efforts to improve the economic performance of the firm. Unfortunately, some managers have overemphasized the economic dimension and have engaged in unethical and illegal actions. Many of these actions have relied on the management accounting system to bring about and even support that unethical behavior. To emphasize the importance of the ever-present constraint of ethical behavior on profit-maximizing behavior, this text presents ethical issues in many of the problems appearing at the end of each chapter.

Three of the major types of certifications are the CMA, the CPA, and the CIA. The CMA is a certification designed especially for management accountants. The prestige of the CMA has increased significantly over the years and is now well regarded by the industrial world. The CPA is primarily intended for those practicing public accounting; however, because this certification is highly regarded, many management accountants also hold it. The CIA serves internal auditors and is also well regarded.

KEY TERMS

Certified Internal Auditor (CIA), 17

Certified Management Accountant (CMA), 16

Certified Public Accountant (CPA), 17

Continuous improvement, 11

Controller, 13

Controlling, 6

Decision making, 6

Ethical behavior, 14

Financial accounting, 6

Line positions, 12

Management accounting, 4

Planning, 5

Staff positions, 12

Total quality management, 11

Treasurer, 13

Value chain, 9

DISCUSSION QUESTIONS

1. What is management accounting?
2. What are the three broad objectives of management accounting?
3. Who are the users of management accounting information?
4. Should a management accounting system provide both financial and nonfinancial information? Explain.
5. What is meant by controlling?
6. Describe the connection between planning, feedback, and controlling.
7. How do management accounting and financial accounting differ?
8. Explain the role of financial reporting in the development of management accounting. Why has this changed in recent years?
9. Explain the meaning of customer value. How is focusing on customer value changing management accounting?
10. Explain why today's management accountant must have a cross-functional perspective.

11. What is the value chain? Why is it important?
12. What is the difference between a staff position and a line position?
13. The controller should be a member of the top management staff. Do you agree or disagree? Explain.
14. What is ethical behavior? Is it possible to teach ethical behavior in a management accounting course?
15. Identify the three forms of accounting certification discussed. Which form of certification do you believe is best for a management accountant? Why?

MULTIPLE-CHOICE EXERCISES

1-1 The provision of accounting information for internal users is known as

a. management accounting.
b. accounting.
c. financial accounting.
d. information provision.
e. accounting for planning and control.

1-2 The users of management accounting information include

a. for-profit companies.
b. not-for-profit organizations.
c. city governments.
d. educational institutions.
e. all of the above.

1-3 Setting objectives and identifying methods to achieve those objectives is

a. controlling.
b. decision making.
c. planning.
d. performance evaluation.
e. none of the above.

1-4 The process of choosing among competing alternatives is called

a. controlling.
b. decision making.
c. planning.
d. performance evaluation.
e. none of the above.

1-5 Which of the following is a characteristic of management accounting?

a. Internal focus
b. Subjective information may be used
c. Emphasis on the future
d. Broad-based and multidisciplinary
e. All of the above

1-6 Which of the following is a characteristic of financial accounting?

a. Internal focus
b. Subjective information may be used
c. Historical orientation
d. Broad-based and multidisciplinary
e. None of the above

1-7 In terms of strategic positioning, which two general strategies may be chosen by a company?

a. Activity-based costing and value-chain emphasis
b. Revenue production and cost enhancement
c. Cost leadership and product differentiation
d. Increasing customer value and decreasing supplier orientation
e. Product differentiation and cost enhancement

1-8 Management accountants in an organization are typically

a. line positions.
b. marketing positions.
c. staff positions.
d. production positions.
e. selling positions.

1-9 The chief accounting officer for a firm is the

a. chief executive officer (CEO).
b. chief operating officer (COO).
c. vice president of sales.
d. production head.
e. controller.

1-10 Which of the following is typically found in a corporation's code of ethics?

a. Respect for others
b. Integrity
c. Honesty
d. Competence
e. All of the above

EXERCISES

Exercise 1-1 *The Managerial Process*

Each of the following scenarios requires the use of accounting information to carry out one or more of the three managerial objectives: planning, control (including performance evaluation), or decision making.

a. **Laboratory Manager:** An HMO approached me recently and offered us its entire range of blood tests. It provided a price list revealing the amount it is willing to pay for each test. In many cases, the prices are below what we normally charge. I need to know the costs of the individual tests to assess the feasibility of accepting its offer and perhaps suggest some price adjustments on some of the tests.

b. **Operating Manager:** This report indicates that we have 30 percent more defects than originally targeted. An investigation into the cause has revealed the problem. We were using a lower-quality material than expected, and the waste has been higher than normal. By switching to the quality level originally specified, we can reduce the defects to the planned level.

c. **Divisional Manager:** Our market share has increased because of higher-quality products. Current projections indicate that we should sell 25 percent more units than last year. I want a projection of the effect this increase in sales will have on profits. I also want to know our expected cash receipts and cash expenditures on a month-by-month basis. I have a feeling that some short-term borrowing may be necessary.

d. **Plant Manager:** Foreign competitors are producing goods with lower costs and delivering them more rapidly than we can to customers in our markets. We need to decrease the cycle time and increase the efficiency of our manufacturing process. There are two proposals that should help us accomplish these goals, both of which involve investing in computer-aided manufacturing. I need to know the future cash flows associated with each system and the effect each system has on unit costs and cycle time.

e. **Manager:** At the last board meeting, we established an objective of earning a 25-percent return on sales. I need to know how many units of our product we need to sell to meet this objective. Once I have the estimated sales in units, we need to outline a promotional campaign that will take us where we want to be. However, in order to compute the targeted sales in units, I need to know the expected unit price and a lot of cost information.

f. **Manager:** Perhaps the Harrison Medical Clinic should not offer a full range of medical services. Some services seem to be having a difficult time showing any kind of profit. I am particularly concerned about the mental health service. It has not shown a profit since the clinic opened. I want to know what costs can be avoided if I drop the service. I also want some assessment of the impact on the other services we offer. Some of our patients may choose this clinic because we offer a full range of services.

Required:

Select the management accounting objective(s) that are applicable for each scenario: planning, controlling, or decision making.

Exercise 1-2 *Differences between Management Accounting and Financial Accounting*

 OBJECTIVE 2

Jenna Suarez, the controller for Arben Company, has faced the following situations in the past two weeks:

a. Ben Heald, head of production, wondered whether it would be more cost effective to buy parts already partially assembled or to buy individual parts and assemble them at the Arben factory.

b. The president of Arben reminded Jenna that the stockholders' meeting was coming up, and he needed her to prepare a PowerPoint presentation showing the income statement and balance sheet information for last year.

c. Ellen Johnson, vice president of sales, has decided to expand the sales offices for next year. She sent Jenna the information on next year's rent and depreciation information for budgeting purposes.

d. Jenna's assistant, Mike, received the information from Ellen on depreciation and added it to depreciation expenses and accumulated depreciation on office equipment.

e. Jenna compared the budgeted spending on materials used in production with the actual spending on materials used in production. Materials spending was significantly higher than expected. She set up a meeting to discuss this outcome with Ben Heald, head of production, so that he could explain it.

Required:

Determine whether each request is relatively more *management accounting oriented* or *financial accounting oriented*.

Exercise 1-3 *Customer Value, Strategic Positioning*

 OBJECTIVE 3

Adriana Alvarado has decided to purchase a personal computer. She has narrowed the choices to two: Drantex and Confiar. Both brands have the same processing speed, 6.4 gigabytes of hard-disk capacity, a 3.5-inch disk drive, a CD-ROM drive, and each comes with the same basic software support package. Both come from mail-order companies with good reputations. The selling price for each is identical. After some review, Adriana discovers that the cost of operating and maintaining Drantex over a 3-year period is estimated to be $300. For Confiar, the operating and maintenance cost is $600.

The sales agent for Drantex emphasized the lower operating and maintenance costs. The agent for Confiar, however, emphasized the service reputation of the product and the faster delivery time (Confiar can be purchased and delivered one week sooner than Drantex). Based on all the information, Adriana has decided to buy Confiar.

Required:
1. What is the total product purchased by Adriana?
2. How does the strategic positioning differ for the two companies?
3. When asked why she decided to buy Confiar, Adriana responded, "I think that Confiar offers more value than Drantex." What are the possible sources of this greater value? What implications does this have for the management accounting information system?
4. Suppose that Adriana's decision was prompted mostly by the desire to receive the computer quickly. Informed that it was losing sales because of the longer time to produce and deliver its products, the management of the company producing Drantex decided to improve delivery performance by improving its internal processes. These improvements decreased the number of defective units and the time required to produce its product. Consequently, delivery time and costs both decreased, and the company was able to lower its prices on Drantex. Explain how these actions translate into strengthening the competitive position of the Drantex PC relative to the Confiar PC. Also discuss the implications for the management accounting information system.

Exercise 1-4 *Line versus Staff*

The job responsibilities of two employees of Barney Manufacturing follow.

Joan Dennison, Cost Accounting Manager. Joan is responsible for measuring and collecting costs associated with the manufacture of the garden hose product line. She is also responsible for preparing periodic reports comparing the actual costs with planned costs. These reports are provided to the production line managers and the plant manager. Joan helps explain and interpret the reports.

Steven Swasey, Production Manager. Steven is responsible for the manufacture of the high-quality garden hose. He supervises the line workers, helps develop the production schedule, and is responsible for seeing that production quotas are met. He is also held accountable for controlling manufacturing costs.

Required:
Identify Joan and Steven as line or staff and explain your reasons.

Exercise 1-5 *Ethical Behavior*

Consider the following true scenario between Dave, a printer, and Steve, an assistant in the local university's athletic department.

Steve: Dave, our department needs to have 10,000 posters printed for the basketball team for next year. Here's the mock-up, we'll need them in a month. How much will you charge?

Dave: Well, given the costs I have for ink and paper, I can come in around $5,000.

Steve: Great, here's what I want you to do. Print me up an invoice for $7,500, that's our budget. Then, when they pay you, you give me a check for $2,500. I'll make sure you get the job.

Required:
Is this ethical? What should Dave do?

Exercise 1-6 *Ethical Behavior*

 **OBJECTIVE 5**

Manager: If I can reduce my costs by $40,000 during this last quarter, my division will show a profit that is 10 percent above the planned level, and I will receive a $10,000 bonus. However, given the projections for the fourth quarter, it does not look promising. I really need that $10,000. I know one way I can qualify. All I have to do is lay off my three most expensive salespeople. After all, most of the orders are in for the fourth quarter, and I can always hire new sales personnel at the beginning of the next year.

Required:

What is the right choice for the manager to make? Why did the ethical dilemma arise? Is there any way to redesign the accounting reporting system to discourage the type of behavior the manager is contemplating?

Exercise 1-7 *Ethical Issues*

 **OBJECTIVE 5**

The following statements have appeared in newspaper editorials:

1. Business students come from all segments of society. If they have not been taught ethics by their families and by their elementary and secondary schools, a business school can have little effect.
2. Sacrificing self-interest for the collective good won't happen unless a majority of Americans also accept this premise.
3. Competent executives manage people and resources for the good of society. Monetary benefits and titles are simply the by-products of doing a good job.
4. Unethical firms and individuals, like high rollers in Las Vegas, are eventually wiped out financially.

Required:

Assess and comment on each of the above statements.

Exercise 1-8 *Ethical Issues*

 **OBJECTIVE 5**

The Bedron Company is a closely held investment service group that has been very successful over the past five years, consistently providing most members of the top management group with 50-percent bonuses. In addition, both the chief financial officer and the chief executive officer have received 100-percent bonuses. Bedron expects this trend to continue.

Recently, Bedron's top management group, which holds 35 percent of the outstanding shares of common stock, has learned that a major corporation is interested in acquiring Bedron. The other corporation's initial offer is attractive and is several dollars per share higher than Bedron's current share price. One member of management told a group of employees under him about the potential offer. He suggested that they might want to purchase more Bedron stock at the current price in anticipation of the takeover offer.

Required:

Do you think the employees should take the action suggested by their boss? Suppose the action was prohibited by Bedron's code of ethics? Now suppose that it is not prohibited by Bedron's code of ethics. Is the action acceptable in that case?

BASIC MANAGEMENT ACCOUNTING CONCEPTS

After studying Chapter 2, you should be able to:

1. Explain the meaning of cost and how costs are assigned to products and services.
2. Define the various costs of producing products and services, as well as the costs of selling and administration.
3. Prepare income statements for manufacturing and service organizations.

Courtney and Ted Weller are a couple in their late 30s. Courtney has just landed her dream job as head chef at a gourmet restaurant in the city. Ted is an architect. Last Monday, when Courtney stormed into their apartment, Ted was concerned. He knew Courtney was to meet with her manager for a performance evaluation. Evidently, it did not go well.

Ted: How was your evaluation meeting? Did your boss like the new menu items you introduced?

Courtney: Oh, yes, that was fine. He was enthusiastic about the improvements in the dessert menu and my use of local fruits and vegetables in season. Customers love knowing that the foods I serve are really fresh.

Ted: Then what's wrong? What did he not like?

Courtney: Nothing's wrong with my performance; he likes everything I've done. It's just that I have to start doing some new things that I don't know how to do. He says profits are down and we need to be "more efficient." So, he wants all department managers to keep track of their costs and report them each week. As the head chef, I'm also the kitchen manager. So I have to do this! And, he doesn't just want overall costs, he wants the costs broken down in a number of ways—direct costs, indirect costs, prime costs, overhead, and gross margin. I don't even know what those terms mean! How am I going to do all this? Why doesn't he realize that I'm a chef—NOT an accountant!

Ted: Boy, that's a lot to unload on you! Still, your boss really needs that information. Believe me, I spend at least a quarter of my time costing out my designs and making sure that they come in on budget. Everyone in business today has to keep an eye on costs. Maybe I can help. I took some accounting classes as part of my business minor. I still have some of those old texts. Let's relax tonight, and tomorrow, I'll find those books and we can look up some definitions.

Courtney: OK, I like that idea. This is the job I've dreamed of having and I want to keep it—even if it means turning into Super Courtney—Chef and Kitchen Accountant!

THE MEANING AND USES OF COST

One of the most important objectives of management accounting is to determine the cost of products, services, customers, and other items of interest to managers. Therefore, we need to understand the meaning of cost and the ways in which costs can be used to make decisions. For example, a local bank looked at the cost of providing basic checking account services to students. On the face of it, these accounts were losing money; that is, the accounts cost more to service than they yielded in fees and interest revenue. However, the bank then evaluated the closely related student loan business and found that students already banking there were more likely to take out one of its student loans. These loans were very profitable. The bank eventually decided to expand its offerings to students. Now, let's define "cost" and more fully describe its managerial importance.

OBJECTIVE 1

Explain the meaning of cost and how costs are assigned to products and services.

Cost

Cost is the amount of cash or cash equivalent sacrificed for goods and/or services that are expected to bring a current or future benefit to the organization. Suppose a wood furniture manufacturer buys lumber for $10,000; then the cost of that lumber is $10,000 cash. Sometimes, one asset is traded for another asset. In this case, the cost of the new asset is measured by the value of the asset given up (the cash equivalent). For example, suppose that the same manufacturer trades office equipment valued at $8,000 for a forklift; then the cost of the forklift is the $8,000 value of the office equipment traded for it. Cost is a dollar measure of the resources used to achieve a given benefit. Managers strive to minimize the cost of achieving benefits. Reducing the cost required to achieve a given benefit means that a firm is becoming more efficient.

Costs are incurred to produce future benefits. In a profit-making firm, those benefits usually mean revenues. As costs are used up in the production of revenues, they are said to expire. Expired costs are called **expenses**. On the income statement, expenses are deducted from revenues to determine income (also called profit). For a company to remain in business, revenues must be larger than expenses. In addition, the income earned must be large enough to satisfy the firm's owners.

We can look more closely at the relationship between cost and revenue by focusing on the units sold. The revenue per unit is called **price**. In everyday conversations, we tend to use *cost* and *price* as synonyms because the price of an item, say a CD, is the cost to us. However, accounting courses view such terms from a company owner's perspective. In that case, cost and price are *not* the same. Price must be greater than cost in order for the firm to earn income. Hence, managers need to know cost and trends in cost.

Accumulating and Assigning Costs

Accumulating costs is the way that costs are measured and recorded. The accounting system does this job quite well. When a telephone bill comes into the company, the bookkeeper records an addition to the telephone expense account and an addition to the liability account, Accounts Payable. In this way, the cost is *accumulated*. It would be easy to tell, at the end of the year, what the total spending on telephone expense was. Accumulating costs tells the company what was spent. However, that usually is not enough information. The company also wants to know why the money was spent. In other words, it wants to know how costs are assigned to cost objects.

Assigning costs involves the way that a cost is linked to some cost object. A cost object is simply something for which a company wants to know the cost. For example, of the total telephone expense, how much was for the sales department, and how much was for manufacturing? Assigning costs tells the company why the money was spent. In this case, cost assignment tells whether the money spent on telephone expense was to support making the product or selling it.

HERE'S THE REAL KICKER

Kicker collects and analyzes many types of costs. In the manufacturing area, the company keeps track of direct materials, direct labor, and overhead. These costs, of course, make up the cost of goods sold that goes on Kicker's monthly income statement. Nonmanufacturing costs include the costs of marketing and administration. However, this information is decomposed into a series of accounts that helps Kicker's management in budgeting and decision making.

The marketing function, for example, is broken down into three areas: selling, customer service, and marketing. Selling works directly with dealers and outside sales representatives. Customer service handles calls from dealers and decides whether or not a problem is covered under warranty. Marketing is responsible for advertising, promotions, and tent shows. One of the largest marketing events is Kicker's annual Big Air Bash, an extravaganza of music, food, cars, and extreme sports demonstrations. Held in conjunction with the Specialty Equipment Market Association (SEMA) show, the Big Air Bash is held outside the Hard Rock Hotel and Casino in Las Vegas. The expenses associated with the show include the modification of show cars in Kicker's in-house garage. For the 2004 Big Bash, Kicker mechanics customized a new Dodge Neon. The trunk and back seat area were virtually gutted to make room for 12 speakers and heavy-duty amps. With a souped-up engine, new fiberglass exterior, and trick paint, the car was ready for show. Other "veteran" show cars and pickup trucks were refreshed with additional trick paint, larger tires, and Kicker's newest amps and speakers. You can feel the music from outside the truck.

Tent shows are smaller scale affairs held several times a year in the central and south-central United States. Kicker brings its semitrailer full of products and sound equipment, as well as a couple of show trucks. Then, a large tent is set up to sell Kicker merchandise, explain products, and sell at greatly reduced prices the previous year's models. Fun and relaxed, the tent shows appeal to Kicker's customer base and provide a chance for a look at the new models. The cost of each tent show is carefully tracked and compared with that show's revenue. Sites that don't provide sales revenue greater than cost are not booked for the coming year.

Like many companies today, Kicker tracks costs carefully for use in decision making. The general cost categories in Chapter 2 help the company to organize cost information and relate it to decision making.

Cost Objects

Management accounting systems are structured to measure and assign costs to entities called *cost objects*. A **cost object** is any item such as products, customers, departments, regions, and so on, for which costs are measured and assigned. For example, if a bank wants to determine the cost of a platinum credit card, then the cost object is the platinum credit card. All costs related to the platinum card are added in, such as the cost of mailings to potential customers, the cost of telephone lines dedicated to the card, the portion of the computer department that processes platinum card transactions and bills, and so on. In a more personal example, suppose that you are considering taking a course during the summer session. Taking the course is the cost object, and the cost would include tuition, books, fees, transportation, and (possibly) housing. Notice that you could also include the foregone earnings from a summer job, and that would be an opportunity cost. (The concept of opportunity cost will be discussed more fully in Chapter 12.)

Assigning Costs to Cost Objects

Costs can be assigned to cost objects in a number of ways. Relatively speaking, some methods are more accurate and others are quite simple. Our choice of method depends on a number of factors such as the need for accuracy. The notion of accuracy is not evaluated based on knowledge of some underlying "true" cost. Rather, it is a relative concept and has to do with the reasonableness and logic of the cost assignment methods used. The objective is to measure and assign costs as well as possible, given management objectives. For example, suppose you and three of your good friends go out to dinner at a local pizza parlor. When the bill comes, everything has been added together for a total of $36. How much is your share? One easy way to figure out is to divide the bill evenly among you and your friends. In that case, you each owe $9 ($36/4). But suppose that one of you had a small salad and drink (totaling $5), while another had a specialty pizza, appetizer, and beer (totaling $15). Clearly, it is possible to identify what each person had and assign cost that way. The second method is more accurate but also more work. Which method you choose will depend on how important it is to you to assign the specific meal costs to each individual. It is the same way in accounting. A number of ways can be used to assign costs to products, customers, and so on. Some methods are quick and easy but may be inaccurate. Other methods are far more accurate but also involve much more work (in business, more work equals more expense).

Tracing Direct Costs

Costs are directly or indirectly associated with cost objects. **Direct costs** are those costs that can be easily and accurately traced to a cost object. When we say that a cost is easy to trace, we often mean that the relationship between the cost and the object can be physically observed and is thus easy to track. The more costs that can be traced to the object, the more accurate are the cost assignments. For example, suppose that Courtney, from the opening scenario, wanted to know the cost of emphasizing fresh, in-season fruits and vegetables in her entrees. The purchase cost of the fruits and vegetables would be relatively easy to determine. Some costs, however, are hard to trace. **Indirect costs** are costs that cannot be easily and accurately traced to a cost object. For example, Courtney incurs additional costs in scouting the outlying farms and farmers' markets (as opposed to simply ordering fruits and vegetables from a distributor). She must use her own time and automobile to make the trips. Farmers' markets may not deliver so Courtney must arrange for a coworker with a van to pick up the produce. By definition, fruits and vegetables that are currently in season, will be out of season (i.e., unavailable) in a few weeks. This means that Courtney must spend much more time revising menus and developing new recipes that can be adapted to restaurant conditions. In addition, waste and spoilage may increase until Courtney and the kitchen staff learn just how much to order. These costs are difficult to assign to the meals prepared and sold. Therefore, they are indirect costs. Exhibit 2-1 shows direct and indirect costs being assigned to cost objects.

Object Costing

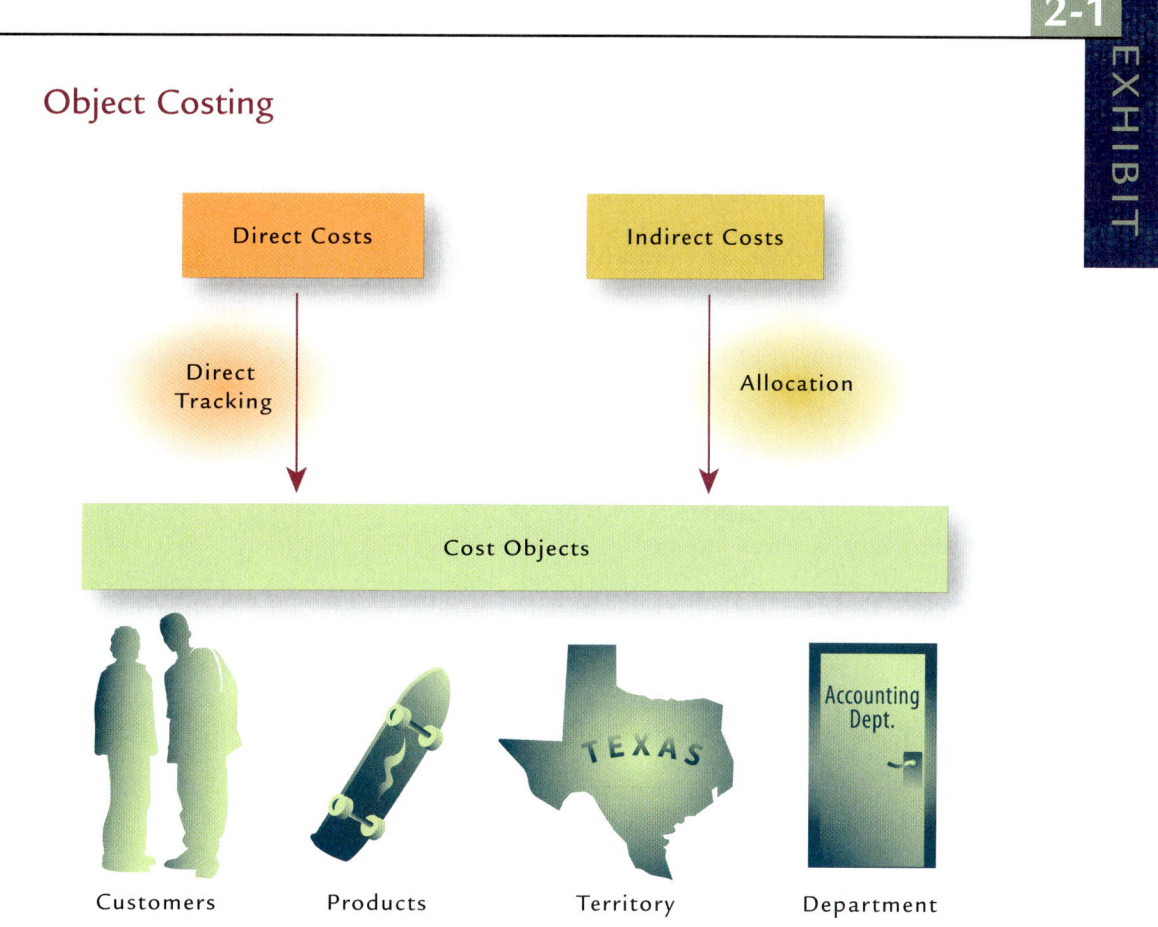

Assigning Indirect Costs

Assigning Indirect Costs

Even though indirect costs cannot be traced to cost objects, it is still important to assign them. This is usually done using allocation. **Allocation** means that an indirect cost is assigned to a cost object using a reasonable and convenient method. Since no causal relationship exists, allocating indirect costs is based on convenience or some assumed linkage. For example, consider the cost of heating and lighting a plant in which five products are manufactured. Suppose that this utility cost is to be assigned to the five products. Clearly, it is difficult to see any causal relationship. A convenient way to allocate this cost is simply to assign it in proportion to the direct labor hours used by each product. This is relatively easy and accomplishes the purpose of ensuring that all costs are assigned to units produced. Allocating indirect costs may be important for a variety of purposes. For example, allocating indirect costs to products is needed to determine the value of inventory and cost of goods sold.

Direct and indirect costs occur in service businesses as well. For example, a bank's cost of printing and mailing monthly statements to checking account holders is a direct cost of the product—checking accounts. However, the cost of office furniture in the bank is an indirect cost for the checking accounts.

Other Categories of Cost

We will further discuss other categories of costs in later chapters including variable costs, fixed costs, and opportunity costs. A **variable cost** is one that increases as output increases and decreases as output decreases. For example, the denim used in making jeans is a variable cost. As the company makes more jeans, it needs more denim. A **fixed cost** is a cost that does not increase as output increases and does not decrease as output decreases. For example, the cost of property taxes on the factory building stays the same no matter how many pairs of jeans the company makes. Some of you might be wondering how that can be since property taxes can change. They can and do change, but not because output changes. Rather, it is because the city or county government decides to raise taxes. Variable and fixed costs are covered more extensively in Chapter 3.

An **opportunity cost** is the benefit given up or sacrificed when one alternative is chosen over another. For example, an opportunity cost of your being in accounting class may be the wages you would have earned during that time if you were working rather than going to school. Opportunity cost differs from accounting costs in that the opportunity cost is never included in the accounting records—because it is the cost of something that did not occur. Opportunity costs are important to decision making, and we will see that more clearly in Chapter 12.

We will discuss various methods of assigning costs to cost objects in the succeeding chapters.

> ## Concept Q & A
>
> Make a list of the costs you are incurring for your classes this term. Which costs are direct costs for your college course(s)? Which costs are indirect? Now, from your list of total costs, which ones are direct costs of this course? Which are indirect?
>
> **Answers will vary.**

PRODUCT AND SERVICE COSTS

> **OBJECTIVE 2**
>
> Define the various costs of producing products and services, as well as the costs of selling and administration.

The output of organizations represents one of the most important cost objects. There are two types of output: tangible products and services. **Tangible products** are goods produced by converting raw materials through the use of labor and capital inputs, such as plant, land, and machinery. Televisions, hamburgers, automobiles, computers, clothes, and furniture are examples of tangible products. **Services** are tasks or activities performed for a customer or an activity performed by a customer using an organization's products or facilities. Services are also produced using materials, labor, and capital inputs. Insurance coverage, medical care, dental care, funeral care, and accounting are examples of service activities performed for customers. Car rental, video rental, and skiing are examples of services where the customer uses an organization's products or facilities.

Services differ from tangible products in a number of ways. First, of course, a service is intangible. The buyer of services cannot see, feel, hear, or taste a service before it is bought. Second, services are perishable; they cannot be stored for future use by a consumer but must be consumed when performed. Inventory valuation, so important for tangible products, is not an issue for services. Third, producers of services and buyers of services must usually be in direct contact for an exchange to take place. For example, an eye examination requires both the patient and the optometrist to be present. However, producers of tangible products need not have direct contact with the buyers of their goods. Thus, buyers of automobiles never need to have contact with the engineers and assembly line workers that produced their automobiles. Finally, there is a greater chance of variation in the performance of services than in the production of products. Service workers can be affected by the job undertaken, the mix of other individuals with whom they work, their education and experience, and personal factors such as home life. These factors make providing a consistent level of service more difficult. The measurement of productivity and quality in a service company must be ongoing and sensitive to these factors.

APPLICATIONS IN BUSINESS

Hospitals are service organizations that need much more detailed information costs now than they once did. One large Oklahoma medical center, for example, has detailed data on the costs of every procedure done in the hospital. A knowledge of costs by procedure is necessary so that the hospital can negotiate with insurance companies. For example, a cardiac catheterization procedure is relatively profitable (the price charged exceeds the cost).

Knowing this, the vice president in charge of negotiating with insurance companies and HMOs has the flexibility to reduce the price on this procedure. He does not have this flexibility for physical therapy, which is already priced such that price equals cost.

This example comes from the authors' personal interviews with controllers of large service and manufacturing firms.

Organizations that produce tangible products are called **manufacturing organizations**. Those that produce intangible products are called **service organizations**. Managers of both types of organizations need to know how much individual products cost. Accurate product costs are vital for profitability analysis and strategic decisions concerning product design, pricing, and product mix.

The ways in which services differ from tangible products can affect the types of information needed for planning, controlling, and decision making. As we run across those differences in succeeding chapters, we will point them out. For now, however, the overall way in which a company costs services is very similar to the way in which it costs products. The main difference in costing is that tangible products often have inventories and services do not.

Determining Product Cost

When companies provide cost information for outside parties, external reporting rules require that costs be classified in terms of the special purposes, or functions, they serve. Costs are subdivided into two major functional categories: production and nonproduction. **Product (manufacturing) costs** are those costs associated with the manufacture of goods or the provision of services. A key feature of product costs is that they can be inventoried. In fact, product costs are initially added to an inventory account and remain in inventory until they are sold. Exhibit 2-2 shows how direct materials, direct labor, and overhead become product costs.

All other costs, called nonproduction costs, are associated with designing, developing, marketing, and distributing the product, as well as customer service and general administration. The costs of marketing, distribution, and customer service are often placed into one general category called *selling costs*.

The costs of designing, developing, and general administration are placed into a second general category called *administrative costs*. For tangible goods, production and nonproduction costs are often referred to as *manufacturing costs* and *nonmanufacturing costs*, respectively. Production costs can be further classified as direct materials, direct labor, and overhead. Only these three cost elements can be assigned to products for external financial reporting.

Direct Materials

Direct materials are those materials that are a part of the final product and can be directly traced to the goods or services being produced. The cost of these materials can be directly charged to products because physical observation can be used to measure the quantity used by each product. Materials that become part of a tangible product or those that are used in providing a service are usually classified as direct materials. For example, tires on a new automobile, wood in a dining room table, alcohol in

Product Costs Include Direct Materials, Direct Labor, and Overhead

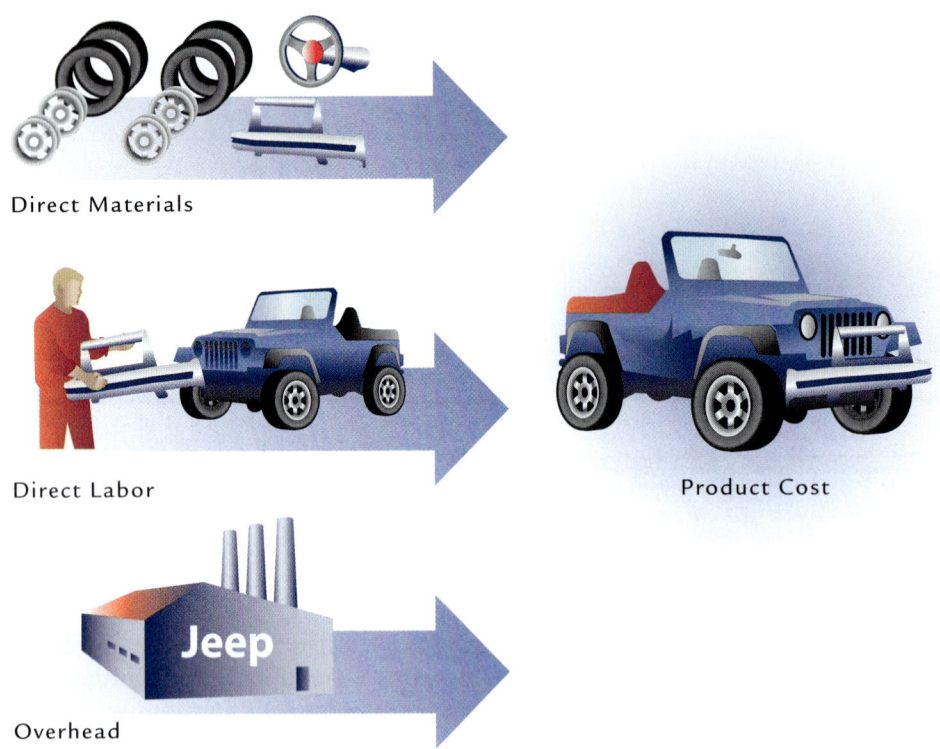

Direct Materials

Direct Labor

Overhead

Product Cost

cologne, and denim in jeans are all part of direct materials for manufacturers of these products. Service companies also recognize direct materials. For example, a surgical center would show that surgical gauze and anesthesia are direct materials used for an operation; a beauty shop would consider shampoo and scrunching gel direct costs of hair styling.

A closely related term is *raw materials*, and the inventory of materials is often called the *raw materials account*. Materials in that account do not become *direct materials* until they are withdrawn from inventory for use in production. The inventory of the raw materials account may include both direct and indirect materials. Indirect materials are included in overhead and will be discussed further in that section.

Direct Labor

Direct labor is the labor that can be directly traced to the goods or services being produced. Physical observation can be used to measure the amount of labor used to produce a product or service. Those employees who convert direct materials into a product or who provide a service to customers are classified as direct labor. Workers on an assembly line at Dell Computers are classified as direct labor, as are a chef in a restaurant, a surgical nurse attending an open-heart operation, and a pilot for Southwest Airlines.

Classifying all workers who actually make the product or service simplifies the accounting. Then, the total labor can be expressed in direct labor hours. So, a computer manufacturer's employees may include assembly workers, hardware testing and software loading workers, and packaging workers. The contribution of all of these groups to the final product can be added together as total direct labor hours.

Just as there were indirect materials in a company, there may also be indirect labor. This labor is not direct labor since these workers do not actually perform the service or make the product. Indirect labor is included in overhead.

Overhead

All product costs other than direct materials and direct labor are put into one category called **overhead**. In a manufacturing firm, overhead is also known as *factory burden* or *manufacturing overhead*. The overhead cost category contains a wide variety of items. Many inputs other than direct labor and direct materials are needed to provide services and produce products. Examples of costs included in overhead are depreciation on buildings and equipment, janitorial and maintenance labor, supplies, supervision, materials handling, power, property taxes, landscaping of factory grounds, security for the factory, and the rental of a Santa suit for the annual factory Christmas party. The important thing to remember is that all costs in the factory are classified as direct materials, direct labor, or overhead. No cost can be omitted from classification, no matter how far removed you might think it is from the actual production of a product (e.g., hotdogs for the factory's summer cookout).

Earlier, we mentioned that indirect materials and indirect labor are included in overhead. Indirect materials can include supplies as well as certain direct materials that are such a small part of the overall product or service that they do not warrant the effort to account for them as direct materials. **Supplies** are generally those materials necessary for production that do not become part of the finished product or are not used in providing a service. Dishwasher detergent in a fast-food restaurant and oil to lubricate manufacturing equipment are examples of supplies. Direct materials that form an insignificant part of the final product are usually lumped into the overhead category as a special kind of indirect material. This is justified on the basis of cost and convenience. The cost of the tracing is greater than the benefit of increased accuracy. In manufacturing, the glue used in furniture or toys is an example, as is the cost of oil to grease cookie sheets. In service companies, insignificant amounts of some direct materials are also treated as overhead. For example, paper used by a law firm to file briefs or court documents may well be treated as overhead.

Indirect labor is also part of overhead. For example, lawyers in a law firm are direct labor because they actually provide the service for which clients pay. The receptionist, however, does not provide legal services and would be considered overhead. Similarly, suppose that the paralegals spend 75 percent of their time researching law books and LEXIS/NEXIS (an online legal reference) for particular cases and the remaining 25 percent ordering supplies and performing other duties designed to make the office function more smoothly. Then, 75 percent of their salaries would be direct labor, and the remaining 25 percent would be overhead (indirect labor).

Concept Q & A

Look up and focus on any object in the room. What do you think the direct materials might include? What kind of direct labor might have worked on that item? Finally, what types of overhead costs might have been incurred by the company that produced it?

Answers will vary.

Total Product Cost

The total cost of providing a service or producing a product is the sum of direct materials, direct labor, and manufacturing overhead. The unit cost is simply the total product cost divided by the number of units.

Product costs include direct materials, direct labor, and overhead. Once the product is finished, no more costs attach to it. That is, any costs associated with storing, selling, and delivering the product are not product costs. We will cover them shortly in the section on period costs. Cornerstone 2-1 shows how to calculate total product cost and per-unit product cost.

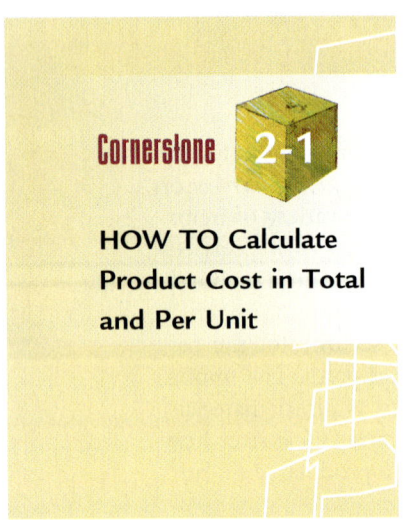

Cornerstone 2-1

HOW TO Calculate Product Cost in Total and Per Unit

Information: BlueDenim Company makes blue jeans. Last week, direct materials (denim, thread, zippers, and rivets) costing $48,000 were put into production. Direct labor of $30,000 (50 workers × 40 hours × $15 per hour) was incurred. Overhead equaled $72,000. By the end of the week, the company had manufactured 30,000 pairs of jeans.

Required: Calculate the total product cost for last week. Calculate the cost of one pair of jeans that was produced last week.

Calculation:

Direct materials	$ 48,000
Direct labor	30,000
Overhead	72,000
Total product cost	$150,000

Per-unit product cost = $150,000/30,000 = $5

Therefore, one pair of jeans costs $5 to produce.

Prime and Conversion Costs

Product costs of direct materials, direct labor, and overhead are sometimes grouped into prime cost and conversion cost. **Prime cost** is the sum of direct materials cost and direct labor cost. **Conversion cost** is the sum of direct labor cost and overhead cost. For a manufacturing firm, conversion cost can be interpreted as the cost of converting raw materials into a final product. Cornerstone 2-2 shows how to calculate prime cost and conversion cost for a manufactured product.

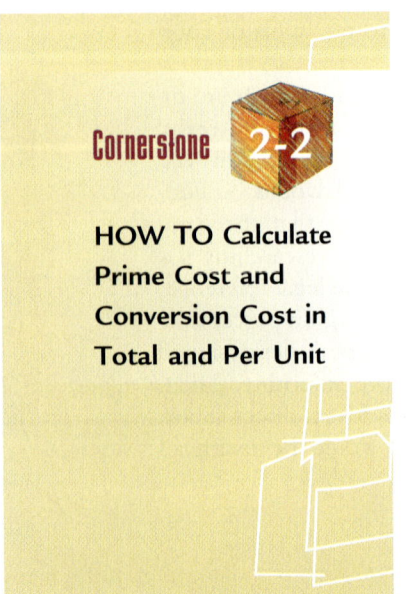

Cornerstone 2-2

HOW TO Calculate Prime Cost and Conversion Cost in Total and Per Unit

Information: BlueDenim Company makes blue jeans. Last week, direct materials (denim, thread, zippers, and rivets) costing $48,000 were put into production. Direct labor of $30,000 (50 workers × 40 hours × $15 per hour) was incurred. Overhead equaled $72,000. By the end of the week, the company had manufactured 30,000 pairs of jeans.

Required: Calculate the total prime cost for last week. Calculate the per-unit prime cost. Calculate the total conversion cost for last week. Calculate the per-unit conversion cost.

Calculation:

Direct materials	$48,000
Direct labor	30,000
Total prime cost	$78,000

Per-unit prime cost = $78,000/30,000 = $2.60

Direct labor	$ 30,000
Overhead	72,000
Total conversion cost	$102,000

Per-unit conversion cost = $102,000/30,000 = $3.40

Note: Remember that prime cost and conversion cost do NOT total product cost. This is because direct labor is part of BOTH prime cost and conversion cost.

Service firms may be particularly interested in dividing product cost into direct materials and conversion cost. This is because, many times, the same workers are both direct labor and indirect labor. The work involved in separating direct from indirect labor may not be worth the time involved. For example, suppose that beauticians in a beauty shop cut, color, and style hair (direct labor) and they also answer the phone and make appointments for each other (indirect labor). Including this labor in conversion cost may well satisfy the decision-making needs of the shop owner. Similarly, manufacturing plants that have set up cells devoted to the production of one product from start to finish find that the cell labor not only assembles and finishes the product, but it also performs routine maintenance on manufacturing equipment and cleans the cell. Here again, classifying cell labor in conversion cost may be the best approach.

Analytical Q & A

A company produced and sold 1,000 units last month. Direct materials totaled $4,000, direct labor totaled $5,000, and overhead amounted to $10,000. (1) What is total prime cost for last month? (2) What is conversion cost per unit?

Answer:
(1) Total prime cost = Direct materials + Direct labor
                    = $4,000 + $5,000 = $9,000
(2) Conversion cost per unit = (Direct labor + Overhead)/Number of units
                    = ($5,000 + $10,000)/1,000 = $15

Period Costs

Product costs are carried in inventory until the goods are sold. However, certain other costs of running a company are not carried in inventory. These are called *selling costs* and *administrative costs*. For external financial reporting, selling and administrative costs are called *period costs*. **Period costs** are expensed in the period in which they are incurred; they are not inventoried. Thus, none of these costs can be assigned to products or appear as part of the reported values of inventories on the balance sheet. In a manufacturing organization, the level of these costs can be significant (often greater than 25 percent of sales revenue), and controlling them may bring greater cost savings than the same effort exercised in controlling production costs. For example, firms that develop, market, produce, and deliver software often find that the bulk of their costs are in development and marketing. Producing CD-ROMs or making the software available for download over the Internet accounts for very little cost. As a result, most of the cost control activity is exercised over period costs. For service organizations, the relative importance of selling and administrative costs depends on the nature of the service produced. Physicians and dentists, for example, do relatively little marketing and thus have very low selling costs. On the other hand, a grocery chain may incur substantial marketing costs.

Selling Costs

Those costs necessary to market, distribute, and service a product or service are **selling (marketing) costs**. They are often referred to as *order-getting* and *order-filling* costs. Examples of selling costs include salaries and commissions of sales personnel, advertising, warehousing, shipping, and customer service. The first two items are examples of order-getting costs; the last three are order-filling costs.

Sometimes, the same cost can be counted as production or selling cost depending on the function that is served. Going back to the opening scenario, Courtney expanded the dessert menu. Each afternoon, to entice customers to order dessert, she prepares one serving of each dessert and arranges them on a dessert cart to be presented to customers at the end of the meal. After three or four hours on the dessert cart, the dessert samples are not edible. The cost of the sample desserts would be marketing expense, not production, because they are not sold to customers.

Administrative Costs

All costs associated with research, development, and general administration of the organization that cannot reasonably be assigned to either selling or production are **administrative costs**. General administration has the responsibility of ensuring that the various activities of the organization are properly integrated so that the overall mission of the firm is realized. The president of the firm, for example, is concerned with the efficiency of selling, production, and research and development activities. Proper integration of these activities is essential to maximizing the overall profits of a firm. Examples of general administrative costs are top executive salaries, legal fees, expenses of printing the annual report, and general accounting. Research and development costs are the costs associated with designing and developing new products.

APPLICATIONS IN BUSINESS

© GEORGE HALL/CORBIS

Given the deep financial trouble many airlines are in, you might wonder just how they actually spend their money. The Air Transport Association (ATA), which represents most U.S. air carriers, has kept track of overall expenses by cost category since 1978. In mid-2002, the ATA reported airline spending in a number of categories as a percentage of total operating expenses. For example, food accounts for 2.3 percent of operating expenses. So there is some potential for decreasing food expense but not much. (If you have flown recently, you are probably surprised that the percentage was even that high!) Interestingly, airlines spend even less on travel agent commissions than food. Fuel costs 11.6 percent, down from 1986, when fuel was 15.5 percent of operating cost. While fuel costs vary with the price of oil, the long-term reduction in fuel cost is partially due to the introduction of more fuel-efficient planes. The biggest expense category is labor. It accounts for nearly 40 percent of operating cost, but some of that amount applies to clerical staff and management. Basically, what we can see from this is that much expense has been cut from the selling and administrative expenses. The largest amount is labor, and that is where most airlines are focusing their cost-cutting efforts.

Source: Scott McCartney, "Which Costs Airlines More: Fuel, Labor or (Ugh) Meals?" The Middle Seat, *The Wall Street Journal Online* (November 5, 2002).

PREPARING INCOME STATEMENTS

OBJECTIVE 3
Prepare income statements for manufacturing and service organizations.

The definitions given earlier of product, selling, and administrative costs are a good overview of the concepts of these costs. However, actually figuring these costs in practice is a bit more complicated. Let's take a closer look at just how costs are calculated for purposes of preparing the external financial statements.

Cost of Goods Manufactured

The **cost of goods manufactured** represents the total product cost of goods completed during the current period. The only costs assigned to goods completed are the manufacturing costs of direct materials, direct labor, and overhead. So, why don't we just add the costs of direct materials, direct labor, and overhead? The reason is, quite simply, inventories. These can be inventories of materials or work in process.

Let's take a look at direct materials. Suppose a company had no materials on hand at the beginning of the month, bought $15,000 of direct materials during the month, and used all of them in production. Then the entire $15,000 would be properly called direct materials. Usually, though, the company does have some materials on hand at the beginning of the month. These materials are the beginning inventory of materials. Let's say that this beginning inventory of materials cost $2,500. During the month, the company would have a total of $17,500 of materials that could be used in production ($2,500 from beginning inventory and $15,000 purchased during the month). Typically, the company would not use the entire amount of materials on hand in production. Perhaps only $12,000 of materials is used. Then, the cost of direct materials is $12,000, and the remaining $5,500 of materials is the ending inventory of materials. This reasoning can be easily expressed in a formula.

$$\begin{array}{c}\text{Beginning} \\ \text{inventory} \\ \text{of materials}\end{array} + \text{Purchases} - \begin{array}{c}\text{Direct materials} \\ \text{used in production}\end{array} = \begin{array}{c}\text{Ending inventory} \\ \text{of materials}\end{array}$$

While the above computation is logical and simple, it does not express the result for which we are usually looking. We are usually trying to figure out the amount of direct materials used in production, not the amount of ending inventory. Cornerstone 2-3 shows how to compute the amount of direct materials used in production.

Cornerstone 2-3

HOW TO Calculate the Direct Materials Used in Production

Information: BlueDenim Company makes blue jeans. On May 1, BlueDenim had $68,000 of materials in inventory. During the month of May, the company purchased $210,000 of materials. On May 31, materials inventory equaled $22,000.
Required: Calculate the direct materials used in production for the month of May.
Calculation:

Materials inventory, May 1	$ 68,000
Purchases	210,000
Materials inventory, May 31	(22,000)
Direct materials used in production	$256,000

Once the direct materials are calculated, the direct labor and overhead for the time period can be added to get the total manufacturing cost for the period. Now we need to consider the second type of inventory—work in process. **Work in process (WIP)** is the cost of the partially completed goods that are still on the factory floor at the end of a time period. These units have been started but not finished. They have value but not as much as they will when they are done. Just as there are beginning and ending inventories of materials, there are beginning and ending inventories of WIP. We must adjust the total manufacturing cost for the time period for the inventories of WIP. When that is done, we will have the total cost of the goods that were completed during the time period. Cornerstone 2-4 shows how to calculate the cost of goods manufactured for a particular time period.

Cornerstone 2-4

HOW TO Calculate Cost of Goods Manufactured

Information: Recall that BlueDenim Company makes blue jeans. During the month of May, the company purchased $210,000 of materials. On May 31, materials inventory equaled $22,000. During the month of May, BlueDenim Company incurred direct labor cost of $135,000 and overhead of $150,000. Inventory information is as follows:

	May 1	May 31
Materials	$68,000	$22,000
Work in process	50,000	16,000

Required: Calculate the cost of goods manufactured for the month of May. Calculate the cost of one pair of jeans assuming that 115,000 pairs of jeans were completed during May.

Calculation:

Direct materials*	$256,000
Direct labor	135,000
Overhead	150,000
Total manufacturing cost for May	$541,000
Work in process, May 1	50,000
Work in process, May 31	(16,000)
Cost of goods manufactured	$575,000

*Direct materials = $68,000 + $210,000 − $22,000 = $256,000
This was calculated in Cornerstone 2-3.

Per-unit cost of goods manufactured = $575,000/115,000 units = $5

We are almost ready to prepare the income statement for the manufacturing firm. To meet external reporting requirements, costs must be classified into three categories: production, selling, and administration. Remember that product costs are initially put into inventory. They become expenses only when the products are sold. Therefore, the expense of manufacturing is not the cost of goods manufactured; rather, it is the cost of the goods that are sold. **Cost of goods sold** is the total product cost (direct materials, direct labor, and overhead) for the units sold during a period. Cornerstone 2-5 shows how to calculate the cost of goods sold.

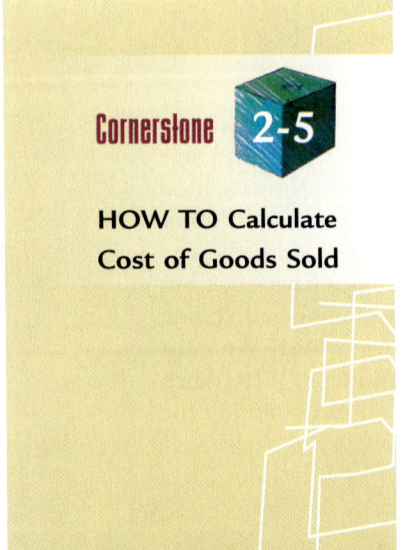

Cornerstone 2-5

HOW TO Calculate Cost of Goods Sold

Information: Recall that BlueDenim Company makes blue jeans. During the month of May, 115,000 pairs of jeans were completed at a cost of goods manufactured of $575,000. Suppose that on May 1 BlueDenim had 10,000 units in finished goods inventory costing $50,000, and on May 31 the company had 26,000 units in finished goods inventory costing $130,000.

Required: Calculate the cost of goods sold for the month of May. Calculate the number of pairs of jeans that were sold during May.

Calculation:

Cost of goods manufactured	$575,000
Finished goods inventory, May 1	50,000
Finished goods inventory, May 31	(130,000)
Cost of goods sold	$495,000

Number of units sold:	
Finished goods inventory, May 1	10,000
Units finished during May	115,000
Finished goods inventory, May 31	(26,000)
Units sold during May	99,000

The ending inventories of materials, WIP, and finished goods are important because they are assets and appear on the balance sheet (as current assets). The cost of goods sold is an expense, and it appears on the income statement. Selling and administrative costs are also on the income statement. They are period costs and are expensed in the period incurred.

Income Statement: Manufacturing Firm

The income statement for a manufacturing firm is displayed in Cornerstone 2-6. This income statement follows the traditional format taught in an introductory financial accounting course. Notice that the income statement covers a certain period of time. In Cornerstone 2-6, that time period is a month, the month of May. However, the time period may well be a quarter or a year. The key point is that all sales revenue and expenses attached to that period of time appear on the income statement.

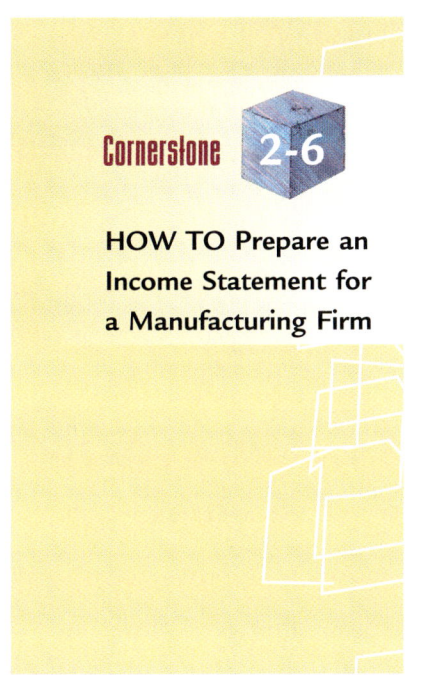

Cornerstone 2-6

HOW TO Prepare an Income Statement for a Manufacturing Firm

Information: Recall that BlueDenim Company sold 99,000 pairs of jeans during the month of May at a total cost of $495,000. Each pair sold at a price of $8. BlueDenim also incurred two types of selling costs: commissions equal to 10 percent of the sales price and other selling expense of $120,000. Administrative expense totaled $85,000.
Required: Prepare an income statement for BlueDenim for the month of May.
Calculation:

BlueDenim Company
Income Statement
For the Month of May

Sales revenue (99,000 × $8)		$792,000
Cost of goods sold		495,000
Gross margin		$297,000
Less:		
Selling expense:		
Commissions (0.10 × $792,000)	$ 79,200	
Fixed selling expense	120,000	199,200
Administrative expense		85,000
Operating income		$ 12,800

Let's take a closer look at the income statement in Cornerstone 2-6. First, the heading tells us what type of statement it is, for what firm, and for what period of time. Then, the income statement itself always begins with "sales revenue" (or "sales" or "revenue"). The sales revenue is simply the price multiplied by the units sold. After the sales revenue is determined, the firm must calculate expenses for the period.

Notice that the expenses are indeed separated into three categories: production (cost of goods sold), selling, and administrative. The first type of expense is the cost of producing the units sold, or the cost of goods sold. This amount was computed and explained in Cornerstone 2-5. Remember that the cost of goods sold is the cost of producing the units that were sold during the time period. It includes direct materials, direct labor, and overhead. It does *not* include any selling or administrative expenses. In the case of a retail firm, the cost of goods sold is simply the total cost of the units sold when they were purchased from an outside supplier.

Gross margin is the difference between sales revenue and cost of goods sold. It shows how much the firm is making over and above the cost of the units sold. Gross margin does *not* equal operating income or profit. Selling and administrative expenses have not been subtracted yet. However, gross margin does give useful information. If gross margin is positive, we know that the firm at least charges prices that cover the product cost. In addition, the firm can figure its gross margin percentage (see Cornerstone 2-7) and compare it with the average gross margin percentage for the industry to see if its experience is in the ballpark with other firms in the industry.

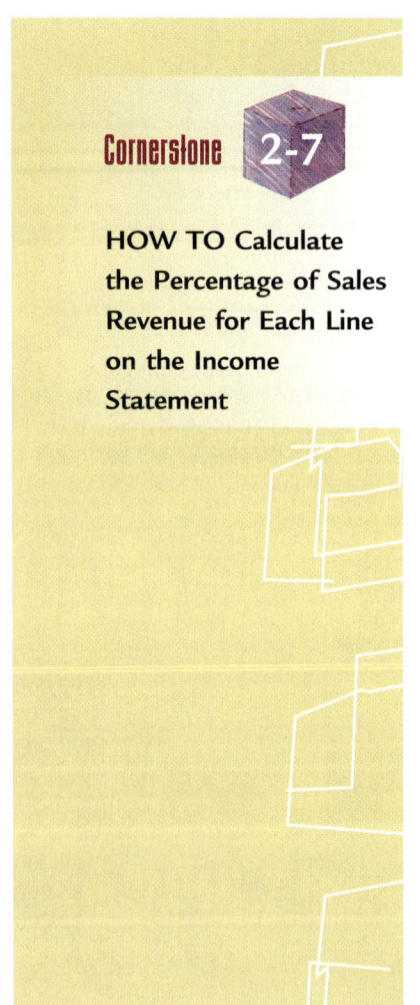

Cornerstone 2-7

HOW TO Calculate the Percentage of Sales Revenue for Each Line on the Income Statement

Information: Recall that BlueDenim Company's income statement for the month of May was shown in Cornerstone 2-6.

Required: Calculate the percentage of sales revenue represented by each line of the income statement.

Calculation:

BlueDenim Company
Income Statement
For the Month of May

			Percent*
Sales revenue (99,000 × $8)		$792,000	100.0%
Cost of goods sold		495,000	62.5
Gross margin		$297,000	37.5%
Less:			
Selling expense:			
Commissions (0.10 × $792,000)	$ 79,200		
Fixed selling expense	120,000	199,200	25.2
Administrative expense		85,000	10.7
Operating income		$ 12,800	1.6%

*Steps in calculating the percentages:

1. Sales revenue percent = $792,000/$792,000 = 1.00, or 100% (sales revenue is always 100% of sales revenue).
2. Cost of goods sold percent = $495,000/$792,000 = 0.625, or 62.5%.
3. Gross margin percent = $297,000/$792,000 = 0.375, or 37.5%.
4. Selling expense percent = $199,200/$792,000 = 0.252, or 25.2% (this has been rounded).
5. Administrative expense percent = $85,000/$792,000 = 0.107, or 10.7% (this has been rounded).
6. Operating income expense percent = $12,800/$792,000 = 0.016, or 1.6% (this has been rounded).

Finally, selling expense and administrative expense for the period are determined and subtracted from gross margin to get operating income. This is the key figure from the income statement; it is profit and shows how much the owners are actually earning from the company. Again, calculating the percentage of operating income and comparing it to the average for the industry gives the owners valuable information about relative profitability.

Analytical Q & A

Suppose your friend, Ted, mentions that Nordstrom's department store marks up sweaters by 100 percent. "Wow," said Ted, "That means a sweater that costs them $25 is sold for $50. They're making $25 in profit!" Is the $25 markup profit (operating income)? Refer to the income statement from Cornerstone 2-7. What line would include the $50 price of the sweater? What line would include the $25 original cost (to the store) of the sweater? What line would include the $25 that is over and above the cost?

Answer:
No, the $25 markup is not operating income. The $50 price is included in revenue; the $25 original cost is included in cost of goods sold; and the $25 over and above the cost to the store is in gross margin.

We have seen that the income statement can be analyzed further by calculating the percentage of sales revenue represented by each line of the statement. This was done in Cornerstone 2-7. How can management use this information? The first thing that jumps out is that operating income is less than 2 percent of sales revenue. That's a very small percentage! Unless this is common for the blue jeans manufacturing business, BlueDenim's management should work hard to increase the percentage. Selling expense is a whopping 25.2 percent of sales! Do commissions really need to be that high? Or, is the price too low (compared to competitors' prices)? Can cost of goods sold be reduced? Is 62.5 percent reasonable? These are questions that are suggested by Cornerstone 2-7, not answered. Answering the questions is the job of management.

Income Statement: Service Organization

In a service organization, the cost of services sold is typically just the materials, labor, and overhead used to provide the services sold. Since services cannot be stored, there are no beginning or ending finished goods inventories. Thus, in a direct comparison with manufacturing firms, cost of services sold would always correspond to cost of goods manufactured. An income statement for a service firm is shown in Cornerstone 2-8.

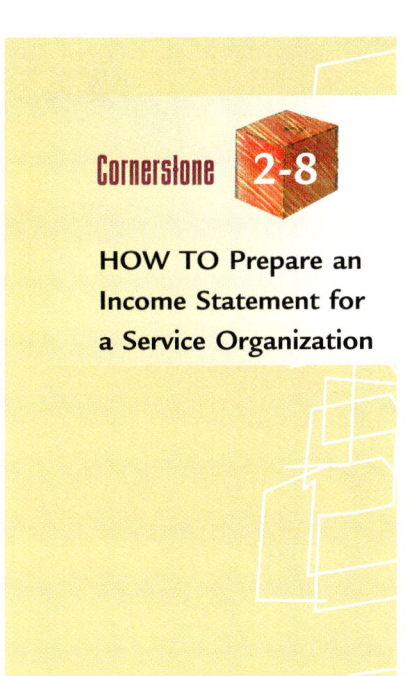

Cornerstone 2-8

HOW TO Prepare an Income Statement for a Service Organization

Information: Komala Information Systems designs and installs human resources software for small companies. Last month, Komala had materials costs of $5,000, direct labor (computer technicians, software designers) of $35,000, and overhead of $55,000. Selling expenses were $5,000, and administrative expenses equaled $7,000. Sales totaled $130,000.

Required: Prepare an income statement for Komala Information Systems for the past month.

Calculation:

Komala Information Systems		
Income Statement		
For the Past Month		
Sales		$130,000
Cost of services sold:		
Direct materials	$ 5,000	
Direct labor	35,000	
Overhead	55,000	95,000
Gross margin		$ 35,000
Less:		
Selling expenses		5,000
Administrative expenses		7,000
Operating income		$ 23,000

Recall that Courtney had to start keeping track of kitchen costs. What were the direct costs, indirect costs, prime costs, overhead, gross margin, and so on? Basically, the restaurant is a blend of production and service. The kitchen produces food. Therefore, the concepts of direct materials (food and supplies), direct labor (Courtney, the head chef, her sous-chefs, and clean-up labor), and overhead would apply. Courtney would have learned that rags, sponges, detergent, disinfectant, etc., would be part of overhead. Utilities to run the stoves and ovens, the depreciation on kitchen appliances and facilities, and the cost of the pots and pans would also be included in overhead.

Once she understood the basics of product costing, Courtney could use that information to consider new menu offerings. For example, she might decide to emphasize salmon entrees. Not only is salmon healthy (it is high in omega-3's and low in calories), but it is cheap. However, she might (regretfully) pass on the opportunity to offer an assortment of crème brulés, since they would require the purchase of special ovenproof individual-sized pots and another broiler. In that case, overhead would go up but would only be used for one type of dish.

Courtney could combine the information on costs with the menu price to see if the gross margin and gross margin percentage seemed reasonable compared to restaurant industry averages. In sum, she would be both an outstanding head chef and an excellent businesswoman.

SUMMARY OF LEARNING OBJECTIVES

Cost is the cash or cash-equivalent value sacrificed for goods and services that are expected to bring a current or future benefit to the organization. Managers and others are very interested in finding out what costs are assigned to cost objects such as products, projects, plants, and customers. Direct tracing is more accurate because it is based on cause-and-effect relationships. Direct tracing relies on physical observation to assign costs. Allocation relies on assumed relationships and convenience to assign costs.

Output can be tangible or intangible. Tangible products are goods that are produced by converting raw materials through the use of labor and capital inputs such as plant, land, and machinery. Services, or intangible products, are tasks or activities performed for a customer or an activity performed by a customer using an organization's products or facilities. Product cost is defined as cost assigned to a product that satisfies a particular managerial objective. Since managerial objectives can differ, product cost definitions can differ—each depending on the managerial objective being served.

After costs have been assigned according to function (production, marketing, and administration), they can be deducted from revenues. The result is an income statement. For manufacturing firms, the major functional classifications are manufacturing and nonmanufacturing; for service organizations, the categories are production and nonproduction. For manufacturing firms, the cost of goods manufactured must be calculated. No such requirement exists for a service firm.

Cornerstones for Chapter 2

KEY TERMS

Accumulating costs, 28
Administrative costs, 38
Allocation, 31
Assigning costs, 28
Conversion cost, 36
Cost, 28
Cost object, 29
Cost of goods manufactured, 39
Cost of goods sold, 40
Direct costs, 30

Direct labor, 34
Direct materials, 33
Expenses, 28
Fixed cost, 32
Gross margin, 42
Indirect costs, 30
Manufacturing organizations, 33
Opportunity cost, 32
Overhead, 35
Period costs, 37

Price, 28
Prime cost, 36
Product (manufacturing) cost, 33
Selling (marketing) costs, 38
Service organizations, 33
Services, 32
Supplies, 35
Tangible products, 32
Variable cost, 32
Work in process (WIP), 39

DISCUSSION QUESTIONS

1. What is a cost object? Give some examples.
2. What is the difference between accumulating cost and assigning cost?
3. What is a direct cost? An indirect cost? Can the same cost be direct for one purpose and indirect for another? Give an example.
4. What is the cost of goods manufactured?
5. Define *prime cost* and *conversion cost*. Why can't you add prime cost to conversion cost to get total product cost?
6. What is the difference between a tangible product and an intangible product? Give an example of each.
7. Explain the difference between cost and expense.
8. How does a period cost differ from a product cost?
9. What is allocation?
10. Define overhead and explain why it is sometimes referred to as a "catchall" category.
11. Explain the difference between direct materials purchases in a month and direct materials for the month.
12. Why do firms like to calculate a percentage column on the income statement (in which each line item is expressed as a percentage of sales)?

13. What is the difference between the income statement for a manufacturing firm and an income statement for a service firm?
14. Define *marketing* (or *selling*) *cost*. Give five examples of marketing cost.
15. What is the difference between cost of goods manufactured and cost of goods sold?

MULTIPLE-CHOICE EXERCISES

2-1 Accumulating costs means that

a. costs must be summed and entered on the income statement.
b. each cost must be linked to some cost object.
c. costs must be measured and tracked.
d. costs must be allocated to units of production.
e. costs have expired and must be transferred from the balance sheet to the income statement.

2-2 Product (or manufacturing) costs consist of

a. direct materials, direct labor, and selling costs.
b. direct materials, direct labor, overhead, and operating expense.
c. prime costs and conversion costs.
d. prime costs and overhead.
e. selling and administrative costs.

Use the following information for Multiple-Choice Exercises 2-3 and 2-4.

Wachman Company produces a product with the following per-unit costs:

Direct materials $15
Direct labor   6
Overhead   10

Last year, Wachman produced and sold 1,000 units at a price of $75 each. Total selling and administrative expense was $30,000.

2-3 Conversion cost per unit was

a. $15.
b. $21.
c. $31.
d. $16.
e. none of the above.

2-4 Total gross profit for last year was

a. $75,000.
b. $44,000.
c. $61,000.
d. $9,000.
e. $31,000.

2-5 The accountant in a factory that produces biscuits for fast-food restaurants wants to assign costs to boxes of biscuits. Which of the following costs can be traced directly to boxes of biscuits?

a. The cost of flour and baking soda
b. The wages of the mixing labor
c. The cost of the boxes
d. The cost of packing labor
e. All of the above

2-6 Which of the following is an indirect cost?

a. The cost of denim in a jeans factory
b. The cost of mixing labor in a factory that makes over-the-counter pain relievers
c. The cost of restriping the parking lot at a perfume factory
d. The cost of bottles in a shampoo factory
e. All of the above

2-7 Bobby Dee's is an owner-operated company that details (thoroughly cleans—inside and out) automobiles. Bobby Dee's is which of the following?

a. Retailer
b. Wholesaler
c. Manufacturing firm
d. Service firm
e. None of the above

2-8 Kellogg's makes a variety of breakfast cereals. Kellogg's is which of the following?

a. Retailer
b. Wholesaler
c. Manufacturing firm
d. Service firm
e. None of the above

2-9 Wal-Mart is which of the following?

a. Retailer
b. Wholesaler
c. Manufacturing firm
d. Service firm
e. None of the above

2-10 Stone, Inc., is a company that purchases goods from overseas (e.g., chess sets, pottery) and resells them to gift shops in the United States. Stone, Inc., is which of the following?

a. Retailer
b. Wholesaler
c. Manufacturing firm
d. Service firm
e. None of the above

2-11 Flame-Glo Company produces novelty candles for gift shops. Flame-Glo estimated the following average costs per candle:

Direct materials	$1.50
Direct labor	0.75
Overhead	2.00

Prime cost per unit is

a. $1.50.
b. $0.75.
c. $2.00.
d. $2.25.
e. $2.75.

2-12 Which of the following is a period expense?

a. Advertising
b. Factory supervision
c. Factory maintenance
d. Direct labor
e. All of the above

Use the following information for Multiple-Choice Exercises 2-13 through 2-18.

Last year, Barnard Company incurred the following costs:

Direct materials	$ 50,000
Direct labor	20,000
Overhead	130,000
Selling expense	40,000
Administrative expense	36,000

Barnard produced and sold 10,000 units at a price of $31 each.

2-13 Prime cost per unit was

a. $7.00.
b. $20.00.
c. $15.00.
d. $5.00.
e. $27.60.

2-14 Conversion cost per unit was

a. $7.00.
b. $20.00.
c. $15.00.
d. $5.00.
e. $27.60.

2-15 Cost of goods sold per unit was

a. $7.00.
b. $20.00.
c. $15.00.
d. $5.00.
e. $27.60.

2-16 Gross margin per unit was

a. $24.00.
b. $11.00.
c. $16.00.
d. $26.00.
e. $3.40.

2-17 Total period expense was

a. $276,000.
b. $200,000.
c. $76,000.
d. $40,000.
c. $36,000.

2-18 Operating income was

a. $34,000.
b. $110,000.
c. $234,000.
d. $270,000.
e. $74,000.

EXERCISES

Exercise 2-1 *Cost Assignment*

OBJECTIVE 1

The sales staff of Central Media (a locally owned radio and cable television station) consists of two salespeople, Derek and Lawanna. During March, the following salaries and commissions were paid:

	Derek	Lawanna
Salary	$25,000	$30,000
Commissions	6,000	1,500

Derek spends 100 percent of his time selling advertising. Lawanna spends two-thirds of her time selling advertising and the remaining one-third on administrative work. Commissions are paid only on sales.

Required:

1. Accumulate these costs by account by filling in the following table.

	Salaries	Commissions
Derek		
Lawanna		
Total		

2. Assign the costs of salaries and commissions to selling expense and administrative expense by filling in the following table.

	Selling Costs	Administrative Costs
Derek's salary		
Lawanna's salary		
Commissions		
Total		

Exercise 2-2 *Products versus Services, Cost Assignment*

OBJECTIVE 1

Holmes Company produces wooden playhouses. When a customer orders a playhouse, it is delivered in pieces with detailed instructions on how to put it together. Some customers prefer that Holmes put the playhouse together, and they purchase the playhouse plus the installation package. Holmes then pulls two workers off the production line and sends them to construct the playhouse on site.

Required:

1. What two products does Holmes sell? Classify each one as a tangible product or a service.
2. Do you think Holmes would assign costs to each individual product? Why or why not?
3. Describe the opportunity cost of the installation process.

Exercise 2-3 *Assigning Costs to a Cost Object, Direct and Indirect Costs*

OBJECTIVE 1

Hummer Company uses manufacturing cells to produce its products (a cell is a manufacturing unit dedicated to the production of subassemblies or products). One manufacturing cell produces small motors for lawn mowers. Suppose that the motor manufacturing cell is the cost object. Assume that all or a portion of the following costs must be assigned to the cell.

a. Salary of cell supervisor
b. Power to heat and cool the plant in which the cell is located

c. Materials used to produce the motors
d. Maintenance for the cell's equipment (provided by the maintenance department)
e. Labor used to produce motors
f. Cafeteria that services the plant's employees
g. Depreciation on the plant
h. Depreciation on equipment used to produce the motors
i. Ordering costs for materials used in production
j. Engineering support (provided by the engineering department)
k. Cost of maintaining the plant and grounds
l. Cost of the plant's personnel office
m. Property tax on the plant and land

Required:
Classify each of the above costs as a direct cost or an indirect cost to the motor manufacturing cell.

Exercise 2-4 *Total and Unit Product Cost*

  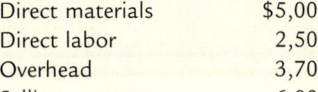

Weibring Manufacturing, Inc., showed the following costs for last month:

Direct materials	$5,000
Direct labor	2,500
Overhead	3,700
Selling expense	6,000

Last month, 8,000 units were produced and sold.

Required:
1. Classify the above four costs as product cost or period cost.
2. What is total product cost for last month?
3. What is the unit product cost for last month?

Exercise 2-5 *Cost Classification*

Loring Company incurred the following costs last year:

Direct materials	$216,000
Factory rent	24,000
Direct labor	120,000
Factory utilities	6,300
Supervision in the factory	50,000
Indirect labor in the factory	30,000
Depreciation on factory equipment	9,000
Sales commissions	27,000
Sales salaries	65,000
Advertising	37,000
Depreciation on the headquarters building	10,000
Salary of the corporate receptionist	30,000
Other administrative costs	175,000
Salary of the factory receptionist	28,000

Required:
1. Classify each of the above costs using the table format given below. Be sure to total the amounts in each column.

Example: Direct materials $216,000

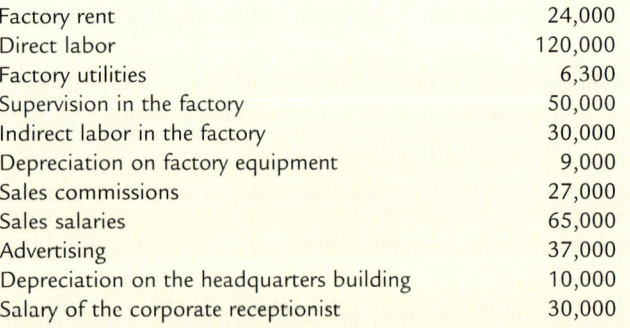

	Product Cost			Period Cost	
Costs	Direct Materials	Direct Labor	Overhead	Selling Expense	Administrative Expense
Direct materials	$216,000				

2. What was the total product cost for last year?
3. What was the total period cost for last year?
4. If 30,000 units were produced last year, what was the unit product cost?

Exercise 2-6 *Classifying Cost of Production*

A factory manufactures jelly. The jars of jelly are packed six to a box, and the boxes are sold to grocery stores. The following types of cost were incurred:

Jars
Sugar
Fruit
Pectin (thickener used in jams and jellies)
Boxes
Depreciation on the factory building
Cooking equipment operators' wages
Filling equipment operators' wages
Packers' wages
Janitors' wages
Receptionist's wages
Telephone
Utilities
Rental of Santa Claus suit (for the annual Christmas party for factory children)
Supervisory labor salaries
Insurance on factory building
Depreciation on factory equipment
Oil to lubricate filling equipment

Required:
Classify each of the above costs as direct materials, direct labor, or overhead by using the following table. The row for "Jars" is filled in as an example.

Costs	Direct Materials	Direct Labor	Overhead
Jars	X		

Exercise 2-7 *Product Cost in Total and Per Unit*

Kyoto Company manufactures digital cameras. In January, Kyoto produced 10,000 cameras with the following costs:

Direct materials	$560,000
Direct labor	96,000
Overhead	220,000

There were no beginning or ending inventories of work in process (WIP).

Required:
1. What was total product cost in January?
2. What was product cost per unit in January?

Exercise 2-8 *Prime Cost and Conversion Cost*

Refer to **Exercise 2-7**.

Required:
1. What was total prime cost in January?
2. What was prime cost per unit in January?

(continued)

3. What was total conversion cost in January?
4. What was conversion cost per unit in January?

Exercise 2-9 *Direct Materials Used by a Service Company*

Colbyville Insurance Company sells automobile and life insurance policies. As a service to its agents, the manager provides complimentary calendars that agents can give as gifts to clients and prospective clients. The calendars cost $0.50 each. Early in February, the manager wanted to know how many calendars had been given out in January. Sue Ellen, the office assistant, gathered the following information:

1. On January 1, there were 150 calendars on hand.
2. An order for 1,000 additional calendars was placed on January 3. It arrived on January 10.
3. On January 31, there were 614 calendars on hand.

Required:
1. How many calendars did agents take to give to clients during January?
2. What is the cost of the calendars given out?
3. What is the cost of the ending inventory of calendars on hand?

Exercise 2-10 *Direct Materials Used*

Better Baker Company makes biscuits for fast-food restaurants. In July, Better Baker Company purchased $12,700 of materials. On July 1, the materials inventory was $2,300. On July 31, $4,900 of materials remained in materials inventory.

Required:
What is the cost of the direct materials that were used in production during July?

Exercise 2-11 *Cost of Goods Sold*

Portman Company makes tricycles. During the year, Portman manufactured 114,000 tricycles. Finished goods inventory had the following units:

January 1	1,430
December 31	2,650

Required:
1. How many tricycles did Portman sell during the year?
2. If each tricycle had a product cost of $15, what was the cost of goods sold last year?

Exercise 2-12 *Direct Materials Used, Cost of Goods Manufactured*

In March, Chilton Company purchased materials costing $14,000 and incurred direct labor cost of $20,000. Overhead totaled $36,000 for the month. Information on inventories was as follows:

	March 1	March 31
Materials	$8,600	$2,300
Work in process	1,700	9,000
Finished goods	7,000	6,500

Required:
1. What was the cost of direct materials for March?
2. What was total manufacturing cost in March?
3. What was the cost of goods manufactured for March?

Exercise 2-13 *Cost of Goods Sold*

Refer to **Exercise 2-12**.

Required:

What was the cost of goods sold for March?

Exercise 2-14 *Cost of Goods Sold, Sales Revenue, Income Statement*

Landes Company provided the following information for last year:

Sales in units	200,000
Selling price	$14
Direct materials	$145,000
Direct labor	$335,000
Overhead	$670,000
Selling expense	$367,000
Administrative expense	$415,000

Required:

Calculate the cost of goods sold for last year.

Exercise 2-15 *Income Statement*

Refer to **Exercise 2-14**.

Required:

1. Calculate the sales revenue for last year.
2. Prepare an income statement for Landes Company for last year.

Exercise 2-16 *Income Statement*

Refer to the income statement calculated in Requirement 2 of **Exercise 2-15**.

Required:

Using the income statement for Landes Company for last year, calculate the percentage of sales for each line item on the income statement. Carry out your calculations to three digits.

PROBLEMS

(Note: Whenever you see a [image] next to a requirement, it signals a "building on a cornerstone" requirement. Assigning this requirement will usually entail additional work, such as a group project, analytical reasoning, Internet research, decision making, and the use of written communication skills.)

Problem 2-1 *Manufacturing, Cost Classification, Income Statement Service Firm Product Costs and Selling and Administrative Costs, Income Statement*

Pop's Drive-Thru Burger Heaven produces and sells quarter-pound hamburgers. Each burger is wrapped and put in a "burger bag," which also includes a serving of fries and a soft drink. The price for the burger bag is $3.50. During December, 10,000

burger bags were sold. The restaurant employs college students part time to cook and fill orders. There is one supervisor (the owner, John Peterson). Pop's maintains a pool of part-time employees so that the number of employees scheduled can be adjusted to the changes in demand. Demand varies on a weekly as well as a monthly basis.

A janitor is hired to clean the building early each morning. Cleaning supplies are used by the janitor, as well as the staff, to wipe counters, wash cooking equipment, and so on. The building is leased from a local real estate company; it has no seating capacity. All orders are filled on a drive-thru basis.

The supervisor schedules work, opens the building, counts the cash, advertises, and is responsible for hiring and firing. The following costs were incurred during December:

Hamburger meat	$4,500	Rent	$1,800
Buns, lettuce, pickles, and onions	800	Depreciation, cooking equipment and fixtures	600
Frozen potato strips	1,250		
Wrappers, bags, and condiment packages	600	Advertising	500
Other ingredients	660	Janitor's wages	520
Part-time employees' wages	7,250	Janitorial supplies	150
John Peterson's salary	3,000	Accounting fees	1,500
Utilities	1,500	Taxes	4,250

Pop's accountant, Elena DeMarco, does the bookkeeping, handles payroll, and files all necessary taxes. To simplify accounting for costs, Elena assumed that all part-time employees are production employees and that John Peterson's salary is selling and administrative expense. She further assumed that all rent and depreciation expense on the building and fixtures are part of product cost. Finally, she decided to put all taxes into one category, taxes, and to treat them as administrative expense.

Required:

1. Fill out the following table and classify the costs for Pop's December operations in one of the following categories: direct materials, direct labor, overhead, or selling and administrative. Be sure to insert the cost for each item and total the categories.

Cost	Direct Materials	Direct Labor	Overhead	Selling and Administrative
Hamburger meat				
Buns, lettuce, pickles, onions				
Frozen potato strips				
Wrappers, bags, condiment packages				
Other ingredients				
Part-time employees' wages				
John Peterson's salary				
Utilities				
Rent				
Depreciation, cooking equipment and fixtures				
Advertising				
Janitor's wages				
Janitorial supplies				
Accounting fees				
Taxes				
Total				

2. Prepare an absorption-costing income statement for the month of December.

3. Elena made some simplifying assumptions. Were those reasonable? Suppose a good case could be made that the portion of the employees' time spent selling the burger bags was really a part of sales. In that case, would it be better to divide their time between production and selling? Should the cash register be classified as product cost or selling and administrative cost? Should John Peterson's time be divided between marketing and administrative duties? What difference (if any) would that make on the income statement?

Problem 2-2 *Services, Cost of Services, and Income Statement*

Celestial Funeral Home offers a full range of services. Last year, Celestial conducted 1,000 funerals, yielding total revenue of $6,000,000. While for a given funeral, the cost of direct materials and direct labor ranged widely, on average, direct materials cost $2,000 and direct labor costs $750. Overhead totaled $250,000. Celestial incurs annual selling expenses of $250,000 and administrative expenses of $375,000.

Required:

1. Does Celestial sell a tangible or intangible product? Explain.
2. Calculate the average overhead cost for one funeral for the past year.
3. Calculate the product cost for one funeral for the past year.
4. Prepare an income statement for Celestial for last year. (*Hint*: Use Cornerstone 2-8.)

Problem 2-3 *Cost Assignment, Direct Costs*

Harry Whipple, owner of an ink jet printer, has agreed to allow Mary and Natalie, two friends who are pursuing master's degrees, to print several papers for their graduate courses. However, he has imposed two conditions. First, they must supply their own paper. Second, they must pay Harry a fair amount for the usage of the ink cartridge. Harry's printer takes two types of cartridges, a black one and a color one that contains the inks necessary to print in color. Black replacement cartridges cost $25.50 each and print approximately 850 pages. The color cartridge replacement cost $31 and prints approximately 310 color pages. One ream of paper costs $2.50 and contains 500 sheets. Mary's printing requirements are for 500 pages, while Natalie's are for 1,000 pages.

Required:

1. Assuming that both women write papers using text only (i.e., black ink), what is the total amount owed to Harry by Mary? By Natalie?
2. What is the total cost of printing (ink and paper) for Mary? For Natalie?
3. Now suppose that Natalie illustrates her writing with many large colorful pie charts and pictures and that about 20 percent of her total printing is primarily color. Mary uses no color illustrations. What is the total amount owed to Harry by Natalie? What is the total cost of printing (ink and paper) for Natalie?

Problem 2-4 *Cost of Direct Materials, Cost of Goods Manufactured, Cost of Goods Sold*

Bisby Company manufactures fishing rods. At the beginning of July, the following information was supplied by its accountant:

Raw materials inventory	$40,000
Work-in-process inventory	21,000
Finished goods inventory	23,200

During July, the direct labor cost was $43,500, raw materials' purchases were $64,000, and the total overhead cost was $108,750. The inventories at the end of July were:

Raw materials inventory	$19,800
Work-in-process inventory	32,500
Finished goods inventory	22,100

Required:
1. What is the cost of the direct materials used in production during July?
2. What is the cost of goods manufactured for July?
3. What is the cost of goods sold for July?

Problem 2-5 *Preparation of Income Statement: Manufacturing Firm*

 OBJECTIVE 3

Laworld, Inc., manufactures small camping tents. Last year, 200,000 tents were made and sold for $60 each. Each tent includes the following costs:

Direct materials	$18
Direct labor	12
Overhead	16

The only selling expenses were a commission of $2 per unit sold and advertising totaling $100,000. Administrative expenses, all fixed, equaled $300,000. There were no beginning or ending finished goods inventories. There were no beginning or ending work-in-process inventories.

Required:
1. Calculate the product cost for one tent. Calculate the total product cost for last year.
2. Prepare an income statement for external users. Did you need to prepare a supporting statement of cost of goods manufactured? Explain.
3. Suppose 200,000 tents were produced (and 200,000 sold) but that the company had a beginning finished goods inventory of 10,000 tents produced in the prior year at $40 per unit. The company follows a first-in, first-out policy for its inventory (meaning that the units produced first are sold first for purposes of cost flow). What effect does this have on the income statement? Show the new statement.

Problem 2-6 *Cost of Goods Manufactured, Cost of Goods Sold*

 OBJECTIVE 3

Spreadsheet

Hayward Company, a manufacturing firm, has supplied the following information from its accounting records for the month of May:

Direct labor cost	$10,500
Purchases of raw materials	15,000
Supplies used	675
Factory insurance	350
Commissions paid	2,500
Factory supervision	2,225
Advertising	800
Material handling	3,750
Work-in-process inventory, May 1	12,500
Work-in-process inventory, May 31	14,250
Materials inventory, May 1	3,475
Materials inventory, May 31	9,500
Finished goods inventory, May 1	6,685
Finished goods inventory, May 31	4,250

Required:
1. Prepare a statement of cost of goods manufactured.
2. Prepare a statement of cost of goods sold.

Problem 2-7 *Cost of Direct Materials, Prime Cost, Conversion Cost, Income Statement, Services versus Manufacturing*

Lance Peckam owns and operates three Confiable Muffler outlets in Tucson, Arizona. Confiable is a franchise popular throughout the Southwest; it specializes in replacing old mufflers with new mufflers that have a lifetime guarantee. In April, purchases of materials equaled $200,000, the beginning inventory of materials was $26,300, and the ending inventory of materials was $14,250. Payments to direct labor during the month totaled $53,000. Overhead incurred was $120,000. The Tucson outlets also spent $15,000 on advertising during the month. A franchise fee of $3,000 per outlet is paid every month. Revenues for April were $500,000.

Required:
1. What was the cost of materials used for muffler-changing services during April?
2. What was the prime cost for April?
3. What was the conversion cost for April?
4. What was the total cost of services for April?
5. Prepare an income statement for the month of April.
6. Confiable purchases all its mufflers from Remington Company, a manufacturer of mufflers. Discuss the differences between the products offered by Remington and Confiable.

Problem 2-8 *Cost Identification*

Following is a list of cost items described in the chapter and a list of brief descriptive settings for each item.

Cost terms:
a. Opportunity cost
b. Period cost
c. Product cost
d. Direct labor cost
e. Selling cost
f. Conversion cost
g. Prime cost
h. Direct materials cost
i. Overhead cost
j. Administrative cost

Settings:
1. Marcus Armstrong, manager of Timmins Optical, estimated that the cost of plastic, wages of the technician producing the lenses, and overhead totaled $30 per pair of single-vision lenses.
2. Linda was having a hard time deciding whether to return to school. She was concerned about the salary she would have to give up for the next four years.
3. Randy Harris is the finished goods warehouse manager for a medium-sized manufacturing firm. He is paid a salary of $90,000 per year. As he studied the financial statements prepared by the local CPA firm, he wondered how his salary was treated.
4. Jamie Young is in charge of the legal department at company headquarters. Her salary is $95,000 per year. She reports to the chief executive officer.
5. All factory costs that are not classified as direct materials or direct labor.

6. The new product required machining, assembly, and painting. The design engineer asked the accounting department to estimate the labor cost of each of the three operations. The engineer supplied the estimated labor hours for each operation.
7. After obtaining the estimate of direct labor cost, the design engineer estimated the cost of the materials that would be used for the new product.
8. The design engineer totaled the costs of materials and direct labor for the new product.
9. The design engineer also estimated the cost of converting the raw materials into its final form.
10. The auditor for a soft drink bottling plant pointed out that the depreciation on the delivery trucks had been incorrectly assigned to product cost (through overhead). Accordingly, the depreciation charge was reallocated on the income statement.

Required:
Match the items with the settings. More than one cost classification may be associated with each setting; however, select the setting that seems to fit the item best. When you are done, each cost term will be used just once.

Problem 2-9 *Income Statement, Cost of Services Provided, Service Attributes*

Berry Company is an architectural firm located in Detroit, Michigan. The company works with small and medium-size construction businesses to prepare building plans according to client contract. Berry employs 10 professionals and five staff. The following data are provided for last year.

Number of designs completed and sold	700
Beginning inventory of designs in process	$60,000
Ending inventory of designs in process	$100,000
Beginning inventory of direct materials	$20,000
Ending inventory of direct materials	$0
Purchases, direct materials	$40,000
Direct labor	$800,000
Overhead	$100,000
Administrative expense	$150,000
Selling expense	$60,000

Required:
1. Calculate the cost of services sold.
2. Assume that the average fee for a design is $2,100. Prepare an income statement for Berry Company.

3. Refer to the cost of services sold (calculated in Requirement 1). What is the dominant cost? Will this always be true of service organizations? If not, provide an example of an exception.
4. Why does Berry Company show zero inventory of finished plans? What change(s) in the company could result in a positive finished goods inventory?

Problem 2-10 *Cost of Goods Manufactured, Income Statement*

W. W. Phillips Company produced 4,000 leather recliners during the year. These recliners sell for $400 each. Phillips had 500 recliners in finished goods inventory at the beginning of the year. At the end of the year, there were 700 recliners in finished goods inventory. Phillips' accounting records provide the following information:

Purchases of raw materials	$320,000
Beginning materials inventory	46,800

Ending materials inventory	$ 66,800
Direct labor	200,000
Indirect labor	40,000
Rent, factory building	42,000
Depreciation, factory equipment	60,000
Utilities, factory	11,900
Salary, sales supervisor	90,000
Commissions, salespersons	180,000
General administration	300,000
Beginning work-in-process inventory	13,040
Ending work-in-process inventory	14,940
Beginning finished goods inventory	80,000
Ending finished goods inventory	114,100

Required:

1. Prepare a statement of cost of goods manufactured.
2. Compute the average cost of producing one unit of product in the year.
3. Prepare an income statement for external users.

Problem 2-11 *Cost Information and Ethical Behavior, Service Organization*

OBJECTIVES
1, 2

Jean Erickson, manager and owner of an advertising company in Charlotte, North Carolina, had arranged a meeting with Leroy Gee, the chief accountant of a large, local competitor. The two are lifelong friends. They grew up together in a small town and attended the same university. Leroy was a competent, successful accountant but currently was experiencing some personal financial difficulties. The problems were created by some investments that had turned sour, leaving him with a $15,000 personal loan to pay off—just at the time that his oldest son was scheduled to enter college.

Jean, on the other hand, was struggling to establish a successful advertising business. She had recently acquired the rights to open a branch office of a large regional advertising firm headquartered in Atlanta, Georgia. During her first two years, she had managed to build a small, profitable practice; however, the chance to gain a significant foothold in the Charlotte advertising community hinged on the success of winning a bid to represent the state of North Carolina in a major campaign to attract new industry and tourism. The meeting she had scheduled with Leroy concerned the bid she planned to submit.

Jean: Leroy, I'm at a critical point in my business venture. If I can win the bid for the state's advertising dollars, I'll be set. Winning the bid will bring $600,000 to $700,000 of revenues into the firm. On top of that, I estimate that the publicity will bring another $200,000 to $300,000 of new business.

Leroy: I understand. My boss is anxious to win that business as well. It would mean a huge increase in profits for my firm. It's a competitive business, though. As new as you are, I doubt that you'll have much chance of winning.

Jean: You may be wrong. You're forgetting two very important considerations. First, I have the backing of all the resources and talent of a regional firm. Second, I have some political connections. Last year, I was hired to run the publicity side of the governor's campaign. He was impressed with my work and would like me to have this business. I am confident that the proposals I submit will be very competitive. My only concern is to submit a bid that beats your firm. If I come in with a lower bid and with good proposals, the governor can see to it that I get the work.

Leroy: Sounds promising. If you do win, however, there will be a lot of upset people. After all, they are going to claim that the business should have been given to local advertisers, not to some out-of-state firm. Given the size of your office, you'll have to get support from Atlanta. You could take a lot of heat.

Jean: True. But I am the owner of the branch office. That fact alone should blunt most of the criticism. Who can argue that I'm not a local? Listen, with your help, I think I can win this bid. Furthermore, if I do win it, you can reap some direct benefits. With that kind of business, I can afford to hire an accountant, and I'll make it worthwhile for you to transfer jobs. I can offer you an up-front bonus of $15,000. On top of that, I'll increase your annual salary by 20 percent. That should solve most of your financial difficulties. After all, we have been friends since day one—and what are friends for?

Leroy: Jean, my wife would be ecstatic if I were able to improve our financial position as quickly as this opportunity affords. I certainly hope that you win the bid. What kind of help can I provide?

Jean: Simple. To win, all I have to do is beat the bid of your firm. Before I submit my bid, I would like you to review it. With the financial skills you have, it should be easy for you to spot any excessive costs that I may have included. Or perhaps I included the wrong kind of costs. By cutting excessive costs and eliminating costs that may not be directly related to the project, my bid should be competitive enough to meet or beat your firm's bid.

Required:

1. What would you do if you were Leroy? Fully explain the reasons for your choice. What do you suppose the code of conduct for Leroy's company would say about this situation?
2. What is the likely outcome if Leroy agrees to review the bid? Is there much risk to him personally if he reviews the bid? Should the degree of risk have any bearing on his decision?

Problem 2-12 *Cost Definitions*

Luisa Giovanni is a student at New York University. To help pay her way through college, Luisa started a dog walking service. She has 12 client dogs—six are walked on the first shift (6:30 A.M. and 5:00 P.M.) and six are walked on the second shift (7:30 A.M. and 6:00 P.M.).

Last month, Luisa noted the following:

1. Purchase of three leashes at $10 each (she carries these with her in case a leash breaks during a walk).
2. Internet service costs her $40 a month. This enables her to keep in touch with the owners, bill them by e-mail, and so on.
3. Dog treats of $50 to reward each dog at the end of each walk.
4. A heavy duty raincoat and hat for $100.
5. Partway through the month, Luisa's friend, Jason, offered her a chance to play a bit role in a movie that was shooting on location in New York City. The job paid $100 and would have required Luisa to be on location at 6 A.M. and to remain for 12 hours. Regretfully, Luisa turned it down.
6. The owners pay Luisa $250 per month per dog for her services.

Required:

1. At the end of the month, how would Luisa classify her Internet payment of $40—as a cost on the balance sheet or as an expense on the income statement?
2. Which of the above is an opportunity cost? Why?
3. What price is charged? What is Luisa's total revenue for a month?

Problem 2-13 *Cost Identification and Analysis, Cost Assignment, Income Statement*

Melissa Vassar has decided to open a printing shop. She has secured two contracts. One is a 5-year contract to print a popular regional magazine. This contract calls for

5,000 copies each month. The second contract is a 3-year agreement to print tourist brochures for the state. The state tourist office requires 10,000 brochures per month.

Melissa has rented a building for $1,400 per month. Her printing equipment was purchased for $40,000 and has a life expectancy of 20,000 hours with no salvage value. Depreciation is assigned to a period based on the hours of usage. Melissa has scheduled the delivery of the products so that two production runs are needed. In the first run, the equipment is prepared for the magazine printing. In the second run, the equipment is reconfigured for brochure printing. It takes twice as long to configure the equipment for the magazine setup as it does for the brochure setup. The total setup costs per month are $600.

Insurance costs for the building and equipment are $140 per month. Power to operate the printing equipment is strongly related to machine usage. The printing equipment causes virtually all the power costs. Power costs will run $350 per month. Printing materials will cost $0.40 per copy for the magazine and $0.08 per copy for the brochure. Melissa will hire workers to run the presses as needed (part-time workers are easy to hire). She must pay $10 per hour. Each worker can produce 20 copies of the magazine per printing hour or 100 copies of the brochure. Distribution costs are $500 per month. Melissa will receive a salary of $1,500 per month. She is responsible for personnel, accounting, sales, and production—in effect, she is responsible for administering all aspects of the business.

Required:

1. What are the total monthly manufacturing costs?
2. What are the total monthly prime costs? Total monthly prime costs for the regional magazine? For the brochure?
3. What are the total monthly conversion costs? Suppose Melissa wants to determine monthly conversion costs for each product. Assign monthly conversion costs to each product using direct tracing and driver tracing whenever possible. For those costs that cannot be assigned using a tracing approach, you may assign them using direct labor hours.
4. If Melissa receives $1.80 per copy of the magazine and $0.45 per brochure, how much will her income be for the first month of operations? (Prepare an income statement.)

Problem 2-14 *Costs of Production in a Service Firm*

OBJECTIVES
1, 2, 3

Recall from the Opening Scenario that Courtney, the head chef of a restaurant, needed to learn basic costing. It is now two months later. She has accumulated the following information on kitchen costs for the past month:

Food purchases	$80,000
Salaries:	
Courtney	2,500
Assistant chefs (2 @ $2,000)	4,000
Preparers (5 @ $1,800)	9,000
Clean-up workers	3,000
Gasoline and depreciation on van	1,000
Depreciation on kitchen equipment	2,000
Dish/cookware purchases	500
Cleaning supplies	350

Required:

1. Classify all kitchen and kitchen-related costs as direct materials, direct labor, and overhead.
2. Calculate each of the following for the past month: total prime cost and total conversion cost.

3. Do you suppose there are any inventories? If so, of what? Should Courtney figure beginning and ending inventories in calculating the cost of meals sold in a month? Why or why not?
4. Assume sales for the past month were $243,000. Front room and bar costs equaled $80,000, and shared restaurant costs equaled $45,000. Prepare an income statement for the restaurant for last month.

Problem 2-15

OBJECTIVES
1, 2

Five to six times a year, Kicker puts on tent sales in various cities throughout Oklahoma and the surrounding states. The tent sales are designed to show Kicker customers new products, engender enthusiasm about those products, and sell soon to be out-of-date products at greatly reduced prices. Each tent sale lasts one day and requires parking lot space to set up the Kicker semitrailer; a couple of show cars; a deejay playing music; and a tent to sell Kicker merchandise, distribute brochures, and so on.

Last year, the Austin tent sale was held in a far corner of the parking lot outside the city exhibition hall where the automotive show was in progress. Because most customers were interested more in the new model cars than in the refurbishment of their current cars, foot traffic was low. In addition, customers did not want to carry speakers and amplifiers all the way back to where they had originally parked. Total direct costs for this tent sale amounted to $14,300. Direct costs included gasoline and fuel for three pickup trucks and the semitrailer; wages and per diem for the five Kicker personnel who traveled to the show; rent on the parking lot space; depreciation on the semitrailer, pickups, tent, tables (in tent), sound equipment; and so on. Revenue was $20,000. Cost of goods sold for the speakers was $7,000.

Required:

1. How do you suppose Kicker accounts for the costs of the tent sales? What income statement items are affected by the tent sales?
2. What was the profit (loss) from the Austin tent show? What do you think Kicker might do to make it more profitable in the future?

COST BEHAVIOR

© BRAND X PICTURES/GETTY IMAGES

After studying Chapter 3, you should be able to:

1. Explain the meaning of cost behavior and define and describe fixed and variable costs.
2. Define and describe mixed and step costs.
3. Separate mixed costs into their fixed and variable components using the high-low method, the scattergraph method, and the method of least squares.
4. (Appendix) Use a personal computer spreadsheet program to perform the method of least squares.

Li Ming Yuan and Tiffany Shaden are the department heads for the accounting department and human resources department, respectively, at a large textile firm in the southern United States. They have just returned from an executive meeting at which the necessity of cutting costs and gaining efficiency has been stressed.

Tiffany: I'd love to cut costs, but where can I? We're already stretched so thin, I don't see that I can lay off anyone.

Li Ming: You've already cut the fat out of your budget. I can see how you have improved over the past few quarters. Your department is really one of our shining stars!

Tiffany: Thanks, I appreciate that! Still, I've got to do something—change something—to meet these new directives.

Li Ming: Hey, maybe there's a way. Your people spend a lot of time processing employee health insurance claims.

Tiffany: That's right. We are self-insured, so we have to process our own claims.

Li Ming: Well, maybe you could outsource it—you know, hire an outside company to process the claims. I could do a study of the cost of in-house processing versus outsourcing it. I suspect there are a lot of fixed costs involved. I propose that we identify those and see if they could be streamlined and made variable. It could actually be less expensive to outsource.

Tiffany: Sounds great—let me know what information you need!

Chapter 2 discussed various types of costs and took a close look at manufacturing and service costs. However, at that time, the primary concern was organizing costs into production, selling, and administrative costs. Related schedules of the cost of goods manufactured, cost of goods sold, and income statements were built. Now, it is time to focus on cost behavior—the way costs change as the related activity changes.

Costs can be variable, fixed, or mixed. Knowing how costs change as output changes is essential to planning, controlling, and decision making. For example, suppose that BlueDenim Jeans Company expects demand for its product to increase by 10 percent next year. How will that affect the total costs budgeted for the factory? Clearly, BlueDenim will need 10 percent more raw materials (denim, thread, zippers, and so on). In addition, it will need more cutting and sewing labor, since someone will need to make the additional jeans. But the factory building will probably not need to be expanded. Nor will the factory need an additional receptionist or plant manager. So those costs are fixed. As long as BlueDenim's accountant understands the behavior of the fixed and variable costs, it will be possible to develop a fairly accurate budget for the next year.

Budgeting, deciding to keep or drop a product line, and evaluating the performance of a segment all benefit from knowledge of cost behavior. In fact, not knowing and understanding cost behavior can lead to poor—even disastrous—decisions. This chapter discusses cost behavior in depth so that a proper foundation is laid for its use in studying other cost management topics.

BASICS OF COST BEHAVIOR

Cost behavior is the general term for describing whether a cost changes when the level of output changes. A cost that does not change as output changes is a *fixed cost*. A *variable cost*, on the other hand, increases in total with an increase in output and decreases in total with a decrease in output. Let's first review the basics of cost and output measures. Then, we will look at fixed and variable costs.

> **OBJECTIVE 1**
>
> Explain the meaning of cost behavior and define and describe fixed and variable costs.

Measures of Output and the Relevant Range

In order to determine the behavior of a cost, we need to have a good grasp of the cost under consideration and a measure of the output associated with the activity. The terms *fixed cost* and *variable cost* do not exist in a vacuum; they only have meaning when related to some output measure. In other words, a cost is fixed or variable with respect to some output measure or driver. In order to understand the behavior of costs, we must first determine the underlying business activity and ask ourselves "What causes the cost of this particular activity to go up (or down)?" A **driver** is a factor that causes or leads to a change in a cost or activity. The driver is the output measure for which we are looking.

Let's look at some examples. Suppose that BlueDenim Jeans Company wants to classify its product costs as either variable or fixed with respect to the number of jeans produced. In this case, the number of jeans produced is the driver. Clearly, the use of raw materials (denim, thread, zippers, and buttons) varies with the number of jeans produced. So we could say that materials costs are variable with respect to the number of units produced. How about electricity to run the sewing machines? That, too, is variable with respect to the number of jeans produced, since the more jeans are produced, the more sewing machine time is needed, and the more electricity it takes. Finally, what about the cost of supervision for the sewing department? Whether the company produces many pairs of jeans, or fewer pairs of jeans, the cost of supervision is unchanged. So, we would say that supervision is fixed with respect to the number of jeans produced.

How does the relevant range fit into cost relationships? The **relevant range** is the range of output over which the assumed cost relationship is valid for the normal operations of a firm. The relevant range limits the cost relationship to the range of operations that the firm normally expects to occur. Let's consider BlueDenim's cost relationships more carefully. We said that the salary of the supervisor is strictly fixed. But is that true? If the company produced just a few pairs of jeans a year, it would not even need a supervisor. Surely the owner could handle that task (and probably a good number of other tasks as well). On the other hand, suppose BlueDenim increased its current production by two or three times, perhaps by adding a second and third shift. One supervisor could not possibly handle three shifts. So, when we talk about supervision cost, we are implicitly talking about it for the range of production that normally occurs.

We now take a closer look at fixed, variable, and mixed costs. In each case, the cost is related to only one driver and defined within the relevant range.

HERE'S THE REAL KICKER

Kicker uses information on cost behavior to guide new programs. For example, the variable cost of manufacturing speakers led Kicker to work with its manufacturers to both increase quality and decrease cost. Fixed costs at the Stillwater location also received attention. For example, eight years ago Safety Director Terry Williams faced a problem with worker safety. Cost information based on a number of indicators revealed the problem:

- The cost of workmen's compensation insurance was high.
- The workmen's compensation experience rating was high.
- The number of injuries was up.
- The number of injuries requiring time off was up.
- The number of back injuries (the most serious type) was up.
- The average cost per injury was up.

Terry looked for the root cause of the problem and discovered that improper lifting led to the more serious back injuries. He instituted a comprehensive safety program emphasizing 20 minutes of stretching exercises each day (five minutes before work, five minutes after each break, and five minutes after lunch).

Was the program a success? At first, the workers resisted the stretching. So Terry got them weight belts. Workers hated them. So, they went back to stretching. But this time, any worker who refused to stretch had to wear the weight belt for 30 days. This was a highly visible sign of failure to adhere to the program. In addition, Kicker's president was a big proponent of the safety program. He explained the impact of the increased insurance premiums and lost work time on the Kicker profit sharing program. The profit sharing program is an important extra for Kicker employees; each one makes it his job to contribute to the bottom line whenever possible.

Over several months, workers bought into the program. The indicators decreased dramatically. The cost of workmen's compensation insurance decreased by nearly 50 percent, the average cost per injury is less than 5 percent of the pre-safety program cost, and there is no lost work time.

Fixed Costs

Fixed costs are costs that *in total* are constant within the relevant range as the level of output increases or decreases. For example, Southwest Airlines has a fleet of 737s. The cost of these planes represents a fixed cost to the airline because, within the relevant range, the cost does not change as the number of flights or the number of passengers changes. Similarly, the rental cost of warehouse space by a wholesaler is fixed for the term of the lease. If the wholesaler's sales go up or down, the cost of the leased warehouse stays the same.

To illustrate fixed cost behavior, consider a factory operated by Colley Computers, Inc., a company that produces unlabelled personal computers for small computer stores across the Midwest. The assembly department of the factory assembles components into a completed personal computer. Assume that Colley Computers want to look at the cost relationship between supervision cost and the number of computers processed. The assembly department can process up to 50,000 computers per year. The assemblers (direct labor) are supervised by a production-line manager who is paid $32,000 per year. The company was established five years ago. Currently, the factory produces 40,000 to 50,000 computers per year. Production has never fallen below 20,000 computers in a year. The cost of supervision for several levels of production is as follows:

Colley Computers, Inc.
Cost of Supervision

Number of Computers Produced	Total Cost of Supervision	Unit Cost
20,000	$32,000	$1.60
30,000	32,000	1.07
40,000	32,000	0.80
50,000	32,000	0.64

The cost relationship considered is between supervision cost and the number of computers processed. The number of computers processed is called the output measure, or driver. Since Colley Computers has been processing between 20,000 and 50,000 computers per year, the relevant range is 20,000 to 50,000. Notice that the *total* cost of supervision remains constant within this range as more computers are processed. Colley Computers pays $32,000 for supervision regardless of whether it processes 20,000, 40,000, or 50,000 computers.

Pay particular attention to the words *in total* in the definition of fixed costs. While the total cost of supervision remains unchanged as more computers are processed, the unit cost does change as the level of output changes. As the example in the table shows, within the relevant range, the unit cost of supervision decreases from $1.60 to $0.64. Because of the behavior of per-unit fixed costs, it is easy to get the impression that the fixed costs themselves are affected by changes in the level of output. But that is not true. Instead, higher output means that the fixed costs can be spread over more units and are thus smaller per unit. Unit fixed costs can often be misleading and may lead to poor decisions. It is often safer to work with total fixed costs.

APPLICATIONS IN BUSINESS

England, Inc., is a furniture company based in New Tazewell, Tennessee. England is making great strides in compressing the time it takes to make a custom furniture order from eight or more months to one or two months. To do this, England has revamped its production methods to be sure that all processes are scheduled to proceed smoothly on orders. Deliveries of fabric and other raw materials are scheduled to the hour. Fixed costs are spread over as many units as possible. For example, England groups units to be produced by style. That way, fabric cutters don't have to cut the fabric for each sofa at a time; instead, they can stack the layers of fabric and cut a stack of 50. Similarly, workers who program the automatic wood routers can cut up to 50 frames instead of just one. (*Note:* The cutting of fabric and the programming of the router are essentially fixed so increasing the number of units helps to spread that fixed cost over more units.)

Source: Dan Morse, "Tennessee Producer Tries New Tactic in Sofas: Speed," *The Wall Street Journal* (November 19, 2002): 1.

Let's take a look at the graph of fixed costs given in Exhibit 3-1. We see that, for the relevant range, fixed cost behavior is described by a horizontal line. Notice that at 40,000 computers processed, supervision cost is $32,000; at 50,000 computers processed, supervision is also $32,000. This line visually demonstrates that cost remains unchanged as the level of the activity driver varies. For the relevant range, total fixed costs are simply an amount. For Colley Computers, supervision cost amounted to $32,000 for any level of output between 20,000 and 50,000 computers processed. Thus, supervision is a fixed cost and can be expressed as:

$$\text{Supervision cost} = \$32,000$$

Strictly speaking, this equation assumes that the fixed costs are $32,000 for all levels (as if the line extends to the vertical axis as indicated by the dashed portion in Exhibit 3-1). Although this assumption is not true, it is harmless if the operating decisions are confined to the relevant range.

Analytical Q & A

In Exhibit 3-1, the fixed cost of supervision is drawn at $32,000. If the supervisor's salary is raised to $34,000 per year, can you draw in the new fixed cost line on Exhibit 3-1?

Answer:
The new line is above and parallel to the original one. The new line intersects the vertical axis at $34,000.

Can fixed costs change? Of course, but this does not make them variable. They are fixed at a new higher (or lower) rate. Going back to Colley Computers, suppose that the company gives a raise to the assembly department supervisor. Instead of being paid $32,000 per year, the salary is $34,000 per year. The cost of supervision within the relevant range is $34,000 per year. However, supervision cost is still *fixed* with respect to the number of computers produced.

By their nature, fixed costs are difficult to change quickly—that is why they are considered fixed. Two types of fixed costs are commonly recognized: discretionary fixed costs and committed fixed costs. **Dis-**

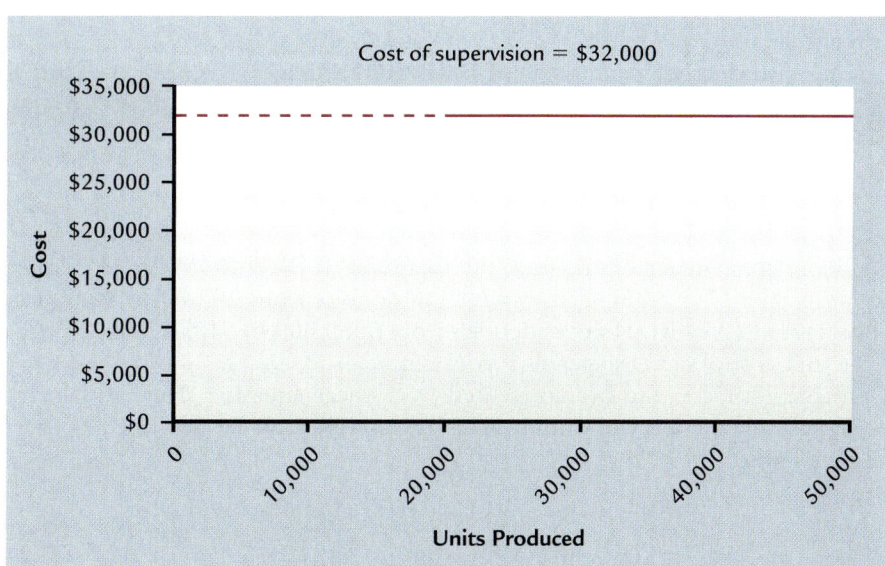

3-1 EXHIBIT

Colley Computers Fixed Cost of Supervision

cretionary **fixed costs** are fixed costs that can be changed relatively easily at management discretion. For example, advertising is a discretionary fixed cost. Advertising cost depends on the decision by management to purchase print, radio, or video advertising. The cost of this may depend on the size of the ad or the number of times it runs, but it does *not* depend on the number of units produced and sold. Management can easily decide to increase or decrease dollars spent on advertising. A **committed fixed cost**, on the other hand, is a fixed cost that cannot be easily changed. Often, committed fixed costs are those that involve a long-term contract (e.g., leasing of machinery or warehouse space) or the purchase of property, plant, and equipment. For example, a construction company may lease heavy-duty earth moving equipment for a period of three years. The lease cost is a committed fixed cost.

Variable Costs

Variable costs are defined as costs that in total vary in direct proportion to changes in output within the relevant range. In the Opening Scenario, we saw that the human resources department processes health insurance forms. The cost of blank forms is a variable cost because it varies with the number of claims processed. In a dentist's office, certain supplies, such as the disposable bib used on each patient, floss, and x-ray film, vary with the number of patients seen. Binney & Smith, the maker of Crayola crayons, finds that the cost of wax and pigments varies with the number of crayons produced.

To illustrate, let's expand the Colley Computers example to include the cost of the DVD-ROM drive that is inserted in each computer. Here, the cost is the cost of direct materials—the DVD-ROM drive, and the output measure is the number of computers processed. Each computer requires one DVD-ROM drive costing $40. The cost of DVD-ROM drives for various levels of production is as follows:

Concept Q & A

Consider the cost of a wedding reception. What costs are fixed? What costs are variable? What output measure did you use in classifying the costs as fixed or variable?

Answer:
Often, the number of guests is the output measure for a wedding reception. The cost of food and drinks varies with the number of guests. The relevant range for a wedding might be the approximate size—perhaps small (less than 100 guests), medium (100–200 guests), and large (200+ guests). Within a relevant range, fixed costs might include rental of the facility, flowers, and the cake.

Colley Computers, Inc.
Cost of DVD-ROM Drives

Number of Computers Produced	Total Cost of DVD-ROM Drives	Unit Cost
20,000	$ 800,000	$40
30,000	1,200,000	40
40,000	1,600,000	40
50,000	2,000,000	40

As more computers are produced, the total cost of DVD-ROM drives increases in direct proportion. For example, as production doubles from 20,000 to 40,000 units, the *total* cost of DVD-ROM drives doubles from $800,000 to $1,600,000. Notice also that the unit cost of direct materials is constant.

Variable costs can also be represented by a linear equation. Here, total variable costs depend on the level of output. This relationship can be described by the following equation:

Total variable costs = Variable rate × Amount of output

The relationship that describes the cost of disk drives is:

Total variable cost = $40 × Number of computers.

Colley Computers Variable Cost of DVD-ROM Drives

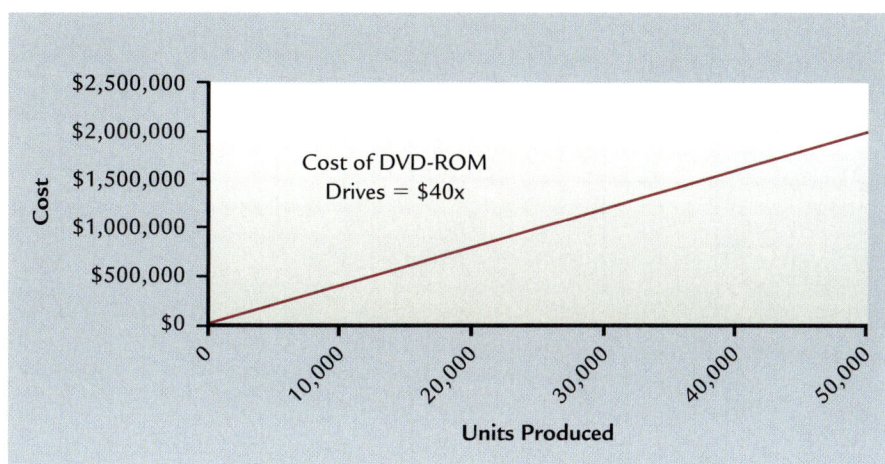

Exhibit 3-2 shows graphically that variable cost behavior is represented by a straight line extending out from the origin. Notice that at zero units processed, total variable cost is zero. However, as units produced increase, the total variable cost also increases. Here, it can be seen that total cost increases in direct proportion to increases in the number of computers processed; the rate of increase is measured by the slope of the line. At 50,000 computers processed, the total cost of disk drives is $2,000,000 (or $40 × 50,000 computers processed); at 80,000 computers processed, the total cost would be $3,200,000. Exhibit 3-2 illustrates variable cost behavior for the DVD-ROM drives.

The Reasonableness of Straight-Line Cost Relationships

The graphs of fixed and variable costs that were just reviewed show cost relationships that are straight lines. Is this reasonable; are real world cost relationships linear?

In the Colley Computers example, the DVD-ROM drives cost $40 each—no matter how many were purchased. However, if only a couple drives were bought, surely the cost would be higher—perhaps more than double. So there are quantity discounts. When quantity discounts are present, the true cost function is increasing at a decreasing rate as shown in Exhibit 3-3.

When unit costs change in this way, how do we choose the correct variable rate? Fortunately, the relevant range can help us out. Recall that the relevant range is defined as the range of activity for which the assumed cost relationships are valid. Exhibit 3-3 shows us how the relevant range can be used to see how well a straight line approximates variable cost. Note that for units of output before 20,000 on the x-axis, the approximation appears to break down.

MIXED COSTS AND STEP COSTS

OBJECTIVE 2

Define and describe mixed and step costs.

While strictly fixed and variable costs are easy to handle, many costs do not fall into those categories. Often, they are a combination of fixed and variable costs (mixed costs) or have an increased fixed component at specified intervals (step costs).

Nonlinearity of Variable Costs

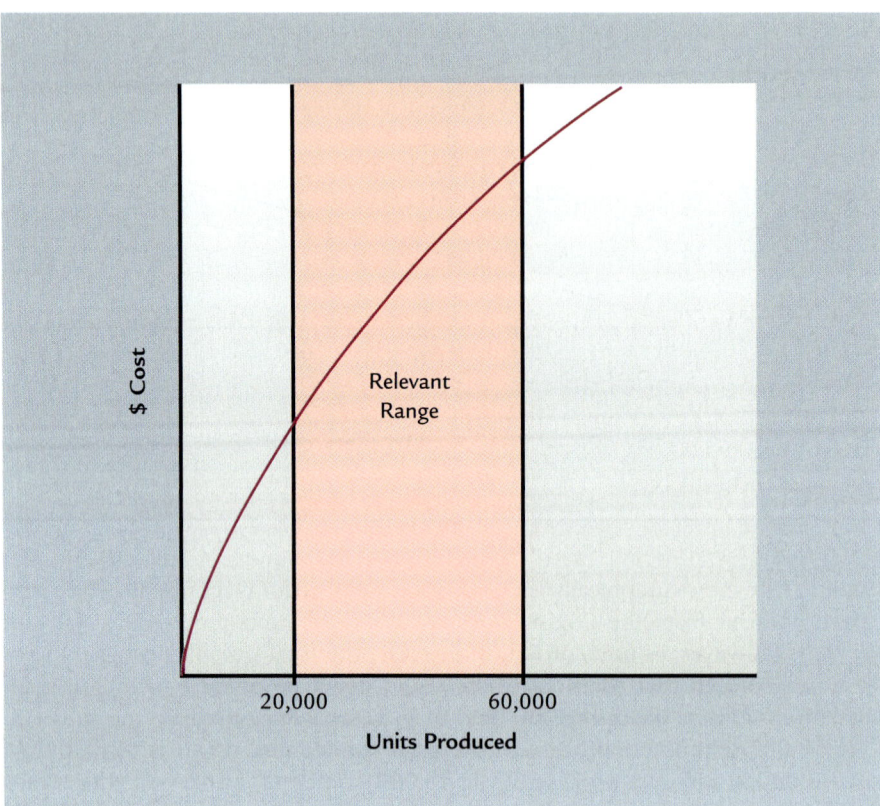

Mixed Costs

Mixed costs are costs that have both a fixed and a variable component. For example, sales representatives are often paid a salary plus a commission on sales. Suppose that Colley Computers has 10 sales representatives, each earning a salary of $30,000 per year, plus a commission of $25 per computer sold. The activity is selling, and the output measure is units sold. If 50,000 computers are sold, then the total cost associated with the sales representatives is $1,550,000—the sum of the fixed salary cost of $300,000 (10 × $30,000) and the variable cost of $1,250,000 ($25 × 50,000).

The formula for a mixed cost is as follows:

$$\text{Total cost} = \text{Total fixed cost} + \text{Total variable cost}$$

For Colley Computers, the cost of the sales representatives is represented by the following equation:

$$\text{Total cost} = \$300,000 + (\$25 \times \text{Number of computers sold})$$

The following table shows the selling cost for different levels of sales activity:

Colley Computers

Fixed Cost of Selling	Variable Cost of Selling	Total Cost	Computers Sold	Selling Cost per Unit
$300,000	$ 500,000	$ 800,000	20,000	$40.00
300,000	750,000	1,050,000	30,000	35.00
300,000	1,000,000	1,300,000	40,000	32.50
300,000	1,250,000	1,550,000	50,000	31.00

The graph for our mixed cost example is given in Exhibit 3-4 (assuming a relevant range of 0 to 50,000 units). Mixed costs are represented by a line that intercepts the vertical axis (at $300,000 for this example). The y-intercept corresponds to the fixed cost, and the slope of the line gives the variable cost per unit of activity driver (slope is $25 for this example).

Step-Cost Behavior

So far in our discussion of cost behavior, we have assumed that the cost function is continuous. In reality, some cost functions may be discontinuous; these costs are known as step costs. A **step cost** displays a constant level of cost for a range of output and then jumps to a higher level of cost at some point, where it remains for a similar range of output. Items that display a step-cost behavior must be purchased in chunks. The width of the step defines the range of output for which a particular amount of the resource applies.

Exhibit 3-5 illustrates step costs. Exhibit 3-5a shows a step cost with relatively narrow steps. This means that the cost changes in response to fairly small changes in output.

3-4

EXHIBIT

Mixed Cost Behavior

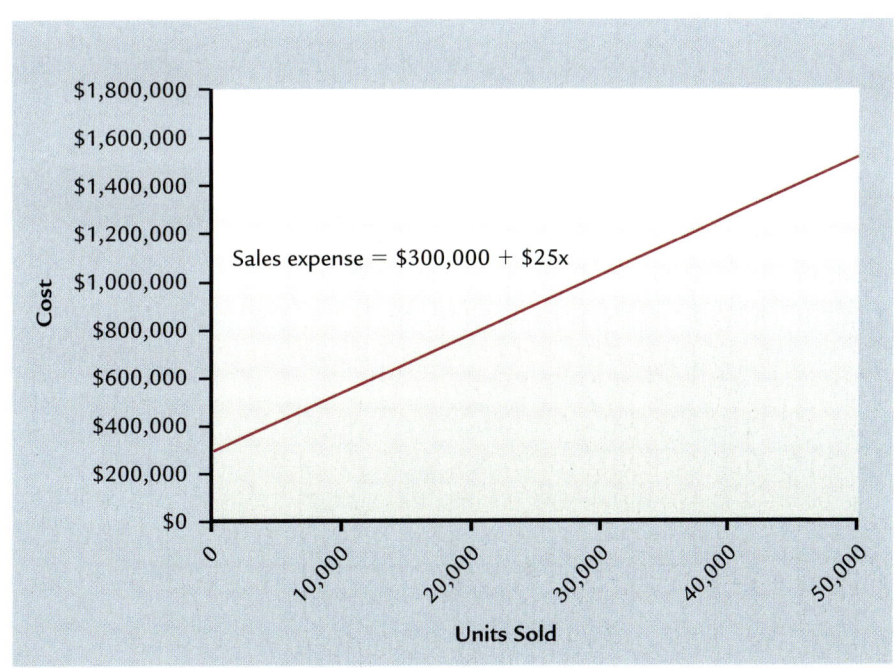

Sales expense = $300,000 + $25x

Step Costs

A: Step Cost with Narrow Steps

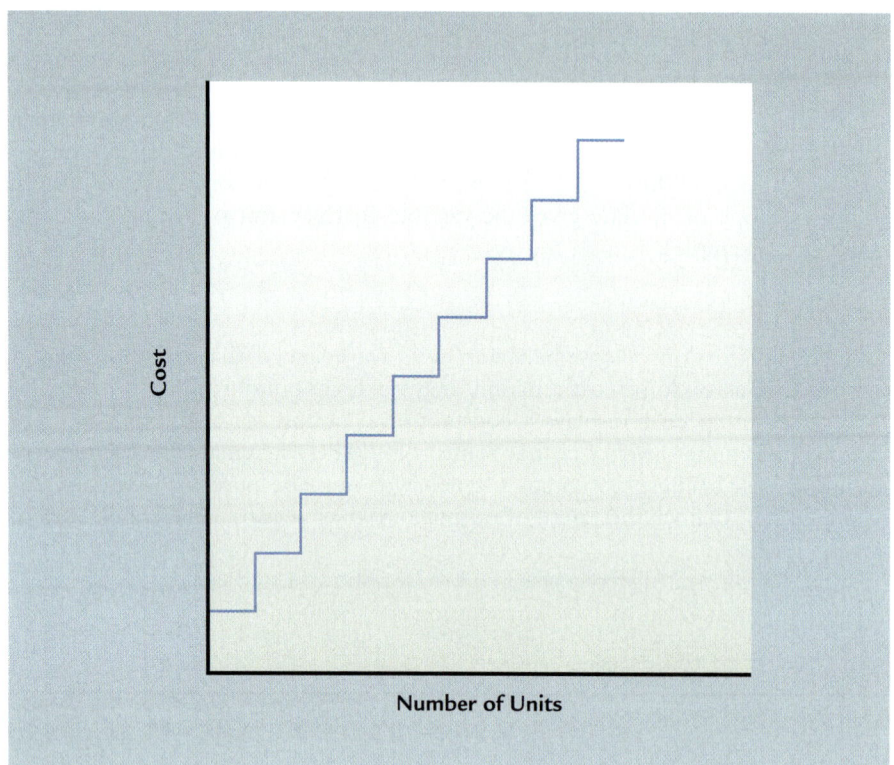

B: Step Cost with Wide Steps

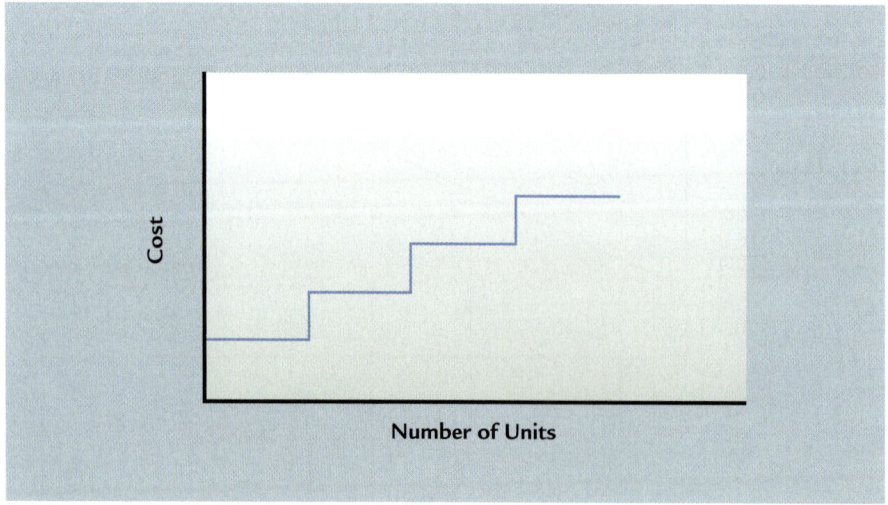

Often, if the steps are very narrow, we can approximate the step cost as a strictly variable cost. For example, Copy-2-Go, a photocopying shop, buys copy paper by the 20-ream box. The shop typically uses three boxes per day. The cost of copy paper is a step cost with very narrow steps. Exhibit 3-5b, however, shows a step cost with relatively wide steps. An example of this type of cost would be a factory that leases production machinery. Suppose that each machine can produce 1,000 units per month. If production ranges from 0 to 1,000 units, only one machine is needed. However, if production increases to amounts between 1,001 and 2,000 units, a second machine must be leased. Many so-called fixed costs may be, in reality, step costs.

Accounting Records and Mixed Costs

Sometimes it is easy to identify the variable and fixed components of a mixed cost, as in the example given earlier for Colley Computers' sales representatives. Many times, however, the only information available is the total cost and a measure of output. For example, the accounting system will usually record both the total cost of maintenance and the number of maintenance hours provided during a given period of time. How much of the total maintenance cost represents a fixed charge and how much represents a variable charge is not revealed by the accounting records. (In fact, the accounting records may not even reveal the breakdown of costs in the sales representative example.) Often, the total cost is simply recorded with no attempt to segregate the fixed and variable costs.

Need for Cost Separation

Accounting records typically show only the total cost and the associated amount of activity of a mixed cost item. Therefore, it is necessary to separate the total cost into its fixed and variable components. Only through a formal effort to separate costs can all costs be classified into the appropriate cost behavior categories.

If mixed costs are a very small percentage of total costs, formal cost separation may be more trouble than it's worth. In this case, mixed costs could be assigned to either the fixed or variable cost category without much concern for the classification error or its effect on decision making. Alternatively, the total mixed cost could be arbitrarily divided between the two cost categories. This option is seldom available though. Mixed costs for many firms are large enough to call for separation.

METHODS FOR SEPARATING MIXED COSTS INTO FIXED AND VARIABLE COMPONENTS

OBJECTIVE 3

Separate mixed costs into their fixed and variable components using the high-low method, the scattergraph method, and the method of least squares.

Three methods of separating a mixed cost into its fixed and variable components are commonly used: the high-low method, the scattergraph method, and the method of least squares. Each method requires the simplifying assumption of a linear cost relationship. Therefore, before we examine each of these methods more closely, let's review the expression of cost as an equation for a straight line.

$$\text{Total cost} = \text{Fixed cost} + \text{Variable rate} \times \text{Output}$$

The **dependent variable** is a variable whose value depends on the value of another variable. In the above equation, total cost is the dependent variable; it is the cost we are trying to predict. The **independent variable** is a variable that measures output and explains changes in the cost. A good independent variable is one that causes or is closely associated with the dependent variable; it is a driver. The **intercept** corresponds to fixed cost. Graphically, the intercept is the point at which the cost line intercepts the cost (vertical) axis. The **slope** corresponds to the variable rate (the variable cost per unit of output); it is the slope of the cost line. Cornerstone 3-1 shows how to create and use a cost formula.

Cornerstone 3-1

HOW TO Create and Use a Cost Formula

Information: The art and graphics department of State College decided to equip each faculty office with an inkjet color printer (computers were already in place). Sufficient color printers had monthly depreciation of $250. The department purchased paper in boxes of 10,000 sheets (20 reams of 500 sheets each) for $35 per box. Ink cartridges cost $30 and will print, on average, 300 pages.

Required:
1. Create a formula for the monthly cost of inkjet printing in the art and graphics department.
2. If the department expects to print 4,400 pages next month, what is the expected fixed cost? Total variable cost? Total printing cost?

Calculation:
1. The cost formula takes the following form:

$$\text{Total cost} = \text{Fixed cost} + (\text{Variable rate} \times \text{Number of pages})$$

The monthly fixed cost is $250 (the cost of printer depreciation) since it does not vary according to the number of pages printed. The variable costs are paper and ink since both do vary with the number of pages printed.

Cost of paper per page = $35/10,000 = $0.0035
Cost of ink per page = $30/300 = $0.10

Variable rate per page = $0.0035 + $0.10 = $0.1035

The cost formula is:

$$\text{Total cost of printing} = \$250 + (\$0.1035 \times \text{Number of pages})$$

2. Expected fixed cost for next month = $250
   Expected variable cost for next month = $0.1035 × 4,400 pages = $455.40
   Expected total printing cost for next month = $250 + $455.40 = $705.40

Since the accounting records reveal only total cost and output, those values must be used to estimate the fixed cost and variable rate. Three methods can be used to accomplish this: the high-low method, the scattergraph method, and the method of least squares.

The following example with the same data will be used with each method so that comparisons among them can be made. The example focuses on materials handling cost for Anderson Company, a manufacturer of household cleaning products. Materials handling involves moving materials from one area of the factory, say the raw materials storeroom, to another area, such as workstation #6. Large, complex organizations have found that the cost of moving materials can be very large. Understanding the behavior of this cost is an important part of deciding how to reduce the cost.

Anderson's controller has accumulated data for the materials handling activity. The plant manager believes that the number of material moves is a good activity driver for the activity. Assume that the accounting records of Anderson Company disclose the following material handling costs and number of material moves for the past 10 months:

Month	Material Handling Cost	Number of Moves
January	$2,000	100
February	3,090	125
March	2,780	175

Month	Material Handling Cost	Number of Moves
April	$1,990	200
May	7,500	500
June	5,300	300
July	3,800	250
August	6,300	400
September	5,600	475
October	6,240	425

The High-Low Method

From basic geometry, we know that two points are needed to determine a line. Once we know two points on a line, then its equation can be determined. Recall that the fixed cost is the *intercept* of the total cost line and that the variable rate is the *slope* of the line. Given two points, the slope and the intercept can be determined. The **high-low method** is a method of separating mixed costs into fixed and variable components by using just the high and low data points. Four steps must be taken in the high-low method.

Analytical Q & A

When working high-low problems, it helps to circle the high and low points so you don't get confused. Right now, go to the data given for materials handling cost and number of moves and circle the high point and low point.

Answer:
The high point is May, with cost of $7,500 and 500 moves; the low point is January, with cost of $2,000 and 100 moves.

Step 1: Find the high point and the low point for a given data set. The *high point* is defined as the point with the *highest activity* or *output level*. The *low point* is defined as the point with the *lowest activity* or *output level*. In the data for maintenance cost, the high output occurred in May, with 500 material moves and total cost of $7,500. The low output was in January with 100 material moves and total cost of $2,000.

Step 2: Using the high and low points, calculate the variable rate. To do this, we recognize that the variable rate, or slope, is the change in the total cost divided by the change in output.

$$\text{Variable rate} = \frac{\text{High point cost} - \text{Low point cost}}{\text{High point output} - \text{Low point output}}$$

Using the high and low points for our example, that would be as follows:

Variable rate = ($7,500 − $2,000)/(500 − 100) = $5,500/400 = $13.75

Step 3: Calculate the fixed cost using the variable rate (from step 2) and either the high point or the low point.

Fixed cost = Total cost at high point − (Variable rate × Output at high point)

OR

Fixed cost = Total cost at low point − (Variable rate × Output at low point)

Let's use the high point to calculate fixed cost.

Fixed cost = $7,500 − ($13.75 × 500) = $625

Step 4: Form the cost formula for materials handling based on the high-low method.

Total cost = $625 + $13.75 × Number of moves

Cornerstone 3-2 shows how to use the high-low method to construct a cost formula. Once we have the cost formula, we can use it in budgeting and in performance control. For example, suppose that the number of moves for November is expected to be 350. Budgeted materials handling cost would be $5,437.50, or $625 + ($13.75 × 350). Alternatively, suppose the controller wondered whether or not October's materials handling cost of $6,240 was reasonably close to what would have been predicted. Our cost formula would predict October's cost of $6,469 (rounded). (This amount is found by multiplying $13.75 times the 425 actual moves and then adding fixed cost of $625.) The actual cost is just $229 different from the predicted cost and probably would be judged to be reasonably close to budgeted cost. Cornerstone 3-3 shows how to use the high-low method to calculate predicted total variable cost and total cost for budgeted output.

Analytical Q & A

Right now, calculate the fixed cost by using the low point and the variable rate calculated in step 2. (You will get the same fixed cost, $625.)

Answer:
Fixed cost = $2,000 − $13.75(100) = $625

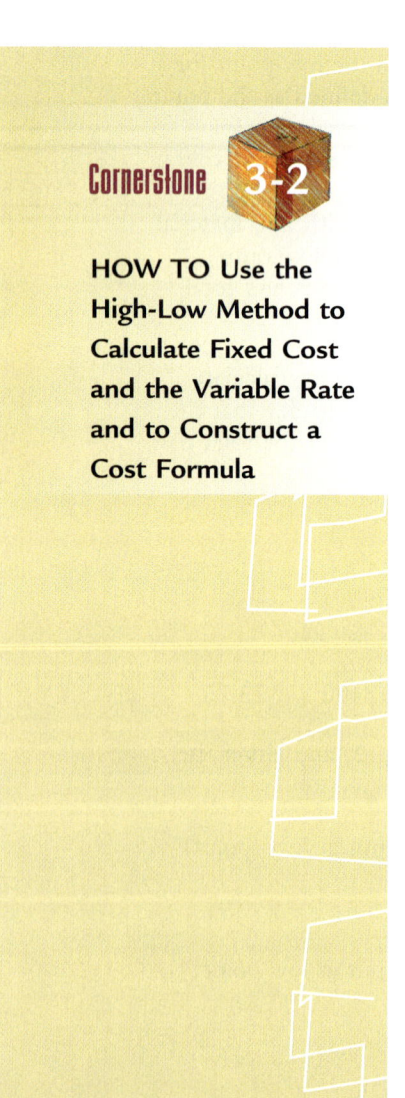

Cornerstone 3-2

HOW TO Use the High-Low Method to Calculate Fixed Cost and the Variable Rate and to Construct a Cost Formula

Information: BlueDenim Company makes blue jeans. The company controller wants to calculate the fixed and variable costs associated with electricity used in the factory. Data for the past nine months were collected:

Month	Electricity Cost	Machine Hours
January	$3,255	460
February	3,485	500
March	**4,100**	**600**
April	3,300	470
May	3,312	470
June	**2,575**	**350**
July	3,910	570
August	4,200	590

Required: Using the high-low method, calculate the fixed cost of electricity, calculate the variable rate per machine hour, and construct the cost formula for total electricity cost.

Calculation:

Step 1—Find the high and low points: The high number of machine hours is in March, and the low number of machine hours is in June. (*Hint:* Did you notice that the high cost of $4,200 was for August? Yet, August is not the high point because its number of machine hours is not the highest activity level. Remember, the high point is associated with the highest activity level; the low point is associated with the lowest activity level.)

Step 2—Calculate the variable rate:

Variable rate = (High cost − Low cost)/(High machine hours − Low machine hours)
= ($4,100 − $2,575)/(600 − 350) = $1,525/250
= $6.10 per machine hour

Step 3—Calculate the fixed cost:

Fixed cost = Total cost − (Variable rate × Machine hours)

Let's choose the high point with cost of $4,100 and machine hours of 600.

Fixed cost = $4,100 − ($6.10 × 600) = $4,100 − $3,660
= $440

(*Hint:* Check your work by computing fixed cost using the low point.)

Step 4—Construct a cost formula: If the variable rate is $6.10 per machine hour and fixed cost is $440 per month, then the formula for monthly electricity cost is:

Total electricity cost = $440 + ($6.10 × Machine hours)

Cornerstone 3-3

HOW TO Use the High-Low Method to Calculate Predicted Total Variable Cost and Total Cost for Budgeted Output

Information: Recall that BlueDenim Company constructed the following formula for monthly electricity cost. (Refer to Cornerstone 3-2 to see how the fixed cost per month and the variable rate were computed.)

$$\text{Total electricity cost} = \$440 + (\$6.10 \times \text{Machine hours})$$

Required: Assume that 550 machine hours are budgeted for the month of September. Use the above cost formula for the following calculations:
1. Calculate total variable electricity cost for October.
2. Calculate total electricity cost for October.

Calculation:
1. Total variable electricity cost = Variable rate × Machine hours
$$= \$6.10 \times 550$$
$$= \$3,355$$
2. Total electricity cost = Fixed cost + (Variable rate × Machine hours)
$$= \$440 + (\$6.10 \times 550)$$
$$= \$440 + \$3,355$$
$$= \$3,795$$

Let's look at one last point. Notice that monthly data were used to find the high and low points and to calculate the fixed cost and variable rate. This means that the cost formula is the fixed cost *for the month*. Suppose, however, that the company wants to use that formula to predict cost for a different period of time, say a year. In that case, the variable cost rate is just multiplied by the budgeted amount of the independent variable for the year. The intercept, or fixed cost, however, must be adjusted. To convert monthly fixed cost to yearly fixed cost, simply multiply the monthly fixed cost by 12 (because there are 12 months in a year). If weekly data were used to calculate the fixed and variable costs, one would multiply the weekly fixed cost by 52 to convert it to yearly fixed cost, and so on. Cornerstone 3-4 shows how to use the high-low method to calculate predicted total variable cost and total cost for budgeted output.

Cornerstone 3-4

HOW TO Use the High-Low Method to Calculate Predicted Total Variable Cost and Total Cost for a Time Period That Differs from the Data Period

Information: Recall that BlueDenim Company constructed the following formula for *monthly* electricity cost. (Refer to Cornerstone 3-2 to see how the fixed cost per month and variable rate were computed.)

$$\text{Total electricity cost} = \$440 + (\$6.10 \times \text{Machine hours})$$

Required: Assume that 6,500 machine hours are budgeted for the coming year. Use the above cost formula to make the following calculations:
1. Calculate total variable electricity cost for the year.
2. Calculate total fixed electricity cost for the year.
3. Calculate total electricity cost for the coming year.

Calculation:
1. Total variable electricity cost = Variable rate × Machine hours
$$= \$6.10 \times 6,500$$
$$= \$39,650$$

2. There's a trick here; the cost formula is for the month, but we are being asked to budget electricity for the year. So, we will need to multiply the fixed cost for the month by 12 (the number of months in a year).

Total fixed electricity cost = Fixed cost × 12 months in a year
$$= \$440 \times 12$$
$$= \$5,280$$

3. Total electricity cost = 12($440) + ($6.10 × 6,500)
$$= \$5,280 + \$39,650$$
$$= \$44,930$$

The high-low method has the advantage of objectivity. That is, any two people using the high-low method on a particular data set will arrive at the same answer. In addition, the high-low method allows a manager to get a quick fix on a cost relationship using only two data points. For example, a manager may have only two months of data. Sometimes this will be enough to get a crude approximation of the cost relationship.

The high-low method is usually not as good as the other methods. Why? First, the high and low points often can be what are known as outliers. They may represent atypical cost-activity relationships. If so, the cost formula computed using these two points will not represent what usually takes place. The scattergraph method can help a manager avoid this trap by selecting two points that appear to be representative of the general cost-activity pattern. Second, even if these points are not outliers, other pairs of points may clearly be more representative. Again, the scattergraph method allows the choice of more representative points.

Scattergraph Method

The **scattergraph method** is a way to see the cost relationship by plotting the data points on a graph. The first step in applying the scattergraph method is to plot the data points so that the relationship between materials handling costs and activity output can be seen. This plot is referred to as a scattergraph and is shown in Exhibit 3-6a. The vertical axis is total cost (materials handling cost), and the horizontal axis is the driver or output measure (number of moves). Looking at Exhibit 3-6a, we see that the relationship between materials handling costs and number of moves is reasonably linear; cost goes up as the number of moves goes up, and vice versa.

Now let's examine Exhibit 3-6b, to see if the line determined by the high and low points is representative of the overall relationship. Notice that three points lie above the

3-6a

EXHIBIT

Anderson Company's Materials Handling Cost

Scattergraph Showing Data Points

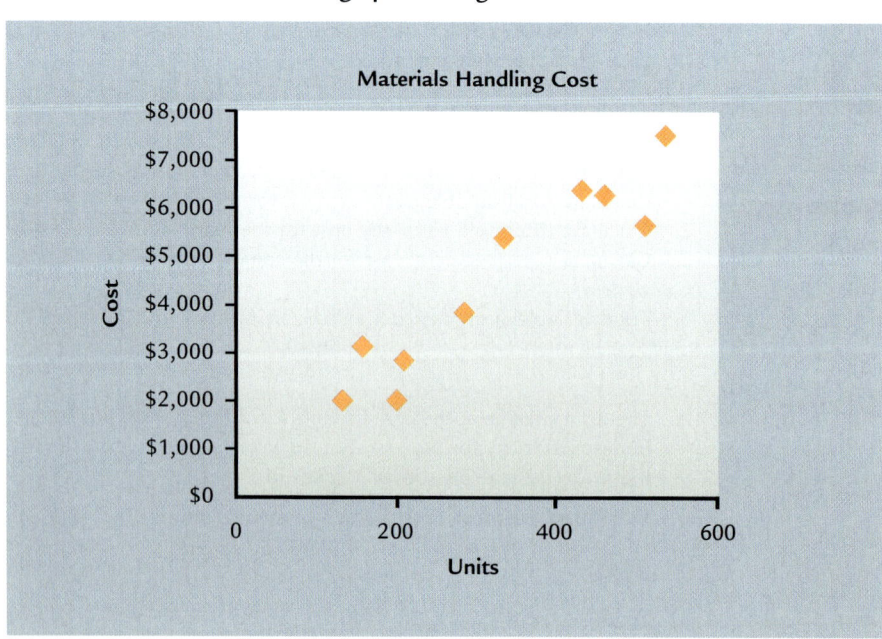

Scattergraph with the High-Low Cost Line

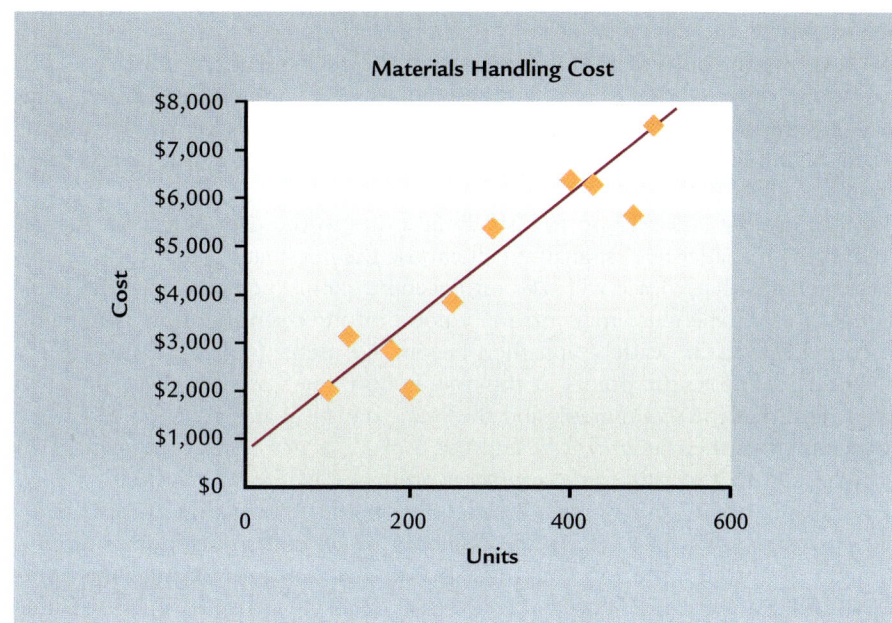

Scattergraph with the Cost Line Fitted by Visual Inspection

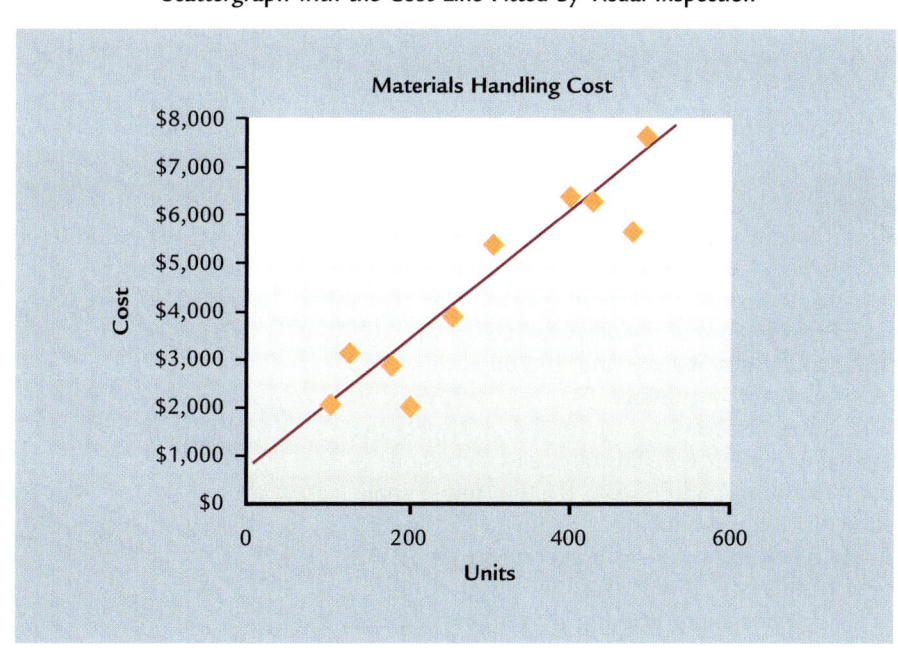

high-low line and five lie below it. This does not give us confidence in the high-low results for fixed and variable costs. In particular, we might wonder if the variable cost (slope) is somewhat higher than it should be and the fixed cost is somewhat lower than it should be.

Thus, one purpose of a scattergraph is to see whether or not a straight line reasonably describes the cost relationship. Additionally, inspecting the scattergraph may reveal one or more points that do not seem to fit the general pattern of behavior. Upon investigation, it may be discovered that these points (the outliers) were due to some irregular occurrences that are not expected to happen again. This knowledge might justify their elimination and perhaps lead to a better estimate of the underlying cost function.

We can use the scattergraph to visually fit a line to the data points on the graph. Of course, the manager or cost analyst will choose the line that appears to fit the points the best, perhaps that choice will take into account past experience with the behavior of the cost item. Experience may provide a good intuitive sense of how materials handling costs behave; the scattergraph then becomes a useful tool to quantify this intuition. Fitting a line to the points in this way is how the scattergraph method works. Keep in mind that the scattergraph and the other statistical aids are tools that can help managers improve their judgment. Using the tools does not restrict the manager from using judgment to alter any of the estimates produced by formal methods.

Examine Exhibit 3-6 carefully. Based only on the information contained in the graph, how would you fit a line to the points in it? Of course, an infinite number of lines might go through the data, but let's choose one that goes through the point for January (100, $2,000) and intersects the y-axis at $800. Now, we have the straight line shown in Exhibit 3-6c. The fixed cost, of course, is $800, the intercept. We can use the high-low method to determine the variable rate.

First, remember that our two points are (100, $2,000) and (0, $800). Next, use these two points to compute the variable rate (the slope):

$$\text{Variable rate} = \frac{\text{High cost} - \text{Low cost}}{\text{High number of moves} - \text{Low number of moves}}$$
$$= (\$2,000 - \$800)/(100 - 0)$$
$$= \$1,200/100$$
$$= \$12$$

Thus, the variable rate is $12 per material move.

The fixed cost and variable rate for materials handling cost have now been identified. The cost formula for the materials handling activity can be expressed as:

$$\text{Total cost} = \$800 + \$12 \times \text{Number of moves}$$

Using this formula, the total cost of materials handling for between 100 and 500 moves can be predicted and then broken down into fixed and variable components. For example, assume that 350 moves are planned for November. Using the cost formula, the predicted cost is $5,000 [$800 + ($12 × 350)]. Of this total cost, $800 is fixed and $4,200 is variable.

A significant advantage of the scattergraph method is that it allows a cost analyst to inspect the data visually. Exhibit 3-7 illustrates cost behavior situations that are not appropriate for the simple application of the high-low method. Exhibit 3-7a shows a nonlinear relationship between cost and output. An example of this is a volume discount given on direct materials or evidence of learning by workers (e.g., as more hours are worked, the total cost increases at a decreasing rate due to the increased efficiency of the

Concept Q & A

Draw a straight line through the high and low points on each graph in Exhibit 3-7. Can you see that these lines, the high-low lines, could give misleading information on fixed and variable costs?

Answer:
Yes, it is very important to consider the relevant range.

Scattergraphs with Nonlinear Cost

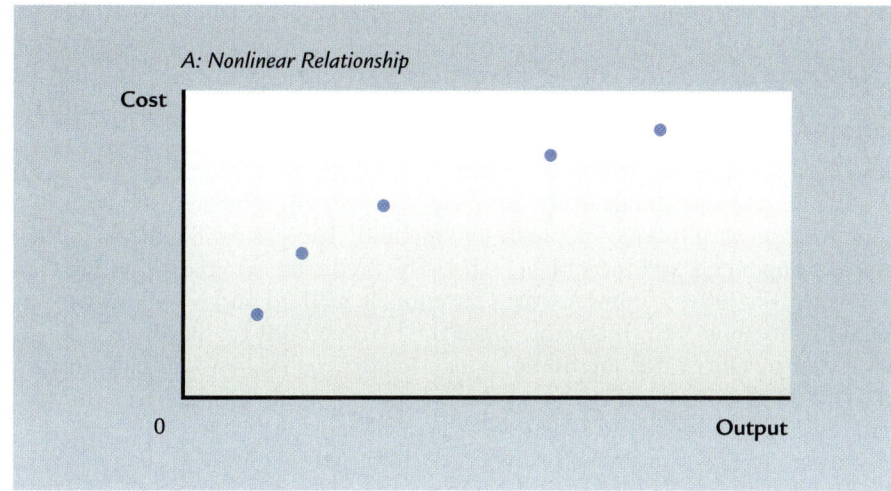

A: Nonlinear Relationship

Cost

0　　　　　　　　　　　　　　　　**Output**

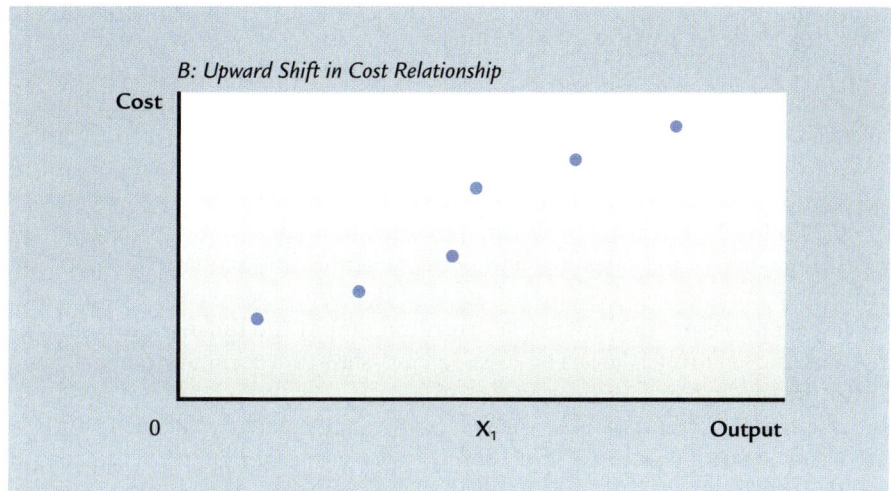

B: Upward Shift in Cost Relationship

Cost

0　　　　　　　**X₁**　　　　　**Output**

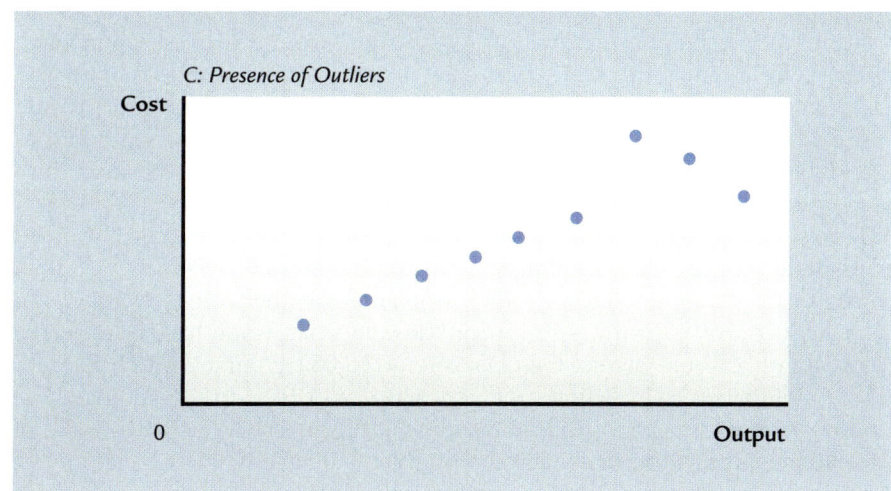

C: Presence of Outliers

Cost

0　　　　　　　　　　　　　　　　**Output**

workers). Exhibit 3-7b shows an upward shift in cost if more than X_1 units are made—perhaps because an additional supervisor must be hired or a second shift run. Exhibit 3-7c shows outliers that do not represent the overall cost relationship.

The cost formula for materials handling was obtained by fitting a line to two points [(0, $800) and (100, $2,000)] in Exhibit 3-6c. Judgment was used to select the line. Whereas one person may decide that the best-fitting line is the one passing through those points, others, using their own judgment, may decide that the best line passes through other pairs of points.

The scattergraph method suffers from the lack of any objective criterion for choosing the best-fitting line. The quality of the cost formula depends on the quality of the subjective judgment of the analyst. The high-low method removes the subjectivity in the choice of the line. Regardless of who uses the method, the same line will result.

Looking again at Exhibits 3-6b and 3-6c, we can compare the results of the scattergraph method with those of the high-low method. There is a difference between the fixed cost components and the variable rates. The predicted materials handling cost for 350 moves is $5,000 according to the scattergraph method and $5,438 according to the high-low method. Which is right? Since the two methods can produce significantly different cost formulas, the question of which method is the best naturally arises. Ideally, a method that is objective and, at the same time, produces the best-fitting line is needed. Let's take a look at the method of least squares.

The Method of Least Squares

The **method of least squares (regression)** is a statistical way to find the *best-fitting* line through a set of data points. One advantage of the method of least squares is that, for a given set of data, it will always produce the same cost formula. Basically, the best-fitting line is the one in which the data points are closer to the line than to any other line. What do we mean by closest? Let's take a look at Exhibit 3-8. Notice that there are a series of data points and a line—we'll assume it is the regression line calculated by the method of least squares. The data points do not all lie directly on the line; this is typical. However, the regression line better describes the pattern of the data than other possible lines. This is because the squared deviations between the regression line and each data point are, in total, smaller than the sum of the squared deviations of the data points and any other line. The least squares statistical formulas can find the one line with the smallest sum of squared deviations.

Formerly, the method of least squares had to be calculated by hand. It was a complicated and lengthy process. Today, spreadsheet programs for personal computers have regression packages. It is easy to use them to input data and let the programs calculate the fixed cost and variable rate. Exhibit 3-9 shows a printout from an Excel® spreadsheet regression that was run on the data from Anderson Company. Notice that the intercept term is the fixed cost and it is $789 (rounded). The variable rate is shown as "X Variable 1"; in other words, it is the first independent variable. So, the variable rate is $12.38 (rounded). We can use the output of regression in budgeting and control the same way that we used the results of the high-low and scattergraph methods.

Suppose that Anderson Company expects the number of moves for November to be 350. Budgeted materials handling cost would be $5,122, or $789 + ($12.38 × 350). Alternatively, suppose the controller wondered whether or not October's materials handling cost of $6,240 was reasonably close to what would have been predicted. Our cost formula would predict October cost of $6,051 (rounded). (This amount is found by multiplying $12.38 times the 425 actual moves and then adding the fixed cost of $789.) The actual cost is just $189 different from the predicted cost and probably would be judged to be reasonably close to the budgeted cost. Cornerstone 3-5 on page 86 shows how to use results of regression to construct a cost formula.

Line Deviations

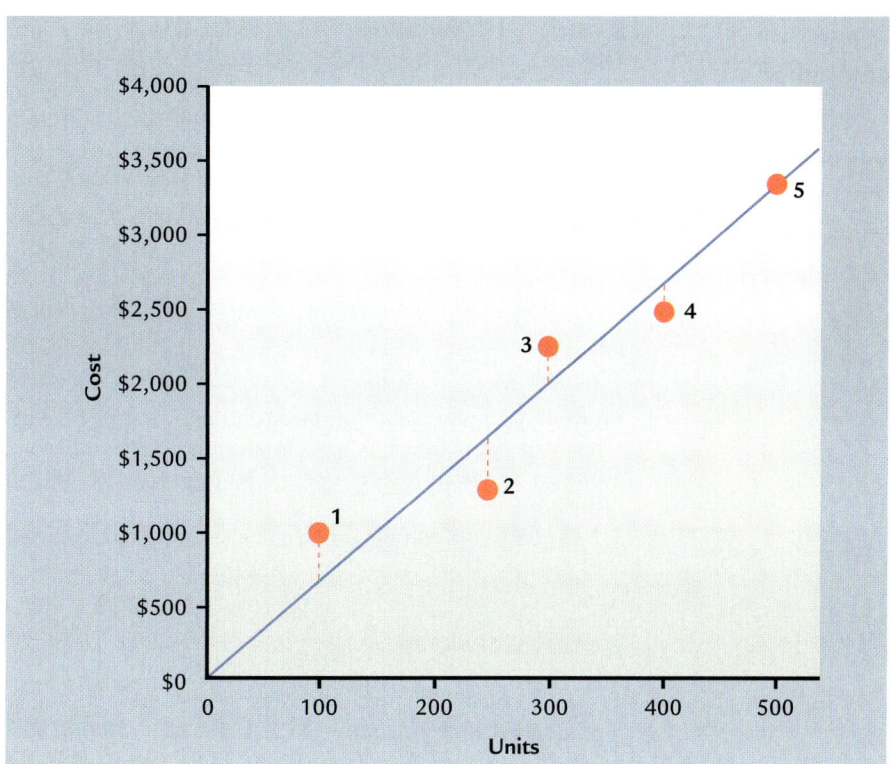

A Portion of the Summary Output from Excel for Anderson Company

	A	B	C	D	E	F	G	H
	Anderson Company.xls							
1	Coefficients:							
2	Intercept	788.7806						
3	X Variable 1	12.38058						
4								
5								
6								
7								
8								
9								
10								
11								
12								
13								
14								
15								

Sheet1 / Sheet2 / Sheet3 /

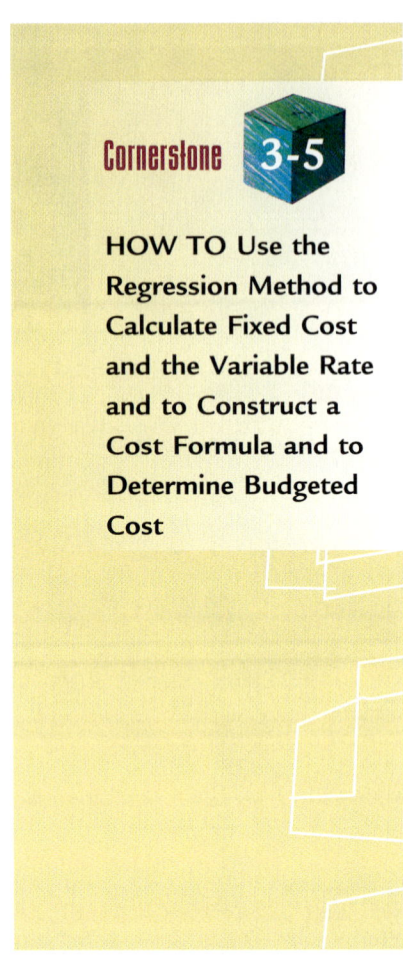

Cornerstone **3-5**

HOW TO Use the Regression Method to Calculate Fixed Cost and the Variable Rate and to Construct a Cost Formula and to Determine Budgeted Cost

Information: BlueDenim Company makes blue jeans. The company controller wanted to calculate the fixed and variable costs associated with electricity used in the factory. Data for the past nine months were collected:

Month	Electricity Cost	Machine Hours
January	$3,255	460
February	3,485	500
March	4,100	600
April	3,300	470
May	3,312	470
June	2,575	350
July	3,910	570
August	4,200	590

Coefficients shown by a regression program are:

Intercept	321
X Variable 1	6.38

Required: Using the results of regression, calculate the fixed cost of electricity and the variable rate per machine hour. Construct the cost formula for total electricity cost. Calculate the budgeted cost for next month assuming that 550 machine hours are budgeted.

Calculation:

1. The fixed cost and the variable rate are given directly by regression.

$$\text{Fixed cost} = \$321$$
$$\text{Variable rate} = \$6.38$$

2. The cost formula is:

$$\text{Total electricity cost} = \$321 + (\$6.38 \times \text{Machine hours})$$

3. Budgeted electricity cost $= \$321 + (\$6.38 \times 550) = \$3,830$

Managerial Judgment

Managerial judgment is critically important in determining cost behavior and is by far the most widely used method in practice. Many managers simply use their experience and past observation of cost relationships to determine fixed and variable costs. This method, however, may take a number of forms. Some managers simply assign some costs to the fixed category and others to the variable category. They ignore the possibility of mixed costs. Thus, a chemical firm may regard materials and utilities as strictly variable, with respect to pounds of chemical produced, and all other costs as fixed. Even labor, the textbook example of a strictly variable cost, may be fixed for this firm. The appeal of this method is simplicity. Before opting for this course, management would do well to make sure that each cost is predominantly fixed or variable and that the decisions being made are not highly sensitive to errors in classifying costs as fixed or variable.

To illustrate the use of judgment in assessing cost behavior, consider Elgin Sweeper Company, a leading manufacturer of motorized street sweepers. Using production volume as the measure of activity output, Elgin revised its chart of accounts to organize costs into fixed and variable components. Elgin's accountants used their knowledge of the company to assign expenses to either a fixed or variable category, using a decision rule that categorized an expense as fixed if it were fixed 75 percent of the time and as variable if it were variable 75 percent of the time.[1]

[1]John P. Callan, Wesley N. Tredup, and Randy S. Wissinger, "Elgin Sweeper Company's Journey Toward Cost Management," *Management Accounting* (July 1991): 24–27.

Concept Q & A

Suppose that you owned a small business with a photocopier that neighboring businesses asked to use occasionally. How would you figure out the average cost of copying one page? What cost items do you think you would include? How would you find the cost? Now consider Kinkos: What cost items do you think they would include?

Answer:

If a neighboring business owner only needed a copy rarely, you might just consider it a favor and not charge at all. If it happened several times a month, for a few pages, you might charge the variable cost of paper and toner. Finally, if the neighboring business owner used your copier frequently, you might just charge 10¢ to 20¢ per page—something in keeping with the cost of an outside photocopying shop. Alternatively, the neighbor might buy you a ream a paper from time to time. Kinkos must include all costs in considering cost—including paper, toner, depreciation on equipment, cost of electricity and utilities, wages of staff, and so on.

Management may instead identify mixed costs and divide these costs into fixed and variable components by deciding just what the fixed and variable parts are; that is, they may use experience to say that a certain amount of a cost is fixed and that the rest therefore must be variable. Suppose that a small business had a photocopier with a fixed cost of $3,000 per year. The variable component could be computed using one or more cost/volume data points. This has the advantage of accounting for mixed costs but is subject to a similar type of error as the strict fixed/variable dichotomy. That is, management may be wrong in its assessment.

Finally, management may use experience and judgment to refine statistical estimation results. Perhaps the experienced manager might "eyeball" the data and throw out several points as being highly unusual or revise results of estimation to take account of projected changes in cost structure or technology. For example, Tecnol Medical Products, Inc., radically changed its method of manufacturing medical face masks. Traditionally, face-mask production was very labor intensive, requiring hand stitching. Tecnol developed its own highly automated equipment and became the industry's low cost supplier—besting both Johnson & Johnson and 3M. Tecnol's rapid expansion into new product lines and European markets means that historical data on costs and revenues are, for the most part, irrelevant. Tecnol's management must look forward, not back, to predict the impact of changes on profit.[2] Statistical techniques are highly accurate in depicting the past, but they cannot foresee the future, which of course is what management really wants.

The advantage of using managerial judgment to separate fixed and variable costs is its simplicity. In situations in which the manager has a deep understanding of the firm and its cost patterns, this method can give good results. However, if the manager does not have good judgment, errors will occur. Therefore, it is important to consider the experience of the manager, the potential for error, and the effect that error could have on related decisions.

APPLICATIONS IN BUSINESS

IBM is promoting its sale of various computer services as an "e-utility." For example, IBM wants to provide health insurance claims processing for companies. Companies using this service would be able to outsource their insurance claims processing, converting what is now a mixed cost with heavy doses of fixed cost into a variable cost based on the number of claims processed. IBM estimates that the outsourcing could save some companies as much as 50 percent in reduced administrative costs.

Many other service companies provide these types of services. For example, many mid-sized and large banks offer their client businesses the option of having their customers send their checks (to pay accounts receivable) directly to the bank. The bank then opens the mail, sorts it, cashes and deposits the checks, and updates both the client's checking account balance and the accounts receivable file. The clients pay based on amount of usage. This allows the client to reduce office staff and excess capacity.

Source: William M. Bulkeley, "IBM Wins Contract to Reduce Health-Claim Processing Costs," *The Wall Street Journal online* (June 13, 2002).

[2]Stephanie Anderson Forest, "Who's Afraid of J&J and 3M," *Business Week* (December 5, 1994): 66, 68.

Let's go back to Tiffany and Li Ming to see what happened next. The two of them are in Li Ming's office:

Li Ming: I've studied your health insurance claims process and discovered that there's a considerable amount of fixed cost involved. You have two paralegals on staff who work full time on processing claims. While some of their time is spent in the routine processing of uncontested claims, much is spent on the claims that have incomplete documentation or are contested. One of my people works half time on cutting checks and accounting for claims processing. That cost does seem to vary with the number of claims processed. Then there is computer time—we had actually been thinking of buying another server and you know how that increases the computer department's costs, not to mention the forms and supplies. I talked to the outsourcing company and figure we could easily save at least 20 percent of our processing costs if we use them instead. My only problem now is what to do with those three people. I hate to tell someone they have to go.

Tiffany: Actually, Li Ming, you won't have to do that. Our hiring is frozen right now, but we still have employees moving away or retiring. I figure at least seven people from the administrative staff will be leaving for one reason or another next month. We could absorb those three employees into one of those jobs! Thanks so much, we're both going to come out ahead on the new efficiency directive!

SUMMARY OF LEARNING OBJECTIVES

Cost behavior is the way in which a cost changes in relation to changes in activity output. The time horizon is important in determining cost behavior because costs can change from fixed to variable depending on whether the decision takes place over the short run or the long run. Variable costs are those which change in total as the driver, or output measure, changes. Usually, we assume that variable costs increase in direct proportion to increases in activity output. Fixed costs are those which do not change in total as activity output changes. Mixed costs have both a variable and a fixed component. The resource usage model adds additional understanding of cost behavior.

Three formal methods can be used to decompose mixed costs: the high-low method, the scattergraph method, and the method of least squares. In the high-low method, the two points chosen from the scattergraph are the high point and the low point with respect to activity level. These two points are then used to compute the intercept and the slope of the line on which they lie. The high-low method is objective and easy. However, if either the high or low point is not representative of the true cost relationship, the relationship will be incorrectly estimated.

The scattergraph method involves inspecting a graph showing total mixed cost at various output levels and selecting two points that seem best to represent the relationship between cost and output. Since two points determine a line, the two selected points can be used to determine the intercept and the slope of the line on which they lie. The intercept gives an estimate of the fixed cost component and the slope an estimate of the variable cost per unit of activity. The scattergraph method is a good way to identify nonlinearity, the presence of outliers, and the presence of a shift in the cost relationship. Its disadvantage is that it is subjective.

The method of least squares uses all of the data points (except outliers) on the scattergraph and produces a line that best fits all of the points. The line is best fitting in the sense that it is closest to all the points as measured by the sum of the squared deviations of the points from the line. The method of least squares produces the line that best fits the data points and is therefore recommended over the high-low and scattergraph methods.

The least squares method has the advantage of offering methods to assess the reliability of cost equations. The coefficient of determination allows an analyst to compute the amount of cost variability explained by a particular activity driver. The standard error of estimate can be used to build a prediction interval for cost. If the interval is too wide, it may suggest that the equation is not very useful for prediction, even if the driver explains a high percentage of the cost variability. The least squares method can also be used to build a cost equation using more than one activity output. Equations built using multiple regression can also be evaluated for their reliability.

Managerial judgment can be used alone or in conjunction with the high-low, scattergraph, or least squares methods. Managers use their experience and knowledge of cost and activity-level relationships to identify outliers, understand structural shifts, and adjust parameters due to anticipated changing conditions.

Cornerstones for Chapter 3

KEY TERMS

Coefficient of determination (R^2), 92

Committed fixed cost, 70

Cost behavior, 66

Dependent variable, 75

Discretionary fixed costs, 70

Driver, 66

Fixed costs, 67

High-low method, 77

Independent variable, 75

Intercept, 75

Method of least squares (regression), 84

Mixed costs, 72

Relevant range, 66

Scattergraph method, 80

Slope, 75

Step cost, 73

Variable costs, 70

APPENDIX

Using the Regression Programs

Computing the regression formula manually is tedious, even with only a few data points. As the number of data points increases, manual computation becomes impractical. Fortunately, spreadsheet packages such as Lotus 1-2-3®, Quattro Pro®, and Microsoft Excel® have regression routines that will perform the computations. All you need to do is input the data. The spreadsheet regression program supplies more than the estimates of the coefficients. It also provides information that can be used to see how reliable the cost equation is—a feature that is not available for the scattergraph and high-low methods.

The first step in using the computer to calculate regression coefficients is to enter the data. Exhibit 3-10 shows the computer screen you would see if you entered the Anderson Company data on setups into a spreadsheet. It is a good idea to label your variables as is done here. That is, the months are labeled, as is column B for setup costs and column C for number of setup hours. The next step is to run the regression. In Excel, the regression routine is located under the tools menu (located toward the top right of the screen). When you pull down the tools menu, you will see other menu possibilities. Choose add in and then add the data analysis tools. When the data analysis tools have been added, data analysis will appear at the bottom of the tools menu; click on data analysis, and then on regression.

OBJECTIVE 4

Use a personal computer spreadsheet program to perform the method of least squares.

3-10 EXHIBIT

Spreadsheet Data for Anderson Company

	A	B	C	D	E	F	G	H
	Month	Cost	# Moves					
1								
2	January	$2,000	100					
3	February	3,090	125					
4	March	2,780	175					
5	April	1,990	200					
6	May	7,500	500					
7	June	5,300	300					
8	July	3,800	250					
9	August	6,300	400					
10	September	5,600	475					
11	October	6,240	425					
12								
13								
14								

Sheet1 / Sheet2 / Sheet3

When the regression screen pops up, you can tell the program where the dependent and independent variables are located. It is easy to simply place the cursor at the beginning of the independent rectangle and then (again using the cursor) block the values under the independent variable column, in this case, cells c2 through c11. Then, move the cursor to the beginning of the dependent rectangle and block the values in cells b2 through b11. Finally, you need to tell the computer where to place the output. Block a nice-sized rectangle, say cells a13 through f20 and click on OK. In less than the blink of an eye, the regression output is complete. The regression output is shown in Exhibit 3-11.

Now, let's take a look at the output in Exhibit 3-11. First, let's locate the fixed cost and variable rate coefficients. At the bottom of the exhibit, the intercept and X Variable 1 are shown, and the next column gives their coefficients. Rounding, the fixed cost is 789, and the variable rate is 12.38. Now, we can construct the cost formula for materials handling cost. It is:

$$\text{Materials handling cost} = \$789 + (\$12.38 \times \text{Number of moves})$$

We can use this formula to predict the materials handling cost for future months as we did with the formulas for the high-low and scattergraph methods.

Since the regression cost formula is the best-fitting line, it should produce better predictions of materials handling costs. For 350 moves, the total materials handling cost predicted by the least squares line is $5,122 [$789 + ($12.38 × 350)], with a fixed component of $789 plus a variable component of $4,333. Using this prediction as a standard, the scattergraph line most closely approximates the least squares line.

While the computer output in Exhibit 3-11 can give us the fixed and variable cost coefficients, its major usefulness lies in its ability to provide information about how reliable the estimated cost formula is. This is a feature not provided by either the scattergraph or high-low methods.

Goodness of Fit

Regression routines provide information on goodness of fit. Goodness of fit tells us how well the independent variable predicts the dependent variable. This information

3-11

EXHIBIT

Regression Output for Anderson Company

Regression Output for Anderson Company.xls

	A	B	C	D	E	F	G	H
1	SUMMARY OUTPUT							
2								
3	*Regression Statistics*							
4	Multiple R	0.92436						
5	R Square	0.854442						
6	Standard Error	810.1969						
7	Observations	9						
8								
9								
10		*Coefficients*						
11	Intercept	788.7806						
12	X Variable 1	12.38058						
13								
14								
15								

Sheet1 / Sheet2 / Sheet3

can be used to assess how reliable the estimated cost formula is, a feature not provided by either the scattergraph or high-low methods. The printout in Exhibit 3-11 provides a wealth of statistical information. However, we will look at just one more feature—the coefficient of determination or R^2. (The remaining information is discussed in statistics classes and higher level accounting classes.)

The Anderson Company example suggests that the number of moves can explain changes in materials handling costs. The scattergraph shown in Exhibit 3-6a confirms this belief because it reveals that materials handling costs and activity output (as measured by number of moves) seem to move together. It is quite likely that a significant percentage of the total variability in cost is explained by our output variable. We can determine statistically just how much variability is explained by looking at the coefficient of determination. The percentage of variability in the dependent variable explained by an independent variable (in this case, a measure of activity output) is called the **coefficient of determination (R^2)**. The higher the percentage of cost variability explained, the better job the independent variable does of explaining the dependent variable. Since R^2 is the percentage of variability explained, it always has a value between 0 and 1.00. In the printout in Exhibit 3-11, the coefficient of determination is labeled R Square (R^2). The value given is 0.85 (rounded), which means that 85 percent of the variability in the materials handling cost is explained by the number of moves. How good is this result? There is no cut-off point for a good versus a bad coefficient of determination. Clearly, the closer R^2 is to 1.00, the better. Is 85 percent good enough? How about 73 percent? Or even 46 percent? The answer is that it depends. If your cost equation yields a coefficient of determination of 75 percent, you know that your independent variable explains three-fourths of the variability in cost. You also know that some other factor or combination of factors explains the remaining one-fourth. Depending on your tolerance for error, you may want to improve the equation by trying different independent variables (for example, materials handling hours worked rather than number of moves) or by trying multiple regression. (Multiple regression uses two or more independent variables. This topic is saved for later courses.)

We note from the computer output in Exhibit 3-11 that the R^2 for materials handling cost is 0.85 In other words, material moves explain about 85 percent of the variability in the materials handling cost. This is not bad. However, something else explains the remaining 15 percent. Anderson Company's controller may want to keep this in mind when using the regression results.

DISCUSSION QUESTIONS

1. Why is knowledge of cost behavior important for managerial decision making? Give an example to illustrate your answer.
2. What is a driver? Give an example of a cost and its corresponding output measure or driver.
3. Suppose a company finds that shipping cost is $3,560 each month plus $6.70 per package shipped. What is the cost formula for monthly shipping cost? Identify the independent variable, the dependent variable, the fixed cost per month, and the variable rate.
4. Some firms assign mixed costs to either the fixed or variable cost categories without using any formal methodology to separate them. Explain how this practice can be defended.
5. Explain the difference between committed and discretionary fixed costs. Give examples of each.
6. Explain why the concept of relevant range is important when dealing with step costs.

7. Why do mixed costs pose a problem when it comes to classifying costs into fixed and variable categories?
8. Describe the cost formula for a strictly fixed cost such as depreciation of $15,000 per year.
9. Describe the cost formula for a strictly variable cost such as electrical power cost of $1.15 per machine hour (that is, every hour the machinery is run, electrical power cost goes up by $1.15).
10. What is the scattergraph method, and why is it used? Why is a scattergraph a good first step in separating mixed costs into their fixed and variable components?
11. Describe how the scattergraph method breaks out the fixed and variable costs from a mixed cost. Now describe how the high-low method works. How do the two methods differ?
12. What are the advantages of the scattergraph method over the high-low method? The high-low method over the scattergraph method?
13. Describe the method of least squares. Why is this method better than either the high-low method or the scattergraph method?
14. What is meant by the best-fitting line?
15. Explain the meaning of the coefficient of determination.

MULTIPLE-CHOICE EXERCISES

3-1 A factor that causes or leads to a change in a cost or activity is a(n)

a. driver.
b. intercept.
c. slope.
d. variable term.
e. ratchet.

3-2 Which of the following would probably be a variable cost in a soda bottling plant?

a. Direct labor
b. Bottles
c. Carbonated water
d. Power to run the bottling machine
e. All of the above

3-3 Which of the following would probably be a fixed cost in an automobile insurance company?

a. Application forms
b. Time spent by adjusters to evaluate accidents
c. The salary of customer service representatives
d. All of the above

3-4 The following cost formula was developed using monthly data for a hospital.

Total cost = $41,670 + ($350 × Number of patient days)

The term $41,670

a. is the independent variable.
b. is the dependent variable.
c. is the intercept.
d. is the variable rate.
e. cannot be determined from the above formula.

3-5 The following cost formula was developed using monthly data for a hospital.

Total cost = $41,670 + ($350 × Number of patient days)

The term $350

a. is the independent variable.
b. is the dependent variable.
c. is the intercept.
d. is the variable rate.
e. cannot be determined from the above formula.

3-6 The following cost formula was developed using monthly data for a hospital.

Total cost = $41,670 + ($350 × Number of patient days)

The term "Number of patient days"

a. is the independent variable.
b. is the dependent variable.
c. is the intercept.
d. is the variable rate.
e. cannot be determined from the above formula.

3-7 The following cost formula was developed using monthly data for a hospital.

Total cost = $41,670 + ($350 × Number of patient days)

The term "Total cost"

a. is the independent variable.
b. is the dependent variable.
c. is the intercept.
d. is the variable rate.
e. cannot be determined from the above formula.

3-8 The following cost formula for total purchasing cost in a factory was developed using monthly data.

Purchasing cost = $56,000 + ($2 × Number of purchase orders)

Next month, 800 purchase orders are predicted. The total cost predicted for the purchasing department next month

a. is $56,000.
b. is $1,600.
c. is $57,600.
d. is $800.
e. cannot be determined from the above formula.

3-9 An advantage of the high-low method is that it

a. is objective.
b. is subjective.
c. is the most accurate method.
d. removes outliers.
e. is descriptive of nonlinear data.

3-10 The following six months of data were collected on maintenance cost and the number of machine hours in a factory:

Month	Maintenance Cost	Machine Hours
January	$16,900	5,600
February	13,900	4,500
March	10,900	3,800

Month	Maintenance Cost	Machine Hours
April	11,450	3,700
May	13,050	4,215
June	16,990	4,980

Select the independent and dependent variables.

	Independent Variable	Dependent Variable
a.	maintenance cost	machine hours
b.	machine hours	maintenance cost
c.	maintenance cost	month
d.	machine hours	month
e.	month	maintenance cost

3-11 The following six months of data were collected on maintenance cost and the number of machine hours in a factory:

Month	Maintenance Cost	Machine Hours
January	$16,900	5,600
February	13,900	4,500
March	10,900	3,800
April	11,450	3,700
May	13,050	4,215
June	16,990	4,980

Select the correct set of high and low months.

	High	Low
a.	January	April
b.	January	March
c.	June	March
d.	June	April

3-12 An advantage of the scattergraph method is that it

a. is objective.
b. is easier to use than the high-low method.
c. is the most accurate method.
d. removes outliers.
e. is descriptive of nonlinear data.

3-13 The cost formula for monthly supervisory cost in a factory is:

Total cost = $4,500

This cost

a. is strictly variable.
b. is strictly fixed.
c. is a mixed cost.
d. is a step cost.
e. cannot be determined from this information.

3-14 (Appendix) In the method of least squares, the coefficient that tells the percentage of variation in the dependent variable that is explained by the independent variable is

a. the intercept term.
b. the x-coefficient.
c. the coefficient of correlation.
d. the coefficient of determination.
e. none of the above.

EXERCISES

Exercise 3-1 *Variable and Fixed Costs*

OBJECTIVE 1

Listed below are a number of resources that are used by a manufacturer of futons. Assume that the output measure or cost driver is the number of futons produced. All direct labor is paid on an hourly basis, and hours worked can be easily changed by management. All other factory workers are salaried.

a. Power to operate a drill (to drill holes in the wooden frames of the futons)
b. Cloth to cover the futon mattress
c. Salary of the factory receptionist
d. Cost of food and decorations for the annual 4th of July party for all factory employees
e. Fuel for a forklift used to move materials in a factory
f. Depreciation on the factory
g. Depreciation on a forklift used to move partially completed goods
h. Wages paid to workers who assemble the futon frame
i. Wages paid to workers who maintain the factory equipment
j. Cloth rags used to wipe the excess stain off the wooden frames

Required:
Classify the resource costs as variable or fixed.

Exercise 3-2 *Cost Behavior, Classification*

OBJECTIVE 1

Smith Concrete Company owns enough ready-mix trucks to deliver up to 100,000 cubic yards of concrete per year (considering each truck's capacity, weather, and distance to each job). Total truck depreciation is $200,000 per year. Raw materials (cement, gravel, and so on) cost about $25 per cubic yard of cement.

Required:
1. Prepare a graph for truck depreciation. Use the vertical axis for cost and the horizontal axis for cubic yards of cement.
2. Prepare a graph for raw materials. Use the vertical axis for cost and the horizontal axis for cubic yards of cement.
3. Assume that the normal operating range for the company is 90,000 to 96,000 cubic yards per year. Classify truck depreciation and raw materials as variable or fixed costs.

Exercise 3-3 *Classifying Costs as Fixed and Variable in a Service Organization*

OBJECTIVE 1

Alva Community Hospital has five laboratory technicians who are responsible for doing a series of standard blood tests. Each technician is paid a salary of $30,000. The lab facility represents a recent addition to the hospital and cost $300,000. It is expected to last 20 years. Equipment used for the testing cost $10,000 and has a life expectancy of five years. In addition to the salaries, facility, and equipment, Alva expects to spend $200,000 for chemicals, forms, power, and other supplies. This $200,000 is enough for 200,000 blood tests.

Required:
Assuming that the driver (measure of output) for each type of cost is the number of blood tests run, classify the costs by completing the following table. Put a check mark in the appropriate box for variable cost, discretionary fixed cost, or committed fixed cost.

Cost Category	Variable Cost	Discretionary Fixed Cost	Committed Fixed Cost
Technician salaries			
Laboratory facility			
Laboratory equipment			
Chemicals and other supplies			

Exercise 3-4 *Cost Behavior*

Carson Company manufactures digital thermometers. Based on past experience, Carson has found that its total maintenance costs can be represented by the following formula: Maintenance cost = $24,000 + $0.30X, where X = Number of digital thermometers. Last year, Carson produced 200,000 thermometers. Actual maintenance costs for the year were as expected.

Required:
1. What is the total maintenance cost incurred by Carson last year?
2. What is the total fixed maintenance cost incurred by Carson last year?
3. What is the total variable maintenance cost incurred by Carson last year?
4. What is the maintenance cost per unit produced?
5. What is the fixed maintenance cost per unit?
6. What is the variable maintenance cost per unit?

Exercise 3-5 *Cost Behavior*

Refer to **Exercise 3-4**. Now assume that Carson Company produced 100,000 thermometers.

Required:
1. What is the total maintenance cost incurred by Carson last year?
2. What is the total fixed maintenance cost incurred by Carson last year?
3. What is the total variable maintenance cost incurred by Carson last year?
4. What is the maintenance cost per unit produced?
5. What is the fixed maintenance cost per unit?
6. What is the variable maintenance cost per unit?

Exercise 3-6 *Step Costs, Relevant Range*

Bellati, Inc., produces large industrial machinery. Bellati has a machining department and a group of direct laborers called machinists. Each machinist is paid $50,000 and can machine up to 500 units per year. Bellati also hires supervisors to develop machine specification plans and to oversee production within the machining department. Given the planning and supervisory work, a supervisor can oversee at most three machinists. Bellati's accounting and production history shows the following relationships between number of units produced and the costs of materials handling and supervision (measured on an annual basis):

Units Produced	Direct Labor	Supervision
0–500	$ 36,000	$ 40,000
501–1,000	72,000	40,000
1,001–1,500	108,000	40,000
1,501–2,000	144,000	80,000
2,001–2,500	180,000	80,000
2,501–3,000	216,000	80,000
3,001–3,500	252,000	120,000
3,501–4,000	288,000	120,000

Required:

1. Prepare a graph that illustrates the relationship between direct labor cost and number of units produced in the machining department. (Let cost be the vertical axis and number of units produced the horizontal axis.) Would you classify this cost as a strictly variable cost, a fixed cost, or a step cost?
2. Prepare a graph that illustrates the relationship between the cost of supervision and the number of units produced. (Let cost be the vertical axis and number of units produced the horizontal axis.) Would you classify this cost as a strictly variable cost, a fixed cost, or a step cost?
3. Suppose that the normal range of activity is between 1,400 and 1,500 units and that the exact number of machinists are currently hired to support this level of activity. Further suppose that production for the next year is expected to increase by an additional 500 units. By how much will the cost of direct labor increase? Cost of supervision?

Exercise 3-7 *Mixed Costs*

Ben Palman owns an art gallery. He accepts paintings and sculpture on consignment and then receives 20 percent of the price of each piece as his fee. Space is limited, and there are costs involved, so Ben is careful about accepting artists. When he does accept one, he arranges for an opening show (usually for three hours on a weekend night) and sends out invitations to his customer list. At the opening, he serves wine, soft drinks, and casual munchies to create a comfortable environment for prospective customers to view the new works and chat with the artist. On average, each opening costs $500. Ben has given as many as 20 opening shows in a year. The total cost of running the gallery, including rent, furniture and fixtures, utilities, and a part-time assistant, amounts to $80,000 per year.

Required:

1. Prepare a graph that illustrates the relationship between the cost of giving opening shows and the number of opening shows given. (Let opening show cost be the vertical axis and number of opening shows given the horizontal axis.) Would you classify this cost as a strictly variable cost, a fixed cost, or a mixed cost?
2. Prepare a graph that illustrates the relationship between the cost of running the gallery and the number of opening shows given. (Let gallery cost be the vertical axis and number of opening shows given the horizontal axis.) Would you classify this cost as a strictly variable cost, a fixed cost, or a mixed cost?
3. Prepare a graph that illustrates the relationship between Ben's total costs (the sum of the costs of giving opening shows and running the gallery) and the number of opening shows given. Let the cost be the vertical axis and number of opening shows given the horizontal axis. Would you classify this cost as a strictly variable cost, a fixed cost, or a mixed cost?

Exercise 3-8 *Mixed Costs and Cost Formula*

Refer to **Exercise 3-7**.

Required:

1. Assume that the cost driver is number of opening shows. Develop the cost formula for the gallery's costs for a year.
2. Using the formula developed in Requirement 1, what is the total cost for Ben in a year with 12 opening shows? With 14 opening shows?

Exercise 3-9 *High-Low Method*

Luisa Crimini has been operating a beauty shop in a college town for the past 10 years. Recently, Luisa rented space next to her shop and opened a tanning salon. She

anticipated that the costs for the tanning service would be primarily fixed but found that tanning salon costs increased with the number of appointments. Costs for this service over the past eight months are as follows:

Month	Tanning Appointments	Total Cost
January	700	$1,758
February	2,000	2,140
March	3,100	2,790
April	2,500	2,400
May	1,500	1,800
June	2,300	2,275
July	2,150	2,200
August	3,000	2,640

Required:
1. Which month represents the high point? The low point?
2. Using the high-low method, compute the variable rate for tanning. Compute the fixed cost per month.
3. Using your answers to Requirement 2, write the cost formula for tanning services.
4. Calculate the total predicted cost of tanning services for September for 2,500 appointments using the formula found in Requirement 3. Of that total cost, how much is the total fixed cost for September? How much is the total predicted variable cost for September?

Exercise 3-10 *Scattergraph Method*

Refer to **Exercise 3-9** for data on Luisa Crimini's tanning salon.

Required:
Prepare a scattergraph based on Luisa's data. Use cost for the vertical axis and number of tanning appointments for the horizontal. Based on an examination of the scattergraph, does there appear to be a linear relationship between the cost of tanning services and the number of appointments?

Exercise 3-11 *Method of Least Squares*

Refer to **Exercise 3-9**. Now assume that Luisa's accountant used an Excel spreadsheet program to run ordinary least squares on the data in **Exercise 3-9**; the following results were produced.

Intercept	1,290
X Variable	0.45

Required:
1. Compute the cost formula for tanning services using the results from the method of least squares.
2. Using the formula computed in Requirement 1, what is the predicted cost of tanning services for September for 2,500 appointments?

Exercise 3-12 *High-Low Method, Cost Formulas*

During the past year, the high and low use of three different resources in a factory occurred in May and November. The resources are machine depreciation, power, and maintenance. Number of machine hours is the driver. The total costs of the three resources and the related number of machine hours are as follows:

Resource	Machine Hours	Total Cost
Machine depreciation:		
High	75,000	$165,000
Low	20,000	165,000
Power:		
High	75,000	4,500
Low	20,000	1,200
Maintenance:		
High	75,000	53,800
Low	20,000	19,700

Required:

Use the high-low method to answer the following:

1. What is the variable rate for machine depreciation? The fixed cost?
2. What is the cost formula for machine depreciation?
3. What is the variable rate for power? The fixed cost?
4. What is the cost formula for power?
5. What is the variable rate for maintenance? The fixed cost?
6. What is the cost formula for maintenance?
7. Using the three cost formulas you developed, predict the cost of each resource in a month with 40,000 machine hours.

Exercise 3-13 *Changing the Cost Formula for a Month to the Cost Formula for a Year*

Refer to **Exercise 3-12**.

Required:

1. Take the monthly cost formulas developed in Requirements 2, 4, and 6 and change them into cost formulas for a year. (You will have a separate annual cost formula for machine depreciation, power, and maintenance.)
2. Using the three annual cost formulas you developed, predict the cost of each resource in a year with 630,000 machine hours.

Exercise 3-14 *Method of Least Squares, Developing and Using the Cost Formula*

The method of least squares was used to develop a cost equation to predict the cost of receiving. Eighty data points from monthly data were used for the regression. The following computer output was received:

Intercept	17,350
Slope	16

The driver used was number of receiving orders.

Required:

1. What is the cost formula?
2. Using the cost formula from Requirement 1, identify each of the following: independent variable, dependent variable, variable rate, and fixed cost per month.
3. Using the cost formula, predict the cost of receiving for a month in which 1,000 orders are processed.

Exercise 3-15 *Method of Least Squares, Budgeted Time Period Is Different from Time Period Used to Generate Results*

Refer to **Exercise 3-14**.

Required:

1. What is the cost formula for a year?
2. Using the cost formula from Requirement 1, predict the cost of receiving for a year in which 12,500 orders are processed.

Exercise 3-16 *Identifying the Parts of the Cost Formula, Calculating Monthly, Quarterly, and Yearly Costs Using a Cost Formula Based on Monthly Data*

Landring Company's controller estimated the following formula, based on monthly data, for overhead cost:

$$\text{Overhead cost} = \$7,344 + (\$10.50 \times \text{Machine hours})$$

Required:

1. Link each term in column A to the corresponding term in column B.

Column A	Column B
Overhead cost	Variable rate (slope)
$7,344	Independent variable
$10.50	Fixed cost (intercept)
Machine hours	Dependent variable

2. If next month's budgeted machine hours equal 10,000, what is the budgeted overhead cost?
3. If next quarter's budgeted machine hours equal 31,000, what is the budgeted overhead cost?
4. If next year's budgeted machine hours equal 125,000, what is the budgeted overhead cost?

Exercise 3-17 *(Appendix) Method of Least Squares Using Computer Spreadsheet Program*

The controller for Beckham Company believes that the number of direct labor hours is associated with overhead cost. He collected the following data on the number of direct labor hours and associated factory overhead cost for the months of January through August.

Month	Number of Direct Labor Hours	Overhead Cost
January	689	$5,550
February	700	5,590
March	720	5,650
April	690	5,570
May	680	5,570
June	590	5,410
July	750	5,720
August	675	5,608

Required:

1. Using a computer spreadsheet program such as Excel, run a regression on these data. Print out your results.
2. Using your results from Requirement 1, write the cost formula for overhead cost. (You may round the fixed cost to the nearest dollar and the variable rate to the nearest cent.)
3. What is R^2 based on your results? Do you think that the number of direct labor hours is a good predictor of factory overhead cost?
4. Assuming that expected September direct labor hours are 700, what is expected factory overhead cost using the cost formula in Requirement 2?

Exercise 3-18 *(Appendix) Method of Least Squares Using Computer Spreadsheet Program*

Susan Lewis, owner of a florist shop, is interested in predicting the cost of delivering floral arrangements. She collected monthly data on the number of deliveries and the total monthly delivery cost (depreciation on the van, wages of the driver, and fuel) for the past year.

Month	Number of Deliveries	Delivery Cost
January	100	$1,200
February	550	1,800
March	85	1,100
April	115	1,050
May	160	1,190
June	590	1,980
July	500	1,800
August	520	1,700

Month	Number of Deliveries	Delivery Cost
September	100	$1,100
October	200	1,275
November	260	1,400
December	450	2,200

Required:

1. Using a computer spreadsheet program such as Excel, run a regression on these data. Print out your results.
2. Using your results from Requirement 1, write the cost formula for delivery cost. (You may round the fixed cost to the nearest dollar and the variable rate to the nearest cent.)
3. What is R^2 based on your results? Do you think that the number of direct labor hours is a good predictor of delivery cost?
4. Using the cost formula in Requirement 2, what would predicted delivery cost be for a month with 300 deliveries?

PROBLEMS

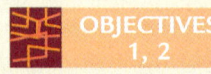

(Note: Whenever you see a ⬛ next to a requirement, it signals a "building on a cornerstone" requirement. Assigning this requirement will usually entail additional work, such as a group project, analytical reasoning, Internet research, decision making, and the use of written communication skills.)

Problem 3-1 *Identifying Fixed, Variable, Mixed, and Step Costs*

OBJECTIVES 1, 2

Consider each of the following independent situations:

a. A computer service agreement in which a company pays $150 per month and $15 per hour of technical time.
b. Fuel cost of the company's fleet of motor vehicles.
c. The cost of beer for a bar.
d. The cost of computer and copy paper in your college.
e. Rent for a dental office.
f. The salary of a receptionist in a law firm.
g. The wages of counter help in a fast-food restaurant.
h. The salaries of dental hygienists in a 3-dentist office. One hygienist can take care of 120 cleanings per month.
i. Electricity cost, which includes a $15 per month billing charge and an additional amount depending on the number of kilowatt-hours used.

Required:

1. For each situation, describe the cost as one of the following: fixed cost, variable cost, mixed cost, or step cost. (*Hint:* First consider what the driver or output measure is. If additional assumptions are necessary to support your cost type decision, be sure to write them down.)

    Example: Raw materials used in production—Variable cost

2. Change your assumption(s) for each situation so that the cost type changes to a different cost type. List the new cost type and the changed assumption(s) that gave rise to it.

    Example: Raw materials used in production. Changed assumption—the materials are difficult to obtain and a year's worth must be contracted for in advance. Now, this is a fixed cost. (This is the case with diamond sales by DeBeers Inc. to its sightholders. See the following Web site for information: **http://www .keyguide.net/sightholders/**.)

Problem 3-2 *Identifying Use of the High-Low, Scattergraph, and Least Squares Methods*

Consider each of the following independent situations:

a. Shaniqua Boyer just started her new job as controller for St. Matthias General Hospital. She wants to get a feel for the cost behavior of various departments of the hospital. Shaniqua first looks at the radiology department. She has annual data on total cost and the number of procedures that have been run for the past 15 years. However, she knows that the department upgraded its equipment substantially two years ago and is doing a wider variety of tests. So, Shaniqua decides to use just the past two years.
b. Francis Hidalgo is a summer intern in the accounting department of a manufacturing firm. His boss assigned him a special project to determine the cost of manufacturing a special order. Francis needs information on variable and fixed overhead so he gathers monthly data on overhead cost and machine hours for the past 60 months and enters them into his personal computer. A few keystrokes later, he has information on fixed and variable overhead costs.
c. Ron Wickstead sighed and studied his computer printout again. The results made no sense to him. He seemed to recall that sometimes it helped if you could visualize the cost relationships. He reached for some graph paper and a pencil.
d. Lois March had hoped that she could find information on the actual cost of promoting new products. Unfortunately, she had spent the weekend going through the files and was only able to find data on the total cost of the sales department by month for the past three years. She was also able to figure out the number of new product launches by month for the same time period. Now, she had just 15 minutes before a staff meeting in which she needed to give the vice president of sales an expected cost of the average new product launch. A light bulb went off in her head, and she reached for paper, pencil, and a calculator.

Required:
Determine which of the following cost separation methods is being used: the high-low method, the scattergraph method, or the method of least squares.

Problem 3-3 *Identifying Variable Costs, Committed Fixed Costs, and Discretionary Fixed Costs*

Required:

Classify each of the following costs for a jeans manufacturing company as a variable cost, committed fixed cost, or discretionary fixed cost.

a. The cost of buttons.
b. The cost to lease warehouse space for completed jeans. The lease contract runs for two years at $5,000 per year.

c. The salary of a summer intern.
d. The cost of landscaping and mowing the grass. The contract with a local mowing company runs from month to month.
e. Advertising in a national magazine for teenage girls.
f. Electricity to run the sewing machines.
g. Oil and spare needles for the sewing machines.
h. Quality training for employees—typically given for four hours at a time, every six months.
i. Food and beverages for the company 4th of July picnic.
j. Natural gas to heat the factory during the winter.

Problem 3-4 *Scattergraph, High-Low Method, and Predicting Cost for a Different Time Period from the One Used to Develop a Cost Formula*

Spreadsheet

Farnsworth Company has gathered data on its overhead activities and associated costs for the past 10 months. Tracy Heppler, a member of the controller's department, has convinced management that overhead costs can be better estimated and controlled if the fixed and variable components of each overhead activity are known. One such activity is receiving raw materials (unloading incoming goods, counting goods, and inspecting goods), which she believes is driven by the number of receiving orders. Ten months of data have been gathered for the receiving activity and are as follows:

Month	Receiving Orders	Receiving Cost
1	1,000	$18,000
2	700	15,000
3	1,500	28,000
4	1,200	17,000
5	1,300	25,000
6	1,100	21,000
7	1,600	29,000
8	1,400	24,000
9	1,700	27,000
10	900	16,000

Required:

1. Prepare a scattergraph based on the 10 months of data. Does the relationship appear to be linear?
2. Using the high-low method, prepare a cost formula for the receiving activity. Using this formula, what is the predicted cost of receiving for a month in which 1,475 receiving orders are processed?
3. Prepare a cost formula for the receiving activity for a quarter. Based on this formula, what is the predicted cost of receiving for a quarter in which 4,650 receiving orders are anticipated? Prepare a cost formula for the receiving activity for a year. Based on this formula, what is the predicted cost of receiving for a year in which 18,000 receiving orders are anticipated?

Problem 3-5 *Method of Least Squares, Predicting Cost for Different Time Periods from the One Used to Develop a Cost Formula*

Refer to **Problem 3-4**. Now assume that Tracy has used the method of least squares on the receiving data and gotten the following results:

Intercept   3,212
Slope   15.15

Required:

1. Using the results from the method of least squares, prepare a cost formula for the receiving activity.

2. Using the formula from Requirement 1, what is the predicted cost of receiving for a month in which 1,475 receiving orders are processed? (Round your answer to the nearest dollar.)

3. Prepare a cost formula for the receiving activity for a quarter. Based on this formula, what is the predicted cost of receiving for a quarter in which 4,650 receiving orders are anticipated? Prepare a cost formula for the receiving activity for a year. Based on this formula, what is the predicted cost of receiving for a year in which 18,000 receiving orders are anticipated? (Round your answers to the nearest dollar.)

Problem 3-6 *(Appendix) Method of Least Squares*

Refer to **Problem 3-4** for the first 10 months of data on receiving orders and receiving cost. Now suppose that Tracy has gathered two more months of data:

Month	Receiving Orders	Receiving Cost
11	1,200	$28,000
12	950	17,500

Required:

1. Run two regressions using a computer spreadsheet program such as Excel. First, use the method of least squares on the 10 months of data from Problem 3-4. Then, use the method of least squares on the 12 months of data (10 months from Problem 3-4 and the additional two months given in this problem). Write down the results for the intercept, slope, and R^2 for each regression. Compare the results.

2. Prepare a scattergraph using all 12 months of data. Do any points appear to be outliers? Suppose Tracy has learned that the factory suffered severe storm damage during month 11 that required extensive repairs to the receiving area—including major repairs on a forklift. These expenses, included in month 11 receiving costs, are not expected to recur. What step might Tracy, using her judgment, take to amend the results from the method of least squares?

3. Rerun the method of least squares, using all the data except for month 11. (You should now have 11 months of data.) Prepare a cost formula for receiving based on these results and calculate the predicted receiving cost for a month with 1,475 receiving orders. Discuss the results from this regression versus those from the regression for 12 months of data.

Problem 3-7 *(Appendix) Scattergraph, High-Low Method, Method of Least Squares, Use of Judgment*

The management of Wheeler Company has decided to develop cost formulas for its major overhead activities. Wheeler uses a highly automated manufacturing process, and power costs are a significant manufacturing cost. Cost analysts have decided that power costs are mixed; thus, they must be broken into their fixed and variable elements so that the cost behavior of the power usage activity can be properly described. Machine hours have been selected as the activity driver for power costs. The following data for the past eight quarters have been collected:

Quarter	Machine Hours	Power Cost
1	20,000	$26,000
2	25,000	38,000
3	30,000	42,500
4	22,000	37,000
5	21,000	34,000
6	18,000	29,000
7	24,000	36,000
8	28,000	40,000

Required:
1. Prepare a scattergraph by plotting power costs against machine hours. Does the scattergraph show a linear relationship between machine hours and power cost?
2. Using the high and low points, compute a power cost formula.
3. Use the method of least squares to compute a power cost formula. Evaluate the coefficient of determination.
4. Rerun the regression and drop the point (20,000, $26,000) as an outlier. Compare the results from this regression to those for the regression in Requirement 3. Which is better?

Problem 3-8 *Cost Behavior, High-Low Method, Pricing Decision*

Fonseca, Ruiz and Dunn is a large, local accounting firm located in a southwestern city. Carlos Ruiz, one of the firm's founders, appreciates the success his firm has enjoyed and wants to give something back to his community. He believes that an inexpensive accounting services clinic could provide basic accounting services for small businesses located in the barrio. He wants to price the services at cost.

Since the clinic is brand new, it has no experience to go on. Carlos decided to operate the clinic for two months before determining how much to charge per hour on an ongoing basis. As a temporary measure, the clinic adopted an hourly charge of $25, half the amount charged by Fonseca, Ruiz and Dunn for professional services.

The accounting services clinic opened on January 1. During January, the clinic had 120 hours of professional service. During February, the activity was 150 hours. Costs for these two levels of activity usage are as follows:

	120 Professional Hours	150 Professional Hours
Salaries:		
Senior accountant	$2,500	$2,500
Office assistant	1,200	1,200
Internet and software subscriptions	700	850
Consulting by senior partner	1,200	1,500
Depreciation (equipment)	2,400	2,400
Supplies	905	1,100
Administration	500	500
Rent (offices)	2,000	2,000
Utilities	332	365

Required:
1. Classify each cost as fixed, variable, or mixed, using hours of professional service as the activity driver.
2. Use the high-low method to separate the mixed costs into their fixed and variable components.
3. Luz Mondragon, the chief paraprofessional of the clinic, has estimated that the clinic will average 140 professional hours per month. If the clinic is to be operated as a nonprofit organization, how much will it need to charge per professional hour? How much of this charge is variable? How much is fixed?
4. Suppose the accounting center averages 170 professional hours per month. How much would need to be charged per hour for the center to cover its costs? Explain why the per-hour charge decreased as the activity output increased.

Problem 3-9 *Separating Fixed and Variable Costs, Service Setting*

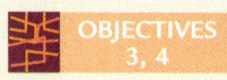

Louise McDermott, controller for the Galvin plant of Veromar, Inc., wanted to determine the cost behavior of moving materials throughout the plant. She accumulated the following data on the number of moves (from 100 to 800 in increments of 100) and the total cost of moving materials at those levels of moves:

Number of Moves	Total Cost
100	$ 3,000
200	4,650
300	3,400
400	8,500
500	10,000
600	12,600
700	13,600
800	14,560

Required:

1. Prepare a scattergraph based on these data. Use cost for the vertical axis and number of moves for the horizontal. Based on an examination of the scattergraph, does there appear to be a linear relationship between the total cost of moving materials and the number of moves?
2. Compute the cost formula for moving materials using the high-low method. Calculate the predicted cost for a month with 550 moves using the high-low formula.
3. Compute the cost formula for moving materials using the method of least squares. Using the regression cost formula, what is the predicted cost for a month with 550 moves? What does the coefficient of determination tell you about the cost formula computed by regression?
4. Evaluate the cost formula using the least squares coefficients. Could it be improved? Try dropping the third data point (300, $3,400) and rerun the regression.

Problem 3-10 *Flexible and Committed Resources, Capacity Usage for a Service*

Jana Morgan is about to sign up for cellular telephone service. She is primarily interested in the safety aspect of the phone; that is, she wants to have one available for emergencies. She does not want to use it as her primary phone. Jana has narrowed her options down to two plans:

	Plan 1	Plan 2
Monthly fee	$20	$ 30
Free local minutes	60	120
Additional charges per minute:		
Airtime	$ 0.40	$ 0.30
Long distance	0.15	—
Regional roaming	0.60	—
National roaming	0.60	0.60

Both plans are subject to a $25 activation fee and a $120 cancellation fee if the service is cancelled before one year. Jana's brother will give her a cell phone that he no longer needs. It is not the latest version (and is not Internet capable) but will work well with both plans.

Required:

1. Classify the charges associated with the cellular phone service as (a) committed resources or (b) flexible resources.
2. Assume that Jana will use, on average, 45 minutes per month in local calling. For each plan, split her minute allotment into used and unused capacity. Which plan would be most cost effective? Why?
3. Assume that Jana loves her cell phone and ends up talking frequently with friends while traveling within her region. On average, she uses 60 local minutes a

month and 30 regional minutes. For each plan, split her minute allotment into used and unused capacity. Which plan would be most cost effective? Why?

4. Analyze your own cellular phone plan by comparing it with other possible options.

Problem 3-11 *Suspicious Acquisition of Data, Ethical Issues*

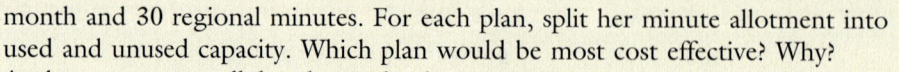

OBJECTIVE 1

Bill Lewis, manager of the Thomas Electronics Division, called a meeting with his controller, Brindon Peterson, and his marketing manager, Patty Fritz. The following is a transcript of the conversation that took place during the meeting:

Bill: Brindon, the variable costing system that you developed has proved to be a big plus for our division. Our success in winning bids has increased, and as a result, our revenues have increased by 25 percent. However, if we intend to meet this year's profit targets, we are going to need something extra—am I not right, Patty?

Patty: Absolutely. While we have been able to win more bids, we still are losing too many, particularly to our major competitor, Kilborn Electronics. If we knew more about their bidding strategy, we could be more successful at competing with them.

Brindon: Would knowing their variable costs help?

Patty: Certainly. It would give me their minimum price. With that knowledge, I'm sure we could find a way to beat them on several jobs, particularly for those jobs where we are at least as efficient. It would also help us identify where we are not cost competitive. With this information, we might be able to find ways to increase our efficiency.

Brindon: Well, I have good news. I've been talking with Carl Penobscot, Kilborn's assistant controller. Carl doesn't feel appreciated by Kilborn and wants to make a change. He could easily fit into our team here. Plus, Carl has been preparing for a job switch by quietly copying Kilborn's accounting files and records. He's already given me some data that reveal bids that Kilborn made on several jobs. If we can come to a satisfactory agreement with Carl, he'll bring the rest of the information with him. We'll easily be able to figure out Kilborn's prospective bids and find ways to beat them. Besides, I could use another accountant on my staff. Bill, would you authorize my immediate hiring of Carl with a favorable compensation package?

Bill: I know you need more staff, Brindon, but is this the right thing to do? It sounds like Carl is stealing those files, and surely Kilborn considers this information confidential. I have real ethical and legal concerns about this. Why don't we meet with Laurie, our attorney, and determine any legal problems?

Required:
1. Is Carl's behavior ethical? What would Kilborn think?
2. Is Bill correct in supposing that there are ethical and/or legal problems involved with the hiring of Carl? (Reread the section on corporate codes of conduct in Chapter 1 of this text.) What would you do if you were Bill? Explain.

Problem 3-12 *Variable and Fixed Costs, Cost Formula, High-Low Method*

OBJECTIVES 1, 3

Recall from the Opening Scenario that Li Ming, head of accounting, studied the costs of processing health insurance claims in the department of human resources. After talking with Tiffany and some of her staff members, as well as his own staff members, he discovered that there were a number of costs associated with the claims processing activity. These costs included the salaries of the two paralegals who worked full time on claims processing, the salary of the accountant who cut the checks, the cost of claims forms, checks, envelopes, and postage, and depreciation on the office equipment dedicated to the processing. Some of the paralegals' time is spent in the routine processing of uncontested claims, but much time is spent on the claims that have incomplete documentation or are contested. The accountant's time appears to vary with the number of claims processed.

Li Ming was able to separate the costs of processing claims from the costs of running the departments of accounting and human resources. He gathered the data on claims processing cost and the number of claims processed per month for the past six months. These data are as follows:

Month	Claims Processing Cost	Number of Claims Processed
February	$34,907	5,700
March	31,260	4,900
April	37,950	6,100
May	38,250	6,500
June	44,895	7,930
July	44,055	7,514

Required:

1. Classify the claims processing costs Li Ming identified as variable and fixed.
2. What is the independent variable? The dependent variable?
3. Use the high-low method to find the fixed cost per month and the variable rate. What is the cost formula?
4. Suppose that an outside company bids on the claims processing business. The bid price is $4.60 per claim. If Tiffany expects 75,600 claims next year, should she outsource the claims processing or continue to do it in house?

Problem 3-13 *Cost Separation*

About eight years ago, Kicker faced the problem of rapidly increasing costs associated with workplace accidents. The costs included:

State unemployment insurance premiums	$100,000
Average cost per injury	$1,500
Number of injuries per year	15
Number of serious injuries	4
Number of workdays lost	30

A safety program was implemented with the following features: hiring a safety director, new employee orientation, stretching required four times a day, and systematic monitoring of adherence to the program by directors and supervisors. A year later, the indicators were:

State unemployment insurance premiums	$50,000
Average cost per injury	$50
Number of injuries per year	10
Number of serious injuries	0
Number of workdays lost	0
Safety director's starting salary	$60,000

Required:

1. Discuss the safety-related costs listed. Are they variable or fixed with respect to speakers sold? With respect to other independent variables (describe)?
2. Did the safety program pay for itself? Discuss your reasoning.

COST-VOLUME-PROFIT ANALYSIS:
A MANAGERIAL PLANNING TOOL

© PHOTODISC/GETTY IMAGES

After studying Chapter 4, you should be able to:

1. Determine the break-even point in number of units and in total sales dollars.
2. Determine the number of units that must be sold, and the amount of revenue required, to earn a targeted profit.
3. Prepare a profit-volume graph and a cost-volume-profit graph and explain the meaning of each.
4. Apply cost-volume-profit analysis in a multiple-product setting.
5. Explain the impact of risk, uncertainty, and changing variables on cost-volume-profit analysis.

For years, Janet McFarland's friends and family raved about her homemade jellies and salsas. Janet traditionally canned several gallons of salsa, ladled it into decorative pint jars, wrapped them, and sent them as gifts. Her friends said, "You ought to sell this stuff—you'd make a fortune!" So, Janet decided to give it a try.

First, she decided to concentrate on one product, a green cactus salsa that had gotten rave reviews. She scouted sources of jars, lids, and labels. In addition, Janet got in touch with her local agricultural extension office and learned a considerable amount about laws regulating food sales. One source of surprise was that she was required to obtain an expert confirmation of the ingredients in her salsa. Usually, Janet added a little of this and a little of that until it tasted right. She found out that this casual approach would not work. Foods were required to be labeled with the name of each ingredient in order of amount. Suddenly, it mattered whether ancho or poblano chilis were used and in what proportion. Janet needed a standardized recipe. She located a professional food chemist to analyze the recipe and certify the proportion of ingredients.

Janet traveled to a number of grocery stores and gift shops in the area. Several were willing to stock her product on consignment, placing a few jars by the cash register; others guaranteed shelf space but required a shelf charge for it. She figured that traveling to the stores, checking on sales and stock, and visiting prospective customers would take about one day a week.

Before starting production, Janet consulted with her family accountant, Bob Ryan.

Janet: Bob, I'm really excited about this opportunity; it all seems to be falling into place.

Bob: I'm happy for you, too, Janet. But first, let's do some planning. I need to take a look at the costs and selling price you anticipate.

Janet: I think I can charge $3.50 per jar. It's a new product, and I want to build a market for it. The costs I've come up with are on this sheet. They aren't as high as they could be since I'm going to start slowly and cook small batches at a time in our kitchen.

Bob: (After a couple of minutes of figuring) Janet, do you realize that at a price of $3.50 and with the variable costs that you described, you'll lose money! You can't do that.

Janet: What if I sell more jars? Will that help?

Bob: No, since the price is less than the variable cost, selling more jars will just make it worse. Let's go back to the drawing board and see if there's a way to decrease those variable costs. If that isn't possible, you will need to see if there is a market for your product at a higher price. Otherwise, you would be better off never getting involved with this business.

BREAK-EVEN POINT IN UNITS AND IN SALES DOLLARS

Cost-volume-profit analysis (CVP analysis) is a powerful tool for planning and decision making. Managers become very interested in CVP analysis during times of economic trouble. You may have heard or read of various companies trying to break even. CVP analysis can help managers pinpoint problems and fix on the necessary solution.

CVP analysis can address many other issues as well, such as the number of units that must be sold to break even, the impact of a given reduction in fixed costs on the break-even point, and the impact of an increase in price on profit. Additionally, CVP analysis allows managers to do sensitivity analysis by examining the impact of various price or cost levels on profit.

Since CVP analysis shows how revenues, expenses, and profits behave as volume changes, it is natural to begin by finding the firm's break-even point in units sold. The **break-even point** is the point where total revenue equals total cost, the point of zero profit.

> **OBJECTIVE 1**
>
> Determine the break-even point in number of units and in total sales dollars.

Kicker separates cost into fixed and variable components by using judgment. Because the bulk of manufacturing is outsourced, the cost of the speakers starts with the purchase price from the manufacturer. This is a strictly variable cost. Also variable are the cost of duty (ranging from 9–30 percent—electronics are at the high end) and freight, as all units are shipped to Stillwater, Oklahoma, for distribution to customers. In-house labor may be needed at Kicker's Stillwater facilities, and that cost has both fixed (salaried workers) and variable (temporary workers) components.

The entire salaried staff in Stillwater, research and development, depreciation on property, plant and equipment, utilities, and so on, are all fixed.

These fixed and variable costs are used in cost-volume-profit analysis (done monthly) and in management decision making. For example, the monthly cost-volume-profit figures can be used to monitor the effect of changing volume on profit and spotlight increases in fixed and variable costs. If costs are going up, management finds out about the problem early and can make adjustments.

HERE'S THE REAL KICKER

Using Operating Income in CVP Analysis

Remember from Chapter 2 that operating income is total revenue minus total expense. For the income statement, expenses were classified according to function, that is, the manufacturing (or service provision) function, the selling function, and the administrative function. For CVP analysis, however, it is much more useful to organize costs into fixed and variable components. The focus is on the firm as a whole. Therefore, the costs refer to all costs of the company—production, selling, and administration. So variable costs are all costs that increase as more units are sold, including direct materials, direct labor, variable overhead, and variable selling and administrative costs. Similarly, fixed cost includes fixed overhead and fixed selling and administrative expenses. The income statement format that is based on the separation of costs into fixed and variable components is called the **contribution margin income statement**. Exhibit 4-1 shows the format for the contribution margin income statement.

The contribution margin income statement in Exhibit 4-1 contains a new term, *contribution margin*. **Contribution margin** is the difference between sales and variable expense. It is the amount left from sales after all the variable expenses are covered that can be used to contribute to fixed expense and operating income. The contribution margin can be calculated in total (as it was in Exhibit 4-1) or per unit.

Let's use Whittier Company, a manufacturer of mulching lawn mowers, for an example. Whittier's controller has budgeted the following production costs for the coming year:

4-1

The Contribution Margin Income Statement

Sales	$XXX
Less: Total variable expense	(XXX)
Total contribution margin	$XXX
Less: Total fixed expense	(XXX)
Operating income	$XXX

EXHIBIT 4-1

Direct materials per mower	$ 180
Direct labor per mower	100
Variable overhead per mower	25
Total fixed factory overhead	15,000

Whittier also has $30,000 in fixed selling and administrative expense, as well as a $20 sales commission on each mower sold. In the coming year, Whittier Company plans to produce and sell 1,000 mowers at a price of $400 each.

The total variable cost per mower includes direct materials, direct labor, variable overhead per unit, and the sales commission. Thus, variable cost per unit is $325 ($180 + $100 + $25 + $20). The total fixed expense includes fixed factory overhead and fixed selling and administrative expense; the total fixed expense is $45,000 ($15,000 + $30,000). Notice that both the variable cost per mower and the total fixed expense include all types of cost—both product and selling cost.

The contribution margin income statement for Whittier Company for the coming year is shown in Cornerstone 4-1.

Cornerstone 4-1

HOW TO Prepare a Contribution Margin Income Statement

Information: Whittier Company plans to sell 1,000 mowers at $400 each in the coming year. Product costs include:

Direct materials per mower	$ 180
Direct labor per mower	100
Variable overhead per mower	25
Total fixed factory overhead	15,000

Variable selling expense is a commission of $20 per mower; fixed selling and administrative expense totals $30,000.

Required:
1. Calculate the total variable cost per unit.
2. Calculate the total fixed expense for the year.
3. Prepare a contribution margin income statement for Whittier Company for the coming year.

Calculation:
1. Variable cost per unit = Direct materials + Direct labor + Variable overhead + Variable selling expense
   = $180 + $100 + $25 + $20 = $325
2. Total fixed expense = $15,000 + $30,000 = $45,000

3.

	Total	Per Unit
Whittier Company		
Contribution Margin Income Statement		
For the Coming Year		
Sales ($400 × 1,000 mowers)	$400,000	$400
Total variable expense ($325 × 1,000)	325,000	325
Total contribution margin	$ 75,000	$ 75
Total fixed expense	45,000	
Operating income	$ 30,000	

Notice that the contribution margin income statement shown in Cornerstone 4-1 shows total contribution margin of $75,000. The per-unit contribution margin is $75($400 − $325). That is, every mower sold contributes $75 toward fixed expense and operating income.

What does Whittier's contribution margin income statement show? First, of course, we notice that Whittier will more than break even at sales of 1,000 mowers. In fact, it expects operating income of $30,000. Clearly, Whittier would just break even if total contribution margin equaled the total fixed cost. Let's see how to calculate the break-even point.

Break-Even Point in Units

If the contribution margin income statement is recast as an equation, it becomes more useful for solving CVP problems. The operating income equation is:

$$\text{Operating income} = \text{Sales} - \text{Total variable expenses} - \text{Total fixed expenses}$$

Notice that all we have done is remove the total contribution margin line, since it is identical to sales minus total variable expense. This equation is the basis of all our coming work on CVP. We can think of it as the basic CVP equation.

We can expand the operating income equation by expressing sales revenues and variable expenses in terms of unit dollar amounts and the number of units sold. Specifically, sales revenue is equal to the unit selling price times the number of units sold, and total variable costs are the unit variable cost times the number of units sold. With these expressions, the operating income equation becomes:

$$\text{Operating income} = (\text{Price} \times \text{Number of units sold}) - (\text{Variable cost per unit} \times \text{Number of units sold}) - \text{Total fixed cost}$$

At the break-even point, of course, operating income equals $0. Let's see how we can use the operating income equation to find the break-even point in units for Whittier Company. Recall that Whittier Company sells mowers at $400 each, and variable cost per mower is $325. Total fixed cost equals $45,000.

$$(\$400 \times \text{Break-even units}) - (\$325 \times \text{Break-even units}) - \$45,000 = \$0$$
$$\$75 \times \text{Break-even units} - \$45,000 = \$0$$
$$\text{Break-even units} = \frac{\$45,000}{\$75}$$
$$\text{Break-even units} = 600$$

It is easy to see that a contribution margin income statement for Whittier Company, with sales of 600 mowers, does result in zero operating income.

Sales ($400 × 600 mowers)	$240,000
Total variable expense ($325 × 600)	195,000
Total contribution margin	$ 45,000
Total fixed expense	45,000
Operating income	$ 0

When Whittier breaks even, total contribution margin is just equal to total fixed cost. Exhibit 4-2 illustrates this.

In solving for the number of units at break-even, the following break-even units equation is obtained:

$$\text{Break-even units} = \frac{\text{Total fixed cost}}{\text{Price} - \text{Variable cost per unit}}$$

In other words, the break-even units are equal to the fixed cost divided by the contribution margin per unit. So, if a company sells enough units for the contribution margin to just cover fixed cost, it will earn zero operating income. In other words, it will break even. It is quicker to solve break-even problems using this equation than it is using the operating income equation. Cornerstone 4-2 shows how to use the break-even units equation to solve for the break-even point for Whittier Company.

Contribution Margin and Fixed Cost at Break-Even for Whittier Company

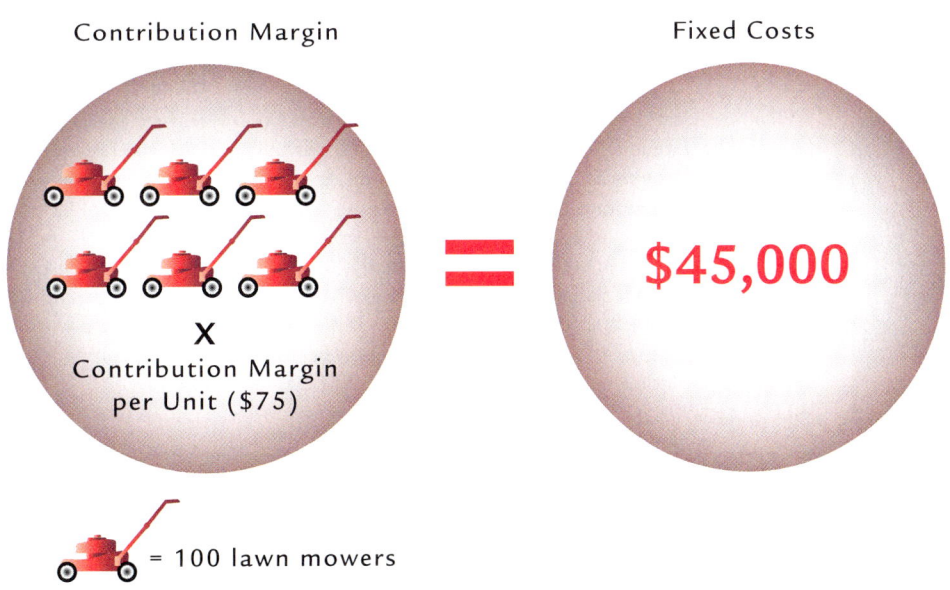

Contribution Margin   Fixed Costs

X
Contribution Margin
per Unit ($75)

= $45,000

= 100 lawn mowers

Cornerstone 4-2

HOW TO Solve for the Break-Even Point in Units

Information: Whittier Company plans to sell 1,000 mowers at $400 each in the coming year. Product costs include:

Direct materials per mower	$ 180
Direct labor per mower	100
Variable overhead per mower	25
Total fixed factory overhead	15,000

Variable selling expense is a commission of $20 per mower; fixed selling and administrative expense totals $30,000.

Required:
1. Calculate the total variable cost per unit.
2. Calculate the total fixed expense for the year.
3. Calculate the number of mowers that Whittier Company must sell to break even.
4. Check your answer by preparing a contribution margin income statement based on the break-even point.

Calculation:
1. Variable cost per unit = $180 + $100 + $25 + $20 = $325
2. Total fixed expense = $15,000 + $30,000 = $45,000
3. Break-even number of mowers = $45,000/($400 − $325) = 600
4. Contribution margin income statement based on 600 mowers.

Sales ($400 × 600 mowers)	$240,000
Total variable expense ($325 × 600)	195,000
Total contribution margin	$ 45,000
Total fixed expense	45,000
Operating income	$ 0

Indeed, selling 600 units does yield a zero profit.

APPLICATIONS IN BUSINESS

CVP analysis can be a valuable tool to identify the extent and magnitude of the economic trouble a company is facing and to help pinpoint the necessary solution. For example, SAAB was on the brink of collapse in 1990 when GM bought a 50-percent share in the company. Within five years, SAAB had cut costs dramatically and lowered its break-even point from 130,000 cars to 80,000 cars. By 2002, SAAB turned a modest profit. GM learned many lessons from this experience. In the late 1990s, GM restructured all of its operations to eliminate many fixed costs and decrease variable costs, thereby lowering the break-even point. Why would the company do that when 1997 profits were at record levels? As auto analyst Stephen Girsky pointed out to GM executives, "Volume distorts everything." When volume decreases, profits turn down in a hurry. GM needs to aggressively contain costs to compete with rivals like Toyota and DaimlerChrysler.

Source: James Bennet, "Eurocars: On the Road Again," *New York Times* (August 20, 1995): Sec. 3, pp. 1, 10. Paul A. Eisenstein, "Saab Making Big Plans: New 9-3 is Key to Expansion—and Profitability," *The Car Connection* (July 7, 2002), http://www.thecarconnection.com/index.asp?article=5108. Gregory White, "For GM, Hard Line on Strike Has Become a Matter of Necessity," *The Wall Street Journal* (June 12, 1998): A1 and A4.

Break-Even Point in Sales Dollars

In some cases when using CVP analysis, managers may prefer to use sales revenue as the measure of sales activity instead of units sold. A units sold measure can be converted to a sales revenue measure simply by multiplying the unit selling price by the units sold. For example, the break-even point for Whittier Company is 600 mulching mowers. Since the selling price for each lawn mower is $400, the break-even volume in sales revenue is $240,000 ($400 × 600).

Any answer expressed in units sold can be easily converted to one expressed in sales revenues, but the answer can be computed more directly by developing a separate formula for the sales revenue case. In this case, the important variable is sales dollars, so both the revenue and the variable costs must be expressed in dollars instead of units. Since sales revenue is always expressed in dollars, measuring that variable is no problem. Let's look more closely at variable costs and see how they can be expressed in terms of sales dollars.

To calculate the break-even point in sales dollars, total variable costs are defined as a percentage of sales rather than as an amount per-unit sold. For example, suppose that a company sells a product for $10 per unit and incurs variable cost of $6 per unit. Of course, the remainder is contribution margin of $4 ($10 − $6). If 10 units are sold, total variable costs are $60 ($6 × 10 units). Alternatively, since each unit sold earns $10 of revenue and has $6 of variable cost, one could say that 60 percent of each dollar of revenue earned is attributable to variable cost ($6/$10). Thus, sales revenues of $100 would result in total variable costs of $60 (0.60 × $100).

This 60 percent is the variable cost ratio. The **variable cost ratio** is simply the proportion of each sales dollar that must be used to cover variable costs. The variable cost ratio can be computed by using either total data or unit data. Of course, the percentage of sales dollars remaining after variable costs are covered is the contribution margin ratio. The **contribution margin ratio** is the proportion of each sales dollar available to cover fixed costs and provide for profit. In the above example, if the variable cost ratio is 60 percent of sales, then the contribution margin ratio must be the remaining 40 percent of sales. It makes sense that the complement of the variable cost ratio is the contribution margin ratio. After all, total variable costs and total contribution margin sum to sales revenue.

Just as the variable cost ratio can be computed using total or unit figures, the contribution margin ratio, 40 percent in our example, can also be computed in these two ways. That is, one can divide the total contribution margin by total sales ($40/$100), or one can use the unit contribution margin divided by price ($4/$10). Naturally, if the variable cost ratio is known, it can be subtracted from 1 to yield the contribution margin ratio (1 − 0.60 = 0.40). Cornerstone 4-3 shows how the income statement can be expanded to yield the variable cost ratio and the contribution margin ratio.

Cornerstone  **4-3**

HOW TO Calculate the Variable Cost Ratio and the Contribution Margin Ratio

Information: Whittier Company plans to sell 1,000 mowers at $400 each in the coming year. Variable cost per unit is $325. Total fixed cost is $45,000.

Required:
1. Calculate the variable cost ratio.
2. Calculate the contribution margin ratio using unit figures.
3. Prepare a contribution margin income statement based on the budgeted figures for next year. In a column next to the income statement, show the percentages based on sales for sales, total variable costs, and total contribution margin.

Calculation:
1. Variable cost ratio = $325/$400 = 0.8125, or 81.25%
2. Contribution margin per unit = $400 − $325 = $75
   Contribution margin ratio = $75/$400 = 0.1875, or 18.75%
3. Contribution margin income statement based on budgeted figures.

		Percent of Sales
Sales ($400 × 1,000 mowers)	$400,000	100.00
Total variable expense (0.8125 × $400,000)	325,000	81.25
Total contribution margin	$ 75,000	18.75
Total fixed expense	45,000	
Operating income	$ 30,000	

Notice in Cornerstone 4-3, Requirement 3, that sales revenue, variable costs, and contribution margin have been expressed as a percent of sales. The variable cost ratio is 0.8125 ($325,000/$400,000); the contribution margin ratio is 0.1875 (computed either as 1 − 0.8125, or $75,000/$400,000).

How do fixed costs relate to the variable cost ratio and contribution margin ratio? Since the total contribution margin is the revenue remaining after total variable costs are covered, it must be the revenue available to cover fixed costs and contribute to profit. How does the relationship of fixed cost to contribution margin affect operating income? There are three possibilities: fixed cost can equal contribution margin; fixed cost can be less than contribution margin; or fixed cost can be greater than contribution margin. If fixed cost equals contribution margin, then operating income is $0 (the company is at break-even). If fixed cost is less than contribution margin, the company earns a positive operating income. Finally, if fixed cost is greater than contribution margin, then the company faces an operating loss.

Now let's turn to the equation for calculating the break-even point in sales dollars. One way of calculating break-even sales revenue is to simply multiply the break-even units by the price. However, often the company is a multiple-product firm, and it can be difficult to figure the break-even point for each product sold. The operating income equation can be used to solve for break-even sales for Whittier as follows:

Concept Q & A

1. If the contribution margin ratio is 30 percent, what is the variable cost ratio?
2. If the contribution margin ratio is 42 percent, what is the variable cost ratio?
3. If the variable cost ratio is 77 percent, what is the contribution margin ratio?
4. Explain why the contribution margin ratio and the variable cost ratio always total 100 percent.

Answer:
1. If the contribution margin ratio is 30 percent, then the variable cost ratio is 1.00 − 0.3 = 0.7, or 70 percent.
2. If the contribution margin ratio is 42 percent, then the variable cost ratio is 1.00 − 0.42 = 0.58, or 58 percent.
3. If the variable cost ratio is 77 percent, then the contribution margin ratio is 1.00 − 0.77 = 0.23, or 23 percent.
4. The contribution margin ratio and the variable cost ratio always precisely equal 100 percent of sales revenue. This is because total variable cost and total contribution margin, by definition, sum to sales revenue.

$$\text{Operating income} = \text{Sales} - \text{Total variable expenses} - \text{Total fixed expenses}$$

$$\text{Break-even sales} - 0.8125 \times \text{Break-even sales} - \$45,000 = \$0$$

$$\text{Break-even sales} = \$45,000/(1.00 - 0.8125)$$

$$\text{Break-even sales} = \$240,000$$

So, Whittier Company has sales of $240,000 at the break-even point.

Just as it was quicker to use an equation to calculate the break-even units directly, it is helpful to have an equation to figure the break-even sales dollars. This equation is:

$$\text{Break-even sales} = \text{Total fixed expenses}/\text{Contribution margin ratio}$$

Cornerstone 4-4 shows how to obtain the break-even point in sales dollars for Whittier Company.

Cornerstone 4-4

HOW TO Solve for the Break-Even Point in Sales Dollars

Information: Whittier Company plans to sell 1,000 mowers at $400 each in the coming year. Total variable expense per unit is $325. Total fixed expense is $45,000.

Required:

1. Calculate the contribution margin ratio.
2. Calculate the sales revenue that Whittier Company must make to break even by using the break-even point in sales equation.
3. Check your answer by preparing a contribution margin income statement based on the break-even point in sales dollars.

Calculation:

1. Contribution margin per unit = $400 − $325 = $75

   Contribution margin ratio = Contribution margin per unit/Price

   = $75/$400 = 0.1875, or 18.75%

   [*Hint:* The contribution margin ratio comes out cleanly to four decimal places. Don't round it, and your break-even point in sales dollars will yield an operating income of $0 (rather than being a few dollars off due to rounding).]

   Notice that the variable cost ratio equals 0.8125, or the difference between 1.0000 and the contribution margin ratio.

2. Calculate the break-even point in sales dollars:

   Break-even sales dollars = $45,000/0.1875 = $240,000

3. Contribution margin income statement based on sales of $240,000:

Sales	$240,000
Total variable expense (0.8125 × $240,000)	195,000
Total contribution margin	$ 45,000
Total fixed expense	45,000
Operating income	$ 0

Indeed, sales equal to $240,000 does yield a zero profit.

UNITS AND SALES DOLLARS NEEDED TO ACHIEVE A TARGET INCOME

OBJECTIVE 2

Determine the number of units that must be sold, and the amount of revenue required, to earn a targeted profit.

While the break-even point is useful information, most firms would like to earn operating income greater than $0. CVP analysis gives us a way to determine how many units must be sold, or how much sales revenue must be earned, to earn a particular target income. Let's look first at the number of units that must be sold to earn a targeted operating income.

Units to Be Sold to Achieve a Target Income

Remember that at the break-even point, operating income is $0. Now, how could positive operating income affect that? The answer is that we add the target income amount to the fixed costs. Let's try it two different ways—with the operating income equation and with the basic break-even equation.

The equation for the operating income is:

Operating income = (Price × Units sold) − (Unit variable cost × Units sold) − Fixed cost

To solve for positive operating income, simply replace the operating income term with the target income. Recall that Whittier Company sells mowers at $400 each, incurs variable cost per unit of $325, and has total fixed expense of $45,000. Suppose that

Whittier wants to make a target operating income of $37,500. The number of units that must be sold to achieve that target income is calculated as follows:

$$\$37{,}500 = (\$400 \times \text{Number of units}) - (\$325 \times \text{Number of units}) - \$45{,}000$$

$$\text{Number of units} = (\$37{,}500 + \$45{,}000)/(\$400 - \$325) = 1{,}100$$

Does the sale of 1,100 units really result in operating income of $37,500? The contribution margin income statement provides a good check.

Sales ($400 × 1,100)	$440,000
Total variable expense ($325 × 1,100)	357,500
Total contribution margin	$ 82,500
Total fixed expense	45,000
Operating income	$ 37,500

Indeed, selling 1,100 units does yield operating income of $37,500.

The operating income equation can be used to find the number of units to sell to earn a targeted income. However, it is quicker to simply adjust the break-even units equation by adding target income to the fixed cost. This results in the following equation:

$$\text{Number of units to earn target income} = \frac{\text{Fixed cost} + \text{Target income}}{\text{Price} - \text{Variable cost per unit}}$$

This equation was used when calculating the 1,100 units needed to earn operating income of $37,500. Cornerstone 4-5 shows how Whittier Company can use this approach.

Cornerstone 4-5

HOW TO Solve for the Number of Units to Be Sold to Earn a Target Operating Income

Information: Whittier Company sells mulching mowers at $400 each. Variable cost per unit is $325, and total fixed costs are $45,000.

Required:
1. Calculate the number of units that Whittier Company must sell to earn operating income of $37,500.
2. Check your answer by preparing a contribution margin income statement based on the number of units calculated.

Calculation:
1. Number of units = ($45,000 + $37,500)/($400 − $325) = 1,100
2. Contribution margin income statement based on sales of 1,100 units.

Sales ($400 × 1,100)	$440,000
Total variable expense ($325 × 1,100)	357,500
Total contribution margin	$ 82,500
Total fixed expense	45,000
Operating income	$ 37,500

Indeed, selling 1,100 units does yield operating income of $37,500.

Another way to check the number of units to be sold to yield a target operating income is to use the break-even point. As shown in Cornerstone 4-5, Whittier must sell 1,100 lawn mowers, or 500 more than the break-even volume of 600 units, to earn a profit of $37,500. The contribution margin per lawn mower is $75. Multiplying $75 by the 500 lawn mowers above break-even produces the operating income of $37,500 ($75 × 500). This outcome demonstrates that contribution margin per unit for each unit above break-even is equivalent to operating income per unit. Since the break-even point had already been computed, the number of lawn mowers to be sold to yield a $37,500 operating income could have been calculated by dividing the unit contribution margin into the target income and adding the resulting amount to the break-even volume.

In general, assuming that fixed costs remain the same, the impact on a firm's income resulting from a change in the number of units sold can be assessed by multiplying the unit contribution margin by the change in units sold. For example, if 1,400 lawn mowers instead of 1,100 are sold, how much more operating income will be earned? The change in units sold is an increase of 300 lawn mowers, and the unit contribution margin is $75. Thus, operating income will increase by $22,500 ($75 × 300) over the $37,500 initially calculated, and total operating income will be $60,000.

Sales Revenue to Achieve a Target Income

Consider the following question: How much sales revenue must Whittier generate to earn operating income of $37,500? This question is similar to the one we asked earlier in terms of units, but phrases the question directly in terms of sales revenue. To answer the question, add the targeted operating income of $37,500 to the $45,000 of fixed cost and divide by the contribution margin ratio. Then the equation is the following:

$$\text{Sales dollars to earn target income} = \frac{\text{Fixed cost} + \text{Target income}}{\text{Contribution margin ratio}}$$

Cornerstone 4-6 shows how to calculate the sales revenue needed to earn a target operating income of $37,500.

Cornerstone 4-6

HOW TO Solve for the Sales Needed to Earn a Target Operating Income

Information: Whittier Company sells mulching mowers at $400 each. Variable cost per unit is $325, and total fixed costs are $45,000.

Required:
1. Calculate the contribution margin ratio.
2. Calculate the sales that Whittier Company must make to earn operating income of $37,500.
3. Check your answer by preparing a contribution margin income statement based on the sales dollars calculated.

Calculation:
1. Contribution margin ratio = ($400 − $325)/$400 = 0.1875
2. Sales dollars = ($45,000 + $37,500)/0.1875 = $440,000
3. Contribution margin income statement based on sales revenue of $440,000.

Sales	$440,000
Total variable expense (0.8125 × $440,000)	357,500
Total contribution margin	$ 82,500
Total fixed expense	45,000
Operating income	$ 37,500

Indeed, sales revenue of $440,000 does yield operating income of $37,500.

Whittier must earn revenues equal to $440,000 to achieve a profit target of $37,500. Since break-even sales equals $240,000, additional sales of $200,000 ($440,000 − $240,000) must be earned above break-even. Notice that multiplying the contribution margin ratio by revenues above break-even yields the profit of $37,500 (0.1875 × $200,000). Above break-even, the contribution margin ratio is a profit ratio; therefore, it represents the proportion of each sales dollar assignable to profit. For Whittier Company, every sales dollar earned above break-even increases profits by $0.1875.

Concept Q & A

Lorna makes and sells decorative candles through gift shops. Lorna knows that she must sell 200 candles a month to break even. Every candle has a contribution margin of $1.50. So far this month, Lorna has sold 320 candles. How much has Lorna earned so far this month in operating income? If she sells 10 more candles, by how much will income increase?

Answer:

320 candles sold − 200 candles at break-even = 120 candles above break-even, 120 × $1.50 = $180

So Lorna has earned operating income of $180 so far during the month.

An additional 10 candles contribute $15 to operating income ($1.50 × 10).

In general, assuming that fixed costs remain unchanged, the contribution margin ratio can be used to find the profit impact of a change in sales revenue. To obtain the total change in profits from a change in revenues, simply multiply the contribution margin ratio times the change in sales. For example, if sales revenues are $400,000 instead of $440,000, how will the expected profits be affected? A decrease in sales revenues of $40,000 will cause a decrease in profits of $7,500 (0.1875 × $40,000).

GRAPHS OF CVP RELATIONSHIPS

It may be helpful in understanding CVP relationships to see them portrayed visually. A graphical representation can help managers see the difference between variable cost and revenue. It may also help them understand quickly what impact an increase or decrease in sales will have on the break-even point. Two basic graphs, the profit-volume graph and the cost-volume-profit graph, are presented here.

> **OBJECTIVE 3**
>
> Prepare a profit-volume graph and a cost-volume-profit graph and explain the meaning of each.

The Profit-Volume Graph

A **profit-volume graph** visually portrays the relationship between profits (operating income) and units sold. The profit-volume graph is the graph of the operating income equation [Operating income = (Price × Units) − (Unit variable cost × Units) − Total fixed cost]. In this graph, operating income is the dependent variable, and units is the independent variable. Usually, values of the independent variable are measured along the horizontal axis and values of the dependent variable along the vertical axis.

To make this discussion more concrete, a simple set of data will be used. Assume that Tyson Company produces a single product with the following cost and price data:

Total fixed costs	$100
Variable costs per unit	5
Selling price per unit	10

Using these data, operating income can be expressed as:

$$\text{Operating income} = (\$10 \times \text{Units}) - (\$5 \times \text{Units}) - \$100$$
$$= (\$5 \times \text{Units}) - \$100$$

This relationship can be graphed by plotting units along the horizontal axis and operating income (or loss) along the vertical axis. Two points are needed to graph a linear equation. While any two points will do, the two points often chosen are those that correspond to zero units sold and zero profits. When units sold are 0, Tyson experiences an operating loss of $100 (or an operating income of −$100). The point corresponding to zero sales volume, therefore, is (0, −$100). When no sales take place,

Profit-Volume Graph

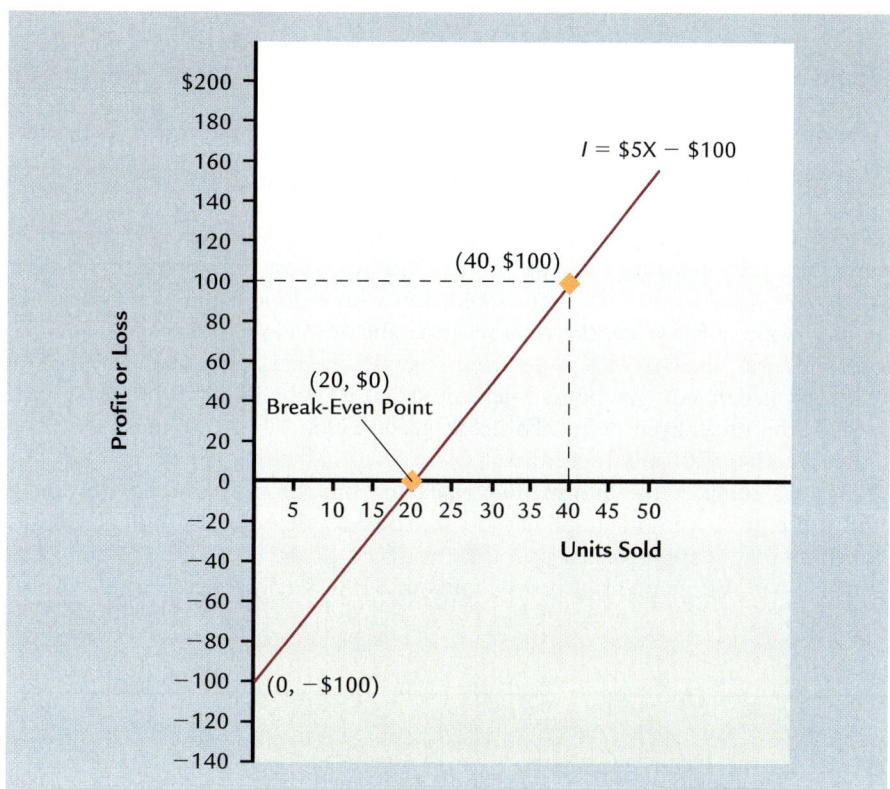

the company suffers a loss equal to its total fixed costs. When operating income is $0, the units sold are equal to 20. The point corresponding to zero profits (break-even) is (20, $0). These two points, plotted in Exhibit 4-3, define the profit graph.

The graph in Exhibit 4-3 can be used to assess Tyson's profit (or loss) at any level of sales activity. For example, the profit associated with the sale of 40 units can be read from the graph by (1) drawing a vertical line from the horizontal axis to the profit line and (2) drawing a horizontal line from the profit line to the vertical axis. As illustrated in Exhibit 4-3, the profit associated with sales of 40 units is $100. The profit-volume graph, while easy to interpret, fails to reveal how costs change as sales volume changes. An alternative approach to graphing can provide this detail.

The Cost-Volume-Profit Graph

The **cost-volume-profit graph** depicts the relationships among cost, volume, and profits (operating income) by plotting the total revenue line and the total cost line on a graph. To obtain the more detailed relationships, it is necessary to graph two separate lines: the total revenue line and the total cost line. These two lines are represented by the following two equations:

$$\text{Revenue} = \text{Price} \times \text{Units}$$
$$\text{Total cost} = (\text{Unit variable cost} \times \text{Units}) + \text{Fixed cost}$$

Using the Tyson Company example, the revenue and cost equations are:

$$\text{Revenue} = \$10 \times \text{Units}$$
$$\text{Total cost} = (\$5 \times \text{Units}) + \$100$$

To portray both equations in the same graph, the vertical axis is measured in dollars and the horizontal axis in units sold.

Again, two points are needed to graph each equation. For the revenue equation, setting number of units equal to 0 results in revenue of \$0; setting number of units equal to 20 results in revenue of \$200. Therefore, the two points for the revenue equation are (0, \$0) and (20, \$200). For the cost equation, units sold of 0 and units sold of 20 produce the points (0, \$100) and (20, \$200). The graph of each equation appears in Exhibit 4-4.

Notice that the total revenue line begins at the origin and rises with a slope equal to the selling price per unit (a slope of 10). The total cost line intercepts the vertical axis at a point equal to total fixed costs and rises with a slope equal to the variable cost per unit (a slope of 5). When the total revenue line lies below the total cost line, a loss region is defined. Similarly, when the total revenue line lies above the total cost line, a profit region is defined. The point where the total revenue line and the total cost line intersect is the break-even point. To break even, Tyson Company must sell 20 units and, thus, receive \$200 total revenues.

Now let's compare the information available from the CVP graph with that available from the profit-volume graph. To do so, consider the sale of 40 units. Recall that the profit-volume graph revealed that this produced profits of \$100. Examine Exhibit 4-4 again. The CVP graph also shows profits of \$100, but it reveals more as well. The

EXHIBIT 4-4

Cost-Volume-Profit Graph

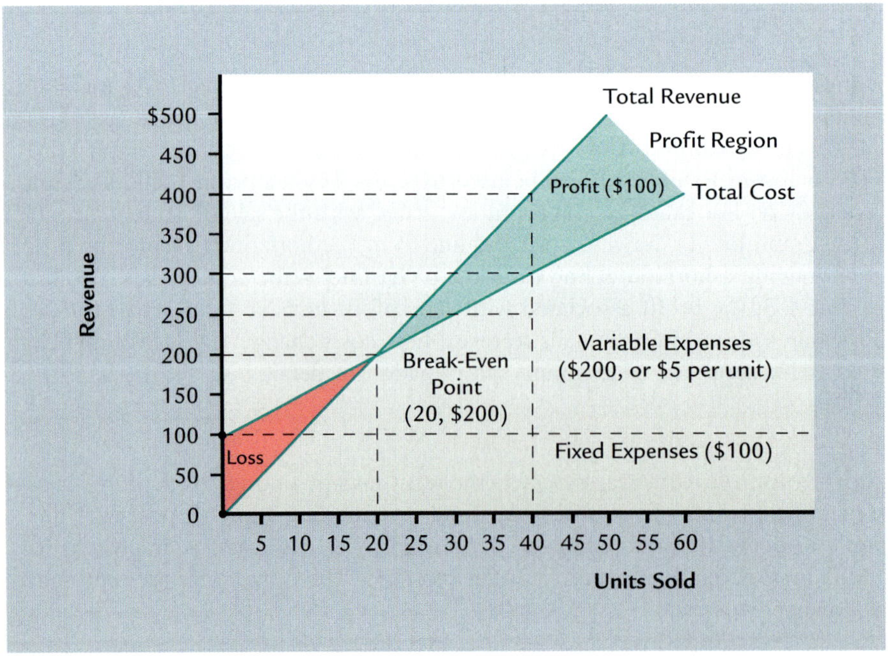

CVP graph discloses that total revenues of $400 and total costs of $300 are associated with the sale of 40 units. Furthermore, the total costs can be broken down into fixed costs of $100 and variable costs of $200. The CVP graph provides revenue and cost information not provided by the profit-volume graph. Unlike the profit-volume graph, some computation is needed to determine the profit associated with a given sales volume. Nonetheless, because of the greater information content, managers are likely to find the CVP graph a more useful tool.

Assumptions of Cost-Volume-Profit Analysis

The profit-volume and cost-volume-profit graphs just shown rely on some important assumptions. Some of these assumptions are as follows:

1. The analysis assumes a linear revenue function and a linear cost function.
2. The analysis assumes that price, total fixed costs, and unit variable costs can be accurately identified and remain constant over the relevant range.
3. The analysis assumes that what is produced is actually sold.
4. For multiple-product analysis, the sales mix is assumed to be known.
5. The selling prices and costs are assumed to be known with certainty.

Linear Cost and Revenue Functions

The first assumption is that cost and revenue functions are linear; that is, they are straight lines. But, as was discussed in Chapter 3 on cost behavior, these functions are often not linear. They may be curved or step functions. Fortunately, it is not necessary to consider all possible ranges of production and sales for a firm. Remember that CVP analysis is a short-run decision-making tool. (We know that it is short run in orientation because some costs are fixed.) It is only necessary for us to determine the current operating range, or relevant range, for which the linear cost and revenue relationships are valid. The second assumption is linked to the determination of the relevant range. Once a relevant range has been identified, then the cost and price relationships are assumed to be known and constant.

Concept Q & A

Suppose that the revenue line in Exhibit 4-4 had a steeper slope (e.g., if the price were $12 rather than $10). What would that imply for the break-even point? For the amount of operating income (profit) for units sold above break-even?

Now suppose that the revenue line remains unchanged, but that variable cost per unit increases. How would that affect the total cost line? What would that imply for the break-even point? For the amount of operating income (profit) for units sold above break-even?

Answer:

A steeper slope for the revenue line would mean that it would intersect the total cost line sooner. Thus, the break-even point would be lower and operating income above break-even would be higher. Try drawing in a steeper line for revenue on Exhibit 4-4 to see. (Remember, revenue still starts at the origin. Zero units sold means zero total revenue.)

Increased variable cost per unit means a steep slope for the total cost line. Thus, the break-even point would be higher, and the operating income above break-even would be lower.

Production Equal to Sales

The third assumption is that what is produced is actually sold. There is no change in inventory over the period. The idea that inventory has no impact on break-even analysis makes sense. Break-even analysis is a short-run decision-making technique; so, we are looking to cover all costs of a particular period of time. Inventory embodies costs of a previous period and is not considered.

Constant Sales Mix

In single-product analysis, the sales mix is obviously constant—100 percent of sales is the one product. Multiple-product break-even analysis requires a constant sales mix. However, it is virtually impossible to predict with certainty the sales mix. Typically, this constraint is handled in practice through sensitivity analysis. By using the capabilities of spreadsheet analysis, the sensitivity of variables to a variety of sales mixes can be readily assessed.

Prices and Costs Known with Certainty

In actuality, firms seldom know prices, variable costs, and fixed costs with certainty. A change in one variable usually affects the value of others. Often, there is a probability distribution to contend with. Furthermore, there are formal ways of explicitly building uncertainty into the CVP model. These issues are explored in the section on incorporating risk and uncertainty into CVP analysis.

MULTIPLE-PRODUCT ANALYSIS

Cost-volume-profit analysis is fairly simple in the single-product setting. However, most firms produce and sell a number of products or services. Even though CVP analysis becomes more complex with multiple products, the operation is reasonably straightforward. Let's see how we can adapt the formulas used in a single-product setting to the multiple-product setting by expanding the Whittier Company example.

OBJECTIVE 4

Apply cost-volume-profit analysis in a multiple-product setting.

Whittier Company has decided to offer two models of lawn mowers: a mulching mower to sell for $400 and a riding mower to sell for $800. The marketing department is convinced that 1,200 mulching mowers and 800 riding mowers can be sold during the coming year. The controller has prepared the following projected income statement based on the sales forecast:

	Mulching Mower	Riding Mower	Total
Sales	$480,000	$640,000	$1,120,000
Less: Variable expenses	390,000	480,000	870,000
Contribution margin	$ 90,000	$160,000	$ 250,000
Less: Direct fixed expenses	30,000	40,000	70,000
Product margin	$ 60,000	$120,000	$ 180,000
Less: Common fixed expenses			26,250
Operating income			$ 153,750

Note that the controller has separated direct fixed expenses from common fixed expenses. The **direct fixed expenses** are those fixed costs that can be traced to each segment and would be avoided if the segment did not exist. The **common fixed expenses** are the fixed costs that are not traceable to the segments and would remain even if one of the segments was eliminated.

Break-Even Point in Units

The owner of Whittier is somewhat apprehensive about adding a new product line and wants to know how many of each model must be sold to break even. If you were given the responsibility of answering this question, how would you respond? One possible response is to use the equation developed earlier in which fixed costs were divided by the contribution margin. This equation presents a problem, however; it was developed for single-product analysis. For two products, there are two prices and two variable costs per unit. The variable cost per unit is derived from the income statement. For the mulching mower, total variable costs are $390,000 based on sales of 1,200 units, yielding a per-unit variable cost of $325 ($390,000/1,200). For the riding mower, total variable costs are $480,000 based on sales of 800 units, yielding a per-unit variable cost of $600 ($480,000/800). Then, the mulching mower has a contribution margin per unit of $75 ($400 − $325); the riding mower has a contribution margin per unit of $200 ($800 − $600).

One possible solution is to apply the analysis separately to each product line. It is possible to obtain individual break-even points when income is defined as product margin. Break-even for the mulching mower is as follows:

$$\text{Mulching mower break-even units} = \text{Fixed cost}/(\text{Price} - \text{Unit variable cost})$$
$$= \$30,000/\$75$$
$$= 400 \text{ units}$$

Break-even for the riding mower can be computed as well:

$$\text{Riding mower break-even units} = \text{Fixed cost}/(\text{Price} - \text{Unit variable cost})$$
$$= \$40,000/\$200$$
$$= 200 \text{ units}$$

Thus, 400 mulching mowers and 200 riding mowers must be sold to achieve a break-even product margin. But a break-even product margin covers only direct fixed costs; the common fixed costs remain to be covered. Selling these numbers of lawn mowers would result in a loss equal to the common fixed costs. This is not the break-even point for the firm as a whole; somehow the common fixed costs must be factored into the analysis.

Allocating the common fixed costs to each product line before computing a break-even point may resolve this difficulty. The problem with this approach is that allocation of the common fixed costs is arbitrary. Thus, no meaningful break-even volume is readily apparent.

Another possible solution is to convert the multiple-product problem into a single-product problem. If this can be done, then all of the single-product CVP methodology can be applied directly. The key to this conversion is to identify the expected sales mix, in units, of the products being marketed. **Sales mix** is the relative combination of products being sold by a firm.

Determining the Sales Mix

The sales mix is measured in units sold. For example, if Whittier plans on selling 1,200 mulching mowers and 800 riding mowers, then the sales mix in units is 1,200:800. Usually, the sales mix is reduced to the smallest possible whole numbers. Thus, the relative mix, 1,200:800, can be reduced to 12:8, and further reduced to 3:2. That is, Whittier expects that for every three mulching mowers sold, two riding mowers will be sold.

A number of different sales mixes can be used to define the break-even volume. For example, a sales mix of 2:1 will define a break-even point of 550 mulching mowers and 275 riding mowers. The total contribution margin produced by this mix is $96,250 [($75 × 550) + ($200 × 275)]. Similarly, if 350 mulching mowers and 350 riding mowers are sold (corresponding to a 1:1 sales mix), then the total contribution margin is also $96,250 [($75 × 350) + ($200 × 350)]. Since total fixed costs are $96,250, both sales mixes define break-even points. Fortunately, every sales mix need not be considered. Can Whittier really expect a sales mix of 2:1 or 1:1? For every two mulching mowers sold, does Whittier expect to sell a riding mower? Or for every mulching mower, can Whittier really sell one riding mower?

According to Whittier's marketing study, a sales mix of 3:2 can be expected. This is the ratio that should be used; all others can be ignored. The sales mix that is expected to prevail should be used for CVP analysis.

Sales Mix and CVP Analysis

Defining a particular sales mix allows the conversion of a multiple-product problem into a single-product CVP format. Since Whittier expects to sell three mulching mowers for every two riding mowers, it can define the single product it sells as a package containing three mulching mowers and two riding mowers. By defining the product as a package, the multiple-product problem is converted into a single-product one. To use the approach of break-even point in units, the package selling price and the variable cost per package must be known. To compute these package values, the sales mix, individual product prices, and individual variable costs are needed. Cornerstone 4-7 shows how the overall break-even point for each product can be determined.

Cornerstone 4-7

HOW TO Calculate the Break-Even Units for a Multiple-Product Firm

Information: Recall that Whittier Company sells two products: mulching mowers priced at $400 and riding mowers priced at $800. The variable costs per unit are $325 per mulching mower and $600 per riding mower. Total fixed expense is $96,250. Whittier's expected sales mix is three mulching mowers to two riding mowers.

Required:

1. Form a package of mulching and riding mowers based on the sales mix and calculate the package contribution margin.
2. Calculate the break-even point in units for mulching mowers and for riding mowers.
3. Check your answers by preparing a contribution margin income statement.

Calculation:

1. Each package consists of three mulching mowers and two riding mowers:

Product	Price	Unit Variable Cost	Unit Contribution Margin	Sales Mix	Package Unit Contribution Margin
Mulching	$400	$325	$ 75	3	$225
Riding	800	600	200	2	400
Package total					$625

The three mulching mowers in the package yield $225 (3 × $75) in contribution margin. The two riding mowers in the package yield $400 (2 × $200) in contribution margin. Thus, a package of five mowers (three mulching and two riding) has a total contribution margin of $625.

2. Break-even packages = Fixed cost/Package contribution margin
   = $96,250/$625
   = 154 packages

   Mulching mower break-even units = 154 × 3 = 462
   Riding mower break-even units = 154 × 2 = 308

3. Income statement—break-even solution:

	Mulching Mower	Riding Mower	Total
Sales	$184,800	$246,400	$431,200
Less: Variable expenses	150,150	184,800	334,950
Contribution margin	$ 34,650	$ 61,600	$ 96,250
Less: Total fixed expenses			96,250
Operating income			$ 0

Concept Q & A

Suppose that Macy's department store sells two brands of suits: designer suits with a contribution margin of $600 each and regular suits with a contribution margin of $500 each. At break-even, the store must sell a total of 100 suits a month. Last month, the store sold 100 suits in total but incurred an operating loss. There was no change in fixed cost, variable cost, or price. What happened?

Answer:
In all probability, the sales mix shifted toward the low contribution margin suits. That is, relatively more of the low contribution margin suits (the regulars) were sold than the high contribution margin suits. Suppose that the break-even point for regular suits was 80 and the break-even point for designer suits was 20. If the mix shifted to 90 regular and 10 designer, it is easy to see that less total contribution margin (and, hence, operating income) would be realized.

The complexity of the approach of break-even point in units increases dramatically as the number of products increases. Imagine performing this analysis for a firm with several hundred products. This observation seems more overwhelming than it actually is. Computers can easily handle a problem with so much data. Furthermore, many firms simplify the problem by analyzing product groups rather than individual products. Another way to handle the increased complexity is to switch from the units sold to the sales revenue approach. This approach can accomplish a multiple-product CVP analysis using only the summary data found in an organization's income statement. The computational requirements are much simpler.

Break-Even Point in Sales Dollars

To illustrate the break-even point in sales dollars, the same examples will be used. However, the only information needed is the projected income statement for Whittier Company as a whole.

Sales	$1,120,000
Less: Variable costs	870,000
Contribution margin	$ 250,000
Less: Fixed costs	96,250
Operating income	$ 153,750

Notice that this income statement corresponds to the total column of the more detailed income statement examined previously. The projected income statement rests on the assumption that 1,200 mulching mowers and 800 riding mowers will be sold (a 3:2 sales mix). The break-even point in sales revenue also rests on the expected sales mix. (As with the units sold approach, different sales mixes will produce different results.)

With the income statement, the usual CVP questions can be addressed. For example, how much sales revenue must be earned to break even? Cornerstone 4-8 shows how to calculate the break-even point in sales dollars for a multiple-product firm.

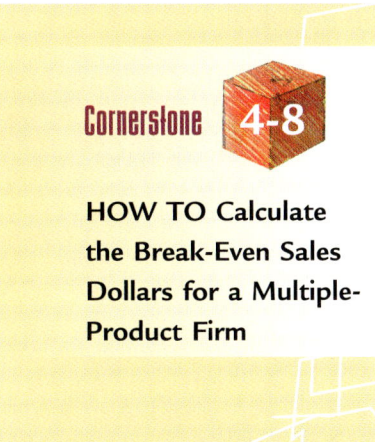

Cornerstone 4-8

HOW TO Calculate the Break-Even Sales Dollars for a Multiple-Product Firm

Information: Recall that Whittier Company sells two products that are expected to produce total revenue next year of $1,120,000 and total variable costs of $870,000. Total fixed costs are expected to equal $96,250.

Required:
1. Calculate the break-even point in sales dollars for Whittier Company.
2. Check your answer by preparing a contribution margin income statement.

Calculation:
1. The contribution margin ratio = $250,000/$1,120,000 = 0.22

$$\text{Break-even sales} = \text{Fixed cost/Contribution margin ratio}$$
$$= \$96,250/0.22$$
$$= \$437,500$$

2. Income statement—break-even solution:

Sales	$437,500
Less: Variable costs (0.78 × $437,500)	341,250
Contribution margin	$ 96,250
Less: Fixed costs	96,250
Operating income	$ 0

The break-even point in sales dollars implicitly uses the assumed sales mix but avoids the requirement of building a package contribution margin. No knowledge of individual product data is needed. The computational effort is similar to that used in the single-product setting. Moreover, the answer is still expressed in sales revenue. Unlike the break-even point in units, the answer to CVP questions using sales dollars is still expressed in a single summary measure. The sales revenue approach, however, does sacrifice information concerning individual product performance.

CVP ANALYSIS AND RISK AND UNCERTAINTY

Because firms operate in a dynamic world, they must be aware of changes in prices, variable costs, and fixed costs. They must also account for the effect of risk and uncertainty. The break-even point can be affected by changes in price, unit contribution margin, and fixed cost. Managers can use CVP analysis to handle risk and uncertainty.

For a given sales mix, CVP analysis can be used as if the firm were selling a single product. However, when the prices of individual products change, the sales mix can be affected because consumers may buy relatively more or less of the product. Keep in mind that a new sales mix will affect the units of each product that need to be sold in order to achieve a desired profit target. If the sales mix for the coming period is uncertain, it may be necessary to look at several different mixes. In this way, a manager gains insight into the possible outcomes facing the firm.

Suppose that Whittier Company recently conducted a market study of the mulching lawn mower that revealed three different alternatives:

1. *Alternative 1*: If advertising expenditures increase by $8,000, then sales will increase from 1,600 units to 1,725 units.
2. *Alternative 2*: A price decrease from $400 to $375 per lawn mower will increase sales from 1,600 units to 1,900 units.
3. *Alternative 3*: Decreasing price to $375 and increasing advertising expenditures by $8,000 will increase sales from 1,600 units to 2,600 units.

Should Whittier maintain its current price and advertising policies, or should it select one of the three alternatives described by the marketing study?

The first alternative, increasing advertising costs by $8,000 with a resulting sales increase of 125 units, is summarized in Exhibit 4-5. This alternative can be analyzed by using the contribution margin per unit of $75. Since units sold increase by 125, the increase in total contribution margin is $9,375 ($75 × 125 units). However, since fixed costs increase by $8,000, profits only increase by $1,375 ($9,375 − $8,000). Notice that we need to look only at the incremental increase in total contribution margin and fixed expenses to compute the increase in total operating income.

For the second alternative, the price is dropped to $375 (from $400), and the units sold increase to 1,900 (from 1,600). The effects of this alternative are summarized in Exhibit 4-6. Here, fixed expenses do not change, so only the change in total contribution margin is relevant. For the current price of $400, the contribution margin per unit is $75 ($400 − $325), and the total contribution margin is $120,000 ($75 × 1,600). For the new price, the contribution margin drops to $50 per unit ($375 − $325). If 1,900 units are sold at the new price, then the new total contribution margin is $95,000 ($50 × 1,900). Dropping the price results in a profit decline of $25,000 ($120,000 − $95,000).

The third alternative calls for a decrease in the unit selling price and an increase in advertising costs. Like the first alternative, the profit impact can be assessed by looking at the incremental effects on contribution margin and fixed expenses. The incremental profit change can be found by (1) computing the incremental change in total contribution margin, (2) computing the incremental change in fixed expenses, and (3) adding the two results. As shown in Exhibit 4-7, the current total contribution margin (for

Summary of the Effects of Alternative 1

	Before the Increased Advertising	With the Increased Advertising
Units sold	1,600	1,725
Unit contribution margin	× $75	× $75
Total contribution margin	$120,000	$129,375
Less: Fixed expenses	45,000	53,000
Operating income	$ 75,000	$ 76,375

	Difference in Profit
Change in sales volume	125
Unit contribution margin	× $75
Change in contribution margin	$9,375
Less: Change in fixed expenses	8,000
Increase in operating income	$1,375

Summary of the Effects of Alternative 2

	Before the Proposed Price Decrease	With the Proposed Price Decrease
Units sold	1,600	1,900
Unit contribution margin	× $75	× $50
Total contribution margin	$120,000	$95,000
Less: Fixed expenses	45,000	45,000
Operating income	$ 75,000	$50,000

	Difference in Profit
Change in contribution margin ($95,000 − $120,000)	$(25,000)
Less: Change in fixed expenses	—
Decrease in operating income	$(25,000)

Summary of the Effects of Alternative 3

	Before the Proposed Price and Advertising Changes	With the Proposed Price Decrease and Advertising Increase
Units sold	1,600	2,600
Unit contribution margin	× $75	× $50
Total contribution margin	$120,000	$130,000
Less: Fixed expenses	45,000	53,000
Profit	$ 75,000	$ 77,000

	Difference in Profit
Change in contribution margin ($130,000 − $120,000)	$10,000
Less: Change in fixed expenses ($53,000 − $45,000)	8,000
Increase in profit	$ 2,000

1,600 units sold) is $120,000. Since the new unit contribution margin is $50, the new total contribution margin is $130,000 ($50 × 2,600 units). Thus, the incremental increase in total contribution margin is $10,000 ($130,000 − $120,000). However, to achieve this incremental increase in contribution margin, an incremental increase of $8,000 in fixed costs is needed. The net effect is an incremental increase in operating income of $2,000.

Of the three alternatives identified by the marketing study, the one that promises the most benefit is the third. It increases total operating income by $2,000. The first alternative increases operating income by only $1,375, and the second actually decreases operating income by $25,000.

These examples are all based on a units sold approach. However, we could just as easily have applied a sales revenue approach. The answers would be the same.

Introducing Risk and Uncertainty

An important assumption of CVP analysis is that prices and costs are known with certainty. This is seldom the case. Risk and uncertainty are a part of business decision making and must be dealt with somehow. Formally, risk differs from uncertainty in that under risk the probability distributions of the variables are known; under uncertainty, they are not known. For purposes of CVP analysis, however, the terms will be used interchangeably.

How do managers deal with risk and uncertainty? There are a variety of methods. First, of course, is that management must realize the uncertain nature of future prices, costs, and quantities. Next, managers move from consideration of a break-even point to what might be called a "break-even band." In other words, given the uncertain nature of the data, perhaps a firm might break even when 1,800 to 2,000 units are sold instead of the point estimate of 1,900 units. Further, managers may engage in sensitivity or what-if analysis. In this instance, a computer spreadsheet is helpful, as managers set up the break-even (or targeted profit) relationships and then check to see the impact that varying costs and prices have on quantity sold. Two concepts useful to management are *margin of safety* and *operating leverage*. Both of these may be considered measures of risk. Each requires knowledge of fixed and variable costs.

Margin of Safety

The **margin of safety** is the units sold or the revenue earned above the break-even volume. Exhibit 4-8 shows the margin of safety. For example, if the break-even volume for a company is 200 units and the company is currently selling 500 units, then the margin of safety is 300 units (500 − 200). The margin of safety can be expressed in sales revenue as well. If the break-even volume is $200,000 and current revenues are $350,000, then the margin of safety is $150,000. Cornerstone 4-9 shows the expected margin of safety for Whittier Company.

Cornerstone 4-9

HOW TO Compute the Margin of Safety

Information: Recall that Whittier Company plans to sell 1,000 mowers at $400 each in the coming year. Whittier has variable cost of $325 and fixed cost of $45,000. Break-even units were previously calculated as 600.

Required:
1. Calculate the margin of safety for Whittier Company in terms of the number of units.
2. Calculate the margin of safety for Whittier Company in terms of sales revenue.

Calculation:
1. Margin of safety in units = 1,000 − 600 = 400
2. Margin of safety in sales revenue = $400(1,000) − $400(600) = $160,000

The Margin of Safety

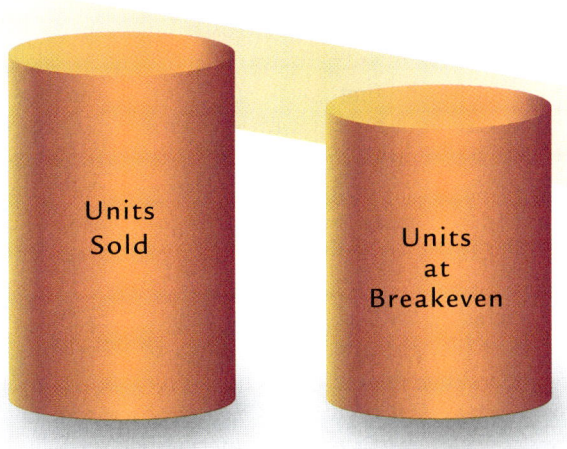

Units Sold

Units at Breakeven

Margin of Safety in Units
X
Price
—————————
Margin of Safety in Sales Revenue

APPLICATIONS IN BUSINESS

A good margin of safety can provide a comfortable cushion for a company in a volatile industry. The restaurant business is considered to be relatively risky. About 27 percent of restaurants fail within one year; about 60 percent fail within five years. "One mistake here or there can cost you your whole profit," according to the founder of a restaurant consulting firm. Typically, the margin of safety is razor thin. Savvy restaurateurs learn to increase it by cutting back on costs. For example, the owners of Don-ley's Old West Steakhouse and Buffet in Union, Illinois, saved unused kale from the salad bar at the end of each day to decorate the buffet the next day. They also made the desserts in-house rather than buying them from a bakery, a move that saved $500 per week. As a result, both fixed and variable costs decreased, and the margin of safety increased. This cushions Donley's in the event of economic downturns or increases in other costs such as beef.

Source: Stephanie N. Mehta, "Restaurant Novices Learn to Turn Popularity into Profit," *The Wall Street Journal* (August 9, 1996): B1 and B2.

The margin of safety can be viewed as a crude measure of risk. There are always events, unknown when plans are made, that can lower sales below the original expected level. If a firm's expected margin of safety is large, then the risk of suffering losses should sales take a downward turn is less than if the margin of safety is small. Managers who face a low margin of safety may wish to consider actions to increase sales or decrease costs. These steps will increase the margin of safety and lower the risk of incurring losses.

Operating Leverage

In physics, a lever is a simple machine used to multiply force. Basically, the lever multiplies the effort applied to create more work. The larger the load moved by a given amount of effort, the greater is the mechanical advantage. In financial terms, operating leverage is concerned with the relative mix of fixed costs and variable costs in an organization. It is sometimes possible to trade off fixed costs for variable costs. As variable costs decrease, the unit contribution margin increases, making the contribution of each unit sold that much greater. In such a case, fluctuations in sales have an increased effect on profitability. Thus, firms that have realized lower variable costs by increasing the proportion of fixed costs will benefit with greater increases in profits as sales increase than will firms with a lower proportion of fixed costs. Fixed costs are being used as leverage to increase profits. Unfortunately, it is also true that firms with a higher operating leverage will experience greater reductions in profits as sales decrease. **Operating leverage** is the use of fixed costs to extract higher percentage changes in profits as sales activity changes.

The greater the degree of operating leverage, the more that changes in sales will affect operating income. Because of this phenomenon, the mix of costs that an organization chooses can have a considerable influence on its operating risk and profit level.

The **degree of operating leverage (DOL)** can be measured for a given level of sales by taking the ratio of contribution margin to operating income, as follows:

Degree of operating leverage = Contribution margin/Operating income

Concept Q & A

Two companies have identical operating incomes of $15 million. Is it true that both have the same operating income and the same margin of safety? Is it possible that one company has a higher margin of safety?

Answer:

It is not necessarily true that the two companies make the same operating income. If one company has lower variable costs per unit and/or a lower total fixed cost, then its operating income would be higher. The differences in variable cost per unit and total fixed cost would lead to different break-even revenues. Of course, the company with the lower break-even sales would have a higher margin of safety.

If fixed costs are used to lower variable costs such that contribution margin increases and operating income decreases, then the degree of operating leverage increases—signaling an increase in risk. Cornerstone 4-10 shows how to compute the degree of operating leverage for Whittier Company.

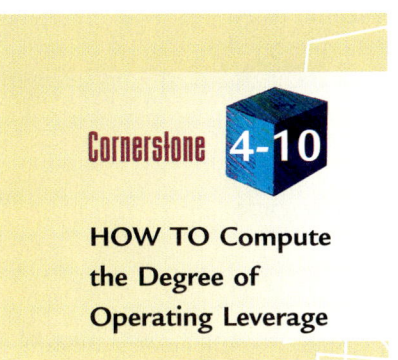

Cornerstone 4-10

HOW TO Compute the Degree of Operating Leverage

Information: Recall that Whittier Company plans to sell 1,000 mowers at $400 each in the coming year. Whittier has variable cost of $325 and fixed cost of $45,000. Operating income at that level of sales was previously computed as $30,000.

Required: Calculate the degree of operating leverage for Whittier Company.

Calculation:

$$\text{Degree of operating leverage} = \text{Contribution margin/Operating income}$$
$$= (\$400 - \$325)/\$30,000$$
$$= 2.5\%$$

To illustrate the impact of these concepts on management decision making, consider a firm that is planning to add a new product line. In adding the line, the firm can choose to rely heavily on automation or on labor. If the firm chooses to emphasize automation rather than labor, fixed costs will be higher and unit variable costs will be lower. Relevant data for a sales level of 10,000 units follow:

	Automated System	Manual System
Sales	$1,000,000	$1,000,000
Less: Variable costs	500,000	800,000
Contribution margin	$ 500,000	$ 200,000
Less: Fixed costs	375,000	100,000
Operating income	$ 125,000	$ 100,000
Unit selling price	$100	$100
Unit variable cost	50	80
Unit contribution margin	50	20

The degree of operating leverage for the automated system is 4.0 ($500,000/$125,000). The degree of operating leverage for the manual system is 2.0 ($200,000/$100,000). What happens to profit in each system if sales increase by 40 percent? We can generate the following income statements to see:

	Automated System	Manual System
Sales	$1,400,000	$1,400,000
Less: Variable costs	700,000	1,120,000
Contribution margin	$ 700,000	$ 280,000
Less: Fixed costs	375,000	100,000
Operating income	$ 325,000	$ 180,000

Profits for the automated system would increase by $200,000 ($325,000 − $125,000) for a 160-percent increase. In the manual system, profits increase by only $80,000 ($180,000 − $100,000) for an 80-percent increase. The automated system has a greater percentage increase because it has a higher degree of operating leverage.

The degree of operating leverage can be used directly to calculate the change in operating income that would result from a given percentage change in sales.

Percentage change in operating income = DOL × Percent change in sales

Since sales are predicted to increase by 40 percent and the DOL for the automated system is 4.0, operating income increases by 160 percent. Since operating income based on the original sales level is $125,000, the operating income based on the increased sales level would be $325,000 [$125,000 + ($125,000 × 1.6)]. Similarly for the manual system, increased sales of 40 percent and DOL of 2.0 imply increased operating income of 80 percent. Therefore, operating income based on the increased sales level would be $180,000 [$100,000 + ($100,000 × 0.8)]. Cornerstone 4-11 illustrates the impact of increased sales on operating income using the degree of operating leverage.

Cornerstone 4-11

HOW TO Compute the Impact of Increased Sales on Operating Income Using the Degree of Operating Leverage

Information: Recall that Whittier Company had expected to sell 1,000 mowers and earn operating income equal to $30,000 next year. Whittier's degree of operating leverage is equal to 2.5. Now, the company plans to increase sales by 20 percent next year.

Required:
1. Calculate the percent change in operating income expected by Whittier Company for next year using the degree of operating leverage.
2. Calculate the operating income expected by Whittier Company next year using the percent change in operating income calculated in Requirement 1.

Calculation:
1. Percent change in operating income = DOL × % change in sales
                                       = 2.5 × 20% = 50%
2. Expected operating income = $30,000 + (0.5 × $30,000) = $45,000

In choosing between the two systems, the effect of operating leverage is a valuable piece of information. Higher operating leverage multiplies the impact of increased sales on income. However, the effect is a two-edged sword. As sales decrease, the automated system will also show much higher percentage decreases. Moreover, the increased operating leverage is available under the automated system because of the presence of increased fixed costs. The break-even point for the automated system is 7,500 units ($375,000/$50), whereas the break-even point for the manual system is 5,000 units ($100,000/$20). Thus, the automated system has greater operating risk. The increased risk, of course, provides a potentially higher profit level as long as units sold exceed 9,167. Why 9,167? Because that is the quantity for which the operating income for the automated system equals the operating income for the manual system. This number of units is computed by setting the operating income equations of the two systems equal and solving for number of units:

$$50 \text{ (Units)} - 375,000 = 20 \text{ (Units)} - 100,000$$
$$\text{Units} = 9,167$$

In choosing between the automated and manual systems, the manager must consider the likelihood that sales will exceed 9,167 units. If, after careful study, there is a strong belief that sales will easily exceed this level, then the choice is obviously the automated system. On the other hand, if sales are unlikely to exceed 9,167 units, then the manual system is preferable. Exhibit 4-9 summarizes the relative differences between the manual and automated systems in terms of some of the CVP concepts.

Differences between a Manual and an Automated System

	Manual System	**Automated System**
Price	Same	Same
Variable cost	Relatively higher	Relatively lower
Fixed cost	Relatively lower	Relatively higher
Contribution margin	Relatively lower	Relatively higher
Break-even point	Relatively lower	Relatively higher
Margin of safety	Relatively higher	Relatively lower
Degree of operating leverage	Relatively lower	Relatively higher
Down-side risk	Relatively lower	Relatively higher
Up-side potential	Relatively lower	Relatively higher

Sensitivity Analysis and CVP

The widespread use of personal computers and spreadsheets has placed *sensitivity analysis* within reach of most managers. An important tool, **sensitivity analysis** is a "what-if" technique that examines the impact of changes in underlying assumptions on an answer. It is relatively simple to input data on prices, variable costs, fixed costs, and sales mix and to set up formulas to calculate break-even points and expected profits. Then, the data can be varied as desired to see how changes impact the expected profit.

In the example on operating leverage, a company analyzed the impact on profit of using an automated versus a manual system. The computations were essentially done by hand, and too much variation is cumbersome. Using the power of a computer, it would be an easy matter to change the sales price in $1 increments between $75 and $125, with related assumptions about quantity sold. At the same time, variable and fixed costs could be adjusted. For example, suppose that the automated system has fixed costs of $375,000 but that those costs could easily double in the first year and come back down in the second and third years as bugs are worked out of the system and workers learn to use it. Again, the spreadsheet can effortlessly handle the many computations.

Finally, a spreadsheet, while wonderful for cranking out numerical answers, cannot do the most difficult job in CVP analysis. That job is determining the data to be entered in the first place. The accountant must be aware of the cost and price distributions of the firm, as well as of the impact of changing economic conditions on these variables. The fact that variables are seldom known with certainty is no excuse for ignoring the impact of uncertainty on CVP analysis. Fortunately, sensitivity analysis can also give managers a feel for the degree to which a poorly forecast variable will affect an answer. That is also an advantage.

In the opening scenario, Janet was discouraged to learn that her original cost and price figures would not produce income—ever! Fortunately, there is a way out. By focusing on the CVP variables, Bob (her accountant) was able to work with her to reduce variable costs, increase fixed costs, and increase price. To do this, her strategy had to change. Janet had to scale up her expected production to take advantage of economies of scale. This was a risky strategy, but it was the only one that had a chance of working.

First, Janet had to increase price to $5 to make her salsa fall into a gourmet category. She also had to decrease variable cost per unit by purchasing tomatoes, spices, and jars at wholesale rather than retail. Finally, Janet increased her fixed costs by renting kitchen space in a restaurant during the times when they were closed. This gave her the equipment and room to hire some part-time help. These changes allowed Janet to produce many more jars of salsa. They also increased her operating leverage (higher fixed costs). By the end of the year, Janet was thrilled with her new enterprise; her company was more than breaking even. She looked forward to even higher income in the year after.

SUMMARY OF LEARNING OBJECTIVES

In a single-product setting, the break-even point can be computed in units by dividing the total fixed costs by the contribution margin per unit. In essence, sufficient units must be sold to just cover all fixed and variable costs of the firm.

Break-even revenue is computed by dividing the total fixed costs by the contribution margin ratio. Targeted profit is added to fixed costs in determining the amount of revenue needed to yield the targeted profit.

Multiple-product analysis requires that an assumption be made concerning the expected sales mix. Given a particular sales mix, a multiple-product problem can be converted into a single-product analysis. However, it should be remembered that the answers change as the sales mix changes. If the sales mix changes in a multiple-product firm, then the break-even point will also change. In general, increases in the sales of high contribution margin products will decrease the break-even point, while increases in the sales of low contribution margin products will increase the break-even point.

CVP is based on several assumptions that must be considered in applying it to business problems. The analysis assumes linear revenue and cost functions, no finished goods ending inventories, and a constant sales mix. CVP analysis also assumes that selling prices and fixed and variable costs are known with certainty. These assumptions form the basis for simple graphical analysis using the profit-volume graph and the cost-volume-profit graph.

4-10

EXHIBIT

Summary of Important Equations

1. Sales revenue = Price $\times$ Units sold
2. Operating income = (Price $\times$ Units sold) $-$ (Unit variable cost $\times$ Units sold) $-$ Fixed cost
3. Break-even point in units = Fixed cost/(Price $-$ Unit variable cost)
4. Contribution margin ratio = Contribution margin/Sales

   $\qquad\qquad$ or

   $\qquad\qquad$ = (Price $-$ Unit variable cost)/Price
5. Variable cost ratio = Total variable cost/Sales

   $\qquad\qquad$ or

   $\qquad\qquad$ = Unit variable cost/Price
6. Break-even point in sales dollars = Fixed cost/Contribution margin ratio

   $\qquad\qquad$ or

   $\qquad\qquad$ = Fixed cost/(1 $-$ Variable cost ratio)
7. Margin of safety = Sales $-$ Break-even sales
8. Degree of operating leverage = Total contribution margin/Operating income
9. Percentage change in profits = Degree of operating leverage $\times$ Percent change in sales

---

Measures of risk and uncertainty, such as the margin of safety and operating leverage, can be used to give managers more insight into CVP answers. Sensitivity analysis gives still more insight into the effect of changes in underlying variables on CVP relationships.

The subject of cost-volume-profit analysis naturally lends itself to the use of numerous equations. Some of the more common equations used in this chapter are summarized in Exhibit 4-10.

Cornerstones for Chapter 4

Cornerstone 4-1 How to prepare a contribution margin income statement, page 113
Cornerstone 4-2 How to solve for the break-even point in units, page 116
Cornerstone 4-3 How to calculate the variable cost ratio and the contribution margin ratio, page 117
Cornerstone 4-4 How to solve for the break-even point in sales dollars, page 119
Cornerstone 4-5 How to solve for the number of units to be sold to earn a target operating income, page 120
Cornerstone 4-6 How to solve for the sales needed to earn a target operating income, page 121
Cornerstone 4-7 How to calculate the break-even units for a multiple-product firm, page 128
Cornerstone 4-8 How to calculate the break-even sales dollars for a multiple-product firm, page 129
Cornerstone 4-9 How to compute the margin of safety, page 133
Cornerstone 4-10 How to compute the degree of operating leverage, page 135
Cornerstone 4-11 How to compute the impact of increased sales on operating income using the degree of operating leverage, page 136

KEY TERMS

DISCUSSION QUESTIONS

1. Explain how CVP analysis can be used for managerial planning.
2. Describe the difference between the units sold approach to CVP analysis and the sales revenue approach.
3. Define the term *break-even point*.
4. Explain why contribution margin per unit becomes profit per unit above the break-even point.
5. What is the variable cost ratio? The contribution margin ratio? How are the two ratios related?
6. Suppose a firm with a contribution margin ratio of 0.3 increased its advertising expenses by $10,000 and found that sales increased by $30,000. Was it a good decision to increase advertising expenses? Suppose that the contribution margin ratio is now 0.4. Would it be a good decision to increase advertising expenses?
7. Define the term *sales mix* and give an example to support your definition.
8. Explain how CVP analysis developed for single products can be used in a multiple-product setting.
9. Since break-even analysis focuses on making zero profit, it is of no value in determining the units a firm must sell to earn a targeted profit. Do you agree or disagree with this statement? Why?
10. How does target profit enter into the break-even units equation?
11. Explain how a change in sales mix can change a company's break-even point.
12. Define the term *margin of safety*. Explain how it can be used as a crude measure of operating risk.
13. Explain what is meant by the term *operating leverage*. What impact does increased leverage have on risk?
14. How can sensitivity analysis be used in conjunction with CVP analysis?
15. Why is a declining margin of safety over a period of time an issue of concern to managers?

MULTIPLE-CHOICE EXERCISES

4-1 If the variable cost per unit goes up,

	Contribution margin	Break-even point
a.	increases	increases
b.	increases	decreases
c.	decreases	decreases
d.	decreases	increases
e.	decreases	remains unchanged

4-2 The amount of revenue required to earn a targeted profit is equal to

a. fixed cost divided by contribution margin.
b. fixed cost divided by contribution margin ratio.
c. fixed cost plus targeted profit divided by contribution margin ratio.
d. targeted profit divided by contribution margin ratio.
e. targeted profit divided by variable cost ratio.

4-3 Break-even revenue for the multiple-product firm can

a. be calculated by dividing total fixed cost by the overall contribution margin ratio.
b. be calculated by dividing segment fixed cost by the overall contribution margin ratio.
c. be calculated by dividing total fixed cost by the package contribution margin.
d. be calculated by multiplying total fixed cost by the contribution margin ratio.
e. not be calculated; break-even revenue can only be computed for a single-product firm.

4-4 In the cost-volume-profit graph,

a. the break-even point is found where the total revenue curve crosses the x-axis.
b. the area of profit is to the left of the break-even point.
c. the area of loss cannot be determined from this graph.
d. both the total revenue curve and the total cost curve appear on this graph.
e. neither the total revenue curve and the total cost curve appear on this graph.

4-5 An important assumption of cost-volume-profit analysis is that

a. both costs and revenues are linear functions.
b. all cost and revenue relationships are analyzed within the relevant range.
c. there is no change in inventories.
d. sales mix remains constant.
e. All of the above are assumptions of cost-volume-profit analysis.

4-6 The use of fixed costs to extract higher percentage changes in profits as sales activity changes involves

a. margin of safety.
b. operating leverage.
c. degree of operating leverage.
d. sensitivity analysis.
e. variable cost reduction.

4-7 If the margin of safety is 0, then

a. the company is operating at a loss.
b. the company is precisely breaking even.
c. the company is earning a small profit.
d. the margin of safety cannot be less than or equal to 0; it must be positive.
e. none of the above is true.

4-8 The contribution margin is the

a. amount by which sales exceed fixed cost.
b. difference between sales and total expenses.
c. difference between sales and operating income.
d. difference between sales and total variable expense.
e. difference between variable expense and fixed expense.

Use the following information for 4-9 and 4-10.

Corleone Company produces a single product with a price of $15, variable cost per unit of $12, and fixed costs of $9,000.

4-9 Corleone's break-even point in units

a. is 600.
b. is 750.
c. is 9,000.
d. is 3,000.
e. cannot be determined from the information given.

4-10 The variable cost ratio and the contribution margin ratio for Corleone are

	Variable cost ratio	Contribution margin ratio
a.	80%	80%
b.	20%	80%
c.	20%	20%
d.	80%	20%

e. The contribution margin ratio cannot be determined from the information given.

4-11 If a company's fixed costs rise by $10,000, which of the following will be true?

a. The break-even point will decrease.
b. The variable cost ratio will increase.
c. The break-even point will be unchanged.
d. The variable cost ratio will decrease.
e. The contribution margin ratio will be unchanged.

4-12 Solemon Company has fixed costs of $15,000, variable cost per unit of $5, and a price of $8. If Solemon wants to earn a targeted profit of $3,600, how many units must be sold?

a. 6,200
b. 5,000
c. 1,200
d. 3,720
e. 1,875

EXERCISES

Exercise 4-1 *Basic Break-Even Calculations*

Suppose that Adams Company sells a product for $16. Unit costs are as follows:

Direct materials	$3.90
Direct labor	1.40
Variable overhead	2.10
Variable selling and administrative expense	1.60

Total fixed overhead is $52,000 per year, and total fixed selling and administrative expense is $37,950.

Required:

1. Calculate the variable cost per unit and the contribution margin per unit.
2. Prepare a contribution margin income statement assuming that 13,000 units are sold.
3. Calculate the contribution margin ratio and the variable cost ratio.
4. Calculate the break-even units.

Exercise 4-2 *Break-Even in Units*

The controller of Greenbrough Company prepared the following projected income statement:

Sales (5,000 units @ $12)	$60,000
Less: Variable cost	45,000
Contribution margin	$15,000
Less: Fixed cost	6,900
Operating income	$ 8,100

Required:

1. Calculate the unit variable cost. Calculate the break-even number of units.
2. Prepare an income statement for Greenbrough at break-even.

Exercise 4-3 *Contribution Margin Ratio, Variable Cost Ratio, Break-Even in Sales Revenue*

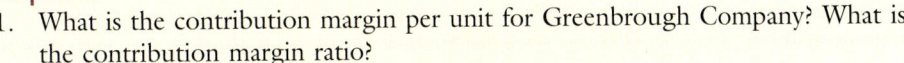

Refer to **Exercise 4-2** for data.

Required:

1. What is the contribution margin per unit for Greenbrough Company? What is the contribution margin ratio?
2. What is the variable cost ratio for Greenbrough Company?
3. Calculate the break-even revenue.

Exercise 4-4 *Units Needed to Earn Target Income*

 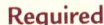
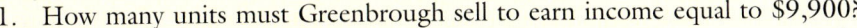

Refer to **Exercise 4-2** for data.

Required:

1. How many units must Greenbrough sell to earn income equal to $9,900?
2. How much sales revenue must Greenbrough make to earn income equal to $9,900?
3. Prepare an income statement based on the number of units you calculated in Requirement 1 (or the revenue you calculated in Requirement 2) to prove your answer.

Exercise 4-5 *Units Sold to Break Even, Unit Variable Cost, Unit Manufacturing Cost*

Prachi Company produces and sells disposable foil baking pans to retailers for $2.45 per pan. The variable costs per pan are as follows:

Direct materials	$0.27
Direct labor	0.58
Variable overhead	0.63
Variable selling	0.17

Fixed manufacturing costs total $131,650 per year. Administrative costs (all fixed) total $18,350.

Required:

1. Compute the number of pans that must be sold for Prachi to break even.
2. What is the unit variable cost? What is the unit variable manufacturing cost? Which is used in cost-volume-profit analysis and why?

Exercise 4-6 *Units and Sales to Earn Target Income*

Refer to **Exercise 4-5** for data.

Required:
1. How many pans must be sold for Prachi to earn operating income of $12,600?
2. How much sales revenue must Prachi have to earn operating income of $12,600?

Exercise 4-7 *Margin of Safety*

Refer to **Exercise 4-5** for data and suppose that Prachi expects to sell 215,000 pans.

Required:
1. What is the margin of safety in pans?
2. What is the margin of safety in dollars?

Exercise 4-8 *Contribution Margin, Unit Amounts, Break-Even Units*

Information on four independent companies follows. Calculate the correct amount for each question mark.

	A	B	C	D
Sales	$5,000	$?	$?	$9,000
Total variable costs	4,000	11,700	9,750	?
Total contribution margin	$1,000	$ 3,900	$?	$?
Total fixed costs	?	4,000	?	750
Operating income (loss)	$ 500	$?	$ 400	$2,850
Units sold	?	1,300	125	90
Price per unit	$ 5	?	$ 130	?
Variable cost per unit	?	$ 9	?	?
Contribution margin per unit	?	$ 3	?	?
Contribution margin ratio	?	?	40%	?
Break-even in units	?	?	?	?

Exercise 4-9 *Sales Revenue Approach, Variable Cost Ratio, Contribution Margin Ratio*

Rezler Company's controller prepared the following budgeted income statement for the coming year:

Sales	$315,000
Less: Variable expenses	141,750
Contribution margin	$173,250
Less: Fixed expenses	63,000
Profit before taxes	$110,250
Less: Taxes	33,075
Profit after taxes	$ 77,175

Required:
1. What is Rezler's variable cost ratio? What is its contribution margin ratio?
2. Suppose Rezler's actual revenues are $30,000 more than budgeted. By how much will operating income increase? Give the answer without preparing a new income statement.
3. How much sales revenue must Rezler earn to break even? Prepare a contribution margin income statement to verify the accuracy of your answer.

Exercise 4-10 *Margin of Safety*

Refer to **Exercise 4-9** for data.

Required:

1. What is Rezler's expected margin of safety?
2. What is Rezler's margin of safety if sales revenue is $280,000?

Exercise 4-11 *Multiple-Product Break-Even*

Switzer Company produces and sells yoga-training products: how-to videotapes and a basic equipment set (blocks, strap, and small pillows). Last year, Switzer sold 10,000 videos and 5,000 equipment sets. Information on the two products is as follows:

	Videotape	Equipment Set
Price	$12	$15
Variable cost per unit	4	6

Total fixed costs are $70,000.

Required:

1. What is the sales mix of videotapes and equipment sets?
2. Compute the break-even quantity of each product.

Exercise 4-12 *Contribution Margin Ratio, Break-Even Sales Revenue, and Margin of Safety for Multiple-Product Firm*

Refer to **Exercise 4-11** for data.

Required:

1. Prepare an income statement for Switzer for last year. What is the overall contribution margin ratio? The overall break-even sales revenue?
2. Compute the margin of safety for last year.

Exercise 4-13 *Multiple-Product Break-Even, Break-Even Sales Revenue*

Refer to **Exercise 4-11**. Suppose that in the coming year, Switzer plans to produce an extra thick yoga mat for sale to health clubs. The company estimates that 20,000 mats can be sold at a price of $18 and variable cost per unit of $13. Fixed cost must be increased by $48,350 (making total fixed cost of $118,350). Assume that anticipated sales of the other products, as well as their prices and variable costs, remain the same.

Required:

1. What is the sales mix of videotapes, equipment sets, and yoga mats?
2. Compute the break-even quantity of each product.
3. Prepare an income statement for Switzer for the coming year. What is the overall contribution margin ratio? The overall break-even sales revenue?
4. Compute the margin of safety for the coming year in sales dollars. (Round the contribution margin ratio to three significant digits; round the break-even sales revenue to the nearest dollar.)

Exercise 4-14 *CVP Graphs*

Lotts Company produces and sells one product. The selling price is $10, and the unit variable cost is $6. Total fixed costs are $10,000.

Required:

1. Prepare a CVP graph with "Units Sold" as the horizontal axis and "$ Profit" as the vertical axis. Label the break-even point on the horizontal axis.

2. Prepare CVP graphs for each of the following independent scenarios:
   a. Fixed costs increase by $5,000.
   b. Unit variable cost increases to $7.
   c. Unit selling price increases to $12.
   d. Assume that fixed costs increase by $5,000 and unit variable cost is $7.

Exercise 4-15 *Basic CVP Concepts*

Berry Company produces a single product. The projected income statement for the coming year is as follows:

Sales (50,000 units @ $45)	$2,250,000
Less: Variable costs	1,305,000
Contribution margin	$ 945,000
Less: Fixed costs	812,700
Operating income	$ 132,300

Required:

1. Compute unit contribution margin and the units that must be sold to break even.
2. Suppose 30,000 units are sold above break-even. What is the operating income?
3. Compute the contribution margin ratio and the break-even point in dollars. Suppose that revenues are $200,000 more than expected. What would the total operating income be?

Exercise 4-16 *Margin of Safety and Operating Leverage*

Refer to **Exercise 4-15** for data.

Required:

1. Compute the margin of safety in sales dollars.
2. Compute the degree of operating leverage (rounded to two decimal places).
3. Compute the new profit level if sales are 20 percent higher than expected.

Exercise 4-17 *Multiple-Product Break-Even*

Parker Pottery produces a line of vases and a line of ceramic figurines. Each line uses the same equipment and labor; hence, there are no traceable fixed costs. Common fixed costs equal $30,000. Parker's accountant has begun to assess the profitability of the two lines and has gathered the following data for last year:

	Vases	Figurines
Price	$40	$70
Variable cost	30	42
Contribution margin	$10	$28
Number of units	1,000	500

Required:

1. Compute the number of vases and the number of figurines that must be sold for the company to break even.
2. Parker Pottery is considering upgrading its factory to improve the quality of its products. The upgrade will add $5,260 per year to total fixed costs, and if it is successful, the projected sales of vases will be 1,500 and figurine sales will increase to 1,000 units. What is the new break-even point in units for each of the products?

PROBLEMS

(Note: Whenever you see a next to a requirement, it signals a "building on a cornerstone" requirement. Assigning this requirement will usually entail additional work, such as a group project, analytical reasoning, Internet research, decision making, and the use of written communication skills.)

Problem 4-1 *Break-Even Units, Contribution Margin Ratio, Margin of Safety*

**OBJECTIVES
1, 2, 5**

Cutlass Company's projected profit for the coming year is as follows:

	Total	Per Unit
Sales	$200,000	$20
Less: Variable expenses	120,000	12
Contribution margin	$ 80,000	$ 8
Less: Fixed expenses	64,000	
Operating income	$ 16,000	

Required:
1. Compute the break-even point in units.
2. How many units must be sold to earn a profit of $30,000?
3. Compute the contribution margin ratio. Using that ratio, compute the additional profit that Cutlass would earn if sales were $25,000 more than expected.
4. For the projected level of sales, compute the margin of safety in units.

Problem 4-2 *Break-Even Units, Operating Income, Margin of Safety*

**OBJECTIVES
1, 5**

Dory Manufacturing Company produces T-shirts screen-printed with the logos of various sports teams. Each shirt is priced at $10 and has a unit variable cost of $5. Total fixed costs are $96,000.

Required:
1. Compute the break-even point in units.
2. Suppose that Dory could reduce its fixed costs by $13,500 by reducing the amount of setup and engineering time needed. How many units must be sold to break even in this case?

3. How does the reduction in fixed costs affect the break-even point? Operating income? The margin of safety?

Problem 4-3 *Contribution Margin, Break-Even Units, Break-Even Sales, Margin of Safety, Degree of Operating Leverage*

**OBJECTIVES
1, 2, 5**

Sohrwide Company produces a variety of chemicals. One division makes reagents for laboratories. The division's projected income statement for the coming year is:

Sales (128,000 units @ $50)	$6,400,000
Less: Variable expenses	4,480,000
Contribution margin	$1,920,000
Less: Fixed expenses	1,000,000
Operating income	$ 920,000

Required:
1. Compute the contribution margin per unit and calculate the break-even point in units (round to the nearest unit). Calculate the contribution margin ratio and the break-even sales revenue.

(continued)

2. The divisional manager has decided to increase the advertising budget by $100,000. This will increase sales revenues by $1 million. By how much will operating income increase or decrease as a result of this action?
3. Suppose sales revenues exceed the estimated amount on the income statement by $315,000. Without preparing a new income statement, by how much are profits underestimated?
4. Compute the margin of safety based on the original income statement.
5. Compute the degree of operating leverage based on the original income statement. If sales revenues are 20 percent greater than expected, what is the percentage increase in profits?

Problem 4-4 *Multiple-Product Analysis, Changes in Sales Mix, Sales to Earn Target Operating Income*

 OBJECTIVE 4

Gosnell Company produces two products: squares and circles. The projected income for the coming year, segmented by product line, follows:

	Squares	Circles	Total
Sales	$300,000	$2,500,000	$2,800,000
Less: Variable expenses	100,000	500,000	600,000
Contribution margin	$200,000	$2,000,000	$2,200,000
Less: Direct fixed expenses	28,000	1,500,000	1,528,000
Product margin	$172,000	$ 500,000	$ 672,000
Less: Common fixed expenses			100,000
Operating income			$ 572,000

The selling prices are $30 for squares and $50 for circles.

Required:
1. Compute the number of units of each product that must be sold for Gosnell Company to break even.
2. Assume that the marketing manager changes the sales mix of the two products so that the ratio is three squares to five circles. Repeat Requirement 1.
3. Refer to the original data. Suppose that Gosnell can increase the sales of squares with increased advertising. The extra advertising would cost an additional $245,000, and some of the potential purchasers of circles would switch to squares. In total, sales of squares would increase by 25,000 units, and sales of circles would decrease by 5,000 units. Would Gosnell be better off with this strategy?

Problem 4-5 *CVP Equation, Basic Concepts, Solving for Unknowns*

 OBJECTIVES 1, 2, 5

Tressa Company produces combination shampoos and conditioners in individual-use bottles for hotels. Each bottle sells for $0.36. The variable costs for each bottle (materials, labor, and overhead) total $0.27. The total fixed costs are $54,000. During the most recent year, 830,000 bottles were sold.

Required:
1. What is the break-even point in units for Tressa? What is the margin of safety in units for the most recent year?
2. Prepare an income statement for the most recent year for Tressa.
3. How many units must be sold for Tressa to earn a profit of $36,000?

Problem 4-6 *Contribution Margin Ratio, Break-Even Sales, Operating Leverage*

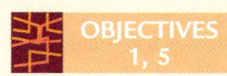 OBJECTIVES 1, 5

Doerhing Company produces plastic mailboxes. The projected income statement for the coming year follows:

Sales	$560,400
Less: Variable costs	257,784
Contribution margin	$302,616
Less: Fixed costs	150,000
Operating income	$152,616

Required:

1. Compute the contribution margin ratio for the mailboxes.
2. How much revenue must Doerhing earn in order to break even?
3. What is the effect on the contribution margin ratio if the unit selling price and unit variable cost each increase by 10 percent?
4. Suppose that management has decided to give a 3-percent commission on all sales. The projected income statement does not reflect this commission. Recompute the contribution margin ratio assuming that the commission will be paid. What effect does this have on the break-even point?
5. If the commission is paid as described in Requirement 4, management expects sales revenues to increase by $80,000. How will this affect operating leverage? Is it a sound decision to implement the commission? Support your answer with appropriate computations.

Problem 4-7 *CVP with Multiple Products, Sales Mix Changes, Changes in Fixed and Variable Costs*

OBJECTIVES
1, 4

Artistic Woodcrafting, Inc., began several years ago as a one-person cabinet-making operation. Employees were added as the business expanded. Last year, sales volume totaled $850,000. Volume for the first five months of the current year totaled $600,000, and sales were expected to be $1.6 million for the entire year. Unfortunately, the cabinet business in the region where Artistic Woodcrafting is located is highly competitive. More than 200 cabinet shops are all competing for the same business.

Artistic currently offers two different quality grades of cabinets: Grade I and Grade II, with Grade I being the higher quality. The average unit selling prices, unit variable costs, and direct fixed costs are as follows:

	Unit Price	Unit Variable Cost	Direct Fixed Cost
Grade I	$3,400	$2,686	$95,000
Grade II	1,600	1,328	95,000

Common fixed costs (fixed costs not traceable to either cabinet) are $35,000. Currently, for every three Grade I cabinets sold, seven Grade II cabinets are sold.

Required:

1. Calculate the Grade I and Grade II cabinets that are expected to be sold during the current year.
2. Calculate the number of Grade I and Grade II cabinets that must be sold for the company to break even.
3. Artistic Woodcrafting can buy computer-controlled machines that will make doors, drawers, and frames. If the machines are purchased, the variable costs for each type of cabinet will decrease by 9 percent, but common fixed costs will increase by $44,000. Compute the effect on operating income and also calculate the new break-even point. Assume the machines are purchased at the beginning of the sixth month. Fixed costs for the company are incurred uniformly throughout the year.
4. Refer to the original data. Artistic Woodcrafting is considering adding a retail outlet. This will increase common fixed costs by $70,000 per year. As a result of adding the retail outlet, the additional publicity and emphasis on quality will

allow the firm to change the sales mix to 1:1. The retail outlet is also expected to increase sales by 30 percent. Assume that the outlet is opened at the beginning of the sixth month. Calculate the effect on the company's expected profits for the current year and calculate the new break-even point. Assume that fixed costs are incurred uniformly throughout the year.

Problem 4-8 *Multiple Products, Break-Even Analysis, Operating Leverage*

OBJECTIVES
4, 5

Carlyle Lighting Products produces two different types of lamps, a floor lamp and a desk lamp. Floor lamps sell for $30 and desk lamps for $20. The projected income statement for the coming year follows:

Sales	$600,000
Less: Variable costs	400,000
Contribution margin	$200,000
Less: Fixed costs	150,000
Operating income	$ 50,000

The owner of Carlyle estimates that 60 percent of the sales revenues will be produced by floor lamps and the remaining 40 percent by desk lamps. Floor lamps are also responsible for 60 percent of the variable expenses. Of the fixed expenses, one-third are common to both products, and one-half are directly traceable to the floor lamp product line.

Required:
1. Compute the sales revenue that must be earned for Carlyle to break even.
2. Compute the number of floor lamps and desk lamps that must be sold for Carlyle to break even.
3. Compute the degree of operating leverage for Carlyle Lighting Products. Now assume that the actual revenues will be 40 percent higher than the projected revenues. By what percentage will profits increase with this change in sales volume?

Problem 4-9 *Multiple-Product Break-Even*

OBJECTIVES
1, 4

Polaris, Inc., manufactures two types of metal stampings for the automobile industry: door handles and trim kits. Fixed costs equal $146,000. Each door handle sells for $12 and has variable costs of $9; each trim kit sells for $8 and has variable costs of $5.

Required:
1. What are the contribution margin per unit and the contribution margin ratio for door handles and for trim kits?
2. If Polaris sells 20,000 door handles and 40,000 trim kits, what is the operating income?
3. How many door handles and how many trim kits must be sold for Polaris to break even?
4. Assume that Polaris has the opportunity to rearrange its plant to produce only trim kits. If this is done, fixed costs will decrease by $35,000 and 70,000 trim kits can be produced and sold. Is this a good idea? Explain.

Problem 4-10 *CVP, Margin of Safety*

OBJECTIVES
1, 5

Victoria Company produces a single product. Last year's income statement is as follows:

Sales (29,000 units)	$1,218,000
Less: Variable costs	812,000
Contribution margin	$ 406,000
Less: Fixed costs	300,000
Operating income	$ 106,000

Required:

1. Compute the break-even point in units and sales dollars.
2. What was the margin of safety for Victoria Company last year?
3. Suppose that Victoria Company is considering an investment in new technology that will increase fixed costs by $250,000 per year but will lower variable costs to 45 percent of sales. Units sold will remain unchanged. Prepare a budgeted income statement assuming that Victoria makes this investment. What is the new break-even point in units and sales dollars, assuming that the investment is made?

Problem 4-11 *CVP, Margin of Safety*

OBJECTIVES
1, 5

Isaac Company had revenues of $930,000 last year with total variable costs of $353,400 and fixed costs of $310,000.

Required:

1. What is the variable cost ratio for Isaac? What is the contribution margin ratio?
2. What is the break-even point in sales revenue?
3. What was the margin of safety for Isaac last year?
4. Isaac is considering starting a multimedia advertising campaign that is supposed to increase sales by $7,500 per year. The campaign will cost $5,000. Is the advertising campaign a good idea? Explain.

Problem 4-12 *Using the Break-Even Equations to Solve for Price and Variable Cost per Unit*

OBJECTIVE 1

Solve the following independent problems.

Required:

1. Sarah Company's break-even point is 1,500 units. Variable cost per unit is $300; total fixed costs are $120,000 per year. What price does Sarah charge?
2. Jesper Company charges a price of $3.50; total fixed costs are $160,000 per year, and the break-even point is 128,000 units. What is the variable cost per unit?

Problem 4-13 *Contribution Margin, CVP, Margin of Safety*

OBJECTIVES
1, 2, 5

Candyland, Inc., produces a particularly rich praline fudge. Each 10-ounce box sells for $5.60. Variable unit costs are as follows:

Pecans	$0.70
Sugar	0.35
Butter	1.85
Other ingredients	0.34
Box, packing material	0.76
Selling commission	0.20

Fixed overhead cost is $32,300 per year. Fixed selling and administrative costs are $12,500 per year. Candyland sold 35,000 boxes last year.

Required:

1. What is the contribution margin per unit for a box of praline fudge? What is the contribution margin ratio?
2. How many boxes must be sold to break even? What is the break-even sales revenue?
3. What was Candyland's operating income last year?
4. What was the margin of safety?

(continued)

5. Suppose that Candyland, Inc., raises the price to $6.20 per box but anticipated sales drop to 31,500 boxes. What will the new break-even point in units be? Should Candyland raise the price? Explain.

Problem 4-14 *Break-Even Sales, Operating Leverage, Change in Income*

Income statements for two different companies in the same industry are as follows:

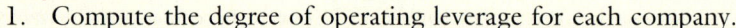

	Company A	Company B
Sales	$500,000	$500,000
Less: Variable costs	400,000	200,000
Contribution margin	$100,000	$300,000
Less: Fixed costs	50,000	250,000
Operating income	$ 50,000	$ 50,000

Required:
1. Compute the degree of operating leverage for each company.
2. Compute the break-even point for each company. Explain why the break-even point for Company B is higher.
3. Suppose that both companies experience a 50-percent increase in revenues. Compute the percentage change in profits for each company. Explain why the percentage increase in Company B's profits is so much larger than that of Company A.

Problem 4-15 *Ethics and a CVP Application*

Danna Lumus, the marketing manager for a division that produces a variety of paper products, was considering the divisional manager's request for a sales forecast for a new line of paper napkins. The divisional manager was gathering data so that he could choose between two different production processes. The first process would have a variable cost of $10 per case produced and fixed costs of $100,000. The second process would have a variable cost of $6 per case and fixed costs of $200,000. The selling price would be $30 per case. Danna had just completed a marketing analysis that projected annual sales of 30,000 cases.

Danna was reluctant to report the 30,000 forecast to the divisional manager. She knew that the first process was labor-intensive, whereas the second was largely automated with little labor and no requirement for an additional production supervisor. If the first process were chosen, Jerry Johnson, a good friend, would be appointed as the line supervisor. If the second process were chosen, Jerry and an entire line of laborers would be laid off. After some consideration, Danna revised the projected sales downward to 22,000 cases.

She believed that the revision downward was justified. Since it would lead the divisional manager to choose the manual system, it showed a sensitivity to the needs of current employees—a sensitivity that she was afraid her divisional manager did not possess. He was too focused on quantitative factors in his decision making and usually ignored the qualitative aspects.

Required:
1. Compute the break-even point for each process.
2. Compute the sales volume for which the two processes are equally profitable. Identify the range of sales for which the manual process is more profitable than the automated process. Identify the range of sales for which the automated process is more profitable than the manual process. Why did the divisional manager want the sales forecast?
3. Discuss Danna's decision to alter the sales forecast. Do you agree with it? Did she act ethically? Was her decision justified since it helped a number of employ-

ees retain their employment? Should the impact on employees be factored into decisions? In fact, is it unethical not to consider the impact of decisions on employees?

Problem 4-16

Suppose that Kicker had the following sales and cost experience (in thousands of dollars) for May of the current year and for May of the prior year:

	May, Current Year	May, Prior Year
Total sales	$43,560	$41,700
Less:		
Purchase price paid	(17,000)	(16,000)
Additional labor and supplies	(1,400)	(1,200)
Commissions	(1,250)	(1,100)
Contribution margin	$23,910	$23,400
Less:		
Fixed warehouse cost	(680)	(500)
Fixed administrative cost	(4,300)	(4,300)
Fixed selling cost	(5,600)	(5,000)
Research and development	(9,750)	(4,000)
Operating income	$ 3,580	$ 9,600

In August of the prior year, Kicker started an intensive quality program designed to enable it to build original equipment manufacture (OEM) speaker systems for a major automobile company. The program was housed in research and development. In the beginning of the current year, Kicker's accounting department exercised tighter control over sales commissions, ensuring that no dubious (e.g., double) payments were made. The increased sales in the current year required additional warehouse space that Kicker rented in town.

Required:
1. Calculate the contribution margin ratio for May of both years.
2. Calculate the break-even point in sales dollars for both years.
3. Calculate the margin of safety in sales dollars for both years.
4. Analyze the differences shown by your calculations in Requirements 1, 2, and 3.

JOB-ORDER COSTING

© BOHEMIAN NOMAD PICTUREMAKERS/CORBIS

After studying Chapter 5, you should be able to:

1. Describe the differences between job-order costing and process costing and identify the types of firms that would use each method.
2. Compute the predetermined overhead rate and use the rate to assign overhead to units or services produced.
3. Identify and set up the source documents used in job-order costing.
4. Describe the cost flows associated with job-order costing.
5. (Appendix) Prepare the journal entries associated with job-order costing.

Applegate Construction Company[1] was established in 1957. For more than 30 years, the company specialized in building subdivisions. Applegate could be described as a small, successful business with a good reputation for building quality homes. Recently, Walter Applegate, founder and owner of the company, retired and his son, Jay Applegate, assumed control of the company.

Jay decided that the company needed to expand into custom-built homes and non-residential construction. As he began to explore these possibilities, he encountered some problems with the company's current accounting system. Accordingly, he requested a meeting with his aunt, Bonnie Barlow, who is the financial manager. She was responsible for bookkeeping and payroll. A local CPA firm prepared all financial reports and filed the company's tax returns.

Jay: Bonnie, as you know, I want our company to become one of the largest in this region. To accomplish this, I am convinced that we need to expand our operations to include both custom homes and industrial buildings. I think we can gain business in both of these areas by capitalizing on our reputation for quality. However, I am afraid that as we enter these markets, we are going to have to change our accounting system. I'm going to need your help in making the changes.

Bonnie: I'm not sure why you want to change our accounting procedures. They are simple and accurate. I keep track of all costs and subtract them from sales to get our profit. It's worked well for 30 years.

Jay: In the past, our company has built houses that were basically the same. We've had slight variations in design so that they didn't look like carbon copies, but each house has required essentially the same work and materials. The cost of each home has been computed by simply accumulating the actual costs incurred over the period of time it took to build all the homes and then dividing this total by the number of units constructed. We priced our houses to stay competitive with the market. But, this approach will not work when we enter the market for custom-built homes or industrial units.

Bonnie: I think I see the problem. Custom-built homes, for example, may require different cement work, different carpentry work, and may use more expensive materials, like a jacuzzi instead of a regular bathtub. They may also differ significantly in size from our standard units. If we simply divide the total construction costs for the year by the number of houses produced, we don't get a very accurate picture of what it's costing to build an individual home. Besides, pricing for custom houses is typically cost plus. We'll need individual costs to calculate the price we charge. Industrial units would cause even worse problems. It sounds like we do need a different method to accumulate our construction costs.

Jay: I agree. We need some way of tracking the labor, materials, and overhead used by each job. In addition, by moving into custom home building, we'll be working much more closely with the customers and their architects. I know there will be times when the customer doesn't go through with building the house, but we will have spent a considerable amount of time on design. How will we measure the cost of our consulting service?

Bonnie: Jay, these costing issues are more complicated than what we are used to dealing with. Let me talk to our CPA and see what advice she can give us. I am sure she can suggest a cost system that will address these issues.

---

[1] This scenario is based on the actual experiences of a mid-sized construction firm. The names of the company and people involved have been changed to preserve confidentiality.

CHARACTERISTICS OF THE JOB-ORDER ENVIRONMENT

Companies can be divided into two major types depending on whether or not their products/services are unique. Manufacturing and service firms producing unique products or services require a job-order accounting system. Applegate Construction, from the Opening Scenario, falls into this category. On the other hand, those firms producing very similar products or services can use a process-costing accounting system. As Jay and Bonnie noted in the Opening Scenario, the characteristics of the actual production process give rise to the accounting system needed.

HERE'S THE REAL KICKER

In the 1970s, Kicker began operations in Steve Irby's garage. Steve was an engineering student at Oklahoma State University and also a keyboard player with a local band. The band needed speakers but couldn't afford new ones. Steve and his father built wooden boxes and fitted them with second-hand components. Word spread and other bands asked for speakers. Steve partnered with a friend to fill the orders. Then, one friend who worked in the oil fields asked if Steve could rig up speakers for his pickup truck. Long days bouncing over rough fields went more smoothly with music, but the built-in "audio" systems at the time were awful. Steve designed and built a speaker to fit behind the driver's seat, and Kicker was born.

At first, each job was made to order to fit a particular truck or car. The price Steve charged depended heavily on the cost of the job. Since each job was different, the various costs had to be computed for each job. Clearly, the costs of wood, fabric, glue, and components were traceable to the individual job. Steve could also trace labor time. But the other costs of design time, use of power tools, and space were lumped together to create an overhead rate. To the extent that the price of a job was greater than its costs, Steve earned a profit.

Job-Order Production and Costing

Firms operating in job-order industries produce a wide variety of services or products that are quite distinct from each other. Customized or built-to-order products fit into this category, as do services that vary from customer to customer. A **job**, then, is one distinct unit or set of units. For example, a job may be a remodeling job for the Ruiz family, or a set of 12 tables for the children's reading room of the local library. Common job-order processes include printing, construction, furniture making, medical and dental services, automobile repair, and beautician services. Often, a job is associated with a particular customer order. The key feature of job-order costing is that the cost of one job differs from that of another job and must be kept track of separately.

For job-order production systems, costs are accumulated by job. This approach to assigning costs is called a **job-order costing system**. In a job-order firm, collecting costs by job provides vital information for management. For example, frequently, prices are based on costs in a job-order environment.

Process Production and Costing

Firms in process industries mass-produce large quantities of similar or homogeneous products. Examples of process manufacturers include food, cement, petroleum, and chemical firms. One gallon of paint is the same as another gallon; one bottle of aspirin is the same as another bottle. The important point here is that the cost of one unit of a product is identical to the cost of another. Service firms can also use a process-costing approach. For example, check-clearing departments of banks incur a uniform cost to clear a check, no matter the size of the check or the name of the payee.

Process firms accumulate production costs by process or by department for a given period of time. The output for the process for that period of time is measured. Unit costs are computed by dividing the process costs for the given period by the output of

APPLICATIONS IN BUSINESS

© ROGER RESSMEYER/CORBIS

iRobot, Inc., is an engineering contractor based in Massachusetts. Founded in the late 1980s, iRobot's mission statement is to build "cool stuff" while making money and changing the world for the better. The founders were accustomed to the academic environment of MIT's Artificial Intelligence Lab. They worked for large companies or governments that wanted them "to do something they (the clients) found interesting but only wanted one of. . . . It was like being an artist working on commission." Contracts included diverse projects like "a crab-walking minesweeper for the Department of Defense, [and] a rugged oil-well-repair bot for Halliburton." Clearly, job-order costing was appropriate for these projects.

In the mid-1990s, iRobot pitched an idea for a story-telling machine to toy maker Hasbro, Inc. The machine, a plastic-molded tableau with little characters surrounding a child's book, could actually act out the story, with dialogue and gestures. It was "unbelievably cool." Unfortunately, it was also unbelievably costly—total direct materials alone cost $3,000. Clearly, this toy was not destined for Toys "R" Us with a $19.95 price point. Hasbro turned thumbs down on the project. The result was that CEO Colin Angle began to pay close attention to cost control, and by 2000, he had a good understanding of the cost control needed for consumer products. His company developed the roomba, a small, disk-shaped vacuum cleaner. Currently in production, the roomba reflects iRobot's shift, for this type of project, from "high-cost prototype design to every-penny-counts mass production." Before, the total bid cost of the project was important, but mass production requires attention to every component's cost.

Source: Leigh Buchanan, "Death to Cool: How an R&D Boutique that Made Only Elite, Sexy Products Became a Big-Time Mass Marketer of the Mundane," *Inc.* (July 2003): 82–87 and 104, **http://www.irobot.com**.

the period. This approach to cost accumulation is known as a **process-costing system**. A comparison of job-order costing and process costing is given in Exhibit 5-1.

Production Costs in Job-Order Costing

While the variety of product cost definitions discussed in Chapter 2 applies to both job-order and process costing, we will use the traditional product-costing definition to illustrate job-order costing procedures. That is, production costs consist of direct materials, direct labor, and overhead. Direct materials and direct labor are typically fairly easy to trace to individual jobs. In fact, this tracing will be considered a little later in this chapter in the section on source documents. It is overhead that presents the problem. By definition, overhead is all production costs other than direct materials and direct labor. Some of these might be easily traced to jobs, but most cannot be. The

5-1

EXHIBIT

Comparison of Job-Order and Process Costing

Job-Order Costing	Process Costing
1. Wide variety of distinct products	1. Homogeneous products
2. Costs accumulated by job	2. Costs accumulated by process or department
3. Unit cost computed by dividing total job costs by units produced on that job	3. Unit cost computed by dividing process costs of the period by the units produced in the period

solution is to apply overhead to production. The next section examines in detail the way overhead is treated.

NORMAL COSTING AND OVERHEAD APPLICATION

The opening scenario shows how important unit costs can be. Applegate Construction needs accurate cost information on materials, labor, and overhead involved in the construction of each building. Since the construction industry typically bills the client at set points throughout construction, it is important that the unit cost be generated in a timely fashion. Job-order costing using a normal cost system will give the company the unit cost information it needs.

> **OBJECTIVE 2**
>
> Compute the predetermined overhead rate and use the rate to assign overhead to units or services produced.

Actual Costing versus Normal Costing

Two ways are commonly used to measure the costs associated with production: actual costing and normal costing. Actual costing requires the firm to use the actual cost of all direct materials, direct labor, and overhead used in production to determine unit cost. While intuitively reasonable, this method has drawbacks. Normal costing requires the firm to assign actual costs of direct materials and direct labor to units produced and to apply overhead to units based on a predetermined estimate. Normal costing is more widely used in practice.

Actual Costing

In an **actual cost system**, only *actual* costs of direct materials, direct labor, and overhead are used to determine unit cost. Strict actual cost systems are rarely used because they cannot provide accurate unit cost information on a timely basis. Per-unit computation of the direct materials and direct labor costs is not the problem. The main problem with using actual costing is overhead. Overhead items do not have the direct relationship that direct materials and direct labor do. For example, how much of a security guard's salary should be assigned to a unit of product or service? Even if the firm averages overhead cost by totaling manufacturing overhead costs for a given period and then divides this total by the number of units produced, distorted costs can occur. The distortion can be traced to uneven incurrence of overhead costs and uneven production from period to period.

The first problem is that many overhead costs are not incurred uniformly throughout the year. For example, property taxes on the factory are typically billed once a year. This can make overhead costs in the month of property tax billing higher than in other months. The second problem, nonuniform production levels, can mean that low production in one month would give rise to high unit overhead costs, and high production in another month would give rise to low unit overhead costs. Yet, the production process and total overhead costs may remain unchanged. Clearly, a solution would be to wait until the end of the year to total the actual overhead costs and divide by the total actual production.

Unfortunately, waiting until the end of the year to compute a unit overhead cost is unacceptable. A company needs unit cost information throughout the year. This information is needed on a timely basis both for interim financial statements and to help managers make decisions such as pricing. Most decisions requiring unit cost information simply cannot wait until the end of the year. Managers must react to day-to-day conditions in the marketplace in order to maintain a sound competitive position.

Normal Costing

Normal costing solves the problems associated with actual costing. A **normal cost system** determines unit cost by adding actual direct materials, actual direct labor, and estimated overhead. Overhead can be estimated by approximating the year's actual overhead at the *beginning* of the year and then using a predetermined rate throughout the year to obtain the needed unit cost information. Virtually all firms use normal costing.

Concept Q & A

The popular reality series "Trading Spaces" involves two pairs of homeowners who, with the guidance of an interior designer and the help of a professional carpenter, redo one room in each other's house. Each pair has only 48 hours and $1,000 to accomplish their renovation. At the end of each show, the host and interior designer total up the "costs" of the redecoration project. Typically, the cost comes in at pennies under $1,000. What costs are included in the $1,000? What costs are not? Does each redecoration really cost under $1,000? (*Hint:* Use the cost categories of direct materials, direct labor, and overhead in your answer.)

Possible Answer:
The $1,000 is used to cover the cost of furniture, fabrics, and materials. It does not cover the services of the designer or carpentry labor. In addition, there is clearly a good deal of overhead involved that includes the power tools, carpentry supplies (nails, glue), hand tools, sewing machine(s), and so on. The completed room costs considerably more than $1,000. (This answer does not consider the labor, materials, and overhead involved in putting on the show.)

Importance of Unit Costs to Manufacturing Firms

Unit cost is a critical piece of information for a manufacturer. Unit costs are essential for valuing inventory, determining income, and making a number of important decisions.

Disclosing the cost of inventories and determining income are financial reporting requirements that a firm faces at the end of each period. In order to report the cost of its inventories, a firm must know the number of units on hand and the unit cost. The cost of goods sold, used to determine income, also requires knowledge of the units sold and their unit cost.

It should be pointed out that full cost information is useful as an input for a number of important internal decisions as well as for financial reporting. In the long run, for any product to be viable, its price must cover its full cost. Decisions to introduce a new product, to continue a current product, and to analyze long-run prices are examples of important internal decisions that rely on full unit cost information.

Importance of Unit Costs to Service Firms

Service and nonprofit firms also require unit cost information. Conceptually, the way companies accumulate and assign costs is the same whether or not the firm is a manufacturing firm. The service firm must first identify the service "unit" being provided. A hospital would accumulate costs by patient, patient day, and type of procedure (e.g., X-ray, complete blood count test). A governmental agency must also identify the service provided. For example, city government might provide household trash collection and calculate the cost by truck run or by number of houses served.

Service firms use cost data in much the same way that manufacturing firms do. They use costs to determine profitability, the feasibility of introducing new services, and so on. However, because service firms do not produce physical products, they do not need to value work-in-process and finished goods inventories. Of course, they may have supplies, and the inventory of supplies is simply valued at historical cost.

Nonprofit firms must track costs to be sure that they provide their services in a cost-efficient way. Governmental agencies have a fiduciary responsibility to taxpayers to use funds wisely. This requires accurate accounting for costs.

A cost accounting system measures and assigns costs so that the unit cost of a product or service can be determined. Unit cost is a critical piece of information for both manufacturing and service firms. For example, bidding is a common requirement in the markets for specialized products and services (consider bids for special tools, audits, and medical tests and procedures). It is virtually impossible to submit a meaningful bid without knowing the unit costs of the products or services to be produced. Because unit cost information is so vital, its accuracy is essential.

Normal Costing and Estimating Overhead

In normal costing, overhead must be estimated and applied to production. The basics of overhead application can be described in three steps. The first step is to calculate the predetermined overhead rate. The second step is to apply overhead to production throughout the year. The third step is to reconcile the difference between the total actual overhead incurred during the year and the total overhead applied to production.

Calculating the Predetermined Overhead Rate

The **predetermined overhead rate** is calculated at the beginning of the year by dividing the total estimated annual overhead by the total estimated level of associated activity or cost driver. Estimated overhead is simply the firm's best estimate of the amount of overhead (utilities, indirect labor, depreciation, etc.) to be incurred in the coming year. The estimate is often based on last year's figures and adjusted for anticipated changes in the coming year.

The associated activity level depends on which particular activity is best associated with overhead. Often, the activity chosen is the number of direct labor hours, or the direct labor cost. This makes sense when much of overhead cost is associated with direct labor (e.g., fringe benefits, worker safety training programs, the cost of running the personnel department). The number of machine hours could be a good choice for a company with automated production. Then, much of the overhead cost might consist of equipment maintenance, depreciation on machinery, electricity to run the machinery, and so on. The estimated activity level is simply the number of direct labor hours, or machine hours, expected for that activity in the coming year.

Then, the predetermined overhead rate is calculated using the following formula:

$$\text{Overhead rate} = \text{Estimated annual overhead/Estimated annual activity level}$$

Notice that the predetermined overhead rate includes estimated amounts in *both* the numerator and the denominator. This is because the predetermined overhead rate is calculated in advance, usually at the beginning of the year. It is impossible to use actual overhead or actual activity level for the year, because at that time, the company does not know what the actual levels will be. Therefore, only estimated or budgeted amounts are used in calculating the predetermined overhead rate.

Applying Overhead to Production

Once the overhead rate has been computed, the company can begin to apply overhead to production. **Applied overhead** is found by multiplying the predetermined overhead rate by the actual use of the associated activity for the period. Suppose that a company had an overhead rate of $5 per machine hour. In the first week of January, the company used 9,000 hours of machine time. Then, the overhead applied to the week's production would be $45,000 ($5 × 9,000). The total cost of product for that first week would be the actual direct materials and direct labor, plus the applied overhead. The concept is the same for any time period. So, if the company runs its machines for 50,000 hours in the month of January, applied overhead for January would be $250,000 ($5 × 50,000). Cornerstone 5-1 shows how to calculate the predetermined overhead rate and use that rate to apply overhead to production.

Cornerstone 5-1

HOW TO Calculate the Predetermined Overhead Rate and Apply Overhead to Production

Information: At the beginning of the year, Argus Company estimated the following costs:

Overhead	$360,000
Direct labor cost	720,000

Argus uses normal costing and applies overhead on the basis of direct labor cost. (Direct labor cost is equal to total direct labor hours worked multiplied by the wage rate.) For the month of February, direct labor cost was $56,000.

Required:
1. Calculate the predetermined overhead rate for the year.
2. Calculate the overhead applied to production in February.

Calculation:
1. Predetermined overhead rate = $360,000/$720,000
   = 0.50, or 50 percent of direct labor cost

2. Overhead applied to February production = 0.50 × $56,000 = $28,000

Reconciling Applied Overhead with Actual Overhead

Recall that two types of overhead must be taken into consideration. One is actual overhead, and those costs are kept track of throughout the year in the overhead account. The second type is applied overhead. Overhead applied to production is computed throughout the year and added to actual direct materials and actual direct labor to get total product cost. At the end of the year, however, it is time to reconcile any difference between actual and applied overhead and to correct the cost of goods sold account to reflect actual overhead spending.

Suppose that Proto Company had actual overhead of $400,000 for the year but had applied $390,000 to production. Notice that the amount of overhead applied to production ($390,000) differs from the actual overhead ($400,000). Since the predetermined overhead rate is based on estimated data, applied overhead will rarely equal actual overhead. Since only $390,000 was applied in our example, the firm has *underapplied* overhead by $10,000. If applied overhead had been $410,000, then too much overhead would have been applied to production. The firm would have *overapplied* overhead by $10,000. The difference between actual overhead and applied overhead is called an **overhead variance**. If actual overhead is greater than applied overhead, then the variance is called **underapplied overhead**. If actual overhead is less than applied overhead, then the variance is called **overapplied overhead**. If overhead has been underapplied, then product cost has been understated; in this case, the cost appears lower than it really is. Conversely, if overhead has been overapplied, then product cost has been overstated; in this case, the cost appears higher than it really is. Exhibit 5-2 illustrates the concepts of over- and under-applied overhead.

Overhead variances occur because it is impossible to estimate perfectly future overhead costs and production activity. The presence of overhead variances is virtually inevitable. A problem arises if the overhead variances are not corrected. At year-end, costs reported on the financial statements must be actual, not estimated, amounts. Thus,

Actual and Applied Overhead

Underapplied + Cost of Goods Sold

Actual Overhead 2005

Applied Overhead 2005

Overapplied − Cost of Goods Sold

Actual Overhead 2006

Applied Overhead 2006

something must be done with the overhead variance. Most often, the entire overhead variance is assigned to cost of goods sold. This practice is justified on the basis of materiality, the same principle used to justify expensing the entire cost of a pencil sharpener in the period acquired rather than depreciating its cost over the life of the sharpener. Since the overhead variance is usually relatively small, the method of disposition is not a critical matter. All production costs should appear in cost of goods sold eventually. Thus, the overhead variance is added to the cost of goods sold, if underapplied, and subtracted from cost of goods sold, if overapplied. For example, assume that Proto Company has an ending balance in its cost of goods sold account equal to $607,000. The underapplied overhead variance of $10,000 would be added to produce a new, adjusted balance of $617,000. (This makes sense because applied overhead was $390,000, while actual overhead was $400,000. Thus, production costs were *under*stated by $10,000, and cost of goods sold must be increased to correct the problem.) If the variance had been overapplied, it would have been subtracted from cost of goods sold to produce a new balance of $597,000. Cornerstone 5-2 shows how to reconcile actual overhead with applied overhead for the Argus Company example.

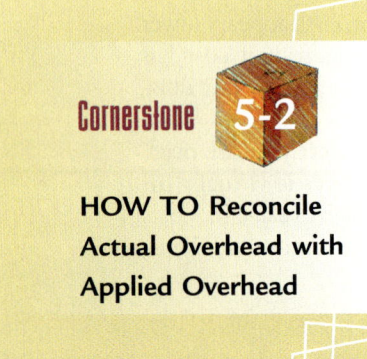

Cornerstone 5-2

HOW TO Reconcile Actual Overhead with Applied Overhead

Information: At the beginning of the year, Argus Company estimated the following:

Overhead	$360,000
Direct labor cost	720,000

By the end of the year, actual data are:

| Overhead | $375,400 |
| Direct labor cost | 750,000 |

Argus uses normal costing and applies overhead on the basis of direct labor cost. At the end of the year, Cost of Goods Sold (before adjusting for any overhead variance) is $632,000.

Required:

1. Calculate the overhead variance for the year.
2. Dispose of the overhead variance by adjusting Cost of Goods Sold.

Calculation:

1. Predetermined overhead rate = $360,000/$720,000 = 0.50 of direct labor cost
   Overhead applied for the year = 0.50 × $750,000 = $375,000

2.
Actual overhead	$375,400
Applied overhead	375,000
Overhead variance—underapplied	$ 400

Unadjusted COGS	$632,000
Add: Overhead variance—underapplied	400
Adjusted COGS	$632,400

If the overhead variance is material, or large, another approach would be taken. That approach, allocating the variance among the ending balances of Work in Process, Finished Goods, and Cost of Goods Sold, is discussed in more detail in later accounting courses.

Departmental Overhead Rates

The description of overhead application so far has emphasized the plantwide overhead rate. A **plantwide overhead rate** is a single overhead rate calculated using all estimated overhead for a factory divided by the estimated activity level across the entire factory. However, some companies believe that multiple overhead rates give more accurate costing information. Service firms, or service departments of manufacturing firms, can also use separate overhead rates to charge out their services.

APPLICATIONS IN BUSINESS

A floor-care products manufacturing firm produces a wide variety of electrical devices used in floor care. These include sanders, polishers, and vacuum cleaners. In addition, the factory produces pressure washers. The floor-care products are assembled from purchased parts. The pressure washers, on the other hand, involve drums that must be painted and dried before the pressure washer can be assembled. The painting and drying area is literally a room-sized oven. Once the pressure washers are painted, direct labor employees leave the area and turn on gas heaters. It takes 25–48 hours to complete the drying process. Clearly, the overhead associated with the pressure washers (the heaters, natural gas for heating) is different from the overhead associated with the floor-care products assembly operation. In this case, two different departmental overhead rates are computed. One overhead rate is applied to the pressure washers; the other overhead rate is applied to the floor-care products.

Source: Based on interviews with the controller for an actual manufacturing firm.

Departmental overhead rates are a widely used type of multiple overhead rate. A **departmental overhead rate** is simply estimated overhead for a department divided by the estimated activity level for that same department. The steps involved in calculating and applying overhead are the same as those involved for one plantwide overhead rate. The company has as many overhead rates as it has departments. Cornerstone 5-3 shows how to calculate and apply departmental overhead rates.

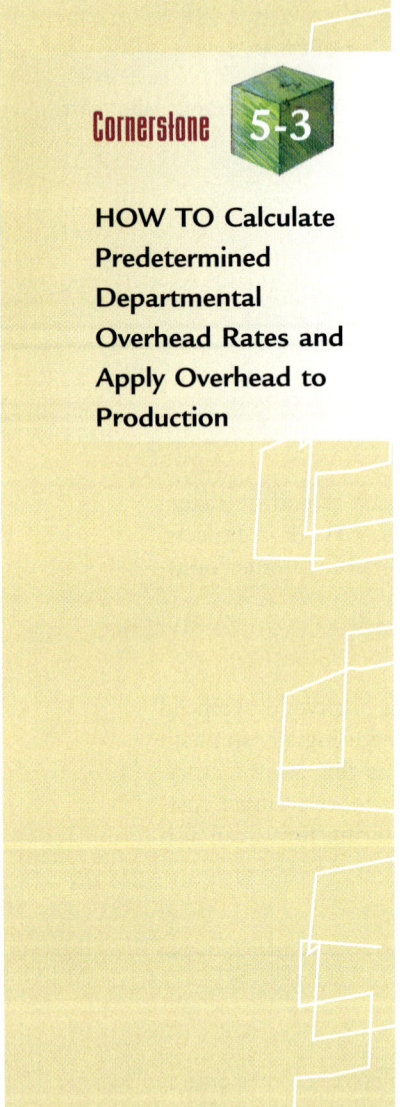

Cornerstone 5-3

HOW TO Calculate Predetermined Departmental Overhead Rates and Apply Overhead to Production

Information: At the beginning of the year, Sorrel Company estimated the following:

	Machining Department	Assembly Department	Total
Overhead	$240,000	$360,000	$600,000
Direct labor hours	135,000	240,000	375,000
Machine hours	200,000	—	200,000

Sorrel uses departmental overhead rates. In the machining department, overhead is applied on the basis of machine hours. In the assembly department, overhead is applied on the basis of direct labor hours. Actual data for the month of June are as follows:

	Machining Department	Assembly Department	Total
Overhead	$22,500	$30,750	$53,250
Direct labor hours	11,000	20,000	31,000
Machine hours	17,000	—	17,000

Required:

1. Calculate the predetermined overhead rates for the machining and assembly departments.
2. Calculate the overhead applied to production in each department for the month of June.
3. By how much has each department's overhead been overapplied? Underapplied?

Calculation:

1. Machining department overhead rate = $240,000/200,000 = $1.20 per machine hour

   Assembly department overhead rate = $360,000/240,000 = $1.50 per direct labor hour

2. Overhead applied to machining in June = $1.20 × 17,000 = $20,400

   Overhead applied to assembly in June = $1.50 × 20,000 = $30,000

3.

	Machining Department	Assembly Department
Actual overhead	$22,500	$30,750
Applied overhead	20,400	30,000
Underapplied overhead	$ 2,100	$ 750

It is important to realize that departmental overhead rates simply carve total overhead into two or more parts. The departments can be added back to get plantwide overhead. Cornerstone 5-4 shows how this is done.

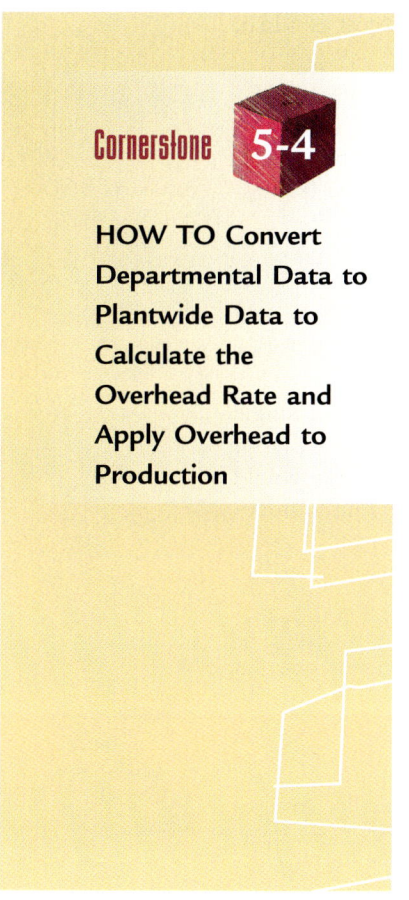

Cornerstone 5-4

HOW TO Convert Departmental Data to Plantwide Data to Calculate the Overhead Rate and Apply Overhead to Production

Information: At the beginning of the year, Sorrel Company estimated the following:

	Machining Department	Assembly Department	Total
Overhead	$240,000	$360,000	$600,000
Direct labor hours	135,000	240,000	375,000
Machine hours	200,000	—	200,000

Sorrel has decided to use a plantwide overhead rate based on direct labor hours. Actual data for the month of June are as follows:

	Machining Department	Assembly Department	Total
Overhead	$22,500	$30,750	$53,250
Direct labor hours	11,000	20,000	31,000
Machine hours	17,000	—	17,000

Required:
1. Calculate the predetermined plantwide overhead rate.
2. Calculate the overhead applied to production for the month of June.
3. Calculate the overhead variance for the month of June.

Calculation:
1. Predetermined plantwide overhead rate = $600,000/375,000 = $1.60 per direct labor hour
2. Overhead applied in June = $1.60 × 31,000 = $49,600
3. Overhead variance = Actual overhead − Applied overhead
$$= \$53,250 - \$49,600$$
$$= \$3,650 \text{ underapplied}$$

Considerable emphasis has been placed on describing how overhead costs are treated because this is the key to normal costing. Now it is time to see how normal costing is used to develop unit costs in the job-order costing system.

Unit Costs in the Job-Order System

In a job-order environment, predetermined overhead rates are always used, since the completion of a job rarely coincides with the completion of a fiscal year. Therefore, in the remainder of this chapter, normal costing is used.

The unit cost of a job is simply the total cost of materials used on the job, labor worked on the job, and applied overhead. Although the concept is simple, the practical reality of the computation can be somewhat more complex, because of the record keeping involved. Let's look at a simple example.

Suppose that Stan Johnson forms a new company, Johnson Leathergoods, which specializes in the production of custom leather products. Stan believes that there is a market for one-of-a-kind leather purses, briefcases, and backpacks. In its first month of operation, January, he obtains two orders: the first is for 20 leather backpacks for a local sporting goods store; the second is for 10 distinctively tooled briefcases for the coaches of a local college. Stan agrees to provide these orders at a price of cost plus 50 percent.

The first order, the backpacks, will require direct materials (leather, thread, buckles), direct labor (cutting, sewing, assembling), and overhead. Assume that overhead is applied using direct labor hours. Suppose that the materials cost $1,000 and the direct labor costs $1,080 (120 hours at $9 per hour). If the predetermined overhead rate is $2 per direct labor hour, then the overhead applied to this job is $240 (120 hours at

$2 per hour). The total cost of the backpacks is $2,320, and the unit cost is $116, computed as follows:

Direct materials	$1,000
Direct labor	1,080
Overhead	240
Total cost	$2,320
÷ Number of units	÷ 20
Unit cost	$ 116

Since cost is so closely linked to price in this case, it is easy to see that Stan will charge the sporting goods store $3,480 (cost of $2,320 plus 50 percent of $2,320), or $174 per backpack.

This is a simplified example of how Stan would arrive at the total cost of a single job. But how did he know that actual materials cost $1,000, or that actual direct labor for this particular job came to $1,080? In order to determine those figures, Stan would need to keep track of costs using a variety of source documents. These source documents are described in the next section.

KEEPING TRACK OF JOB COSTS WITH SOURCE DOCUMENTS

Accounting for job-order production begins by preparing the source documents that are used to keep track of the costs of jobs.

OBJECTIVE 3

Identify and set up the source documents used in job-order costing.

Job-Order Cost Sheet

Every time a new job is started, a job-order cost sheet is prepared. The earlier computation for Stan's backpack job, which lists the total cost of materials, labor, and overhead for a single job, is the simplest example of a job-order cost sheet. The **job-order cost sheet** is prepared for every job; it is subsidiary to the work-in-process account and is the primary document for accumulating all costs related to a particular job. Exhibit 5-3 illustrates a simple job-order cost sheet.

The job-order cost sheet contains all information pertinent to a job. For a simple job, the job-order cost sheet is quite brief, containing only the job description (backpacks) and cost of materials, labor, and overhead added during the month.

5-3 EXHIBIT

Job-Order Cost Sheet

Johnson Leathergoods
Job-Order Cost Sheet

Job Name: <u>Backpacks</u>　　　Date Started: <u>Jan. 3, 2005</u>　　　Date Completed: <u>Jan. 29, 2005</u>

Direct materials	$1,000
Direct labor	1,080
Applied overhead	240
Total cost	$2,320
÷ Number of units	÷ 20
Unit cost	$ 116

Concept Q & A

Job-order cost sheets are subsidiary to the work-in-process account. Can you think of other accounts that have subsidiary accounts? (*Hint:* Consider Accounts Receivable or Accounts Payable. What might their respective subsidiary accounts be?)

Possible Answer:
Accounts Receivable is a control account; its subsidiary accounts are named (or numbered) by customers having an account with the company. Similarly, Accounts Payable has subsidiary accounts for each person/company to which money is owed.

Johnson Leathergoods had only two jobs in January; these could be easily identified by calling them "Backpacks" and "Briefcases." Some companies may find that the customer's name is sufficient to identify a job. For example, a construction company may identify its custom houses as the "Smith residence" or the "Malkovich residence." As more and more jobs are produced, a company will usually find it most convenient to number them. Thus, you will see Job 13, Job 22, Job 44, etc. Perhaps the job number starts with the year so that the first job of 2005 is 2005-1, the second is 2005-2, and so on. The key point is that each job is unique and must have a uniquely identifiable name. This name, or job-order number, heads the job-order cost sheet.

Work in Process consists of all incomplete work. In a job-order system, this would be all of the unfinished jobs. The balance in Work in Process at the end of the month would be the total of all the job-order cost sheets for the incomplete jobs.

A job-order costing system must have the ability to identify the quantity of direct materials, direct labor, and overhead consumed by each job. In other words, documentation and procedures are needed to associate the manufacturing inputs used by a job with the job itself. This need is satisfied through the use of materials requisitions for direct materials, time tickets for direct labor, and source documents for other activity drivers that might be used in applying overhead.

Materials Requisitions

The cost of direct materials is assigned to a job by the use of a source document known as a **materials requisition form**, which is illustrated in Exhibit 5-4. Notice that the form asks for the type, quantity, and unit price of the direct materials issued and, most

5-4

EXHIBIT

Materials Requisition Form

Materials Requisition Number: 012

Date: January 11, 2005
Department: Assembly
Job: Briefcases

Description	Quantity	Cost/Unit	Total Cost
Buckles	10	$3	$30

Authorized Signature ___*Jim Lawson*___

importantly, for the number of the job. Using this form, the cost accounting department can enter the cost of direct materials onto the correct job-order cost sheet.

If the accounting system is automated, this posting may entail directly entering the data at a computer terminal, using the materials requisition forms as source documents. A program enters the cost of direct materials into the record for each job.

In addition to providing essential information for assigning direct materials costs to jobs, the materials requisition form may also have other data items, such as a requisition number, a date, and a signature. These data items are useful for maintaining proper control over a firm's inventory of direct materials. The signature, for example, transfers responsibility for the materials from the storage area to the person receiving the materials, usually a production supervisor.

No attempt is made to trace the cost of other materials, such as supplies, lubricants, and so on, to a particular job. You will recall that these indirect materials are assigned to jobs through the predetermined overhead rate.

Job Time Tickets

Direct labor also must be associated with each particular job. The means by which direct labor costs are assigned to individual jobs is the source document known as a **time ticket** (see Exhibit 5-5). Each day, the employee fills out a time ticket that identifies his or her name, wage rate, and the hours worked on each job. These time tickets are collected and transferred to the cost accounting department where the information is used to post the cost of direct labor to individual jobs. Again, in an automated system, posting involves entering the data into the computer.

Time tickets are used only for direct laborers. Since indirect labor is common to all jobs, these costs belong to overhead and are allocated using one or more predetermined overhead rates.

5-5

EXHIBIT

Job Time Ticket

Job Time Ticket #: _008_

Employee Name: _Ed Wilson_
Date: _January 12, 2005_

Start Time	Stop Time	Total Time	Hourly Rate	Amount	Job Number
8:00	10:00	2	$9	$18	Backpacks
10:00	11:00	1	9	9	Briefcases
11:00	12:00	1	9	9	Backpacks
1:00	5:00	4	9	36	Backpacks

Approved by: ___*Jim Lawson*___
(Department Supervisor)

Other Source Documents

The company may use an overhead application base other than direct labor hours. In that case, other source documents may be required. For example, machine hours may be used to apply overhead. Then, a new source document must be developed. A source document that will track the machine hours used by each job can be modeled on job time tickets.

All completed job-order cost sheets of a firm can serve as a subsidiary ledger for the finished goods inventory. Then, the work-in-process account consists of all of the job-order cost sheets for the unfinished jobs. The finished goods inventory account consists of all the job-order cost sheets for jobs that are complete but not yet sold. As finished goods are sold and shipped, the cost records would be pulled (or deleted) from the finished goods inventory file. These records then form the basis for calculating a period's cost of goods sold. We will examine the flow of costs through these accounts next.

THE FLOW OF COSTS THROUGH THE ACCOUNTS

OBJECTIVE 4

Describe the cost flows associated with job-order costing.

Cost flow describes the way costs are accounted for from the point at which they are incurred to the point at which they are recognized as an expense on the income statement. The principal interest in a job-order costing system is the flow of manufacturing costs. Accordingly, we begin with a description of exactly how the three manufacturing cost elements—direct materials, direct labor, and overhead—flow through the work-in-process account, into Finished Goods, and, finally, into Cost of Goods Sold.

The simplified job-shop environment provided by Johnson Leathergoods will continue to serve as an example. To start the business, Stan leased a small building and bought the necessary production equipment. Recall that he finalized two orders for January: one for 20 backpacks for a local sporting goods store and a second for 10 briefcases for the coaches of a local college. Both orders will be sold for manufacturing costs plus 50 percent. Stan expects to average two orders per month for the first year of operation.

Stan created two job-order cost sheets, one for each order. The first job-order cost sheet is for the backpacks; the second is for the briefcases.

Accounting for Materials

Since the company is just starting business, it has no beginning inventories. To produce the backpacks and briefcases in January and have a supply of materials on hand at the beginning of February, Stan purchases, on account, $2,500 of raw materials (leather, webbing for backpack straps, heavy-duty thread, buckles). Physically, the materials are put in a materials storeroom. In the accounting records, the raw materials and the accounts payable accounts are each increased by $2,500. Raw Materials is an inventory account (it appears on the balance sheet under current assets). It also is the controlling account for all raw materials. Any purchase increases the raw materials account.

When the production supervisor needs materials for a job, materials are removed from the storeroom. The cost of the materials is removed from the raw materials account and added to the work-in-process account. Of course, in a job-order environment, the materials moved from the storeroom to work stations on the factory floor must be "tagged" with the appropriate job name. Suppose that Stan needs $1,000 of materials for the backpacks and $500 for the briefcases. Then the job-order cost sheet for the backpacks would show $1,000 for direct materials, and the job-order cost sheet for the briefcases would show $500 for direct materials. Exhibit 5-6 summarizes the raw materials cost flow into these two jobs.

The raw materials account increased by $2,500 due to purchases and decreased by $1,500 as materials were withdrawn for use in production. So, what is the balance in the raw materials account after these two transactions? It is $1,000. This is calculated by taking the beginning balance in the raw materials account of $0, adding $2,500 of purchases, and subtracting $1,500 of materials used in production.

Accounting for Direct Labor Cost

Since two jobs were in progress during January, Stan must determine not only the total number of direct labor hours worked but also the time worked on each job. The backpacks required 120 hours at an average wage rate of $9 per hour, for a total direct labor cost of $1,080. For the briefcases, the total was $450, based on 50 hours at an average hourly wage of $9. These amounts are posted to each job's cost sheet. The summary of the labor cost flows is given in Exhibit 5-7. Notice that the direct labor costs assigned to the two jobs exactly equal the total labor costs assigned to Work in Process. Remember that the labor cost flows reflect only direct labor cost. Indirect labor is assigned as part of overhead.

More accounts are involved in this transaction than meets the eye in Exhibit 5-6. Accounting for labor cost is a complex process, since the company must keep track of FICA, Medicare, federal and state unemployment taxes, vacation time, and so on. We will concentrate on the concept that direct labor adds to the cost of the product or service and not on the details of the various labor-related accounts.

Accounting for Overhead

The use of normal costing means that actual overhead costs are not assigned directly to jobs. Overhead is applied to each individual job using a predetermined rate. Actual

EXHIBIT 5-6

Summary of Materials Cost Flows

Microsoft Excel - Summary of Materials Cost Flows.xls

	A	C	E	G
1	Raw Materials Account			
2	Beginning balance	$ 0		
3	Add: Purchases	2,500		
4	Less: Direct materials charged to jobs	1,500		
5	Ending balance	$1,000		
6				
7		Work-in-Process Account		
8	Job: Backpacks		Job: Briefcases	
9	Direct materials	$1,000	Direct materials	$500
10	Direct labor		Direct labor	
11	Applied overhead		Applied overhead	
12	Total cost		Total cost	
13	Number of units	÷ 20	Number of units	÷ 10
14	Unit cost		Unit cost	
15				

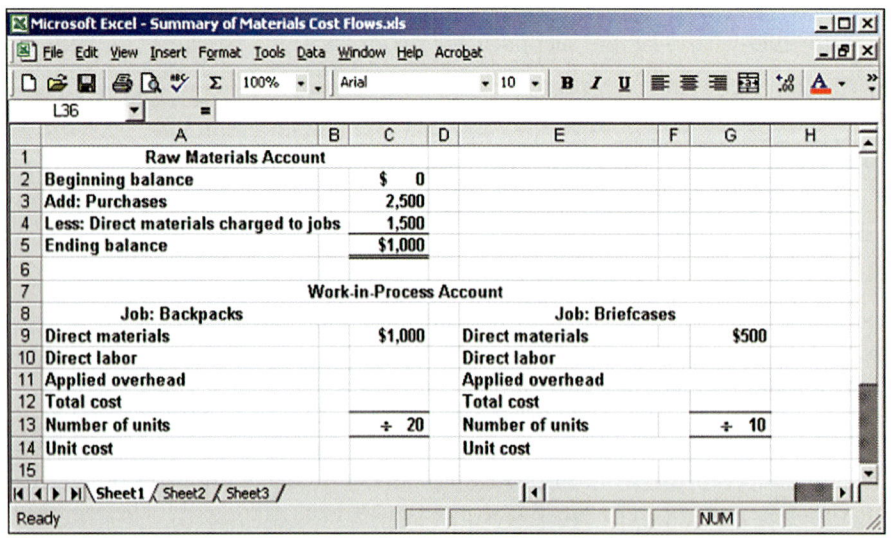

Summary of Direct Labor Cost Flows

	A	B	C	D	E	F	G	H
1	Wages Payable Account							
2	Direct labor hours for backpacks		120					
3	Direct labor hours for briefcases		50					
4	Total direct labor hours		170					
5	Wage rate		× $9					
6	Total direct labor		$1,530					
7								
8			Work-in-Process Account					
9	Job: Backpacks				Job: Briefcases			
10	Direct materials		$1,000		Direct materials		$500	
11	Direct labor		1,080		Direct labor		450	
12	Applied overhead				Applied overhead			
13	Total cost				Total cost			
14	Number of units		÷ 20		Number of units		÷ 10	
15	Unit cost				Unit cost			
16								

overhead costs incurred must be accounted for as well, but on an overall (not a job-specific) basis.

Overhead costs can be assigned using a single plantwide overhead rate or departmental rates. Typically, direct labor hours is the measure used to calculate a plantwide overhead rate, and departmental rates are based on drivers such as direct labor hours, machine hours, or direct materials dollars. The use of a plantwide rate has the virtue of being simple and reduces data collection requirements. To illustrate these two features, assume that total estimated overhead cost for Johnson Leathergoods is $9,600, and the estimated direct labor hours total 4,800 hours. Accordingly, the predetermined overhead rate is:

$$\text{Overhead rate} = \$9,600/4,800 = \$2 \text{ per direct labor hour}$$

For the backpacks, with a total of 120 hours worked, the amount of applied overhead cost posted to the job-order cost sheet is $240 ($2 × 120). For the briefcases, the applied overhead cost is $100 ($2 × 50). Note also that assigning overhead to jobs only requires a rate and the direct labor hours used by the job. Since direct labor hours are already being collected to assign direct labor costs to jobs, overhead assignment would not demand any additional data collection.

Accounting for Actual Overhead Costs

Overhead has been applied to the jobs, but what about the actual overhead incurred? To illustrate how actual overhead costs are recorded, assume that Johnson Leathergoods incurred the following indirect costs for January:

Lease payment	$200
Utilities	50
Equipment depreciation	100
Indirect labor	65
Total overhead costs	$415

It is important to understand that the actual overhead costs never enter the work-in-process account. The usual procedure is to record actual overhead to the overhead control account. Then, at the end of a period (typically a year), actual overhead is reconciled with applied overhead, and, if the variance is immaterial, it is closed to the cost of goods sold account.

For Johnson Leathergoods at the end of January, actual overhead incurred is $415, while applied overhead is $340. Therefore, the overhead variance of $75 ($415 − $340) means that overhead is underapplied for the month of January.

The flow of overhead costs is summarized in Exhibit 5-8. Notice that the total overhead applied from all jobs is entered in the work-in-process account.

Let's take a moment to recap. The cost of a job includes direct materials, direct labor, and applied overhead. These costs are entered on the job-order cost sheet. Work in Process, at any point in time, is the total of the costs on all open job-order cost sheets. When the job is complete, it must leave Work in Process and be entered into Finished Goods or Cost of Goods Sold.

Accounting for Finished Goods

When a job is complete, direct materials, direct labor, and applied overhead amounts are totaled to yield the manufacturing cost of the job. Simultaneously, the costs of the completed job are transferred from the work-in-process account to the finished goods account.

For example, assume that the backpacks were completed in January with the completed cost sheet shown in Exhibit 5-8. Since the backpacks are completed, the total manufacturing costs of $2,320 must be transferred from the work-in-process account to the finished goods account. A summary of the cost flows occurring when a job is finished is shown in Exhibit 5-9.

The completion of a job is an important step in the flow of manufacturing costs. The cost of the completed job must be removed from work in process, added to fin-

5-8

EXHIBIT

Summary of Overhead Cost Flows

	A	B	C	D	E	F	G	H
1	**Actual Overhead Account**				**Applied Overhead Account**			
2	Lease		$200		Direct labor hours		170	
3	Utilities		50		Overhead rate		× $2	
4	Equipment depreciation		100		Total applied overhead		340	
5	Indirect labor		65					
6	Total actual overhead		$415					
7								
8					**Work-in-Process Account**			
9	**Job: Backpacks**				**Job: Briefcases**			
10	Direct materials		$1,000		Direct materials		$500	
11	Direct labor		1,080		Direct labor		450	
12	Applied overhead		240		Applied overhead		100	
13	Total cost				Total cost			
14	Number of units		÷ 20		Number of units		÷ 10	
15	Unit cost				Unit cost			
16								

Summary of Cost Flows from Work in Process to Finished Goods

	Microsoft Excel - Summary of Cost Flows from Work in Process to Finished Goods.xls							

File Edit View Insert Format Tools Data Window Help Acrobat

Arial   10   **B** *I* <u>U</u>

J37   =

	A	B	C	D	E	F	G	H
1	Work-in-Process Account BEFORE Transfer of Backpacks to Finished Goods							
2	Job: Backpacks				Job: Briefcases			
3	Direct materials		$1,000		Direct materials		$ 500	
4	Direct labor		1,080		Direct labor		450	
5	Applied overhead		240		Applied overhead		100	
6	Total cost		$2,320		Total cost		$1,050	
7	Number of units		÷ 20		Number of units			
8	Unit cost*		$ 116		Unit cost*			
9								
10	Work-in-Process Account AFTER Transfer of Backpacks to Finished Goods							
11	Job: Briefcases							
12	Direct materials		$ 500					
13	Direct labor		450					
14	Applied overhead		100					
15	Total cost		$1,050					
16	Number of units							
17	Unit cost							
18								
19	Finished Goods Account							
20	Beginning balance		$ 0					
21	Add: Completed backpacks		2,320					
22	Less: Jobs sold		0					
23	Ending balance		$2,320					
24								

Sheet1

Ready   NUM

*Unit cost information is included for backpacks because they are complete. The briefcases are still in process, so no unit cost is calculated.

ished goods, and, eventually, added to cost of goods sold expense on the income statement. To ensure accuracy in computing these costs, a cost of goods manufactured statement is prepared. The schedule of the cost of goods manufactured presented in Exhibit 5-10 summarizes the production activity of Johnson Leathergoods for January. It is important to note that applied overhead is used to arrive at the cost of goods manufactured. Both work-in-process and finished goods inventories are carried at normal cost rather than actual cost.

Notice that ending work in process is $1,050. Where did this figure come from? Of the two jobs, the backpacks were finished and transferred to finished goods. The briefcases are still in process, however, and the manufacturing costs assigned thus far are direct materials, $500; direct labor, $450; and overhead applied, $100. The total of these costs gives the cost of ending work in process. You may want to check these figures against the job-order cost sheet for briefcases shown at the top right of Exhibit 5-9.

Accounting for Cost of Goods Sold

In a job-order firm, units can be produced for a particular customer or they can be produced with the expectation of selling the units later. If a job is produced especially for a customer (as with the backpacks) and then shipped to the customer, then the cost of the finished job becomes the cost of goods sold. When the backpacks are completed,

Schedule of Cost of Goods Manufactured

Johnson Leathergoods Schedule of Cost of Goods Manufactured For the Month of January		
Direct materials:		
Beginning raw materials inventory	$ 0	
Purchases of raw materials	2,500	
Total raw materials available	$2,500	
Ending raw materials	1,000	
Total raw materials used		$1,500
Direct labor		1,530
Overhead:		
Lease	$ 200	
Utilities	50	
Depreciation	100	
Indirect labor	65	
	$ 415	
Less: Underapplied overhead	75	
Overhead applied		340
Current manufacturing costs		$3,370
Add: Beginning work in process		0
Total manufacturing costs		$3,370
Less: Ending work in process		1,050
Cost of goods manufactured		$2,320

Cost of Goods Sold increases by $2,320, while Work in Process decreases by the same amount (the job is no longer incomplete so its costs cannot stay in Work in Process). Then, the sale is recognized by increasing both Sales Revenue and Accounts Receivable by $3,480 (cost plus 50 percent of cost or $2,320 + $1,160).

A schedule of cost of goods sold usually is prepared at the end of each reporting period (for example, monthly and quarterly). Exhibit 5-11 presents such a schedule for Johnson Leathergoods for January. Typically, the overhead variance is not material and, therefore, is closed to the cost of goods sold account. The cost of goods sold before an adjustment for an overhead variance is called **normal cost of goods sold**. After the adjustment for the period's overhead variance takes place, the result is called the **adjusted cost of goods sold**. It is this latter figure that appears as an expense on the income statement.

However, closing the overhead variance to the cost of goods sold account is not done until the end of the year. Variances are expected each month because of nonuniform production and nonuniform actual overhead costs. As the year unfolds, these monthly variances should, by and large, offset each other so that the year-end variance is small. Nonetheless, to illustrate how the year-end overhead variance would be treated, we will close out the overhead variance experienced by Johnson Leathergoods in January.

Statement of Cost of Goods Sold

Statement of Cost of Goods Sold	
Beginning finished goods inventory	$ 0
Cost of goods manufactured	2,320
Goods available for sale	$2,320
Less: Ending finished goods inventory	0
Normal cost of goods sold	$2,320
Add: Underapplied overhead	75
Adjusted cost of goods sold	$2,395

Notice that there are two cost of goods sold figures in Exhibit 5-11. The first is normal cost of goods sold and is equal to actual direct materials, actual direct labor, and applied overhead for the jobs that were sold. The second figure is adjusted cost of goods sold. The adjusted cost of goods sold is equal to normal cost of goods sold plus or minus the overhead variance. In this case, overhead has been underapplied (actual overhead of $415 is $75 higher than the applied overhead of $340) so this amount is added to normal cost of goods sold. If the overhead variance shows overapplied overhead, then that amount would be subtracted from normal cost of goods sold.

Suppose that the backpacks had not been ordered by a customer but had been produced with the expectation that they could be sold through a subsequent marketing effort. Then all 20 units might not be sold at the same time. Assume that on January 31, there were 15 backpacks sold. In this case, the cost of goods sold figure is the unit cost times the number of units sold ($116 × 15, or $1,740). The unit cost figure is found on the cost sheet in Exhibit 5-9.

Sometimes, it is simpler to use a briefer version of the job-order cost sheet in order to calculate ending Work in Process, Finished Goods, and Cost of Good Sold. (This is particularly true when working homework and test questions.) Cornerstone 5-5 shows how to set up a briefer version to calculate account balances.

Cornerstone 5-5

HOW TO Prepare Brief Job-Order Cost Sheets

Information: At the beginning of June, Galway Company had two jobs in process, Job 78 and Job 79, with the following accumulated cost information:

	Job 78	Job 79
Direct materials	$1,000	$ 800
Direct labor	600	1,000
Applied overhead	750	1,250
Balance, June 1	$2,350	$3,050

During June, two more jobs (80 and 81) were started. The following direct materials and direct labor costs were added to the four jobs during the month of June:

	Job 78	Job 79	Job 80	Job 81
Direct materials	$500	$1,110	$ 900	$100
Direct labor	400	1,400	2,000	320

At the end of June, Jobs 78, 79, and 80 were completed. Only Job 79 was sold. On June 1, the balance in Finished Goods was zero.

Required:

1. Calculate the overhead rate based on direct labor cost.
2. Prepare a brief job-order cost sheet for the four jobs. Show the balance as of June 1 as well as direct materials and direct labor added in June. Apply overhead to the four jobs for the month of June and show the ending balances.
3. Calculate the ending balances of Work in Process and Finished Goods as of June 30.
4. Calculate the Cost of Goods Sold for June.

Calculation:

1. Ordinarily, the predetermined overhead rate is calculated using estimated overhead and, in this case, estimated direct labor cost. Those figures were not given. However, it is possible to work backward from the applied overhead by the beginning of June for Jobs 78 and 79.

$$\text{Applied overhead} = \text{Predetermined overhead rate} \times \text{Actual activity level}$$

For Job 78,

$$\$750 = \text{Predetermined overhead rate} \times \$600$$

Predetermined overhead rate = $750/$600 = 1.25, or 125 percent of direct labor cost

(The predetermined overhead rate using Job 79 is identical.)

2.

	Job 78	Job 79	Job 80	Job 81
Beginning balance, June 1	$2,350	$3,050	$ 0	$ 0
Direct materials	500	1,110	900	100
Direct labor	400	1,400	2,000	320
Applied overhead	500	1,750	2,500	400
Total, June 30	$3,750	$7,310	$5,400	$820

3. By the end of June, Jobs 78, 79, and 80 have been transferred out of Work in Process. Therefore, the ending balance in Work in Process consists only of Job 81.

Work in process, June 30 $820

While three jobs (78, 79, and 80) were transferred out of Work in Process and into Finished Goods during June, only two jobs remain (Jobs 78 and 80).

Finished goods, June 1	$ 0
Job 78	3,750
Job 80	5,400
Finished goods, June 30	$9,150

4. One job, Job 79, was sold during June.

Cost of goods sold $7,310

Accounting for Nonmanufacturing Costs

Manufacturing costs, however, are not the only costs experienced by a firm. Nonmanufacturing costs are also incurred. Recall that costs associated with selling and general administrative activities are period costs. Selling and administrative costs are never assigned to the product; they are not part of the manufacturing cost flows.

To illustrate how these costs are accounted for, assume Johnson Leathergoods had the following additional transactions in January:

Advertising circulars	$ 75
Sales commission	125
Office salaries	500
Depreciation, office equipment	50

The first two transactions fall in the category of selling expense and the last two into the category of administrative expense. So, the selling expense account would increase by $200 ($75 + $125), and the administrative expense account would increase by $550 ($500 + $50).

Controlling accounts accumulate all of the selling and administrative expenses for a period. At the end of the period, all of these costs flow to the period's income statement. An income statement for Johnson Leathergoods is shown in Exhibit 5-12.

With the preparation of the income statement, the flow of costs through the manufacturing, selling, and administrative expense accounts is complete. A more detailed look at the actual accounting for these cost flows is undertaken in the appendix to this chapter.

5-12

EXHIBIT

Income Statement

Johnson Leathergoods Income Statement For the Month Ended January 31, 2005		
Sales		$3,480
Less: Cost of goods sold		2,395
Gross margin		$1,085
Less selling and administrative expenses:		
Selling expenses	$200	
Administrative expenses	550	750
Net operating income		$ 335

A few months later, Jay and Bonnie were discussing the new accounting system over coffee.

Jay: Bonnie, thanks for taking care of implementing the new accounting system. The job-costing system has made it easier for me to keep our custom homeowners up-to-date on the costs. It is easy for all of us to see what progress has been made to date and how much is left. They are better able to plan on the right size mortgage.

Bonnie: That's great! I was a little skeptical at first—filing all materials and labor by job is a lot of work. But now, it is easy to see at the end of each month just how much to bill each custom homeowner. I can bill the actual materials bought directly to the houses for which they were bought. Our cash flow has improved significantly!

SUMMARY OF LEARNING OBJECTIVES

Most firms use normal costing systems to assign costs to units of product or service. Normal costing includes actual direct materials, actual direct labor, and applied overhead. Overhead is applied on the basis of a predetermined rate that is computed at the beginning of the year. Then, overhead is applied throughout the year by multiplying the predetermined overhead rate by the actual amount of the base used. Finally, at the end of the year, actual overhead costs are reconciled with applied overhead. Typically, the difference between the two is not large, and the variance can be closed to Cost of Goods Sold.

Job-order costing and process costing are two major cost assignment systems. Job-order costing is used in firms that produce a wide variety of heterogeneous (unique) products. Process costing is used by firms that mass-produce a homogeneous product. In job-order costing, the key document or record for accumulating manufacturing costs is the job-order cost sheet. Materials requisition forms (for direct materials), time tickets (for direct labor), and source documents for manufacturing activities are the source documents needed to assign manufacturing costs to jobs.

In job-order costing, the cost of each job is accumulated on the job-order cost sheet. The total job cost consists of actual direct materials, actual direct labor, and overhead applied using a predetermined rate (or rates). The balance in Work in Process consists of the balances of all incomplete jobs. When a job is finished, its cost is transferred from Work in Process to Finished Goods, and then, when sold, to Cost of Goods Sold.

Cornerstones for Chapter 5

Cornerstone 5-1 How to calculate the predetermined overhead rate and apply overhead to production, page 161

Cornerstone 5-2 How to reconcile actual overhead with applied overhead, page 162

Cornerstone 5-3 How to calculate predetermined departmental overhead rates and apply overhead to production, page 164

Cornerstone 5-4 How to convert departmental data to plantwide data to calculate the overhead rate and apply overhead to production, page 165

Cornerstone 5-5 How to prepare brief job-order cost sheets, page 175

KEY TERMS

Actual cost system, 158

Adjusted cost of goods sold, 174

Applied overhead, 160

Departmental overhead rate, 164

Job, 156

Job-order cost sheet, 166

Job-order costing system, 156

Materials requisition form, 167

Normal cost of goods sold, 174

Normal cost system, 159

Overapplied overhead, 161

Overhead variance, 161

Plantwide overhead rate, 163

Predetermined overhead rate, 160

Process-costing system, 157

Time ticket, 168

Underapplied overhead, 161

APPENDIX: JOURNAL ENTRIES ASSOCIATED WITH JOB-ORDER COSTING

OBJECTIVE 5

Prepare the journal entries associated with job-order costing.

How are the transactions that flow through the accounts in job-order costing actually entered into the accounting system? This is done by making journal entries and posting them to the accounts.

Let's summarize the various transactions that occurred during the month of January for Johnson Leathergoods.

1. Purchased raw materials costing $2,500 on account.
2. Requisitioned materials costing $1,500 for use in production.
3. Recognized direct labor costing $1,530 (that is, it was not paid in cash, but shown as a liability in the wages payable account).
4. Applied overhead to production at the rate of $2 per direct labor hour. A total of 170 direct labor hours were worked.
5. Incurred actual overhead costs of $415.
6. Completed the backpack job and transferred it to Finished Goods.
7. Sold the backpack job at cost plus 50 percent.
8. Closed underapplied overhead to Cost of Goods Sold.

The journal entries for each of the above transactions are as follows:

1. Raw Materials   2,500
       Accounts Payable   2,500

2. Work in Process   1,500
       Raw Materials   1,500

3. Work in Process	1,530	
Wages Payable		1,530
4. Work in Process	340	
Overhead Control		340
5. Overhead Control	415	
Lease Payable		200
Utilities Payable		50
Accumulated Depreciation		100
Wages Payable		65
6. Finished Goods	2,320	
Work in Process		2,320
7. Cost of Goods Sold	2,320	
Finished Goods		2,320
Accounts Receivable	3,480	
Sales Revenue		3,480
8. Cost of Goods Sold	75	
Overhead Control		75

Journal entry (1) shows that the purchase of materials increases the raw materials account as well as the accounts payable account. In other words, the company has increased both assets (materials on hand) and liabilities (through Accounts Payable).

Entry (2) shows the transfer from the materials storeroom to the factory floor. In other words, the materials are no longer awaiting requisition; they are being used. Therefore, the work-in-process account goes up, but the raw materials account goes down.

Entry (3) recognizes the contribution of direct labor. The amount of direct labor wages is added to Work in Process and also added to the liability account, Wages Payable.

Entry (4) recognizes the application of overhead to the jobs. Since 170 hours of direct labor were worked, and the overhead rate is $2 per direct labor hour, then $340 has been applied to overhead. Notice that this overhead application increases the work-in-process account and shows as a credit to Overhead Control.

Entry (5) shows that the actual overhead incurred is debited to Overhead Control. The credit is to the various payable accounts.

Entry (6) shows the transfer of the backpack job from Work in Process to Finished Goods. We find the appropriate cost by referring to the job-order cost sheet in Exhibit 5-9.

Entry (7) consists of two journal entries. First, we recognize the cost of the backpack job by debiting Cost of Goods Sold for the cost and crediting Finished Goods. This entry mirrors the physical movement of the backpacks out of the warehouse and to the customer. The second entry shows the sales price. It is very important here to separate the cost of the job from the sale. This always requires two entries.

Finally, in entry (8), we check the overhead control account. It has a debit balance of $75, indicating that the overhead variance is $75 underapplied. To bring the balance to zero, then, Overhead Control must be credited $75 and Cost of Goods Sold debited $75.

Exhibit 5-13 summarizes theses journal entries and posts them to the appropriate accounts.

Posting of Journal Entries to the Accounts

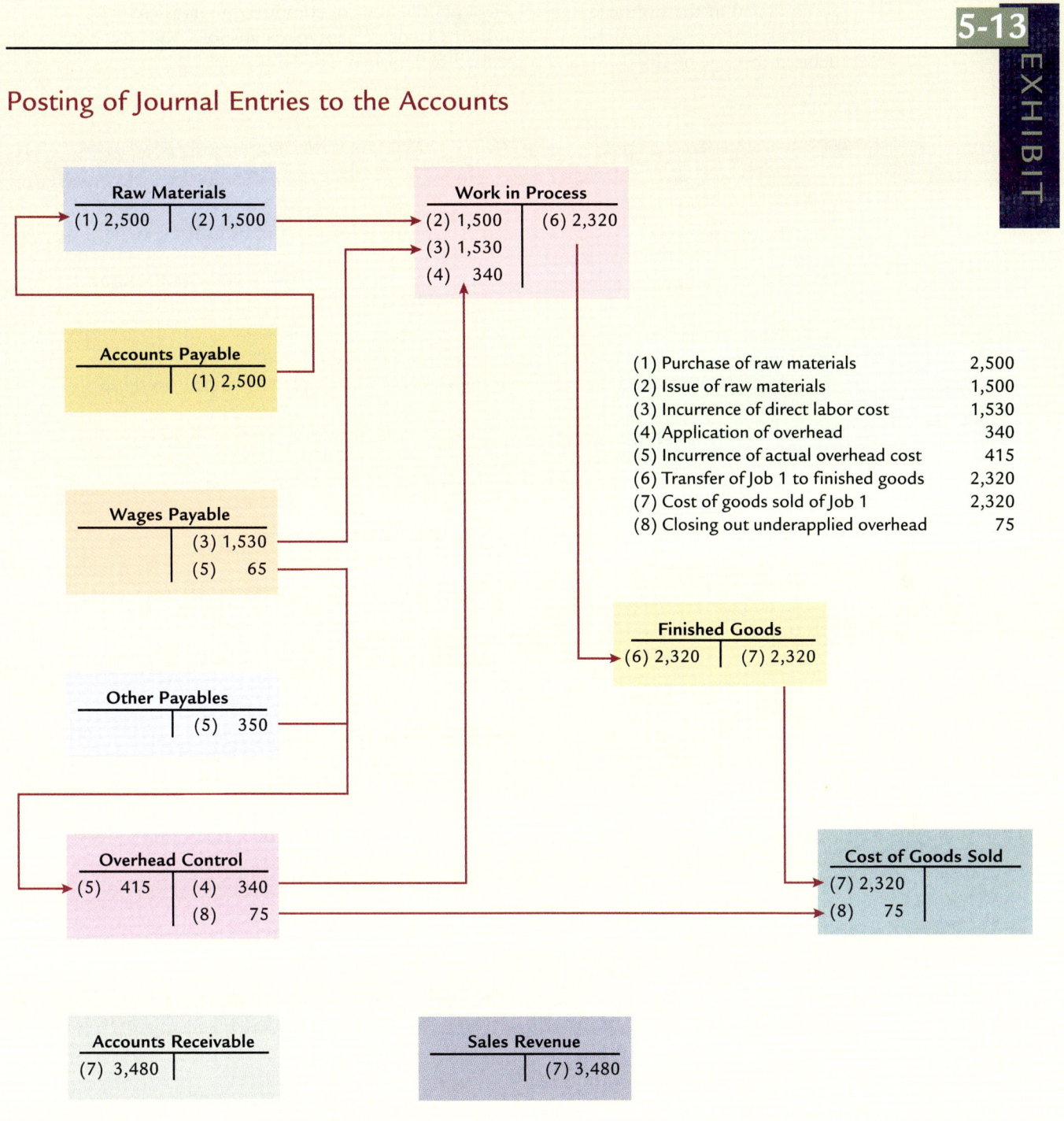

(1) Purchase of raw materials	2,500
(2) Issue of raw materials	1,500
(3) Incurrence of direct labor cost	1,530
(4) Application of overhead	340
(5) Incurrence of actual overhead cost	415
(6) Transfer of Job 1 to finished goods	2,320
(7) Cost of goods sold of Job 1	2,320
(8) Closing out underapplied overhead	75

SUMMARY OF APPENDIX

In job-order costing, materials and direct labor are charged to the work-in-process account (Raw Materials and Wages Payable are credited, respectively). Overhead costs are assigned to Work in Process using a predetermined rate. Actual overhead costs are accumulated in the overhead control account. The cost of completed units is credited to Work in Process and debited to Finished Goods. When goods are sold, the cost is debited to Cost of Goods Sold and credited to Finished Goods.

DISCUSSION QUESTIONS

1. What are job-order costing and process costing? What types of firms use job-order costing? Process costing?
2. Give some examples of service firms that might use job-order costing and explain why it is used there.
3. What is normal costing? How does it differ from actual costing?
4. Why are actual overhead rates seldom used in practice?
5. Explain how overhead is assigned to production when a predetermined overhead rate is used.
6. What is underapplied overhead? When Cost of Goods Sold is adjusted for underapplied overhead, will the cost increase or decrease? Why?
7. What is overapplied overhead? When Cost of Goods Sold is adjusted for overapplied overhead, will the cost increase or decrease? Why?
8. Suppose that you and a friend decide to set up a lawn mowing service next summer. Describe the source documents that you would need to account for your activities.
9. Why might a company decide to use departmental overhead rates instead of a plantwide overhead rate?
10. What is the role of materials requisition forms in a job-order costing system? Time tickets? Predetermined overhead rates?
11. Carver Company uses a plantwide overhead rate based on direct labor cost. Suppose that, during the year, Carver raises its wage rate for direct labor. How would that affect overhead applied? The total cost of jobs?
12. What is an overhead variance? How is it accounted for typically?
13. Is the cost of a job related to the price charged? Explain.
14. If a company decides to increase advertising expense by $25,000, how will that affect the predetermined overhead rate? Eventual cost of goods sold?
15. How can a departmental overhead system be converted to a plantwide overhead system?

MULTIPLE-CHOICE EXERCISES

5-1 Which of the following statements is true?

a. Job-order costing is used only in manufacturing firms.
b. The job cost sheet is subsidiary to the work-in process account.
c. Job-order costing is simpler to use than process costing because the record-keeping requirements are less.
d. Process costing is used only for services.
e. All of the above are true.

5-2 The ending balance of which of the following accounts is calculated by summing the totals of the open (unfinished) job-order cost sheets?

a. Raw Materials
b. Work in Process

   c. Finished Goods
   d. Cost of Goods Sold
   e. Overhead Control

5-3 In a normal costing system, the cost of a job includes

   a. actual direct materials, actual direct labor, and actual overhead.
   b. estimated direct materials, estimated direct labor, and estimated overhead.
   c. actual direct materials, actual direct labor, actual overhead, and actual selling cost.
   d. actual direct materials, actual direct labor, and estimated (applied) overhead.
   e. Job-order costing requires the use of actual, not normal, costing.

5-4 The predetermined overhead rate is

   a. calculated at the end of each month.
   b. calculated at the end of the year.
   c. equal to actual overhead divided by actual activity level for a period.
   d. equal to estimated overhead divided by actual activity level for a period.
   e. calculated at the beginning of the year.

5-5 The predetermined overhead rate equals

   a. actual overhead divided by actual activity level for a period.
   b. estimated overhead divided by estimated activity level for a period.
   c. actual overhead minus estimated overhead.
   d. actual overhead multiplied by actual activity level for a period.
   e. one-twelfth of estimated overhead.

5-6 Applied overhead is

   a. an important part of normal costing.
   b. never used in normal costing.
   c. an important part of actual costing.
   d. the predetermined overhead rate multiplied by estimated activity level.
   e. the predetermined overhead rate multiplied by estimated activity level for the month.

5-7 The overhead variance is overapplied if

   a. actual overhead is less than applied overhead.
   b. actual overhead is more than applied overhead.
   c. applied overhead is less than actual overhead.
   d. estimated overhead is less than applied overhead.
   e. estimated overhead is more than applied overhead.

5-8 Which of the following is typically a job-order costing firm?

   a. Paint manufacturer
   b. Pharmaceutical manufacturer
   c. A large regional medical center
   d. Cement manufacturer
   e. Cleaning products' manufacturer

5-9 Which of the following is typically a process-costing firm?

   a. Paint manufacturer
   b. Custom cabinetmaker
   c. A large regional medical center
   d. A law office
   e. Custom framing shop

5-10 When materials are requisitioned for use in production in a job-order costing firm, the cost of materials is added to the

a. raw materials account.
b. work-in-process account.
c. finished goods account.
d. accounts payable account.
e. cost of goods sold account.

5-11 When a job is completed, the total cost of the job is

a. subtracted from the raw materials account.
b. subtracted from the work-in-process account.
c. subtracted from the finished goods account.
d. added to the accounts payable account.
e. subtracted from the cost of goods sold account.

5-12 The costs of a job are accounted for on the

a. materials requisition sheet.
b. labor time ticket.
c. requisition for overhead application.
d. job-order cost sheet.
e. sales invoice.

5-13 Wilson Company has a predetermined overhead rate of $5 per direct labor hour. The job-order cost sheet for Job 145 shows 1,000 direct labor hours costing $10,000 and materials requisitions totaling $7,500. Job 145 had 500 units completed and transferred to finished goods. What is the cost per unit for Job 145?

a. $35
b. $135
c. $30
d. $45
e. $22,500

5-14 (Appendix) When a job costing $2,000 is finished, the following journal entry is made:

a.	Cost of Goods Sold	2,000	
	Finished Goods		2,000
b.	Finished Goods	2,000	
	Cost of Goods Sold		2,000
c.	Finished Goods	2,000	
	Work in Process		2,000
d.	Work in Process	2,000	
	Finished Goods		2,000
e.	Cost of Goods Sold	2,000	
	Sales		2,000

EXERCISES

Exercise 5-1 *Job-Order Costing versus Process Costing*

OBJECTIVE 1

a. Paint manufacturing
b. Auto manufacturing
c. Toy manufacturing
d. Custom cabinet making
e. Airplane manufacturing (e.g., 767s)

f. Personal computer assembly
g. Furniture making
h. Custom furniture making
i. Dental services
j. Hospital services
k. Paper manufacturing
l. Auto repair
m. Architectural services
n. Landscape design services
o. Light bulb manufacturing

Required:
Identify each of these types of businesses as either job-order or process costing.

Exercise 5-2 *Job-Order versus Process*

a. Auto manufacturing
b. Dental services
c. Auto repair
d. Costume making

Required:
For each of the given types of industries, give an example of a firm that would use job-order costing. Then give an example of a firm that would use process costing.

Exercise 5-3 *Calculating the Predetermined Overhead Rate, Applying Overhead to Production*

At the beginning of the year, Jeffords Company estimated the following:

Overhead	$450,000
Direct labor hours	90,000

Jeffords uses normal costing and applies overhead on the basis of direct labor hours. For the month of March, direct labor hours equaled 7,300.

Required:
1. Calculate the predetermined overhead rate for Jeffords.
2. Calculate the overhead applied to production in March.

Exercise 5-4 *Calculating the Predetermined Overhead Rate, Applying Overhead to Production*

At the beginning of the year, Badiyan Company estimated the following:

Overhead	$270,000
Direct labor hours	90,000

Badiyan uses normal costing and applies overhead on the basis of direct labor hours. For the month of January, direct labor hours equaled 8,150.

Required:
1. Calculate the predetermined overhead rate for Badiyan.
2. Calculate the overhead applied to production in January.

Exercise 5-5 *Reconciling Overhead at the End of the Year, Adjusting Cost of Goods Sold for Under- and Overapplied Overhead*

Refer to **Exercise 5-4**. By the end of the year, Badiyan showed the following actual amounts:

Overhead	$308,000
Direct labor hours	102,600

Assume that unadjusted Cost of Goods Sold for Badiyan was $235,670.

Required:

1. Calculate the total overhead applied for the year. Was overhead over- or under-applied, and by how much?
2. Calculated adjusted Cost of Goods Sold after adjusting for the overhead variance.

Exercise 5-6 *Calculating Departmental Overhead Rates and Applying Overhead to Production*

At the beginning of the year, Videosym Company estimated the following:

	Assembly Department	Testing Department	Total
Overhead	$620,000	$180,000	$800,000
Direct labor hours	155,000	20,000	175,000
Machine hours	80,000	120,000	200,000

Videosym uses departmental overhead rates. In the assembly department, overhead is applied on the basis of direct labor hours. In the testing department, overhead is applied on the basis of machine hours. Actual data for the month of March are as follows:

	Assembly Department	Testing Department	Total
Overhead	$53,000	$15,500	$68,500
Direct labor hours	13,000	1,680	14,680
Machine hours	6,800	13,050	19,850

Required:

1. Calculate the predetermined overhead rates for the assembly and testing departments.
2. Calculate the overhead applied to production in each department for the month of March.
3. By how much has each department's overhead been overapplied? Underapplied?

Exercise 5-7 *Job-Order Cost Sheet*

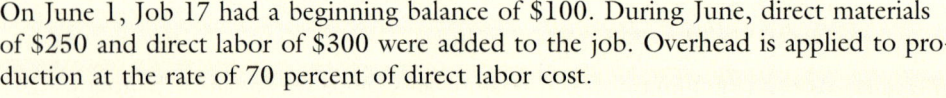

On June 1, Job 17 had a beginning balance of $100. During June, direct materials of $250 and direct labor of $300 were added to the job. Overhead is applied to production at the rate of 70 percent of direct labor cost.

Required:

1. Set up a simple job-order cost sheet for Job 17. What is the total cost of Job 17?
2. If Job 17 consisted of five units, what is the unit cost?

Exercise 5-8 *Source Documents*

Required:

For each of the following independent situations, give the source document that would be referred to for the necessary information.

1. Direct materials costing $460 are requisitioned for use on a job.
2. Greiner's Garage uses a job-order costing system. Overhead is applied to jobs based on direct labor hours. Which source document gives the number of direct labor hours worked on Job 2005-276?

3. Pasilla Investigative Services bills clients on a monthly basis for costs to date. Job 3-48 involved an investigator following the client's business partner for a week by automobile. Mileage is billed at number of miles times $0.75.
4. The foreman on the Jackson job wonders what the actual direct materials cost was for that job.

Exercise 5-9 *Applying Overhead to Jobs, Costing Jobs*

LaSalle, Inc., designs and builds sheds and outbuildings for individual customers. On August 1, there were two jobs in process: Job 214 with a beginning balance of $13,400, and Job 215 with a beginning balance of $9,670. LaSalle applies overhead at the rate of $16 per direct labor hour. Direct labor wages average $10 per hour.

During August, Jobs 216 and 217 were started. Data on August costs for all jobs are as follows:

	Job 214	Job 215	Job 216	Job 217
Direct materials	$2,200	$9,000	$1,500	$3,450
Direct labor cost	1,800	4,000	150	800

Required:
1. Calculate the number of direct labor hours that were worked on each job in August.
2. Calculate the overhead applied to each job during the month of August.
3. Prepare job-order cost sheets for each job as of the end of August.

Exercise 5-10 *Work in Process Balance, Job Cost*

Refer to **Exercise 5-9**. Job 214 was completed on August 22, and the client was billed at cost plus 30 percent. All other jobs remained in process.

Required:
1. Calculate the balance in Work in Process on August 31.
2. What is the price of Job 214?

Exercise 5-11 *Applying Overhead to Jobs, Costing Jobs*

Perrine Company builds internal conveyor equipment to client specifications. On October 1, Job 877 was in process with a cost of $20,520 to date.

During October, Jobs 878, 879, and 880 were started. Data on costs added during October for all jobs are as follows:

	Job 877	Job 878	Job 879	Job 880
Direct materials	$13,960	$ 7,000	$ 350	$4,800
Direct labor	13,800	10,000	1,500	4,000

Overhead is applied to production at the rate of 85 percent of direct labor cost. Job 878 was completed on October 28, and the client was billed at cost plus 50 percent. All other jobs remained in process.

Required:
1. Prepare a brief job-order cost sheet showing the October 1 balances of all four jobs, plus the direct materials and direct labor costs during October. (There is no need to calculate applied overhead at this point or to total the costs.)
2. Calculate the overhead applied during October and complete the job-order cost sheet for each job as of the end of October.
3. Calculate the balance in Work in Process on October 31.
4. What is the price of Job 878?

Exercise 5-12 *Balance of Work in Process and Finished Goods, Cost of Goods Sold*

Grenelin Company uses job-order costing. At the end of the month, the following information was gathered:

Job #	Total Cost	Complete?	Sold?
301	$450	yes	no
302	300	yes	yes
303	500	no	no
304	670	yes	no
305	800	yes	no
306	230	no	no
307	150	yes	yes
308	700	no	no
309	915	no	no
310	103	no	no

The beginning balance of Finished Goods was zero.

Required:

1. Calculate the balance in Work in Process at the end of the month.
2. Calculate the balance in Finished Goods at the end of the month.
3. Calculate Cost of Goods Sold for the month.

Exercise 5-13 *Job-Order Cost Sheets, Balance in Work in Process and Finished Goods*

Geneva Company, a job-order costing firm, worked on three jobs in July. Data are as follows:

	Job 37	Job 38	Job 39
Balance, 7/1	$12,450	$ 0	$0
Direct materials	$6,900	$7,900	$15,350
Direct labor	$10,000	$8,500	$23,000
Machine hours	200	150	1,000

Overhead is applied to jobs at the rate of $20 per machine hour. By July 31, Jobs 37 and 39 were completed. Jobs 35 and 37 were sold. Job 38 remained in process. On July 1, the balance in Finished Goods was $49,000 (consisting of Job 35 for $19,000 and Job 36 for $30,000).

Required:

1. Prepare job-order cost sheets for all jobs in process during July, showing all costs through July 31.
2. Calculate the balance in Work in Process on July 31.
3. Calculate the balance in Finished Goods on July 31.
4. Calculate Cost of Goods Sold for July.

Exercise 5-14 *Income Statement for the Job-Order Costing Firm*

Refer to **Exercise 5-13**. Geneva prices its jobs at cost plus 40 percent. During July, variable marketing expenses were 10 percent of sales and fixed marketing expenses were $2,000; administrative expenses were $3,500.

Required:

Prepare an income statement for Geneva Company for the month of July.

Exercise 5-15 *Cost Flows*

Consider the following independent jobs. Overhead is applied in Department 1 at the rate of $6 per direct labor hour. Overhead is applied in Department 2 at the rate of $8 per machine hour. Direct labor wages average $10 per hour in each department.

	Job 213	Job 214	Job 217	Job 225
Total sales revenue	$?	$4,375	$5,600	$1,150
Price per unit	$12	$?	$14	$5
Materials used in production	$365	$?	$488	$207
Direct labor cost, Department 1	$?	$700	$2,000	$230
Machine hours, Department 1	15	35	50	12
Direct labor cost, Department 2	$50	$100	$?	$0
Machine hours, Department 2	25	50	?	?
Overhead applied, Department 1	$90	$?	$1,200	$138
Overhead applied, Department 2	$?	$400	$160	$0
Total manufacturing cost	$855	$3,073	$?	$575
Number of units	?	350	400	?
Unit cost	$8.55	$?	$9.87	$?

Required:

Fill in the missing data for each job.

Exercise 5-16 *Job Cost Flows*

Timter Company uses a normal job-order costing system. The company has two departments through which most jobs pass. Overhead is applied using a plantwide overhead rate of $10 per direct labor hour. During the year, several jobs were completed. Data pertaining to one such job, Job 10, follow:

Direct materials	$20,000
Direct labor cost:	
Department A (5,000 hours @ $6)	$30,000
Department B (1,000 hours @ $6)	$6,000
Machine hours used:	
Department A	100
Department B	1,200
Units produced	10,000

Required:

1. Compute the total cost of Job 10.
2. Compute the per-unit manufacturing cost for Job 10.

Exercise 5-17 *Departmental Overhead Rates and Job Cost*

Refer to **Exercise 5-16**. Suppose that Timter no longer used a plantwide overhead rate. Instead, an overhead rate is calculated for each department. In Department A, overhead is applied at the rate of $2 per direct labor hour. In Department B, overhead is applied at the rate of $10 per machine hour.

Required:

1. Compute the total cost of Job 10.
2. Compute the per-unit manufacturing cost for Job 10.

Exercise 5-18 *Calculation of Work in Process and Cost of Goods Sold with Multiple Jobs*

Greenthumb Landscape Design designs landscape plans and plants the material for clients. On April 1, there were three jobs in process, Jobs 68, 69, and 70. During April, two more jobs were started, Jobs 71 and 72. By April 30, Jobs 69, 70, and 72 were completed. The following data were gathered:

	Job 68	Job 69	Job 70	Job 71	Job 72
Balance, April 1	$540	$1,230	$990	–	–
Direct materials	700	560	75	$3,500	$2,750
Direct labor	500	600	90	2,500	2,000

Overhead is applied at the rate of 120 percent of direct labor cost. Jobs are sold at cost plus 40 percent. Selling and administrative expenses for April totaled $3,670.

Required:

1. Prepare job-order cost sheets for each job as of April 30.
2. Calculate the ending balance in Work in Process (as of April 30) and Cost of Goods Sold for April.
3. Construct an income statement for Greenthumb Landscape Design for the month of April.

Exercise 5-19 *(Appendix) Journal Entries*

 OBJECTIVE 5

Kaycee, Inc., uses a job-order costing system. During the month of May, the following transactions occurred:

a. Purchased materials on account for $23,175.
b. Requisitioned materials totaling $19,000 for use in production. Of the total, $8,200 was for Job 62, $7,100 for Job 63, and the remainder for Job 64.
c. Incurred direct labor for the month of $22,500, with an average wage of $15 per hour. Job 62 used 700 hours; Job 63, 500 hours; Job 64, 300 hours.
d. Incurred and paid actual overhead of $15,500 (credit various payables).
e. Charged overhead to production at the rate of $8 per direct labor hour.
f. Completed and transferred Jobs 62 and 63 to Finished Goods.
g. Sold Job 58 (see beginning balance of Finished Goods) and Job 62 to their respective clients on account for a price of cost plus 30 percent.

Beginning balances as of May 1 were:

Materials	$ 5,170
Work in Process	0
Finished Goods (Job 58)	23,000

Required:

1. Prepare the journal entries for events (a) through (g).
2. Prepare brief job-order cost sheets for Jobs 62, 63, and 64.
3. Calculate the ending balance of Raw Materials.
4. Calculate the ending balance of Work in Process.
5. Calculate the ending balance of Finished Goods.

PROBLEMS

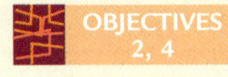

(Note: Whenever you see a   next to a requirement, it signals a "building on a cornerstone" requirement. Assigning this requirement will usually entail additional work, such as a group project, analytical reasoning, Internet research, decision making, and the use of written communication skills.)

Problem 5-1 *Overhead Application and Job-Order Costing*

OBJECTIVES 2, 4

Zavner Company is a job-order costing firm that uses a plantwide overhead rate based on direct labor hours. Estimated information for the year is as follows:

Overhead	$450,000
Direct labor hours	40,000

Zavner worked on five jobs in July. Data are as follows:

	Job 60	Job 61	Job 62	Job 63	Job 64
Balance, July 1	$32,450	$40,770	$29,090	$0	$0
Direct materials	$26,000	$37,900	$25,350	$11,000	$13,560
Direct labor cost	$40,000	$38,500	$43,000	$20,900	$18,000
Direct labor hours	2,500	2,400	2,600	1,200	1,100

By July 31, Jobs 60 and 62 were completed and sold. The remaining jobs were in process.

Required:
1. Calculate the plantwide overhead rate for Zavner Company.
2. Prepare job-order cost sheets for each job showing all costs through July 31.
3. Calculate the balance in Work in Process on July 31.
4. Calculate Cost of Goods Sold for July.

Problem 5-2 *Job Cost, Source Documents*

Spade Millhone Detective Agency performs investigative work for a variety of clients. Recently, Reliance Insurance Company asked Spade Millhone to investigate a series of suspicious claims for whiplash. In each case, the claimant was driving on a freeway and was suddenly rear-ended by a Reliance-insured client. The claimants were all driving old, uninsured automobiles. The Reliance clients reported that the claimants suddenly changed lanes in front of them, and the accidents were unavoidable. Reliance suspected that these "accidents" were the result of insurance fraud. Basically, the claimants cruised the freeways in virtually worthless cars, attempting to cut in front of expensive late-model cars that would surely be insured. Reliance believed that the injuries were faked.

Scott Spade spent 40 hours shadowing the claimants and taking pictures as necessary. His surveillance methods located the office of a doctor used by all claimants. He also took pictures of claimants performing tasks that they had sworn were now impossible to perform, due to whiplash injuries. Kris Millhone spent 25 hours using the Internet to research court records in surrounding states to locate the names of the claimants and their doctor. She found a pattern of similar insurance claims for each of the claimants.

Spade Millhone Detective Agency bills clients for detective time at $100 per hour. Mileage is charged at $0.40 per mile. The agency logged in 430 miles on the Reliance job. The film and developing amounted to $80.

Required:
1. Prepare a job-order cost sheet for the Reliance job.
2. Why is overhead not specified in the charges? How does Spade Millhone charge clients for the use of overhead (e.g., the ongoing costs of their office—supplies, paper for notes and reports, telephone, utilities)?
3. The mileage is tallied from a source document. Design a source document for this use and make up data for it that would total the 430 miles driven on the Reliance job.

Problem 5-3 *Calculating Ending Work in Process, Income Statement*

Brandt Company produces unique metal sculptures. On January 1, three jobs were in process with the following costs:

	Job 35	Job 36	Job 37
Direct materials	$100	$ 340	$ 780
Direct labor	350	700	1,050
Applied overhead	420	840	1,260
Total	$870	$1,880	$3,090

During the month of January, two more jobs were started, Jobs 38 and 39. Materials and labor costs incurred by each job in January are as follows:

	Materials	Direct Labor
Job 35	$400	$300
Job 36	150	200
Job 37	260	150
Job 38	800	650
Job 39	760	700

Jobs 37 and 38 were completed and sold by January 31.

Required:

1. If overhead is applied on the basis of direct labor dollars, what is the overhead rate?
2. Prepare simple job-order cost sheets for each of the five jobs in process during January.
3. What is the ending balance of Work in Process on January 31? What is the Cost of Goods Sold in January?
4. Suppose that Brandt Company prices its jobs at cost plus 50 percent. In addition, during January, marketing and administrative costs of $1,200 were incurred. Prepare an income statement for the month of January.

Problem 5-4 *Overhead Assignment: Actual and Normal Activity Compared*

OBJECTIVES
1, 2

Reynolds Printing Company specializes in wedding announcements. Reynolds uses an actual job-order costing system. An actual overhead rate is calculated at the end of each month using actual direct labor hours and overhead for the month. Once the actual cost of a job is determined, the customer is billed at actual cost plus 50 percent.

During April, Mrs. Lucky, a good friend of owner Jane Reynolds, ordered three sets of wedding announcements to be delivered May 10, June 10, and July 10, respectively. Reynolds scheduled production for each order on May 7, June 7, and July 7, respectively. The orders were assigned job numbers 115, 116, and 117, respectively.

Reynolds assured Mrs. Lucky that she would attend each of her daughters' weddings. Out of sympathy and friendship, she also offered a lower price. Instead of cost plus 50 percent, she gave her a special price of cost plus 25 percent. Additionally, she agreed to wait until the final wedding to bill for the three jobs.

On August 15, Reynolds asked her accountant to bring her the completed job-order cost sheets for Jobs 115, 116, and 117. She also gave instructions to lower the price as had been agreed upon. The cost sheets revealed the following information:

	Job 115	Job 116	Job 117
Cost of direct materials	$250.00	$250.00	$250.00
Cost of direct labor (5 hours)	25.00	25.00	25.00
Cost of overhead	200.00	400.00	400.00
Total cost	$475.00	$675.00	$675.00
Total price	$593.75	$843.75	$843.75
Number of announcements	500	500	500

Reynolds could not understand why the overhead costs assigned to Jobs 116 and 117 were so much higher than those for Job 115. She asked for an overhead cost summary sheet for the months of May, June, and July, which showed that actual overhead costs were $20,000 each month. She also discovered that direct labor hours worked on all jobs were 500 hours in May and 250 hours each in June and July.

Required:

1. How do you think Mrs. Lucky will feel when she receives the bill for the three sets of wedding announcements?
2. Explain how the overhead costs were assigned to each job.
3. Assume that Reynolds's average activity is 500 hours per month and that the company usually experiences overhead costs of $240,000 each year. Can you recommend a better way to assign overhead costs to jobs? Recompute the cost of each job and its price given your method of overhead cost assignment. Which method do you think is best? Why?

Problem 5-5 *Overhead Applied to Jobs, Departmental Overhead Rates*

Watson Products, Inc., uses a normal job-order costing system. Currently, a plantwide overhead rate based on machine hours is used. Marlon Burke, the plant manager, has heard that departmental overhead rates can offer significantly better cost assignments than a plantwide rate can offer. Watson has the following data for its two departments for the coming year:

	Department A	Department B
Overhead costs (expected)	$50,000	$22,000
Normal activity (machine hours)	20,000	16,000

Required:

1. Compute a predetermined overhead rate for the plant as a whole based on machine hours.
2. Compute predetermined overhead rates for each department using machine hours. (Carry your calculations out to three decimal places.)
3. Job 73 used 20 machine hours from Department A and 50 machine hours from Department B. Job 74 used 50 machine hours from Department A and 20 machine hours from Department B. Compute the overhead cost assigned to each job using the plantwide rate computed in Requirement 1. Repeat the computation using the departmental rates found in Requirement 2. Which of the two approaches gives the fairer assignment? Why?
4. Repeat Requirement 3 assuming the expected overhead cost for Department B is $40,000. For this company, would you recommend departmental rates over a plantwide rate?

Problem 5-6 *Overhead Rates, Unit Costs*

Lacy Company manufactures specialty tools to customer order. There are three producing departments. Departmental information on budgeted overhead and various activity measures for the coming year is as follows:

Spreadsheet

	Department 1	Department 2	Department 3
Estimated overhead	$40,000	$25,000	$25,000
Direct labor hours	9,000	5,000	15,000
Direct labor cost	$180,000	$20,000	$200,000
Machine hours	5,000	3,000	2,000

Currently, overhead is applied on the basis of machine hours using a plantwide rate. However, Jennifer, the controller, has been wondering whether it might be worthwhile to use departmental overhead rates. She has analyzed the overhead costs and drivers for the various departments and decided that Departments 1 and 3 should base their overhead rates on machine hours and that Department 2 should base its overhead rate on direct labor hours.

Jennifer has been asked to prepare bids for two jobs with the following information:

	Job 1	Job 2
Direct materials	$4,500	$8,600
Direct labor cost	$1,000	$2,000
Direct labor hours:		
Department 1	10	20
Department 2	60	20
Department 3	30	80
Number of machine hours:		
Department 1	50	30
Department 2	40	5
Department 3	110	165

The typical bid price includes a 30-percent markup over full manufacturing cost.

Required:

1. Calculate a plantwide rate for Lacy Company based on machine hours. What is the bid price of each job using this rate?
2. Calculate departmental overhead rates for the departments. What is the bid price of each job using these rates? (Round all answers to the nearest dollar.)

Problem 5-7 *(Appendix) Unit Cost, Ending Work in Process, Journal Entries*

OBJECTIVES
4, 5

During August, Pamell, Inc., worked on two jobs. Data relating to these two jobs follow:

	Job 64	Job 65
Units in each order	50	100
Units sold	50	—
Materials requisitioned	$1,240	$985
Direct labor hours	410	583
Direct labor cost	$6,150	$8,745

Overhead is assigned on the basis of direct labor hours at a rate of $12. During August, Job 64 was completed and transferred to Finished Goods. Job 65 was the only unfinished job at the end of the month.

Required:

1. Calculate the per-unit cost of Job 64.
2. Compute the ending balance in the work-in-process account.
3. Prepare the journal entries reflecting the completion and sale on account of Job 64. The selling price is 160 percent of cost.

Problem 5-8 *(Appendix) Journal Entries, Job Costs*

OBJECTIVES
4, 5

The following transactions occurred during the month of April for Kearney Company.

a. Purchased materials costing $3,000 on account.
b. Requisitioned materials totaling $1,700 for use in production, $500 for Job 443 and the remainder for Job 444.
c. Recorded 50 hours of direct labor on Job 443 and 100 hours on Job 444 for the month. Direct laborers are paid at the rate of $8 per hour.
d. Applied overhead using a plantwide rate of $7.50 per direct labor hour.
e. Incurred and paid in cash actual overhead for the month of $1,230.

f. Completed and transferred Job 443 to Finished Goods.
g. Sold on account Job 442, which had been completed and transferred to Finished Goods in March, for cost ($2,000) plus 25 percent.

Required:
1. Prepare journal entries for transactions (a) through (e).
2. Prepare job-order cost sheets for Jobs 443 and 444. Prepare journal entries for transactions (f) and (g).
3. Prepare a statement of cost of goods manufactured for April. Assume that the beginning balance in the raw materials account was $1,400 and the beginning balance in the work-in-process account was zero.

Problem 5-9 *(Appendix) Predetermined Overhead Rates, Variances, Cost Flows*

Barrymore Costume Company, located in New York City, sews costumes for plays and musicals. Barrymore considers itself primarily a service firm, as it never produces costumes without a pre-existing order and only purchases materials to the specifications of the particular job. Any finished goods ending inventory is temporary and is zeroed out as soon as the show producer pays for the order. Overhead is applied on the basis of direct labor cost. During the first quarter of the year, the following activity took place in each of the accounts listed:

Work in Process					Finished Goods		
Bal.	17,000	DM	245,000		Bal.	40,000	210,000
DL	80,000					245,000	
OH	140,000				Bal.	75,000	
DM	40,000						
Bal.	32,000						

Overhead				Cost of Goods Sold	
	138,500		140,000	210,000	
		Bal.	1,500		

Job 32 was the only job in process at the end of the first quarter. A total of 1,000 direct labor hours at $10 per hour were charged to Job 32.

Required:
1. Assuming that overhead is applied on the basis of direct labor cost, what was the overhead rate used during the first quarter of the year?
2. What was the applied overhead for the first quarter? The actual overhead? The under- or overapplied overhead?
3. What was the cost of the goods manufactured for the quarter?
4. Assume that the overhead variance is closed to the cost of goods sold account. Prepare the journal entry to close out the overhead control account. What is the adjusted balance in Cost of Goods Sold?
5. For Job 32, identify the costs incurred for direct materials, direct labor, and overhead.

Problem 5-10 *(Appendix) Overhead Application, Journal Entries, Job Cost*

At the beginning of the year, Paxton Company budgeted overhead of $180,000 and budgeted 15,000 direct labor hours. During the year, Job K456 was completed with the following information: direct materials cost, $2,340; direct labor cost, $3,600. The average wage for Paxton Company employees is $10 per hour.

By the end of the year, 15,400 direct labor hours had actually been worked, and Paxton Company incurred the following actual overhead costs for the year:

Equipment lease	$ 5,000
Depreciation on building	20,000
Indirect labor	100,000
Utilities	15,000
Other overhead	45,000

Required:
1. Calculate the overhead rate for the year.
2. Calculate the total cost of Job K456.
3. Prepare the journal entries to record actual overhead and to apply overhead to production for the year.
4. Is overhead overapplied or underapplied? By how much?
5. Assuming that the normal cost of goods sold for the year is $700,000, what is the adjusted cost of goods sold?

Problem 5-11 *(Appendix) Journal Entries, T-Accounts*

OBJECTIVES
1, 4, 5

Lowder, Inc., builds custom conveyor systems for warehouses and distribution centers. During the month of July, the following occurred:

a. Purchased materials on account for $42,630.
b. Requisitioned materials totaling $27,000 for use in production: $12,500 for Job 703 and the remainder for Job 704.
c. Recorded direct labor payroll for the month of $26,320 with an average wage of $14 per hour. Job 703 required 780 direct labor hours; Job 704 required 1,100 direct labor hours.
d. Incurred and paid actual overhead of $19,950.
e. Charged overhead to production at the rate of $10 per direct labor hour.
f. Completed Job 703 and transferred it to finished goods.
g. Kept Job 704, which was started during July, in process at the end of the month.
h. Sold Job 700, which had been completed in May, on account for cost plus 30 percent.

Beginning balances as of July 1 were:

Raw Materials	$ 6,070
Work in process (for Job 703)	10,000
Finished goods (for Job 700)	6,240

Required:
1. Prepare the journal entries for events (a) through (e).
2. Prepare simple job-order cost sheets for Jobs 703 and 704.
3. Prepare the journal entries for events (f) and (h).
4. Calculate the ending balances of:
    a. Raw Materials
    b. Work in Process
    c. Finished Goods

Problem 5-12 *Assigning Overhead to Jobs Ethical Issues*

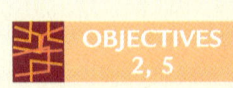

OBJECTIVES
2, 5

Tonya Martin, CMA and controller of the Parts Division of Gunderson, Inc., was meeting with Doug Adams, manager of the division. The topic of discussion was the assignment of overhead costs to jobs and their impact on the division's pricing decisions. Their conversation was as follows:

Tonya: Doug, as you know, about 25 percent of our business is based on government contracts, with the other 75 percent based on jobs from private sources won through bidding. During the last several years, our private business has declined. We have been losing more bids than usual. After some careful investigation, I have concluded that we are overpricing some jobs because of improper assignment of overhead costs. Some jobs are also being underpriced. Unfortunately, the jobs being overpriced are coming from our higher-volume, labor-intensive products; thus, we are losing business.

Doug: I think I understand. Jobs associated with our high-volume products are being assigned more overhead than they should be receiving. Then, when we add our standard 40-percent markup, we end up with a higher price than our competitors, who assign costs more accurately.

Tonya: Exactly. We have two producing departments, one labor-intensive and the other machine-intensive. The labor-intensive department generates much less overhead than the machine-intensive department. Furthermore, virtually all of our high-volume jobs are labor-intensive. We have been using a plantwide rate based on direct labor hours to assign overhead to all jobs. As a result, the high-volume, labor-intensive jobs receive a greater share of the machine-intensive department's overhead than they deserve. This problem can be greatly alleviated by switching to departmental overhead rates. For example, an average high-volume job would be assigned $100,000 of overhead using a plantwide rate and only $70,000 using departmental rates. The change would lower our bidding price on high-volume jobs by an average of $42,000 per job. By increasing the accuracy of our product costing, we can make better pricing decisions and win back much of our private-sector business.

Doug: Sounds good. When can you implement the change in overhead rates?

Tonya: It won't take long. I can have the new system working within four to six weeks—certainly by the start of the new fiscal year.

Doug: Hold it. I just thought of a possible complication. As I recall, most of our government contract work is done in the labor-intensive department. This new overhead assignment scheme will push down the cost on the government jobs, and we will lose revenues. They pay us full cost plus our standard markup. This business is not threatened by our current costing procedures, but we can't switch our rates for only the private business. Government auditors would question the lack of consistency in our costing procedures.

Tonya: You do have a point. I thought of this issue also. According to my estimates, we will gain more revenues from the private sector than we will lose from our government contracts. Besides, the costs of our government jobs are distorted; in effect, we are overcharging the government.

Doug: They don't know that and never will unless we switch our overhead assignment procedures. I think I have the solution. Officially, let's keep our plantwide overhead rate. All of the official records will reflect this overhead costing approach for both our private and government business. Unofficially, I want you to develop a separate set of books that can be used to generate the information we need to prepare competitive bids for our private-sector business.

Required:
1. Do you believe that the solution proposed by Doug is ethical? Explain.
2. Suppose that Tonya decides that Doug's solution is not right and objects strongly. Further suppose that, despite Tonya's objections, Doug insists strongly on implementing the action. What should Tonya do?

Problem 5-13 *Calculate Job Cost and Use It to Calculate Price*

OBJECTIVES
2, 4

Suppose that back in the 1970s, Steve was asked to build speakers for two friends. The first friend, Jan, needed a speaker for her band. The second friend, Ed, needed a speaker built into the back of his hatchback automobile. Steve figured the following costs for each:

	Jan's Job	Ed's Job
Materials	$50	$75
Labor hours	10	20

Steve knew that Jan's job would be easier, since he had experience in building the type of speaker she needed. Her job would not require any special equipment, nor would it require specialized fitting. Ed's job, on the other hand, required specialized design and precise fitting. Steve thought he might need to build a mock-up of the speaker first, to fit it into the space. In addition, he might have to add to his tool collection to complete the job. Normally, Steve figured a wage rate of $6 per hour and charged 20 percent of labor and materials as an overhead rate.

Required:

1. Prepare job-order cost sheets for the two jobs, showing total cost.
2. Which cost do you think is more likely to be accurate? How might Steve build in some of the uncertainty of Ed's job into a budgeted cost?

PROCESS COSTING

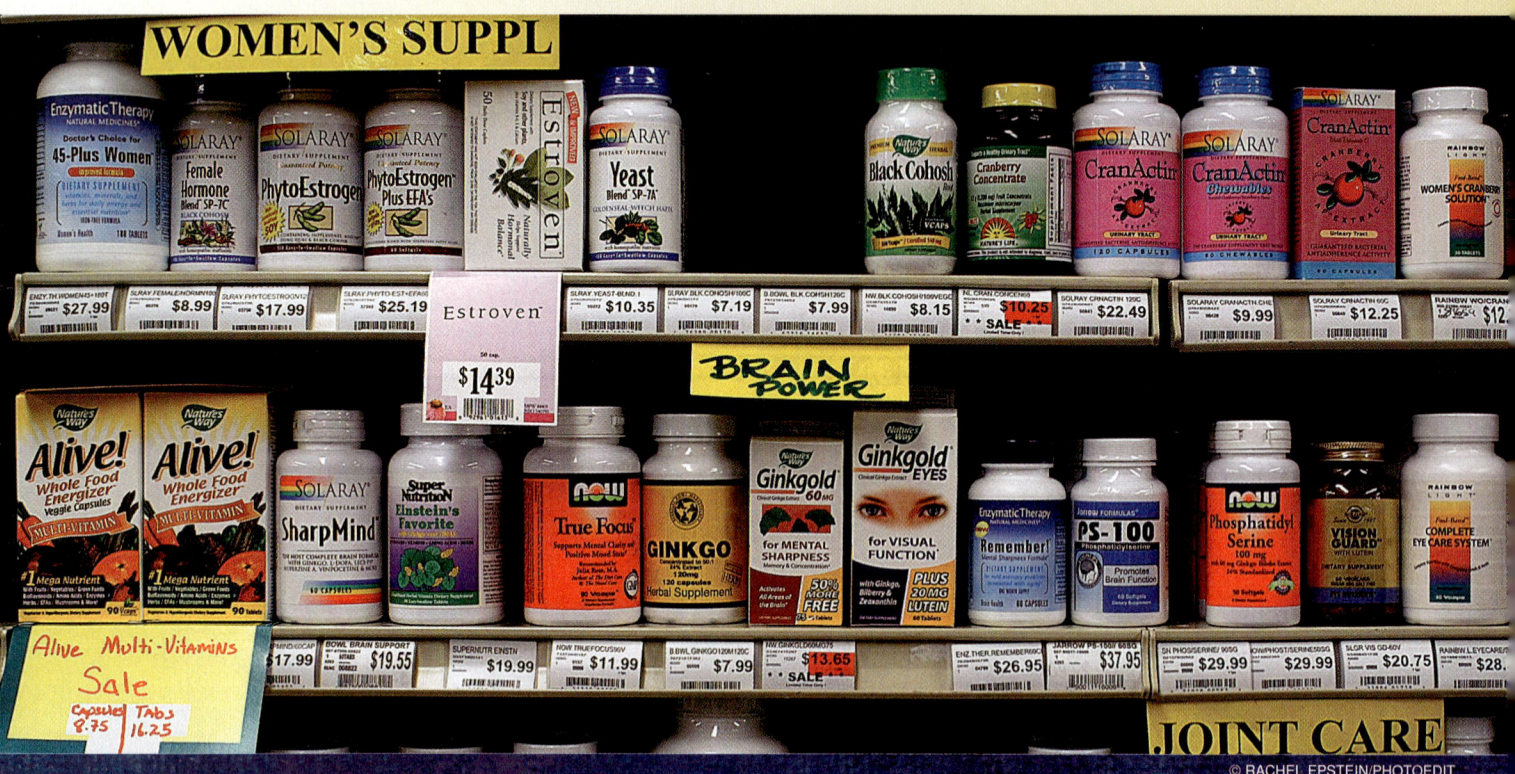

© RACHEL EPSTEIN/PHOTOEDIT

After studying Chapter 6, you should be able to:

1. Describe the basic characteristics and cost flows associated with process manufacturing.
2. Define *equivalent units* and explain their role in process costing. Explain the differences between the weighted average method and the FIFO method of accounting for process costs.
3. Prepare a departmental production report using the weighted average method.
4. Explain how nonuniform inputs and multiple processing departments affect process costing.
5. (Appendix) Prepare a departmental production report using the FIFO method.

Makenzie Gibson, owner of Healthblend Nutritional Supplements, was reviewing last year's income statement. Net income was up 33 percent over last year's, and Makenzie was pleased. The company she had begun in the basement of her home 10 years ago was now a multimillion-dollar business housed in a modern facility with more than 60 employees.

Despite her business success, Makenzie was convinced that she could not afford to be complacent. Recently, the owner of a health food store had told her that some other suppliers had dropped competing lines because they were no longer profitable. This comment made Makenzie realize that she did not know whether all of her products were profitable—in fact, she didn't even know the manufacturing cost of each individual product. All she knew was that overall profits were high.

After some reflection, she decided that knowing individual product costs would be useful for decisions regarding production methods, prices, and the mix of products. So, she contacted Judith Manesfield, manager of a regional CPA firm's small business practice section, for help. After several visits by Judith and her staff, Makenzie received the following preliminary report:

Makenzie Gibson
Healthblend Nutritional Supplements
Tucson, Arizona

Dear Ms. Gibson:

As you know, your current accounting system does not collect the necessary data for costing out the various products that you produce. You currently manufacture three major product lines: mineral, herb, and vitamin. Each product, regardless of the type, passes through three processes: picking, encapsulating, and bottling. In picking, the ingredients are measured, sifted, and blended. In encapsulating, the powdered mix from the first process is put into capsules. The capsules are then transferred to the bottling department where they are bottled, and the bottles are labeled and fitted with safety seals and lids.

Each bottle contains 50 capsules, and the capsules are of equal size for all three product lines. The cost of materials among the three product lines differs, but within a product line, the cost of materials for different products does not vary significantly. The layout of the plant is structured so that all three product lines are produced simultaneously; thus, there are three different picking departments, one for each major product line.

Based on the nature of the manufacturing processes, our tentative recommendation is to accumulate costs of manufacturing by process for a given period of time and measure the output for that same period. By dividing the costs accumulated for the period by the output for the period, a good measure of individual product cost can be obtained.

The cost system we recommend will require a minimal increase in your bookkeeping activities. With your permission, we will proceed with the development of the cost system. As part of this development, we will conduct several training seminars so that your financial staff will be able to operate the system once it is implemented.

CHARACTERISTICS OF PROCESS MANUFACTURING

Makenzie Gibson hired a consultant to help her decide how best to cost out Health-blend's products. The consultant first studied Healthblend's methods of production. This is vital, since the production process helps determine the best way of accounting for costs. The study showed that a large number of similar products pass through an identical set of processes. Since each product within a product line passing through the three processes would receive similar "doses" of materials, labor, and overhead, Judith Manesfield saw no need to accumulate costs by batches (a job-order costing system). Instead, she recommended accumulating costs by process.

Process costing works well whenever relatively homogeneous products pass through a series of processes and they receive similar amounts of manufacturing costs. Large manufacturing plants, such as chemical, food, and tire manufacturers, use process costing.

Let's consider the Healthblend example in more detail. From the consultant's letter, it can be seen that there are three processes each centered in a producing department: picking, encapsulation, and bottling. In the picking department, direct labor selects the appropriate herbs, vitamins, minerals, and inert materials (typically some binder such as cornstarch) for the product to be manufactured. Then, the materials are measured and combined in a mixer to blend them thoroughly. When the mix is complete, the resulting mixture is sent to the encapsulation department. In encapsulating, the vitamin, mineral, or herb blend is loaded into a machine that fills one-half of a gelatin capsule. The filled half is matched to another half of the capsule, and a safety seal is applied. This process is entirely mechanized. Overhead in this department consists of depreciation on machinery, maintenance of machinery, supervision, fringe benefits, lights, and power. The final department is bottling. Filled capsules are transferred to this department, loaded into a hopper, and automatically counted into bottles. Filled bottles are mechanically capped, and direct labor then manually packs the correct number of bottles into boxes to ship to retail outlets.

Types of Processes

Production at Healthblend Nutritional Supplements is an example of sequential processing. In **sequential processing**, units must pass through one process before they can

OBJECTIVE 1

Describe the basic characteristics and cost flows associated with process manufacturing.

APPLICATIONS IN BUSINESS

Alcoa, Inc., leads the world in production of aluminum. Aluminum production begins with bauxite ore, which has a value of about $0.01 per pound. Bauxite is first crushed and then mixed with lime and caustic soda. This mix is then transferred to a process where it is heated under high pressure. Out of this process comes a white powder called alumina (aluminum oxide, which has a value of about $0.10 per pound). Alumina becomes aluminum by passing through a subsequent smelting process. Here alumina is dissolved in a cryolite bath and then a powerful electrical current is passed through the bath. Aluminum separates and is then siphoned off and transferred to furnaces where it is mixed with other metals to form alloys. These alloys are then purified in a fluxing process. Finally, the metal is cast directly into ingots. At this stage, the value of aluminum is about $0.70 per pound. Notice the sequential nature of the manufacturing processes. Also, take note of the vital role of cost information. For the operation to be profitable, the cost per pound must be less than the value per pound.

Source: **http://www.alcoa.com/**. Accessed January 4, 2003.

be worked on in later processes. Exhibit 6-1 shows the sequential pattern of the manufacture of Healthblend's minerals, herbs, and vitamins.

Sequential Processing Illustrated

Summarizing, in a process firm, units typically pass through a series of manufacturing or producing departments; in each department or process is an operation that brings a product one step closer to completion. In each department, materials, labor, and overhead may be needed. Upon completion of a particular process, the partially completed goods are transferred to the next department. After passing through the final department, the goods are completed and transferred to the warehouse.

Another processing pattern is **parallel processing**, in which two or more sequential processes are required to produce a finished good. Partially completed units (for example, two subcomponents) can be worked on simultaneously in different processes and then brought together in a final process for completion. Consider, for example, the manufacture of hard disk drives for personal computers. In one series of processes, write-heads and cartridge disk drives are produced, assembled, and tested. In a second series of processes, printed circuit boards are produced and tested. These two major subcomponents then come together for assembly in the final process. Exhibit 6-2 portrays this type of process pattern. Notice that processes 1 and 2 can occur independently of (or parallel to) processes 3 and 4.

Other forms of parallel processes also exist. However, regardless of which processing pattern exists within a firm, all units produced share a common property. Since units are homogeneous and subjected to the same operations for a given process, each unit produced in a period should receive the same unit cost. Understanding how unit costs are computed requires an understanding of the manufacturing cost flows that take place in a process-costing firm.

Parallel Processing Illustrated

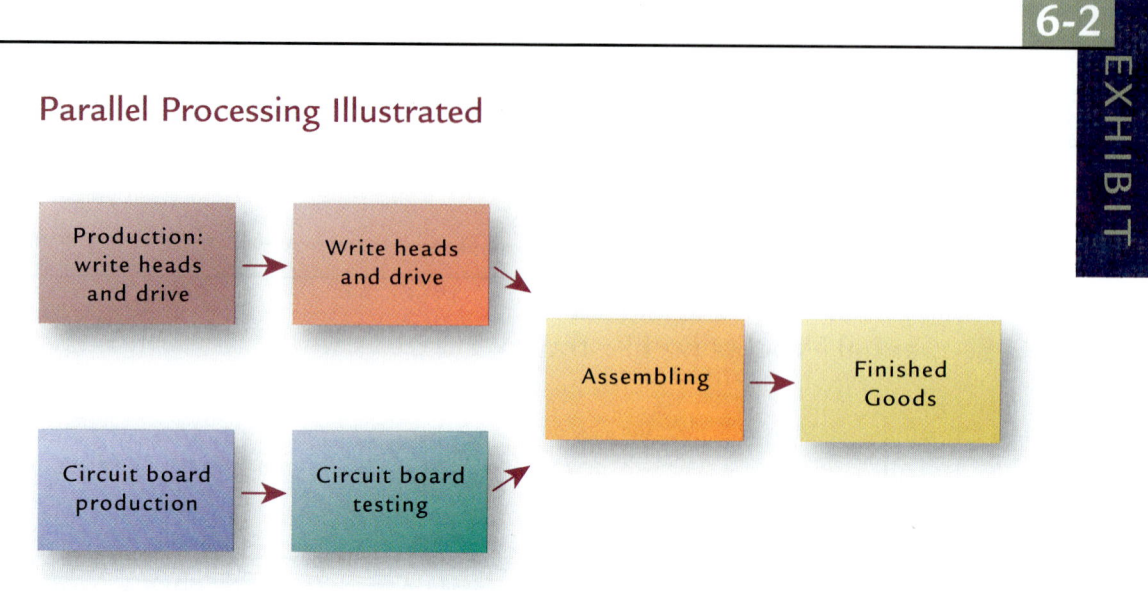

How Costs Flow Through the Accounts in Process Costing

The manufacturing cost flows for a process-costing system are generally the same as those for a job-order system. As raw materials are purchased, the cost of these materials flows into a raw materials inventory account. Similarly, raw materials, direct labor, and applied overhead costs flow into a work-in-process account. When goods are completed, the cost of the completed goods is transferred from Work in Process to the finished goods account. Finally, as goods are sold, the cost of the finished goods is transferred to the cost of goods sold account. The journal entries generally parallel those described in a job-order costing system.

Although job-order and process cost flows are generally similar, some differences exist. In process costing, each producing department has its own work-in-process account. As goods are completed in one department, they are transferred to the next department. Exhibit 6-3 illustrates this process for Healthblend. Notice that a product (let's say multivitamins) starts out in the picking department, where the proper amounts of vitamin, mineral, and inert materials are mixed. Picking direct labor and applied overhead are recognized and added to the picking WIP account. When the mixture is

Concept Q & A

Will process costing be the same for sequential and parallel processing systems?

Answer:
Yes. Process-costing procedures are the same for both process settings. Costs are collected by process and assigned to units produced by the process. Each process undergoes this costing action regardless of whether it is a member of a sequential or a parallel process system. Once goods are costed, they are transferred out to the next process.

Flow of Manufacturing Costs Through the Accounts of a Process-Costing Firm

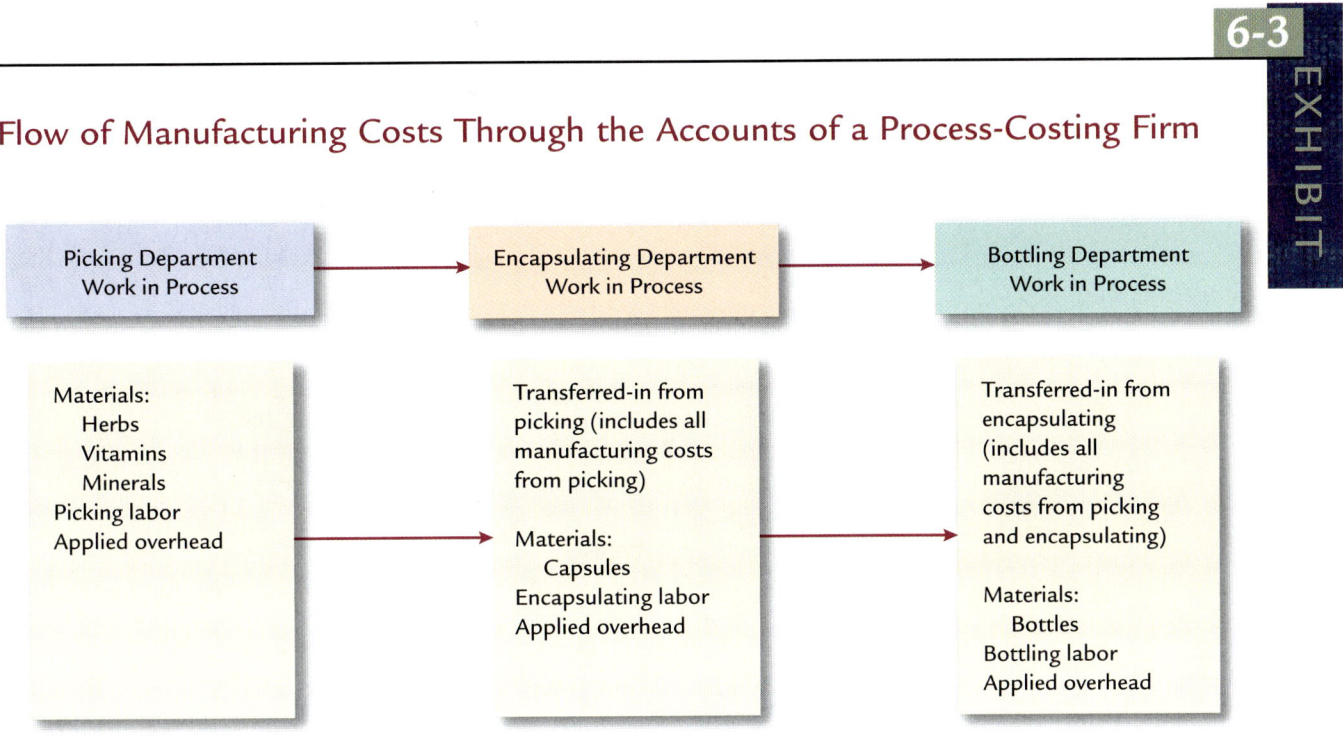

properly blended, it is transferred to the encapsulating department, where capsules are filled. The filled capsules are transferred out to the bottling department. In bottling, the capsules are bottled, and the bottles are packaged. The important point is that as the product is transferred from one department to another, so are all of the costs attached to the product. By the end of the process, all manufacturing costs end up in the final department (here, bottling) with the final product. Let's attach some costs to the various departments and follow them through the accounts. Cornerstone 6-1 shows how cost flows are computed when there are no work-in-process (WIP) inventories.

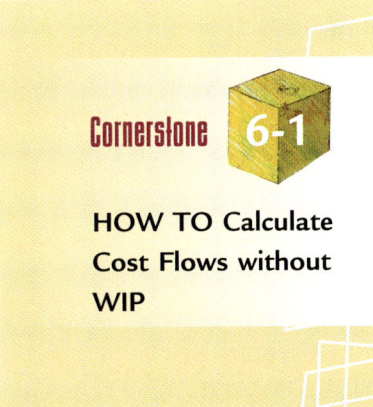

Cornerstone 6-1

HOW TO Calculate Cost Flows without WIP

Information: Suppose that Healthblend decides to produce 2,000 bottles of multivitamins with the following costs:

	Picking Department	Encapsulating Department	Bottling Department
Direct materials	$1,700	$1,000	$800
Direct labor	50	60	300
Applied overhead	450	500	600

Required:
1. Calculate the costs transferred out of each department.
2. Prepare journal entries that reflect these cost transfers.

Calculation:

1.

	Picking Department	Encapsulating Department	Bottling Department
Direct materials	$1,700	$1,000	$ 800
Direct labor	50	60	300
Applied overhead	450	500	600
Costs added	$2,200	$1,560	$1,700
Costs transferred in	0	2,200	3,760
Costs transferred out	$2,200	$3,760	$5,460

2. Journal entries:

Work in Process (Encapsulating)	2,200	
Work in Process (Picking)		2,200
Work in Process (Bottling)	3,760	
Work in Process (Encapsulating)		3,760
Finished Goods	5,460	
Work in Process (Bottling)		5,460

Cornerstone 6-1 shows that when the multivitamin mixture is transferred from the picking department to the encapsulating department, it takes $2,200 of cost along with it. The costs transferred from a prior process to a subsequent process are referred to as **transferred-in costs**. From the viewpoint of the subsequent process, transferred-in costs are a type of raw material cost. The same relationship exists between the encapsulating and bottling departments. The completed bottles of multivitamins are transferred to the finished goods warehouse at a total cost of $5,460.

Accumulating Costs in the Production Report

In process costing, costs are accumulated by department for a period of time. The **production report** is the document that summarizes the manufacturing activity that takes place in a process department for a given period of time. A production report contains information on costs transferred in from prior departments as well as costs added in the department such as direct materials, direct labor, and overhead; it is subsidiary to the work-in-process account, just as the job-order cost sheet is subsidiary to the work-in-process account in a job-order costing system.

A production report provides information about the physical units processed in a department and also about the manufacturing costs associated with them. Thus, a production report is divided into a unit information section and a cost information section. The unit information section has two major subdivisions: (1) units to account for and (2) units accounted for. Similarly, the cost information section has two major subdivisions: (1) costs to account for and (2) costs accounted for. A production report traces the flow of units through a department, identifies the costs charged to the department, shows the computation of unit costs, and reveals the disposition of the department's costs for the reporting period.

Analytical Q & A

Encapsulating transferred $5,000 of partially completed goods to bottling. Bottling added $3,000 of manufacturing cost and then transferred the completed goods to the finished goods warehouse. What two journal entries would be made for these transactions?

Answer:

Work in Process (Bottling)	5,000	
Work in Process (Encapsulating)		5,000
Finished Goods	8,000	
Work in Process (Bottling)		8,000

Service and Manufacturing Firms

Any product or service that is basically homogeneous and repetitively produced can take advantage of a process-costing approach. Let's look at three possibilities: services, manufacturing firms with a JIT orientation, and traditional manufacturing firms.

Check processing in a bank, teeth cleaning by a hygienist, air travel between Dallas and Los Angeles, sorting mail by zip code, and laundering and pressing shirts are examples of homogeneous services that are repetitively produced. Although services cannot be stored, it is possible for firms engaged in service production to have work-in-process inventories. For example, a batch of tax returns can be partially completed at the end of a period. However, many services are provided so quickly that there are no work-in-process inventories. Teeth cleaning, funerals, surgical operations, sonograms, and carpet cleaning are a few examples where work-in-process inventories would be virtually nonexistent. Therefore, process costing for services is relatively simple. The total costs for the period are divided by the number of services provided to compute unit cost.

Manufacturing firms may also operate without significant work-in-process inventories. Specifically, firms that have adopted a JIT (just-in-time) approach to manufacturing view the carrying of unnecessary inventories as wasteful. These firms try to reduce work-in-process inventories to very low levels. Furthermore, JIT firms usually structure their manufacturing so that process costing can be used to determine product costs.

In many JIT firms, work cells are created that produce a product or subassembly from start to finish. Costs are collected by cell for a period of time, and output for the cell is measured for the same period. Unit costs are computed by dividing the costs of the period by output of the period. There is no ambiguity concerning what costs belong to the period and how output is measured. One of the objectives of JIT manufacturing is simplification. Keep this in mind as you study the process-costing requirements of manufacturing firms that carry work-in-process inventories. The difference between the two settings is impressive and illustrates one of the significant benefits of JIT.

Finally, traditional manufacturing firms may have significant beginning and ending work-in-process inventories. It is the presence of these inventories that leads to much of the complication surrounding process costing. These complications are due to several factors such as the presence of beginning and ending work-in-process inventories and different approaches to the treatment of beginning inventory cost. These complicating factors are discussed in the following sections.

THE IMPACT OF WORK-IN-PROCESS INVENTORIES ON PROCESS COSTING

OBJECTIVE 2

Define *equivalent units* and explain their role in process costing. Explain the differences between the weighted average method and the FIFO method of accounting for process costs.

The computation of unit cost for the work performed during a period is a key part of the production report. This unit cost is needed both to compute the cost of goods transferred out of a department and to value ending work-in-process inventory. Conceptually, calculating the unit cost is easy—just divide total cost by the number of units produced. However, the presence of work-in-process inventories causes two problems. First, defining the units produced can be difficult, given that some units produced during a period are complete, while those in ending inventory are not. This is handled through the concept of equivalent units of production. Second, how should the costs and work of beginning work in process be treated? Should they be counted with the current period work and costs or treated separately? Two methods have been developed to solve this problem: the weighted average method and the FIFO method.

Equivalent Units of Production

By definition, ending work in process is not complete. Thus, a unit completed and transferred out during the period is not identical (or equivalent) to one in ending work-in-process inventory, and the cost attached to the two units should not be the same. In computing the unit cost, the output of the period must be defined. A major problem of process costing is making this definition.

To illustrate the output problem of process costing, assume that Department A had the following data for October:

Units in beginning work in process	—
Units completed	1,000
Units in ending work in process (25 percent complete)	600
Total manufacturing costs	$11,500

What is the output in October for this department? 1,000? 1,600? If the answer is 1,000 units, the effort expended on the units in ending work in process is ignored. Furthermore, the manufacturing costs incurred in October belong to both the units completed and to the partially completed units in ending work in process. On the other hand, if the answer is 1,600 units, the fact that the 600 units in ending work in process are only partially completed is ignored. Somehow output must be measured so that it reflects the effort expended on both completed and partially completed units.

The solution is to calculate equivalent units of output. **Equivalent units of output** are the complete units that could have been produced given the total amount of manufacturing effort expended for the period under consideration. Determining equivalent units of output for transferred-out units is easy; a unit would not be transferred out unless it were complete. Thus, every transferred-out unit is an equivalent unit. Units remaining in ending work-in-process inventory, however, are not complete. Thus, someone in production must "eyeball" ending work in process to estimate its degree of completion. Cornerstone 6-2 illustrates how to calculate equivalent units of production.

Analytical Q & A

In March, a company completed 8,000 tons of aluminum ingots and had 2,500 tons of ingots in ending work in process (EWIP), 60 percent complete. Calculate the equivalent units for March.

Answer:
Equivalent units = 8,000 + (0.6 × 2,500) = 9,500.

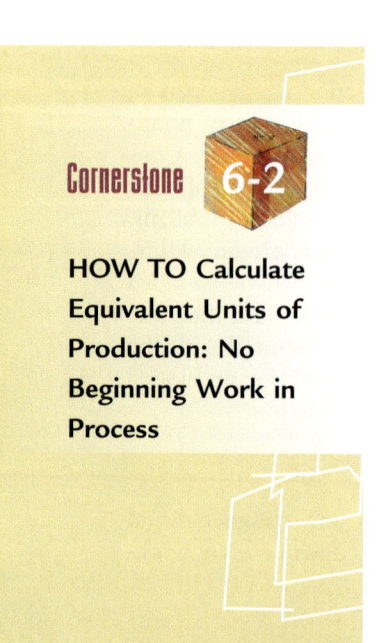

Cornerstone 6-2

HOW TO Calculate Equivalent Units of Production: No Beginning Work in Process

Concept:

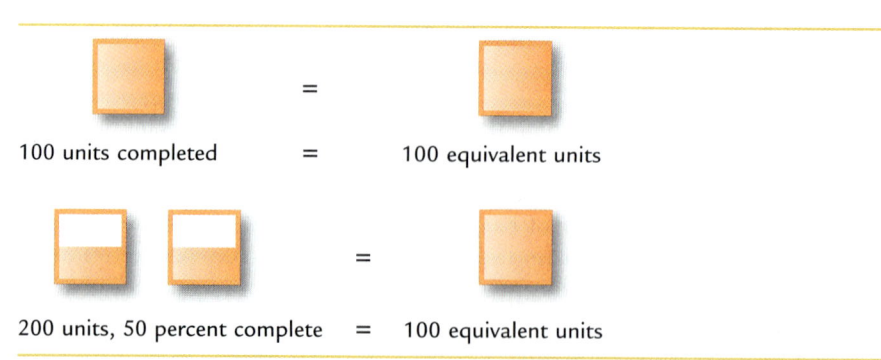

100 units completed   =   100 equivalent units

200 units, 50 percent complete   =   100 equivalent units

Information: October data: 1,000 units completed, 600 units, 25 percent complete
Required: Calculate the equivalent units for October.

Calculation:

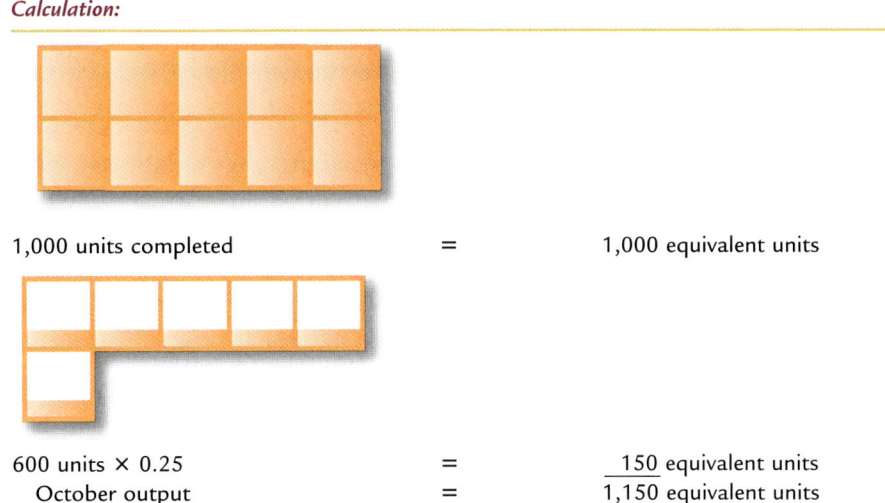

1,000 units completed	=	1,000 equivalent units
600 units × 0.25	=	150 equivalent units
October output	=	1,150 equivalent units

Knowing the output for a period and the manufacturing costs for the department for that period, a unit cost can be calculated. The unit cost can then be used to determine the cost of units transferred out and the cost of the units in ending work in process. Cornerstone 6-3 shows how the calculations are done when there is no beginning work in process. The unit cost of $10 is used to assign a cost of $10,000 ($10 × 1,000) to the 1,000 units transferred out and a cost of $1,500 ($10 × 150) to the 600 units in ending work in process. Notice that the cost of the ending work in process is obtained by multiplying the unit cost by the equivalent units, not the actual number of partially completed units.

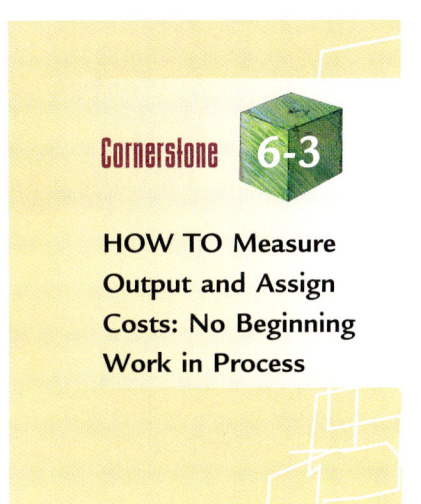

Cornerstone 6-3

HOW TO Measure Output and Assign Costs: No Beginning Work in Process

Information: Manufacturing costs of the period, $11,500; units transferred out, 1,000; units in ending work in process, 600 (25 percent complete).

Required:
1. Calculate the unit cost.
2. Calculate the cost of goods transferred out and the cost of ending work in process.

Calculation:
1. Equivalent units:

Units completed	1,000
Units in EWIP × 25 percent (600 × 0.25)	150
Equivalent units	1,150

Cost assignment:
Cost per equivalent unit = $11,500/1,150
$\qquad\qquad\qquad\qquad\quad$ = $10

2. Cost of goods transferred out = $10 per unit × 1,000 equivalent units = $10,000
Cost of ending work in process = $10 per unit × 150 equivalent units = $1,500

Two Methods of Treating Beginning Work-in-Process Inventory

The calculations illustrated by Cornerstones 6-2 and 6-3 become more complicated when there are beginning work-in-process inventories. The work done on these partially completed units represents prior-period work, and the costs assigned to them are prior-period costs. In computing a current-period unit cost for a department, two approaches have evolved for dealing with the prior-period output and prior-period costs found in beginning work in process: the weighted average method and the first-in, first-out (FIFO) method.

The **weighted average costing method** combines beginning inventory costs and work done with current-period costs and work to calculate this period's unit cost. In essence, the costs and work carried over from the prior period are counted as if they belong to the current period. Thus, beginning inventory work and costs are pooled with current work and costs, and an average unit cost is computed and applied to both units transferred out and units remaining in ending inventory.

The **FIFO costing method**, on the other hand, separates work and costs of the equivalent units in beginning inventory from work and costs of the equivalent units produced during the current period. Only current work and costs are used to calculate this period's unit cost. It is assumed that units from beginning inventory are completed first and transferred out. The costs of these units include the costs of the work done in the prior period as well as the current-period costs necessary to complete the units. Units started in the current period are divided into two categories: units started and completed and units started but not finished (ending work in process). Units in both of these categories are valued using the current period's cost per equivalent unit.

If product costs do not change from period to period, or if there is no beginning work-in-process inventory, the FIFO and weighted average methods yield the same results. The weighted average method is discussed in more detail in the next section. Further discussion of the FIFO method is found in the chapter appendix.

WEIGHTED AVERAGE COSTING

The weighted average costing method treats beginning inventory costs and the accompanying equivalent output as if they belong to the current period. This is done for costs by adding the manufacturing costs in beginning work in process to the manufacturing costs incurred during the current period. The total cost is treated as if it were the current period's total manufacturing cost. Similarly, beginning inventory output and current-period output are merged in the calculation of equivalent units. Under the weighted average method, equivalent units of output are computed by adding units completed to equivalent units in ending work in process. Notice that the equivalent units in beginning work in process are included in the computation. Consequently, these units are counted as part of the current period's equivalent units of output.

Overview of the Weighted Average Method

The essential conceptual and computational features of the weighted average method are illustrated by Cornerstone 6-4. The example uses production data for Healthblend's picking department for July. The objective is to calculate a unit cost for July and use this unit cost to value goods transferred out and ending work in process. Unit cost is simply costs of the period divided by output of the period. Thus, output needs to be calculated and costs defined for July to value goods transferred out and ending work in process.

Analytical Q & A

During March, a molding process transferred out 9,000 equivalent units to grinding and had 1,250 equivalent units in ending work in process. The cost per equivalent unit for March was $8.00. Calculate the cost of goods transferred out and the cost of the ending work in process.

Answer:
Cost of goods transferred out: $8.00 × 9,000 = $72,000; ending WIP = $8.00 × 1,250 = $10,000.

OBJECTIVE 3

Prepare a departmental production report using the weighted average method.

Concept Q & A

What is the key difference between FIFO and the weighted average costing methods?

Answer:
FIFO treats work and costs in beginning work in process separately from the work and costs of the current period. Weighted average rolls back and picks up the work and costs of beginning work in process and counts them as if they belong to the current period's work and costs.

Cornerstone 6-4

HOW TO Measure Output and Assign Costs: Weighted Average Method

Information:

Production:

Units in process, July 1, 75 percent complete	20,000 gallons
Units completed and transferred out	50,000 gallons
Units in process, July 31, 25 percent complete	10,000 gallons

Costs:

Work in process, July 1	$ 3,525
Costs added during July	10,125

Required:

1. Calculate an output measure for July.
2. Assign costs to units transferred out and ending work in process using the weighted average method.

Calculation:

1. Equivalent units:

Key: = 10,000 units completed   = 10,000 units, 25 percent complete

Output for July:
  60,000 total units ———▶ Become 52,500 equivalent units

Units completed:
BWIP:

= 20,000

Units started and completed:

= 30,000   50,000

+ EWIP, 25 percent complete:

= 2,500
= 52,500

2. Cost assignment:
   Costs for July:

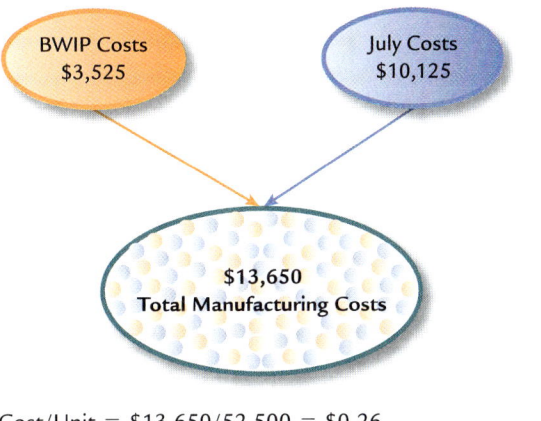

Cost/Unit = $13,650/52,500 = $0.26

Transferred out ($0.26 × 50,000)	$13,000
EWIP ($0.26 × 2,500)	650
Total cost assigned	$13,650

Cornerstone 6-4 illustrates that costs from beginning work in process (BWIP) are pooled with costs added to production during July. These total pooled costs ($13,650) are averaged and assigned to units transferred out and to units in ending work in process. On the output side, it is necessary to concentrate on the degree of completion of all units at the end of the period. There is no need to be concerned with the percentage of completion of beginning work-in-process inventory. The only issue is whether these units are complete or not by the end of July. Thus, equivalent units are computed by pooling manufacturing efforts from June and July.

Analytical Q & A

The weighted average cost per equivalent unit for April is $10. There were 3,800 units completed and transferred out during April and 750 units in ending work in process, 40 percent complete. Calculate the cost of goods transferred out and the cost assigned to EWIP.

Answer:
Cost of goods transferred out: $10 × 3,800 = $38,000; EWIP = $10 × 0.4 × 750 = $3,000.

Five Steps in Preparing a Production Report

The elements of Cornerstone 6-4 are used to prepare a production report. Recall that the production report summarizes cost and manufacturing activity for a producing department for a given period of time. The production report is subsidiary to the work-in-process account for a department. The following five steps describe the general pattern of a process-costing production report:

1. Physical flow analysis.
2. Calculation of equivalent units.
3. Computation of unit cost.
4. Valuation of inventories (goods transferred out and ending work in process).
5. Cost reconciliation.

These five steps provide structure to the method of accounting for process costs.

Step 1: Physical Flow Analysis

The purpose of step 1 is to trace the physical units of production. Physical units are not equivalent units; they are units that may be in any stage of completion. The analysis of physical flow of units is usually accomplished by preparing a **physical flow schedule** like the one shown by Cornerstone 6-5 for Healthblend's picking department. To construct the schedule from the information given in the example, two calculations are needed. First, units started and completed in this period are obtained by subtracting the units in beginning work in process from the total units completed. Next, the units started are obtained by adding the units started and completed to the units in ending work in process. Notice that the "Total units to account for" must equal the "Total units accounted for." The physical flow schedule is important because it contains the information needed to calculate equivalent units (step 2).

Cornerstone 6-5

HOW TO Prepare a Physical Flow Schedule

Information:

Production:

Units in process, July 1, 75 percent complete	20,000 gallons
Units completed and transferred out	50,000 gallons
Units in process, July 31, 25 percent complete	10,000 gallons

Required: Prepare a physical flow schedule.

Calculation:

Units started and completed = Units completed − Units, BWIP
= 50,000 − 20,000
= 30,000

Units started = Units started and completed + Units, EWIP
= 30,000 + 10,000
= 40,000

Physical flow schedule:

Units to account for:

Units in beginning work in process (75 percent complete)		20,000
Units started during the period		40,000
Total units to account for		60,000

Units accounted for:

Units completed and transferred out:		
Started and completed	30,000	
From beginning work in process	20,000	50,000
Units in ending work in process (25 percent complete)		10,000
Total units accounted for		60,000

Analytical Q & A

The following data are provided for the month of April:

Units in process, April 1, 40 percent complete	6,000 cases
Units completed and transferred out	20,000 cases

How many units were started and completed during April?

Answer:
Units started and completed:
20,000 − 6,000 = 14,000.

Step 2: Calculation of Equivalent Units

Given the information in the physical flow schedule, the weighted average equivalent units for July can be calculated as follows:

Units completed	50,000
Add: Units in ending work in process × Fraction complete	
(10,000 units × 25 percent)	2,500
Equivalent units of output	52,500

Notice that July's output is measured as 52,500 units, 50,000 units completed and transferred out and 2,500 equivalent units from ending inventory (10,000 × 25 percent). What about beginning inventory? There were 20,000 units in beginning inventory, 75 percent complete. These units are included in the 50,000 units completed and transferred out during the month. Thus, the weighted average method treats beginning inventory units as if they were started and completed during the current period. Because of this, the equivalent unit schedule shown in step 2 shows only the total units completed. There is no need to show whether the units completed are from July or from beginning work in process as was done by Cornerstone 6-4.

Step 3: Computation of Unit Cost

In addition to July output, July manufacturing costs are needed to compute a unit cost. The weighted average method rolls back and includes the manufacturing costs associated with the units in beginning work in process and counts these costs as if they belong to July. Thus, as Cornerstone 6-4 illustrated, these costs are pooled to define total manufacturing costs for July as $13,650 ($3,525 + $10,125). The manufacturing costs carried over from the prior period ($3,525) are treated as if they were current-period costs. The unit cost for July is July's pooled costs divided by the equivalent output for July:

$$\text{Unit cost} = \$13,650/52,500$$
$$= \$0.26 \text{ per equivalent unit}$$

Step 4: Valuation of Inventories

Cornerstone 6-4 also showed how to value goods transferred out and ending work in process. Using the unit cost of $0.26, the cost of goods transferred to the encapsulating department is $13,000 (50,000 units × $0.26 per unit), and the cost of ending work in process is $650 (2,500 equivalent units × $0.26 per unit). Notice that units completed (from step 1), equivalent units in ending work in process (from step 2), and the unit cost (from step 3) were all needed to value both goods transferred out and ending work in process.

Analytical Q & A

During June, 5,000 units were completed and transferred out and there were 1,500 units in EWIP, 80 percent complete. How many equivalent units were completed in June, using the weighted average method?

Answer:
Equivalent units = 5,000 + (0.8 × 1,500) = 6,200

Analytical Q & A

June had the following costs to account for:

BWIP: $4,000

Incurred in June: $27,000

There were 6,200 equivalent units produced in June. What is the unit cost for June using the weighted average method?

Answer:
Unit cost = $31,000/6,200 = $5.00

APPLICATIONS IN BUSINESS

By now, you may have the impression that process-costing calculations can be demanding and complex. Fortunately, advances in information technology facilitate these calculations. Consider Wells' Dairy, Inc., America's largest family-owned dairy. Wells' Dairy is recognized as one of the most technically advanced companies in its industry. It has used technology to increase its efficiency and reduce costs. Recently, Wells' Dairy implemented Oracle's process manufacturing software package, allowing it quick and precise product cost calculations while simultaneously enabling it to better reduce costs and increase profitability.

Source: **http://www.oracle.com/customers**. Accessed January 4, 2003.

Step 5: Cost Reconciliation

The total manufacturing costs assigned to inventories are as follows:

Goods transferred out	$13,000
Goods in ending work in process	650
Total costs accounted for	$13,650

The manufacturing costs to account for are also $13,650.

Beginning work in process	$ 3,525
Incurred during the period	10,125
Total costs to account for	$13,650

Thus, the costs to account for are exactly assigned to inventories, and you have the necessary **cost reconciliation**. Remember, the total costs assigned to goods transferred out and to ending work in process must agree with the total costs in beginning work in process and the manufacturing costs incurred during the current period.

Production Report

Steps 1 through 5 provide all of the information needed to prepare a production report for the picking department for July. The method for preparing this report is shown in Cornerstone 6-6.

Cornerstone 6-6

HOW TO Prepare a Production Report: Weighted Average Method

Information: Steps 1-5 of the Healthblend Company example.
Required: Prepare a production report.
Calculation:

Healthblend Company
Picking Department
Production Report for July 2007
(Weighted Average Method)

UNIT INFORMATION

Physical Flow

Units to account for:		Units accounted for:	
Units in beginning work in process	20,000	Units completed	50,000
Units started	40,000	Units in ending work in process	10,000
Total units to account for	60,000	Total units accounted for	60,000

Equivalent Units

Units completed	50,000
Units in ending work in process	2,500
Total equivalent units	52,500

COST INFORMATION

Costs to account for:	
Beginning work in process	$ 3,525
Incurred during the period	10,125
Total costs to account for	$13,650
Cost per equivalent unit	$ 0.26

	Transferred Out	Ending Work in Process	Total
Costs accounted for:			
Goods transferred out ($0.26 × 50,000)	$13,000	—	$13,000
Goods in ending work in process			
($0.26 × 2,500)	—	$650	650
Total costs accounted for	$13,000	$650	$13,650

Evaluation of the Weighted Average Method

The major benefit of the weighted average method is simplicity. By treating units in beginning work in process as belonging to the current period, all equivalent units belong to the same category when it comes to calculating unit costs. Thus, unit cost computations are simplified. The main disadvantage of this method is reduced accuracy in computing unit costs for current-period output and for units in beginning work in process. If the unit cost in a process is relatively stable from one period to the next, the weighted average method is reasonably accurate. However, if the price of manufacturing inputs increases significantly from one period to the next, the unit cost of current output is understated, and the unit cost of beginning work-in-process units is overstated. If greater accuracy in computing unit costs is desired, a company should use the FIFO method to determine unit costs.

HERE'S THE REAL KICKER

Stillwater Designs builds a limited number of items on site. The manufacturing activities include designing and building prototypes and rebuilding of warranty returns (only of certain models such as the square L7s). Rebuilding of warranty returns follows a process manufacturing structure. All units are alike and go through the same steps. First, the woofers are removed from the cabinet and the cabinet is stripped and cleaned. The speaker is torn down to its structures with all chemicals and glues removed. The speaker is passed through a demagnetizing process so that all metal pieces and shavings can be removed. The speaker is rebuilt using a recone kit to replace damaged and defective parts. Once the cabinets and speakers are ready, they are assembled, tested, and boxed. Assembly involves placing the speakers in the enclosures (cabinets) and connecting the wire harnesses. There are two tests: the in-phase test and the air-leak test. The in-phase test is to make sure that the power is hooked up correctly. Overall checking for air leaks is the final test. The product must be properly sealed because an air leak can damage the woofer.

Notice that the rebuilding and assembly processes are sequential. When finished, the rebuilt speakers and cabinets are transferred from the rebuilding process to the assembly process. Also, note that the cost of the final product is the cost of the materials transferred in from the rebuilding process, plus the cost of the other components and materials added, plus the assembly conversion cost. For example, at the end of the assembly process, the assembled product is packaged for delivery. In this simple process application, it is easy to see that some materials are added at the beginning of the assembly process (the cabinet and components) and some at end of the process (packaging). The Kicker example also makes it possible to catch a glimpse of how process costing handles multiple departments.

MULTIPLE INPUTS AND MULTIPLE DEPARTMENTS

OBJECTIVE 4

Explain how nonuniform inputs and multiple processing departments affect process costing.

Accounting for production under process costing is complicated by nonuniform application of manufacturing inputs and the presence of multiple processing departments. How process-costing methods address these complications will now be discussed.

Nonuniform Application of Manufacturing Inputs

Up to this point, we have assumed that work in process being 60 percent complete meant that 60 percent of materials, labor, and overhead needed to complete the process have been used and that another 40 percent are needed to finish the units. In other words, we have assumed that manufacturing inputs are applied uniformly as the manufacturing process unfolds.

Assuming uniform application of conversion costs (direct labor and overhead) is not unreasonable. Direct labor input is usually needed throughout the process, and overhead is normally assigned on the basis of direct labor hours. Direct materials, on the other hand, are not as likely to be applied uniformly. In many instances, materials are added at either the beginning or the end of the process.

For example, look at the differences in Healthblend's three departments. In the picking and encapsulating departments, all materials are added at the beginning of the process. However, in the bottling department, materials are added both at the beginning (filled capsules and bottles) and at the end (bottle caps and boxes).

Work in process in the picking department that is 50 percent complete with respect to conversion inputs would be 100 percent complete with respect to the material inputs. But work in process in bottling that is 50 percent complete with respect to conversion would be 100 percent complete with respect to bottles and transferred-in capsules, but 0 percent complete with respect to bottle caps and boxes.

Different percentage completion figures for manufacturing inputs pose a problem for the calculation of equivalent units, unit cost, and valuation of ending work in process (steps 2-4). Fortunately, the solution is relatively simple. Equivalent unit calculations are done for each category of manufacturing input. Thus, equivalent units are calculated for each category of materials and for conversion cost. Next, a unit cost for each category is computed. The individual category costs are then used in step 4 to cost out ending work in process. The total unit cost is used to calculate the cost of goods transferred out in the same way as when there was only one input category. Cornerstone 6-7 shows how to calculate steps 2-4 with nonuniform inputs, using the weighted average method.

Cornerstone 6-7

HOW TO Calculate Equivalent Units, Unit Costs, and Value Inventories with Nonuniform Inputs

Information: The picking department of Healthblend has the following data for September:

Production:	
Units in process, September 1, 50 percent complete*	10,000
Units completed and transferred out	60,000
Units in process, September 30, 40 percent complete*	20,000
Costs:	
Work in process, September 1:	
Materials	$ 1,600
Conversion costs	200
Total	$ 1,800
Current costs:	
Materials	$12,000
Conversion costs	3,200
Total	$15,200

*With respect to conversion costs, all materials are added at the beginning of the process.

Required: Calculate steps 2-4 using the weighted average method.

Calculation:

Step 2: Calculation of equivalent units: nonuniform application:

	Materials	Conversion
Units completed	60,000	60,000
Add: Units in ending work in process × Fraction complete:		
20,000 × 100 percent	20,000	—
20,000 × 40 percent	0	8,000
Equivalent units of output	80,000	68,000

Step 3: Calculation of unit costs:

$$\text{Unit materials cost} = (\$1,600 + \$12,000)/80,000$$
$$= \$0.17$$
$$\text{Unit conversion cost} = (\$200 + \$3,200)/68,000$$
$$= \$0.05$$
$$\text{Total unit cost} = \text{Unit materials cost} + \text{Unit conversion cost}$$
$$= \$0.17 + \$0.05$$
$$= \$0.22 \text{ per completed unit}$$

Step 4: Valuation of EWIP and goods transferred out:

The cost of ending work in process is as follows:

Materials: $0.17 × 20,000	$3,400
Conversion: $0.05 × 8,000	400
Total cost	$3,800

Valuation of goods transferred out:

$$\text{Cost of goods transferred out} = \$0.22 \times 60,000 = \$13,200$$

For illustrative purposes, a production report, based on Cornerstone 6-7, is shown in Exhibit 6-4. As the example shows, applying manufacturing inputs at different stages of a process poses no serious problems. However, the effort required has increased.

Multiple Departments

In process manufacturing, some departments receive partially completed goods from prior departments. The usual approach is to treat transferred-in goods as a separate material category when calculating equivalent units. Thus, the department receiving transferred-in goods would have *three* input categories: one for the transferred-in materials, one for materials added, and one for conversion costs.

In dealing with transferred-in goods, two important points should be remembered. First, the cost of this material is the cost of the goods transferred out as computed in the prior department. Second, the units started in the subsequent department correspond to the units transferred out from the prior department (assuming that there is a one-to-one relationship between the output measures of both departments). Cornerstone 6-8 shows how to calculate the first three process-costing steps when there are transferred-in goods, where steps 2 and 3 are restricted to the transferred-in category.

Analytical Q & A

A mixing process produced 200 equivalent units of material and 500 equivalent units of conversion activity during the month. If the materials cost was $400 and the conversion cost was $1,000, what is the cost per equivalent unit for the month?

Answer:

Unit cost = Unit materials cost + Unit conversion cost = ($400/200) + ($1,000/500) = $2 + $2 = $4

Production Report: Weighted Average Method

Healthblend Company
Picking Department
Production Report for September 2007
(Weighted Average Method)

UNIT INFORMATION

Units to account for:		Units accounted for:	
Units in beginning work in process	10,000	Units completed	60,000
Units started during the period	70,000	Units in ending work in process	20,000
Total units to account for	80,000	Total units accounted for	80,000

Equivalent Units

	Materials	Conversion Cost
Units completed	60,000	60,000
Units in ending work in process	20,000	8,000
Total equivalent units	80,000	68,000

COST INFORMATION

	Materials	Conversion Cost	Total
Costs to account for:			
Beginning work in process	$ 1,600	$ 200	$ 1,800
Incurred during the period	12,000	3,200	15,200
Total costs to account for	$13,600	$3,400	$17,000
Cost per equivalent unit	$0.17	$0.05	$0.22

	Transferred Out	Ending Work in Process	Total
Costs accounted for:			
Goods transferred out ($0.22 × 60,000)	$13,200	—	$13,200
Goods in ending work in process:			
Materials ($0.17 × 20,000)	—	$3,400	3,400
Conversion ($0.05 × 8,000)	—	400	400
Total costs accounted for	$13,200	$3,800	$17,000

Cornerstone 6-8

HOW TO Calculate the Physical Flow Schedule, Equivalent Units, and Unit Costs with Transferred-In Goods

Information: For September, Heathblend's encapsulating department had 15,000 units in beginning inventory (with transferred-in costs of $3,000) and completed 70,000 units during the month. Further, the picking department completed and transferred out 60,000 units at a cost of $13,200 in September.

Required:
1. Prepare a physical flow schedule with transferred-in goods.
2. Calculate equivalent units for the transferred-in category.
3. Calculate unit cost for the transferred-in category.

Calculation:
1. In constructing a physical flow schedule for the encapsulating department, its dependence on the picking department must be considered:

Units to account for:	
Units in beginning work in process	15,000
Units transferred in during September	60,000
Total units to account for	75,000
Units accounted for:	
Units completed and transferred out:	
Started and completed	55,000
From beginning work in process	15,000
Units in ending work in process	5,000
Total units accounted for	75,000

2. Equivalent units for the transferred-in category only:

Transferred in:	
Units completed	70,000
Add: Units in ending work in process ×	5,000
Fraction complete (5,000 × 100 percent)*	
Equivalent units of output	75,000

*Remember that the EWIP is 100 percent complete with respect to transferred-in costs, not to all costs of the encapsulating department.

3. To find the unit cost for the transferred-in category, we add the cost of the units transferred in from picking in September to the transferred-in costs in beginning work in process and divide by transferred-in equivalent units:

$$\text{Unit cost (transferred-in category)} = (\$13,200 + \$3,000)/75,000$$
$$= \$16,200/75,000$$
$$= \$0.216$$

The only additional complication introduced in the analysis for a subsequent department is the presence of the transferred-in category. As has just been shown, dealing with this category is similar to handling any other category. However, it must be remembered that the current cost of this special type of raw material is the cost of the units transferred in from the prior process and that the units transferred in are the units started.

Concept Q & A

How are transferred-in goods viewed and treated by the department receiving them?

Answer:
Transferred-in goods are viewed as materials added at the beginning of the process. They are treated as a separate input category, and equivalent units and a unit cost are calculated for transferred-in materials.

It is now possible to see how Makenzie Gibson and Healthblend Nutritional Supplements benefited by installing a formal cost accounting system. Typically, as a business begins and is small, an entrepreneurial owner can track the costs and revenues using his or her own memory and abilities. However, as a business grows, and the number of products and supporting activities increases, an informal tracking system is no longer practical. Procedures for tracking and assigning costs to products must be formalized. Makenzie responded to the consultant's recommendation and installed a process-costing system.

Process-costing systems are specifically designed to support costing out homogeneous products that are mass-produced, exactly the situation faced by Makenzie's company. The herbal and vitamin products pass through sequential processes and receive essentially similar doses of manufacturing inputs from each process. Thus, costs need to be collected by process for a period of time, and output needs to be measured for that same period. Unit costs can then be calculated. Makenzie found that after implementing the recommended system, she was able to compare unit costs with selling prices and, thus, determine which products were profitable. She then dropped some product lines as her competitors had done because the market was no longer willing to pay a price that justified the required manufacturing cost.

SUMMARY OF LEARNING OBJECTIVES

Cost flows under process costing are similar to those under job-order costing. Raw materials are purchased and debited to the raw materials account. Direct materials used in production, direct labor, and applied overhead are charged to the work-in-process account. In a production process with several processes, there is a work-in-process account for each department or process. Goods completed in one department are transferred out to the next department. When units are completed in the final department or process, their cost is credited to Work in Process and debited to Finished Goods.

Equivalent units of production are the complete units that could have been produced given the total amount of manufacturing effort expended during the period. The number of physical units is multiplied by the percentage of completion to calculate equivalent units. Two approaches have evolved for dealing with beginning work-in-process inventory costs. The weighted average costing method combines beginning inventory costs with current-period costs to compute unit costs. The FIFO costing method separates units in beginning inventory from those produced during the current period. The production report summarizes the manufacturing activity occurring in a department for a given period. It discloses information concerning the physical flow of units, equivalent units, unit costs, and the disposition of the manufacturing costs associated with the period.

Nonuniform inputs and multiple departments are easily handled by process-costing methods. When inputs are added nonuniformly, equivalent units and unit cost are calculated for each separate input category. The adjustment for multiple departments is also relatively simple. The goods transferred from a prior department to a subsequent department are treated as a material added at the beginning of the process. Thus, there is a separate transferred-in materials category, where the equivalent units and unit cost are calculated.

The FIFO method separates the cost of beginning work in process from the cost of the current period. The units in beginning Work in Process are assumed to be completed and transferred out first. Costs from BWIP are not pooled with the current-period costs in computing unit cost. Additionally, equivalent units of production exclude work done in the prior period.

Cornerstones for Chapter 6

KEY TERMS

Cost reconciliation, 215
Equivalent units of output, 208
FIFO costing method, 210
Parallel processing, 203
Physical flow schedule, 212
Production report, 206
Sequential processing, 202
Transferred-in costs, 206
Weighted average costing method, 210

APPENDIX: PRODUCTION REPORT—FIFO COSTING

OBJECTIVE 5
Prepare a departmental production report using the FIFO method.

Under the FIFO costing method, the equivalent units and manufacturing costs in beginning work in process are excluded from the current-period unit cost calculation. This method recognizes that the work and costs carried over from the prior period legitimately belong to that period.

Differences between the FIFO and Weighted Average Methods

If changes occur in the prices of the manufacturing inputs from one period to the next, then FIFO produces a more accurate (that is, more current) unit cost than does the weighted average method. A more accurate unit cost means better cost control, better pricing decisions, and so on. Keep in mind that if the period is as short as a week or a month, however, the unit costs calculated under the two methods are not likely to differ much. In that case, the FIFO method has little, if anything, to offer over the weighted average method. Perhaps for this reason, many firms use the weighted average method.

Since FIFO excludes prior-period work and costs, it is necessary to create two categories of completed units. FIFO assumes that units in beginning work in process are completed first, before any new units are started. Thus, one category of completed units is beginning work-in-process units. The second category is for those units started and completed during the current period.

For example, assume that a department had 20,000 units in beginning work in process and completed and transferred out a total of 50,000 units. Of the 50,000 completed units, 20,000 are the units initially found in work in process. The remaining 30,000 were started and completed during the current period.

These two categories of completed units are needed in the FIFO method so that each category can be costed correctly. For the units started and completed, the unit cost is obtained by dividing total current manufacturing costs by the current-period equivalent output. However, for the beginning work-in-process units, the total associated manufacturing costs are the sum of the prior-period costs plus the costs incurred in the current period to finish the units.

Example of the FIFO Method

Cornerstone 6-9 shows how FIFO handles output and cost calculations. The computations of Cornerstone 6-9 are based on the same Healthblend data used for the weighted average method (see Cornerstone 6-4). Using the same data highlights the differences between the two methods. Cornerstone 6-9 shows that the equivalent unit calculation measures only the output for the current period. Cornerstone 6-9 also reveals that costs from the current period and costs carried over from June (beginning inventory costs) are not pooled to calculate July's unit cost. The unit cost calculation uses only July (current-period) costs. The five steps to cost out production follow.

Cornerstone 6-9

HOW TO Calculate Output and Cost Assignments: FIFO Method

Information:

Production:

Units in process, July 1, 75 percent complete	20,000 gallons
Units completed and transferred out	50,000 gallons
Units in process, July 31, 25 percent complete	10,000 gallons

Costs:

Work in process, July 1	$ 3,525
Costs added during July	10,125

Required:

1. Calculate the output measure for July.
2. Assign costs to units transferred out and ending work in process using the FIFO method.

Calculation:

1. Equivalent units:

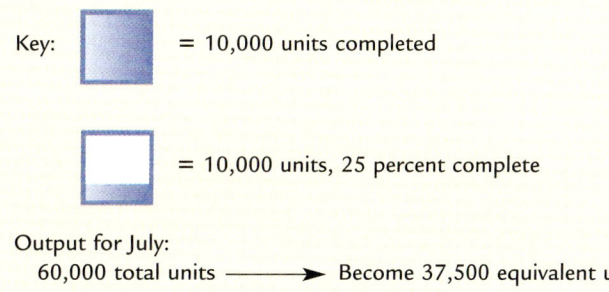

Key: = 10,000 units completed

 = 10,000 units, 25 percent complete

Output for July:
60,000 total units ———→ Become 37,500 equivalent units

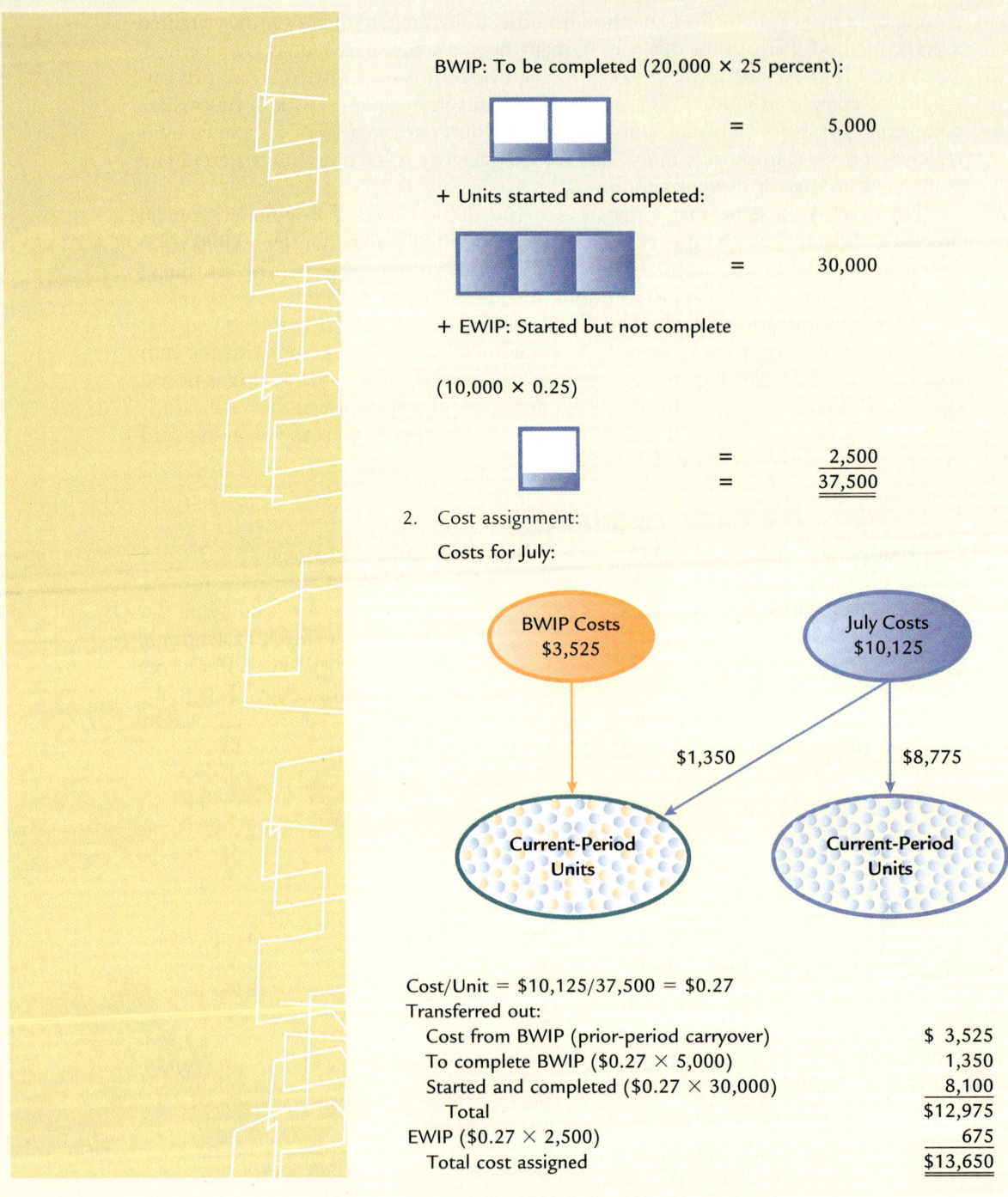

BWIP: To be completed (20,000 × 25 percent):

=   5,000

+ Units started and completed:

=   30,000

+ EWIP: Started but not complete

(10,000 × 0.25)

=   2,500
=   37,500

2. Cost assignment:

Costs for July:

BWIP Costs
$3,525

July Costs
$10,125

$1,350 $8,775

Current-Period
Units

Current-Period
Units

Cost/Unit = $10,125/37,500 = $0.27
Transferred out:
  Cost from BWIP (prior-period carryover) $ 3,525
  To complete BWIP ($0.27 × 5,000)   1,350
  Started and completed ($0.27 × 30,000)   8,100
    Total $12,975
EWIP ($0.27 × 2,500)   675
  Total cost assigned $13,650

Step 1: Physical Flow Analysis

The purpose of step 1 is to trace the physical units of production. As with the weighted average method, in the FIFO method, a physical flow schedule is prepared. This schedule is identical for both methods. (See Cornerstone 6-5 for details on how to prepare this schedule.)

Step 2: Calculation of Equivalent Units

Cornerstone 6-9 illustrates the calculation of equivalent units under the FIFO method and is summarized below without the graphic detail:

Physical Flow Schedule

Units to account for:		
Units in beginning work in process (75 percent complete)		20,000
Units started during the period		40,000
Total units to account for		60,000
Units accounted for:		
Units completed:		
Started and completed	30,000	
From beginning work in process	20,000	50,000
Units in ending work in process (25 percent complete)		10,000
Total units accounted for		60,000

Units started and completed	30,000
Add: Units in beginning work in process × Fraction to be completed (20,000 × 25 percent)	5,000
Add: Units in ending work in process × Fraction complete (10,000 × 25 percent)	2,500
Equivalent units of output	37,500

From the equivalent unit computation, one difference between weighted average and FIFO becomes immediately apparent. Under FIFO, the equivalent units in beginning work in process (work done in the prior period) are not counted as part of the total equivalent work. Only the equivalent work to be completed this period is counted. The equivalent work to be completed for the units from the prior period is computed by multiplying the number of units in beginning work in process by the percentage of work remaining. Since in this example the percentage of work done in the prior period is 75 percent, the percentage left to be completed this period is 25 percent, or an equivalent of 5,000 additional units of work.

The effect of excluding prior-period effort is to produce the current-period equivalent output. Recall that under the weighted average method, 52,500 equivalent units were computed for this month. Under FIFO, only 37,500 units are calculated for the same month. These 37,500 units represent current-period output. The difference, of course, is explained by the fact that the weighted average method rolls back and counts the 15,000 equivalent units of prior-period work (20,000 units BWIP × 75 percent) as belonging to this period.

Analytical Q & A

For August, there are 40,000 units in BWIP, 30 percent complete and 20,000 units in EWIP, 60 percent complete. There were 80,000 units started and completed. How many equivalent units were produced in August, using the FIFO method?

Answer:
Equivalent units = 80,000 + (0.70 × 40,000) + (0.60 × 20,000) = 120,000

Step 3: Computation of Unit Cost

The additional manufacturing costs incurred in the current period are $10,125. Thus, the current-period unit manufacturing cost is $10,125/37,500, or $0.27. Notice that the costs of beginning inventory are excluded from this calculation. Only current-period manufacturing costs are used.

Step 4: Valuation of Inventories

Cornerstone 6-9 shows FIFO values for ending work in process and goods transferred out. Since all equivalent units in ending work in process are current-period units, the cost of ending work in process is simply $0.27 \times 2,500$, or $675, the same value that the weighted average method would produce. However, when it comes to valuing goods transferred out, a significant difference emerges between the weighted average method and FIFO.

Under weighted average, the cost of goods transferred out is simply the unit cost times the units completed. Under FIFO, however, there are two sources of completed units: 20,000 units from beginning inventory and 30,000 units started and completed. The cost of the 30,000 units that were started and completed in the current period and transferred out is $8,100 ($0.27 \times 30,000$). For these units, the use of the current-period unit cost is entirely appropriate. However, the cost of the beginning work-in-process units that were transferred out is another matter. These units started the period with $3,525 of manufacturing costs already incurred and 15,000 units of equivalent output already completed. To finish these units, the equivalent of 5,000 units were needed. The cost of finishing the units in beginning work in process is $1,350 ($0.27 \times 5,000$). Adding this $1,350 to the $3,525 in cost carried over from the prior period gives a total manufacturing cost for these units of $4,875. The unit cost of these 20,000 units, then, is about $0.244 ($4,875/20,000$).

Concept Q & A

The FIFO cost per equivalent unit for July was $12. The beginning work in process had 25,000 units, 20 percent complete, with $50,000 of costs carried over from June. What is the total cost that these 25,000 units will contribute to the cost of goods transferred out?

Answer:
($12 \times 25,000 \times 0.8) + ($50,000) = $290,000.

Step 5: Cost Reconciliation

The total costs assigned to production are as follows:

Goods transferred out:	
Units in beginning work in process	$ 4,875
Units started and completed	8,100
Goods in ending work in process	675
Total costs accounted for	$13,650

The total manufacturing costs to account for during the period are:

Beginning work in process	$ 3,525
Incurred during the period	10,125
Total costs to account for	$13,650

The costs assigned, thus, equal the costs to account for. With the completion of step 5, the production report can be prepared. Cornerstone 6-10 shows how to prepare this report for FIFO.

Cornerstone 6-10

HOW TO Prepare a Production Report: FIFO Method

Information: The five steps for the Healthblend Company.
Required: Prepare a production report for July 2007 (FIFO method).
Calculation:

**Healthblend Company
Picking Department
Production Report for July 2007
(FIFO Method)**

UNIT INFORMATION

Units to account for:

Units in beginning work in process	20,000
Units started during the period	40,000
Total units to account for	60,000

Units accounted for:	Physical Flow	Equivalent Units
Units started and completed	30,000	30,000
Units completed from beginning work in process	20,000	5,000
Units in ending work in process	10,000	2,500
Total units accounted for	60,000	37,500

COST INFORMATION

Costs to account for:

Beginning work in process	$ 3,525
Incurred during the period	10,125
Total costs to account for	$13,650

Cost per equivalent unit	$ 0.27

Costs accounted for:	Transferred Out	Ending Work in Process	Total
Units in beginning work in process:			
From prior period	$ 3,525	—	$ 3,525
From current period ($0.27 × 5,000)	1,350	—	1,350
Units started and completed			
($0.27 × 30,000)	8,100	—	8,100
Goods in ending work in process			
($0.27 × 2,500)	—	$675	675
Total costs accounted for	$12,975	$675	$13,650

APPENDIX SUMMARY

A production report prepared according to the FIFO method separates the cost of beginning work in process from the cost of the current period. BWIP is assumed to be completed and transferred out first. Costs from BWIP are not pooled with the current period costs in computing unit cost. Additionally, equivalent units of production exclude work done in the prior period. When calculating the cost of goods transferred out, the prior period costs are added to the costs of completing the units in beginning work in process and then these costs are added to the costs of units started and completed.

Cornerstones for Appendix to Chapter 6

Cornerstone 6-9   How to calculate output and cost assignments: FIFO method, page 223
Cornerstone 6-10   How to prepare a production report: FIFO method, page 227

DISCUSSION QUESTIONS

1. Distinguish between sequential processing and parallel processing.
2. Describe the differences between process costing and job-order costing.
3. What are equivalent units? Why are they needed in a process-costing system?
4. Under the weighted average method, how are prior-period costs and output treated? How are they treated under the FIFO method?
5. Under what conditions will the weighted average and FIFO methods give the same results?
6. How is the equivalent unit calculation affected when materials are added at the beginning or end of the process rather than uniformly throughout the process?
7. Explain why transferred-in costs are a special type of raw material for the receiving department.
8. What are the similarities in and differences between the manufacturing cost flows for job-order firms and process firms?
9. What journal entry would be made as goods are transferred out from one department to another department? From the final department to the warehouse?
10. Describe the five steps in accounting for the manufacturing activity of a processing department and explain how they interrelate.
11. What is a production report? What purpose does this report serve?
12. In assigning costs to goods transferred out, how do the weighted average and FIFO methods differ?
13. Describe the effect of automation on the process accounting system.
14. How does the adoption of a JIT (just-in-time) approach to manufacturing affect process costing?
15. How would process costing for services differ from process costing for manufactured goods?

MULTIPLE-CHOICE EXERCISES

6-1 Process costing works well whenever

a. heterogeneous products pass through a series of processes and receive similar doses of materials, labor, and overhead.
b. homogeneous products pass through a series of processes and receive similar amounts of materials, labor, and overhead.

c. homogeneous products pass through a series of processes and receive similar doses of conversion inputs and different doses of material inputs.

d. material cost is accumulated by process and conversion cost is accumulated by process.

e. None of the above.

6-2 Operation costing works well whenever

a. heterogeneous products pass through a series of processes and receive similar doses of materials, labor, and overhead.

b. homogeneous products pass through a series of processes and receive similar doses of materials, labor, and overhead.

c. homogeneous products pass through a series of processes and receive similar doses of conversion inputs and different doses of material inputs.

d. material cost is accumulated by process and conversion cost is accumulated by process.

e. None of the above.

6-3 Sequential processing is characterized by

a. a pattern where partially completed units are worked on simultaneously.

b. a pattern where different partially completed units must pass through parallel processes before being brought together in a final process.

c. a pattern where partially completed units must pass through one process before they can be worked on in later processes.

d. a pattern where partially completed units must be purchased from outside suppliers and delivered to the final process in a sequential time mode.

e. None of the above.

6-4 To record the transfer of costs from a prior process to a subsequent process, the following entry would be made:

a. debit Finished Goods and credit Work in Process.

b. debit Work in Process (subsequent department) and credit Transferred-In Materials.

c. debit Work in Process (prior department) and credit Work in Process (subsequent department).

d. debit Work in Process (subsequent department) and credit Conversion Cost Control.

e. None of the above.

6-5 The costs transferred from a prior process to a subsequent process

a. are treated as another type of material cost.

b. are referred to as transferred-in costs (for the receiving department).

c. are referred to as the cost of goods transferred out (for the transferring department).

d. All of the above.

e. None of the above.

6-6 During the month of May, the grinding department produced and transferred out 2,000 units. Ending work in process had 500 units, 60 percent complete. There was no beginning work in process. The equivalent units of output for May are

a. 2,000.

b. 2,500.

c. 2,300.

d. 2,200.

e. None of the above.

Questions 7 through 9 are based on the following information:
The drilling department incurred $24,000 of manufacturing costs during the month of October. The department transferred out 2,000 units and had 400 equivalent units in ending work in process. There was no beginning work in process.

6-7 The unit cost for the month of October is

a. $12.
b. $10.
c. $24.
d. $120.
e. $100.

6-8 The cost of goods transferred out is

a. $20,000.
b. $24,000.
c. $28,800.
d. $18,000.
e. None of the above.

6-9 The cost of ending work in process is

a. $400.
b. $4,800.
c. $4,000.
d. $8,800.
e. None of the above.

6-10 During May, Kimbrell Manufacturing completed and transferred out 100,000 units. In ending work in process, there were 25,000 units, 80 percent complete. Using the weighted average method, the equivalent units are

a. 100,000 units.
b. 125,000 units.
c. 105,000 units.
d. 110,000 units.
e. 120,000 units.

6-11 During June, Kimbrell Manufacturing completed and transferred out 100,000 units. In ending work in process, there were 25,000 units, 40 percent complete. Using the weighted average method, the equivalent units are

a. 100,000 units.
b. 125,000 units.
c. 105,000 units.
d. 110,000 units.
e. 120,000 units.

6-12 For August, Kimbrell Company has costs in beginning work in process equal to $50,000. During August, the cost incurred was $450,000. Using the weighted average method, Kimbrell had 125,000 equivalent units for August. There were 100,000 units transferred out during the month. The cost of goods transferred out is

a. $500,000.
b. $400,000.
c. $450,000.
d. $360,000.
e. $50,000.

6-13 For September, Murphy Company has manufacturing costs in beginning work in process equal to $100,000. During September, the manufacturing costs incurred were $650,000. Using the weighted average method, Murphy had 100,000 equivalent units for September. The equivalent unit cost for September is

a. $1.00.
b. $7.50.
c. $6.50.
d. $6.00.
e. $6.62.

6-14 During June, Faust Manufacturing started and completed 80,000 units. In beginning work in process there were 25,000 units, 60 percent complete. In ending work in process, there were 25,000 units, 40 percent complete. Using FIFO, the equivalent units are

a. 80,000 units.
b. 100,000 units.
c. 90,000 units.
d. 105,000 units.
e. 85,000 units.

6-15 During July, Faust Manufacturing started and completed 80,000 units. In beginning work in process, there were 25,000 units, 20 percent complete. In ending work in process, there were 25,000 units, 80 percent complete. Using FIFO, the equivalent units are

a. 80,000 units.
b. 85,000 units.
c. 65,000 units.
d. 120,000 units.
e. 100,000 units.

6-16 Assume for August that Faust Manufacturing has manufacturing costs equal to $80,000. During August, the cost incurred was $720,000. Using the FIFO method, Faust had 120,000 equivalent units for August. The cost per equivalent unit for August is

a. $6.12.
b. $6.50.
c. $5.60.
d. $6.67.
e. $6.00.

6-17 For August, Lanny Company had 25,000 units in beginning work in process, 40 percent complete, with costs equal to $36,000. During August, the cost incurred was $450,000. Using the FIFO method, Lanny had 125,000 equivalent units for August. There were 100,000 units transferred out during the month. The cost of goods transferred out is

a. $500,000.
b. $400,000.
c. $450,000.
d. $360,000.
e. $50,000.

6-18 When materials are added either at the beginning or the end of the process, a unit cost should be calculated for

a. materials and labor categories.
b. materials category only.
c. materials and conversion categories.
d. conversion category only.
e. labor category only.

6-19 With nonuniform inputs, the cost of ending working in process is calculated by

a. multiplying the unit cost in each input category by the equivalent units of each input found in ending work in process.
b. subtracting the cost of goods transferred out from the total cost of materials.
c. adding the materials cost to the conversion cost.
d. multiplying the total unit cost by the units in ending work in process.
e. None of the above.

6-20 Transferred-in goods are treated by the receiving department as

a. units started for the period.
b. a material added at the beginning of the process.
c. a category of materials separate from conversion costs.
d. All of the above.
e. None of the above.

EXERCISES

Exercise 6-1 *Basic Cost Flows*

Burnham Company produces a metal component for farm tractors. The component is produced in three departments: molding, grinding, and finishing. The following data are available for the month of September:

	Molding Department	Grinding Department	Finishing Department
Direct materials	$15,400	$ 1,900	$1,225
Direct labor	1,150	2,800	1,900
Applied overhead	1,750	13,600	1,900

During September, 1,500 components were completed. There is no beginning or ending work in process in any department.

Required:

1. Prepare a schedule showing, for each department, the cost of direct materials, direct labor, applied overhead, product transferred in from a prior department, and total manufacturing cost.
2. Calculate the unit cost.

Exercise 6-2 *Journal Entries, Basic Cost Flows*

In the month of October, Burnham Company had the following cost flows:

	Molding Department	Grinding Department	Finishing Department
Direct materials	$17,400	$ 2,500	$ 1,800
Direct labor	1,500	2,900	2,400
Applied overhead	1,600	14,600	2,300
Transferred-in cost:			
From molding		20,500	
From grinding			40,500
Total cost	$20,500	$40,500	$47,000

Required:

Prepare the journal entries to transfer costs from (a) molding to grinding, (b) grinding to finishing, and (c) finishing to finished goods.

Exercise 6-3 *Equivalent Units, No BWIP*

The sewing department of a clothing plant had the following data for May:

Units in beginning work in process	—
Units completed	2,500
Units in ending work in process (40 percent complete)	600

Required:

Calculate May's output for the sewing department in equivalent units of production.

Exercise 6-4 *Equivalent Units, Unit Cost, Valuation of Goods Transferred Out and EWIP*

The mixing department had the following data for the month of December:

Units in beginning work in process	—
Units completed	5,850
Units in ending work in process (30 percent complete)	500
Total manufacturing costs	$3,900

Required:

1. What is the output in equivalent units for December?
2. What is the unit manufacturing cost for December?
3. Calculate the cost of goods transferred out for December.
4. Calculate the value of December's ending work in process.

Exercise 6-5 *Weighted Average Method, Equivalent Units*

Lawson Company produces a product where all manufacturing inputs are applied uniformly. The company produced the following physical flow schedule for March:

Units to account for:	
Units in beginning work in process (40 percent complete)	15,000
Units started	35,000
Total units to account for	50,000
Units accounted for:	
Units completed:	
From BWIP	10,000
Started and completed	32,000
	42,000
Units, ending work in process (75 percent complete)	8,000
Total units accounted for	50,000

Required:

Prepare a schedule of equivalent units using the weighted average method.

Exercise 6-6 *Weighted Average Method, Unit Cost, Valuing Inventories*

Loren, Inc., manufactures products that pass through two or more processes. During April, equivalent units were computed using the weighted average method:

Units completed	6,000
Units in ending work in process × Fraction complete:	
4,000 × 60 percent	2,400
Equivalent units of output	8,400

April's costs to account for are as follows:

Beginning work in process (40 percent complete)	$ 1,120
Materials	10,000
Conversion cost	4,000
Total	$15,120

Required:

1. Calculate the unit cost for April using the weighted average method.
2. Using the weighted average method, determine the cost of ending work in process and the cost of the goods transferred out.

Exercise 6-7 *Weighted Average Method, Unit Costs, Valuing Inventories*

Orley, Inc., produces a product that passes through two processes. During February, equivalent units were calculated using the weighted average method:

Units completed	60,000
Add: Units in EWIP × Fraction complete:	
20,000 × 40 percent	8,000
Equivalent units of output (weighted average)	68,000
Less: Units in BWIP × Fraction complete:	
10,000 × 70%	7,000
Equivalent units of output (FIFO)	61,000

The costs that Orley had to account for during the month of February were as follows:

Beginning work in process	$ 42,000
Costs added	397,200
Total	$439,200

Required:

1. Using the weighted average method, calculate unit cost.
2. Under the weighted average method, what is the total cost of units transferred out? What is the cost assigned to units in ending inventory?

Exercise 6-8 *Physical Flow Schedule*

The following information was obtained for the first department of LPZ Company for April:

a. Beginning work in process had 30,500 units, 30 percent complete with respect to manufacturing costs.
b. Ending work in process had 8,400 units, 25 percent complete with respect to manufacturing costs.
c. LPZ started 33,000 units in April.

Required:
Prepare a physical flow schedule.

Exercise 6-9 *Physical Flow, Weighted Average Method*

Nelrok Company manufactures fertilizer. Department 1 mixes the chemicals required for the fertilizer. The following data are for the year:

Beginning work in process	25,000
(40 percent complete)	
Units started	142,500
Units in ending work in process	
(60 percent complete)	35,000

Required:
Prepare a physical flow schedule.

Exercise 6-10 *Production Report, Weighted Average*

Mino, Inc., manufactures chocolate syrup in three departments: cooking, mixing, and bottling. Mino uses the weighted average method. The following are cost and production data for the cooking department for April (assume that units are measured in gallons):

Production:
Units in process, April 1, 60 percent complete	20,000
Units completed and transferred out	50,000
Units in process, April 30, 20 percent complete	10,000

Costs:
Work in process, April 1	$ 93,600
Costs added during April	314,600

Required:
Prepare a production report for the cooking department.

Exercise 6-11 *Nonuniform Inputs, Equivalent Units*

Terry Linens, Inc., manufactures bed and bath linens. The bath linens department sews terry cloth into towels of various sizes. Terry uses the weighted average method. All materials are added at the beginning of the process. The following data are for the bath linens department for August:

Production:
Units in process, August 1, 25 percent complete*	10,000
Units completed and transferred out	60,000
Units in process, August 31, 60 percent complete*	20,000

*With respect to conversion costs.

Required:
Calculate equivalent units of production for the bath linens department for August.

Exercise 6-12 *Unit Cost and Cost Assignment, Nonuniform Inputs*

Millard, Inc., had the following equivalent units schedule and cost for its fabrication department during the month of September:

	Materials	Conversion
Units completed	120,000	120,000
Add: Units in ending WIP ×		
Fraction complete (40,000 × 60%)	40,000	24,000
Equivalent units of output	160,000	144,000
Costs:		
Work in process, September 1:		
Materials	$ 98,000	
Conversion costs	5,250	
Total	$103,250	
Current costs:		
Materials	$702,000	
Conversion costs	157,470	
Total	$859,470	

Required:

1. Calculate the unit cost for materials, for conversion, and in total for the fabrication department for September.
2. Calculate the cost of units transferred out and the cost of ending work in process.

Exercise 6-13 *Nonuniform Inputs, Transferred-In Cost*

Drysdale Dairy produces a variety of dairy products. In Department 12, cream (transferred in from Department 6) and other materials (sugar and flavorings) are mixed and churned to make ice cream. The following data are for Department 12 for August:

Production:

Units in process, August 1, 25 percent complete*	40,000
Units completed and transferred out	120,000
Units in process, August 31, 60 percent complete*	30,000

*With respect to conversion costs.

Required:

1. Prepare a physical flow schedule for the month.
2. Calculate equivalent units for the following categories: transferred-in, materials, and conversion.

Exercise 6-14 *Transferred-In Cost*

Golding's finishing department had the following data for the month of July:

	Transferred-In	Materials	Conversion
Units transferred out	60,000	60,000	60,000
Units in ending WIP	15,000	15,000	9,000
Equivalent units	75,000	75,000	69,000

Costs:

Work in process, July 1:	
Transferred-in from fabricating	$ 2,100
Materials	1,500
Conversion costs	3,000
Total	$ 6,600
Current costs:	
Transferred-in from fabricating	$30,900
Materials	22,500
Conversion costs	45,300
Total	$98,700

Required:

1. Calculate unit costs for the following categories: transferred-in, materials, and conversion.
2. Calculate total unit cost.

Exercise 6-15 *(Appendix) FIFO Method, Equivalent Units*

Lawson Company produces a product where all manufacturing inputs are applied uniformly. The company produced the following physical flow schedule for March:

Units to account for:	
Units in beginning work in process (40 percent complete)	15,000
Units started	35,000
Total units to account for	50,000

Units accounted for:	
Units completed:	
From BWIP	10,000
Started and completed	32,000
	42,000
Units, ending work in process (75 percent complete)	8,000
Total units accounted for	50,000

Required:

Prepare a schedule of equivalent units using the FIFO method.

Exercise 6-16 *(Appendix) FIFO Method, Unit Cost, Valuing Inventories*

Loren, Inc., manufactures products that pass through two or more processes. During April, equivalent units were computed using the FIFO method:

Units started and completed	4,600
Units in BWIP × Fraction to complete (60 percent)	840
Units in ending work in process × Fraction complete:	
4,000 × 60 percent	2,400
Equivalent units of output (FIFO)	7,840
April's costs to account for are as follows:	
Beginning work in process (40 percent complete)	$ 1,120
Materials	10,000
Conversion cost	4,000
Total	$15,120

Required:

1. Calculate the unit cost for April using the FIFO method.
2. Using the FIFO method, determine the cost of ending work in process and the cost of the goods transferred out.

PROBLEMS

(Note: Whenever you see a  next to a requirement, it signals a "building on a cornerstone" requirement. Assigning this requirement will usually entail additional work, such as a group project, analytical reasoning, Internet research, decision making, and the use of written communication skills.)

Problem 6-1 *Basic Flows, Equivalent Units*

Lapp Company produces a pain medication that passes through two departments: mixing and tableting. Lapp uses the weighted average method. Data for November for mixing is as follows: beginning work in process was zero; ending work in process had 600 units, 50 percent complete; and 7,000 units were started.

Tableting's data for November is as follows: beginning work in process was 400 units, 20 percent complete; and 200 units were in ending work in process, 40 percent complete.

Required:

1. For mixing, calculate the following:
   a. Number of units transferred to tableting.
   b. Equivalent units of production.
2. For tableting, calculate the number of units transferred out to Finished Goods.

(continued)

3. Suppose that the units in the mixing department are measured in ounces, while the units in tableting are measured in bottles of 100 tablets, with a total weight of eight ounces (excluding the bottle). Decide how you would treat units that are measured differently and then repeat Requirement 2 using this approach.

Problem 6-2 *Steps in Preparing a Cost of Production Report*

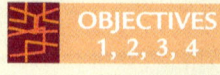

Stillwater Designs is expanding its market by becoming an original equipment supplier to DaimlerChrysler. DaimlerChrysler will offer a higher-end Kicker audio package for its Dodge Neon SRT4 line. As part of this effort, Stillwater Designs will produce the plastic cabinet prototypes that will house the Kicker speakers and amplifiers. After producing the prototype cabinets, their production will be outsourced. However, assembly will remain in-house. Stillwater Designs will assemble the product by placing the speakers and amplifiers (produced according to specifications by outside manufacturers) in the plastic cabinets. Plastic cabinets and Kicker speaker and amplifier components are added at the beginning of the assembly process.

Assume that Stillwater Designs uses the weighted average method to cost out the audio package. The following are cost and production data for the assembly process for April:

Production:	
Units in process, April 1, 60 percent complete	40,000
Units completed and transferred out	100,000
Units in process, April 30, 20 percent complete	20,000
Costs:	
Work in process, April 1:	
Plastic cabinets	$ 800,000
Kicker components	8,400,000
Conversion costs	3,600,000
Costs added during April:	
Plastic cabinets	$ 1,600,000
Kicker components	16,800,000
Conversion costs	5,760,000

Required:

1. Prepare a physical flow analysis for the assembly department for the month of April.
2. Calculate equivalent units of production for the assembly department for the month of April.
3. Calculate unit cost for the assembly department for the month of April.
4. Calculate the cost of units transferred out and the cost of ending work-in-process inventory.
5. Prepare a cost reconciliation for the assembly department for the month of April.

Problem 6-3 *Steps for a Cost of Production Report*

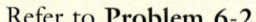

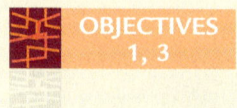

Refer to **Problem 6-2**.

Required:

1. Prepare a cost of production report for the assembly department for the month of April.
2. Write a one-page report that compares the purpose and content of the cost of production report with the job-order cost sheet.

Problem 6-4 *Equivalent Units, Unit Cost, Weighted Average*

Fino Linens, Inc., manufactures bed and bath linens. The bath linens department sews terry cloth into towels of various sizes. Fino uses the weighted average method. All materials are added at the beginning of the process. The following data are for the bath linens department for August:

Production:	
Units in process, August 1, 60 percent complete	20,000
Units completed and transferred out	60,000
Units in process, August 31, 60 percent complete	20,000
Costs:	
Work in process, August 1	$11,520
Current costs	72,000
Total	$83,520

Required:

1. Prepare a physical flow analysis for the bath linens department for August.
2. Calculate equivalent units of production for the bath linens department for August.
3. Calculate the unit cost for the bath linens department for August.
4. Show that the cost per unit calculated in Requirement 3 is a weighted average of the cost per equivalent unit in beginning work in process and the current (FIFO) cost per equivalent unit. (*Hint:* The weights are in proportion to the number of units from each source.)

Problem 6-5 *Cost of Production Report*

Refer to **Problem 6-4**.

Required:

Prepare a cost of production report for the bath linens department for August using the weighted average method.

Problem 6-6 *Weighted Average Method, Physical Flow, Equivalent Units, Unit Costs, Cost Assignment*

Yomasca, Inc., manufactures various Halloween masks. Each mask is shaped from a piece of rubber in the molding department. The masks are then transferred to the finishing department where they are painted and have elastic bands attached. Yomasca uses the weighted average method. In April, the molding department reported the following data:

a. Beginning work in process consisted of 6,000 units, 20 percent complete. Cost in beginning inventory totaled $552.
b. Costs added to production during the month were $8,698.
c. At the end of the month, 18,000 units were transferred out to finishing. Then 2,000 units remained in ending work in process, 25 percent complete.

Required:

1. Prepare a physical flow schedule.
2. Calculate equivalent units of production.
3. Compute unit cost.
4. Calculate the cost of goods transferred to finishing at the end of the month. Calculate the cost of ending inventory.
5. Assume that at the end of the molding process, the masks are inspected. Of the 18,000 units inspected, 1,000 are rejected as faulty and discarded. Thus, only 17,000 units are transferred to the finishing department. The manager of

Yomasca considers all such spoilage as abnormal and does not want to assign any of this cost to the 17,000 good units produced and transferred to finishing. Your task is to determine the cost of this spoilage of 1,000 units and then discuss how you would account for this spoilage cost. Now suppose that the manager feels that this spoilage cost is just part of the cost of producing the good units transferred out. Therefore, he wants to assign this cost to the good production. Explain how this would be handled. (*Hint:* Spoiled units are a type of output, and equivalent units of spoilage can be calculated.)

Problem 6-7 *Weighted Average Method, Single-Department Analysis*

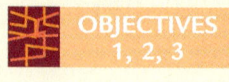

Jbooth Company produces a product that passes through an assembly process and a finishing process. All manufacturing costs are added uniformly for both processes. The following information was obtained for the assembly department for March:

a. Work in process, March 1, had 48,000 units (60 percent completed) and the following costs:

Direct materials	$186,256
Direct labor	64,864
Overhead applied	34,400

b. During March, 138,400 units were completed and transferred to the finishing department, and the following costs were added to production:

Direct materials	$267,880
Direct labor	281,280
Overhead applied	117,144

c. On March 31, there were 21,600 partially completed units in process. These units were 70 percent complete.

Required:

Prepare a production report for the assembly department for March using the weighted average method of costing. The report should disclose the physical flow of units, equivalent units, and unit costs and should track the disposition of manufacturing costs.

Problem 6-8 *(Appendix) FIFO Method, Single-Department Analysis, One Cost Category*

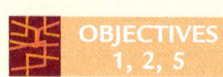

Refer to the data in **Problem 6-7**.

Spreadsheet

Required:

Prepare a production report for the assembly department for March using the FIFO method of costing. The report should contain the same schedules described in **Problem 6-7**. (*Hint:* Carry the unit cost computation to four decimal places.)

Problem 6-9 *Weighted Average Method, Separate Materials Cost*

Tyrone Company produces a variety of stationery products. One product, sealing wax sticks, passes through two processes: blending and molding. The weighted average method is used to account for the costs of production. After blending, the resulting product is sent to the molding department, where it is poured into molds and cooled. The following information relates to the blending process for August:

a. Work in process, August 1, had 20,000 pounds, 20 percent complete. Costs associated with partially completed units were:

Materials	$220,000
Direct labor	30,000
Overhead applied	10,000

b. Work in process, August 31, had **30,000** pounds, 70 percent complete.
c. Units completed and transferred out totaled 500,000 pounds. Costs added during the month were (all inputs are added uniformly):

Materials	$5,610,000
Direct labor	3,877,500
Overhead applied	1,292,500

Required:

1. Prepare (a) a physical flow schedule and (b) an equivalent unit schedule.
2. Calculate the unit cost.
3. Compute the cost of ending work in process and the cost of goods transferred out.
4. Prepare a cost reconciliation.
5. Suppose that the materials added uniformly in blending are paraffin and pigment and that the manager of the company wants to know how much each of these materials costs per equivalent unit produced. The costs of the materials in beginning work in process are as follows:

Paraffin	$120,000
Pigment	100,000

The costs of the materials added during the month are also given:

Paraffin	$3,060,000
Pigment	2,550,000

Prepare an equivalent unit schedule with cost categories for each material. Calculate the cost per unit for each type of material.

Problem 6-10 *Weighted Average Method, Journal Entries*

OBJECTIVES
1, 2, 3, 4

Seacrest Company uses a process-costing system. The company manufactures a product that is processed in two departments, A and B. As work is completed, it is transferred out. The following summarizes the production activity and costs for November:

	Department A	Department B
Beginning inventories:		
Physical units	5,000	8,000
Costs:		
Transferred in	—	$45,320
Direct materials	$10,000	—
Conversion costs	$6,900	$16,800
Current production:		
Units started	25,000	?
Units transferred out	28,000	33,000
Costs:		
Transferred in	—	?
Direct materials	$57,800	$37,950
Conversion costs	$95,220	$128,100
Percentage completion:		
Beginning inventory	40%	50%
Ending inventory	80%	50%

Required:

1. Using the weighted average method, prepare the following for Department A:
    a. A physical flow schedule.
    b. An equivalent unit calculation.
    c. Calculation of unit costs.
    d. Cost of ending work in process and cost of goods transferred out.
    e. A cost reconciliation.

2. Prepare journal entries that show the flow of manufacturing costs for Department A. Use a conversion cost control account for conversion costs. Many firms are now combining direct labor and overhead costs into one category. They are not tracking direct labor separately. Offer some reasons for this practice.

Problem 6-11 *(Appendix) FIFO Method, Journal Entries*

Refer to the data in **Problem 6-10**.

Required:

Repeat the requirements in **Problem 6-10** using the FIFO method.

Problem 6-12 *Weighted Average Method, Nonuniform Inputs, Multiple Departments*

Benson Pharmaceuticals uses a process-costing system to compute the unit costs of the over-the-counter cold remedies that it produces. It has three departments: picking, encapsulating, and bottling. In picking, the ingredients for the cold capsules are measured, sifted, and blended. The mix is transferred out in gallon containers. The encapsulating department takes the powdered mix and places it in capsules. One gallon of powdered mix converts into 1,500 capsules. After the capsules are filled and polished, they are transferred to bottling where they are placed in bottles, which are then affixed with a safety seal, lid, and label. Each bottle receives 50 capsules.

During March, the following results are available for the first two departments:

	Picking	Encapsulating
Beginning inventories:		
Physical units	10 gallons	4,000
Costs:		
Materials	$252	$32
Labor	$282	$20
Overhead	?	?
Transferred in	—	$140
Current production:		
Transferred out	140 gallons	208,000
Ending inventory	20 gallons	6,000
Costs:		
Materials	$3,636	$1,573
Transferred in	—	?
Labor	$4,618	$1,944
Overhead	?	?
Percentage of completion:		
Beginning inventory	40%	50%
Ending inventory	50%	40%

Overhead in both departments is applied as a percentage of direct labor costs. In the picking department, overhead is 200 percent of direct labor. In the encapsulating department, the overhead rate is 150 percent of direct labor.

Required:

1. Prepare a production report for the picking department using the weighted average method. Follow the five steps outlined in the chapter.
2. Prepare a production report for the encapsulating department using the weighted average method. Follow the five steps outlined in the chapter.
3. Explain why the weighted average method is easier to use than FIFO. Explain when weighted average will give about the same results as FIFO.

Problem 6-13 *(Appendix) FIFO Method*

Refer to the data in **Problem 6-12**.

Required:

Prepare a production report for each department using the FIFO method. (*Hint:* For the second department, you must convert gallons to capsules.)

Problem 6-14 *Production Report, Ethical Behavior*

Consider the following conversation between Gary Means, manager of a division that produces industrial machinery, and his controller, Donna Simpson, a CMA and CPA:

Gary: Donna, we have a real problem. Our operating cash is too low, and we are in desperate need of a loan. As you know, our financial position is marginal, and we need to show as much income as possible—and our assets need bolstering as well.

Donna: I understand the problem, but I don't see what can be done at this point. This is the last week of the fiscal year, and it looks like we'll report income just slightly above break-even.

Gary: I know all this. What we need is some creative accounting. I have an idea that might help us, and I wanted to see if you would go along with it. We have 200 partially finished machines in process, about 20 percent complete. That compares with the 1,000 units that we completed and sold during the year. When you computed the per-unit cost, you used 1,040 equivalent units, giving us a manufacturing cost of $1,500 per unit. That per-unit cost gives us cost of goods sold equal to $1.5 million and ending work in process worth $60,000. The presence of the work in process gives us a chance to improve our financial position. If we report the units in work in process as 80 percent complete, this will increase our equivalent units to 1,160. This, in turn, will decrease our unit cost to about $1,345 and cost of goods sold to $1.345 million. The value of our work in process will increase to $215,200. With those financial stats, the loan would be a cinch.

Donna: Gary, I don't know. What you're suggesting is risky. It wouldn't take much auditing skill to catch this one.

Gary: You don't have to worry about that. The auditors won't be here for at least six to eight more weeks. By that time, we can have those partially completed units completed and sold. I can bury the labor cost by having some of our more loyal workers work overtime for some bonuses. The overtime will never be reported. And, as you know, bonuses come out of the corporate budget and are assigned to overhead—next year's overhead. Donna, this will work. If we look good and get the loan to boot, corporate headquarters will treat us well. If we don't do this, we could lose our jobs.

Required:

1. Should Donna agree to Gary's proposal? Why or why not? To assist in deciding, review the corporate code of ethics standards described in Chapter 1. Do any apply?
2. Assume that Donna refuses to cooperate and that Gary accepts this decision and drops the matter. Does Donna have any obligation to report the divisional manager's behavior to a superior? Explain.
3. Assume that Donna refuses to cooperate; however, Gary insists that the changes be made. Now what should she do? What would you do?
4. Suppose that Donna is age 63 and that the prospects for employment elsewhere are bleak. Assume again that Gary insists that the changes be made. Donna also knows that his supervisor, the owner of the company, is his father-in-law. Under these circumstances, would your recommendations for Donna differ? If you were Donna, what would you do?

ACTIVITY-BASED COSTING AND MANAGEMENT

© DIGITAL VISION/GETTY IMAGES

After studying Chapter 7, you should be able to:

1. Explain why functional-based costing approaches may produce distorted costs.
2. Explain how an activity-based costing system works for product costing.
3. Describe activity-based customer and supplier costing.
4. Explain how activity-based management can be used for cost reduction.
5. (Appendix) Explain the basics of quality cost management.
6. (Appendix) Explain the basics of environmental cost management.

Russell Gumbrecht, president of Rio Novo Corporation, a Brazilian manufacturer of refrigerators, freezers, dishwashers, and washing machines, had just returned from a seminar on product costing and continuous improvement, excited and encouraged by what he had heard. He had attended the meeting for ideas on how to improve the company's competitive position given the recent sales explosion in appliances being experienced by Brazil. He immediately called a meeting with Carlos Lacerda, the company's controller and financial vice president.

Russell: I am convinced that we can become more competitive by carefully reviewing the mix of products and customers that we are emphasizing and by reducing costs by managing our activities. I am concerned that our current costing method is giving us the wrong information about the profitability of our various products. Something needs to be done given the pressure on our profit margins because of increased competition.

Carlos: I agree that we need to do something. I also agree that our current costing approach is deficient. I just completed a pilot study relating to activity-based costing in one of our large plants. Thirty to 40 percent of our cost allocations using direct labor hours did not correlate with the cost and profitability of the products. Products reported as very profitable were in an exact opposite state. It seems that many of our low-volume products that require complex manufacturing procedures are actually losing money while the high-volume and less-complex products are actually earning a high margin. This is just the opposite message of our direct labor-based allocation cost system. According to the pilot study, 20 percent of the products are producing 80 percent of the profits.

Russell: This is exactly the message of the seminar. I am pleased that we have a head start. I would like you to implement this ABC system throughout the company, and let's get the information that we need to determine what products we should be producing and emphasizing. Out product mix may need to change. I also understand that ABC can be used to help us identify the best customer mix. Finally, I want to analyze the activities that we are doing. I would bet that some are unnecessary and can be eventually eliminated.

Carlos: I agree. We not only need to worry about accuracy in assigning costs, but we need to reduce costs by eliminating waste.

Russell: Exactly. If we expect to improve our profitability and remain competitive, we need to know what our product costs are and how to take measures to reduce those costs so that our prices can be lowered. Lower prices will help us capture more market share and increase our profitability.

LIMITATIONS OF FUNCTIONAL-BASED COST ACCOUNTING SYSTEMS

Plantwide and departmental rates based on direct labor hours, machine hours, or other volume-based measures have been used for decades to assign overhead costs to products and continue to be used successfully by many organizations. However, for many settings, such as that of Rio Novo, this approach to costing is equivalent to an averaging approach and may produce distorted costs. Distorted costs can be a real problem in extremely competitive environments like the one Rio Novo was facing in Brazil. To understand why average costing can cause difficulties, consider the case where two individuals go out for dinner. One orders steak and lobster, costing $40, and the other orders a chef salad, costing $10. Thus, the total cost of the food is $50. If the bill is split evenly between the two, each would pay $25. The $25 would be the average cost of the meals, but it doesn't represent well the actual cost of each individual's meal. One meal is overstated by $15 and the other is understated by $15. If it is important to know the meal cost for each individual (for example, the one ordering steak and lobster can be reimbursed by his company), then the averaging approach will not be suitable.

> **OBJECTIVE 1**
>
> Explain why functional-based costing approaches may produce distorted costs.

In the same way, plantwide and departmental rates can produce average costs that severely under- or overstate individual product costs. Product cost distortions can be damaging, particularly for those firms characterized by intense or increasing competitive pressures (often on a worldwide level), continuous improvement, total quality management, total customer satisfaction, and sophisticated technology. As firms operating in this competitive environment adopt new strategies to achieve competitive excellence, their cost accounting systems often must change to keep pace. Specifically, the need for more accurate product costs has forced many companies to take a serious look at their costing procedures. At least two major factors impair the ability of unit-based plantwide and departmental rates to assign overhead costs accurately: (1) the proportion of non-unit-related overhead costs to total overhead costs is large, and (2) the degree of product diversity is great.

Non-Unit-Related Overhead Costs

The use of either plantwide rates or departmental rates assumes that a product's consumption of overhead resources is related strictly to the units produced. For **unit-level activities**, activities that are performed each time a unit is produced, this assumption makes sense. But what if there are *non-unit-level activities*—activities that are not performed each time a unit of product is produced? Consider, for example, two activities: setting up equipment and reengineering products. Often, the same equipment is used to produce different products. Setting up equipment is simply preparing it for the particular type of product being made. For example, a vat may be used to dye tee shirts. After completing a batch of 1,000 red tee shirts, the vat must be carefully cleaned before a batch of 3,000 green tee shirts is produced. Thus, setup costs are incurred each time a batch of products is produced. A batch may consist of 1,000 or 3,000 units, and the cost of setup is the same. Yet, as more setups are done, setup costs increase. The number of setups, not the number of units produced, is a much better measure of the consumption of the setup activity. At times, based on customer feedback, firms face the necessity of redesigning their products. This product reengineering activity is authorized by a document called an engineering work order. For example, Rio Novo, the Brazilian appliance manufacturer, may issue engineering work orders to correct design flaws of their refrigerators, freezers, and washers. Product reengineering costs may depend on the number of different engineering work orders rather than the units produced of any given product. Thus, *non-unit-level drivers* such as setups and engineering orders are needed for accurate

Concept Q & A

One department inspects every product produced. A second department inspects a small sample of every batch of products produced. Which inspection activity is unit-level, and which is non-unit-level?

Answer:

A unit-level activity is performed each time a unit is produced, whereas a non-unit-level activity is performed at times that do not correspond to individual unit production. Thus, inspection is unit-level for the first department and non-unit-level for the second department.

cost assignment of non-unit-level activities. **Non-unit-level activity drivers** are factors that measure the consumption of non-unit-level activities by products and other cost objects, whereas **unit-level activity drivers** measure the consumption of unit-level activities. **Activity drivers**, then, are factors that measure the consumption of activities by products and other cost objects and can be classified as either *unit-level* or *non-unit-level*.

Using only unit-based activity drivers to assign non-unit-related overhead costs can create distorted product costs. The severity of this distortion depends on what proportion of total overhead costs these non-unit-based costs represent. For many companies, this percentage can be significant. This suggests that some care should be exercised in assigning non-unit-based overhead costs. If non-unit-based overhead costs are only a small percentage of total overhead costs, then the distortion of product costs would be quite small. In such a case, using unit-based activity drivers to assign overhead costs would be acceptable.

Product Diversity

The presence of significant nonunit overhead costs is a necessary but not sufficient condition for plantwide and departmental rate failure. For example, if products consume the non-unit-level overhead activities in the same proportion as the unit-level overhead activities, then no product-costing distortion will occur (with the use of traditional overhead assignment methods). The presence of product diversity is also necessary. **Product diversity** simply means that products consume overhead activities in systematically different proportions. Products might consume overhead in different proportions for several reasons. For example, differences in product size, product complexity, setup time, and size of batches all can cause products to consume overhead at different rates. Regardless of the nature of the product diversity, product cost will be distorted whenever the quantity of unit-based overhead that a product consumes does not vary in direct proportion to the quantity consumed of non-unit-based overhead. The proportion of each activity consumed by a product is defined as the **consumption ratio**. How non-unit-level overhead costs and product diversity can produce distorted product costs is best illustrated with an example.

An Example Illustrating the Failure of Unit-Based Overhead Rates

To illustrate how traditional unit-based overhead rates can distort product costs, we will provide detailed information for Rio Novo's Porto Belho plant. The Porto Belho plant produces two models of washers: a deluxe and a regular model. The detailed data are provided in Exhibit 7-1 (assume that the measures are expected and actual outcomes). Because the quantity of regular models produced is 10 times greater than that of the deluxe, we can label the regular model a high-volume product and the deluxe model a low-volume product. The models are produced in batches.

For simplicity, only four types of overhead activities, performed by four distinct support departments, are assumed: setting up the equipment for each batch (different configurations are needed for the electronic components associated with each model), moving a batch, machining, and assembly. Assembly is performed after each department's operations.

Problems with Costing Accuracy

The activity usage data in Exhibit 7-1 reveal some serious problems with either plantwide or departmental rates for assigning overhead costs. The main problem with either procedure is the assumption that unit-level drivers such as machine hours or direct labor hours drive or cause all overhead costs.

From Exhibit 7-1, it be seen that regular models, the high-volume product, use four times as many direct labor hours as deluxe models, the low-volume product (80 hours versus 20 hours). Thus, if a plantwide rate is used, the regular models will be assigned four times more overhead cost than the deluxe models. But is this reasonable? Do unit-based drivers explain the consumption of all overhead activities? In particular, is it reasonable to assume that each product's consumption of overhead increases in direct proportion to the direct labor hours used? Now consider the four overhead activities to see if the unit-level drivers accurately reflect the demands of regular and deluxe model production.

Examination of the data in Exhibit 7-1 suggests that a significant portion of overhead costs is not driven or caused by direct labor hours. For example, each product's demands for setup and material-moving activities are more logically related to the setup hours and the number of moves, respectively. These nonunit activities represent 50 percent ($2,000/$4,000) of the total overhead costs—a significant percentage. Notice that the low-volume product, deluxe models, uses three times more setup hours than the regular models (3/1) and one and a half as many moves (6/4). However, using a plantwide rate based on direct labor hours, a unit-based activity driver, assigns four times more setup and material-moving costs to the regular models than to the deluxe. Thus, product diversity exists, and we should expect product cost distortion because

7-1

EXHIBIT

Product-Costing Data

Activity Usage Measures	Deluxe	Regular	Total
Units produced	10	100	110
Prime costs	$800	$8,000	$8,800
Direct labor hours	20	80	100
Machine hours	10	40	50
Setup hours	3	1	4
Number of moves	6	4	10

Activity Cost Data (Overhead Activities)	
Activity	Activity Cost
Setting up equipment	$1,200
Moving goods	800
Machining	1,500
Assembly	500
Total	$4,000

the quantity of unit-based overhead that each product consumes does not vary in direct proportion to the quantity consumed of non-unit-based overhead.

How to calculate the consumption ratios for the two products is illustrated in Cornerstone 7-1. Consumption ratios are simply the proportion of each activity consumed by a product. The consumption ratios suggest that a plantwide rate based on direct labor hours will overcost the regular models and undercost the deluxe models.

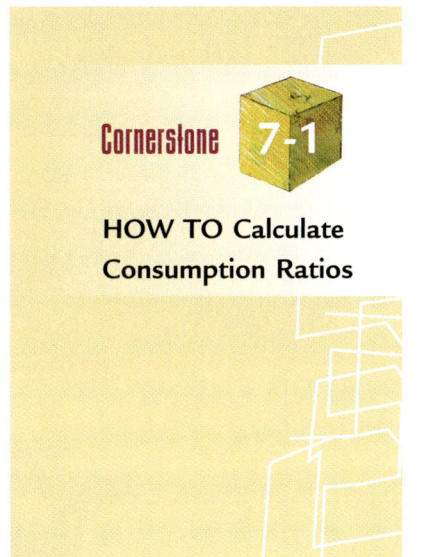

Cornerstone 7-1

HOW TO Calculate Consumption Ratios

Information: Activity usage information, Exhibit 7-1.
Required: Calculate the consumption ratios for each product.
Calculation: First, we must identify the activity driver for each activity. Next, divide the amount of driver used for each product by the total driver quantity. We obtain the following:

	Consumption Ratios		
Overhead Activity	Deluxe Model	Regular Model	Activity Driver
Setting up equipment	0.75[a]	0.25[a]	Setup hours
Moving goods	0.60[b]	0.40[b]	Number of moves
Machining	0.20[c]	0.80[c]	Machine hours
Assembly	0.20[d]	0.80[d]	Direct labor hours

[a] 3/4 (deluxe) and 1/4 (regular).
[b] 6/10 (deluxe) and 4/10 (regular).
[c] 10/50 (deluxe) and 40/50 (regular).
[d] 20/100 (deluxe) and 80/100 (regular).

Analytical Q & A

The activity driver for the receiving activity is number of orders processed. Product A uses 10 orders, and Product B uses 30 orders. Calculate the consumption ratios for Product A and Product B.

Answer:
Product A = 10/40 = 0.25; Product B = 30/40 = 0.75.

Solving the Problem of Cost Distortion

The cost distortion just described can be solved by the use of activity rates. That is, rather than assigning the overhead costs using a single, plantwide rate, why not calculate a rate for each overhead activity and then use this activity rate to assign overhead costs? How to calculate these rates is shown in Cornerstone 7-2.

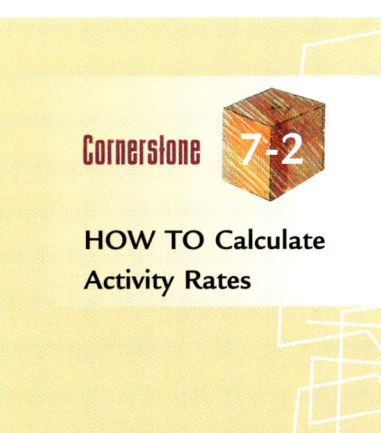

Cornerstone 7-2

HOW TO Calculate Activity Rates

Information: (from Exhibit 7-1)

Activity	Activity Cost	Driver	Driver Quantity
Setting up equipment	$1,200	Setup hours	4
Moving goods	800	Number of moves	10
Machining	1,500	Machine hours	50
Assembly	500	Direct labor hours	100

Required: Calculate activity rates.

Calculation: The rates are obtained by dividing the activity cost by the total driver quantity:

Setup rate	$1,200/4 setup hours = $300 per setup hour
Materials handling rate	$800/10 moves = $80 per move
Machining rate	$1,500/50 machine hours = $30 per machine hour
Assembly rate	$500/100 direct labor hours = $5.00 per direct labor hour

To assign overhead costs, the amount of activity consumed by each product is needed along with the activity rates. How to calculate the unit cost for each product using activity rates is given in Cornerstone 7-3. A visual summary is provided in Exhibit 7-2.

Analytical Q & A

Inspecting provides 4,000 inspection hours and costs $80,000 per year. What is the activity rate for inspecting?

Answer:
Rate = $80,000/4,000 inspection hours = $20 per inspection hour.

7-2

EXHIBIT

Visual Summary of Cornerstones 7-2 and 7-3

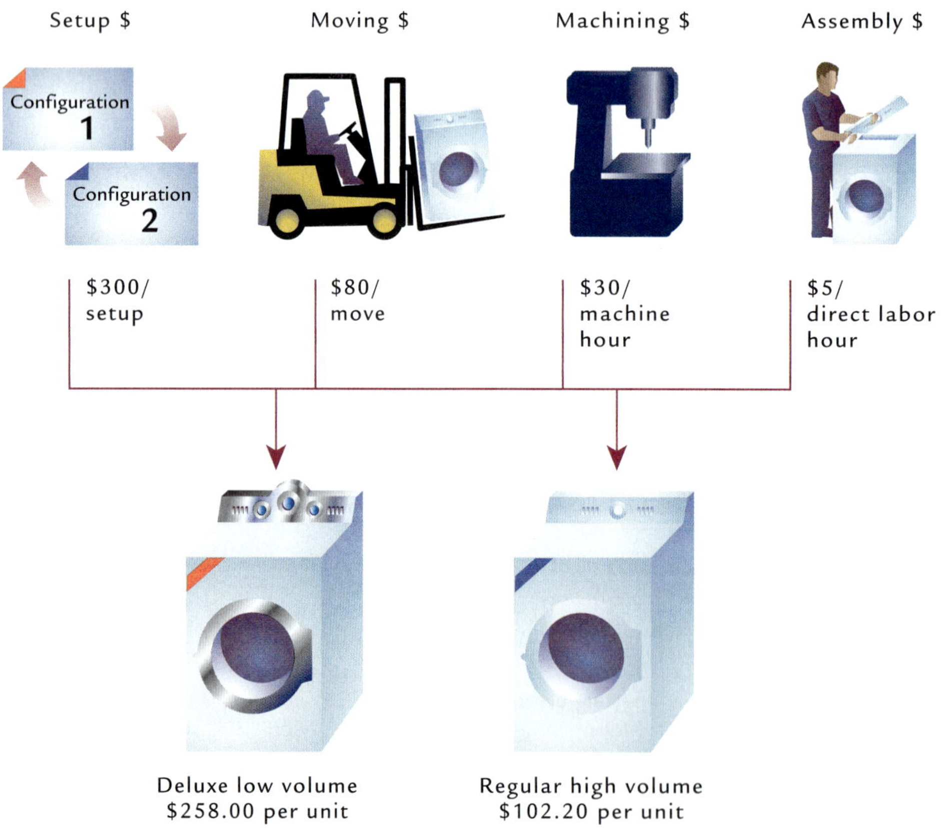

Setup $	Moving $	Machining $	Assembly $

Configuration 1 → Configuration 2

$300/ setup	$80/ move	$30/ machine hour	$5/ direct labor hour

Deluxe low volume
$258.00 per unit

Regular high volume
$102.20 per unit

Cornerstone 7-3

HOW TO Calculate Activity-Based Unit Costs

Information:

	Deluxe	Regular	Activity Rate
Units produced per year	10	100	
Prime costs	$800	$8,000	
Setup hours	3	1	$300.00
Number of moves	6	4	80.00
Machine hours	10	40	30.00
Direct labor hours	20	80	5.00

Required: Calculate the unit cost for deluxe and regular models.

Calculation:

	Deluxe	Regular
Prime costs	$ 800	$ 8,000
Overhead costs:		
Setups:		
$300 × 3	900	
$300 × 1		300
Moving materials:		
$80 × 6	480	
$80 × 4		320
Machining:		
$30 × 10	300	
$30 × 40		1,200
Assembly:		
$5 × 20	100	
$5 × 80		400
Total manufacturing costs	$2,580	$10,220
Units produced	÷ 10	÷ 100
Unit cost (Total costs/Units)	$ 258	$102.20

Comparison of Functional-Based and Activity-Based Product Costs

A plantwide rate based on direct labor hours is calculated by dividing the total overhead costs by the total direct labor hours: $4,000/100 = $40 per direct labor hour. The product cost for each product using this single unit-level overhead rate is calculated as follows:

	Deluxe	Regular
Prime costs	$ 800	$ 8,000
Overhead costs:		
$40 × 20	800	
$40 × 80		3,200
Total cost	$ 1,600	$11,200
Units produced	÷ 10	÷ 100
Unit cost	$160.00	$112.00

Now compare these product costs with the ABC cost of Cornerstone 7-3. This comparison clearly illustrates the effects of using only unit-based activity drivers to assign overhead costs. The activity-based cost assignment reflects the pattern of overhead consumption and is, therefore, the most accurate. Activity-based product costing reveals that functional-based costing under-costs the deluxe models and overcosts the regular models. In fact, the ABC assignment increase the cost of the deluxe models by $98 per unit and decreases the cost of the regular models by almost $10 per unit—a movement in the right direction given the pattern of overhead consumption. In a diverse product environment, ABC promises greater accuracy, and given the importance of making decisions based on correct facts, a detailed look at ABC is certainly merited.

Analytical Q & A

Producing 5,000 units of a DVD player requires $150,000 of prime costs, uses 1,000 machine hours, and takes 600 setup hours. The activity rates are $20 per machine hour and $50 per setup hour. What is the unit cost of a DVD player?

Answer:
Unit cost = [$150,000 + ($20 × 1,000) + ($50 × 600)]/5,000 = $40.

ACTIVITY-BASED PRODUCT COSTING: DETAILED DESCRIPTION

Functional-based overhead costing involves two major stages: first, overhead costs are assigned to an organizational unit (plant or department), and second, overhead costs are then assigned to products. As Exhibit 7-3 illustrates, an **activity-based costing (ABC) system** first traces costs to activities and then to products. The underlying assumption is that activities consume resources, and products, in turn, consume activities. Thus, activity-based costing is also a two-stage process. An ABC costing system, however, emphasizes direct tracing and driver tracing (exploiting cause-and-effect relationships), while a volume-based costing system tends to be allocation-intensive (largely ignoring cause-and-effect relationships). As the Exhibit 7-3 model reveals, the focus of activity-based costing is activities. Thus, identifying activities must be the first step in designing an activity-based costing system.

OBJECTIVE 2

Explain how an activity-based costing system works for product costing.

Identifying Activities and Their Attributes

Since an activity is action taken or work performed by equipment or people for other people, identifying activities is usually accomplished by interviewing managers or representatives of functional work areas (departments). A set of key questions is asked whose answers provide much of the data needed for an activity-based costing system. These interview-derived data are used to prepare an *activity dictionary*. An **activity dictionary** lists the activities in an organization along with some critical activity attributes. **Activity attributes** are financial and nonfinancial information items that describe individual activities. What attributes are used depends on the purpose. Examples of activity attributes associated with a costing objective include types of resources consumed, amount (percentage) of time spent on an activity by workers, cost objects that consume the activity output (reason for performing the activity), a measure of the activity output (activity driver), and the activity name.

Concept Q & A

What are some key differences between ABC and volume-based costing?

Answer:
ABC uses cause-and-effect relationships to assign overhead costs. Volume-based costing uses unit-based drivers such as direct labor hours, which often have nothing to do with the actual overhead resources consumed by a product.

Key Set of Questions

Interview questions can be used to identify activities and activity attributes needed for costing purposes. The information derived from these questions serves as the basis for constructing an activity dictionary as well as providing data helpful for assigning resource costs to individual activities. The list is not exhaustive but serves to illustrate the nature of the information gathering process.

ABC: Two-Stage Assignment

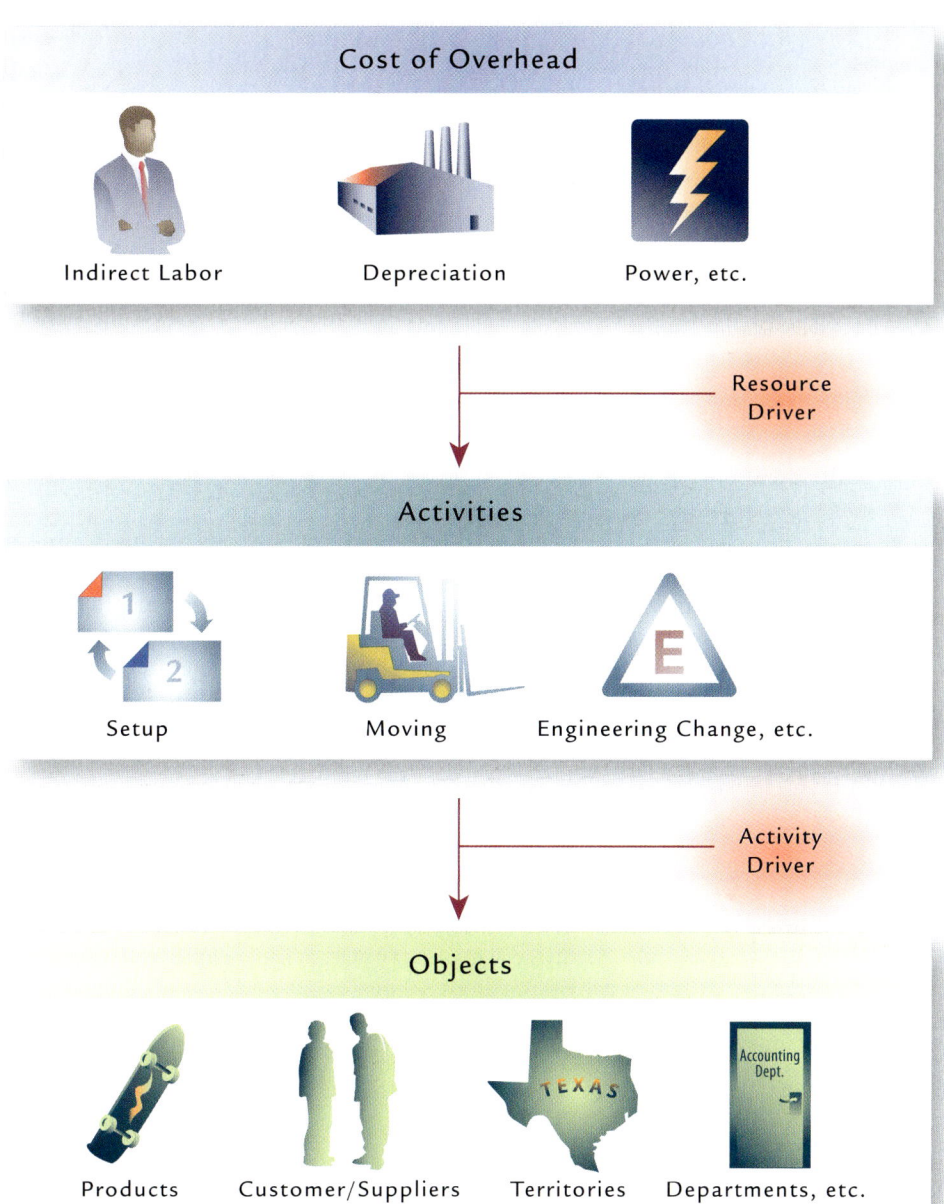

1. How many employees are in your department? (Activities consume labor.)
2. What do they do (please describe)? (Activities are people doing things for other people.)
3. Do customers outside your department use any equipment? (Activities also can be equipment working for other people.)

4. What resources are used by each activity (equipment, materials, energy)? (Activities consume resources in addition to labor.)
5. What are the outputs of each activity? (Helps identify activity drivers.)
6. Who or what uses the activity output? (Identifies the cost object: products, other activities, customers, etc.)
7. How much time do workers spend on each activity? By equipment? (Information needed to assign the cost of labor and equipment to activities.)

Illustrative Example: Service Firm

Suppose, for example, that a manager of a bank's credit card department is interviewed and presented the seven questions just listed. Consider the purpose and response to each question, in the order indicated.

- *Question 1 (labor resource):* There are five employees.
- *Question 2 (activity identification):* There are three major activities: processing credit card transactions, issuing customer statements, and answering customer questions.
- *Question 3 (activity identification):* Yes. Automatic bank tellers service customers who require cash advances.
- *Question 4 (resource identification):* Every employee has their own computer, printer, and desk. Paper and other supplies are needed to operate the printers. Of course, each employee has a telephone as well.
- *Question 5 (potential activity drivers):* Processing transactions produces a posting for each transaction in our computer system and serves as a source for preparing the monthly statements. The number of monthly customer statements has to be the product for the issuing activity, and I suppose that customers served is the output for the answering activity. The number of cash advances would measure the product of the automatic teller activity, although the teller really generates more transactions for other products such as checking accounts. So perhaps the number of teller transactions is the real output.
- *Question 6 (potential cost objects identified):* We have three products: classic, gold, and platinum credit cards. Transactions are processed for these three types of cards, and statements are sent to clients holding these cards. Similarly, answers to questions are all directed to clients who hold these cards.
- *Question 7 (identifying resource drivers):* I just completed a work survey and have the percentage of time calculated for each worker. All five clerks work on each of the three departmental activities. About 40 percent of their time is spent processing transactions, with the rest of their time split evenly between preparing statements and answering questions. Phone time is used only for answering client questions, and computer time is 70 percent transaction processing, 20 percent statement preparation, and 10 percent answering questions. Furthermore, my own time and that of my computer are 100 percent administrative.

Concept Q & A

What is the purpose of the interview questions?

Answer:
The purpose is to identify activities, drivers, and other important attributes essential for activity-based costing.

Activity Dictionary

Based on the answers to the survey, an activity dictionary can now be prepared. Exhibit 7-4 illustrates the dictionary for the credit card department. The activity dictionary names the activity (usually by using an action verb and an object that receives the action), describes the tasks that make up the activity, lists the users (cost objects), and identifies a measure of activity output (activity driver). The three products, classic, gold,

Activity Dictionary: Credit Card Department

Activity Name	Activity Description	Cost Object(s)	Activity Driver
Processing	Sorting, keying, and transactions verifying	Credit cards	Number of transactions
Preparing statements	Reviewing, printing, stuffing, and mailing	Credit cards	Number of statements
Answering questions	Answering, logging, reviewing database, and making call backs	Credit cards	Number of calls
Providing automatic tellers	Accessing accounts, withdrawing funds	Credit cards, checking and savings accounts	Number of teller transactions

and platinum credit cards, in turn, consume the activities. It is not unusual for a typical organization to produce an activity dictionary containing 200 to 300 activities.

Assigning Costs to Activities

Once activities are identified and described, the next task is determining how much it costs to perform each activity. This requires identification of the resources being consumed by each activity. Activities consume resources such as labor, materials, energy, and capital. The cost of these resources is found in the general ledger, but how much is spent on each activity is not revealed. Thus, it becomes necessary to assign the resource costs to activities using direct and driver tracing. For labor resources, a *work distribution matrix* is often used. A work distribution matrix simply identifies the amount of labor consumed by each activity and is derived from the interview process (or a written survey). Exhibit 7-5 provides an example of a work distribution matrix supplied by the manager of the credit card department for individual activities (see Question 7).

The time spent on each activity is the basis for assigning the labor costs to the activity. If the time is 100 percent, then labor is exclusive to the activity and the

Work Distribution Matrix

Activity	Percentage of Time on Each Activity
Processing transactions	40%
Preparing statements	30%
Answering questions	30%

assignment method is direct tracing. If the resource is shared by several activities (as is the case of the clerical resource), then the assignment is driver tracing and the drivers are called *resource drivers*. **Resource drivers** are factors that measure the consumption of resources by activities. Once resource drivers are identified, then the costs of the resource can be assigned to the activity. Cornerstone 7-4 shows how resource drivers and direct tracing are used to assign labor cost to the credit department activities.

Cornerstone 7-4

HOW TO Assign Resource Costs Using Direct Tracing and Resource Drivers

Information: Assume that each clerk is paid a salary of $30,000 ($150,000 total clerical cost for 5 clerks). Refer also to the work distribution matrix of Exhibit 7-4.
Required: Assign the cost of labor to each of the activities in the credit department.
Calculation: The amount of labor cost assigned to each activity is given below. The percentages come from the work distribution matrix.

Processing transactions	$60,000 (0.4 × $150,000)
Preparing statements	$45,000 (0.3 × $150,000)
Answering questions	$45,000 (0.3 × $150,000)

Labor, of course, is not the only resource consumed by activities. Activities also consume materials, capital, and energy. The interview, for example, reveals that the activities within the credit card department use computers (capital), phones (capital), desks (capital), and paper (materials). The automatic teller activity uses the automatic teller (capital) and energy. The cost of these other resources must also be assigned to the various activities. They are assigned in the same way as was described for labor (using direct tracing and resource drivers). The cost of computers, for example, could be assigned using direct tracing (for the supervising activity) and hours of usage for the remaining activities. From the interview, we know the relative usage of computers by each activity. The general ledger reveals that the cost per computer is $1,200 per year. Thus, an additional $6,000 (5 × $1,200) would be assigned to three activities based on relative usage: 70 percent to processing transactions ($4,200), 20 percent to preparing statements ($1,200), and 10 percent to answering questions ($600). Repeating this process for all resources, the total cost of each activity can be calculated. Exhibit 7-6 gives the cost of the activities associated with the credit card department under the assumption that all resource costs have been assigned (these numbers are assumed because all resource data are not given for their calculation).

Assigning Costs to Products

From Cornerstone 7-3, we know that activity costs are assigned to products by multiplying a predetermined activity rate by the usage of the activity, as measured by activity drivers. Exhibit 7-4 identifies the activity drivers for each of the four credit card activities: number of transactions for processing transactions, number of statements for preparing statements, number of calls for answering questions, and number of teller

Activity Costs, First Stage: Credit Card Department

Processing transactions	$130,000
Preparing statements	102,000
Answering questions	92,400
Providing automatic tellers	250,000

transactions for the activity of providing automatic tellers. To calculate an activity rate, the practical capacity of each activity must be determined. To assign costs, the amount of each activity consumed by each product must also be known. Assuming that the practical activity capacity is equal to the total activity usage by all products, the following actual data have been collected for the credit card example:

	Classic Card	Gold Card	Platinum Card	Total
Number of cards	5,000	3,000	2,000	10,000
Transactions processed	600,000	300,000	100,000	1,000,000
Number of statements	60,000	36,000	24,000	120,000
Number of calls	10,000	12,000	8,000	30,000
Number of teller transactions*	15,000	3,000	2,000	20,000

*The number of teller transactions for the cards is 10 percent of the total transactions from all sources. Thus, teller transactions total 200,000 (10 × 20,000).

Applying Cornerstone 7-2 by using the data and costs from Exhibit 7-6, the activity rates are calculated as follows:

Rate calculations:
  Processing transactions $130,000/1,000,000 = $0.13 per transaction
  Preparing statements $102,000/120,000 = $0.85 per statement
  Answering questions $92,400/30,000 = $3.08 per call
  Providing automatic tellers $250,000/200,000 = $1.25 per transaction

APPLICATIONS IN BUSINESS

ABC has been used to analyze the profitability of products in the dairy case of food retailers. Milk was found to be the most profitable item, taking up just 23 percent of the space in the dairy case yet providing 25 percent of the revenues and 34 percent of the profits. The unit activity-based cost for dairy items was calculated using distribution activities, handling activities, space, and time on the shelf. The average activity-based cost for a dairy-case item was $0.11, with juice costing $0.23 and milk less than $0.05. ABC also revealed that per-unit cost is affected by the type of handling activities used. Costs can be lowered by an appropriate choice of a stocking activity. For example, front-loading, hand stacking costs 5.5 cents per item whereas using a roll-in cart for stocking costs only 2.7 cents per unit.

Source: Jerry Dryer, "ABC's of Milk Selling," *Dairy Foods* (May 1999): 31.

Assigning Costs: Final Stage

	Classic	Gold	Platinum
Processing transactions:			
$0.13 × 600,000	$ 78,000		
$0.13 × 300,000		$ 39,000	
$0.13 × 100,000			$13,000
Preparing statements:			
$0.85 × 60,000	51,000		
$0.85 × 36,000		30,600	
$0.85 × 24,000			20,400
Answering questions:			
$3.08 × 10,000	30,800		
$3.08 × 12,000		36,960	
$3.08 × 8,000			24,640
Providing automatic tellers:			
$1.25 × 15,000	18,750		
$1.25 × 3,000		3,750	
$1.25 × 2,000			2,500
Total costs	$178,550	$110,310	$60,540
Units	÷ 5,000	÷ 3,000	÷ 2,000
Unit cost	$ 35.71	$ 36.77	$ 30.27

These rates provide the price charged for activity usage. Using these rates, costs are assigned as shown in Exhibit 7-7. However, we now know the whole story behind the development of the activity rates and usage measures. Furthermore, the banking setting emphasizes the utility of activity-based costing in service organizations.

ACTIVITY-BASED CUSTOMER AND SUPPLIER COSTING

OBJECTIVE 3

Describe activity-based customer and supplier costing.

In an activity-based costing system, product-costing accuracy is improved by tracing activity costs to the products that consume the activities. ABC can also be used to accurately determine the costs of customers and suppliers. Knowing the costs of customers and suppliers can be vital information for improving a company's profitability. LSI Logic, a high-tech producer of semiconductors, implemented ABC customer costing and discovered that 10 percent of its customers were responsible for about 90 percent of its profits. LSI also discovered that it was actually losing money on about 50 percent of its customers. It worked to convert its unprofitable customers into profitable ones and invited those who would not provide a fair return to take their business elsewhere. As a consequence, LSI's sales decreased, but its profit tripled.[1]

[1] Gary Cokins, "Are All of Your Customers Profitable (To You)?" (June 14, 2001), **http://www.bettermanagment .com/Library**.

© AP/WIDE WORLD PHOTOS

APPLICATIONS IN BUSINESS

In a 1998 survey conducted by Ohio State University's Supply Chain Management Research Group, about one-fourth of the respondents indicated that the need to measure customer profitability was their primary motivation for implementing ABC. They also pointed out that measuring customer profitability has assumed more importance because customers are demanding more logistics services without commensurate increases in prices. Interest was also expressed in applying ABC across the entire supply chain to determine how activity costs are driven by the services requested by other supply chain members.

Source: Thomas A. Foster, "Time to Learn the ABC's of Logistics," *Logistics Management and Distribution Report*, Vol. 38, Issue 2, 67–70.

Activity-Based Customer Costing

Customers are thus cost objects of fundamental interest. As the LSI Logic experience illustrates, customer management can produce significant gains in profit. It is possible to have customer diversity just as it is possible to have product diversity. Customers can consume customer-driven activities in different proportions. Sources of customer diversity include such things as order frequency, delivery frequency, geographic distance, sales and promotional support, and engineering support requirements. Knowing how much it costs to service different customers can be vital information for such purposes as pricing, determining customer mix, and improving profitability. Furthermore, because of diversity of customers, multiple drivers are needed to trace costs accurately. This outcome means that ABC can be useful to organizations that may have only one product, homogeneous products, or a JIT structure where direct tracing diminishes the value of ABC for product costing.

Customer Costing versus Product Costing

Assigning the costs of customer service to customers is done in the same way that manufacturing costs are assigned to products. Customer-driven activities such as order entry, order picking, shipping, making sales calls, and evaluating a client's credit are identified and listed in an activity dictionary. The cost of the resources consumed is assigned to activities, and the cost of the activities is assigned to individual customers. The same model and procedures that apply to products apply to customers as well. Cornerstone 7-5 illustrates how ABC assigns costs to customers.

Cornerstone 7-5

HOW TO Calculate Activity-Based Customer Costs

Information: Milan Company produces precision parts for 11 major buyers. Of the 11 customers, one accounts for 50 percent of the sales, with the remaining 10 accounting for the rest of the sales. The 10 smaller customers purchase parts in roughly equal quantities. Orders placed by the smaller customers are about the same size. Data concerning Milan's customer activity follow:

	Large Customer	Ten Smaller Customers
Units purchased	500,000	500,000
Orders placed	2	200
Number of sales calls	10	210
Manufacturing costs	$3,000,000	$3,000,000
Order filling costs allocated*	$202,000	$202,000
Sales force costs allocated*	$110,000	$110,000

*Allocated based on sales volume.

Currently, customer-driven costs are assigned to customers based on units sold, a unit-level driver.

Required: Assign costs to customers using an ABC approach.

Calculation: The appropriate drivers are orders placed and number of sales calls. The activity rates are:

$$\$404,000/202 \text{ orders} = \$2,000 \text{ per order}$$
$$\$220,000/220 \text{ calls} = \$1,000 \text{ per call}$$

Using this information, the customer-driven costs can be assigned to each group of customers as follows:

	Large Customer	Ten Smaller Customers
Order filling costs:		
($2,000 × 2)	$ 4,000	
($2,000 × 200)		$400,000
Sales force costs:		
($1,000 × 10)	10,000	
($1,000 × 210)		210,000

The ABC cost assignments reveal a much different picture of the cost of servicing each type of customer. The smaller customer is costing more, attributable to smaller, more frequent orders and the evident need of the sales force to engage in more negotiations to make a sale.

What does this tell management that it didn't know before? First, the large customer costs much less to service than the smaller customers and perhaps should be charged less. Second, it raises some significant questions relative to the smaller customers. Is it possible, for example, to encourage larger, less frequent orders? Perhaps offering discounts for larger orders would be appropriate. Why is it more difficult to sell to the smaller customers? Why are more calls needed? Are they less informed than the larger customer about the products? Can we improve profits by influencing our customers to change their buying behavior?

Concept Q & A

How are costs assigned to customers using the ABC approach?

Answer:
Costs are traced to activities and then assigned to customers based on their usage of these activities.

Activity-Based Supplier Costing

Activity-based costing can also help a manager identify the true cost of a firm's suppliers. The cost of a supplier is much more than the purchase price of the components or materials acquired. Just like customers, suppliers can affect many internal activities of a firm and significantly increase the cost of purchasing. A more correct view is one where the costs associated with quality, reliability, and late deliveries are added to the purchase costs. Managers are then required to evaluate suppliers based on total cost, not just purchase price. Activity-based costing is the key to tracing costs relating to purchase, quality, reliability, and delivery performance to suppliers.

Supplier Costing Methodology

Assigning the costs of supplier-related activities to suppliers follows the same pattern as ABC product and customer costing. Supplier-driven activities such as purchasing, receiving, inspection of incoming components, reworking products (because of defective components), expediting products (because of late deliveries of suppliers), and warranty work (due to defective supplier components) are identified and listed in an activity dictionary. The cost of the resources consumed is assigned to these activities, and the cost of the activities is assigned to individual suppliers. Cornerstone 7-6 illustrates how to use ABC for supplier costing.

Cornerstone 7-6

HOW TO Calculate Activity-Based Supplier Costs

Information: Assume that a purchasing manager uses two suppliers, Murray Inc. and Plata Associates, as the source of two machine parts: Part A1 and Part B2. Consider two activities: repairing products (under warranty) and expediting products. Repairing products occurs because of part failure (bought from suppliers). Expediting products occurs because suppliers are late in delivering needed parts. Activity cost information and other data needed for supplier costing follow:

I. Activity Costs Caused by Suppliers (e.g., failed parts or late delivery)

Activity	Costs
Repairing products	$800,000
Expediting products	200,000

II. Supplier Data

	Murray Inc.		Plata Associates	
	Part A1	Part B2	Part A1	Part B2
Unit purchase price	$20	$52	$24	$56
Units purchased	80,000	40,000	10,000	10,000
Failed units	1,600	380	10	10
Late shipments	60	40	0	0

Required: Determine the cost of each supplier using ABC.

Calculation: Using the above data, the activity rates for assigning costs to suppliers are computed as follows:

$$\text{Repair rate} = \$800{,}000/2{,}000^*$$
$$= \$400 \text{ per failed part}$$
$$^*(1{,}600 + 380 + 10 + 10).$$

$$\text{Expediting rate} = \$200{,}000/100^{**}$$
$$= \$2{,}000 \text{ per late delivery}$$
$$^{**}(60 + 40).$$

Using these rates and the activity data, the total purchasing cost per unit of each component is computed:

	Murray, Inc.		Plata Associates	
	Part A1	Part B2	Part A1	Part B2
Purchase cost:				
$20 × 80,000	$1,600,000			
$52 × 40,000		$2,080,000		
$24 × 10,000			$240,000	
$56 × 10,000				$560,000
Repairing products:				
$400 × 1,600	640,000			
$400 × 380		152,000		
$400 × 10			4,000	
$400 × 10				4,000
Expediting products:				
$2,000 × 60	120,000			
$2,000 × 40		80,000		
Total costs	$2,360,000	$2,312,000	$244,000	$564,000
Units	÷ 80,000	÷ 40,000	÷ 10,000	÷ 10,000
Total unit cost	$ 29.50	$ 57.80	$ 24.40	$ 56.40

The example in Cornerstone 7-6 shows that Murray, the "low-cost" supplier (as measured by the purchase price of the two parts), actually costs more when the supplier-related activities of repairing and expediting are considered. If all costs are considered, then the choice becomes clear: Plata Associates is the better supplier with a higher-quality product, more on-time deliveries, and, consequently, a lower overall cost per unit.

PROCESS-VALUE ANALYSIS

Process-value analysis is fundamental to **activity-based management**, focuses on cost reduction instead of cost assignment, and emphasizes the maximization of systemwide performance. As the model in Exhibit 7-8 illustrates, process-value analysis is concerned with (1) *driver analysis*, (2) *activity analysis*, and (3) *performance measurement*.

OBJECTIVE 4

Explain how activity-based management can be used for cost reduction.

Driver Analysis: The Search for Root Causes

Managing activities requires an understanding of what causes activity costs. Every activity has inputs and outputs. **Activity inputs** are the resources consumed by the activity in producing its output. **Activity output** is the result or product of an activity. For example, if the activity is moving materials, the inputs would be such things as a forklift, a forklift driver, fuel (for the forklift), and crates. The output would be moved goods and materials. An **activity output measure** is the number of times the activity is performed. It is the quantifiable measure of the output. For example, the number of moves or distance moved are possible output measures for the material moving activity.

The output measure effectively is a measure of the demands placed on an activity and is what we have been calling an *activity driver*. As the demands for an activity change, the cost of the activity can change. For example, as the number of programs written increases, the activity of writing programs may need to consume more inputs (labor, disks, paper, and so on). However, output measures, such as the number of programs, may not (and usually don't) correspond to the root causes of activity costs; rather, they are the consequences of the activity being performed. The purpose of driver analysis is to reveal root causes. Thus, **driver analysis** is the effort expended to identify those factors that are the root causes of activity costs. For example, an analysis may reveal that the root cause of the cost of moving materials is plant layout. Once the root cause is known, then action can be taken to improve the activity. Specifically, reorganizing plant layout can reduce the cost of moving materials.

Often, the root cause of the cost of an activity is also the root cause of other related activities. For example, the costs of inspecting purchased parts and reordering may

7-8

EXHIBIT

Process-Value Analysis Model

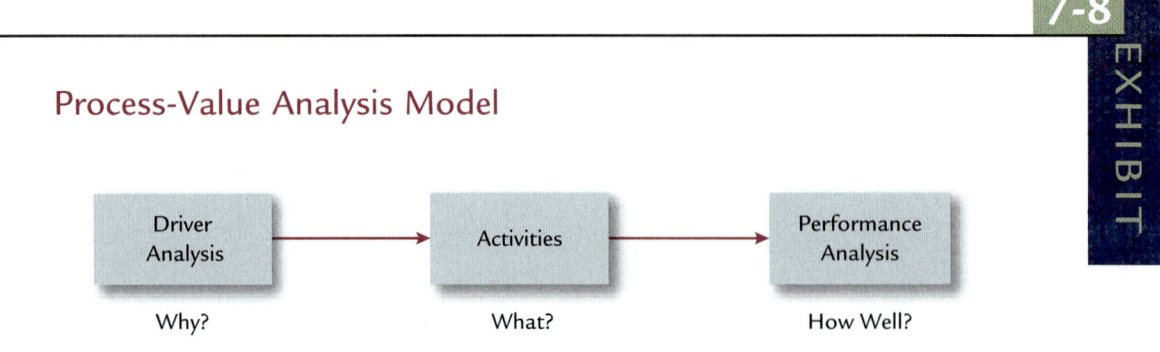

Driver Analysis → Activities → Performance Analysis

Why?　　What?　　How Well?

both be caused by poor supplier quality. By working with suppliers to reduce the number of defective components supplied (or choosing suppliers that have fewer defects), the demand for both activities may then decrease, allowing the company to save money.

Activity Analysis: Identifying and Assessing Value Content

The heart of process-value analysis is activity analysis. **Activity analysis** is the process of identifying, describing, and evaluating the activities an organization performs. Activity analysis should produce four outcomes: (1) what activities are done, (2) how many people perform the activities, (3) the time and resources required to perform the activities, and (4) an assessment of the value of the activities to the organization, including a recommendation to select and keep only those that add value. Steps 1–3 have been described earlier and are common to the information needed for determining and assigning activity costs. Knowing how much an activity costs is clearly an important part of activity-based management. Step 4, determining the value-added content of activities, is concerned with cost reduction rather than cost assignment. Thus, some feel that this is the most important part of activity analysis. Activities can be classified as *value-added* or *non-value-added*.

Value-Added Activities

Those activities necessary to remain in business are called **value-added activities**. Some activities—required activities—are necessary to comply with legal mandates. Activities needed to comply with the reporting requirements of the SEC and the filing requirements of the IRS are examples. These activities are value-added by *mandate*. The remaining activities in the firm are *discretionary*. A discretionary activity is classified as value-added provided it simultaneously satisfies three conditions: (1) the activity produces a change of state, (2) the change of state was not achievable by preceding activities, and (3) the activity enables other activities to be performed.

For example, consider the production of rods used in hydraulic cylinders. The first activity, cutting rods, cuts long rods into the correct lengths for the cylinders. Next, the cut rods are welded to cut plates. The cutting rod activity is value-added because (1) it causes a change of state—uncut rods become cut rods, (2) no prior activity was supposed to create this change of state, and (3) it enables the welding activity to be performed. Though the value-added properties are easy to see for an operational activity like cutting rods, what about a more general activity like supervising production workers? A managerial activity is specifically designed to manage other value-added activities—to ensure that they are performed in an efficient and timely manner. Supervision certainly satisfies the enabling condition. Is there a change in state? There are two ways of answering in the affirmative. First, supervising can be viewed as an enabling resource that is consumed by the operational activities that do produce a change of state. Thus, supervising is a secondary activity that serves as an input that is needed to help bring about the change of state expected for value-added primary activities. Second, it could be argued that the supervision brings order by changing the state from uncoordinated activities to coordinated activities. Once value-added activities are identified, we can define value-added costs. **Value-added costs** are the costs to perform value-added activities with perfect efficiency.

Non-Value-Added Activities

All activities other than those that are absolutely essential to remain in business, and therefore considered unnecessary, are referred to as **non-value-added activities**. A non-value-added activity can be identified by its failure to satisfy any one of the three previous defining conditions. Violation of the first two is the usual case for non-value-added activities. Inspecting cut rods (for correct length), for example, is a non-value-added activity. Inspection is a state-detection activity, not a state-changing activity (it tells us the state of the cut rod—whether it is the right length or not). Thus, it fails the first condition. Consider the activity of reworking goods or subassemblies. Rework is designed to bring a good from a nonconforming state to a conforming state. Thus, a change of state occurs. Yet, the activity is non-value-added because it repeats work; it is doing something that should have been done by preceding activities (Condition 2 is violated).

Non-value-added costs are costs that are caused either by non-value-added activities or the inefficient performance of valued-added activities. For non-value-added activities, the non-value-added cost is simply the cost of the activity itself. For inefficient value-added activities, the activity cost must be broken into its value-added and non-value-added components. For example, if receiving should use 10,000 receiving orders but uses 20,000, then half the cost of receiving is value-added and half is non-value-added. The value-added component is the waste-free component of the value-added activity and is, therefore, the *value-added standard*. Due to increased competition, many firms are attempting to eliminate non-value-added activities because they add unnecessary cost and impede performance; firms are also striving to optimize value-added activities. Thus, activity analysis identifies and eventually eliminates all unnecessary activities and, simultaneously, increases the efficiency of necessary activities.

> ## Concept Q & A
>
> How can a value-added activity have non-value-added costs?
>
> **Answer:**
> If a value-added activity is performed inefficiently, the inefficient component is waste and is the non-value-added cost.

The theme of activity analysis is waste elimination. As waste is eliminated, costs are reduced. The cost reduction *follows* the elimination of waste. Note the value of managing the causes of the costs rather than the costs themselves. Though managing costs may increase the efficiency of an activity, if the activity is unnecessary, what does it matter if it's performed efficiently? An unnecessary activity is wasteful and should be eliminated. For example, moving raw materials and partially finished goods is often cited as a non-value-added activity. Installing an automated materials handling system may increase the efficiency of this activity, but changing to cellular manufacturing with on-site, just-in-time delivery of raw materials could virtually eliminate the activity. It's easy to see which is preferable.

Examples of Non-Value-Added Activities

Reordering parts, expediting production, and rework because of defective parts are all examples of non-value-added activities. Other examples include warranty work, handling customer complaints, and reporting defects. Non-value-added activities can exist anywhere in the organization. In the manufacturing operation, five major activities are often cited as wasteful and unnecessary:

1. *Scheduling.* An activity that uses time and resources to determine when different products have access to processes (or when and how many setups must be done) and how much will be produced.
2. *Moving.* An activity that uses time and resources to move raw materials, work in process, and finished goods from one department to another.

3. *Waiting.* An activity in which raw materials or work in process use time and resources by waiting on the next process.
4. *Inspecting.* An activity in which time and resources are spent ensuring that the product meets specifications.
5. *Storing.* An activity that uses time and resources while a good or raw material is held in inventory.

None of these activities adds any value for the customer. (Note that inspection would not be necessary if the product were produced correctly the first time, and therefore, adds no value for the customer.) The challenge of activity analysis is to find ways to produce the good without using any of these activities.

HERE'S THE REAL KICKER

For Stillwater Designs, warranty work is a significant cost. Warranty work associated with defective products is typically labeled a non-value-added cost. Stillwater Designs recognizes the non-value-added nature of this activity and takes measures to eliminate the causes of the defective units. The company tracks return failures (over time) and provides this information to its research and development department. R&D then uses this information to make design improvements on existing models (running changes) as well to change the design on future models. The objective of the design changes is to reduce the demand for the warranty activity, thus reducing warranty cost.

However, not all Kicker warranty costs can be classified as non-value-added. When products are returned, customer service decides whether the problem is covered under warranty. Sometimes problems are covered even though they are not attributable to a defective product. When the company decides to replace a nondefective product, it is making a conscious decision to increase customer satisfaction and brand loyalty. This part of the warranty cost is a "marketing warranty cost" and could be classified as a value-added cost. For example, customers sometimes buy amplifiers that are more powerful than the subwoofers can handle, resulting in burnt voice coils. By replacing the product (even though technically it is the customer's fault), the customer will be more likely to buy again and to provide good word-of-mouth advertising for Kicker products.

Cost Reduction

Activity management carries with it the objective of cost reduction. Competitive conditions dictate that companies must deliver products the customers want, on time, and at the lowest possible cost. This means that an organization must continually strive for cost improvement. Activity management can reduce costs in four ways:[2]

1. Activity elimination
2. Activity selection
3. Activity reduction
4. Activity sharing

Activity elimination focuses on non-value-added activities. Once activities that fail to add value are identified, measures must be taken to rid the organization of these activities. For example, the activity of inspecting incoming parts seems necessary to ensure that the product using the parts functions according to specifications. Use of a bad part can produce a bad final product. Yet, this activity is necessary only because of the poor-quality performance of the supplying firms. Selecting suppliers who are able to supply high-quality parts or who are willing to improve their quality performance to achieve this objective will eventually allow the elimination of incoming inspection. Cost reduction then follows.

[2]Peter B. B. Turney, "How Activity-Based Costing Helps Reduce Cost," *Journal of Cost Management* (Winter 1991): 29–35.

Activity selection involves choosing among different sets of activities that are caused by competing strategies. Different strategies cause different activities. Different product design strategies, for example, can require significantly different activities. Activities, in turn, cause costs. Each product design strategy has its own set of activities and associated costs. All other things being equal, the lowest-cost design strategy should be chosen. In a kaizen cost framework, redesign of existing products and processes can lead to a different, cheaper set of activities. Thus, activity selection can have a significant effect on cost reduction.

Activity reduction decreases the time and resources required by an activity. This approach to cost reduction should be primarily aimed at improving the efficiency of necessary activities or a short-term strategy for improving non-value-added activities until they can be eliminated. Setup activity is a necessary activity that is often cited as an example for which less time and fewer resources need to be used. Finding ways to reduce setup time—and thus lower the cost of setups—is another example of the concept of gradual reductions in activity costs.

Activity sharing increases the efficiency of necessary activities by using economies of scale. Specifically, the quantity of the cost driver is increased without increasing the total cost of the activity itself. This lowers the per-unit cost of the cost driver and the amount of cost traceable to the products that consume the activity. For example, a new product can be designed to use components already being used by other products. By using existing components, the activities associated with these components already exist, and the company avoids the creation of a whole new set of activities.

Cornerstone 7-7 shows how to determine the non-value-added cost of activities. Determining the cost is followed by a root-cause analysis and then by the selection of an approach to reduce the waste found in the activity. For example, defective products cause warranty work. Defective products, in turn, are caused by such factors as defective internal processes, poor product design, and defective supplier components. Correcting the causes will lead to the elimination of the warranty activity. Inefficient purchasing could be attributable to such root causes as poor product design (too many components), orders that are incorrectly filled out, and defective supplier components (producing additional orders). Correcting the causes will reduce the demand for the purchasing activity, and as the activity is reduced, cost reduction will follow.

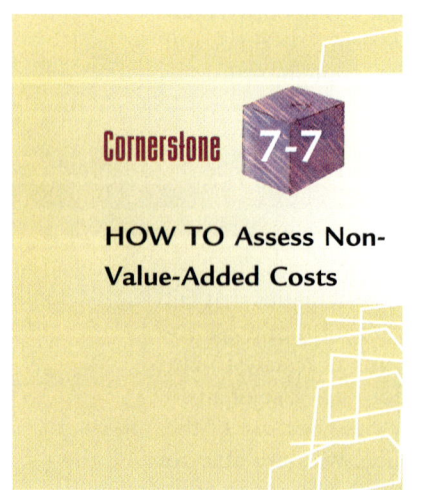

Cornerstone 7-7

HOW TO Assess Non-Value-Added Costs

Information: Consider the following two activities: (1) Performing warranty work, cost: $120,000. The warranty cost of the most efficient competitor is $20,000. (2) Purchasing components, cost: $200,000 (10,000 purchase orders). A benchmarking study reveals that the most efficient level would use 5,000 purchase orders and entail a cost of $110,000.

Required: Determine the non-value-added cost of each activity.

Calculation: Determine the value content of each activity: Is the activity non-value-added or value-added? Performing warranty work is non-value-added; it is done to correct something that wasn't done right the first time. Thus, the non-value-added cost of performing warranty work is $120,000. The cost of the competitor is also non-value-added and has no bearing on the analysis. Root causes for warranty work are defective products. Purchasing components is necessary so that materials are available to produce products and, thus, is value-added. However, the activity is not performed efficiently as revealed by the benchmarking study. The non-value-added cost is $90,000 ($200,000 − $110,000).

Activity Performance Measurement

Assessing how well activities (and processes) are performed is fundamental to management's efforts to improve profitability. Activity performance measures exist in both financial and nonfinancial forms. These measures are designed to assess how well an activity was performed and the results achieved. They are also designed to reveal if constant improvement is being realized. Measures of activity performance center on three major dimensions: (1) efficiency, (2) quality, and (3) time.

Efficiency focuses on the relationship of activity inputs to activity outputs. For example, one way to improve activity efficiency is to produce the same activity output with lower cost for the inputs used. Thus, cost and trends in cost become important measures of efficiency. *Quality* is concerned with doing the activity right the first time it is performed. If the activity output is defective, then the activity may need to be repeated, causing unnecessary cost and reduction in efficiency. Quality cost management is a major topical area and is treated in detail in the appendix to this chapter. The *time* required to perform an activity is also critical. Longer times usually mean more resource consumption and less ability to respond to customer demands. Time measures of performance tend to be nonfinancial, whereas efficiency and quality measures are both financial and nonfinancial.

Cycle time and *velocity* are two operational measures of time-based performance. Cycle time can be applied to any activity or process that produces an output, and it measures how long it takes to produce an output from start to finish. Consider, for example, the manufacturing process. In this case, **cycle time** is the length of time it takes to produce a unit of output from the time raw materials are received (starting point of the cycle) until the good is delivered to finished goods inventory (finishing point of the cycle). Thus, cycle time is the time required to produce one unit of a product (time/units produced). **Velocity** is the number of units of output that can be produced in a given period of time (units produced/time). Notice that velocity is the reciprocal of cycle time. For the cycle time example, the velocity is 2 units per hour. Cornerstone 7-8 demonstrates how to compute cycle time and velocity.

Concept Q & A

What are the three dimensions of performance for activities? Explain why they are important.

Answer:
Efficiency, quality, and time are the three performance dimensions. All three relate to the ability of a manager to reduce activity cost.

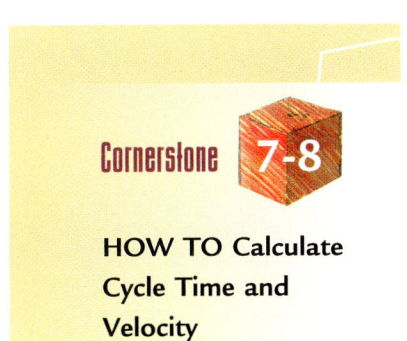

Cornerstone 7-8

HOW TO Calculate Cycle Time and Velocity

Information: Assume that a company takes 10,000 hours to produce 20,000 units of a product.

Required: What is the velocity? Cycle time?

Calculation: Velocity = 20,000/10,000 = 2 units per hour; Cycle time = 10,000/20,000 = 1/2 hour.

SCENARIO REVISITED

Russell Gumbrecht's enthusiasm relating to some of the newer management accounting methods appears to be well justified. Activity-based costing can help a company become more competitive by providing more accurate cost data. Accurate product costs help managers improve profitability by allowing them to make better decisions. Product mix decisions and pricing decisions are but two examples of possible impact. What Russell perhaps did not fully appreciate was the potential for ABC to help with other important cost objects such as customers and suppliers. Managing costs across the supply chain can be greatly enhanced by accurate cost information.

Russell also was on target with his belief that managing activities can be beneficial. Activity-based management promises cost reduction by identifying non-value-added activities and eliminating them. Value-added activities can also be improved by increasing their efficiency. In both cases, significant cost savings are available through waste elimination.

SUMMARY OF LEARNING OBJECTIVES

Overhead costs have increased in significance over time and in many firms represent a much higher percentage of product costs than direct labor. At the same time, many overhead activities are unrelated to the units produced. Functional-based costing systems are not able to assign the costs of these non-unit-related overhead activities properly. These overhead activities are consumed by products in different proportions than are unit-based overhead activities. Because of this, assigning overhead using only unit-based drivers can distort product costs. This can be a serious matter if the non-unit-based overhead costs are a significant proportion of total overhead costs.

Activities are identified and defined through the use of interviews and surveys. This information allows an activity dictionary to be constructed. The activity dictionary lists activities and potential activity drivers, classifies activities as primary or secondary, and provides any other attributes deemed to be important. Resource costs are assigned to activities by using direct tracing and resource drivers. The costs of secondary activities are ultimately assigned to primary activities using activity drivers. Finally, the costs of primary activities are assigned to products, customers, and other cost objects. Thus, the cost assignment process is described by the following general steps: (1) identifying the major activities and building an activity dictionary, (2) determining the cost of those activities, (3) identifying a measure of consumption for activity costs (activity drivers), (4) calculating an activity rate, (5) measuring the demands placed on activities by each product, and (6) calculating product costs.

Tracing customer-driven costs to customers can provide significant information to managers. Accurate customer costs allow managers to make better pricing decisions, customer-mix decisions, and other customer-related decisions that improve profitability. Similarly, tracing supplier-driven costs to suppliers can enable managers to choose the true low-cost suppliers, producing a stronger competitive position and increased profitability.

Assigning costs accurately is vital for good decision making. However, assigning the costs of an activity accurately does not address the issue of whether or not the activity should be performed or whether it is being performed efficiently. Activity-based management focuses on process-value analysis. Process-value analysis has three components: driver analysis, activity analysis, and performance evaluation. These three steps determine what activities are being done, why they are being done, and how well they are done. Understanding the root causes of activities provides the opportunities to manage activities so that costs can be reduced.

Cornerstones for Chapter 7

KEY TERMS

APPENDIX: QUALITY AND ENVIRONMENTAL COSTING

Quality Cost Management

Quality costs can be substantial and a source of significant savings. Improving quality can produce significant improvements in profitability and overall efficiency. Quality improvement can increase profitability in two ways: (1) by increasing customer demand and (2) by decreasing costs. In a tightly competitive market, increased demand and cost savings can mean the difference between surviving and thriving. The U.S. government has recognized the importance of quality in today's economy. One indication is the creation in 1987 of the Malcolm Baldrige National Quality Award. The Baldrige award was created to recognize U.S. companies that excel in quality management and achievement. The award categories include manufacturing, small business, service, educational, and health entities. Since no more than two awards are given per category, they are difficult to achieve and highly sought after. For example, winners in 2003 included Dana Corporation—Spicer Driveshaft Division (manufacturing category), Karlee Company, Inc. (manufacturing category), Operations Management International, Inc. (service category), and Los Alamos Bank (small business category). Winners in earlier years included STMicroelectronics, Inc.—Region Americas, BI, The Ritz-Carlton Hotel Company, LLC, Sunny Fresh Foods, Boeing Airlift and Tanker Programs, Solar Turbines Incorporated, and Texas Nameplate Company, Inc.

As companies implement quality improvement programs, a need arises to monitor and report on the progress of these programs. Managers need to know what quality costs are and how they are changing over time. Reporting and measuring quality performance is absolutely essential to the success of an ongoing quality improvement program. A fundamental prerequisite for this reporting is measuring the costs of quality. But to measure those costs, an operational definition of quality is needed.

OBJECTIVE 5
Explain the basics of quality cost management.

Quality Defined

Operationally, a **quality product** or **service** is one that meets or exceeds customer expectations. In effect, quality is customer satisfaction. But what is meant by "customer expectations"? Customers can be concerned with such product attributes as reliability, durability, fitness for use, and conformance to specifications. Although many important attributes can affect customer satisfaction, the quality attributes that are measurable tend to receive more emphasis. Conformance, in particular, is strongly emphasized. In fact, many quality experts believe that "quality is conformance" is the best operational definition. There is some logic to this position. Product specifications should explicitly consider such things as reliability, durability, and fitness for use. Implicitly, a conforming product is reliable, durable, fit for use, and performs well. The product should be produced as the design specifies it; specifications should be met. Conformance is the basis for defining what is meant by a nonconforming, or *defective*, product.

A **defective product** is one that does not conform to specifications. **Zero defects** means that all products conform to specifications. But what is meant by "conforming to specifications"? The *traditional view* of conformance assumes that there is an acceptable range of values for each specification or quality characteristic. A target value is defined, and upper and lower limits are set that describe acceptable product variation for a given quality characteristic. Any unit that falls within the limits is deemed nondefective. For example, losing or gaining zero minutes per month may be the target value for a watch, and any watch that keeps time correctly within plus or minus two minutes per month is judged acceptable. On the other hand, the *robust quality* view of conformance emphasizes fitness of use. *Robustness* means hitting the target value every time.

Concept Q & A

What is a defective product using the robust quality view?

Answer:
A defective product is one that does not conform to specifications. The robust quality view does not allow any deviation from the ideal specification.

There is no range in which variation is acceptable. A nondefective watch in the robust setting would be one that does not gain or lose any minutes during the month. Since evidence exists that product variation can be costly, the robust quality definition of conformance is superior to the traditional definition.

Costs of Quality Defined

Quality-linked activities are those activities performed because poor quality may or does exist. The costs of performing these activities are referred to as *costs of quality*. Thus, the **costs of quality** are the costs that exist because poor quality may or does exist. This definition implies that quality costs are associated with two subcategories of quality-related activities: *control activities* and *failure activities*. **Control activities** are performed by an organization to prevent or detect poor quality (because poor quality may exist). Therefore, control activities are made up of prevention and appraisal activities. **Control costs** are the costs of performing control activities. **Failure activities** are performed by an organization or its customers in response to poor quality (poor quality does exist). If the response to poor quality occurs before delivery of a bad (nonconforming, unreliable, not durable, and so on) product to a customer, the activities are classified as internal failure activities; otherwise, they are classified as external failure activities. **Failure costs** are the costs incurred by an organization because failure activities are performed. Notice that the definitions of failure activities and failure costs imply that customer response to poor quality can impose costs on an organization. The definitions of quality-related activities also imply four categories of quality costs: (1) prevention costs, (2) appraisal costs, (3) internal failure costs, and (4) external failure costs.

Prevention costs are incurred to prevent poor quality in the products or services being produced. As prevention costs increase, we would expect the costs of failure to decrease. Examples of prevention costs are quality engineering, quality training programs, quality planning, quality reporting, supplier evaluation and selection, quality audits, quality circles, field trials, and design reviews.

Appraisal costs are incurred to determine whether products and services are conforming to their requirements or customer needs. Examples include inspecting and testing raw materials, packaging inspection, supervising appraisal activities, product acceptance, process acceptance, measurement (inspection and test) equipment, and outside endorsements. Two of these terms require further explanation.

Product acceptance involves sampling from batches of finished goods to determine whether they meet an acceptable quality level; if so, the goods are accepted. *Process acceptance* involves sampling goods while in process to see if the process is in control and producing nondefective goods; if not, the process is shut down until corrective action can be taken. The main objective of the appraisal function is to prevent nonconforming goods from being shipped to customers.

Internal failure costs are incurred when products and services do not conform to specifications or customer needs. This nonconformance is detected prior to being shipped or delivered to outside parties. These are the failures detected by appraisal activities. Examples of internal failure costs are scrap, rework, downtime (due to defects), reinspection, retesting, and design changes. These costs disappear if no defects exist.

External failure costs are incurred when products and services fail to conform to requirements or satisfy customer needs after being delivered to customers. Of all the costs of quality, this category can be the most devastating. Costs of recalls, for example, can run into the hundreds of millions of dollars. Other examples include lost sales because of poor product performance, returns and allowances because of poor quality, warranties, repairs, product liability, customer dissatisfaction, lost market share, and complaint adjustment. External failure costs, like internal failure costs, disappear if no defects exist.

Concept Q & A

Which quality costs will totally disappear in a zero-defects environment?

Answer:
Both internal and external failure costs will vanish. Most, if not all, of the appraisal costs should also disappear.

Quality Cost Reports

A quality cost reporting system is essential to an organization serious about improving and controlling quality costs. The first and simplest step in creating such a system is assessing current actual quality costs. A detailed listing of actual quality costs by category can provide two important insights. First, it reveals the magnitude of the quality costs in each category, allowing managers to assess their financial impact. Second, it shows the distribution of quality costs by category, allowing managers to assess the relative importance of each category.

The financial significance of quality costs can be assessed more easily by expressing these costs as a percentage of actual sales. Cornerstone 7-9, for example, reports Jensen Products' quality costs as representing almost 12 percent of sales for fiscal 2007. Given the rule of thumb that quality costs should be no more than about 2.5 percent, Jensen Products has ample opportunity to improve profits by decreasing quality costs. Understand, however, that reduction in costs should come through improvement of quality. Reduction of quality costs without any effort to improve quality could prove to be a disastrous strategy.

Cornerstone 7-9

HOW TO Prepare a Quality Cost Report

Information: Jensen Products had total sales of $2,800,000 for fiscal 2007. Jensen's costs of quality-related activities are as follows:

Warranty	$25,000
Scrap	50,000
Process acceptance	38,000
Repair	15,000
Reliability engineering	80,000
Rework	35,000
Quality training	35,000
Product acceptance	10,000
Customer complaints	25,000
Materials inspection	20,000

Required: Prepare a quality cost report, classifying costs by category and expressing each category as a percentage of sales.

Calculation:

Quality Cost Report
Jensen Products
For the Year Ended March 31, 2007

	Quality Costs		Percentage of Sales[a]
Prevention costs:			
Quality training	$35,000		
Reliability engineering	80,000	$115,000	4.11%
Appraisal costs:			
Materials inspection	$20,000		
Product acceptance	10,000		
Process acceptance	38,000	68,000	2.43

Internal failure costs:			
Scrap	$50,000		
Rework	35,000	$ 85,000	3.04
External failure costs:			
Customer complaints	$25,000		
Warranty	25,000		
Repair	15,000	65,000	2.32
Total quality costs		$333,000	11.90%[b]

[a]Actual sales of $2,800,000.
[b]$333,000/$2,800,000 = 11.89 percent; difference is rounding error.

Additional insight concerning the relative distribution of quality costs can be realized by constructing a pie chart. Exhibit 7-9 provides such a chart, using the quality costs reported in Cornerstone 7-9. Managers, of course, have the responsibility of assessing the optimal level of quality and determining the relative amount that should be spent in each category. Understanding the nature of how quality costs behave should help with this objective.

Activity-Based Management and Optimal Quality Costs

Activity-based management is useful for understanding how quality costs can be managed. Appraisal and failure activities and their associated costs are non-value-added and should be eliminated. Prevention activities—performed efficiently—can be classified as value-added and should be retained. Initially, however, prevention activities may not be performed efficiently, and activity reduction and activity selection (and perhaps even

7-9

EXHIBIT

Relative Distribution of Quality Costs

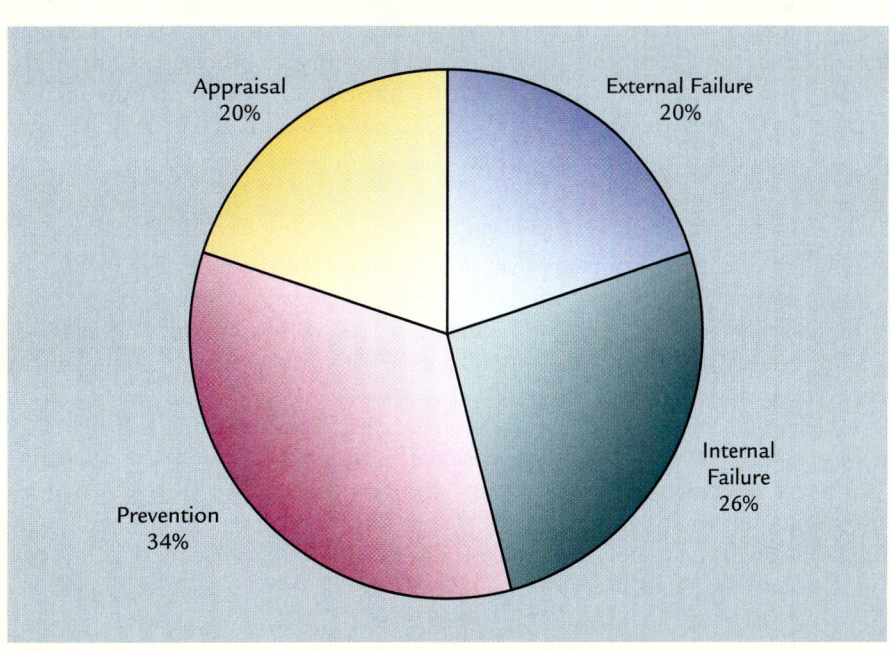

activity sharing) can be used to achieve the desired value-added state. Grede Foundries, Inc., of Milwaukee, the world's largest foundry company, has been tracking all four categories of quality costs for more than 15 years. However, it does not report prevention costs as part of its final cost-of-quality figures because it does not want its managers reducing quality costs by cutting prevention activities. It feels strongly that spending money on prevention activities pays off. For example, it has found that a 1-percent reduction in scrap reduces external defects by about 5 percent.[3]

Once the activities are identified for each category, resource drivers can be used to assign costs to the individual activities. Root (cost) drivers can also be identified, especially for failure activities, and used to help managers understand what is causing the costs of the activities. This information can then be used to select ways of reducing quality costs to the lowest level possible. In effect, activity-based management supports the robust zero-defect view of quality costs. There is no optimal trade-off between control and failure costs; the latter are non-value-added costs and should be reduced to zero. Some control activities are non-value-added and should be eliminated. Other control activities are value-added but may be performed inefficiently, and the costs caused by the inefficiency are non-value-added. Thus, costs for these categories may also be reduced to lower levels.

> ## Concept Q & A
>
> What is the purpose of a quality cost report?
>
> **Answer:**
> A quality cost report allows managers to assess the financial importance of quality costs, both in absolute as well as in relative terms.

> ## Concept Q & A
>
> Why are failure costs regarded as non-value-added costs?
>
> **Answer:**
> Failure costs can be eliminated by producing nondefective products, and, hence, are unnecessary and wasteful.

ENVIRONMENTAL COST MANAGEMENT

For many organizations, management of environmental costs is becoming a matter of high priority and intense interest. Successful treatment of environmental concerns is becoming a significant competitive issue. Corporations are discovering that meeting sound business objectives and resolving environmental concerns are not mutually exclusive. In fact, many now believe that improving environmental quality may actually reduce environmental costs rather than increase them. To understand this critical observation, it is important to examine a concept known as *ecoefficiency*.

> **OBJECTIVE 6**
>
> Explain the basics of environmental cost management.

The Benefits of Ecoefficiency

Ecoefficiency essentially maintains that organizations can produce more useful goods and services while *simultaneously* reducing negative environmental impacts, resource consumption, and costs. This concept conveys at least three important messages. First, improving ecological and economic performance can and should be complementary. Second, improving environmental performance should no longer be viewed as a matter of charity and goodwill but rather as a matter of competitiveness. Third, ecoefficiency is complementary and supportive of *sustainable development*. **Sustainable development** is defined as development that meets the needs of the present without compromising the ability of future generations to meet their own needs. Although absolute sustainability may not be attainable, progress toward its achievement certainly seems to have some merit.

---

[3]Nancy Chase, "Counting Costs, Reaping Returns," *Quality Magazine* (October 1998), **http://www.qualitymag .com/articles/oct98/1098fl.html**.

Ecoefficiency implies that increased efficiency comes from improving environmental performance. Environmental costs can be a significant percentage of total operating costs, and interestingly, many of these costs can be reduced or eliminated through effective management. Knowledge of environmental costs and their causes may lead to a redesign of a process that, as a consequence, reduces the raw materials used and the pollutants emitted to the environment (an interaction between the innovation and cost reduction incentives). Thus, current and future environmental costs are reduced, and the firm becomes more competitive. For example, between 1992 and 1999, Baxter International, Incorporated, a producer of medical products, reduced toxic wastes emitted to air, water, and soil; increased recycling activity; and, as a consequence, reported environmental savings for the 7-year period of $98 million.[4] Similarly, Interface, Inc., over a 4-year period, saved $50 million in reduced materials costs, reduced energy costs, and reduced waste.[5]

Concept Q & A

What is ecoefficiency, and why is it important?

Answer:
Ecoefficiency maintains that a firm can simultaneously improve environmental performance and economic efficiency. If true, then improving environmental performance is a competitive requirement and not just a social responsibility.

Effective cost management leading to cost reduction like that described for Baxter and Interface means that environmental cost information must be provided to management. To provide this financial information, it is necessary to define, measure, classify, and assign environmental costs to processes, products, and other cost objects of interest. Environmental costs should be reported as a separate classification so managers can assess their impact on firm profitability. Furthermore, assigning environmental costs to products and processes reveals the sources of these costs and helps identify their fundamental causes so that they can be controlled.

Environmental Quality Cost Model

Before environmental cost information can be provided to management, environmental costs must be defined. Various possibilities exist; however, an appealing approach is to adopt a definition consistent with a total environmental quality model. In the total environmental quality model, the ideal state is that of zero damage to the environment (analogous to the zero-defects state of total quality management). Damage is defined as direct degradation of the environment such as the emission of solid, liquid, or gaseous residues into the environment (e.g., water contamination and air pollution), or indirect degradation such as *unnecessary* usage of materials and energy.

Accordingly, environmental costs can be referred to as *environmental quality costs*. Similar to quality costs, **environmental costs** are costs that are incurred because poor environmental quality exists or because poor environmental quality *may* exist. In other words, environmental costs are associated with the creation, detection, remediation, and prevention of environmental degradation. With this definition, environmental costs can be classified into four categories: prevention costs, detection costs, internal failure costs, and external failure costs. External failure costs, in turn, can be subdivided into realized and unrealized categories.

Environmental prevention costs are the costs of activities carried out to prevent the production of contaminants and/or waste that could cause damage to the environment. Examples of prevention activities include the following: evaluating and selecting suppliers, evaluating and selecting equipment to control pollution, designing processes and products to reduce or eliminate contaminants, training employees, studying

---

[4]Baxter Environmental Financial Statement, 1999, at **http://www.baxter.com/sustainability** (October 9, 2002).
[5]Charles Fishman, "Sustainable Growth—Interface, Inc.," *The Magazine* (April 1998), **http://www.fastcompany .com/online/14/sustaing.html**. See also Interface's own description of its sustainability program at **http://www .ifsia.com/us/company/sustainability**.

environmental impacts, auditing environmental risks, undertaking environmental research, developing environmental management systems, recycling products, and obtaining ISO 14001 certification.[6]

Environmental detection costs are the costs of activities executed to determine if products, processes, and other activities within the firm are in compliance with appropriate environmental standards. The environmental standards and procedures that a firm seeks to follow are defined in three ways: (1) regulatory laws of governments, (2) voluntary standards (ISO 14001) developed by the International Standards Organization, and (3) environmental policies developed by management. Examples of detection activities are auditing environmental activities, inspecting products and processes (for environmental compliance), developing environmental performance measures, carrying out contamination tests, verifying supplier environmental performance, and measuring levels of contamination.

Environmental internal failure costs are costs of activities performed because contaminants and waste have been produced but not discharged into the environment. Thus, internal failure costs are incurred to eliminate and manage contaminants or waste once produced. Internal failure activities have one of two goals: (1) to ensure that the contaminants and waste produced are not released to the environment or (2) to reduce the level of contaminants released to an amount that complies with environmental standards. Examples of internal failure activities include operating equipment to minimize or eliminate pollution, treating and disposing of toxic materials, maintaining pollution equipment, licensing facilities for producing contaminants, and recycling scrap.

Environmental external failure costs are the costs of activities performed after discharging contaminants and waste into the environment. **Realized external failure costs** are those incurred and paid for by the firm. **Unrealized external failure costs (societal costs)** are caused by the firm but are incurred and paid for by parties outside the firm. Societal costs can be further classified as (1) those resulting from environmental degradation and (2) those associated with an adverse impact on the property or welfare of individuals. In either case, the costs are borne by others and not by the firm, even though they are caused by the firm. Of the four environmental cost categories, the external failure category is the most devastating. For example, a report by the Environmental Protection Agency indicates that private cleanup costs, under the Comprehensive Environmental Response, Compensation and Liability Act of 1980, have run into the tens of billions of dollars and are projected to eventually amount to several hundred billion dollars. Furthermore, cleanup costs that must be borne by taxpayers will also run into the hundreds of billions of dollars. Cleanup of defense wastes alone are estimated at $500 billion.[7] Examples of realized external failure activities are cleaning up a polluted lake, cleaning up oil spills, cleaning up contaminated soil, using materials and energy inefficiently, settling personal injury claims from environmentally unsound practices, settling property damage claims, restoring land to its natural state, and losing sales from a bad environmental reputation. Ex-

Concept Q & A

Why are there two categories of external failure costs?

Answer:
One category represents those external environmental costs that the firm causes and pays for, and the other category is those external environmental costs caused by the firm but paid for by parties outside the firm.

[6]ISO 14001 certification is obtained when an organization installs an environmental management system that satisfies specific privately set international standards. These standards are concerned with environmental *management* procedures and do not directly indicate acceptable levels of environmental performance. The certification, therefore, functions primarily as a signal that a firm is interested and willing to improve its environmental performance.
[7]"The United States Experience with Economic Incentives for Protecting the Environment," EPA-240-R-01-001 (January 2001). The report is available at **http://www.epa.gov/economics**. The cost estimates reported above are in Section 3.32 of the report.

amples of societal costs include receiving medical care because of polluted air (individual welfare), losing a lake for recreational use because of contamination (degradation), losing employment because of contamination (individual welfare), and damaging ecosystems from solid waste disposal (degradation).

Exhibit 7-10 summarizes the four environmental cost categories and lists specific activities for each category. Within the external failure cost category, societal costs are labeled with an "S." The costs for which the firm is financially responsible are called **private costs**. All costs without the "S" label are private costs.

Environmental Cost Report

Environmental cost reporting is essential if an organization is serious about improving its environmental performance and controlling environmental costs. A good first step is a report that details the environmental costs by category. Reporting environmental costs by category reveals two important outcomes: (1) the impact of environmental costs on firm profitability and (2) the relative amounts expended in each category. Cornerstone 7-10 provides an example of how to prepare a simple environmental cost report.

7-10 EXHIBIT

Classification of Environmental Costs by Activity

Prevention Activities

Evaluating and selecting suppliers
Evaluating and selecting pollution control equipment
Designing processes
Designing products
Carrying out environmental studies
Auditing environmental risks
Developing environmental management systems
Recycling products
Obtaining ISO 14001 certification

Detection Activities

Auditing environmental activities
Inspecting products and processes
Developing environmental performance measures
Testing for contamination
Verifying supplier environmental performance
Measuring contamination levels

Internal Failure Activities

Operating pollution control equipment
Treating and disposing of toxic waste
Maintaining pollution equipment
Licensing facilities for producing contaminants
Recycling scrap

External Failure Activities

Cleaning up a polluted lake
Cleaning up oil spills
Cleaning up contaminated soil
Settling personal injury claims (environmentally related)
Restoring land to natural state
Losing sales due to poor environmental reputation
Using materials and energy inefficiently
Receiving medical care due to polluted air (S)
Losing employment because of contamination (S)
Losing a lake for recreational use (S)
Damaging ecosystems from solid waste disposal (S)

Cornerstone 7-10

HOW TO Prepare an Environmental Cost Report

Information: Operating costs for Numade Corporation as of December 31, 2005, are $20,000,000. Environmental costs are as follows:

Maintaining pollution equipment	$200,000
Developing measures	80,000
Property damage claim	400,000
Selecting equipment	40,000
Operating pollution equipment	400,000
Designing products	180,000
Training employees	60,000
Restoring land	500,000
Inspecting processes	240,000
Cleaning up lake	900,000

Required: Prepare an environmental cost report, classifying costs by quality category and expressing each as a percentage of total operating costs.

Calculation:

Numade Corporation
Environmental Cost Report
For the Year Ended December 31, 2005

	Environmental Costs		Percentage of Operating Costs
Prevention costs:			
Training employees	$ 60,000		
Designing products	180,000		
Selecting equipment	40,000	$ 280,000	1.40%
Detection costs:			
Inspecting processes	$240,000		
Developing measures	80,000	320,000	1.60
Internal failure costs:			
Operating pollution equipment	$400,000		
Maintaining pollution equipment	200,000	600,000	3.00
External failure costs:			
Cleaning up lake	$900,000		
Restoring land	500,000		
Property damage claim	400,000	1,800,000	9.00
Totals		$3,000,000	15.00%

The report in Cornerstone 7-10 highlights the importance of environmental costs by expressing them as a percentage of total operating costs. In this report, environmental costs are 15 percent of total operating costs, seemingly a significant amount. From a practical point of view, environmental costs will receive managerial attention only if they represent a significant amount. Although environmental managerial cost reporting is in its infancy, some evidence exists concerning this issue. After six months of investigation, Amoco concluded that environmental costs at its Yorktown refinery were at least 22 percent of operating costs.[8] Other evidence from case studies by the World Resources Institute suggests that environmental costs are 20 percent or more of a firm's

[8]Daniel Baker, "Environmental Accounting's Conflicts and Dilemmas," *Management Accounting* (October 1996): 46–48.

Concept Q & A

What are two important outcomes achieved by an environmental cost report?

Answer:
It allows managers to (1) assess the impact of environmental costs on profitability and (2) determine the relative distribution of costs by category.

total operating costs.[9] It appears that environmental costs can significantly affect a firm's profitability.

The cost report also provides information relating to the relative distribution of the environmental costs. Of the total environmental costs, only 20 percent are from the prevention and detection categories. Thus, eighty percent of the environmental costs are failure costs—costs that exist because of poor environmental performance.

Reducing Environmental Costs: More Activity-Based Management

Fortunately, evidence suggests that environmental failure costs can be reduced by investing more in prevention and detection activities. Reducing and eventually eliminating non-value-added activities can produce significant cost reduction. Ford Motor Company, for example, has made a commitment to improve its environmental performance. As part of this overall commitment, Ford has resolved to obtain ISO 14001 certification in all its plants throughout the world. Some of its plants in Germany and England have already received this certification. In these certified plants, Ford has already saved hundreds of thousands of dollars in environmental costs.[10] In the organic chemical industrial sector, studies concerned with efforts to prevent toxic waste have shown that for every dollar spent on prevention activities, $3.49 was saved from environmental failure activities (per year).[11] For a typical project, savings were $351,000 per year, and an average of 1.6 million pounds of chemical were eliminated.[12]

It is possible that the environmental cost reduction model will behave in a very similar way to the total quality cost model. Perhaps the lowest environmental costs are attainable at the *zero-damage point*, much like the zero-defects point of the total quality cost model. This point of view is certainly compatible with the notion of ecoefficiency. The idea underlying the zero-damage view is that *prevention is cheaper than the cure*. In Phillips Petroleum, this concept is referred to as the *rule of 1-10-100*.[13] This rule states that if a problem is solved in its own area of work, it costs $1; if the problem is solved outside the originating area but within the company, it costs $10; if the problem is solved outside the company, it costs $100. The rule suggests that zero damage is the lowest cost point for environmental costs.

In reality, it may be that zero degradation is the low cost point for many types of contaminating activities. For example, Numar, a Costa Rican producer of margarines and cooking oils, managed to reduce its emission of contaminated water effluents to zero.[14] The actions taken by Numar were in response to a new environmental law that prohibited the dumping of these effluents into rivers and streams. Numar invested in a new system that treated the water and allowed it to recover usable materials and, at the same time, reuse the treated water. The annual costs of the investment, including depreciation, purchase of bacteria, electricity, and maintenance, were $116,350. Three benefits were observed. First, the amount of water required on a daily basis was reduced

[9]Daryl Ditz, Janet Ranganathan, and R. Daryl Banks, *Green Ledgers: Case Studies in Corporate Environmental Accounting* (World Resources Institute, May 1995).

[10]Michael Prince, "ISO Now Offering Voluntary Standards," *Business Insurance* (November 11, 1996): 21–23.

[11]Michael E. Porter and Claus van der Linde, "Green and Competitive: Ending the Stalemate," *Harvard Business Review* (September/October 1995): 120–134.

[12]See also *Cutting Chemical Waste* (1985) and *Environmental Dividends: Cutting More Chemical Waste* (1991), INFORM, New York. (INFORM is a not-for-profit group that conducted a study of 29 chemical companies.)

[13]Blair W. Felmate, "Making Sustainable Development a Corporate Reality," *CMA Magazine* (March 1997): 9–16.

[14]Arnoldo Rodriguez, "Grupo Numar," *INCAE* (June 1997).

from 950 cubic meters to 200 cubic meters (because of the ability to recycle water). This produced savings of $391,500 per year. Second, the materials recovered from the treated water were worth $30,000 per year (cost only). Third, the company avoided stiff environmental fines and possible closure costs. Thus, the zero-degradation state for solid residues was achieved at a cost of $116,350 per year, but *benefits* of at least $421,500 were produced. The approach taken to obtain zero emissions actually increased the profitability of the firm! It is curious that a legal incentive was required for the company to seek the more efficient approach. Part of the reason can be attributed to the common view that improving environmental performance is a charitable act. It is also true that most firms do not have the necessary environmental cost information. Knowing environmental costs and how they relate to products, for example, can be a strong incentive for innovating and increasing efficiency.

Concept Q & A

What is the key to reducing environmental failure costs?

Answer:
Investing more in prevention and detection activities should produce a significant reduction in the demand for failure activities. As with quality, the low cost point may be one of zero degradation.

Assigning Environmental Costs

The environmental costs of processes that produce, market, and deliver products and the environmental postpurchase costs caused by the use and disposal of the products are examples of *environmental product costs*. Assigning environmental costs to products can produce valuable managerial information. For example, it may reveal that a particular product is responsible for much more toxic waste than other products. This information may lead to a more efficient and environmentally friendly alternative design for the product or its associated processes. It could also reveal that with the environmental costs correctly assigned, the product is not profitable. This could mean something as simple as dropping the product to achieve significant improvement in environmental performance and economic efficiency. Many opportunities for improvement may exist, but knowledge of the environmental product costs is the key. Moreover, it is critical that environmental costs be assigned accurately.

Activity-based costing facilitates environmental costing. Tracing the environmental costs to the products responsible for those costs is a fundamental requirement of a sound environmental accounting system. Each environmental activity is assigned costs, activity rates are computed, and the rates are then used to assign environmental costs to products based on usage of the activity. Cornerstone 7-11 shows how to assign environmental costs to two different types of industrial cleaners. This cost assignment allows managers to see the relative environmental economic impact of the two products, and to the extent that environmental costs reflect environmental damage, the unit environmental cost can also act as an index or measure of product cleanliness. The "dirtier" products can then be the focus of efforts to improve environmental performance and economic efficiency. Cornerstone 7-11 reveals, for example, that Cleanser B has more environmental problems than Cleanser A. Cleanser B's environmental costs total $370,000 ($3.70 × 100,000) and are 18.5 percent of the total manufacturing costs. Furthermore, its environmental failure costs (maintenance plus toxic waste) are $310,000, representing 83.8 percent of the total environmental costs. Cleanser A portrays a much better picture. Its environmental costs total $80,000, which is 8.0 percent of the total manufacturing costs, and the failure costs are 18.75 percent of the total environmental costs. It is evident that Cleanser B offers the most environmental and economic potential for improvement.

Concept Q & A

How are environmental costs assigned to products using the ABC approach?

Answer:
The costs of environmental activities are assigned to products using drivers based on causal relationships.

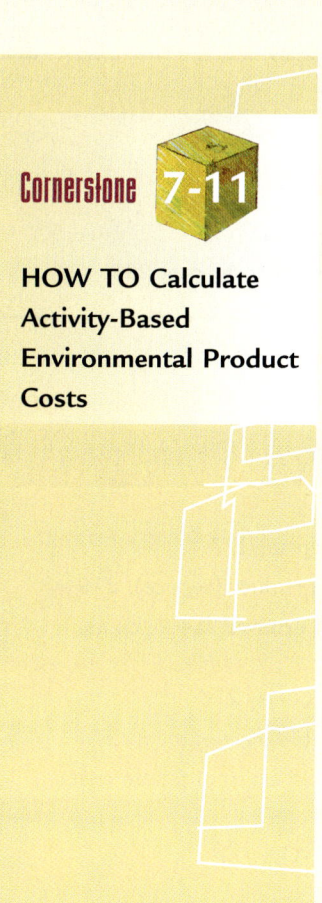

Cornerstone 7-11

HOW TO Calculate Activity-Based Environmental Product Costs

Information:

I.   Environmental activity costs

Activity	Costs
Design processes (to reduce pollution)	$ 45,000
Inspect processes (for pollution problems)	80,000
Maintain environmental equipment	125,000
Toxic waste disposal	200,000

II.   Driver data

	Cleanser A	Cleanser B
Design hours	2,000	1,000
Inspection hours	1,750	2,250
Maintenance hours	200	4,800
Pounds of waste	1,000	19,000

III. Other production data

	Cleanser A	Cleanser B
Nonenvironmental production costs	$920,000	$1,630,000
Units produced	100,000	100,000

Required: Determine the unit environmental and unit cost of each product using ABC.

Calculation:

Rates:

Design process: $45,000/3,000 = $15 per design hour
Inspection: $80,000/4,000 = $20 per inspection hour
Maintaining equipment: $125,000/5,000 = $25 per maintenance hour
Waste disposal: $200,000/20,000 = $10 per pound

Product costs:

Activities	Cleanser A	Cleanser B
Design processes ($15 × 2,000; $15 × 1,000)	$ 30,000	$ 15,000
Inspect processes ($20 × 1,750; $20 × 2,250)	35,000	45,000
Maintain equipment ($25 × 200; $25 × 4,800)	5,000	120,000
Toxic waste disposal ($10 × 1,000; $10 × 19,000)	10,000	190,000
Total environmental cost	$ 80,000	$ 370,000
Other manufacturing costs (nonenvironmental)	920,000	1,630,000
Total cost (environmental + other)	$1,000,000	$2,000,000
Unit environmental cost	$ 0.80	$ 3.70
Unit cost (environmental + other)	$ 10.00	$ 20.00

SUMMARY OF APPENDIX

Quality and environmental activities are particularly susceptible to activity-based management. Quality and environmental costs are costs that exist because poor product or environmental quality exist or may exist. With the exception of the prevention activity costs, virtually all quality and environmental cost are non-value-added. Providing quality and environmental quality cost reports to management can help them identify the potential savings and provide an incentive for action to reduce these costs. Eliminating non-value-added quality and environmental activities can produce significant cost reductions. Assigning environmental costs to products can help managers assess which products are the sources of environmental concerns.

Cornerstones for the Appendix to Chapter 7

APPENDIX KEY TERMS

Appraisal costs, 271

Control activities, 271

Control costs, 271

Costs of quality, 271

Defective product, 270

Ecoefficiency, 274

Environmental costs, 275

Environmental detection costs, 276

Environmental external failure costs, 276

Environmental internal failure costs, 276

Environmental prevention costs, 275

External failure costs, 271

Failure activities, 271

Failure costs, 271

Internal failure costs, 271

Prevention costs, 271

Private costs, 277

Quality product (service), 270

Realized external failure costs, 276

Societal costs, 276

Sustainable development, 274

Unrealized external failure costs, 276

Zero defects, 270

DISCUSSION QUESTIONS

1. Describe the two-stage process associated with plantwide overhead rates.
2. Describe the two-stage process for departmental overhead rates.
3. What are non-unit-level overhead activities? Non-unit-based cost drivers? Give some examples.
4. What is meant by "product diversity"?
5. What is an overhead consumption ratio?
6. What is activity-based product costing?
7. What is an activity dictionary?
8. Explain how costs are assigned to activities.
9. Describe the value of activity-based customer costing.
10. Explain how activity-based costing can help a firm identify its true low-cost suppliers.
11. What is driver analysis? What role does it play in process-value analysis?
12. What are value-added activities? Value-added costs?
13. What are non-value-added activities? Non-value-added costs? Give an example of each.
14. Identify and define four different ways to manage activities so that costs can be reduced.
15. What is cycle time? Velocity?

MULTIPLE-CHOICE EXERCISES

7-1 A unit-level driver is consumed by a product each and every time that

a. a batch of products is produced.
b. a purchase order is issued.
c. a unit is produced.
d. a customer complains.
e. None of the above.

7-2 Which of the following is a non-unit-level driver?

a. Direct labor hours
b. Machine hours
c. Setup hours
d. Direct materials
e. Assembly hours

7-3 Consider the information given on two products and their activity usage:

	Laser Printer	Dot Matrix Printer
Units produced	1,000	4,000
Setup hours	800	400
Inspection hours	500	500
Machine hours	200	1,000

The consumption ratios for the setup activity for each product are

a. 0.167; 0.833.
b. 0.333; 0.667.
c. 0.500; 0.500.
d. 0.20; 0.80.
e. None of the above.

7-4 Refer to the data for 7-3. Suppose that machine hours are used to assign all overhead costs to the two products. Select the best answer from the following.

a. Laser printers are undercosted, and dot matrix printers are overcosted.
b. Laser printers and dot matrix printers are accurately costed.
c. Laser printers are overcosted, and dot matrix printers are undercosted.
d. Using inspection hours to assign overhead costs is the most accurate approach.
e. None of the above.

7-5 The first stage of activity-based costing entails the assignment of

a. resource costs to departments.
b. activity costs to products or customers.
c. resource costs to a plantwide pool.
d. resource costs to individual activities.
e. resource costs to distribution channels.

7-6 The second stage of activity-based costing entails the assignment of

a. resource costs to departments.
b. activity costs to products or customers.
c. resource costs to a plantwide pool.
d. resource costs to individual activities.
e. resource costs to distribution channels.

7-7 Interview questions are asked to determine

a. what activities are being performed.
b. who performs the activities.
c. the relative amount of time spent on each activity by individual workers.
d. possible activity drivers for assigning costs to products.
e. All of the above.

7-8 The receiving department employs one worker who spends 75 percent of his time on the receiving activity and 25 percent of his time on inspecting products. His salary is $40,000. The amount of cost assigned to the receiving activity is

a. $34,000.
b. $40,000.
c. $10,000.
d. $30,000.
e. None of the above.

7-9 Assume that the moving activity has an expected cost of $80,000. Expected direct labor hours are 20,000, and expected number of moves is 40,000. The best activity rate for moving is

a. $4 per move.
b. $1.33 per hour-move.
c. $4 per hour.
d. $2 per move.
e. None of the above.

7-10 Which of the following is a true statement about ABC customer costing?

a. Customer diversity requires multiple drivers to trace costs accurately to customers.
b. Customers can consume customer-driven activities in different proportions.
c. It often produces changes in the company's customer mix.
d. It often improves profitability.
e. All of the above.

7-11 Which of the following is a true statement about ABC supplier costing?

a. The cost of a supplier is simply the purchase price of the components or materials acquired.
b. Suppliers can affect many internal activities of a firm and significantly increase the cost of purchasing.
c. It encourages managers to evaluate suppliers based on purchase cost.
d. It encourages managers to increase the number of suppliers.
e. All of the above.

7-12 This year, Lambert Company will ship 1,500,000 pounds of goods to customers at a cost of $1,200,000. If an individual customer orders 10,000 pounds and produces $200,000 of revenue (total revenue is $20 million), the amount of shipping cost assigned to the customer using ABC would be

a. Cannot be determined.
b. $24,000 (2 percent of the shipping cost).
c. $8,000 ($0.80 per pound shipped).
d. $12,000 (1 percent of the shipping cost).
e. None of the above.

7-13 Lambert Company has two suppliers: Deming and Leming. The cost of warranty work due to defective components is $2,000,000. The total units repaired under warranty average 100,000, of which 90,000 have components from Deming and 10,000 have components from Leming. Select the items below that represent true statements.

a. Components purchased from Deming cost $200,000 more than their purchase price.
b. Components purchased from Leming cost $1,800,000 more than their purchase price.
c. Components from Deming appear to be of higher quality.
d. All of the above.
e. None of the above.

7-14 A forklift and its driver used for moving materials are examples of

a. activity outputs.
b. activity output measures.
c. resource drivers.
d. activity inputs.
e. root causes.

7-15 Which of the following are non-value-added activities?

a. Moving goods
b. Storing goods
c. Inspecting finished goods
d. Reworking a defective product
e. All of the above.

7-16 Suppose that a company is spending $50,000 per year for inspecting, $40,000 for purchasing, and $60,000 for reworking products. A good estimate of non-value-added costs would be

a. $110,000.
b. $50,000.
c. $60,000.
d. $90,000.
e. $100,000.

7-17 The cost of inspecting incoming parts is most likely to be reduced by

a. activity sharing.
b. activity selection.
c. activity reduction.
d. activity elimination.
e. None of the above.

7-18 Thom Company produces 100 units in 5 hours. The cycle time for Thom is

a. 20 units per hour.
b. 5 hours per unit.
c. 3 minutes per unit.
d. 1 hour per 20 units.
e. Cannot be calculated.

7-19 Thom Company produces 100 units in 5 hours. The velocity for Thom is

a. 20 units per hour.
b. 5 hours per unit.
c. 3 minutes per unit.
d. 1 hour per 20 units.
e. Cannot be calculated.

7-20 Striving to produce the same activity output with lower costs for the input used is concerned with which of the following dimensions of activity performance?

a. Quality
b. Time
c. Activity sharing
d. Efficiency
e. Effectiveness

7-21 (Appendix) Which of the following is a quality prevention cost?

a. Quality planning
b. Supplier evaluation and selection
c. Quality audits
d. Field trials
e. All of the above.

7-22 (Appendix) Which of the following is an appraisal cost (quality)?

a. Design reviews
b. Quality reporting
c. Manager of an inspection team
d. Warranties
e. Retesting

7-23 (Appendix) Which of the following is an internal failure cost (quality)?

a. Supplier evaluation and selection
b. Scrapped units
c. Packaging inspection
d. Product liability
e. Complaint adjustment

7-24 (Appendix) Which of the following is an external failure cost (quality)?

a. Lost market share
b. Retesting
c. Rework
d. Design reviews
e. All of the above.

7-25 (Appendix) Which of the following are considered non-value-added activities?

a. Prevention activities
b. Appraisal activities
c. Internal control activities
d. External control activities
e. All of the above except for (a).

7-26 (Appendix) Which item represents environmental detection costs?

a. Developing environmental performance measures
b. Recycling products
c. Disposing of toxic materials
d. Carrying out contamination tests
e. None of the above.

7-27 (Appendix) An example of an environmental internal failure cost is

a. cleaning up oil spills.
b. damaging ecosystems from solid waste disposal.
c. verifying supplier environmental performance.
d. measuring levels of contamination.
e. None of the above.

7-28 (Appendix) An example of a societal cost is

a. maintaining pollution equipment.
b. recycling scrap.
c. disposing of toxic materials.
d. medical care due to polluted air.
e. All of the above.

7-29 (Appendix) An example of an environmental prevention cost is

a. restoring land to its natural state.
b. developing environmental management systems.
c. licensing facilities for producing contaminants.
d. auditing environmental activities.
e. treating toxic materials.

EXERCISES

Exercise 7–1 *Consumption Ratios*

Gladmark Company produces two types of get-well cards: scented and regular. Drivers for the four activities are as follows:

	Scented Cards	Regular Cards
Inspection hours	40	160
Setup hours	50	50
Machine hours	200	600
Number of moves	225	75

Required:

1. Calculate the consumption ratios for the four drivers.
2. Is there evidence of product diversity? Explain.

Exercise 7–2 *Activity Rates*

Refer to **Exercise 7–1.** The following activity data have been collected:

Inspecting products	$2,000
Setting up equipment	2,500
Machining	4,000
Moving materials	900

Required:

1. Calculate the activity rates that would be used to assign costs to each product.
2. Suppose that the activity rate for inspecting products is $20 per inspection hour. How many hours of inspection are expected for the coming year?

Exercise 7–3 *Activity-Based Product Costing*

Suppose that a cardiology ward has gathered the following information for four nursing activities and two types of patients:

	Driver	Patient Category Normal	Patient Category Intensive	Activity Rate
Treating patients	Treatments	5,000	20,000	$4.00
Providing hygienic care	Hygienic hours	5,000	11,000	5.00
Responding to requests	Requests	30,000	50,000	2.00
Monitoring patients	Monitoring hours	20,000	180,000	0.75

Required:

1. Determine the total nursing costs assigned to each patient category.
2. Output is measured in patient days. Assuming that the normal patient category uses 10,000 patient days and the intensive patient category uses 8,000 patient days, calculate the nursing cost per patient day for each type of patient.

Exercise 7–4 *Assigning Costs to Activities, Resource Drivers*

Receiving has three activities: unloading, counting goods, and inspecting. Unloading uses a forklift that is leased for $12,000 per year. The forklift is used only for unloading. The fuel for the forklift is $2,400 per year. Other operating costs (maintenance) for the forklift total $1,000 per year. Inspection uses some special testing equipment that has a depreciation of $800 per year and an operating cost of $500. Receiving has three employees who have an average salary of $40,000 per year. The work distribution matrix for the receiving personnel is as follows:

Activity	Percentage of Time on Each Activity
Unloading	40%
Counting	25
Inspecting	35

No other resources are used for these activities.

Required:

1. Calculate the cost of each activity.
2. Explain the two methods used to assign costs to activities.

Exercise 7–5 *Activity-Based Customer-Driven Costs*

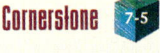

Suppose that Stillwater Designs has two classes of distributors: JIT distributors and non-JIT distributors. The JIT distributor places small, frequent orders, and the non-JIT distributor tends to place larger, less frequent orders. Both types of distributors are buying the same product. Stillwater Designs provides the following information about customer-related activities and costs for the most recent quarter:

	JIT Distributors	Non-JIT Distributors
Sales orders	200	20
Sales calls	20	20
Service calls	100	50
Average order size	500	5,000
Manufacturing cost/unit	$100	$100
Customer costs:		
Processing sales orders	$ 880,000	
Selling goods	320,000	
Servicing goods	300,000	
Total	$1,500,000	

Required:

1. Calculate the total revenues per distributor category and assign the customer costs to each distributor type using revenues as the allocation base.
2. Calculate the customer cost per distributor type using activity-based cost assignments. Discuss the merits of offering the non-JIT distributors a $3 price decrease (assume that they are agitating for a price concession).

3. Assume that the JIT distributors are simply imposing the frequent orders on Stillwater Designs. No formal discussion has taken place between JIT customers and Stillwater Designs regarding the supply of goods on a just-in-time basis. The sales pattern has simply evolved over time. As an independent consultant, what would you suggest to Stillwater Designs' management?

Exercise 7–6 *Activity-Based Supplier Costing*

Lumus Company manufactures refrigerators. Lumus produces all the parts necessary for its product except for one electronic component, which is purchased from two local suppliers: Vance, Inc., and Foy Company. Both suppliers are reliable and seldom deliver late; however, Vance sells the component for $24 per unit, while Foy sells the same component for $21.50. Lumus purchases 80 percent of its components from Foy because of its lower price. The total annual demand is 2,000,000 components.

To help assess the cost effect of the two components, the following data were collected for supplier-related activities and suppliers:

I. Activity data:

	Activity Cost
Inspecting components (sampling only)	$ 120,000
Reworking products (due to failed component)	1,521,000
Warranty work (due to failed component)	2,400,000

II. Supplier data:

	Vance, Inc.	Foy Company
Unit purchase price	$24	$21.50
Units purchased	400,000	1,600,000
Sampling hours*	40	1,960
Rework hours	180	2,820
Warranty hours	400	7,600

*Sampling inspection for Vance's product has been reduced because the reject rate is so low.

Required:

1. Calculate the cost per component for each supplier, taking into consideration the costs of the supplier-related activities and using the current prices and sales volume. (Assume that prices are cost plus 25 percent.)
2. Suppose that Lumus loses $1,000,000 in sales per year because of the reputation effect of defective units attributable to failed components. Using warranty hours, assign the cost of lost sales to each supplier. By how much would this change the cost of each supplier's component?

Exercise 7–7 *Non-Value-Added Costs*

The following six situations are independent.

a. A manual insertion process takes 30 minutes and eight pounds of material to produce a product. Automating the insertion process requires 15 minutes of machine time and 7.5 pounds of material. The cost per labor hour is $12, the cost per machine hour is $8, and the cost per pound of materials is $10.
b. With its original design, a gear requires eight hours of setup time. By redesigning the gear so that the number of different groves needed is reduced by 50 percent, the setup time is reduced by 75 percent. The cost per setup hour is $50.
c. A product currently requires six moves. By redesigning the manufacturing layout, the number of moves can be reduced from six to zero. The cost per move is $20.

d. Inspection time for a plant is 16,000 hours per year. The cost of inspection consists of salaries of eight inspectors, totaling $320,000. Inspection also uses supplies costing $5 per inspection hour. The company eliminated most defective components by eliminating low-quality suppliers. The number of production errors was reduced dramatically by installing a system of statistical process control. Further quality improvements were realized by redesigning the products, making them easier to manufacture. The net effect was to achieve a close to zero-defect state and eliminate the need for any inspection activity.

e. Each unit of a product requires six components. The average number of components is 6.5 due to component failure, requiring rework and extra components. Developing relations with the right suppliers and increasing the quality of the purchased component can reduce the average number of components to six components per unit. The cost per component is $500.

f. A plant produces 100 different electronic products. Each product requires an average of eight components that are purchased externally. The components are different for each part. By redesigning the products, it is possible to produce the 100 products so that they all have four components in common. This will reduce the demand for purchasing, receiving, and paying bills. Estimated savings from the reduced demand are $900,000 per year.

Required:

Estimate the non-value-added cost for each situation.

Exercise 7–8 *Driver Analysis*

Refer to the six situations in **Exercise 7–7.**

Required:

For each situation, identify the possible root cause(s) of the activity cost (such as plant layout, process design, and product design).

Exercise 7–9 *Type of Activity Management*

Refer to the six situations in **Exercise 7–7.**

Required:

For each situation, identify the cost reduction measure: activity elimination, activity reduction, activity sharing, or activity selection.

Exercise 7–10 *Cycle Time and Velocity*

A manufacturing cell produces 90,000 stereo speakers per quarter. A total of 15,000 production hours are used within the cell per quarter.

Required:

1. Compute the velocity (per hour).
2. Compute the cycle time (minutes per unit produced).

Exercise 7–11 *Product-Costing Accuracy, Consumption Ratios*

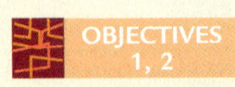

Plata Company produces two products: a mostly handcrafted soft leather briefcase under the label Maletin Elegant and a leather briefcase produced largely through automation and sold under the label Maletin Fina. The two products use two overhead activities, with the following costs:

Setting up equipment	$ 3,000
Machining	18,000

The controller has collected the expected annual prime costs for each briefcase, the machine hours, the setup hours, and the expected production.

	Elegant	Fina
Direct labor	$9,000	$3,000
Direct materials	$3,000	$3,000
Units	3,000	3,000
Machine hours	500	4,500
Setup hours	100	100

Required:

1. Do you think that the direct labor costs and direct materials costs are accurately traced to each briefcase? Explain.
2. Calculate the consumption ratios for each activity.
3. Calculate the overhead cost per unit for each briefcase, using a plantwide rate based on direct labor costs. Comment on this approach to assigning overhead.
4. Calculate the overhead cost per unit for each briefcase using overhead rates based on machine hours and setup hours. Explain why these assignments are more accurate than using the direct labor costs.

Exercise 7–12 *Product-Costing Accuracy, Consumption Ratios, Activity Rates, Activity Costing*

Tristar Manufacturing produces two types of battery-operated toy soldiers: infantry and special forces. The soldiers are produced using one continuous process. Four activities have been identified: machining, setups, receiving, and packing. Resource drivers have been used to assign costs to each activity. The overhead activities, their costs, and the other related data are as follows:

Product	Machine Hours	Setups	Receiving Orders	Packing Orders
Infantry	20,000	300	900	1,600
Special forces	20,000	100	100	800
Costs	$80,000	$24,000	$18,000	$30,000

Required:

1. Calculate the total overhead assigned to each product using only machine hours to calculate a plantwide rate.
2. Calculate consumption ratios for each activity.
3. Calculate a rate for each activity using the associated driver.
4. Assign the overhead costs to each product using the activity rates computed in Requirement 3. Comment on the difference between the assignment in Requirement 1 and the activity-based assignment.

Exercise 7–13 *Formation of an Activity Dictionary*

A hospital is in the process of implementing an ABC system. A pilot study is being done to assess the effects of the costing changes on specific products. Of particular interest is the cost of caring for patients who receive in-patient recovery treatment for illness, surgery (noncardiac), and injury. These patients are housed on the third and fourth floors of the hospital (the floors are dedicated to patient care and have only nursing stations and patient rooms). A partial transcript of an interview with the hospital's nursing supervisor is as follows:

1. How many nurses are in the hospital?
   There are 101 nurses, including me.
2. Of these 100 nurses, how many are assigned to the third and fourth floors?
   Fifty nurses are assigned to these two floors.

3. What do these nurses do (please describe)?
   Provide nursing care for patients, which, as you know, means answering questions, changing bandages, administering medicine, changing clothes, etc.

4. And what do you do?
   I supervise and coordinate all the nursing activity in the hospital. This includes surgery, maternity, the emergency room, and the two floors you mentioned.

5. What other lodging and care activities are done for the third and fourth floors by persons other than the nurses?
   The patients must be fed. The hospital cafeteria delivers meals. The laundry department picks up dirty clothing and bedding once each shift. The floors also have a physical therapist assigned to provide care on a physician-directed basis.

6. Do patients use any equipment?
   Yes. Mostly monitoring equipment.

7. Who or what uses the activity output?
   Patients. But there are different kinds of patients. On these two floors, we classify patients into three categories according to severity: intensive care, intermediate care, and normal care. The more severe the illness, the more activity is used. Nurses spend much more time with intermediate care patients than with normal care. The more severe patients tend to use more of the laundry service as well. Their clothing and bedding need to be changed more frequently. On the other hand, severe patients use less food. They eat fewer meals. Typically, we measure each patient type by the number of days of hospital stay. And you have to realize that the same patient contributes to each type of product.

Required:

Prepare an activity dictionary with three categories: activity name, activity description, and activity driver.

Exercise 7–14 *Activity Rates and Activity-Based Product Costing*

Hammer Company produces a variety of electronic equipment. One of its plants produces two laser printers: the deluxe and the regular. At the beginning of the year, the following data were prepared for this plant:

	Deluxe	Regular
Quantity	100,000	800,000
Selling price	$900	$750
Unit prime cost	$529	$483

In addition, the following information was provided so that overhead costs could be assigned to each product:

Activity Name	Activity Driver	Activity Cost	Deluxe	Regular
Setups	Number of setups	$ 2,000,000	300	200
Machining	Machine hours	80,000,000	100,000	300,000
Engineering	Engineering hours	6,000,000	50,000	100,000
Packing	Packing orders	1,000,000	100,000	400,000

Required:

1. Calculate the overhead rates for each activity.
2. Calculate the per-unit product cost for each product.

Exercise 7–15 *Value and Non-Value-Added Costs*

River Technology produces transmissions for snowmobiles. Because of competitive pressures, the company was making an effort to reduce costs. As part of this effort,

management implemented an activity-based management system and began focusing its attention on processes and activities. Purchasing was among the processes (activities) that were carefully studied. The study revealed that the number of purchase orders was a good driver for purchasing costs. During the last year, the company incurred fixed purchasing costs of $420,000 (salaries of 10 employees). These fixed costs provide a capacity of processing 48,000 orders (4,800 per employee at practical capacity). Management decided that the efficient level for purchasing should use 24,000 purchase orders.

Required:

1. Explain why purchasing would be viewed as a value-added activity. List all possible reasons. Also, list some possible reasons that explain why the demand for purchasing is more than the efficient level of 24,000 orders.
2. Break the cost of purchasing into its value-added and non-value-added components.

Exercise 7–16 *(Appendix) Quality Cost Report*

During 2007 and 2008, Wilmington Company reported sales of $6,000,000 (for each year). Wilmington listed the following quality costs for the past two years. Assume that all changes in the quality costs are due to a quality improvement program.

	2007	2008
Design review	$ 150,000	$ 300,000
Recalls	200,000	100,000
Reinspection	100,000	50,000
Materials inspection	60,000	40,000
Quality training	40,000	100,000
Process acceptance	—	50,000
Scrap	145,000	35,000
Lost sales (estimated)	300,000	200,000
Product inspection	50,000	30,000
Returned goods	155,000	95,000
Total	$1,200,000	$1,000,000

Required:

1. Prepare a quality cost report for each year (2007 and 2008).
2. How much were the additional resources invested in prevention and appraisal activities (control costs) from one year to the next? What return did this investment generate? (What reduction in failure costs was achieved?)
3. The management of Wilmington believes that it is possible to reduce quality costs to 2.5 percent of sales. Assuming sales continue at the $6,000,000 level, calculate the additional profit potential facing Wilmington. Is the expectation of improving quality and reducing quality costs to 2.5 percent of sales realistic? Explain.

Exercise 7–17 *(Appendix) Environmental Cost Report*

At the end of 2007, Booth Pharmaceuticals (BP) implemented an environmental quality management program. As a first step, BP identified the following costs for the year just ended in its accounting records as environmentally related:

	2007
Inefficient materials usage	$ 600,000
Treating and disposing of toxic waste	2,400,000
Cleanup of chemically contaminated soil	900,000
Testing for contamination	300,000

(continued)

	2007
Operating pollution control equipment	$420,000
Maintaining pollution control equipment	180,000
Performing environmental studies	60,000
Verifying supplier environmental performance	30,000
Training (environmentally related)	37,500

Required:

1. Prepare an environmental cost report by category. Assume that total operating costs are $30,000,000.
2. Calculate the relative distribution percentages for each environmental cost category (the percentage of the total environmental cost represented by each category). Comment on the distribution.
3. Suppose that the newly hired environmental manager examines the report and makes the following comment: "This report understates the total environmental costs. It fails to consider the costs that we are imposing on the local community. For example, we have polluted the river and lake so much that swimming and fishing are no longer possible. I have heard rumblings from the local citizens, and I'll bet that we will be facing a big cleanup bill in a few years."

    Assume that subsequent to the comment, engineering estimated that cleanup costs for the river and lake would amount to $3,000,000, assuming the cleanup is required within five years. To pay for the cleanup, annual contributions of $525,000 will be invested with the expectation that the fund will grow to $3,000,000 by the end of the fifth year. Assume, also, that the loss of recreational opportunities is costing the local community $1,200,000 per year. How would this information alter the report in Requirement 1?

Exercise 7–18 *(Appendix) ABC Environmental Costing*

Gosney Chemical produces two chemical products: a dyestuff intermediate and an adhesive for rubber. The controller and environmental manager have identified the following environmental activities and costs associated with the two products:

	Dyestuff Intermediate	Rubber Adhesive
Pounds produced	10,000,000	25,000,000
Packaging materials (pounds)	3,000,000	1,500,000
Energy usage (kilowatt-hours)	1,000,000	500,000
Toxin releases (pounds into air)	2,500,000	500,000
Pollution control (machine hours)	400,000	100,000
Costs of activities:		
Using packaging materials	$4,500,000	
Using energy	1,200,000	
Releasing toxins (fines)	600,000	
Operating pollution control equipment	1,400,000	

Required:

1. Calculate the environmental cost per pound for each product. Which of the two appears to cause the most degradation to the environment?
2. In which environmental category would you classify excessive use of materials and energy?
3. Suppose that the toxin releases cause health problems for those who live near the chemical plant. The costs, due to missed work and medical treatments, are estimated at $2,700,000 per year. How would assignment of these costs change the unit cost? Should they be assigned?

PROBLEMS

(Note: Whenever you see a  next to a requirement, it signals a "building on a cornerstone" requirement. Assigning this requirement will usually entail additional work, such as a group project, analytical reasoning, Internet research, decision making, and the use of written communication skills.)

Problem 7–1 *Functional-Based versus Activity-Based Costing*

OBJECTIVES 1, 2

Tamarindo Company for years produced only one product: backpacks. Recently, the company decided to add a line of duffel bags. With this addition, the company began assigning overhead costs using departmental rates. (Prior to this, the company used a predetermined plantwide rate based on *units produced*.) Departmental rates meant that overhead costs had to be assigned to each producing department to create overhead pools so that predetermined departmental rates could be calculated. Surprisingly, after the addition of the duffel-bag line and the switch to departmental rates, the costs to produce the backpacks increased and their profitability dropped.

The marketing manager and the production manager both complained about the increase in the production cost of backpacks. The marketing manager was concerned because the increase in unit costs led to pressure to increase the unit price of backpacks. She was resisting this pressure because she was certain that the increase would harm the company's market share. The production manager was receiving pressure to cut costs also, yet he was convinced that nothing different was being done in the way the backpacks were produced. He was also convinced that further efficiency in the manufacture of the backpacks was unlikely. After some discussion, the two managers decided that the problem had to be connected to the addition of the duffel-bag line.

Upon investigation, they were informed that the only real change in product-costing procedures was in the way overhead costs are assigned. A two-stage procedure was now in use. First, overhead costs are assigned to the two producing departments, patterns and finishing. Some overhead costs are assigned to the producing departments using direct tracing, and some are assigned using driver tracing. For example, the salaries of the producing department's supervisors are assigned using direct tracing, whereas the costs of the factory's accounting department are assigned using driver tracing (the driver being the number of transactions processed for each department). Second, the costs accumulated in the producing departments are assigned to the two products using direct labor hours as a driver (the rate in each department is based on direct labor hours). The managers were assured that great care was taken to associate overhead costs with individual products. So that they could construct their own example of overhead cost assignment, the controller provided them with the information necessary to show how accounting costs are assigned to products:

| | Department | | |
	Patterns	Finishing	Total
Accounting cost	$48,000	$72,000	$120,000
Transactions processed	32,000	48,000	80,000
Total direct labor hours	10,000	20,000	30,000
Direct labor hours per backpack*	0.10	0.20	0.30
Direct labor hours per duffel bag*	0.40	0.80	1.20

*Hours required to produce one unit of each product.

The controller remarked that the cost of operating the accounting department had doubled with the addition of the new product line. The increase came because of the need to process additional transactions, which had also doubled in number.

During the first year of producing duffel bags, the company produced and sold 100,000 backpacks and 25,000 duffel bags. The 100,000 backpacks matched the prior year's output for that product.

Required:

1. Compute the amount of accounting cost assigned to a backpack before the duffel-bag line was added using a plantwide rate approach based on units produced. Is this assignment accurate? Explain.

2. Suppose that the company decided to assign the accounting costs directly to the product lines using the number of transactions as the activity driver. What is the accounting cost per unit of backpacks? Per unit of duffel bags?

3. Compute the amount of accounting cost assigned to each backpack and duffel bag using departmental rates based on direct labor hours.

4. Which way of assigning overhead does the best job—the functional-based approach using departmental rates or the activity-based approach using transactions processed for each product? Explain. Discuss the value of activity-based costing before the duffel-bag line was added.

Problem 7–2 *Plantwide versus Departmental Rates, Product-Costing Accuracy: ABC*

Ramsey Company produces speakers (Model A and Model B). Both products pass through two producing departments. Model A's production is much more labor-intensive than Model B. Model B is also the most popular of the two speakers. The following data have been gathered for the two products:

	Product Data	
	Model A	Model B
Units produced per year	30,000	300,000
Prime costs	$100,000	$1,000,000
Direct labor hours	140,000	300,000
Machine hours	20,000	200,000
Production runs	40	60
Inspection hours	800	1,200
Maintenance hours	10,000	90,000
Overhead costs:		
Setup costs	$180,000	
Inspection costs	140,000	
Machining	160,000	
Maintenance	180,000	
Total	$660,000	

Required:

1. Compute the overhead cost per unit for each product using a plantwide rate based on direct labor hours.

2. Compute the overhead cost per unit for each product using activity-based costing.

3. Suppose that Ramsey decides to use departmental overhead rates. There are two departments: Department 1 (machine intensive) with a rate of $2.33 per machine hour and Department 2 (labor intensive) with a rate of $0.60 per direct labor hour. The consumption of these two drivers is as follows:

	Department 1 Machine Hours	Department 2 Direct Labor Hours
Model A	10,000	130,000
Model B	170,000	270,000

Compute the overhead cost per unit for each product using departmental rates.

4. Using the activity-based product costs as the standard, comment on the ability of departmental rates to improve the accuracy of product costing. (Did the departmental rates do better than the plantwide rate?)

Problem 7–3 *Production-Based Costing versus Activity-Based Costing, Assigning Costs to Activities, Resource Drivers*

OBJECTIVES 1, 2

Willow Company produces lawn mowers. One of its plants produces two versions of mowers: a basic model and a deluxe model. The deluxe model has a sturdier frame, a higher horsepower engine, a wider blade, and mulching capability. At the beginning of the year, the following data were prepared for this plant:

	Basic Model	Deluxe Model
Expected quantity	40,000	20,000
Selling price	$180	$360
Prime costs	$80	$160
Machine hours	5,000	5,000
Direct labor hours	10,000	10,000
Engineering support (hours)	1,500	4,500
Receiving (orders processed)	250	500
Materials handling (number of moves)	1,200	4,800
Purchasing (number of requisitions)	100	200
Maintenance (hours used)	1,000	3,000
Paying suppliers (invoices processed)	250	500
Setting up equipment (number of setups)	16	64

Additionally, the following overhead activity costs are reported:

Maintaining equipment	$114,000
Engineering support	120,000
Materials handling	?
Setting up equipment	96,000
Purchasing materials	60,000
Receiving goods	40,000
Paying suppliers	30,000
Providing space	20,000
Total	$?

Facility-level costs are allocated in proportion to machine hours (provides a measure of time the facility is used by each product). Materials handling uses three inputs: two forklifts, gasoline to operate the forklift, and three operators. The three operators are paid a salary of $40,000 each. The operators spend 25 percent of their time on the receiving activity and 75 percent on moving goods (materials handling). Gasoline costs $3 per move. Depreciation amounts to $6,000 per forklift per year.

Required:
1. Calculate the cost of the materials handling activity. Label the cost assignments as driver tracing or direct tracing. Identify the resource drivers.
2. Calculate the cost per unit for each product using direct labor hours to assign all overhead costs.
3. Calculate activity rates and assign costs to each product. Calculate a unit cost for each product and compare these costs with those calculated in Requirement 2.
4. Calculate consumption ratios for each activity.
5. Explain how the consumption ratios calculated in Requirement 4 can be used to reduce the number of rates. Calculate the rates that would apply under this approach.

Problem 7–4 *Activity Costing, Assigning Resource Costs, Primary and Secondary Activities*

OBJECTIVES 1, 2

Trinity Clinic has identified three activities for daily maternity care: occupancy and feeding, nursing, and nursing supervision. The nursing supervisor oversees 150 nurses, 25 of whom are maternity nurses (the other nurses are located in other care areas such as the emergency room and intensive care). The nursing supervisor has three assistants, a secretary, several offices, computers, phones, and furniture. The three assistants spend 75 percent of their time on the supervising activity and 25 percent of their time as surgical nurses. They each receive a salary of $48,000. The nursing supervisor has a salary of $70,000. She spends 100 percent of her time supervising. The secretary receives a salary of $22,000 per year. Other costs directly traceable to the supervisory activity (depreciation, utilities, phone, etc.) average $100,000 per year.

Daily care output is measured as "patient days." The clinic has traditionally assigned the cost of daily care by using a daily rate (a rate per patient day). Different kinds of daily care are provided, and rates are structured to reflect these differences. For example, a higher daily rate is charged for an intensive care unit than for a maternity care unit. Within units, however, the daily rates are the same for all patients. Under the traditional, functional approach, the daily rate is computed by dividing the annual costs of occupancy and feeding, nursing, and a share of supervision by the unit's capacity expressed in patient days. The cost of supervision is assigned to each care area based on the number of nurses. A single driver (patient days) is used to assign the costs of daily care to each patient.

A pilot study has revealed that the demands for nursing care vary within the maternity unit, depending on the severity of a patient's case. Specifically, demand for nursing services per day increases with severity. Assume the maternity unit has three levels of increasing severity: normal patients, cesarean patients, and patients with complications. The pilot study provided the following activity and cost information:

Activity	Annual Cost	Activity Driver	Annual Quantity
Occupancy and feeding	$1,000,000	Patient days	10,000
Nursing care (maternity)	950,000	Hours of nursing care	50,000
Nursing supervision	?	Number of nurses	150

The pilot study also revealed the following information concerning the three types of patients and their annual demands:

Patient Type	Patient Days Demanded	Nursing Hours Demanded
Normal	7,000	17,500
Cesarean	2,000	12,500
Complications	1,000	20,000
Total	10,000	50,000

Required:

1. Calculate the cost per patient day using a functional-based approach.
2. Calculate the cost per patient day using an activity-based approach.
3. The hospital processes 1,000,000 pounds of laundry per year. The cost for the laundering activity is $500,000 per year. In a functional-based cost system, the cost of the laundry department is assigned to each user department in proportion to the pounds of laundry produced. Typically, maternity produces 200,000 pounds per year. How much would this change the cost per patient day calculated in Requirement 1? Now describe what information you would need to modify the calculation made in Requirement 2. Under what conditions would this activity calculation provide a more accurate cost assignment?

Problem 7–5 *Customers as a Cost Object*

Oaklawn National Bank has requested an analysis of checking account profitability by customer type. Customers are categorized according to the size of their account: low balances, medium balances, and high balances. The activities associated with the three different customer categories and their associated annual costs are as follows:

Opening and closing accounts	$ 200,000
Issuing monthly statements	300,000
Processing transactions	2,050,000
Customer inquiries	400,000
Providing ATM services	1,120,000
Total cost	$4,070,000

Additional data concerning the usage of the activities by the various customers are also provided:

	Account Balance		
	Low	Medium	High
Number of accounts opened/closed	15,000	3,000	2,000
Number of statements issued	450,000	100,000	50,000
Processing transactions	18,000,000	2,000,000	500,000
Number of telephone minutes	1,000,000	600,000	400,000
Number of ATM transactions	1,350,000	200,000	50,000
Number of checking accounts	38,000	8,000	4,000

Required:

1. Calculate a cost per account per year by dividing the total cost of processing and maintaining checking accounts by the total number of accounts. What is the average fee per month that the bank should charge to cover the costs incurred because of checking accounts?
2. Calculate a cost per account by customer category using activity rates.
3. Currently, the bank offers free checking to all its customers. The interest revenues average $90 per account; however, the interest revenues earned per account by category are $80, $100, and $165 for the low, medium, and high balance accounts, respectively. Calculate the average profit per account (average revenue less average cost from Requirement 1). Now calculate the profit per account using the revenue per customer type and the unit cost per customer type calculated in Requirement 2.
4. After the analysis in Requirement 3, a vice president recommended eliminating the free checking feature for low-balance customers. The bank president expressed reluctance to do so, arguing that the low-balance customers more than made up for the loss through cross sales. He presented a survey that showed that 50 percent of the customers would switch banks if a checking fee were imposed. Explain how you could verify the president's argument using activity-based costing.

Problem 7–6 *ABC and Customer-Driven Costs*

OBJECTIVES
2, 3

Sorensen Manufacturing produces several types of bolts used in aircrafts. The bolts are produced in batches according to customer orders. Although there are a variety of bolts, they can be grouped into three product families. Because the product families are used in different kinds of aircraft, customers also can be grouped into three categories, corresponding to the product family they purchase. The number of units sold to each customer class is the same. The selling prices for the three product families range from $0.50 to $0.80 per unit. Historically, the costs of order entry, processing, and handling were expensed and not traced to individual customer groups. These costs are not trivial and totaled $4,500,000 for the most recent year. Furthermore, these costs had been increasing over time. Recently, the company started emphasizing a cost reduction strategy; however, any cost reduction decisions had to contribute to the creation of a competitive advantage.

Because of the magnitude and growth of order-filling costs, management decided to explore the causes of these costs. They discovered that order-filling costs were driven by the number of customer orders processed. Further investigation revealed the following cost behavior for the order-filling activity:

Step-fixed cost component: $50,000 per step (2,000 orders define a step)*
Variable cost component: $20 per order

*Sorensen currently has sufficient steps to process 100,000 orders.

The expected customer orders for the year total 100,000. The expected usage of the order-filling activity and the average size of an order by customer category follow:

	Category I	Category II	Category III
Number of orders	50,000	30,000	20,000
Average order size	600	1,000	1,500

As a result of cost behavior analysis, the marketing manager recommended the imposition of a charge per customer order. The president of the company concurred. The charge was implemented by adding the cost per order to the price of each order (computed using the projected ordering costs and expected orders). This ordering cost was then reduced as the size of the order increased and eliminated as the order size reached 2,000 units (the marketing manager indicated that any penalties imposed for orders greater than this size would lose sales from some of the smaller customers). Within a short period of communicating this new price information to customers, the average order size for all three product families increased to 2,000 units.

Required:
1. Sorensen traditionally has expensed order-filling costs. What is the most likely reason for this practice?
2. Calculate the cost per order for each customer category.
3. Calculate the reduction in order-filling costs produced by the change in pricing strategy (assume that resource spending is reduced as much as possible and that the total units sold remain unchanged). Explain how exploiting customer activity information produced this cost reduction. Would any other internal activities benefit from this pricing strategy?

Problem 7–7 *Activity-Based Supplier Costing*

OBJECTIVES
2, 3

Levy, Inc., manufactures tractors for agricultural usage. Levy purchases the engines needed for its tractors from two sources: Johnson Engines and Watson Company. The Johnson engine is the more expensive of the two sources and has a price of $1,000. The Watson engine is $900 per unit. Levy produces and sells 22,000 tractors. Of the 22,000 engines needed for the tractors, 4,000 are purchased from Johnson Engines and 18,000 are purchased from Watson Company. The production manager, Jamie Murray, prefers the Johnson engine. However, Jan Booth, purchasing manager, maintains that the price difference is too great to buy more than the 4,000 units currently purchased. Booth also wants to maintain a significant connection with the Johnson source just in case the less expensive source cannot supply the needed quantities. Even though Jamie understands the price argument, he is convinced that the quality of the Johnson engine is worth the price difference.

Frank Wallace, the controller, has decided to use activity costing to resolve the issue. The following activity cost and supplier data have been collected:

Activity	Cost
Replacing engines[a]	$ 800,000
Expediting orders[b]	1,000,000
Repairing engines[c]	1,800,000

[a]All units are tested after assembly, and some are rejected because of engine failure. The failed engines are removed and replaced, with the supplier replacing any failed engine. The replaced engine is retested before being sold. Engine failure often causes collateral damage, and other parts often need to be replaced.

[b]Due to late or failed delivery of engines.

[c]Repair work is for units under warranty and almost invariably is due to engine failure. Repair usually means replacing the engine. This cost plus labor, transportation, and other costs make warranty work very expensive.

	Watson	Johnson
Engines replaced by source	1,980	20
Late or failed shipments	198	2
Warranty repairs (by source)	2,440	60

Required:

1. Calculate the activity-based supplier cost per engine (acquisition cost plus supplier-related activity costs). Which of the two suppliers is the low-cost supplier? Explain why this is a better measure of engine cost than the usual purchase costs assigned to the engines.

2. Consider the supplier cost information obtained in Requirement 1. Suppose further that Johnson can only supply a total of 20,000 units. What actions would you advise Levy to undertake with its suppliers?

Problem 7–8 *Activity-Based Management, Non-Value-Added Costs*

OBJECTIVE 4

Danna Martin, president of Mays Electronics, was concerned about the end-of-the year marketing report that she had just received. According to Larry Savage, marketing manager, a price decrease for the coming year was again needed to maintain the company's annual sales volume of integrated circuit boards (CBs). This would make a bad situation worse. The current selling price of $18 per unit was producing a $2-per-unit profit—half the customary $4-per-unit profit. Foreign competitors kept reducing their prices. To match the latest reduction would reduce the price from $18 to $14. This would put the price below the cost to produce and sell it. How could these firms sell for such a low price? Determined to find out if there were problems with the company's operations, Danna decided to hire a consultant to evaluate the way in which the CBs were produced and sold. After two weeks, the consultant had identified the following activities and costs:

Setting up equipment	$ 125,000
Materials handling	180,000
Inspecting products	122,000
Engineering support	120,000
Handling customer complaints	100,000
Filling warranties	170,000
Storing goods	80,000
Expediting goods	75,000
Using materials	500,000
Using power	48,000
Manual insertion labor[a]	250,000
Other direct labor	150,000
Total costs	$1,920,000[b]

[a]Diodes, resistors, and integrated circuits are inserted manually into the circuit board.

[b]This total cost produces a unit cost of $16 for last year's sales volume.

The consultant indicated that some preliminary activity analysis shows that per-unit costs can be reduced by at least $7. Since the marketing manager had indicated that the market share (sales volume) for the boards could be increased by 50 percent if the price could be reduced to $12, Danna became quite excited.

Required:
1. What is activity-based management? What phases of activity analysis did the consultant provide? What else remains to be done?
2. Identify as many non-value-added costs as possible. Compute the cost savings per unit that would be realized if these costs were eliminated. Was the consultant correct in his preliminary cost reduction assessment? Discuss actions that the company can take to reduce or eliminate the non-value-added activities.
3. Compute the unit cost required to maintain current market share, while earning a profit of $4 per unit. Now compute the unit cost required to expand sales by 50 percent. How much cost reduction would be required to achieve each unit cost?
4. Assume that further activity analysis revealed the following: switching to automated insertion would save $60,000 of engineering support and $90,000 of direct labor. Now what is the total potential cost reduction per unit available from activity analysis? With these additional reductions, can Mays achieve the unit cost to maintain current sales? To increase it by 50 percent? What form of activity analysis is this: reduction, sharing, elimination, or selection?
5. Calculate income based on current sales, prices, and costs. Now calculate the income using a $14 price and a $12 price, assuming that the maximum cost reduction possible is achieved (including Requirement 4's reduction). What price should be selected?

Problem 7–9 *Non-Value-Added Costs, Activity Costs, Activity Cost Reduction*

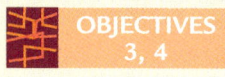

OBJECTIVES
3, 4

John Thomas, vice president of Mallett Company (a producer of a variety of plastic products), has been supervising the implementation of an activity-based cost management system. One of John's objectives is to improve process efficiency by improving the activities that define the processes. To illustrate the potential of the new system to the president, John has decided to focus on two processes: production and customer service.

Within each process, one activity will be selected for improvement: materials usage for production and sustaining engineering for customer service (sustaining engineers are responsible for redesigning products based on customer needs and feedback). Value-added standards are identified for each activity (the level of efficiency so that no waste exists). For materials usage, the value-added standard calls for six pounds per unit of output (although the plastic products differ in shape and function, their size—as measured by weight—is uniform). The value-added standard is based on the elimination of all waste due to defective molds. The standard price of materials is $5 per pound. For sustaining engineering, the standard is 58 percent of current practical activity capacity. This standard is based on the fact that about 42 percent of the complaints have to do with design features that could have been avoided or anticipated by the company.

Current practical capacity (at the end of 2005) is defined by the following requirements: 6,000 engineering hours for each product group that has been on the market or in development for five years or less and 2,400 hours per product group of more than five years. Four product groups have less than five years' experience, and 10 product groups have more. Each of the 24 engineers is paid a salary of $60,000. Each engineer can provide 2,000 hours of service per year. No other significant costs are incurred for the engineering activity.

Actual materials usage for 2006 was 25 percent above the level called for by the value-added standard; engineering usage was 46,000 hours. A total of 80,000 units of output were produced. John and the operational managers have selected some improvement measures that promise to reduce non-value-added activity usage by 40 percent in 2007. Selected actual results achieved for 2007 are as follows:

Units produced	80,000
Materials used	584,800
Engineering hours	35,400

The actual prices paid for materials and engineering hours are identical to the standard or budgeted prices.

Required:

1. For 2006, calculate the non-value-added usage and costs for materials usage and sustaining engineering.
2. Using the budgeted improvements, calculate the expected activity usage levels for 2007. Now compute the 2007 usage variances (the difference between the expected and actual values), expressed in both physical and financial measures, for materials and engineering. Comment on the company's ability to achieve its targeted reductions. In particular, discuss what measures the company must take to capture any realized reductions in resource usage.

Problem 7–10 *Cycle Time, Velocity, Product Costing*

Silverman Company has a JIT system in place. Each manufacturing cell is dedicated to the production of a single product or major subassembly. One cell, dedicated to the production of binoculars, has four operations: machining, finishing, assembly, and qualifying (testing).

For the coming year, the binocular cell has the following budgeted costs and cell time (both at theoretical capacity):

Budgeted conversion costs	$2,500,000
Budgeted raw materials	$3,000,000
Cell time	4,000 hours
Theoretical output	30,000 binoculars

During the year, the following actual results were obtained:

Actual conversion costs	$2,500,000
Actual materials	$2,600,000
Actual cell time	4,000 hours
Actual output	25,000 binoculars

Required:

1. Compute the velocity (number of binoculars per hour) that the cell can theoretically achieve. Now compute the theoretical cycle time (number of hours or minutes per binocular) that it takes to produce one binocular.
2. Compute the actual velocity and the actual cycle time.

3. Compute the budgeted conversion costs per minute. Using this rate, compute the conversion costs per binocular if theoretical output is achieved. Using this measure, compute the conversion costs per binocular for actual output. Does this product-costing approach provide an incentive for the cell manager to reduce cycle time? Explain.

Problem 7–11 *(Appendix) Trade-Offs among Quality Cost Categories, Gainsharing*

Piura Company has sales of $10 million and quality costs of $2,000,000. The company is embarking on a major quality improvement program. During the next three years, Piura intends to attack failure costs by increasing its appraisal and prevention costs. The "right" prevention activities will be selected, and appraisal costs will be reduced according to the results achieved. For the coming year, management is considering six specific activities: quality training, process control, product inspection, supplier evaluation, redesign of two major products, and prototype testing. To encourage managers to focus on reducing non-value-added quality costs and select the right activities, a bonus pool is established relating to reduction of quality costs. The bonus pool is equal to 10 percent of the total reduction in quality costs.

Current quality costs and the costs of these six activities are given in the following table. Each activity is added sequentially so that its effect on the cost categories can be assessed. For example, after quality training is added, the control costs increase to $400,000 and the failure costs drop to $1,300,000. Even though the activities are presented sequentially, they are totally independent of each other. Thus, only beneficial activities need be selected.

	Control Costs	Failure Costs
Current quality costs*	$ 200,000	$1,800,000
Quality training	400,000	1,300,000
Process control	650,000	900,000
Product inspection	750,000	820,000
Supplier evaluation	900,000	250,000
Prototype testing	1,200,000	150,000
Engineering redesign	1,250,000	50,000

*All current control costs are appraisal costs.

Required:

1. Identify the control activities that should be implemented and calculate the total quality costs associated with this selection. Assume that an activity is selected only if it increases the bonus pool.
2. Given the activities selected in Requirement 1, calculate the following:
   a. The reduction in total quality costs.
   b. The percentage distribution for control and failure costs.
   c. The amount for this year's bonus pool.

3. Suppose that a quality engineer complained about the gainsharing incentive system. Basically, he argued that the bonus should be based only on reductions of failure and appraisal costs. In this way, investment in prevention activities would be encouraged and failure and appraisal costs would eventually be eliminated. After eliminating the non-value-added costs, focus could then be placed on the level of prevention costs. If this approach were adopted, what activities would be selected? Do you agree with this approach? Explain.

Problem 7–12 *(Appendix) Quality Cost Summary, Gainsharing*

Linda Wise, president of Troy Company, has recently returned from a conference on quality and productivity. At the conference, she learned that many American firms have made significant progress in improving quality and reducing quality costs. Many of these firms have been able to reduce quality costs from 20 to 30 percent of sales to 2 to 3 percent of sales. She was skeptical, however, about this statistic. But even if the quality gurus were right, she was sure that her company's quality costs were much lower—probably less than 5 percent. On the other hand, if she was wrong, she would be passing up an opportunity to improve profits significantly and simultaneously strengthen her competitive position. In fact, she reflected on the comment of one of the quality experts: "Quality has become a condition of entrance to the market. If the product is not good, you will quickly go out of business." The quality issue was at least worth exploring. Moreover, she decided that it might be too risky not to assess her company's quality performance. She knew that her company produced most of the information needed for quality cost reporting, but there never had been a need to bother with any formal quality data gathering and analysis.

This conference, however, had convinced her that a firm's profitability can increase significantly by improving quality—provided the potential for improvement exists. Thus, before committing the company to a quality improvement program, Linda contacted her controller and requested a preliminary estimate of the total quality costs currently being incurred. She also instructed the controller to classify quality costs into four categories: prevention, appraisal, internal failure, and external failure costs. The controller has gathered the following information from the past year, 2007:

a. Sales revenue is $20,000,000; net income is $4,000,000.
b. During the year, customers returned 60,000 units needing repair. Repair cost averages $7 per unit.
c. Ten inspectors are employed, each earning an annual salary of $30,000. These 10 inspectors are involved only with final inspection (product acceptance).
d. Total scrap is 60,000 units. All scrap is quality related. The cost of scrap is about $15 per unit.
e. Each year, approximately 300,000 units are rejected in final inspection. Of these units, about 80 percent can be recovered through rework. The cost of rework is $3 per unit.
f. A customer cancelled an order that would have increased profits by $500,000. The customer's reason for cancellation was poor product performance. The accounting and marketing departments agree that the company loses at least this much each year for the same reason.
g. The company employs eight full-time employees in its complaint department. Each earns $25,000 a year.
h. The company gave sales allowances totaling $250,000 due to substandard products being sent to the customer.
i. The company requires all new employees to take its 3-hour quality training program. The estimated annual cost of the program is $160,000.
j. Inspection of the final product requires testing equipment. The annual cost of operating and maintaining this equipment is $240,000.

Required:

1. Prepare a simple quality cost report, classifying costs by category. Comment on the quality costs/sales ratio.
2. Discuss the distribution of quality costs among the four categories. Are they properly distributed? Explain.
3. Suppose Troy Company decides a 5-year program will reduce quality costs to 2.5 percent of sales and that control costs will be 80 percent of total quality costs. Calculate the income increase that will occur if sales remain at $20,000,000. Also, calculate the total amount spent on control and failure costs.
4. Refer to Requirements 1 and 3. Suppose that Linda decides to create a bonus pool to allow employees to share in the benefits from quality improvements. The bonus pool is 20 percent of quality cost reductions. How much will be put in the bonus pool for the 5-year period? Why establish such a pool? Suppose Linda's quality manager suggests that the bonus be based only on reductions of appraisal and failure costs. Explain why he might suggest this modification. Do you agree?

Problem 7–13 *(Appendix) Classification of Environmental Costs*

Consider the following independent environmental activities.

a. A company takes actions to reduce the amount of material in its packages.

b. After its useful life, a soft-drink producer returns the activated carbon used for purifying water for its beverages to the supplier. The supplier reactivates the carbon for a second use in nonfood applications. As a consequence, many tons of material are prevented from entering landfills.

c. An evaporator system is installed to treat wastewater and collect usable solids for other uses.

d. The inks used to print snack packages (for chips) contain heavy metals.

e. Processes are inspected to ensure compliance with environmental standards.

f. Delivery boxes are used five times and then recycled. This prevents 112 million pounds of cardboard from entering landfills and saves two million trees per year.

g. Scrubber equipment is installed to ensure that air emissions are less than the level permitted by law.

h. Local residents are incurring medical costs from illnesses caused by air pollution from automobile exhaust pollution.

i. As part of implementing an environmental perspective for the Balanced Scorecard, environmental performance measures are developed.

j. Because of liquid and solid residues being discharged into a local lake, it is no longer fit for swimming, fishing, and other recreational activities.

k. To reduce energy consumption, magnetic ballasts are replaced with electronic ballasts, and more efficient light bulbs and lighting sensors are installed. As a result, 2.3 million kilowatt-hours of electricity are saved per year.

l. Because of a legal settlement, a chemical company must spend $20,000,000 to clean up contaminated soil.

m. A soft-drink company uses the following practice: In all bottling plants, packages damaged during filling are collected and recycled (glass, plastic, and aluminum).

n. Products are inspected to ensure that the gaseous emissions produced during operation follow legal and company guidelines.

o. Costs are incurred to operate pollution control equipment.

p. An internal audit is conducted to verify that environmental policies are being followed.

Required:

Classify these environmental activities as prevention costs, detection costs, internal failure costs, or external failure costs. For external failure costs, classify the costs as societal or private. Also, label those activities that are compatible with sustainable development with "SD."

Problem 7–14 *(Appendix) ABC Assignment of Environmental Costs*

The following environmental cost report is for 2005, 2006, and 2007 for the Communications Products Division of Hepworth Company, a telecommunications company. In 2005, Hepworth committed itself to a continuous environmental improvement program, which was implemented throughout the company.

Environmental Activity	2005	2006	2007
Disposing of hazardous waste	$ 800,000	$600,000	$ 200,000
Measuring contaminant releases	40,000	400,000	280,000
Releasing air contaminants	2,000,000	1,600,000	1,000,000
Producing scrap (nonhazardous)	700,000	600,000	500,000
Operating pollution equipment	1,040,000	800,000	520,000
Designing processes and products	200,000	1,200,000	400,000
Using energy	720,000	648,000	576,000
Training employees (environmental)	40,000	80,000	160,000
Remediation (cleanup)	1,600,000	1,200,000	760,000
Inspecting processes	0	400,000	320,000

In 2005, Jack Carter, president of Hepworth, requested that environmental costs be assigned to the two major products produced by the company. He felt that knowledge of the environmental product costs would help guide the design decisions that would be necessary to improve environmental performance. The products represent two different models of a cellular phone (Model XA2 and Model KZ3). The models use different processes and materials. To assign the costs, the following data were gathered for 2005:

Activity	Model XA2	Model KZ3
Disposing hazardous waste (tons)	80	720
Measuring contaminant releases (transactions)	4,000	16,000
Releasing air contaminants (tons)	100	900
Producing scrap (pounds of scrap)	100,000	100,000
Operating pollution equipment (hours)	480,000	1,600,000
Designing processes and products (hours)	6,000	2,000
Using energy (BTUs)	2,400,000	4,800,000
Training employees (hours)	200	200
Remediation (labor hours)	20,000	60,000

During each of the three years (2005 to 2007), Hepworth's division produced 800,000 units of Model XA2 and 1,200,000 units of Model KZ3.

The marketing vice president and the environmental manager estimated that annual sales revenue had increased $800,000 by 2007 because of an improved public image relative to environmental performance (the company was able to charge higher prices because of the perception of "greener products"). The company's finance department also estimated that Hepworth saved $80,000 in 2007 because of reduced finance and insurance costs, all attributable to improved environmental performance. All reductions in environmental costs from 2005 to 2007 are attributable to improvement efforts. Furthermore, any reductions represent ongoing savings.

Required:

1. Using the activity data, calculate the environmental cost per unit for each model. How will this information be useful?

2. Upon examining the cost data produced in Requirement 1, an environmental engineer made the following suggestions: (1) Substitute a new plastic for a raw material that appeared to be the source of much of the hazardous waste (the new material actually cost less than the contaminating material it would replace). (2) Redesign the processes to reduce the amount of air contaminants produced. This option will involve a $1,000,000 one-time expenditure and a $200,000 recurring expense (increased operating cost of the new processes).

   As a result of the first suggestion, by 2007, the amount of hazardous waste produced had diminished to 200 tons, 40 tons for Model XA2 and 160 tons for Model KZ3. The second suggestion reduced the contaminants released by 50 percent by 2007 (50 tons for Model XA2 and 450 tons for Model KZ3). The need for pollution equipment also diminished, and the hours required for Model XA2 and Model KZ3 were reduced to 240,000 and 800,000, respectively. Calculate the unit cost reductions for the two models associated with the actions and outcomes described. Do you think the efforts to reduce the environmental cost per unit were economically justified? Explain.

PROFIT PLANNING

PHOTODISC RED/GETTY IMAGES

After studying Chapter 8, you should be able to:

1. Define budgeting and discuss its role in planning, control, and decision making.
2. Define and prepare the operating budget, identify its major components, and explain the interrelationships of its various components.
3. Define and prepare the financial budget, identify its major components, and explain the interrelationships of its various components.
4. Describe the behavioral dimension of budgeting.

By all outward appearances, Dr. Roger Jones was a successful dentist. He owned his office building, which he leased to the professional corporation housing his dental practice (he owned all shares in the professional corporation). His professional corporation provided annual revenues of more than $750,000 and paid him a salary of $150,000.

However, Dr. Jones recently received a registered letter from the IRS threatening to impound his business and sell its assets for the corporation's failure to pay payroll taxes for the past six months. Furthermore, the professional corporation has had difficulty paying its suppliers. The corporation owed one supplier more than $200,000 and had arranged to pay the interest but has missed even those payments. These same kinds of difficulty have been experienced repeatedly for the past five years.

In the past, Dr. Jones had solved similar problems by borrowing money on the equity in either his personal residence or his office building so that additional capital could be infused into the corporation. This time, however, Dr. Jones was determined to get to the root of the financial difficulties faced by the business. He called Lawson, Johnson, and Smith, a local CPA firm, and requested that a consultant determine the cause of the corporation's recurring financial difficulties. John Smith, a partner in the CPA firm, spent a week examining the records of the practice and extensively interviewing Dr. Jones. He delivered the following report:

Dr. Roger Jones
1091 West Apple Avenue
Reno, Nevada

Dear Dr. Jones:

The cause of your professional corporation's financial difficulties is the absence of proper planning and control. Currently, many spending decisions are made in a haphazard and arbitrary manner. Resources are often committed beyond the capabilities of the practice. To meet these additional commitments, your bookkeeper has been forced to postpone payments for essential operating expenses such as payroll taxes, supplies, and laboratory services.

The following examples illustrate some of the decisions that have contributed to the corporation's financial troubles:

1. *Salary increases*. You have granted 5 percent increases each year whether or not the business could successfully absorb them. Also, your salary is 10 percent higher than dentists with comparable practices.

2. *Cash withdrawals*. For the past five years, cash withdrawals have averaged approximately $1,000 in cash per month. These withdrawals have been treated as a loan from the corporation to you, the president of the corporation.

3. *Equipment purchases*. During the past five years, the corporation has acquired a van, a video recorder, a refrigerator, a microwave, and an in-house stereo system. Some items were purchased for cash, and some are still being paid for in installments. None of them was essential to the mission of your corporation.

These decisions, and others like them, have adversely affected the financial well-being of your dental practice. To solve the corporation's financial problems, I recommend the installation of a formal budgetary system. A comprehensive financial plan is needed so that you know where you are going and what you are capable of doing.

My firm would be pleased to assist you in designing and implementing the recommended system. For it to be successful, you and your staff need to be introduced to the elementary principles of budgeting. We offer three 2-hour seminars on budgeting. The first will describe the basic philosophy of budgeting, the second will teach you how to prepare budgets, and the third will explore the use of budgets for planning, control, and performance evaluation.

Sincerely,
John Smith, CPA

DESCRIPTION OF BUDGETING

All businesses should prepare budgets; all large businesses do. Business entities come in a variety of forms: sole proprietorships (single-owner businesses), partnerships, and corporations. As Dr. Jones's experience vividly points out, even small, professional corporations like his dental practice can benefit from budgeting. In reality, every for-profit and not-for-profit entity can benefit from the planning and control provided by budgets.

> **OBJECTIVE 1**
>
> Define budgeting and discuss its role in planning, control, and decision making.

Budgeting and Planning and Control

Planning and control are tied together in an important and vital way. Planning is looking ahead to see what actions should be taken to realize particular goals. Control is looking backward, determining what actually happened and comparing it with the previously planned outcomes. This comparison can then be used to adjust the budget, looking forward once more. Exhibit 8-1 illustrates the cycle of planning, control, and budgets.

A key component of planning, **budgets** are financial plans for the future; they identify objectives and the actions needed to achieve them. Before a budget is prepared, an organization should develop a strategic plan. The **strategic plan** identifies strategies for future activities and operations, generally covering at least five years. The organization can translate the overall strategy into long- and short-term objectives. These objectives form the basis of the budget. The budget and the strategic plan should be tightly linked. This linkage helps management to ensure that all attention is not focused on the short run. This is important because budgets, as 1-year period plans, are short run in nature.

Advantages of Budgeting

A budgetary system gives an organization several advantages.

1. It forces managers to plan.
2. It provides information that can be used to improve decision making.
3. It provides a standard for performance evaluation.
4. It improves communication and coordination.

Planning, Control, and Budgets

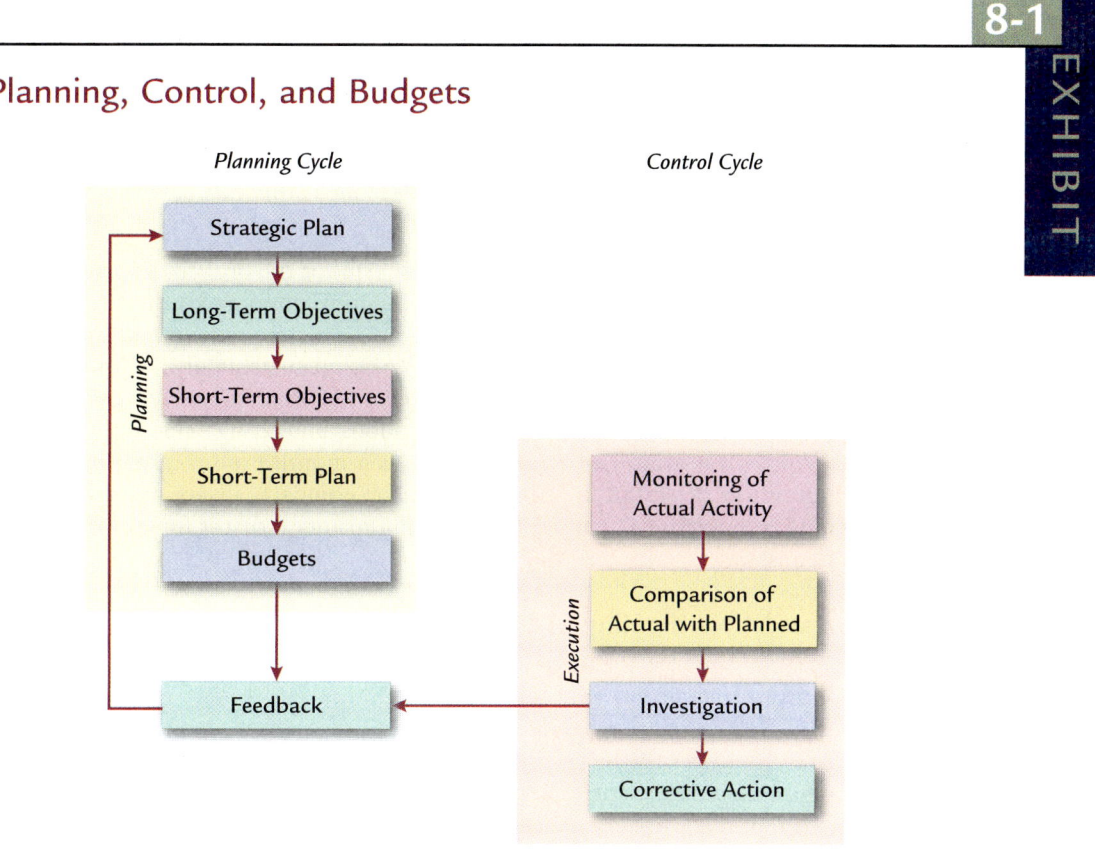

Budgeting forces management to plan for the future. It encourages managers to develop an overall direction for the organization, foresee problems, and develop future policies.

Budgets improve decision making. For example, if Dr. Jones had known the expected revenues and the costs of supplies, lab fees, utilities, salaries, and so on, he might have lowered the rate of salary increases, avoided borrowing money from the corporation, and limited the purchase of nonessential equipment. These better decisions, in turn, might have prevented the problems that arose and resulted in a better financial status for both the business and Dr. Jones.

Budgets set standards that can control the use of a company's resources and motivate employees. A vital part of the budgetary system, **control** is achieved by comparing actual results with budgeted results on a periodic basis (for example, monthly). A large difference between actual and planned results is feedback revealing that the system is out of control. Steps should be taken to find out why and then to correct the situation. For example, if Dr. Jones knows how much amalgam should be used in a filling and what the cost should be, he can evaluate his use of this resource. If more amalgam is being used than expected, Dr. Jones may discover that he is often careless in its use and that extra care will produce savings. The same principle applies to other resources used by the corporation. In total, the savings could be significant.

Budgets also serve to communicate and coordinate. Budgets formally communicate the plans of the

Concept Q & A

How can a budget help in planning and control?

Answer:
A budget requires a plan. It also sets benchmarks that can be used to evaluate performance.

organization to each employee. Accordingly, all employees can be aware of their particular role in achieving those objectives. Since budgets for the various areas and activities of the organization must all work together to achieve organizational objectives, coordination is promoted. Managers can see the needs of other areas and are encouraged to subordinate their individual interests to those of the organization. The role of communication and coordination becomes more significant as an organization increases in size.

The Master Budget

The **master budget** is the comprehensive financial plan for the organization as a whole. Typically, the master budget is for a 1-year period corresponding to the fiscal year of the company. Yearly budgets are broken down into quarterly and monthly budgets. The use of smaller time periods allows managers to compare actual data with budgeted data more frequently, so problems may be noticed and solved sooner.

Some organizations have developed a continuous budgeting philosophy. A **continuous budget** is a moving 12-month budget. As a month expires in the budget, an additional month in the future is added so that the company always has a 12-month plan on hand. Proponents of continuous budgeting maintain that it forces managers to plan ahead constantly.

Directing and Coordinating

Most organizations prepare the master budget for the coming year during the last four or five months of the current year. The **budget committee** reviews the budget, provides policy guidelines and budgetary goals, resolves differences that arise as the budget is prepared, approves the final budget, and monitors the actual performance of the organization as the year unfolds. The president of the organization appoints the members of the committee, who are usually the president, vice president for marketing, vice president for manufacturing, other vice presidents, and the controller. The controller usually serves as the **budget director**, the person responsible for directing and coordinating the organization's overall budgeting process.

Major Components of the Master Budget

A master budget can be divided into operating and financial budgets. **Operating budgets** describe the income-generating activities of a firm: sales, production, and finished goods inventories. The ultimate outcome of the operating budgets is a pro forma or budgeted income statement. **Financial budgets** detail the inflows and outflows of cash and the overall financial position. Planned cash inflows and outflows appear in the cash budget. The expected financial position at the end of the budget period is shown in a budgeted, or pro forma, balance sheet. Since many of the financing activities are not known until the operating budgets are known, the operating budget is prepared first. Describing and illustrating the individual budgets that make up the master budget will make apparent the interdependencies of the component budgets. A diagram displaying these interrelationships is shown in Exhibit 8-2. Details of the capital budget are covered in a separate chapter.

> ## Concept Q & A
>
> What is the main objective of continuous budgeting?
>
> **Answer:**
> It forces managers to plan ahead constantly—something especially needed when firms operate in rapidly changing environments.

> **OBJECTIVE 2**
>
> Define and prepare the operating budget, identify its major components, and explain the interrelationships of its various components.

PREPARING THE OPERATING BUDGET

The operating budget consists of a budgeted income statement accompanied by the following supporting schedules:

The Master Budget and Its Interrelationships

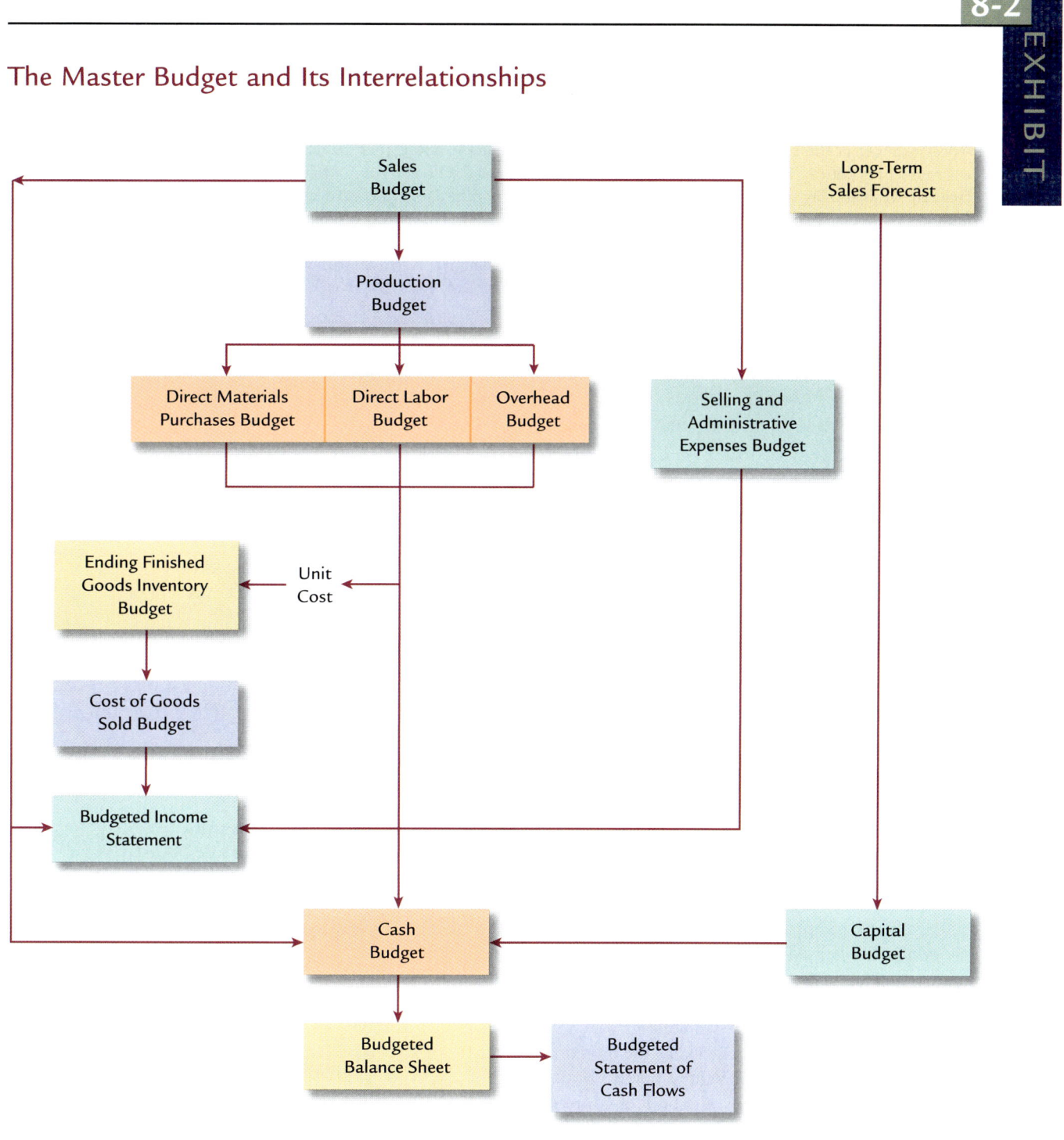

1. Sales budget
2. Production budget
3. Direct materials purchases budget
4. Direct labor budget

5. Overhead budget
6. Selling and administrative expenses budget
7. Ending finished goods inventory budget
8. Cost of goods sold budget

APPLICATIONS IN BUSINESS

The concept of continuous budgeting is driven by the need to make dynamic adjustments to budgets. Firms operate in continuously changing environments, and the ability to reflect changes in the budgets based on changes in the environment is critical. Budgeting and planning software facilitate this flexibility requirement. For example, Huntsman Corporation, a chemical company, uses budgeting and forecasting software to meet the demands of external and internal users for various snapshots of the future. The company uses rolling monthly forecasts to recalibrate results for the balance of the year. Huntsman's director of corporate finance indicated that prices of raw materials (such as those for ethylene and crude oil) can change quickly, noting that the most recent three months may be quite different from what you thought they'd be four months ago. The controller of Children's Hospital Los Angeles (CHLA) made a similar observation. CHLA uses budgeting and planning software to run various budgetary scenarios, such as assessing the impact of new Blue Cross rates on units throughout the hospital.

Source: Tim Reason, "Partial Clearing: Budgeting Software Isn't the Key to Corporate Finance Reform, But It Can Help CFOs Manage Expectations in a Sinking Economy," *CFO: Magazine for Senior Financial Executives* (December 2002), **http://www.CFO.com**. Select "Browse Back Issues."

To illustrate the master budgeting process, we will use an example based on the activities of Texas Rex, Inc., a trendy restaurant in the Southwest that sells t-shirts with the Texas Rex logo (a dinosaur who engages in a variety of adventures while eating the Mexican food for which the restaurant is known). The example focuses on the Texas Rex clothing manufacturing plant.

Sales Budget

The **sales budget** is the projection approved by the budget committee that describes expected sales in units and dollars. Because the sales budget is the basis for all of the other operating budgets and most of the financial budgets, it is important that the sales budget be as accurate as possible.

The first step in creating a sales budget is to develop the sales forecast. This is usually the responsibility of the marketing department. One approach to forecasting sales is the *bottom-up approach*, which requires individual salespeople to submit sales predictions. These are aggregated to form a total sales forecast. The accuracy of this sales forecast may be improved by considering other factors such as the general economic climate, competition, advertising, pricing policies, and so on. Some companies supplement the bottom-up approach with other, more formal approaches, such as time-series analysis, correlation analysis, and econometric modeling.

The sales forecast is merely the initial estimate. The sales forecast is presented to the budget committee for consideration. The budget committee may decide that the forecast is too pessimistic or too optimistic and revise it appropriately. For example, if the budget committee decides that the forecast is too pessimistic and not in harmony with the strategic plan of the organization, it may recommend specific actions to increase sales beyond the forecast level, such as increasing promotional activities and hiring additional salespeople.

Concept Q & A

Why is the sales budget not necessarily the same as the sales forecast?

Answer:
The sales forecast is a starting point and an important input to the budgetary process; however, it is usually adjusted up or down depending on the strategic objectives and plans of management.

Cornerstone 8-1 shows how to prepare the sales budget for Texas Rex's standard t-shirt line. For simplicity, we assume that Texas Rex has only one product: a standard short-sleeved t-shirt with the Texas Rex logo screen printed on the back. (For a multiple-product firm, the sales budget reflects sales for each product in units and sales dollars.)

Cornerstone 8-1

HOW TO Prepare a Sales Budget

Information: Budgeted units to be sold for each quarter: 1,000, 1,200, 1,500, and 2,000. Selling price is $10 per t-shirt.
Required: Prepare a sales budget for each quarter and for the year.
Calculation:

Texas Rex, Inc.
Sales Budget
For the Year Ended December 31, 2007

	\multicolumn{4}{c}{Quarter}			
	1	2	3	4	Year
Units	1,000	1,200	1,500	2,000	5,700
Unit selling price	× $10	× $10	× $10	× $10	× $10
Budgeted sales	$10,000	$12,000	$15,000	$20,000	$57,000

Notice that the sales budget in Cornerstone 8-1 reveals that Texas Rex's sales fluctuate seasonally. Most sales take place in the summer and fall quarters. This is due to the popularity of the t-shirts in the summer and the sales promotions that Texas Rex puts on for "back to school" and Christmas.

HERE'S THE REAL KICKER

Stillwater Designs has 14 departments. Each department is given a budget for the coming fiscal year. The budgeting process begins with a sales forecast prepared by the president and vice presidents. The fiscal year for the company is October 1 through September 30. The budget is prepared during August and September, the last two months of the fiscal year. The fiscal year is driven by the seasonal nature of the business. In January of each year, there is a consumer electronics show in Las Vegas, Nevada. New products are introduced, and initial orders from distributors are taken. The sales season starts earnestly in March, reaches its peak in June or July, and drops to its lowest level in the fall. The sales season is driven by the anticipation of warm weather. The young men buying the Kicker speakers and amplifiers want to drive with windows down—with the apparent hope of impressing the girls!

Each department is given a percentage of sales as its budget. The amount ultimately decided upon is not simply a top-down decision. Department managers submit a request for their desired budget. Negotiation takes place between the department managers and their associated vice president (each departmental manager is answerable to a specific vice president). Whether or not the desired levels are provided depends on how well the departmental manager can justify the expenditures. A very important criterion is the notion that resources are expended to make profits.

The budget is reviewed monthly. Any large deviations from the budget are investigated (usually more than a 10-percent deviation is required for an investigation). However, no formal incentive system is tied to budgetary performance. The budget is viewed as a guideline. If more resources are needed, then they can be obtained provided the request is backed up with a good idea and a promising payout.

Production Budget

The **production budget** describes how many units must be produced in order to meet sales needs and satisfy ending inventory requirements. For example, a production budget for Texas Rex would reveal how many t-shirts are needed to satisfy sales demand for each quarter and for the year. If there were no beginning or ending inventories, the t-shirts to be produced would exactly equal the units to be sold. This would be the case in a JIT firm. However, many manufacturing firms use inventories as a buffer against uncertainties in demand or production. Thus, they need to plan for inventory levels as well as sales.

To compute the units to be produced, both unit sales and units of beginning and ending finished goods inventory are needed:

Units to be produced = Expected unit sales + Units in ending inventory (DEI)
− Units in beginning inventory (BI)

Cornerstone 8-2 illustrates how to prepare a production budget using this formula. Consider the first column (quarter 1) of the budget in Cornerstone 8-2. Texas Rex anticipates sales of 1,000 t-shirts. In addition, the company wants 240 t-shirts in ending inventory at the end of the first quarter (0.20 × 1,200). Thus, 1,240 t-shirts are needed during the first quarter. Where will these 1,240 t-shirts come from? Beginning inventory can provide 180 of them, leaving 1,060 t-shirts to be produced during the quarter. Notice that the production budget is expressed in terms of units.

Cornerstone 8-2

HOW TO Prepare the Production Budget

Information: The sales budget (see Cornerstone 8-1). Further, assume that company policy requires 20 percent of the next quarter's sales in ending inventory and that beginning inventory of t-shirts for the first quarter of the year was 180. Assume also that sales for the first quarter of 2008 are estimated at 1,000 units.

Required: Prepare a production budget for each quarter and for the year.

Calculation:

Texas Rex, Inc.
Production Budget
For the Year Ended December 31, 2007

| | \multicolumn{5}{c}{Quarter} | | | | |
	1	2	3	4	Year
Sales (Cornerstone 8-1)	1,000	1,200	1,500	2,000	5,700
Desired ending inventory	240	300	400	200*	200
Total needs	1,240	1,500	1,900	2,200	5,900
Less: Beginning inventory	(180)	(240)	(300)	(400)	(180)
Units to be produced	1,060	1,260	1,600	1,800	5,720

*0.20 × 1,000.

Two important points should be emphasized. First, the beginning inventory for one quarter is always equal to the ending inventory of the previous quarter. For quarter 2, the beginning inventory is 240 t-shirts, which is identical to the desired ending inventory of quarter 1. Second, the column for the year is not simply the addition of the amounts for the four quarters. Notice that the desired ending inventory for the year is 200 t-shirts, which is, of course, equal to the desired ending inventory for the fourth quarter.

Analytical Q & A

Assume that the expected sales for January and February are 2,000 units and 2,500 units, respectively. The desired ending inventory is 20 percent of the next month's expected sales. If the inventory on hand at the beginning of January is 150 units, how many units should be budgeted for production?

Answer:
Budgeted units = Sales + DEI − BI = 2,000 + (0.20 × 2,500) − 150 = 2,350.

Direct Materials Purchases Budget

After the production budget is completed, the budgets for direct materials, direct labor, and overhead can be prepared. The **direct materials purchases budget** tells the amount and cost of raw materials to be purchased in each time period; it depends on the expected use of materials in production and the raw materials inventory needs of the firm. The company needs to prepare a separate direct materials purchases budget for every type of raw material used. The formula used for calculating purchases is as follows:

$$\text{Purchases} = \text{Direct materials needed for production} + \text{Desired direct materials in ending inventory} - \text{Direct materials in beginning inventory}$$

The quantity of direct materials in inventory is determined by the firm's inventory policy.

Texas Rex uses two types of raw materials: plain t-shirts and ink. The direct materials purchases budgets for these two materials are presented in Cornerstone 8-3. Notice how similar the direct materials purchases budget is to the production budget. Consider the first quarter, starting with the plain t-shirts. It takes one plain t-shirt for every logo tee, so the 1,060 logo t-shirts to be produced are multiplied by one to obtain the number of plain t-shirts needed for production. Next, the desired ending inventory of 126 (10 percent of the next quarter's production needs) is added. Thus, 1,186 plain t-shirts are needed during the first quarter. Of this total, 58 are already in beginning inventory, meaning the remaining 1,128 must be purchased. Multiplying the 1,128 plain t-shirts by the cost of $3 each gives Texas Rex the $3,384 expected cost of plain t-shirt purchases for the first quarter of the year.

The second section of the direct materials purchases budget is for ink. Again, the first quarter will be used for illustration. It takes five ounces of ink for every logo tee, so the 1,060 logo t-shirts to be produced are multiplied by five to obtain the 5,300 ounces of ink needed for production. Next, the desired ending inventory of 630 ounces (10 percent of the next quarter's production needs) is added, yielding a requirement of 5,930 ounces of ink for the first quarter. Of this total, 390 ounces are already in beginning inventory, meaning the remaining 5,540 ounces must be purchased. Multiplying the 5,540 ounces of ink by the cost of $0.20 per ounce gives Texas Rex the $1,108 expected cost of ink purchases for the first quarter of the year.

The total direct materials purchases of $4,492 for the first quarter is the sum of the $3,384 plain t-shirt purchases and the $1,108 ink purchases. As you can see, there is a separate direct materials purchases budget for each type of raw material in a firm.

Cornerstone 8-3

HOW TO Prepare a Direct Materials Purchases Budget

Information: The production budget (see Cornerstone 8-2). Plain t-shirts cost $3 each and ink (for the screen printing) costs $0.20 per ounce. On a per-unit basis, the factory needs one plain t-shirt and five ounces of ink for each logo t-shirt that it produces. Texas Rex's policy is to have 10 percent of the following quarter's production needs in ending inventory. The factory has 58 plain t-shirts and 390 ounces of ink on hand on January 1. At the end of the year, the desired ending inventory is 106 plain t-shirts and 530 ounces of ink.

Required: Prepare a direct materials purchases budget for plain t-shirts and one for ink.

Calculation:

Texas Rex, Inc.
Direct Materials Purchases Budget
For the Year Ended December 31, 2007

Plain T-Shirts:

	Quarter				
	1	2	3	4	Year
Units to be produced (Cornerstone 8-2)	1,060	1,260	1,600	1,800	5,720
Direct materials per unit	× 1	× 1	× 1	× 1	× 1
Production needs	1,060	1,260	1,600	1,800	5,720
Desired ending inventory (DEI)	126	160	180	106	106
Total needs	1,186	1,420	1,780	1,906	5,826
Less: Beginning inventory (BI)	(58)	(126)	(160)	(180)	(58)
Direct materials to be purchased	1,128	1,294	1,620	1,726	5,768
Cost per pound	× $3	× $3	× $3	× $3	× $3
Total purchase cost plain t-shirts	$3,384	$3,882	$4,860	$5,178	$17,304

Ink:

	Quarter				
	1	2	3	4	Year
Units to be produced (Cornerstone 8-2)	1,060	1,260	1,600	1,800	5,720
Direct materials per unit	× 5	× 5	× 5	× 5	× 5
Production needs	5,300	6,300	8,000	9,000	28,600
Desired ending inventory (DEI)	630	800	900	530	530
Total needs	5,930	7,100	8,900	9,530	29,130
Less: Beginning inventory (BI)	(390)	(630)	(800)	(900)	(390)
Direct materials to be purchased	5,540	6,470	8,100	8,630	28,740
Cost per pound	×$0.20	×$0.20	×$0.20	×$0.20	× $0.20
Total purchase cost of ink	$ 1,108	$ 1,294	$ 1,620	$ 1,726	$ 5,748
Total direct materials purchase cost	$ 4,492	$ 5,176	$ 6,480	$ 6,904	$23,052

Direct Labor Budget

The **direct labor budget** shows the total direct labor hours needed and the associated cost for the number of units in the production budget. As with direct materials, the budgeted hours of direct labor are determined by the relationship between labor and output. For example, if a batch of 100 logo t-shirts requires 12 direct labor hours, then the direct labor time per logo t-shirt is 0.12 hour.

Given the direct labor used per unit of output and the units to be produced from the production budget, the way to prepare the direct labor budget is shown by Cornerstone 8-4. In the direct labor budget, the wage rate ($10 per hour in this example) is the average wage paid the direct laborers associated with the production of the t-shirts. Since it is an average, it allows for the possibility of differing wage rates paid to individual laborers.

Analytical Q & A

Assume that a product uses 10 pounds of plastic per unit. Expected production for the year is 1,250 units, and the desired ending inventory is 500 pounds. If the inventory on hand at the beginning of the year is 250 pounds, how many pounds of plastic should be budgeted for purchase?

Answer:
Purchases = Needs + DEI − BI = (10 × 1,250) + 500 − 250 = 12,750.

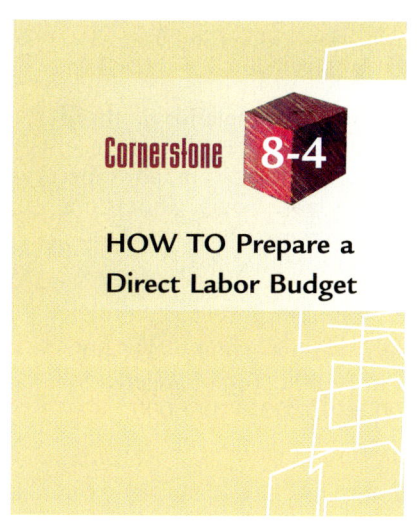

Cornerstone 8-4

HOW TO Prepare a Direct Labor Budget

Information: The production budget (See Cornerstone 8-2). It takes 0.12 hour to produce one t-shirt. The average wage cost per hour is $10.
Required: Prepare a direct labor budget.
Calculation:

Texas Rex, Inc.
Direct Labor Budget
For the Year Ended December 31, 2007

	Quarter				
	1	2	3	4	Year
Units to be produced (Cornerstone 8-2)	1,060	1,260	1,600	1,800	5,720
Direct labor time per unit (hr.)	× 0.12	× 0.12	× 0.12	× 0.12	× 0.12
Total hours needed	127.2	151.2	192	216	686.4
Average wage per hour	× $10	× $10	× $10	× $10	× $10
Total direct labor cost	$1,272	$1,512	$1,920	$2,160	$6,864

Analytical Q & A

Assume that a product uses two hours of direct labor per unit. Expected production for the year is 1,250 units. The average wage cost per hour is $8. What is the budget for direct labor cost?

Answer:
Budget = (2 × 1,250) × $8 = $20,000.

Overhead Budget

The **overhead budget** shows the expected cost of all production costs other than direct materials and direct labor. Unlike direct materials and direct labor, there is no readily identifiable input-output relationship for overhead items. Instead, there are a series of activities and related drivers. These drivers are used to separate overhead costs into fixed and variable components. Past experience can be used as a guide to determine how these overhead activities vary with their drivers. Although multiple drivers may be used, many companies use only one driver (direct labor hours being the most common). Individual items that vary with the selected driver(s) are identified. These items are pooled, and a variable overhead rate is calculated. For example, the rate may be $5 per direct labor hour. Those items whose costs do not vary with direct labor hours are collected into one pool. For our example, assume that two overhead cost pools are created, one for overhead activities that vary with direct labor hours and one for all other activities, which are fixed. The method for preparing an overhead budget using this approach to cost behavior is shown in Cornerstone 8-5.

Cornerstone 8-5

HOW TO Prepare an Overhead Budget

Information: Direct labor budget (see Cornerstone 8-4). The variable overhead rate is $5 per direct labor hour; fixed overhead is budgeted at $1,645 per quarter.
Required: Prepare an overhead budget.
Calculation:

Texas Rex, Inc.
Overhead Budget
For the Year Ended December 31, 2007

	Quarter				
	1	2	3	4	Year
Budgeted direct labor hours	127.2	151.2	192	216	686.4
Variable overhead rate	× $5	× $5	× $5	× $5	× $5
Budgeted variable overhead	$ 636	$ 756	$ 960	$1,080	$ 3,432
Budgeted fixed overhead*	1,645	1,645	1,645	1,645	6,580
Total overhead	$2,281	$2,401	$2,605	$2,725	$10,012

*Includes $540 of depreciation in each quarter.

Ending Finished Goods Inventory Budget

The **ending finished goods inventory budget** supplies information needed for the balance sheet and also serves as an important input for the preparation of the cost of goods sold budget. To prepare this budget, the unit cost of producing each t-shirt must be calculated using information from the direct materials, direct labor, and overhead budgets. The way to calculate the unit cost of a t-shirt and the cost of the planned ending inventory is shown in Cornerstone 8-6.

Analytical Q & A

Assume that the budget formula for overhead costs (OH) is OH = $2,000 + $3X, where X = total direct labor hours. If the company expects to work 5,000 direct labor hours, what is the budgeted variable overhead? Budgeted fixed overhead? Budgeted total overhead?

Answer:
Variable overhead = $3 × 5,000 = $15,000; Fixed overhead = $2,000. Total budgeted overhead = $15,000 + $2,000 = $17,000.

Cornerstone 8-6

HOW TO Prepare the Ending Finished Goods Inventory Budget

Information: Direct materials, direct labor, and overhead budgets (see Cornerstones 8-3, 8-4, and 8-5).

Required: Prepare an ending finished goods inventory budget.

Calculation:

Texas Rex, Inc.
Ending Finished Goods Inventory Budget
For the Year Ended December 31, 2007

Unit cost computation:	
Direct materials ($3 + $1)	$4.00
Direct labor (0.12 hr. @ $10)	1.20
Overhead:	
Variable (0.12 hr. @ $5)	0.60
Fixed (0.12 hr. @ $9.59)*	1.15
Total unit cost	$6.95

*Budgeted fixed overhead/Budgeted direct labor hours = $6,580/686.4 = $9.59.

	Units	Unit Cost	Total
Finished goods: Logo t-shirts	200	$6.95	$1,390

Cost of Goods Sold Budget

Assuming that the beginning finished goods inventory is valued at $1,251, the budgeted cost of goods sold schedule can be prepared using information from Cornerstones 8-3 to 8-6. The **cost of goods sold budget** reveals the expected cost of the goods to be sold and is shown in Cornerstone 8-7.

Concept Q & A

What operating budgets are needed to calculate a budgeted unit cost?

Answer:
Materials, labor, and overhead budgets. You could argue that sales and production budgets are needed also because the three budgets just listed cannot be developed until those are known.

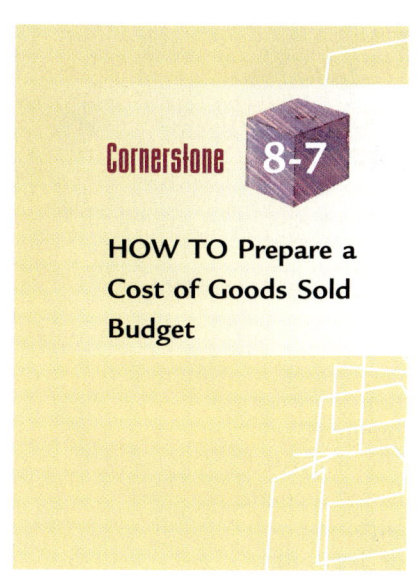

Cornerstone 8-7

HOW TO Prepare a Cost of Goods Sold Budget

Information: Direct materials, direct labor, overhead, and ending finished goods budgets (see Cornerstones 8-3 to 8-6).

Required: Prepare a cost of goods sold budget.

Calculation:

Texas Rex, Inc.
Cost of Goods Sold Budget
For the Year Ended December 31, 2007

Direct materials used (Cornerstone 8-3)*	$22,880
Direct labor used (Cornerstone 8-4)	6,864
Overhead (Cornerstone 8-5)	10,012
Budgeted manufacturing costs	$39,756
Beginning finished goods	1,251
Goods available for sale	$41,007
Less: Ending finished goods (Cornerstone 8-6)	(1,390)
Budgeted cost of goods sold	$39,617

*Production needs = (5,720 plain t-shirts × $3) + (28,600 oz. ink × $0.20).

Analytical Q & A

Assume that the budgeted cost of goods sold is $700. There is no beginning finished goods inventory. Budgeted manufacturing costs are $1,000. What is the budgeted finished goods inventory?

Answer:
Ending finished goods = Goods available for sale − Cost of goods sold = $1,000 − $700 = $300.

Selling and Administrative Expenses Budget

The next budget to be prepared, the **selling and administrative expenses budget**, outlines planned expenditures for nonmanufacturing activities. As with overhead, selling and administrative expenses can be broken down into fixed and variable components. Such items as sales commissions, freight, and supplies vary with sales activity. The selling and administrative expenses budget is illustrated in Cornerstone 8-8.

Cornerstone 8-8

HOW TO Prepare a Selling and Administrative Expenses Budget

Information: Sales budget (see Cornerstone 8-1). Variable expenses are $0.10 per unit sold. Salaries average $1,420 per quarter; utilities, $50 per quarter; and depreciation, $150 per quarter. Advertising for quarters 1 through 4 is $100, $200, $300, and $500, respectively. Insurance is $500 and is paid in the third quarter.

Required: Prepare a selling and administrative expenses budget.

Calculation:

Texas Rex, Inc.
Selling and Administrative Expenses Budget
For the Year Ended December 31, 2007

	Quarter				
	1	2	3	4	Year
Planned sales in units (Cornerstone 8-1)	1,000	1,200	1,500	2,000	5,700
Variable selling and administrative expenses per unit	×$0.10	×$0.10	×$0.10	×$0.10	×$0.10
Total variable expenses	$ 100	$ 120	$ 150	$ 200	$ 570
Fixed selling and administrative expenses:					
Salaries	$ 1,420	$ 1,420	$ 1,420	$ 1,420	$ 5,680
Utilities	50	50	50	50	200
Advertising	100	200	300	500	1,100
Depreciation	150	150	150	150	600
Insurance	—	—	500	—	500
Total fixed expenses	$ 1,720	$ 1,820	$ 2,420	$ 2,120	$ 8,080
Total selling and administrative expenses	$ 1,820	$ 1,940	$ 2,570	$ 2,320	$ 8,650

Concept Q & A

Assume that sales agents are paid a commission of 2 percent of sales revenue. Further, the only fixed selling expense is advertising, which is expected to be $10,000. If sales revenue is budgeted at $500,000, what is the budgeted selling expense?

Answer:
Budgeted selling expense = $10,000 + (0.02 × $500,000) = $20,000.

Budgeted Income Statement

With the completion of the budgeted cost of goods sold schedule and the budgeted selling and administrative expenses budget, Texas Rex has all the operating budgets needed to prepare an estimate of *operating* income. The way to prepare this budgeted income statement is shown in Cornerstone 8-9. The eight budgets already prepared, along with the budgeted operating income statement, define the operating budget for Texas Rex.

Operating income is *not* equivalent to the net income of a firm. To yield net income, interest expense and taxes must be subtracted from operating income. The interest expense deduction is taken from the cash budget for Texas Rex (see Cornerstone 8-10), a budget discussed in the section on financial budgets. The taxes owed depend on the current federal and state tax laws. For simplicity, a combined rate of 40 percent is assumed.

Cornerstone 8-9

HOW TO Prepare a Budgeted Income Statement

Information: The sales budget, the cost of goods sold budget, the selling and administrative expenses budget, and the cash budget (see Cornerstones 8-1, 8-7, 8-8, and 8-10). Assume the tax rate is 40 percent.
Required: Prepare a budgeted income statement.
Calculation:

Texas Rex, Inc.
Budgeted Income Statement
For the Year Ended December 31, 2007

Sales (Cornerstone 8-1)	$57,000
Less: Cost of goods sold (Cornerstone 8-7)	(39,617)
Gross margin	$17,383
Less: Selling and administrative expenses (Cornerstone 8-8)	(8,650)
Operating income	$ 8,733
Less: Interest expense (Cornerstone 8-10)	(60)
Income before taxes	$ 8,673
Less: Income taxes (0.40 × $8,673)	(3,469)
Net income	$ 5,204

Concept Q & A

Why is it not possible to prepare a budgeted income statement using only operating budgets?

Answer:
Interest expense comes from the financial budgets. Only operating income can be computed using operating budgets.

PREPARING THE FINANCIAL BUDGET

OBJECTIVE 3

Define and prepare the financial budget, identify its major components, and explain the interrelationships of its various components.

The remaining budgets found in the master budget are the financial budgets. The usual financial budgets prepared are:

1. The cash budget
2. The budgeted balance sheet
3. The budget for capital expenditures

The master budget also contains a plan for acquiring long-term assets—assets that have a time horizon that extends beyond the 1-year operating period. Some of these assets may be purchased during the coming year; plans to purchase others may be detailed for future periods. This part of the master budget is typically referred to as the *capital budget*. Decision making for capital expenditures is considered in Chapter 13. Accordingly, only the cash budget and the budgeted balance sheet will be illustrated here.

Cash Budget

Knowledge of cash flows is critical to managing a business. Often, a business is successful in producing and selling a product but fails because of timing problems associated with cash inflows and outflows. By knowing when cash deficiencies and surpluses are likely to occur, a manager can plan to borrow cash when needed and to repay the loans during periods of excess cash. Bank loan officers use a company's **cash budget** to document the need for cash, as well as determine the ability to repay. Because cash flow is the lifeblood of an organization, the cash budget is one of the most important budgets in the master budget. The basic structure of a cash budget is illustrated in Exhibit 8-3.

Cash available consists of the beginning cash balance and the expected cash receipts. Expected cash receipts include all sources of cash for the period being considered. The principal source of cash is from sales. Because a significant proportion of sales is usually on account, a major task of an organization is to determine the pattern of collection for its accounts receivable. If a company has been in business for a while, it can use past experience in creating an accounts receivable aging schedule. In other words, the company can determine, on average, what percentages of its accounts receivable are paid in the months following sales. For example, assume a company, Patton Hardware, has the following accounts receivable payment experience:

Percent paid in the month of sale	30%
Percent paid in the month after the sale	60
Percent paid in the second month after the sale	10

The Cash Budget

Beginning cash balance	$ 1,000
Add: Cash receipts	10,000
Cash available	$11,000
Less: Cash disbursements	9,000
Less: Minimum cash balance	1,000
Cash surplus (deficiency)	$ 1,000
Add: Cash from loans	0
Less: Loan repayments	500
Add: Minimum cash balance	1,000
Ending cash balance	$ 1,500

8-3

EXHIBIT

If Patton sells $100,000 worth of goods on account in the month of May, then it would expect to receive $30,000 cash from May credit sales in the month of May, $60,000 cash from May credit sales in June, and $10,000 from May credit sales in July. (Notice that Patton expects to receive all of its accounts receivable. This is not typical. If a company experiences, let's say, 3 percent uncollectible accounts, then this 3 percent of sales is ignored for the purpose of cash budgeting—because no cash is received from customers who default.)

The cash disbursements section lists all planned cash outlays for the period. All expenses not resulting in a cash outlay are excluded from the list (depreciation, for example, is never included in the disbursements section). A disbursement that is typically not included in this section is interest on short-term borrowing. This interest expenditure is reserved for the section on loan repayments.

The cash excess or deficiency line compares the cash available with the cash needed. Cash needed is the total cash disbursements plus the minimum cash balance required by company policy. The minimum cash balance is simply the lowest amount of cash on hand that the firm finds acceptable. Consider your own checking account. You probably try to keep at least some cash in the account, perhaps because by having a minimum balance you avoid service charges, or because a minimum balance allows you to make an unplanned purchase. Similarly, companies also require minimum cash balances. The amount varies from firm to firm and is determined by each company's partic-

> ## Concept Q & A
>
> Why would a company want a minimum cash balance? Suppose that the minimum cash balance is $1,000 and that the projected cash surplus is $500. What would a company have to do to achieve the desired minimum?
>
> **Answer:**
> Borrow the difference.

ular needs and policies. If the total cash available is less than the cash needed, a deficiency exists. In such a case, a short-term loan will be needed. On the other hand, with a cash excess (cash available is greater than the firm's cash needs), the firm has the ability to repay loans and perhaps make some temporary investments.

The final section of the cash budget consists of borrowings and repayments. If there is a deficiency, this section shows the necessary amount to be borrowed. When excess cash is available, this section shows planned repayments, including interest expense.

The last line of the cash budget is the planned ending cash balance. Remember that the minimum cash balance was subtracted to find the cash excess or deficiency. However, the minimum cash balance is not a disbursement so it must be added back to yield the planned ending balance. The way to prepare a cash budget is illustrated by Cornerstone 8-10.

Cornerstone 8-10

HOW TO Prepare a Cash Budget

Information: Cornerstones 8-1, 8-3, 8-4, 8-5, 8-8, and 8-9, and the following specific details:

a. A $1,000 minimum cash balance is required for the end of each quarter. Money can be borrowed and repaid in multiples of $1,000. Interest is 12 percent per year. Interest payments are made only for the amount of the principal being repaid. All borrowing takes place at the beginning of a quarter, and all repayment takes place at the end of a quarter.

b. One-quarter of all sales are for cash, 90 percent of credit sales are collected in the quarter of sale, and the remaining 10 percent are collected in the following quarter. The sales for the fourth quarter of 2006 were $18,000.

c. Purchases of raw materials are made on account; 80 percent of purchases are paid for in the quarter of purchase. The remaining 20 percent are paid for in the following quarter. The purchases for the fourth quarter of 2006 were $5,000.

d. Budgeted depreciation is $540 per quarter for overhead and $150 per quarter for selling and administrative expenses (see Cornerstones 8-5 and 8-8).

e. The capital budget for 2007 revealed plans to purchase additional screen-printing equipment. The cash outlay for the equipment, $6,500, will take place in the first

quarter. The company plans to finance the acquisition of the equipment with operating cash, supplementing it with short-term loans as necessary.

f.   Corporate income taxes are approximately $3,469 and will be paid at the end of the fourth quarter (Cornerstone 8-9).

g.   Beginning cash balance equals $5,200.

h.   All amounts in the budget are rounded to the nearest dollar.

Required: Prepare a cash budget for Texas Rex.

Calculation:

Texas Rex, Inc.
Cash Budget
For the Year Ended December 31, 2007

| | Quarter | | | | | |
	1	2	3	4	Year	Source[a]
Beginning cash balance	$ 5,200	$ 1,023	$ 1,611	$ 3,762	$ 5,200	g
Collections:						
Cash sales	2,500	3,000	3,750	5,000	14,250	b,1
Credit sales:						
Current quarter	6,750	8,100	10,125	13,500	38,475	b,1
Prior quarter	1,350	750	900	1,125	4,125	b,1
Total cash available	$ 15,800	$ 12,873	$ 16,386	$ 23,387	$ 62,050	
Less disbursements:						
Raw materials:						
Current quarter	$ (3,594)	$ (4,141)	$ (5,184)	$ (5,523)	$(18,442)	c,3
Prior quarter	(1,000)	(898)	(1,035)	(1,296)	(4,229)	c,3
Direct labor	(1,272)	(1,512)	(1,920)	(2,160)	(6,864)	4
Overhead	(1,741)	(1,861)	(2,065)	(2,185)	(7,852)	d,5
Selling and administrative	(1,670)	(1,790)	(2,420)	(2,170)	(8,050)	d,8
Income taxes	—	—	—	(3,469)	(3,469)	f,9
Equipment	(6,500)	—	—	—	(6,500)	e
Total disbursements	$(15,777)	$(10,202)	$(12,624)	$(16,803)	$(55,406)	
Minimum cash balance	(1,000)	(1,000)	(1,000)	(1,000)	(1,000)	a
Total cash needs	$(16,777)	$(11,202)	$(13,624)	$(17,803)	$(56,406)	
Excess (deficiency) of cash available over needs	$ (977)	$ 1,671	$ 2,762	$ 5,584	$ 5,644	
Financing:						
Borrowings	1,000	—	—	—	1,000	
Repayments	—	(1,000)	—	—	(1,000)	a
Interest[b]	—	(60)	—	—	(60)	a
Total financing	$ 1,000	$ (1,060)		—	$ (1,060)	
Ending cash balance[c]	$ 1,023	$ 1,611	$ 3,762	$ 6,584	$ 6,584	

[a]Letters refer to the detailed information above. Numbers refer to Cornerstone schedules.
[b]Interest payment is $6/12 \times 0.12 \times \$1,000$. Since borrowings occur at the beginning of the quarter and repayments at the end of the quarter, the principal repayment takes place after six months.
[c]Total cash available minus total disbursements plus (or minus) total financing.

Concept Q & A

Sales for a month total $10,000. Cash receipts for the same month were $15,000. How is it possible for cash receipts to be more than sales?

Answer:
Money can be collected from credit sales of prior month(s).

APPLICATIONS IN BUSINESS

Cash budgeting can mean the difference between success and failure. From 1957 to 1990, 14,352 dealerships left the retail automotive business. The major reason for these failures is significant profit declines attributable in large part to poor cash management. Surveys have revealed a significant desire by dealers to develop better and more reliable cash management practices. In one survey of 500 dealers, 61 percent of those responding indicated that they use a cash budget. The respondents also indicated that a monthly cash budget is the most useful, followed by weekly and daily cash budgets. They expressed the view that the most critical factor in building a good cash budget is a good sales forecast. Poor cash budgeting and sales forecasting can lead to serious managerial and financial problems. The majority of the dealers thus felt that a need for a cash budget was highly critical.

Source: Nasrollah Ahadiat and Misty Wright, "Cash Budgeting Practices and Computer Use by Automobile Dealerships," *International Journal of Retail and Distribution Management* (September/October 1992): 31–36; Nasrollah Ahadiat, "Sales Forecasting and Cash Budgeting for Automobile Dealerships," *The Journal of Business Forecasting Methods and Systems* (Fall 1992): 18–20.

Cornerstone 8-10 reveals that much of the information needed to prepare the cash budget comes from the operating budgets. However, these operating budgets by themselves do not supply all of the needed information. The collection pattern for revenues and the payment pattern for materials must be known before the cash flow for sales and purchases on credit can be budgeted. Exhibit 8-4 displays the specific pattern of cash inflows from both cash and credit sales. For example, cash sales for the first quarter are budgeted for $2,500 (0.25 × $10,000; Cornerstone 8-1). Collections on account for the first quarter relate to credit sales made during the last quarter of the previous year and the first quarter of 2007. Quarter 4, 2006, credit sales equaled $13,500 (0.75 × $18,000), and $1,350 of those sales (0.10 × $13,500) remain to be collected in quarter 1, 2007. Quarter 1, 2007, credit sales are budgeted at $7,500, and 90 percent will be collected in that quarter. Therefore, $6,750 will be collected on account

8-4

EXHIBIT

Texas Rex's Cash Receipts Pattern for 2007

Source	Quarter 1	Quarter 2	Quarter 3	Quarter 4
Cash sales	$ 2,500	$ 3,000	$ 3,750	$ 5,000
Received on account from:				
Quarter 4, 2006	1,350			
Quarter 1, 2007	6,750	750		
Quarter 2, 2007		8,100	900	
Quarter 3, 2007			10,125	1,125
Quarter 4, 2007	—	—	—	13,500
Total cash receipts	$10,600	$11,850	$14,775	$19,625

for credit sales made in that quarter. Similar computations are made for the remaining quarters.

Similar computations are done for purchases. In both cases, patterns of collection and payment are needed in addition to the information supplied by the operating budgets. Additionally, all noncash expenses, such as depreciation, need to be removed from the total amounts reported in the expense budgets. Thus, the budgeted expenses in Cornerstones 8-5 and 8-8 were reduced by the budgeted depreciation for each quarter. Overhead expenses in Cornerstone 8-5 were reduced by depreciation of $540 per quarter. Selling and administrative expenses in Cornerstone 8-8 were reduced by $150 per quarter. The net amounts are what appear in the cash budget.

The cash budget underscores the importance of breaking down the annual budget into smaller time periods. The cash budget for the year gives the impression that sufficient operating cash will be available to finance the acquisition of the new equipment. Quarterly information, however, shows the need for short-term borrowing ($1,000) because of both the acquisition of the new equipment and the timing of the firm's cash flows. Most firms prepare monthly cash budgets, and some even prepare weekly and daily budgets.

Another significant piece of information emerges from Texas Rex's cash budget. By the end of the third quarter, the firm has more cash ($3,762) than necessary to meet operating needs. The management of Texas Rex should consider investing the excess cash in an interest-bearing account. Once plans are finalized for use of the excess cash, the cash budget should be revised to reflect those plans. Budgeting is a dynamic process. As the budget is developed, new information becomes available, and better plans can be formulated.

Budgeted Balance Sheet

The budgeted balance sheet depends on information contained in the current balance sheet and in the other budgets in the master budget. Cornerstone 8-11 shows how the budgeted balance sheet for December 31, 2007, is prepared. Explanations for the budgeted figures are provided in the footnotes.

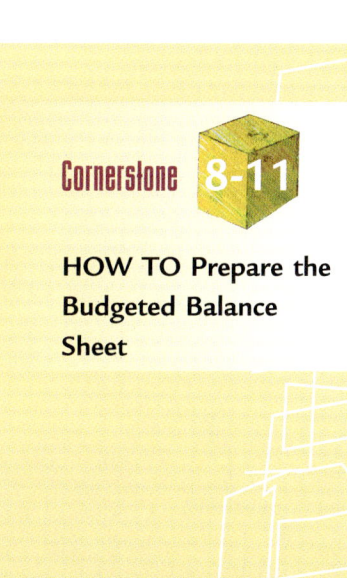

Cornerstone 8-11

HOW TO Prepare the Budgeted Balance Sheet

Information:

1. Last year's balance sheet:

Texas Rex, Inc.
Balance Sheet
December 31, 2006

Assets

Current assets:		
Cash	$ 5,200	
Accounts receivable	1,350	
Raw materials inventory	252	
Finished goods inventory	1,251	
Total current assets		$ 8,053
Property, plant, and equipment (PP&E):		
Land	$ 1,100	
Building and equipment	30,000	
Accumulated depreciation	(5,000)	
Total PP&E		26,100
Total assets		$34,153

Liabilities and Owner's Equity

Current liabilities:		
Accounts payable		$ 1,000
Owner's equity:		
Retained earnings	33,153	
Total owner's equity		33,153
Total liabilities and owner's equity		$34,153

2. Cornerstones 8-1, 8-3, 8-5, 8-6, 8-8, 8-9, and 8-10.

Required: Prepare a budgeted balance sheet for 2007.

Calculation:

Texas Rex, Inc.
Budgeted Balance Sheet
December 31, 2007

Assets

Current assets:		
Cash	$ 6,584[a]	
Accounts receivable	1,500[b]	
Raw materials inventory	424[c]	
Finished goods inventory	1,390[d]	
Total current assets		$ 9,898
Property, plant, and equipment (PP&E):		
Land	$ 1,100[e]	
Building and equipment	36,500[f]	
Accumulated depreciation	(7,760)[g]	
Total PP&E		29,840
Total assets		$39,738

Liabilities and Owner's Equity

Current liabilities:		
Accounts payable		$ 1,381[h]
Owner's equity:		
Retained earnings	$38,557[i]	
Total owner's equity		38,357
Total liabilities and owner's equity		$39,738

[a]Ending balance from Cornerstone 8-10.
[b]10 percent of fourth-quarter credit sales ($0.75 \times \$20,000$)—see Cornerstones 8-1 and 8-10.
[c]From Cornerstone 8-3 [$(106 \times \$3) + (530 \times \$0.20)$].
[d]From Cornerstone 8-6.
[e]From the December 31, 2006, balance sheet.
[f]December 31, 2006, balance ($30,000) plus new equipment acquisition of $6,500 (see the 2006 ending balance sheet and Cornerstone 8-10).
[g]From the December 31, 2006, balance sheet, Cornerstone 8-5, and Cornerstone 8-8 ($5,000 + $2,160 + $600).
[h]20 percent of fourth-quarter purchases ($0.20 \times \$6,904$)—see Cornerstones 8-3 and 8-10.
[i]$33,153 + $5,204 (December 31, 2006, balance plus net income from Cornerstone 8-9).

USING BUDGETS FOR PERFORMANCE EVALUATION

Budgets are often used to judge the performance of managers. Bonuses, salary increases, and promotions are all affected by a manager's ability to achieve or beat budgeted goals. Since a manager's financial status and career can be affected, budgets can have a significant behavioral effect. Whether that effect is positive or negative depends in large part on how budgets are used.

Positive behavior occurs when the goals of individual managers are aligned with the goals of the organization and the manager has the drive to achieve them. The alignment of managerial and organizational goals is often referred to as **goal congru-**

OBJECTIVE 4

Describe the behavioral dimension of budgeting.

ence. If the budget is improperly administered, subordinate managers may subvert the organization's goals. **Dysfunctional behavior** is individual behavior that is in basic conflict with the goals of the organization.

An ideal budgetary system is one that achieves complete goal congruence and, simultaneously, creates a drive in managers to achieve the organization's goals in an ethical manner. While an ideal budgetary system probably does not exist, research and practice have identified some key features that promote a reasonable degree of positive behavior. These features include frequent feedback on performance, monetary and nonmonetary incentives, participative budgeting, realistic standards, controllability of costs, and multiple measures of performance.

Frequent Feedback on Performance

Managers need to know how they are doing as the year unfolds. Providing them with frequent, timely performance reports allows them to know how successful their efforts have been, to take corrective actions, and to change plans as necessary.

Monetary and Nonmonetary Incentives

A sound budgetary system encourages goal-congruent behavior. The means an organization uses to influence a manager to exert effort to achieve an organization's goal are called **incentives**. Traditional organizational theory assumes that individuals are primarily motivated by monetary rewards, resist work, and are inefficient and wasteful. Thus, **monetary incentives** are used to control a manager's tendency to shirk and waste resources by relating budgetary performance to salary increases, bonuses, and promotions. The threat of dismissal is the ultimate economic sanction for poor performance. In reality, individuals are motivated by more than economic factors. Individuals are also motivated by intrinsic psychological and social factors, such as the satisfaction of a job well done, recognition, responsibility, self-esteem, and the nature of the work itself. Thus, **nonmonetary incentives**, including job enrichment, increased responsibility and autonomy, nonmonetary recognition programs, and so on, can be used to enhance a budgetary control system.

Participative Budgeting

Rather than imposing budgets on subordinate managers, **participative budgeting** allows subordinate managers considerable say in how the budgets are established. Typically, overall objectives are communicated to the manager, who helps develop a budget that will accomplish these objectives. Participative budgeting communicates a sense of responsibility to subordinate managers and fosters creativity. Since the subordinate manager creates the budget, the budget's goals will more likely become the manager's personal goals, resulting in greater goal congruence. The increased responsibility and challenge inherent in the process provide nonmonetary incentives that lead to a higher level of performance.

Participative budgeting has three potential problems:

1. Setting standards that are either too high or too low.
2. Building slack into the budget (often referred to as padding the budget).
3. Pseudoparticipation.

The Art of Standard Setting

Standard Set Too Loose
Goals Too Easily Achieved

Standard Set Too Tight
Frustration

Some managers may tend to set the budget either too loose or too tight. Since budgeted goals tend to become the manager's goals when participation is allowed, making this mistake in setting the budget can result in decreased performance levels. If goals are too easily achieved, a manager may lose interest, and performance may actually drop. Challenge is important to aggressive and creative individuals. Similarly, setting the budget too tight ensures failure to achieve the standards and frustrates the manager. This frustration, too, can lead to poorer performance. The trick is to get managers in a participative setting to set high, but achievable, goals.

The second problem with participative budgeting is the opportunity for managers to build slack into the budget. **Budgetary slack** (or *padding the budget*) exists when a manager deliberately underestimates revenues or overestimates costs. Either approach increases the likelihood that the manager will achieve the budget and consequently reduces the risk that the manager faces. Top management should carefully review budgets proposed by subordinate managers and provide input, where needed, in order to decrease the effects of building slack into the budget. (See Exhibit 8-5.)

Concept Q & A

Assume that a company evaluates and rewards its managers based on their ability to achieve budgeted goals. Why would the same company ask its managers to participate in setting their budgeted standards?

Answer:
Participation encourages managers to internalize the goals and make them their own, leading to improved performance.

The third problem with participation occurs when top management assumes total control of the budgeting process, seeking only superficial participation from lower-level managers. This practice is termed **pseudoparticipation**. Top management is simply obtaining formal acceptance of the budget from subordinate managers, not seeking real input. Accordingly, none of the behavioral benefits of participation will be realized.

Realistic Standards

Budgeted objectives are used to gauge performance; accordingly, they should be based on realistic conditions and expectations. Budgets should reflect operating realities such as actual levels of activity, seasonal variations, efficiencies, and general economic trends. Flexible budgets are used to ensure that budgeted costs can be realistically compared to costs for actual levels of activity. Interim budgets should reflect seasonal effects. Toys "R" Us, for example, would expect much higher sales in the quarter that includes Christmas than in other quarters. Budgetary cuts should be based on *planned* increases in efficiency and not simply arbitrary across-the-board reductions. Across-the-board cuts without any formal evaluation may impair the ability of some units to carry out their missions. General economic conditions also need to be considered. Budgeting for a significant increase in sales when a recession is projected is not only foolish but also potentially dangerous.

Controllability of Costs

Ideally, managers are held accountable only for costs they can control. **Controllable costs** are costs whose level a manager can influence. For example, divisional managers have no power to authorize such corporate-level costs as research and development and salaries of top managers. Therefore, they should not be held accountable for the incurrence of those costs. If noncontrollable costs are put in the budgets of subordinate managers to help them understand that these costs also need to be covered, then they should be separated from controllable costs and labeled as *noncontrollable*.

Multiple Measures of Performance

Often, organizations make the mistake of using budgets as their only measure of managerial performance. While financial measures of performance are important, overemphasis can lead to a form of dysfunctional behavior called *milking the firm* or *myopia*. **Myopic behavior** occurs when a manager takes actions that improve budgetary performance in the short run but bring long-run harm to the firm. For example, to meet budgeted cost objectives or profits, managers can fail to promote promotable employees or reduce expenditures for preventive maintenance, advertising, and new product development. Using measures that are both financial and nonfinancial and that are long term and short term can alleviate this problem. Budgetary measures by themselves are inadequate.

Dr. Roger Jones clearly did not have any formal means of controlling his finances. At the time he requested help from his CPA, he did not have any real idea what the financial capabilities of his practice were. As a consequence, his practice was suffering, and his personal financial situation was being stressed. After receiving the report from his CPA, John Smith, Dr. Jones decided to follow the recommendation and installed a formal budgetary system.

He discovered that budgeting revenues and expenses was an interesting and revealing exercise—one that helped him gain control of his practice. By budgeting revenue, he was forced to consider the revenue earning ability of his practice. Similarly, by examining and planning carefully the expenses that must be paid, he obtained a good understanding of what it takes to generate the current level of revenues. He found that the difference between the revenues and business expenses and the amount available for his own personal income and the amount needed for future capital expenditures was not sufficient—especially for the level of personal income that he desired.

Given that the amount being provided by the practice for his personal income was not at the level he wanted, he then took steps to increase the income. Specifically, he took two actions. First, he increased revenues by working Friday afternoons and Saturday mornings. Second, he also invested in equipment and training that allowed him to offer new procedures. Both actions proved to be fruitful and increased income more than expected. These favorable outcomes were a product of knowing and understanding the financial issues of his practice, made possible by a formal budgetary system.

SUMMARY OF LEARNING OBJECTIVES

Budgeting is the creation of a plan of action expressed in financial terms. Budgeting plays a key role in planning, control, and decision making. Budgets also serve to improve communication and coordination, a role that becomes increasingly important as organizations grow in size. The master budget, the comprehensive financial plan of an organization, is made up of the operating and financial budgets.

The operating budget is the budgeted income statement and all supporting budgets. The sales budget consists of the anticipated quantity and price of all products to be sold. The production budget gives the expected production in units to meet forecasted sales and desired ending inventory goals; expected production is supplemented by beginning inventory. The direct materials purchases budget gives the necessary purchases during the year for every type of raw material to meet production and desired ending inventory goals. The direct labor budget and overhead budget give the amounts of these resources necessary for the coming year's production. The overhead budget may be broken down into fixed and variable components to facilitate preparation of the budget. The selling and administrative expenses budget gives the forecasted costs for these functions. The finished goods inventory budget and the cost of goods sold budget detail production costs for the expected ending inventory and the units sold, respectively. The budgeted income statement outlines the net income to be realized if budgeted plans come to fruition.

The financial budget includes the cash budget, the capital expenditures budget, and the budgeted balance sheet. The cash budget is simply the beginning balance in the cash account, plus anticipated receipts, minus anticipated disbursements, plus or minus any necessary borrowing. The budgeted (or pro forma) balance sheet gives the anticipated ending balances of the asset, liability, and equity accounts if budgeted plans hold.

The success of a budgetary system depends on how seriously human factors are considered. To discourage dysfunctional behavior, organizations should avoid overemphasizing budgets as a control mechanism. Other areas of performance should be evaluated in addition to budgets. Budgets can be improved as performance measures by using participative budgeting and other nonmonetary incentives, providing frequent feedback on performance, using flexible budgeting, ensuring that the budgetary objectives reflect reality, and holding managers accountable for only controllable costs.

Cornerstones for Chapter 8

Cornerstone 8–1   How to prepare a sales budget, page 315
Cornerstone 8–2   How to prepare the production budget, page 316
Cornerstone 8–3   How to prepare a direct materials purchases budget, page 317
Cornerstone 8–4   How to prepare a direct labor budget, page 319
Cornerstone 8–5   How to prepare an overhead budget, page 319
Cornerstone 8–6   How to prepare the ending finished goods inventory budget, page 320
Cornerstone 8–7   How to prepare a cost of goods sold budget, page 321
Cornerstone 8–8   How to prepare a selling and administrative expenses budget, page 321
Cornerstone 8–9   How to prepare a budgeted income statement, page 322
Cornerstone 8–10 How to prepare a cash budget, page 324
Cornerstone 8–11 How to prepare the budgeted balance sheet, page 327

KEY TERMS

Budget committee, 312
Budget director, 312
Budgetary slack, 330
Budgets, 310
Cash budget, 323
Continuous budget, 312
Control, 311
Controllable costs, 331
Cost of goods sold budget, 320
Direct labor budget, 318

Direct materials purchases budget, 317
Dysfunctional behavior, 329
Ending finished goods inventory budget, 320
Financial budgets, 312
Goal congruence, 328
Incentives, 329
Master budget, 312
Monetary incentives, 329
Myopic behavior, 331

Nonmonetary incentives, 329
Operating budgets, 312
Overhead budget, 319
Participative budgeting, 329
Production budget, 316
Pseudoparticipation, 331
Sales budget, 314
Selling and administrative expenses budget, 321
Strategic plan, 310

DISCUSSION QUESTIONS

1. Define the term budget. How are budgets used in planning?
2. Define control. How are budgets used to control?
3. Explain how both small and large organizations can benefit from budgeting.

4. Discuss some reasons for budgeting.
5. What is a master budget? An operating budget? A financial budget?
6. Explain the role of a sales forecast in budgeting. What is the difference between a sales forecast and a sales budget?
7. All budgets depend on the sales budget. Is this true? Explain.
8. Why is goal congruence important?
9. Why is it important for a manager to receive frequent feedback on his or her performance?
10. Discuss the roles of monetary and nonmonetary incentives. Do you believe that nonmonetary incentives are needed? Why?
11. What is participative budgeting? Discuss some of its advantages.
12. A budget too easily achieved will lead to diminished performance. Do you agree? Explain.
13. What is the role of top management in participative budgeting?
14. Explain why a manager has an incentive to build slack into the budget.
15. Explain how a manager can milk the firm to improve budgetary performance.

MULTIPLE-CHOICE EXERCISES

8-1 A budget

a. is a long-term plan.
b. covers at least two years.
c. is only a control tool.
d. is necessary only for large firms.
e. is a short-term financial plan.

8-2 Which of the following is *not* part of the control process?

a. Monitoring of actual activity
b. Comparison of actual with planned activity
c. Investigating
d. Developing a strategic plan
e. Taking corrective action

8-3 Which of the following is *not* an advantage of budgeting?

a. It forces managers to plan.
b. It provides information for decision making.
c. It guarantees an improvement in organizational efficiency.
d. It provides a standard for performance evaluation.
e. It improves communication and coordination.

8-4 The budget committee

a. reviews the budget.
b. resolves differences that arise as the budget is prepared.
c. approves the final budget.
d. is directed (typically) by the controller.
e. does all of the above.

8-5 A moving, 12-month budget, updated monthly, is

a. a waste of time and effort.
b. a continuous budget.
c. a master budget.
d. not used by industrial firms.
e. always used by firms that prepare a master budget.

8-6 Which of the following is *not* part of the operating budget?

a. The capital budget
b. The cost of goods sold budget
c. The production budget
d. The direct labor budget
e. The selling and administrative expenses budget

8-7 Before a direct materials purchases budget can be prepared, you should first

a. prepare a sales budget.
b. prepare a production budget.
c. decide on the desired ending inventory of materials.
d. obtain the expected price of each type of material.
e. do all of the above.

8-8 The first step in preparing the sales budget is to

a. talk with past customers.
b. review the production budget carefully.
c. assess the desired ending inventory of finished goods.
d. prepare a sales forecast.
e. increase sales beyond the forecast level.

8-9 Which of the following is needed to prepare the production budget?

a. Direct materials needed for production
b. Expected unit sales
c. Direct labor needed for production
d. Units of materials in ending inventory
e. None of the above

8-10 A company requires 100 pounds of plastic to meet the production needs of a small toy. It currently has 10 pounds of plastic inventory. The desired ending inventory of plastic is 30 pounds. How many pounds of plastic should be budgeted for purchasing during the coming period?

a. 100 pounds
b. 120 pounds
c. 130 pounds
d. 140 pounds
e. None of the above

8-11 A company plans on selling 200 units. The selling price per unit is $12. There are 20 units in beginning inventory, and the company would like to have 50 units in ending inventory. How many units should be produced for the coming period?

a. 250
b. 200
c. 230
d. 220
e. None of the above

8-12 Which of the following is needed to prepare a budgeted income statement?

a. The production budget
b. The budgeted balance sheet
c. Budgeted selling and administrative expenses
d. The capital expenditures budget
e. None of the above

8-13 Select the one budget below that is not a financial budget.

a. The cost of goods sold budget
b. The cash budget
c. The budgeted balance sheet
d. The capital expenditures budget
e. None of the above

8-14 The cash budget serves which of the following purposes?

a. Documents the need for liberal inventory policies
b. Provides information about the ability to repay loans
c. Reveals the amount lost due to uncollectible accounts
d. Reveals the amount of depreciation expense
e. None of the above

8-15 Assume that a company has the following accounts receivable collection pattern:

Month of sale   40%
Month following sale   60

All sales are on credit. If credit sales for January and February are $100,000 and $200,000, respectively, the cash collections for February are

a. $140,000.
b. $300,000.
c. $120,000.
d. $160,000.
e. $80,000.

8-16 The percentage of accounts receivable uncollectible can be ignored for cash budgeting because

a. for most companies, it is not a material amount.
b. it is included in cash sales.
c. it appears on the budgeted income statement.
d. no cash is received from an account that defaults.
e. none of the above.

8-17 An ideal budgetary system is one that

a. encourages dysfunctional behavior.
b. encourages myopic behavior.
c. encourages goal-congruent behavior.
d. encourages subversion of an organization's goals.
e. does none of the above.

8-18 Some key budgetary features that tend to promote positive managerial behavior are

a. frequent feedback on performance.
b. participative budgeting.
c. realistic standards.
d. well-designed monetary and nonmonetary incentives.
e. all of the above.

8-19 Which of the following is *not* an advantage of participative budgeting?

a. It fosters a sense of creativity in managers.
b. It encourages budgetary slack.
c. It fosters a sense of responsibility.
d. It encourages greater goal congruence.
e. It tends to lead to a higher level of performance.

8-20 Which of the following items is *not* a possible example of myopic behavior?

a. Promotion of deserving employees
b. Reducing expenditures on preventive maintenance
c. Cutting back on new product development
d. Laying off top sales personnel so that budgeted income can be achieved
e. Buying cheaper, lower-quality materials so that the company does not exceed the materials purchases budget

EXERCISES

Exercise 8-1 *Planning and Control*

a. Dr. Jones, a dentist, wants to increase the size and profitability of his business by building a reputation for quality and timely service.
b. To achieve this, he plans on adding a dental laboratory to his building so that crowns, bridges, and dentures can be made in-house.
c. To add the laboratory, he needs additional money, which he decides must be obtained by increasing revenues. After some careful calculation, Dr. Jones concludes that annual revenues must be increased by 10 percent.
d. Dr. Jones finds that his fees for fillings and crowns are below the average in his community and decides that the 10-percent increase can be achieved by increasing these fees.
e. He then identifies the quantity of fillings and crowns expected for the coming year, the new per-unit fee, and the total fees expected.
f. As the year unfolds (on a month-by-month basis), Dr. Jones compares the actual revenues received with the budgeted revenues. For the first three months, actual revenues were less than planned.
g. Upon investigating, he discovered that he had some reduction in the number of patients because he had also changed his available hours of operation.
h. He returned to his old schedule and found out that the number of patients was restored to the original expected levels.
i. However, to make up the shortfall, he also increased the price of some of his other services.

Required:
Match each statement with the following planning and control elements (a letter may be matched to more than one item):

1. Corrective action
2. Budgets
3. Feedback
4. Investigation
5. Short-term plan
6. Comparison of actual with planned
7. Monitoring of actual activity
8. Strategic plan
9. Short-term objectives
10. Long-term objectives

Exercise 8-2 *Sales Budget*

Assume that Stillwater Designs produces two automotive subwoofers: S12L7 and S12L5. The S12L7 sells for $500, and the S12L5 sells for $300. Projected sales (number of speakers) for the coming five quarters are as follows:

	S12L7	S12L5
First quarter, 2007	1,000	500
Second quarter, 2007	2,000	1,000
Third quarter, 2007	8,000	4,000
Fourth quarter, 2007	4,000	2,000
First quarter, 2008	1,200	700

The vice president of sales believes that the projected sales are realistic and can be achieved by the company.

Required:

1. Prepare a sales budget for each quarter of 2007 and for the year in total. Show sales by product and in total for each time period.
2. How will Stillwater Designs use this sales budget?

Exercise 8-3 *Production Budget*

Refer to **Exercise 8-2**. Stillwater Designs needs a production budget for each product (representing the amount that must be outsourced to manufacturers located in Asia). Beginning inventory of S12L7 for the first quarter, 2007, was 500 boxes. The company's policy is to have 50 percent of the next quarter's sales of S12L7 in ending inventory. Beginning inventory of S12L5 was 200 boxes. The company's policy is to have 40 percent of the next quarter's sales of S12L5 in ending inventory.

Required:

Prepare a production budget for each quarter for 2007 and for the year in total.

Exercise 8-4 *Production Budget*

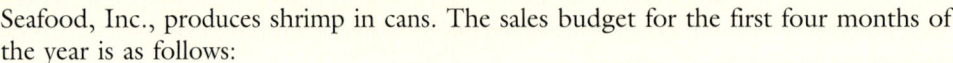

Seafood, Inc., produces shrimp in cans. The sales budget for the first four months of the year is as follows:

	Unit Sales	Dollar Sales
January	200,000	$150,000
February	240,000	180,000
March	220,000	165,000
April	200,000	150,000

Company policy requires that ending inventories for each month be 35 percent of next month's sales. At the beginning of January, the inventory of shrimp is 36,000 cans.

Required:

Prepare a production budget for the first quarter of the year. Show the number of cans that should be produced each month as well as for the quarter in total.

Exercise 8-5 *Direct Materials Purchases Budget*

Refer to **Exercise 8-4**. The two raw materials needed are shrimp and cans. Each can of shrimp requires one can and four ounces of shrimp. Company policy requires that ending inventories of raw materials for each month be 20 percent of the next month's production needs. That policy was met on January 1.

Required:

Prepare separate direct materials purchases budgets for cans and for shrimp for the months of January and February.

Exercise 8-6 *Production Budget*

Carson, Inc., produces office supplies, including pencils. Pencils are bundled in packages of four and sold for $0.50. The sales budget for the first four months of the year for this product is as follows:

	Unit Sales	Dollar Sales
January	200,000	$100,000
February	240,000	120,000
March	220,000	110,000
April	200,000	100,000

Company policy requires that ending inventories for each month be 15 percent of next month's sales. However, at the beginning of January, due to greater sales in December than anticipated, the beginning inventory of pencils is only 18,000 packages.

Required:
Prepare a production budget for the first quarter of the year. Show the number of units that should be produced each month as well as for the quarter in total.

Exercise 8-7 *Direct Materials Purchases Budget*

Lester Company produces a variety of labels, including iron-on name labels, which are sold to parents of camp-bound children. (The camps require campers to have their name on every article of clothing.) The labels are sold in a roll of 1,000, which requires about 25 yards of paper strip. Each yard of paper strip costs $0.17. Lester has budgeted production of the label rolls for the next four months as follows:

	Units
March	5,000
April	25,000
May	35,000
June	6,000

Inventory policy requires that sufficient paper strip be in ending monthly inventory to satisfy 20 percent of the following month's production needs. The inventory of paper strip at the beginning of March equals exactly the amount needed to satisfy the inventory policy.

Required:
Prepare a direct materials purchases budget for March, April, and May, showing purchases in units and in dollars for each month and in total.

Exercise 8-8 *Direct Labor Budget*

Refer to the production budget in **Exercise 8-7**. Each roll of labels produced requires (on average) 0.03 direct labor hour. The average cost of direct labor is $8 per hour.

Required:
Prepare a direct labor budget for March, April, and May, showing the hours needed and the direct labor cost for each month and in total.

Exercise 8-9 *Sales Budget*

Norton, Inc., manufactures six models of leaf blowers and weed eaters. Norton's budgeting team is finalizing the sales budget for the coming year. Sales in units and dollars for last year follow:

Product	Number Sold	Price	Revenue
LB-1	16,800	$29	$ 487,200
LB-2	18,000	15	270,000
WE-6	25,200	13	327,600
WE-7	16,200	10	162,000
WE-8	2,400	22	52,800
WE-9	1,000	26	26,000
Total			$1,325,600

In looking over the previous year's sales figures, Norton's sales budgeting team recalled the following:

a. Model LB-1 is a newer version of the leaf blower with a gasoline engine. The LB-1 is mounted on wheels, instead of being carried. This model is designed for the commercial market and did better than expected its first year. As a result, the number of units of Model LB-1 to be sold was forecast at 300 percent of the previous year's units.

b. Models WE-8 and WE-9 were introduced on October 1 last year. They are lighter versions of the traditional weed eater and designed for smaller households or condo units. Norton estimates that demand for both models will continue at the previous year's rate.

c. A competitor has announced plans to introduce an improved version of model WE-6, Norton's traditional weed eater. Norton believes that the model WE-6 price must be cut 20 percent to maintain unit sales at the previous year's level.

d. It was assumed that unit sales of all other models would increase by 10 percent, prices remaining constant.

Required:

Prepare a sales budget by product and in total for Norton, Inc., for the coming year.

Exercise 8-10 *Production Budget*

Raylene Webber, owner of Raylene's Flowers and Gifts, produces gift baskets for various special occasions. Each gift basket includes fruit or assorted small gifts (e.g., a coffee mug, deck of cards, novelty cocoa mixes, scented soap) in a basket that is wrapped in colorful cellophane. Raylene has estimated the following sales of the standard gift basket for the rest of the year and January of next year.

September	200
October	150
November	180
December	250
January	100

Raylene likes to have 10 percent of the next month's sales needs on hand at the end of each month. This requirement was met on August 31.

Required:

Prepare a production budget for September, October, November, and December for gift baskets.

Exercise 8-11 *Direct Materials Purchases Budget*

Refer to **Exercise 8-10**. Assume that Raylene's Flowers and Gifts has the following production budget for gift baskets for the last four months of its fiscal year:

September	October	November	December
195	153	187	235

Two materials needed for each fruit basket are as follows:

Fruit	1 pound
Small gifts	5 items

The materials inventory policy is to have 5 percent of the next month's fruit needs on hand and 50 percent of the next month's production needs of small gifts. (The relatively low inventory amount for fruit is designed to prevent spoilage.) Materials inventory on September 1 met this company policy.

Required:

Prepare a direct materials purchases budget for the two types of materials used in the production of gift baskets for the months of September, October, and November. (Round all answers to the nearest whole unit.)

Exercise 8-12 *Cash Budget*

Johnson, Inc., found that about 10 percent of its sales during the month were for cash. Johnson has the following accounts receivable payment experience:

Percent paid in the month of sale	30%
Percent paid in the month after the sale	60
Percent paid in the second month after the sale	7

Johnson's anticipated sales for the next few months are as follows:

April	$200,000
May	240,000
June	230,000
July	246,000
August	250,000

Required:

1. Calculate credit sales for May, June, July, and August.
2. Prepare a schedule of cash receipts for July and August.

Exercise 8-13 *Cash Budget*

Janzen, Inc., sells all of its product on account. Janzen has the following accounts receivable payment experience:

Percent paid in the month of sale	20%
Percent paid in the month after the sale	60
Percent paid in the second month after the sale	15

To encourage payment in the month of sale, Janzen gives a 2-percent cash discount. Janzen's anticipated sales for the next few months are as follows:

April	$200,000
May	220,000
June	230,000
July	210,000
August	250,000

Required:

1. Prepare a schedule of cash receipts for July.
2. Prepare a schedule of cash receipts for August.

Exercise 8-14 *Cash Budget*

Kasper Company provided the following information relating to cash payments:

a. Kasper purchased direct materials on account in the following amounts:

June	20,000
July	25,000
August	30,000

Kasper pays 25 percent of accounts payable in the month of purchase and the remaining 75 percent in the following month.

b. In July, direct labor cost $40,000. August direct labor cost was $50,000. The company finds that typically 90 percent of direct labor cost is paid in cash during the month, with the remainder paid in the following month.

c. August overhead amounted to $70,000, including $5,500 of depreciation.

d. Kasper had taken out a loan of $10,000 on May 1. Interest, due with payment of principle, accrued at the rate of 12 percent per year. The loan and all interest were repaid on August 31.

Required:

Prepare a schedule of cash payments for Kasper Company for the month of August.

Exercise 8-15 *Cash Budget*

The owner of a small mining supply company has requested a cash budget for June. After examining the records of the company, you find the following:

a. Cash balance on June 1 is $345.

b. Actual sales for April and May are as follows:

	April	May
Cash sales	$10,000	$15,000
Credit sales	25,000	35,000
Total sales	$35,000	$50,000

c. Credit sales are collected over a 3-month period: 50 percent in the month of sale, 30 percent in the second month, and 15 percent in the third month. The sales collected in the third month are subject to a 1.5-percent late fee, but only half of the affected customers pay the late fee, and the owner does not think it is worth his while to try to collect from the other half. The remaining sales are uncollectible.

d. Inventory purchases average 60 percent of a month's total sales. Of those purchases, 40 percent are paid for in the month of purchase. The remaining 60 percent are paid for in the following month.

e. Salaries and wages total $8,700 a month, including a $4,500 salary paid to the owner.

f. Rent is $1,200 per month.

g. Taxes to be paid in June are $5,500.

The owner also tells you that he expects cash sales of $20,000 and credit sales of $40,000 for June. No minimum cash balance is required. The owner of the company does not have access to short-term loans.

Required:

1. Prepare a cash budget for June. Include supporting schedules for cash collections and cash payments.

2. Did the business show a negative cash balance for June? Assuming that the owner has no hope of establishing a line of credit for the business, what recommendations would you give the owner for dealing with a negative cash balance?

PROBLEMS

(Note: Whenever you see a next to a requirement, it signals a "building on a cornerstone" requirement. Assigning this requirement will usually entail additional work, such as a group project, analytical reasoning, Internet research, decision making, and the use of written communication skills.)

Problem 8-1 *Cash Budget*

Kendall Law Firm has found from past experience that 30 percent of its services are for cash. The remaining 70 percent are on credit. An aging schedule for accounts receivable reveals the following pattern:

a. Ten percent of fees on credit are paid in the month service is rendered.
b. Seventy percent of fees on credit are paid in the month following legal service.
c. Seventeen percent of fees on credit are paid in the second month following the legal service.
d. Three percent of fees on credit are never collected.

Fees (on credit) that have not been paid until the second month following performance of the legal service are considered overdue and are subject to a 2-percent late charge.

Kendall has developed the following forecast of fees:

May	$228,000
June	255,000
July	204,000
August	240,000
September	300,000

Required:
Prepare a schedule of cash receipts for August and September.

Problem 8-2 *Operating Budget, Comprehensive Analysis*

Spreadsheet

Woodruff Manufacturing produces a subassembly used in the production of jet aircraft engines. The assembly is sold to engine manufacturers and to aircraft maintenance facilities. Projected sales for the coming four months follow:

January	40,000
February	50,000
March	60,000
April	60,000

The following data pertain to production policies and manufacturing specifications followed by Woodruff Manufacturing:

a. Finished goods inventory on January 1 is 32,000 units, each costing $148.71. The desired ending inventory for each month is 80 percent of the next month's sales.
b. The data on materials used are as follows:

Direct Material	Per-Unit Usage	Unit Cost
Metal	10 lbs.	$8
Components	6	2

Inventory policy dictates that sufficient materials be on hand at the beginning of the month to produce 50 percent of that month's estimated sales. This is exactly the amount of material on hand on January 1.

c. The direct labor used per unit of output is four hours. The average direct labor cost per hour is $9.25.

d. Overhead each month is estimated using a flexible budget formula. (Activity is measured in direct labor hours.)

	Fixed-Cost Component	Variable-Cost Component
Supplies	—	$1.00
Power	—	0.50
Maintenance	$ 30,000	0.40
Supervision	16,000	—
Depreciation	200,000	—
Taxes	12,000	—
Other	80,000	1.50

e. Monthly selling and administrative expenses are also estimated using a flexible budgeting formula. (Activity is measured in units sold.)

	Fixed Costs	Variable Costs
Salaries	$50,000	—
Commissions	—	$2.00
Depreciation	40,000	—
Shipping	—	1.00
Other	20,000	0.60

f. The unit selling price of the subassembly is $180.

g. All sales and purchases are for cash. The cash balance on January 1 equals $400,000. If the firm develops a cash shortage by the end of the month, sufficient cash is borrowed to cover the shortage. Any cash borrowed is repaid at the end of the quarter, as is the interest due (cash borrowed at the end of the quarter is repaid at the end of the following quarter). The interest rate is 12 percent per annum. No money is owed at the beginning of January.

Required:

1. Prepare a monthly operating budget for the first quarter with the following schedules:
   a. Sales budget.
   b. Production budget.
   c. Direct materials purchases budget.
   d. Direct labor budget.
   e. Overhead budget.
   f. Selling and administrative expenses budget.
   g. Ending finished goods inventory budget.
   h. Cost of goods sold budget.
   i. Budgeted income statement.
   j. Cash budget.

2. Form a group of three or four. Locate a manufacturing plant in your community that has headquarters elsewhere. Interview the controller for the plant regarding the master budgeting process. Ask when the process starts each year, what schedules and budgets are prepared at the plant level, how the controller forecasts the amounts, and how those schedules and budgets fit in with the overall corporate budget. Is the budgetary process participative? Also, find out how budgets are used for performance analysis. Write a summary of the interview.

Problem 8-3 *Cash Budget, Pro Forma Balance Sheet*

OBJECTIVE 3

Ryan Richards, controller for Grange Retailers, has assembled the following data to assist in the preparation of a cash budget for the third quarter of 2007:

a. Sales:

May (actual)	$100,000
June (actual)	120,000
July (estimated)	90,000
August (estimated)	100,000
September (estimated)	135,000
October (estimated)	110,000

b. Each month, 30 percent of sales are for cash and 70 percent are on credit. The collection pattern for credit sales is 20 percent in the month of sale, 50 percent in the following month, and 30 percent in the second month following the sale.

c. Each month, the ending inventory exactly equals 50 percent of the cost of next month's sales. The markup on goods is 25 percent of cost.

d. Inventory purchases are paid for in the month following the purchase.

e. Recurring monthly expenses are as follows:

Salaries and wages	$10,000
Depreciation on plant and equipment	4,000
Utilities	1,000
Other	1,700

f. Property taxes of $15,000 are due and payable on July 15, 2007.

g. Advertising fees of $6,000 must be paid on August 20, 2007.

h. A lease on a new storage facility is scheduled to begin on September 2, 2007. Monthly payments are $5,000.

i. The company has a policy to maintain a minimum cash balance of $10,000. If necessary, it will borrow to meet its short-term needs. All borrowing is done at the beginning of the month. All payments on principal and interest are made at the end of a month. The annual interest rate is 9 percent. The company must borrow in multiples of $1,000.

j. A partially completed balance sheet as of June 30, 2007, follows. (Accounts payable is for inventory purchases only.)

Cash	$?		
Accounts receivable	?		
Inventory	?		
Plant and equipment	425,000		
Accounts payable		$?	
Common stock		210,000	
Retained earnings		268,750	
Total	$?	$?	

Required:

1. Complete the balance sheet given in item j.

2. Prepare a cash budget for each month in the third quarter and for the quarter in total (the third quarter begins on July 1). Provide a supporting schedule of cash collections.

3. Prepare a pro forma balance sheet as of September 30, 2007.

4. Form a group of three or four. Discuss why a bank might require a cash budget for businesses seeking short-term loans. Determine what other financial reports might be useful for a loan decision. Also, discuss how the reliability of cash budgets and other financial information can be determined.

Problem 8-4 *Participative Budgeting, Not-for-Profit Setting*

Dwight D. Eisenhower was the 34th President of the United States and the Supreme Commander of the Allied Forces during World War II. Much of his army career was spent in planning. He once said that "planning is everything; the plan is nothing." What do you think he meant by this? Consider his comment with respect to the master budget. Do you agree or disagree? Be sure to include the impact of the master budget on planning and control.

Problem 8-5 *Cash Budget*

The controller of Minota Company is gathering data to prepare the cash budget for July 2007. He plans to develop the budget from the following information:

a.   Of all sales, 30 percent are cash sales.
b.   Of credit sales, 60 percent are collected within the month of sale. Half of the credit sales collected within the month receive a 2-percent cash discount (for accounts paid within 10 days). Twenty percent of credit sales are collected in the following month; remaining credit sales are collected the month thereafter. There are virtually no bad debts.
c.   Sales for the second two quarters of the year follow. (The first three months are actual sales, and the last three months are estimated sales.)

	Sales
April	$ 460,000
May	600,000
June	1,000,000
July	1,140,000
August	1,200,000
September	1,134,000

d.   The company sells all that it produces each month. The cost of raw materials equals 24 percent of each sales dollar. The company requires a monthly ending inventory equal to the coming month's production requirements. Of raw materials purchases, 50 percent are paid for in the month of purchase. The remaining 50 percent is paid for in the following month.
e.   Wages total $110,000 each month and are paid in the month incurred.
f.   Budgeted monthly operating expenses total $336,000, of which $50,000 is depreciation and $6,000 is expiration of prepaid insurance (the annual premium of $72,000 is paid on January 1).
g.   Dividends of $140,000, declared on June 30, will be paid on July 15.
h.   Old equipment will be sold for $25,200 on July 4.
i.   On July 13, new equipment will be purchased for $168,000.
j.   The company maintains a minimum cash balance of $20,000.
k.   The cash balance on July 1 is $27,000.

Required:
Prepare a cash budget for July. Give a supporting schedule that details the cash collections from sales.

Problem 8-6 *Master Budget, Comprehensive Review*

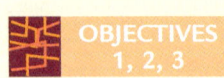

Optima Company is a high-technology organization that produces a mass-storage system. The design of Optima's system is unique and represents a breakthrough in the industry. The units Optima produces combine positive features of both floppy and hard disks. The company is completing its fifth year of operations and is preparing to build its master budget for the coming year (2007). The budget will detail each quarter's activity and the activity for the year in total. The master budget will be based on the following information:

a.   Fourth-quarter sales for 2006 are 55,000 units.
b.   Unit sales by quarter (for 2007) are projected as follows:

First quarter	65,000
Second quarter	70,000
Third quarter	75,000
Fourth quarter	90,000

The selling price is $400 per unit. All sales are credit sales. Optima collects 85 percent of all sales within the quarter in which they are realized; the other 15 percent is collected in the following quarter. There are no bad debts.

c. There is no beginning inventory of finished goods. Optima is planning the following ending finished goods inventories for each quarter:

First quarter	13,000 units
Second quarter	15,000
Third quarter	20,000
Fourth quarter	10,000

d. Each mass-storage unit uses five hours of direct labor and three units of direct materials. Laborers are paid $10 per hour, and one unit of direct materials costs $80.

e. There are 65,700 units of direct materials in beginning inventory as of January 1, 2007. At the end of each quarter, Optima plans to have 30 percent of the direct materials needed for next quarter's unit sales. Optima will end the year with the same level of direct materials found in this year's beginning inventory.

f. Optima buys direct materials on account. Half of the purchases are paid for in the quarter of acquisition, and the remaining half are paid for in the following quarter. Wages and salaries are paid on the 15th and 30th of each month.

g. Fixed overhead totals $1 million each quarter. Of this total, $350,000 represents depreciation. All other fixed expenses are paid for in cash in the quarter incurred. The fixed overhead rate is computed by dividing the year's total fixed overhead by the year's expected actual units produced.

h. Variable overhead is budgeted at $6 per direct labor hour. All variable overhead expenses are paid for in the quarter incurred.

i. Fixed selling and administrative expenses total $250,000 per quarter, including $50,000 depreciation.

j. Variable selling and administrative expenses are budgeted at $10 per unit sold. All selling and administrative expenses are paid for in the quarter incurred.

k. The balance sheet as of December 31, 2006, is as follows:

Assets

Cash	$ 250,000
Direct materials inventory	5,256,000
Accounts receivable	3,300,000
Plant and equipment	33,500,000
Total assets	$42,306,000

Liabilities and Stockholders' Equity

Accounts payable	$ 7,248,000*
Capital stock	27,000,000
Retained earnings	8,058,000
Total liabilities and stockholders' equity	$42,306,000

*For purchase of direct materials only.

l. Optima will pay quarterly dividends of $300,000. At the end of the fourth quarter, $2 million of equipment will be purchased.

Required:

Prepare a master budget for Optima Company for each quarter of 2007 and for the year in total. The following component budgets must be included:

1. Sales budget.
2. Production budget.
3. Direct materials purchases budget.
4. Direct labor budget.

(continued)

5. Overhead budget.
6. Selling and administrative expenses budget.
7. Ending finished goods inventory budget.
8. Cost of goods sold budget.
9. Cash budget.
10. Pro forma income statement (using absorption costing).
11. Pro forma balance sheet.

Problem 8-7 *Budgetary Performance, Rewards, Ethical Behavior*

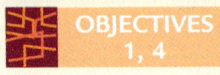

OBJECTIVES
1, 4

Linda Ellis, division manager, is evaluated and rewarded on the basis of budgetary performance. She, her assistants, and the plant managers are all eligible to receive a bonus if actual divisional profits are between budgeted profits and 120 percent of budgeted profits. The bonuses are based on a fixed percentage of actual profits. Profits above 120 percent of budgeted profits earn a bonus at the 120-percent level (in other words, there is an upper limit on possible bonus payments). If the actual profits are less than budgeted profits, no bonuses are awarded. Now consider the following actions taken by Linda:

a. Linda tends to overestimate expenses and underestimate revenues. This approach facilitates the ability of the division to attain budgeted profits. Linda believes the action is justified because it increases the likelihood of receiving bonuses and helps keep the morale of the managers high.

b. Suppose that toward the end of the fiscal year, Linda saw that the division would not achieve budgeted profits. Accordingly, she instructed the sales department to defer the closing of a number of sales agreements to the following fiscal year. She also decided to write off some inventory that was nearly worthless. Deferring revenues to next year and writing off the inventory in a no-bonus year increased the chances of a bonus for next year.

c. Assume that toward the end of the year, Linda saw that actual profits would likely exceed the 120-percent limit. She took actions similar to those described in item b.

Required:

1. Comment on the ethics of Linda's behavior. Are her actions right or wrong? What role does the company play in encouraging her actions?
2. Suppose that you are the marketing manager for the division and you receive instructions to defer the closing of sales until the next fiscal year. What would you do?
3. Suppose that you are a plant manager and you know that your budget has been padded by the division manager. Further, suppose that the padding is common knowledge among the plant managers, who support it because it increases the ability to achieve the budget and receive a bonus. What would you do?
4. Suppose that you are the division controller and you receive instructions from the division manager to accelerate the recognition of some expenses that legitimately belong to a future period. What would you do?

Problem 8-8 *Cash Budget*

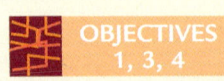

OBJECTIVES
1, 3, 4

According to the analysis of a local consultant, the financial difficulties facing Dr. Roger Jones have been caused by the absence of proper planning and control. (Review the introduction to the chapter for a description of the financial difficulties that Dr. Jones faces on a recurring basis.) Budgetary control is sorely needed. To assist you in preparing a plan of action that will help his dental practice regain financial stability, Dr. Jones has made available the financial information describing a typical month in the following table.

Revenues		
	Average Fee	Quantity
Fillings	$ 50	90
Crowns	300	19
Root canals	170	8
Bridges	500	7
Extractions	45	30
Cleaning	25	108
X-rays	15	150

Costs

Salaries:		
Two dental assistants	$1,900	
Receptionist/bookkeeper	1,500	
Hygienist	1,800	
Public relations (Mrs. Jones)	1,000	
Personal salary	6,500	
Total salaries		$12,700
Benefits		1,344
Building lease		1,500
Dental supplies		1,200
Janitorial		300
Utilities		400
Phone		150
Office supplies		100
Lab fees		5,000
Loan payments		570
Interest payments		500
Miscellaneous		500
Depreciation		700
Total costs		$24,964

Benefits include Dr. Jones's share of Social Security and a health insurance premium for all employees. Although all revenues billed in a month are not collected, the cash flowing into the business is approximately equal to the month's billings because of collections from prior months. The dental office is open Monday through Thursday from 8:30 A.M. to 4:00 P.M. and on Friday from 8:30 A.M. to 12:30 P.M. A total of 32 hours are worked each week. Additional hours could be worked, but Dr. Jones is reluctant to do so because of other personal endeavors that he enjoys.

Dr. Jones has noted that the two dental assistants and the receptionist are not fully utilized. He estimates that they are busy about 65 to 70 percent of the time. Dr. Jones's wife spends about five hours each week on a monthly newsletter that is sent to all patients; she also maintains a birthday list and sends cards to patients on their birthdays.

Dr. Jones spends about $2,400 yearly on informational seminars. These seminars, targeted especially for dentists, teach them how to increase their revenues. It is from one of these seminars that Dr. Jones decided to invest in promotion and public relations (the newsletter and the birthday list).

Required:

1. Prepare a monthly cash budget for Dr. Jones. Does Dr. Jones have a significant cash flow problem? How would you use the budget to show Dr. Jones why he is having financial difficulties?
2. Using the cash budget prepared in Requirement 1 and the information given in the case, recommend actions to solve Dr. Jones's financial problems. Prepare a

cash budget that reflects these recommendations and demonstrates to Dr. Jones that the problems can be corrected. Do you think that Dr. Jones will accept your recommendations? Do any of the behavioral principles discussed in the chapter have a role in this type of setting? Explain.

Problem 8-9 *Budgeting in the Government Sector, Internet Research*

OBJECTIVES
1, 2

In a similar sense as companies, the U.S. government must prepare a budget each year. However, unlike private, for-profit companies, the budget and its details are available to the public. The entire budgetary process is established by law. The government makes available a considerable amount of information concerning the federal budget. Most of this information can be found on the Internet. Using Internet resources (e.g., consider accessing the Office of Management and Budget) **http://www.whitehouse.gov/omb/**, answer the following questions:

Required:
1. When is the federal budget prepared?
2. Who is responsible for preparing the federal budget?
3. How is the final federal budget determined? Explain in detail how the government creates its budget.
4. What percentage of the gross domestic product (GDP) is represented by the federal budget?
5. What are the revenue sources for the federal budget? Indicate the percentage contribution of each of the major sources.
6. How does U.S. spending as a percentage of GDP compare to other countries?
7. How are deficits financed?

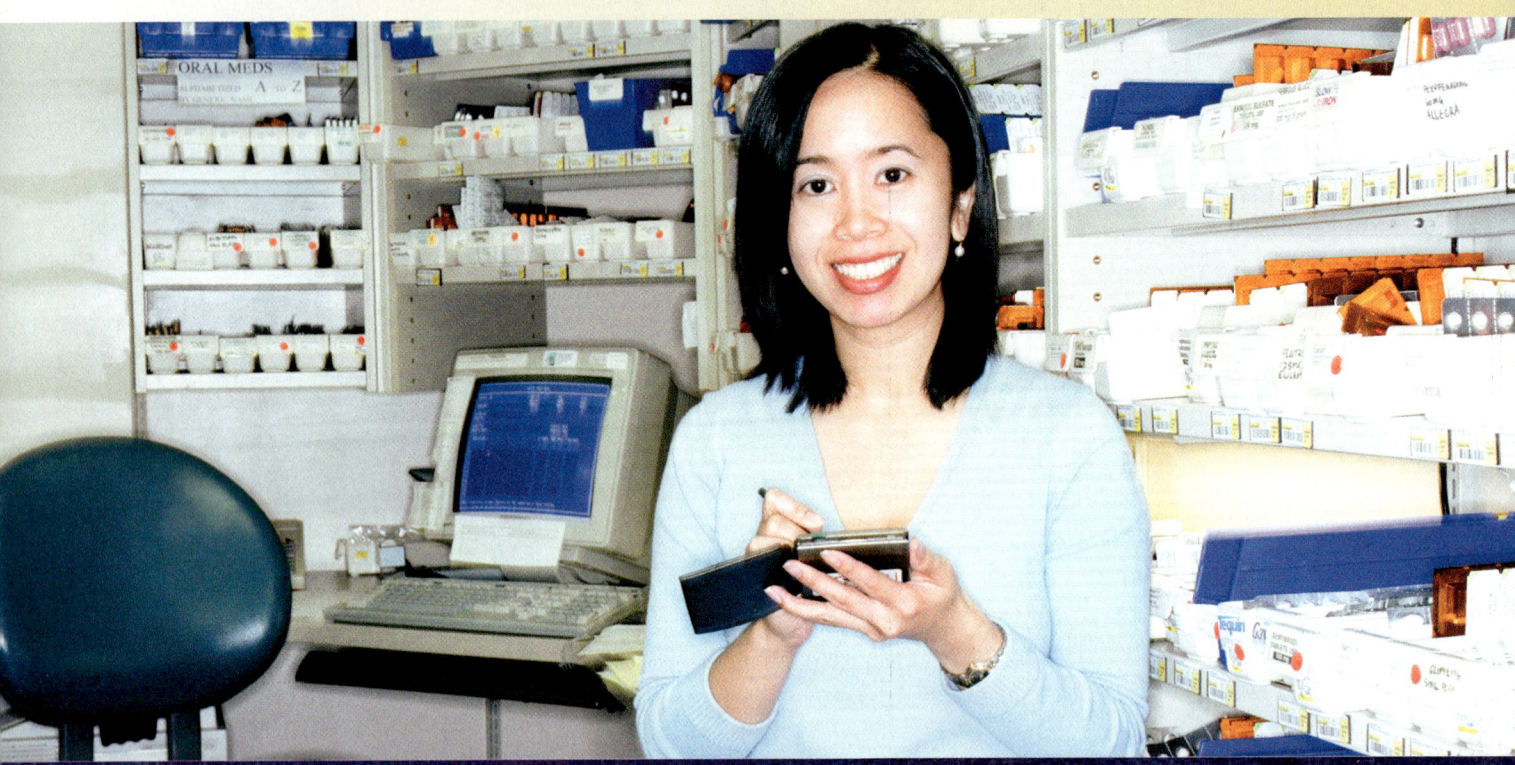

© PHOTODISC/GETTY IMAGES

STANDARD COSTING: A MANAGERIAL CONTROL TOOL

After studying Chapter 9, you should be able to:

1. Explain how unit standards are set and why standard cost systems are adopted.
2. Explain the purpose of a standard cost sheet.
3. Describe the basic concepts underlying variance analysis and explain when variances should be investigated.
4. Compute the materials variances and explain how they are used for control.
5. Compute the labor variances and explain how they are used for control.
6. (Appendix 9A) Prepare journal entries for materials and labor variances.
7. (Appendix 9B) Define kaizen and target costing and explain their relationship to traditional standard costing.

Millie Anderson, manager of Honley Medical's IV Products Division, was more than satisfied with her division's performance last year. At the start of the year, the division had introduced a new line of polyurethane catheters, replacing the old teflon catheters, and sales had more than tripled. The market reaction to the new catheter was a virtual replay of the company's history: Honley Medical was establishing a dominant position in the IV market.

Nearly 30 years ago, Lindell Honley, founder of Honley Medical, had perceived the need for something other than a metal needle for long-term insertion into veins. Metal needles were irritating and could damage the vein. Based on this, Honley had developed a catheter using teflon, a lubricated plastic, which was easy to insert into the vein. The development was well received by the medical community and produced a new and successful company, one with expanded activities into a variety of medical products.

For years, the new technology allowed Honley to dominate the market, but when the patent expired, other companies entered the market with their own teflon catheters, increasing competition. Prices had been driven down, and profit margins were eroding.

The eroding profit margins had prompted Millie and other high-level managers to examine the continued viability of the teflon catheters. After many years, the medical profession had noted that after 24 hours of use, an infection tended to develop around the point of insertion. Researchers at Honley Medical had discovered that the problem was one of incompatibility of blood and tissue with teflon. Further studies showed that different plastics produced different reactions. Researchers began immediately to search for a material that was more biocompatible than teflon. The outcome was polyurethane catheters. The new catheter could be left in for 72 hours, compared to the 24 hours for teflon catheters.

Millie also knew that history would repeat itself in the later stages—the time would come when other firms would produce catheters with the same degree of biocompatibility. In fact, Honley's research scientists estimated that competitors would have a competing catheter on the market within three years. This time, however, Millie was determined to protect the division's market share. Since most patients had little need for a catheter beyond 72 hours, further improvements in biocompatibility were not likely to yield the same market benefits as in the past. Price competition would become more important. Competing on price meant that cost control would become critical. In the past, because of its dominant position, the division had not been too concerned with manufacturing costs. By implementing cost control measures now, she believed that the division could better compete on price when competition resurfaced in a few years.

After some research, Millie discovered that most firms use a standard cost system for controlling the costs of their manufacturing inputs. She found that firms using standard cost systems specify standards for materials, labor, and overhead. Using the unit price and quantity standards, budgeted costs for labor, materials, and overhead are established for each unit produced. The standards are based on efficiency expectations and can be used to monitor performance by comparing actual costs to standard costs. Using this approach, operating managers would be held responsible for meeting standards.

UNIT STANDARDS

In the opening scenario, Millie recognized the need to encourage operating managers to control costs. Cost control often means the difference between success and failure or between above-average profits and lesser profits. Millie was convinced that cost control meant that her managers had to be cost-conscious and they had to assume responsibility for this important objective.

OBJECTIVE 1

Explain how unit standards are set and why standard cost systems are adopted.

In Chapter 8, we learned that budgets set standards that are used to control and evaluate managerial performance. However, budgets are aggregate measures of performance; they identify the revenues and costs in total that an organization should experience if plans are executed as expected. By comparing the actual costs and actual revenues with the corresponding budgeted amounts at the same level of activity, a measure of managerial efficiency emerges.

Although the process just described provides significant information for control, developing standards for unit amounts as well as for total amounts can enhance control. To determine the unit standard cost for a particular input, two decisions must be made: (1) the amount of input that should be used per unit of output (the quantity decision) and (2) the amount that should be paid for the quantity of the input to be used (the pricing decision). The quantity decision produces **quantity standards**, and the pricing decision produces **price standards**. The unit standard cost can be computed by multiplying these two standards: Quantity standard × Price standard.

For example, a soft-drink bottling company may decide that five ounces of fructose should be used for every 16-ounce bottle of cola (the quantity standard), and the price of the fructose should be $0.05 per ounce (the price standard). The standard cost of the fructose per bottle of cola is then $0.25 (5 × $0.05). The standard cost per unit of fructose can be used to predict what the total cost of fructose should be as the activity level varies; thus, it becomes a flexible budget formula. If 10,000 bottles of cola are produced, then the total expected cost of fructose is $2,500 ($0.25 × 10,000); if 15,000 bottles are produced, then the total expected cost of fructose is $3,750 ($0.25 × 15,000).

Analytical Q & A

If the unit quantity standard for a raw material is 10 pounds per unit, and the cost per pound of this material is $8, what is the standard cost per unit of product for the material?

Answer:
Standard cost = 10 × $8 = $80.

How Standards Are Developed

Historical experience, engineering studies, and input from operating personnel are three potential sources of quantitative standards. Although historical experience may provide an initial guideline for setting standards, it should be used with caution. Often, processes are operating inefficiently; adopting input–output relationships from the past thus perpetuates these inefficiencies. The IV Products Division of Honley Medical, for example, had never emphasized cost control and had operated in a resource-rich environment. The division manager was convinced that significant inefficiencies existed. Engineering studies can determine the most efficient way to operate and can provide very rigorous guidelines; however, engineered standards are often too rigorous. They may not be achievable by operating personnel. Since operating personnel are accountable for meeting standards, they should have significant input in setting standards. The same principles governing participative budgeting pertain to setting unit standards.

Price standards are the joint responsibility of operations, purchasing, personnel, and accounting. Operating personnel determine the quality of the inputs required; personnel and purchasing have the responsibility of acquiring the labor and materials quality requested at the lowest price. Market forces, trade unions, and other external forces limit the range of choices for price standards. In setting price standards, purchasing must consider discounts, freight, and quality; personnel, on the other hand, must consider payroll taxes, fringe benefits, and qualifications. Accounting is responsible for recording the price standards and preparing reports that compare actual performance to the standard.

Types of Standards

Standards are generally classified as either *ideal* or *currently attainable*. **Ideal standards** demand maximum efficiency and can be achieved only if everything operates perfectly. No machine breakdowns, slack, or lack of skill (even momentarily) are allowed. **Currently attainable standards** can be achieved under efficient operating conditions. Allowance is made for normal breakdowns, interruptions, less than perfect skill, and so on. These standards are demanding but achievable. Exhibit 9-1 provides a visual and conceptual portrayal of the two standards.

Of the two types, currently attainable standards offer the most behavioral benefits. If standards are too tight and never achievable, workers become frustrated and performance levels decline. However, challenging but achievable standards tend to extract higher performance levels—particularly when the individuals subject to the standards have participated in their creation.

Concept Q & A

What is the difference between an ideal standard and a currently attainable standard?

Answer:
An ideal standard is a standard of perfection—absolute efficiency is required. A currently attainable standard is rigorous but achievable and reflects a reasonable level of efficiency.

9-1

EXHIBIT

Types of Standards

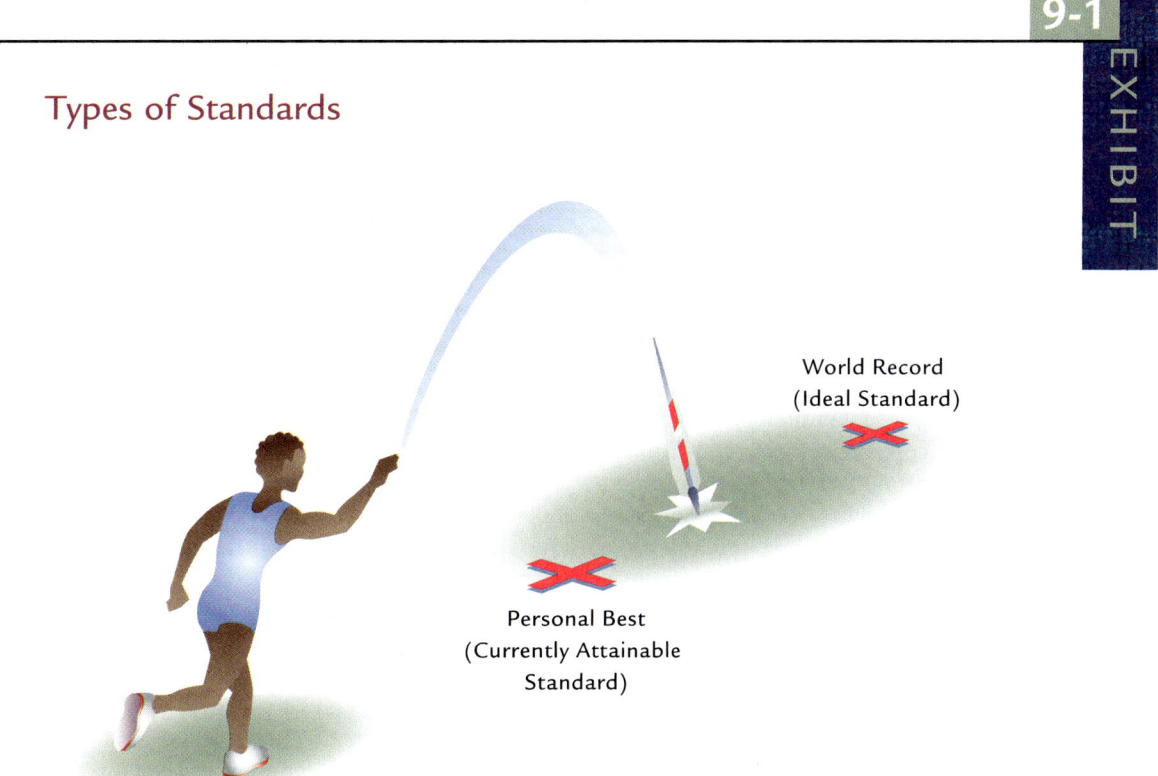

World Record
(Ideal Standard)

Personal Best
(Currently Attainable
Standard)

APPLICATIONS IN BUSINESS

Standard cost systems are widely used. Adoption rates range from 65 to 85 percent in countries such as Japan, the United States, New Zealand, and the United Kingdom. Standard setting techniques tend to involve a variety of techniques. Surveys reveal that engineering studies and historical usage are the two most widely used approaches for setting standards. Companies also tend to involve accounting, human resources, industrial engineering, purchasing, top management, and line managers in the standard setting process. In a similar vein, the issue of achievability of standards has also been explored. The same surveys reveal that currently attainable (difficult but achievable) and historical standards are both widely used. Currently attainable standards are used slightly more than historical standards in the United States and New Zealand and in about equal proportions in the United Kingdom.

Source: Chris Guilding, Dawne Lamminmaki, and Colin Drury, "Budgeting and Standard Costing Practices in New Zealand and the United Kingdom," *The International Journal of Accounting*, Vol. 33, No. 5 (1998): 569–588.

Why Standard Cost Systems Are Adopted

Two reasons for adopting a standard cost system are frequently mentioned: to improve planning and control and to facilitate product costing.

Planning and Control

Standard costing systems enhance planning and control and improve performance measurement. Unit standards are a fundamental requirement for a flexible budgeting system, which is a key feature of a meaningful planning and control system. Budgetary control systems compare actual costs with budgeted costs by computing variances, the difference between the actual and planned costs for the actual level of activity. By developing unit price and quantity standards, an overall variance can be decomposed into a price variance and a usage or efficiency variance.

By performing this decomposition, a manager has more information. If the variance is unfavorable, a manager can tell whether it is attributable to discrepancies between planned prices and actual prices, to discrepancies between planned usage and actual usage, or to both. Since managers have more control over the usage of inputs than over their prices, efficiency variances provide specific signals regarding the need for corrective action and where that action should be focused. Thus, in principle, the use of efficiency variances enhances operational control. Additionally, by breaking out the price variance, over which managers potentially have less control, the system provides an improved measure of managerial efficiency.

The benefits of operational control, however, may not extend to the manufacturing environments that are emphasizing continuous improvement and just-in-time (JIT) purchasing and manufacturing. The use of a standard cost system for operational control in these settings can produce dysfunctional behavior. For example, materials price variance reporting may encourage the purchasing department to buy in large quantities to take advantage of discounts. Yet, this may lead to holding significant inventories, something not desired by JIT firms. Therefore, the detailed computation of variances—at least at the operational level—is discouraged in this new environment. Nonetheless, standards in this newer manufacturing environment are still useful for planning, for example, in the creation of bids. Also, variances may still be computed and presented in reports to higher-level managers so that the financial dimension can be monitored.

Finally, it should be mentioned that many firms operate with conventional manufacturing systems. Standard cost systems are widely used. According to one survey, 87 percent of the firms responding used a standard cost system.[1] Furthermore, the survey revealed that significant numbers of respondents were calculating variances at the operational level. For example, about 40 percent of the firms using a standard costing system reported labor variances for small work crews or individual workers.

Product Costing

In a standard costing system, costs are assigned to products using quantity and price standards for all three manufacturing costs: direct materials, direct labor, and overhead. In contrast, a normal costing system predetermines overhead costs for the purpose of product costing but assigns direct materials and direct labor to products by using actual costs. Overhead is assigned using a budgeted rate and actual activity. At the other end of the cost assignment spectrum, an actual costing system assigns the actual costs of all three manufacturing inputs to products. Exhibit 9-2 summarizes these three cost assignment approaches. Standard product costing has several advantages over normal costing and actual costing. One, of course, is the greater capacity for control. Standard costing systems also provide readily available unit cost information that can be used for pricing decisions. This is particularly helpful for companies that do a significant amount of bidding and that are paid on a cost-plus basis.

Other simplifications are also possible. For example, if a process-costing system uses standard costing to assign product costs, there is no need to compute a unit cost for each equivalent unit cost category. A standard unit cost would exist for each category. Additionally, there is no need to distinguish between the FIFO and weighted average methods of accounting for beginning inventory costs. Usually, a standard process-costing system will follow the equivalent unit calculation of the FIFO approach. That is, current equivalent units of work are calculated. By calculating

Concept Q & A

Why would a firm adopt a standard costing system?

Answer:
Standard costing enhances planning and control and improves performance evaluation. It also simplifies product costing. Having a readily available product cost facilitates pricing decisions.

9-2 EXHIBIT

Cost Assignment Approaches

	Manufacturing Costs		
	Direct Materials	Direct Labor	Overhead
Actual costing system	Actual	Actual	Actual
Normal costing system	Actual	Actual	Budgeted
Standard costing system	Standard	Standard	Standard

[1]Bruce R. Gaumnitz and Felix P. Kollaritsch, "Manufacturing Variances: Current Practice and Trends," *Journal of Cost Management* (Spring 1991): 59–64. Similar widespread usage is also reported by Carole B. Cheatham and Leo R. Cheatham, "Redesigning Cost Systems: Is Standard Costing Obsolete?" *Accounting Horizons* (December 1996): 23–31. Furthermore, a survey of UK firms revealed that 76 percent of them use a standard cost system (see Colin Drury, "Standard Costing: A Technique at Variance with Modern Management," *Management Accounting* (London, November 1999): 56–58.

current equivalent work, current actual production costs can be compared with standard costs for control purposes.

STANDARD PRODUCT COSTS

In manufacturing firms, standard costs are developed for direct materials, direct labor, and overhead. Using these costs, the **standard cost per unit** is computed. The **standard cost sheet** provides the production data needed to calculate the standard unit cost. To illustrate, a standard cost sheet will be developed for a 16-ounce bag of corn chips produced by Crunchy Chips, Inc. The production of corn chips begins by steaming and soaking corn kernels overnight in a lime solution. This process softens the kernels so that they can be shaped into a sheet of dough. The dough is then cut into small triangular chips. Next, the chips are toasted in an oven and dropped into a deep fryer. After cooking, the chips pass under a salting device and are inspected for quality. Substandard chips are sorted and discarded; the chips that pass inspection are bagged by a packaging machine. The bagged chips are manually packed into boxes for shipping.

Four materials are used to process corn chips: yellow corn, cooking oil, salt, and lime. The package in which the chips are placed is also classified as a direct material. Crunchy Chips has two types of direct laborers: machine operators and inspectors (or sorters). Variable overhead is made up of three costs: gas, electricity, and water. Both variable and fixed overhead are applied using direct labor hours. The standard cost sheet is given in Exhibit 9-3. Note that it should cost $0.88 to produce a 16-ounce package of corn chips. Also, notice that the company uses 18 ounces of corn to produce a 16-ounce package of chips. There are two reasons for this. First, some chips are discarded during the inspection process. The company plans on a normal amount of waste. Second, the company wants to have more than 16 ounces in each package to increase customer satisfaction with its product and avoid any problems with fair packaging laws.

Exhibit 9-3 also reveals other important insights. The standard usage for variable and fixed overhead is tied to the direct labor standards. For variable overhead, the rate is $4.00 per direct labor hour. Since one package of corn chips uses 0.02 direct labor hour, the variable overhead cost assigned to a package of corn chips is $0.08 ($4.00 × 0.02). For fixed overhead, the rate is $15.00 per direct labor hour, making the fixed

OBJECTIVE 2

Explain the purpose of a standard cost sheet.

A P P L I C A T I O N S   I N   B U S I N E S S

Although standards are widely used for manufacturing operations, the concept of using them for other types of operations is also valid. For example, Smith Dairy is a family-owned producer of milk and milk products that operates in Ohio, Indiana, and Kentucky. It uses a fleet of delivery trucks to deliver its products throughout its sales region. Distribution cost is the second highest cost in a dairy, exceeded only by production cost. Cost control for distribution thus becomes a natural focus. Standards are set for such things as truck speed, shifting patterns, idling time, braking intensity, temperature in transit, Department of Transportation (DOT) log compliance, and unloading rates. Low unloading rates and excessive amounts of speed, shifting, idling time, and braking can significantly increase delivery costs. Furthermore, incorrect temperatures can ruin a load of goods.

To better monitor and improve compliance with delivery performance standards, Smith installed onboard computers in each of its delivery trucks. These computers monitor and report on speed, shifting, and temperature in transit; they record hard braking, and they have reduced idle time and lowered fuel costs. The standard cost system has not only increased cost efficiency, but it has also improved driver safety by capturing how vehicles are operated on a real-time basis.

Source: Jack Mans, "High-Tech Cost Management," *Dairy Foods* (March 2000): 51–53.

Standard Cost Sheet for Corn Chips

Description	Standard Price	Standard Usage	Standard Cost*	Subtotal
Direct materials:				
Yellow corn	$ 0.01	18 oz.	$0.18	
Cooking oil	0.03	2 oz.	0.06	
Salt	0.01	1 oz.	0.01	
Lime	0.50	0.04 oz.	0.02	
Bags	0.05	1 bag	0.05	
Total direct materials				$0.32
Direct labor:				
Inspection	8.00	0.01 hr.	$0.08	
Machine operators	10.00	0.01 hr.	0.10	
Total direct labor				0.18
Overhead:				
Variable overhead	4.00	0.02 hr.	$0.08	
Fixed overhead	15.00	0.02 hr.	0.30	
Total overhead				0.38
Total standard unit cost				$0.88

*Calculated by multiplying price times usage.

overhead cost per package of corn chips $0.30 ($15.00 × 0.02). About one-third of the cost of production is fixed, indicating a capital-intensive production effort. Indeed, much of the operation is mechanized.

The standard cost sheet also reveals the quantity of each input that should be used to produce one unit of output. The unit quantity standards can be used to compute the total amount of inputs allowed for the actual output. This computation is an essential component in computing efficiency variances. A manager should be able to compute the **standard quantity of materials allowed (SQ)** and the **standard hours allowed (SH)** for the actual output. This computation must be done for every class of direct material and every class of direct labor. How to compute these quantities is shown in Cornerstone 9-1 using one type of material and one class of labor.

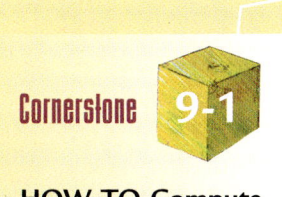

Cornerstone 9-1

HOW TO Compute Standard Quantities Allowed (SQ and SH)

Information: Assume that 100,000 packages of corn chips are produced during the first week of March. The unit quantity standard is 18 ounces of yellow corn per package (Exhibit 9-2). The unit quantity standard for machine operators is 0.01 hour per package produced (Exhibit 9-2).

Required: How much yellow corn and how many operator hours should have been used for the actual output of 100,000 packages?

Calculation:
Corn allowed:

$$SQ = \text{Unit quantity standard} \times \text{Actual output}$$
$$= 18 \times 100{,}000$$
$$= 1{,}800{,}000 \text{ ounces}$$

Operator hours allowed:

$$SH = \text{Unit labor standard} \times \text{Actual output}$$
$$= 0.01 \times 100{,}000$$
$$= 1{,}000 \text{ direct labor hours}$$

Analytical Q & A

A product is allowed three ounces of silver per unit and 0.5 hour of labor. If 3,000 units are produced, what is the standard quantity of silver allowed? Standard quantity of labor?

Answer:
$SQ = 3 \times 3{,}000 = 9{,}000$ ounces; $SH = 0.5 \times 3{,}000 = 1{,}500$ direct labor hours.

HERE'S THE REAL KICKER

About 15 percent of the defective Kicker speakers returned to Stillwater Designs can be rebuilt. The other 85 percent are sold as metal scrap. Speakers are candidates for rebuilding if the cost of direct materials and labor is less than the sum of the speaker's purchase cost, shipping cost, and duty (the production of Kicker speakers is outsourced to mostly Asian producers). This is true, for example, of the square S12L7 speakers.

To rebuild a square S12L7, the returned speaker is torn down to its basic structures, chemical and glue residues are removed, and the speaker is demagnetized so that it is possible to get rid of metal shavings and pieces. After this preparatory work, recone kits are used to replace the stripped-out components. The rebuilt woofer is then placed in a cabinet and sealed. The completed unit undergoes two tests—one to ensure that the power is hooked up correctly and a second that checks for air leaks.

Every two years, standard costs for materials and labor are set. Time studies are used to determine the time required for rebuilding, and, thus, the labor content. The cost of the recone kit is the major material cost. These standard costs are used for two purposes: (1) to determine if rebuilding is feasible for a given model and (2) to assign costs to the rebuilt product on an ongoing basis if rebuilding is the decision.

VARIANCE ANALYSIS: GENERAL DESCRIPTION

It is possible to calculate the costs that should have been incurred for the actual level of activity. This figure is obtained by multiplying the amount of input allowed (either materials or labor) for the actual output by the standard price of the input. Letting SP be the standard unit price of an input and SQ the standard quantity of input allowed for the actual output, the planned or budgeted input cost is $SP \times SQ$. The actual input cost is $AP \times AQ$, where AP is the actual price per unit of the input and AQ is the actual quantity of input used. The **total budget variance** is simply the difference between the actual cost of the input and its planned cost. For simplicity, the total budget variance will be simply called the *total variance*:

$$\text{Total variance} = \text{Actual cost} - \text{Planned cost}$$
$$= (AP \times AQ) - (SP \times SQ)$$

OBJECTIVE 3

Describe the basic concepts underlying variance analysis and explain when variances should be investigated.

Because responsibility for deviations from planned prices tends to be located in the purchasing or personnel department and responsibility for deviations from planned usage of inputs tends to be located in the production department, it is important to separate the total variance into price and usage (quantity) variances.

Price and Usage Variances

Exhibit 9-4 provides a general model for calculating price and quantity variances for materials and labor.[2] For labor, the price variance is usually called a rate variance, and the usage (quantity) variance is called an efficiency variance. **Price (rate) variance** is the difference between the actual and standard unit price of an input multiplied by the number of inputs used: $(AP - SP)AQ$. **Usage (efficiency) variance** is the difference between the actual and standard quantity of inputs multiplied by the standard unit price of the input: $(AQ - SQ)SP$.

Unfavorable (U) variances occur whenever actual prices or actual usage of inputs are greater than standard prices or standard usage. When the opposite occurs, **favorable (F) variances** are obtained. Favorable and unfavorable variances are not equivalent to good and bad variances. The terms merely indicate the relationship of the actual prices or quantities to the standard prices and quantities. Whether or not the variances are good or bad depends on why they occurred. Determining why requires managers to do some investigation.

9-4

EXHIBIT

Variance Analysis: General Description

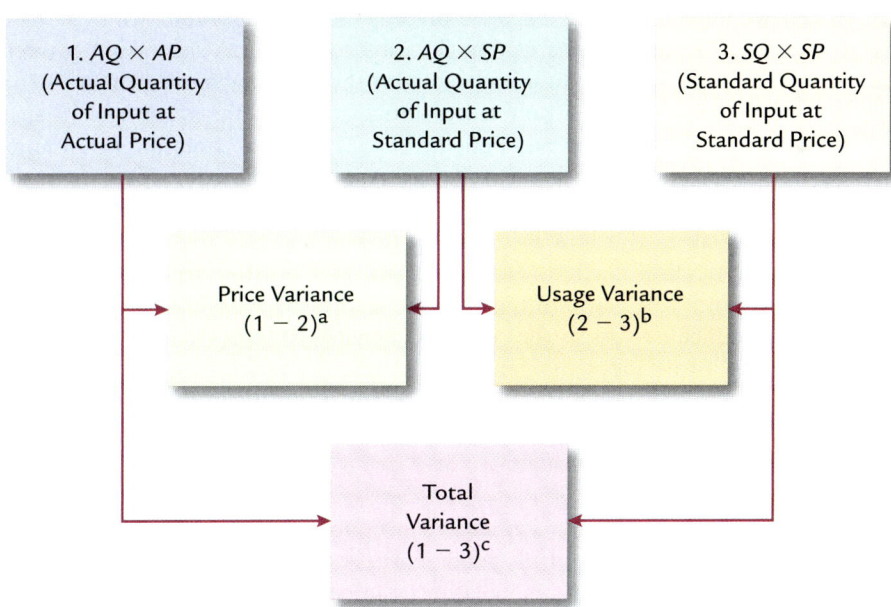

[a]Price variance = $(AQ \times AP) - (AQ \times SP) = (AP - SP)AQ$
[b]Usage variance = $(AQ \times SP) - (SQ \times SP) = (AQ - SQ)SP$
[c]Total variance = $(AQ \times AP) - (SQ \times SP)$

[2]Overhead variance analysis is discussed in Chapter 10.

The Decision to Investigate

Rarely will actual performance exactly meet the established standards, and management does not expect it to do so. Random variations around the standard are expected. Because of this, management should have in mind an acceptable range of performance. When variances are within this range, they are assumed to be caused by random factors. When a variance falls outside this range, the deviation is likely to be caused by nonrandom factors, either factors that managers can control or factors they cannot control. In the noncontrollable case, managers need to revise the standard.

An example from the pharmaceutical industry may drive home the importance of variance investigation.[3] Drugs must contain a certain amount of the active ingredient, plus or minus a small percent (for example, aspirin claiming to have five grains per tablet must really have somewhere between 90 and 110 percent of the specified amount). The FDA is responsible for ensuring the safety and efficacy of drugs manufactured at home and abroad. An anonymous letter alerted the FDA to manufacturing problems with an antibiotic produced by a Canadian firm, Novopharm Ltd. Basically, the drug was too strong and could potentially destroy beneficial bacteria along with the harmful bacteria. Upon investigation, the FDA found the blending process to be "out of control." The result was that the firm stopped shipping that drug until the process could be corrected. Another FDA investigation centered on Haimen Pharmaceutical Factory in China. There, the FDA found the samples of an antileukemia drug to be too weak. Again, large variances from standard triggered an investigation. Interestingly, the question of what to do about the company and the drug was not clear-cut. In this case, the FDA did not withdraw its approval because the drug was in short supply.

Now that we understand why variance investigation is important, we need to understand when to investigate. Investigating the cause of variances and taking corrective action, like all activities, have a cost associated with them. As a general principle, an investigation should be undertaken only if the anticipated benefits are greater than the expected costs. Assessing the costs and benefits of a variance investigation is not an easy task, however. A manager must consider whether a variance will recur. If so, the process may be permanently out of control, meaning that periodic savings may be achieved if corrective action is taken. But how is it possible to know if the variance is going to recur unless an investigation is conducted? And how is it possible to know the cost of corrective action unless the cause of the variance is known?

Because it is difficult to assess the costs and benefits of variance analysis on a case-by-case basis, many firms adopt the general guideline of investigating variances only if they fall outside of an acceptable range. They are not investigated unless they are large enough to be of concern. They must be large enough to be caused by something other than random factors and large enough (on average) to justify the costs of investigating and taking corrective action.

How do managers determine whether variances are significant? How is the acceptable range established? The acceptable range is the standard, plus or minus an allowable deviation. The top and bottom measures of the allowable range are called the **control limits**. The upper control limit is the standard plus the allowable deviation, and the lower control limit is the standard minus the allowable deviation. Current practice sets the control limits subjectively: based on past experience, intuition, and judg-

---

[3]The examples given here are taken from an article by Christopher Drew, "Medicines from Afar Raise Safety Concerns," *The New York Times* (October 29, 1995): A1 and A16.

ment, management determines the allowable deviation from standard.[4] The actual deviations from standard are often plotted over time against the upper and lower limits to allow managers to see the significance of the variance. Cornerstone 9-2 shows how control limits are used to trigger an investigation. The control chart graphically illustrates the concept of control limits. The assumed standard is $100,000, and the allowable deviation is plus or minus $10,000. The upper limit is $110,000, and the lower limit is $90,000. Investigation occurs whenever an observation falls outside of these limits (as would be the case for the sixth observation). Trends can also be important.

The control limits are often expressed both as a percentage of the standard and as an absolute dollar amount. For example, the allowable deviation may be expressed as the lesser of 10 percent of the standard amount, or $10,000.

Cornerstone 9-2

HOW TO Use Control Limits to Trigger a Variance Investigation

Information: Standard cost: $100,000; allowable deviation: ±10,000; actual costs for six months:

June	$ 97,500	September	$102,500
July	105,000	October	107,500
August	95,000	November	112,500

Required: Plot the actual costs over time against the upper and lower control limits. Determine when a variance should be investigated.

Calculation:

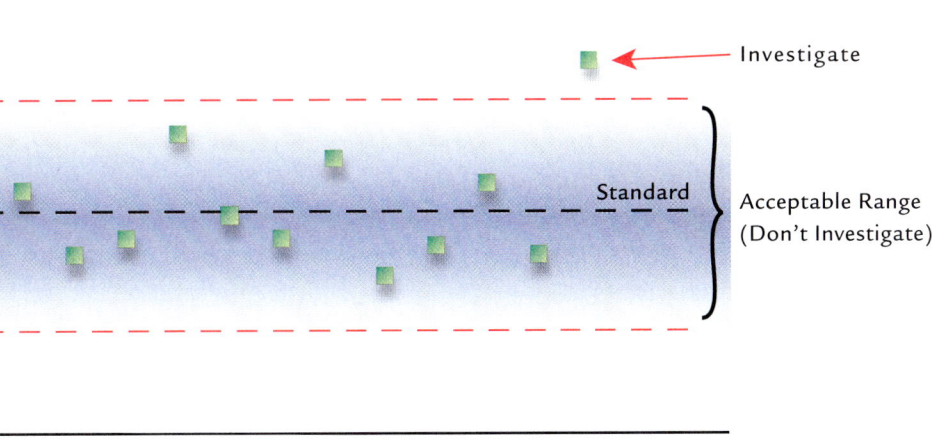

The control chart reveals that the last variance should be investigated. The chart also reveals a short-term increasing trend that suggests the process is moving out of control. A nongraphical approach is to calculate the difference between the actual cost and the upper or lower limit and see if it exceeds $10,000.

In other words, management will not accept a deviation of more than $10,000 even if that deviation is less than 10 percent of the standard. Alternatively, even if the dollar amount is less than $10,000, an investigation is required if the deviation is more than 10 percent of the standard amount.

[4]Gaumnitz and Kollaritsch, "Manufacturing Variances: Current Practices and Trends," reports that about 45–47 percent of the firms use dollar or percentage control limits. Most of the remaining firms use judgment rather than any formal identification of limits.

Concept Q & A

Refer to the control chart in Cornerstone 9-2. What action would you take for an actual value of $89,750?

Answer:
This would produce a value below the lower control limit so there should be an investigation to find the cause or causes of the deviation. Corrective action could then be taken.

VARIANCE ANALYSIS: MATERIALS

The total variance measures the difference between the actual costs of materials and their budgeted costs for the actual level of activity. How to calculate the total variance for materials is illustrated in Cornerstone 9-3, using selected data from Crunchy Chips for the first week of March. To keep the example simple, only one material (corn) is illustrated.

OBJECTIVE 4

Compute the materials variances and explain how they are used for control.

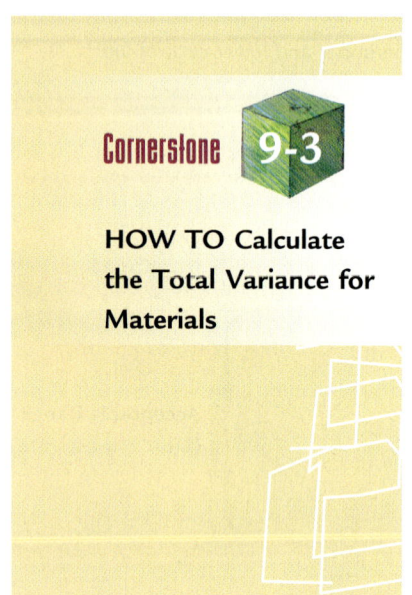

Cornerstone 9-3

HOW TO Calculate the Total Variance for Materials

Information: Unit standards from Exhibit 9-3; the actual results for the first week in March:

Actual production	48,500 bags of corn chips
Actual cost of corn	780,000 ounces at $0.015 = $11,700
Actual cost of inspection labor	360 hours at $8.35 = $3,006

Required: Calculate the total variance for corn for the first week in March.
Calculation:

	Actual Costs	Budgeted Costs*	Total Variance
	$AQ \times AP$	$SQ \times SP$	$(AQ \times AP) - (SQ \times SP)$
Corn	$11,700	$8,730	$2,970 U

*The standard quantities for materials and labor are computed as unit quantity standards from Exhibit 9-3:

$$\text{Corn: } SQ = 18 \times 48,500 = 873,000 \text{ ounces}$$

Multiplying these standard quantities by the unit standard prices given in Exhibit 9-3 produces the budgeted amounts appearing in this column:

$$\text{Corn: } \$0.01 \times 873,000 = \$8,730$$

Direct Materials Variances

To help control the cost of materials, price and usage variances are calculated. However, the sum of the price and usage variances will add up to the total materials variance calculated in Cornerstone 9-3 *only if the materials purchased equal the materials used.* The materials price variance is computed using the actual quantity of materials *purchased,* and the materials usage variances is computed using the actual quantity of materials *used.*

Since it is better to have information on variances earlier rather than later, the materials price variance uses the actual quantity of materials purchased rather than the actual quantity of materials used. The more timely the information, the more likely that proper managerial action can be taken. Old information is often useless information. Materials may sit in inventory for weeks or months before they are needed in production. By the time the materials price variance is computed, signaling a problem, it may be too late to take corrective action. Or, even if corrective action is still possible, the delay may cost the company thousands of dollars. For example, suppose a new purchasing agent is unaware of the availability of a quantity discount on a raw material. If the materials price variance that ignores the discount is computed when a new purchase is made, the resulting unfavorable signal would lead to quick corrective action. (In this case, the action would be to use the discount for future purchases.) If the materials price variance is not computed until the material is issued to production, it may be several weeks or even months before the problem is discovered.

Materials price and usage variances normally should be calculated using variance formulas. However, the 3-pronged (columnar) approach is used when the materials purchased equal the materials used. Cornerstone 9-4 shows how to use the materials variance formulas, which we now specifically state and define.

The **materials price variance (*MPV*)** measures the difference between what should have been paid for raw materials and what was actually paid. The formula for computing this variance is:

$$MPV = (AP \times AQ) - (SP \times AQ)$$

or, factoring, we have:

$$MPV = (AP - SP)AQ$$

where

$$AP = \text{The actual price per unit}$$
$$SP = \text{The standard price per unit}$$
$$AQ = \text{The actual quantity of material } \textit{purchased}$$

The **materials usage variance (*MUV*)** measures the difference between the direct materials actually used and the direct materials that should have been used for the actual output. The formula for computing this variance is:

$$MUV = (SP \times AQ) - (SP \times SQ)$$

or, factoring:

$$MUV = (AQ - SQ)SP$$

where

$$AQ = \text{The actual quantity of materials } \textit{used}$$
$$SQ = \text{The standard quantity of materials allowed for the actual output}$$
$$SP = \text{The standard price per unit}$$

How to calculate the materials price and usage variances using either a columnar approach or a formula approach is shown for the Crunchy Chips example in Cornerstone 9-4 (for corn only).

Concept Q & A

When is the total materials variance the sum of the price variance and the usage variance?

Answer:
When the materials purchased equal the materials used.

Cornerstone 9-4

HOW TO Calculate Materials Variances: Formula and Columnar Approaches

Information: Unit standards from Exhibit 9-3; the actual results for the first week in March:

Actual production	48,500 bags of corn chips
Actual cost of corn	780,000 ounces @ $0.015

Required: Calculate the materials price and usage variances using the 3-pronged (columnar) and formula approaches.

Calculation:

A. Formulas (recommended approach for materials variances because materials purchased may differ from materials used):

$$MPV = (AP - SP)AQ$$
$$= (\$0.015 - \$0.01)780,000$$
$$= \$3,900 \text{ U}$$

$$MUV = (AQ - SQ)SP$$
$$= (780,000 - 873,000)(\$0.01)$$
$$= \$930 \text{ F}$$

B. Columnar (this approach is possible only if the materials purchased = materials used):

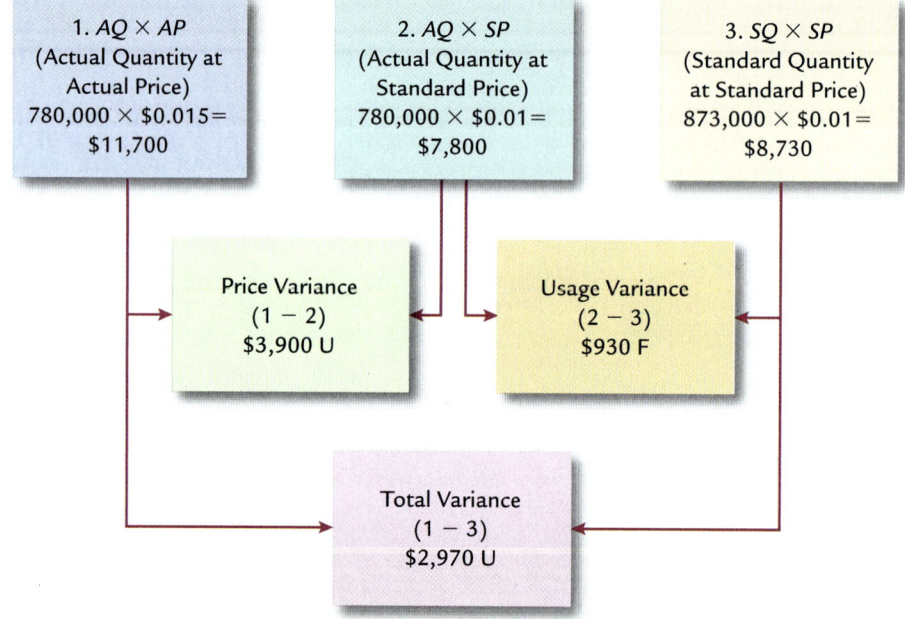

Analytical Q & A

Assume that $SP = \$3$ and $AP = \$2$. If 100 units are purchased, what is the materials price variance?

Answer:
$MPV = (\$2.00 - \$3.00)100 = \$100$ F.

Using Materials Variance Information

Calculating materials variances is only the first step. Using the variance information to exercise control is fundamental to a standard cost system. Responsibility must be assigned, variance significance must be assessed, and the variances must be accounted for and disposed of at the end of the year.

Responsibility for the Materials Price Variance

The responsibility for controlling the materials price variance usually belongs to the purchasing agent. Admittedly, the price of materials is largely beyond his or her control; however, the price variance can be influenced by such factors as quality, quantity discounts, distance of the source from the plant, and so on. These factors are often under the control of the agent.

Using the price variance to evaluate the performance of purchasing has some limitations. Emphasis on meeting or beating the standard can produce some undesirable outcomes. For example, if the purchasing agent feels pressured to produce favorable variances, materials of lower quality than desired may be purchased or too much inventory may be acquired to take advantage of quantity discounts.

Analysis of the Materials Price Variance

The first step in variance analysis is deciding whether the variance is significant or not. If it is judged insignificant, no further steps are needed. The materials price variance is $3,900 unfavorable, which is about 45 percent of standard cost ($3,900/$8,730). Most would judge this variance to be significant. The next step is to find out why it occurred.

For the Crunchy Chips example, the investigation revealed that a higher-quality corn was purchased because of a shortage of the usual grade in the market. Once the reason is known, corrective action can be taken if necessary—and if possible. In this case, no corrective action is needed. The firm has no control over the supply shortage; it will simply have to wait until market conditions improve.

Responsibility for the Materials Usage Variance

The production manager is generally responsible for materials usage. Minimizing scrap, waste, and rework are all ways in which the manager can ensure that the standard is met. However, at times, the cause of the variance is attributable to others outside the production area, as the next section shows.

As with the price variance, using the usage variance to evaluate performance can lead to undesirable behavior. For example, a production manager feeling pressure to produce a favorable variance might allow a defective unit to be transferred to finished goods. While this avoids the problem of wasted materials, it may create customer-relation problems.

Analysis of the Materials Usage Variance

The materials usage variance is about 11 percent of standard cost ($930/$8,730). A deviation greater than 10 percent is likely to be judged significant. Thus, investigation is needed. Investigation revealed that the favorable materials usage variance was the result of the higher-quality corn acquired by the purchasing department. In this case, the favorable variance is essentially assignable to purchasing. Since the materials usage variance is favorable—but smaller than the unfavorable price variance—the overall result of the change in purchasing is unfavorable. In the future, management should try to resume purchasing of the normal-quality corn.

If the overall variance had been favorable, a different response would be expected. If the favorable variance was expected to persist, the higher-quality corn should be purchased regularly and the price and quantity standards revised to reflect it. As this possibility reveals, standards are not static. As improvements in production take place and conditions change, standards may need to be revised to reflect the new operating environment.

Accounting and Disposition of Materials Variances

Recognizing the price variance for materials at the point of purchase also means that the raw materials inventory is carried at standard cost. In general, materials variances are not inventoried. Typically, materials variances are added (subtracted) to cost of goods sold if unfavorable (favorable). The journal entries associated with the purchase and usage of raw materials for a standard cost system are illustrated in Appendix 9A.

VARIANCE ANALYSIS: DIRECT LABOR

The total variance measures the difference between the actual costs of labor and their budgeted costs for the actual level of activity. How to calculate the total variance for labor is illustrated in Cornerstone 9-5, using selected data from Crunchy Chips for the first week of March. To keep the example simple, only inspection labor is illustrated.

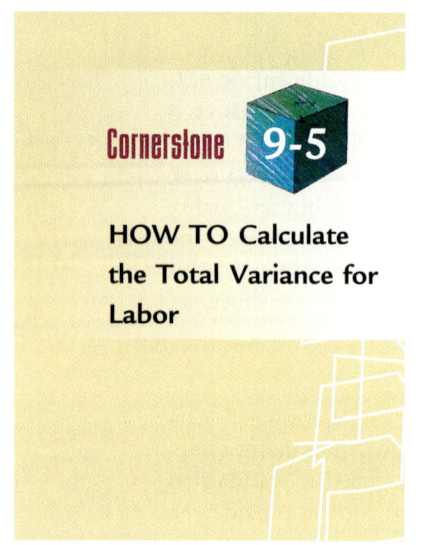

Cornerstone 9-5

HOW TO Calculate the Total Variance for Labor

Information: Unit standards from Exhibit 9-3; the actual results for the first week in March:

Actual production	48,500 bags of corn chips
Actual cost of inspection labor	360 hours at $8.35 = $3,006

Required: Calculate the total variance for inspection labor for the first week in March.

Calculation:

	Actual Costs $AQ \times AP$	Budgeted Costs* $SQ \times SP$	Total Variance $(AQ \times AP) - (SQ \times SP)$
Inspection labor	$3,006	$3,880	$874 F

*The standard quantities for inspection labor are computed as unit quantity standards from Exhibit 9-3:

$$\text{Labor: } SH = 0.01 \times 48,500 = 485 \text{ hours}$$

Multiplying these standard quantities by the unit standard prices given in Exhibit 9-3 produces the budgeted amounts appearing in this column:

$$\text{Labor: } \$8.00 \times 485 = \$3,880$$

Direct Labor Variances

Unlike the total materials variance, the labor rate and labor efficiency variances will always add up to the total variance as calculated in Cornerstone 9-5. Thus, the rate (price) and efficiency (usage) variances for labor can be calculated using either the columnar approach or the associated formulas. Which to use is a matter of taste. The formulas are adapted to reflect the specific terms used for labor prices (rates) and usage (efficiency).

The **labor rate variance** (*LRV*) computes the difference between what was paid to direct laborers and what should have been paid:

$$LRV = (AR \times AH) - (SR \times AH)$$

or, factoring:

$$LRV = (AR - SR)AH$$

where

$$AR = \text{The actual hourly wage rate}$$
$$SR = \text{The standard hourly wage rate}$$
$$AH = \text{The actual direct labor hours used}$$

The **labor efficiency variance** (*LEV*) measures the difference between the labor hours that were actually used and the labor hours that should have been used:

$$LEV = (AH \times SR) - (SH \times SR)$$

or, factoring:

$$LEV = (AH - SH)SR$$

where

AH = The actual direct labor hours used
SH = The standard direct labor hours that should have been used
SR = The standard hourly wage rate

How to calculate the labor rate and efficiency variances using either a columnar approach or a formula approach is shown for the Crunchy Chips example in Cornerstone 9-6 (for inspection labor only).

Cornerstone 9-6

HOW TO Calculate Labor Variances: Formula and Columnar Approaches

Information: Unit standards from Exhibit 9-3; the actual results for the first week in March:

| Actual production | 48,500 bags of corn chips |
| Actual cost of inspection labor | 360 hours @ $8.35 |

Required: Calculate the labor rate and efficiency variances using the 3-pronged (columnar) and formula approaches.

Calculation:

Formulas:

$LRV = (AR - SR)AH$
$= (\$8.35 - \$8.00)360$
$= \$126$ U

$LEV = (AH - SH)SR$
$= (360 - 485)(\$8.00)$
$= \$1,000$ F

Columnar:

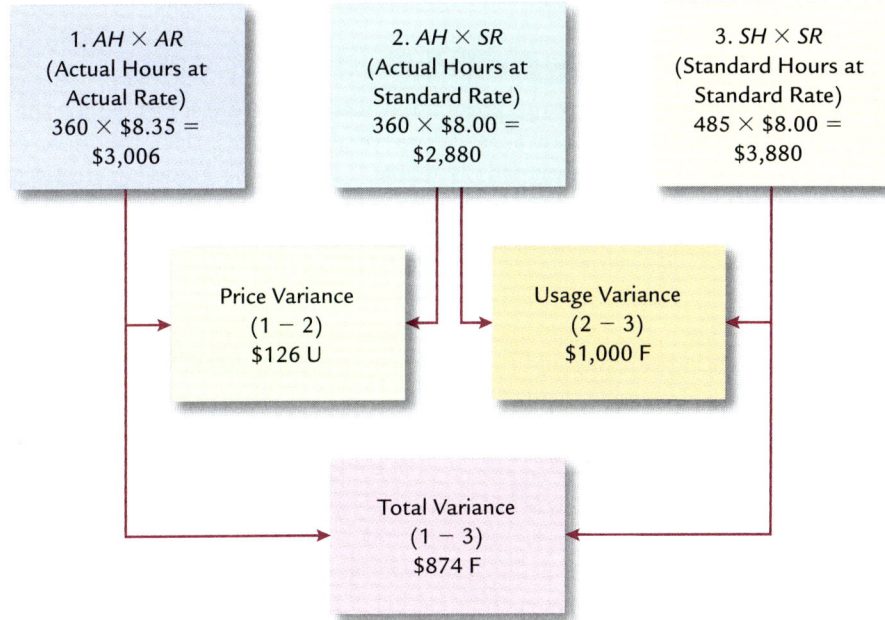

| 1. $AH \times AR$ (Actual Hours at Actual Rate) $360 \times \$8.35 = \$3,006$ | 2. $AH \times SR$ (Actual Hours at Standard Rate) $360 \times \$8.00 = \$2,880$ | 3. $SH \times SR$ (Standard Hours at Standard Rate) $485 \times \$8.00 = \$3,880$ |

Price Variance (1 − 2) $126 U

Usage Variance (2 − 3) $1,000 F

Total Variance (1 − 3) $874 F

Using Labor Variance Information

As with materials variances, calculating labor variances initiates the feedback process. Using the labor variance information to exercise control is fundamental. Responsibility must be assigned, variance significance must be assessed, and the variances must be accounted for and disposed of at the end of the year.

Responsibility for the Labor Rate Variance

Labor rates are largely determined by such external forces as labor markets and union contracts. The actual wage rate rarely departs from the standard rate. When labor rate variances do occur, they usually do so because an average wage rate is used for the rate standard and because more skilled and more highly paid laborers are used for less skilled tasks. Unexpected overtime can also be the cause of a labor rate variance.

Wage rates for a particular labor activity often differ among workers because of differing levels of seniority. Rather than selecting labor rate standards reflecting those different levels, an average wage rate is often chosen. As the seniority mix changes, the average rate changes. This will give rise to a labor rate variance; it also calls for a new standard to reflect the new seniority mix. Controllability is not assignable for this cause of a labor rate variance.

However, the use of labor is controllable by the production manager. The use of more skilled workers to perform less skilled tasks (or vice versa) is a decision that a production manager consciously makes. For this reason, responsibility for the labor rate variance is generally assigned to the individuals who decide how labor will be used.

Analysis of the Labor Rate Variance

The labor rate variance is only 3 percent of the standard cost ($126/$3,880). Although a 3-percent variance is not likely to be judged significant, for illustrative purposes, assume that an investigation is conducted. The cause of the variance is found to be the use of more highly paid and skilled machine operators as inspectors, which occurred because two inspectors quit without formal notice. The corrective action is to hire and train two new inspectors.

Responsibility for the Labor Efficiency Variance

Generally speaking, production managers are responsible for the productive use of direct labor. However, as is true of all variances, once the cause is discovered, responsibility may be assigned elsewhere. For example, frequent breakdowns of machinery may cause interruptions and nonproductive use of labor. But the responsibility for these breakdowns may be faulty maintenance. If so, the maintenance manager should be charged with the unfavorable labor efficiency variance.

Production managers may be tempted to engage in dysfunctional behavior if too much emphasis is placed on the labor efficiency variance. For example, to avoid losing hours or using additional hours because of possible rework, a production manager could deliberately transfer defective units to finished goods.

Analysis of the Labor Efficiency Variance

The labor efficiency variance is 26 percent of standard cost ($1,000/$3,880). This favorable variance is judged to be significant, and an investigation is undertaken. The investigation revealed that inspections flowed more smoothly because of the higher quality of materials. This additional benefit of the higher-quality materials should be factored into whether Crunchy should return to purchasing its normal quality of corn when it is available again or whether the higher-quality material should again be purchased. Unfortunately, even with this additional benefit, the materials price variance is so large that the correct action is to acquire the normal-quality material when it again becomes available.

It is often true that a company making a healthy profit may not be concerned as much as it should be with controlling costs. Honley Medical is an example of such a company. It had a proprietary product and used that position to dominate the market. During this period of time, little attention was paid to cost efficiency. With the patent on its product soon to expire, Honley was about to face a competitive environment—one that would likely threaten the level of profitability that had been enjoyed for many years.

Using standards to identify efficient but achievable levels of performance and encouraging managers and workers to meet these standards is certainly a sound approach to prepare for the coming competitive pressures. The curious aspect of this case is the implication that Honley could have been operating more efficiently during its dominating period. For years, higher levels of profits had been lost because of the dominating position that was generating profits at an apparently satisfactory level. Perhaps one message is that standard costing systems should be used even when a company is earning very good levels of profits. Satisfactory levels of profits because of a dominant market position may serve to hide inefficiencies.

SUMMARY OF LEARNING OBJECTIVES

A standard cost system budgets quantities and costs on a unit basis. These unit budgets are for labor, materials, and overhead. Standard costs, therefore, are the amount that should be expended to produce a product or service. Standards are set using historical experience, engineering studies, and input from operating personnel, marketing, and accounting. Currently attainable standards are those that can be achieved under efficient operating conditions. Ideal standards are those achievable under maximum efficiency, or ideal operating conditions. Standard cost systems are adopted to improve planning and control and to facilitate product costing. By comparing actual outcomes with standards and breaking the variance into price and quantity components, detailed feedback is provided to managers. This information allows managers to exercise a greater degree of cost control than that found in a normal or actual cost system. Decisions such as bidding are also made easier when a standard costing system is in place.

The standard cost sheet provides the details for computing the standard cost per unit. It shows the standard costs for materials, labor, and variable and fixed overhead. It also reveals the quantity of each input that should be used to produce one unit of output. Using these unit quantity standards, the standard quantity of materials allowed and the standard hours allowed can be computed for the actual output. These computations play an important role in variance analysis.

The total variance is the difference between actual costs and planned costs. In a standard costing system, the total variance is broken down into price and usage variances. By breaking the total variances into price and usage variances, managers have more ability to analyze and control the total variance. Variances should be investigated if they are material and if the benefits of corrective action are greater than the costs of investigation. Because of the difficulty of assessing cost and benefits on a case-by-case basis, many firms set up formal control limits—either a dollar amount, a percentage, or both. Others use judgment to assess the need to investigate.

The materials price and usage variances are computed using either a 3-pronged (columnar) approach or formulas. The materials price variance is the difference between what should have been paid for materials and what was paid (generally associated with the purchasing activity). The materials usage variance is the difference between the cost of the materials that should have been used and the amount that was used (generally associated with the production activity). When a significant variance is signaled, an investigation is undertaken to find the cause. Corrective action is taken, if possible, to put the system back in control. The labor variances are computed using either a 3-pronged approach or formulas. The labor rate variance is caused by the actual wage rate differing from the standard wage rate. It is the difference between the wages that were paid and those that should have been paid. The labor efficiency variance is the difference between the cost of the labor that was used and the cost of the labor that should have been used. When a significant variance is signaled, investigation is called for and corrective action should be taken, if possible, to put the system back in control.

Assuming that the materials price variance is computed at the point of purchase, all inventories are carried at standard cost. Actual costs are never entered into an inventory account. Accounts are created for materials price and usage variances and for labor rate and efficiency variances. Unfavorable variances are always debits; favorable variances are always credits.

Cornerstones for Chapter 9

Cornerstone 9-1 How to compute standard quantities allowed (*SQ* and *SH*), page 359
Cornerstone 9-2 How to use control limits to trigger a variance investigation, page 363
Cornerstone 9-3 How to calculate the total variance for materials, page 364
Cornerstone 9-4 How to calculate materials variances: formula and columnar approaches, page 366
Cornerstone 9-5 How to calculate the total variance for labor, page 368
Cornerstone 9-6 How to calculate labor variances: formula and columnar approaches, page 369

KEY TERMS

Control limits, 362

Currently attainable standards, 355

Favorable (F) variances, 361

Ideal standards, 355

Labor efficiency variance (*LEV*), 368

Labor rate variance (*LRV*), 368

Materials price variance (*MPV*), 365

Materials usage variance (*MUV*), 365

Price standards, 354

Price (rate) variance, 361

Quantity standards, 354

Standard cost per unit, 358

Standard cost sheet, 358

Standard hours allowed (*SH*), 359

Standard quantity of materials allowed (*SQ*), 359

Total budget variance, 360

Unfavorable (U) variances, 361

Usage (efficiency) variance, 361

APPENDIX 9A: ACCOUNTING FOR VARIANCES

OBJECTIVE 6

Prepare journal entries for materials and labor variances.

To illustrate recording variances, we will assume that the materials price variance is computed at the time materials are purchased. With this assumption, we can state a general rule for a firm's inventory accounts: all inventories are carried at standard cost. Actual costs are never entered into an inventory account. In recording variances, unfavorable variances are always debits, and favorable variances are always credits.

Entries for Direct Materials Variances

Materials Price Variance

The entry to record the purchase of materials follows (assuming an unfavorable *MPV* and that *AQ* is materials purchased):

Materials	$SP \times AQ$	
Materials Price Variance	$(AP - SP)AQ$	
Accounts Payable		$AP \times AQ$

For example, if *AP* is \$0.0069 per ounce of corn, *SP* is \$0.0060 per ounce, and 780,000 ounces of corn are purchased, the entry would be:

Materials	4,680	
Materials Price Variance	702	
Accounts Payable		5,382

Notice that the raw materials are carried in the inventory account at standard cost.

Materials Usage Variance

The general form for the entry to record the issuance and usage of materials, assuming a favorable *MUV*, is as follows:

Work in Process	$SQ \times SP$	
Materials Usage Variance		$(AQ - SQ)SP$
Materials		$AQ \times SP$

Here *AQ* is the materials issued and used, not necessarily equal to the materials purchased. Notice that only standard quantities and standard prices are used to assign costs to Work in Process; no actual costs enter this account.

    For example, if *AQ* is 780,000 ounces of corn, *SQ* is 873,000 ounces, and *SP* is \$0.006, then the entry would be:

Work in Process	5,238	
Materials Usage Variance		558
Materials		4,680

Notice that the favorable usage variance appears as a credit entry.

Entries for Direct Labor Variances

Unlike the materials variances, the entry to record both types of labor variances is made simultaneously. The general form of this entry follows (assuming an unfavorable labor rate variance and an unfavorable labor efficiency variance).

Work in Process	$SH \times SR$	
Labor Efficiency Variance	$(AH - SH)SR$	
Labor Rate Variance	$(AR - SR)AH$	
Accrued Payroll		$AH \times AR$

Again, notice that only standard hours and standard rates are used to assign costs to Work in Process. Actual prices or quantities are not used.

To give a specific example, assume that *AH* is 360 hours of inspection, *SH* is 339.5 hours, *AR* is $7.35 per hour, and *SR* is $7.00 per hour. The following journal entry would be made:

Work in Process	2,376.50	
Labor Efficiency Variance	143.50	
Labor Rate Variance	126.00	
Accrued Payroll		2,646.00

Disposition of Materials and Labor Variances

At the end of the year, the variances for materials and labor are usually closed to Cost of Goods Sold. (This practice is acceptable provided that variances are not material in amount.) Using the previous data, the entries would take the following form:

Cost of Goods Sold	971.50	
Materials Price Variance		702.00
Labor Efficiency Variance		143.50
Labor Rate Variance		126.00
Materials Usage Variance	558.00	
Cost of Goods Sold		558.00

If the variances are material, they must be prorated among various accounts. For the materials price variance, it is prorated among Materials Inventory, Materials Usage Variance, Work in Process, Finished Goods, and Cost of Goods Sold. The remaining materials and labor variances are prorated among Work in Process, Finished Goods, and Cost of Goods Sold. Typically, materials variances are prorated on the basis of the materials balances in each of these accounts and the labor variances on the basis of the labor balances in the accounts.

SUMMARY OF APPENDIX 9A

Assuming that the materials price variance is computed at the point of purchase, all inventories are carried at standard cost. Actual costs are never entered into an inventory account. Accounts are created for materials price and usage variances and for labor rate and efficiency variances. Unfavorable variances are always debits; favorable variances are always credits.

APPENDIX 9B: KAIZEN AND TARGET COSTING

The Role of Kaizen Standards

Kaizen costing is concerned with reducing the costs of existing products and processes. In operational terms, this translates into reducing nonvalue-added costs. Controlling this cost reduction process is accomplished through the repetitive use of two major subcycles: (1) the kaizen or continuous improvement cycle and (2) the maintenance cycle. The kaizen subcycle is defined by a Plan-Do-Check-Act sequence. Thus, if a company emphasizes reducing nonvalue-added costs, the amount of improvement planned for the coming period (month, quarter, etc.) is set (the *Plan* step). A **kaizen standard** reflects the planned improvement for the upcoming period. The planned improvement is assumed to be attainable; thus, kaizen standards are a type of currently attainable standard. Actions are taken to implement the planned improvements (the *Do* step). Next, actual results (e.g., costs) are compared with the kaizen standard to provide a measure of the level of improvement attained (the *Check* step). Setting this new level as a min-

OBJECTIVE 7

Define kaizen and target costing and explain their relationship to traditional standard costing.

imum standard for future performance locks in the realized improvements and initiates simultaneously the maintenance cycle and a search for additional improvement opportunities (the *Act* step). The maintenance cycle follows a traditional Standard-Do-Check-Act sequence. A *standard* is set based on prior improvements (locking in these improvements). Next, actions are taken (the *Do* step) and the results checked to ensure that performance conforms to this new level (the *Check* step). If not, then corrective actions are taken to restore performance (the *Act* step). The kaizen cost reduction process is summarized in Exhibit 9-5.

Kaizen Cost Reduction Process

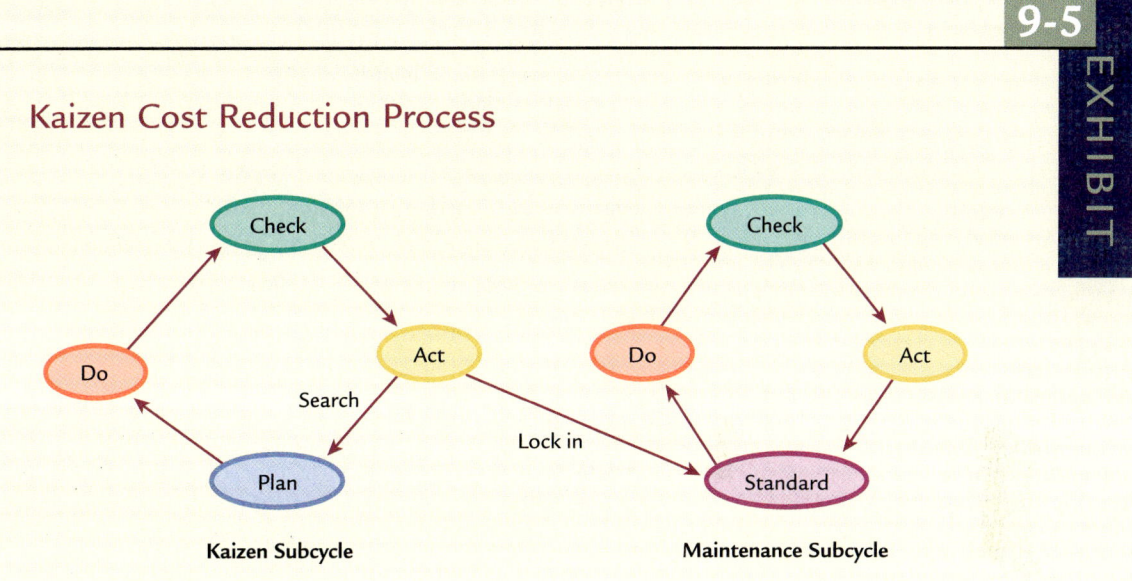

EXHIBIT 9-5

Cornerstone 9-7 shows how to apply kaizen costing for a particular example. A Medical Products Division inspects every unit produced of a particular surgical instrument. The unit-level, value-added standard for this product calls for zero inspection hours per unit and a value-added inspection cost of $0 per unit. The company currently uses 15 minutes to inspect each instrument at a cost of $15 per inspection hour. Therefore, the actual inspection cost per unit is $3.75 ($15 × 1/4 hr.). This is also the non-value-added cost. The objective ultimately is to reduce the inspection cost to zero. Each successive reduction is locked in, and a new maintenance standard is set. Thus, kaizen costing differs from traditional standard costing in that the standard changes frequently, reflecting continuous improvement efforts.

Cornerstone 9-7

HOW TO Apply Kaizen Costing

Information:

a. *Current state*: A Medical Products Division inspects every unit produced of a surgical instrument. The standard labor cost is $15 per inspection hour. The maintenance standard at the beginning of the quarter is 15 minutes per instrument.

b. *Planned improvement*: At the beginning of the first quarter, a new production process will be installed that is expected to increase the precision with which the surgical instrument is produced. This new process is expected to reduce the inspection time from 15 minutes to 10 minutes. At the beginning of the second quarter, implementation of a statistical process control system is expected to reduce the inspection time by an additional three minutes.

c. *Actual (realized) improvement*: Inspection time was reduced from 15 minutes to 12 minutes as a result of the new process.

Required:

1. Identify the kaizen and maintenance labor (inspection) standards in place at the beginning of the first quarter. Express the standard in both physical and financial terms. Calculate the expected and actual cost reductions.
2. Identify the kaizen and maintenance labor (inspection) standards in place at the end of the first quarter. Express the standard in both physical and financial terms. Calculate the expected cost reduction.

Calculation:

1. Beginning of first quarter:

    Maintenance:

    Physical standard: 15 minutes
    Financial standard: $3.75 ($15 × 15/60 hr.)

    Kaizen:

    Physical standard: 10 minutes
    Financial: $2.50 ($15 × 10/60)

    Expected cost reduction: $3.75 − $2.50 = $1.25 per unit

    Actual cost reduction: $3.75 − $3.00 = $0.75 per unit

2. End of first quarter:

    Maintenance:

    Physical standard: 12 minutes
    Financial standard: $3.00 ($15 × 12/60 hr.)

    Kaizen:

    Physical standard: 9 minutes
    Financial: $2.25 ($15 × 9/60)

    Expected cost reduction (second quarter): $3.00 − $2.25 = $0.75 per unit

The Role of Target Costing

Target costing is a particularly useful tool for establishing cost reduction goals for products that are in the design stage. A **target cost** is the difference between the sales price needed to capture a predetermined market share and the desired per-unit profit. The sales price reflects the product specifications or functions valued by the customer (referred to as *product functionality*). If the target cost is less than what is currently achievable, then management must find cost reductions that move the actual cost toward the target cost. Finding those cost reductions is the principal challenge of target costing.

Three cost reduction methods are typically used: (1) reverse engineering, (2) value analysis, and (3) process improvement. Reverse engineering tears down the competitors' products with the objective of discovering more design features that create cost reductions. Value analysis attempts to assess the value placed on various product functions by customers. If the price customers are willing to pay for a particular function is less than its cost, the function is a candidate for elimination. Value analysis also may involve other interested parties such as suppliers, who may be able to suggest design modifications in certain components that might reduce costs, e.g., using common (commodity) components. Both reverse engineering and value analysis focus on product design to achieve cost reductions. The processes used to produce and market the product are also sources of potential cost reductions. Thus, redesigning processes to improve their efficiency can also contribute to achieving the needed cost reductions. The target-costing model is summarized in Exhibit 9-6.

Cornerstone 9-8 shows how to implement the target-costing concepts described by Exhibit 9-6. Notice how the expected cost of the initial design exceeds the target cost. Calculating the target cost is clearly a simple matter, although generating the tar-

Target-Costing Model

```
┌──────────────────┐         ┌──────────────┐         ┌──────────────────┐
│  Market Share    │ ──────▶ │ Target Price │ ◀────── │     Product      │
│   Objective      │         │              │         │  Functionality   │
└──────────────────┘         └──────┬───────┘         └──────────────────┘
                                    │
                                    ▼
                             ┌──────────────┐
                             │ Target Profit│
                             └──────┬───────┘
                                    │
                                    ▼
                             ┌──────────────┐
                             │ Target Cost  │
                             └──────┬───────┘
                                    │
          ┌─────────────────────▶  ▼
          │                  ┌──────────────┐
          │                  │ Product and  │
          │                  │Process Design│
          │                  └──────┬───────┘
          │                         │
          │                         ▼
          │                    ╱──────────╲
       NO │                   │   Target   │
          └───────────────────│  Cost Met? │
                               ╲──────────╱
                                    │
                                   YES
                                    │
                                    ▼
                             ┌──────────────┐
                             │ Market Share │
                             │  Objective   │
                             └──────────────┘
```

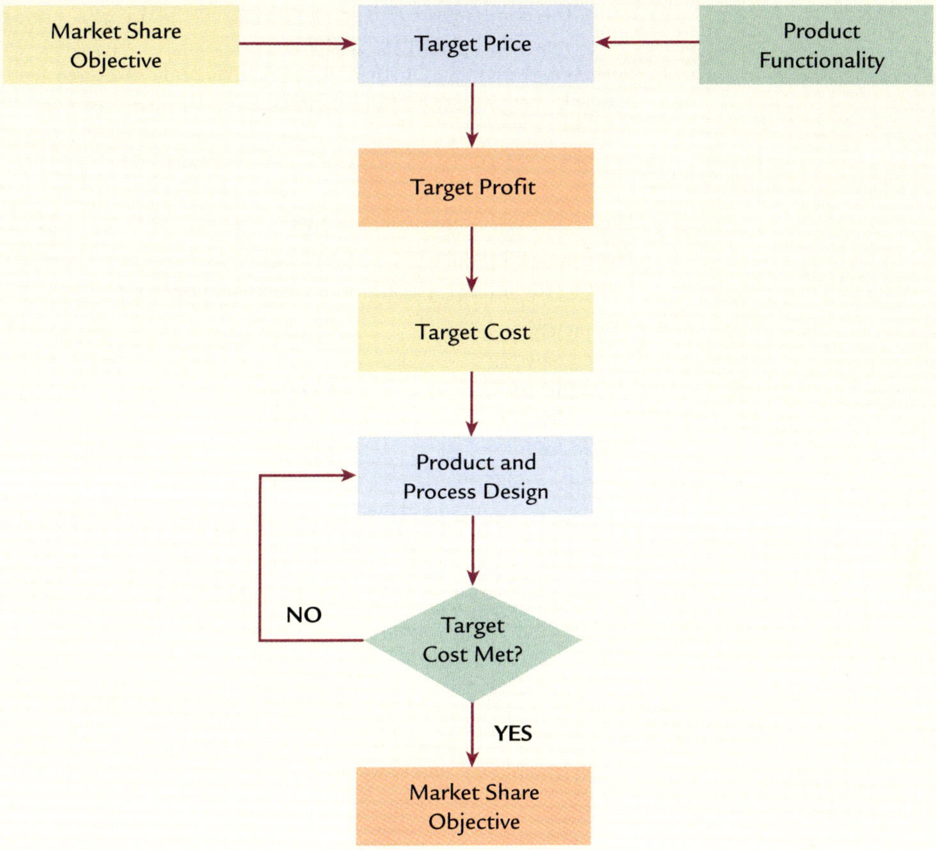

get price and target profit for the calculation requires some careful analysis by managers. The real value of target costing is that, once calculated, it becomes an incentive to find ways to reduce the expected cost. Target costs are a type of currently attainable standard. However, target costs are conceptually different from traditional standards because of the motivating force. Traditional currently attainable standards are motivated by the objective of moving toward an efficient operating level generated *internally* by industrial engineers and production managers. Target costs, on the other hand, are *externally* driven, generated by an analysis of markets and competitors.

Cornerstone 9-8

HOW TO Implement Target Costing

Information: A company is considering the production of a new trencher:

a.   Financial data:
    Target price: $250,000
    Target profit: $50,000
    Estimated cost given current product and process designs: $225,000

b.   Other:
    • A tear-down analysis of a competitor's trencher revealed a design improvement that
      promised to save $5,000 per unit (over current design).

- A marketing study of customer reactions to product functions revealed that the extra trenching speed in the current design was relatively unimportant. Changing the design to reflect a lower trenching speed saved $10,000.
- The design team was able to change the process design and reduce the test time by 50 percent. This saved $6,000 per unit.
- The company's supplier also proposed the use of a standardized component, reducing costs by another $7,000.

Required: Determine whether the company should produce the new trencher by calculating the target cost and assessing whether the expected cost is acceptable.

Calculation:

$$\text{Target cost} = \$250{,}000 - \$50{,}000$$
$$= \$200{,}000$$

The current expected cost ($225,000) exceeds the target cost by $25,000.

The proposed reductions from reverse engineering, value analysis, and process redesign promise the following additional cost reductions:

Reverse engineering	$ 5,000
Value analysis:	
Customers	10,000
Suppliers	7,000
Process redesign	6,000
Total savings	$28,000

Total cost reduction enables the expected cost to be reduced below the target cost so the new trencher should be produced.

Cornerstones for Chapter 9 Appendix

Cornerstone 9-7   How to apply kaizen costing, page 375
Cornerstone 9-8   How to implement target costing, page 377

APPENDIX KEY TERMS

Kaizen standard, 374   Target cost, 376

DISCUSSION QUESTIONS

1. Discuss the difference between budgets and standard costs.
2. Describe the relationship that unit standards have with flexible budgeting.
3. Why is historical experience often a poor basis for establishing standards?
4. What are ideal standards? Currently attainable standards? Of the two, which is usually adopted? Why?
5. Explain why standard costing systems are adopted.
6. How does standard costing improve the control function?
7. Discuss the differences among actual costing, normal costing, and standard costing.
8. What is the purpose of a standard cost sheet?

9. The budget variance for variable production costs is broken down into quantity and price variances. Explain why the quantity variance is more useful for control purposes than the price variance.
10. When should a standard cost variance be investigated?
11. What are control limits, and how are they set?
12. Explain why the materials price variance is often computed at the point of purchase rather than at the point of issuance.
13. The materials usage variance is always the responsibility of the production supervisor. Do you agree or disagree? Why?
14. The labor rate variance is never controllable. Do you agree or disagree? Why?
15. Suggest some possible causes of an unfavorable labor efficiency variance.
16. (Appendix 9B) What is a kaizen standard? Describe the kaizen and maintenance subcycles.
17. (Appendix 9B) What is target costing? Describe how costs are reduced so that the target cost can be met.

MULTIPLE-CHOICE EXERCISES

9-1 Historical experience should be used with caution in setting standards because

a. most companies have very poor records.
b. ideal standards are always better than historical standards.
c. they may not be achievable by operating personnel.
d. they may perpetuate operating inefficiencies.
e. none of the above.

9-2 Standards set by engineering studies

a. can determine the most efficient way of operating.
b. can provide very rigorous guidelines.
c. may not be achievable by operating personnel.
d. often do not allow operating personnel to have much input.
e. all of the above.

9-3 The standard cost per unit of output for a particular input is calculated using the equation

a. Actual input price per unit × Actual input used per unit.
b. Standard input price × Inputs allowed for the actual output.
c. Standard input price × Actual inputs.
d. Standard price per unit × Standard units produced.
e. Standard input price × Standard input allowed per unit of output produced.

9-4 A currently attainable standard is one that

a. relies on maximum efficiency.
b. uses only historical experience.
c. can be achieved under efficient operating conditions.
d. is based on ideal operating conditions.
e. none of the above.

9-5 An ideal standard is one that

a. relies on maximum efficiency.
b. uses only historical experience.
c. can be achieved under efficient operating conditions.
d. makes allowances for normal breakdowns, interruptions, less than perfect skill, and so on.
e. none of the above.

9-6 Reasons for adopting a standard cost system include

a. to enhance operational control.
b. to imitate most other firms.
c. to encourage purchasing managers to purchase cheap materials.
d. so that the weighted average method can be used for process manufacturers.
e. none of the above.

9-7 Standard costs are developed for

a. direct materials.
b. direct labor.
c. variable overhead.
d. fixed overhead.
e. all of the above.

9-8 The underlying details for the standard cost per unit are provided in

a. the balance sheet.
b. the standard production budget.
c. the standard cost sheet.
d. the standard work-in-process account.
e. none of the above.

9-9 The standard quantity of materials allowed is computed by the equation

a. Unit quantity standard $\times$ Standard output.
b. Unit quantity standard $\times$ Actual output.
c. Unit quantity standard $\times$ Practical output.
d. Unit quantity standard $\times$ Normal output.
e. none of the above.

9-10 The standard direct labor hours allowed is given by the equation

a. Unit labor standard $\times$ Normal output.
b. Unit labor standard $\times$ Practical output.
c. Unit labor standard $\times$ Standard output.
d. Unit labor standard $\times$ Actual output.
e. Unit labor standard $\times$ Theoretical output.

9-11 The total (budget) variance is given by the equation

a. $(AP \times AQ) - (SP \times SQ)$.
b. $(SP \times AQ) - (AP \times SQ)$.
c. $(SP \times AQ) - (SP \times SQ)$.
d. $(AP \times SP) - (AQ \times SQ)$.
e. none of the above.

9-12 Investigating variances from standard is

a. always done.
b. done if the variance is outside an acceptable range.
c. not done if the variance is expected to recur.
d. done if the variance is less than 10 percent of standard cost.
e. none of the above.

9-13 Responsibility for the materials price variance typically belongs to

a. production.
b. marketing.
c. purchasing.
d. personnel.
e. the CEO.

9-14 The materials price variance is usually computed

a. when materials are purchased.
b. when materials are issued to production.
c. when goods are finished.
d. after suppliers are paid.
e. none of the above.

9-15 Responsibility for the materials usage variance is usually assigned to

a. production.
b. marketing.
c. purchasing.
d. personnel.
e. the CEO.

9-16 Responsibility for the labor rate variance typically is assigned to

a. labor unions.
b. labor markets.
c. personnel.
d. production.
e. engineering.

9-17 Responsibility for the labor efficiency variance typically is assigned to

a. labor unions.
b. personnel.
c. production.
d. engineering.
e. outside trainers.

9-18 Which of the following items describes practices surrounding the recording of variances?

a. All inventories are typically carried at standard.
b. Unfavorable variances appear as debits.
c. Favorable variances appear as credits.
d. Immaterial variances are typically closed to Cost of Goods Sold.
e. All of the above.

9-19 (Appendix 9A) Which of the following is true concerning significantly large labor variances?

a. They are prorated among Work in Process, Finished Goods, and Cost of Goods Sold.
b. They are closed to Cost of Goods Sold.
c. They are prorated among Materials, Work in Process, Finished Goods, and Cost of Goods Sold.
d. They are reported on the balance sheet at the end of the year.
e. All of the above.

9-20 (Appendix 9B) Kaizen costing can also be described as

a. a form of target costing.
b. continuous improvement costing.
c. a variant of the maintenance subcycle.
d. superior to target costing.
e. none of the above.

9-21 (Appendix 9B) Which of the following is used to help bring expected costs in line with targeted costs?

a. Value analysis
b. Reverse engineering

c. Process improvements
d. All of the above
e. None of the above

EXERCISES

Exercise 9-1 *Standard Quantities of Labor and Materials*

Stillwater Designs rebuilds defective units of its S12L7 Kicker speaker model. During the year, Stillwater rebuilt 3,000 units. Materials and labor standards for performing the repairs are as follows:

Direct materials (1 recon kit @ $120.00)	$120.00
Direct materials (1 cabinet @ $30)	30.00
Direct labor (6 hrs. @ $12)	72.00

Required:

1. Compute the standard hours allowed for a volume of 3,000 rebuilt units.
2. Compute the standard number of kits and cabinets allowed for a volume of 3,000 rebuilt units.

Exercise 9-2 *Investigation of Variances*

Foresome Company uses the following rule to determine whether materials usage variances ought to be investigated: A materials usage variance will be investigated anytime the amount exceeds the lesser of $8,000 or 10 percent of the standard cost. Reports for the past five weeks provided the following information:

Week	MUV	Standard Materials Cost
1	$7,000 F	$80,000
2	7,800 U	75,000
3	6,000 F	80,000
4	9,000 U	85,000
5	7,000 U	69,000

Required:

1. Using the rule provided, identify the cases that will be investigated.
2. Suppose investigation reveals that the cause of an unfavorable materials usage variance is the use of lower-quality materials than are usually used. Who is responsible? What corrective action would likely be taken?
3. Suppose investigation reveals that the cause of a significant unfavorable materials usage variance is attributable to a new approach to manufacturing that takes less labor time but causes more material waste. Examination of the labor efficiency variance reveals that it is favorable and larger than the unfavorable materials usage variance. Who is responsible? What action should be taken?

Exercise 9-3 *Budget Variances, Materials and Labor*

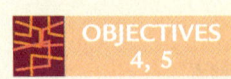

Cordero Corporation produces high-quality leather purses. The company uses a standard cost system and has set the following standards for materials and labor:

Leather (6 strips @ $8)	$48
Direct labor (1.5 hrs. @ $12)	18
Total prime cost	$66

During the year, Cordero produced 10,000 leather purses. Actual leather purchased was 61,000 strips at $7.96 per strip. There were no beginning or ending inventories of leather. Actual direct labor was 15,600 hours at $12.50 per hour.

Required:
1. Compute the costs of leather and direct labor that should have been incurred for the production of 10,000 leather purses.
2. Compute the total budget variances for materials and labor.

Exercise 9-4 *Materials Variances*

Refer to **Exercise 9-3.**

Required:
Break down the total variance for materials into a price variance and a usage variance.

Exercise 9-5 *Labor Variances*

Refer to **Exercise 9-3**.

Required:
Break down the total variance for labor into a rate variance and an efficiency variance.

Exercise 9-6 *Materials Variances*

Jugo Company produces fruit juices, sold in gallons. Recently, the company adopted the following material standard for one gallon of its cranberry juice:

Direct materials (128 oz. @ $0.03) = $3.84

During the first week of operation, the company experienced the following actual results:
a. Gallon units produced: 40,000.
b. Ounces of materials purchased and used: 5,200,000 ounces at $0.04.
c. No beginning or ending inventories of raw materials.

Required:
1. Compute the materials price variance.
2. Compute the materials usage variance

Exercise 9-7 *Labor Variances*

Green Enterprises produces small engines for lawn mowers. During the year, 110,000 engines were produced. The actual labor used was 60,000 hours @ $9.50 per hour. Green has the following labor standard: 0.5 hour @ $10.

Required:
1. Compute the labor rate variance.
2. Compute the labor efficiency variance.

Exercise 9-8 *Materials and Labor Variances*

At the beginning of the year, Lewis Company had the following standard cost sheet for one of its chemical products:

Direct materials (5 lbs. @ $3.20)	$16.00
Direct labor (2 hrs. @ $9.00)	18.00
Standard prime cost per unit	$34.00

The actual results for the year are as follows:

a. Units produced: 140,000.
b. Materials purchased: 744,000 pounds @ $3.30.
c. Materials used: 740,000 pounds.
d. Direct labor: 290,000 hours @ $9.05.

Required:

1. Compute price and usage variances for materials.
2. Compute the labor rate and labor efficiency variances.

Exercise 9-9 *Variances, Evaluation, and Behavior*

OBJECTIVE 1

Jackie Iverson was furious. She was about ready to fire Tom Rich, her purchasing agent. Just a month ago, she had given him a salary increase and a bonus for his performance. She had been especially pleased with his ability to meet or beat the price standards. But now she had found out that it was because of a huge purchase of raw materials. It would take months to use that inventory, and there was hardly space to store it. In the meantime, where could the other materials supplies that would be ordered and processed on a regular basis be put? Additionally, it was a lot of capital to tie up in inventory—money that could have been used to help finance the cash needs of the new product just coming on line.

Her interview with Tom had been frustrating. He was defensive, arguing that he thought that she wanted those standards met and that the means were not that important. He also pointed out that quantity purchases were the only way to meet the price standards. Otherwise, an unfavorable variance would have been realized.

Required:

1. Why did Tom Rich purchase the large quantity of raw materials? Do you think that this behavior was the objective of the price standard? If not, what is the objective(s)?
2. Suppose that Tom is right and that the only way to meet the price standards is through the use of quantity discounts. Also, assume that using quantity discounts is not a desirable practice for this company. What would you do to solve this dilemma?
3. Should Tom be fired? Explain.

Exercise 9-10 *Materials and Labor Variances*

OBJECTIVES 4, 5

Camisa Company produces single-colored t-shirts. Materials for the shirts are dyed in large vats. After dying the materials for a given color, the vats must be cleaned and prepared for the next batch of materials to be colored. The following standards for changeover for a given batch have been established:

Direct materials (2.5 lbs. @ $0.90)	$2.25
Direct labor (0.75 hr. @ $7.00)	5.25
Standard prime cost	$7.50

During the year, 53,000 pounds of material were purchased and used for the changeover activity. There were 20,000 batches produced, with the following actual prime costs:

Direct materials	$ 42,000
Direct labor	102,000 (for 14,900 hrs.)

Required:

Compute the materials and labor variances associated with the changeover activity, labeling each variance as favorable or unfavorable.

Exercise 9-11 *(Appendix 9A) Journal Entries*

OBJECTIVE 6

Refer to **Exercise 9-10**.

Required:
1. Prepare a journal entry for the purchase of raw materials.
2. Prepare a journal entry for the issuance of raw materials.
3. Prepare a journal entry for the addition of labor to Work in Process.
4. Prepare a journal entry for the closing of variances to Cost of Goods Sold.

Exercise 9-12 *(Appendix 9A) Materials Variances, Journal Entries*

OBJECTIVES 4, 6

Cornerstone 9-4

Esteban Products produces instructional aids. Among the company's products are white boards, which use colored markers instead of chalk. They are particularly popular for conference rooms in educational institutions and executive offices of large corporations. The standard cost of materials for this product is 12 pounds at $8.25 per pound.

During the first month of the year, 3,200 boards were produced. Information concerning actual costs and usage of materials follows:

Materials purchased	38,000 lbs @ $8.35
Materials used	37,500 lbs

Required:
1. Compute the materials price and usage variances.
2. Prepare journal entries for all activity relating to materials.

Exercise 9-13 *(Appendix 9A) Labor Variances, Journal Entries*

OBJECTIVES 5, 6

Cornerstone 9-6

Escribir Products, producer of white boards, has established a labor standard for its product—direct labor: 4 hrs @ $9.65. During January, Escribir produced 3,200 boards. The actual direct labor used was 12,520 hours at a total cost of $122,696.

Required:
1. Compute the labor rate and efficiency variances.
2. Prepare journal entries for all activities relating to labor.

Exercise 9-14 *(Appendix 9B) Kaizen Costing*

OBJECTIVE 7

Cornerstone 9-7

Nabors Motors Division had been charged to reduce the delivery time of its tractor motors from three days to one day. To help achieve this goal, engineering and production workers had made the commitment to reduce setup time. Current setup time was 12 hours. Setup cost was $50 per setup hour. For the first quarter, engineering developed a new process design that it believed would reduce the setup time from 12 to 8 hours. After implementing the design, the actual setup time dropped from 12 to 7 hours, one hour more than expected. In the second quarter, production workers suggested a new setup procedure. Engineering's evaluation of the suggestion was positive, and it projected that the new approach would save an additional hour of setup time. Setup labor was trained to perform new setup procedures. The actual reduction in setup time based on the suggested changes was 1.5 hours.

Required:
1. What kaizen setup standard would be used at the beginning of each quarter?
2. Describe the kaizen subcycle using the two quarters of data provided by Nabors.
3. Describe the maintenance subcycle using the two quarters of data provided by Nabors.
4. How much non-value-added cost was eliminated by the end of two quarters?
5. How does kaizen costing differ from standard costing?

Exercise 9-15 *(Appendix 9B) Target Costing*

Leishman Toys' product development department was in the process of developing a new video game player. The product life cycle is estimated at 27 months. Estimated sales over its life cycle are 500,000 units. For the current design, the development, production, and logistics costs for the life cycle are estimated at $60,000,000. The product specifications and the targeted market share call for a price of $150 per unit. The target profit per unit is $40. Postpurchase costs for the current design are estimated to be $12 per unit.

Required:
1. What is the target cost?
2. How much must costs be reduced per unit and in total for this target to be met? Describe three approaches available to reduce costs so that the target cost is met.

PROBLEMS

(*Note:* Whenever you see a   next to a requirement, it signals a "Building on a Cornerstone" requirement. Assigning this requirement will usually entail additional work, such as a group project, analytical reasoning, Internet research, decision making, and the use of written communication skills.)

Problem 9-1 *Setting Standards and Assigning Responsibility*

Cabanarama, Inc., designs and manufactures easy-to-set-up beach cabanas. The cabanas come in a kit including canvas, lacing, and aluminum support poles. Families can easily transport the cabanas to the beach, set them up, and have a protected place to change clothing, store picnic hampers, etc. Cabanarama has expanded rapidly from a essentially a two-person operation to one involving over a hundred employees. The founder and owner of Cabanarama, Frank Love, understands that a more formal approach to standard setting and control is needed to ensure that the consistent quality the company is known for continues to exist.

Frank and Annette Wilson, his financial vice president, divided the company into departments and designated each department as a cost center. Sales, Quality Control, and Design report directly to Frank. The Production, Shipping, Finance and Accounting departments report to Annette. In the Production Department, one of the supervisors was assigned the materials purchasing function; the job included purchasing all raw materials, overseeing inventory handling (receiving, storage, and so on), and tracking materials purchases and use.

Frank felt that control would be better achieved if there was a way for his employees to continue to perform in such a way that quality was maintained and cost reduction achieved. Annette suggested that Cabanarama institute a standard costing system. Variances for materials and labor could then be calculated and reported directly to her and she could alert Frank to any problems or opportunities for improvement.

Required:
1. a. When Annette designs the standard costing system for Cabanarama, who should be involved in setting the standards for each cost component?
   b. What factors should be considered in establishing the standards for each cost component?
2. Assume that Cabanarama develops the standards for materials use, materials price, labor use, and labor wages. Who will be assigned responsibility for each and for any resulting variances? Why?

Problem 9-2 *Basics of Variance Analysis, Variable Inputs*

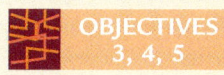

Guanamo Waste Disposal Company has a long-term contract with several large cities to collect garbage and trash from residential customers. To facilitate the collection, Guanamo places a large plastic container with each household. Because of wear and tear, growth, and other factors, Guanamo places about 200,000 new containers each year (about 20 percent of the total households). Several years ago, Guanamo decided to manufacture its own containers as a cost-saving measure. A strategically located plant involved in this type of manufacturing was acquired. To help ensure cost efficiency, a standard cost system was installed in the plant. The following standards have been established for the product's variable inputs:

	Standard Quantity	Standard Price (Rate)	Standard Cost
Direct materials	12 lbs.	$ 3.00	$36.00
Direct labor	1.60 hrs.	10.00	16.00
Variable overhead	1.60 hrs.	2.50	4.00
Total			$56.00

During the first week, the company had the following actual results:

Units produced	4,000
Actual labor costs	$70,000
Actual labor hours	6,600
Materials purchased and used	46,000 lbs. @ $3.05
Actual variable overhead costs	$26,500

The purchasing agent located a new source of slightly higher-quality plastic, and this material was used during the first week in January. Also, a new manufacturing process was implemented on a trial basis. The new process required a slightly higher level of skilled labor. The higher-quality material has no effect on labor utilization. However, the new manufacturing process was expected to reduce materials usage by 0.25 pound per can.

Required:

1. Compute the materials price and usage variances. Assume that the 0.25-pound per can reduction of materials occurred as expected and that the remaining effects are all attributable to the higher-quality material. Would you recommend that the purchasing agent continue to buy this quality? Or should the usual quality be purchased? Assume that the quality of the end product is not affected significantly.

2. Compute the labor rate and efficiency variances. Assuming that the labor variances are attributable to the new manufacturing process, should it be continued or discontinued? In answering, consider the new process's materials reduction effect as well. Explain.

3. Refer to Requirement 2. Suppose that the industrial engineer argued that the new process should not be evaluated after only one week. His reasoning was that it would take at least a week for the workers to become efficient with the new approach. Suppose that the production is the same the second week and that the actual labor hours were 6,000 and the labor cost was $62,000. Should the new process be adopted? Assume the variances are attributable to the new process. Assuming production of 4,000 units per week, what would be the projected annual savings? (Include the materials reduction effect.)

Problem 9-3 *Setting Standards, Materials and Labor Variances*

Tom Belford and Tony Sorrentino own a small business devoted to kitchen and bath granite installations. Recently, building contractors have insisted on up-front bid prices for a house rather than the cost plus system Tom and Tony had been used to.

They worry because natural flaws in the granite make it impossible to tell in advance exactly how much granite will be used on a particular job. In addition, granite can be easily broken, meaning that Tom or Tony could ruin a slab and need to start over with a new one. Sometimes the improperly cut pieces could be used for smaller installations, sometimes not. All their accounting is done by a local CPA firm headed by Charlene Davenport. Charlene listened to their concerns and suggested that it might be time to implement tighter controls by setting up a standard costing system.

Charlene reviewed the invoices pertaining to a number of Tom and Tony's previous jobs to determine the average amount of granite and glue needed per square foot. She then updated prices on both materials to reflect current conditions. The standards she developed for one square foot of counter installed were as follows:

Granite, per square foot	$50.00
Glue (10 oz. @ $0.15 per ounce)	1.50
Direct labor hours:	
Cutting labor (0.10 hr. @ $15)	1.50
Installation labor (0.25 hr. @ $25)	6.25

These standards assumed that one seamless counter requires one sink cut (the space into which the sink will fit) as well as cutting the counter to fit the space available.

Charlene tracked the actual costs incurred by Tom and Tony for granite installation for the next six months. She found that they completed 50 jobs with an average of 32 square feet of granite installed in each one. The following information on actual amounts used and cost was gathered:

Granite purchased and used (1,640 sq. ft.)	$79,048
Glue purchased and used (16,000 oz.)	$2,560
Actual hours cutting labor	180 hours
Actual hours installation labor	390 hours

The actual wage rate for cutting and installation labor remained unchanged from the standard rate.

Required:
1. Calculate the materials price variances and materials usage variances for granite and for glue for the past six months.
2. Calculate the labor rate variances and labor efficiency variances for cutting labor and for installation labor for the past six months.
3. Would it worthwhile for Charlene to establish standards for atypical jobs (e.g., those with more than one sink cut or wider than 24″)?

Problem 9-4 *Setting a Direct Labor Standard, Learning Curve Effects, Service Company*

Mantenga Company provides routine maintenance services for heavy moving and transportation vehicles. Although the vehicles vary, the maintenance services provided follow a fairly standard pattern. Recently, a potential new customer has approached the company and requested a new maintenance service for a radically different type of vehicle. New servicing equipment and some new labor skills will be needed to provide the maintenance service. The customer is placing an initial order to service 150 vehicles and has indicated that if the service is satisfactory, several additional orders of the same size will be placed every three months over the next three to five years.

Mantenga uses a standard costing system and wants to develop a set of standards for the new part. The usage standards for direct materials such as oil, lubricants, and transmission fluids were easily established. The usage standard is 25 quarts per servicing with a standard cost of $4.00 per quart. Management has also decided on standard rates for labor and overhead: the standard labor rate is $15 per direct labor hour, the standard variable overhead rate is $8 per direct labor hour, and the standard fixed overhead rate is $12 per hour. The only remaining decision is the standard for labor usage. To assist in developing this standard, the engineering department has estimated the following relationship between units serviced and average direct labor hours used:

Units Serviced	Cumulative Average Time per Unit
40	2.500 hrs.
80	2.000 hrs.
160	1.600 hrs.
320	1.280 hrs.
640	1.024 hrs.

As the workers learn more about servicing the new vehicles, they become more efficient, and the average time needed to service one unit declines. Engineering estimates that all of the learning effects will be achieved by the time 320 units are produced. No further improvement will be realized past this level.

Required:

1. Assume that the average labor time is 0.768 hour per unit, after the learning effects are achieved. Using this information, prepare a standard cost sheet that details the standard service cost per unit.
2. Given the per-unit labor standard set, would you expect a favorable or an unfavorable labor efficiency? Explain. Calculate the labor efficiency variance for servicing the first 320 units.
3. Assuming no further improvement in labor time per unit is possible past 320 units, explain why the cumulative average time per unit at 640 is lower than the time at 320 units. Show that the standard labor time should be 0.768 hour per unit. Explain why this value is a good choice for the per-unit labor standard.

Problem 9-5 *Unit Costs, Multiple Products, Variance Analysis, Service Setting*

OBJECTIVES
2, 4, 5

Spreadsheet

The maternity wing of the city hospital has two types of patients: normal and cesarean. The standard quantities of labor and materials per delivery for 2007 are:

	Normal	Cesarean
Direct materials (lbs.)	8	20
Nursing labor (hrs.)	2	4

The standard price paid per pound of direct materials is $10. The standard rate for labor is $16. Overhead is applied on the basis of direct labor hours. The variable overhead rate for maternity is $30 per hour, and fixed overhead rate is $40 per hour.

Actual operating data for 2007 are as follows:

a. Patient days produced: normal, 3,500; cesarean, 7,000.
b. Direct materials purchased and used: 172,000 pounds at $9.50—30,000 for normal maternity patients and 142,000 for the cesarean patients; no beginning or ending raw materials inventories.
c. Nursing labor: 36,500 hours—7,200 hours for normal patients and 29,300 hours for the cesarean; total cost of labor, $580,350.

Required:

1. Prepare a standard cost sheet showing the unit cost per patient day for each type of patient.
2. Compute the materials price and usage variances for each type of patient.
3. Compute the labor rate and efficiency variances.

(continued)

4. Assume that you know only the total direct materials used for both products and the total direct labor hours used for both products. Can you compute the total materials usage and labor efficiency variances? Explain.

5. Standard costing concepts have been applied in the health care industry. For example, diagnostic related groups (DRGs) are used for prospective payments for Medicare patients. Select a search engine (such as Yahoo! or Google) and conduct a search to see what information you can obtain about DRGs. You might try "Medicare DRGs" as a possible search topic. Write a memo that answers the following questions:
   a. What is a DRG?
   b. How are DRGs established?
   c. How many DRGs are used?
   d. How does the DRG concept relate to standard costing concepts discussed in the chapter? Can hospitals use DRGs to control their costs? Explain.

Problem 9-6 *Control Limits, Variance Investigation*

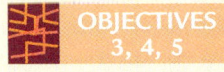

**OBJECTIVES
3, 4, 5**

Goodsmell Company produces a well-known cologne. The standard manufacturing cost of the cologne is described by the following standard cost sheet:

Direct materials:	
Liquids (4.2 oz. @ $0.25)	$1.05
Bottles (1 @ $0.05)	0.05
Direct labor (0.2 hr. @ $12.50)	2.50
Variable overhead (0.2 hr. @ $4.70)	0.94
Fixed overhead (0.2 hr. @ $1.00)	0.20
Standard cost per unit	$4.74

Management has decided to investigate only those variances that exceed the lesser of 10 percent of the standard cost for each category or $20,000.

During the past quarter, 250,000 four-ounce bottles of cologne were produced. Descriptions of actual activity for the quarter follow:

a. A total of 1.15 million ounces of liquids was purchased, mixed, and processed. Evaporation was higher than expected (no inventories of liquids are maintained). The price paid per ounce averaged $0.27.
b. Exactly 250,000 bottles were used. The price paid for each bottle was $0.048.
c. Direct labor hours totaled 48,250 with a total cost of $622,425.

Normal production volume for Goodsmell is 250,000 bottles per quarter. The standard overhead rates are computed using normal volume. All overhead costs are incurred uniformly throughout the year.

Required:

1. Calculate the upper and lower control limits for each manufacturing cost category.
2. Compute the total materials variance and then break it into price and usage variances. Would these variances be investigated?
3. Compute the total labor variance and break it into rate and efficiency variances. Would these variances be investigated?

Problem 9-7 *Control Limits, Variance Investigation*

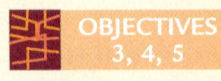

**OBJECTIVES
3, 4, 5**

The management of Golding Company has determined that the cost to investigate a variance produced by its standard cost system ranges from $2,000 to $3,000. If a problem is discovered, the average benefit from taking corrective action usually outweighs the cost of investigation. Past experience from the investigation of variances has revealed that corrective action is rarely needed for deviations within 8 percent of the standard cost. Golding produces a single product, which has the following standards for materials and labor:

Direct materials (8 lbs. @ $0.25) $2
Direct labor (0.4 hr. @ $7.50)   3

Actual production for the past three months with the associated actual usage and costs for materials and labor follow. There were no beginning or ending raw materials inventories.

	April	May	June
Production (units)	90,000	100,000	110,000
Direct materials:			
Cost	$189,000	$218,000	$230,000
Usage (lbs.)	723,000	870,000	885,000
Direct labor:			
Cost	$270,000	$323,000	$360,000
Usage (hrs.)	36,000	44,000	46,000

Required:

1. What upper and lower control limits would you use for materials variances? For labor variances?
2. Compute the materials and labor variances for April, May, and June. Identify those that would require investigation.
3. Let the horizontal axis be time and the vertical axis be variances measured as a percentage deviation from standard. Draw horizontal lines that identify upper and lower control limits. Plot the labor and material variances for April, May, and June. Prepare a separate graph for each type of variance. Explain how you would use these graphs (called control charts) to assist your analysis of variances.

Problem 9-8 *Standard Costing, Planned Variances*

OBJECTIVES
2, 4, 5

Ogundipe Company manufactures a plastic toy cell phone. The following standards have been established for the toy's materials and labor inputs:

	Standard Quantity	Standard Price (Rate)	Standard Cost
Direct materials	0.5 lb.	$ 1	$0.50
Direct labor	0.1 hr.	10	1.00

During the first week of July, the company had the following actual results:

Units produced	40,000
Actual labor costs	$42,000
Actual labor hours	4,100
Materials purchased and used	19,500 lbs @ $1.05 per pound

Other information: The purchasing agent located a new source of slightly higher-quality plastic, and this material was used during the first week in July. Also, a new manufacturing layout was implemented on a trial basis. The new layout required a slightly higher level of skilled labor. The higher-quality material has no effect on labor utilization. Similarly, the new manufacturing approach has no effect on material usage.

Required:

1. Compute the materials price and usage variances. Assuming that the materials variances are essentially attributable to the higher quality of materials, would you recommend that the purchasing agent continue to buy this quality? Or should the usual quality be purchased? Assume that the quality of the end product is not affected significantly.
2. Compute the labor rate and efficiency variances. Assuming that the labor variances are attributable to the new manufacturing layout, should it be continued or discontinued? Explain.

(continued)

3. Refer to Requirement 2. Suppose that the industrial engineer argued that the new layout should not be evaluated after only one week. His reasoning was that it would take at least a week for the workers to become efficient with the new approach. Suppose that the production is the same the second week and that the actual labor hours were 3,900 and the labor cost was $39,000. Should the new layout be adopted? Assume the variances are attributable to the new layout. If so, what would be the projected annual savings?

Problem 9-9 *Standard Costing*

OBJECTIVES
1, 4, 5

Whitecotton Company produces plastic bottles. The unit for costing purposes is a case of eighteen bottles. The following standards for producing one case of bottles have been established:

Direct materials (5 lbs @ $0.80)	$ 4
Direct labor (1.5 hours @ $16.00)	24
Standard prime cost	$28

During December, 52,000 pounds of material were purchased and used in production. There were 10,000 cases produced, with the following actual prime costs:

Direct materials	$ 40,000
Direct labor	236,910 (for 14,900 hours)

Required:
1. Compute the materials variances
2. Compute the labor variances.
3. What are the advantages and disadvantages that can result from the use of a standard costing system.

Problem 9-10 *Establishment of Standards, Variance Analysis*

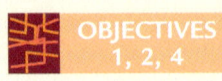
OBJECTIVES
1, 2, 4

Paul Golding and his wife, Nancy, established Crunchy Chips in 1938. (Nancy sold her piano to help raise capital to start the business.) Paul assumed responsibility for buying potatoes and selling chips to local grocers; Nancy assumed responsibility for production. Since Nancy was already known for her delicious thin potato chips, the business prospered.

Over the past 60 years, the company has established distribution channels in 11 western states, with production facilities in Utah, New Mexico, and Colorado. In 1980, Paul Golding died, and his son, Edward, took control of the business. By 2007, the company was facing stiff competition from national snack-food companies. Edward was advised that the company's plants needed to gain better control over production costs. To assist in achieving this objective, he hired a consultant to install a standard costing system. To help the consultant in establishing the necessary standards, Edward sent her the following memo:

To: Diana Craig, CMA
From: Edward Golding, President, Crunchy Chips
Subject: Description and Data Relating to the Production of Our Plain Potato Chips
Date: September 28, 2007

The manufacturing process for potato chips begins when the potatoes are placed into a large vat in which they are automatically washed. After washing, the potatoes flow directly to an automatic peeler. The peeled potatoes then pass by inspectors who manually cut out deep eyes or other blemishes. After inspection, the potatoes are automatically sliced and dropped into the cooking oil. The frying process is closely monitored by an employee. After they are cooked, the chips pass under a salting device and then pass by more inspectors, who sort out the unacceptable finished chips (those that are discolored or too small). The chips then continue on the conveyor belt to a bagging machine that bags them in 1-pound bags. After bagging, the bags are placed in a box and shipped. The box holds 15 bags.

The raw potato pieces (eyes and blemishes), peelings, and rejected finished chips are sold to animal feed producers for $0.16 per pound. The company uses this revenue to reduce the cost of potatoes; we would like this reflected in the price standard relating to potatoes.

Crunchy Chips purchases high-quality potatoes at a cost of $0.245 per pound. Each potato averages 4.25 ounces. Under efficient operating conditions, it takes four potatoes to produce one 16-ounce bag of plain chips. Although we label bags as containing 16 ounces, we actually place 16.3 ounces in each bag. We plan to continue this policy to ensure customer satisfaction. In addition to potatoes, other raw materials are the cooking oil, salt, bags, and boxes. Cooking oil costs $0.04 per ounce, and we use 3.3 ounces of oil per bag of chips. The cost of salt is so small that we add it to overhead. Bags cost $0.11 each and boxes $0.52.

Our plant produces 8.8 million bags of chips per year. A recent engineering study revealed that we would need the following direct labor hours to produce this quantity if our plant operates at peak efficiency:

Raw potato inspection	3,200
Finished chip inspection	12,000
Frying monitor	6,300
Boxing	16,600
Machine operators	6,300

I'm not sure that we can achieve the level of efficiency advocated by the study. In my opinion, the plant is operating efficiently for the level of output indicated if the hours allowed are about 10 percent higher.

The hourly labor rates agreed upon with the union are:

Raw potato inspectors	$15.20
Finished chip inspectors	10.30
Frying monitor	14.00
Boxing	11.00
Machine operators	13.00

Overhead is applied on the basis of direct labor dollars. We have found that variable overhead averages about 116 percent of our direct labor cost. Our fixed overhead is budgeted at $1,135,216 for the coming year.

Required:

1. Discuss the benefits of a standard costing system for Crunchy Chips.
2. Discuss the president's concern about using the result of the engineering study to set the labor standards. What standard would you recommend?
3. Form a group of three or four. Develop a standard cost sheet for Crunchy Chips' plain potato chips.
4. Suppose that the level of production was 8.8 million bags of potato chips for the year as planned. If 9.5 million pounds of potatoes were used, compute the materials usage variance for potatoes.

Problem 9-11 *Standard Costing, Ethical Behavior, Usefulness of Standard Costing*

Pat James, the purchasing agent for a local plant of the Oakden Electronics Division, was considering the possible purchase of a component from a new supplier. The component's purchase price, $0.90, compared favorably with the standard price of $1.10. Given the quantity that would be purchased, Pat knew that the favorable price variance would help offset an unfavorable variance for another component. By offsetting the unfavorable variance, his overall performance report would be impressive and good enough to help him qualify for the annual bonus. More importantly, a good performance rating this year would help him secure a position at division headquarters at a significant salary increase.

Purchase of the part, however, presented Pat with a dilemma. Consistent with his past behavior, Pat made inquiries regarding the reliability of the new supplier and the part's quality. Reports were basically negative. The supplier had a reputation for making the first two or three deliveries on schedule, but being unreliable from then on. Worse, the part itself was of questionable quality. The number of defective units was only slightly higher than that for other suppliers, but the life of the component was 25 percent less than what normal sources provided.

If the part were purchased, no problems with deliveries would surface for several months. The problem of shorter life would cause eventual customer dissatisfaction and perhaps some loss of sales, but the part would last at least 18 months after the final product began to be used. If all went well, Pat expected to be at headquarters within six months. He saw very little personal risk associated with a decision to purchase the part from the new supplier. By the time any problems surfaced, they would belong to his successor. With this rationalization, Pat decided to purchase the component from the new supplier.

Required:

1. Do you agree with Pat's decision? Why or why not? How important do you think Pat's assessment of his personal risk was in the decision? Should it be a factor?

2. Do you think that the use of standards and the practice of holding individuals accountable for their achievement played major roles in Pat's decision?

3. Review the discussion on corporate ethical standards in Chapter 1. Identify the standards that might apply to Pat's situation.

   Should every company adopt a set of ethical standards that apply to its employees, regardless of their specialty?

4. The usefulness of standard costing has been challenged in recent years. Some claim that its use is an impediment to the objective of continuous improvement (an objective that many feel is vital in today's competitive environment). Write a short paper (individually or in a small group of three or four) that analyzes the role and value of standard costing in today's manufacturing environment. Address the following questions:
   a. What are the major criticisms of standard costing?
   b. Will standard costing disappear, or is there still a role for it in the new manufacturing environment? If so, what is the role?
   c. Given the criticisms, can you explain why its use continues to be so prevalent? Will this use eventually change?

   In preparing your paper, the following references may be useful; however, do not restrict your literature search to these references. They are simply to help you get started.

   a. Robin Cooper and Robert S. Kaplan, "Activity-Based Systems: Measuring the Costs of Resource Usage," *Accounting Horizons* (September 1992): 1–13.
   b. Forrest B. Green and Felix E. Amenkhienan, "Accounting Innovations: A Cross-Sectional Survey of Manufacturing Firms," *Journal of Cost Management* (Spring 1992): 59–64.
   c. Bruce R. Gaumnitz and Felix P. Kollaritsch, "Manufacturing Variances: Current Practice and Trends," *Journal of Cost Management* (Spring 1991): 59–64.
   d. Chris Guilding, Dane Lamminmaki, and Colin Drury, "Budgeting and Standard Costing Practices in New Zealand and the United Kingdom," *Journal of International Accounting*, Vol. 33, No. 5 (1998): 569–588.

Problem 9-12 *(Appendix 9A) Variance Analysis, Revision of Standards, Journal Entries*

OBJECTIVES 4, 5, 6

The Lubbock plant of Morril's Small Motor Division produces a major subassembly for a 6.0 horsepower motor for lawn mowers. The plant uses a standard costing system for production costing and control. The standard cost sheet for the subassembly follows:

Direct materials (6.0 lbs. @ $5.00)	$30.00
Direct labor (1.6 hrs. @ $12.00)	19.20

During the year, the Lubbock plant had the following actual production activity:

a. Production of motors totaled 50,000 units.
b. A total of 260,000 pounds of raw materials was purchased at $4.70 per pound.
c. There were 60,000 pounds of raw materials in beginning inventory (carried at $5 per pound). There was no ending inventory.
d. The company used 82,000 direct labor hours at a total cost of $1,066,000.

The Lubbock plant's practical activity is 60,000 units per year. Standard overhead rates are computed based on practical activity measured in standard direct labor hours.

Required:

1. Complete the materials price and usage variances. Of the two materials variances, which is viewed as the most controllable? To whom would you assign responsibility for the usage variance in this case? Explain.
2. Compute the labor rate and efficiency variances. Who is usually responsible for the labor efficiency variance? What are some possible causes for this variance?
3. Assume that the purchasing agent for the small motors plant purchased a lower-quality raw material from a new supplier. Would you recommend that the plant continue to use this cheaper raw material? If so, what standards would likely need revision to reflect this decision? Assume that the end product's quality is not significantly affected.
4. Prepare all possible journal entries.

Problem 9-13 *(Appendix 9B) Kaizen Standards, Process Improvement, Non-Value-Added Costs*

OBJECTIVE 7

Ryan Hepworth, an outside consultant working for Briggs Company (a producer of a variety of plastic products), has been supervising the implementation of an activity-based cost management system. One of Ryan's objectives is to improve process efficiency by improving the activities that define the processes. To illustrate the potential of the new system to the president, Ryan has decided to focus on two processes: production and customer service.

Within each process, one activity will be selected for improvement: materials usage for production and redesigning products for customer service. Waste-free standards are identified for each activity. For materials usage, the waste-free standard calls for six pounds per unit of output (although the plastic products differ in shape and function, their size—as measured by weight—is uniform). The waste-free materials standard is based on the elimination of all waste due to defective molds. The standard price of materials is $8 per pound. For redesigning products, the waste-free standard is 60 percent of current practical activity capacity. This standard is based on the fact that about 40 percent of the customer complaints have to do with design features that could have been avoided or anticipated by the company.

Current practical capacity (at the end of 2006) is defined by 24 engineers, where each engineer provides 2,000 hours of service per year. Each engineer is paid a salary of $60,000. There are no other significant costs for the engineering activity.

Actual materials usage for 2006 was 30 percent above the level called for by the waste-free standard; engineering usage was 50,000 hours. There were 80,000 units of output produced. Ryan and the operational managers have selected some improvement measures that promise to reduce non-value-added activity usage by 40 percent in 2007. Selected actual results achieved for 2007 are as follows:

Units produced	80,000
Materials used	580,000
Engineering hours	34,000

The actual prices paid for materials and engineering hours are identical to the standard or budgeted prices.

Required:

1. For 2006, calculate the non-value-added usage and costs for materials usage and redesigning products.
2. Using the targeted reduction, establish kaizen standards for materials and engineering (for 2007).
3. Using the kaizen standards prepared in Requirement 2, compute the 2007 usage variances, expressed in both physical and financial measures, for materials and engineering (for engineering, compare actual resource usage with the kaizen standard). Comment on the company's ability to achieve its targeted reductions. In particular, discuss what measures the company must take to capture any realized reductions in resource usage.

Problem 9-14 *(Appendix 9B) Target Costing*

Marvel Products has two plants that manufacture a line of high quality wheelchairs. One is located in Pocatello and the other in Boise. Each plant is set up as a profit center. During the past year, both plants sold the regular model for $900. Sales volume averages 20,000 units per year in each plant. Recently, the Boise plant reduced the price of the regular model to $800. Discussion with the Boise manager revealed that the price reduction was possible because the plant had reduced its manufacturing and selling costs by decreasing "non-value-added costs." The Boise plant manufacturing and selling costs for the regular chair were $700 per unit. The Boise manager offered to loan the Pocatello plant his cost accounting manager to help it achieve similar results. The Pocatello plant manager readily agreed, knowing that his plant must keep pace—not only with the Boise plant but also with competitors. A local competitor had also reduced its price on a similar model, and Pocatello's marketing manager had indicated that the price must be matched or sales would drop dramatically. In fact, the marketing manager suggested that if the price were dropped to $780 by the end of the year, the plant could expand its share of the market by 20 percent. The plant manager agreed but insisted that the current profit per unit must be maintained, and he wants to know if the plant can at least match the $700-per-unit cost of the Boise plant. He also wants to know if the plant can achieve the cost reduction using the approach of the Boise plant.

    The plant controller and the Boise cost accounting manager have assembled the following data for the most recent year. The actual cost of inputs, their value-added (ideal) quantity levels, and the actual quantity levels are provided (for production of 20,000 units). Assume there is no difference between actual prices of activity units and standard prices.

	SQ	AQ	Actual Cost
Materials (lb.)	475,000	500,000	$10,500,000
Labor (hr.)	114,000	120,000	1,500,000
Setups (hr.)	—	8,000	600,000
Material handling (moves)	—	20,000	1,400,000
Warranties (no. repaired)	—	20,000	2,000,000
Total			$16,000,000

Required:

1. Calculate the target cost for expanding the Pocatello market share by 20 percent, assuming that the per-unit profitability is maintained as requested by the plant manager.
2. Calculate the non-value-added cost per unit. Assuming that non-value-added costs can be reduced to zero, can the Lincoln plant match the Boise plant's per-unit cost? Can the target cost for expanding market share be achieved? What actions would you take if you were the plant manager?

FLEXIBLE BUDGETS AND OVERHEAD ANALYSIS

© LARRY DALE GORDON/THE IMAGE BANK/GETTY IMAGES

After studying Chapter 10, you should be able to:

1. Prepare a flexible budget and use it for performance reporting.
2. Calculate the variable overhead variances and explain their meaning.
3. Calculate the fixed overhead variances and explain their meaning.
4. Prepare an activity-based flexible budget.

Bill Hardy, manager of a large hotel, was facing that time of the year when he had to forecast what the coming year was going to look like financially. Bill was worried about several matters. First, he had to figure out how to maintain net operating income with lower average daily rates and lower occupancy rates. Second, he really needed to know the costs at various levels of occupancy. This issue became very clear when Beta Alpha Phi, a local university accounting honor society, had hosted a national meeting and asked for a room and meal package quote. The quote was accepted, and the hotel hosted a large group of out-of-state students. The quote produced the expected extra revenues but also caused increases in costs greater than expected (especially utility and housekeeping costs). Third, operating results needed to be analyzed to assess how well the hotel had done for the entire year. Unfortunately, Bill was having difficulty doing so because the projected occupancy for the year was so often different from the actual occupancy. The Beta Alpha Phi group was but one example that contributed to an increase in occupancy beyond the levels projected at the beginning of the year. Fourth, he was convinced that to maintain income, costs must be reduced. Knowing how to allocate the hotel's scarce resources was something that he had to resolve. Bill had expressed these concerns to his controller, Rick Linsenmeyer. Rick sent him the following memo in response.

MEMO

To: William Hardy, Hotel Manager
From: Rick Linsenmeyer, Controller
Date: October 1, 2007
Subject: Profit Planning Issues

To maintain our current net operating income, we need to have a good system in place that can focus your attention on what needs to be done to drive performance throughout the year. We also need to be able to assess performance more accurately during the year.

I have three key recommendations. First, we need to implement flexible or variable budgeting. This approach allows us to assess what costs should be for various levels of occupancy, given our underlying cost structure. This before-the-fact planning capability is critical for the environment that we currently have. It makes it much easier to do the what-if scenarios to manage performance. Flexible budgeting will also allow us to more accurately assess performance after the fact because it allows us to calculate what the costs should have been for the actual level of activity. Second, with improved benchmarks, we are able to do a detailed variance analysis. We particularly need to evaluate our overhead costs because they are such a large percentage of total operating costs. Third, we should consider using activity-based budgeting (ABB). Activity-based budgeting is a good approach for assessing where costs can be reduced. It sheds light on alternative uses of resources—an important benefit in an era of scarce resources. It will also help us understand capacity and capacity utilization.

I would like to schedule a meeting with you soon so that we can discuss the possibility of implementing these procedures for the coming year. I am confident that they will prove to be valuable tools for addressing the concerns that you have expressed.

USING BUDGETS FOR PERFORMANCE EVALUATION

Budgets are useful for both planning and control. Budgets are often used as benchmarks for performance evaluation. Determining how budgeted amounts should be compared with actual results is a major consideration that must be addressed.

OBJECTIVE 1

Prepare a flexible budget and use it for performance reporting.

Static Budgets versus Flexible Budgets

In Chapter 8, we learned how companies prepare a master budget based on their best estimate of the level of sales and production activity for the coming period (the best estimate is the budgeted level for the period). We also discussed some behavioral issues associated with performance reporting. However, no detailed discussion was provided on how to prepare budgetary *performance reports*. A **performance report** compares actual costs with budgeted costs. Two possibilities exist for making this comparison: (1) comparison of actual costs with the budgeted costs for the budgeted level of activity and (2) comparison of actual costs with the actual level of activity. The first choice is a report based on *static budgets*, whereas the second choice is for a report based on *flexible budgets*. The two approaches for variance calculation are illustrated in Exhibit 10-1.

Static Budgets and Performance Reports

A **static budget** is a budget for a particular level of activity. Master budgets are generally created for a particular level of activity. Thus, one way to prepare a performance report is to compare the actual costs with the budgeted costs from the master budget. To illustrate, the production of Texas Rex t-shirts will again be considered. Corner-

10-1

EXHIBIT

Static and Flexible Budget Variances

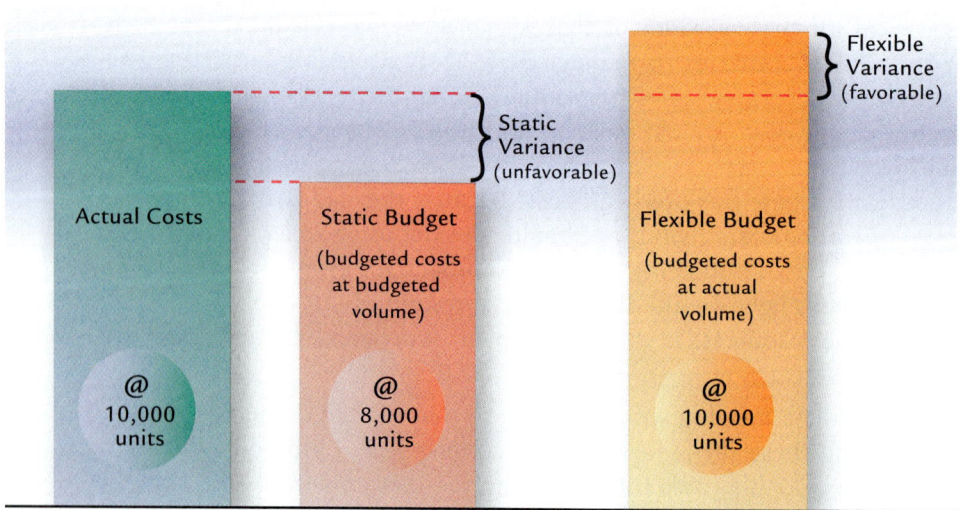

stone 10-1 shows how to prepare a performance report based on a static budget for the Texas Rex clothing manufacturing plant for its first quarter of operations. For simplicity, the report only considers production costs.

Cornerstone 10-1

HOW TO Prepare a Performance Report Based on a Static Budget (Using Budgeted Production)

Information:

Relationships from the Master Budget	Actual Data for Quarter 1
Budgeted production for Quarter 1: 1,060	Production: 1,200 units
Materials:	
1 plain t-shirt @ $3.00	Materials cost: $4,380
5 ounces of ink @ $0.20	
Labor:	
0.12 hr. @ $10.00	Labor cost: $1,500
Variable overhead:	
Maintenance:	
0.12 hr. @ $3.75	Maintenance cost: $535
Power:	
0.12 hr. @ $1.25	Power cost: $170
Fixed overhead:	
Grounds keeping: $1,200 per quarter	Grounds keeping: $1,050
Depreciation: $600 per quarter	Depreciation: $600

Required: Prepare a performance report using a budget based on expected production.
Calculation:

	Actual	Budgeted	Variance
Units produced	1,200	1,060	140 F[a]
Direct materials cost	$4,830	$4,240[b]	$590 U[c]
Direct labor cost	1,500	1,272[d]	228 U
Variable overhead:			
Maintenance	535	477[e]	58 U
Power	170	159[f]	11 U
Fixed overhead:			
Grounds keeping	1,050	1,200	(150) F
Depreciation	600	600	0
Total	$8,685	$7,948	$737 U

[a]F means the variance is favorable.
[b][(1,060 × $3) + (1,060 × 5 × $0.20)].
[c]U means the variance is unfavorable.
[d]0.12 × 1,060 × $10.00.
[e]0.12 × 1,060 × $3.75.
[f]0.12 × 1,060 × $1.25.

According to the report, there were unfavorable variances for direct materials, direct labor, maintenance, and power. However, there is something fundamentally wrong with the report. Actual costs for production of 1,200 t-shirts are being compared with planned costs for production of 1,060. Because direct materials, direct labor, and variable overhead are variable costs, they should be greater at a higher level of production. Thus, even if cost control were perfect for the production of 1,200 units, unfavorable variances would be produced for at least some of the variable costs. To create a meaningful performance report, actual costs and expected costs must be compared at the *same* level of activity. Since actual output often differs from planned output, a method is needed to compute what the costs should have been for the actual output level.

Flexible Budgets

The budget that enables a firm to compute expected costs for a range of activity levels is called a **flexible budget**. The key to flexible budgeting is knowledge of fixed and variable costs. The two types of flexible budgets are:

1. *Before-the-fact.* This type of flexible budget helps managers deal with uncertainty by allowing them to see the expected outcomes for a range of activity levels. It can be used to generate financial results for a number of plausible scenarios.
2. *After-the-fact.* This flexible budget is the budget for the actual level of activity. This type of budget is used to compute what costs should have been for the actual level of activity. Those expected costs are then compared with the actual costs in order to assess performance.

Flexible budgeting is the key to providing the frequent feedback that managers need to exercise control and effectively carry out the plans of an organization.

Concept Q & A

Why are static budgets usually not a good choice for benchmarks in preparing a performance report?

Answer:
The actual output may differ from the budgeted output, thus causing significant differences in cost. Comparing planned costs for one level of activity with the actual costs of a different level of activity does not provide good control information.

Stillwater Designs has a Product Steering Committee whose charge is to decide on the timing for upgrades and redesigns for its various Kicker speaker models. About every four years, a complete redesign is done for a Kicker speaker. A complete redesign takes about 16 to 18 months. A specification workshop is held that identifies features, benefits, customers, and competitors. Additionally, the costs of the new model, including the design costs (research and development), acquisition costs, freight, and duties, are estimated for various sales volumes. During this phase, the company will work closely with the manufacturers to control the design so that manufacturing costs are carefully set. A financial analysis is run over the expected life cycle of the new product (two to three years) to see what the profit potential is. Thus, both expected revenues and costs for various levels of activity are assessed. This before-the-fact flexible budgeting analysis is especially done for those products with which the company has less experience. At times, a new product may be produced even if at the most likely volume, the product is not expected to be profitable. The reason? The new product may complete a line or may enhance the overall image of the Kicker speakers.

HERE'S THE REAL KICKER

To illustrate the before-the-fact capability of flexible budgeting, suppose that the management of Texas Rex wants to know the cost of producing 1,000 t-shirts, 1,200 t-shirts, and 1,400 t-shirts. To compute the expected cost for these different levels of output, the cost behavior pattern of each item in the budget needs to be known. Knowing the variable cost per unit and the total fixed costs allows the calculation of the expected costs for various levels of activity. Cornerstone 10-2 shows how budgets can be prepared for different levels of activity, using cost formulas for each item.

Notice in Cornerstone 10-2 that total budgeted production costs increase as the production level increases. Budgeted costs change because total variable costs go up as output increases. Because of this, flexible budgets are sometimes referred to as **variable budgets**. Since Texas Rex has a mix of variable and fixed costs, the overall cost of producing one t-shirt goes *down* as production goes *up*. This makes sense. As production increases, there are more units over which to spread the fixed production costs.

It should also be pointed out that the flexible budget formulas often are based on direct labor hours instead of units. This is easy to do because direct labor hours are correlated with units produced. For example, the variable cost formulas for variable overhead are $3.75 and $1.25 per direct labor hour ($5.00 per direct labor hour in total) for maintenance and power, respectively. However, two choices are available for hours: standard hours allowed for the units produced and actual hours used for the units produced. The output levels for hours allowed would be 120 (0.12 × 1,000), 144 (0.12 × 1,200), and 168 (0.12 × 1,400).

Cornerstone 10-2

HOW TO Prepare a Flexible Production Budget

Information:

Levels of output: 1,000, 1,200, and 1,400.
Materials:
   1 plain t-shirt @ $3.00
   5 ounces of ink @ $0.20
Labor:
   0.12 hr. @ $10.00
Variable overhead:
   Maintenance:
      0.12 hr. @ $3.75
   Power:
      0.12 hr. @ $1.25
Fixed overhead:
   Grounds keeping: $1,200 per quarter
   Depreciation: $600 per quarter

Required: Prepare a budget for three levels of output: 1,000, 1,200, and 1,400 units.
Calculation:

Production Costs	Variable Cost per Unit	Range of Production (units) 1,000	1,200	1,400
Variable:				
Direct materials	$4.00[a]	$4,000	$4,800	$5,600
Direct labor	1.20[b]	1,200	1,440	1,680
Variable overhead:				
Maintenance	0.45[c]	450	540	630
Power	0.15[d]	150	180	210
Total variable costs	$5.80	$5,800	$6,960	$8,120
Fixed overhead:				
Grounds keeping		$1,200	$1,200	$1,200
Depreciation		600	600	600
Total fixed costs		$1,800	$1,800	$1,800
Total production costs		$7,600	$8,760	$9,920

[a][($3.00 × 1) + ($0.20 × 5)].
[b]($10.00 × 0.12).
[c]($3.75 × 0.12).
[d]($1.25 × 0.12).

Analytical Q & A

What is the budgeted cost of maintenance if 2,000 t-shirts are produced?

Answer:
$0.45 × 2,000 = $900.

Flexible budgets are powerful control tools because they allow management to compute what the costs should be for the level of output that actually occurred. Cornerstone 10-2 also reveals what the costs should have been for the actual level of activity (1,200 units). It is now possible to provide management with a useful performance report, one that compares actual and budgeted costs for the actual level of activity. This is the second type of flexible budget and preparation of this report is shown by Cornerstone 10-3. The revised performance report in Cornerstone 10-3 paints a much different picture from the one in Cornerstone 10-1. All of the variances are fairly small. Had they been larger, management would have searched for the cause and tried to correct the problems.

Cornerstone 10-3

HOW TO Prepare a Performance Report using a Flexible Budget

Information: Budgeted costs for the actual level of activity (Cornerstone 10-2); actual costs (Cornerstone 10-1).
Required: Prepare a performance report using budgeted costs for the actual level of activity.
Calculation:

	Actual	Budget	Variance
Units produced	1,200	1,200	—
Production costs:			
Direct materials	$4,830	$4,800	$ 30 U
Direct labor	1,500	1,440	60 U
Variable overhead:			
Maintenance	535	540	(5) F
Power	170	180	(10) F
Total variable costs	$7,035	$6,960	$ 75 U
Fixed overhead:			
Grounds keeping	$1,050	$1,200	$ (150) F
Depreciation	600	600	(0)
Total fixed costs	$1,650	$1,800	$ (150) F
Total production costs	$8,685	$8,760	$ (75) F

A difference between the actual amount and the flexible budget amount is the **flexible budget variance**. The flexible budget provides a measure of the efficiency of a manager. In other words, given the level of production achieved, how well did the manager control costs? To measure whether or not a manager accomplishes his or her goals, the static budget is used. The static budget represents certain goals that the firm wants to achieve. A manager is effective if the goals described by the static budget are achieved or exceeded. In the Texas Rex example, production volume was 140 units greater than the original budgeted amount; the manager exceeded the original budgeted goal. Therefore, the effectiveness of the manager is not in question.

APPLICATIONS IN BUSINESS

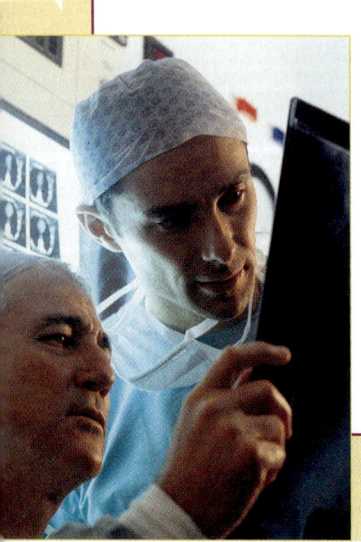

In formulating the budget for the coming year, LRL Radiology Clinic used the prior year's actual work load with its volume and mix of patients served, adjusted for changes in forecasted demand. This process produced a budget of 60,000 imaging procedures for the year (5,000 per month). At the end of the year, the budgeted costs for this level of patient load were compared with the actual costs incurred on a month-by-month basis. Significant variances were analyzed to determine the causes. For example, in the month of August, large unfavorable variances were reported for x-ray technicians and x-ray film. Investigation revealed that the cause of the variances was attributable mostly to a significant increase in the volume of imaging procedures (the increase in volume resulted from the closure of a competitor's clinic). Thus, unfavorable variances occurred because budgeted costs were compared for a static volume with the actual costs of a larger than expected actual output! This example emphasizes the importance of using flexible budgeting to better monitor and understand the consumption of resources.

Source: C. L. Bautista, "Meeting the Challenge of Cost Containment: A Case Study Using Variance Analysis," *Journal of Health Care Finance* (Fall 1994): 13–24.

VARIABLE OVERHEAD ANALYSIS

OBJECTIVE 2

Calculate the variable overhead variances and explain their meaning.

In Chapter 9, total variances for direct materials and direct labor were broken down into price and efficiency variances. In a standard cost system, the total overhead variance, the difference between applied and actual overhead, is also broken down into component variances. How many component variances are computed depends on the method of variance analysis used. One method only is described in this chapter. First, overhead is divided into fixed and variable categories. Next, component variances are calculated for each category. The total variable overhead variance is divided into two components: the variable overhead spending variance and the variable overhead efficiency variance. Similarly, the total fixed overhead variance is divided into two components: the fixed overhead spending variance and the fixed overhead volume variance.

Total Variable Overhead Variance

To illustrate the variable overhead variances, the first quarter data for Texas Rex will be used again. The unit prices and quantities used for the flexible budget are assumed to be the standards associated with Texas Rex's standard cost system. Cornerstone 10-4 illustrates how to calculate the total variable overhead variance. The total variable overhead variance is simply the difference between the total actual variable overhead and applied variable overhead. Variable overhead is applied using hours allowed in a standard cost system. The total variable overhead variance can be divided into spending and efficiency variances. Variable overhead spending and efficiency variances can be calculated using either the 3-pronged (columnar) approach or formulas. The best approach to use seems to be a matter of taste. However, the formulas first need to be expressed specifically for variable overhead.

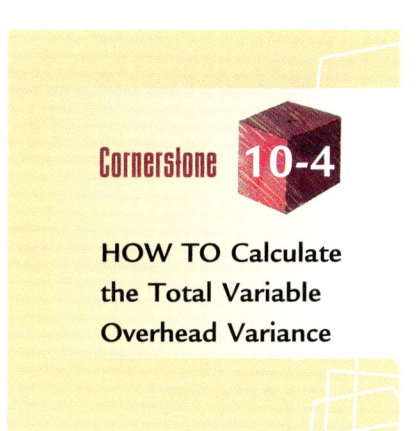

Cornerstone 10-4

HOW TO Calculate the Total Variable Overhead Variance

Information:

Standard variable overhead rate (*SVOR*)	\$5.00 per direct labor hour
Actual variable overhead costs	150 hours (*AH*) @\$4.70 (*AVOR*)
Standard hours allowed per unit	0.12 hour
Actual production	1,200 units

Required: Calculate the total variable overhead variance.

Calculation:

Actual Costs	Applied Costs*	Total Variance
$AH \times AVOR$	$SH \times SVOR$	$(AH \times AVOR) - (SH \times SVOR)$
\$705	\$720	\$(15)

*$SH \times SVOR = 0.12 \times 1{,}200 \times \$5.$

Variable Overhead Spending Variance

The **variable overhead spending variance** measures the aggregate effect of differences between the actual variable overhead rate (*AVOR*) and the standard variable overhead rate (*SVOR*). The actual variable overhead rate is simply actual variable overhead divided by actual hours. For our example, this rate is \$4.70 per hour (\$705/150 hours). The formula for computing the variable overhead spending variance is:

$$\text{Variable overhead spending variance} = (AVOR \times AH) - (SVOR \times AH)$$
$$= (AVOR - SVOR)AH$$

Variable Overhead Efficiency Variance

Variable overhead is assumed to vary as the production volume changes. Thus, variable overhead changes in proportion to changes in the direct labor hours used. The **variable**

overhead efficiency variance measures the change in variable overhead consumption that occurs because of efficient (or inefficient) use of direct labor. The efficiency variance is computed using the following formula:

$$\text{Variable overhead efficiency variance} = (AH - SH)SVOR$$

How to calculate the variable overhead variances using either a columnar or formula approach is shown for the Texas Rex example in Cornerstone 10-5.

Cornerstone 10-5

HOW TO Calculate Variable Overhead Variances: Columnar and Formula Approaches

Information:

Standard variable overhead rate (*SVOR*)	$5.00 per direct labor hour
Actual variable overhead rate (*AVOR*)	$4.70
Actual hours worked (*AH*)	150 hours
Number of t-shirts produced	1,200 units
Hours allowed for production (*SH*)	144 hours[a]

[a]0.12 × 1,200.

Required: Calculate the variable overhead spending and efficiency variances.
Calculation:
Columnar:

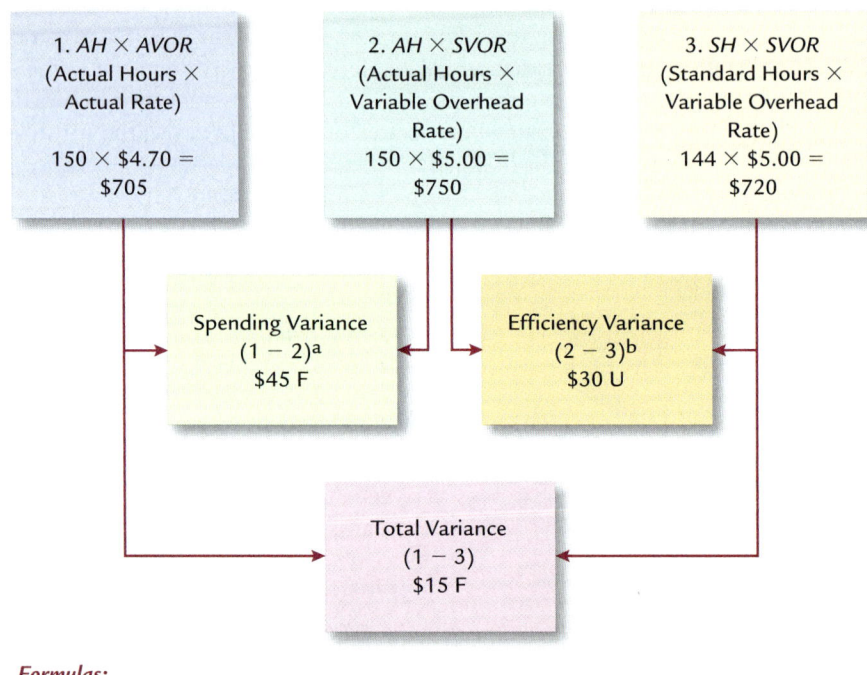

Formulas:
[a]*VOH* spending variance = (*AVOR* − *SVOR*)*AH*
= ($4.70 − $5.00)150
= $45 F
[b]*VOH* efficiency variance = (*AH* − *SH*)*SVOR*
= (150 − 144)($5.00)
= $30 U

Analytical Q & A

If *AH* = 100, *SH* = 90, and *SVOR* = $6, what is the variable overhead efficiency variance?

Answer
VOH efficiency variance = (*AH* − *SH*)*SVOR* = (100 − 90)$6 = $60.

Comparison of the Spending Variance with the Price Variances of Materials and Labor

The variable overhead spending variance is similar but not identical to the price variances of materials and labor; there are some conceptual differences. Variable overhead is not a homogeneous input—it is made up of a large number of individual items, such as indirect materials, indirect labor, electricity, maintenance, and so on. The standard variable overhead rate represents the weighted cost per direct labor hour that should be incurred for all variable overhead items. The difference between what should have been spent per hour and what actually was spent per hour is a type of price variance.

A variable overhead spending variance can arise because prices for individual variable overhead items have increased or decreased. Assume, for the moment, that the price changes of individual overhead items are the only cause of the spending variance. If the spending variance is unfavorable, price increases for individual variable overhead items are the cause; if the spending variance is favorable, price decreases are dominating.

If the only source of the variable overhead spending variance were price changes, then it would be completely analogous to the price variances of materials and labor. Unfortunately, the spending variance is also affected by how efficiently overhead is used. Waste or inefficiency in the use of variable overhead increases the actual variable overhead cost. This increased cost, in turn, is reflected in an increased actual variable overhead rate. Thus, even if the actual prices of the individual overhead items were equal to the budgeted or standard prices, an unfavorable variable overhead spending variance could still take place. For example, more kilowatt-hours of power may be used than should be—yet, this is not captured by any change in direct labor hours. However, the effect is reflected by an increase in the total cost of power and, thus, the total cost of variable overhead. Similarly, efficiency can decrease the actual variable overhead cost and decrease the actual variable overhead rate. Efficient use of variable overhead items contributes to a favorable spending variance. If the waste effect dominates, then the net contribution will be unfavorable; if efficiency dominates, then the net contribution is favorable. Therefore, the variable overhead spending variance is the result of both price and efficiency.

Concept Q & A

How does the variable overhead spending variance differ from the materials and labor price variances?

Answer:
The variable overhead spending variance is affected by both price changes of individual items as well as efficiency issues.

Responsibility for the Variable Overhead Spending Variance

Many variable overhead items are affected by several responsibility centers. For example, utilities are a joint cost. To the extent that consumption of variable overhead can be traced to a responsibility center, responsibility can be assigned. Consumption of indirect materials is an example of a traceable variable overhead cost.

Controllability is a prerequisite for assigning responsibility. Price changes of variable overhead items are essentially beyond the control of supervisors. If price changes are small (as they often are), then the spending variance is primarily a matter of the efficient use of overhead in production, which is controllable by production supervisors. Accordingly, responsibility for the variable overhead spending variance is generally assigned to production departments.

Responsibility for the Variable Overhead Efficiency Variance

The variable overhead efficiency variance is directly related to the direct labor efficiency or usage variance. If variable overhead is truly proportional to direct labor consumption, then like the labor usage variance, the variable overhead efficiency variance is caused by efficient or inefficient use of direct labor. If more (or fewer) direct labor hours are used than the standard calls for, then the total variable overhead cost will increase (or decrease). The validity of the measure depends on how valid the relationship is between variable overhead costs and direct labor hours. In other words, do variable overhead costs really change in proportion to changes in direct labor hours? If so, responsibility for the variable overhead efficiency variance should be assigned to the individual who has responsibility for the use of direct labor: the production manager.

A Performance Report for the Variable Overhead Spending and Efficiency Variances

Cornerstone 10-5 shows a favorable $45 spending variance and an unfavorable $30 efficiency variance. The $45 F spending variance means that overall Texas Rex spent less than expected on variable overhead. The reasons for the $30 unfavorable variable overhead efficiency variance are the same as those offered for an unfavorable labor usage variance. An unfavorable variance means that more hours were used than called for by the standard. Since these variances are aggregate measures, they reveal nothing about how individual variable overhead items were controlled. Even if the variances are insignificant, they reveal nothing about how well costs of *individual* variable overhead items were controlled. It is possible for two large variances of opposite sign to cancel each other out. Control of variable overhead requires line-by-line analysis for each individual item. Cornerstone 10-6 shows how to prepare a performance report that supplies the line-by-line information essential for detailed analysis of the variable overhead variances.

The analysis on a line-by-line basis reveals no unusual problems such as two large individual item variances with opposite signs. No individual item variance is greater than 10 percent of its budgeted amount. Thus, no variance at the individual item level appears to be of a large enough magnitude to be of concern.

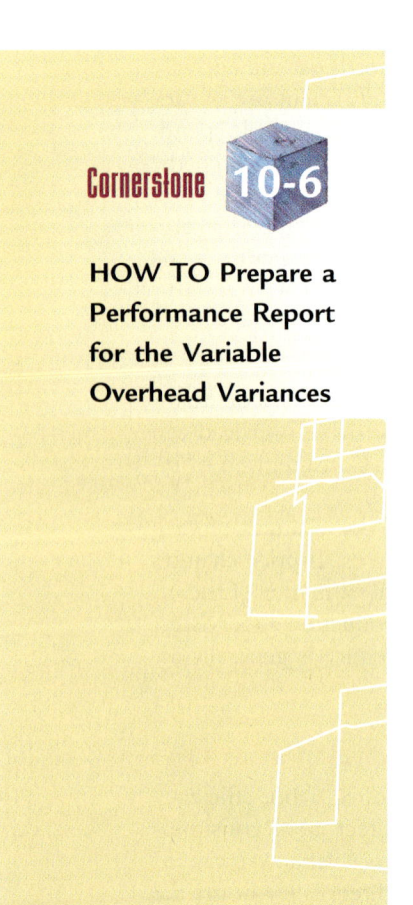

Cornerstone 10-6

HOW TO Prepare a Performance Report for the Variable Overhead Variances

Information:

Standard variable overhead rate (*SVOR*)	$5.00 per direct labor hour
Actual costs:	
Maintenance	$535
Power	$170
Actual hours worked (*AH*)	150 hours
Number of t-shirts produced	1,200 units
Hours allowed for production (*SH*)	144 hours[a]
Variable overhead:	
Maintenance	0.12 hr. @ $3.75
Power	0.12 hr. @ $1.25

[a]0.12 × 1,200.

Required: Prepare a performance report that shows the variances on an item-by-item basis.
Calculation:

Performance Report
For the Quarter Ended March 31, 2007

Cost	Cost Formula[a]	Actual Costs	Budget for Actual Hours[b]	Budget for Spending Variance[c]	Budget for Standard Hours[d]	Budget for Efficiency Variance[e]
Maintenance	$3.75	$535	$562.50	$27.50 F	$540	$22.50 U
Power	1.25	170	187.50	17.50 F	180	7.50 U
Total	$5.00	$705	$750.00	$45.00 F	$720	$30.00 U

[a]Per direct labor hour.
[b]Computed using the cost formula and 150 actual hours.
[c]Spending variance = Actual costs − Budget for actual hours.
[d]Computed using the cost formula and an activity level of 144 standard hours.
[e]Efficiency variance = Budget for actual hours − Budget for standard hours.

Concept Q & A

Why are the labor efficiency and variable overhead efficiency variances similar in nature?

Answer:
Both depend on the difference between actual and standard direct labor hours.

Fixed Overhead Analysis

OBJECTIVE 3

Calculate the fixed overhead variances and explain their meaning.

Fixed overhead costs are capacity costs. They represent manufacturing activity capacity acquired in advance of usage. The standard fixed overhead rate is calculated as follows:

$$SFOR = \text{Budgeted fixed overhead costs/Practical capacity}$$

For example, if Texas Rex can produce 1,500 t-shirts per quarter under efficient operating conditions, then practical capacity measured in standard hours (SH_p) is calculated by the following formula:

$$\begin{aligned} SH_p &= \text{Unit standard} \times \text{Units of practical capacity} \\ &= 0.12 \times 1{,}500 \\ &= 180 \text{ hours} \end{aligned}$$

Using Texas Rex's budgeted fixed overhead costs (from Cornerstone 10-2), the standard fixed overhead rate is calculated as follows:

$$\begin{aligned} SFOR &= \$1{,}800/180 \\ &= \$10 \text{ per direct labor hour} \end{aligned}$$

From the calculation for *SFOR*, it is easy to see how the budgeted fixed overhead (*BFOH*) can be expressed as the product of the rate and practical capacity as follows:

$$\begin{aligned} BFOH &= SFOR \times SH_p \\ &= \$10 \times 180 \\ &= \$1{,}800 \end{aligned}$$

Some firms use average or expected capacity instead of practical capacity to calculate fixed overhead rates. In this case, the standard hours used to calculate the fixed overhead rate will typically be less than SH_p.

Analytical Q & A

If the budgeted fixed overhead is $10,000 and the standard fixed overhead rate is $100 per direct labor hour (calculated using practical capacity), what is the practical capacity, measured in direct labor hours?

Answer:
Practical capacity = $10,000/$100 = 100 direct labor hours.

Total Fixed Overhead Variances

The total fixed overhead variance is the difference between actual fixed overhead and applied fixed overhead, when applied fixed overhead is obtained by multiplying the standard fixed overhead rate times the standard hours allowed for the actual output. Thus, the applied fixed overhead (*ApFOH*) is:

$$ApFOH = SFOR \times SH$$

The total fixed overhead variance is the difference between the actual fixed overhead (*AFOH*) and the applied fixed overhead:

$$\text{Total variance} = \text{Actual fixed overhead} - \text{Applied fixed overhead}$$
$$= AFOH - ApFOH$$

Cornerstone 10-7 illustrates how to calculate the total fixed overhead variance, using the Texas Rex example. The total fixed overhead variance can be divided into spending and volume variances. Spending and volume variances can be calculated using either the 3-pronged (columnar) approach or formulas. The best approach to use seems to be a matter of taste. However, the formulas first need to be expressed specifically for fixed overhead.

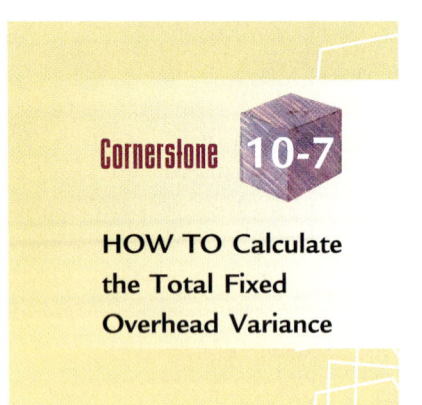

Cornerstone 10-7

HOW TO Calculate the Total Fixed Overhead Variance

Information:

Standard fixed overhead rate (*SFOR*)	$10.00 per direct labor hour
Actual fixed overhead costs	$1,650
Standard hours allowed per unit	0.12 hour
Actual production	1,200 units

Required: Calculate the total fixed overhead variance.

Calculation:

Actual Costs	Applied Fixed Overhead*	Total Variance
AFOH	*SH* × *SFOR*	*AFOH* − *ApFOH*
$1,650	$1,440	$210 U

*SH × SFOR = 0.12 × 1,200 × $10.

Fixed Overhead Spending Variance

The **fixed overhead spending variance** is defined as the difference between the actual fixed overhead and the budgeted fixed overhead:

$$\text{FOH spending variance} = AFOH - ApFOH$$

Fixed Overhead Volume Variance

The **fixed overhead volume variance** is the difference between budgeted fixed overhead and applied fixed overhead:

$$\text{Volume variance} = \text{Budgeted fixed overhead} - \text{Applied fixed overhead}$$
$$= BFOH - ApFOH$$
$$= (SH_p \times SFOR) - (SH \times SFOR)$$
$$= (SH_p - SH)SFOR$$

The volume variance measures the effect of the actual output differing from the output used at the beginning of the year to compute the predetermined standard fixed overhead rate. If you think of the output used to calculate the fixed overhead rate as the activity capacity acquired (practical capacity) and the actual output as the activity capacity used, then the volume variance is the cost of unused activity capacity. Cornerstone 10-8 illustrates how to calculate the fixed overhead variances using either a columnar or a formula approach.

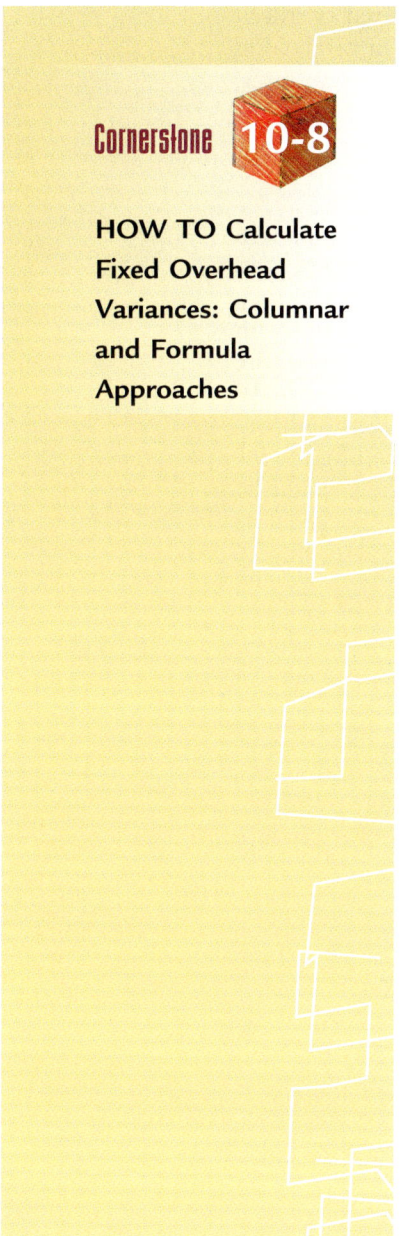

Cornerstone 10-8

HOW TO Calculate Fixed Overhead Variances: Columnar and Formula Approaches

Information:

Standard fixed overhead rate ($SFOR$)	$10.00 per direct labor hour
Budgeted fixed overhead ($BFOH$)	$1,800
Number of t-shirts produced	1,200 units
Hours allowed for production (SH)	144 hours[a]

[a]$0.12 \times 1,200$.

Required: Calculate the fixed overhead spending and volume variances.
Calculation:
Columnar:

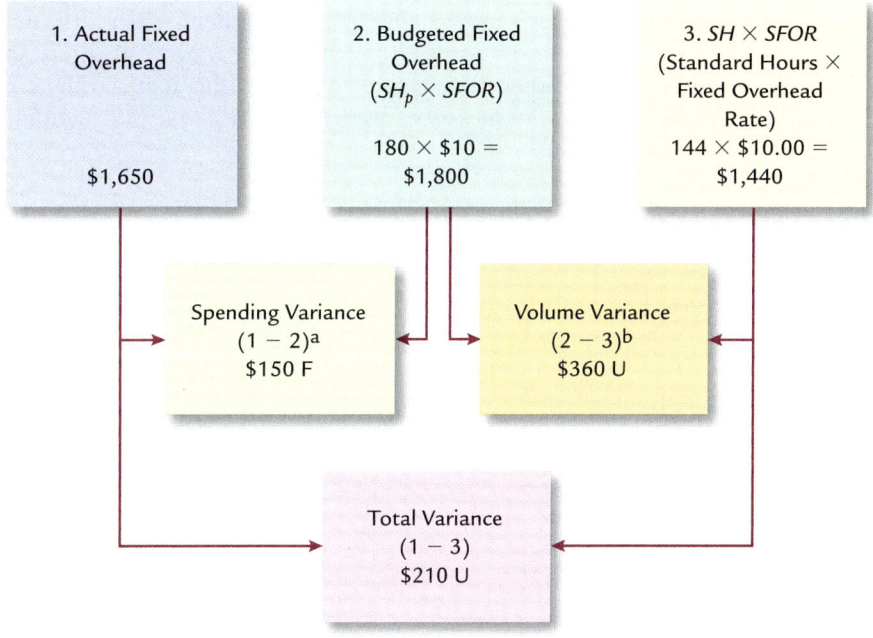

Formulas:
[a]FOH spending variance $= AFOH - BFOH$
$$= \$1,650 - \$1,800$$
$$= \$150 \text{ F}$$
[b]FOH volume variance $= BFOH - ApFOH$
$$= (SH_p - SH)SFOR$$
$$= (180 - 144)(\$10.00)$$
$$= \$360 \text{ U}$$

Analytical Q & A

If $BFOH = \$10,000$, $SFOR = \$8.00$, and $SH = 1,200$, what is the volume variance?

Answer:
Volume variance $= BFOH - ApFOH = \$10,000 - (\$8 \times 1,200) = \$400$ Unfavorable.

Responsibility for the Fixed Overhead Spending Variance

Fixed overhead is made up of a number of individual items such as salaries, depreciation, taxes, and insurance. Many fixed overhead items—long-run investments, for instance—are not subject to change in the short run; consequently, fixed overhead costs are often beyond the immediate control of management. Since many fixed overhead costs are affected primarily by long-run decisions, and not by changes in production levels, the budget variance is usually small. For example, depreciation, salaries, taxes, and insurance costs are not likely to be much different from planned.

Analysis of the Fixed Overhead Spending Variance

Because fixed overhead is made up of many individual items, a line-by-line comparison of budgeted costs with actual costs provides more information concerning the causes of the spending variance. The fixed overhead section of Cornerstone 10-3 provides such a report. The report reveals that the fixed overhead spending variance is out of line with expectations. Less was spent on grounds keeping than expected. In fact, the entire spending variance is attributable to this one item. Since the amount is more than 10 percent of budget, it merits an investigation. An investigation, for example, might reveal that the weather was especially wet and thus reduced the cost of watering for the period involved. In this case, no action is needed, as a natural correction would be forthcoming.

Responsibility for the Fixed Overhead Volume Variance

Assuming that volume variance measures capacity utilization implies that the general responsibility for this variance should be assigned to the production department. At times, however, investigation into the reasons for a significant volume variance may reveal the cause to be factors beyond the control of production. In this instance, specific responsibility may be assigned elsewhere. For example, if purchasing acquires a raw material of lower quality than usual, significant rework time may result, causing lower production and an unfavorable volume variance. In this case, responsibility for the variance rests with purchasing, not production.

Analysis of the Volume Variance

The $360 U variance (from Cornerstone 10-8) occurs because the production capacity is 180 hours and only 144 hours should have been used. Why the company failed to use all of its capacity is not specifically revealed. Given that unutilized capacity is about 20 percent of the total, investigation seems merited. Exhibit 10-2 graphically illustrates the volume variance. Notice that the volume variance occurs because fixed overhead is treated as if it were a variable cost. In reality, fixed costs do not change as activity changes as a predetermined fixed overhead rate allows.

ACTIVITY-BASED BUDGETING

OBJECTIVE 4
Prepare an activity-based flexible budget.

In Chapter 8, the budgetary process used a traditional approach, especially with respect to the overhead and selling and administrative expenses budgets. Traditional, functional-based budgeting is concerned with budgeting the costs of resources associated with organizational units, such as departments and plants. Companies that have implemented an ABC system may also wish to install an *activity-based budgeting system*. A budgetary system at the activity level can be a useful approach to support continuous improvement and process management. Furthermore, because activities are what consume resources and, thus, are the causes of costs, activity-based budgeting may prove to be a much more powerful planning and control tool than the traditional, functional-based budgeting approach. An activity-based budgetary approach can be used to emphasize cost reduction through the elimination of wasteful activities and improving the efficiency of necessary activities.

Graphical Analysis of the Volume Variance

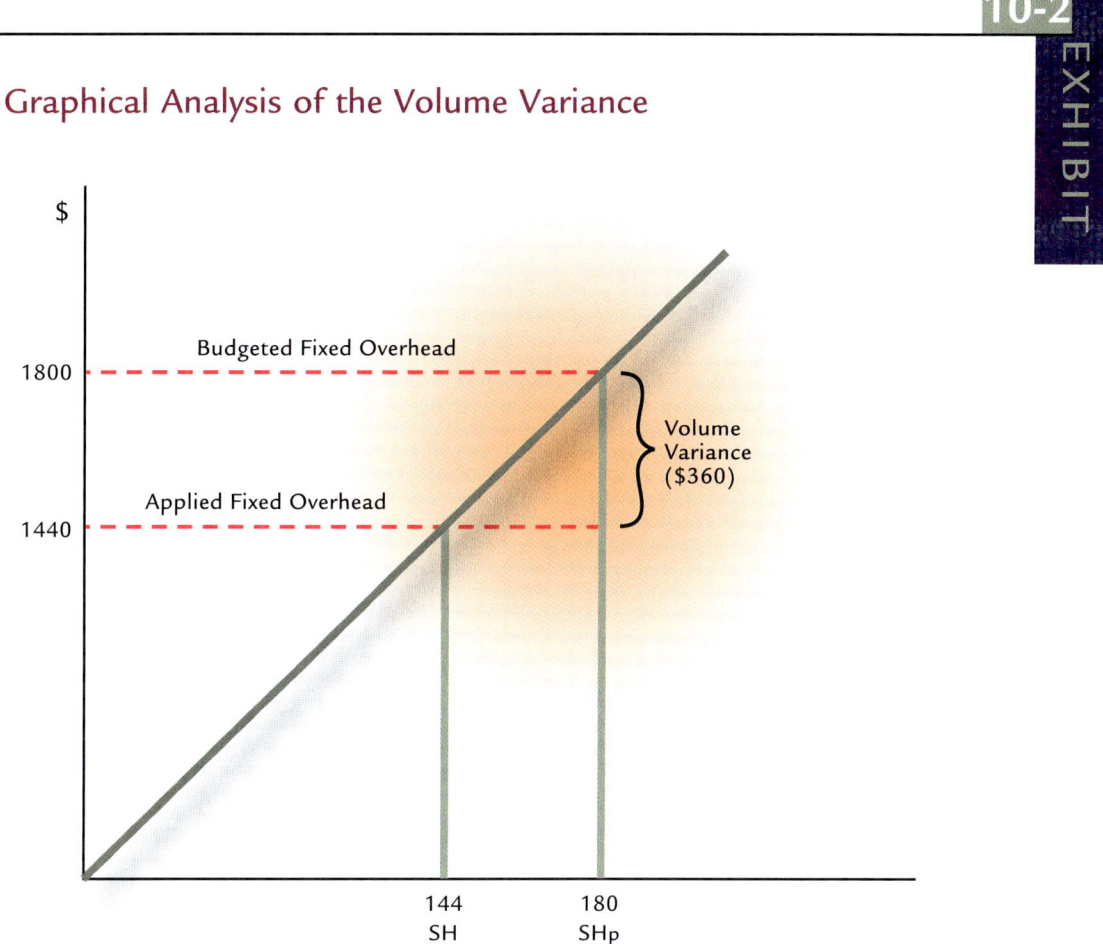

Static Activity Budgets

Activities cause costs by consuming resources; however, the amount of resources consumed depends on the demand for the activity's output. Building an **activity-based budget** requires three steps: (1) the activities within an organization must be identified, (2) the demand for each activity's output must be estimated, and (3) the cost of resources required to produce this activity output must be assessed. If an organization has implemented an ABC or ABM system, then step 1 will already have been accomplished. Assuming that ABC has been implemented, the major emphasis for activity-based budgeting is estimating the workload (demand) for each activity and then budgeting the resources required to sustain this workload. The workload for each activity must be set to support the sales and production activities expected for the coming period.

As with traditional, functional-based budgeting, activity-based budgeting begins with sales and production budgets. Direct materials and direct labor budgets are also compatible with an ABC framework because these production inputs are directly traceable to the individual products. The major differences between functional and activity-based budgeting are found within the overhead and selling and administration categories. In a functional-based approach, budgets within these categories are typically detailed by cost elements. These cost elements are classified as variable or fixed, using production or sales output measures as the basis for determining cost behavior. Furthermore, these budgets are usually constructed by budgeting for a cost item within a department (function) and then rolling these items up into the master overhead budget. For example, the cost of supervision in an overhead budget is the sum of all the supervision costs of the various departments. Activity-based budgeting, on the other hand, identifies the overhead, selling, and administrative *activities* and then builds a budget for each activity, based on the resources needed to provide the required activity output levels. Costs are classified as variable or fixed with respect to the *activity* output measure.

Consider, for example, the activity of purchasing materials. The demand for this activity is a function of the materials requirements for the various products and services produced. An activity driver, such as number of purchase orders, measures the activity output demand. Cornerstone 10-9 illustrates how to prepare a budget at the activity level for the purchasing activity.

Cornerstone 10-9

HOW TO Prepare a Static Budget for an Activity

Information:
1. Demand for purchase orders based on materials requirements: 15,000 purchase orders.
2. Resources needed:
   a. Five purchasing agents, each capable of processing 3,000 orders per year; salary, $40,000 each.
   b. Supplies (forms, paper, stamps, envelopes, etc.), projected to cost $1.00 per purchase order.
   c. Desks and computers: depreciation, $5,000 per year.
   d. Office space, rent, and utilities, $6,000.

Required: Prepare a budget for the purchasing activity.

Calculation: Purchasing budget:

Salaries	Depreciation	Supplies	Occupancy	Total
$200,000	$5,000	$15,000	$6,000	$226,000

Of the resources consumed by the purchasing activity in Cornerstone 10-9, supplies is a flexible resource and, therefore, a variable cost, whereas the other resources consumed are committed resources and display a fixed cost behavior (a step-fixed cost behavior in the case of salaries and depreciation). However, one important difference should be mentioned: Fixed and variable purchasing costs are defined with respect to the *number of purchase orders* and not direct labor hours or units produced or other measures of production output. In budgeting at the activity level, the cost behavior of each activity is defined with respect to *its* output measure (which is often different from the production-based drivers used in functional-based budgeting). Knowing the output measure provides significant insights for controlling activity costs. In an activity framework, controlling costs translates into managing activities. For example, by redesigning products so that they use more common components, the number of purchase orders can be decreased. By decreasing the number of purchase orders demanded, flexible resource demand is reduced; furthermore, decreasing the number of purchase orders demanded also reduces the activity capacity needed. Thus, activity costs will decrease.

Concept Q & A

What are the main differences between activity-based budgeting and traditional budgeting?

Answer:
Activity-based budgeting (ABB) differs primarily with overhead and selling and administrative budgets. ABB builds a budget for each activity based on the demands of the activity for resources, whereas traditional budgeting focuses on cost items required by organizational units such as departments.

APPLICATIONS IN BUSINESS

In fiscal 2001, the Small Business Administration (SBA) began to use activity-based budgeting (ABB) with the objective of showing the relationship between the resources needed to support the outputs that it plans to produce. The SBA begins ABB by identifying the services that customers expect to receive from its various offices. These services constitute the outputs of the SBA. Once the outputs are identified, then the SBA identifies the activities needed to produce the outputs. Since activities consume resources, it is then possible to determine the level of funding needed for the various outputs. This information is then used to decide which outputs can be produced given the funding provided. The objective is to manage resources to maximize the agency's outputs so that America's small businesses are best served.

Source: **http://www.sba.gov/cfo/abb.html** as of July 25, 2003.

Activity Flexible Budgeting

The ability to identify changes in activity costs as activity output changes allows managers to more carefully plan and monitor activity improvements. **Activity flexible budgeting** is the prediction of what activity costs will be as activity output changes. Variance analysis within an activity framework makes it possible to improve traditional budgetary performance reporting. It also enhances the ability to manage activities.

In a functional-based approach, budgeted costs for the actual level of activity are obtained by assuming that a single unit-based driver (units of product or direct labor hours) drives all costs. A cost formula is developed for each cost item as a function of units produced or direct labor hours. Exhibit 10-3 illustrates a traditional flexible budget based on direct labor hours. If, however, costs vary with respect to more than one driver, and the drivers are not highly correlated with direct labor hours, then the predicted costs can be misleading.

The solution, of course, is to build flexible budget formulas for more than one driver. Cost estimation procedures (high-low method, the method of least squares, and so on) can be used to estimate and validate the cost formulas for each activity. In

10-3

EXHIBIT

Flexible Budget: Direct Labor Hours

	Cost Formula		Direct Labor Hours	
	Fixed	Variable	10,000	20,000
Direct materials	—	$10	$100,000	$200,000
Direct labor	—	8	80,000	160,000
Maintenance	$ 20,000	3	50,000	80,000
Machining	15,000	1	25,000	35,000
Inspections	120,000	—	120,000	120,000
Setups	50,000	—	50,000	50,000
Purchasing	220,000	—	220,000	220,000
Total	$425,000	$22	$645,000	$865,000

principle, the variable cost component for each activity should correspond to resources acquired as needed (flexible resources) and the fixed cost component should correspond to resources acquired in advance of usage (committed resources). This multiple-formula approach allows managers to predict more accurately what costs ought to be for different levels of activity usage, as measured by the activity output measure. These costs can then be compared with the actual costs to help assess budgetary performance. Cornerstone 10-10 illustrates how to prepare an activity flexible budget. The approach for calculating this budget follows that illustrated earlier in Cornerstone 10-2. The principal difference is that flexible budgets are computed for *each driver*. Notice that the budgeted amounts for materials and labor are the same as those reported in Exhibit 10-3; they use the same activity output measure. The budgeted amounts for the other items differ significantly from the traditional amounts because the activity output measures differ by driver.

Cornerstone 10-10

HOW TO Prepare an Activity Flexible Budget

Information: For simplicity, the full set of information is not listed, but the individual activities, drivers, their cost formulas, and the output levels are the inputs needed to prepare the budget. To illustrate, the maintenance activity would require the following information for its role in the budget:

Activity: Maintenance
Driver: Machine hours
Fixed activity cost: $20,000
Variable activity rate: $5.50 per machine hour

Required: Prepare an activity-based flexible budget.
Calculation:

	Formula		Level of Activity	
Driver: Direct Labor Hours				
	Fixed	Variable	10,000	20,000
Direct materials	$ —	$ 10	$100,000	$200,000
Direct labor	—	8	80,000	160,000
Subtotal	$ 0	$ 18	$180,000	$360,000
Driver: Machine Hours				
	Fixed	Variable	8,000	16,000
Maintenance	$ 20,000	$ 5.50	$ 64,000	$108,000
Machining	15,000	2.00	31,000	47,000
Subtotal	$ 35,000	$ 7.50	$ 95,000	$155,000
Driver: Number of Setups				
	Fixed	Variable	25	30
Setups	$ —	$1,800	$ 45,000	$ 54,000
Inspections	80,000	2,100	132,500	143,000
Subtotal	$ 80,000	$3,900	$177,500	$197,000
Driver: Number of Orders				
	Fixed	Variable	15,000	25,000
Purchasing	$211,000		$226,000	$236,000

Assume that the first activity level for each driver in Cornerstone 10-10 corresponds to the actual activity usage levels. Cornerstone 10-11 illustrates how to prepare a performance report using activity-based flexible budgeting. Notice that the report compares the budgeted costs for the actual activity usage levels with the actual costs. One item is on target, and the other six items are mixed. The net outcome is a favorable variance of $21,500. The performance report in Cornerstone 10-11 compares total budgeted costs for the actual level of activity with the total actual costs for each activity. The preparation of the performance report follows the pattern and approach in Cornerstone 10-3. The difference is that the comparison is for *each* activity. It is also possible to compare the actual fixed activity costs with the budgeted fixed activity costs and the actual variable activity costs with the budgeted variable costs. For example, assume that the actual fixed inspection costs are $82,000 (due to a midyear salary adjustment, reflecting a more favorable union agreement than anticipated) and that the actual variable inspection costs are $43,500. The variable and fixed budget variances for the inspection activity are computed as follows:

Activity	Actual Cost	Budgeted Cost	Variance
Inspection			
Fixed	$ 82,000	$ 80,000	$2,000 U
Variable	43,500	52,500	9,000 F
Total	$125,500	$132,500	$7,000 F

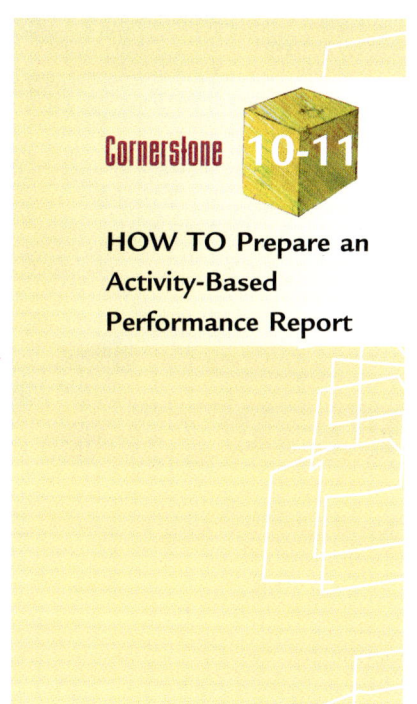

Cornerstone 10-11

HOW TO Prepare an Activity-Based Performance Report

Information: Actual activity level is the first one for each activity listed in Cornerstone 10-10.

Actual costs:

Direct materials	$101,000
Direct labor	80,000
Maintenance	55,000
Machining	29,000
Inspections	125,500
Setups	46,500
Purchases	220,000

Required: Prepare an activity-based performance report.
Calculation:

	Actual Costs	Budgeted Costs	Budget Variance
Direct materials	$101,000	$100,000	$ 1,000 U
Direct labor	80,000	80,000	—
Maintenance	55,000	64,000	9,000 F
Machining	29,000	31,000	2,000 F
Inspections	125,500	132,500	7,000 F
Setups	46,500	45,000	1,500 U
Purchases	220,000	226,000	6,000 F
Total	$657,000	$678,500	$21,500 F

Breaking each variance into fixed and variable components provides more insight into the source of the variation in planned and actual expenditures.

Concept Q & A

Why does activity-based flexible budgeting provide a more accurate prediction of costs?

Answer:
Activity-based flexible budgeting is more accurate if costs vary with more than one driver and the drivers are not highly correlated with direct labor hours (which is often the case).

Bill Hardy was struggling with issues related to managing costs and profits in the hotel business. He was faced with considerable uncertainty regarding the level of occupancy. He did not have a good understanding of how to highlight critical issues during the year nor what to do to drive performance. He also needed a better understanding of how to evaluate performance during the year. Finally, how to allocate resources and reduce costs were items of critical importance as well.

Flexible budgeting resolves many of the issues Bill faces. First, it allows him to deal with uncertainty by assessing what revenues and costs are at various levels of occupancy. Second, it allows him to assess what the efficiency was after the fact by comparing the actual costs with the budgeted costs for the actual occupancy. Analyzing the causes of the significant variances also helps in managing the performance of the organization.

Activity-based budgeting is perhaps the icing on the cake. In a highly competitive environment, knowing which activities consume which resources provides Bill with the opportunity to make sound resource allocation decisions. Some activities are more critical than others, and understanding these relationships should help Bill decide how to reduce costs so that the mission of the organization is met and overall efficiency increases.

SCENARIO REVISITED

SUMMARY OF LEARNING OBJECTIVES

Static budgets provide expected cost for a given level of activity. If the actual level of activity differs from the level associated with the static budget level, then comparing actual costs with budgeted costs does not make any sense. The solution is flexible budgeting.

Flexible budgets divide costs into costs that vary with units of production (or direct labor hours) and those that are fixed with respect to these unit-level drivers. These relationships allow the identification of a cost formula for each item in the budget. The cost formulas are the means for calculating expected costs for various level of activity. There are two applications of flexible budgets: Before-the-fact and after-the-fact. Before-the-fact applications allow managers to see what costs will be for different levels of activity, thus helping in planning. After-the-fact applications allow managers to see what the cost should have been for the actual level of activity. Knowing these after-the-fact expected or budgeted costs then provides the opportunity to evaluate efficiency by comparing actual costs with budgeted costs.

Overhead costs are often a significant proportion of costs in a budget. Comparing actual variable and fixed overhead costs with applied overhead costs yields a total overhead variance. In a standard cost system, it is possible to break down these overhead variances into component variances. For variable overhead, the two component variances are the spending variance and the efficiency variance. For fixed overhead, the two component variances are the spending variance and the volume variance. The spending variances are the result of comparing the actual costs with budgeted costs. The variable overhead efficiency variance is the result of efficient or inefficient use of labor—because variable overhead is assumed to vary with direct labor hours. The fixed overhead volume variance is the result of producing a level different than that used to calculate the predetermined fixed overhead rate. It can be interpreted as a measure of capacity utilization.

Activity-based budgeting is done at the activity level. First, demand for products is assessed. Next, the level of activity output needed to support the expected production level is estimated. Finally, the resources needed to support the required activity output are estimated. This then becomes the activity budget. It is also possible to define activity flexible budgets. These budgets differ from traditional flexible budgeting because the cost formulas are based on the activity drivers for the respective activities rather than being based only on direct labor hours.

Cornerstones for Chapter 10

Cornerstone 10-1	How to prepare a performance report based on a static budget (using budgeted production, page 401
Cornerstone 10-2	How to prepare a flexible production budget, page 403
Cornerstone 10-3	How to prepare a performance report using a flexible budget, page 404
Cornerstone 10-4	How to calculate the total variable overhead variance, page 405
Cornerstone 10-5	How to calculate variable overhead variances: columnar and formula approaches, page 406
Cornerstone 10-6	How to prepare a performance report for the variable overhead variances, page 408
Cornerstone 10-7	How to calculate the total fixed overhead variance, page 410
Cornerstone 10-8	How to calculate fixed overhead variances: columnar and formula approaches, page 411
Cornerstone 10-9	How to prepare a static budget for an activity, page 414
Cornerstone 10-10	How to prepare an activity flexible budget, page 416
Cornerstone 10-11	How to prepare an activity-based performance report, page 417

KEY TERMS

Activity flexible budgeting, 415

Activity-based budget, 413

Fixed overhead spending variance, 410

Fixed overhead volume variance, 410

Flexible budget, 402

Flexible budget variance, 404

Performance report, 400

Static budget, 400

Variable budgets, 402

Variable overhead efficiency variance, 406

Variable overhead spending variance, 405

DISCUSSION QUESTIONS

1. Discuss the differences between static and flexible budgets.
2. Why are flexible budgets superior to static budgets for performance reporting?
3. Explain why mixed costs must be broken down into their fixed and variable components before a flexible budget can be developed.
4. What is the purpose of a before-the-fact flexible budget?

5. What is the purpose of an after-the-fact flexible budget?
6. Explain how an activity-based budget is prepared.
7. What is the difference between an activity flexible budget and a functional-based (traditional) flexible budget?
8. Why would an activity-based performance report be more accurate than a report based on a traditional flexible budget?
9. Explain why the variable overhead spending variance is not a pure price variance.
10. The variable overhead efficiency variance has nothing to do with efficient use of variable overhead. Do you agree or disagree? Why?
11. Describe the difference between the variable overhead efficiency variance and the labor efficiency variance.
12. Explain why the fixed overhead spending variance is usually very small.
13. What is the cause of an unfavorable volume variance?
14. Does the volume variance convey any meaningful information to managers?
15. Which do you think is more important for control of fixed overhead costs: the spending variance or the volume variance? Explain.

MULTIPLE-CHOICE EXERCISES

10-1 For performance reporting, it is best to compare actual costs with budgeted costs using

a. flexible budgets.
b. static budgets.
c. master budgets.
d. short-term budgets.
e. None of the above.

10-2 To create a meaningful performance report, actual costs and expected costs should be compared

a. at the budgeted level of activity.
b. weekly.
c. at the actual level of activity.
d. at the average level of activity.
e. hourly.

10-3 To help deal with uncertainty, managers should use

a. a static budget.
b. a master budget.
c. an after-the-fact flexible budget.
d. a before-the-fact flexible budget.
e. None of the above.

10-4 To help assess performance, managers should use

a. a static budget.
b. a master budget.
c. an after-the-fact flexible budget.
d. a before-the-fact flexible budget.
e. None of the above.

10-5 A firm comparing the actual variable costs of producing 10,000 units with the total variable costs of a static budget based on 9,000 units would probably see

a. no variances.
b. small favorable variances.

c. small unfavorable variances.
d. large favorable variances.
e. large unfavorable variances.

10-6 The total variable overhead variance is the difference between

a. the budgeted variable overhead and the actual variable overhead.
b. the actual variable overhead and the applied variable overhead.
c. the budgeted variable overhead and the applied variable overhead.
d. the applied variable overhead and the budgeted total overhead.
e. None of the above.

10-7 A variable overhead spending variance can occur because

a. prices for individual overhead items have increased.
b. prices for individual overhead items have decreased.
c. more of an individual overhead item was used than expected.
d. less of an individual overhead item was used than expected.
e. All of the above.

10-8 Because the calculation of both variances is based on direct labor hours, an unfavorable labor efficiency variance implies that

a. the variable overhead efficiency variance will also be unfavorable.
b. the variable overhead efficiency variance will be favorable.
c. there will be no variable overhead efficiency variance.
d. the variable overhead spending variance will be unfavorable.
e. the variable overhead is overapplied.

10-9 The total variable overhead variance can be expressed as the sum of

a. the underapplied variable overhead and the spending variance.
b. the efficiency variance and the overapplied variable overhead.
c. the spending and efficiency variances.
d. the spending, efficiency, and volume variances.
e. None of the above.

10-10 In a performance report that details the spending and efficiency variances, which of the following columns will be found?

a. A cost formula for each item
b. A budget for actual hours for each item
c. A budget of standard hours for each item
d. All of the above.
e. Only a and b.

10-11 The total fixed overhead variance is

a. the difference between actual and budgeted fixed overhead costs.
b. the difference between budgeted and applied fixed overhead costs.
c. the difference between budgeted fixed and variable overhead costs.
d. the difference between actual and applied fixed overhead costs.
e. None of the above.

10-12 The total fixed overhead variance can be expressed as the sum of

a. the spending and efficiency variances.
b. the spending and volume variances.
c. the efficiency and volume variances.
d. the flexible budget and the volume variances.
e. None of the above.

10-13 Because of the nature of fixed overhead items, the difference between the actual fixed overhead cost and the budgeted fixed overhead is

a. likely to be small.
b. likely to be large.
c. usually a major concern.
d. often attributable to labor inefficiency.
e. None of the above.

10-14 An unfavorable volume variance can occur because

a. too much finished goods inventory was held.
b. the company overproduced.
c. the actual output was less than expected or practical capacity.
d. the actual output was greater than expected or practical capacity.
e. All of the above.

10-15 Responsibility for the volume variance usually is assigned to

a. the purchasing department.
b. the receiving department.
c. the shipping department.
d. the manufacturing department.
e. None of the above.

10-16 If ABC has been implemented, then activity-based budgeting must

a. estimate the demand for each activity's output.
b. estimate the resources required to support the activity output demanded.
c. assign activity costs to individual suppliers.
d. Only a and b.
e. None of the above.

10-17 In activity-based budgeting, costs are classified as variable or fixed with respect to

a. the activity driver.
b. only the units produced.
c. only the units sold.
d. only the direct labor hours.
e. None of the above.

10-18 Activity flexible budgeting makes it possible to

a. predict what activity costs will be as activity output changes.
b. improve traditional budgetary performance reporting.
c. enhance the ability to manage activities.
d. All of the above.
e. Only a and c.

10-19 In activity-based budgeting, flexible budget formulas are created

a. using only unit-level drivers.
b. using only nonunit-level drivers.
c. using both unit-level and nonunit-level drivers.
d. using only direct labor hours.
e. All of the above.

10-20 For activity-based budgeting, the variable component in a flexible budget cost formula corresponds to

a. resources acquired as needed and used (flexible resources).
b. resources acquired in advance of usage (committed resources).

c. the cost of capital resources.
d. the cost of depreciation.
e. All of the above.

EXERCISES

Exercise 10-1 *Performance Report*

Thorndark, Inc., produces sandals. Data for the second quarter are as follows:

Master Budget	Actual Data
Budgeted production: 1,000	Actual production: 1,100 units
Materials:	
2 leather strips @ $5.00	Materials cost: $11,200
Labor:	
0.5 hr. @ $8.00	Labor cost: $4,400

Required:

1. Prepare a performance report using a budget based on expected production.
2. Comment on the limitations of this report.

Exercise 10-2 *Overhead Budget for a Particular Level of Activity*

Regina Johnson, controller for Pet-Care Company, has been instructed to develop a flexible budget for overhead costs. The company produces two types of dog food. One, BasicDiet, is a standard mixture for healthy dogs. The second, SpecDiet, is a reduced protein formulation for older dogs with health problems. The two dog foods use common raw materials in different proportions. The company expects to produce 100,000 50-pound bags of each product during the coming year. BasicDiet requires 0.25 direct labor hour per bag, and SpecDiet requires 0.30. Regina has developed the following fixed and variable costs for each of the four overhead items:

Overhead Item	Fixed Cost	Variable Rate per DLH
Maintenance	$17,000	$0.40
Power		0.50
Indirect labor	26,500	1.60
Rent	18,000	

Required:

Prepare an overhead budget for the expected activity level for the coming year.

Exercise 10-3 *Flexible Budget*

Refer to the information in **Exercise 10-2**.

Required:

Prepare an overhead budget that reflects production that is 10 percent higher than expected (for both products) and one for production that is 20 percent lower than expected.

Exercise 10-4 *Performance Report*

Refer to the information given in **Exercise 10-2**. Assume that Pet-Care actually produced 120,000 bags of BasicDiet and 100,000 of SpecDiet. The actual overhead costs incurred were as follows:

Maintenance	$40,500	Indirect labor	$119,000
Power	31,700	Rent	18,000

Required:

1. Prepare a performance report for the period.
2. Based on the report, would you judge any of the variances to be significant? Can you think of some possible reasons for the variances?

Exercise 10-5 *Activity-Based Budgeting: Static*

Jamison, Inc., uses three forklifts to move materials from receiving to stores. The forklifts are also used to move materials from stores to the production area. The forklifts are obtained through an operating lease that costs $8,000 per year per forklift. Each move requires the use of a crate (costing $1 per unit). The crates are used to store the parts and are only emptied when used in production. Crates are disposed of after one cycle (two moves), where a cycle is defined as moving from receiving to stores to production. Forklifts can make three moves per hour and are used for 280 days per year, 24 hours per day (the remaining time is downtime for various reasons).

Required:

Prepare an annual budget for the activity, moving materials, assuming that all of the capacity of the activity is used. Identify which resources you would treat as fixed costs and which would be viewed as variable costs.

Exercise 10-6 *Activity-Based Flexible Budgeting*

Refer to the information in **Exercise 10-5**. Assume that the company uses only 90 percent of the activity capacity. The actual costs incurred at this level were as follows:

Lease	$24,000
Crates	50,000

Required:

1. What is the budget for this level of activity?
2. Prepare a performance report.

Exercise 10-7 *Performance Report and Activity-Based Budgeting*

Refer to the information in **Exercise 10-5**. Suppose that a redesign of the plant layout reduces the demand for moving materials by 75 percent.

Required:

What would be the budget for this new activity level?

Exercise 10-8 *Performance Report for Variable Overhead Variances*

Larsen Company had the data below for its most recent year, ending December 2007:

Actual costs:		Variable overhead standards:	
Indirect labor	$3,000	Indirect labor	0.10 hr. @ $8.00
Supplies	$700	Supplies	0.10 hr. @ $2.00
Actual hours worked	400 hours	Standard variable	
Number of units produced	5,000 units	overhead rate	$10.00 per direct labor hour
Hours allowed for			
production	500 hours		

Required:
Prepare a performance report that shows the variances on an item-by-item basis.

Exercise 10-9 *Variable Overhead Variances, Service Company*

Joven, Inc., operates a delivery service for over 70 restaurants. Joven has a fleet of vehicles and has invested in a sophisticated computerized communications system to coordinate its deliveries. Joven has gathered the following data on last year's operations:

Deliveries made: 42,000
Direct labor: 30,000 delivery hours @ $7.00
Actual variable overhead: $138,000

Joven employs a standard costing system. During the year, a variable overhead rate of $4.05 per hour was used. The labor standard requires 0.75 hour per delivery.

Required:
Compute the variable overhead spending and efficiency variances.

Exercise 10-10 *Fixed Overhead Variances*

Refer to **Exercise 10**-9. Assume that the actual fixed overhead was $420,000 and that the standard fixed overhead rate is $12 per delivery hour. The fixed overhead rate was calculated using practical capacity of 33,750 delivery hours.

Required:
Compute the fixed overhead spending and volume variances.

Exercise 10-11 *Fixed Overhead Application, Variances*

Tules Company is planning to produce 2,400,000 power drills for the coming year. Each drill requires 0.5 standard hour of labor for completion. The company uses direct labor hours to assign overhead to products. The total fixed overhead budgeted for the coming year is $1,320,000. Predetermined overhead rates are calculated using expected production, measured in direct labor hours. Actual results for the year are:

Actual production (units)   2,360,000
Actual direct labor hours   1,190,000
Actual fixed overhead $1,260,000

Required:
1. Compute the applied fixed overhead.
2. Compute the fixed overhead spending and volume variances.

Exercise 10-12 *Variable Overhead Application, Variances*

Refer to the information in **Exercise 10**-11. The total budgeted overhead was $2,700,000. Actual variable overhead incurred was $1,410,000.

Required:
1. Compute the applied variable overhead.
2. Compute the variable overhead spending and efficiency variances.

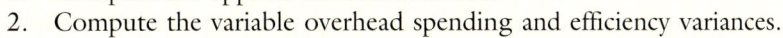

Exercise 10-13 *Overhead Variances*

At the beginning of the year, Raydom Company had the following standard cost sheet for one of its chemical products:

Direct materials (5 lbs. @ $6.40)	$32.00
Direct labor (2 hrs. @ $18.00)	36.00
Fixed overhead (2 hrs. @ $4.00)	8.00
Variable overhead (2 hrs. @ $1.50)	3.00
Standard cost per unit	$79.00

Raydom computes its overhead rates using practical volume, which is 144,000 units. The actual results for the year are as follows:

a. Units produced: 140,000
b. Direct labor: 290,000 hours at $9.05
c. Fixed overhead: $1,160,000
d. Variable overhead: $436,000

Required:

1. Compute the fixed overhead spending and volume variances.
2. Compute the variable overhead spending and efficiency variances.

PROBLEMS

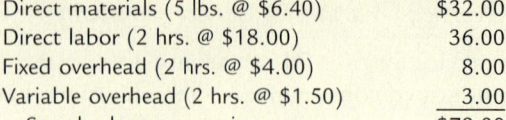

(Note: Whenever you see a next to a requirement, it signals a "building on a cornerstone" requirement. Assigning this requirement will usually entail additional work, such as a group project, analytical reasoning, internet research, decision making, and the use of written communication skills.)

Problem 10-1 *Overhead Budget, Flexible Budget*

Torino, Inc., manufactures machine parts in its Alva plant. Torino has developed the following flexible budget for overhead for the coming year. Activity level is measured in direct labor hours.

		Activity Level (hours)		
	Variable Cost Formula	10,000	20,000	30,000
Variable costs:				
Maintenance	$1.20	$12,000	$ 24,000	$ 36,000
Supplies	0.80	8,000	16,000	24,000
Power	0.10	1,000	2,000	3,000
Total variable costs	$2.10	$21,000	$ 42,000	$ 63,000
Fixed costs:				
Depreciation		$ 7,800	$ 7,800	$ 7,800
Salaries		66,000	66,000	66,000
Total fixed costs		$73,800	$ 73,800	$ 73,800
Total overhead costs		$94,800	$115,800	$136,800

The Alva plant produces two different types of parts. The production budget for November is 40,000 units for Part A23 and 20,000 units for Part B14. Part A23 requires 15 minutes of direct labor time, and Part B14 requires 24 minutes. Fixed overhead costs are incurred uniformly throughout the year.

Required:

1. Calculate the number of direct labor hours needed in November to produce Part A23 and the number of direct labor hours needed in November to produce Part B14. What are the total direct labor hours budgeted for November?
2. Prepare an overhead budget for November.

Problem 10-2 *Kicker Speakers, Before-the-Fact Flexible Budgeting, Flexible Budgeting for the New Solo X18 Model*

Stillwater Designs is considering a new Kicker speaker model: Solo X18, which is a very large and expensive subwoofer (projected price is $760 to distributors). Stillwater Designs controls the design specifications of the model and contracts with manufacturers in mainland China to produce the model. Stillwater Designs pays the freight and custom duties. The product is shipped to Stillwater and then sold to distributors throughout the United States.

The market for this type of subwoofer is small and very competitive. It is expected to have a 3-year life cycle. Market test reviews were encouraging. One potential customer noted that the speaker could make a deaf person hear again. Another remarked that the bass could be heard two miles away. Another customer was simply impressed by the size and watts of the subwoofer (a maximum of 10,000 watts capability). Encouraged by the results of market tests, the Product Steering Committee also wanted to review the financial analysis. The projected revenues and costs at three levels of sales volume are as follows (for the 3-year life cycle):

	Pessimistic	Most Likely	Optimistic
Sales volume (units)	72,000	150,000	250,000
Variable costs (total):			
Acquisition cost	$43,200,000	$ 90,000,000	$150,000,000
Freight	4,320,000	9,000,000	15,000,000
Duties	1,800,000	3,750,000	6,250,000
Total	$49,320,000	$102,750,000	$171,250,000
Fixed costs (total):			
Engineering (R&D)	$10,000,000	$ 10,000,000	$ 10,000,000
Overhead	3,000,000	3,000,000	3,000,000
Total	$13,000,000	$ 13,000,000	$ 13,000,000

Required:
1. Prepare flexible budget formulas for the cost items listed for the Solo X18 model. Also, provide a flexible budget formula for total costs.
2. Prepare an income statement for each of the three levels of sales volume. Discuss the value of before-the-fact flexible budgeting and relate this to the current example.

3. Form a small group of three to five. Assume you are acting as a Product Steering Committee. Evaluate the feasibility of producing the Solo X18 model (using the given financial data and the results of Requirements 1 and 2.) If the financial performance of the model is questionable, discuss possible courses of action that the company might take to improve the financial performance of the product. Also, discuss some reasons why the company might wish to produce the model even if it does not promise a good financial return.

Problem 10-3 *Flexible Budgeting*

Quarterly budgeted overhead costs for two different levels of activity follow. The 2,000 level was the expected level from the master budget.

	Cost Formula		Direct Labor Hours	
	Fixed	Variable	1,000	2,000
Maintenance	$ 4,000	$6.00	$10,000	$16,000
Depreciation	5,000	—	5,000	5,000
Supervision	15,000	—	15,000	15,000
Supplies	—	1.40	1,400	2,800
Power	—	0.75	750	1,500
Other	8,000	0.10	8,100	8,200

The actual activity level was 1,650 hours.

Required:
1. Prepare a flexible budget for an activity level of 1,650 direct labor hours.
2. Suppose that the formulas for each item are all missing. All you have are the budgeted costs for each level of activity. Show how you can obtain the formulas for each item using the information given for the budgeted costs for the two levels.

Problem 10-4 *Flexible Budgeting*

OBJECTIVE 1

Spreadsheet

Fruta, Inc., purchases fruit from numerous growers and packs fruit boxes and fruit baskets for sale. Fruta has developed the following flexible budget for overhead for the coming year. Activity level is measured in direct labor hours.

		Activity Level (hours)		
		2,000	2,500	3,000
Variable costs:				
Maintenance	$0.80	$ 1,600	$ 2,000	$ 2,400
Supplies	0.20	400	500	600
Power	0.40	800	1,000	1,200
Total variable costs	$1.40	$ 2,800	$ 3,500	$ 4,200
Fixed costs:				
Depreciation		$ 4,800	$ 4,800	$ 4,800
Salaries		18,000	18,000	18,000
Total fixed costs		$22,800	$22,800	$22,800
Total overhead costs		$25,600	$26,300	$27,000

Two products produced by Fruta during May are the standard fruit box (contains 12–15 large blemish-free apples and oranges) and the Mother's Day gift basket (a basket packed with various types of fruit and a box of chocolate truffles, wrapped in cellophane and tied with a large pink bow). The production budget for May is 1,500 units for the standard fruit box and 1,000 units for the gift basket. The standard fruit box requires five minutes of direct labor time, and the gift basket requires 15 minutes. Fixed overhead costs are incurred uniformly throughout the year.

Required:
1. Prepare an overhead budget for May.
2. The Cushing High School PTA ordered 200 gift baskets from Fruta to be given to high school teachers and support staff as a thank you for a successful school year. These gift baskets must be ready by May 31 and were not included in the original production budget for May. Without preparing a new overhead budget, what is Fruta's new total budgeted overhead for May?

Problem 10-5 *Performance Reporting*

OBJECTIVE 1

Fernando's is a hole-in-the-wall sandwich shop just off the State University campus. Customers enter off the street into a small counter area to order one of ten varieties of sandwiches and a soft drink. All orders must be taken out because there is no space for dining in.

The owner of Fernando's is Luis Azaria, son of Fernando Azaria who founded the shop. Luis is attempting to construct a series of budgets. He has accumulated the following information:

a. The average sandwich (which sells for $4.50) requires 1 roll, 4 ounces of meat, 2 ounces of cheese, 0.05 head of lettuce, 0.25 of a tomato, and a healthy squirt (1 ounce) of secret sauce. (We can't reveal the recipe here, but it includes Serrano pepper and hoisin sauce.)

b.   Each customer typically orders one soft drink (average price $1.50) consisting of a cup and twelve ounces of soda. Refills on the soda are free, but this offer is seldom taken advantage of because the typical customer carries his/her sandwich and soda back to the office or commons area.
c.   Use of paper supplies (napkins, bag, sandwich wrap, cups) varies somewhat from customer to customer but averages $1,650 per month.
d.   Fernando's is open for two 4-hour shifts. The noon shift on Monday through Friday requires two workers earning $10 per hour. The evening shift is only worked on Friday, Saturday, and Sunday nights. The two evening shift employees also earn $10 per hour. There are 4.3 weeks in a month.
e.   Rent is $575 per month. Other monthly cash expenses average $1,800.
f.   Food costs are:

Meat	$7.00/lb
Cheese	$6.00/lb
Rolls	$28.80/gross
Lettuce (a box contains 24 heads)	$12.00/box
Tomatoes (a box contains about 20 tomatoes)	$4/box
Secret sauce	$6.40/gallon
Soda (syrup and carbonated water)	$2.56/gallon

In a normal month when school is in session, Fernando's sells 5,000 sandwiches and 5,000 sodas. In October, State U holds its homecoming celebration. Therefore, Luis figured that if he added a noon shift on Saturday and Sunday of homecoming weekend, October sales would be 30 percent higher than normal. To advertise his noon shifts during homecoming weekend, Luis bought cups emblazoned with the State U Homecoming schedule. This added $200 to paper costs for the month. Last year, he did add the two additional shifts, and his sales goal was realized.

Required:
1.   Prepare a flexible budget for a normal school month.
2.   Prepare a flexible budget for October.
3.   Do you think it was worthwhile for Luis to add the additional shifts for homecoming weekend last October?

Problem 10-6 *Functional versus Activity Flexible Budgeting*

Amy Bunker, production manager, was upset with the latest performance report, which indicated that she was $100,000 over budget. Given the efforts that she and her workers had made, she was confident that they had met or beat the budget. Now she was not only upset but also genuinely puzzled over the results. Three items—direct labor, power, and setups—were over budget. The actual costs for these three items follow:

Direct labor	$210,000
Power	135,000
Setups	140,000
Total	$485,000

Amy knew that her operation had produced more units than originally had been budgeted so more power and labor had naturally been used. She also knew that the uncertainty in scheduling had led to more setups than planned. When she pointed this out to Gary Grant, the controller, he assured her that the budgeted costs had been adjusted for the increase in productive activity. Curious, Amy questioned Gary about the methods used to make the adjustment.

Gary: If the actual level of activity differs from the original planned level, we adjust the budget by using budget formulas—formulas that allow us to predict the costs for different levels of activity.

Amy: The approach sounds reasonable. However, I'm sure something is wrong here. Tell me exactly how you adjusted the costs of direct labor, power, and setups.

Gary: First, we obtain formulas for the individual items in the budget by using the method of least squares. We assume that cost variations can be explained by variations in productive activity where activity is measured by direct labor hours. Here is a list of the cost formulas for the three items you mentioned. The variable X is the number of direct labor hours.

$$\text{Direct labor cost} = \$10X$$
$$\text{Power cost} = \$5,000 + \$4X$$
$$\text{Setup cost} = \$100,000$$

Amy: I think I see the problem. Power costs don't have a lot to do with direct labor hours. They have more to do with machine hours. As production increases, machine hours increase more rapidly than direct labor hours. Also,. . .

Gary: You know, you have a point. The coefficient of determination for power cost is only about 50 percent. That leaves a lot of unexplained cost variation. The coefficient for labor, however, is much better—it explains about 96 percent of the cost variation. Setup costs, of course, are fixed.

Amy: Well, as I was about to say, setup costs also have very little to do with direct labor hours. And I might add that they certainly are not fixed—at least not all of them. We had to do more setups than our original plan called for because of the scheduling changes. And we have to pay our people when they work extra hours. It seems like we are always paying overtime. I wonder if we simply do not have enough people for the setup activity. Also, there are supplies that are used for each setup, and these are not cheap. Did you build these extra costs of increased setup activity into your budget?

Gary: No, we assumed that setup costs were fixed. I see now that some of them could vary as the number of setups increases. Amy, let me see if I can develop some cost formulas based on better explanatory variables. I'll get back to you in a few days.

Assume that after a few days' work, Gary developed the following cost formulas, all with a coefficient of determination greater than 90 percent:

$$\text{Direct labor cost} = \$10X, \text{ where } X = \text{Direct labor hours}$$
$$\text{Power cost} = \$68,000 + 0.9Y, \text{ where } Y = \text{Machine hours}$$
$$\text{Setup cost} = \$98,000 + \$400Z, \text{ where } Z = \text{Number of setups}$$

The actual measure of each activity driver is as follows:

Direct labor hours	20,000
Machine hours	90,000
Number of setups	110

Required:

1. Prepare a performance report for direct labor, power, and setups using the direct labor-based formulas.
2. Prepare a performance report for direct labor, power, and setups using the multiple cost driver formulas that Gary developed.

3. Of the two approaches, which provides the more accurate picture of Amy's performance? Why?

Problem 10-7 *Activity Flexible Budgeting*

 OBJECTIVE 4

Billy Adams, controller for Westcott, Inc., prepared the following budget for manufacturing costs at two different levels of activity for 2007:

DIRECT LABOR HOURS

	Level of Activity	
	50,000	100,000
Direct materials	$ 300,000	$ 600,000
Direct labor	200,000	400,000
Depreciation (plant)	100,000	100,000
Subtotal	$ 600,000	$1,100,000

MACHINE HOURS

	Level of Activity	
	200,000	300,000
Maintaining equipment	$ 360,000	$ 510,000
Machining	112,000	162,000
Subtotal	$ 472,000	$ 672,000

MATERIAL MOVES

	Level of Activity	
	20,000	40,000
Materials handling	$ 165,000	$ 290,000

NUMBER OF BATCHES INSPECTED

	Level of Activity	
	100	200
Inspecting products	$ 125,000	$ 225,000
Total	$1,362,000	$2,287,000

During 2007, Westcott employees worked a total of 80,000 direct labor hours, used 250,000 machine hours, made 32,000 moves, and performed 120 batch inspections. The following actual costs were incurred:

Direct materials	$440,000
Direct labor	355,000
Depreciation	100,000
Maintenance	425,000
Machining	142,000
Materials handling	232,500
Inspecting products	160,000

Westcott applies overhead using rates based on direct labor hours, machine hours, number of moves, and number of batches. The second level of activity (the far right column in the preceding table) is the practical level of activity (the available activity for resources acquired in advance of usage) and is used to compute predetermined overhead pool rates.

Required:

1. Prepare a performance report for Westcott's manufacturing costs in 2007.
2. Assume that one of the products produced by Westcott is budgeted to use 10,000 direct labor hours, 15,000 machine hours, and 500 moves and will be produced in five batches. A total of 10,000 units will be produced during the year. Calculate the budgeted unit manufacturing cost.
3. One of Westcott's managers said the following: "Budgeting at the activity level makes a lot of sense. It really helps us manage costs better. But the above

budget really needs to provide more detailed information. For example, I know that the materials handling activity involves the usage of forklifts and operators, and this information is lost with simply reporting the total cost of the activity for various levels of output. We have four forklifts, each capable of providing 10,000 moves per year. We lease these forklifts for five years, at $10,000 per year. Furthermore, for our two shifts, we need up to eight operators if we run all four forklifts. Each operator is paid a salary of $30,000 per year. Also, I know that fuel costs us about $0.25 per move."

Based on these comments, explain how this additional information may help Westcott better manage its costs. Also, assuming that these are the only three items, expand the detail of the flexible budget for materials handling to reveal the cost of these three resource items for 20,000 moves and 40,000 moves, respectively. You may wish to review the concepts of flexible, committed, and discretionary resources found in Chapter 3.

Problem 10-8 *Flexible Budgeting*

 At the beginning of last year, Jean Bingham, controller for Thorpe, Inc., prepared the following budget for conversion costs at two levels of activity for the coming year:

| | Direct Labor Hours | |
	100,000	120,000
Direct labor	$1,000,000	$1,200,000
Supervision	180,000	180,000
Utilities	18,000	21,000
Depreciation	225,000	225,000
Supplies	25,000	30,000
Maintenance	240,000	284,000
Rent	120,000	120,000
Other	60,000	70,000
Total manufacturing cost	$1,868,000	$2,130,000

During the year, the company worked a total of 112,000 direct labor hours and incurred the following actual costs:

Direct labor	$963,200
Supervision	190,000
Utilities	20,500
Depreciation	225,000
Supplies	24,640
Maintenance	237,000
Rent	120,000
Other	60,500

Thorpe applied overhead on the basis of direct labor hours. Normal volume of 120,000 direct labor hours is the activity level to be used to compute the predetermined overhead rate.

Required:

1. Determine the cost formula for each of Thorpe's conversion costs. (Hint: Use the high-low method.)
2. Prepare a performance report for Thorpe's conversion costs for last year. Should any cost item be given special attention? Explain.

Problem 10-9 *Overhead Application, Overhead Variances*

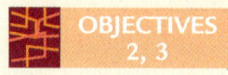 Tavera Company uses a standard cost system. The direct labor standard indicates that six direct labor hours should be used for every unit produced. Tavera produces one

product. The normal production volume is 120,000 units of this product. The budgeted overhead for the coming year is as follows:

Fixed overhead	$2,160,000*
Variable overhead	1,440,000

*At normal volume.

Tavera applies overhead on the basis of direct labor hours.

During the year, Tavera produced 119,000 units, worked 731,850 direct labor hours, and incurred actual fixed overhead costs of $2.25 million and actual variable overhead costs of $1.425 million.

Required:
1. Calculate the standard fixed overhead rate and the standard variable overhead rate.
2. Compute the applied fixed overhead and the applied variable overhead. What is the total fixed overhead variance? Total variable overhead variance?
3. Break down the total fixed overhead variance into a spending variance and a volume variance. Discuss the significance of each.
4. Compute the variable overhead spending and efficiency variances. Discuss the significance of each.

5. Journal entries for overhead variances were not discussed in the chapter. Typically, the overhead variance entries happen at the end of the year. Assume that applied fixed (variable) overhead is accumulated on the credit side of the fixed (variable overhead) control account. Actual fixed (variable) overhead costs are accumulated on the debit side of the respective control accounts. At the end of the year, the balance in each control account is the total (fixed) variable variance. Create accounts for each of the four overhead variances and close out the total variances to each of these four variance accounts. These four variance accounts are then usually disposed of by closing them to Cost of Goods Sold. Form groups of three to five and prepare the journal entries that isolate the four variances. Finally, prepare the journal entries that close these variances to Cost of Goods Sold.

Problem 10-10 *Overhead Variance Analysis*

OBJECTIVES
2, 3

Spreadsheet

The Lubbock plant of Morril's Small Motor Division produces a major subassembly for a 6.0 horsepower motor for lawn mowers. The plant uses a standard costing system for production costing and control. The standard cost sheet for the subassembly follows:

Direct materials (6.0 lbs. @ $5.00)	$30.00
Direct labor (1.6 hrs. @ $12.00)	19.20
Variable overhead (1.6 hrs. @ $10.00)	16.00
Fixed overhead (1.6 hrs. @ $6.00)	9.60
Standard unit cost	$74.80

During the year, the Lubbock plant had the following actual production activity:

a. Production of motors totaled 50,000 units.
b. The company used 82,000 direct labor hours at a total cost of $1,066,000.
c. Actual fixed overhead totaled $556,000.
d. Actual variable overhead totaled $860,000.

The Lubbock plant's practical activity is 60,000 units per year. Standard overhead rates are computed based on practical activity measured in standard direct labor hours.

Required:
1. Compute the variable overhead spending and efficiency variances.
2. Compute the fixed overhead spending and volume variances. Interpret the volume variance. What can be done to reduce this variance?

Problem 10-11 *Fixed Overhead Spending and Volume Variances, Capacity Management*

Lorale Company, a producer of recreational vehicles, recently decided to begin producing a major subassembly for jet skis. The subassembly would be used by Lorale's jet ski plants and also would be sold to other producers. The decision was made to lease two large buildings in two different locations: Little Rock, Arkansas, and Athens, Georgia. The company agreed to a 10-year, renewable lease contract. The plants were of the same size, and each had 10 production lines. New equipment was purchased for each line and workers hired to operate the equipment. The company also hired production line supervisors for each plant. A supervisor is capable of directing up to two production lines per shift. Two shifts are run for each plant. The practical production capacity of each plant was 300,000 subassemblies per year. Two standard direct labor hours are allowed for each subassembly. The costs for leasing, equipment depreciation, and supervision for a single plant are as follows (the costs are assumed to be the same for each plant):

Supervision (10 supervisors @ $50,000)	$ 500,000
Building lease (annual payment)	800,000
Equipment depreciation (annual)	1,100,000
Total fixed overhead costs*	$2,400,000

*For simplicity, assume these are the only fixed overhead costs.

After beginning operations, Lorale discovered that demand for the product in the region covered by the Little Rock plant was less than anticipated. At the end of the first year, only 240,000 units were sold. The Athens plant sold 300,000 units as expected. The actual fixed overhead costs at the end of the first year were $2,500,000 (for each plant).

Required:
1. Calculate a fixed overhead rate based on standard direct labor hours.
2. Calculate the fixed overhead spending and volume variances for the Little Rock and Athens plants. What is the most likely cause of the spending variance? Why are the volume variances different for the two plants?

3. Suppose that from now on the sales for the Little Rock plant are expected to be no more than 240,000 units. What actions would you take to manage the capacity costs (fixed overhead costs)?
4. Calculate the fixed overhead cost per subassembly for each plant. Do they differ? Should they differ? Explain. Do activity-based costing concepts help in analyzing this issue?

Problem 10-12 *Incomplete Data, Overhead Analysis*

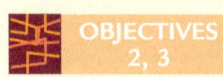

Lynwood Company produces surge protectors. To help control costs, Lynwood employs a standard costing system and uses a flexible budget to predict overhead costs at various levels of activity. For the most recent year, Lynwood used a standard overhead rate of $18 per direct labor hour. The rate was computed using practical activity. Budgeted overhead costs are $396,000 for 18,000 direct labor hours and $540,000 for 30,000 direct labor hours. During the past year, Lynwood generated the following data:

a. Actual production: 100,000 units
b. Fixed overhead volume variance: $20,000 U
c. Variable overhead efficiency variance: $18,000 F
d. Actual fixed overhead costs: $200,000
e. Actual variable overhead costs: $310,000

Required:
1. Calculate the fixed overhead rate.
2. Determine the fixed overhead spending variance.
3. Determine the variable overhead spending variance.
4. Determine the standard hours allowed per unit of product.

Problem 10-13 *Flexible Budget, Overhead Variances*

Shumaker Company manufactures a line of high-top basketball shoes. At the beginning of the year, the following plans for production and costs were revealed:

Pairs of shoes to be produced and sold	55,000
Standard cost per unit:	
Direct materials	$15
Direct labor	12
Variable overhead	6
Fixed overhead	3
Total unit cost	$36

During the year, a total of 50,000 units were produced and sold. The following actual costs were incurred:

Direct materials	$775,000
Direct labor	590,000
Variable overhead	310,000
Fixed overhead	180,000

There were no beginning or ending inventories of raw materials. In producing the 50,000 units, 63,000 hours were worked, 5 percent more hours than the standard allowed for the actual output. Overhead costs are applied to production using direct labor hours.

Required:
1. Using a flexible budget, prepare a performance report comparing expected costs for the actual production with actual costs.
2. Determine the following:
    a. Fixed overhead spending and volume variances.
    b. Variable overhead spending and efficiency variances.

PERFORMANCE EVALUATION, VARIABLE COSTING, AND DECENTRALIZATION

© TOM STEWART/CORBIS

After studying Chapter 11, you should be able to:

1. Explain how and why firms choose to decentralize.
2. Explain the difference between absorption and variable costing. Prepare segmented income statements.
3. Compute and explain return on investment (ROI).
4. Compute and explain residual income and economic value added (EVA).
5. Explain the role of transfer pricing in a decentralized firm.
6. (Appendix) Explain the uses of the Balanced Scorecard and compute cycle time, velocity, and manufacturing cycle efficiency (MCE).

Geoff Maslow was concerned. He had long been interested in software development, particularly music and video players. After several years of developing software programs on his own and with several college friends, he created his own firm, Galactic-Media, Inc., or GMI. Geoff was president and CEO, and a college friend, Luz Pacheco, served as chief financial officer and COO. Luz handled day-to-day operations and Geoff dealt with outside sales and product development. Over a 4-year period, GMI grew rapidly as its bread and butter program, an integrated music/video player, was adopted by college students and young professionals across the country. Employment stood at 250, with departmental managers in sales, player software design, content interface, and streaming media. The growing size of the company meant that Geoff and Luz could no longer keep hands-on control of the departments. This bothered them, so one sunny morning Geoff and Luz went out for coffee to discuss the future direction of the company.

Luz: Geoff, I'm concerned. Our latest quarterly financials show operating income is flat. Meanwhile, our capital spending is increasing. I'm afraid we're stalling.

Geoff: I know what you mean about the income being flat, but we need to buy the latest hardware. It's crucial to stay on top of the competition. After all, it takes money to make money.

Luz: It also takes increasing expenses and flat sales to go out of business. Besides, sometimes I think our developers have lost the big picture—new hardware is only valuable when it's materially different from the old—when it can do things we need to do better. You understand that. Some of the newbies don't—they think new hardware is some kind of perk.

Geoff: You may be right about that, but we can't spend all our time reviewing every capital spending request. How can we get our people to have the same vision that we do? A healthy net income is critically important to the survival of this company. I know some of them think that any extra income just fattens my wallet.

Luz: (laughing) Hey, mine too! Seriously, though, maybe we need to restructure the incentive schemes around here. It may be time to start decentralizing the company. Look, we're both being run ragged by trying to control everything and being in charge of all aspects of the company. I can't control production, online delivery, and software development by myself. And don't get me started on the move into India and the European Union. You can't be spending most of each day in sales meetings with record and movie companies and still have time and energy left to work on strategy and R&D.

Geoff: You are so right about that, besides, I really want to do more with animation. *Toy Story* was great in its time, same with *Finding Nemo*. Ragmar and I have been fiddling around with some new types of animation—if this takes off—we'll be the next Pixar!

Luz: That is just the strategic thinking I was talking about! Now let's get you some help. I'll look into ways of changing the corporate structure. Give me a couple of days.

[Two days later, same shop, more coffee.]

Luz: I talked with Carla Verdugo, a friend of mine at MediaGiant. She's head of their movie distribution division. Carla runs the division and is evaluated on the basis of both operating income and ROI. She said it has really started her thinking like an owner of the business instead of an employee.

Geoff: OK, I give up. What's ROI?

Luz: It's short for return on investment. You get it by dividing income by capital investment. It's your rate of return—similar to an interest rate. If we divide GMI into divisions, evaluate each division on the basis of ROI, and reward the new managers appropriately, I think our capital spending problem will solve itself.

Geoff: I see what you mean! Some capital spending is good; too much is bad. The division managers will work harder to be sure that the spending they OK is spending that will increase creativity *and* income! I like it!

DECENTRALIZATION AND RESPONSIBILITY CENTERS

OBJECTIVE 1

Explain how and why firms choose to decentralize.

In general, a company is organized along lines of responsibility. The traditional organizational chart, with its pyramid shape, illustrates the lines of responsibility flowing from the CEO down through the vice presidents to middle- and lower-level managers. As the Opening Scenario indicates, as organizations grow larger, these lines of responsibility become longer and more numerous. The structure becomes cumbersome. Contemporary practice is moving toward a flattened hierarchy. This structure—emphasizing teams—is consistent with decentralization. GE Capital, for example, is essentially a group of smaller businesses. A strong link exists between the structure of an organization and its responsibility accounting system. Ideally, the responsibility accounting system mirrors and supports the structure of an organization.

Firms with multiple responsibility centers usually choose one of two decision-making approaches to manage their diverse and complex activities: *centralized* or *decentralized*. In centralized decision making, decisions are made at the very top level, and lower-level managers are charged with implementing these decisions. On the other hand, decentralized decision making allows managers at lower levels to make and implement key decisions pertaining to their areas of responsibility. **Decentralization** is the practice of delegating decision-making authority to the lower levels of management in a company. Exhibit 11-1 illustrates the difference between centralized and decentralized companies.

Organizations range from highly centralized to strongly decentralized. Most firms fall somewhere in between, with the majority tending toward decentralization. The reasons for the popularity of decentralization and the ways in which a company may choose to decentralize are discussed next.

Reasons for Decentralization

Firms decide to decentralize for several reasons, including (1) ease of gathering and using local information; (2) focusing of central management; (3) training and motivating of segment managers; and (4) enhanced competition, exposing segments to market forces.

Gathering and Using Local Information

The quality of decisions is affected by the quality of information available. As a firm grows in size and operates in different markets and regions, central management may not understand local conditions. Lower-level managers, however, are in contact with immediate operating conditions (such as the strength and nature of local competition, the nature of the local labor force, and so on). As a result, they are often better positioned to make local decisions. For example, McDonald's has restaurants around the world. The tastes of people in China or France differ from those of people in the United States. So, McDonald's tailors its menu to different countries. The

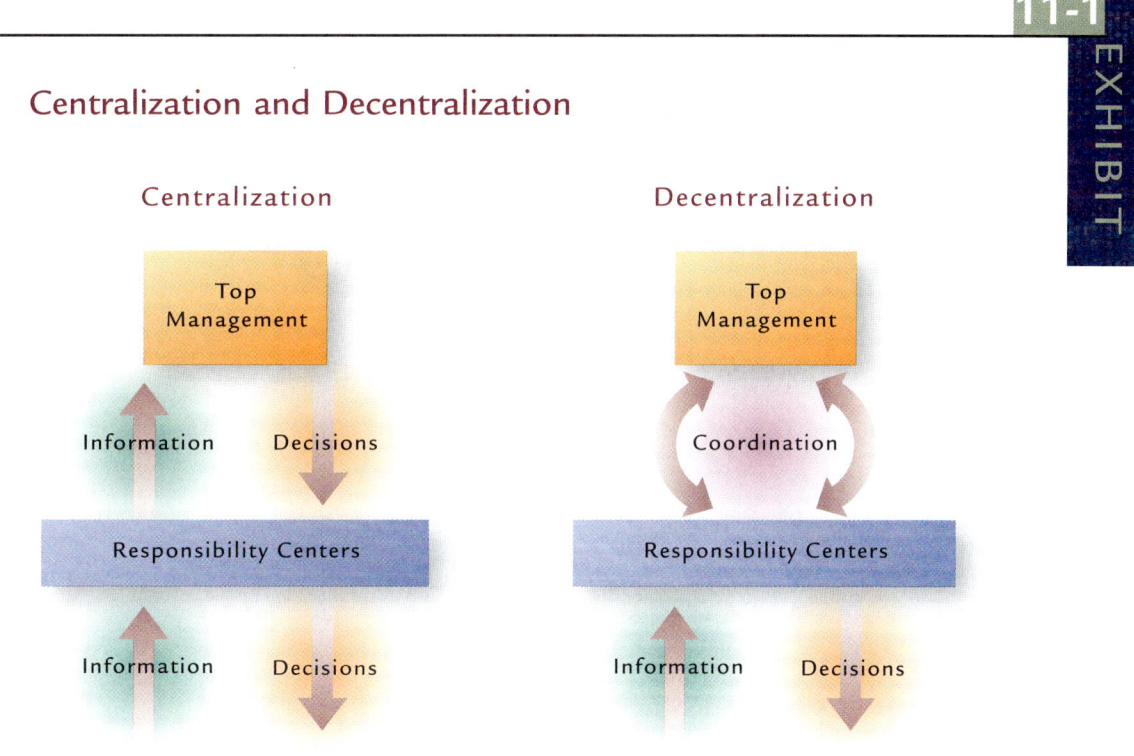

Centralization and Decentralization

result is that the McDonald's in each country can differentiate to meet the needs of its local market.

Focusing of Central Management

By decentralizing the operating decisions, central management is free to engage in strategic planning and decision making. The long-run survival of the organization should be of more importance to central management than day-to-day operations.

Training and Motivating of Managers

Organizations always need well-trained managers to replace higher-level managers who leave to take advantage of other opportunities. What better way to prepare a future generation of higher-level managers than by providing them the opportunity to make significant decisions? These opportunities also enable top managers to evaluate local managers' capabilities. Those who make the best decisions are the ones who can be promoted.

Enhanced Competition

In a highly centralized company, overall profit margins can mask inefficiencies within the various subdivisions. Large companies now find that they cannot afford to keep a noncompetitive division. One of the best ways to improve performance of a division or factory is to expose it more fully to market forces. At Koch Industries, Inc., each unit is expected to act as an autonomous business unit and set prices both externally and internally. Units whose services are not required by other Koch units will die on the vine.

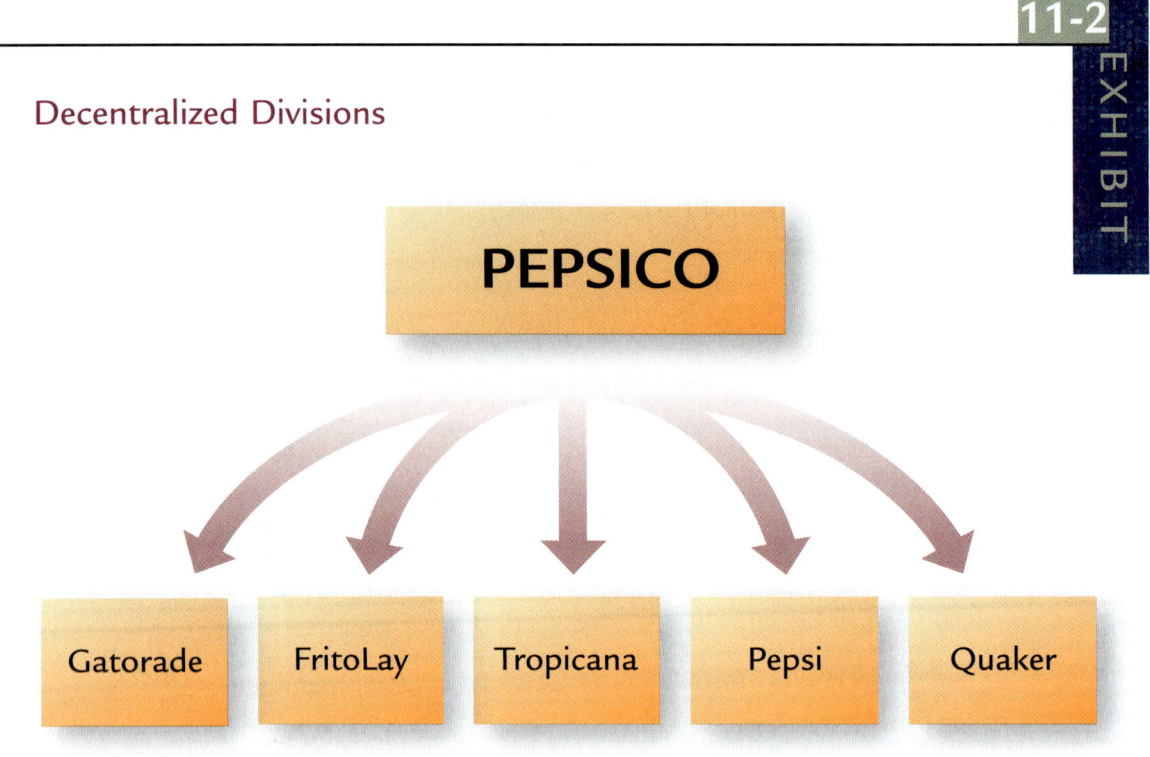

Decentralized Divisions

Divisions in the Decentralized Firm

Decentralization is usually achieved by creating units called *divisions*. One way in which divisions are differentiated is by the types of goods or services produced. For example, divisions of PepsiCo include the Snack Ventures Europe Division (a joint venture with General Mills), Frito-Lay, Inc., and Tropicana, as well as its flagship soft-drink division. Exhibit 11-2 shows decentralized divisions of Pepsico. These divisions are organized on the basis of product lines. Notice that some divisions depend on other divisions. For example, PepsiCo spun off its restaurant divisions to YUM. As a result, the cola you drink at Pizza Hut, Taco Bell, and KFC will be Pepsi—not Coke. In a decentralized setting, some interdependencies usually exist; otherwise, a company would merely be a collection of totally separate entities.

Divisions may also be created along geographic lines. For example, UAL, Inc. (parent of United Airlines) has a number of regional divisions: Asia/Pacific, Caribbean, European, Latin American, and North American. The presence of divisions spanning one or more regions creates the need for performance evaluation that can take into account differences in divisional environments.

A third way divisions differ is by the type of responsibility given to the divisional manager. As a firm grows, top management typically creates areas of responsibility, known as responsibility centers, and assigns subordinate managers to those areas. A **responsibility center** is a segment of the business

Concept Q & A

Think about summer jobs you and your friends have held. To what extent did you or your friends work in a centralized or decentralized decision-making environment?

Answer:
If you worked at a Taco Bell or Pizza Hut, you were working for a decentralized company, YUM. This company owns many Taco Bells and Pizza Huts. Some decision making is pushed down to lower-level managers. On the other hand, suppose you worked for a small local law or accounting firm, which has only the local office. Then you were working for a centralized company, and the owner probably made all important operating and strategic decisions.

whose manager is accountable for specified sets of activities. The results of each responsibility center can be measured according to the information managers need to operate their centers. The four major types of responsibility centers are as follows:

1. **Cost center**: A responsibility center in which a manager is responsible only for costs.
2. **Revenue center**: A responsibility center in which a manager is responsible only for sales.
3. **Profit center**: A responsibility center in which a manager is responsible for both revenues and costs.
4. **Investment center**: A responsibility center in which a manager is responsible for revenues, costs, and investments.

The way that responsibility centers are assigned mirrors the actual situation and the type of information available to the manager. Information is the key to appropriately holding managers responsible for outcomes. For example, a production department manager is held responsible for departmental costs but not for sales. This is because the production department manager not only directly controls some of these costs but also knows and understands them. Any difference between actual and expected costs can best be explained at this level. Exhibit 11-3 displays these centers along with the type of information they need to manage their operations. Investment centers represent the greatest degree of decentralization (followed by profit centers and finally by cost and revenue centers) because their managers have the freedom to make the greatest variety of decisions.

A production department within the factory, such as assembly or finishing, is an example of a cost center. The supervisor of a production department controls manufacturing costs but does not set a price or make marketing decisions. Therefore, the production department supervisor is evaluated on the basis of how well costs are controlled.

The marketing department manager sets the price and projected sales. Therefore, the marketing department may be evaluated as a revenue center. Direct costs of the marketing department and overall sales are the responsibility of the sales manager.

In some companies, plant managers are given the responsibility for manufacturing and marketing their products. These plant managers control both costs and revenues, putting them in control of a profit center. Operating income would be an important performance measure for profit center managers.

11-3

EXHIBIT

Types of Responsibility Centers and Accounting Information Used to Measure Performance

	Cost	Sales	Capital Investment	Other
Cost center	X			
Revenue center		X		
Profit center	X	X		
Investment center	X	X	X	X

APPLICATIONS IN BUSINESS

Manufacturing companies are not the only companies that decentralize and measure performance. Service industries also break down performance by area of business. For example, the Texas Rangers baseball team, based in Arlington, Texas, implicitly recognizes spring training as a profit center. The Rangers moved their spring training to Surprise, a suburb of Phoenix, Arizona, for the 2003 training season. That first year in Arizona, the club earned a $300,000 profit. This compares to the roughly $700,000 lost in Port Charlotte, Florida, the previous year.

What, in addition to the weather, are the benefits of training in small desert towns? Surprise invested in a $48 million spring training complex to lure the Texas Rangers and the Kansas City Royals. The complex has a 10,500-seat stadium and 12 practice diamonds.

Fans travel from across the United States and beyond to spend weeks following their favorite teams in spring training. Local communities, like Surprise, invest in state-of-the-art facilities. Tickets and concessions are major revenue sources. Less directly, increased hotel and rental car taxes fill city coffers.

Source: Mark Hyman, "If You Build It, They Will Train," *Business Week* (March 24, 2003): 77.

Finally, divisions are often cited as examples of investment centers. In addition to having control over cost and pricing decisions, divisional managers have the power to make investment decisions, such as plant closings and openings, and decisions to keep or drop a product line. As a result, both operating income and some type of return on investment are important performance measures for investment center managers.

It is important to realize that while the responsibility center manager has responsibility for only the activities of that center, decisions made by that manager can affect other responsibility centers. For example, the sales force at a floor care products firm routinely offers customers price discounts at the end of the month. Sales increase dramatically, which is good for revenue and the sales force. However, the factory is forced to institute overtime shifts to keep up with demand; this increases the costs of the factory as well as the cost per unit of product.

Organizing divisions as responsibility centers creates the opportunity to control the divisions through the use of responsibility accounting. Revenue center control is achieved by evaluating the efficiency and the effectiveness of divisional managers on the basis of sales revenue. Cost center control is based on control of costs and frequently employs variance analysis as described in Chapters 9 and 10. This chapter will focus on the evaluation of profit centers and investment centers.

MEASURING THE PERFORMANCE OF PROFIT CENTERS USING VARIABLE AND ABSORPTION INCOME STATEMENTS

Profit centers are evaluated based on income statements. However, the overall income statement for the company would be of little use for this purpose. Instead, it is important to develop a segmented income statement for each profit center. Two methods of computing income have been developed, one based on variable costing and the other based on full or absorption costing. These are costing methods because they refer to the way in which product costs are determined. Recall that *product costs* are inventoried; they include direct materials, direct labor, and overhead. *Period costs*, such as selling and administrative expense, are expensed in the period incurred. The difference between variable and absorption costing hinges on the treatment of one particular cost: fixed factory overhead.

OBJECTIVE 2

Explain the difference between absorption and variable costing. Prepare segmented income statements.

Variable costing stresses the difference between fixed and variable manufacturing costs. **Variable costing** assigns only variable manufacturing costs to the product; these costs include direct materials, direct labor, and variable overhead. Fixed overhead is treated as a period expense and is excluded from the product cost. The rationale for this is that fixed overhead is a cost of capacity, or staying in business. Once the period is over, any benefits provided by capacity have expired and should not be inventoried. Under variable costing, fixed overhead of a period is seen as expiring that period and is charged in total against the revenues of the period.

Absorption costing assigns *all* manufacturing costs to the product. Direct materials, direct labor, variable overhead, and fixed overhead define the cost of a product. Thus, under absorption costing, fixed overhead is viewed as a product cost, not a period cost. Under this method, fixed overhead is assigned to the product through the use of a predetermined fixed overhead rate and is not expensed until the product is sold. In other words, fixed overhead is an inventoriable cost. Exhibit 11-4 illustrates the classification of costs as product or period costs under absorption and variable costing.

Generally accepted accounting principles (GAAP) require absorption costing for external reporting. The Financial Accounting Standards Board (FASB), the Internal Revenue Service (IRS), and other regulatory bodies do not accept variable costing as a product-costing method for external reporting. Yet, variable costing can supply vital cost information for decision making and control, information not supplied by absorption costing. For *internal* application, variable costing is an invaluable managerial tool.

Inventory Valuation

Inventory is valued at product or manufacturing cost. Under absorption costing, that product cost includes direct materials, direct labor, variable overhead, and fixed overhead. Under variable costing, the product cost includes only direct materials, direct labor, and variable overhead. Cornerstone 11-1 shows how to compute inventory cost under both methods.

11-4 EXHIBIT

Classification of Costs as Product or Period Costs Under Absorption and Variable Costing

	Absorption Costing	**Variable Costing**
Product costs	Direct materials	Direct materials
	Direct labor	Direct labor
	Variable overhead	Variable overhead
	Fixed overhead	
Period costs	Selling expenses	Fixed overhead
	Administrative expenses	Selling expenses
		Administrative expenses

Cornerstone 11-1

HOW TO Compute Inventory Cost Under Absorption and Variable Costing

Information: During the most recent year, Fairchild Company had the following data associated with the product it makes:

Units in beginning inventory	—
Units produced	10,000
Units sold ($300 per unit)	8,000
Variable costs per unit:	
Direct materials	$ 50
Direct labor	100
Variable overhead	50
Fixed costs:	
Fixed overhead per unit produced	25
Fixed selling and administrative	100,000

Required:

1. How many units are in ending inventory?
2. Using absorption costing, calculate the per-unit product cost. What is the value of ending inventory?
3. Using variable costing, calculate the per-unit product cost. What is the value of ending inventory?

Calculation:

1. Units ending inventory = Units beginning inventory + Units produced − Units sold
   = 0 + 10,000 − 8,000
   = 2,000

2. Absorption costing:

Direct materials	$ 50
Direct labor	100
Variable overhead	50
Fixed overhead	25
Unit product cost	$225

   Value of ending inventory = 2,000 × $225 = $450,000

3. Variable costing:

Direct materials	$ 50
Direct labor	100
Variable overhead	50
Unit product cost	$200

   Value of ending inventory = 2,000 × $200 = $400,000

Notice that the only difference between the two approaches is the treatment of fixed factory overhead. Thus, the unit product cost under absorption costing is always greater than the unit product cost under variable costing.

Income Statements Using Variable and Absorption Costing

Because unit product costs are the basis for cost of goods sold, the variable- and absorption-costing methods can lead to different operating income figures. The difference arises because of the amount of fixed overhead recognized as an expense under the two methods. Cornerstone 11-2 shows how to develop cost of goods sold and income statements for both variable and absorption costing.

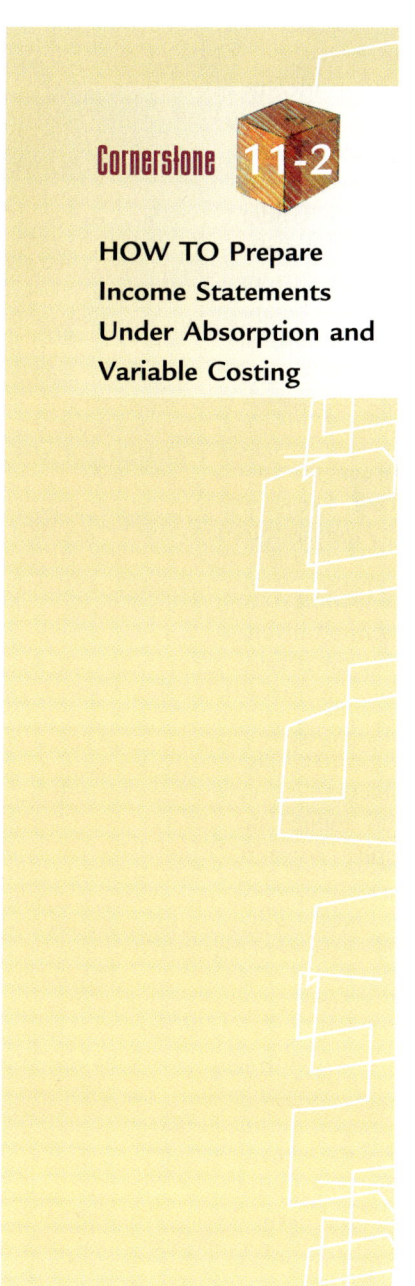

Cornerstone 11-2

HOW TO Prepare Income Statements Under Absorption and Variable Costing

Information: During the most recent year, Fairchild Company had the following data associated with the product it makes:

Units in beginning inventory	—
Units produced	10,000
Units sold ($300 per unit)	8,000

Variable costs per unit:	
Direct materials	$ 50
Direct labor	100
Variable overhead	50

Fixed costs:	
Fixed overhead per unit produced	25
Fixed selling and administrative	100,000

Required:

1. Calculate the cost of goods sold under absorption costing.
2. Calculate the cost of goods sold under variable costing.
3. Prepare an income statement using absorption costing.
4. Prepare an income statement using variable costing.

Calculation:

1. Cost of goods sold = Absorption unit product cost $\times$ Units sold
   = $225 $\times$ 8,000 = $1,800,000
2. Cost of goods sold = Variable unit product cost $\times$ Units sold
   = $200 $\times$ 8,000 = $1,600,000

3.
Fairchild Company
Absorption-Costing Income Statement

Sales ($300 $\times$ 8,000)		$2,400,000
Less: Cost of goods sold		1,800,000
Gross margin		$ 600,000
Less: Selling and administrative expenses		100,000
Net income		$ 500,000

4.
Fairchild Company
Variable-Costing Income Statement

Sales ($300 $\times$ 8,000)		$2,400,000
Less variable expenses:		
Variable cost of goods sold		1,600,000
Contribution margin		$ 800,000
Less fixed expenses:		
Fixed overhead	$250,000	
Fixed selling and administrative	100,000	350,000
Net income		$ 450,000

Cornerstone 11-2 demonstrates that absorption-costing income is $50,000 higher than variable-costing income. This difference is due to some of the period's fixed overhead flowing into inventory when absorption costing is used. This occurred because less fixed overhead cost flowed into the absorption-costing cost of goods sold. In fact, only $200,000 ($25 $\times$ 8,000) of fixed overhead was included in cost of goods sold for absorption costing; the remaining $50,000 ($25 $\times$ 2,000) was added to inventory. Under variable costing, however, all of the $250,000 of fixed overhead cost for the period was added to expense on the income statement.

Notice that selling and administrative expenses are never included in product cost. They are always expensed on the income statement and never appear on the balance sheet.

Production, Sales, and Income Relationships

The relationship between variable-costing income and absorption-costing income changes as the relationship between production and sales changes. If more is sold than was produced, variable-costing income is greater than absorption-costing income. This situation is just the opposite of that for the Fairchild example. Selling more than was produced means that beginning inventory and units produced are being sold. Under absorption costing, units coming out of inventory have attached to them fixed overhead from a prior period. In addition, units produced and sold have all of the current period's fixed overhead attached. Thus, the amount of fixed overhead expensed by absorption costing is greater than the current period's fixed overhead by the amount of fixed overhead flowing out of inventory. Accordingly, variable-costing income is greater than absorption-costing income by the amount of fixed overhead flowing out of beginning inventory.

If production and sales are equal, of course, no difference exists between the two reported incomes. Since the units produced are all sold, absorption costing, like variable costing, will recognize the total fixed overhead of the period as an expense. No fixed overhead flows into or out of inventory.

The relationships between production, sales, and the two reported incomes are summarized in Exhibit 11-5. Note that if production is greater than sales, then inventory has increased. If production is less than sales, then inventory must have decreased. If production is equal to sales, then beginning inventory is equal to ending inventory.

The difference between absorption and variable costing centers on the recognition of expense associated with fixed factory overhead. Under absorption costing, fixed factory overhead must be assigned to units produced. This presents two problems that we have not explicitly considered. First, how do we convert factory overhead applied on the basis of direct labor hours or machine hours into factory overhead applied to units produced? Second, what is done when actual factory overhead does not equal applied factory overhead? The solution to these problems is reserved for a more advanced accounting course.

Evaluating Profit-Center Managers

The evaluation of managers is often tied to the profitability of the units they control. How income changes from one period to the next and how actual income compares to planned income are frequently used as signals of managerial ability. To be meaningful signals, however, income should reflect managerial effort. For example, if a manager has worked hard and increased sales while holding costs in check, income should increase over the prior period, signaling success. In general terms, if income perfor-

Production, Sales, and Income Relationships

	If	Then
1.	Production > Sales	Absorption net income > Variable net income
2.	Production < Sales	Absorption net income < Variable net income
3.	Production = Sales	Absorption net income = Variable net income

EXHIBIT 11-5

mance is expected to reflect managerial performance, then managers have the right to expect the following:

1. As sales revenue increases from one period to the next, all other things being equal, income should increase.
2. As sales revenue decreases from one period to the next, all other things being equal, income should decrease.
3. As sales revenue remains unchanged from one period to the next, all other things being equal, income should remain unchanged.

Variable costing does ensure that the above relationships hold, however, absorption costing may not.

Segmented Income Statements Using Variable Costing

Variable costing is useful in preparing segmented income statements because it gives useful information on variable and fixed expenses. A **segment** is a subunit of a company of sufficient importance to warrant the production of performance reports. Segments can be divisions, departments, product lines, customer classes, and so on. In segmented income statements, however, fixed expenses are broken down into two categories: *direct fixed expenses* and *common fixed expenses*. This additional subdivision highlights controllable versus noncontrollable costs and enhances the manager's ability to evaluate each segment's contribution to overall firm performance.

Direct fixed expenses are fixed expenses that are directly traceable to a segment. These are sometimes referred to as *avoidable fixed expenses* or *traceable fixed expenses* because they vanish if the segment is eliminated. For example, if the segments were sales regions, a direct fixed expense for each region would be the rent for the sales office, salary of the sales manager of each region, and so on. If one region were to be eliminated, then those fixed expenses would disappear.

Common fixed expenses are jointly caused by two or more segments. These expenses persist even if one of the segments to which they are common is eliminated. For example, depreciation on the corporate headquarters building, the salary of the CEO, and the cost of printing and distributing the annual report to shareholders are common fixed expenses for Walt Disney Company. If Walt Disney Company were to sell a theme park or open a new one, then those common expenses would not be affected.

Cornerstone 11-3 shows how to prepare a segmented income statement where the segments are product lines. In the example, Audiomatronics produces both MP3 players and DVD players.

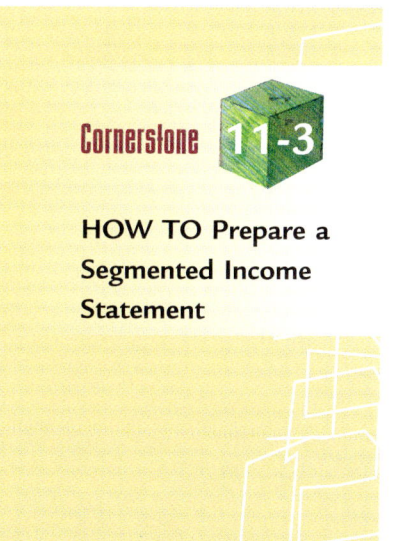

Cornerstone 11-3

HOW TO Prepare a Segmented Income Statement

Information: Audiomatronics, Inc., produces MP3 players and DVD players in a single factory. The following information was provided for the coming year.

	MP3 Players	DVD Players
Sales	$400,000	$290,000
Variable cost of goods sold	200,000	150,000
Direct fixed overhead	30,000	20,000

A sales commission of 5 percent of sales is paid for each of the two product lines. Direct fixed selling and administrative expense was estimated to be $10,000 for the MP3 line and $15,000 for the DVD line.

Common fixed overhead for the factory was estimated to be $100,000; common selling and administrative expense was estimated to be $20,000.

Required: Prepare a segmented income statement for Audiomatronics, Inc., for the coming year, using variable costing.

Calculation:

Audiomatronics, Inc.
Segmented Income Statement
For the Coming Year

	MP3 Players	DVD Players	Total
Sales	$400,000	$290,000	$690,000
Variable cost of goods sold	(200,000)	(150,000)	(350,000)
Variable selling expense	(20,000)	(14,500)	(34,500)
Contribution margin	$180,000	$125,500	$305,500
Less direct fixed expenses:			
Direct fixed overhead	(30,000)	(20,000)	(50,000)
Direct selling and administrative	(10,000)	(15,000)	(25,000)
Segment margin	$140,000	$ 90,500	$230,500
Less common fixed expenses:			
Common fixed overhead			(100,000)
Common selling and administrative			(20,000)
Net income			$110,500

Notice that Cornerstone 11-3 shows that both MP3 players and DVD players have large positive contribution margins ($180,000 for MP3 players and $125,500 for DVD players). Both products are providing revenue above variable costs that can be used to help cover the firm's fixed costs. However, some of the firm's fixed costs are caused by the segments themselves. Thus, the real measure of the profit contribution of each segment is what is left over after these direct fixed costs are covered.

The profit contribution each segment makes toward covering a firm's common fixed costs is called the **segment margin**. A segment should at least be able to cover both its own variable costs and direct fixed costs. A negative segment margin drags down the firm's total profit, making it time to consider dropping the product. Ignoring any effect a segment may have on the sales of other segments, the segment margin measures the change in a firm's profits that would occur if the segment were eliminated.

MEASURING THE PERFORMANCE OF INVESTMENT CENTERS USING ROI

Typically, investment centers are evaluated on the basis of return on investment. Other measures, such as residual income and economic value added, are discussed in the following section.

Return on Investment

Divisions that are investment centers will have an income statement and a balance sheet. So, could those divisions be ranked on the basis of net income? Suppose, for example, that a company has two divisions—Alpha and Beta. Alpha's net income is $100,000, and Beta's is $200,000. Did Beta perform better than Alpha? What if Alpha used an investment of $500,000 to produce the contribution of $100,000, while Beta used an investment of $2 million to produce the $200,000 contribution? Does your response change? Clearly, relating the reported operating profits to the assets used to produce them is a more meaningful measure of performance.

One way to relate operating profits to assets employed is to compute the **return on investment (ROI)**, which is the profit earned per dollar of investment. ROI is the most common measure of performance for an investment center. It can be defined as follows:

$$\text{ROI} = \text{Operating income/Average operating assets}$$

Operating income refers to earnings before interest and taxes. **Operating assets** are all assets acquired to generate operating income, including cash, receivables, inventories, land, buildings, and equipment. The figure for average operating assets is computed as follows:

$$\text{Average operating assets} = (\text{Beginning net book value} + \text{Ending net book value})/2$$

Opinions vary regarding how long-term assets (plant and equipment) should be valued (for example, gross book value versus net book value or historical cost versus current cost). Most firms use historical cost and net book value.[1]

Going back to our example, Alpha's ROI is 0.20 ($100,000/$500,000), while Beta's ROI is only 0.10 ($200,000/$2,000,000). The formula for ROI is quick and easy to use. However, the decomposition of ROI into margin and turnover ratios gives additional information. Cornerstone 11-4 shows how to calculate these ratios.

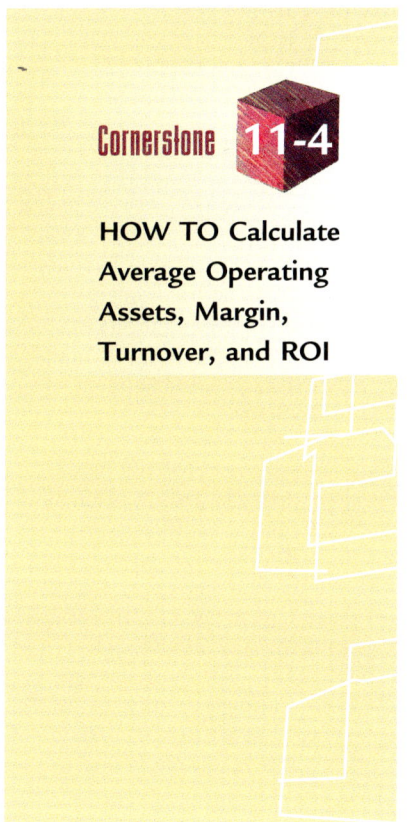

Cornerstone 11-4

HOW TO Calculate Average Operating Assets, Margin, Turnover, and ROI

Information: Celimar Company's Western Division earned operating income last year as shown in the following income statement:

Sales	$480,000
Cost of goods sold	222,000
Gross margin	$258,000
Selling and administrative expense	210,000
Operating income	$ 48,000

At the beginning of the year, the net book value of operating assets was $277,000. At the end of the year, the net book value of operating assets was $323,000.

Required: For the Western Division, calculate:
1. Average operating assets.
2. Margin.
3. Turnover.
4. Return on investment.

Calculation:
1. Average operating assets = (Beginning assets + Ending assets)/2
   = ($277,000 + $323,000)/2
   = $300,000
2. Margin = Operating income/Sales = $48,000/$480,000 = 0.10, or 10 percent
3. Turnover = Sales/Average operating assets = $480,000/$300,000 = 1.6
4. ROI = Margin × Turnover = 0.10 × 1.6 = 0.16, or 16 percent

Alternatively,

ROI = Operating income/Average operating assets
   = $48,000/$300,000
   = 0.16, or 16 percent

Margin and Turnover

A second way to calculate ROI is to separate the formula (Operating income/Average operating assets) into margin and turnover.

[1]There is no one correct way to calculate ROI. The important thing is to be sure that one method is applied consistently over time. This allows the company to compare the ROIs among divisions and over time.

$$\text{ROI} = \overset{\textbf{Margin}}{\frac{\text{Operating income}}{\text{Sales}}} \times \overset{\textbf{Turnover}}{\frac{\text{Sales}}{\text{Average operating assets}}}$$

Notice that "Sales" in the above formula can be cancelled out to yield the original ROI formula of Operating income/Average operating assets.

Margin is the ratio of operating income to sales. It tells how many cents of operating income result from each dollar of sales; it expresses the portion of sales that is available for interest, taxes, and profit. **Turnover** is a different measure; it is found by dividing sales by average operating assets. Turnover tells how many dollars of sales result from every dollar invested in operating assets; it shows how productively assets are being used to generate sales.

Suppose, for example, that Alpha had sales of $400,000. Then, margin would be 0.25 ($100,000/$400,000), and turnover would be 0.80 ($400,000/$500,000). Alpha's ROI would still be 0.20 (0.25 × 0.80).

While both approaches yield the same ROI, the calculation of margin and turnover gives a manager valuable information. To illustrate this additional information, consider the data presented in Exhibit 11-6. The Electronics Division improved its ROI from 18 percent in year 1 to 20 percent in year 2. The Medical Supplies Division's ROI, however, dropped from 18 to 15 percent. Computing the margin and turnover ratios for each division gives a better picture of what caused the change in rates. These ratios are also presented in Exhibit 11-6.

Notice that the margins for both divisions dropped from year 1 to year 2. In fact, the divisions experienced the *same* percentage of decline (16.67 percent). A declining margin could be explained by increasing expenses, by competitive pressures (forcing a decrease in selling prices), or both.

In spite of the declining margin, the Electronics Division was able to increase its rate of return. The reason is that the increase in turnover more than compensated for the decline in margin. One explanation for the increased turnover could be a deliberate policy to reduce inventories. (Notice that the average assets employed remained the same for the Electronics Division even though sales increased by $10 million.)

The experience of the Medical Supplies Division was less favorable. Because its turnover rate remained unchanged, its ROI dropped. This division, unlike the Electronics Division, could not overcome the decline in margin.

Concept Q & A

Think about some stores in your town, such as a jewelry store, fast-food outlet, or grocery store. How do you suppose their margins and turnover ratios compare to each other? Explain your thinking.

Answer:
Fast-food outlets and groceries probably have low margins and high turnover. This is because they deal in perishables and must have continual turnover, or the food will go bad. A jewelry store, on the other hand, has high margin and relatively low turnover. This is because the goods are not perishable and there is relatively less competition in this market. (The existence of competition, of course, changes as more jewelry stores enter a market and as consumers become more confident about buying jewelry online.)

Advantages of ROI

At least three positive results stem from the use of ROI:

1. It encourages managers to focus on the relationship among sales, expenses, and investment, as should be the case for a manager of an investment center.
2. It encourages managers to focus on cost efficiency.
3. It encourages managers to focus on operating asset efficiency.

These advantages are illustrated by the following three scenarios.

Comparison of Divisional Performance

	Comparison of ROI	
	Electronics Division	Medical Supplies Division
Year 1:		
Sales	$30,000,000	$117,000,000
Operating income	1,800,000	3,510,000
Average operating assets	10,000,000	19,510,000
ROI[a]	18%	18%
Year 2:		
Sales	$40,000,000	$117,000,000
Operating income	2,000,000	2,925,000
Average operating assets	10,000,000	19,500,000
ROI[a]	20%	15%

	Margin and Turnover Comparisons			
	Electronics Division		Medical Supplies Division	
	Year 1	Year 2	Year 1	Year 2
Margin[b]	6.0%	5.0%	3.0%	2.5%
Turnover[c]	× 3.0	× 4.0	× 6.0	× 6.0
ROI	18.0%	20.0%	18.0%	15.0%

[a]Operating income divided by average operating assets.
[b]Operating income divided by sales.
[c]Sales divided by average operating assets.

Focus on ROI Relationships

Della Barnes, manager of the Plastics Division, is mulling over a suggestion from her marketing vice president to increase the advertising budget by $100,000. The marketing vice president is confident that this increase will boost sales by $200,000. Della realizes that the increased sales will also raise expenses. She finds that the increased variable cost will be $80,000. The division will also need to purchase additional machinery to handle the increased production. The equipment will cost $50,000 and will add $10,000 of depreciation expense. As a result, the proposal will add $10,000 ($200,000 − $80,000 − $10,000 − $100,000) to operating income. Currently, the division has sales of $2 million, total expenses of $1,850,000, and net operating income of $150,000. Operating assets equal $1 million.

	Without Increased Advertising	With Increased Advertising
Sales	$2,000,000	$2,200,000
Less: Expenses	1,850,000	2,040,000
Operating income	$ 150,000	$ 160,000
Operating assets	$1,000,000	$1,050,000

ROI:

$150,000/$1,000,000 = 0.15, or 15 percent

$160,000/$1,050,000 = 0.1524, or 15.24 percent

The ROI without the additional advertising is 15 percent; the ROI with the additional advertising and $50,000 investment in assets is 15.24 percent. Since ROI is increased by the proposal, Della decides to authorize the increased advertising. In effect, the current ROI, without the proposal, is the "hurdle rate." This term is frequently used to indicate the minimum ROI necessary to accept an investment.

Focus on Cost Efficiency

Kyle Chugg, manager of Turner's Battery Division, groaned as he reviewed the projections for the last half of the current fiscal year. The recession was hurting his division's performance. Adding the projected operating income of $200,000 to the actual operating income of the first half produced expected annual earnings of $425,000. Kyle then divided the expected operating income by the division's average operating assets to obtain an expected ROI of 12.15 percent. "This is awful," muttered Kyle. "Last year our ROI was 16 percent. And I'm looking at a couple more bad years before business returns to normal. Something has to be done to improve our performance."

Kyle directed all operating managers to identify and eliminate nonvalue-added activities. As a result, lower-level managers found ways to reduce costs by $150,000 for the remaining half of the year. This reduction increased the annual operating income from $425,000 to $575,000, increasing ROI from 12.15 percent to 16.43 percent as a result. Interestingly, Kyle found that some of the reductions could be maintained after business returned to normal.

Focus on Operating Asset Efficiency

The Electronic Storage Division prospered during its early years. In the beginning, the division developed portable external disk drives for storing data; sales and return on investment were extraordinarily high. However, during the past several years, competitors had developed competing technology, and the division's ROI had plunged from 30 to 15 percent. Cost cutting had helped initially, but the fat had all been removed, making further improvements from cost reductions impossible. Moreover, any increase in sales was unlikely—competition was too stiff. The divisional manager searched for some way to increase the ROI by at least 3 to 5 percent. Only by raising the ROI so that it compared favorably to that of the other divisions could the division expect to receive additional capital for research and development.

The divisional manager initiated an intensive program to reduce operating assets. Most of the gains were made in the area of inventory reductions; however, one plant was closed because of a long-term reduction in market share. By installing a just-in-time purchasing and manufacturing system, the division was able to reduce its asset base without threatening its remaining market share. Finally, the reduction in operating assets meant that operating costs could be decreased still further. The end result was a 50-percent increase in the division's ROI, from 15 percent to more than 22 percent.

Disadvantages of the ROI Measure

Overemphasis on ROI can produce myopic behavior. Two negative aspects associated with ROI are frequently mentioned:

1. It can produce a narrow focus on divisional profitability at the expense of profitability for the overall firm.
2. It encourages managers to focus on the short run at the expense of the long run.

These disadvantages are illustrated by the following two scenarios:

Narrow Focus on Divisional Profitability

A Cleaning Products Division has the opportunity to invest in two projects for the coming year. The outlay required for each investment, the dollar returns, and the ROI are as follows:

	Project I	**Project II**
Investment	$10,000,000	$4,000,000
Operating income	1,300,000	640,000
ROI	13%	16%

The division currently earns ROI of 15 percent, with operating assets of $50 million and operating income on current investments of $7.5 million. The division has approval to request up to $15 million in new investment capital. Corporate headquarters requires that all investments earn at least 10 percent (this rate represents the corporation's cost of acquiring the capital). Any capital not used by a division is invested by headquarters, and it earns exactly 10 percent.

The divisional manager has four alternatives: (1) invest in Project I, (2) invest in Project II, (3) invest in both Projects I and II, or (4) invest in neither project. The divisional ROI was computed for each alternative.

	Alternatives			
	Select Project I	**Select Project II**	**Select Both Projects**	**Select Neither Project**
Operating income	$8,800,000	$8,140,000	$9,440,000	$7,500,000
Operating assets	$60,000,000	$54,000,000	$64,000,000	$50,000,000
ROI	14.67%	15.07%	14.75%	15.00%

The divisional manager chose to invest only in Project II, since it would boost ROI from 15.00 percent to 15.07 percent.

While the manager's choice maximized divisional ROI, it actually cost the company profit. If Project I had been selected, the company would have earned $1.3 million. By not selecting Project I, the $10 million in capital is invested at 10 percent, earning only $1 million (0.10 × $10,000,000). The single-minded focus on divisional ROI, then, cost the company $300,000 in profits ($1,300,000 − $1,000,000).

Encourages Short-Run Optimization

Ruth Lunsford, manager of a Small Tools Division, was displeased with her division's performance during the first three quarters. Given the expected income for the fourth quarter, the ROI for the year would be 13 percent, at least two percentage points below where she had hoped to be. Such an ROI might not be strong enough to justify the early promotion she wanted. With only three months left, drastic action was needed. Increasing sales for the last quarter was unlikely. Most sales were booked at least two to three months in advance. Emphasizing extra sales activity would benefit next year's performance. What was needed were some ways to improve this year's performance.

After careful thought, Ruth decided to take the following actions:

1. Lay off five of the highest paid salespeople.
2. Cut the advertising budget for the fourth quarter by 50 percent.

3. Delay all promotions within the division for three months.
4. Reduce the preventive maintenance budget by 75 percent.
5. Use cheaper raw materials for fourth-quarter production.

In the aggregate, these steps would reduce expenses, increase income, and raise the ROI to about 15.2 percent.

While Ruth's actions increase the profits and ROI in the short run, they have some long-run negative consequences. Laying off the highest paid (and possibly the best) salespeople may harm the division's future sales-generating capabilities. Future sales could also be hurt by cutting back on advertising and using cheaper raw materials. Delaying promotions could hurt employee morale, which could, in turn, lower productivity and future sales. Finally, reducing preventive maintenance will likely increase downtime and decrease the life of the productive equipment.

MEASURING THE PERFORMANCE OF INVESTMENT CENTERS USING RESIDUAL INCOME AND ECONOMIC VALUE ADDED

To compensate for the tendency of ROI to discourage investments that are profitable for the company but that lower a division's ROI, some companies have adopted alternative performance measures such as residual income. Economic value added is an alternate way to calculate residual income and is being used in a number of companies.

OBJECTIVE 4

Compute and explain residual income and economic value added (EVA).

Residual Income

Residual income is the difference between operating income and the minimum dollar return required on a company's operating assets:

Residual income = Operating income −
(Minimum rate of return × Average operating assets)

Cornerstone 11-5 shows how to calculate residual income.

Cornerstone 11-5

HOW TO Calculate Residual Income

Information: Celimar Company's Western Division earned operating income last year as shown in the following income statement:

Sales	$480,000
Cost of goods sold	222,000
Gross margin	$258,000
Selling and administrative expense	210,000
Operating income	$ 48,000

At the beginning of the year, the net book value of operating assets was $277,000. At the end of the year, the net book value of operating assets was $323,000. Celimar Company requires a minimum rate of return of 12 percent.

Required: For the Western Division, calculate:
1. Average operating assets.
2. Residual income.

Calculation:
1. Average operating assets = (Beginning assets + Ending assets)/2
= ($277,000 + $323,000)/2
= $300,000
2. Residual income = Operating income − (Minimum rate of return × Average operating assets)
= $48,000 − (0.12 × $300,000)
= $48,000 − $36,000
= $12,000

The minimum rate of return is set by the company and is the same as the hurdle rate mentioned in the section on ROI. If residual income is greater than zero, then the division is earning more than the minimum required rate of return (or hurdle rate). If residual income is less than zero, then the division is earning less than the minimum required rate of return. Finally, if residual income is just equal to zero, then the division is earning precisely the minimum required rate of return.

Advantage of Residual Income

Recall that the manager of the Cleaning Products Division rejected Project I because it would have reduced divisional ROI; however, that decision cost the company $300,000 in profits. The use of residual income as the performance measure would have prevented this loss. The residual income for each project is computed as follows:

Project I
Residual income = Operating income − (Minimum rate of return × Average
                operating assets)
            = $1,300,000 − (0.10 × $10,000,000)
            = $1,300,000 − $1,000,000
            = $300,000

Project II
Residual income = $640,000 − (0.10 × $4,000,000)
            = $640,000 − $400,000
            = $240,000

Notice that both projects have positive residual income. For comparative purposes, the divisional residual income for each of the four alternatives identified follows:

	Alternatives			
	Select Only Project I	Select Only Project II	Select Both Projects	Select Neither Project
Operating assets	$60,000,000	$54,000,000	$64,000,000	$50,000,000
Operating income	$ 8,800,000	$ 8,140,000	$ 9,440,000	$ 7,500,000
Minimum return*	6,000,000	5,400,000	6,400,000	5,000,000
Residual income	$ 2,800,000	$ 2,740,000	$ 3,040,000	$ 2,500,000

*0.10 × Operating assets.

As shown above, selecting both projects produces the greatest increase in residual income. The use of residual income encourages managers to accept any project that earns above the minimum rate.

Disadvantages of Residual Income

Residual income, like ROI, can encourage a short-run orientation. If Ruth Lunsford were being evaluated on the basis of residual income, she could have taken the same actions.

Another problem with residual income is that, unlike ROI, it is an absolute measure of profitability. Thus, direct comparison of the performance of two different investment centers becomes difficult, since the level of investment may differ. For example, consider the residual income computations for Division A and Division B, where the minimum required rate of return is 8 percent.

	Division A	**Division B**
Average operating assets	$15,000,000	$2,500,000
Operating income	$ 1,500,000	$ 300,000
Minimum return[a]	(1,200,000)	(200,000)
Residual income	$ 300,000	$ 100,000
Residual return[b]	2%	4%

[a]0.08 × Operating assets.
[b]Residual income divided by operating assets.

It is tempting to claim that Division A is outperforming Division B since its residual income is three times higher. Notice, however, that Division A is considerably larger than Division B and has six times as many assets. One possible way to correct this disadvantage is to compute both return on investment and residual income and use both measures for performance evaluation. ROI could then be used for interdivisional comparisons.

Economic Value Added (EVA)

A specific way of calculating residual income is *economic value added*. **Economic value added (EVA)**[2] is net income (operating income minus taxes) minus the total annual cost of capital. Basically, EVA is residual income with the cost of capital equal to the actual cost of capital for the firm (as opposed to some minimum rate of return desired by the company for other reasons). It is said that if EVA is positive, then the company is creating wealth; if EVA is negative, then the company is destroying wealth. Consider the old saying, "It takes money to make money." EVA helps the company to determine whether the money it makes is more than the money it takes to make it. Over the long term, only those companies creating capital, or wealth, can survive.

As a form of residual income, EVA is a dollar figure, not a percentage rate of return. However, it does bear a resemblance to rates of return such as ROI because it links net income (return) to capital employed. The key feature of EVA is its emphasis on *after-tax* operating profit and the *actual* cost of capital. Residual income, on the other hand, uses a minimum expected rate of return. Investors like EVA because it relates profit to the amount of resources needed to achieve it. A number of companies have been evaluated on the basis of EVA. In 2003, for example, economic value added for General Electric was $5,983 million, for Wal-Mart Stores it was $2,928 million, and for Merck & Co. it was $3,872 million.[3] Among large companies showing negative EVA were IBM at ($8,032) million, Verizon Communications at ($5,612) million, and Disney Company at ($2,072) million. Smaller companies also differed in terms of their economic value added. Pixar's was positive at $31 million while Jetblue Airways Corp. came in with a $15 million.

Calculating EVA

EVA is after-tax operating income minus the dollar cost of capital employed. The dollar cost of capital employed is the actual percentage cost of capital[4] multiplied by the total capital employed. The equation for EVA is expressed as follows:

$$\text{EVA} = \text{After-tax operating income} - (\text{Actual percentage cost of capital} \times \text{Total capital employed})$$

Cornerstone 11-6 shows how to calculate EVA.

[2]EVA was developed by Stern Stewart & Company. More information can be found on the firm's Web site at **http://www.sternstewart.com/evaabout/whatis.php.**

[3]Stephen Taub, "MVPs of MVA," CFO Magazine (July 1, 2003). **http://www.cfo.com/article/1,5309,9854% 7C22%7CA%7C14%7C,00.html**

[4]The computation of a company's actual cost of capital is reserved for later accounting courses.

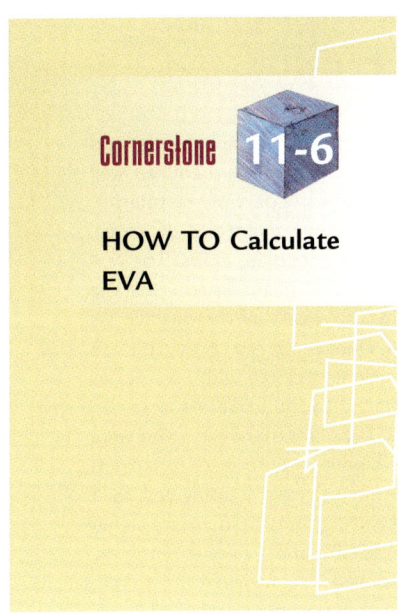

Cornerstone 11-6

HOW TO Calculate EVA

Information: Celimar Company's Western Division earned net income last year as shown in the following income statement:

Sales	$480,000
Cost of goods sold	222,000
Gross margin	$258,000
Selling and administrative expense	210,000
Operating income	$ 48,000
Less: Income taxes (@ 30%)	14,400
Net income	$ 33,600

Total capital employed equaled $300,000. Celimar Company's actual cost of capital is 10 percent.

Required: Calculate EVA for the Western Division.

Calculation:

EVA = After-tax operating income − (Actual percentage cost of capital × Total capital employed)

= $33,600 − (0.10 × $300,000)

= $33,600 − $30,000

= $3,600

Concept Q & A

What are the differences and similarities between the basic residual income calculation and EVA?

Answer:
Residual income can use either before-tax income (operating income) or after-tax income. In addition, residual income uses a minimum required rate of return set by upper management. EVA, on the other hand, uses after-tax income and requires the company to compute its actual cost of capital.

Behavioral Aspects of EVA

A number of companies have discovered that EVA helps to encourage the right kind of behavior from their divisions in a way that emphasis on operating income alone cannot. The underlying reason is EVA's reliance on the true cost of capital. In many companies, the responsibility for investment decisions rests with corporate management. As a result, the cost of capital is considered a corporate expense. If a division builds inventories and investment, the cost of financing that investment is passed along to the overall income statement and does not show up as a reduction from the division's operating income. The result is to make investment seem free to the divisions, and of course, they want more.

TRANSFER PRICING

OBJECTIVE 5

Explain the role of transfer pricing in a decentralized firm.

In many decentralized organizations, the output of one division is used as the input of another. This raises an accounting issue. How is the transferred good valued? When divisions are treated as responsibility centers, they are evaluated on the basis of operating income, return on investment, and residual income or EVA. As a result, the value of the transferred good is revenue to the selling division and cost to the buying division. This value, or internal price, is called the *transfer price*. In other words, a **transfer price** is the price charged for a component by the selling division to the buying division of

APPLICATIONS IN BUSINESS

© CORBIS SYGMA

Quaker Oats is a strong believer in the value of EVA. Prior to 1991, Quaker Oats evaluated its business segments on the basis of quarterly profits. In order to keep quarterly earnings on an upward march, segment managers offered sharp discounts on products at the end of each quarter. This resulted in huge orders from retailers and sharp surges in production at Quaker's plants at the end of each 3-month period. This practice is called *trade loading* because it "loads up the trade" (retail stores) with product. It is not inexpensive, however, because trade loading requires massive amounts of capital—e.g., working capital, inventories, and warehouses—to store the quarterly spikes in output. Quaker's plant in Danville, Illinois, produces snack foods and breakfast cereals. Before EVA, the Danville plant ran well below capacity throughout the early part of the quarter. Purchasing, however, bought huge quantities of boxes, plastic wrappers, granola, and chocolate chips. The raw materials purchases buildup was in anticipation of the production surge of the last six weeks of the quarter. As the products were finished, Quaker packed 15 warehouses with finished goods. All costs associated with inventories were absorbed by corporate headquarters. As a result, they appeared to be free to the plant managers, who were encouraged to build ever higher inventories. The advent of EVA and the cancellation of trade loading led to a smoothing of production throughout the quarter, higher overall production (and sales), and lower inventories. Quaker's Danville plant reduced inventories from $15 million to $9 million. Quaker has closed one-third of its 15 warehouses, saving $6 million annually in salaries and capital costs.

Source: Shawn Tully, "The Real Key to Creating Wealth," *Fortune* (September 20, 1993): 38–50.

the same company. Transfer pricing is a complex issue. The impact of transfer prices on divisions and the company as a whole, as well as methods of setting transfer prices, will be explored in the following sections.

Impact of Transfer Pricing on Divisions and the Firm as a Whole

When one division of a company sells to another division, both divisions as well as the company as a whole are affected. The price charged for the transferred good affects the costs of the buying division and the revenues of the selling division. Thus, the profits of both divisions, as well as the evaluation and compensation of their managers, are affected by the transfer price. Since profit-based performance measures of the two divisions are affected (for example, ROI and residual income), transfer pricing can often be a very emotionally charged issue. Exhibit 11-7 illustrates the effect of the transfer price on two divisions of ABC, Inc. Division A produces a component and sells it to another division of the same company, Division C. The $30 transfer price is revenue to Division A; clearly, Division A wants the price to be as high as possible. Conversely, the $30 transfer price is cost to Division C, just like the cost of any raw material. Division C prefers as low a transfer price as possible.

While the actual transfer price nets out for the company as a whole, transfer pricing can affect the level of profits earned by the multinational company through corporate income taxes and other legal requirements set by the countries in which the various divisions operate. For example, if the selling division operates in a low-tax country and the buying division operates in a high-tax country, the transfer price may be set quite high. Then, the profits would accrue to the division in the low-tax country and the cost would be assigned to the division in the high-tax country. This has the result of reducing overall corporate income taxes. The international transfer pricing situation is examined in detail in more advanced courses.

Impact of Transfer Price on Transferring Divisions and the Company, ABC, Inc., as a Whole

Division A	Division C
Produces component and transfers it to C for transfer price of $30 per unit	Purchases component from A at transfer price of $30 per unit and uses it in production of final product
Transfer price = $30 per unit	Transfer price = $30 per unit
Revenue to A	Cost to C
Increases net income	Decreases net income
Increases ROI	Decreases ROI

Note: Transfer price revenue = Transfer price cost; zero dollar impact on ABC, Inc.

Transfer Pricing Policies

Recall that a decentralized company allows much more authority for decision making at lower management levels. It would be counterproductive for the decentralized company to then decide on the actual transfer prices between two divisions. As a result, top management sets the transfer pricing policy, but the divisions still decide whether to transfer or not. For example, top management at Verybig, Inc., may set the corporate transfer pricing policy at full manufacturing cost. Then, if Mediumbig Division wants to transfer a product to Somewhatbig Division, the transfer price would be the product cost. However, neither division is forced to transfer the product internally. The transfer pricing policy only says that *if* the product is transferred, it must be at cost.

Several transfer pricing policies are used in practice. These transfer pricing policies include market price, cost-based transfer prices, and negotiated transfer prices.

Market Price

If there is a competitive outside market for the transferred product, then the best transfer price is the market price. In such a case, divisional managers' actions will simultaneously optimize divisional profits and firmwide profits. Furthermore, no division can benefit at the expense of another. In this setting, top management will not be tempted to intervene.

Suppose that the Furniture Division of a corporation produces hide-a-beds. The Mattress Division of that same corporation produces mattresses, including a mattress model that fits into the hide-a-bed. If mattresses are transferred from the Mattress division to the Furniture division, a transfer pricing opportunity exists. In this case, the Mattress Division is the selling division, and the Furniture Division is the buying division. Suppose that the mattresses can be sold to outside buyers at $50 each; this $50 is the market price. Clearly, the Mattress Division would not sell the mattresses to the Furniture Division for less than $50 each. Just as clearly, the Furniture Division would not pay more than $50 for the mattresses. The transfer price is easily set at the market price.

The market price, if available, is the best approach to transfer pricing. Since the selling division can sell all that it produces at the market price, transferring internally at a lower price would make the division worse off. Similarly, the buying division can always acquire the good at the market price, so it would be unwilling to pay more for an internally transferred good.

Will the two divisions transfer at the market price? It really does not matter, since the divisions and the company as a whole will be as well off whether or not the transfer takes place internally. However, if the transfer is to occur, it will be at the market price.

Cost-Based Transfer Prices

Frequently, there is no good outside market price. This may occur because the transferred product uses patented designs owned by the parent company. Then, a company may use a cost-based transfer pricing approach. For example, suppose that the mattress company uses a high-density foam padding in the hide-a-bed mattress and that outside companies do not produce this type of mattress in the appropriate size. If the company has set a cost-based transfer pricing policy, then the Mattress Division will charge the full cost of producing the mattress. (Recall that full cost includes the cost of direct materials, direct labor, variable overhead, and a portion of fixed overhead.) Suppose that the full cost of the mattress is as follows:

Direct materials	$15
Direct labor	5
Variable overhead	3
Fixed overhead	5
Full cost	$28

Now, the transfer price is $28 per mattress. This amount will be paid to the Mattress Division by the Furniture Division. Notice that this transfer price does not allow for any profit for the selling division (here, the Mattress Division). The Mattress Division may well try to scale back production of the hide-a-bed mattress and increase production of mattresses available for sale to outside parties. To reduce this desire, top management may define cost as "cost plus." In this case, suppose that the company allows transfer pricing at cost plus 10 percent. Then, the transfer price is $30.80 [$28 + (0.10 × $28)].

If the policy is cost-based transfer pricing, will the transfer take place? That depends. Suppose that the Furniture Division wants to purchase lower-quality mattresses in the external market for $25 each? Then no transfer will occur. Similarly, suppose that the Mattress Division is producing at capacity and can sell the special mattresses for $40 each. The Mattress Division will refuse to transfer any mattresses to the Furniture Division, and instead, will sell all it can produce to outside parties.

Negotiated Transfer Prices

Finally, top management may allow the selling and buying division managers to negotiate a transfer price. This approach is particularly useful in cases with market imperfections, such as the ability of an in-house division to avoid selling and distribution costs. Then, the cost saved can be shared by the two divisions.

Using the example of the Mattress and Furniture divisions, suppose that the hide-a-bed mattress typically sells for $50 and has full product cost of $28. Normally, a sales commission of $5 is paid to the salesperson, but that cost will not be incurred for any internal transfers. Now, a bargaining range exists. That range goes from the minimum transfer price to the maximum.

1. The minimum transfer price is the transfer price that would leave the selling division no worse off if the good were sold to an internal division than if the good

were sold to an external party. This is sometimes referred to as the "floor" of the bargaining range.

2. The maximum transfer price is the transfer price that would leave the buying division no worse off if an input were purchased from an internal division than if the same good were purchased externally. This is sometimes referred to as the "ceiling" of the bargaining range.

In the example, the minimum transfer price is $45 ($50 market price less the $5 selling commission that can be avoided on internal sales). The maximum transfer price is $50 (the outside market price that the Furniture Division would have to pay if the mattresses were bought externally). What is the actual transfer price? That depends on the negotiating skills of the Mattress and Furniture division managers. Any transfer price between $45 and $50 is possible. Cornerstone 11-7 shows how to calculate several types of transfer prices.

Cornerstone 11-7

HOW TO Calculate Transfer Prices

Information: Omni, Inc., has a number of divisions, including Alpha Division, producer of circuit boards, and Delta Division, a heating and air conditioning manufacturer.

Alpha Division produces the cb-117 model that can be used by Delta Division in the production of thermostats that regulate the heating and air conditioning systems. The market price of the cb-117 is $14, and the full cost of the board is $9.

Required:

1. If Omni, Inc., has a transfer pricing policy that requires transfer at full cost, what would the transfer price be? Do you suppose that Alpha and Delta divisions would choose to transfer at that price?

2. If Omni, Inc., has a transfer pricing policy that requires transfer at market price, what would the transfer price be? Do you suppose that Alpha and Delta divisions would choose to transfer at that price?

3. Now suppose that Omni, Inc., allows negotiated transfer pricing and that Alpha Division can avoid $3 of selling expense by selling to Delta Division. Which division sets the minimum transfer price, and what is it? Which division sets the maximum transfer price, and what is it? Do you suppose that Alpha and Delta divisions would choose to transfer somewhere in the bargaining range?

Calculation:

1. The full cost transfer price is $9. Delta Division would be delighted with that price, but Alpha Division would refuse to transfer since $14 could be earned in the outside market.

2. The market price is $14. Both Delta and Alpha divisions would be willing to transfer at that price (since neither division would be worse off than if it bought/sold in the outside market).

3. Minimum transfer price = $14 − $3 = $11
   This price is set by Alpha Division, the selling division.
   Maximum transfer price = $14
   This price is the market price and is set by Delta Division, the buying division.

   Yes, both divisions would be willing to accept a transfer price within the bargaining range. Precisely what the transfer price would be depends on the negotiating skills of the Alpha and Delta division managers.

HERE'S THE REAL KICKER

Kicker's top management is closely involved in all aspects of the company, from design and development, through production, sales, delivery, and after-market activities. Profit performance, as measured by periodic income statements, is an important measure. In addition, Kicker keeps track of a number of other measures of performance.

For example, financial information is very important. Financial statements are presented to the president and vice presidents every month. These are reviewed carefully for trends and are compared with the budgeted amounts. Worrisome increases in expenses or decreases in revenue are analyzed to see what the underlying factors might be. This leads to the next perspective.

Customer satisfaction is also continually measured. Kicker has two major types of customers—dealers who sell Kicker products and end users who have Kicker speakers installed in the car. Each customer type has specific needs. For example, dealers have the exclusive right to sell Kicker products. Theoretically, you must buy from a dealer to get a new set of speakers, amplifier, etc. Kicker offers a 1-year warranty on speakers sold through a dealer. However, end users want as low a price as possible. Speakers are available on the Internet, which are called "gray market" speakers (that is, the seller is not authorized to sell them). In the past, no warranty was available on nondealer-sold speakers. Problems arose when customers purchased obviously new products through the Internet, something went wrong, and they were not covered under warranty. It was very difficult to explain the no-warranty policy. Finally, Kicker decided to offer a shorter warranty for new products sold by unauthorized sellers. The objective of keeping the customer base happy and increasing satisfaction was achieved.

Kicker focuses on strategic objectives for the long term. For example, engineers in research and development take continuing education to stay current in their fields. When Kicker approached producing and selling original equipment manufacture (OEM) speakers to a major automobile maker, a number of employees had to learn ISO-quality concepts quickly. They took classes, met with consultants, and traveled to the site of other ISO-qualified firms to learn how to meet quality standards.

Over a 6-month period, Geoff and Luz developed clear-cut divisions that were evaluated as investment centers. A series of meetings were held with all staff to explain the importance of financial measures and the way in which they are computed. All division managers received bonuses based on meeting ROI and operating income goals. All full-time staff were made part of a profit-sharing plan once they had been employed at least six months.

A year later, Geoff and Luz met again to assess the changes. Of the four new centers, three had ROI of just over of 10 percent, and the fourth had ROI of 20 percent.

Geoff: I'm delighted with the changes taking place here. Slowly, it's become a better place to work—with more enthusiasm than I've seen in a long time!

Luz: I like the changes, too. It has made my job easier and more fun. With the division managers' attention focused on goals that are important to the overall company, we can devote our time to long-range planning and strategy. Looks like we're out of the doldrums and well into the black and headed for a terrific return on investment.

SUMMARY OF LEARNING OBJECTIVES

To increase overall efficiency, many companies choose to decentralize. The essence of decentralization is decision-making freedom. In a decentralized organization, lower-level managers make and implement decisions, whereas in a centralized organization, lower-level managers are responsible only for implementing decisions. Reasons for decentralization are numerous. Companies decentralize because local managers can make better decisions using local information. Local managers can also provide a more timely response to changing conditions. Additionally, decentralization for large, diversified companies is necessary because of cognitive limitations—it is impossible for any one central manager to be fully knowledgeable about all products and markets. Other reasons include training and motivating local managers and freeing top management from day-to-day operating conditions so that they can spend time on more long-range activities, such as strategic planning.

A decentralized company sets up responsibility centers. The four types of responsibility centers are cost centers, revenue centers, profit centers, and investment centers. The actual results for each responsibility center can be compared with expected results.

Variable and absorption costing differ in their treatment of fixed factory overhead. Variable costing treats fixed factory overhead as a period expense. Thus, unit production cost under variable costing consists of direct materials, direct labor, and variable factory overhead. Absorption costing treats fixed factory overhead as a product cost. Thus, unit production cost under absorption costing consists of direct materials, direct labor, variable factory overhead, and a share of fixed factory overhead.

A variable-costing income statement divides expenses according to cost behavior. First, variable expenses of manufacturing, marketing, and administration are subtracted from sales to yield the contribution margin. Then, all fixed expenses are subtracted from the contribution margin to yield variable-costing net income. An absorption-costing income statement divides expenses according to function. First, the cost of goods sold is subtracted from sales to yield gross profit (or gross margin). Then, selling and administrative expenses are subtracted from gross profit to yield absorption-costing net income. A segmented income statement allows management to properly evaluate each segment's contribution to overall firm performance.

ROI is the ratio of operating income to average operating assets. This ratio can be broken down into two components: margin (the ratio of operating income to sales) and turnover (the ratio of sales to average operating assets). Residual income is the difference between income and the minimum rate of return required by a company times the capital employed. EVA is very similar to residual income, but after-tax income and the actual percentage cost of capital are used in the computation.

Return on investment is the most common measure of performance for managers of decentralized units. Return on investment encourages managers to focus on improving their divisions' profitability by improving sales, controlling costs, and using assets efficiently. Unfortunately, the measure can also encourage managers to increase ROI by sacrificing the long run for short-run benefits (for example, encouraging managers to forego investments that are profitable for the firm but that would lower the divisional ROI).

Residual income is operating income minus some minimum percentage cost of capital times capital employed. Positive residual income means that the division is earning more than the minimum cost of capital. Negative residual income means that the division is earning less than the minimum cost of capital. Residual income precisely equal to zero indicates that the division is earning precisely the minimum cost of capital.

Economic value added is after-tax operating profit minus the total annual cost of capital. If EVA is positive, then the company is creating wealth. If it is negative, then the company is destroying capital. EVA is a dollar figure, not a percentage rate of return. The key feature of EVA is its emphasis on *after-tax* operating profit and the *actual* cost of capital. Investors like EVA because it relates profit to the amount of resources needed to achieve it.

Decentralized firms may encourage goal congruence by constructing management compensation programs that reward managers for taking actions that benefit the firm. Possible reward systems include cash compensation and noncash benefits.

When one division of a company produces a product that can be used in production by another division, transfer pricing exists. The transfer price is revenue to the selling division and cost to the buying division; thus, the price charged for the intermediate good affects the operating income of both divisions. Since both divisions are evaluated on their profitability, the price charged for the intermediate good can be a point of serious contention. Three transfer pricing policies are generally used: market price, cost-based transfer price, and negotiated transfer price.

KEY TERMS

APPENDIX: THE BALANCED SCORECARD: BASIC CONCEPTS

OBJECTIVE 6

Explain the uses of the Balanced Scorecard and compute cycle time, velocity, and manufacturing cycle efficiency (MCE).

Segment income, ROI, residual income, and EVA are important measures of managerial performance. As such, the temptation exists for managers to focus only on dollar figures. This focus may not tell the whole story for the company. In addition, lower-level managers and employees may feel helpless to affect net income or investment. As a result, nonfinancial operating measures have been developed. For example, top management could look at such factors as market share, customer complaints, personnel turnover ratios, and personnel development. By letting lower-level managers know that attention to long-run factors is also vital, the tendency to overemphasize financial measures is reduced.

Managers in an advanced manufacturing environment are especially likely to use multiple measures of performance and to include nonfinancial as well as financial measures. For example, in 2002, Robert Lutz, head of product development at General Motors, was evaluated on the basis of 12 criteria. These included how well he used existing parts in new vehicles and how many engineering hours he cut from the development process.[5]

The *Balanced Scorecard* is a strategic management system that defines a strategic-based responsibility accounting system. The **Balanced Scorecard** *translates* an organization's mission and strategy into operational objectives and performance measures for four different perspectives: the financial perspective, the customer perspective, the internal business process perspective, and the learning and growth (infrastructure) perspective. The **financial perspective** describes the economic consequences of actions

[5]David Welch and Kathleen Kerwin, "Rick Wagoner's Game Plan," *Business Week* (February 10, 2003): 52–60.

taken in the other three perspectives. The **customer perspective** defines the customer and market segments in which the business unit will compete. The **internal business process perspective** describes the internal processes needed to provide value for customers and owners. Finally, the **learning and growth (infrastructure) perspective** defines the capabilities that an organization needs to create long-term growth and improvement. This last perspective is concerned with three major *enabling factors*: employee capabilities, information systems capabilities, and employee attitudes (motivation, empowerment, and alignment).

Strategy Translation

Strategy, according to the creators of the Balanced Scorecard framework, is defined as:[6]

> . . . *choosing the market and customer segments the business unit intends to serve, identifying the critical internal and business processes that the unit must excel at to deliver the value propositions to customers in the targeted market segments, and selecting the individual and organizational capabilities required for the internal, customer, and financial objectives.*

Strategy specifies management's desired relationships among the four perspectives. *Strategy translation*, on the other hand, means specifying objectives, measures, targets, and initiatives for each perspective. Consider, for example, the financial perspective. For the financial perspective, a company's *objective* may be to grow revenues by introducing new products. The *performance measure* may be the percentage of revenues from the sale of new products. The *target* or *standard* for the coming year for the measure may be 20 percent (that is, 20 percent of the total revenues for the coming year must be from the sale of new products). The *initiative* describes *how* this is to be accomplished. The "how," of course, involves the other three perspectives. The company must now identify the customer segments, internal processes, and individual and organizational capabilities that will permit the realization of the revenue growth objective. This illustrates the fact that the financial objectives serve as the focus for the objectives, measures, and initiatives of the other three perspectives.

The Role of Performance Measures

The Balanced Scorecard is not simply a collection of critical performance measures. The performance measures are derived from a company's vision, strategy, and objectives. These measures must be *balanced* between outcome measures and lead measures (performance drivers), between objective and subjective measures, between external and internal measures, and between financial and nonfinancial measures. The performance measures must also be carefully *linked* to the organization's strategy. Doing so creates significant advantages for an organization. For example, each quarter, Analog Devices' senior managers gather to discuss Balanced Scorecard results for the various divisions. On one occasion, managers noted problems with their new-product ratios—used to measure the effectiveness of R&D spending. They quickly discovered that one division lagged in developing new products. The division's manager focused more on R&D by investing more money and exploring new market segments, new product sales, and marketing strategies. Analog Devices' corporate vice president for marketing, quality, and planning noted that they wouldn't have been able to catch the problem so early if they just looked at financials.[7] Other companies, such as Hilton Hotels Corporation, Verizon Communications, Duke University Children's Hospital, City of Charlotte, NatWest

---

[6]Robert S. Kaplan and David P. Norton, *The Balanced Scorecard* (Boston: Harvard Business School Press, 1996), p. 37.

[7]Joel Kurtzman, "Is Your Company Off Course: Now You Can Find Out Why," *Fortune* (February 17, 1997), **http://www.fortune.com/fortune/articles/0,15114,375247,00.html.**

Bancorp, and AT&T Canada LDS, have had similar success. The rapid and widespread adoption of this strategic management system is a strong testimonial of its worth.

Linking Performance Measures to Strategy

Balancing outcome measures with performance drivers is essential to linking with the organization's strategy. Performance drivers make things happen and are indicators of how the outcomes are going to be realized. Thus, they tend to be unique to a particular strategy. Outcome measures are also important because they reveal whether the strategy is being implemented successfully with the desired economic consequences. For example, if the number of defective products is decreased, does this produce a greater market share? Does this, in turn, produce more revenues and profits? These questions suggest that the most important principle of linkage is the usage of cause-and-effect relationships. In fact, a **testable strategy** can be defined as a set of linked objectives aimed at an overall goal. The testability of the strategy is achieved by restating the strategy into a set of cause-and-effect hypotheses that are expressed by a sequence of if-then statements.[8] Consider, for example, the following sequence of if-then statements that link quality training with increased profitability:

> *If design engineers receive quality training, then they can redesign products to reduce the number of defective units; if the number of defective units is reduced, then customer satisfaction will increase; if customer satisfaction increases, then market share will increase; if market share increases, then sales will increase; if sales increase, then profits will increase.*

Exhibit 11-8 illustrates the quality improvement strategy described by a sequence of if-then statements. First, notice how each of the four perspectives is linked through the cause-and-effect relationships hypothesized. The learning and growth perspective is present through the training dimension; the process perspective is represented by the redesign and manufacturing processes; the customer perspective is represented by customer satisfaction and market share; and, finally, the financial perspective is present because of revenues and profits. Second, viability of the strategy is testable. Strategic feedback is available that allows managers to test the reasonableness of the strategy. Hours of training, the number of products redesigned, the number of defective units, customer satisfaction, market share, revenues, and profits are all observable measures. Thus, the claimed relationships can be checked to see if the strategy produces the expected results. If not, it could be due to one of two causes: (1) implementation problems or (2) an invalid strategy. First, it is possible that key *performance drivers* such as training and redesign of products did not achieve their targeted levels (that is, fewer hours of training and fewer products redesigned than planned). In this case, the failure to produce the targeted *outcomes* for defects, customer satisfaction, market share, revenues, and profits could be merely an implementation problem. On the other hand, if the targeted levels of performance drivers were achieved and the expected outcomes did not materialize, then the problem could very well lie with the strategy itself. This is an example of *double-loop feedback*. **Double-loop feedback** occurs whenever managers receive information about both the *effectiveness* of strategy implementation as well as the *validity* of the assumptions underlying the strategy. In a functional-based responsibility accounting system, typically only *single-loop feedback* is provided. **Single-loop feedback** emphasizes only effectiveness of implementation. In single-loop feedback, actual results deviating from planned results are a signal to take corrective action so that the plan (strategy) can be executed as intended. The validity of the assumptions underlying the plan is usually not questioned.

---

[8]Robert S. Kaplan and David P. Norton, *The Balanced Scorecard*, p. 149. (Kaplan and Norton describe the sequence of if-then statements only as a strategy. Calling it a testable strategy distinguishes it from the earlier, more general definition offered, and, in our opinion, properly so.)

Testable Strategy Illustrated

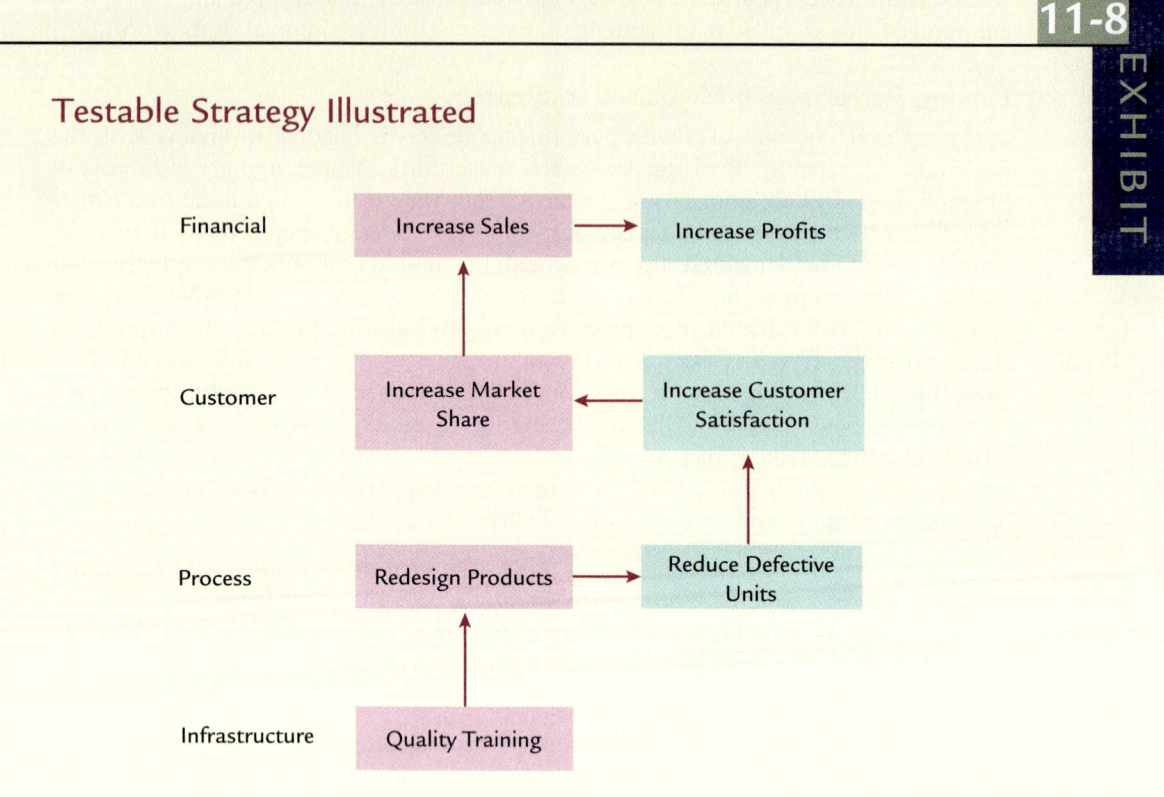

THE FOUR PERSPECTIVES AND PERFORMANCE MEASURES

The four perspectives define the strategy of an organization. Furthermore, the example of if-then statements illustrates that the four perspectives provide the structure or framework for developing an integrated, cohesive set of performance measures. These measures, once developed, become the means for articulating and communicating the strategy of the organization to its employees and managers. The measures also serve the purpose of aligning individual objectives and actions with organizational objectives and initiatives. Given the role the four perspectives play in development of performance measures, a more detailed examination of the perspectives is warranted.

The Financial Perspective

The financial perspective establishes the long- and short-term financial performance objectives. The financial perspective is concerned with the global financial consequences of the other three perspectives. Thus, the objectives and measures of the other perspectives must be linked to the financial objectives. The financial perspective has three strategic themes: revenue growth, cost reduction, and asset utilization. These themes serve as the building blocks for the development of specific operational objectives and measures.

Revenue Growth

Several possible objectives are associated with revenue growth, including to (1) increase the number of new products, (2) create new applications for existing products, (3) develop new customers and markets, and (4) adopt a new pricing strategy. Once operational objectives are known, performance measures can be designed. For example, possible measures for the above list of objectives (in the order given) are percentage of revenue from new products, percentage of revenue from new applications, percentage of revenue from new customers and market segments, and profitability by product or customer.

Cost Reduction

Reducing the cost per unit of product, per customer, or per distribution channel are examples of cost reduction objectives. The appropriate measure is obvious: the cost per unit of the particular cost object. Trends in this measure will tell whether the costs are being reduced or not. For these objectives, the accuracy of cost assignments is especially important. Activity-based costing can play an essential measurement role, especially for selling and administrative costs—costs not usually assigned to cost objects like customers and distribution channels.

Asset Utilization

Improving asset utilization is the principal objective. Financial measures such as return on investment and economic value added are used. The objectives and measures for the financial perspective are summarized in Exhibit 11-9.

Customer Perspective

The customer perspective is the source of the revenue component for the financial objectives. This perspective defines and selects the customer and market segments in which the company chooses to compete.

Core Objectives and Measures

Once the customers and segments are defined, then *core objectives and measures* are developed. **Core objectives and measures** are those that are common across all organizations. The five key core objectives are to (1) increase market share, (2) increase

11-9

EXHIBIT

Summary of Objectives and Measures: Financial Perspective

Objectives	Measures
Revenue Growth:	
Increase the number of new products	Percentage of revenue from new products
Create new applications	Percentage of revenue from new applications
Develop new customers and markets	Percentage of revenue from new sources
Adopt a new pricing strategy	Product and customer profitability
Cost Reduction:	
Reduce unit product cost	Unit product cost
Reduce unit customer cost	Unit customer cost
Reduce distribution channel cost	Cost per distribution channel
Asset Utilization:	
Improve asset utilization	Return on investment
	Economic value added

customer retention, (3) increase customer acquisition, (4) increase customer satisfaction, and (5) increase customer profitability. Possible core measures for these objectives, respectively, are market share (percentage of the market), percentage growth of business from existing customers and percentage of repeating customers, number of new customers, ratings from customer satisfaction surveys, and individual and segment profitability. Activity-based costing is a key tool in assessing customer profitability (see Chapter 7). Notice that customer profitability is the only financial measure among the core measures. This measure, however, is critical because it emphasizes the importance of the *right* kind of customers. What good is it to have customers if they are not profitable? The obvious answer spells out the difference between being customer focused and customer obsessed.

Customer Value

In addition to the core measures and objectives, measures are needed that drive the creation of *customer value* and, thus, drive the core outcomes. For example, increasing customer value builds customer loyalty (increases retention) and increases customer satisfaction. **Customer value** is the difference between realization and sacrifice, where realization is what the customer receives and sacrifice is what is given up in return. Realization includes such things as product functionality (features), product quality, reliability of delivery, delivery response time, image, and reputation. Sacrifice includes product price, time to learn to use the product, operating cost, maintenance cost, and disposal cost. The costs incurred by the customer *after* purchase are called **postpurchase costs**.

The attributes associated with the realization and sacrifice value propositions provide the basis for the objectives and measures that will lead to improving the core outcomes. The objectives for the sacrifice value proposition are the simplest: decrease price and decrease postpurchase costs. Selling price and postpurchase costs are important measures of value creation. Decreasing these costs decreases customer sacrifice and, thus, increases customer value. Increasing customer value should impact favorably on most of the core objectives. Similar favorable effects can be obtained by increasing realization. Realization objectives, for example, would include the following: improve product functionality, improve product quality, increase delivery reliability, and improve product image and reputation. Possible measures for these objectives include, respectively, feature satisfaction ratings, percentage of returns, on-time delivery percentage, and product recognition ratings. Of these objectives and measures, delivery reliability will be used to illustrate how measures can affect managerial behavior, indicating the need to be careful in the choice and use of performance measures.

Delivery reliability means that output is delivered on time. On-time delivery is a commonly used operational measure of reliability. To measure on-time delivery, a firm sets delivery dates and then calculates on-time delivery performance by dividing the orders delivered on time by the total number of orders delivered. The goal, of course, is to achieve a ratio of 100 percent. Some, however, have found that this measure used by itself may produce undesirable behavioral consequences.[9] Specifically, plant managers were giving priority to filling orders not yet late over orders that were already late. The performance measure was encouraging managers to have one very late shipment rather than several moderately late shipments! A chart measuring the age of late deliveries could help mitigate this problem. Exhibit 11-10 summarizes the objectives and measures for the customer perspective.

Process Perspective

Processes are the means for creating customer and shareholder value. Thus, the process perspective entails the identification of the processes needed to achieve the customer

---

[9]Joseph Fisher, "Nonfinancial Performance Measures," *Journal of Cost Management* (Spring 1992): 31–38.

and financial objectives. To provide the framework needed for this perspective, a *process value chain* is defined. The **process value chain** is made up of three processes: the *innovation process*, the *operations process*, and the *postsales service process*. The **innovation process** anticipates the emerging and potential needs of customers and creates new products and services to satisfy those needs. It represents what is called the *long-wave* of value creation. The **operations process** produces and delivers *existing* products and services to customers. It begins with a customer order and ends with the delivery of the product or service. It is the *short-wave* of value creation. The **postsales service process** provides critical and responsive services to customers after the product or service has been delivered.

Innovation Process: Objectives and Measures

Objectives for the innovation process include the following: (1) increase the number of new products, (2) increase percentage of revenue from proprietary products, and (3) decrease the time to develop new products. Associated measures are actual new products developed versus planned products, percentage of total revenues from new products, percentage of revenues from proprietary products, and development cycle time (time to market).

Operations Process: Objectives and Measures

The three operations process objectives that are almost always mentioned and emphasized include the following: (1) increase process quality, (2) increase process efficiency, and (3) decrease process time. Examples of process quality measures are quality costs, output yields (good output/good input), and percentage of defective units (good output/total output). Measures of process efficiency are concerned mainly with process cost and process productivity. Activity-based costing and process-value analysis facilitate measuring and tracking process costs. Common process time measures are cycle time, velocity, and manufacturing cycle effectiveness (MCE).

11-10

EXHIBIT

Summary of Objectives and Measures: Customer Perspective

Objectives	Measures
Core:	
Increase market share	Market share (percentage of market)
Increase customer retention	Percentage growth of business from existing customers
	Percentage of repeating customers
Increase customer acquisition	Number of new customers
Increase customer satisfaction	Ratings from customer surveys
Increase customer profitability	Customer profitability
Performance Value:	
Decrease price	Price
Decrease postpurchase costs	Postpurchase costs
Improve product functionality	Ratings from customer surveys
Improve product quality	Percentage of returns
Increase delivery reliability	On-time delivery percentage
	Aging schedule
Improve product image and reputation	Ratings from customer surveys

Cycle Time and Velocity

The time to respond to a customer order is referred to as *responsiveness. Cycle time* and *velocity* are two operational measures of responsiveness. **Cycle time** is the length of time it takes to produce a unit of output from the time raw materials are received (starting point of the cycle) until the good is delivered to finished goods inventory (finishing point of the cycle). Thus, cycle time is the time required to produce a product (time/units produced). **Velocity** is the number of units of output that can be produced in a given period of time (units produced/time). Cornerstone 11-8 shows how to compute cycle time and velocity.

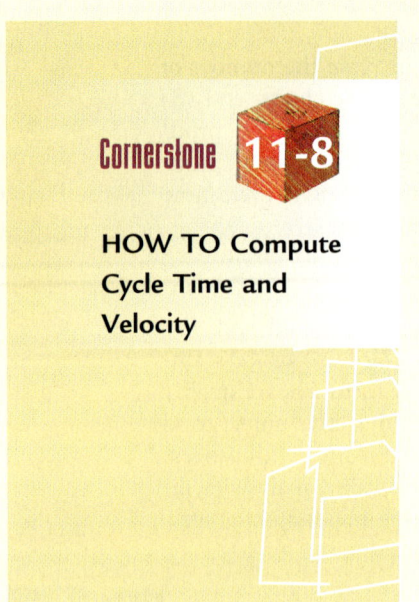

Cornerstone 11-8

HOW TO Compute Cycle Time and Velocity

Information: A company has the following data for one of its manufacturing cells:

Maximum units produced in a quarter (3-month period): 200,000 units
Actual units produced in a quarter (3-month period): 160,000 units
Productive hours in one quarter: 40,000 hours

Required:
1. Compute the theoretical cycle time (in minutes).
2. Compute the actual cycle time (in minutes).
3. Compute the theoretical velocity in units per hour.
4. Compute the actual velocity in units per hour.

Computation:
1. Theoretical cycle time = (40,000 hours)(60 minutes per hour)/200,000 units
                   = 12 minutes per unit
2. Actual cycle time = (40,000 hours)(60 per hour)/160,000 units
                   = 15 minutes per unit
3. Theoretical velocity = 60 minutes per hour/12 minutes per unit
                   = 5 units per hour
4. Actual velocity = 60 minutes per hour/15 minutes per unit
                   = 4 units per hour

Incentives can be used to encourage operational managers to reduce manufacturing cycle time or to increase velocity, thus improving delivery performance. A natural way to accomplish this objective is to tie product costs to cycle time and reward operational managers for reducing product costs. For example, in a JIT firm, conversion costs of the cell can be assigned to products on the basis of the time that it takes a product to move through the cell. Using the theoretical productive time available for a period (in minutes), a value-added standard cost per minute can be computed.

Standard cost per minute = Cell conversion costs/Minutes available

To obtain the conversion cost per unit, this standard cost per minute is multiplied by the actual cycle time used to produce the units during the period. By comparing the unit cost computed using the actual cycle time with the unit cost possible using the theoretical or optimal cycle time, a manager can assess the potential for improvement. Note that the more time it takes a product to move through the cell, the greater the unit product cost. With incentives to reduce product cost, this approach to product costing encourages operational managers and cell workers to find ways to decrease cycle time or increase velocity.

Manufacturing Cycle Efficiency (MCE)

Another time-based operational measure calculates **manufacturing cycle efficiency (MCE)**. MCE is measured as value-added time divided by total time. Total time includes both value-added time (the time spent efficiently producing the product) and non-value-added time (such as move time, inspection time, and waiting time) The formula for computing MCE is:

$$MCE = \frac{\text{Processing time}}{\text{Processing time} + \text{Move time} + \text{Inspection time} + \text{Waiting time}}$$

In this equation, processing time is the time it takes to convert raw materials into a finished good. The other activities and their times are viewed as wasteful, and the goal is to reduce those times to zero. If this is accomplished, the value of MCE would be 1.0, or 100 percent. As MCE improves (moves toward 1.0), cycle time decreases. Furthermore, since the only way MCE can improve is by decreasing waste, cost reduction must also follow. Cornerstone 11-9 shows how to calculate MCE.

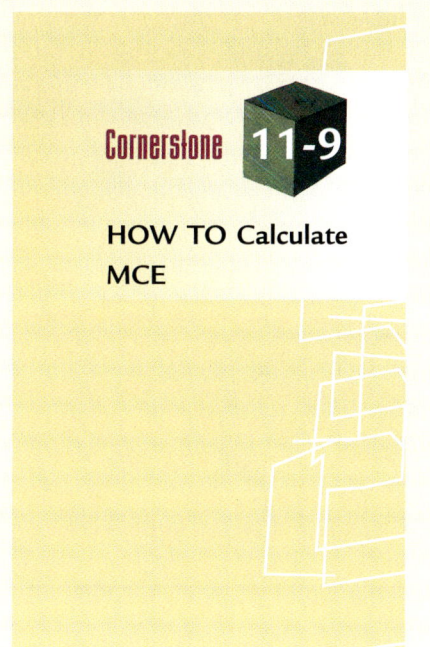

Cornerstone 11-9

HOW TO Calculate MCE

Information: A company provided the following information:

Maximum units produced in a quarter (3-month period): 200,000 units
Actual units produced in a quarter (3-month period): 160,000 units
Productive hours in one quarter: 40,000 hours
Actual cycle time = 15 minutes
Theoretical cycle time = 12 minutes

Required:

1. Calculate the amount of processing time and the amount of nonprocessing time.
2. Calculate MCE.

Calculation:

1. Processing time is equal to theoretical cycle time. That is, if everything goes smoothly and there is no wasted time, it takes 12 minutes to produce one unit. Nonprocessing time, therefore, must be the difference between actual cycle time (which includes some waste) and theoretical cycle time.

   Processing time = Theoretical cycle time = 12 minutes

   Nonprocessing time = Actual cycle time − Theoretical cycle time
   $\qquad\qquad\qquad\quad$ = 15 − 12 = 3 minutes

2. MCE = Processing time/(Processing time + Nonprocessing time)
   $\qquad$ = 12/(12 + 3) = 0.8, or 80 percent

Actually, Cornerstone 11-9 illustrates a fairly efficient process, as measured by MCE. Many manufacturing companies have MCEs less than 0.05.[10]

Postsales Service Process: Objectives and Measures

Increasing quality, increasing efficiency, and decreasing process time are also objectives that apply to the postsales service process. Service quality, for example, can be measured by first-pass yields, where first-pass yields are defined as the percentage of customer requests resolved with a single service call. Efficiency can be measured by cost trends and productivity measures. Process time can be measured by cycle time, where the starting point of the cycle is defined as the receipt of a customer request and the finishing point is when the customer's problem is solved. The objectives and measures for the process perspective are summarized in Exhibit 11-11.

Learning and Growth Perspective

The learning and growth perspective is the source of the capabilities that enable the accomplishment of the other three perspectives' objectives. This perspective has three major objectives: (1) increase employee capabilities; (2) increase motivation, empowerment, and alignment; and (3) increase information systems capabilities.

---

[10]Robert S. Kaplan and David P. Norton, *The Balanced Scorecard*, p. 117.

Summary of Objectives and Measures: Process Perspective

Objectives	Measures
Innovation:	
Increase the number of new products	Number of new products vs. planned
Increase proprietary products	Percentage revenue from proprietary products
Decrease new product development time	Time to market (from start to finish)
Operations:	
Increase process quality	Quality costs
	Output yields
	Percentage of defective units
Increase process efficiency	Unit cost trends
	Output/input(s)
Decrease process time	Cycle time and velocity
	MCE
Postsales Service:	
Increase service quality	First-pass yields
Increase service efficiency	Costs trends
	Output/input
Decrease service time	Cycle time

Employee Capabilities

Three core *outcome* measurements for employee capabilities are employee satisfaction ratings, employee turnover percentages, and employee productivity (e.g., revenue per employee). Examples of lead measures or performance drivers for employee capabilities are hours of training and strategic job coverage ratios (percentage of critical job requirements filled). As new processes are created, new skills are often required. Training and hiring are sources of these new skills. Furthermore, the percentage of the employees needed in certain key areas with the requisite skills signals the capability of the organization to meet the objectives of the other three perspectives.

Motivation, Empowerment, and Alignment

Employees must not only have the necessary skills, but they must also have the freedom, motivation, and initiative to use those skills effectively. The number of suggestions per employee and the number of suggestions implemented per employee are possible measures of motivation and empowerment. Suggestions per employee provide a measure of the degree of employee involvement, whereas suggestions implemented per employee signal the quality of the employee participation. The second measure also signals to employees whether or not their suggestions are being taken seriously.

Information Systems Capabilities

Increasing information system capabilities means providing more accurate and timely information to employees so that they can improve processes and effectively execute

Summary of Objectives and Measures: Learning and Growth Perspective

Objectives	Measures
Increase employee capabilities	Employee satisfaction ratings
	Employee turnover percentages
	Employee productivity (revenue/employee)
	Hours of training
	Strategic job coverage ratio (percentage of critical job requirements filled)
Increase motivation and alignment	Suggestions per employee
	Suggestions implemented per employee
Increase information systems capabilities	Percentage of processes with real-time feedback capabilities
	Percentage of customer-facing employees with online access to customer and product information

new processes. Measures should be concerned with the *strategic information availability.* For example, possible measures include percentage of processes with real-time feedback capabilities and percentage of customer-facing employees with online access to customer and product information. Exhibit 11-12 summarizes the objectives and measures for the learning and growth perspective.

APPENDIX: SUMMARY OF LEARNING OBJECTIVES

The Balanced Scorecard is a strategic management system that translates the vision and strategy of an organization into operational objectives and measures. Objectives and measures are developed for each of four perspectives: the financial perspective, the customer perspective, the process perspective, and the learning and growth perspective. The objectives and measures of the four perspectives are linked by a series of cause-and-effect hypotheses. This produces a testable strategy that provides strategic feedback to managers. The Balanced Scorecard is compatible with activity-based responsibility accounting because it focuses on processes and requires the use of activity-based information to implement many of its objectives and measures.

Nonfinancial measures evaluated by the Balanced Scorecard include velocity, cycle time, and MCE. Velocity is the number of units produced in a period of time. Cycle time is the time needed to produce one unit. MCE is manufacturing cycle efficiency; it is measured as value-added time divided by total time. The higher the MCE, the more efficient the firm is.

Cornerstones for the Appendix to Chapter 11

Cornerstone 11-8 How to compute cycle time and velocity, page 472
Cornerstone 11-9 How to calculate MCE, page 473

APPENDIX: KEY TERMS

Balanced Scorecard, 465

Core objectives and measures, 469

Customer perspective, 466

Customer value, 470

Cycle time, 472

Double-loop feedback, 467

Financial perspective, 465

Innovation process, 471

Internal business process perspective, 466

Learning and growth (infrastructure) perspective, 466

Manufacturing cycle efficiency (MCE), 472

Operations process, 471

Postpurchase costs, 470

Postsales service process, 471

Process value chain, 471

Single-loop feedback, 467

Strategy, 466

Testable strategy, 467

Velocity, 472

DISCUSSION QUESTIONS

1. Discuss the differences between centralized and decentralized decision making.
2. What is decentralization?
3. Explain why firms choose to decentralize.
4. What are margin and turnover? Explain how these concepts can improve the evaluation of an investment center.
5. What are the three benefits of ROI? Explain how each can lead to improved profitability.
6. What is residual income? What is EVA? How does EVA differ from the general definition of residual income?
7. Can residual income or EVA ever be negative? What is the meaning of negative residual income or EVA?
8. What is a transfer price?
9. If the minimum transfer price of the selling division is less than the maximum transfer price of the buying division, then the intermediate product should be transferred internally. Do you agree? Why or why not?
10. What is the difference between unit cost of a product under absorption costing and variable costing?
11. If a company produces 10,000 units and sells 8,000 units during a period, which method of computing operating income (absorption costing or variable costing) will result in the higher operating income? Why?
12. What is a segment?
13. What is the difference between contribution margin and segment margin?
14. (Appendix) What is the Balanced Scorecard?
15. (Appendix) Describe the four perspectives of the Balanced Scorecard.

MULTIPLE-CHOICE EXERCISES

11-1 The practice of delegating authority to division-level managers by top management is

a. centralization.
b. good business practice.
c. decentralization.
d. autonomy.
e. never done in business today.

11-2 Which of the following is *not* a reason for decentralizing?

a. Training and motivating managers
b. Unmasking inefficiencies in subdivisions of an overall profitable company
c. Allowing top management to focus on strategic decision making
d. Allowing top management to make all key operating decisions throughout the company
e. All of the above are reasons for decentralizing.

11-3 A responsibility center in which a manager is responsible only for controlling costs is a(n)

a. cost center.
b. profit center.
c. revenue center.
d. investment center.

11-4 A responsibility center in which a manager is responsible for revenues, costs, and investments is a(n)

a. cost center.
b. profit center.
c. revenue center.
d. investment center.

11-5 If sales and average operating assets for year 2 are identical to their values in year 1, yet operating income is higher, year 2 ROI (compared to year 1 ROI) will

a. increase.
b. decrease.
c. stay the same.
d. The direction of change in ROI cannot be determined by this information.

11-6 If sales and average operating assets for year 2 are identical to their values in year 1, yet operating income is higher, year 2 turnover (compared to year 1 turnover) will

a. increase.
b. decrease.
c. stay the same.
d. The direction of change in turnover cannot be determined by this information.

11-7 A key difference between residual income and economic value added (EVA) is that EVA

a. uses the actual cost of capital for the company rather than a minimum required cost of capital.
b. uses the minimum required cost of capital for a company rather than the actual percentage cost of capital.
c. is a ratio rather than an absolute dollar amount.
d. cannot be negative.
e. There is no difference between residual income and EVA.

11-8 If ROI for a division is 15 percent and the company's minimum required cost of capital is 18 percent, then

a. residual income for the division is negative.
b. residual income for the division takes on a value between zero and positive one.
c. residual income cannot be computed.
d. EVA must be negative.
e. residual income is positive.

11-9 Division A, operating at full capacity, manufactures component 98-2 with unit variable product cost of $26 and market price of $40. Division A incurs shipping costs of $2 per unit for sales to outside parties only. Division B uses component 98-2 in the manufacture of its own products. Top management allows negotiated transfer pricing. The maximum transfer price (the ceiling of the bargaining range) is

a. $26.
b. $40.
c. $33.
d. $38.
e. There is no bargaining range.

11-10 Division A, operating at less than full capacity, manufactures component 98-2 with unit variable product cost of $26 and market price of $40. Division A incurs shipping costs of $2 per unit for sales to outside parties only. Division B uses component 98-2 in the manufacture of its own products. Top management allows negotiated transfer pricing. The minimum transfer price (the floor of the bargaining range) is

a. $26.
b. $40.
c. $33.
d. $38.
e. There is no bargaining range.

11-11 A company shows the following unit costs for its product:

Direct materials	$40
Direct labor	30
Variable overhead	2
Fixed overhead	5

The company started the year with 8,000 units in inventory, produced 50,000 units during the year, and sold 55,000 units. The value of ending inventory is

a. greater under absorption costing than variable costing.
b. greater under variable costing than absorption costing.
c. the same under both variable and absorption costing.
d. There is no ending inventory.
e. This situation cannot happen.

11-12 In a segmented income statement, which of the following statements is true?

a. Segment margin is greater than contribution margin.
b. Common fixed expenses must be allocated to each segment.
c. Contribution margin is equal to sales less all variable and direct fixed expenses of a segment.
d. Segment margin is equal to contribution margin less direct fixed expenses.
e. Segment margin is equal to contribution margin less direct and common fixed expenses.

11-13 (Appendix) Which of the following is *not* a perspective of the Balanced Scorecard?

a. Learning and growth (infrastructure)
b. Internal business process
c. Customer
d. Financial
e. All of the above are perspectives of the Balanced Scorecard.

11-14 (Appendix) The number of units of output that can be produced in a given period of time is called

a. velocity.
b. cycle time.
c. manufacturing cycle efficiency.
d. theoretical cycle time.
e. theoretical MCE.

EXERCISES

Exercise 11-1 *Types of Responsibility Centers*

Consider each of the following independent scenarios:

a. Terrin Belson, plant manager for the laser printer factory of Compugear, Inc., brushed his hair back and sighed. December had been a bad month; two machines had broken down, and some factory production workers (all on salary) were idled for part of the month. Materials prices increased, and insurance premiums on the factory increased. No way out of it; costs were going up. He hoped that the marketing vice president would be able to push through some price increases, but that really wasn't his department.

b. Joanna Pauly was delighted to see that her ROI figures had increased for the third straight year. She was sure that her campaign to lower costs and use machinery more efficiently (enabling her factories to sell several older machines) was the reason why. Joanna planned to take full credit for the improvements at her semiannual performance review.

c. Gil Rodriguez, sales manager for ComputerWorks, was not pleased with a memo from headquarters detailing the recent cost increases for the laser printer line. Headquarters suggested raising prices. "Great," thought Gil, "an increase in price will kill sales and revenue will go down. Why can't the plant shape up and cut costs like every other company in America is doing? Why turn this into my problem?"

d. Susan Whitehorse looked at the quarterly profit/loss statement with disgust. Revenue was down and cost was up—what a combination! Then she had an idea. If she cut back on maintenance of equipment and let a product engineer go, expenses would decrease—perhaps enough to reverse the trend in income.

e. Shonna had just been hired to improve the fortunes of the Southern Division of ABC, Inc. She met with top staff and hammered out a 3-year plan to improve the situation. A centerpiece of the plan is the retiring of obsolete equipment and the purchasing of state-of-the-art, computer-assisted machinery. The new machinery would take time for the workers to learn to use, but once that was done, waste would be virtually eliminated.

Required:

For each of the above independent scenarios, indicate the type of responsibility center involved (cost, revenue, profit, or investment).

Exercise 11-2 *Inventory Valuation under Absorption Costing*

Abile Company produced 15,000 units during its first year of operations and sold 13,800 at $22 per unit. The company chose practical activity—at 15,000 units—to compute its predetermined overhead rate. Manufacturing costs are as follows:

Direct materials	$ 79,500
Direct labor	105,000
Variable overhead	15,900
Fixed overhead	51,000

Required:

1. Calculate the unit cost for each of these four costs.
2. Calculate the cost of one unit of product under absorption costing.
3. How many units are in ending inventory?
4. Calculate the cost of ending inventory under absorption costing.

Exercise 11-3 *Inventory Valuation under Variable Costing*

Refer to **Exercise 11-2**.

Required:

1. Calculate the cost of one unit of product under variable costing.
2. Calculate the cost of ending inventory under variable costing.

Exercise 11-4 *Inventory Valuation under Absorption and Variable Costing*

The following information pertains to Gabon, Inc., for last year:

Beginning inventory in units	—
Units produced	20,000
Units sold	17,200
Costs per unit:	
Direct materials	$8.00
Direct labor	$4.00
Variable overhead	$1.50
Fixed overhead*	$4.15
Variable selling expenses	$3.00
Fixed selling and administrative costs	$24,300

*Fixed overhead totals $83,000 per year.

Required:

1. Calculate the cost of one unit of product under absorption costing.
2. Calculate the cost of one unit of product under variable costing.
3. How many units are in ending inventory?
4. Calculate the cost of ending inventory under absorption costing.
5. Calculate the cost of ending inventory under variable costing.

Exercise 11-5 *Income Statements under Absorption and Variable Costing*

Refer to **Exercise 11-4**. Assume the selling price is $32 per unit.

Required:

1. Prepare an income statement using absorption costing.
2. Prepare an income statement using variable costing.

Exercise 11-6 *Margin, Turnover, ROI*

Shryock Company had sales of $100,000, expenses of $83,000, and operating assets of $80,000.

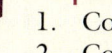

Required:
1. Compute the operating income.
2. Compute the margin and turnover ratios.
3. Compute the ROI.

Exercise 11-7 *Margin, Turnover, ROI, Average Operating Assets*

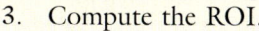 OBJECTIVE 3

Park Company provided the following income statement for last year:

Sales	$80,000
Less: Variable expenses	55,000
Contribution margin	$25,000
Less: Fixed expenses	19,800
Operating income	$ 5,200

At the beginning of last year, Park had $38,650 in operating assets. At the end of the year, Park had $41,350 in operating assets.

Required:
1. Compute average operating assets.
2. Compute the margin and turnover ratios for last year.
3. Compute ROI.

Exercise 11-8 *ROI, Margin, Turnover*

 OBJECTIVE 3

Data follow for the Southern Division of Loring Company:

	Year 1	Year 2
Sales	$20,000,000	$20,000,000
Net operating income	1,800,000	1,640,000
Average operating assets	10,000,000	8,000,000

Required:
1. Compute the margin and turnover ratios for each year.
2. Compute the ROI for the Southern Division for each year.

Exercise 11-9 *Residual Income*

 OBJECTIVE 4

The Home Products Division of Schipper Company had operating income last year of $112,500 and operating assets of $750,000. Schipper's minimum acceptable rate of return is 10 percent.

Required:
1. Calculate the residual income for the Home Products Division.
2. Was the ROI for the Home Products Division greater than, less than, or equal to 10 percent?

Exercise 11-10 *EVA*

 OBJECTIVE 4

Kando Company had net (after-tax) income last year of $400,000 and operating assets of $920,000. Kando's actual cost of capital was 12 percent.

Required:
1. Calculate EVA for Kando Company.
2. Is Kando creating or destroying wealth?

Exercise 11-11 *EVA*

 OBJECTIVE 4

Messier Company has two divisions, the Northern Division and the Southern Division. The following information pertains to last year's results:

	Northern Division	Southern Division
Net (after-tax) income	$125,000	$550,000
Operating assets	850,000	990,000

Messier's actual cost of capital was 15 percent.

Required:
1. Calculate EVA for the Northern Division.
2. Calculate EVA for the Southern Division.
3. Is each division creating or destroying wealth?

Exercise 11-12 *Residual Income*

Refer to **Exercise 11-11**. Now assume that Messier Company's top management has set a minimum acceptable rate of return equal to 10 percent.

Required:
1. Calculate residual income for the Northern Division.
2. Calculate residual income for the Southern Division.

Exercise 11-13 *Transfer Pricing*

Aulman, Inc., has a number of divisions including a Furniture Division and a Motel Division. The Motel Division owns and operates a line of budget motels located along major highways. Each year, the Motel Division purchases furniture for the motel rooms. Currently, it purchases a basic dresser from an outside supplier for $40. The manager of the Furniture Division has approached the manager of the Motel Division about selling dressers to the Motel Division. The full product cost of a dresser is $29. The Furniture Division can sell all the dressers it makes to outside companies for $40. The Motel Division needs 10,000 dressers per year; the Furniture Division can make up to 50,000 dressers per year.

Required:
1. Which division sets the maximum transfer price? Which division sets the minimum transfer price?
2. Suppose the company policy is that all transfers take place at full cost. What is the transfer price?
3. Do you think that the transfer will occur at the company-mandated transfer price? Why or why not?

Exercise 11-14 *Transfer Pricing*

Refer to **Exercise 11-13**. Now suppose that the company policy is that all transfer prices are negotiated by the divisions involved.

Required:
1. What is the maximum transfer price? Which division sets it?
2. What is the minimum transfer price? Which division sets it?
3. If the transfer takes place, what will the transfer price be? Does it matter whether or not the transfer takes place?

Exercise 11-15 *Transfer Pricing*

Recall from **Exercise 11-13** that the Motel Division buys dressers from outside companies for $40 each. While the Furniture Division has been operating at capacity (50,000 dressers per year) and selling them for $40 each, it expects to produce and sell only 40,000 dressers (with a full manufacturing cost of $29 each) for $40 next year. The Furniture Division incurs variable costs of $14 per dresser. The company policy is that all transfer prices are negotiated by the divisions involved.

1. What is the maximum transfer price? Which division sets it?
2. What is the minimum transfer price? Which division sets it?
3. Suppose that the two divisions agree on a transfer price of $35. What is the change in operating income for the Furniture Division? For the Motel Division? For Aulman, Inc., as a whole?

Exercise 11-16 *(Appendix) Cycle Time and Velocity*

Prakesh Company has the following data for one of its manufacturing cells:

Maximum units produced in a month: 50,000 units
Actual units produced in a month: 40,000 units
Hours of production labor in one month: 10,000 hours

Required:
1. Compute the theoretical cycle time (in minutes).
2. Compute the actual cycle time (in minutes).
3. Compute the theoretical velocity in units per hour.
4. Compute the actual velocity in units per hour.

Exercise 11-17 *(Appendix) Cycle Time and Velocity*

Lasker Company divided its tool production factory into manufacturing cells. Each cell produces one product. The cordless drill cell had the following data for last quarter:

Maximum units produced in a quarter: 90,000 units
Actual units produced in a quarter: 75,000 units
Hours of cell production labor in a quarter: 30,000 hours

Required:
1. Compute the theoretical cycle time (in minutes).
2. Compute the actual cycle time (in minutes).
3. Compute the theoretical velocity in units per hour.
4. Compute the actual velocity in units per hour.

Exercise 11-18 *(Appendix) Manufacturing Cycle Efficiency (MCE)*

Ventris Company found that one of its manufacturing cells had actual cycle time of 15 minutes per unit. The theoretical cycle time for this cell was nine minutes per unit.

Required:
1. Calculate the amount of processing time per unit and the amount of nonprocessing time per unit.
2. Calculate MCE.

Exercise 11-19 *(Appendix) Manufacturing Cycle Efficiency (MCE)*

Kurena Company provided the following information on one of its factories:

Maximum units produced in a quarter: 180,000 units
Actual units produced in a quarter: 112,500 units
Hours of cell production labor in a quarter: 30,000 hours
Theoretical cycle time: 10 minutes per unit
Actual cycle time: 16 minutes per unit

Required:
1. Calculate the amount of processing time per unit and the amount of nonprocessing time per unit.
2. Calculate MCE.

PROBLEMS

(Note: Whenever you see a  next to a requirement, it signals a "building on a cornerstone" requirement. Assigning this requirement will usually entail additional work, such as a group project, analytical reasoning, Internet research, decision making, and the use of written communication skills.)

Problem 11-1 *Variable- and Absorption-Costing Income*

OBJECTIVE 2

Spicer Company produces and sells wooden pallets that are used in moving and stacking materials. The operating costs for the past year were as follows:

Variable costs per unit:	
Direct materials	$ 2.45
Direct labor	2.10
Variable overhead	0.25
Variable selling	0.30
Fixed costs per year:	
Fixed overhead	180,000
Selling and administrative	56,000

During the year, Spicer produced 200,000 wooden pallets and sold 208,000 at $9 each. Spicer had 11,300 pallets in beginning finished goods inventory; costs have not changed from last year to this year. An actual cost system is used for product costing.

Required:
1. What is the per-unit inventory cost that will be reported on Spicer's balance sheet at the end of the year? How many units are in ending inventory? What is the total cost of ending inventory?
2. Calculate absorption-costing income.
3. What would the per-unit inventory cost be under variable costing? Does this differ from the unit cost computed in Requirement 1? Why?
4. Calculate variable-costing income.
5. Suppose that Spicer Company had sold 196,700 pallets during the year. What would absorption-costing income have been? Variable-costing income?

Problem 11-2 *Variable Costing, Absorption Costing, Segmented Income Statements, Inventory Valuation*

OBJECTIVE 2

During its first year of operations, Sugarsmooth, Inc., produced 55,000 jars of hand cream based on a formula containing 10 percent glycolic acid. Unit sales were 53,500 jars. Fixed overhead totaled $27,500 and was applied at the rate of $0.50 per unit produced. The results of the year's operations are as follows (on an absorption-costing basis):

Sales (53,500 units @ $8.50)	$454,750
Less: Cost of goods sold	160,500
Gross margin	$294,250
Less: Selling and administrative (all fixed)	120,000
Operating income	$174,250

At the end of the first year of operations, Sugarsmooth is considering expanding its customer base. In its first year, it sold to small drugstores and supermarkets. Now, Sugarsmooth wants to add large discount stores and small beauty shops. Working together, the company controller and marketing manager have accumulated the following information:

a. Anticipated sales to discount stores would be 20,000 units at a discounted price of $6.75. Higher costs of shipping and return penalties would be incurred. Shipping would amount to $45,000 per year, and return penalties would average 1 percent of sales. In addition, a clerk would need to be hired solely to handle the discount stores' accounts. The clerk's salary and benefits would be $30,000 per year.

b. Anticipated sales to beauty shops would be 10,000 units at a price of $9. A commission of 10 percent of sales would be paid to independent jobbers who sell to the shops. In addition, an extra packing expense of $0.50 per unit would be incurred because the shops require fewer bottles per carton.

c. The fixed overhead and selling and administrative expenses would remain unchanged and are treated as common costs.

Required:

1. Calculate the cost of Sugarsmooth's ending inventory at the end of the first year under absorption costing.
2. Calculate the cost of Sugarsmooth's ending inventory at the end of the first year under variable costing. What is operating income for the first year using variable costing?
3. Prepare a segmented variable-costing income statement for next year. The segments correspond to customer groups: drugstores and supermarkets, discount stores, and beauty shops.
4. Are all three customer groups profitable? Should Sugarsmooth expand its marketing base?

Problem 11-3 *ROI and Investment Decisions*

OBJECTIVES 3, 4

Spreadsheet

Leslie Blandings, division manager of Audiotech, Inc., was debating the merits of a new product—a weather radio that would put out a warning if the county in which the listener lived was under a severe thunderstorm or tornado alert.

The budgeted income of the division was $3,960,000 with operating assets of $18,000,000. The proposed investment would add income of $450,000 and would require an additional investment in equipment of $3,000,000. The minimum required return on investment for the company is 14 percent.

Required:

1. Compute the ROI of:
   a. The division if the radio project is not undertaken.
   b. The radio project alone.
   c. The division if the radio project is undertaken.
2. Compute the residual income of:
   a. The division if the radio project is not undertaken.
   b. The radio project alone.
   c. The division if the radio project is undertaken.
3. Do you suppose that Leslie will decide to invest in the new radio? Why or why not?

Problem 11-4 *ROI, Margin, Turnover*

OBJECTIVE 3

Ready Electronics is facing stiff competition from imported goods. Its operating income margin has been declining steadily for the past several years; the company has been forced to lower prices so that it can maintain its market share. The operating results for the past three years are as follows:

	Year 1	Year 2	Year 3
Sales	$10,000,000	$ 9,500,000	$ 9,000,000
Net operating income	1,200,000	1,045,000	945,000
Average assets	15,000,000	15,000,000	15,000,000

For the coming year, Ready's president plans to install a JIT purchasing and manufacturing system. She estimates that inventories will be reduced by 70 percent during the first year of operations, producing a 20-percent reduction in the average operating assets of the company, which would remain unchanged without the JIT system. She also estimates that sales and operating income will be restored to year 1 levels because of simultaneous reductions in operating expenses and selling prices. Lower selling prices will allow Ready to expand its market share.

Required:

1. Compute the ROI, margin, and turnover for years 1, 2, and 3.
2. Suppose that in year 4 the sales and operating income were achieved as expected but inventories remained at the same level as in year 3. Compute the expected ROI, margin, and turnover. Explain why the ROI increased over the year 3 level.
3. Suppose that the sales and net operating income for year 4 remained the same as in year 3 but inventory reductions were achieved as projected. Compute the ROI, margin, and turnover. Explain why the ROI exceeded the year 3 level.
4. Assume that all expectations for year 4 were realized. Compute the expected ROI, margin, and turnover. Explain why the ROI increased over the year 3 level.

Problem 11-5 *ROI for Multiple Investments, Residual Income*

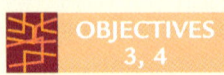

OBJECTIVES
3, 4

The manager of a division that produces add-on products for the automobile industry has just been presented the opportunity to invest in two independent projects. The first is an air conditioner for the back seats of vans and minivans. The second is a turbocharger. Without the investments, the division will have average assets for the coming year of $28.9 million and expected operating income of $4.335 million. The outlay required for each investment and the expected operating incomes are as follows:

	Air Conditioner	Turbocharger
Outlay	$750,000	$540,000
Operating income	90,000	82,080

Required:

1. Compute the ROI for each investment project.
2. Compute the budgeted divisional ROI for each of the following four alternatives:
   a. The air conditioner investment is made.
   b. The turbocharger investment is made.
   c. Both investments are made.
   d. Neither additional investment is made.

   Assuming that divisional managers are evaluated and rewarded on the basis of ROI performance, which alternative do you think the divisional manager will choose?

3. Suppose that the company sets a minimum required rate of return equal to 14 percent. Calculate the residual income for each of the following four alternatives:
   a. The air conditioner investment is made.
   b. The turbocharger investment is made.
   c. Both investments are made.
   d. Neither additional investment is made.

Which option will the manager choose based on residual income? Explain.

4. Suppose that the company sets a minimum required rate of return equal to 10 percent. Calculate the residual income for each of the following four alternatives:
   a. The air conditioner investment is made.
   b. The turbocharger investment is made.
   c. Both investments are made.
   d. Neither additional investment is made.

   Based on residual income, are the investments profitable? Why does your answer differ from your answer in Requirement 3?

Problem 11-6 *ROI and EVA Calculations with Varying Assumptions*

Knitpix Products is a division of Parker Textiles, Inc. During the coming year, it expects to earn income of $310,000 based on sales of $3.45 million; without any new investments, the division will have average net operating assets of $3 million. The division is considering a capital investment project—adding knitting machines to produce gaiters—that requires an additional investment of $600,000 and increases net income by $57,500 (sales would increase by $575,000). If made, the investment would increase beginning net operating assets by $600,000 and ending net operating assets by $400,000. Assume that the actual cost of capital for the company is 7 percent.

Required:
1. Compute the ROI for the division without the investment.
2. Compute the margin and turnover ratios without the investment. Show that the product of the margin and turnover ratios equals the ROI computed in Requirement 1.
3. Compute the ROI for the division with the new investment. Do you think the divisional manager will approve the investment?
4. Compute the margin and turnover ratios for the division with the new investment. Compare these with the old ratios.
5. Compute the EVA of the division with and without the investment. Should the manager decide to make the knitting machine investment?

Problem 11-7 *Transfer Pricing*

GreenWorld, Inc., is a nursery products firm. It has three divisions that grow and sell plants: the Western Division, the Southern Division, and the Canadian Division. Recently, the Southern Division of GreenWorld acquired a plastics factory that manufactures green plastic pots. These pots can be sold both externally and internally. Company policy permits each manager to decide whether to buy or sell internally. Each divisional manager is evaluated on the basis of return on investment and EVA.

The Western Division had bought its plastic pots in lots of 100 from a variety of vendors. The average price paid was $75 per box of 100 pots. However, the acquisition made Rosario Sanchez-Ruiz, manager of the Western Division, wonder whether or not a more favorable price could be arranged. She decided to approach Lorne Matthews, manager of the Southern Division, to see if he wanted to offer a better price for an internal transfer. She suggested a transfer of 3,500 boxes at $70 per box.

Lorne gathered the following information regarding the cost of a box of 100 pots:

Direct materials	$35
Direct labor	8
Variable overhead	10
Fixed overhead*	10
Total unit cost	$63

*Fixed overhead is based on $200,000/20,000 boxes.

Selling price	$75
Production capacity	20,000 boxes

Required:

1. Suppose that the plastics factory is producing at capacity and can sell all that it produces to outside customers. How should Lorne respond to Rosario's request for a lower transfer price?
2. Now assume that the plastics factory is currently selling 16,000 boxes. What are the minimum and maximum transfer prices? Should Lorne consider the transfer at $70 per box?
3. Suppose that GreenWorld's policy is that all transfer prices be set at full cost plus 20 percent. Would the transfer take place? Why or why not?

Problem 11-8 *Setting Transfer Prices—Market Price versus Full Cost*

Lansing Electronics, Inc., manufactures a variety of printers, scanners, and fax machines in its two divisions: the PSF Division and the Components Division. The Components Division produces electronic components that can be used by the PSF Division. All the components this division produces can be sold to outside customers; however, from the beginning, nearly 90 percent of its output has been used internally. The current policy requires that all internal transfers of components be transferred at full cost.

Recently, Cam DeVonn, the chief executive officer of Lansing Electronics, decided to investigate the transfer pricing policy. He was concerned that the current method of pricing internal transfers might force decisions by divisional managers that would be suboptimal for the firm. As part of his inquiry, he gathered some information concerning Component Y34, which is used by the PSF Division in its production of a basic scanner, Model SC67.

The PSF Division sells 40,000 units of Model SC67 each year at a unit price of $42. Given current market conditions, this is the maximum price that the division can charge for Model SC67. The cost of manufacturing the scanner follows:

Component Y34	$ 6.50
Direct materials	12.50
Direct labor	3.00
Variable overhead	1.00
Fixed overhead	15.00
Total unit cost	$38.00

The scanner is produced efficiently, and no further reduction in manufacturing costs is possible.

The manager of the Components Division indicated that she could sell 40,000 units (the division's capacity for this part) of Component Y34 to outside buyers at $12 per unit. The PSF Division could also buy the part for $12 from external suppliers. She supplied the following details on the manufacturing cost of the component:

Direct materials	$2.50
Direct labor	0.50
Variable overhead	1.00
Fixed overhead	2.50
Total unit cost	$6.50

Required:

1. Compute the firmwide contribution margin associated with Component Y34 and Model SC67. Also, compute the contribution margin earned by each division.
2. Suppose that Cam DeVonn abolishes the current transfer pricing policy and gives divisions autonomy in setting transfer prices. Can you predict what transfer price the manager of the Components Division will set? What should the minimum transfer price for this part be? The maximum transfer price?

3. Given the new transfer pricing policy, predict how this will affect the production decision for Model SC67 of the PSF Division manager. How many units of Component Y34 will the manager of the PSF Division purchase, either internally or externally?
4. Given the new transfer price set by the Components Division and your answer to Requirement 3, how many units of Y34 will be sold externally?
5. Given your answers to Requirements 3 and 4, compute the firmwide contribution margin. What has happened? Was Cam's decision to grant additional decentralization good or bad?

Problem 11-9 *Full Cost-Plus Pricing and Negotiation*

Technovia, Inc., has two divisions: Auxiliary Components and Audio Systems. Divisional managers are encouraged to maximize return on investment and EVA. Managers are essentially free to determine whether goods will be transferred internally and what internal transfer prices will be. Headquarters has directed that all internal prices be expressed on a full cost-plus basis. The markup in the full cost pricing arrangement, however, is left to the discretion of the divisional managers. Recently, the two divisional managers met to discuss a pricing agreement for a subwoofer that would be sold with a personal computer system. Production of the subwoofers is at capacity. Subwoofers can be sold for $31 to outside customers. The Audio Systems Division can also buy the subwoofer from external sources for the same price; however, the manager of this division is hoping to obtain a price concession by buying internally. The full cost of manufacturing the subwoofer is $20. If the manager of the Auxiliary Components Division sells the subwoofer internally, $5 of selling and distribution costs can be avoided. The volume of business would be 250,000 units per year, well within the capacity of the producing division.

After some discussion, the two managers agreed on a full cost-plus pricing scheme that would be reviewed annually. Any increase in the outside selling price would be added to the transfer price by simply increasing the markup by an appropriate amount. Any major changes in the factors that led to the agreement could initiate a new round of negotiation; otherwise, the full cost-plus arrangement would continue in force for subsequent years.

Required:
1. Calculate the minimum and maximum transfer prices.
2. Assume that the transfer price agreed upon between the two managers is halfway between the minimum and maximum transfer prices. Calculate this transfer price. What markup over full cost is implied by this transfer price?
3. Refer to Requirement 2. Assume that in the following year, the outside price of subwoofers increases to $32. What is the new full cost-plus transfer price?
4. Assume that two years after the initial agreement, the market for subwoofers has softened considerably, causing excess capacity for the Auxiliary Components Division. Would you expect a renegotiation of the full cost-plus pricing arrangement for the coming year? Explain.

Problem 11-10 *(Appendix) Cycle Time, Velocity, Conversion Cost*

The theoretical cycle time for a product is 30 minutes per unit. The budgeted conversion costs for the manufacturing cell are $2,700,000 per year. The total labor minutes available are 600,000. During the year, the cell was able to produce 1.5 units of the product per hour. Suppose also that production incentives exist to minimize unit product costs.

Required:
1. Compute the theoretical conversion cost per unit.

2. Compute the applied conversion cost per unit (the amount of conversion cost actually assigned to the product).
3. Discuss how this approach to assigning conversion costs can improve delivery time performance.

Problem 11-11 *(Appendix) Balanced Scorecard*

The following list gives a number of measures associated with the Balanced Score-card:

a. Number of new customers.
b. Percentage of customer complaints resolved with one contact.
c. Unit product cost.
d. Cost per distribution channel.
e. Suggestions per employee.
f. Warranty repair costs.
g. Consumer satisfaction (from surveys).
h. Cycle time for solving a customer problem.
i. Strategic job coverage ratio.
j. On-time delivery percentage.
k. Percentage of revenues from new products.

Required:
1. Classify each performance measure as belonging to one of the following perspectives: financial, customer, internal business process, or learning and growth.
2. Suggest an additional measure for each of the four perspectives.

Problem 11-12 *ROI Ethical Considerations*

Jason Kemp was torn between conflicting emotions. On the one hand, things were going so well. He had just completed six months as the assistant financial manager in the Electronics Division of Med-Products, Inc. The pay was good, he enjoyed his coworkers, and he felt that he was part of a team that was making a difference in American health care. On the other hand, his latest assignment was causing some sleepless nights. Mel Cravens, his boss, had asked him to "refine" the figures on the division's latest project—a portable imaging device code—named ZM. The original estimates called for investment of $15.6 million and projected annual income of $1.87 million. Med-Products required an ROI of at least 15 percent for new project approval; so far, ZM's rate of return was nowhere near that hurdle rate. Mel encouraged him to show increased sales and decreased expenses in order to get the projected income above $2.34 million. Jason asked for a meeting with Mel to voice his concerns.

Jason: Mel, I've gone over the figures for the new project and can't find any way to get the income above $1.9 million. The salespeople have given me the most likely revenue figures, and production feels that the expense figures are solid.

Mel: Jason, those figures are just projections. Sales doesn't really know what the revenue will be. In fact, when I talked with Sue Harris, our sales vice president, she said that sales could range from $1.5 million to $2.5 million. Use the higher figure. I'm sure this product will justify our confidence in it!

Jason: I know the range of sales was that broad, but Sue felt the $2.5 million estimate was pretty unlikely. She thought that during the first five years or so that ZM sales would stay in the lower end of the range.

Mel: Again, Sue doesn't know for sure. She's just estimating. Let's go with the higher estimate. We really need this product to expand our line and to give our division a chance to qualify for sales-based bonuses. If ZM sells at all, our revenue will go up, and we'll all share in the bonus pool!

Jason: I don't know, Mel. I feel pretty bad signing off on ROI projections that I have so little confidence in.

Mel: (frustrated) Look, Jason, just prepare the report. I'll back you up.

Required:
1. What is the ROI of project ZM based on the initial estimates? What would ROI be if the income rose to $2.34 million?
2. Do you agree that Jason has an ethical dilemma? Explain. Is there any way that Mel could ethically justify raising the sales estimates and/or lowering expense estimates?
3. What do you think Jason should do? Explain.

Problem 11-13 *Cycle Time and Velocity, MCE*

OBJECTIVE 6

A company like Kicker performs warranty repair work on speakers in a manufacturing cell. The typical warranty repair involves taking the defective speaker apart, testing the components, and replacing the defective components. The maximum capacity of the cell is 1,000 repairs per month. There are 500 production hours available per month.

Required:
1. Compute the theoretical velocity (per hour) and the theoretical cycle time (minutes per unit repaired).
2. Speaker repair uses four minutes of move time, 10 minute of wait time, and six minutes of inspection time. Calculate MCE.
3. Using the information from Requirement 2, calculate the actual cycle time and the actual velocity for speaker repair.

SHORT-RUN DECISION MAKING: RELEVANT COSTING AND INVENTORY MANAGEMENT

© TONY FREEMAN/PHOTO EDIT

After studying Chapter 12, you should be able to:

1. Describe the short-run decision-making model and explain how cost behavior affects the information used to make decisions.
2. Apply relevant costing and decision-making concepts in a variety of business situations.
3. Choose the optimal product mix when faced with one constrained resource.
4. Explain the impact of cost on pricing decisions.
5. Discuss inventory management under the economic order quantity and JIT models.

Bill McCormick, founder and president of Audio-Blast, Inc., hung up the phone and let out an excited "Yesss!" A major automobile manufacturer wanted to meet with him to discuss installing Audio-Blast's main product—the mega-blast speaker system—into its new sports car. That way, Audio-Blast speakers would be installed at the factory on all units of the sports car. Bill quickly assembled his management team: Carol Maldonado, controller; Gene Bickford, vice president of sales; and Harry Lester, production head. After Bill briefed them on his phone conversation, the following conversation took place:

Gene: This is the break we've been hoping for! How many units do they need? 20,000? 50,000? Our sales will go through the roof!

Harry: That's great, Bill, but I'm worried about our production line handling a big increase in volume. This order could easily double our current volume—maybe triple it! We're cramped for space as it is. At the beginning of every month, raw materials are stacked in the aisles and the break room; at the end of the month, those materials are used up, and we're stacking finished product all over the place. We don't have enough space right now, and we'll need to hire more people, maybe put on an additional shift.

Gene: Even so, triple the sales equals triple the profit. We've been talking about growing our business. I say, let's go for this.

Carol: Hold on, Gene, triple the sales does NOT necessarily mean triple the profit. Harry has a great point—we may need to significantly increase our fixed costs by adding warehouse space for finished product as well as space for increased inventory of materials. In addition, we'll need to check out better venting methods for painting and drying the speaker boxes. Our hazardous emissions from painting are getting close to a critical level.

Gene: Carol's right—we need more sophisticated venting equipment—the EPA is starting to require it. I can hardly stand to walk back to the drying room. Plus, we owe it to our people to make sure we're not making them sick.

Bill: Those are good points. Harry, why don't you go on the assumption of 10,000 more units per year and work with our engineering consultant to outline any changes necessary. I want you to come up with several alternatives that would work for increases in production from 20,000 to 50,000 units per year. Carol, if you can work with Harry to estimate costs of the various alternatives that would be great. Then, Gene, you and I will prepare for the meeting. With the production and cost data, we'll be better able to talk price and quantity with the automobile manufacturer.

Decision making is a key part of management. Often, it is useful to consider decision making as either long run or short run. Long-run decision making, often involving investment in property, plant, and equipment, is referred to as capital budgeting. That topic is covered in Chapter 13. The use of cost and revenue data in making short-run decisions, such as the acceptance of special orders or setting an optimal level of inventory, is the focus of this chapter.

SHORT-RUN DECISION MAKING

Short-run decision making consists of choosing among alternatives with an immediate or limited end in view. Accepting a special order for less than the normal selling price to utilize idle capacity and increase this year's profits is an example. Thus, some decisions tend to be *short run* in nature; however, it should be emphasized that short-run decisions often have long-run consequences. Consider a second example. Suppose that a company is considering producing a component instead of buying it from suppliers. The immediate objective may be to lower the cost of making the main product. Yet, this decision may be a small part of the overall strategy of establishing a cost leadership position for the firm. Therefore, short-run decisions are often *small-scale actions* that serve a larger purpose.

OBJECTIVE 1

Describe the short-run decision-making model and explain how cost behavior affects the information used to make decisions.

The Decision-Making Model

How does a company go about making good short-run decisions? A **decision model**, a specific set of procedures that produces a decision, can be used to structure your thinking and organize the information to make a good decision. Here is an outline of one decision-making model.

1. Recognize and define the problem.
2. Identify alternatives as possible solutions to the problem; eliminate alternatives that are clearly not feasible.
3. Identify the costs and benefits associated with each feasible alternative. Classify costs and benefits as relevant or irrelevant and eliminate irrelevant ones from consideration.
4. Total the relevant costs and benefits for each alternative.
5. Assess qualitative factors.
6. Select the alternative with the greatest overall benefit.

The decision-making model described above has six steps. Nothing is special about this particular listing. You may find it more useful to break down the steps into eight or 10 segments. Alternatively, you may find it useful to aggregate them into a shorter list. For example, you could use a 3-step model: (1) identify the decision, (2) identify alternatives and their associated relevant costs, and (3) make the decision. The key point is to find a comfortable way for you to remember the important steps in the decision-making model.

Two years ago, the loan officer at Kicker's bank left for another job out of state. This was an excellent time for Kicker to reevaluate its banking relationship. The company took a number of bids from the four major banks in town. In the process, Kicker executives learned a great deal about various banking services and the way that banks charged for them. Some examples include Internet service, loan rates, credit card transactions, returned check fees, and wire fees. Qualitative factors played a role in the ultimate decision. For example, how quickly does the bank respond? Does Kicker feel comfortable with its banking officer (is she or he knowledgeable about the speaker and electronics industry and attuned to Kicker's special needs)? After weighing both the monetary and nonmonetary factors, Kicker switched banks.

HERE'S

THE REAL

KICKER

Suppose that Audio-Blast, Inc., decides to pursue the speaker order from the automobile manufacturer. Clearly, the company does not currently have sufficient productive and storage capacity to fulfill the order. How might the decision-making model help Audio-Blast find the best way of getting that capacity?

Step 1: Define the Problem

The first step is to recognize and define a specific problem. For example, the members of Audio-Blast's management team recognized the need for additional productive capacity, as well as increased space for raw materials and finished goods inventories. The number of workers and the amount of space needed, the reasons for the need, and how the additional space would be used are all important dimensions of the problem. However, the central question is *how* to acquire the additional capacity.

Step 2: Identify the Alternatives

Step 2 is to list and consider possible solutions. Suppose that the production head, Harry, and the consulting engineer identified the following possible solutions:

1. Build a new factory with sufficient capacity to handle current and foreseeable needs.
2. Lease a larger facility and sublease its current facility.
3. Lease an additional, similar facility.
4. Institute a second shift in the main factory and lease an additional building that would be used for storage of raw materials and finished goods inventories only, thereby freeing up space for expanded production.
5. Outsource production to another company and resell the speakers to the auto manufacturer.

As part of this step, Harry met with Carol and Bill to eliminate alternatives that were clearly not feasible. The first alternative was eliminated because it carried too much risk for the company. The order had not even been secured, and the popularity of the new sports car model was not proven. Bill refused to "bet the company" on such a risky proposition. The second alternative was rejected because the economy in Audio-Blast's small town was such that subleasing a facility of its size was not possible. The third alternative was eliminated because it went too far in solving the space problem and, presumably, was too expensive. The fourth and fifth alternatives were feasible; they were within the cost and risk constraints and solved the needs of the company. Notice that Bill linked the short-run decision (increase productive capacity) to the company's overall growth strategy by rejecting alternatives that involved too much risk at this stage of the company's development.

Step 3: Identify the Costs and Benefits Associated with Each Feasible Alternative

In step 3, the costs and benefits associated with each feasible alternative are identified. At this point, clearly irrelevant costs can be eliminated from consideration. (It is fine to include irrelevant costs and benefits in the analysis as long as they are included for all alternatives. The reason we usually do not is that focusing only on the relevant costs and benefits reduces the amount of data to be collected.) Carol, the controller, is responsible for gathering necessary data.

Assume that Audio-Blast determines that the costs of making 20,000 speakers include the following:

Direct materials	$ 60,000
Direct labor	110,000
Variable overhead	10,000
Total variable production cost	$180,000

In addition, a second shift must be put in place and a warehouse must be leased to store raw materials and finished goods inventories if Audio-Blast continues to manufacture the speakers internally. Additional costs of the second shift, including a production supervisor and part-time maintenance and engineering, amount to $90,000 per year. A building that could serve as a warehouse is sitting empty across the street and can be rented for $20,000 per year. Costs of operating the building for inventory storage, including telephone and Internet access, as well as salaries of materials handlers, would amount to $80,000 per year. The second alternative is to purchase the speakers externally and use the freed-up production space for inventory. An outside supplier has offered to supply sufficient volume for $360,000 per year.

It should be mentioned that when the cash flow patterns become complicated for competing alternatives, it becomes difficult to produce a stream of equal cash flows for each alternative. In such a case, more sophisticated procedures can and should be used for the analysis. These procedures are discussed in the next chapter, which deals with the long-run investment decisions referred to as *capital expenditure decisions*.

Step 4: Total the Relevant Costs and Benefits for Each Feasible Alternative

We now see that alternative 4—continue producing internally and lease more space—costs $370,000, while alternative 5—purchase outside and use internal space—costs $360,000. The comparison follows:

Alternative 4		**Alternative 5**	
Variable cost of production	$180,000	Purchase price	$360,000
Added second shift costs	90,000		
Building lease and operating costs	100,000		
Total	$370,000		

The **differential cost** is the difference in total cost between the alternatives in a decision. Notice that the differential cost is $10,000 in favor of alternative 5. Emphasis on differential cost allows decision makers to occasionally include an irrelevant cost in the alternatives. This is just fine as long as *all irrelevant costs are included for each alternative*. For example, suppose that Carol had included fixed manufacturing cost that must be paid whether or not the speakers are made internally or externally. Then the total cost of each alternative would increase, but the differential cost would still be $10,000.

Step 5: Assess the Qualitative Factors

While the costs and revenues associated with the alternatives are important, they do not tell the whole story. Qualitative factors can significantly affect the manager's decision. Qualitative factors are simply those factors that are hard to put a number on. For example, Audio-Blast's president, Bill, likely would be concerned with such qualitative considerations as the quality of the speakers purchased externally, the reliability of supply sources, the expected stability of prices over the next several years, labor relations, community image, and so on. To illustrate the possible impact of qualitative factors on Audio-Blast's decision, consider the first two factors, quality and reliability of supply.

If the quality of speakers is significantly less when purchased externally from what is available internally, then the quantitative advantage from purchasing may be more fictitious than real. Reselling lower-quality speakers to such a high-profile buyer could permanently damage Audio-Blast's reputation. Because of this, Audio-Blast may choose to continue to produce the speakers internally.

Similarly, if supply sources are not reliable, production schedules could be interrupted, and customer orders could arrive late. These factors can increase labor costs and overhead and hurt sales. Again, depending on the perceived trade-offs, Audio-Blast may decide that producing the speakers internally is better than purchasing them, even if relevant cost analysis gives the initial advantage to purchasing.

How should qualitative factors be handled in the decision-making process? First, they must be identified. Secondly, the decision maker should try to quantify them. Often, qualitative factors are simply more difficult to quantify—not impossible. For example, possible unreliability of the outside supplier might be quantified as the probable number of days late multiplied by the penalty to be charged by the auto manufacturer for later delivery. Finally, truly qualitative factors, such as the impact of late orders on customer relations, must be taken into consideration in the final step of the decision-making model—the selection of the alternative with the greatest overall benefit.

Step 6: Make the Decision

Once all relevant costs and benefits for each alternative have been assessed and the qualitative factors weighed, a decision can be made.

Concept Q & A

Apply the decision-making model outlined in this section to a problem you have faced. For example, the problem might be whether or not to go to college, or which car to buy. Include all steps. Would the application of the decision-making model have helped you make the decision? Why or why not?

Answer:
Suppose that you were deciding between keeping your old car or getting a new one.

Step 1—*Recognize and define the problem*. The old car breaks down at least twice a month. It costs at least $100 to fix each problem, and you see no end to the potential problems. The problem is the unreliability of the car.

Step 2—*Identify alternatives*. Fixing the car once and for all is unfeasible (too costly and you don't trust it anymore). Alternative 1 is to buy a new Honda Civic. Alternative 2 is to buy a 2-year-old Ford F-150 pickup. Unfeasible alternatives might include public transportation, which is nonexistent in your small college town; riding with friends (you hate to be at the mercy of their schedules); or buying other more expensive cars (right now that's more fantasy than reality).

Steps 3 and 4—*Identify the costs and benefits for each feasible alternative*.

	Civic	F-150 Pickup
Asking price	$16,000	$10,500
Additional repair	0	2,500
Independent mechanic appraisal	0	50
Additional insurance/year	550	500
Total	$16,550	$13,550

Step 5—*Assess qualitative factors*. Perhaps some of your friends prefer riding inside the car and the Civic can hold four passengers plus the driver inside. Other friends think the pickup would be more useful for hauling gear to the beach, mountains, etc. You like the ride and handling of the Civic. You like sitting higher in the pickup cab. Resale value is a toss-up.

Step 6—*Select the alternative with the greatest overall benefit*. You choose.

Ethics in Decision Making

Ethical concerns revolve around the way in which decisions are implemented and the possible sacrifice of long-run objectives for short-run gain. Relevant costs are used in making short-run decisions. However, decision makers should always maintain an ethical framework. Reaching objectives is important, but how you get there is perhaps more important. Unfortunately, many managers have the opposite view. Part of the reason for the problem is the extreme pressure to perform that many managers feel. Often, the individual who is not a top performer may be laid off or demoted. Under such conditions, the temptation is often great to engage in questionable behavior today and let the future take care of itself.

Recall that Carol and Gene, in the opening Scenario, mentioned the need for more sophisticated emissions equipment. This is not just a question of satisfying EPA requirements, but it also involves ensuring a safe working environment for employees.

The company should send a consistent message throughout all its departments on its mission and goals. For example, if marketing enthusiastically touts the product's high quality and reliability, while engineering and production are busily reducing the quality of the materials and reliability of the design, then problems are sure to surface. Customers will see this inconsistency as an ethical lapse.

Whenever relevant costing is used, it is important to include all costs that are relevant—including those involving ethical ramifications.

Relevant Costs Defined

The decision-making approach just described emphasized the importance of identifying and using relevant costs. **Relevant costs** are future costs that differ across alternatives. All decisions relate to the future; accordingly, only future costs can be relevant to decisions. However, to be relevant, a cost must not only be a future cost but must also differ from one alternative to another. If a future cost is the same for more than one alternative, then it has no effect on the decision. Such a cost is *irrelevant*. The ability to identify relevant and irrelevant costs is an important decision-making skill.

Relevant Costs Illustrated

To illustrate the concept of relevant costs, consider Audio-Blast's make-or-buy alternatives. The cost of direct labor to produce the additional 20,000 speakers is $110,000. Is the direct labor cost a future cost that differs across the two alternatives? It is certainly a future cost. Producing the speakers for the auto manufacturer requires the services of direct laborers, who must be paid. But does it differ across the two alternatives? If the speakers are purchased from an external supplier, then a second shift, with its direct labor, would not be needed. Thus, the cost of direct labor differs across alternatives ($110,000 for the make alternative and $0 for the buy alternative). It is, therefore, a relevant cost.

Implicit in this analysis is the use of a past cost to estimate a future cost. The most recent cost of direct labor has averaged $5.50 per speaker; for 20,000 speakers, the direct labor would cost $110,000. This past cost was used as the estimate of next year's cost. Although past costs are never relevant, they are often used to predict what future costs will be.

Another type of relevant cost is opportunity cost. *Opportunity cost* is the benefit sacrificed or foregone when one alternative is chosen over another. While an opportunity cost is never an accounting cost, because accountants do not record the cost of what does not happen, it is an important consideration in decision making. For example, if you are deciding whether to work full time or to go to school full time, the opportunity cost of going to school would be the wages you give up by not working.

Illustration of an Irrelevant Past Cost

Audio-Blast uses large power saws to cut the lumber that forms the housings for speakers. These saws were purchased three years ago and are being depreciated at an annual rate of $25,000. Is this $25,000 a relevant cost? In other words, is depreciation a future cost that differs across the two alternatives?

Depreciation represents an allocation of a cost already incurred. It is a sunk cost, a cost that cannot be affected by any future action. Although we allocate this sunk cost to future periods and call that allocation depreciation, none of the original cost is avoidable. **Sunk costs** are past costs that cannot be affected by future decisions. They are always the same across alternatives and are, therefore, always irrelevant.

In choosing between the two alternatives, the original cost of the power saws and their associated depreciation are not factors. However, it should be noted that salvage value of the machinery is a relevant cost for certain decisions. For example, if Audio-Blast decided to transform itself into a distributor, not a producer, of speakers, the amount that could be realized from sale of the power equipment would be relevant and would be included as a benefit of the switch to distributor status.

Illustration of an Irrelevant Future Cost

Suppose that Audio-Blast currently pays an Internet provider $5,000 per year to store its Web site on the server. Since Audio-Blast intends to keep the Web page no matter what is decided regarding the potential speaker order, that cost is not relevant to the decision.

The same concepts apply to benefits. One alternative may produce an amount of future benefits different from another alternative (for example, differences in future revenues). If future benefits differ across alternatives, then they are relevant and should be included in the analysis.

Cost Behavior and Relevant Costs

Most short-run decisions require extensive consideration of cost behavior. It is easy to fall into the trap of believing that variable costs are relevant and fixed costs are not. But this is not so. For example, the variable costs of production were relevant to Audio-Blast's decision. The fixed costs associated with the existing factory were not relevant. However, the additional fixed cost of the supervisor for a second shift was relevant to the decision.

The key point is that changes in supply and demand for resources must be considered when assessing relevance. If changes in demand and supply for resources across alternatives bring about changes in spending, then the changes in resource spending are the relevant costs that should be used in assessing the relative desirability of the two alternatives.

Flexible resources can be easily purchased in the amount needed and at the time of use. For example, electricity used to run stoves that boil fruit in the production of jelly is a resource that can be acquired as used and needed. Thus, if the jelly manufacturer wants to increase production of jelly, electricity will increase just enough to satisfy that demand. This type of resource is typically referred to as a strictly variable cost.

Some resources are purchased before they are used. Clearly, investment in a factory of a particular size falls into this category; so does a year-to-year lease of office space or equipment. These are usually treated as fixed costs. If the decision covers a situation shorter than the time that the resource is fixed, this cost is usually not relevant.

Still other resources are acquired in advance of usage through implicit contracting; they are usually acquired in lumpy amounts. In Chapter 2, these were shown as step costs. This category may include an organization's salaried and hourly employees. The implicit understanding is that the organization will maintain employment levels even though there may be temporary downturns in the quantity of an activity used. This means that an activity may have unused capacity available. Recall that the relevant range is important in considering step costs. As long as a company remains within the relevant range, it will not go up or down a step; so the cost is for all intents and purposes fixed. For example, assume a company has three purchasing agents who can process 15,000 purchase orders a year. This means that the existing staff can handle 45,000 purchase orders a year. If the company is only processing 40,000 purchase orders, then there is some unused capacity in purchasing. If the company is considering a special order that would require an additional 2,000 purchase orders, then there is no increased cost to purchasing. However, if the company considers an expansion that would require an additional 8,000 purchase orders per year, then additional staffing will be needed in purchasing.

SOME COMMON RELEVANT COST APPLICATIONS

Relevant costing is of value in solving many different types of problems. Traditionally, these applications include decisions to make or buy a component, to keep or drop a segment or product line, and to accept a special order at less than the usual price. Though by no means an exhaustive list, many of the same decision-making principles apply to a variety of problems.

OBJECTIVE 2

Apply relevant costing and decision-making concepts in a variety of business situations.

Make-or-Buy Decisions

Managers are often faced with the decision of whether to make a particular product or service, or to buy it from an outside supplier. A manufacturer may need to consider whether to make or buy components used in manufacturing. A manager of a service firm may need to decide whether to provide a service in house or to outsource it. Many services traditionally performed within the company, such as payroll processing or human resources, are now being outsourced. **Make-or-buy decisions** are those decisions involving a choice between internal and external production. Exhibit 12-1 illustrates the make or buy decision.

12-1
EXHIBIT

Make or Buy

OR

To illustrate more fully the cost analysis of a make-or-buy problem, assume that Swasey Manufacturing currently produces an electronic component used in one of its printers. In one year, Swasey will switch production to another type of printer, and the electronic component will not be used. However, for the coming year, Swasey must produce 10,000 of these parts to support the production requirements for the old printer.

A potential supplier has approached Swasey about the component. The supplier will build the electronic component to Swasey's specifications for $4.75 per unit. The offer sounds very attractive since the full manufacturing cost per unit is $8.20. Should Swasey Manufacturing make or buy the component?

The problem and the feasible alternatives are both readily identifiable. Since the horizon for the decision is only one period, there is no need to be concerned about periodically recurring costs. Relevant costing is particularly useful for short-run analysis. We simply need to identify the relevant costs, total them, and make a choice (assuming no overriding qualitative concerns).

The full absorption cost of the component is computed as follows:

	Total Cost	Unit Cost
Direct materials	$10,000	$1.00
Direct labor	20,000	2.00
Variable overhead	8,000	0.80
Fixed overhead	44,000	4.40
Total	$82,000	$8.20

Fixed overhead consists of common factory costs that are allocated to each product line. No matter what happens to the component line, overall fixed overhead will not be affected. As a result, the fixed overhead is all irrelevant; it can be safely ignored in structuring the problem.

All other costs are relevant. The costs of direct materials and direct labor are relevant since they will not be needed if the part is bought externally. Similarly, variable overhead is relevant, since its cost would not be incurred if the component were bought externally.

Now, what about the purchase of the component? Of course, the purchase price is relevant. If the component were made, this cost would not be incurred. Are there any other costs associated with an outside purchase? A check with the purchasing department and receiving dock confirmed that there was sufficient slack in the system to easily handle the additional purchase. Cornerstone 12-1 shows how to structure this make-or-buy problem.

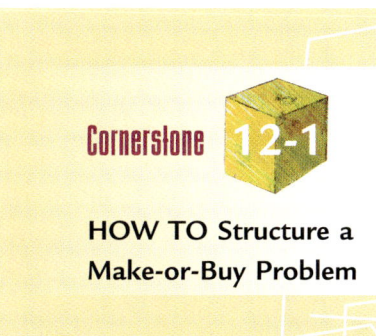

Cornerstone 12-1

HOW TO Structure a Make-or-Buy Problem

Information: Swasey Manufacturing needed to determine if it would be cheaper to make 10,000 units of a component in house or purchase them from an outside supplier for $4.75 each. Absorption-costing information on internal production includes the following:

	Total Cost	Unit Cost
Direct materials	$10,000	$1.00
Direct labor	20,000	2.00
Variable overhead	8,000	0.80
Fixed overhead	44,000	4.40
Total	$82,000	$8.20

Fixed overhead will continue whether the component is produced internally or externally. No additional costs of purchasing will be incurred beyond the purchase price.

Required:

1. What are the alternatives for Swasey Manufacturing?
2. List the relevant cost(s) of internal production and of external purchase.
3. Which alternative is more cost effective, and by how much?
4. Now assume that the fixed overhead includes $10,000 of cost that can be avoided if the component is purchased externally. Which alternative is more cost effective, and by how much?

Calculation:

1. There are two alternatives: make the component in house or purchase it externally.
2. Relevant costs of making the component inhouse include direct materials, direct labor, and variable overhead. Relevant costs of purchasing the component externally include the purchase price.

3.

| | Alternatives | | Differential |
	Make	**Buy**	**Cost to Make**
Direct materials	$10,000	—	$10,000
Direct labor	20,000	—	20,000
Variable overhead	8,000	—	8,000
Purchase cost	—	$47,500	(47,500)
Total relevant cost	$38,000	$47,500	$ (9,500)

It is cheaper to make the component in house. This alternative is better by $9,500.

4.

| | Alternatives | | Differential |
	Make	**Buy**	**Cost to Make**
Direct materials	$10,000	—	$10,000
Direct labor	20,000	—	20,000
Variable overhead	8,000	—	8,000
Avoidable fixed overhead	10,000	—	10,000
Purchase cost	—	$47,500	(47,500)
Total relevant cost	$48,000	$47,500	$ 500

Now, it is cheaper to purchase the component. This alternative is better by $500.

Be sure to read the analysis in Cornerstone 12-1 carefully. At first, the fixed overhead remains whether or not the component is made internally. In this case, fixed overhead is not relevant, and making the product is $9,500 cheaper than buying it. Later, in Requirement 4, part of the fixed overhead is avoidable. This means that purchasing the component externally will save $10,000 in fixed cost. Now, the $10,000 of fixed cost is relevant and the offer of the supplier should be accepted; it is $500 cheaper to buy the component.

The same analysis can be done on a unit-cost basis. Once the relevant costs are identified, relevant unit costs can be compared. For this example, these costs are $3.80 ($38,000/10,000) for the make alternative and $4.75 ($47,500/10,000) for the buy alternative.

Concept Q & A

You also have make-or-buy decisions to make. For example, do you change the oil in your car yourself, or do you take it to the shop? Do you make your own clothing? Or do home improvement projects? Choose one such decision and explain why you have chosen to "make it" or "buy it." What factors could change that might make you change your mind?

Answer:
Suppose you choose the oil change decision. You might decide to change it yourself because (1) you know how to, (2) you have the appropriate tools to do the job, (3) you have the time, and (4) you don't mind messing around under the hood. Alternatively, you might decide to have it done because (1) you don't have confidence in your ability to do it, (2) you don't own the equipment (nozzle, pan to hold oil), (3) you are unsure which oil to choose, or (4) you don't want to do the job.

A factor that could make you go from changing your own oil to taking it to a shop might be that you have graduated from college and are working full time and really don't want to mess with oil changes in the few hours of free time you do have.

Special-Order Decisions

From time to time, a company may consider offering a product or service at a price different from the usual price. For example, bid prices can vary to customers in the same market, and firms often have the opportunity to consider special orders from potential customers in markets not ordinarily served. **Special-order decisions** focus on whether a specially priced order should be accepted or rejected. These orders often can be attractive, especially when the firm is operating below its maximum productive capacity. Exhibit 12-2 illustrates the special-order decision.

Suppose, for example, that an ice cream company produces only premium ice cream. Its factory has a capacity of 20 million half-gallon units but only plans to produce 16 million units. The total costs associated with producing and selling 16 million units are as follows (in thousands of dollars):

12-2

EXHIBIT

Accept or Reject a Special Order

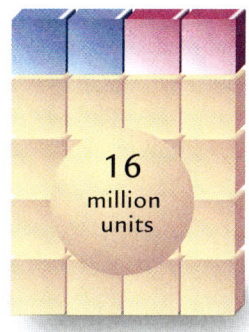
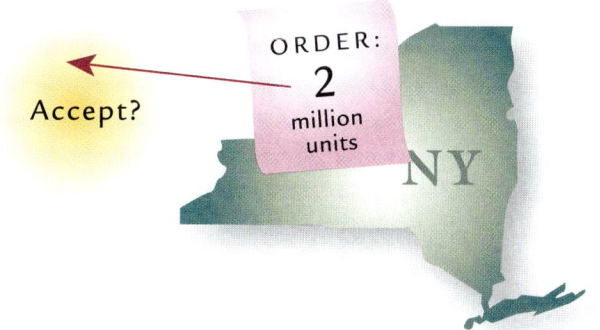

Capacity: **20** million units

	Total	Unit Cost
Variable costs:		
Ingredients	$15,200	$ 0.95
Packaging	3,200	0.20
Direct labor	4,000	0.25
Variable overhead	1,280	0.08
Selling commission	320	0.02
Total variable costs	$24,000	$ 1.50
Total fixed costs	$ 1,552	$0.097
Total costs	$25,552	$1.597
Selling price		$ 2.00

An ice cream distributor from a geographic region not normally served by the company has offered to buy 2 million units at $1.55 per unit, provided its own label can be attached to the product. Since the distributor approached the company directly, there is no sales commission. As the manager of the ice cream company, would you accept or reject this order?

The offer of $1.55 is well below the normal selling price of $2.00; in fact, it is even below the total unit cost. Even so, accepting the order may be profitable. The company does have idle capacity, and the order will not displace other units being produced to sell at the normal price. Additionally, many of the costs are not relevant; fixed costs will continue regardless of whether the order is accepted or rejected.

If the order is accepted, a benefit of $1.55 per unit will be realized that otherwise wouldn't be. However, all of the variable costs except for commissions ($0.02) also will be incurred, producing a cost of $1.48 per unit. The net benefit is $0.07 ($1.55 – $1.48) per unit. The relevant cost analysis can be summarized as follows:

	Accept	Reject	Differential Benefit to Accept
Revenues	$3,100,000	$—	$3,100,000
Ingredients	(1,900,000)	—	(1,900,000)
Packaging	(400,000)	—	(400,000)
Direct labor	(500,000)	—	(500,000)
Variable overhead	(160,000)	—	(160,000)
Profit	$ 140,000	$ 0	$ 140,000

We see that for this company, accepting the special order will increase profits by $140,000 ($0.07 × 2,000,000).

Cornerstone 12-2 shows how to apply relevant costing to a special-order problem.

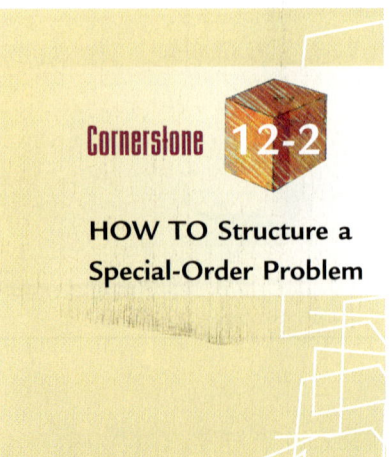

Cornerstone 12-2

HOW TO Structure a Special-Order Problem

Information: Leibnitz Company has been approached by a new customer with an offer to purchase 20,000 units of model TR8 at a price of $9 each. The new customer is geographically separated from the company's other customers, and existing sales would not be affected. Leibnitz normally produces 100,000 units of TR8 per year but only plans to produce and sell 75,000 in the coming year. The normal sales price is $14 per unit. Unit cost information is as follows:

Direct materials	$3.00
Direct labor	2.80
Variable overhead	1.50
Fixed overhead	2.00
Total	$9.30

Fixed overhead will not be affected whether or not the special order is accepted.

Required:

1. What are the relevant costs and benefits of the two alternatives (accept or reject the special order)?
2. By how much will operating income increase or decrease if the order is accepted?

Calculation:

1. Relevant costs and benefits of accepting the special order include the sales price of $9, direct materials, direct labor, and variable overhead. No relevant costs or benefits are attached to rejecting the order.
2. If the problem is done on a unit basis:

	Accept	Reject	Differential Benefit to Accept
Price	$9.00	$—	$9.00
Direct materials	(3.00)	—	(3.00)
Direct labor	(2.80)	—	(2.80)
Variable overhead	(1.50)	—	(1.50)
Increase in operating income	$1.70	$0	$1.70

Operating income will increase by $34,000 ($1.70 × 20,000 units) if the special order is accepted.

Keep-or-Drop Decisions

Often, a manager needs to determine whether or not a segment, such as a product line, should be kept or dropped. Segmented reports prepared on a variable-costing basis provide valuable information for these **keep-or-drop decisions**. Both the segment's contribution margin and its segment margin are useful in evaluating the performance of segments. However, while segmented reports provide useful information for keep-or-drop decisions, relevant costing describes how the information should be used to arrive at a decision.

To illustrate, consider Norton Materials, Inc., which produces concrete blocks, bricks, and roofing tile. The controller has prepared the following estimated segment income statement for next year (in thousands of dollars):

	Blocks	Bricks	Tile	Total
Sales revenue	$500	$800	$150	$1,450
Less: Variable expenses	250	480	140	870
Contribution margin	$250	$320	$ 10	$ 580
Less direct fixed expenses:				
Advertising	(10)	(10)	(10)	(30)
Salaries	(37)	(40)	(35)	(112)
Depreciation	(53)	(40)	(10)	(103)
Segment margin	$150	$230	$(45)	$ 335

The projected performance of the roofing tile line shows a negative segment margin. This would be the third consecutive year of poor performance for that line. The president of Norton Materials, Tom Blackburn—concerned about this poor performance—is trying to decide whether to drop or keep the roofing tile line.

His first reaction is to try to increase the sales revenue of roofing tiles, possibly through an aggressive sales promotion coupled with an increase in the selling price. The marketing manager thinks that this approach would be fruitless, however; the market is saturated and the level of competition too keen to hold out any hope for increasing the firm's market share.

Increasing the product line's profits through cost cutting is not feasible either. Costs were cut the past two years to reduce the loss to its present anticipated level. Any further reductions would lower the quality of the product and adversely affect sales.

With no hope for improving the profit performance of the line beyond its projected level, Tom has decided to drop it. He reasons that the firm will lose a total of $10,000 in contribution margin but save $45,000 by dismissing the line's supervisor and eliminating its advertising budget. (The depreciation cost of $10,000 is not relevant since it represents an allocation of a sunk cost.) Thus, dropping the product line has a $35,000 advantage over keeping it. Cornerstone 12-3 shows how to structure this information as a keep-or-drop product line problem.

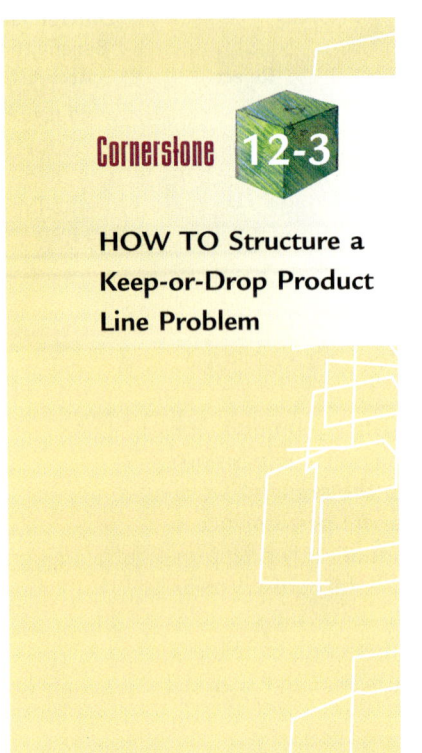

Cornerstone 12-3

HOW TO Structure a Keep-or-Drop Product Line Problem

Information: The roofing tile line has a contribution margin of $10,000 (sales of $150,000 less total variable costs of $140,000). All variable costs are relevant. Relevant fixed costs associated with this line include $10,000 in advertising and $35,000 in supervision.

Required:
1. List the alternatives being considered.
2. List the relevant benefits and costs for each alternative.
3. Which alternative is more cost effective, and by how much?

Calculation:
1. The two alternatives are to keep the roofing tile line or to drop it.
2. The relevant benefits and costs of keeping the roofing tile line include sales of $150,000, variable costs of $140,000, advertising cost of $10,000, and supervision cost of $35,000.
   None of the relevant benefits and costs of keeping the roofing tile line would occur under the drop alternative.
3.

	Keep	Drop	Differential Amount to Keep
Sales	$150,000	$—	$150,000
Less: Variable expenses	140,000	—	140,000
Contribution margin	$ 10,000	$—	$ 10,000
Less: Advertising	(10,000)	—	(10,000)
Cost of supervision	(35,000)	—	(35,000)
Total relevant benefit (loss)	$ (35,000)	$ 0	$ (35,000)

The difference is $35,000 in favor of dropping the roofing tile line.

Keep or Drop with Complementary Effects

Suppose that dropping the roofing tile line would lower sales of blocks by 10 percent and of bricks by 8 percent since many customers buy roofing tile at the same time they purchase blocks or bricks. Some will go elsewhere if they cannot buy both products at the same location. How does this information affect the keep-or-drop decision? Cornerstone 12-4 shows the impact on all product lines.

Cornerstone 12-4

HOW TO Structure a Keep-or-Drop Product Line Problem with Complementary Effects

Information: Dropping the product line reduces sales of blocks by 10 percent and sales of bricks by 8 percent. All other information remains the same.

Required:
1. If the roofing tile line is dropped, what is the contribution margin for the block line? For the brick line?
2. Now which alternative (keep or drop the roofing tile line) is more cost effective, and by how much?

Calculation:

1. Previous contribution margin of blocks was $250,000. A 10-percent decrease in sales implies a 10-percent decrease in total variable costs so contribution margin decreases by 10 percent.

    New contribution margin for blocks = $250,000 – 0.10($250,000) = $225,000.

    The reasoning is the same for the brick line, but the decrease is 8 percent.

    New contribution margin for bricks = $320,000 – 0.08($320,000) = $294,400.

2.

	Keep	Drop	Differential Amount to Keep
Contribution margin	$580,000	$519,400	$60,600
Less: Advertising	(30,000)	(20,000)	(10,000)
Cost of supervision	(112,000)	(77,000)	(35,000)
Total	$438,000	$422,400	$15,600

Notice that the contribution margin for the drop alternative equals the new contribution margins of the block and brick lines ($225,000 + $294,400). Also, advertising and supervision remain relevant across these alternatives.

Now the analysis favors keeping the roofing tile line. In fact, company income will be $15,600 higher if all three lines are kept as opposed to dropping the roofing tile line.

The example provides some insights beyond the simple application of the decision model. The initial analysis, which focused on two feasible alternatives, led to a tentative decision to drop the product line. Additional information provided by the marketing manager led to a reversal of the first decision. Perhaps other feasible alternatives exist as well. These would require still more analysis.

APPLICATIONS IN BUSINESS

Many of us base our impression of hospital emergency rooms on the long-running television drama, "ER." Its emergency room is crowded and functional; the décor runs to green and white (with occasional splashes of red). Where do the patient's family and friends wait? Who knows—they are typically relegated to some cramped, uncomfortable waiting area. Some hospitals, however, have taken steps to improve the ambience of the ER waiting area.

St. Vincent's Hospital in New York City worked with a furniture design company to install warm colors and lighting in its ER waiting area. The ob-

jective was to create a "warm glow." Charlotte, North Carolina's Presbyterian Hospital just opened a pediatric ER with video games and beach murals on the ceilings. The waiting room attached to the ER at Emory Crawford Long Hospital resembles an upscale hotel lobby, with contemporary décor and comfortable armchairs.

Why the new emphasis on improved ER waiting areas? Hospitals have found out that many patients' first contact with their hospital is through the emergency room. If that contact was brusque and unpleasant, patients and their families look elsewhere for a hospital to perform elective surgery or more extensive medical procedures. Since the vast majority of ER patients have health insurance, a poor experience in the ER can negatively affect the bottom line for the hospital's more profitable departments.

Source: Peter Landers, "Hospital Chic: The ER Gets a Makeover," *The Wall Street Journal* (July 8, 2003): D1 and D3.

Further Processing of Joint Products

Joint products have common processes and costs of production up to a split-off point. At that point, they become distinguishable. For example, certain minerals such as copper and gold may both be found in a given ore. The ore must be mined, crushed, and treated before the copper and gold are separated. The point of separation is called the **split-off point**. The costs of mining, crushing, and treatment are common to both products.

Many joint products are sold at the split-off point. However, sometimes it is more profitable to process a joint product further, beyond the split-off point, prior to selling it. A **sell-or-process-further decision** is an important decision that a manager must make.

To illustrate, consider Appletime Corporation, a large corporate farm that specializes in growing apples. Each plot produces approximately one ton of apples. The trees in each plot must be sprayed, fertilized, watered, and pruned. When the apples are ripened, workers are hired to pick them. The apples are then transported to a warehouse, where they are washed and sorted. The approximate cost of all these activities (including processing) is $300 per ton per year.

Apples are sorted into three grades (A, B, and C), determined by size and blemishes. Large apples without blemishes (bruises, cuts, wormholes, and so on) are sorted into one bin and classified as Grade A. Small apples without blemishes are sorted into a second bin and classified as Grade B. All remaining apples are placed in a third bin and classified as Grade C. Every ton of apples produces 800 pounds of Grade A, 600 pounds of Grade B, and 600 pounds of Grade C.

Grade A apples are sold to large supermarkets for $0.40 per pound. Grade B apples are packaged in 5-pound bags and sold to supermarkets for $1.30 per bag. (The cost of each bag is $0.05.) Grade C apples are processed further and made into applesauce. The sauce is sold in 16-ounce cans for $0.75 each. The cost of processing is $0.10 per pound of apples. The final output is 500 sixteen-ounce cans.

A large supermarket chain recently requested that Appletime supply 16-ounce cans of apple pie filling for which the chain is willing to pay $0.90 per can. Appletime determined that the Grade B apples would be suitable for this purpose and estimated that it would cost $0.24 per pound to process the apples into pie filling. The output would be 500 cans. Exhibit 12-3 illustrates the decision to sell grade B apples at the split-off point or process them further into pie filling.

In deciding whether to sell Grade B apples at split-off or to process them further and sell them as pie filling, the common costs of spraying, pruning, and so on, are not relevant. The company must pay the $300 per ton for these activities regardless of whether it sells at split-off or processes further. However, the revenues earned at split-off are likely to differ from the revenues that would be received if the Grade B apples were sold as pie filling. Therefore, revenues are a relevant consideration. Similarly, the processing costs occur only if further processing takes place. Hence, processing costs are relevant. Cornerstone 12-5 shows how to structure the sell-or-process-further decision for the Grade B apples.

Cornerstone 12-5

HOW TO Structure the Sell-or-Process-Further Decision

Information: Appletime must decide whether to sell the Grade B apples at split-off or process them into apple pie filling. The company normally sells the Grade B apples in 120 five-pound bags at a net per-unit price of $1.25. If the apples are processed into pie filling, the result would be 500 cans of filling with additional costs of $0.24 per can. The buyer will pay $0.90 per can.

Required:
1. What is the contribution to income from selling the Grade B apples in 5-pound bags?
2. What is the contribution to income from processing the Grade B apples into pie filling?

Further Processing of Joint Products

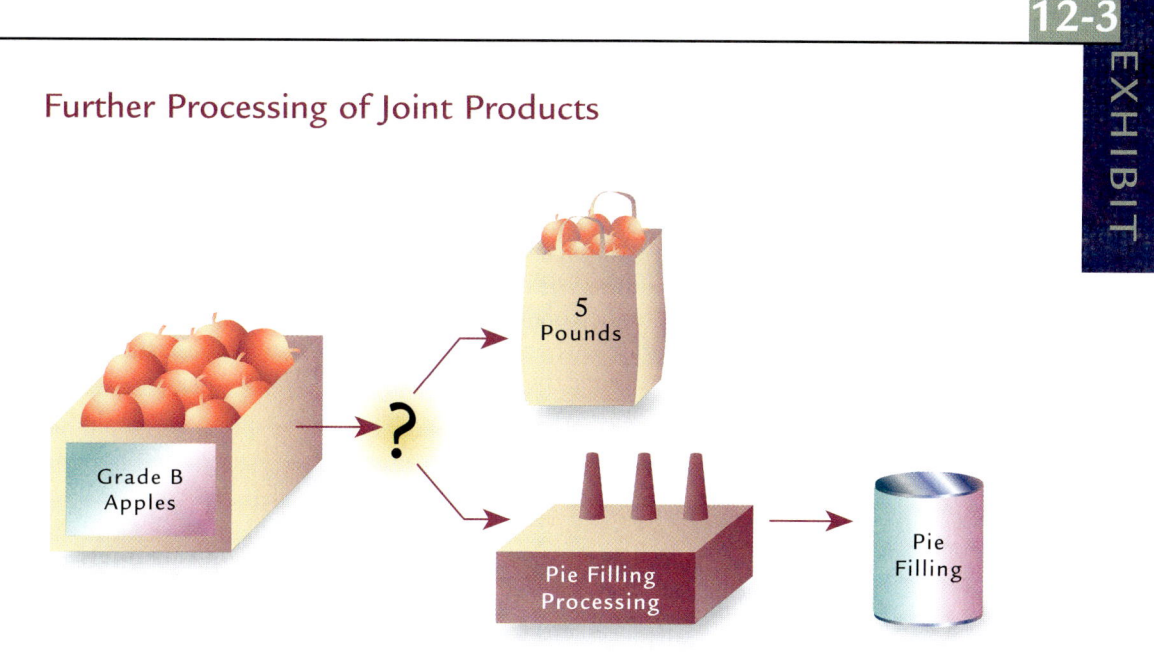

3. Should Appletime continue to sell the Grade B apples in bags, or process them further into pie filling?

Calculation:

1. Revenue from apples in bags = ($1.25 × 120) = $150.
2. Revenue from further processing = $0.90 × 500 = $450.
    Further processing cost = $0.24 × 500 = $120.
    Income from further processing = $450 – $120 = $330.
3. Appletime should process the Grade B apples into pie filling since it will make $330 versus the $150 it would make by selling them in bags.

PRODUCT MIX DECISIONS

OBJECTIVE 3

Choose the optimal product mix when faced with one constrained resource.

Most of the time, organizations have wide flexibility in choosing their product mix. Decisions about product mix can have a significant impact on an organization's profitability.

Each mix represents an alternative that carries with it an associated profit level. A manager should choose the alternative that maximizes total profits. Since fixed costs do not vary with activity level, the total fixed costs of a firm would be the same for all possible mixes and, therefore, are not relevant to the decision. Thus, a manager needs to choose the alternative that maximizes total contribution margin.

Assume, for example, that Jorgenson Company produces two types of gears: X and Y, with unit contribution margins of $25 and $10, respectively. If the firm possesses unlimited resources and the demand for each product is unlimited, then the product mix decision is simple—produce an infinite number of each product. Unfortunately, every firm faces limited resources and limited demand for each product. These limitations are called **constraints**. A manager must choose the optimal mix given the constraints found within the firm.

Assuming that Jorgenson can sell all that is produced, some may argue that only Gear X should be produced and sold—it has the larger contribution margin. However, this solution is not necessarily the best. The selection of the optimal mix can be significantly affected by the relationships of the constrained resources to the individual products. These relationships affect the quantity of each product that can be produced and, consequently, the total contribution margin that can be earned. This point is most vividly illustrated when faced with one resource constraint. Cornerstone 12-6 shows how to determine the optimal product mix with one constrained resource.

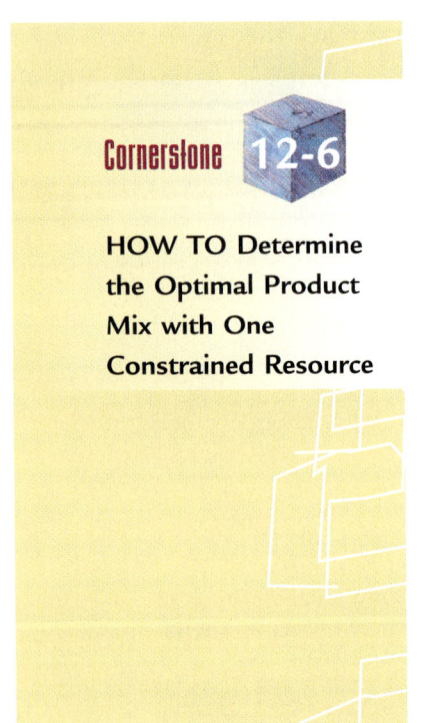

Cornerstone 12-6

HOW TO Determine the Optimal Product Mix with One Constrained Resource

Information: Jorgenson Company produces two types of gears, X and Y, with unit contribution margins of $25 and $10, respectively. Each gear must be notched by a special machine. The firm owns eight machines that together provide 40,000 hours of machine time per year. Gear X requires two hours of machine time, and Gear Y requires 0.5 hour of machine time. There are no other constraints.

Required:
1. What is the contribution margin per hour of machine time for each gear?
2. What is the optimal mix of gears?
3. What is the total contribution margin earned for the optimal mix?

Calculation:

1.

	Gear X	Gear Y
Contribution margin per unit	$ 25	$ 10
÷ Hours of machine time	÷ 2	÷ 0.5
Contribution margin per hour of machine time	$12.50	$ 20

2. Since Gear Y yields $20 of contribution margin per hour of machine time, all machine time should be devoted to the production of Gear Y.

   Units Gear Y = 40,000 total hours/0.5 hour per Gear Y = 80,000 units.

   The optimal mix is Gear Y—80,000 units and Gear X—0 units.

3. Total contribution margin of optimal mix = (80,000 units Gear Y) × $10
   = $800,000

The contribution margin per unit of each product is not the critical concern. The contribution margin per unit of a scarce resource is the deciding factor. The product yielding the highest contribution margin per machine hour should be selected. Gear X earns $12.50 per machine hour ($25/2), but Gear Y earns $20 per machine hour ($10/0.5). Thus, the optimal mix is 80,000 units of Gear Y and none of Gear X.

Suppose, however, that there is also a demand constraint. Only 60,000 units of Gear Y can be sold. Cornerstone 12-7 shows how to incorporate this additional constraint.

Cornerstone 12-7

HOW TO Determine the Optimal Product Mix with One Constrained Resource and a Sales Constraint

Information: Jorgenson Company produces two types of gears, X and Y, with unit contribution margins of $25 and $10, respectively. Each gear must be notched by a special machine. The firm owns eight machines that together provide 40,000 hours of machine time per year. Gear X requires two hours of machine time, and Gear Y requires 0.5 hour of machine time. A maximum of 60,000 units of each gear can be sold.

Required:
1. What is the contribution margin per hour of machine time for each gear?
2. What is the optimal mix of gears?
3. What is the total contribution margin earned for the optimal mix?

Calculation:

1.

	Gear X	Gear Y
Contribution margin per unit	$ 25	$ 10
÷ Hours of machine time	÷ 2	÷ 0.5
Contribution margin per hour of machine time	$12.50	$ 20

2. Since Gear Y yields $20 of contribution margin per hour of machine time, the first priority is to produce all of Gear Y that the market will take.

   Machine time required for maximum amount of Gear Y = 60,000 × 0.5
   = 30,000 hours

   Remaining machine time for Gear X = 40,000 – 30,000
   = 10,000 hours

   Units of Gear X to be produced in 10,000 hours = 10,000/2
   = 5,000 units

   Now the optimal mix is 60,000 units of Gear Y and 5,000 units of Gear X. This will precisely exhaust the machine time available.

3. Total contribution margin of optimal mix
   = (60,000 units Gear Y × $10) + (5,000 units Gear X × $25)
   = $725,000

Concept Q & A

Consider your cell phone plan (or that of a friend). Often, there are different types of minutes—priced at different levels. For example, a plan might include 300 "anytime" minutes and 1,000 "night and weekend minutes." Discuss these as constraints. What do they constrain? Do these constraints affect the decision to phone a friend?

Answer:
They constrain the amount of time you can talk per month. Early in the month, you might phone friends regularly. Later in the month, you might try to figure out how many minutes you have left and try harder to time your calls. For example, calls that must be made at a particular time are made (e.g., to set up a job interview appointment between 9 A.M. and 5 P.M.), while calls to friends and family might be postponed to later in the evening or on the weekend.

Multiple Constrained Resources

The presence of only one constrained resource may not be realistic. Organizations face multiple constraints: limitations of raw materials, limitations of skilled labor, limited demand for each product, and so on. The solution of the product mix problem in the presence of multiple constraints is considerably more complicated and requires the use of a specialized mathematical technique known as linear programming, which is reserved for advanced cost management courses.

THE USE OF COSTS IN PRICING DECISIONS

One of the more difficult decisions faced by a company is pricing. This section examines the impact of cost on price and the role of the accountant in gathering the needed information.

OBJECTIVE 4

Explain the impact of cost on pricing decisions.

Cost-Based Pricing

Demand is one side of the pricing equation; supply is the other side. Since revenue must cover cost for the firm to make a profit, many companies start with cost to determine price. That is, they calculate product cost and add the desired profit. The mechanics of this approach are straightforward. Usually, there is some cost base and a markup. The **markup** is a percentage applied to the base cost; it includes desired profit and any costs not included in the base cost. Companies that bid for jobs routinely base bid price on cost. Cornerstone 12-8 shows how to apply a markup percentage to cost to obtain price.

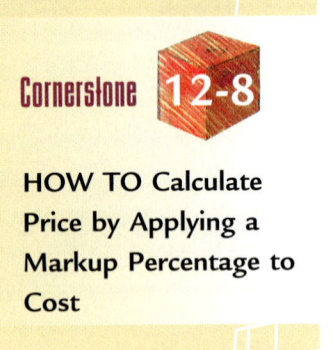

Cornerstone 12-8

HOW TO Calculate Price by Applying a Markup Percentage to Cost

Information: Elvin Company assembles and installs computers to customer specifications. Elvin has decided to price its jobs at the cost of direct materials and direct labor plus 20 percent. The job for a local vocational-technical school included the following costs:

Direct materials	$65,000
Direct labor (assembly and installation)	4,000

Required: Calculate the price charged by Elvin Company to the vocational-technical school.

Calculation:

$$\text{Price} = \text{Cost} + \text{Markup percentage} \times \text{Cost}$$
$$= \$69,000 + 0.20(\$69,000)$$
$$= \$69,000 + \$13,800$$
$$= \$82,800$$

Notice in Cornerstone 12-8 that the markup of 20 percent is not pure profit. Instead, it includes other costs not specified, such as overhead (including Elvin's offices and management salaries), as well as any marketing and administrative expenses. The markup percentage can be calculated using a variety of bases.

Concept Q & A

Consider a situation in which you want to buy something, but it is quite expensive. Suppose that the salesperson says the price of the item is high because the cost to the store is high. (That is, price is related to cost.) Suppose, on the other hand, that the salesperson says the price is high because the demand for the item is strong. (That is, price is not related to cost.) Which explanation would make you happier to buy the item?

Possible Answer:
You would probably be more likely to buy the item when the reason for the high price is high cost to the store. This situation makes the high price seem "fairer" to you, since the store is not gouging you, but simply trying to make a normal profit.

Retail stores often use markup pricing, and typical markup is 100 percent of cost. Thus, if Graham Department Store purchases a sweater for $24, the retail price marked is $48 [$24 + (1.00 × $24)]. Again, the 100-percent markup is not pure profit—it goes toward the salaries of the clerks, payment for space and equipment (cash registers, furniture, and fixtures), utilities, advertising, and so on. A major advantage of markup pricing is that standard markups are easy to apply. Consider the difficulty of setting a price for every piece of merchandise in a hardware or department store. It is much simpler to apply a uniform markup to cost and then adjust prices as needed if demand is less than anticipated.

Target Costing and Pricing

Many American and European firms set the price of a new product as the sum of the costs and the desired profit. The rationale is that the company must earn sufficient revenues to cover all costs and yield a profit. Peter Drucker writes, "This is true but irrelevant: Customers do not see it as their job to ensure manufacturers a profit. The only sound way to price is to start out with what the market is willing to pay."[1]

Target costing is a method of determining the cost of a product or service based on the price (target price) that customers are willing to pay. The marketing department determines what characteristics and price for a product are most acceptable to consumers; then, it is the job of the company's engineers to design and develop the product such that cost and profit can be covered by that price. Japanese firms have been doing this for years; American companies are beginning to use target costing.

For example, Digitime Company is developing a wristwatch that incorporates a PDA (personal digital assistant). The "cool factor" on this item is high, but actually inputting data on the watch is difficult. So, the company expects to be able to charge a premium price to a relatively small number of early adopters. The marketing vice president's price estimate is $200. Digitime's management requires a 15-percent profit on new products. Cornerstone 12-9 shows how to calculate a target cost.

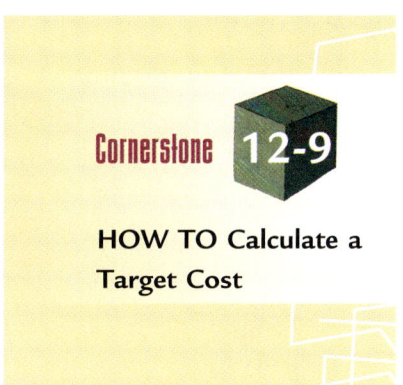

Cornerstone 12-9

HOW TO Calculate a Target Cost

Information: Digitime's new wristwatch plus PDA has a target price of $200. Management requires a 15-percent profit on new products.

Required:
1. Calculate the amount of desired profit.
2. Calculate the target cost.

Calculation:
1. Desired profit = 0.15 × Target price
                    = 0.15 × $200
                    = $30
2. Target cost = Target price − Desired profit
               = $200 − $30
               = $170

Target costing involves much more up-front work than cost-based pricing. If Digitime can't make the watch for $170, then the engineers and designers will have to go back to the drawing board and find a way to get it done on budget. However, let's not forget the additional work that must be done if the cost-based price turns out to be higher than what customers will accept. Then the arduous task of bringing costs into line to support a lower price, or the opportunity cost of missing the market altogether, begins. For example, in the 1980s, the U.S. consumer electronics market became virtually nonexistent because cost-based pricing led to increasingly higher prices. Japanese

[1]Peter Drucker, "The Five Deadly Business Sins," *The Wall Street Journal* (October 21, 1993): A22.

APPLICATIONS IN BUSINESS

Convenience stores constantly balance the need to offer a wide selection of products with the need to streamline offerings so that they can fit into the small-store format. In the past, stores determined which products to stock based on each one's profitability. Profit was calculated as the difference between wholesale and retail prices. While this sounds reasonable, it completely ignores the additional costs associated with carrying and stocking each product line. In early 2001, the American Wholesale Marketers Association and the National Association of Convenience Stores presented the results of a study of new software designed to "assess each item's profitability by factoring in the operating, labor, inventory, and overhead costs of each item." In the past, the cost of handling a product was not considered in determining per-product costs. However, handling costs are a significant part of the total cost structure.

One owner of a chain of convenience stores tested the software and learned that every auto fuse and bulb sold resulted in a loss of 50 cents. He surveyed customers and found that they were willing to pay a higher price. As a result, he raised the price by a dollar. This achieved two goals. The bulbs and fuses now make money, and customers still appreciate the opportunity to pop into the convenience store for suddenly needed products. The same chain determined that three kinds of laundry detergent were two too many. It pared its offering to one brand and displayed it more prominently. Sales increased by 20 percent, while costs fell because the sole brand could be ordered by the case.

Source: Ann Zimmerman, "Convenience Stores Create Software to Boost Profitability and Cut Costs," *The Wall Street Journal Interactive Edition* (February 15, 2001).

(and later Korean) firms practicing target costing offered lower prices and just the features consumers wanted to win the market.

Target costing can be used most effectively in the design and development stage of the product life cycle. At that point, the features of the product as well as its costs are still fairly easy to adjust.

DECISION MAKING FOR INVENTORY MANAGEMENT

Other types of short-run decisions relate to inventories of raw materials, work in process, and finished goods. Audio-Blast, in the opening Scenario, experienced ongoing problems with raw materials and finished goods inventories. Lack of storage for these inventories had a spill-over effect on productive capacity and warehouse costs.

OBJECTIVE 5

Discuss inventory management under the economic order quantity and JIT models.

Inventory-Related Costs

When the demand for a product or material is known with near certainty for a given period of time (usually a year), two major costs are associated with inventory. If the inventory is a material or good purchased from an outside source, then these inventory-related costs are known as *ordering costs* and *carrying costs*. (If the material or good is produced internally, then the costs are called *setup costs* and *carrying costs*.)

Ordering costs are the costs of placing and receiving an order. Examples include order processing costs (clerical costs and documents), the cost of insurance for shipment, and unloading costs. **Carrying costs** are the costs of carrying inventory. Examples include insurance, inventory taxes, obsolescence, the opportunity cost of funds tied up in inventory, handling costs, and storage space.

If demand is not known with certainty, then a third category of inventory costs—called *stockout costs*—exists. **Stockout costs** are the costs of not having a product available when demanded by a customer or the cost of not having a raw material available when needed for production. Examples are lost sales (both current and future), the costs of expediting (increased transportation charges, overtime, and so on), and the costs of interrupted production (e.g., idled workers).

Concept Q & A

Has a store ever been out of an item you wanted to buy? What did you do? What is the impact of the stockout on the store?

Answer:
You might have gone to another store or tried to buy the item from a catalog or online. The stockout cost the first store not only the profit to be made from selling to you, but also, potentially, your future business.

It is important to realize that the purchase price of raw materials is not a part of the total cost associated with carrying inventory. That price must be paid anyway.

Exhibit 12-4 summarizes the reasons typically offered for carrying inventory. It's important to realize that these reasons are given to *justify* carrying inventories. A host of other reasons can be offered that *encourage* the carrying of inventories. For example, performance measures such as measures of machine and labor efficiency may promote the buildup of inventories.

Economic Order Quantity: The Traditional Inventory Model

Once a company decides to carry inventory, two basic questions must be addressed:

1. How much should be ordered?
2. When should the order be placed?

The first question needs to be addressed before the second can be answered. Assume that demand is known. In choosing an order quantity, managers need be concerned only with ordering and carrying costs. The formulas for calculating these are as follows:

$$\text{Total inventory-related cost} = \text{Ordering cost} + \text{Carrying cost}$$

$$\text{Ordering cost} = \text{Number of orders per year} \times \text{Cost of placing an order}$$

$$\text{Carrying cost} = \text{Average number of units in inventory} \times \text{Cost of carrying one unit in inventory}$$

The cost of carrying inventory can be computed for any organization that carries inventories, including retail, service, and manufacturing organizations. Cornerstone 12-10 illustrates the application for a service organization and shows how to calculate total ordering cost, carrying cost, and inventory cost.

12-4

EXHIBIT

Traditional Reasons for Carrying Inventory

1. To balance ordering or setup costs and carrying costs.
2. To satisfy customer demand (for example, meet delivery dates).
3. To avoid shutting down manufacturing facilities because of:
   a. Machine failure.
   b. Defective parts.
   c. Unavailable parts.
   d. Late delivery of parts.
4. To buffer against unreliable production processes.
5. To take advantage of discounts.
6. To hedge against future price increases.

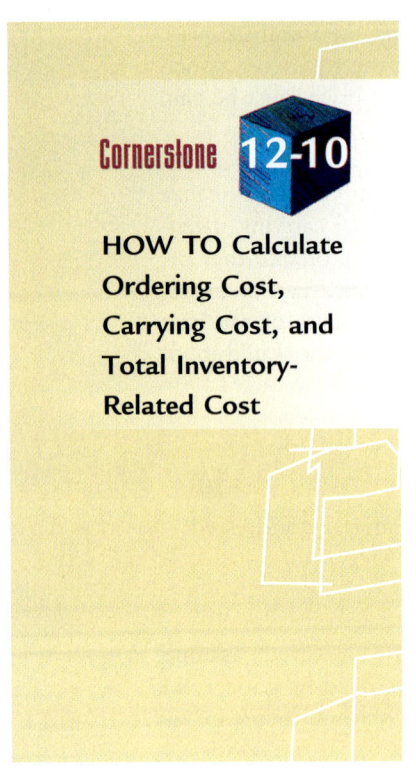

Cornerstone 12-10

HOW TO Calculate Ordering Cost, Carrying Cost, and Total Inventory-Related Cost

Information: Mall-o-Cars, Inc., sells a number of automotive brands and provides service after the sale for those brands. Part X7B is used in the repair of water pumps (the part is purchased from external suppliers). Each year, 10,000 units of Part X7B are used; they are currently purchased in lots of 1,000 units. It costs Mall-o-Cars $25 to place the order, and carrying cost is $2 per part per year.

Required:

1. How many orders for Part X7B does Mall-o-Cars place per year?
2. What is the total ordering cost of Part X7B per year?
3. What is the total carrying cost of Part X7B per year?
4. What is the total cost of Mall-o-Cars's inventory policy for Part X7B per year?

Calculation:

1. Number of orders = Annual number of units used/Number of units in an order
   = 10,000/1,000
   = 10 orders per year
2. Total ordering cost = Number of orders × Cost per order
   = 10 orders × $25
   = $250
3. Total carrying cost = Average number of units in inventory × Cost of carrying one unit in inventory
   = (1,000/2) × $2
   = $1,000
4. Total inventory-related cost = Total ordering cost + Total carrying cost
   = $250 + $1,000
   = $1,250

The total carrying cost for the year is figured by multiplying the average number of units on hand by the cost of carrying one unit in inventory for a year. But what is the average number of units on hand? Given the policy of ordering 1,000 units at a time, the maximum number on hand would be 1,000 units—the amount on hand just after an order is delivered. The minimum amount on hand would be zero, ideally, the amount seconds before the new order arrives. Therefore, the average amount in inventory is the maximum plus the minimum divided by two.

The total cost of Mall-o-Cars's current policy is $1,250 ($250 + $1,000). An order quantity of 1,000 with a total cost of $1,250, however, may not be the best choice. Some other order quantity may produce a lower total cost. The objective is to find the order quantity that minimizes the total cost. The number of units in the optimal size order quantity is called the **economic order quantity (EOQ)**.

The Economic Order Quantity (EOQ)

Since EOQ is the quantity that minimizes total inventory-related costs, a formula[2] for computing this quantity can be stated as:

$$EOQ = \sqrt{\frac{2 \times CO \times D}{CC}}$$

where:

EOQ = The number of units to be ordered at one time
CO = The cost of placing one order
D = The annual demand for the item in units
CC = The cost of carrying one unit in inventory for a year

Cornerstone 12-11 shows how to use the EOQ formula.

[2]This formula is derived using calculus. Its derivation is reserved for a later course.

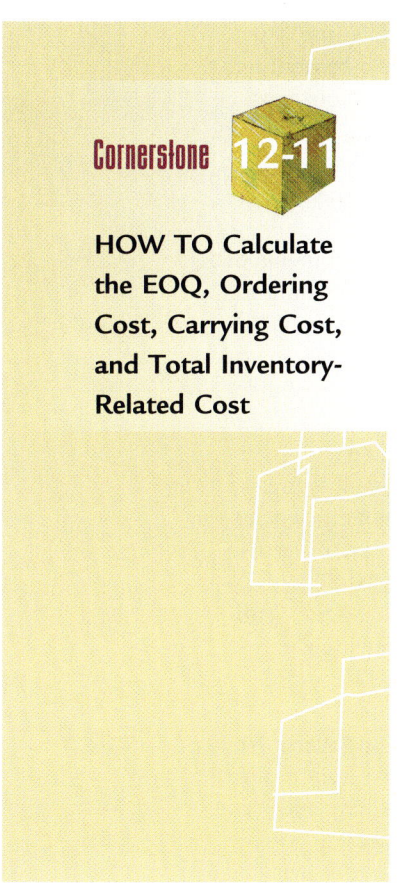

Cornerstone 12-11

HOW TO Calculate the EOQ, Ordering Cost, Carrying Cost, and Total Inventory-Related Cost

Information: Mall-o-Cars, Inc., provides service after the sale for a variety of automotive makes and models. Part X7B is used in the repair of water pumps (the part is purchased from external suppliers). Each year, 10,000 units of Part X7B are used; they are currently purchased in lots of 1,000 units. It costs Mall-o-Cars $25 to place the order, and carrying cost is $2 per part per year.

Required:

1. What is the EOQ for Part X7B?
2. How many orders per year for Part X7B will Mall-o-Cars place under the EOQ policy?
3. What is the total annual ordering cost of Part X7B for a year under the EOQ policy?
4. What is the total annual carrying cost of Part X7B per year under the EOQ policy?
5. What is the total annual inventory-related cost for Part X7B under the EOQ?

Calculation:

1. $EOQ = \sqrt{2 \times 10,000 \times \$25/\$2}$
   $= \sqrt{500,000/2}$
   $= 500$ units

2. Number of orders = Annual number of units used/Number of units in an order
   $= 10,000/500$
   $= 20$ orders per year

3. Total ordering cost = Number of orders × Cost per order
   $= 20$ orders $\times \$25$
   $= \$500$

4. Total carrying cost = Average number of units in inventory × Cost of carrying one unit in inventory
   $= (500/2) \times \$2$
   $= \$500$

5. Total inventory-related cost = Total ordering cost + Total carrying cost
   $= \$500 + \$500$
   $= \$1,000$

Notice that at the EOQ the carrying cost equals the ordering cost. This is always true for the simple EOQ model described here. Also, notice that an order quantity of 500 is less costly than an order quantity of 1,000 ($1,000 versus $1,250).

EOQ and Inventory Management

The EOQ model is very useful in identifying the optimal trade-off between inventory ordering costs and carrying costs. It also is useful in helping to deal with uncertainty by using safety stock. The historical importance of the EOQ model in many American industries can be better appreciated by understanding the nature of the traditional manufacturing environment. This environment has been characterized by the mass production of a few standardized products that typically have a very high setup cost. The high setup cost encouraged a large batch size. Thus, production runs for these firms tended to be quite long, and the excess production was placed in inventory.

Just-in-Time Approach to Inventory Management

The economic environment for many traditional, large-batch, high setup cost firms has changed dramatically in the past 10 to 20 years. Advances in transportation and communication have contributed significantly to the creation of global competition. Advances in technology have contributed to shorter life cycles for products, and product diversity has increased. These competitive pressures have led many firms to abandon the EOQ model in favor of a JIT approach. In this way, the costs of ordering and carrying inventory are simply not incurred. However, it is still necessary to solve the underlying problems with uncertainty.

The **just-in-time (JIT)** approach maintains that goods should be pulled through the system by present demand rather than pushed through the system on a fixed schedule based on anticipated demand. Many fast-food restaurants, like McDonald's, use a pull system to control their finished goods inventory. When a customer orders a hamburger, it is taken from the rack. When the number of hamburgers gets too low, the cooks make new hamburgers. Customer demand pulls the materials through the system. This same principle is used in manufacturing settings. Each operation produces only what is necessary to satisfy the demand of the succeeding operation. The material or subassembly arrives just in time for production to occur so that demand can be met.

The hallmark of JIT is to reduce all inventories to very low levels. The pursuit of insignificant levels of inventories is vital to the success of JIT. This idea of pursuing insignificant inventories, however, necessarily challenges the traditional reasons for holding inventories (see Exhibit 12-4). These reasons are no longer viewed as valid.

According to the traditional view, inventories solve some underlying problem related to each of the reasons listed in Exhibit 12-4. For example, the problem of resolving the conflict between ordering or setup costs and carrying costs is solved by selecting an inventory level that minimizes the sum of these costs. If demand is greater than expected or if production is reduced by breakdowns and production inefficiencies, then inventories serve as buffers, providing products to customers that may otherwise not have been available. Similarly, inventories can prevent shutdowns caused by late deliveries of materials, defective parts, and failures of machines used to produce subassemblies. Finally, inventories are often the solution to the problem of buying the best raw materials for the least cost through the use of quantity discounts. JIT inventory management offers alternative solutions that do not require high inventories.

Ordering costs are reduced by developing close relationships with suppliers. Negotiating long-term contracts for the supply of outside materials will obviously reduce the number of orders and the associated ordering costs. Some retailers have reduced ordering costs by allowing the manufacturer to handle inventory management for the retailer. The manufacturer tells the retailer when and how much stock to reorder. The retailer reviews the recommendation and approves the order if it makes sense. Wal-Mart and Procter & Gamble, for example, use this arrangement to reduce inventories, as well as stockout problems.

Uncertainty in demand is approached by reducing setup times. Then, manufacturers can literally produce to order. Most shutdowns occur for one of three reasons: machine failure, defective material or subassembly, and unavailability of a raw material or subassembly. Holding inventories is one traditional solution to all three problems. Those espousing the JIT approach claim that inventories do not solve these problems but rather cover up or hide them. JIT solves the three problems by emphasizing total preventive maintenance and total quality control and by building the right kind of relationship with suppliers.

Traditionally, inventories are carried so that a firm can take advantage of quantity discounts and hedge against future price increases of the items purchased. The objective is to lower the cost of inventory. JIT achieves the same objective without carrying inventories. The JIT solution is to negotiate long-term contracts with a few chosen suppliers located as close to the production facility as possible and to establish more extensive supplier involvement. Suppliers are not selected on the basis of price alone. Performance—the quality of the component and the ability to deliver as needed—and commitment to JIT purchasing are vital considerations. Other benefits of long-term contracts exist. They stipulate prices and acceptable quality levels. Long-term contracts also reduce dramatically the number of orders placed, which helps to drive down the ordering cost.

JIT does have limitations. JIT is often referred to as a program of simplification—yet this does not imply that it is simple or easy to implement. Time is required, for example, to build sound relationships with suppliers. Insisting on immediate changes in delivery times and quality may not be realistic and may cause difficult confrontations between a company and its suppliers. Workers also may be affected by JIT. Studies have shown that sharp reductions in inventory buffers may cause a regimented workflow and high levels of stress among production workers. If the workers perceive JIT as a way of simply squeezing more out of them, then JIT efforts may be doomed. Perhaps a better strategy for JIT implementation is one where inventory reductions follow the process improvements that JIT offers. Implementing JIT is not easy, and it requires careful and thorough planning and preparation. Companies should expect some struggle and frustration.

The most glaring deficiency of JIT is the absence of inventory to buffer production interruptions. Current sales are constantly being threatened by an unexpected interruption in production. In fact, if a problem occurs, JIT's approach consists of trying to find and solve the problem before any further production activity occurs. Retailers who use JIT tactics also face the possibility of shortages. (JIT retailers order what they need now—not what they expect to sell—the idea is to flow goods through the channel as late as possible, keeping inventories low and decreasing the need for markdowns.) If demand increases well beyond the retailer's supply of inventory, then the retailer may be unable to make order adjustments quickly enough to avoid lost sales and irritated customers. The JIT manufacturing company is also willing to place current sales at risk to achieve assurance of future sales. This assurance comes from higher quality, quicker response time, and less operating costs. Even so, we must recognize that a sale lost today is a sale lost forever. Installing a JIT system so that it operates with very little interruption is not a short-run project. Thus, losing sales is a real cost of installing a JIT system.

In the opening scenario, Audio-Blast's management team struggled to find ways to improve productive capacity and increase storage space. After a month of fact-finding and intense discussion, the team decided to lease an additional building across the street for warehouse space. The lease was short term so that the company could also experiment with a JIT approach to inventory. The suppliers for Audio-Blast were a diverse group, and the cost of trimming materials inventories by instituting long-term contracts and supplier relationships was seen as more trouble than it was worth. However, trimming the inventory of finished goods was practical. Audio-Blast began converting some of the speaker assembly lines to manufacturing cells. In this way, speakers could be made in response to customer orders. Large amounts of finished goods inventory were no longer needed.

A side benefit of Audio-Blast's exercise in relevant costing was the enthusiasm it engendered in Bill's management team. The team developed a decision-making vocabulary that helped with both job-related and personal decision making. Bill, Gene, Carol, and Harry found ways to use relevant costing in personal decision making—everything from deciding whether or not to buy a car for a newly licensed teenager to handling problems with aging parents.

SUMMARY OF LEARNING OBJECTIVES

The decision-making model described in this chapter consists of six steps: recognizing and defining the problem, identifying alternatives, determining the costs and benefits of each alternative, comparing relevant costs and benefits for each alternative, assessing qualitative factors, and making the decision. In using cost analysis to choose among alternatives, managers should take steps to ensure that all important feasible alternatives are being considered.

It is important to consider relevant cost and benefits in making decisions. Relevant costs are future costs that vary among alternatives. Sunk costs are never relevant costs. In addition, costs that are future costs may be irrelevant if they stay the same across alternatives. Cost behavior is a key consideration in determining whether or not a cost is relevant.

Several examples illustrating the application of the relevant costing model were given within the chapter. Applications were illustrated for make-or-buy decisions, keep-or-drop decisions, and special-order decisions. Product mix decisions were also discussed. The list of applications is by no means exhaustive but was given to illustrate the scope and power of relevant costing analysis.

In dealing with a resource constraint, it is important to phrase the product contribution margin in terms of contribution margin per unit of constrained resource.

Costs are important inputs into the pricing decision. Cost-based pricing uses a markup based on a subset of costs. Target costing works backward from a price acceptable to consumers to find the cost necessary to manufacture the product.

Inventory management involves short-run decision making. The traditional approach uses inventories to manage the trade-offs between ordering (setup) costs and carrying costs. The optimal trade-off defines the economic order quantity (EOQ). Other reasons for inventories are also offered: due-date performance, avoiding shutdowns (protecting sales), hedging against future price increases, and taking advantage of discounts.

JIT, on the other hand, argues that inventories are costly and are used to cover up fundamental problems that need to be corrected so that the organization can become more competitive. JIT uses long-term contracts and supplier relationships to handle materials delivery problems and reduce ordering cost. Similarly, efforts are made to increase the efficiency of production through the reduction in setup times and the creation of manufacturing cells. Maximizing quality and productivity while minimizing lead time become critically important.

Cornerstones for Chapter 12

KEY TERMS

DISCUSSION QUESTIONS

1. What is the difference between tactical and strategic decisions?
2. Explain why depreciation on an existing asset is always irrelevant.
3. Give an example of a future cost that is not relevant.
4. What role do past costs play in relevant costing decisions?
5. Can direct materials ever be irrelevant in a make-or-buy decision? Explain.
6. Discuss the importance of complementary effects in a keep-or-drop decision.
7. What are some ways a manager can expand his or her knowledge of the feasible set of alternatives?
8. Should joint costs be considered in a sell-or-process-further decision? Explain.
9. Suppose that a product can be sold at split-off for $5,000 or processed further at a cost of $1,000 and then sold for $6,400. Should the product be processed further?
10. Suppose that a firm produces two products. Should the firm always place the most emphasis on the product with the largest contribution margin per unit? Explain.
11. Why would a firm ever offer a price on a product that is below its full cost?
12. Does the purchase price of the part being ordered enter into the EOQ equation? Why or why not?
13. What are ordering costs? Carrying costs? Give examples of each.
14. What are stockout costs?
15. What are the reasons for carrying inventory?

MULTIPLE-CHOICE EXERCISES

12-1 Which of the following is not a step in the short-run decision-making model?

a. Defining the problem
b. Identifying alternatives
c. Identifying the costs and benefits of feasible alternatives
d. Assessing qualitative factors
e. All of the above are steps in the short-run decision-making model.

12-2 Costs that cannot be affected by any future action are called

a. differential costs.
b. relevant costs.
c. inventory costs.
d. sunk costs.
e. joint costs.

Use the following information for 12-3, 12-4, and 12-5.

Sandy is considering moving from her apartment into a small house with a fenced yard. The apartment is noisy, and she has difficulty studying. In addition, the fenced yard would be great for her dog. The distance from school is much the same from the house and from the apartment. The apartment costs $750 per month, and she has two months remaining on her lease. The lease cannot be broken so Sandy must pay the last two months of rent, whether she lives there or not. The rent for the house is $450 per month, plus utilities, which should average $100 per month. The apartment is furnished; the house is not. If Sandy moves into the house, she will need to buy a bed, dresser, desk, and chair immediately. She thinks she can pick up some used furniture for a good price.

12-3 Which of the following costs is irrelevant to Sandy's decision to stay in the apartment or move to the house?

a. House rent of $450 per month
b. Utilities for the house of $100 per month
c. The noise in the apartment house
d. The cost of the used furniture
e. The last two months of rent in the apartment

12-4 Which of the following is a qualitative factor?

a. House rent of $450 per month
b. Utilities for the house of $100 per month
c. The noise in the apartment house
d. The cost of the used furniture
e. The last two months of rent in the apartment

12-5 Suppose that the apartment building was within walking distance to campus and the house was five miles away. Sandy does not own a car. How would that affect her decision?

a. It would make the apartment more desirable.
b. It would make the house more desirable.
c. It would make both choices less desirable.
d. It would make both choices more desirable.
e. It would have no effect on the decision; buying or not buying a car is a separate decision.

12-6 Which of the following is a true statement?

a. Fixed costs are always irrelevant.
b. Variable costs are always relevant.
c. Step costs may be relevant if an alternative requires moving outside the existing relevant range.
d. Usually, variable costs are irrelevant.
e. All of the above.

12-7 In a make-or-buy decision,

a. the company must choose between expanding or dropping a product line.
b. the company must choose between accepting or rejecting a special order.
c. the company would consider the purchase price of the externally provided good to be relevant.
d. the company would consider all fixed overhead to be irrelevant.
e. none of the above.

12-8 Carroll Company, a manufacturer of vitamins and minerals, has been asked by a large drugstore chain to provide bottles of vitamin E. The bottles would be labeled with the name of the drugstore chain, and the chain would pay Carroll Company $2.30 per bottle rather than the $3.00 regular price. Which type of a decision is this?

a. Make-or-buy
b. Keep-or-drop
c. Special-order
d. Economic order quantity
e. Markup pricing

12-9 Jennings Hardware Store marks up its merchandise by 80 percent. If a part costs $1.50, which of the following is true?

a. The price is $1.20.
b. The markup is $2.70.

c. The price is $2.70.
d. The markup is pure profit.
e. All of the above.

12-10 The EOQ for Part B-22 is 2,500 units, and four orders are placed each year. The total annual ordering cost is $1,200. Which of the following is true?

a. The total carrying cost is $1,200.
b. The annual demand for the part is 2,500 units.
c. The cost of placing one order is $1,200.
d. The cost of placing one order is $4,800.
e. It is impossible to calculate the annual carrying cost given the above information.

12-11 When a company faces a production constraint or scarce resource (for example, only a certain number of machine hours is available), it is important to

a. produce the product with the highest contribution margin.
b. produce the product with the lowest full manufacturing cost.
c. produce a mix of products.
d. produce the product with the highest contribution margin per unit of scarce resource.
e. The constraint is not relevant to the production problem.

12-12 In the keep-or-drop decision, the company will find which of the following income statement formats most useful?

a. A segmented income statement in the contribution margin format
b. A segmented income statement in the full costing format that is used for financial reporting
c. An overall income statement in the contribution margin format
d. An overall income statement in the full costing format that is used for financial reporting
e. Income statements are of no use in making this type of decision.

12-13 In the sell-or-process-further decision,

a. joint costs are never relevant.
b. total costs of joint processing and further processing are relevant.
c. all costs incurred prior to the split-off point are relevant.
d. only agricultural products can be processed further.
e. none of the above.

12-14 Which of the following is a reason for carrying inventory?

a. To balance setup and carrying costs
b. To satisfy customer demand
c. To avoid shutting down manufacturing facilities
d. To take advantage of discounts
e. All of the above

EXERCISES

Exercise 12-1 *Model for Making Tactical Decisions*

 OBJECTIVE 1

The model for making tactical decisions that was described in your text has six steps. These steps are listed, out of order, below.

Required:
Put the steps in the correct order starting with the step that should be taken first.

1. Select the alternative with the greatest overall benefit.
2. Identify the costs and benefits associated with each feasible alternative.
3. Assess qualitative factors.
4. Recognize and define the problem.
5. Identify alternatives as possible solutions to the problem.
6. Total the relevant costs and benefits for each alternative.

Exercise 12-2 *Model for Making Tactical Decisions*

Austin Porter is a sophomore at a small midwestern university (SMWU). He is considering whether to continue at this university or to transfer to one with a nationally recognized engineering program. Austin's decision-making process included the following:

a. He surfed the Web to check out the sites of a number of colleges and universities with engineering programs.
b. Austin wrote to five of the universities to obtain information on their engineering colleges, tuition and room and board costs, likelihood of his being accepted, and so on.
c. Austin compared costs of the five other schools to the cost of his present school. He totaled the balance in his checking and savings accounts, estimated the earnings from his work-study job, and asked his parents whether or not they would be able to help him out.
d. Austin's high-school sweetheart had a long heart-to-heart talk with him about their future—specifically, that there might be no future if he left town.
e. Austin thought that while he enjoyed his present college, its engineering program did not have the national reputation that would enable him to get a good job on either the East or West coast. Working for a large company on the coast was an important dream of his.
f. Austin's major advisor agreed that a school with a national reputation would make job hunting easier. However, he reminded Austin that small college graduates had occasionally gotten the kind of jobs Austin wanted.
g. Austin had a number of good friends at SMWU, and they were encouraging him to stay.
h. A friend of Austin's from high school returned home for a long weekend. She attends a prestigious university and told Austin of the fun and opportunities available at her school. She encouraged Austin to check out the possibilities elsewhere.
i. A friendly professor outside of Austin's major area ran into him at the student union. She listened to his thinking and reminded him that a degree from SMWU would easily get him into a good graduate program. Perhaps he ought to consider postponing the job hunt until he had his master's degree in hand.
j. Two of the three prestigious universities accepted Austin and offered financial aid. The third one rejected his application.
k. Austin made his decision.

Required:

Classify the above events as one the six steps of the model for making tactical decisions described in your text.

Exercise 12-3 *Make-or-Buy Decision*

LaSalle Manufacturing had always made its components in house. However, Jasper Component Works had recently offered to supply one component, C-430, at a price of $12 each. LaSalle uses 4,100 units of Component C-430 each year. The absorption cost per unit of this component is as follows:

Direct materials	$ 7.42
Direct labor	2.38
Variable overhead	1.75
Fixed overhead	3.00
Total	$14.55

The fixed overhead is an allocated expense; none of it would be eliminated if production of Component C-430 stopped.

Required:

1. What are the alternatives facing LaSalle Manufacturing with respect to production of Component C-430?
2. List the relevant costs for each alternative.
3. If LaSalle decides to purchase the component from Jasper, by how much will operating income increase or decrease? Which alternative is better?

Exercise 12-4 *Make-or-Buy Decision*

Refer to **Exercise 12-3**. Now assume that 40 percent of LaSalle Manufacturing's fixed overhead for Component C-430 would be eliminated if that component would no longer be produced.

Required:

If LaSalle decides to purchase the component from Jasper, by how much will operating income increase or decrease? Which alternative is better?

Exercise 12-5 *Special-Order Decision*

Otonic Company has been approached by a new customer with an offer to purchase 2,300 units of Otonic's product at a price of $6.90 each. The new customer is geographically separated from Otonic's other customers, and existing sales would not be affected. Otonic normally produces 12,000 units but only plans to produce and sell 9,000 in the coming year. The normal sales price is $11 per unit. Unit cost information is as follows:

Direct materials	$1.75
Direct labor	2.80
Variable overhead	1.40
Fixed overhead	2.00
Total	$7.95

If Otonic accepts the order, no fixed manufacturing activities will be affected because there is sufficient excess capacity.

Required:

1. What are the alternatives for Otonic?
2. Should Otonic accept the special order? By how much will profit increase or decrease if the order is accepted?

Exercise 12-6 *Special Order*

Refer to **Exercise 12-5**. Now suppose that the customer wants to have a label with its own name on each unit. Otonic would have to purchase a special labeling machine that will cost $2,300. The machine will be able to label the 2,300 units and then it will be scrapped (with no further value).

Required:

Should Otonic accept the special order? By how much will profit increase or decrease if the order is accepted?

Exercise 12-7 *Keep-or-Drop Decision*

Uintah Company produces three products: A, B, and C. A segmented income statement, with amounts given in thousands, follows:

	A	B	C	Total
Sales revenue	$700	$1,800	$200	$2,700
Less: Variable expenses	350	1,000	140	1,490
Contribution margin	$350	$ 800	$ 60	$1,210
Less: Direct fixed expenses	100	300	70	470
Segment margin	$250	$ 500	$(10)	$ 740

Direct fixed expenses consist of depreciation on equipment dedicated to the product lines. None of the equipment can be sold.

Required:
What impact on profit would result from dropping Product C?

Exercise 12-8 *Keep-or-Drop Decision*

Refer to **Exercise 12-7**. Now suppose that 10 percent of the customers for Product B choose to buy from Uintah because it offers a full range of products, including Product C. If C were no longer available from Uintah, these customers would go elsewhere to purchase B.

Required:
Now what is the impact on profit if Product C is dropped?

Exercise 12-9 *Sell at Split-Off or Process Further*

Crosby Company manufactures two products from a joint production process. The joint process costs $140,000 and yields 1,000 pounds of Alpha-P and 3,000 pounds of Beta-Q. Alpha-P can be sold at split-off for $60 per pound. Beta-Q can be sold at split-off for $45 per pound. A buyer of Beta-Q asked Crosby Company to process Beta-Q further into Beta-Z. If Beta-Q were processed further, it would cost $9,000 to turn 3,000 pounds of Beta-Q into 2,500 pounds of Beta-Z. The Beta-Z would sell for $50 per pound.

Required:
1. What is the contribution to income from selling the 3,000 pounds of Beta-Q at split-off?
2. What is the contribution to income from processing the 3,000 pounds of Beta-Q into 2,500 pounds of Beta-Z? Should Crosby Company continue to sell the Beta-Q at split-off, or process it further into Beta-Z?

Exercise 12-10 *Choosing the Optimal Product Mix with One Constrained Resource*

Billings Company produces two products, Product Reno and Product Tahoe. Each product goes through its own assembly and finishing departments. However, both of them must go through the painting department. The painting department has capacity of 2,460 hours per year. Product Reno has a unit contribution margin of $120 and requires five hours of painting department time. Product Tahoe has a unit contribution margin of $75 and requires three hours of painting department time. There are no other constraints.

Required:

1. What is the contribution margin per hour of painting department time for each product?
2. What is the optimal mix of products?
3. What is the total contribution margin earned for the optimal mix?

Exercise 12-11 *Choosing the Optimal Product Mix with a Constrained Resource and a Demand Constraint*

Refer to **Exercise 12-10**. Now assume that only 500 units of each product can be sold.

Required:

1. What is the optimal mix of products?
2. What is the total contribution margin earned for the optimal mix?

Exercise 12-12 *Calculating Price Using a Markup Percentage of Cost*

Aunt Cecilia's Gift Shop has decided to price the candles it sells at cost plus 70 percent. One type of carved pillar candle costs $5, and scented votive candles cost $0.90 each.

Required:

1. What price will Aunt Cecilia's charge for the pillar candle?
2. What price will Aunt Cecilia's charge for each scented votive candle?

Exercise 12-13 *Target Costing*

Toastalot, Inc., would like to design, produce, and sell versatile toasters for the home kitchen market. The toaster will have four slots that adjust in thickness to accommodate both slim slices of bread and oversized bagels. The target price is $100. Toastalot requires that new products be priced such that 20 percent of the price is profit.

Required:

1. Calculate the amount of desired profit per unit of the new toaster.
2. Calculate the target cost per unit of the new toaster.

Exercise 12-14 *Ordering Cost, Carrying Cost, and Total Inventory-Related Cost*

Aravan Company purchases 4,000 units of Product Beta each year in lots of 400 units per order. The cost of placing one order is $20, and the cost of carrying one unit of product in inventory for a year is $4.

Required:

1. How many orders for Product Beta does Aravan place per year?
2. What is the total ordering cost of Beta per year?
3. What is the total carrying cost of Beta per year?
4. What is the total cost of Aravan's inventory policy for Beta per year?

Exercise 12-15 *EOQ, Ordering Cost, Carrying Cost, and Total Inventory-Related Cost*

Refer to **Exercise 12-14**.

Required:

1. What is the EOQ for Product Beta?

2. How many orders for Product Beta will Aravan place per year under the EOQ policy?
3. What is the total ordering cost of Beta for a year under the EOQ policy?
4. What is the total carrying cost of Beta per year under the EOQ policy?
5. What is the total cost of Aravan's inventory policy for Beta per year under the EOQ policy?

Exercise 12-16 *Keep or Buy, Sunk Costs*

OBJECTIVES 1, 2

Heather Alburty purchased a previously owned, 2-year-old Grand Am for $8,900. Since purchasing the car, she has spent the following amounts on parts and labor:

New stereo system	$1,200
Trick paint	400
New wide racing tires	800
Total	$2,400

Unfortunately, the new stereo doesn't completely drown out the sounds of a grinding transmission. Apparently, the Grand Am needs a considerable amount of work to make it reliable transportation. Heather estimates that the needed repairs include the following:

Transmission overhaul	$2,000
Water pump	400
Master cylinder work	1,100
Total	$3,500

In a visit to a used car dealer, Heather has found a 1-year-old Neon in mint condition for $9,400. Heather has advertised and found that she can sell the Grand Am for only $6,400. If she buys the Neon, she will pay cash, but she would need to sell the Grand Am.

Required:

1. In trying to decide whether to restore the Grand Am or buy the Neon, Heather is distressed because she already has spent $11,300 on the Grand Am. The investment seems too much to give up. How would you react to her concern?
2. Assuming that Heather would be equally happy with the Grand Am or the Neon, should she buy the Neon, or should she restore the Grand Am?

Exercise 12-17 *Make or Buy*

OBJECTIVES 1, 2

Blasingham Company is currently manufacturing Part Q108, producing 35,000 units annually. The part is used in the production of several products made by Blasingham. The cost per unit for Q108 is as follows:

Direct materials	$ 6.00
Direct labor	2.00
Variable overhead	1.50
Fixed overhead	3.50
Total	$13.00

Of the total fixed overhead assigned to Q108, $77,000 is direct fixed overhead (the lease of production machinery and salary of a production line supervisor—neither of which will be needed if the line is dropped). The remaining fixed overhead is common fixed overhead. An outside supplier has offered to sell the part to Blasingham for $11. There is no alternative use for the facilities currently used to produce the part.

Required:
1. Should Blasingham Company make or buy Part Q108?
2. What is the most Blasingham would be willing to pay an outside supplier?
3. If Blasingham bought the part, by how much would income increase or decrease?

Exercise 12-18 *Make or Buy*

Refer to **Exercise 12-17**. Now suppose that all of the fixed overhead is common fixed overhead.

Required:
1. Should Blasingham Company make or buy Part Q108?
2. What is the most Blasingham would be willing to pay an outside supplier?
3. If Blasingham bought the part, by how much would income increase or decrease?

PROBLEMS

(Note: Whenever you see a next to a requirement, it signals a "building on a cornerstone" requirement. Assigning this requirement will usually entail additional work, such as a group project, analytical reasoning, Internet research, decision making, and the use of written communication skills.)

Problem 12-1 *Special-Order Decision*

Rianne Company produces a light fixture with the following unit cost:

Direct materials	$2
Direct labor	1
Variable overhead	3
Fixed overhead	2
Unit cost	$8

The production capacity is 300,000 units per year. Because of a depressed housing market, the company expects to produce only 180,000 fixtures for the coming year. The company also has fixed selling costs totaling $500,000 per year and variable selling costs of $1 per unit sold. The fixtures normally sell for $12 each.

At the beginning of the year, a customer from a geographic region outside the area normally served by the company offered to buy 100,000 fixtures for $7 each. The customer also offered to pay all transportation costs. Since there would be no sales commissions involved, this order would not have any variable selling costs.

Required:
1. Based on a quantitative (numerical) analysis, should the company accept the order?
2. What qualitative factors might impact the decision? Assume that no other orders are expected beyond the regular business and the special order.

Problem 12-2 *Make or Buy, Qualitative Considerations*

Hetrick Dentistry Services operates in a large metropolitan area. Currently, Hetrick has its own dental laboratory to produce porcelain and gold crowns. The unit costs to produce the crowns are as follows:

	Porcelain	Gold
Raw materials	$ 70	$130
Direct labor	27	27
Variable overhead	8	8
Fixed overhead	22	22
Total	$127	$187

Fixed overhead is detailed as follows:

Salary (supervisor)	$26,000
Depreciation	5,000
Rent (lab facility)	32,000

Overhead is applied on the basis of direct labor hours. These rates were computed using 5,500 direct labor hours.

A local dental laboratory has offered to supply Hetrick all the crowns it needs. Its price is $125 for porcelain crowns and $150 for gold crowns; however, the offer is conditional on supplying both types of crowns—it will not supply just one type for the price indicated. If the offer is accepted, the equipment used by Hetrick's laboratory would be scrapped (it is old and has no market value), and the lab facility would be closed. Hetrick uses 2,000 porcelain crowns and 600 gold crowns per year.

Required:

1. Should Hetrick continue to make its own crowns, or should they be purchased from the external supplier? What is the dollar effect of purchasing?
2. What qualitative factors should Hetrick consider in making this decision?
3. Suppose that the lab facility is owned rather than rented and that the $32,000 is depreciation rather than rent. What effect does this have on the analysis in Requirement 1?
4. Refer to the original data. Assume that the volume of crowns used is 3,400 porcelain and 600 gold. Should Hetrick make or buy the crowns? Explain the outcome.

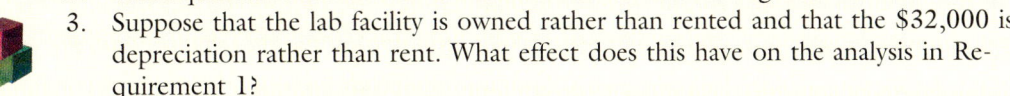

Problem 12-3 *Sell or Process Further*

Zanda Drug Corporation buys three chemicals that are processed to produce two types of analgesics used as ingredients for popular over-the-counter drugs. The purchased chemicals are blended for two to three hours and then heated for 15 minutes. The results of the process are two separate analgesics, depryl and pencol, which are sent to a drying room until their moisture content is reduced to 6 to 8 percent. For every 1,300 pounds of chemicals used, 600 pounds of depryl and 600 pounds of pencol are produced. After drying, depryl and pencol are sold to companies that process them into their final form. The selling prices are $12 per pound for depryl and $30 per pound for pencol. The costs to produce 600 pounds of each analgesic are as follows:

Chemicals	$8,500
Direct labor	6,735
Overhead	9,900

The analgesics are packaged in 20-pound bags and shipped. The cost of each bag is $1.30. Shipping costs $0.10 per pound.

Zanda could process depryl further by grinding it into a fine powder and then molding the powder into tablets. The tablets can be sold directly to retail drug stores as a generic brand. If this route were taken, the revenue received per bottle of tablets would be $4.00, with 10 bottles produced by every pound of depryl. The costs of grinding and tableting total $2.50 per pound of depryl. Bottles cost $0.40 each. Bottles are shipped in boxes that hold 25 at a shipping cost of $1.60 per box.

Required:

1. Should Zanda sell depryl at split-off, or should depryl be processed and sold as tablets?
2. If Zanda normally sells 265,000 pounds of depryl per year, what will be the difference in profits if depryl is processed further?

Problem 12-4 *Keep or Drop*

OBJECTIVES
1, 2

AudioMart is a retailer of radios, stereos, and televisions. The store carries two portable sound systems that have radios, tape players, and speakers. System A, of slightly higher quality than System B, costs $20 more. With rare exceptions, the store also sells a headset when a system is sold. The headset can be used with either system. Variable-costing income statements for the three products follow:

	System A	System B	Headset
Sales	$45,000	$ 32,500	$8,000
Less: Variable expenses	20,000	25,500	3,200
Contribution margin	$25,000	$ 7,000	$4,800
Less: Fixed costs*	10,000	18,000	2,700
Operating income	$15,000	$(11,000)	$2,100

*This includes common fixed costs totaling $18,000, allocated to each product in proportion to its revenues.

The owner of the store is concerned about the profit performance of System B and is considering dropping it. If the product is dropped, sales of System A will increase by 30 percent, and sales of headsets will drop by 25 percent.

Required:

1. Prepare segmented income statements for the three products using a better format.
2. Prepare segmented income statements for System A and the headsets assuming that System B is dropped. Should B be dropped?
3. Suppose that a third system, System C, with a similar quality to System B, could be acquired. Assume that with C the sales of A would remain unchanged; however, C would produce only 80 percent of the revenues of B, and sales of the headsets would drop by 10 percent. The contribution margin ratio of C is 50 percent, and its direct fixed costs would be identical to those of B. Should System B be dropped and replaced with System C?

Problem 12-5 *Accept or Reject a Special Order*

OBJECTIVES
1, 2

Steve Murningham, manager of an electronics division, was considering an offer by Pat Sellers, manager of a sister division. Pat's division was operating below capacity and had just been given an opportunity to produce 8,000 units of one of its products for a customer in a market not normally served. The opportunity involves a product that uses an electrical component produced by Steve's division. Each unit that Pat's division produces requires two of the components. However, the price the customer is willing to pay is well below the price usually charged; to make a reasonable profit on the order, Pat needs a price concession from Steve's division. Pat had offered to pay full manufacturing cost for the parts. So that Steve would know that everything was above board, Pat had supplied the following unit cost and price information concerning the special order, excluding the cost of the electrical component:

Selling price	$32
Less costs:	
Direct materials	(17)
Direct labor	(7)
Variable overhead	(2)
Fixed overhead	(3)
Operating profit	$ 3

The normal selling price of the electrical component is $2.30 per unit. Its full manufacturing cost is $1.85 ($1.05 variable and $0.80 fixed). Pat had argued that paying $2.30 per component would wipe out the operating profit and result in her division showing a loss. Steve was interested in the offer because his division was also operating below capacity (the order would not use all the excess capacity).

Required:
1. Should Steve accept the order at a selling price of $1.85 per unit? By how much will his division's profits be changed if the order is accepted? By how much will the profits of Pat's division change if Steve agrees to supply the part at full cost?
2. Suppose that Steve offers to supply the component at $2. In offering this price, Steve says that it is a firm offer, not subject to negotiation. Should Pat accept this price and produce the special order? If Pat accepts the price, what is the change in profits for Steve's division?
3. Assume that Steve's division is operating at full capacity and that Steve refuses to supply the part for less than the full price. Should Pat still accept the special order? Explain.

Problem 12-6 *Cost-Based Pricing Decision*

Jeremy Costa, owner of Costa Cabinets, Inc., is preparing a bid on a job that requires $1,800 of direct materials, $1,600 of direct labor, and $800 of overhead. Jeremy normally applies a standard markup based on cost of goods sold to arrive at an initial bid price. He then adjusts the price as necessary in light of other factors (for example, competitive pressure). Last year's income statement is as follows:

Sales	$130,000
Cost of goods sold	48,100
Gross margin	$ 81,900
Selling and administrative expenses	46,300
Operating income	$ 35,600

Required:
1. Calculate the markup Jeremy will use.
2. What is Jeremy's initial bid price?

Problem 12-7 *Product Mix Decision, Single Constraint*

Sealing Company manufactures three types of floppy disk storage units. Each of the three types requires the use of a special machine that has a total operating capacity of 15,000 hours per year. Information on the three types of storage units is as follows:

	Basic	Standard	Deluxe
Selling price	$9.00	$30.00	$35.00
Variable cost	$6.00	$20.00	$10.00
Machine hours required	0.10	0.50	0.75

Sealing Company's marketing director has assessed demand for the three types of storage units and believes that the firm can sell as many units as it can produce.

Required:
1. How many of each type of unit should be produced and sold to maximize the company's contribution margin? What is the total contribution margin for your selection?
2. Now suppose that Sealing Company believes that it can sell no more than 12,000 of the deluxe model but up to 50,000 each of the basic and standard models at the selling prices estimated. What product mix would you recommend, and what would be the total contribution margin?

Problem 12-8 *Special-Order Decision, Qualitative Aspects*

OBJECTIVES
1, 2

Randy Stone, manager of Specialty Paper Products Company, was agonizing over an offer for an order requesting 5,000 calendars. Specialty Paper Products was operating at 70 percent of its capacity and could use the extra business; unfortunately, the order's offering price of $4.20 per box was below the cost to produce the calendars. The controller, Louis Barns, was opposed to taking a loss on the deal. However, the personnel manager, Yatika Blaine, argued in favor of accepting the order even though a loss would be incurred; it would avoid the problem of layoffs and would help maintain the company's community image. The full cost to produce a calendar follows:

Direct materials	$1.15
Direct labor	2.00
Variable overhead	1.10
Fixed overhead	1.00
Total	$5.25

Later that day, Louis and Yatika met over coffee. Louis sympathized with Yatika's concerns and suggested that the two of them rethink the special-order decision. He offered to determine relevant costs if Yatika would list the activities to be affected by a layoff. Yatika eagerly agreed and came up with the following activities: an increase in the state unemployment insurance rate from 1 percent to 2 percent of total payroll, notification costs to lay off approximately 20 employees, increased costs of rehiring and retraining workers when the downturn was over. Louis determined that these activities would cost the following amounts:

- Total payroll is $1,460,000 per year.
- Layoff paperwork is $25 per laid-off employee.
- Rehiring and retraining is $150 per new employee.

Required:

1. Assume that the company would accept the order only if it increases total profits. Should the company accept or reject the order? Provide supporting computations.

2. Consider the new information on activity costs associated with the layoff. Should the company accept or reject the order? Provide supporting computations.

Problem 12-9 *Sell or Process Further, Basic Analysis*

OBJECTIVES
1, 2

Shenista, Inc., produces four products (Alpha, Beta, Gamma, and Delta) from a common input. The joint costs for a typical quarter follow:

Direct materials	$95,000
Direct labor	43,000
Overhead	85,000

The revenues from each product are as follows: Alpha, $100,000; Beta, $93,000; Gamma, $30,000; and Delta, $40,000.

Management is considering processing Delta beyond the split-off point, which would increase the sales value of Delta to $75,000. However, to process Delta further means that the company must rent some special equipment costing $15,400 per quarter. Additional materials and labor also needed would cost $8,500 per quarter.

Required:

1. What is the operating profit earned by the four products for one quarter?
2. Should the division process Product Delta further or sell it at split-off? What is the effect of the decision on quarterly operating profit?

Problem 12-10 *Ordering and Carrying Costs*

Zarlon Company uses 24,000 circuit boards each year in its production of stereo units. The cost of placing an order is $125. The cost of holding one unit of inventory for one year is $6. Currently, Zarlon places 12 orders of 2,000 circuit boards per year.

Required:
1. Compute the annual ordering cost.
2. Compute the annual carrying cost.
3. Compute the cost of Zarlon's current inventory policy.
4. Compute the economic order quantity.
5. Compute the ordering cost and the carrying cost for the EOQ.
6. How much money does using the EOQ policy save the company over the policy of purchasing 2,000 circuit boards per order?
7. Suppose that the supplier charges an extra $0.05 per unit to purchase circuit boards in orders of 1,500 or less. Should Zarlon switch to the EOQ policy or not?

Problem 12-11 *Economic Order Quantity*

Italia Pizzeria is a popular pizza restaurant near a college campus. Brandon Thayn, an accounting student, works for Italia Pizzeria. After several months at the restaurant, Brandon began to analyze the efficiency of the business, particularly inventory practices. He noticed that the owner had more than 50 items regularly carried in inventory. Of these items, the most expensive to buy and carry was cheese. Cheese was ordered in blocks at $17.50 per block. Annual usage totals 14,000 blocks.

Upon questioning the owner, Brandon discovered that the owner did not use any formal model for ordering cheese. It took five days to receive a new order when placed, which was done whenever the inventory of cheese dropped to 200 blocks. The size of the order was usually 400 blocks. The cost of carrying one block of cheese is 10 percent of its purchase price. It costs $40 to place and receive an order.

Italia Pizzeria stays open seven days a week and operates 50 weeks a year. The restaurant closes for the last two weeks of December.

Required:
1. Compute the total cost of ordering and carrying the cheese inventory under the current policy.
2. Compute the total cost of ordering and carrying cheese if the restaurant were to change to the economic order quantity. How much would the restaurant save per year by switching policies?
3. If the restaurant uses the economic order quantity, when should it place an order? (Assume that the amount of cheese used per day is the same throughout the year.) How does this compare with the current reorder policy?
4. Suppose that storage space allows a maximum of 600 blocks of cheese. Discuss the inventory policy that should be followed with this restriction.
5. Suppose that the maximum storage is 600 blocks of cheese and that cheese can be held for a maximum of 10 days. The owner will not hold cheese any longer in order to ensure the right flavor and quality. Under these conditions, evaluate the owner's current inventory policy.

Problem 12-12 *Product Mix Decision, Single Constraint*

Norton Company produces two products (Juno and Hera) that use the same material input. Juno uses two pounds of the material for every unit produced, and Hera uses five pounds. Currently, Norton has 16,000 pounds of the material in inventory. All of the material is imported. For the coming year, Norton plans to import an additional 8,000 pounds to produce 2,000 units of Juno and 4,000 units of Hera. The unit contribution margin is $30 for Juno and $60 for Hera.

Norton Company has received word that the source of the material has been shut down by embargo. Consequently, the company will not be able to import the 8,000 pounds it planned to use in the coming year's production. There is no other source of the material.

Required:
1. Compute the total contribution margin that the company would earn if it could manufacture 2,000 units of Juno and 4,000 units of Hera.
2. Determine the optimal usage of the company's inventory of 16,000 pounds of the material. Compute the total contribution margin for the product mix that you recommend.

Problem 12-13 *Sell at Split-Off or Process Further*

OBJECTIVE 2

Eunice Company produces two products from a joint process. Joint costs are $70,000 for one batch, which yields 1,000 liters of germain and 4,000 liters of hastain. Germain can be sold at the split-off point for $24 or be processed further, into geraiten, at a manufacturing cost of $4,100 (for the 1,000 liters) and sold for $33 per liter.

If geraiten is sold, additional distribution costs of $0.80 per liter and sales commissions of 10 percent of sales will be incurred. In addition, Eunice's legal department is concerned about potential liability issues with geraiten—issues that do not arise with germain.

Required:
1. Considering only gross profit, should germain be sold at the split-off point or processed further?
2. Taking a value-chain approach (by considering distribution, marketing, and after-the-sale costs), determine whether or not germain should be processed into geraiten.

Problem 12-14 *Differential Costing*

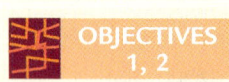
OBJECTIVES 1, 2

As pointed out earlier in "Here's the Real Kicker," Kicker changed banks a couple of years ago since the loan officer at its bank moved out of state. Kicker saw that as an opportunity to take bids for its banking business and to fine-tune the banking services it was using. This problem uses that situation as the underlying scenario but uses three banks: FirstBank, Community Bank, and RegionalOne Bank. A set of representative data was presented to each bank for the purpose of preparing a bid. The data are as follows:

Checking accounts needed: 6
Checks per month:* 2,000
Foreign debits/credits on checking accounts per month:* 200
Deposits per month:* 300
Returned checks:* 25 per month
Credit card charges per month: 4,000
Wire transfers per month: 100, of which 60 are to foreign bank accounts
Monthly credit needs (line of credit availability and cost): $100,000 average monthly usage

Internet banking services?
Knowledgeable loan officer?
Responsiveness of bank?

*These are overall totals for the six accounts during a month.

FirstBank bid:

Checking accounts: $5 monthly maintenance fee per account
$0.10 foreign debit/credit
$0.50 earned for each deposit
$3 per returned check

Credit card fees: $0.50 per item

Wire transfers: $15 to domestic bank accounts, $50 to foreign bank accounts

Line of credit: Yes, this amount is available,
interest charged at prime plus 2 percent,
subject to a 6 percent minimum interest rate

Internet banking services? Yes, full online banking available,
$15 one-time setup fee for each account
$20 monthly fee for software module

The loan officer assigned to the potential Kicker account had 10 years of experience with medium to large business banking and showed an understanding of the audio industry.

Community Bank bid:

Checking accounts: No fees for the accounts, and no credits earned on deposits
$2.00 per returned check

Credit card fees: $0.50 per item,
$7 per batch processed. Only manual processing was available,
Kicker estimated 20 batches per month

Wire transfers: $30 per wire transfer

Line of credit: Yes, this amount is available,
interest charged at prime plus 2 percent,
subject to a 7 percent minimum interest rate

Internet banking services? Not currently, but within the next six months

The loan officer assigned to the potential Kicker account had four years of experience with medium to large business banking, none of which pertained to the audio industry.

RegionalOne Bank bid:

Checking accounts: $5 monthly maintenance fee per account to be waived for Kicker
$0.20 foreign debit/credit
$0.30 earned for each deposit
$3.80 per returned check

Credit card fees: $0.50 per item

Wire transfers: $10 to domestic bank accounts, $55 to foreign bank accounts

Line of credit: Yes, this amount is available,
interest charged at prime plus 2 percent,
subject to a 6.5 percent minimum interest rate

Internet banking services? Yes, full online banking available,
one-time setup fee for each account waived for Kicker
$20 monthly fee for software module

The loan officer assigned to the potential Kicker account had two years of experience with large business banking. Another branch of the bank had had expertise in the audio industry and would be willing to help as needed. This bank was the first one to submit a bid.

Required:

1. Calculate the predicted monthly cost of banking with each bank.
2. Suppose Kicker felt that full online Internet banking was critical. How would that affect your analysis from Requirement 1? How would you incorporate the subjective factors (e.g., experience, access to expertise)?

Problem 12-15 *Make or Buy: Ethical Considerations*

Pamela McDonald, CMA and controller for Murray Manufacturing, Inc., was having lunch with Roger Branch, manager of the company's power department. Over the past six months, Pamela and Roger had developed a romantic relationship and were making plans for marriage. To keep company gossip at a minimum, Pamela and Roger had kept the relationship very quiet, and no one in the company was aware of it. The topic of the luncheon conversation centered on a decision concerning the company's power department that Larry Johnson, president of the company, was about to make.

Pamela: Roger, in our last executive meeting, we were told that a local utility company offered to supply power and quoted a price per kilowatt-hour that they said would hold for the next three years. They even offered to enter into a contractual agreement with us.

Roger: This is news to me. Is the bid price a threat to my area? Can they sell us power cheaper than we make it? And why wasn't I informed about this matter? I should have some input. This burns me. I think I should give Larry a call this afternoon and lodge a strong complaint.

Pamela: Calm down, Roger. The last thing I want you to do is call Larry. Larry made us all promise to keep this whole deal quiet until a decision had been made. He did not want you involved because he wanted to make an unbiased decision. You know that the company is struggling somewhat, and they are looking for ways to save money.

Roger: Yeah, but at my expense? And at the expense of my department's workers? At my age, I doubt that I could find a job that pays as well and has the same benefits. How much of a threat is this offer?

Pamela: Jack Lacy, my assistant controller, prepared an analysis while I was on vacation. It showed that internal production is cheaper than buying, but not by much. Larry asked me to review the findings and submit a final recommendation for next Wednesday's meeting. I've reviewed Jack's analysis, and it's faulty. He overlooked the interactions of your department with other service departments. When these are considered, the analysis is overwhelmingly in favor of purchasing the power. The savings are about $300,000 per year.

Roger: If Larry hears that, my department's gone. Pam, you can't let this happen. I'm three years away from having a vested retirement. And my workers—they have home mortgages, kids in college, families to support. No, it's not right. Pam, just tell him that your assistant's analysis is on target. He'll never know the difference.

Pamela: Roger, what you're suggesting doesn't sound right either. Would it be ethical for me to fail to disclose this information?

Roger: Ethical? Do you think it's right to lay off employees that have been loyal, faithful workers simply to fatten the pockets of the owners of this company? The Murrays already are so rich that they don't know what to do with their money. I think that it's even more unethical to penalize me and my workers. Why should we have to bear the consequences of some bad marketing decisions? Anyway, the effects of those decisions are about gone, and the company should be back to normal within a year or so.

Pamela: You may be right. Perhaps the well-being of you and your workers is more important than saving $300,000 for the Murrays.

Required:

1. Should Pamela have told Roger about the impending decision concerning the power department? What do you think most corporate codes of ethics would say about this?

2. Should Pamela provide Larry with the correct data concerning the power department? Or should she protect its workers? What would you do if you were Pamela?

CAPITAL INVESTMENT DECISIONS

After studying Chapter 13, you should be able to:

1. Explain what a capital investment decision is and distinguish between independent and mutually exclusive capital investment decisions.
2. Compute the payback period and accounting rate of return for a proposed investment and explain their roles in capital investment decisions.
3. Use net present value analysis for capital investment decisions involving independent projects.
4. Use the internal rate of return to assess the acceptability of independent projects.
5. Explain the role and value of postaudits.
6. Explain why NPV is better than IRR for capital investment decisions involving mutually exclusive projects.

TastyFood Corporation, a large food-store chain, is considering a $2 million investment in an automated deposit processing system for its stores. The company's special capital acquisitions committee has just completed a pilot study to test such a system in seven stores for a 9-month period. At the end of the nine months, Earl Wise, chair of the capital acquisitions committee and vice president of finance, scheduled a committee meeting to evaluate the outcome of the pilot study. The committee also included Stan Miller, controller; Ron Thomas, vice president of operations; and Paula Summers, area supervisor for the seven pilot-study stores. Paula began the discussion by providing a summary of the benefits she felt were identifiable from the pilot study.

Paula: The new system has produced some significant benefits. I have four specific benefits that I would like to acknowledge. First, our check processing charges have been reduced because the system now encodes the dollar amount on all checks prior to deposit. Second, there has been a dramatic reduction in forms cost. We have eliminated nearly three million documents used per year under the old manual system. Third, by reducing manual calculations, greater data integrity has been achieved. This has decreased the time spent on correcting incorrect deposit information. Fourth, we have reduced training costs. Since the system is simpler and has fewer forms, new cashiers and new store openings require less training time. By the way, there should be another significant benefit if this system goes company-wide. Processing data through the store computer to the host computer at headquarters will save time to both the sales audit and cash/banking calculations by eliminating manual entries and expediting bank reconciliations.

Ron: After seeing these benefits, I'm convinced that automatic deposits are a good idea. I move that we attach the handout to a recommendation to implement the automated system for the entire company. Then, we can get back to more pressing matters.

Stan: Wait a minute! While the description of the benefits is impressive, we shouldn't be too hasty in our decisions. After all, we are talking about investing $2 million. We need to be certain that this is a sound investment.

Ron: But that's the whole point, Stan. The benefits make it clear that the investment is sound. Why waste any more time deliberating over an obvious conclusion? What do you say, Earl? Can we vote on this matter and adjourn?"

Earl: Well, Ron, we can—if you will first answer the following questions. How much will this investment increase the profits of the firm? What effect will it have on our overall value? Will the investment earn at least the return required by company policy? How long will it take us to recover the investment through the savings alluded to in Paula's handout? Only when we know the answers to these questions can we accurately assess the soundness of the investment. The pilot study provides us with fundamental information needed to estimate future cash savings associated with automation. Once we have these estimates, we can use financial models to assess the proposed investment. Stan, for our next meeting, please bring estimates of cash flows over the life of the proposed system. I will come prepared to discuss some of the financial models that will help us assess the financial merits of the investment.

TYPES OF CAPITAL INVESTMENT DECISIONS

Organizations are often faced with the opportunity (or need) to invest in assets or projects that represent long-term commitments. New production systems, new plants, new equipment, and new product development are examples of assets and projects that fit this category. Usually, many alternatives are available. For example, an organization may be faced with the decision of whether to invest or not invest in a new plant, or whether to invest in a flexible manufacturing system or continue with an existing traditional manufacturing system. These long-range decisions are examples of *capital investment decisions*.

Capital investment decisions are concerned with the process of planning, setting goals and priorities, arranging financing, and using certain criteria to select long-term assets. Because capital investment decisions place large amounts of resources at risk for long periods of time and simultaneously affect the future development of the firm, they are among the most important decisions managers make. Every organization has limited resources, which should be used to maintain or enhance its long-run profitability. Poor capital investment decisions can be disastrous. For example, a failure to invest in automated manufacturing when other competitors do so may result in significant losses in market share because of the inability to compete on the basis of quality, cost, and delivery time. Competitors with more modern facilities may produce more output at lower cost and higher quality. Thus, making the right capital investment decisions is absolutely essential for long-term survival.

The process of making capital investment decisions is often referred to as **capital budgeting**. Two types of capital budgeting projects will be considered: *independent projects* and *mutually exclusive projects*. **Independent projects** are projects that, if accepted or rejected, do not affect the cash flows of other projects. For example, a decision by General Motors to build a new plant for production of the Cadillac line is not affected by its decision to build a new plant for the production of its Saturn line. They are independent capital investment decisions. The second type of capital budgeting project requires a firm to choose among competing alternatives that provide the same basic service. Acceptance of one option precludes the acceptance of another. Thus, **mutually exclusive projects** are those projects that, if accepted, preclude the acceptance of all other competing projects. For example, some time ago, Monsanto's Fibers Division decided to automate its Pensacola, Florida, plant. Thus, Monsanto was faced with the choice of continuing with its existing manual production operation or replacing it with an automated system. In all likelihood, part of the company's deliberation concerned different types of automated systems. If three different automated systems were being considered, this would produce four alternatives: the current system plus the three potential new systems. Once one system is chosen, the other three are excluded; they are mutually exclusive.

Notice that one of the competing alternatives in the Monsanto example is that of maintaining the status quo (the manual system). This emphasizes the fact that new investments replacing existing investments must prove to be economically superior. Of course, at times, replacement of the old system is mandatory and not discretionary if the firm wishes to remain in business (for example, equipment in the old system may be worn out, making the old system not a viable alternative). In such a situation, going out of business could be a viable alternative, especially if none of the new investment alternatives is profitable.

Capital investment decisions often are concerned with investments in long-term capital assets. With the exception of land, these assets depreciate over their lives, and the original investment is used up as the assets are employed. In general terms, a sound capital investment will earn back its original capital outlay over its life and, at the same time, provide a reasonable return on the original investment. Therefore, managers must decide whether or not a capital investment will earn back its original outlay and pro-

OBJECTIVE 1

Explain what a capital investment decision is and distinguish between independent and mutually exclusive capital investment decisions.

vide a reasonable return. By making this assessment, a manager can decide on the acceptability of independent projects and compare competing projects on the basis of their economic merits.

But what is meant by reasonable return? It is generally agreed that any new project must cover the opportunity cost of the funds invested. For example, if a company takes money from a money market fund that is earning 6 percent and invests it in a new project, then the project must provide at least a 6-percent return (the return that could have been earned had the money been left in the money market fund). Of course, in reality, funds for investment often come from different sources—each representing a different opportunity cost. The return that must be earned is a blend of the opportunity costs of the different sources. Thus, if a company uses two sources of funds, one with an opportunity cost of 4 percent and the other with an opportunity cost of 6 percent, then the return that must be earned is somewhere between 4 and 6 percent, depending on the relative amounts used from each source. Furthermore, it is usually assumed that managers should select projects that promise to maximize the wealth of the owners of the firm.

To make a capital investment decision, a manager must estimate the quantity and timing of cash flows, assess the risk of the investment, and consider the impact of the project on the firm's profits. One of the most difficult tasks is to estimate the cash flows. Projections must be made years into the future, and forecasting is far from a perfect science. Obviously, as the accuracy of cash flow forecasts increases, the reliability of the decision improves. In making projections, managers must identify and quantify the benefits associated with the proposed project(s). For example, an automated cash deposit system can produce the following benefits (relative to a manual system): bank charge reductions, productivity gains, forms cost reduction, greater data integrity, lower training costs, and savings in time required to audit and do bank/cash reconciliations. The dollar value of these benefits must be assessed. Although forecasting future cash flows is a critical part of the capital investment process, forecasting methods will not be considered here. Furthermore, the cash flows projected must be *after-tax cash flows*. Taxes have an important role in developing cash flow assessments. However, taxes will not be explicitly considered. Tax effects are either assumed away or the cash flows can be thought of as after-tax cash flows. Forecasting methodologies and tax considerations are issues that are left for more advanced studies. Consequently, after-tax cash flows are assumed to be known; the focus will be on making capital investment decisions *given* these cash flows.

Managers must set goals and priorities for capital investments. They also must identify some basic criteria for the acceptance or rejection of proposed investments. In this chapter, we will study four basic methods to guide managers in accepting or rejecting potential investments. The methods include both nondiscounting and discounting decision approaches (two methods are discussed for each approach). The discounting methods are applied to investment decisions involving both independent and mutually exclusive projects.

Concept Q & A

What is the difference between independent and mutually exclusive investments?

Answer:
Acceptance or rejection of an independent investment does not affect the cash flows of other investments. Acceptance of a mutually exclusive investment precludes the acceptance of any competing project.

OBJECTIVE 2

Compute the payback period and accounting rate of return for a proposed investment and explain their roles in capital investment decisions.

NONDISCOUNTING MODELS

The basic capital investment decision models can be classified into two major categories: *nondiscounting models* and *discounting models*. **Nondiscounting models** ignore the time value of money, whereas **discounting models** explicitly consider it. Although many accounting theorists disparage the nondiscounting models because they ignore the time value of money, many firms continue to use these models in making capital investment decisions. However, the use of discounting models has increased over the years, and few firms use only one model; indeed, most firms seem to use both types.[1] This suggests that both categories supply useful information to managers as they struggle to make a capital investment decision.

Payback Period

One type of nondiscounting model is the *payback period*. The **payback period** is the time required for a firm to recover its original investment. If the cash flows of a project are an equal amount each period, then the following formula can be used to compute its payback period:

$$\text{Payback period} = \text{Original investment/Annual cash flow}$$

If, however, the cash flows are unequal, the payback period is computed by adding the annual cash flows until such time as the original investment is recovered. If a fraction of a year is needed, it is assumed that cash flows occur evenly within each year. Cornerstone 13-1 shows how payback analysis is done for both even and uneven cash flows.

Cornerstone 13-1

HOW TO Calculate Payback

Information: Suppose that a new car wash facility requires an investment of $100,000 and either has:

a. Even cash flows of $50,000 per year or

b. The following expected annual cash flows: $30,000, $40,000, $50,000, $60,000, and $70,000.

Required: Calculate the payback period for each case.

Calculation:

a. Even cash flows:

$$\text{Payback period} = \text{Original investment/Annual cash flow}$$
$$= \$100,000/\$50,000 = 2 \text{ years}$$

b. Uneven cash flows:

Year	Unrecovered Investment (beginning of year)	Annual Cash Flow	Time Needed for Payback
1	$100,000	$30,000	1.0 year
2	70,000	40,000	1.0 year
3	30,000	50,000	0.6 year*
4	0	60,000	0.0 year
5	0	70,000	0.0 year
			2.6 years

*At the beginning of year 3, $30,000 is needed to recover the investment. Since a net cash flow of $50,000 is expected, only 0.6 year ($30,000/$50,000) is needed to recover the remaining $30,000, assuming a uniform cash inflow throughout the year.

One way to use the payback period is to set a maximum payback period for all projects and to reject any project that exceeds this level. Why would a firm use the payback period in this way? Some analysts suggest that the payback period can be used as a rough measure of risk, with the notion that the longer it takes for a project to pay for itself, the riskier it is. Also, firms with riskier cash flows could require a shorter pay-

---

[1]From the mid-1950s to 1988, surveys reveal that the use of discounting models as the primary evaluation method for capital projects went from about 9 to 80 percent. See A. A. Robichek and J. G. McDonald, "Financial Planning in Transition, Long Range Planning Service," Report No. 268 (Menlo Park, Calif., Stanford Research Institute, January 1966) and T. Klammer, B. Koch, and N. Wilner, "Capital Budgeting Practices—A Survey of Corporate Use," Working Paper, North Texas State University.

Analytical Q & A

Suppose that a project requires an investment of $30,000 and produces $8,000 cash per year. What is the payback period?

Answer:
$30,000/$8,000 = 3.75 years

back period than normal. Additionally, firms with liquidity problems would be more interested in projects with quick paybacks. Another critical concern is obsolescence. In some industries, the risk of obsolescence is high; firms within these industries would be interested in recovering funds rapidly.

Another reason, less beneficial to the firm, may also be involved. Many managers in a position to make capital investment decisions may choose investments with quick payback periods out of self-interest. If a manager's performance is measured using such short-run criteria as annual net income, he or she may choose projects with quick paybacks to show improved net income as quickly as possible. Consider that divisional managers often are responsible for making capital investment decisions and are evaluated on divisional profit. The tenure of divisional managers, however, is typically short—three to five years on average. Consequently, the incentive for such managers is to shy away from investments that promise healthy long-run returns but relatively meager returns in the short run. Corporate budgeting policies and a budget review committee can eliminate these problems.

The payback period can be used to choose among competing alternatives. Under this approach, the investment with the shortest payback period is preferred over investments with longer payback periods. However, this use of the payback period is less defensible because this measure suffers from two major deficiencies: (1) it ignores the performance of the investments beyond the payback period, and (2) it ignores the time value of money.

These two significant deficiencies are easily illustrated. Assume that an engineering firm is considering two different types of computer-aided design (CAD) systems: CAD-A and CAD-B. Each system requires an initial outlay of $150,000, has a 5-year life, and displays the following annual cash flows:

Investment	Year 1	Year 2	Year 3	Year 4	Year 5
CAD-A	$90,000	$ 60,000	$50,000	$50,000	$50,000
CAD-B	40,000	110,000	25,000	25,000	25,000

Both investments have payback periods of two years. In other words, if a manager uses the payback period to choose among competing investments, the two investments would be equally desirable. In reality, however, the CAD-A system should be preferred over the CAD-B system for two reasons. First, the CAD-A system provides a much larger dollar return for the years beyond the payback period ($150,000 versus $75,000). Second, the CAD-A system returns $90,000 in the first year, while B returns only $40,000. The extra $50,000 that the CAD-A system provides in the first year could be put to productive use, such as investing it in another project. It is better to have a dollar now than to have it one year from now, because the dollar on hand can be invested to provide a return one year from now.

In summary, the payback period provides information to managers that can be used as follows:

1. To help control the risks associated with the uncertainty of future cash flows.
2. To help minimize the impact of an investment on a firm's liquidity problems.
3. To help control the risk of obsolescence.
4. To help control the effect of the investment on performance measures.

However, the method suffers significant deficiencies: it ignores a project's total profitability and the time value of money. While the computation of the payback period may be useful to a manager, relying on it solely for a capital investment decision would be foolish.

APPLICATIONS IN BUSINESS

A survey of small firms (those with sales less than $5 million and fewer than 1,000 employees) revealed that in the 1990s the payback method was the dominant method of investment selection. Of the firms surveyed, 42.7 percent used the payback method as the primary method of investment analysis. This compares with 27.6 percent of the firms that specifically considered the time value of money as their primary method. Interestingly, 22.4 percent used the accounting rate of return as their primary method of investment analysis. The reason offered for this payback outcome is also interesting. It has been suggested that the widespread use of the payback method among small firms is because of the financial pressures put on the small business owner by financial institutions that are providing the capital. The emphasis is on how quickly a loan can be paid back by an investment and not on how profitable the investment is.

Source: S. Block, "Capital Budgeting Techniques Used by Small Business Firms in the 1990s," *Engineering Economist*, Vol. 42, Issue 4 (Summer 1997): 355–365.

Accounting Rate of Return

The *accounting rate of return* is the second commonly used nondiscounting model. The **accounting rate of return** (ARR) measures the return on a project in terms of income, as opposed to using a project's cash flow. The accounting rate of return is computed by the following formula:

$$\text{Accounting rate of return} = \text{Average income/Initial investment}$$

Income is not equivalent to cash flows because of accruals and deferrals used in its computation. The average income of a project is obtained by adding the net income for each year of the project and then dividing this total by the number of years.

Cornerstone 13-2 shows how to calculate the accounting rate of return. Often, debt contracts require that a firm maintain certain financial accounting ratios, which can be affected by the income reported and by the level of long-term assets. Accordingly, the accounting rate of return may be used as a screening measure to ensure that any new investment will not adversely affect these ratios. Additionally, because bonuses to managers are often based on accounting income or return on assets, managers may have a personal interest in seeing that any new investment contributes significantly to net income. A manager seeking to maximize personal income will select investments that return the highest net income per dollar invested.

Cornerstone 13-2

HOW TO Calculate the Accounting Rate of Return

Information: Assume that an investment requires an initial outlay of $100,000. The life of the investment is five years with the following net income stream: $30,000, $30,000, $40,000, $30,000, and $50,000.

Required: Calculate the accounting rate of return.

Calculation:

Total net income (five years) = $180,000

Average net income = $180,000/5 = $36,000

Accounting rate of return = $36,000/$100,000 = 0.36

Unlike the payback period, the accounting rate of return does consider a project's profitability; like the payback period, it ignores the time value of money. Ignoring the

Concept Q & A

Why would a manager choose only investments that return the highest income per dollar invested?

Answer:
It may be an action that helps the company comply with debt covenants. It also may have something to do with the manager's incentive compensation.

time value of money is a critical deficiency in this method as well; it can lead a manager to choose investments that do not maximize profits. It is because the payback period and the accounting rate of return ignore the time value of money that they are referred to as *nondiscounting models*. Discounting models use **discounted cash flows**, which are future cash flows expressed in terms of their present value. The use of discounting models requires an understanding of the present value concepts. Present value concepts are reviewed in Appendix 13A. You should review these concepts and make sure that you understand them before studying capital investment discount models. Present value tables (Exhibits 13B-1 and 13B-2) are presented in Appendix 13B at the end of this chapter. These tables are referred to and used throughout the rest of this chapter.

DISCOUNTING MODELS: THE NET PRESENT VALUE METHOD

OBJECTIVE 3

Use net present value analysis for capital investment decisions involving independent projects.

Discounting models explicitly consider the time value of money and, therefore, incorporate the concept of discounting cash inflows and outflows. Two discounting models will be considered: *net present value* (NPV) and *internal rate of return* (IRR). The net present value method will be discussed first; the internal rate of return method is discussed in the following section.

NPV Defined

Net present value is the difference between the present value of the cash inflows and outflows associated with a project:

$$
\begin{aligned}
\text{NPV} &= [\textstyle\sum CF_t/(1 + i)^t] - I \\
&= [\textstyle\sum CF_t df_t] - I \\
&= P - I
\end{aligned}
$$

where

$$
\begin{aligned}
I &= \text{The present value of the project's cost (usually the initial outlay)} \\
CF_t &= \text{The cash inflow to be received in period } t, \text{ with } t = 1 \ldots n \\
i &= \text{The required rate of return} \\
t &= \text{The time period} \\
P &= \text{The present value of the project's future cash inflows} \\
df_t &= 1/(1 + i)^t, \text{ the discount factor}
\end{aligned}
$$

Net present value measures the profitability of an investment. If the NPV is positive, it measures the increase in wealth. For a firm, this means that the size of a positive NPV measures the increase in the value of the firm resulting from an investment. To use the NPV method, a *required rate of return* must be defined. The **required rate of return** is the minimum acceptable rate of return. It is also referred to as the *discount rate*, the *hurdle rate*, and the *cost of capital*. In theory, if future cash flows are known with certainty, then the correct required rate of return is the firm's **cost of capital**. In practice, future cash flows are uncertain, and managers often choose a discount rate higher than the cost of capital to deal with the uncertainty. However, if the rate chosen is excessively high, it will bias the selection process toward short-term investments. Because of the risk of being overly conservative, it may be better to use the cost of capital as the discount rate and find other approaches to deal with uncertainty.

If the net present value is positive, it signals that (1) the initial investment has been recovered, (2) the required rate of return has been recovered, and (3) a return in excess of (1) and (2) has been received. Thus, if NPV is greater than zero, the investment is profitable and, therefore, is acceptable. If NPV equals zero, the decision maker will find acceptance or rejection of the investment equal. Finally, if NPV is less than zero, the investment should be rejected. In this case, it is earning less than the required rate of return.

Concept Q & A

Suppose that the NPV of an investment is $2,000. Why does this mean that the investment should be accepted?

Answer:
A NPV greater than zero means that the investment recovers its capital while simultaneously earning a return in excess of the required rate.

An Example Illustrating Net Present Value

Brannon Company has developed new earphones for portable CD and tape players that it believes are superior to anything on the market. The earphones have a projected product life cycle of five years. Although the marketing manager is excited about the new product's prospects, a decision to manufacture the new product depends on whether it can earn a positive net present value given the company's required rate of return of 12 percent. In order to make a decision regarding the earphones, two steps must be taken: (1) the cash flows for each year must be identified, and (2) the NPV must be computed using the cash flows from step 1. How to calculate the NPV is shown in Cornerstone 13-3. Notice that step 2 offers two approaches for computing NPV. Step 2A computes NPV by using discount factors from Exhibit 13B-1. Step 2B simplifies the computation by using a single discount factor from Exhibit 13B-2 for the even cash flows occurring in years 1 through 4.

Cornerstone 13-3

HOW TO Assess Cash Flows and Calculate NPV

Information: A detailed market study revealed expected annual revenues of $300,000 for the new earphones. Equipment to produce the earphones would cost $320,000. After five years, the equipment can be sold for $40,000. In addition to equipment, working capital is expected to increase by $40,000 because of increases in inventories and receivables. The firm expects to recover the investment in working capital at the end of the project's life. Annual cash operating expenses are estimated at $180,000. The required rate of return is 12 percent.

Required: Estimate the annual cash flows and calculate the NPV.

STEP 1. CASH FLOW IDENTIFICATION

Year	Item	Cash Flow
0	Equipment	$(320,000)
	Working capital	(40,000)
	Total	$(360,000)
1–4	Revenues	$ 300,000
	Operating expenses	(180,000)
	Total	$ 120,000
5	Revenues	$ 300,000
	Operating expenses	(180,000)
	Salvage	40,000
	Recovery of working capital	40,000
	Total	$ 200,000

STEP 2A. NPV ANALYSIS

Year	Cash Flow[a]	Discount Factor[b]	Present Value
0	$(360,000)	1.000	$(360,000)
1	120,000	0.893	107,160
2	120,000	0.797	95,640
3	120,000	0.712	85,440
4	120,000	0.636	76,320
5	200,000	0.567	113,400
Net present value			$ 117,960

STEP 2B. NPV ANALYSIS

Year	Cash Flow	Discount Factor[c]	Present Value
0	$(360,000)	1.000	$(360,000)
1–4	120,000	3.037	364,440
5	200,000	0.567	113,400
Net present value			$ 117,840[d]

[a]From step 1.
[b]From Exhibit 13B-1.
[c]Years 1–4 from Exhibit 13B-2; year 5 from Exhibit 13B-1.
[d]This differs from the computation in step 2A because of rounding.

INTERNAL RATE OF RETURN

OBJECTIVE 4

Use the internal rate of return to assess the acceptability of independent projects.

Another discounting model is the *internal rate of return* method. The **internal rate of return (IRR)** is defined as the interest rate that sets the present value of a project's cash inflows equal to the present value of the project's cost. In other words, it is the interest rate that sets the project's NPV at zero. The following equation can be used to determine a project's IRR:

$$I = \sum CF_t/(1 + i)^t$$

where $t = 1, \ldots, n$

The right-hand side of this equation is the present value of future cash flows, and the left-hand side is the investment. I, CF_t, and t are known. Thus, the IRR (the interest rate, i, in the equation) can be found using trial and error. Once the IRR for a project is computed, it is compared with the firm's required rate of return. If the IRR is greater than the required rate, the project is deemed acceptable; if the IRR is equal to the required rate of return, acceptance or rejection of the investment is equal; if the IRR is less than the required rate of return, the project is rejected.

The internal rate of return is the most widely used of the capital investment techniques. One reason for its popularity may be that it is a rate of return, a concept that managers are comfortable with using. Another possibility is that managers may believe (in most cases, incorrectly) that the IRR is the true or actual compounded rate of return being earned by the initial investment. Whatever the reasons for its popularity, a basic understanding of the IRR is necessary.

Example: Multiple-Period Setting with Uniform Cash Flows

Assume initially that the investment produces a series of uniform cash flows. Since the series of cash flows is uniform, a single discount factor from Exhibit 13B-2 can be used to compute the present value of the annuity. Letting *df* be this discount factor and *CF* be the annual cash flow, the IRR equation assumes the following form:

$$I = CF(df)$$

Solving for *df*, we obtain:

$$df = I/CF$$
$$= \text{Investment/Annual cash flow}$$

Assume that the investment is $100 and that it produces a single-period cash flow of $110. The discount factor is I/CF = $100/$110 = 0.909. Looking in Exhibit 13B-2, a discount factor of 0.909 for a single period corresponds to a rate of 10 percent, which is the IRR. In general, once the discount factor is computed, go to Exhibit 13B-2 and find the row corresponding to the life of the project, then move across that row until the computed discount factor is found. The interest rate corresponding to this discount factor is the IRR. Cornerstone 13-4 illustrates how to calculate the IRR for multiple-period uniform cash flows.

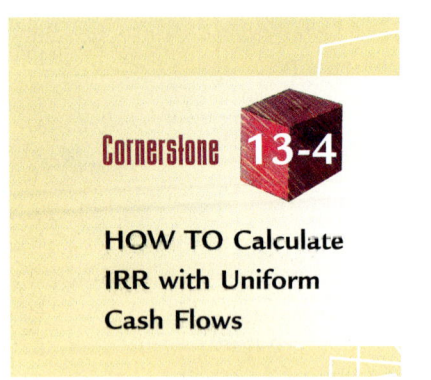

Cornerstone 13-4

HOW TO Calculate IRR with Uniform Cash Flows

Information: Assume that a hospital has the opportunity to invest $120,000 in a new ultrasound system that will produce net cash inflows of $49,950 at the end of each year for the next three years.
Required: Calculate the IRR for the ultrasound system.
Calculation:

$$df = I/CF$$
$$= \$120{,}000/\$49{,}950$$
$$= 2.402$$

Since the life of the investment is three years, find the third row in Exhibit 13B-2 and then move across this row until *df* = 2.402 is found. The interest rate corresponding to 2.402 is 12 percent, which is the IRR.

Exhibit 13B-2 does not provide discount factors for every possible interest rate. To illustrate, assume that the annual cash inflows expected by the hospital (in Cornerstone 13-4) are $51,000 instead of $49,950. The new discount factor is 2.353 ($120,000/ $51,000). Going once again to the third row in Exhibit 13B-2, it is clear that the discount factor—and thus the IRR—lies between 12 and 14 percent. Although it is possible to approximate the IRR by interpolation, for simplicity, simply identify the range for the IRR as indicated by the tabled values. In practice, business calculators or spreadsheet programs like Excel can provide the values of IRR without the use of tables such as Exhibit 13B-2.

Analytical Q & A

Suppose that an investment of $169 produces an annual cash flow of $100 for two years. What is the IRR?

Answer:
df = I/CF = $169/$100 = 1.69; from Exhibit 13B-2, the IRR is 12 percent.

Multiple-Period Setting: Uneven Cash Flows

If the cash flows are not uniform, then the IRR equation must be used. For a multiple-period setting, this equation can be solved by trial and error or by using a business calculator or a spreadsheet program. To illustrate solution by trial and error, assume that a $10,000 investment in a PC system produces clerical savings of $6,000 and $7,200 for each of two years. The IRR is the interest rate that sets the present value of these two cash inflows equal to $10,000:

$$P = [\$6{,}000/(1 + i)] + [\$7{,}200/(1 + i)^2]$$
$$= \$10{,}000$$

To solve this equation by trial and error, start by selecting a possible value for *i*. Given this first guess, the present value of the future cash flows is computed and then com-

APPLICATIONS IN BUSINESS

Many surveys over four decades have indicated that the financial managers of large firms prefer the internal rate of return and the payback method to the net present value method. However, a recent survey of *Fortune* 1000 firms revealed that the net present value method is now the most widely used method for investment analysis. For NPV, 85.1 percent of the respondents used this method always (49.8 percent) or frequently (35.3 percent). For IRR, 76.8 percent of the respondents used this method always (44.6 percent) or frequently (32.2 percent). These results also suggest that firms simultaneously use both discounting methods. For the payback method, 52.6 percent of the respondents used the method always (19.4 percent) or frequently (33.2 percent). The accounting rate of return was the lowest of the four, with only 14.7 percent using the method always (5.2 percent) or frequently (9.5 percent).

Source: P. A. Ryan and G. P. Ryan, "Capital Budgeting Practices of the Fortune 1000: How Have Things Changed?" *Journal of Business and Management* (Fall 2002): 355–365.

© DIGITAL VISION/GETTY IMAGES

pared with the initial investment. If the present value is greater than the initial investment, then the interest rate is too low; if the present value is less than the initial investment, then the interest rate is too high. The next guess is adjusted accordingly.

Assume that the first guess is 18 percent. Using *i* equal to 0.18, Exhibit 13B-1 yields the following discount factors: 0.847 and 0.718. These discount factors produce the following present value for the two cash inflows:

$$P = (0.847 \times \$6,000) + (0.718 \times \$7,200)$$
$$= \$10,252$$

Since *P* is greater than $10,000, the interest rate selected is too low. A higher guess is needed. If the next guess is 20 percent, we obtain the following:

$$P = (0.833 \times \$6,000) + (0.694 \times \$7,200)$$
$$= \$9,995$$

Since this value is reasonably close to $10,000, we can say that the IRR is 20 percent. (The IRR is, in fact, exactly 20 percent; the present value is slightly less than the investment because of rounding error in the discount factors found in Exhibit 13B-1.)

POSTAUDIT OF CAPITAL PROJECTS

OBJECTIVE 5

Explain the role and value of postaudits.

A key element in the capital investment process is a follow-up analysis of a capital project once it is implemented. This analysis is called a *postaudit*. A **postaudit** compares the actual benefits with the estimated benefits and actual operating costs with estimated operating costs; it evaluates the overall outcome of the investment and proposes corrective action if needed. The following real-world case illustrates the usefulness of a postaudit activity.

Honley Medical Company: An Illustrative Application

Allen Manesfield and Jenny Winters were discussing a persistent and irritating problem present in the process of producing intravenous needles (IVs). Both Allen and Jenny are employed by Honley Medical, which specializes in the production of medical products and has three divisions: the IV Products Division, the Critical Care Monitoring

Division, and the Specialty Products Division. Allen and Jenny both are associated with the IV Products Division—Allen as the senior production engineer and Jenny as the marketing manager.

The IV Products Division produces needles of five different sizes. During one stage of the manufacturing process, the needle itself is inserted into a plastic hub and bonded using epoxy glue. According to Jenny, the use of epoxy to bond the needles was causing the division all kinds of problems. In many cases, the epoxy wasn't bonding correctly. The rejects were high, and the division was receiving a large number of complaints from its customers. Corrective action was needed to avoid losing sales. After some discussion and analysis, a recommendation was made to use induction welding in lieu of epoxy bonding. In induction welding, the needles are inserted into the plastic hub, and an RF generator is used to heat the needles. The RF generator works on the same principle as a microwave oven. As the needles get hot, the plastic melts and the needles are bonded.

Switching to induction welding required an investment in RF generators and the associated tooling; the investment was justified by the IV Products Division, based on the savings associated with the new system. Induction welding promised to reduce the cost of direct materials, eliminating the need to buy and use epoxy. Savings of direct labor costs were also predicted because the welding process is much more automated. Adding to these savings were the avoidance of daily clean-up costs and the reduction in rejects. Allen presented a formal NPV analysis showing that the welding system was superior to the epoxy system. Headquarters approved its purchase.

One Year Later

Jenny: Allen, I'm quite pleased with induction welding for bonding needles. In the year since the new process was implemented, we've had virtually no complaints from our customers. The needles are firmly bonded.

Allen: I wish that positive experience were true for all other areas as well. Unfortunately, implementing the process has uncovered some rather sticky and expensive problems that I simply didn't anticipate. The internal audit department recently completed a postaudit of the project, and now my feet are being held to the fire.

Jenny: That's too bad. What's the problem?

Allen: You mean problems. Let me list a few for you. One is that the RF generators interfered with the operation of other equipment. To eliminate this interference, we had to install filtering equipment. But that's not all. We also discovered that the average maintenance person doesn't know how to maintain the new equipment. Now we are faced with the need to initiate a training program to upgrade the skills of our maintenance people. Upgrading skills also implies higher wages. Although the RF bonding process is less messy, it is also more complex. The manufacturing people complained to the internal auditors about that. They maintain that a simple process, even if messy, is to be preferred—especially now that demand for the product is increasing by leaps and bounds.

Jenny: What did the internal auditors conclude?

Allen: They observed that many of the predicted savings did take place, but that some significant costs were not foreseen. Because of some of the unforeseen problems, they have recommended that I look carefully at the possibility of moving back to using epoxy. They indicated that NPV analysis using actual data appears to favor that process. With production expanding, the acquisition of additional RF generators and filtering equipment plus the necessary training is simply not as attractive as returning to epoxy bonding. This conclusion is reinforced by the fact that the epoxy process is simpler and by the auditors' conclusion that the mixing of the epoxy can be automated, avoiding the quality problem we had in the first place.

Jenny: Well, Allen, you can't really blame yourself. You had a real problem and took action to solve it. It's difficult to foresee all the problems and hidden costs of a new process.

Allen: Unfortunately, the internal auditors don't totally agree. In fact, neither do I. I probably jumped too quickly. In the future, I intend to think through new projects more carefully.

Benefits of a Postaudit

In the case of the RF bonding decision, some of the estimated capital investment benefits did materialize: complaints from customers decreased, rejects were fewer, and direct labor and materials costs decreased. However, the investment was greater than expected because filtering equipment was needed, and actual operating costs were much higher because of the increased maintenance cost and the increased complexity of the process. Overall, the internal auditors concluded that the investment was a poor decision. The corrective action they recommended was to abandon the new process and return to epoxy bonding. Based on this recommendation, the firm did abandon inductive welding and returned to epoxy bonding, which was improved by automating the mix.

Firms that perform postaudits of capital projects experience a number of benefits. First, by evaluating profitability, postaudits ensure that resources are used wisely. If the project is doing well, it may call for additional funds and additional attention. If the project is not doing well, corrective action may be needed to improve performance or abandon the project.

A second benefit of the postaudit is its impact on the behavior of managers. If managers are held accountable for the results of a capital investment decision, they are more likely to make such decisions in the best interests of the firm. Additionally, postaudits supply feedback to managers that should help improve future decision making. Consider Allen's reaction to the postaudit of the RF bonding process. Certainly, we would expect him to be more careful and more thorough in making future investment recommendations. In the future, Allen will probably consider more than one alternative, such as automating the mixing of the epoxy. Also, for those alternatives being considered, he will probably be especially alert to the possibility of hidden costs, such as increased training requirements for a new process.

The case also reveals that the postaudit was performed by the internal audit staff. Generally, more objective results are obtainable if the postaudit is done by an independent party. Since considerable effort is expended to ensure as much independence as possible for the internal audit staff, that group is usually the best choice for this task.

Postaudits, however, are costly. Moreover, even though they may provide significant benefits, they have other limitations. Most obvious is the fact that the assumptions driving the original analysis may often be invalidated by changes in the actual operating environment. Accountability must be qualified to some extent by the impossibility of foreseeing every possible eventuality.

Concept Q & A

Why do a postaudit?

Answer:
Postaudits allow a company to assess the quality of capital investment decisions and also produce corrective actions where some of the initial assumptions prove to be wrong. They also encourage managerial accountability and provide useful information for improving future capital budgeting decisions.

MUTUALLY EXCLUSIVE PROJECTS

OBJECTIVE 6

Explain why NPV is better than IRR for capital investment decisions involving mutually exclusive projects.

Up to this point, we have focused on independent projects. Many capital investment decisions deal with mutually exclusive projects. How NPV analysis and IRR are used to choose among competing projects is an interesting question. An even more interesting question to consider is whether NPV and IRR differ in their ability to help managers make wealth-maximizing decisions in the presence of competing alternatives. For example, we already know that the nondiscounting models can produce erroneous choices because they ignore the time value of money. Because of this deficiency, the discounting models are judged superior. Similarly, it can be shown that the NPV model is generally preferred to the IRR model when choosing among mutually exclusive alternatives.

NPV Compared with IRR

NPV and IRR both yield the same decision for independent projects. For example, if the NPV is greater than zero, then the IRR is also greater than the required rate of return; both models signal the correct decision. However, for competing projects, the two methods can produce different results. Intuitively, we believe that, for mutually exclusive projects, the project with the highest NPV or the highest IRR should be chosen. Since it is possible for the two methods to produce different rankings of mutually exclusive projects, the method that consistently reveals the wealth-maximizing project is preferred.

NPV differs from IRR in two major ways. First, NPV assumes that each cash inflow received is reinvested at the required rate of return, whereas the IRR method assumes that each cash inflow is reinvested at the computed IRR. Reinvesting at the required rate of return is more realistic and produces more reliable results when comparing mutually exclusive projects. Second, the NPV method measures profitability in absolute terms, whereas the IRR method measures it in relative terms. NPV measures the amount by which the value of the firm changes. These differences are summarized in Exhibit 13-1.

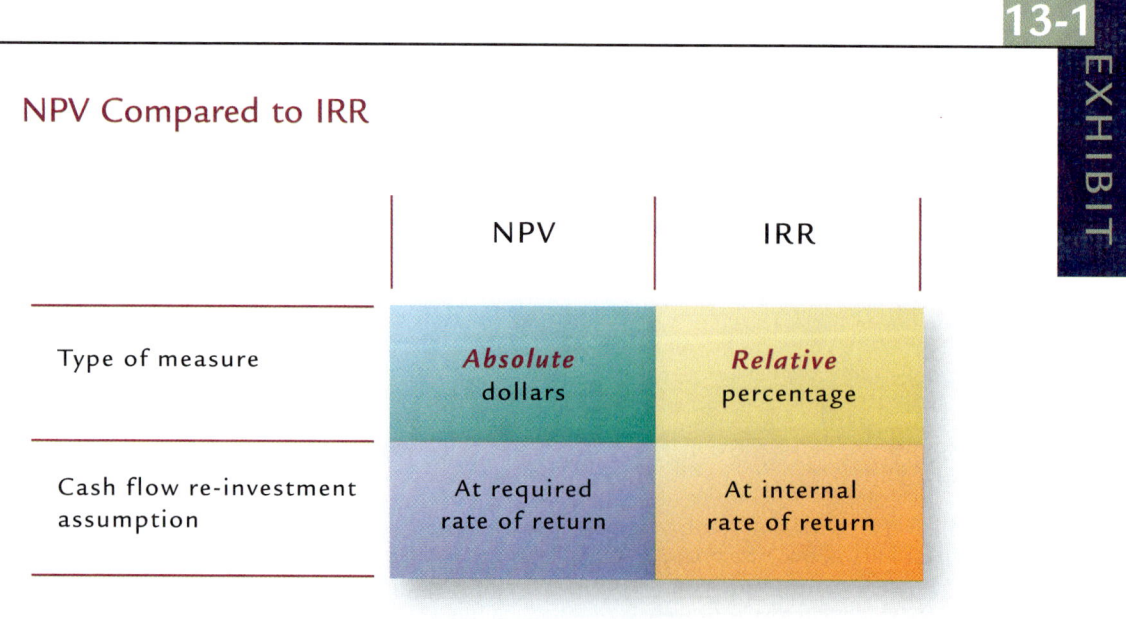

EXHIBIT 13-1

NPV Compared to IRR

	NPV	IRR
Type of measure	*Absolute* dollars	*Relative* percentage
Cash flow re-investment assumption	At required rate of return	At internal rate of return

Since NPV measures the impact that competing projects have on the value of the firm, choosing the project with the largest NPV is consistent with maximizing the wealth of shareholders. On the other hand, IRR does not consistently result in choices that maximize wealth. IRR, as a relative measure of profitability, has the virtue of measuring accurately the rate of return of funds that remain internally invested. However, maximizing IRR will not necessarily maximize the wealth of firm owners because it cannot, by nature, consider the absolute dollar contributions of projects. In the final analysis, what counts are the total dollars earned—the absolute profits—not the relative profits. Accordingly, NPV, not IRR, should be used for choosing among competing, mutually exclusive projects or competing projects when capital funds are limited.

An independent project is acceptable if its NPV is positive. For mutually exclusive projects, the project with the largest NPV is chosen. There are three steps in selecting the best project from several competing projects: (1) assessing the cash flow pattern for each project, (2) computing the NPV for each project, and (3) identifying the project with the greatest NPV. To illustrate NPV analysis for competing projects, an example is provided.

Concept Q & A

Why is NPV better than IRR for choosing among competing projects?

Answer:
NPV uses a more realistic reinvestment assumption, and its signal is consistent with maximizing the wealth of firm owners (IRR does not measure absolute profits).

Example: Mutually Exclusive Projects

Bintley Corporation has committed to improve its environmental performance. One environmental project identified a manufacturing process as being the source of both liquid and gaseous residues. After six months of research activity, the engineering department announced that it is possible to redesign the process to prevent the production of contaminating residues. Two different process designs (A and B) are being considered that prevent the production of contaminants. Both process designs are more expensive to operate than the current process; however, because the designs prevent production of contaminants, significant annual benefits are created. These benefits stem from eliminating the need to operate and maintain expensive pollution control equipment, treat and dispose of toxic liquid wastes, and pay the annual fines for exceeding allowable contaminant releases. Increased sales to environmentally conscious customers are also factored into the benefit estimates. Cornerstone 13-5 shows how NPV and IRR analyses are carried out for this setting.

Based on NPV analysis, Design B is more profitable; it has the larger NPV. Accordingly, the company should select Design B over Design A. Interestingly, Designs A and B have identical internal rates of return. As shown by Cornerstone 13-5, both designs have a discount factor of 3.000. From Exhibit 13B-2, it is easily seen that a discount factor of 3.000 and a life of five years yields an IRR of about 20 percent. Even though both projects have an IRR of 20 percent, the firm should not consider the two designs to be equally desirable. The analysis demonstrates that Design B produces a larger NPV and, therefore, will increase the value of the firm more than Design A. Design B should be chosen. This illustrates the conceptual superiority of NPV over IRR for analysis of competing projects.

Cornerstone 13-5

HOW TO Calculate NPV and IRR for Mutually Exclusive Projects

Information: Consider two pollution prevention designs: Design A and Design B. Both designs have a project life of five years. Design A requires an initial outlay of $180,000 and has a net annual after-tax cash inflow of $60,000 (revenues of $180,000 minus costs of $120,000). Design B, with an initial outlay of $210,000, has a net annual cash inflow of $70,000 ($240,000 − $170,000). The after-tax cash flows are summarized as follows:

CASH FLOW PATTERN

Year	Design A	Design B
0	$(180,000)	$(210,000)
1	60,000	70,000
2	60,000	70,000
3	60,000	70,000
4	60,000	70,000
5	60,000	70,000

The cost of capital for the company is 12 percent.
Required: Calculate the NPV and the IRR for each project.
Calculation:

DESIGN A: NPV ANALYSIS

Year	Cash Flow	Discount Factor*	Present Value
0	$(180,000)	1.000	$(180,000)
1–5	60,000	3.605	216,300
Net present value			$ 36,300

DESIGN A: IRR ANALYSIS

Discount factor = Initial investment/Annual cash flow
= $180,000/$60,000
= 3.000

From Exhibit 13B-2, *df* = 3.000 for five years implies that IRR = 20 percent.

DESIGN B: NPV ANALYSIS

Year	Cash Flow	Discount Factor*	Present Value
0	$(210,000)	1.000	$(210,000)
1–5	70,000	3.605	252,350
Net present value			$ 42,350

DESIGN B: IRR ANALYSIS

Discount factor = Initial investment/Annual cash flow
= $210,000/$70,000
= 3.000

From Exhibit 13B-2, *df* = 3.000 for five years implies that IRR = 20 percent.

*From Exhibit 13B-2.

During the period of 2001–2003, Stillwater Designs experienced high sales of their Kicker products. As a consequence, the levels of inventory filled all storage areas to capacity. Consequently, Stillwater Designs began plans to add another building on existing property with 50,000 square feet of capacity. This new facility had an estimated construction cost between $1 and $1.5 million. During this preliminary planning phase, a shipping strike placed extra storage demands on existing facilities, and Stillwater Designs began looking for a warehousing facility that could be leased on a short-term basis.

They identified a large 250,000-square-foot facility, housed on 22 acres, that was owned by Moore Business Forms. This facility not only was an attractive leasing option, but it also quickly became a competing alternative to adding the 50,000-square-foot facility to Stillwater's current complex of buildings. In fact, the company began looking at the possibility of buying and renovating the Moore facility and moving all of its operations into the one facility. Renovation required such actions as installing a new HVAC system, bringing the building up to current fire codes, painting and resealing the floor, and adding a large number of offices. After careful financial analysis, Stillwater Designs decided that the buy-and-renovate option was more profitable than adding the 50,000-square-foot building to its current complex of buildings. Two economic factors affecting the decision were: (1) Selling the current complex of five buildings would help pay for the needed renovations; and (2) The purchase cost of the nonrenovated Moore facility was less than the cost of building the 50,000-square-foot facility.

Special Considerations for the Advanced Manufacturing Environment

How Investment Differs

Investment in automated manufacturing processes is much more complex than investment in the standard manufacturing equipment of the past. For standard equipment, the direct costs of acquisition represent virtually the entire investment. For automated manufacturing, the direct costs can represent as little as 50 or 60 percent of the total investment; software, engineering, training, and implementation are a significant percentage of the total costs. Thus, great care must be exercised to assess the actual cost of an automated system. It is easy to overlook the peripheral costs, which can be substantial.

How Estimates of Operating Cash Flows Differ

Estimates of operating cash flows from investments in standard equipment have typically relied on directly identifiable tangible benefits, such as direct savings from labor, power, and scrap. However, when investing in automated systems, the intangible and indirect benefits can be material and critical to the viability of the project. Greater quality, more reliability, reduced lead time, improved customer satisfaction, and an enhanced ability to maintain market share are all important intangible benefits of an advanced manufacturing system. Reduction of labor in support areas such as production scheduling and stores are indirect benefits. More effort is needed to measure these intangible and indirect benefits in order to assess more accurately the potential value of investments.

An example can be used to illustrate the importance of considering intangible and indirect benefits. Consider a company that is evaluating a potential investment in a flexible manufacturing system (FMS). The choice facing the company is to continue producing with its traditional equipment, expected to last 10 years, or to switch to the new system, which is also expected to have a useful life of 10 years. The company's discount rate is 12 percent. The data pertaining to the investment are presented in Exhibit 13-2. Notice that for this example, the *incremental cash flows* are used to compare the new project with the old. Instead of calculating the NPV for each alternative and comparing, an equivalent approach is to calculate the NPV of the incremental cash flows of the new system (cash flows of new system less cash flows of old system). If the NPV for the incremental cash flows is positive, then the new equipment is preferred to the old.

Using the incremental data in Exhibit 13-2, the net present value of the proposed system can be computed as follows:

Present value ($4,000,000 × 5.650*)	$22,600,000
Investment	18,000,000
Net present value	$ 4,600,000

*This is the discount factor for an interest rate of 12 percent and a life of 10 years (see Exhibit 13B-2).

The net present value is positive and large in magnitude, and it clearly signals the acceptability of the FMS. This outcome, however, is strongly dependent on explicit recognition of both intangible and indirect benefits. If those benefits are eliminated, then the direct savings total $2.2 million, and the NPV is negative:

13-2
EXHIBIT

Investment Data; Direct, Intangible, and Indirect Benefits

	FMS	Status Quo
Investment (current outlay):		
Direct costs	$10,000,000	—
Software, engineering	8,000,000	—
Total current outlay	$18,000,000	$ 0
Net after-tax cash flow	$ 5,000,000	$1,000,000
Less: After-tax cash flows for status quo	1,000,000	n/a
Incremental benefit	$ 4,000,000	n/a
Incremental Benefit Explained		
Direct benefits:		
Direct labor	$ 1,500,000	
Scrap reduction	500,000	
Setups	200,000	$2,200,000
Intangible benefits (quality savings):		
Rework	$ 200,000	
Warranties	400,000	
Maintenance of competitive position	1,000,000	1,600,000
Indirect benefits:		
Production scheduling	$ 110,000	
Payroll	90,000	200,000
Total		$4,000,000

Present value ($2,200,000 × 5.650)	$12,430,000
Investment	18,000,000
Net present value	$(5,570,000)

The rise of activity-based costing has made identifying indirect benefits easier with the use of cost drivers. Once they are identified, they can be included in the analysis if they are material.

Examination of Exhibit 13-2 reveals the importance of intangible benefits. One of the most important intangible benefits is maintaining or improving a firm's competitive position. A key question is what will happen to the cash flows of the firm if the investment is not made. That is, if the company chooses to forego an investment in technologically advanced equipment, will it be able to continue to compete with other firms on the basis of quality, delivery, and cost? (The question becomes especially relevant if competitors choose to invest in advanced equipment.) If the competitive position deteriorates, the company's current cash flows will decrease.

If cash flows will decrease if the investment is not made, this decrease should show up as an incremental benefit for the advanced technology. In Exhibit 13-2, the company estimates this competitive benefit as $1,000,000. Estimating this benefit requires some serious strategic planning and analysis, but its effect can be critical. If this benefit had been ignored or overlooked, then the net present value would have been negative, and the investment alternative rejected:

Present value ($3,000,000 × 5.650)	$16,950,000
Investment	18,000,000
Net present value	$(1,050,000)

Describing the different types of benefits from the pilot project was a good starting point in the analysis of the proposed automated deposit system for TastyFood Corporation. However, Earl Wise and Stan Miller were on target when they resisted a quick approval for the investment based only on a qualitative description of benefits. The identified benefits did not have any specific projected cash flows associated with them. To correct this deficiency, Stan Miller, the controller, estimated the cash flows associated with the project. Stan provided three estimates of net annual cash savings: $500,000, $800,000, and $1 million, corresponding to pessimistic, most likely, and optimistic scenarios. Stan also indicated that the cost of capital is 10 percent.

Armed with this information, Stan calculated a payback period for each scenario: 4 years, 2.5 years, and 2 years. The project passed the company's payback period criterion of five years or less. Furthermore, the NPV for each of the three scenarios was positive—even when the lowest expected life of five years was used. Based on this very positive assessment, the capital acquisitions committee recommended that the new system be installed throughout the company.

After two years of operations, a postaudit assessment confirmed the wisdom of the decision to invest in the automated system. In fact, the postaudit revealed an even better economic outcome than what was expected. The one criticism found by the postaudit analysis was that the initial analysis failed to estimate and incorporate the cash benefits from interfacing the store's computers with the host computer at headquarters. By eliminating manual entries and expediting bank reconciliations, an additional savings of $100,000 per year were realized—an item not incorporated in the initial analysis.

SUMMARY OF LEARNING OBJECTIVES

Capital investment decisions are concerned with the acquisition of long-term assets and usually involve a significant outlay of funds. The two types of capital investment projects are independent and mutually exclusive. Independent projects are projects that, if accepted or rejected, do not affect the cash flows of other projects. Mutually exclusive projects are those projects that, if accepted, preclude the acceptance of all other competing projects.

Managers make capital investment decisions by using formal models to decide whether to accept or reject proposed projects. These decision models are classified as nondiscounting and discounting, depending on whether they address the question of the time value of money. The two nondiscounting models are the payback period and the accounting rate of return.

The payback period is the time required for a firm to recover its initial investment. For even cash flows, it is calculated by dividing the investment by the annual cash flow. For uneven cash flows, the cash flows are summed until the investment is recovered. If only a fraction of a year is needed, then it is assumed that the cash flows occur evenly within each year. The payback period ignores the time value of money and the profitability of projects because it does not consider the cash inflows available beyond the payback period. However, it does supply some useful information. The payback period is useful for assessing and controlling risk, minimizing the impact of an investment on a firm's liquidity, and controlling the risk of obsolescence.

The accounting rate of return is computed by dividing the average income expected from an investment by either the original or average investment. Unlike the payback period, it does consider the profitability of a project; however, it ignores the time value of money. The payback period may be useful to managers for screening new investments to ensure that certain accounting ratios are not adversely affected (specifically accounting ratios that may be monitored to ensure compliance with debt covenants).

NPV is the difference between the present value of future cash flows and the initial investment outlay. To use the model, a required rate of return must be identified (usually the cost of capital). The NPV method uses the required rate of return to compute the present value of a project's cash inflows and outflows. If the present value of the inflows is greater than the present value of the outflows, then the net present value is greater than zero, and the project is profitable; if the NPV is less than zero, then the project is not profitable and should be rejected.

The IRR is computed by finding the interest rate that equates the present value of a project's cash inflows with the present value of its cash outflows. If the IRR is greater than the required rate of return (cost of capital), then the project is acceptable; if the IRR is less than the required rate of return, then the project should be rejected.

Postauditing of capital projects is an important step in capital investment. Postaudits evaluate the actual performance of a project in relation to its expected performance. A postaudit may lead to corrective action to improve the performance of the project or to abandon it. Postaudits also serve as an incentive for managers to make capital investment decisions prudently.

In evaluating mutually exclusive or competing projects, managers have a choice of using NPV or IRR. When choosing among competing projects, the NPV model correctly identifies the best investment alternative. IRR, at times, may choose an inferior project. Thus, since NPV always provides the correct signal, it should be used.

Cornerstones for Chapter 13

Cornerstone 13-1   How to calculate payback, page 544
Cornerstone 13-2   How to calculate the accounting rate of return, page 546
Cornerstone 13-3   How to assess cash flows and calculate NPV, page 548
Cornerstone 13-4   How to calculate IRR with uniform cash flows, page 550
Cornerstone 13-5   How to calculate NPV and IRR for mutually exclusive projects, page 556

KEY TERMS

APPENDIX 13A: PRESENT VALUE CONCEPTS

An important feature of money is that it can be invested and can earn interest. A dollar today is not the same as a dollar tomorrow. This fundamental principle is the backbone of discounting methods. Discounting methods rely on the relationships between current and future dollars. Thus, to use discounting methods, we must understand these relationships.

Future Value

Suppose a bank advertises a 4-percent annual interest rate. If a customer invests $100, he or she would receive, after one year, the original $100 plus $4 interest [$100 + (0.04)($100)] = (1 + 0.04)$100 = (1.04)($100) = $104. This result can be expressed by the following equation, where F is the future amount, P is the initial or current outlay, and i is the interest rate:

$$F = P(1 + i)$$

For the example, $F = \$100(1 + 0.04) = \$100(1.04) = \$104$.

Now suppose that the same bank offers a 5-percent rate if the customer leaves the original deposit, plus any interest, on deposit for a total of two years. How much will the customer receive at the end of two years? Again assume that a customer invests $100. Using the future value equation, the customer will earn $105 at the end of year 1 [$F = \$100(1 + 0.05) = (\$100 \times 1.05) = \$105$]. If this amount is left in the account for a second year, this equation is used again with P now assumed to be $105. At the end of the second year, then, the total is $110.25 [$F = \$105(1 + 0.05) = (\$105 \times 1.05) = \$110.25$]. In the second year, interest is earned on both the original deposit and the interest earned in the first year. The earning of interest on interest is referred to as **compounding of interest**. The value that will accumulate by the end of an investment's life, assuming a specified compound return, is the **future value**. The future value of the $100 deposit in the second example is $110.25.

A more direct way to compute the future value is possible. Since the first application of the future value equation can be expressed as $F = \$105 = \$100(1.05)$, the second application can be expressed as $F = \$105(1.05) = \$100(1.05)(1.05) = \$100(1.05)^2 = P(1 + i)^2$. This suggests the following compounding interest formula for computing amounts for n periods into the future:

$$F = P(1 + i)^n$$

Present Value

Often, a manager needs to compute not the future value but the amount that must be invested now in order to yield some given future value. The amount that must be invested now to produce the future value is known as the **present value** of the future amount. For example, how much must be invested now in order to yield $363 two years from now, assuming that the interest rate is 10 percent? Or put another way, what is the present value of $363 to be received two years from now?

In this example, the future value, the years, and the interest rate are all known; we want to know the current outlay that will produce that future amount. In the compounding interest equation, the variable representing the current outlay (the present value of F) is P. Thus, to compute the present value of a future outlay, all we need to do is solve the compounding interest equation for P:

$$P = F/(1 + i)^n$$

Using this present value equation, we can compute the present value of $363:

$$P = \$363/(1 + 0.1)^2$$
$$= \$363/1.21$$
$$= \$300$$

The present value, $300, is what the future amount of $363 is worth today. All other things being equal, having $300 today is the same as having $363 two years from now. Put another way, if a firm requires a 10-percent rate of return, the most the firm would be willing to pay today is $300 for any investment that yields $363 two years from now.

The process of computing the present value of future cash flows is often referred to as **discounting**; thus, we say that we have discounted the future value of $363 to its present value of $300. The interest rate used to discount the future cash flow is the **discount rate**. The expression $1/(1 + i)^n$ in the present value equation is the **discount factor**. By letting the discount factor, called *df*, equal $1/(1 + i)^n$, the present value equation can be expressed as $P = F(df)$. To simplify the computation of present value, a table of discount factors is given for various combinations of i and n (see Exhibit 13B-1 in Appendix 13B). For example, the discount factor for $i = 10$ percent and $n = 2$ is 0.826 (simply go to the 10-percent column of the table and move down to the second row). With the discount factor, the present value of $363 is computed as follows:

$$P = F(df)$$
$$= \$363 \times 0.826$$
$$= \$300 \text{ (rounded)}$$

Present Value of an Uneven Series of Cash Flows

Exhibit 13B-1 can be used to compute the present value of any future cash flow or series of future cash flows. A series of future cash flows is called an **annuity**. The present value of an annuity is found by computing the present value of each future cash flow and then summing these values. For example, suppose that an investment is expected to produce the following annual cash flows: $110, $121, and $133.10. Assuming a discount rate of 10 percent, the present value of this series of cash flows is computed in Exhibit 13A-1.

Present Value of a Uniform Series of Cash Flows

If the series of cash flows is even, the computation of the annuity's present value is simplified. Assume, for example, that an investment is expected to return $100 per year for three years. Using Exhibit 13B-1 and assuming a discount rate of 10 percent, the present value of the annuity is computed in Exhibit 13A-2.

13A-1

EXHIBIT

Present Value of an Uneven Series of Cash Flows

Year	Cash Receipt	Discount Factor	Present Value*
1	$110.00	0.909	$100.00
2	121.00	0.826	100.00
3	133.10	0.751	100.00
			$300.00

* Rounded.

Present Value of Uniform Series of Cash Flows

Year	Cash Receipt*	Discount Factor	Present Value*
1	$100	0.909	$ 90.90
2	100	0.826	82.60
3	100	0.751	75.10
		2.486	$248.60

*The annual cash flow of $100 can be multiplied by the sum of the discount factors (2.486) to obtain the present value of the uniform series ($248.60).

As with the uneven series of cash flows, the present value in Exhibit 13A-2 was computed by calculating the present value of each cash flow separately and then summing them. However, in the case of an annuity displaying uniform cash flows, the computations can be reduced from three to one as described in the footnote to the exhibit. The sum of the individual discount factors can be thought of as a discount factor for an annuity of uniform cash flows. A table of discount factors that can be used for an annuity of uniform cash flows is available in Exhibit 13B-2.

APPENDIX 13A KEY TERMS

Annuity, 563

Compounding of interest, 562

Discount factor, 563

Discount rate, 563

Discounting, 563

Future value, 562

Present value, 562

APPENDIX 13B: PRESENT VALUE TABLES

The present value tables are found on pages 565 and 566.

Present Value of $1*

Periods	2%	4%	6%	8%	10%	12%	14%	16%	18%	20%	22%	24%	26%	28%	30%	32%	40%
1	0.980	0.962	0.943	0.926	0.909	0.893	0.877	0.862	0.847	0.833	0.820	0.806	0.794	0.781	0.769	0.758	0.714
2	0.961	0.925	0.890	0.857	0.826	0.797	0.769	0.743	0.718	0.694	0.672	0.650	0.630	0.610	0.592	0.574	0.510
3	0.942	0.889	0.840	0.794	0.751	0.712	0.675	0.641	0.609	0.579	0.551	0.524	0.500	0.477	0.455	0.435	0.364
4	0.924	0.855	0.792	0.735	0.683	0.636	0.592	0.552	0.516	0.482	0.451	0.423	0.397	0.373	0.350	0.329	0.260
5	0.906	0.822	0.747	0.681	0.621	0.567	0.519	0.476	0.437	0.402	0.370	0.341	0.315	0.291	0.269	0.250	0.186
6	0.888	0.790	0.705	0.630	0.564	0.507	0.456	0.410	0.370	0.335	0.303	0.275	0.250	0.227	0.207	0.189	0.133
7	0.871	0.760	0.665	0.583	0.513	0.452	0.400	0.354	0.314	0.279	0.249	0.222	0.198	0.178	0.159	0.143	0.095
8	0.853	0.731	0.627	0.540	0.467	0.404	0.351	0.305	0.266	0.233	0.204	0.179	0.157	0.139	0.123	0.108	0.068
9	0.837	0.703	0.592	0.500	0.424	0.361	0.308	0.263	0.225	0.194	0.167	0.144	0.125	0.108	0.094	0.082	0.048
10	0.820	0.676	0.558	0.463	0.386	0.322	0.270	0.227	0.191	0.162	0.137	0.116	0.099	0.085	0.073	0.062	0.035
11	0.804	0.650	0.527	0.429	0.350	0.287	0.237	0.195	0.162	0.135	0.112	0.094	0.079	0.066	0.056	0.047	0.025
12	0.788	0.625	0.497	0.397	0.319	0.257	0.208	0.168	0.137	0.112	0.092	0.076	0.062	0.052	0.043	0.036	0.018
13	0.773	0.601	0.469	0.368	0.290	0.229	0.182	0.145	0.116	0.093	0.075	0.061	0.050	0.040	0.033	0.027	0.013
14	0.758	0.577	0.442	0.340	0.263	0.205	0.160	0.125	0.099	0.078	0.062	0.049	0.039	0.032	0.025	0.021	0.009
15	0.743	0.555	0.417	0.315	0.239	0.183	0.140	0.108	0.084	0.065	0.051	0.040	0.031	0.025	0.020	0.016	0.006
16	0.728	0.534	0.394	0.292	0.218	0.163	0.123	0.093	0.071	0.054	0.042	0.032	0.025	0.019	0.015	0.012	0.005
17	0.714	0.513	0.371	0.270	0.198	0.146	0.108	0.080	0.060	0.045	0.034	0.026	0.020	0.015	0.012	0.009	0.003
18	0.700	0.494	0.350	0.250	0.180	0.130	0.095	0.069	0.051	0.038	0.028	0.021	0.016	0.012	0.009	0.007	0.002
19	0.686	0.475	0.331	0.232	0.164	0.116	0.083	0.060	0.043	0.031	0.023	0.017	0.012	0.009	0.007	0.005	0.002
20	0.673	0.456	0.312	0.215	0.149	0.104	0.073	0.051	0.037	0.026	0.019	0.014	0.010	0.007	0.005	0.004	0.001
21	0.660	0.439	0.294	0.199	0.135	0.093	0.064	0.044	0.031	0.022	0.015	0.011	0.008	0.006	0.004	0.003	0.001
22	0.647	0.422	0.278	0.184	0.123	0.083	0.056	0.038	0.026	0.018	0.013	0.009	0.006	0.004	0.003	0.002	0.001
23	0.634	0.406	0.262	0.170	0.112	0.074	0.049	0.033	0.022	0.015	0.010	0.007	0.005	0.003	0.002	0.002	0.001
24	0.622	0.390	0.247	0.158	0.102	0.066	0.043	0.028	0.019	0.013	0.008	0.006	0.004	0.003	0.002	0.002	0.000
25	0.610	0.375	0.233	0.146	0.092	0.059	0.038	0.024	0.016	0.010	0.007	0.005	0.003	0.002	0.001	0.001	0.000
26	0.598	0.361	0.220	0.135	0.084	0.053	0.033	0.021	0.014	0.009	0.006	0.004	0.002	0.002	0.001	0.001	0.000
27	0.586	0.347	0.207	0.125	0.076	0.047	0.029	0.018	0.011	0.007	0.005	0.003	0.002	0.001	0.001	0.001	0.000
28	0.574	0.333	0.196	0.116	0.069	0.042	0.026	0.016	0.010	0.006	0.004	0.002	0.002	0.001	0.001	0.000	0.000
29	0.563	0.321	0.185	0.107	0.063	0.037	0.022	0.014	0.008	0.005	0.003	0.002	0.001	0.001	0.000	0.000	0.000
30	0.552	0.308	0.174	0.099	0.057	0.033	0.020	0.012	0.007	0.004	0.003	0.002	0.001	0.001	0.000	0.000	0.000

*$P_n = A/(1 + i)^n$

Present Value of an Annuity of $1 in Arrears*

Periods	2%	4%	6%	8%	10%	12%	14%	16%	18%	20%	22%	24%	26%	28%	30%	32%	40%
1	0.980	0.962	0.943	0.926	0.909	0.893	0.877	0.862	0.847	0.833	0.820	0.806	0.794	0.781	0.769	0.758	0.714
2	1.942	1.886	1.833	1.783	1.736	1.690	1.647	1.605	1.566	1.528	1.492	1.457	1.424	1.392	1.361	1.331	1.224
3	2.884	2.775	2.673	2.577	2.487	2.402	2.322	2.246	2.174	2.106	2.042	1.981	1.923	1.868	1.816	1.766	1.589
4	3.808	3.630	3.465	3.312	3.170	3.037	2.914	2.798	2.690	2.589	2.494	2.404	2.320	2.241	2.166	2.096	1.849
5	4.713	4.452	4.212	3.993	3.791	3.605	3.433	3.274	3.127	2.991	2.864	2.745	2.635	2.532	2.436	2.345	2.035
6	5.601	5.242	4.917	4.623	4.355	4.111	3.889	3.685	3.498	3.326	3.167	3.020	2.885	2.759	2.643	2.534	2.168
7	6.472	6.002	5.582	5.206	4.868	4.564	4.288	4.039	3.812	3.605	3.416	3.242	3.083	2.937	2.802	2.677	2.263
8	7.325	6.733	6.210	5.747	5.335	4.968	4.639	4.344	4.078	3.837	3.619	3.421	3.241	3.076	2.925	2.786	2.331
9	8.162	7.435	6.802	6.247	5.759	5.328	4.946	4.607	4.303	4.031	3.876	3.566	3.366	3.184	3.019	2.868	2.379
10	8.983	8.111	7.360	6.710	6.145	5.650	5.216	4.833	4.494	4.192	3.923	3.682	3.465	3.269	3.092	2.930	2.414
11	9.787	8.760	7.887	7.139	6.495	5.938	5.453	5.029	4.656	4.327	4.035	3.776	3.543	3.335	3.147	2.978	2.438
12	10.575	9.385	8.384	7.536	6.814	6.194	5.660	5.197	4.793	4.439	4.127	3.851	3.606	3.387	3.190	3.013	2.456
13	11.348	9.986	8.853	7.904	7.103	6.424	5.842	5.342	4.910	4.533	4.203	3.912	3.656	3.427	3.223	3.040	2.469
14	12.106	10.563	9.295	8.244	7.367	6.628	6.002	5.468	5.008	4.611	4.265	3.962	3.695	3.459	3.249	3.061	2.478
15	12.849	11.118	9.712	8.559	7.606	6.811	6.142	5.575	5.092	4.675	4.315	4.001	3.726	3.483	3.268	3.076	2.484
16	13.578	11.652	10.106	8.851	7.824	6.974	6.265	5.668	5.162	4.730	4.357	4.033	3.751	3.503	3.283	3.088	2.489
17	14.292	12.166	10.477	9.122	8.022	7.120	6.373	5.749	5.222	4.775	4.391	4.059	3.771	3.518	3.295	3.097	2.492
18	14.992	12.659	10.828	9.372	8.201	7.250	6.467	5.818	5.273	4.812	4.419	4.080	3.786	3.529	3.304	3.104	2.494
19	15.678	13.134	11.158	9.604	8.365	7.366	6.550	5.877	5.316	4.843	4.442	4.097	3.799	3.539	3.311	3.109	2.496
20	16.351	13.590	11.470	9.818	8.514	7.469	6.623	5.929	5.353	4.870	4.460	4.110	3.808	3.546	3.316	3.113	2.497
21	17.011	14.029	11.764	10.017	8.649	7.562	6.687	5.973	5.384	4.891	4.476	4.121	3.816	3.551	3.320	3.116	2.498
22	17.658	14.451	12.042	10.201	8.772	7.645	6.743	6.011	5.410	4.909	4.488	4.130	3.822	3.556	3.323	3.118	2.498
23	18.292	14.857	12.303	10.371	8.883	7.718	6.792	6.044	5.432	4.925	4.499	4.137	3.827	3.559	3.325	3.120	2.499
24	18.914	15.247	12.550	10.529	8.985	7.784	6.835	6.073	5.451	4.937	4.507	4.143	3.831	3.562	3.327	3.121	2.499
25	19.523	15.622	12.783	10.675	9.077	7.843	6.873	6.097	5.467	4.948	4.514	4.147	3.834	3.564	3.329	3.122	2.499
26	20.121	15.983	13.003	10.810	9.161	7.896	6.906	6.118	5.480	4.956	4.520	4.151	3.837	3.566	3.330	3.123	2.500
27	20.707	16.330	13.211	10.935	9.237	7.943	6.935	6.136	5.492	4.964	4.524	4.154	3.839	3.567	3.331	3.123	2.500
28	21.281	16.663	13.406	11.051	9.307	7.984	6.961	6.152	5.502	4.970	4.528	4.157	3.840	3.568	3.331	3.124	2.500
29	21.844	16.984	13.591	11.158	9.370	8.022	6.983	6.166	5.510	4.975	4.531	4.159	3.841	3.569	3.332	3.124	2.500
30	22.396	17.292	13.765	11.258	9.427	8.055	7.003	6.177	5.517	4.979	4.534	4.160	3.842	3.569	3.332	3.124	2.500

*$P_n = (1/i)[1 - 1/(1+i)^n]$

DISCUSSION QUESTIONS

1. Explain the difference between independent projects and mutually exclusive projects.
2. Explain why the timing and quantity of cash flows are important in capital investment decisions.
3. The time value of money is ignored by the payback period and the accounting rate of return. Explain why this is a major deficiency in these two models.
4. What is the payback period? Compute the payback period for an investment requiring an initial outlay of $80,000 with expected annual cash inflows of $30,000.
5. Name and discuss three possible reasons that the payback period is used to help make capital investment decisions.
6. What is the accounting rate of return? Compute the accounting rate of return for an investment that requires an initial outlay of $300,000 and promises an average net income of $100,000.
7. The net present value is the same as the profit of a project expressed in present dollars. Do you agree? Explain.
8. Explain the relationship between NPV and a firm's value.
9. What is the cost of capital? What role does it play in capital investment decisions?
10. What is the role that the required rate of return plays in the NPV model? In the IRR model?
11. Explain how the NPV is used to determine whether a project should be accepted or rejected.
12. The IRR is the true or actual rate of return being earned by the project. Do you agree or disagree? Discuss.
13. Explain what a postaudit is and how it can provide useful input for future capital investment decisions, especially those involving advanced technology.
14. Explain why NPV is generally preferred over IRR when choosing among competing or mutually exclusive projects. Why would managers continue to use IRR to choose among mutually exclusive projects?
15. Suppose that a firm must choose between two mutually exclusive projects, both of which have negative NPVs. Explain how a firm can legitimately choose between two such projects.

MULTIPLE-CHOICE EXERCISES

13-1 Capital investments should

a. earn back their original capital outlay.
b. only be analyzed using the accounting rate of return.
c. always produce an increase in market share.
d. always be done using a payback criterion.
e. do none of the above.

13-2 To make a capital investment decision, a manager must

a. estimate the quantity and timing of cash flows.
b. assess the risk of the investment.
c. consider the impact of the investment on the firm's profits.
d. select investments with a positive NPV.
e. do all of the above.

13-3 Mutually exclusive capital budgeting projects are those that

a. if accepted or rejected do not affect the cash flows of other projects.
b. if accepted will produce a negative NPV.
c. if accepted preclude the acceptance of all other competing projects.
d. if rejected preclude the acceptance of all other competing projects.
e. if rejected imply that all other competing projects have a positive NPV.

13-4 An investment of $1,000 produces a net annual cash inflow of $500 for each of five years. What is the payback period?

a. Two years
b. One-half year
c. Unacceptable
d. Three years
e. Cannot be determined

13-5 An investment of $1,000 produces a net cash inflow of $600 in the first year and $2,000 in the second year. What is the payback period?

a. 1.67 years
b. 0.50 year
c. 2.00 years
d. 1.20 years
e. Cannot be determined

13-6 The payback period suffers from which of the following deficiencies?

a. It is a rough measure of the uncertainty of future cash flows.
b. It helps control the risk of obsolescence.
c. It ignores the time value of money.
d. It ignores the financial performance of a project beyond the payback period.
e. Both c and d.

13-7 The accounting rate of return has one specific advantage not possessed by the payback period in that it

a. considers the time value of money.
b. measures the value added by a project.
c. considers the profitability of a project beyond the payback period.
d. is more widely accepted by financial managers.
e. is always an accurate measure of profitability.

13-8 An investment of $1,000 provides an average net income of $220 with zero salvage value. Depreciation is $20 per year. The accounting rate of return using the original investment is

a. 44 percent.
b. 22 percent.
c. 20 percent.
d. 40 percent.
e. none of the above.

13-9 If the net present value is positive, it signals

a. that the initial investment has been recovered.
b. that the required rate of return has been earned.
c. that the value of the firm has increased.
d. all of the above.
e. both a and b.

13-10 Net present value measures

a.   the profitability of an investment.
b.   the change in wealth.
c.   the change in firm value.
d.   the difference in present value of cash inflows and outflows.
e.   all of the above.

13-11 The net present value is calculated using

a.   accounting income.
b.   the required rate of return.
c.   the internal rate of return.
d.   the future value of cash flows.
e.   none of the above.

13-12 Using NPV, a project is rejected if it is

a.   equal to zero.
b.   positive.
c.   negative.
d.   less than the hurdle rate.
e.   greater than the cost of capital.

13-13 If the present value of future cash flows is $1,200 for an investment that requires an outlay of $1,000, the NPV

a.   is $200.
b.   is $1,000.
c.   is $1,200.
d.   is $2,200.
e.   cannot be determined.

13-14 Assume an investment of $1,000 produces a future cash flow of $1,000. The discount factor for this future cash flow is 0.89. The NPV is

a. $0.
b. $110.
c. $2,000.
d. $911.
e.   none of the above.

13-15 Which of the following is *not* true regarding the IRR?

a.   The IRR is the interest rate that sets the present value of a project's cash inflows equal to the present value of the project's cost.
b.   The IRR is the interest rate that sets the NPV equal to zero.
c.   The IRR is the most reliable of the capital budgeting methods.
d.   If the IRR is greater than the required rate of return, then the project is acceptable.
e.   The popularity of IRR may be attributable to the fact that it is a rate of return, a concept that managers are comfortable with using.

13-16 Using IRR, a project is rejected if the IRR

a.   is less than the required rate of return.
b.   is equal to the required rate of return.
c.   is greater than the cost of capital.
d.   is greater than the required rate of return.
e.   produces a NPV equal to zero.

13-17 A postaudit

a. is a follow-up analysis of a capital project, once implemented.
b. compares the actual benefits with the estimated benefits.
c. evaluates the overall outcome of the investment.
d. proposes corrective action, if needed.
e. does all of the above.

13-18 Postaudits of capital projects are useful because

a. they are not very costly.
b. they help ensure that resources are used wisely.
c. the assumptions underlying the original analyses are often invalidated by changes in the actual working environment.
d. they have no significant limitations.
e. of all of the above.

13-19 For competing projects, NPV is preferred to IRR because

a. maximizing IRR may not maximize the wealth of the owners.
b. in the final analysis, total dollars earned, not relative profitability, are what count.
c. choosing the project with the largest NPV maximizes the wealth of the shareholders.
d. assuming that cash flows are reinvested at the required rate of return is more realistic than assuming that cash flows are reinvested at the computed IRR.
e. of all of the above.

13-20 Assume there are two competing projects: A and B. Project A has a NPV of $1,000 and an IRR of 15 percent; Project B has a NPV of $800 and an IRR of 20 percent. Which of the following is true?

a. It is not possible to use NPV or IRR to choose between the two projects.
b. Project B should be chosen because it has a higher IRR.
c. Project A should be chosen because it has a higher NPV.
d. Neither project should be chosen.
e. None of the above.

EXERCISES

Exercise 13-1 *Payback Period*

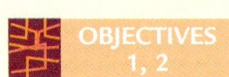

Each of the following situations is independent. Assume all cash flows are after-tax cash flows.

a. Kaylin Hansen has just invested $200,000 in a book and video store. She expects to receive a cash income of $60,000 per year from the investment.
b. Kambry Day has just invested $500,000 in a new biomedical technology. She expects to receive the following cash flows over the next five years: $125,000, $175,000, $250,000, $150,000, and $100,000.
c. Emily Nabors invested in a project that has a payback period of three years. The project brings in $120,000 per year.
d. Joseph Booth invested $250,000 in a project that pays him an even amount per year for five years. The payback period is 2.5 years.
e. Kenzie Hepworth has just invested $100,000 in a company. She expects to receive $16,100 per year for the next eight years. Her cost of capital is 6 percent.

Required:
1. What is the payback period for Kaylin?
2. What is the payback period for Kambry?

3. How much did Emily invest in the project?
4. How much cash does Joseph receive each year?

Exercise 13-2 *Accounting Rate of Return*

Each of the following scenarios is independent. Assume all cash flows are after-tax cash flows.

a. Cameron Company is considering the purchase of new equipment that will speed up the process for extracting copper. The equipment will cost $1,500,000 and have a life of five years with no expected salvage value. The expected cash flows associated with the project are as follows:

Year	Cash Revenues	Cash Expenses
1	$2,500,000	$2,000,000
2	2,500,000	2,000,000
3	2,500,000	2,000,000
4	2,500,000	2,000,000
5	2,500,000	2,000,000

b. Merlene Jensen is considering investing in one of the following two projects. Either project will require an investment of $20,000. The expected revenues less cash expenses for the two projects follow. Assume each project is depreciable.

Year	Project A	Project B
1	$ 6,000	$ 6,000
2	8,000	8,000
3	10,000	12,000
4	20,000	6,000
5	20,000	6,000

c. Suppose that a project has an accounting rate of return of 25 percent (based on average investment) and that the average net income of the project is $100,000.
d. Suppose that a project has an accounting rate of return of 50 percent and that the investment is $200,000.

Required:
1. Compute the accounting rate of return on the new equipment that Cameron Company is considering.
2. Which project should Merlene Jensen choose based on the accounting rate of return?
3. How much did the company in scenario c invest in the project?
4. What is the average income earned by the project in scenario d?

Exercise 13-3 *NPV*

Each of the following scenarios is independent. Assume all cash flows are after-tax cash flows.

1. Modinero Bank is considering the purchase of a new automated teller system. The cash benefits will be $240,000 per year. The system costs $1,360,000 and will last 10 years.
2. Brandon Smith is interested in investing in some tools and equipment so that he can do independent remodeling. The cost of the tools and equipment is $30,000. He estimates that the return from owning his own equipment will be $9,000 per year. The tools and equipment will last six years.

(continued)

3. Golman Company calculated the NPV of a project and found it to be $3,550. The project's life was estimated to be six years. The required rate of return used for the NPV calculation was 10 percent. The project was expected to produce annual after-tax cash flows of $10,000.

Required:

1. Compute the NPV for Moderino Bank assuming a discount rate of 12 percent. Should the bank buy the new automated teller system?
2. Assuming a required rate of return of 8 percent, calculate the NPV for Brandon Smith's investment. Should he invest?
3. What was the required investment for Goldman Company's project?

Exercise 13-4 *IRR*

Required:

1. Collins Company is considering the purchase of new equipment that will speed up the process for producing hard disk drives. The equipment will cost $1,563,500 and have a life of five years with no expected salvage value. The expected cash flows associated with the project follow:

Year	Cash Revenues	Cash Expenses
1	$1,500,000	$1,000,000
2	1,500,000	1,000,000
3	1,500,000	1,000,000
4	1,500,000	1,000,000
5	1,500,000	1,000,000

Calculate the IRR. Should the new equipment be purchased?

2. Pamela Barker is evaluating an investment in an information system that will save $100,000 per year. She estimates that the system will last 10 years. The system will cost $521,600. Her company's cost of capital is 10 percent. Calculate the project's internal rate of return. Should she acquire the new system?
3. Wellington Enterprises just announced that a new plant would be built in Wilmington, Delaware. Wellington told its shareholders that the plant has an expected life of 15 years and an expected IRR equal to 24 percent. The cost of building the plant is expected to be $2,400,000. What is the expected annual cash flow from the plant?

Exercise 13-5 *NPV and Competing Projects*

Heltham Medical Clinic is investigating the possibility of investing in new blood analysis equipment. Two local manufacturers of this equipment are being considered as sources of the equipment. After-tax cash inflows for the two competing projects are as follows:

Year	Marson Equipment	Lawson Equipment
1	$120,000	$ 20,000
2	100,000	20,000
3	80,000	120,000
4	40,000	160,000
5	20,000	180,000

Both projects require an initial investment of $200,000. In both cases, assume the equipment has a life of five years with no salvage value.

Required:

1. Assuming a discount rate of 12 percent, compute the net present value of each piece of equipment.

2. A third option has surfaced for equipment purchased from an out-of-state supplier. The cost is also $200,000, but this equipment will produce even cash flows over its 5-year life. What must the annual cash flow be for this equipment to be selected over the other two? Assume a 12-percent discount rate.

Exercise 13-6 *Payback, Accounting Rate of Return, NPV, IRR*

Wheeler Company wants to buy a numerically controlled (NC) machine to be used in producing specially machined parts for manufacturers of trenching machines. The outlay required is $800,000. The NC equipment will last five years with no expected salvage value. The expected after-tax cash flows associated with the project follow:

Year	Cash Revenues	Cash Expenses
1	$1,300,000	$1,000,000
2	1,300,000	1,000,000
3	1,300,000	1,000,000
4	1,300,000	1,000,000
5	1,300,000	1,000,000

Required:
1. Compute the payback period for the NC equipment.
2. Compute the NC equipment's accounting rate of return.
3. Compute the investment's net present value, assuming a required rate of return of 10 percent.
4. Compute the investment's internal rate of return.

Exercise 13-7 *Payback, Accounting Rate of Return, Present Value, NPV, IRR*

The first two parts are related; the last three are independent of all other parts. Assume all cash flows are after-tax cash flows.

Required:
1. Randy Willis is considering investing in one of the following two projects. Either project will require an investment of $10,000. The expected cash flows for the two projects follow. Assume each project is depreciable.

Year	Project A	Project B
1	$ 3,000	$3,000
2	4,000	4,000
3	5,000	6,000
4	10,000	3,000
5	10,000	3,000

What is the payback period for each project? If rapid payback is important, which project should be chosen? Which would you choose?
2. Calculate the accounting rate of return for each project in Requirement 1 (the expected cash flows are the difference between cash revenues and cash expenses). Which project should be chosen based on the accounting rate of return?
3. Wilma Golding is retiring and has the option to take her retirement as a lump sum of $225,000 or to receive $24,000 per year for 20 years. Wilma's required rate of return is 8 percent. Assuming she will live for another 20 years, should she take the lump sum or the annuity?
4. David Booth is interested in investing in some tools and equipment so that he can do independent dry walling. The cost of the tools and equipment is $20,000. He estimates that the return from owning his own equipment will be

$6,000 per year. The tools and equipment will last six years. Assuming a required rate of return of 8 percent, calculate the NPV of the investment. Should he invest?

5. Patsy Folson is evaluating what appears to be an attractive opportunity. She is currently the owner of a small manufacturing company and has the opportunity to acquire another small company's equipment that would provide production of a part currently purchased externally. She estimates that the savings from internal production would be $25,000 per year. She estimates that the equipment would last 10 years. The owner is asking $130,400 for the equipment. Her company's cost of capital is 10 percent. Calculate the project's internal rate of return. Should she acquire the equipment?

Exercise 13-8 *NPV, Basic Concepts*

Harmony Company is considering an investment that requires an outlay of $200,000 and promises an after-tax cash inflow one year from now of $231,000. The company's cost of capital is 10 percent.

Required:
1. Break the $231,000 future cash inflow into three components: (a) the return of the original investment, (b) the cost of capital, and (c) the profit earned on the investment. Now compute the present value of the profit earned on the investment.
2. Compute the NPV of the investment. Compare this with the present value of the profit computed in Requirement 1. What does this tell you about the meaning of NPV?

Exercise 13-9 *Solving for Unknowns*

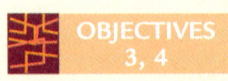

Each of the following cases is independent. (Assume all cash flows are after-tax cash flows.)

Required:
1. Thomas Company is investing $120,000 in a project that will yield a uniform series of cash inflows over the next four years. If the internal rate of return is 14 percent, how much cash inflow per year can be expected?
2. Video Repair has decided to invest in some new electronic equipment. The equipment will have a 3-year life and will produce a uniform series of cash savings. The net present value of the equipment is $1,750 using a discount rate of 8 percent. The internal rate of return is 12 percent. Determine the investment and the amount of cash savings realized each year.
3. A new lathe costing $60,096 will produce savings of $12,000 per year. How many years must the lathe last if an IRR of 18 percent is realized?
4. The NPV of a project is $3,927. The project has a life of four years and produces the following cash flows:

Year 1	$10,000	Year 3	15,000
Year 2	$12,000	Year 4	?

The cost of the project is two times the cash flow produced in year 4. The discount rate is 10 percent. Find the cost of the project and the cash flow for year 4.

Exercise 13-10 *NPV versus IRR*

A company is thinking about two different modifications to its current manufacturing process. The after-tax cash flows associated with the two investments follow:

Year	Project I	Project II
0	$(100,000)	$(100,000)
1	—	63,857
2	134,560	63,857

The company's cost of capital is 10 percent.

Required:

1. Compute the NPV and the IRR for each investment.
2. Explain why the project with the larger NPV is the correct choice for the company.

PROBLEMS

(*Note:* Whenever you see a  next to a requirement, it signals a "building on a cornerstone" requirement. Assigning this requirement will usually entail additional work, such as a group project, analytical reasoning, Internet research, decision making, and the use of written communication skills.)

Problem 13-1 *Basic NPV Analysis*

Camus Blalack, process engineer, knew that the acceptance of a new process design would depend on its economic feasibility. The new process was designed to improve environmental performance. The process design required new equipment and an infusion of working capital. The equipment would cost $300,000, and its cash operating expenses would total $60,000 per year. The equipment would last for seven years but would need a major overhaul costing $30,000 at the end of the fifth year. At the end of seven years, the equipment would be sold for $24,000. An increase in working capital totaling $30,000 would also be needed at the beginning. This would be recovered at the end of the seven years.

On the benefit side, Camus estimated that the new process would save $135,000 per year in environmental costs (fines and cleanup costs avoided). The cost of capital is 10 percent.

Required:

1. Prepare a schedule of cash flows for the proposed project. Assume there are no income taxes.
2. Compute the NPV of the project. Should the new process design be accepted?

Problem 13-2 *NPV Analysis*

Uintah Communications Company is considering the production and marketing of a communications system that will increase the efficiency of messaging for small businesses or branch offices of large companies. Each unit hooked into the system is assigned a mailbox number, which can be matched to a telephone extension number, providing access to messages 24 hours a day. Up to 20 units can be hooked into the system, allowing the delivery of the same message to as many as 20 people. Personal codes can be used to make messages confidential. Furthermore, messages can be reviewed, recorded, cancelled, replied to, or deleted all during the same phone call. Indicators wired to the telephone blink whenever new messages are present.

To produce this product, a $1.1 million investment in new equipment is required. The equipment would last 10 years but would need major maintenance costing $100,000 at the end of its sixth year. The salvage value of the equipment at the end of 10 years is estimated to be $40,000. If this new system is produced, working capital must also be increased by $50,000. This capital will be restored at the end of the product's life cycle, which is estimated to be 10 years. Revenues from the sale of the product are estimated at $1.5 million per year; cash operating expenses are estimated at $1.26 million per year.

Required:

1. Prepare a schedule of cash flows for the proposed project. Assume there are no income taxes.
2. Assuming that Uintah's cost of capital is 12 percent, compute the project's NPV. Should the product be produced?

Problem 13-3 *Basic IRR Analysis*

Lindsey Thompson, owner of Leshow Company, was approached by a local dealer in air conditioning units. The dealer proposed replacing Leshow's old cooling system with a modern, more efficient system. The cost of the new system was quoted at $96,660, but it would save $20,000 per year in energy costs. The estimated life of the new system is 10 years, with no salvage value expected. Excited over the possibility of saving $20,000 per year and having a more reliable unit, Lindsey requested an analysis of the project's economic viability. All capital projects are required to earn at least the firm's cost of capital, which is 10 percent. There are no income taxes.

Required:

1. Calculate the project's internal rate of return. Should the company acquire the new cooling system?
2. Suppose that energy savings are less than claimed. Calculate the minimum annual cash savings that must be realized for the project to earn a rate equal to the firm's cost of capital.
3. Suppose that the life of the new system is overestimated by two years. Repeat Requirements 1 and 2 under this assumption.
4. Explain the implications of the answers from Requirements 1, 2, and 3.

Problem 13-4 *NPV, Uncertainty*

Eden Airlines is interested in acquiring a new aircraft to service a new route. The route would be from Dallas to El Paso. The aircraft would fly one round-trip daily except for scheduled maintenance days. There are 15 maintenance days scheduled each year. The seating capacity of the aircraft is 150. Flights are expected to be fully booked. The average revenue per passenger per flight (one-way) is $200. Annual operating costs of the aircraft follow:

Fuel	$1,400,000
Flight personnel	500,000
Food and beverages	100,000
Maintenance	400,000
Other	100,000
Total	$2,500,000

The aircraft will cost $100,000,000 and has an expected life of 20 years. The company requires a 14-percent return. Assume there are no income taxes.

Required:

1. Calculate the NPV for the aircraft. Should the company buy it?
2. In discussing the proposal, the marketing manager for the airline believes that the assumption of 100-percent booking is unrealistic. He believes that the booking rate will be somewhere between 70 percent and 90 percent, with the most likely rate being 80 percent. Recalculate the NPV using an 80-percent seating capacity. Should the aircraft be purchased?

3. Calculate the average seating rate that would be needed so that NPV will equal zero.
4. Suppose that the price per passenger could be increased by 10 percent without any effect on demand. What is the average seating rate now needed to achieve a NPV equal to zero? What would you now recommend?

Problem 13-5 *Review of Basic Capital Budgeting Procedures*

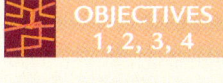

OBJECTIVES
1, 2, 3, 4

Spreadsheet

Dr. Whitley Avard, plastic surgeon, had just returned from a conference in which she learned of a new surgical procedure for removing wrinkles around eyes, reducing the time to perform the normal procedure by 50 percent. Given her patient-load pressures, Dr. Avard was anxious to try out the new technique. By decreasing the time spent on eye treatments or procedures, she could increase her total revenues by performing more services within a work period. Unfortunately, in order to implement the new procedure, some special equipment costing $74,000 was needed. The equipment had an expected life of four years, with a salvage value of $6,000. Dr. Avard estimated that her cash revenues would increase by the following amounts:

Year	Revenue Increases
1	$19,800
2	27,000
3	32,400
4	32,400

She also expected additional cash expenses amounting to $3,000 per year. The cost of capital is 12 percent. Assume there are no income taxes.

Required:

1. Compute the payback period for the new equipment.
2. Compute the accounting rate of return.
3. Compute the NPV and IRR for the project. Should Dr. Avard purchase the new equipment? Should she be concerned about payback or the accounting rate of return in making this decision?

4. Before finalizing her decision, Dr. Avard decided to call two plastic surgeons who had been using the new procedure for the past six months. The conversations revealed a somewhat less glowing report than she received at the conference. The new procedure reduced the time required by about 25 percent rather than the advertised 50 percent. Dr. Avard estimated that the net operating cash flows of the procedure would be cut by one-third because of the extra time and cost involved (salvage value would be unaffected). Using this information, recompute the NPV of the project. What would you now recommend?

Problem 13-6 *NPV and Competing Alternatives*

OBJECTIVES
1, 6

Stillwater Designs has been rebuilding 10″, 12″, and 15″ Kicker subwoofers that were returned for warranty action. Customers returning the subwoofers receive a new replacement. The warranty returns are then rebuilt and resold (as seconds). Tent sales are often used to sell the rebuilt speakers. As part of the rebuilding process, the speakers are demagnetized so that metal pieces and shavings can be removed. A demagnetizing (demag) machine is used to achieve this objective. A product design change has made the most recent 15″ speakers too tall for the demag machine. They no longer fit in the demag machine.

Stillwater Designs has two alternatives that it is currently considering. First, a new demag machine can be bought that has a different design, eliminating the fit problem. The cost of this machine is $100,000, and it will last five years. Second, Stillwater can keep the current machine and sell the 15″ speakers for scrap, using the old demag machine for the 10″ and 12″ speakers only. A rebuilt speaker sells for $295 and costs $274.65 to rebuild (for materials, labor, and overhead cash outlays). The $274.65 outlay includes the annual operating cash effects of the new demag machine. If not rebuilt, the 15″ speakers can be sold for $17 each as scrap. There are 10,000 15″ warranty returns per year. Assume that the required rate of return is 10 percent.

Required:

1. Determine which alternative is the best for Stillwater Designs, using NPV analysis.
2. Determine which alternative is best for Stillwater Designs using an IRR analysis. Explain why NPV analysis is a better approach.

Problem 13-7 *Basic NPV Analysis, Competing Projects*

Kildare Medical Center, a for-profit hospital, has three investment opportunities: (1) adding a wing for in-patient treatment of substance abuse, (2) adding a pathology laboratory, and (3) expanding the out-patient surgery wing. The initial investments and the net present value for the three alternatives are as follows:

	Substance Abuse	Laboratory	Out-Patient Surgery
Investment	$1,500,000	$500,000	$1,000,000
Net Present Value	150,000	140,000	135,000

Although the hospital would like to invest in all three alternatives, only $1.5 million is available.

Required:

1. Rank the projects on the basis of net present value and allocate the funds in order of this ranking. What project or projects were selected? What is the total net present value realized by the medical center using this approach?
2. Assume that the size of the lot on which the hospital is located makes the substance abuse wing and the out-patient surgery wing mutually exclusive. With unlimited capital, which of those two projects would be chosen? With limited capital and the three projects being considered, which projects would be chosen?
3. Form a group of three to five and discuss qualitative considerations that should be considered in capital budgeting evaluations. Identify three such considerations.

Problem 13-8 *Payback, NPV, IRR, Intangible Benefits, Inflation Adjustment*

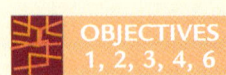

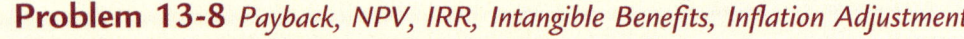

Foster Company wants to buy a numerically controlled (NC) machine to be used in producing specially machined parts for manufacturers of trenching machines (to replace an existing manual system). The outlay required is $3,500,000. The NC equipment will last five years with no expected salvage value. The expected incremental after-tax cash flows (cash flows of the NC equipment less cash flows of the old equipment) associated with the project follow:

Year	Cash Benefits	Cash Expenses
1	$3,900,000	$3,000,000
2	3,900,000	3,000,000
3	3,900,000	3,000,000
4	3,900,000	3,000,000
5	3,900,000	3,000,000

Foster has a cost of capital equal to 10 percent. The above cash flows are expressed without any consideration of inflation.

Required:
1. Compute the payback period.
2. Calculate the NPV and IRR of the proposed project.
3. Inflation is expected to be 5 percent per year for the next five years. The discount rate of 10 percent is composed of two elements: the real rate and the inflationary element. Since the discount rate has an inflationary component, the projected cash flows should also be adjusted to account for inflation. Make this adjustment and recalculate the NPV. Comment on the importance of adjusting cash flows for inflationary effects.

Problem 13-9 *Cost of Capital, NPV*

Leakam Company's product engineering department has developed a new product that has a 3-year life cycle. Production of the product requires development of a new process that requires a current $100,000 capital outlay. The $100,000 will be raised by issuing $60,000 of bonds and by selling new stock for $40,000. The $60,000 in bonds will have net (after-tax) interest payments of $3,000 at the end of each of the three years, with the principal being repaid at the end of year 3. The stock issue carries with it an expectation of a 17.5-percent return, expressed in the form of dividends at the end of each year [($7,000) in dividends is expected for each of the next three years]. The sources of capital for this investment represent the same proportion and costs that the company typically has. Finally, the project will produce after-tax cash inflows of $50,000 per year for the next three years.

Required:
1. Compute the cost of capital for the project. (*Hint*: The cost of capital is a weighted average of the two sources of capital where the weights are the proportion of capital from each source.)
2. Compute the NPV for the project. Explain why it is not necessary to subtract the interest payments and the dividend payments and appreciation from the inflow of $50,000 in carrying out this computation.

Problem 13-10 *Capital Investment, Advanced Manufacturing Environment*

"I know that it's the thing to do," insisted Pamela Kincaid, vice president of finance for Colgate Manufacturing. "If we are going to be competitive, we need to build this completely automated plant."

"I'm not so sure," replied Bill Thomas, CEO of Colgate. "The savings from labor reductions and increased productivity are only $4 million per year. The price tag for this factory—and it's a small one—is $45 million. That gives a payback period of more than 11 years. That's a long time to put the company's money at risk."

"Yeah, but you're overlooking the savings that we'll get from the increase in quality," interjected John Simpson, production manager. "With this system, we can decrease our waste and our rework time significantly. Those savings are worth another million dollars per year."

"Another million will only cut the payback to about nine years," retorted Bill. "Ron, you're the marketing manager—do you have any insights?"

"Well, there are other factors to consider, such as service quality and market share. I think that increasing our product quality and improving our delivery service will make us a lot more competitive. I know for a fact that two of our competitors have decided against automation. That'll give us a shot at their customers, provided our product is of higher quality and we can deliver it faster. I estimate that it'll increase our net cash benefits by another $2.4 million."

"Wow! Now that's impressive," Bill exclaimed, nearly convinced. "The payback is now getting down to a reasonable level."

"I agree," said Pamela, "but we do need to be sure that it's a sound investment. I know that estimates for construction of the facility have gone as high as $48 million. I also know that the expected residual value, after the 20 years of service we expect to get, is $5 million. I think I had better see if this project can cover our 14-percent cost of capital."

"Now wait a minute, Pamela," Bill demanded. "You know that I usually insist on a 20-percent rate of return, especially for a project of this magnitude."

Required:
1. Compute the NPV of the project using the original savings and investment figures. Do the calculation for discount rates of 14 percent and 20 percent. Include salvage value in the computation.
2. Compute the NPV of the project using the additional benefits noted by the production and marketing managers. Also, use the original cost estimate of $45 million. Again, do the calculation for both possible discount rates.
3. Compute the NPV of the project using all estimates of cash flows, including the possible initial outlay of $48 million. Do the calculation using discount rates of 14 percent and 20 percent.
4. If you were making the decision, what would you do? Explain.

Problem 13-11 *Postaudit, Sensitivity Analysis*

OBJECTIVES
5, 6

Newmarge Products, Inc., is evaluating a new design for one of its manufacturing processes. The new design will eliminate the production of a toxic solid residue. The initial cost of the system is estimated at $860,000 and includes computerized equipment, software, and installation. There is no expected salvage value. The new system has a useful life of eight years and is projected to produce cash operating savings of $225,000 per year over the old system (reducing labor costs and costs of processing and disposing of toxic waste). The cost of capital is 16 percent.

Required:
1. Compute the NPV of the new system.
2. One year after implementation, the internal audit staff noted the following about the new system: (1) the cost of acquiring the system was $60,000 more than expected due to higher installation costs, and (2) the annual cost savings were $20,000 less than expected because more labor cost was needed than anticipated. Using the changes in expected costs and benefits, compute the NPV as if this information had been available one year ago. Did the company make the right decision?
3. Upon reporting the results mentioned in the postaudit, the marketing manager responded in a memo to the internal auditing department indicating that revenues had increased by $60,000 per year because of increased purchases by environmentally sensitive customers. Describe the effect this has on the analysis in Requirement 2.
4. Why is a postaudit beneficial to a firm?

Problem 13-12 *Discount Rates, Automated Manufacturing, Competing Investments*

OBJECTIVE 6

A company is considering two competing investments. The first is for a standard piece of production equipment; the second is for some computer-aided manufacturing (CAM) equipment. The investment and after-tax operating cash flows follow:

Year	Standard Equipment	CAM Equipment
0	$(500,000)	$(2,000,000)
1	300,000	100,000
2	200,000	200,000
3	100,000	300,000
4	100,000	400,000
5	100,000	400,000
6	100,000	400,000
7	100,000	500,000
8	100,000	1,000,000
9	100,000	1,000,000
10	100,000	1,000,000

The company uses a discount rate of 18 percent for all of its investments. The company's cost of capital is 10 percent.

Required:
1. Calculate the net present value for each investment using a discount rate of 18 percent.
2. Calculate the net present value for each investment using a discount rate of 10 percent.
3. Which rate should the company use to compute the net present value? Explain.

Problem 13-13 *Quality, Market Share, Automated Manufacturing Environment*

 **OBJECTIVE 6**

Refer to **Problem 13-12**. Assume that the company's cost of capital is 14 percent.

Required:
1. Calculate the NPV of each alternative using the 14-percent rate.
2. Now assume that if the standard equipment is purchased, the competitive position of the firm will deteriorate because of lower quality (relative to competitors who did automate). Marketing estimates that the loss in market share will decrease the projected net cash inflows by 50 percent for years 3 through 10. Recalculate the NPV of the standard equipment given this outcome. What is the decision now? Discuss the importance of assessing the effect of intangible benefits.

SUPPORT DEPARTMENT COST ALLOCATION

© PHOTODISC GREEN/GETTY IMAGES

After studying Chapter 14, you should be able to:

1. Describe the difference between support departments and producing departments.
2. Calculate single and multiple charging rates for a support department.
3. Assign support department costs to producing departments using the direct, sequential, and reciprocal methods.
4. Calculate departmental overhead rates.

Hamilton and Barry, a large regional accounting services firm, consists of three major departments: systems, tax, and management advisory services (MAS). Gary Premark, head of management advisory services, is talking with Jan McAndrews, partner in charge.

Jan: So far, this has been a good year for MAS, Gary. We're very pleased with the way you increased your client base and billing hours. Our only remaining problem is profitability. As you can see, the total costs of your department rose at a faster pace last year than the year before.

Gary: My profitability is just fine—or would be if I weren't forced to use the inefficient services of this firm. Look at my photocopying costs! These are way out of line! I'd be better off using Kopykats a block away.

Jan: Gary, as you know, we went to an in-house photocopying department to provide convenience and security. If it costs a little more, so be it. Besides, the convenience of just walking down the hall to get your reports and bids copied outweighs any small increase in cost allocation.

Gary: Look, Jan, I don't mind paying a little extra for convenience, but this allocation is much more than a little extra. My department is going to boycott photocopying until this problem gets resolved.

Jan: Don't take that step just yet. Carol Morton is in charge of photocopying. Let's get some answers from her first.

Two days later, Gary, Jan, and Carol Morton, executive assistant in charge of the photocopying service, meet in Jan's office.

Carol: Gary, I understand you have some questions about the way photocopying is run. Let me assure you that we work very hard to keep costs down while providing top-notch service. Your department was charged only for the copies you made.

Gary: Carol, I took my total cost allocation and divided it by the number of copies. Do you realize that it comes to $0.10 per page? Why is your department so much higher than outside services?

Carol: Gary, you have to realize that we bought machinery for peak usage. In our firm, that's the month of April when the tax department runs most of their copies. Other months are slower, but I can't trade in the copier on a month-to-month basis. Also, we need at least one person ready to handle your copies or you'll really hit the ceiling. As a result, the per-page charges are higher.

Gary: I think I'm beginning to see what's happening. Still, I'd like to explore different charging systems.

Jan: If there's a problem here, it is a firmwide problem. I can assign Cynthia Bowles, our firm's new intern from State University, to take this on as a special project.

583

The earlier chapters have focused on product costs and the way that they are assigned to products. The complexity of many modern firms leads the accountant to focus particularly on the assignment of overhead. We have learned that there are a variety of ways to assign overhead: plantwide rates, departmental rates, and activity-based costing. Of the three methods, departmental rates require that overhead costs be assigned to individual producing departments. In this chapter, we explain how this is done so that departmental overhead rates can be calculated.

Allocation is simply a means of dividing a pool of costs and assigning it to various subunits. It is important to realize that allocation does not affect the total cost. Total cost is neither reduced nor increased by allocation. However, the amounts of cost assigned to the subunits can be affected by the allocation procedure chosen. Because cost allocation can affect product cost, bid prices, the profitability of individual products, and the behavior of managers, it is an important topic.

AN OVERVIEW OF COST ALLOCATION

When resources are shared in the production of two or more services or products, the costs of these shared resources are typically referred to as **common costs**. For example, the cost of a maintenance department is shared by producing departments that use maintenance services. How to assign these shared costs to individual producing departments is the focus of this chapter.

OBJECTIVE 1
Describe the difference between support departments and producing departments.

Types of Departments

The two categories of departments are producing departments and support departments. **Producing departments** are directly responsible for creating the products or services sold to customers. In the opening scenario's public accounting firm, examples of producing departments are systems, tax, and management advisory services. In a manufacturing setting, producing departments are those that work directly on the products being manufactured such as grinding and assembly departments. **Support departments** provide essential support services for producing departments. Examples include maintenance, grounds, engineering, housekeeping, personnel, and storage. Of course, the photocopying department of Hamilton and Barry is a support department.

Once the producing and support departments have been identified, the overhead costs that belong exclusively to each department are identified. Thus, initially direct costs are identified for each department. A factory cafeteria, for example, would have such direct costs as food costs, salaries of cooks and servers, depreciation on dishwashers and stoves, and supplies (e.g., napkins, plastic forks). Direct costs of a producing department would include such costs as supplies, supervisory salaries, and depreciation on equipment used in that department. Overhead that cannot be easily assigned to a producing or support department is assigned to a catchall department usually referred to as general factory.

Exhibit 14-1 provides examples of producing and support departments for a furniture manufacturing firm and a service firm (bank). The furniture manufacturing plant is departmentalized into two producing departments (assembly and finishing) and four support departments (materials storeroom, cafeteria, maintenance, and general factory). The bank is departmentalized into three producing departments (auto loans, commercial lending, and personal banking) and three support departments (drive-through, data processing, and bank administration). Examples of direct costs are provided for each department.

Concept Q & A

What is the key difference between a producing department and a support department?

Answer:
A producing department works directly on products/services, whereas a support department provides services that enable a producing department to produce the goods.

Examples of Departmentalization for a Manufacturing Firm and a Service Firm

MANUFACTURING FIRM: FURNITURE MAKER	
Producing Departments	**Support Departments**

Assembly:
  Supervisory salaries
  Small tools
  Indirect materials
  Depreciation on machinery
Finishing:
  Sandpaper
  Depreciation on sanders and buffers

Materials storeroom:
  Clerk's salary
  Depreciation on forklift
Cafeteria:
  Food
  Cooks' salaries
  Depreciation on stoves
Maintenance:
  Janitors' salaries
  Cleaning supplies
  Machine oil and lubricants
General factory:
  Depreciation on building
  Security and utilities

SERVICE FIRM: BANK	
Producing Departments	**Support Departments**

Auto loans:
  Loan processors' salaries
  Forms and supplies
Commercial lending:
  Lending officers' salaries
  Depreciation on office equipment
  Bankruptcy prediction software
Personal banking:
  Supplies and postage for statements

Drive-through:
  Tellers' salaries
  Depreciation on equipment
Data processing:
  Personnel salaries
  Software
  Depreciation on hardware
Bank administration:
  Salary of CEO
  Receptionist salary
  Telephone costs
  Depreciation on bank vault

Assigning Costs from Departments to Products

After departmentalizing the company and determining the direct overhead costs of the support and producing departments, the next step is to assign the support department costs to producing departments. Since the producing departments share support department costs, these shared costs are assigned to producing departments using causal factors (drivers) that measure the consumption of the services. The share of the support department costs is added to the direct overhead cost of each producing department. This total estimated overhead is then divided by a unit-level driver to obtain a predetermined overhead rate for each producing department. Overhead rates are calculated only for producing departments because products only pass through producing departments. Overhead rates are used to assign overhead to products. This illustrates the 2-stage cost assignment process of departmental overhead rates: (1) overhead costs are traced to producing departments using direct and driver tracing, and (2) the overhead costs of producing department costs are assigned to products using predetermined rates. Exhibit 14-2 summarizes the steps involved. Steps 1–5 define the first stage, and step 6 corresponds to the second stage.

Types of Drivers

Producing departments require support services; therefore, the costs of support departments are caused by the activities of the producing departments. **Causal factors** are cost drivers within a producing department that measure the consumption of support service costs. In choosing a basis for assigning support department costs, every effort should be made to identify appropriate causal factors (cost drivers). Using causal factors results in more accurate product costs. Furthermore, if the causal factors are known, managers can better control the consumption of support services.

To illustrate the types of cost drivers that can be used, consider the following three support departments: power, personnel, and materials handling. For power costs, a driver choice is kilowatt-hours, which can be measured by separate meters for each department. If separate meters do not exist, perhaps machine hours used by each department would provide a good proxy, or driver. For personnel costs, both the number of producing department employees and the labor turnover (for example, number of new hires) are possible cost drivers. For materials handling, the number of material moves, the hours of materials handling used, and the quantity of material moved are all possible cost drivers. Exhibit 14-3 lists some possible cost drivers that can be used to assign support department costs. When competing cost drivers exist, managers need to decide which provides the most convincing relationship.

While the use of a causal factor to allocate common cost is the best, sometimes an easily measured causal factor cannot be found. In that case, the accountant looks for a good proxy. For example, the common cost of plant depreciation may be allocated to

14-2 EXHIBIT

Steps for Determining Product Costs Using Predetermined Departmental Overhead Rates

1. Departmentalize the firm.
2. Classify each department as a support department or a producing department.
3. Trace all overhead costs in the firm to a support department or producing department.
4. Assign support department costs to the producing departments using drivers that measure the consumption of support department services.
5. Calculate predetermined overhead rates for producing departments.
6. Assign overhead costs to the units of individual products using the predetermined overhead rates.

Examples of Possible Cost Drivers for Support Departments

Accounting:
   Number of transactions
Cafeteria:
   Number of employees
Data processing:
   Number of lines entered
   Number of hours of service
Engineering:
   Number of change orders
   Number of hours
Maintenance:
   Machine hours
   Maintenance hours
Materials storeroom:
   Number of material moves
   Pounds of material moved
   Number of different parts

Payroll:
   Number of employees
Personnel:
   Number of employees
   Number of firings or layoffs
   Number of new hires
   Direct labor cost
Power:
   Kilowatt-hours
   Machine hours
Purchasing:
   Number of orders
   Cost of orders
Shipping:
   Number of orders

Concept Q & A

Why is it important to use appropriate cost drivers to assign support department costs to producing departments?

Answer:
Appropriate drivers are those that accurately measure the consumption of support services by producing departments. More accurate product costs and better control of support service consumption are the usual reasons offered for choosing good drivers to assign the support costs.

producing departments on the basis of square footage. Square footage does not cause depreciation; however, it can be argued that the number of square feet a department occupies is a good proxy for the services provided to it by the factory building. The choice of a good proxy to guide allocation is dependent upon the company's objectives for allocation.

Objectives of Assigning Support Department Costs

A number of important objectives are associated with the assignment of support department costs to producing departments and ultimately to specific products. The following major objectives have been identified by the IMA:[1]

1. To obtain a mutually agreeable price.
2. To compute product line profitability.
3. To predict the economic effects of planning and control.
4. To value inventory.
5. To motivate managers.

[1]Statements of Management Accounting (Statement 4B), *Allocation of Service and Administrative Costs* (Montvale, NJ: NAA, 1985). The NAA is now known as the Institute of Management Accountants (IMA).

Competitive pricing requires an understanding of costs. Only by knowing the costs of each service or product can the firm create meaningful bids. If costs are not accurately allocated, the costs of some services could be overstated, resulting in bids that are too high and a loss of potential business. Alternatively, if the costs are understated, bids could be too low, producing losses on these services.

Closely allied to pricing is profitability. Multiproduct companies need to be sure that all products are profitable and that the overall profitability of the firm is not disguising the poor performance of individual products.

By assessing the profitability of various services, a manager may evaluate the mix of services offered by the firm. From this evaluation, it may be decided to drop some services, reallocate resources from one service to another, reprice certain services, or exercise greater cost control in some areas. These steps would meet the IMA's planning and control objective. Of course, accurate costs are important to determine profit.

For manufacturing organizations, inventory valuation can be important. Generally accepted accounting principles (GAAP) require that direct manufacturing costs and all indirect manufacturing costs be assigned to the products produced. Inventories and cost of goods sold must include direct materials, direct labor, and all manufacturing overhead.

Assigning support department cost can be used to motivate managers. If the costs of support departments are not assigned to producing departments, managers may treat these services as if they were free. In reality, of course, the marginal cost of a service is greater than zero. By assigning the costs and holding managers of producing departments responsible for the economic performance of their units, the organization ensures that managers will use a service until the marginal benefit of the service equals its marginal cost. Thus, allocating service costs helps each producing department select the correct level of service consumption.

There are other behavioral benefits. Assigning support department costs to producing departments encourages managers of those departments to monitor the performance of support departments. Since the costs of the support departments affect the economic performance of their own departments, those managers have an incentive to control service costs through means other than simple usage of the service. We can see this happening in the opening scenario as Gary compared the cost of in-house copying with external copy companies. If a support department is not as cost-effective as an outside source, perhaps the company should discontinue supplying the service internally. For example, many university libraries are moving toward the use of outside contractors for photocopying services. They have found that these contractors are more cost-efficient and provide a higher level of service to library users than did the previous method of using professional librarians to make change, keep the copy machines supplied with paper, fix paper jams, and so on. This possibility of comparison should result in a more efficient internal support department. Monitoring by managers of producing departments will also encourage managers of support departments to be more sensitive to the needs of the producing departments.

Clearly, then, there are good reasons for allocating support department costs. The validity of these reasons, however, depends on the accuracy and fairness of the cost assignments made.

In determining how to allocate support department costs, the guideline of cost-benefit must be considered. In other words, the costs of implementing a particular allocation scheme must be compared to the benefits to be derived. As a result, companies try to use easily measured and understood bases for allocation.

ASSIGNING SERVICE DEPARTMENT COSTS TO PRODUCING DEPARTMENTS

OBJECTIVE 2

Calculate single and multiple charging rates for a support department.

Frequently, the costs of a support department are assigned to other departments by using either single or multiple charging rates. For example, a company's data processing department may serve various other departments. The cost of operating the data processing department is then charged to the user departments based on usage (as measured by the appropriate driver).

A Single Charging Rate

Some companies prefer to develop a single charging rate. A single budgeted charging rate is computed by dividing the total expected service department cost by the expected usage of all producing departments. This budgeted rate is then used to determine the amount of copying costs to be assigned to each producing department. The amount assigned is determined by either one of the following two calculations, depending on the *purpose*:

$$\text{Cost assignment} = \text{Budgeted rate} \times \text{Budgeted usage}$$
$$\text{Cost assignment} = \text{Budgeted rate} \times \text{Actual usage}$$

The first cost assignment is done at the beginning of the year and is the amount that would be added to the budgets of each producing department. This first assignment serves at least two purposes: (1) it enables a predetermined overhead rate to be computed for purposes of product costing (enabling pricing, inventory valuation, and profitability assessments), and (2) it sets a benchmark for comparing actual performance with planned performance. The second cost assignment is done at the end of the year. This provides the actual cost assigned to the producing departments and thus is needed for comparing with planned performance.

To illustrate these concepts, let's return to the case of Hamilton and Barry, the public accounting firm from the opening scenario. Recall that the firm developed an in-house photocopying department to serve its three producing departments (systems, tax, and management advisory services, or MAS). The relationships are portrayed in Exhibit 14-4. Cornerstone 14-1 shows how to calculate and use a single charging rate to assign service costs using either budgeted or actual usage.

14-4

EXHIBIT

Single-Charging Rate

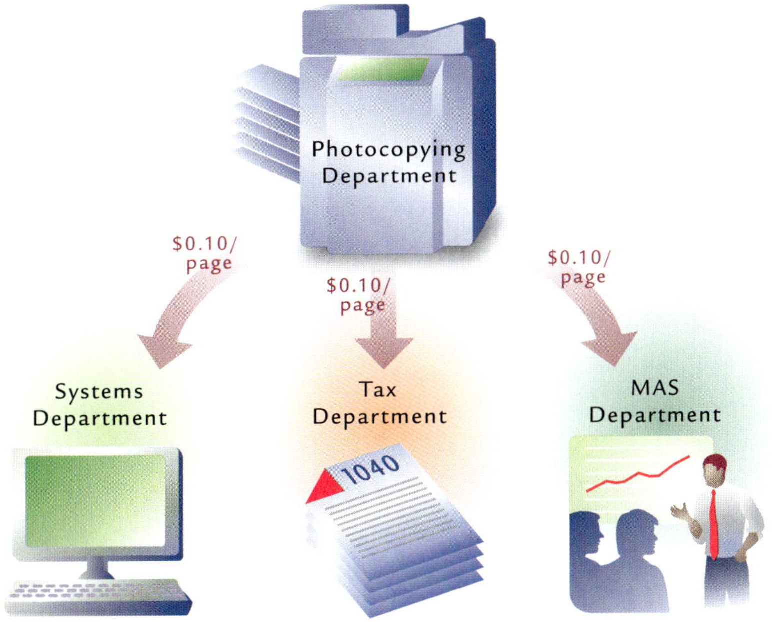

Cornerstone 14-1

HOW TO Calculate and Use a Single Charging Rate

Information: Expected (budgeted) cost of Hamilton and Barry's photocopying department:

Fixed costs: $15,000 per year (machine rental)
Variable costs: $0.04 per page copied (paper and toner)

Estimated (budgeted) usage:

	Pages
Systems department	90,000
Tax department	60,000
MAS department	100,000
Total	250,000

Actual usage:

	Pages
Systems department	96,000
Tax department	55,000
MAS department	105,000
Total	256,000

Required: Calculate a single charging rate and use this rate to assign the costs of the photocopying department to the user departments based on both budgeted and actual usage. Discuss the service usage performance of the producing departments.

Calculation: Single charging rate:

Total expected costs of the photocopying department:

Fixed costs:	$15,000
Variable costs (250,000 × $0.04)	10,000
Total	$25,000

Budgeted single rate = $25,000/250,000 = $0.10 per page

Assignment based on budgeted usage (budgeted service costs—needed as a performance benchmark and for product costing):

The budgeted amount charged to the producing departments is calculated as follows:

	Number of Pages	×	Charge per Page	=	Total Charges
Systems	90,000		$0.10		$ 9,000
Tax	60,000		0.10		6,000
MAS	100,000		0.10		10,000
Total	250,000				$25,000

Assignment based on actual usage (actual service costs—to be compared with the budgeted service costs):

The actual amount charged to the producing departments is calculated as follows:

	Number of Pages	×	Charge per Page	=	Total Charges
Systems	96,000		$0.10		$ 9,600
Tax	55,000		0.10		5,500
MAS	105,000		0.10		10,500
Total	256,000				$25,600

The illustration of Cornerstone 14-1 shows that the use of a single rate results in the fixed cost being treated as if it were variable. In fact, to the producing departments, photocopying is strictly variable. Did the photocopying department need $25,600 to copy 256,000 pages? No, it needed only $25,240 [$15,000 + (256,000 × $0.04)].

Analytical Q & A

Suppose that the charging rate for a maintenance department is $25 per maintenance hour. What is the amount of maintenance cost assigned to a machining department for product-costing purposes given that the actual and budgeted usages are, respectively, 500 hours and 400 hours?

Answer:
Maintenance cost assigned = $25 × 400 = $10,000 (budgeted usage must be used for product costing).

The extra amount charged is due to treating fixed costs as if they were variable. In the next section, we see how multiple charging rates can eliminate this problem.

Multiple Charging Rates

Sometimes a single charging rate masks the variety of causal factors that lead to a support department's total costs. For service departments, variable costs increase as the level of service increases. Thus, it makes sense to charge the variable rate for each unit of service consumed by the producing departments. Fixed costs, however, can be considered capacity costs; they are incurred to provide the capacity necessary to deliver the service units required by the producing departments. When the service department was established, its delivery capability (size) was created based on the peak usage of the producing departments (for a given time period such as a month). Thus, it seems reasonable to assign the fixed costs to producing departments in proportion to their planned peak usage. The fixed cost allocation rate is obtained by dividing the planned peak usage for a producing department divided by the total peak usage. This rate is then multiplied by the budgeted fixed service costs to provide the cost assignment to the producing department. Thus, this approach produces two different rates for assigning service costs: one for variable costs (based on actual usage) and one for fixed costs (based on planned peak usage). Cornerstone 14-2 shows how to assign service costs using this approach for Hamilton and Barry's photocopying department.

Cornerstone 14-2

HOW TO Calculate and Assign Service Costs Using Multiple Charging Rates

Information: Expected (budgeted) cost of Hamilton and Barry's photocopying department:

Fixed costs: $15,000 per year (machine rental)
Variable costs: $0.04 per page copied (paper and toner)

Estimated peak usage (monthly):

	Pages
Systems department	8,800
Tax department	24,000
MAS department	7,200
Total	40,000

Budgeted usage:

	Pages
Systems department	90,000
Tax department	60,000
MAS department	100,000
Total	250,000

Actual usage:

	Pages
Systems department	96,000
Tax department	55,000
MAS department	105,000
Total	256,000

Required: Assign the photocopying cost to the producing departments using variable and fixed rates based on both budgeted and actual usage.

Calculation: Fixed cost assignment (assigned in proportion to peak usage for both budgeted and actual usage cases):

	Peak Number of Pages	Proportion of Peak Usage	Total Fixed Costs	Amount Assigned to Each Department
Systems	8,800	0.22	$15,000	$ 3,300
Tax	24,000	0.60	15,000	9,000
MAS	7,200	0.18	15,000	2,700
Total	40,000			$15,000

Total cost assignment (variable + fixed):

Budgeted usage (Budgeted costs for performance benchmark and product costing):

	Number of Pages	Number of Pages × $0.04	+	Fixed Cost Assignment	=	Total Charges
Systems	90,000	$ 3,600		$ 3,300		$ 6,900
Tax	60,000	2,400		9,000		11,400
MAS	100,000	4,000		2,700		6,700
Total	250,000	$10,000		$15,000		$25,000

Actual usage (Actual costs for comparison with planned performance):

	Number of Pages	Number of Pages × $0.04	+	Fixed Cost Assignment	=	Total Charges
Systems	96,000	$ 3,840		$ 3,300		$ 7,140
Tax	55,000	2,200		9,000		11,200
MAS	105,000	4,200		2,700		6,900
Total	256,000	$10,240		$15,000		$25,240

Now compare the assignments provided in Cornerstones 14-1 and 14-2. Notice that the assignment of photocopying department costs using two rates is very different compared to when a single rate was used. In the 2-rate case, the tax department absorbs a larger proportion of the cost because its peak usage is responsible for the size of the department. Notice, too, that the amount charged of $25,240 is equal to the actual cost of running the department. With the two charging rates, each one based on a strong causal factor, the allocation of cost to the using departments is clearly based on the amount of cost that they actually cause the support department.

Analytical Q & A

A producing department is responsible for 40 percent of the peak usage of a particular support department's service. How much cost will be assigned to the producing department if the corresponding support department has fixed costs of $50,000?

Answer:
Cost assigned = 0.40 × $50,000 = $20,000.

Assigning Budgeted versus Actual Service Costs

When support department costs are assigned to the producing departments, should actual or budgeted costs be used? The answer is budgeted costs. For product costing, the budgeted support department costs are assigned to producing departments as a preliminary step in forming the predetermined overhead rates. Recall that the overhead rate is calculated at the beginning of the period, when actual costs are not known. Thus, budgeted costs must be used. The second usage of allocated support department costs is for performance evaluation. In this case, too, budgeted support department costs are assigned to producing departments.

Managers of support and producing departments usually are held accountable for the performance of their units. Their ability to control costs is an important factor in their performance evaluation. This ability is usually measured by comparing actual costs with planned or budgeted costs. If actual costs exceed budgeted costs, then the department may be operating inefficiently, with the difference between the two costs the measure of that inefficiency. Similarly, if actual costs are less than budgeted costs, then the unit may be operating efficiently.

A general principle of performance evaluation is that managers should not be held responsible for costs or activities over which they have no control. While it is true that managers of producing departments consume services and should be assigned the cost of those services, producing department managers should not be responsible for any inefficiency in producing those services. Thus, actual costs of a support department should not be assigned to producing departments because they may include inefficiencies or an efficient state beyond the planned level. Managers of producing departments have no control over the degree of efficiency achieved by a support department manager. By assigning budgeted costs instead of actual costs, no inefficiencies or efficiencies are transferred from one department to another.

CHOOSING A SUPPORT DEPARTMENT COST ALLOCATION METHOD

So far, we have considered cost allocation from a single support department to several producing departments. The support department costs were assigned directly to the producing departments. This was appropriate because no other support departments existed, and there was no possibility of interaction among support departments. Most companies do have multiple support departments, and they frequently interact. For example, in a factory, personnel and cafeteria serve each other and other support departments as well as the producing departments.

The three methods of assigning costs of multiple support departments to producing departments are the *direct method*, the *sequential method*, and the *reciprocal method*. The direct method ignores interactions and assigns support department costs directly to producing departments. Ignoring these interactions and allocating service costs directly to producing departments may produce unfair and inaccurate cost assignments. For example, power, although a support department, may use 30 percent of the services of the maintenance department. By not assigning some maintenance costs to the power department, its costs are understated. As a result, a producing department that is a heavy user of power and an average or below-average user of maintenance may then receive, under the direct method, a cost allocation that is understated. The sequential method considers some of the interaction effects, and the reciprocal method fully considers all interactions. In determining which support department cost allocation method to use, companies must determine the extent of support department interaction and weigh the individual costs and benefits of each method. In the next three sections, the direct, sequential, and reciprocal methods are discussed.

Direct Method

The **direct method** ignores support department interactions and assigns support department costs *only* to the producing departments. The direct method is the simplest and most straightforward way to assign support department costs. For those choosing to use a single rate to assign service costs, the total service costs are assigned to producing departments in proportion to the producing departments' expected or normal usage. For the dual-rate setting, variable service costs are assigned directly to producing departments in proportion to each department's expected or normal usage of the service. Fixed costs are also assigned directly to the producing department, but in proportion to the producing department's expected peak usage of the service.

Exhibit 14-5 illustrates the lack of support department reciprocity on cost allocation using the direct method. We see that using the direct method, support department cost is assigned to producing departments only. No cost from one support department is given to another support department. Thus, no support department interaction is recognized. Cornerstone 14-3 shows how the direct method is used to assign the costs of two support departments to two producing departments. Notice that the interactions of the service departments are ignored and do not enter the calculations for assigning costs to producing departments.

Illustration of the Direct Method

Suppose there are two support departments, Power and Maintenance, and two producing departments, Grinding and Assembly, each with a "bucket" of directly traceable overhead cost.
Objective: Distribute all maintenance and power costs to Grinding and Assembly using the direct method.

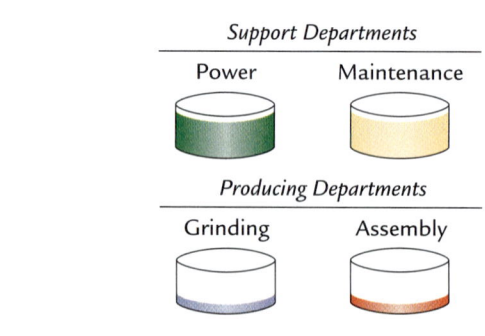

Direct method—Allocate maintenance and power costs only to Grinding and Assembly.

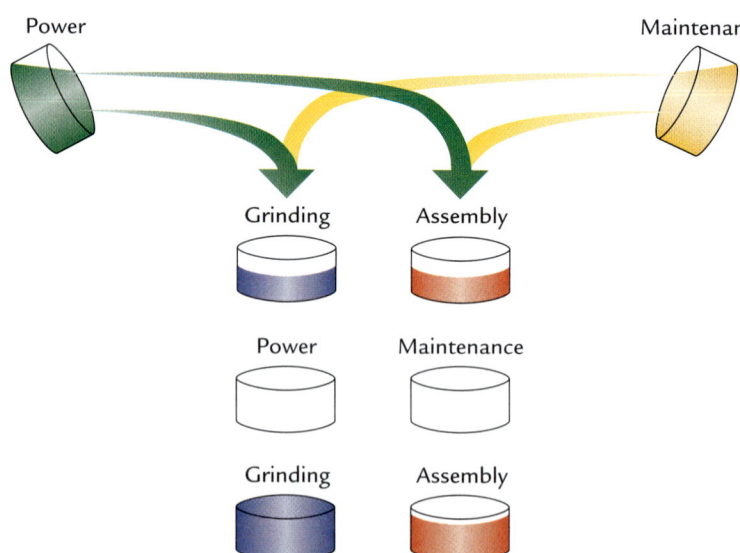

After allocation—Zero cost in maintenance and power; all overhead cost is in Grinding and Assembly.

Cornerstone 14-3

HOW TO Assign Support Department Costs Using the Direct Method

Information: Departmental data:

	Support Departments		Producing Departments	
	Power	Maintenance	Grinding	Assembly
Direct costs:[a]				
Variable	$150,000	$100,000	$75,000	$20,000
Fixed	$100,000	$60,000	$25,000	$40,000
Expected activity:				
Kilowatt-hours	—	200,000	600,000	200,000
Maintenance hours	1,000	—	4,500	4,500
Percent of peak capacity required:[b]				
Power			60%	40%
Maintenance			80%	20%

[a]Overhead costs that are directly traceable to the department.
[b]For the direct method, only the peak capacity of producing departments is used.

Required: Using the direct method, assign the support department costs to the producing departments using both a single-rate and a dual-rate approach.

Calculation: Calculate usage or allocation ratios:

	Grinding	Assembly
Power: 600,000/(600,000 + 200,000)	0.75	—
200,000/(600,000 + 200,000)	—	0.25
Maintenance: 4,500/(4,500 + 4,500)	0.50	—
4,500/(4,500 + 4,500)	—	0.50

Using a single-rate approach:

	Support Departments		Producing Departments	
	Power	Maintenance	Grinding	Assembly
Direct costs	$250,000	$160,000	$100,000	$ 60,000
Power[a]	(250,000)	—	187,500	62,500
Maintenance[b]		(160,000)	80,000	80,000
	$ 0	$ 0	$367,500	$202,500

[a]Using the allocation ratios for power: 0.75 × $250,000; 0.25 × $250,000.
[b]Using the allocation ratios for maintenance: 0.50 × $160,000; 0.50 × $160,000.

Using a dual-rate approach:

	Support Departments		Producing Departments	
	Power	Maintenance	Grinding	Assembly
Direct costs	$250,000	$160,000	$100,000	$ 60,000
Variable cost assignment:				
Power[a]	(150,000)	—	112,500	37,500
Maintenance[b]		(100,000)	50,000	50,000
Fixed cost assignment:				
Power[c]	(100,000)		80,000	20,000
Maintenance[d]	—	(60,000)	36,000	24,000
	$ 0	$ 0	$378,500	$191,500

[a]Using the allocation ratios for power: 0.75 × $150,000; 0.25 × $150,000.
[b]Using the allocation ratios for maintenance: 0.50 × $100,000; 0.50 × $100,000.
[c]Using the peak capacity percentages: 0.80 × $100,000; 0.20 × $100,000.
[d]Using the peak capacity percentages: 0.60 × $60,000; 0.40 × $60,000.

Concept Q & A

What is the major disadvantage of the direct method?

Answer:
It ignores the interactions that may exist among support departments.

HERE'S
THE REAL
KICKER

At the beginning of 2004, Stillwater Designs entered into an agreement with Daimler-Chrysler to provide Kicker systems for the Dodge Neon SRT-4. By becoming an original equipment (OEM) supplier for DaimlerChrysler, Stillwater Designs now has two product lines: the *OEM* line of business (LOB) and the *after-market* LOB. With two lines of business, the management of Stillwater Designs now wants and needs to assess the profitability of each LOB.

To accommodate this profit measurement objective, the account codes have been re-organized so that the direct costs can be traced easily to each LOB. However, after this direct tracing, a large pool of common or shared costs is still unassigned. These are support department costs such as accounting, personnel, quality assurance, and general facility costs. Many of these support cost have increased because of the addition of the new LOB. Jeanne Snyder, chief accountant for Stillwater Designs, indicated that the pool of indirect costs is sufficiently large that they will need to be assigned to each LOB so that the desired profitability measurement can be realized. Furthermore, these costs likely will be assigned to each LOB using the direct method.

Sequential Method of Allocation

The **sequential** (or **step**) **method** of allocation recognizes that interactions among support departments occur. However, the sequential method does not fully account for support department interaction. Cost allocations are performed in a step-down fashion, following a predetermined ranking procedure. Usually, the sequence is defined by ranking the support departments in order of the amount of service rendered, from the greatest to the least, where degree of service is measured by the direct costs of each support department.

Exhibit 14-6 provides a visual portrayal of the sequential method. First, the support departments are ranked, usually in accordance with direct costs; here, power is first, then maintenance. Next, power costs are allocated to maintenance and the two producing departments. Finally, the costs of maintenance are allocated only to producing departments.

The costs of the support department rendering the greatest service are assigned to all support departments below it in the sequence and to all producing departments. The costs of the support department next in sequence are similarly allocated and so on. *In the sequential method, once a support department's costs are allocated, it never receives a subsequent allocation from another support department.* In other words, costs of a support department are never allocated to support departments above it in the sequence. *Also, note that the costs allocated from a support department are its direct costs plus any costs it receives in allocations from other support departments.*

Cornerstone 14-4 shows how to assign support department cost to producing departments using the sequential method. Using cost as a measure of service, the support department rendering more service is power. Thus, its costs will be allocated first, followed by those for maintenance. The first step is to compute the allocation ratios. Note that the allocation ratios for the maintenance department ignore the usage by the power department, since its costs cannot be allocated to a support department above it in the allocation sequence. Thus, when the costs of the maintenance department are allocated,

Illustration of the Sequential Method

Suppose there are two support departments, Power and Maintenance, and two producing departments, Grinding and Assembly, each with a "bucket" of directly traceable overhead cost.

Objective: Distribute all maintenance and power costs to Grinding and Assembly using the sequential method.

Step 1: Rank service departments—#1 Power, #2 Maintenance.

Step 2: Distribute power to Maintenance, Grinding, and Assembly.

Then, distribute maintenance to Grinding and Assembly.

After allocation—Zero cost in Maintenance and Power; all overhead cost is in Grinding and Assembly.

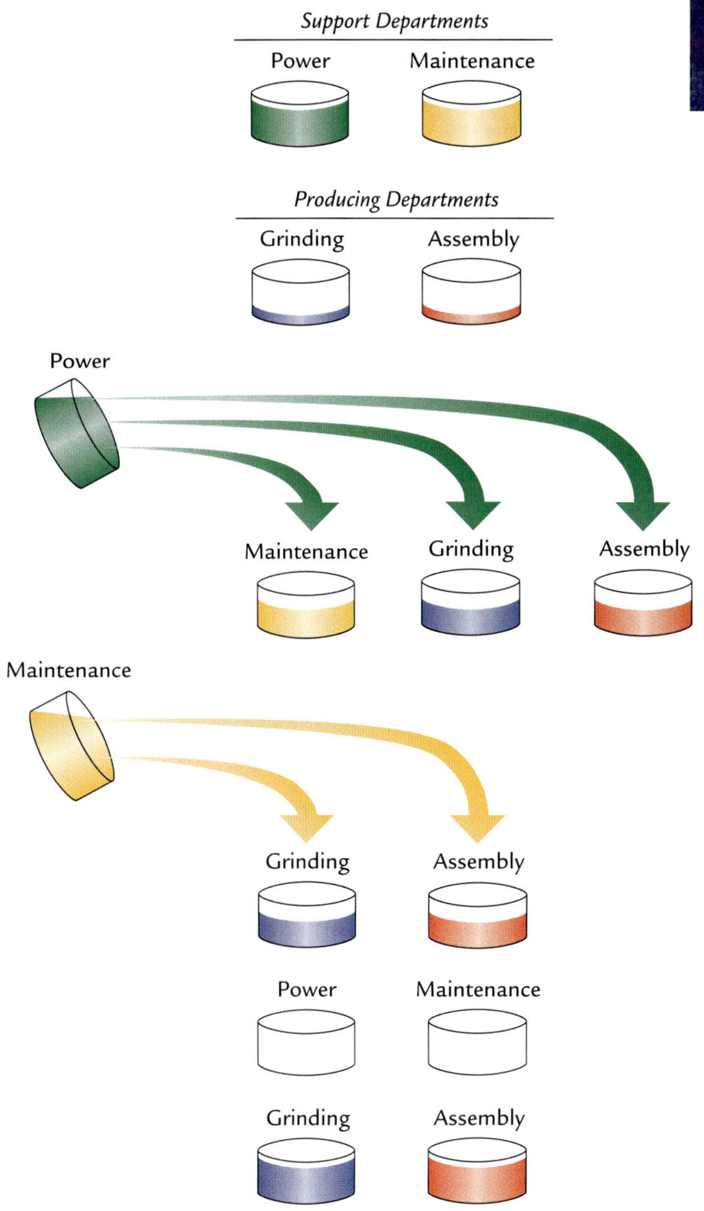

Support Departments

Power   Maintenance

Producing Departments

Grinding   Assembly

Power

Maintenance   Grinding   Assembly

Maintenance

Grinding   Assembly

Power   Maintenance

Grinding   Assembly

no costs are allocated back to the power department, even though it uses 1,000 hours of the output of the maintenance department. For the same reason, when dual rates are used, only the peak load measures are used to assign the fixed costs of the maintenance department. Unlike the direct method, the sequential method recognizes some interactions among the support departments. It does not recognize all interactions, however; no maintenance costs were assigned to the power department even though it used 10 percent of the maintenance department's output. The reciprocal method corrects this deficiency.

Cornerstone 14-4

HOW TO Assign Support Department Costs Using the Sequential Method

Information: Departmental data:

	Support Departments		Producing Departments	
	Power	Maintenance	Grinding	Assembly
Direct costs:[a]				
Variable	$150,000	$100,000	$75,000	$20,000
Fixed	$100,000	$60,000	$25,000	$40,000
Expected activity:				
Kilowatt-hours	—	200,000	600,000	200,000
Maintenance hours	1,000	—	4,500	4,500
Percent of peak capacity required:[b]				
Power		25%	45%	30%
Maintenance	25%		60%	15%

[a]Overhead costs that are directly traceable to the department.
[b]For the sequential method, the peak capacity of all user departments is provided.

Required: Using the sequential method, assign the support department costs to the producing departments using both a single-rate and a dual-rate approach.

Calculate usage ratios:

	Maintenance	Grinding	Assembly
Power: 200,000/(200,000 + 600,000 + 200,000)	0.20	—	—
600,000/(200,000 + 600,000 + 200,000)	—	0.60	—
200,000/(200,000 + 600,000 + 200,000)	—	—	0.20
Maintenance: 4,500/(4,500 + 4,500)	—	0.50	—
4,500/(4,500 + 4,500)	—	—	0.50

Using a single-rate approach:

	Support Departments		Producing Departments	
	Power	Maintenance	Grinding	Assembly
Direct costs	$250,000	$160,000	$100,000	$ 60,000
Power[a]	(250,000)	50,000	150,000	50,000
Maintenance[b]	—	(210,000)	105,000	105,000
	$ 0	$ 0	$355,000	$215,000

[a]Using the usage ratios for power: 0.20 × $250,000; 0.60 × $250,000; 0.20 × $250,000.
[b]Using the usage ratios for maintenance: 0.50 × $210,000; 0.50 × $210,000.

Using a dual-rate approach:

	Support Departments		Producing Departments	
	Power	Maintenance	Grinding	Assembly
Variable direct costs	$150,000	$100,000	$ 75,000	$ 20,000
Variable cost assignment:				
Power[a]	(150,000)	30,000	90,000	30,000
Maintenance[b]		(130,000)	65,000	65,000
Fixed direct costs:	$100,000	$ 60,000	$ 25,000	$ 40,000
Fixed cost assignment:				
Power[c]	(100,000)	25,000	60,000	15,000
Maintenance[d]	—	(85,000)	51,000	34,000
	$ 0	$ 0	$366,000	$204,000

[a]Using the usage ratios for power: 0.20 × $150,000; 0.60 × $150,000; 0.20 × $150,000.
[b]Using the usage ratios for maintenance: 0.50 × $130,000; 0.50 × $130,000.
[c]Using the peak capacity percentages: 0.25 × $100,000; 0.60 × $100,000; 0.15 × $100,000.
[d]Using the peak capacity percentages: 0.60 × $85,000; 0.40 × $85,000, where 0.60 = [0.45/(0.45 + 0.30)] and 0.40 = [0.30/(0.45 + 0.30)]. For the allocation of fixed maintenance costs, only the peak load measures of the producing department are used.

APPLICATIONS IN BUSINESS

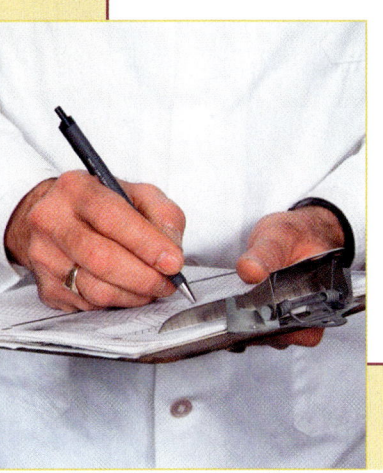

Since 1966, Medicare has required all health care providers to cost service departments to revenue producing departments. The Medicare cost report requires that health care providers use the step-down (sequential) method or the double-apportionment method (which is a 2-stage variation of the step-down method) to calculate operating costs for patient care departments. Health care organizations rarely use the direct method because service departments provide many services to other departments and because the direct method is not allowed on Medicare cost reports. The Medicare guideline for the step-down method requires that the order of the sequence be from the service center that renders the greatest service to the least. The magnitude of service is determined by the *number* of other centers served. If two centers render service to an equal number of centers, then the center with the greatest amount of expense is allocated first.

Source: *Provider Reimbursement Manual: Part I*, Chapter 23, **http://www.cms.hhs.gov**., accessed, June 2004.

Concept Q & A

Why is the sequential method considered to be more accurate than the direct method?

Answer:
The sequential method considers some of the interactions among service departments.

Reciprocal Method of Allocation

The **reciprocal method** of allocation recognizes all interactions among support departments. Under the reciprocal method, one support department's use by another figures in determining the total cost of each support department, where the total cost reflects interactions among the support departments. Then, the new total of support department costs is allocated to the producing departments. This method fully accounts for support department interaction. This is accomplished by using a system of simultaneous linear equations. However, this method will not be illustrated; rather, its complete description is left to a more advanced course. Also, it should be noted that the reciprocal method is not widely used because of its complexity.

It is important to keep a cost-benefit perspective in choosing an allocation method. For example, about 20 years ago, the controller for the IBM Poughkeepsie plant decided that the reciprocal method of cost allocation would do a better job of allocating support department costs. He identified more than 700 support departments and solved the system of equations using a computer. Computationally, he had no problems. However, the producing department managers did not understand the reciprocal method. They were sure that extra cost was being allocated to their departments; they just were not sure how. After months of meetings with the line managers, the controller threw in the towel and returned to the sequential method, which everyone seemed to understand.

Another factor in allocating support department cost is the rapid change in technology. Many firms currently find that support department cost allocation is useful for them. However, the move toward activity-based costing and just-in-time manufacturing can virtually eliminate the need for support department cost allocation.

DEPARTMENTAL OVERHEAD RATES AND PRODUCT COSTING

After assigning support costs to producing departments, an overhead rate can be computed for each department. This rate is computed by adding the assigned support costs to the overhead costs that are directly traceable to the producing department and dividing this total by some measure of activity, usually a unit-level driver such as direct labor hours or machine hours. Cornerstone 14-5 shows how departmental overhead rates are calculated.

OBJECTIVE 4

Calculate departmental overhead rates.

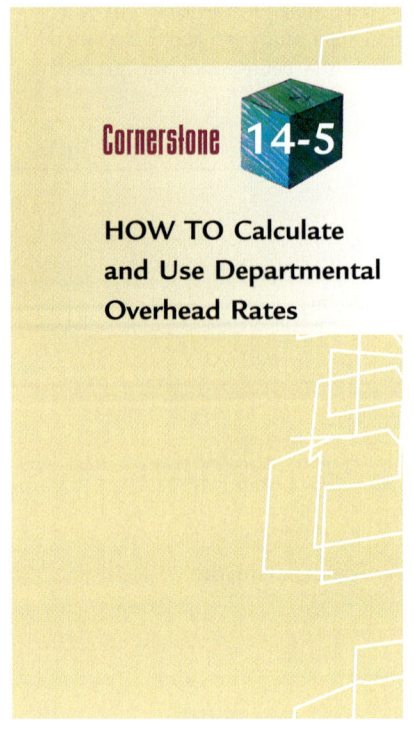

Cornerstone 14-5

HOW TO Calculate and Use Departmental Overhead Rates

Information: Summary of the single-rate sequential cost assignment:

	Producing Departments	
	Grinding	**Assembly**
Direct costs	$100,000	$ 60,000
Power cost assignment	150,000	50,000
Maintenance cost assignment	105,000	105,000
	$355,000	$215,000
Machine hours (expected level)	71,000	
Assembly hours (expected level)		107,500

Usage of one unit of Product A: Grinding, 2 machine hours; Assembly, 3 assembly hours

Required: Calculate departmental overhead rates using machine hours for Grinding and assembly hours for Assembly. Using the rates, determine the overhead cost that is assigned to one unit of Product A.

Calculation:

Overhead rate (Grinding) = $355,000/71,000 machine hours
$\qquad$ = $5 per machine hour

Overhead rate (Assembly) = $215,000/107,500 assembly hours
$\qquad$ = $2 per assembly hour

Product A unit overhead cost = ($5 × 2) + ($2 × 3)
$\qquad$ = $16

Analytical Q & A

The welding department has total overhead costs assigned from service departments of $150,000, direct costs of $50,000, and an expected volume of 50,000 welding hours. What is the overhead rate for the welding department?

Answer:
Rate = ($150,000 + $50,000)/50,000 = $4 per welding hour.

The concerns expressed by Gary Premark about how copying costs were being assigned reveal the importance of assigning service costs correctly and fairly. Although the objectives that were being served by the charge for the copying services were not spelled out, it is clear that Gary felt that the costs were excessive and that they were affecting the profitability of his area of responsibility.

It is also clear that the service costs were being assigned using a single charging rate. Furthermore, this rate was being compared with an outside price for the same service. Apparently, the outside service was cheaper, relative to the inside service price. The explanation for the higher price was centered in the need for a larger copier based on peak usage *caused* mostly by the tax department. This suggests that a more accurate and fair approach to service charges would be a dual-rate system. In fact, when a dual-rate charging system is put into place, the cost per copy drops from $0.10 to $0.067 (as shown by the data in Cornerstones 14-1 and 14-2). Not only does this more accurate assignment reduce the internal cost, but it also makes it much easier to compare and evaluate the cost of outside copying services.

SUMMARY OF LEARNING OBJECTIVES

Producing departments create the products or services that the firm is in business to manufacture and sell. Support departments provide support for the producing departments but do not create a salable product. Because support departments exist to support a variety of producing departments, the costs of the support departments are common to all producing departments.

The reasons for assigning support department cost to producing departments include inventory valuation, product line profitability, pricing, and planning and control. The cost assignment can also be used to encourage favorable managerial behavior. When the costs of one support department are assigned to other departments, a charging rate must be developed. A single rate combines variable and fixed costs of the support department to generate a charging rate.

When multiple rates are used, a separate rate is computed for each type of resource based on a causal factor. Then, actual usage of each type of causal factor is multiplied by the appropriate rate to get the amount of support department cost to be allocated. Budgeted, not actual, costs should be allocated so that the efficiencies or inefficiencies of the support departments are not passed on to the producing departments.

Three methods can be used to allocate support costs to producing departments: the direct method, the sequential method, and the reciprocal method. They differ in the degree of support department interaction considered. By considering support department interactions, more accurate product costing is achieved. The result can be improved planning, control, and decision making. Two methods of allocation recognize interactions among support departments: the sequential (or step) method and the reciprocal method. These methods allocate service costs among some (or all) interacting support departments before allocating costs to the producing departments.

Departmental overhead rates are calculated by adding direct departmental overhead costs to those costs allocated from the support departments and dividing the sum by the budgeted departmental base.

Cornerstones for Chapter 14

Cornerstone 14-1 How to calculate and use a single charging rate, page 590
Cornerstone 14-2 How to calculate and assign service costs using multiple charging rates, page 591
Cornerstone 14-3 How to assign support department costs using the direct method, page 595
Cornerstone 14-4 How to assign support department costs using the sequential method, page 598
Cornerstone 14-5 How to calculate and use departmental overhead rates, page 600

KEY TERMS

Causal factors, 586

Common costs, 584

Direct method, 593

Producing departments, 584

Reciprocal method, 599

Sequential (or step) method, 596

Support departments, 584

DISCUSSION QUESTIONS

1. Describe the difference between producing and support departments.
2. Explain the comment: "Departmental overhead rates are needed only for plants with more than one product."
3. Describe the 2-stage allocation process for assigning support department costs to products in a functional manufacturing environment.
4. Explain how allocating support department costs can be helpful in pricing decisions.
5. Why must support department costs be assigned to products for purposes of inventory valuation?
6. Explain how allocation of support department costs is useful for planning and control.
7. Assume that a company has decided not to allocate any support department costs to producing departments. Describe the likely behavior of the managers of the producing departments. Would this be good or bad? Explain why allocation would correct this type of behavior.
8. Explain how allocating support department costs will encourage support departments to operate more efficiently.
9. Why is it important to identify and use causal factors to allocate support department costs?
10. Identify some possible causal factors for the following support departments:
    a. Cafeteria.
    b. Custodial services.

c. Laundry.
d. Receiving, shipping, and storage.
e. Maintenance.
f. Personnel.
g. Accounting.

11. Explain why dual charging rates are more accurate than single charging rates.
12. Explain why it is better to allocate budgeted support department costs rather than actual support department costs.
13. Explain the difference between the direct method and the sequential method.
14. The reciprocal method of allocation is more accurate than either the direct or sequential methods. Do you agree? Explain.
15. Explain how departmental rates are calculated and used.

MULTIPLE-CHOICE EXERCISES

14-1 Common costs are defined as

a. the costs of shared resources.
b. the wages paid to common laborers.
c. mutually beneficial costs of exclusive resources.
d. those costs that cannot be allocated.
e. none of the above.

14-2 Those departments responsible for creating products or services that are sold to customers are referred to as

a. revenue generating departments.
b. support departments.
c. cost centers.
d. production departments.
e. none of the above.

14-3 Those departments that provide essential services to producing departments are referred to as

a. revenue generating departments.
b. support departments.
c. profit centers.
d. production departments.
e. none of the above.

14-4 An example of a producing department is

a. a materials storeroom.
b. the maintenance department.
c. engineering design.
d. assembly.
e. all of the above.

14-5 An example of a support department is

a. data processing.
b. personnel.
c. a materials storeroom.
d. payroll.
e. all of the above.

14-6 A good driver to assign the cost of the power service center to producing departments would be

a. number of employees.
b. machine hours.
c. maintenance hours.
d. direct labor hours.
e. none of the above.

14-7 Using causal factors (cost drivers) to assign the costs of support departments to producing departments has which of the following potential benefits?

a. More accurate product costs
b. Better control of the consumption of support services
c. Avoids the need to measure service consumption
d. All of the above
e. Both a and b

14-8 Which of the following items represents a step in allocating support cost to products?

a. Trace all overhead costs to support and producing departments
b. Allocate support department costs to producing departments
c. Calculate predetermined overhead rates for the producing departments
d. Assign overhead costs to products using predetermined overhead rates
e. All of the above

14-9 Allocating support department costs to producing departments satisfies which of the following objectives?

a. To encourage managers to monitor the performance of support departments
b. To allow the firm's customers to create meaningful bids
c. To prevent the manager from using external services
d. To encourage managers to use more of the services
e. All of the above

14-10 A maintenance department has direct costs of $400,000 and services two producing departments. The maintenance hours expected to be used by the first and second producing departments are 10,000 and 40,000, respectively. How much of the maintenance cost would be allocated to the first department using the direct method?

a. $0
b. $80,000
c. $320,000
d. $400,000
e. None of the above

14-11 A maintenance department has direct costs of $600,000 and services two producing departments and a power department. The power department has direct costs of $300,000. The power department expects to use 10,000 maintenance hours, and the two producing departments expect to use 20,000 and 30,000 hours each. How much of the maintenance cost would be allocated to the power department using the sequential method?

a. None
b. Cannot be determined
c. $100,000
d. $200,000
e. $300,000

14-12 For product-costing purposes, a dual charging rate usually assigns support costs to production departments using

a. budgeted usage for fixed costs and expected peak usage for variable costs.
b. actual usage for fixed costs and actual peak usage for variable costs.
c. actual usage for variable costs and expected peak usage for fixed costs.
d. budgeted usage for variable costs and expected peak usage for fixed costs.
e. none of the above.

14-13 For performance valuation purposes, service costs are assigned to producing departments using

a. budgeted usage and budgeted costs.
b. budgeted usage and actual costs.
c. actual usage and budgeted costs.
d. actual usage and actual costs.
e. none of the above.

14-14 For product-costing purposes, support department costs are assigned to producing departments using

a. budgeted usage and budgeted costs.
b. budgeted usage and actual costs.
c. actual usage and budgeted costs.
d. actual usage and actual costs.
e. none of the above.

14-15 The method that assigns support department costs only to producing departments in proportion to each department's usage of the service is known as

a. the sequential method.
b. the proportional method.
c. the reciprocal method.
d. the direct method.
e. none of the above.

14-16 The method that assigns support department costs by giving partial recognition to support department interactions is known as

a. the sequential method.
b. the proportional method.
c. the reciprocal method.
d. the direct method.
e. none of the above.

14-17 The method that assigns support department costs by giving full recognition to support department interactions is known as

a. the sequential method.
b. the proportional method.
c. the reciprocal method.
d. the direct method.
e. none of the above.

14-18 The method that assigns support department costs most accurately to producing departments is

a. the sequential method.
b. the proportional method.
c. the reciprocal method.
d. the direct method.
e. none of the above.

14-19 Of the three methods, the two that are the most widely used are

a. the direct and sequential methods.
b. the direct and reciprocal methods.
c. the reciprocal and sequential methods.
d. the proportional and direct methods.
e. none of the above.

14-20 A departmental overhead rate is calculated by

a. using the direct allocation only and dividing by some measure of activity.
b. adding the allocated support cost to the direct costs of the producing department and dividing by some measure of activity.
c. dividing the sequential allocation by some measure of activity.
d. adding the direct costs of the support departments to the direct costs of the producing departments and dividing by direct labor hours.
e. both a and c.

EXERCISES

Exercise 14-1 *Single Charging Rate*

DeMarco Company uses a single rate to charge its three producing departments (molding, grinding, and assembly) for the use of machine maintenance services. Budgeted maintenance costs for the year are $156,000 ($54,000 variable and $102,000 fixed), and budgeted maintenance hours are 3,000. By the end of the year, total actual maintenance hours equal 2,960, and actual cost is $154,500.

Required:
1. Calculate the billing rate for machine maintenance.
2. Assume that the molding department was budgeted to use 1,100 hours but used 1,200 maintenance hours during the year. Calculate the amount assigned to the molding department using budgeted hours and then the amount using actual hours. What is the purpose of each assignment?

Exercise 14-2 *Multiple (Dual) Charging Rates*

Refer to **Exercise 14-1**. Suppose that the $102,000 fixed costs provide the peak capacity of the maintenance department. The expected peak usage percentages for the three departments are as follows:

Molding	30%
Grinding	60
Assembly	10

Required:
1. Calculate the cost assigned to the molding department using two rates: one for variable costs and one for fixed costs. First, make the assignment using budgeted hours (1,100). Next, assign the costs using actual maintenance hours (1,200).
2. Explain why the dual-rate charging system might be preferred to the single-rate approach.

Exercise 14-3 *Single Charging Rate*

Carter Auto Sales has three producing departments: new car sales, used car sales, and service. The service department provides service to both outside customers and to the

new and used car departments. Carter wants to charge the new and used car departments for their use of the service department. It seems fair to charge each department for the cost of actual direct materials used (e.g., oil, engine parts) and to develop a single charging rate for direct labor and overhead.

Assume the following budgeted amounts for the year:

Direct labor cost	$720,000
Direct labor hours	48,000
Overhead cost	$480,000

Actual materials and direct labor hours incurred by the service department during the year are as follows:

	Materials	Actual DLH
New car department	$ 4,200	2,600
Used car department	15,780	9,400
Service department	172,600	38,200
Total	$192,580	50,200

Required:
1. Calculate the single charging rate per hour of labor.
2. Suppose that the used car department gets a 2001 Camry as a trade-in that needs general maintenance and some transmission work. The service department spends eight hours working on the car and uses $478 of parts. Calculate the charge to the used car department by the service department, using actual hours.
3. Calculate the total costs charged by the service department to each of the producing departments for the year (based on actual hours).

Exercise 14-4 *Single Charging Rate*

Lorring Management Company manages five apartment houses in a college town. A local attorney agreed to provide legal services on an as needed basis for $125 per hour. Based on the past two years' experience, Lorring and the attorney estimated that 200 hours would be needed annually for help with matters such as the wording of leases or the pursuit of a court claim against a nonpaying tenant.

Lorring wanted to charge the apartment owners for legal assistance by levying a monthly charge. However, it did not have good information on how many hours each owner would use. Deciding that the number of units in each apartment would be a good proxy for use of legal services, Lorring determined that a single charging rate based on number of units would be reasonable. The number of units for each owner is as follows:

Applewood Court	200
Scholar's Inn	120
Wheaton Arms	100
Varsity View	50
The Loft	30
Total	500

By the end of the first year, the actual usage of legal hours was Applewood Court, 100; Scholar's Inn, 70; Wheaton Arms, 10; Varsity View, 10; and The Loft, 40.

Required:
1. Calculate a charging rate for legal services based on number of apartment units.
2. What was the total amount charged by the attorney to Lorring Management Company by the end of the first year? What was the amount charged to each of

the apartment owners using the charging rate computed in Requirement 1? How much would have been charged to each apartment owner if actual usage of legal hours had been the basis?

3. Which driver is better for charging legal services—number of units or number of hours of legal service? Why?

Exercise 14-5 *Dual Charging Rates*

The engineering department serves three production departments. The costs of this support department are assigned to the production departments as follows:

Variable costs: Engineering hours
Fixed costs: Expected peak usage

The variable costs of the engineering department are $120,000, and the fixed costs are $480,000. The department has 6,000 engineering hours available each year. The expected engineering hours and peak usage data are as follows:

Department	Proportion of Peak Usage	Expected Engineering Hours	Actual Hours
Drilling	20%	1,500	1,600
Cutting	50	2,500	2,200
Welding	30	2,000	2,200

Required:

1. Assign the costs of the engineering department to each producing department using fixed and variable charges. Use expected engineering hours to assign variable costs.
2. Repeat Requirement 1 using actual hours to assign variable support costs.
3. What is the purpose of using budgeted hours for the cost assignment? Actual hours?

Exercise 14-6 *Assigning Support Department Costs Using the Direct Method*

Vanderber Company manufactures a product in a factory that has two producing departments, cutting and sewing, and two support departments, S1 and S2. The activity driver for S1 is number of employees, and the activity driver for S2 is number of maintenance hours. The following data pertain to Vanderber Company:

	Support Departments		Producing Departments	
	S1	S2	Cutting	Sewing
Direct costs	$180,000	$150,000	$122,000	$90,500
Normal activity:				
Number of employees	—	30	63	147
Maintenance hours	1,200	—	16,000	4,000

Required:

1. Calculate the cost assignment ratios to be used under the direct method for S1 and S2. (Each support department will have two ratios—one for cutting and the other for sewing.)
2. Allocate the support department costs to the producing departments using the direct method.

Exercise 14-7 *Allocating Support Department Costs Using the Sequential Method*

Refer to **Exercise 14-6**. Under the sequential method, the S1 costs are allocated first.

Required:

1. Calculate the cost assignment ratios to be used under the sequential method for S1 and S2. Carry your calculations out to four digits. (S1 will have three ratios—one each for S2, cutting, and sewing. S2 will have two allocation ratios—one for each producing department.)
2. Allocate the support department costs to the producing departments using the sequential method.

Exercise 14-8 *Computing Departmental Overhead Rates and Product Cost*

Dulcinea Bakery, Inc., has two producing departments, baking and decorating. In the baking department, ingredients are mixed, poured into the appropriate pans, and baked. In the decorating department, baked goods are iced and decorated (if necessary). At the beginning of the year, the following budgeted information was provided:

	Baking	Decorating
Machine hours	6,250	1,000
Direct labor hours	1,000	6,000
Total overhead	$250,000	$42,000

Overhead in the baking department is based on the number of machine hours; overhead in the decorating department is based on the number of direct labor hours.

Required:

1. Calculate overhead rates for each producing department.
2. Suppose that direct materials cost $170 per batch of 1,000 loaves, and direct labor costs $60 per batch of 1,000 loaves. One batch of bread requires two hours in the baking department and no time in the decorating department. What is the unit cost of one loaf of bread?
3. Susan Sanderson ordered a 5-tier cake for her wedding. It will require one hour in the baking department and 10 hours in the decorating department. Direct materials are estimated at $15, and direct labor cost is estimated at $50. What is the cost of the Sanderson wedding cake? If the cake is priced at 200 percent of cost, what is the price of the wedding cake?

Exercise 14-9 *Direct Method and Overhead Rates*

Lanoka Company manufactures pottery in two producing departments: shaping and firing. Three support departments support the production departments: power, general factory, and human resources. Budgeted data on the five departments are as follows:

	Support Departments			Producing Departments	
	Power	Gen. Factory	HR	Shaping	Firing
Direct overhead costs	$90,000	$167,000	$84,000	$75,000	$234,000
Kilowatt-hours	—	13,000	25,000	30,000	70,000
Square feet	2,000	—	6,000	24,000	8,000
Direct labor hours	—	—	—	4,000	6,000

Power is allocated on the basis of kilowatt-hours, general factory is allocated on the basis of square footage, and human resources is allocated on the basis of direct labor hours. The company does not break overhead into fixed and variable components.

Required:

1. Allocate the overhead costs to the producing departments using the direct method.
2. Using direct labor hours, compute departmental overhead rates.

Exercise 14-10 *Sequential Method and Overhead Rates*

Refer to the data in **Exercise 14-9**. The company has decided to use the sequential method of allocation instead of the direct method.

Required:
1. Allocate the overhead costs to the producing departments using the sequential method.
2. Using direct labor hours, compute departmental overhead rates.

Exercise 14-11 *Direct Method, Overhead Rates, Unit Cost*

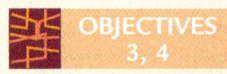

Goodson Company has two support departments—human resources and general factory—and two producing departments—grinding and assembly. Budgeted data for each follows:

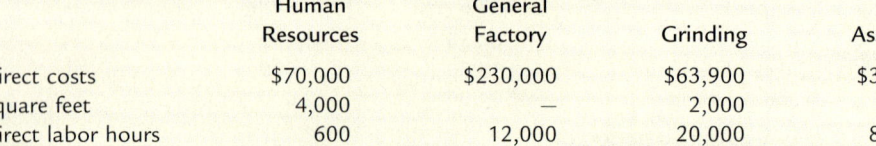

	Human Resources	General Factory	Grinding	Assembly
Direct costs	$70,000	$230,000	$63,900	$39,500
Square feet	4,000	—	2,000	6,000
Direct labor hours	600	12,000	20,000	80,000
Machine hours	—	1,000	4,000	1,000

Human resources is allocated on the basis of direct labor hours; general factory is allocated on the basis of square footage.

Required:
1. Allocate overhead costs to producing departments using the direct method.
2. Calculate departmental overhead rates, using machine hours for grinding and direct labor hours for assembly.
3. If a unit has prime costs of $123 and spends one hour in grinding and 12 hours in assembly, what is the unit cost?

Exercise 14-12 *Sequential Method, Overhead Rates, Unit Cost*

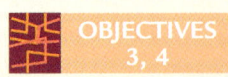

Refer to the data in **Exercise 14-11**.

Required:
1. Allocate the costs of the support departments using the sequential method.
2. Calculate departmental overhead rates, using machine hours for grinding and direct labor hours for assembly.
3. If a unit has prime costs of $123 and spends one hour in grinding and 12 hours in assembly, what is the unit cost?

PROBLEMS

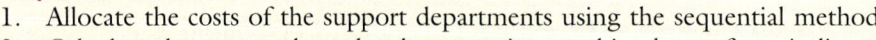

(Note: Whenever you see a  next to a requirement, it signals a "building on a cornerstone" requirement. Assigning this requirement will usually entail additional work, such as a group project, analytical reasoning, Internet research, decision making, and the use of written communication skills.)

Problem 14-1 *Single and Dual Rates; The Emergence of Multiple Lines of Business and the Need to Assign Support Costs*

OBJECTIVE 2

At the beginning of 2004, Stillwater Designs entered into an agreement with Daimler-Chrysler to provide Kicker systems for the Dodge Neon SRT-4. By becoming an

original equipment (OEM) supplier for DaimlerChrysler, Stillwater Designs now has an OEM line of business (LOB) and an *after-market* LOB.

With the addition of the OEM line of business, the role of quality assurance has increased significantly, requiring more rigorous and careful documentation of quality. Design quality and testing procedures are also critical factors. With the added demands, the cost of quality assurance (QA) has increased (e.g., additional testing equipment and salaries). The expected variable QA costs are $80,000, and the expected fixed QA costs are $140,000. Given the amount of support costs (of which quality assurance is but one example), the need to assign the cost to each LOB so that LOB profitability can be determined has also become an important issue. The expected quality assurance hours and expected peak usage are as follows:

LOB	Proportion of Peak Usage	Expected QA Hours
OEM	75%	5,000
After-market	25	3,000

Required:
1. Assign the QA costs to the two LOBs using a single charge rate based on expected QA hours.
2. Assign the QA costs to the two LOBs using dual charging rates.

Problem 14-2 *Direct Method, Dual Rates, Costing and Performance Evaluation*

AirBorne is a small airline operating out of Boise, Idaho. Its three flights travel to Reno, Salt Lake City, and Portland. The owner of the airline wants to assess the full cost of operating each flight. As part of this assessment, the costs of the two support departments (baggage and maintenance) must be allocated to the three flights. The two support departments are located in Boise (any baggage or maintenance costs at the destination airports are directly traceable to the individual flights). Budgeted and actual data for the current year are as follows:

	Support Departments		Flights		
	Maintenance	Baggage	Salt Lake City	Reno	Portland
Budgeted data:					
Fixed overhead	$480,000	$300,000	$20,000	$36,000	$60,000
Variable overhead	$60,000	$126,000	$10,000	$20,000	$12,000
Number of passengers	—	—	10,000	15,000	5,000
Peak load proportions			0.10	0.30	0.60
Hours of flight time			2,000	4,000	2,000
Peak load proportions	—	—	0.20	0.20	0.60
Actual data:					
Fixed overhead	$490,000	$312,000	$44,000	$34,000	$59,000
Variable overhead	$160,000	$100,000	$12,400	$22,000	$11,600
Number of passengers	—	—	8,000	16,000	6,000
Hours of flight time	—	—	1,800	4,200	2,500

Required:
1. Using the direct method, assign the support costs to each flight, assuming that the objective is to determine the cost of operating each flight. Use dual rates.
2. Using the direct method, allocate the service costs to each flight, assuming that the objective is to evaluate performance. Explain why the amount assigned from maintenance to the flights is less than the actual costs of maintenance. Use dual rates.
3. Discuss how activity-based costing could be used to assign the costs of the baggage department more accurately to each flight. In this discussion, identify some of the activities that might be located within the baggage department.

Problem 14-3 *Comparison of Methods of Allocation*

MedServices, Inc., is divided into two operating departments: the laboratory and tissue pathology. The company allocates delivery and accounting costs to each operating department. Delivery costs include the costs of a fleet of vans and drivers that drive throughout the state each day to clinics and doctors' offices to pick up samples and deliver them to the centrally located laboratory and tissue pathology offices. Delivery costs are allocated on the basis of number of samples. Accounting costs are allocated on the basis of the number of transactions processed. No effort is made to separate fixed and variable costs; however, only budgeted costs are allocated. Allocations for the coming year are based on the following data:

| | Support Departments | | Operating Departments | |
	Delivery	Accounting	Laboratory	Pathology
Overhead costs	$240,000	$270,000	$345,000	$456,000
Number of samples	—	—	70,200	46,800
Transactions processed	2,000	200	24,700	13,300

Required:

1. Assign the support department costs using the direct method.
2. Assign the support department costs using the sequential method.
3. Write a memo addressed to the controller explaining when the sequential method is a better choice than either the direct method or the reciprocal method. Provide an example in your memo that shows the sequential method providing at least a 10-percent difference in the costs assigned relative to those of the direct method.

Problem 14-4 *Comparison of Methods of Allocation*

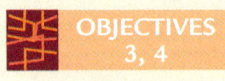

Spreadsheet

Bender Automotive Works, Inc., manufactures a variety of front-end assemblies for automobiles. A front-end assembly is the unified front of an automobile and includes the headlamps, fender, and surrounding metal/plastic. Bender has two producing departments: drilling and assembly. Usually, the front-end assemblies are ordered in batches of 100.

Two support departments provide support for Bender's operating units: maintenance and power. Budgeted data for the coming quarter follow. The company does not separate fixed and variable costs.

| | Support Departments | | Producing Departments | |
	Maintenance	Power	Drilling	Assembly
Overhead costs	$320,000	$400,000	$163,000	$ 90,000
Machine hours	—	22,500	30,000	7,500
Kilowatt-hours	40,000	—	36,000	324,000
Direct labor hours	—	—	5,000	40,000

The predetermined overhead rate for drilling is computed on the basis of machine hours; direct labor hours are used for assembly.

Recently, a truck manufacturer requested a bid on a 3-year contract that would supply front-end assemblies to a nearby factory. The prime costs for a batch of 100 front-end assemblies are $1,817. It takes two machine hours to produce a batch in the drilling department and 50 direct labor hours to assemble the 100 front-end assemblies in the assembly department.

Bender's policy is to bid full manufacturing cost, plus 15 percent.

Required:

1. Prepare bids for Bender Automotive Works using each of the following allocation methods:

a. Direct method.
b. Sequential method.
2. Which method most accurately reflects the cost of producing the front-end assemblies? Why?

3. Using the Internet and library resources, write a memo that addresses the following issues related to hospitals:
    a. Identify and describe at least five support departments found in a hospital.
    b. Identify and describe at least five different revenue producing departments in a hospital.
    c. How do hospitals typically assign support department costs to revenue producing departments? Explain why.
    d. Identify at least five different products in a hospital.
    e. Explain how hospitals assign the costs of the support departments to individual products.

Problem 14-5 *Direct Method and Dual Charging Rates*

OBJECTIVES 2, 3

Lilly Candies has three producing departments—mixing, cooking, and packaging—and five support departments. The following is the basic information on all departments (drivers represent *practical* annual levels):

	Number of Items Processed	Number of Employees	Square Feet Occupied	Machine Hours	Labor Hours
Cafeteria	300	5	5,000	—	—
Personnel	1,000	10	7,000	—	—
Custodial services	200	7	2,000	—	—
Maintenance	2,500	15	16,000	—	—
Cost accounting	—	13	5,000	—	—
Mixing	2,800	20	40,000	4,000	30,000
Cooking	2,700	10	30,000	10,000	20,000
Packaging	3,000	20	20,000	6,000	50,000
Total	12,500	100	125,000	20,000	100,000

The budgeted overhead costs for the department at practical capacity are as follows for the coming year:

	Fixed	Variable	Total
Cafeteria	$ 20,000	$ 40,000	$ 60,000
Personnel	70,000	20,000	90,000
Custodial services	80,000	—	80,000
Maintenance	100,000	100,000	200,000
Cost accounting	130,000	16,500	146,500
Mixing	120,000	20,000	140,000
Cooking	60,000	10,000	70,000
Packaging	25,000	40,000	65,000

Required:

1. Assign the support department costs to the producing departments using the direct method and a dual-rate approach. The practical annual level is used as a measure of peak-load demands for the services.
2. Compute a predetermined fixed overhead rate and a predetermined variable overhead rate. Assume that overhead is applied using direct labor hours for mixing and packaging and machine hours for cooking.

3. Form small groups of three or four and discuss how the initial capacity of a support department is established. In other words, how would you determine the size of a support department? Next, explain why fixed costs are assigned to user departments in proportion to this initial capacity decision rather than in proportion to expected actual usage each year. Explain why practical capacity may serve as a measure of initial capacity.

Problem 14-6 *Direct and Sequential Methods, Cost of Operating a Support Department*

OBJECTIVES
3, 4

Watterman Company has two producing departments (machining and assembly) and two support departments (power and maintenance). The budgeted costs and normal usage are as follows for the coming year:

	Power	Maintenance	Machining	Assembly
Overhead costs*	$50,000	$ 80,000	$120,000	$ 60,000
Kilowatt-hours	—	100,000	300,000	100,000
Machine hours	5,000	—	10,000	5,000

*All overhead costs are variable.

The president of Watterman was approached by a local utility company and offered the opportunity to buy power for $0.11 per kilowatt-hour. The president has asked you to determine the cost of producing the power internally so that a response to the offer can be made.

Required:
1. Compute the unit cost of kilowatts for overall plant usage. Based on this computation, how would you respond to the offer to buy the power externally?
2. Now suppose that you are either the manager of the machining or assembly department and that support costs are allocated using the direct method. From your point of view, how much are you paying per kilowatt-hour (based on internal production)? What would your reaction to the offer be?
3. Consider the same facts as in Requirement 2, except that the sequential method is used to assign the costs of the support department, in the order of highest cost to least cost. This approach recognizes some of the interactions of the two support departments. Based on this sequential information, what is the unit cost of kilowatts for overall plant usage? For usage by the machining and assembly departments? Now what is the decision regarding the power department?
4. Show that the correct decision is to accept the outside offer by following two steps:

   a. Computing the savings realized if the power department is eliminated.
   b. Computing the cost per kilowatt-hour saved by dividing the total savings by the kilowatts needed if the power department is eliminated.

   (*Hint:* Total savings include the direct costs of the power department plus any costs avoided by the maintenance department since it no longer needs to serve the power department. The total kilowatt-hours consumed by the company need to be adjusted, since the power needs of the maintenance department decrease when the amount of service they offer decreases.) What is the implication for the direct and sequential methods?

Problem 14-7 *Direct Method, Sequential Method, Overhead Rates*

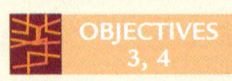
OBJECTIVES
3, 4

Bright, Inc., has two producing departments and four support departments. It currently uses the direct method of support department cost allocation. Data for the company are follows:

	Producing Departments		Support Departments			
	PD1	PD2	SD1	SD2	SD3	SD4
Overhead	$183,000	$212,400	$30,000	$35,000	$40,000	$100,000
Square feet	2,000	2,000	400	5,000	600	—
Employees	15	45	—	12	20	3
DLH	30,000	90,000	—	24,000	20,000	6,000
Machine hours	10,000	20,000	—	—	—	—

Original allocation base:
SD1   Machine hours
SD2   Number of employees
SD3   Direct labor hours
SD4   Square feet

Cara James, controller of Bright, Inc., is considering changing to a more accurate method of support department cost allocation. She has discovered the following:

a. SD1 provides its services only to the producing departments based on machine hours.
b. SD2 provides services to both producing and support departments based on the number of employees.
c. SD3 provides 15 percent of its service to SD1 and the remainder to PD1 and PD2 based on direct labor hours.
d. SD4 provides services to all other departments based on square footage.

Cara has decided to rank the support departments in the following order for purposes of cost allocation: SD4, SD2, SD3, SD1.

Required:

1. Allocate support department costs using the direct method and the original allocation bases.
2. Allocate support department costs using the sequential method as outlined by Cara James.
3. Calculate overhead rates for PD1 (based on machine hours) and PD2 (based on direct labor hours) using total departmental overhead costs as determined by the:
    a. Direct method.
    b. Sequential method.

Problem 14-8 *Fixed and Variable Cost Allocation*

Golden Oaks is a chain of assisted living apartments for retired people who cannot live completely alone, yet do not need 24-hour nursing services. The chain has grown from one apartment complex in 2000 to five complexes located in Texas and Louisiana. In 2007, the owner of the company decided to set up a centralized purchasing department to purchase food and other supplies and to coordinate inventory decisions. The purchasing department was opened in January 2007 by renting space adjacent to corporate headquarters in Shreveport, Louisiana. Each apartment complex has been supplied with personal computers and modems by which to transfer information to central purchasing on a daily basis.

The purchasing department has budgeted fixed costs of $70,000 per year. Variable costs are budgeted at $18 per hour. Actual costs in 2007 equaled budgeted costs. Further information is as follows:

	Actual Revenues		Actual Purchase Orders
	2006	2007	Used in 2007
Baton Rouge	$ 675,000	$ 781,000	1,475
Kilgore	720,000	750,000	1,188
Longview	900,000	912,000	500
Paris	1,125,000	1,098,000	525
Shreveport	1,080,000	1,100,000	562

Required:

1. Suppose the total costs of the purchasing department are allocated on the basis of 2007 revenues. How much will be allocated to each apartment complex?
2. Suppose that Golden Oaks views 2006 revenue figures as a proxy for budgeted capacity of the apartment complexes (they approximate the initial capacity

percentages). Thus, fixed purchasing department costs are allocated on the basis of 2006 revenues, and variable costs are allocated according to 2007 usage multiplied by the variable rate. How much purchasing department cost will be allocated to each apartment complex?

3. Comment on the two allocation schemes. Which is better? Explain.

Problem 14-9 *Plantwide Overhead Rate versus Departmental Rates, Effects on Pricing Decisions*

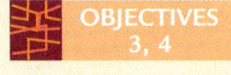

OBJECTIVES
3, 4

Alden Peterson, marketing manager for Retlief Company, had been puzzled by the outcome of two recent bids. The company's policy was to bid 150 percent of the full manufacturing cost. One job (labeled Job SS) had been turned down by a prospective customer, who indicated that the proposed price was $3 per unit higher than the winning bid. A second job (Job TT) had been accepted by a customer, who was amazed that Retlief could offer such favorable terms. This customer revealed that Retlief's price was $43 per unit lower than the next lowest bid.

Alden knew that Retlief Company was more than competitive in terms of cost control. Accordingly, he suspected that the problem was related to cost assignment procedures. Upon investigating, Alden was told that the company used a plantwide overhead rate based on direct labor hours. The rate was computed at the beginning of the year using budgeted data. Selected budgeted data are as follows:

	Department A	Department B	Total
Overhead	$500,000	$2,000,000	$2,500,000
Direct labor hours	200,000	50,000	250,000
Machine hours	20,000	120,000	140,000

The above information led to a plantwide overhead rate of $10 per direct labor hour. In addition, the following specific manufacturing data on Job SS and Job TT were given:

	JOB SS		
	Department A	Department B	Total
Direct labor hours	5,000	1,000	6,000
Machine hours	200	500	700
Prime costs	$100,000	$20,000	$120,000
Units produced	14,400	14,400	14,400

The units produced are correct (above and below)—they pass through each department—14,400 through A and the same 14,400 through B.

	JOB TT		
	Department A	Department B	Total
Direct labor hours	400	600	1,000
Machine hours	200	3,000	3,200
Prime costs	$10,000	$40,000	$50,000
Units produced	1,500	1,500	1,500

This information led to the original bid prices of $18.75 per unit for Job SS and $60 per unit for Job TT.

Then Alden discovered that the overhead costs in department B were higher than those of department A because department B has more equipment, higher maintenance, higher power consumption, higher depreciation, and higher setup costs. So he tried reworking the two bids by using departmental overhead rates. Department A's overhead rate was $2.50 per direct labor hour; department B's overhead rate was $16.67 per machine hour. These rates resulted in unit prices of $14.67 for Job SS and $101.01 for Job TT.

Alden still was not satisfied, however. He did some reading on overhead allocation methods and learned that proper support department cost allocation can lead to more accurate product costs. He decided to create four support departments and recalculate departmental overhead rates. Information on departmental costs and related items follows:

	Maintenance	Power	Setups	General Factory	Department A	Department B
Overhead	$500,000	$225,000	$150,000	$625,000	$200,000	$800,000
Maintenance hours	—	1,500	500	—	1,000	7,000
Kilowatt-hours	4,500	—	—	15,000	10,000	50,000
Direct labor hours	10,000	12,000	6,000	8,000	200,000	50,000
Number of setups	—	—	—	—	40	160
Square feet	25,000	40,000	5,000	15,000	35,360	94,640

The following allocation bases (cost drivers) seemed reasonable:

Support Department	Allocation Base
Maintenance	Maintenance hours
Power	Kilowatt-hours
Setups	Number of setups
General factory	Square feet

Required:

1. Using the direct method, verify the original departmental overhead rates.
2. Using the sequential method, allocate support department costs to the producing departments. Calculate departmental overhead rates using direct labor hours for department A and machine hours for department B. What would the bids for Jobs SS and TT have been if these overhead rates had been in effect?
3. Which method of overhead cost assignment would you recommend to Alden? Why?
4. Suppose that the best competing bid was $4.10 lower than the original bid price (based on a plantwide rate). Does this affect your recommendation in Requirement 3? Explain.

Problem 14-10 *Allocation, Pricing, Ethical Behavior*

OBJECTIVES
1, 2

Emma Hanks, manager of a division that produces valves and castings on a special-order basis, was excited about an order received from a new customer. The customer, a personal friend of Bob Johnson, Emma's supervisor, had placed an order for 10,000 valves. The customer agreed to pay full manufacturing cost plus 25 percent. The order was timely since business was sluggish, and Emma had some concerns about her division's ability to meet its targeted profits. Even with the order, the division would likely fall short in meeting the target by at least $50,000. After examining the cost sheet for the order, however, Emma thought she saw a way to increase the profitability of the job. Accordingly, she called Larry Smith, CMA, the controller of the division.

Emma: Larry, this cost sheet for the new order reflects an allocation of maintenance costs to the grinding department based on maintenance hours used. Currently, 60 percent of our maintenance costs are allocated to grinding on that basis. Can you tell me what the allocation ratio would be if we used machine hours instead of maintenance hours?

Larry: Sure. Based on machine hours, the allocation ratio would increase from 60 percent to 80 percent.

Emma: Excellent. Now tell me what would happen to the unit cost of this new job if we used machine hours to allocate maintenance costs.

Larry: Hold on. That'll take a few minutes. . . . The cost would increase by $10 per unit.

Emma: And with the 25-percent markup, the revenues on that job would jump by $12.50 per unit. That would increase the profitability of the division by $125,000. Larry, I want you to change the allocation base from maintenance hours worked to machine hours.

Larry: Are you sure? After all, if you recall, we spent some time assessing the causal relationships, and we found that maintenance hours reflect the consumption of maintenance cost much better than machine hours. I'm not sure that would be a fair cost assignment. We've used this base for years now.

Emma: Listen, Larry, allocations are arbitrary anyway. Changing the allocation base for this new job will increase its profitability and allow us to meet our targeted profit goals for the year. If we meet or beat those goals, we'll be more likely to get the capital we need to acquire some new equipment. Furthermore, by beating the targeted profit, we'll get our share of the bonus pool. Besides, this new customer has a prosperous business and can easily afford to pay somewhat more for this order.

Required:
1. Evaluate Emma's position. Do you agree with her reasoning? Explain. What should Emma do?
2. If you were the controller, what would you do? Do you think it likely that any corporate standards for ethical conduct for management accountants would apply to the controller (see Chapter 1)? Explain.
3. Suppose Larry refused to change the allocation scheme. Emma then issued the following ultimatum: "Either change the allocation or look for another job!" Larry then made an appointment with Bob Johnson and disclosed the entire affair. Bob, however, was not sympathetic. He advised Larry to do as Emma had requested, arguing that the request represented good business sense. Now what should Larry do?
4. Refer to Requirement 3. Larry decided that he cannot comply with the request to change the allocation scheme. Appeals to higher-level officials have been in vain. Angered, Larry submitted his resignation and called the new customer affected by the cost reassignment. In his phone conversation, Larry revealed Emma's plans to increase the job's costs in order to improve the division's profits. The new customer expressed her gratitude and promptly cancelled her order for 10,000 valves. Evaluate Larry's actions. Should he have informed the customer about Emma's intent? Explain.

Problem 14-11 *Direct Method, Settlement of a Contract Dispute*

OBJECTIVES 3, 4

A state government agency contracted with FlyRite Helicopters to provide helicopter services on a requirements contract. After six months, FlyRite discovered that the agency's original estimates of the number of flying hours needed were grossly overstated. FlyRite Helicopters is now making a claim against the state agency for defective specifications. The state has been advised by its legal advisers that its chances in court on this claim would not be strong, and, therefore, an out-of-court settlement is in order. As a result of the legal advice, the state agency has hired a local CPA firm to analyze the claim and prepare a recommendation for an equitable settlement.

The particulars on which the original bid was based follow. The contract was for three different types of helicopters and had a duration of one year. Thus, the data reflect the original annual expectations. Also, the costs and activity pertain only to the contract.

| | Aircraft Type | | |
	Hughes 500D	206B Jet Ranger	206L-1 Long Ranger
Flying hours	1,200	1,600	900
Direct costs:			
Fixed:			
Insurance	$32,245	$28,200	$55,870
Lease payments	31,000	36,000	90,000
Pilot salaries	30,000	30,000	30,000
Variable:			
Fuel	$24,648	$30,336	$22,752
Minor servicing	6,000	8,000	4,500
Lease	—	—	72,000

In addition to the direct costs, the following indirect costs were expected:

	Fixed Costs	Variable Costs
Maintenance	$ 26,000	$246,667
Hanger rent	18,000	—
General administrative	110,000	—

Maintenance costs and general administrative costs are allocated to each helicopter on the basis of flying hours; hanger rent is allocated on the basis of the number of helicopters. The company has one of each type of aircraft.

During the first six months of the contract, the actual flying hours were as follows:

Type	Flying Hours
500D	299
206B	160
206L-1	204

The state agency's revised projection of total flying hours for the year is as follows:

Type	Flying Hours
500D	450
206B	600
206L-1	800

Required:

1. Assume that FlyRite won the contract with a bid of cost plus 15 percent, where cost refers to cost per flying hour. Compute the original bid price per flying hour for each type of helicopter. Next, compute the original expected profit of the contract.
2. Compute the profit (or loss) earned by FlyRite for the first six months of activity. Assume that the planned costs were equal to the actual costs. Also, assume that 50 percent of the fixed costs for the year have been incurred. Compute the profit that FlyRite should have earned during the first six months, assuming that 50 percent of the hours originally projected (for each aircraft type) had been flown.

3. Compute the profit (or loss) that the contract would provide FlyRite assuming the original price per flying hour and using the state agency's revised projection of hours needed.

4. Assume that the state has agreed to pay what is necessary so that FlyRite receives the profit originally expected in the contract. This will be accomplished by revising the price paid per flying hour based on the revised estimates of flying hours. What is the new price per flying hour?

STATEMENT OF CASH FLOWS

© DIGITAL VISION/GETTY IMAGES

After studying Chapter 15, you should be able to:

1. Explain the basic elements of a statement of cash flows.
2. Prepare a statement of cash flows using the indirect method.
3. Calculate operating cash flows using the direct method.
4. Prepare a statement of cash flows using a worksheet approach.

The president of Golding Company, a large retailer, has called a meeting of the company's executive team to consider the purchase of a small merchandising company located in an area where Golding wants to expand. The following is the discussion that took place:

President: We have the opportunity to acquire Lemmons Company for the same offer we made two years ago. It appears to be a good buy and will contribute to our long-run objective of establishing a strong presence in the West. As you know, we've been trying for some time to convince the owner to sell to us. The location in the city is ideal. I have a nagging suspicion, however, that there's a catch somewhere in this deal. I don't understand why the owner is so eager to sell now when two years ago he was strongly opposed to any deal whatsoever. I wonder if the company is having cash flow problems.

Vice president of operations: That's hard to believe. The income statements for the past several years show stable profits. The most recent balance sheet shows a positive cash balance.

Vice president of finance: The positive cash balance on the balance sheet really doesn't say much about the firm's cash flows—we know nothing about the sources and uses of cash during the reporting period. We need to be very cautious in our interpretation of stable profits. It is possible for a company to report stable profits for a period of time and yet during the same period be a net user rather than a provider of cash.

President: Lemmons may or may not be in this same category, but I want to know more about its cash flows before we commit formally to any acquisition. I want to evaluate Lemmons's current cash flows and assess its future cash flow potential. If the firm is in a cash crisis, acquiring it will cost us more than the purchase price. We still may be able to work out a deal if a cash crisis exists but on much more favorable terms. I want a statement of cash flows from Lemmons for each of the past five years of operations. In that statement, I want the cash flows from operations detailed as well as the cash flows from the firm's financing and investing activities.

As the dialogue reveals, cash flow performance is an important input for the decision concerning the acquisition of Lemmons Company. While the cash flow performance of Lemmons was the focus of the discussion, the cash flow performance of Golding Company is also important. Golding's management needs to know the sources and uses of cash within its own company to assess its financing capabilities. Golding's management might raise a number of questions. Can Golding purchase Lemmons using cash generated from operations? Will Golding need to borrow all or some of the needed cash? If borrowing is necessary, can the debt be serviced? Can some or all of the cash be raised by issuing additional capital stock?

Answers to these questions and others like them are not available in a company's income statement or balance sheet. A third financial statement—the statement of cash flows—does provide this information. All SEC-registered firms must issue a statement of cash flows.

OVERVIEW OF THE STATEMENT OF CASH FLOWS

Cash Defined

Cash is defined as both currency and cash equivalents. **Cash equivalents** are highly liquid investments such as Treasury bills, money market funds, and commercial paper. Many firms, as part of their cash management programs, invest their excess cash in these short-term securities. Because of their high liquidity, these short-term investments are treated as cash for the statement of cash flows. For example, suppose that a company has $100,000 of cash and $200,000 of marketable securities on its beginning balance sheet. The total cash at the beginning of the year would be measured as $300,000.

> **OBJECTIVE 1**
>
> Explain the basic elements of a statement of cash flows.

Sources and Uses of Cash

The **statement of cash flows** provides information regarding the sources and uses of a firm's cash. Activities that increase cash are sources of cash; they are referred to as **cash inflows**. Activities that decrease cash are uses of cash, referred to as **cash outflows**. The statement provides additional information by classifying cash flows into three categories.

1. Cash flows from operating activities.
2. Cash flows from investing activities.
3. Cash flows from financing activities.

This classification, referred to as the **activity format**, is the format that should be followed in preparing the statement of cash flows. Cornerstone 15-1 shows how activities can be classified into the three categories and identified as sources or uses of cash (shown in Exhibit 15-1).

Analytical Q & A

On the beginning balance sheet, a company reports $20,000 cash, $40,000 in Treasury bills, $30,000 in the money market, and $200,000 in accounts receivable. What is the total cash at the beginning of the year?

Answer:
The total cash at the beginning of the year is $90,000. Accounts receivable is not counted as cash.

Cornerstone 15-1

HOW TO Classify Activities and Identify Them as Sources or Uses of Cash

Information:
- **Operating activities** are the ongoing, day-to-day, revenue-generating activities of an organization. Cash inflows from operating activities come from the collection of sales revenues. Cash outflows are caused by payment for operating costs. The difference between the two produces the net cash inflow (outflow) from operations.
- **Investing activities** are those activities that involve the acquisition or sale of long-term assets. Long-term assets may be productive assets (e.g., acquiring new equipment) or long-term activities (e.g., acquiring stock in another company).
- **Financing activities** are those activities that raise (provide) cash from (to) creditors and owners. Although interest payments could be seen as financing outflows, the statement includes these payments in the operating section.

Required: Classify the following major activities as belonging to the operating, investing, or financing categories. Identify them as sources or uses of cash.

1. Issuing long-term debt.
2. Paying cash dividends.
3. Reporting unprofitable operations.
4. Issuing capital stock.
5. Reducing long-term debt.
6. Retiring capital stock.
7. Selling long-term assets (e.g., plant, equipment, and securities).
8. Reporting profitable operations.
9. Purchasing long-term assets.

Calculation:

1. Issuing long-term debt—financing, source of cash.
2. Paying cash dividends—financing, use of cash.
3. Reporting unprofitable operations—operating, use of cash.
4. Issuing capital stock—financing, source of cash.
5. Reducing long-term debt—financing, use of cash.
6. Retiring capital stock—financing, use of cash.
7. Selling long-term assets (e.g., plant, equipment, and securities)—investing, source of cash.
8. Reporting profitable operations—operating, source of cash.
9. Purchasing long-term assets—investing, use of cash.

15-1

EXHIBIT

Sources and Uses of Cash

Sources of Cash

Operating Activities
- Collection of sales revenue

Investing Activities
- Sale of long-term asset

Financing Activities
- Issuance of long-term debt or stock

Uses of Cash

Operating Activities
- Payment of operating expenses

Investing Activities
- Purchase long-term asset

Financing Activities
- Retirement of long-term debt
- Treasury stock purchases
- Dividends

Noncash Exchanges

Occasionally, investing and financing activities take place without affecting cash. These are referred to as **noncash investing and financing activities.** A direct exchange of noncurrent balance sheet items may occur. For example, land may be exchanged for common stock. These noncash transactions must also be disclosed as a supplementary schedule attached to the statement. The requirement to report noncash financing and investing activity is essentially an "all-financial-resources approach." Since the major purpose of the statement is to provide cash flow information, the noncash nature of these transactions should be identified and highlighted. The best way to do so is to report them in a supplementary schedule that is attached to the statement of cash flows.

Methods for Calculating Operating Cash Flows

The two approaches for calculating operating cash flows are the *indirect method* and the *direct method.* The two methods differ only on how the cash flows from *operating activities* are calculated. The **indirect method** computes operating cash flows by *adjusting net income* for items that do not affect cash flows. The **direct method** computes operating cash flows by *adjusting each line on the income statement* to reflect cash flows. For example, revenue on an accrual basis is adjusted to reflect only cash revenue. If the direct method is used, companies must also provide a supplementary schedule showing how net income is reconciled with operating cash flows. This essentially means that direct method users must also provide the information associated with the indirect method. On the other hand, if the indirect method is used, there is no need to provide a line-by-line adjustment as found in the direct method. Not surprisingly, the indirect method is by far the most widely used.

> ## Concept Q & A
>
> Explain why disclosing the sources and uses of cash is so important for potential users of a statement of cash flows?
>
> **Answer:**
> Knowing the sources of cash—especially from operating activities—provides a user with a good idea of a company's financial strength and its long-term viability. The decision to invest in a company is much safer if a potential investor—be it a bank or buyer—knows how much cash is being produced, where it is coming from, and the requirements for using cash. A firm's value is inextricably tied to its cash flows.

PREPARATION OF THE STATEMENT: INDIRECT METHOD

Five basic steps are followed in preparing a statement of cash flows:

OBJECTIVE 2

Prepare a statement of cash flows using the indirect method.

1. *Compute the change in cash for the period.* This figure is the difference between the ending and beginning cash balances shown on the balance sheets. It must equal the net cash inflow or outflow shown on the statement of cash flows.
2. *Compute the cash flows from operating activities.* Use the period's beginning and ending balance sheets and information about other events and transactions to adjust the period's income statement to an operating cash flow basis.
3. *Identify the cash flows from investing activities.* Use the period's beginning and ending balance sheets and information about other events and transactions to identify the cash flows associated with the sale and purchase of long-term assets.
4. *Identify the cash flows from financing activities.* Use the period's beginning and ending balance sheets to identify the cash flows associated with long-term debt and capital stock.
5. *Prepare the statement of cash flows based on the previous four steps.*

An example will be used to illustrate the specific details underlying the application of these five steps. Comparative balance sheets are essential information for preparing a statement of cash flows and are provided in Exhibit 15-2 for Lemmons Company, the acquisition target mentioned in the opening Scenario.

Balance Sheets: Lemmons Company

Lemmons Company
Comparative Balance Sheets
For the Years Ended December 31, 2007 and 2008

			Net Changes	
	2007	2008	Debit	Credit
Assets				
Cash	$ 70,000	$ 175,000	$105,000	
Accounts receivable	140,000	112,500		$ 27,500
Inventories	50,000	60,000	10,000	
Plant and equipment	400,000	410,000	10,000	
Accumulated depreciation	(200,000)	(210,000)		10,000
Land	200,000	287,500	87,500	
Total assets	$ 660,000	$ 835,000		
Liabilities and Stockholders' Equity				
Accounts payable	$ 120,000	$ 95,000	25,000	
Mortgage payable		100,000		100,000
Common stock	75,000	75,000		
Contributed capital in excess of par	100,000	100,000		
Retained earnings	365,000	465,000		100,000
Total liabilities and stockholders' equity	$ 660,000	$ 835,000	$237,500	$237,500

Step One: Compute the Change in Cash Flow

Cornerstone 15-2 shows how to compute the change in cash flow. Notice that the change in cash flow is simply the change in cash, which for Lemmons is an increase of $105,000 from 2007 to 2008. This number serves as a control figure for the statement of cash flows. The sum of the operating, investing, and financing cash flows must equal $105,000.

Cornerstone 15-2

HOW TO Compute the Change in Cash Flow

Information: From Exhibit 15-2, we extract the information on cash and cash equivalents:

Lemmons Company
Comparative Balance Sheets
For the Years Ended December 31, 2007 and 2008

			Net Changes	
Assets	2007	2008	Debit	Credit
Cash	$70,000	$175,000	$105,000	

Required: Calculate the change in cash flow.
Calculation: The change in cash flow is simply the difference in ending and beginning cash flows:

$$\$175,000 - \$70,000 = \$105,000.$$

Step Two: Compute Operating Cash Flows

Income statements are prepared on an accrual basis. Thus, revenues and expenses that involve no cash inflows and outflows may be recognized. Also, cash inflows and outflows that are not recognized on the income statement may occur. The accrual income statement can be converted to an operating cash flow basis by making four adjustments to net income. Cornerstone 15-3 lists these four types of adjustments and illustrates how to calculate operating cash flows using them. Five adjusting items are used to compute operating cash flows for Lemmons Company. These five entries exhibit each of the four types of adjustments.

Cornerstone 15-3

HOW TO Calculate Operating Cash Flows: Indirect Method

Information:

1. Four types of adjustments:
   a. Add to net income any increases in *current* liabilities and decreases in noncash *current* assets.
   b. Deduct from net income any decreases in *current* liabilities and increases in noncash *current* assets.
   c. Add to or deduct from net income the remaining net income items that do affect cash flows (e.g., add back noncash expenses).
   d. Eliminate any income items that belong in either the investing or financing section.
2. Current assets and liabilities extracted from the comparative balance sheets for Lemmons Company (Exhibit 15-2):

Lemmons Company
Comparative Balance Sheets
For the Years Ended December 31, 2007 and 2008

	2007	2008	Net Changes Debit	Net Changes Credit
Current assets				
Accounts receivable	$140,000	$112,500		$27,500
Inventories	50,000	60,000	$10,000	
Current liabilities				
Accounts payable	$120,000	$ 95,000	$25,000	

3. The income statement for Lemmons Company:

Lemmons Company
Income Statement
For the Year Ended December 31, 2008

Revenues	$ 480,000
Gain on sale of equipment	20,000
Less: Cost of goods sold	(260,000)
Less: Depreciation expense	(50,000)
Less: Interest expense	(10,000)
Net income	$ 180,000

Required: Compute operating cash flows using the indirect method.

Calculation:

Operating net income	$180,000
Add (deduct) adjusting items:	
Decrease in accounts receivable	27,500 (Type A adjustment)
Decrease in accounts payable	(25,000) (Type B adjustment)
Increase in inventories	(10,000) (Type B adjustment)
Depreciation expense	50,000 (Type C adjustment)
Gain on sale of equipment	(20,000) (Type D adjustment)
Net cash from operating activities	$202,500

Decrease in Accounts Receivable (Example of Type A Adjustment)

From Cornerstone 15-3, operating income is increased by a $27,500 decrease in accounts receivable. A decrease in accounts receivable represents a decrease in a noncash current asset. It indicates that cash collections from customers were greater than the revenues reported on the income statement by the amount of the decrease. Thus, to compute the operating cash flow, the decrease must be added to net income. To understand fully why this amount is added back to net income, consider the cash collection activity of Lemmons.

At the beginning of the year, the company reported accounts receivable of $140,000 (see Exhibit 15-2). This beginning balance represents revenues recognized during 2007 but not collected. During 2008, additional operating revenues of $480,000 were earned and recognized on the income statement; Lemmons Company, therefore, had a total cash collection potential of $620,000 ($140,000 + $480,000). Since the ending balance of accounts receivable was $112,500, the company collected cash totaling $507,500 ($620,000 – $112,500). The cash collected from operations was $27,500 greater than the amount recognized on the income statement ($507,500 versus $480,000), an amount exactly equal to the decrease in accounts receivable. Thus, the change in accounts receivable can be used to adjust revenues from an accrual to a cash basis.

Decrease in Accounts Payable and Increase in Inventories (Examples of Type B Adjustment)

Cornerstone 15-3 shows that the second adjusting item in the operating section reflects a decrease in accounts payable of $25,000 and the third an increase in inventories of $10,000. Taken together, these two items adjust the cost of goods sold to a cash basis. A decrease in accounts payable means that cash payments to creditors were larger than the purchases made during the period; the difference is the amount that accounts payable decreased. The total cash payment made to creditors, therefore, is equal to the purchases plus the decrease in accounts payable. Since inventories increased, purchases are larger than the cost of goods sold by the amount that inventories increased. Thus, by deducting both the decrease in accounts payable and the increase in inventories, the cost of goods sold figure is increased to reflect the cash outflow for goods during the period.

The effect of the above adjustments is best illustrated with the actual figures from Lemmons Company. From Exhibit 15-2, the following statement of costs of goods sold can be prepared. (In this statement, goods available for sale and purchases are obtained by working backwards from cost of goods sold.)

Beginning inventory	$ 50,000
Purchases	270,000
Goods available for sale	$320,000
Less: Ending inventory	(60,000)
Cost of goods sold	$260,000

Adding purchases to the beginning balance in accounts payable (from Exhibit 15-2) yields the total potential payments to creditors: $390,000 ($270,000 + $120,000). Subtracting the ending balance of accounts payable (see Exhibit 15-2) from the total potential payments gives the total cash payments for the year: $295,000 ($390,000 − $95,000). By deducting the decrease in accounts payable ($25,000) and the increase in inventories ($10,000), an additional $35,000 is deducted, bringing the cost of goods sold figure from $260,000 to $295,000. This is the total cash payment for goods during 2008.

Depreciation Expense (Example of Type C Adjustment)

While depreciation expense is a legitimate deduction from revenues to arrive at net income, it does not require any cash outlay. As a noncash expense, it should be added back to net income as part of the adjustment needed to produce operating cash flow.

Gain on the Sale of Equipment (Example of Type D Adjustment)

The sale of long-term assets is a nonoperating activity and should be classified in the section that reveals the firm's investing activities. Furthermore, the gain on the sale of the equipment does not reveal the total cash received—it gives only the cash received in excess of the equipment's book value. The correct procedure is to deduct the gain and report the full cash inflow from the sale in the investing section of the statement of cash flows.

Analytical Q & A

What adjustment would be made to net income for (a) an increase of $100,000 in accounts receivable? (b) An increase of $30,000 in accounts payable? (c) A decrease in inventories of $10,000? Explain why.

Answer:

(a) Decrease net income by $100,000 because sales were recognized where cash was not collected; (b) Increase net income by $30,000 because cash payments to creditors were less than purchases; and (c) Increase net income by $10,000 because purchases were less than cost of goods sold because inventories decreased.

Step Three: Compute Investing Cash Flows

Investing activities include the purchase and sale of long-term assets (plant and equipment, land, and long-term securities). Cornerstone 15-4 shows how to compute investing cash flows for Lemmons Company. Lemmons Company had three investing transactions in 2008. These transactions are summarized in the investing section that follows.

Cornerstone 15-4

HOW TO Compute Investing Cash Flows

Information:

a.   Equipment with a book value of $50,000 was sold for $70,000 (original purchase cost of $90,000). New equipment was purchased.

b.   Information extracted from the comparative balance sheets of Lemmons Company (from Exhibit 15-2):

Comparative Balance Sheets
For the Years Ended December 31, 2007 and 2008

Long-Term Assets	2007	2008	Net Changes Debit	Net Changes Credit
Plant and equipment	$ 400,000	$ 410,000	$10,000	
Accumulated depreciation	(200,000)	(210,000)		$10,000
Land	200,000	287,500	87,500	

Required: Calculate the investing cash flows.

Calculation:

Sale of equipment	$ 70,000[a]
Purchase of equipment	(100,000)[b]
Purchase of land	(87,500)[c]
Net cash from investing activities	$(117,500)

[a]The sale of long-tem assets is an investing activity. Thus, the receipt of the $70,000 should be reported in the investing section.

[b]There is no explicit information concerning the purchase price of equipment. The purchase price is inferred from the comparative balance information as well as the information about the equipment originally costing $90,000 that was sold and removed from the books. The purchase price of the new equipment can be computed by the following procedure:

Beginning plant and equipment	$400,000
Purchase of equipment	?
Less: Sale of equipment	(90,000)
Ending balance, plant, and equipment	$410,000

The "plug figure" for the equipment purchase must be $100,000. (*Note*: $40,000 of accumulated depreciation was deducted from the books, removing the accumulated depreciation associated with the equipment that was sold, and $50,000 was added to reflect the depreciation expense for 2008, giving a net increase of $10,000.)

[c]The comparative balance sheets reveal that land was purchased for $87,500. This transaction also should appear in the investing section.

Step Four: Cash Flows from Financing

Issuance of long-term debt or capital stock can produce cash inflows; retirement of debt or stock and payment of dividends produce cash outflows. How to compute the financing cash flows for Lemmons Company is shown in Cornerstone 15-5.

Cornerstone 15-5

HOW TO Compute Financing Cash Flows

Information:

a. Net income of $180,000 was earned in 2008.

b. Extraction from comparative balance sheets (Exhibit 15-2):

Comparative Balance Sheets
For the Years Ended December 31, 2007 and 2008

			Net Changes	
	2007	2008	Debit	Credit
Mortgage payable		100,000		100,000
Common stock	75,000	75,000		
Contributed capital in excess of par	100,000	100,000		
Retained earnings	365,000	465,000		100,000

Required: Compute the investing cash flows for 2008.

Calculation: The cash flows associated with the financing activities of Lemmons Company are as follows:

Issuance of mortgage	$100,000[a]
Payment of dividends	(80,000)[b]
Net cash flow from financing	$ 20,000

[a]The comparative balance sheets show that the only change in long-term debt and capital stock accounts is the apparent issue of a mortgage during 2008. The proceeds from this mortgage should be shown as a source of cash in the financing section.

[b]

Retained earnings, end of 2007	$365,000
Net income (2008)	180,000
Total	$545,000
Less retained earnings, end of 2008	465,000
Dividends paid in 2008	$ 80,000

Since dividends represent a return on the funds provided by stockholders, this amount should be shown in the financing section.

Step Five: Prepare the Statement of Cash Flows

The outcomes of steps 2–4 correspond to the individual sections needed for the statement of cash flows. How to prepare this statement is presented in Cornerstone 15-6. Notice that the change in cash flow computed in step 1 from the comparative balance sheets corresponds to the net increase in cash identified in the statement of cash flows. The computation produced by step 1 serves as a control on the accuracy of steps 2–4.

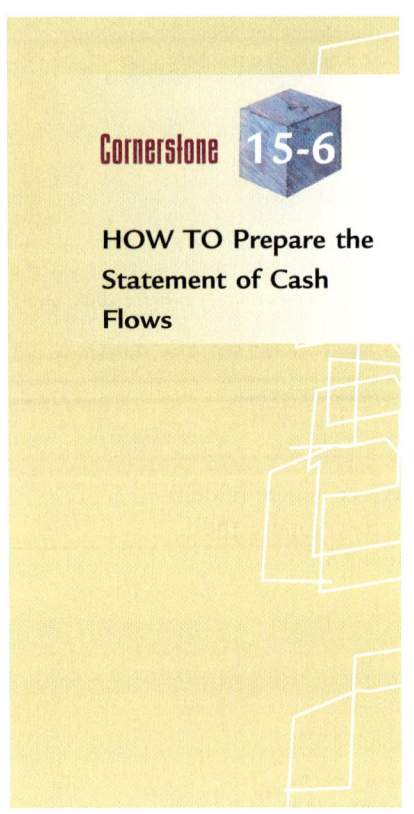

Cornerstone 15-6

HOW TO Prepare the Statement of Cash Flows

Information: Cornerstones 15-2 to 15-5.
Required: Prepare a statement of cash flows for Lemmons Company.
Calculation:

Lemmons Company
Statement of Cash Flows
For the Year Ended December 31, 2008

Cash flows from operating activities:		
Net income	$180,000	
Add (deduct) adjusting items:		
Decrease in accounts receivable	27,500	
Decrease in accounts payable	(25,000)	
Increase in inventories	(10,000)	
Depreciation expense	50,000	
Gain on sale of equipment	(20,000)	
Net operating cash		$202,500
Cash flows from investing activities:		
Sale of equipment	$ 70,000	
Purchase of equipment	(100,000)	
Purchase of land	(87,500)	
Net cash from investing activities		(117,500)
Cash flows from financing activities:		
Issuance of mortgage	$100,000	
Payment of dividends	(80,000)	
Net cash from financing activities		20,000
Net increase in cash		$105,000

APPLICATIONS IN BUSINESS

Many investment analysts believe that cash is the key factor for making a company a "power stock." One analyst noted that cash flow is the same as air for us—without it, a company can't survive. With a healthy cash flow, a company can exercise power across the industry. It can invest in new plants and systems. It can pay more dividends. It can borrow less and thus be more likely to survive hard times. For example, during the economic downturn from 2000 to 2003, companies in the S&P 500 that produced the most cash relative to their share price, produced an average annualized return of 20.7 percent compared to a 12.5-percent loss for the S&P 500 overall. Of course, you must not only have the extra cash, but you must also know how to use it productively. Microsoft and ExxonMobil generate between $10 and $12 billion in free cash annually. Microsoft also produces an average return on capital of 38 percent over the past five years (as of 2003). ExxonMobil has invested in new finding methods that have allowed it to significantly reduce exploration costs.

Source: David Rynecki, "Cash Power," *Fortune,* Vol. 148, Issue 3 (August 11, 2003): 149.

THE DIRECT METHOD: AN ALTERNATIVE APPROACH

OBJECTIVE 3

Calculate operating cash flows using the direct method.

The section of operating cash flows in Cornerstone 15-3 computes cash flows by adjusting net income for items that do not affect cash flows. This approach is known as the indirect method. Some prefer to show operating cash flows as the difference between cash receipts and cash payments. To do so, each item on the accrual income statement is adjusted to reflect cash flows. The same adjustments and the same reasoning behind the indirect method are used to produce the operating cash flows; however, the presentation of the information is different. Each line on the income statement is adjusted to produce a cash flow income statement. How to compute operating cash flows using this approach, known as the direct method, is illustrated in Cornerstone 15-7 using the Lemmons Company example. Either approach to computing and presenting operating cash flows may be used; which to use is a matter of preference. However, if a company chooses the direct method, it must also present the indirect method in a separate schedule.

Cornerstone 15-7

HOW TO Calculate Operating Cash Flows Using the Direct Method

Information:

a. Current assets and liabilities extracted from the comparative balance sheets for Lemmons Company (Exhibit 15-2):

Lemmons Company
Comparative Balance Sheets
For the Years Ended December 31, 2007 and 2008

	2007	2008	Net Changes Debit	Net Changes Credit
Current assets				
Accounts receivable	$140,000	$112,500		$27,500
Inventories	50,000	60,000	$10,000	
Current liabilities				
Accounts payable	$120,000	$95,000	$25,000	

b. The income statement for Lemmons Company:

Lemmons Company
Income Statement
For the Year Ended December 31, 2008

Revenues	$480,000
Gain on sale of equipment	20,000
Less: Cost of goods sold	(260,000)
Less: Depreciation expense	(50,000)
Less: Interest expense	(10,000)
Net income	$180,000

Required: Calculate operating cash flows using the direct method.

Calculation:

	Income Statement	Adjustments	Cash Flows
Revenues	$480,000	$ 27,500[a]	$507,500
Gain on sale of equipment	20,000	(20,000)	
Less: Cost of goods sold	(260,000)	(25,000)[b]	
		(10,000)[c]	(295,000)
Less: Depreciation expense	(50,000)	50,000	
Less: Interest expense	(10,000)		(10,000)
Net income	$180,000		
Net operating cash			$202,500

[a]Decrease in accounts receivable.
[b]Decrease in accounts payable.
[c]Increase in inventories.

The statement of cash flows is a report required of all SEC-registered firms. Stillwater Designs, however, is not a public company and therefore is not subject to the requirement to produce a statement of cash flows. The management of Stillwater Designs does not see any value in producing this statement, and, therefore, the accounting department does not produce it. A daily cash position report is provided to management. Furthermore, it is a very easy matter to identify the source of the cash flows—either they come from operations, investing, or financing activities. Thus, if this information is ever explicitly needed, it can be provided. Interestingly, Stillwater Designs' creditors have not demanded this statement as information needed for granting loans. Income statements and balance sheets have provided the needed information. Stillwater Designs' chief accountant, Jeanne Snyder, noted that bank officers tend to be much more interested in assets that can act as collateral such as accounts receivable and inventory.

HERE'S THE REAL KICKER

WORKSHEET APPROACH TO THE STATEMENT OF CASH FLOWS

As transactions increase in number and complexity, a worksheet becomes a useful and almost necessary aid in preparing the statement of cash flows. The approach minimizes confusion and allows careful consideration of all the details underlying an analysis of cash flows. One advantage of a worksheet is the fact that it uses a spreadsheet format, allowing the preparer to use a PC and spreadsheet software. Furthermore, a worksheet offers the user an efficient, logical means to organize the data needed to prepare a statement of cash flows. Although the worksheet itself is not the statement of cash flows, the statement can be easily extracted from the worksheet. The use of a worksheet is best illustrated with an example. The comparative balance sheets of Portermart Company are presented in Exhibit 15-3.

How to prepare a worksheet for Portermart's statement of cash flows is shown in Cornerstone 15-8. Notice that the worksheet is divided into two major sections, one corresponding to the balance sheet classifications and one corresponding to the classifications of the statement of cash flows. Four columns are needed: two for the beginning and ending balances of the balance sheet and two to analyze the transactions that produced the changes in cash flows. The columns for the analysis of transactions are the focus of the worksheet approach. Generally, a debit or credit in a balance sheet column produces a corresponding credit or debit in a cash flow column. Once all changes are accounted for, the statement of cash flows can be prepared (using the lower half of the worksheet).

OBJECTIVE 4

Prepare a statement of cash flows using a worksheet approach.

Cornerstone 15-8

HOW TO Prepare a Statement of Cash Flows Using a Worksheet Approach

Information:
1. Exhibit 15-3 (comparative balance sheets for Portermart Company).
2. Other (2008) transactions:
   a. Cash dividends of $10,000 were paid.
   b. Equipment was sold for $8,000. It had an original cost of $30,000 and a book value of $15,000. The loss is included in operating expenses.
   c. Land with a fair market value of $40,000 was acquired by issuing common stock with a par value of $10,000.
   d. One thousand shares of preferred stock (no par) were sold for $10 per share.
3. The income statement for 2008 is as follows:

Sales	$400,000
Less: Cost of goods sold	(250,000)
Gross margin	$150,000
Less: Operating expenses	(110,000)
Net income	$ 40,000

Balance Sheets: Portermart Company

Portermart Company
Comparative Balance Sheets
For the Years Ended December 31, 2007 and 2008

	2007	2008	Net Changes Debit	Net Changes Credit
Assets				
Cash	$ 90,000	$ 183,000	$ 93,000	
Accounts receivable	55,000	60,000	5,000	
Inventory	80,000	55,000		$ 25,000
Plant and equipment	130,000	100,000		30,000
Accumulated depreciation	(65,000)	(60,000)	5,000	
Land	25,000	65,000	40,000	
Total assets	$ 315,000	$ 403,000		
Liabilities and Stockholders' Equity				
Accounts payable	$ 40,000	$ 60,000		20,000
Wages payable	5,000	3,000	2,000	
Bonds payable	30,000	20,000	10,000	
Preferred stock (no par)	5,000	15,000		10,000
Common stock	50,000	60,000		10,000
Paid-in capital in excess of par	50,000	80,000		30,000
Retained earnings	135,000	165,000		30,000
Total liabilities and stockholders' equity	$ 315,000	$ 403,000	$155,000	$155,000

Required: Prepare a worksheet for Portermart Company.
Calculation:

Worksheet: Portermart Company

	2007	Transactions Debit	Transactions Credit	2008
Assets				
Cash	$ 90,000	(1) $93,000		$183,000
Accounts receivable	55,000	(2) 5,000		60,000
Inventory	80,000		(3) $25,000	55,000
Plant and equipment	130,000		(4) 30,000	100,000
Accumulated depreciation	(65,000)	(4) 15,000	(5) 10,000	(60,000)
Land	25,000	(6) 40,000		65,000
Total assets	$315,000			$403,000

	2007	Transactions		2008
		Debit	**Credit**	
Liabilities and Stockholders' Equity				
Accounts payable	$ 40,000		(7) $20,000	$ 60,000
Wages payable	5,000	(8) $ 2,000		3,000
Bonds payable	30,000	(9) 10,000		20,000
Preferred stock (no par)	5,000		(10) 10,000	15,000
Common stock	50,000		(11) 10,000	60,000
Paid-in capital in excess of par	50,000		(11) 30,000	80,000
Retained earnings	135,000	(13) 10,000	(12) 40,000	165,000
Total liabilities and stockholders' equity	$315,000			$403,000
Operating cash flows:				
Net income		(12) $40,000		
Depreciation expense		(5) 10,000		
Loss on sale of equipment		(4) 7,000		
Decrease in inventory		(3) 25,000		
Increase in accounts payable		(7) 20,000		
Increase in accounts receivable			(2) 5,000	
Decrease in wages payable			(8) 2,000	
Cash flows from investing:				
Sale of equipment		(4) 8,000		
Cash flows from financing:				
Reduction in bonds payable			(9) 10,000	
Payment of dividends			(13) 10,000	
Issuance of preferred stock		(10) 10,000		
Net increase in cash			(1) 93,000	
Noncash investing and financing activities:				
Land acquired with common stock		(11) 40,000	(6) 40,000	

Analysis of Transactions

The summary transactions on the worksheet will be explained by examining the items on the worksheet in order of their appearance (essentially equivalent to the numerical order of the entries). The entries are developed by considering each balance sheet item and the associated supplementary information.

Change in Cash

Entry (1) identifies the total change in cash during 2008.

(1)   Cash   93,000
         Net Increase in Cash   93,000

The actual cash balance increased from the beginning to the end of the year by $93,000.

Change in Accounts Receivable

Entry (2) reflects the increase in accounts receivable.

(2)   Accounts Receivable   5,000
         Operating Cash   5,000

Increasing accounts receivable means that revenues were recognized on the income statement but not collected. Thus, net income must be adjusted to show that cash inflows from revenues were less by this amount.

Decrease in Inventory

Entry (3) reflects the effect of a decrease of inventory on operating cash flow.

(3) Operating Cash	25,000	
Inventory		25,000

Operating cash should be increased since a decrease in inventory would be included in the cost of goods sold but would not represent a cash outflow.

Sale of Equipment

The sale of equipment affects two balance sheet accounts and two cash flow accounts. The effect is captured in Entry (4).

(4) Operating Cash	7,000	
Cash from Investing Activities	8,000	
Accumulated Depreciation	15,000	
Plant and Equipment		30,000

Operating cash shows an increase because the loss on the sale is a noncash expense and should be added back to net income to arrive at the correct cash provided by operating activities. The equipment is sold for $8,000. This produces a cash inflow that is recognized as a cash flow from investing activities. The other two entries reflect the fact that the original cost of the equipment and the accumulated depreciation have been removed from the company's books.

Depreciation Expense

Entry (5) shows an increase in operating cash flow because depreciation expense, a noncash expense, is added back to net income.

(5) Operating Cash	10,000	
Accumulated Depreciation		10,000

Although the amount of depreciation expense is not explicitly given, it can be easily computed. The net decrease in the accumulated depreciation account is $5,000 (see Exhibit 15-3). The sale of the equipment decreased accumulated depreciation by $15,000 (accumulated depreciation removed is equal to original cost minus book value, or $30,000 − $15,000). Thus, the amount of depreciation expense recognized for the period must be $10,000. Depreciation expense increases accumulated depreciation—an increase of $10,000 and a decrease of $15,000 produce a net decrease of $5,000.

Land for Common Stock

In the noncash transaction that acquires land in exchange for common stock, three balance sheet accounts are affected. To balance the transactions columns, two separate entries [(6) and (11)] are needed.

(6) Land	40,000	
Noncash Investing Activities		40,000
(11) Noncash Investing Activities	40,000	
Common Stock		10,000
Paid-In Capital in Excess of Par		30,000

Accounts Payable

Entry (7) provides the adjusting entry for an increase in accounts payable.

(7)	Operating Cash	20,000	
	Accounts Payable		20,000

An increase in accounts payable means that some of the purchases were not acquired through the use of cash. Accordingly, the amount of the increase needs to be added back to net income.

Wages Payable

Wages payable decreased by $2,000 during 2008. This means that the company had a cash outflow $2,000 larger than the wage expense recognized on the income statement. Entry (8) reflects this $2,000 decrease.

(8)	Wages Payable	2,000	
	Operating Cash		2,000

Bonds Payable

Bonds payable decreased by $10,000 indicating a cash outflow belonging to the financing section. Entry (9) recognizes the reduction of debt and the associated cash outflow.

(9)	Bonds Payable	10,000	
	Cash Flow from Financing Activities		10,000

Preferred Stock

Entry (10) reflects the cash inflow that resulted from the issuance of preferred stock.

(10)	Cash Flow from Financing Activities	10,000	
	Preferred Stock		10,000

Net Income

Net income is assigned to the operating cash flow section by Entry (12).

(12)	Operating Cash	40,000	
	Retained Earnings		40,000

Payment of Dividends

The payment of dividends is given in Entry (13).

(13)	Retained Earnings	10,000	
	Cash Flow from Financing Activities		10,000

The Final Step

Once the worksheet is completed, the final step in preparing the statement of cash flows is relatively straightforward. The lower half of the worksheet contains all of the sections needed. The debit column provides the cash inflows and the credit column the cash outflows. The noncash section is an exception; either column may be used to provide the information. The only additional effort needed is to compute subtotals for each section. The statement of cash flows for Portermart Company is shown in Exhibit 15-4.

Concept Q & A

What are the advantages of a worksheet approach for preparing the statement of cash flows?

Answer:
A worksheet reduces confusion, provides a ready way to track the details of a cash flow analysis, and allows the use of spreadsheet programs.

Worksheet-Derived Statement of Cash Flows

15-4
EXHIBIT

Portermart Company Statement of Cash Flows For the Year Ended December 31, 2008		
Operating cash flows:		
Net income	$40,000	
Add (deduct) adjusting items:		
Depreciation expense	10,000	
Loss on sale of equipment	7,000	
Decrease in inventory	25,000	
Increase in accounts payable	20,000	
Increase in accounts receivable	(5,000)	
Decrease in wages payable	(2,000)	
Net operating cash		$ 95,000
Cash flows from investing activities:		
Sale of equipment		$ 8,000
Cash flows from financing activities:		
Reduction in bonds payable		$(10,000)
Payment of dividends		(10,000)
Issuance of preferred stock		10,000
Total cash flow from financing		$(10,000)
Net increase in cash		$ 93,000
Investing and financing activities not affecting cash:		
Acquisition of land issuing common stock		$ 40,000

Golding Company was on target when it indicated a need to evaluate the cash flows of a potential acquisition. So important is the information that all SEC-registered firms are required to disclose sources and uses of cash. This information is vital for assessing the value and soundness of Lemmons Company, the potential target.

Using the example within the chapter, the statement of cash flows revealed that in the most recent period, Lemmons Company produced more than $200,000 in cash from operations. Golding can use this information to assess whether cash flows being generated signal a viable, ongoing company, and if so, whether the performance is in line with other units of similar size and geographic characteristics. If the performance is below expectations, then Golding can assess the likelihood of improving the performance with better practices. Additionally, operating cash flows can be used to help determine a fair acquisition price.

The analysis of cash flows also can be used to assess how much capability that Lemmons has to withstand a cash crunch should one come—something that might be a factor in negotiating a mutually acceptable purchase price. The cash flow statement will also reveal the capability of local operations to make investments for future expansion and growth. Differences between net income and net cash flow are explained, and the quality of earnings is better understood. Thus, the statement of cash flows provides vital information for the decision faced by Golding.

SUMMARY OF LEARNING OBJECTIVES

Knowing a company's cash flows enables managers, investors, creditors, and others to assess more fully the economic strength and viability of a company by allowing the evaluation of its current cash flows and by assessing future cash flow potential. Cash management is a particularly critical activity for any organization. The FASB, recognizing the need for cash flow information, has recommended that all firms prepare a statement of cash flows. Public companies must prepare this statement as part of their required financial reporting.

The activity format for a statement of cash flows has three sections: cash flows from operating activities, cash flows from investing activities, and cash flows from financing activities. It also reports noncash financing and investing activities. The change in cash for a period is the difference between the beginning and ending balances of the cash account. The change in cash equivalents is also included in the change in cash.

Operating activities are the main revenue-generating activities engaged in by the organization. Operating cash flows are computed by adjusting the period's net income for noncash expenses, accrual effects, and nonoperating revenues or expenses. Investing activities involve the acquisition and sale of long-term assets. Financing activities involve raising outside capital through the issuance of debt and capital stock. Financing activities also involve the retirement of debt and capital stock.

Preparing the statement of cash flows includes five basic steps: (1) computing the change in cash flows, (2) computing operating cash flows, (3) identifying investing cash flows, (4) identifying financing cash flows, and (5) assembling the data into a statement of cash flows. Preparation of the statement relies on the beginning and ending balance sheets and information regarding other activities and events that may not be fully apparent from the balance sheets themselves.

Worksheets can be used to organize the preparation of the statement of cash flows. In addition to increased efficiency in form, worksheets offer the added convenience of the PC and spreadsheet software packages.

Cornerstones for Chapter 15

Cornerstone 15-1 How to classify activities and identify them as sources or uses of cash, page 622

Cornerstone 15-2 How to compute the change in cash flow, page 625

Cornerstone 15-3 How to calculate operating cash flows: indirect method, page 626

Cornerstone 15-4 How to compute investing cash flows, page 628

Cornerstone 15-5 How to compute financing cash flows, page 629

Cornerstone 15-6 How to prepare the statement of cash flows, page 630

Cornerstone 15-7 How to calculate operating cash flows using the direct method, page 631

Cornerstone 15-8 How to prepare a statement of cash flows using a worksheet approach, page 632

KEY TERMS

Activity format, 622

Cash equivalents, 622

Cash inflows, 622

Cash outflows, 622

Direct method, 624

Financing activities, 622

Indirect method, 624

Investing activities, 622

Noncash investing and financing activities, 624

Operating activities, 622

Statement of cash flows, 622

DISCUSSION QUESTIONS

1. Explain why the president of Golding in the opening scenario wanted information on Lemmons's cash flow performance.

2. The activity format calls for three categories on the statement of cash flows. Define each category.

3. Of the three categories on the statement of cash flows, which do you think provides the most useful information? Explain.

4. Explain what is meant by the all-financial-resources approach to reporting financing and investing activities.

5. Why is it better to report the noncash investing and financing activities in a supplemental schedule rather than to include these activities on the body of the statement of cash flows?

6. What are the five steps for preparing the statement of cash flows? What is the purpose of each step?

7. What are cash equivalents? How are cash equivalents treated in preparing a statement of cash flows?

8. What are the advantages in using worksheets when preparing a statement of cash flows?

9. Explain how a company can report a positive net income and yet still have a negative net operating cash flow.

10. Explain how a company can report a loss and still have a positive net operating cash flow.

11. In computing the period's net operating cash flows, why are increases in current liabilities and decreases in current assets added back to net income?

12. In computing the period's net operating cash flows, why are decreases in liabilities and increases in current assets deducted from net income?

13. In computing the period's net cash operating flows, why are noncash expenses added back to net income?

14. Explain the reasoning for including the payment of dividends in the financing section of the statement of cash flows.

15. Explain how the statement of cash flows can be prepared using the worksheet approach.

MULTIPLE-CHOICE EXERCISES

15-1 Cash inflows from operating activities come from

a. payment for raw materials.
b. collection of sales revenues.
c. gains on the sale of operating equipment.
d. issuing capital stock.
e. issuing bonds.

15-2 Cash outflows from operating activities come from

a. payment for raw materials.
b. collection of sales revenues.
c. acquisition of operating equipment.
d. retirement of bonds.
e. none of the above.

15-3 Raising cash by issuing capital stock is an example of

a. an operating activity.
b. an investing activity.
c. a financing activity.
d. a noncash transaction.
e. none of the above.

15-4 Sources of cash include

a. profitable operations.
b. the issuance of long-term debt.
c. the sale of long-term assets.
d. the issuance of capital stock.
e. all of the above.

15-5 Uses of cash include

a. cash dividends.
b. the purchase of long-term assets.
c. the sale of old equipment.
d. only a and b.
e. none of the above.

15-6 The difference between the beginning and ending cash balances shown on the balance sheet

a.   is added to net income to obtain total cash inflows.
b.   is deducted from net income to obtain net cash inflows.
c.   serves as a control figure for the statement of cash flows.
d.   is the source of all investing and financing activities.
e.   both c and d.

15-7 Which of the following adjustments helps convert accrual income to operating cash flows?

a.   Add to net income an increase in inventories.
b.   Deduct from net income a decrease in inventories.
c.   Add to net income a decrease in accounts payable.
d.   Deduct from income an increase in accounts payable.
e.   None of the above.

15-8 Which of the following adjustments to net income is needed to obtain cash flows?

a.   Elimination of gains on sale of equipment
b.   Add to net income all noncash expenses (e.g., depreciation and amortization)
c.   Add to net income any increases in current liabilities
d.   Deduct from net income any increases in inventories
e.   All of the above

15-9 A decrease in accounts receivable is added to net income to obtain operating cash flows because

a.   cash collections from customers were greater than the revenues reported.
b.   cash collections from customers were less than the revenues reported.
c.   cash collections decreased due to declining sales.
d.   cash collections increased due to increasing sales.
e.   none of the above.

15-10 An increase in inventories is deducted from net income to arrive at operating cash flow because

a.   cash payments to customers were larger than the purchases made during the period.
b.   cash payments to customers were less than the purchases made during the period.
c.   purchases are larger than the cost of goods sold by the amount that inventories increased.
d.   purchases are less than the cost of goods sold by the amount that inventories increased.
e.   all of the above.

15-11 The gain on sale of equipment is deducted from net income to arrive at operating cash flows because

a.   the sale of long-term assets is a nonoperating activity.
b.   the gain does not reveal the total cash received.
c.   all of the cash received from the sale is reported in the investing section.
d.   all of the above.
e.   none of the above.

15-12 Which of the following is an investing activity?

a.   Issuance of a mortgage
b.   Purchase of land
c.   Increase in accounts receivable
d.   Increase in inventories
e.   All of the above

15-13 Which of the following is a financing activity?

a. Issuance of a mortgage
b. Purchase of land
c. Increase in accounts receivable
d. Increase in inventories
e. All of the above

15-14 Which method calculates operating cash flows by adjusting the income statement on a line-by-line basis?

a. The working paper approach
b. The indirect method
c. The direct method
d. The income method
e. None of the above

15-15 A worksheet approach to preparing the statement of cash flows

a. is a useful aid.
b. uses a spreadsheet format.
c. offers an efficient and logical way of organizing the data.
d. allows an easy extraction of the needed data.
e. all of the above.

15-16 In a completed worksheet,

a. the debit column contains the cash outflows.
b. the debit column contains the cash inflows.
c. the credit column contains the cash inflows.
d. the credit column contains only operating cash flows.
e. none of the above.

EXERCISES

Exercise 15-1 *Activity Classification*

Stillwater Designs is a private company and outsources production of its Kicker speaker lines. Suppose that Stillwater Designs provided you the following transactions.

a. Sold a warehouse for $750,000.
b. Reported a profit of $100,000.
c. Retired long-term bonds.
d. Paid cash dividends of $350,000.
e. Obtained a mortgage for a new building from a local bank.
f. Purchased a new robotic system.
g. Issued a long-term note payable.
h. Purchased a 40-percent interest in a company.
i. Reported a loss for the year.
j. Negotiated a working capital loan.

Required:
Classify each of these transactions as an operating activity, an investing activity, or a financing activity. Also, indicate whether the activity is a source of cash or a use of cash.

Exercise 15-2 *Adjustments to Net Income*

Consider the following independent events:

a. Amortization of a patent.

b. Increase in accounts receivable.
c. Decrease in prepaid insurance.
d. Depreciation expense.
e. Increase in accounts payable.
f. Uncollectible accounts expense.
g. Decrease in wages payable.
h. Increase in inventory.
i. Gain on sale of an asset.

Required:
Indicate whether each event will be added to or deducted from net income in order to compute cash flow from operations.

Exercise 15-3 *Adjustment for Prepaid Rent*

Jenkins Company showed $12,000 in Prepaid Rent on December 31, 2007. On December 31, 2008, the balance in the prepaid rent account was $14,400. Rent expense for 2008 was $30,000.

Required:
1. What amount of cash was paid for rent in 2008?
2. What adjustment in Prepaid Expenses is needed if the indirect method is used to prepare Jenkins Company's statement of cash flows?

Exercise 15-4 *Operating Cash Flows*

During the year, Inmac Company earned a net income of $12,050. Beginning and ending balances for the year for selected accounts are as follows:

	Account Balance	
	Beginning	Ending
Cash	$24,000	$30,000
Accounts Receivable	15,000	21,500
Inventory	8,000	11,300
Prepaid Expenses	6,000	4,000
Accumulated Depreciation	18,000	19,500
Accounts Payable	10,000	12,250
Wages Payable	6,000	4,000

There were no financing or investing activities for the year. The above balances reflect all of the adjustments needed to adjust net income to operating cash flows.

Required:
Prepare a schedule of operating cash flows using the indirect method.

Exercise 15-5 *Cash Flow from Investing Activities*

During 2007, Danforth Company had the following transactions:

a. Purchased $50,000 of 10-year bonds issued by Martin, Inc.
b. Acquired land valued at $14,000 in exchange for machinery.
c. Sold equipment with original cost of $90,000 for $55,000; accumulated depreciation taken on the equipment to the point of sale was $30,000.
d. Purchased new machinery for $40,000.
e. Purchased common stock in Lemmons Company for $19,000.

Required:
Prepare the net cash flow from investing activities of the statement of cash flows.

Exercise 15-6 *Cash Flow from Financing Activities*

Hobart Company experienced the following during 2007:

a. Sold preferred stock for $98,000.
b. Declared dividends of $50,000 payable on March 1, 2008.
c. Borrowed $120,000 from bank on a 2-year note.
d. Purchased $25,000 of its own common stock to hold as treasury stock.
e. Repaid 5-year bonds issued in 1987 for $250,000 due in December.

Required:
Prepare the net cash flow from financing activities of the statement of cash flows.

Exercise 15-7 *Operating Cash Flows*

Daniels Company revealed the following information for the years 2007 and 2008:

Daniels Company
Income Statement
For the Year Ended December 31, 2008

Sales	$ 45,000
Cost of goods sold	(20,000)
Depreciation expense	(2,000)
Other expenses	(13,000)
Net income	$ 10,000

Daniels Company
Comparative Balance Sheets
For the Years Ended December 31, 2007 and 2008

	2007	2008
Assets		
Cash	$ 12,000	$ 29,800
Accounts receivable	3,700	4,600
Inventory	2,500	3,000
Property, plant, and equipment	80,000	80,000
Accumulated depreciation	(8,000)	(10,000)
Land	10,000	23,500
Total assets	$100,200	$130,900
Liabilities and Equity		
Accounts payable	$ 4,300	$ 5,000
Mortgage payable	—	20,000
Stockholders' equity	95,900	105,900
Total liabilities and equity	$100,200	$130,900

Required:
1. Calculate the change in cash flows that serves as the control figure for the statement of cash flows.
2. Prepare a schedule that provides operating cash flows for the year 2008 using the indirect method.

Exercise 15-8 *Operating Cash Flows*

Refer to the data for Daniels Company in **Exercise 15-7**.

Required:
Prepare a schedule that provides operating cash flows for the year 2008 using the direct method.

Exercise 15-9 *Classification of Transactions*

Consider the following independent activities.

a.   Payment of a cash dividend.
b.   Amortization of intangible asset.
c.   Gain on disposal of equipment.
d.   Exchange of common stock for land.
e.   Increase in accrued wages.
f.   Retirement of preferred stock.
g.   Purchase of a new plant.
h.   Depreciation expense.
i.   Decrease in accounts payable.
j.   Increase in accounts receivable.
k.   Proceeds from the sale of land.
l.   Increase in prepaid expenses.
m. Retirement of a bond.
n.   Purchase of a 60-percent interest in another company.

Required:

Classify the following transaction as operating activities, investing activities, financing activities, or financing/investing not affecting cash. If an activity is an operating activity, indicate whether it will be added to or deducted from net income to compute cash from operations.

Exercise 15-10 *Operating Cash Flows*

The income statement for Riobamba Merchandising Corporation is as follows:

Riobamba Merchandising Corporation
Income Statement
For the Year Ended December 31, 2007

Sales		$375,000
Less: Cost of goods sold		
Beginning inventory	$100,000	
Purchases	200,000	
Ending inventory	(50,000)	
		(250,000)
Less: Depreciation expense		(25,000)
Less: Amortization of patent		(5,000)
Less: Wages expense		(20,000)
Less: Insurance expense		(10,000)
Income before taxes		$ 65,000
Less: Income taxes (all current)		(26,000)
Net income		$ 39,000

Other information is as follows:

a.   Accounts payable decreased by $5,000 during the year.
b.   Accounts receivable increased by $5,000.
c.   All wages were paid at the beginning of the year; at the end of the year, Wages Payable had a balance of $3,000.
d.   Prepaid insurance increased by $6,000 during the year.

Required:

Prepare a schedule that provides the operating cash flows for the year using the indirect method.

Exercise 15-11 *Operating Cash Flows, Direct Method*

Refer to the data given in **Exercise 15-10**.

Required:
Prepare a schedule of operating cash flows using the direct method.

PROBLEMS

(*Note:* Whenever you see a ▨ next to a requirement, it signals a "Building on a Cornerstone" requirement. Assigning this requirement will usually entail additional work, such as a group project, analytical reasoning, Internet research, decision making, and the use of written communication skills.)

Problem 15-1 *Statement of Cash Flows, Indirect Method*

Richmoon Corporation has the following comparative financial statements:

Richmoon Corporation
Comparative Balance Sheets
For the Years Ended December 31, 2007 and 2008

	2007	2008
Assets		
Cash	$ 5,500	$ 9,000
Accounts receivable, net	15,000	12,000
Inventory	3,000	6,000
Plant and equipment	20,000	20,000
Accumulated depreciation	(4,000)	(5,000)
Total assets	$39,500	$42,000
Liabilities and Equity		
Accounts payable	$ 6,400	$ 2,000
Common stock	21,200	23,000
Retained earnings	11,900	17,000
Total liabilities and equity	$39,500	$42,000

Richmoon Corporation
Income Statement
For the Year Ended December 31, 2008

Sales	$ 33,000
Less: Cost of goods sold	(19,500)
Gross margin	$ 13,500
Less: Operating expenses	(6,500)
Net income	$ 7,000

Dividends of $1,900 were paid. No equipment was purchased or retired during the current year.

Required:
Using the indirect method, prepare a statement of cash flows.

Problem 15-2 *Statement of Cash Flows, Direct Method*

Refer to the financial statements and other data in **Problem 15-1**.

Required:
Using the direct method, prepare a statement of cash flows.

Problem 15-3 *Statement of Cash Flows, Indirect Method*

The following financial statements were furnished by Betten Company:

Betten Company
Balance Sheets
For the Years Ended September 30, 2007 and 2008

	2007	2008
Assets		
Cash	$11,000	$ 2,000
Marketable securities	500	1,500
Accounts receivable	3,800	4,800
Inventory	10,400	9,000
Plant and equipment	20,000	30,000
Accumulated depreciation	(5,000)	(8,000)
Total assets	$40,700	$39,300
Liabilities and Equity		
Accounts payable	$ 2,400	$ 1,600
Accrued wages	600	400
Common stock	25,000	25,000
Retained earnings	12,700	12,300
Total liabilities and equity	$40,700	$39,300

Betten Company
Income Statement
For the Year Ended September 30, 2008

Sales		$ 20,000
Less: Cost of goods sold		
Beginning inventory	$10,400	
Purchases	13,000	
Ending inventory	(9,000)	(14,400)
Less: Wages expense		(2,000)
Less: Advertising		(1,000)
Less: Depreciation expense		(3,000)
Net income (loss)		$ (400)

At the end of 2008, Betten purchased some additional equipment for $10,000.

Required:
Prepare a statement of cash flows using the indirect method.

Problem 15-4 *Statement of Cash Flows, Direct Method*

Refer to the data for the Betten Company in **Problem 15-3**.

Required:
Prepare a statement of cash flows using the direct method.

Problem 15-5 *Statement of Cash Flows, Indirect Method*

Booth Manufacturing has provided the financial statements shown at the top of the following page. Other information includes:

a. Equipment with a book value of $125,000 was sold for $175,000 (original cost was $225,000).

b. Dividends of $225,000 were declared and paid.

Booth Manufacturing
Comparative Balance Sheets
For the Years Ended December 31, 2007 and 2008

	2007	2008
Assets		
Cash	$ 112,500	$ 350,000
Accounts receivable	350,000	281,250
Inventories	125,000	150,000
Plant and equipment	1,000,000	1,025,000
Accumulated depreciation	(500,000)	(525,000)
Land	500,000	718,750
Total assets	$1,587,500	$2,000,000
Liabilities and Equity		
Accounts payable	$ 300,000	$ 237,500
Mortgage payable	—	250,000
Common stock	75,000	75,000
Contributed capital in excess of par	300,000	300,000
Retained earnings	912,500	1,137,500
Total liabilities and equity	$1,587,500	$2,000,000

Booth Manufacturing
Income Statement
For the Year Ended December 31, 2008

Revenues	$1,200,000
Gain on sale of equipment	50,000
Less: Cost of goods sold	(640,000)
Less: Depreciation expense	(125,000)
Less: Interest expense	(35,000)
Net income	$ 450,000

Required:

1. Calculate the cash flows from operations using the indirect method.
2. Prepare a statement of cash flows.
3. Search the Internet to find a statement of cash flows. Which method was used—the indirect method or the direct method? How does the net income reported compare to the operating cash flows? To the change in cash flows?

Problem 15-6 *Statement of Cash Flows: Direct Method*

Refer to the information in **Problem 15-5**. Assume that all data are the same except that during 2008, common stock was exchanged for land with a fair market value of $60,000. This transaction changes the balance sheet for 2008 by increasing the land account by $60,000 and the capital stock accounts by $60,000.

Required:

1. Calculate the operating cash flows using the direct method.
2. Prepare a statement of cash flows.

Problem 15-7 *Direct and Indirect Methods*

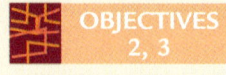

The comparative balance sheets and income statement of Piura Manufacturing are shown on the following page. Additional transactions for 2008 were as follows:

a. Paid cash dividends of $8,000.
b. Acquired equipment by issuing common stock with a par value of $6,000. The fair market value of the equipment is $32,000.

c. Sold equipment with a book value of $12,000 for $6,000. The original cost of the equipment was $24,000. The loss is included in operating expenses.

d. Sold 2,000 shares of preferred stock for $4 per share.

Piura Manufacturing
Comparative Balance Sheets
For the Years Ended June 30, 2007 and 2008

	2007	2008
Assets		
Cash	$ 72,000	$ 146,400
Accounts receivable	44,000	48,000
Inventory	64,000	44,000
Plant and equipment	104,000	112,000
Accumulated depreciation	(52,000)	(48,000)
Land	20,000	20,000
Total assets	$252,000	$322,400

	2007	2008
Liabilities and Equity		
Accounts payable	$ 32,000	$ 48,000
Wages payable	4,000	2,400
Bonds payable	24,000	16,000
Preferred stock (no par)	4,000	12,000
Common stock	30,000	36,000
Paid-in capital in excess of par	50,000	76,000
Retained earnings	108,000	132,000
Total liabilities and equity	$252,000	$322,400

Piura Manufacturing
Income Statement
For the Year Ended June 30, 2008

Sales	$ 320,000
Less: Cost of goods sold	(200,000)
Gross margin	$ 120,000
Less: Operating expenses	(88,000)
Net income	$ 32,000

Required:
1. Prepare a schedule of operating cash flows using the following:
   a. The indirect method.
   b. The direct method.
2. Prepare a statement of cash flows using the indirect method.
3. Form a group of three to five members and discuss the merits of the direct and indirect methods. Which do you think investors might prefer? Should the FASB require all companies to use the direct method?

Problem 15-8 *Statement of Cash Flows, Worksheet*

Refer to the financial statements and other information pertaining to Piura Manufacturing in **Problem 15-7**.

Required:
Using a worksheet similar to the one shown in Cornerstone 15-8, prepare a statement of cash flows.

Problem 15-9 *Statement of Cash Flows: Indirect Method*

Balance sheets for Brierwold Corporation follow:

	Beginning Balances	Ending Balances
Assets		
Cash	$ 100,000	$ 150,000
Accounts receivable	200,000	180,000
Inventory	400,000	410,000
Plant and equipment	700,000	690,000
Accumulated depreciation	(200,000)	(245,000)
Land	100,000	150,000
Total assets	$1,300,000	$1,335,000
Liabilities and Equity		
Accounts payable	$ 300,000	$ 250,000
Mortgage payable		110,000
Preferred stock	60,000	
Common stock	240,000	280,000
Contributed capital in excess of par:		
Preferred stock	40,000	
Common stock	360,000	420,000
Retained earnings	300,000	275,000
Total liabilities and equity	$1,300,000	$1,335,000

Additional transactions were as follows:

a. Purchased equipment costing $50,000.
b. Sold equipment costing $60,000 with a book value of $25,000 for $40,000.
c. Retired preferred stock at a cost of $110,000. The premium is debited to retained earnings.
d. Issued 10,000 shares of its common stock (par value, $4) for $10 per share.
e. Reported a loss of $15,000 for the year.
f. Purchased land for $50,000.

Required:
Prepare a statement of cash flows using the indirect method.

Problem 15-10 *Statement of Cash Flows, Worksheet*

Refer to the financial statements and additional information concerning Brierwold Corporation in **Problem 15-9**.

Required:
Prepare a statement of cash flows using the worksheet approach.

Problem 15-11 *Schedule of Operating Cash Flows: Indirect Method*

The income statement for the Mendelin Corporation is as follows:

Revenues		$ 380,000
Less: Cost of goods sold	$ 50,000	
Beginning inventory	200,000	
Ending inventory	(34,000)	(216,000)
Less: Patent amortization		(20,000)
Advertising		(12,000)
Depreciation expense		(60,000)
Wages expense		(30,000)
Insurance expense		(10,500)
Bad debt expense		(6,400)
Interest expense		(7,600)
Net income		$ 17,500

Additional information is as follows:

a.   Interest expense includes $1,800 of discount amortization.
b.   The prepaid insurance expense account decreased by $2,000 during the year.
c.   Accrued wages decreased by $3,000 during the year.
d.   Accounts payable increased by $7,500 (this account is for purchase of merchandise only).
e.   Accounts receivable increased by $10,000 (net of allowance for doubtful accounts).

Required:
Prepare a schedule of operating cash flows using the indirect method.

Problem 15-12 *Statement of Cash Flows, Indirect Method*

The following balance sheets are taken from the records of Golding Company (numbers are expressed in thousands):

	2007	2008
Assets		
Cash	$130,000	$150,000
Accounts receivable	25,000	20,000
Plant and equipment	50,000	60,000
Accumulated depreciation	(20,000)	(25,000)
Land	10,000	10,000
Total assets	$195,000	$215,000
Liabilities and Equity		
Accounts payable	$ 10,000	$ 5,000
Bonds payable	8,000	18,000
Common stock	120,000	120,000
Retained earnings	57,000	72,000
Total liabilities and equity	$195,000	$215,000

Additional information is as follows:

a.   Equipment costing $10,000,000 was purchased at year-end. No equipment was sold.
b.   Net income for the year was $25,000,000; $10,000,000 in dividends were paid.

Required:

1.   Prepare a statement of cash flows using the indirect method.
2.   Assess Golding's ability to use cash to acquire Lemmons Company. You should consider the information in Exhibit 15-2 and Cornerstone 15-6 as part of your analysis.

Problem 15-13 *Statement of Cash Flows*

The following balance sheets were taken from the records of Blalock Company:

	2007	2008
Assets		
Cash	$150,000	$185,000
Accounts receivable	70,000	80,000
Investments		30,000
Plant and equipment	100,000	105,000
Accumulated depreciation	(30,000)	(32,000)
Land	20,000	30,000
Total assets	$310,000	$398,000

(continued)

	2007	2008
Liabilities and Equity		
Accounts payable	$ 40,000	$ 50,000
Bonds payable	60,000	
Mortgage payable		50,000
Preferred stock	20,000	
Common stock	100,000	160,000
Retained earnings	90,000	138,000
Total liabilities and equity	$310,000	$398,000

Additional transactions were as follows:

a. Sold equipment costing $12,000 with accumulated depreciation of $9,000 for $2,000.
b. Retired bonds at a price of $60,000 on December 31.
c. Earned net income for the year of $68,000; paid cash dividends of $20,000.

Required:
Prepare a statement of cash flows using the indirect method.

Problem 15-14 *Statement of Cash Flows, Worksheet*

Refer to the balance sheets and other information given in **Problem 15-13** concerning Blalock Company.

Required:
Prepare a statement of cash flows using the worksheet approach.

Problem 15-15 *Management of Statement of Cash Flows, Ethical Issues*

Fred Jackson, president of Bailey Company, was concerned about the company's ability to obtain a loan from a major bank. The loan was a key factor in the firm's plan to expand its operations. Demand for the firm's product was high, too high for the current production capacity to handle. Fred was convinced that a new plant was needed. Building the new plant, however, would require an infusion of new capital. Fred called a meeting with Karla Jones, financial vice president.

Fred: Karla, what is the status of our loan application? Do you think that the bank will approve?

Karla: Perhaps, but at this point, there is a real risk. The loan officer has requested a complete set of financials for this year and the past two years. He has indicated that he is particularly interested in the statement of cash flows. As you know, our income statement looks great for all three years, but the statement of cash flows will show a significant increase in receivables, especially for this year. It will also show a significant increase in inventory, and I'm sure that he'll want to know why inventory is increasing if demand is so great that we need another plant. Both of these effects show decreasing cash flows from operating activities.

Fred: Well, it is certainly true that cash flows have been decreasing. One major problem is the lack of operating cash. This loan will solve that problem. Bill Lawson has agreed to build the plant for the amount of the loan but will actually charge me for only 95 percent of the stated cost. We get 5 percent of the loan for operating cash. Bill is willing to pay 5 percent to get the contract.

Karla: The loan may help with operating cash flows, but we can't get the loan without showing some evidence of cash strength. We need to do something about the increases in inventory and receivables that we expect for this year.

Fred: The increased inventory is easy to explain. We had to work overtime and use subcontractors to take care of one of our biggest customers. That inventory will be gone by the first of next year.

Karla: The problem isn't explaining the inventory. The problem is that the increase in inventory decreases our operating cash flows and this shows up on the statement of cash flows. This effect coupled with the increase in receivables reveals us as being cash poor. It'll definitely hurt our chances.

Fred: I see. Well, this can be solved. The inventory is for a customer that I know well. She'll do me a favor. I'll simply get her to take delivery of the inventory early, before the end of our fiscal year. She can pay me next year as originally planned.

Karla: Fred, all that will do is shift the increase from inventory to receivables. It'll still report the same cash position.

Fred: No problem. We'll report the delivery as a cash sale, and I'll have Bill Lawson advance me the cash as a temporary loan. He'll do that to get the contract to build our new plant. In fact, we can do the same with some of our other receivables. We'll report them as collected, and I'll get Bill to cover. If he understands that this is what it takes to get the loan, he'll cooperate. He stands to make a lot of money on the deal.

Karla: Fred, this is getting complicated. The bank will have us audited each year if this loan is approved. If an audit were to reveal some of this manipulation, we could be in big trouble, particularly if the company has any trouble in repaying the loan.

Fred: The company won't have any trouble. Sales are strong, and the problem of collecting receivables can be solved, especially given the extra time that the 5 percent of the loan proceeds will provide.

Required:

1. Form a group of three to five members. Discuss the propriety of the arrangement that Fred has with Bill Lawson concerning the disbursement of the proceeds from the loan.

2. In your group, discuss the propriety of the actions that Fred is proposing to improve the firm's statement of cash flows. Suppose that there is very little risk that the loan will not be repaid. Does this information affect your assessment?

3. Assume that Karla is subject to the IMA (Institute of Management Accountants) code of ethics. Look up this code and identify the standards of ethical conduct that would be violated, if any, by Karla should she agree to cooperate with Fred's scheme.

4. Using the IMA code of ethics, if you were in Karla's position, what would you do (suppose that Fred insists on implementing his plan)? Now answer the question assuming that Fred is willing to consider alternative ways to solve the company's problems.

FINANCIAL STATEMENT ANALYSIS

© TERRI MILLER/E-VISUAL COMMUNICATIONS, INC.

After studying Chapter 16, you should be able to:

1. Analyze financial statements using two forms of common-size analysis: horizontal analysis and vertical analysis.
2. Explain why historical standards and industrial averages are important for ratio analysis.
3. Calculate and use liquidity ratios to assess the ability of a company to meet its current obligations.
4. Calculate and use leverage ratios to assess the ability of a company to meet its long- and short-term obligations.
5. Calculate and use profitability ratios to assess the extent to which a company's resources are being used efficiently.

Doug Litster, president of National Bank, was troubled by the bank's performance in commercial loans and hired Patricia Benson to revamp the commercial loan department. Patricia had been a commercial loan officer with a large regional bank; she had significant experience in commercial loans and could successfully bring in high-quality loan business. Doug offered Patricia a large salary increase and the promise of an opportunity to become part of senior management within a couple of years. After her first month on the job, Patricia briefed Doug on the problems she had encountered so far and recommended some improvements.

Patricia: Doug, after examining the bank's portfolio of loans, I'm appalled at the sloppy procedures used to process commercial loan applications.

Doug: I suppose this shouldn't surprise me, but can you give me some examples?

Patricia: For every commercial loan application, our bank faces two major issues. First, should it grant the loan or not? Second, if the loan is granted, what specific controls can we build into the agreement? In the past, the first decisions were made on some very vague, informal criteria. Furthermore, none of our agreements has any financial controls.

Doug: Patricia, I don't understand. We've always required loan applicants to submit a current financial statement so that we could assess their financial capabilities. Plus, all loan agreements have the standard late penalties and default provisions built in.

Patricia: The problem isn't the submission of the financial statements—it's the analysis of those statements. Currently, there are no guidelines for their analyses. It's basically a seat-of-the-pants approach with a touch of favoritism. Loans are often approved because someone on the loan committee knows the applicant. We need to give more attention to the financial statements and less to favoritism. Plus, what the applicant does after the loan is approved is critical. We have the right to specify what default means, and it should be more than just missing a payment. We need more control over the loans we make. Our loan losses are excessive.

Doug: I know—that's why I hired you. I'm hoping for some major improvements. What do you have in mind?

Patricia: Before any loan is approved, we must seriously evaluate the applicant's financial capabilities. We should compute some specific financial ratios and use them as aids in making a loan decision. Furthermore, certain ratios should be included as part of the loan agreement. Falling below the ratio's specified minimum value or exceeding its specified maximum value is then used to define default. More careful screening and better control of the loans we make should decrease the loan losses we have been experiencing.

Doug: Sounds good. After you identify the ratios and work with our contract people to refine the loan agreements, I want you to schedule some training seminars. I want all commercial loan officers in our branches trained to use this more formal approach.

As the opening scenario illustrates, the formal analysis of financial statements can provide important input for commercial loan managers in making loan decisions. By using ratio analysis, common-size analysis, and other techniques, loan managers can assess the creditworthiness of potential customers. The formal analysis of financial statements can also provide a means to exercise control over outstanding loans.

Managers of commercial loan departments, however, are not the only ones who can benefit from analysis of financial statements. Individuals interested in investing in a company and managers of the company to whom the financial statements belong need this skill as well. Investors need to analyze financial statements to assess the attractiveness of a company as a potential investment. Managers need to analyze their own financial statements so as to assess profitability, liquidity, debt position, and progress toward organizational objectives. The analysis of financial statements is designed to reveal relationships among items on the financial statements and trends of individual items over time. By knowing these relationships and trends, users are in a better position to exercise sound judgment regarding the current or future performance of a company. The two major techniques for financial analysis are common-size analysis and ratio analysis.

COMMON-SIZE ANALYSIS

OBJECTIVE 1

Analyze financial statements using two forms of common-size analysis: horizontal analysis and vertical analysis.

A simple first step in financial statement analysis is comparing two financial statements. For example, the income statement for this year could be compared to the income statement for last year. To make the analysis more meaningful, percentages can be used. **Common-size analysis** expresses line items or accounts in the financial statements as percentages. The two major forms of common-size analysis are horizontal analysis and vertical analysis. Exhibit 16-1 illustrates vertical and horizontal analysis.

Horizontal Analysis

Also called trend analysis, **horizontal analysis** expresses a line item as a percentage of some prior-period amount. This approach allows the trend over time to be assessed. In

Common-Size Analysis

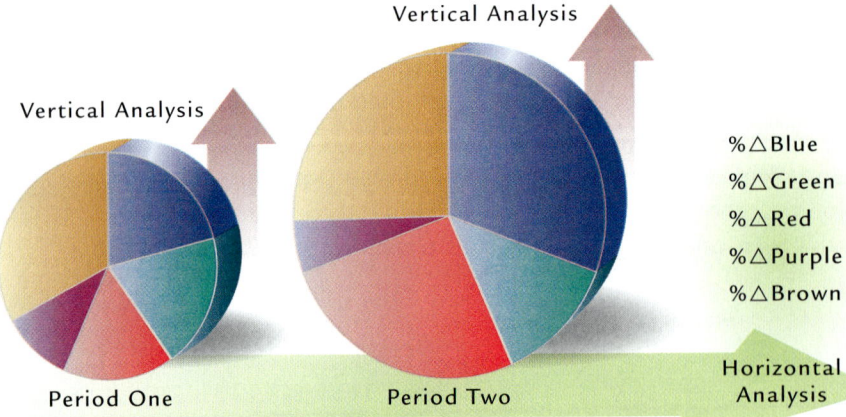

Vertical Analysis

Vertical Analysis

%△ Blue
%△ Green
%△ Red
%△ Purple
%△ Brown

Period One   Period Two   Horizontal Analysis

horizontal analysis, line items are expressed as a percentage of a base period amount. The base period can be the immediately preceding period, or it can be a period further in the past. Cornerstone 16-1 shows how to prepare common-size income statements using the first year as the base period.

Since the base year in Cornerstone 16-1 is year 1, all line amounts in subsequent years are compared to the amount in the base year. For example, year 3 sales are expressed as a percentage of year 1 sales. By comparing each subsequent amount to the base period, trends can be seen. The data reveal that sales have increased by 32 percent over the three years. With such a large increase in sales, many would expect net income likewise to experience a significant increase. The percentage analysis, however, shows that net income has shown no change from the base period. Net income has stayed flat because expenses and taxes have also increased; cost of goods sold has increased by 35 percent, operating expenses by 45 percent, and taxes by 25 percent. As a result of the percentage analysis, the manager of the company may decide to focus more attention on controlling costs.

Cornerstone 16-1

HOW TO Prepare Common-Size Income Statements Using Base Period Horizontal Analysis

Information: Simpson Company provided the following income statements for its first three years of operation:

	Year 1	Year 2	Year 3
Net sales	$100,000	$120,000	$132,000
Less: Cost of goods sold	(60,000)	(75,000)	(81,000)
Gross margin	$ 40,000	$ 45,000	$ 51,000
Less:			
Operating expenses	(20,000)	(24,000)	(29,000)
Income taxes	(8,000)	(9,000)	(10,000)
Net income	$ 12,000	$ 12,000	$ 12,000

Required: Prepare common-size income statements using year 1 as the base period.

Calculation: Year 1 is the base year. Therefore, every dollar amount in year 1 is 100 percent of itself.

Percent for a line item = (Dollar amount of line item/Dollar amount of base year line item) × 100

Percent year 1 net sales = ($100,000/$100,000) × 100 = 100%
Percent year 2 net sales = ($120,000/$100,000) × 100 = 120%
Percent year 3 net sales = ($132,000/$100,000) × 100 = 132%

	Year 1		Year 2		Year 3	
	Dollars	Percent	Dollars	Percent	Dollars	Percent
Net sales	$100,000	100%	$120,000	120.0%	$132,000	132.0%
Less: Cost of goods sold	(60,000)	100	(75,000)	125.0	(81,000)	135.0
Gross margin	$ 40,000	100	$ 45,000	112.5	$ 51,000	127.5
Less:						
Operating expenses	(20,000)	100	(24,000)	120.0	(29,000)	145.0
Income taxes	(8,000)	100	(9,000)	112.5	(10,000)	125.0
Net income	$ 12,000	100	$ 12,000	100.0	$ 12,000	100.0

Vertical Analysis

While horizontal analysis involves relationships among items over time, vertical analysis is concerned with relationships among items within a particular time period. **Vertical analysis** expresses the line item as a percentage of some other line item for the same period. With this approach, within-period relationships can be assessed. Line items on income statements are often expressed as percentages of net sales; items on the balance sheet are often expressed as a percentage of total assets. Cornerstone 16-2 shows how to perform vertical analysis with the same example used in Cornerstone 16-1. Sales is used as the base for computing percentages. Although the main purpose of vertical analysis is to highlight relationships among components of a company's financial statements, changes in these relationships over time can also be informative. For example, Cornerstone 16-1 reveals large increases in cost of goods sold and operating expenses over time. Over the 3-year period, cost of goods sold has increased by 35 percent ($21,000/$60,000), and operating expenses have increased by 45 percent ($9,000/$20,000). Cornerstone 16-2 compares these expenses to sales. This comparison reveals that much of the increase may be tied to increased sales. That is, year 1 operating expenses represented 20 percent of sales, whereas in year 3 they represented 22 percent of sales.

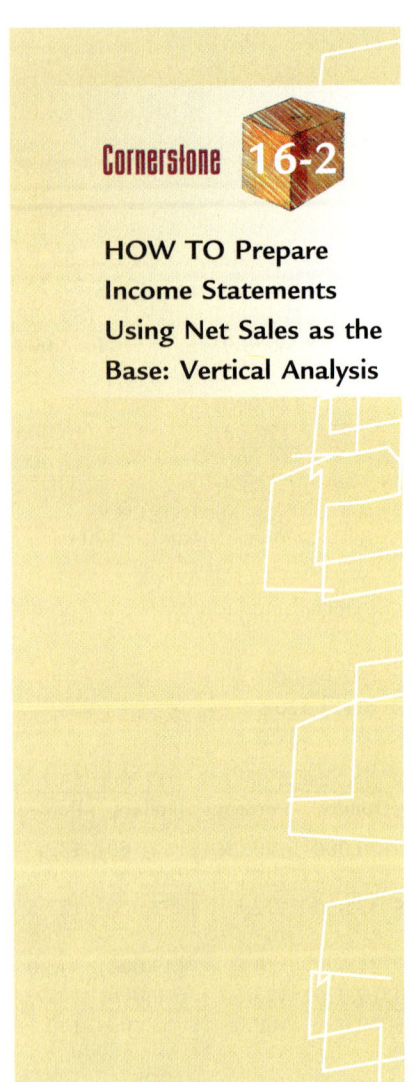

Cornerstone 16-2

HOW TO Prepare Income Statements Using Net Sales as the Base: Vertical Analysis

Information: Simpson Company provided the following income statements for its first three years of operation:

	Year 1	Year 2	Year 3
Net sales	$100,000	$120,000	$132,000
Less: Cost of goods sold	(60,000)	(75,000)	(81,000)
Gross margin	$ 40,000	$ 45,000	$ 51,000
Less:			
Operating expenses	(20,000)	(24,000)	(29,000)
Income taxes	(8,000)	(9,000)	(10,000)
Net income	$ 12,000	$ 12,000	$ 12,000

Required: Prepare common-size income statements using net sales as the base.

Calculation: Since the analysis is based on net sales, net sales in each year equals 100 percent of itself. Then, every line item on the income statement is figured as a percent of that year's net sales.

Percent for a line item = (Dollar amount of line item/Dollar amount of that year's sales) × 100

Percent year 1 net sales (of itself) = ($100,000/$100,000) × 100 = 100%
Percent year 2 net sales (of year 1) = ($120,000/$120,000) × 100 = 100%
Percent year 3 net sales (of year 2) = ($132,000/$132,000) × 100 = 100%

Percent year 1 COGS = ($60,000/$100,000) × 100 = 60%
Percent year 2 COGS = ($75,000/$120,000) × 100 = 62.5%
Percent year 3 COGS = ($81,000/$132,000) × 100 = 61.4%

	Year 1		Year 2		Year 3	
	Dollars	Percent	Dollars	Percent	Dollars	Percent
Net sales	$100,000	100%	$120,000	100.0%	$132,000	100.0%
Less: Cost of goods sold	(60,000)	60	(75,000)	62.5	(81,000)	61.4
Gross margin	$ 40,000	40	$ 45,000	37.5	$ 51,000	38.6
Less:						
Operating expenses	$(20,000)	20	$(24,000)	20.0	$(29,000)	22.0
Income taxes	(8,000)	8	(9,000)	7.5	(10,000)	7.6
Net income	$ 12,000	12	$ 12,000	10.0	$ 12,000	9.1

Percentages and Size Effects

The use of common-size analysis makes comparisons more meaningful because percentages eliminate the effects of size. For example, if one company earns $100,000 and another company earns $1 million, which is the more profitable? The answer depends to a large extent on the assets employed to earn the profits. If the first company used an investment of $1 million to earn the $100,000, then the return expressed as a percentage of dollars is 10 percent ($100,000/$1,000,000). If the second company used an investment of $20 million to earn its $1 million, the percentage return is only 5 percent ($1,000,000/$20,000,000). By using percentages, it is easy to see that the first firm is relatively more profitable than the second.

Concept Q & A

Company A's net income is $1,000 one year and $1,500 the following year. Company B's net income is $10,000 one year and $12,000 the following year. What is the percentage increase from one year to the next for each company? Which company is doing better?

Answer:
Company A's net income has increased by 50 percent, while Company B's net income has increased by 20 percent. It is hard to say which is doing a better job. Because percentages abstract from size, a user must exercise caution in their interpretation, particularly when the numbers involved are small. If the base is small, small changes in line items can produce large percentage changes. The percentage increase in net income is larger for Company A than Company B. However, Company A increased its total earnings by only $500, while Company B increased its earnings by $2,000.

HERE'S THE REAL KICKER

Every month, Kicker holds a company-wide meeting of all employees. In addition to the introduction of new employees and general announcements, Kicker's owner shares financial information. Then, graphs showing the trend in sales and profits are posted on the bulletin board in the break room. Employees can check trends in financial information at their leisure. This information is very important to Kicker employees since all of them are part of a comprehensive profit-sharing plan. Robust monthly sales and income will result in a bonus check to every employee that month. Yearly profits lead to another bonus check at year-end. Finally, Kicker also contributes to employees' 401(K) accounts. Since all of this is dependent on net income, each employee has a vested interest in keeping costs down and sales up.

RATIO ANALYSIS

OBJECTIVE 2

Explain why historical standards and industrial averages are important for ratio analysis.

Ratio analysis is the second major technique for financial statement analysis. Ratios are fractions or percentages computed by dividing one account or line-item amount by another. For example, operating income divided by sales produces a ratio that measures the profit margin on sales.

Standards for Comparison

Ratios by themselves tell little about the financial well-being of a company. For meaningful analysis, the ratios should be compared with a standard. Only through comparison can someone using a financial statement assess the financial health of a company. Two standards commonly used are the past history of the company and industrial averages. Exhibit 16-2 illustrates the way a company might view both types of ratio comparison.

Past History

One way to detect progress or problems is to compare the value of a ratio over time. Doing so allows trends to be assessed. Ratios measuring liquidity, for example, may be

Ratio Analysis

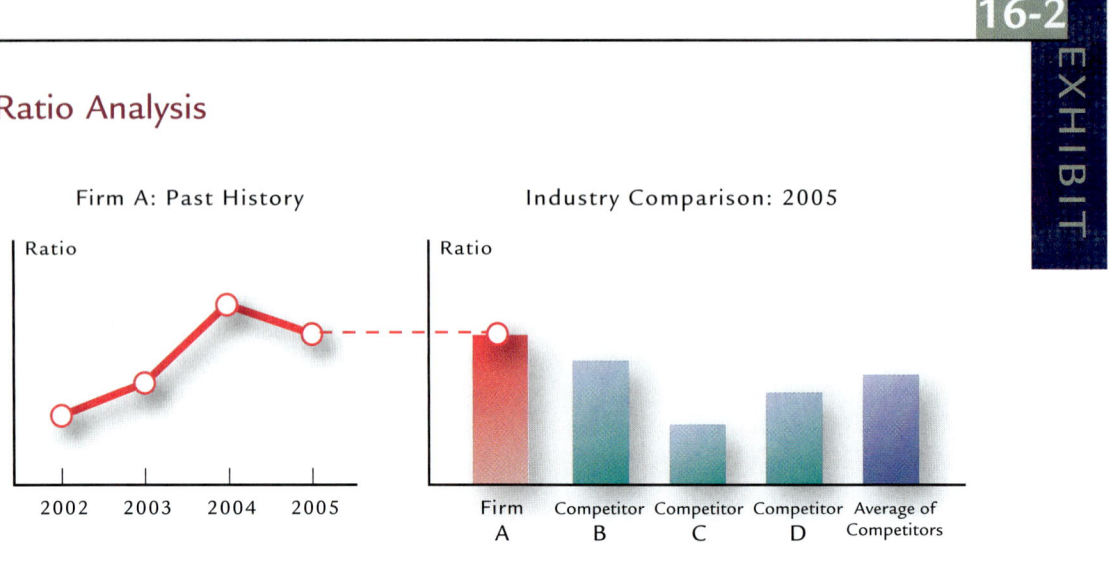

Firm A: Past History   Industry Comparison: 2005

dropping over time, signaling a deteriorating financial condition. The company's management can use this information to take corrective action. Investors and creditors, on the other hand, may use this information to decide whether or not to invest money in the company.

Industrial Averages

Additional insight can be gained by comparing a company's ratios with the same ratios for the companies in the same business. To facilitate the comparison, a number of annual publications provide industrial figures. Dun and Bradstreet, for example, report the median, upper quartile, and lower quartile for 14 commonly used ratios for more than 900 lines of business. The titles and publishers of some of the more common sources of industrial ratios are as follows:

1. *Key Business Ratios,* Dun and Bradstreet
2. *Standard and Poor's Industry Survey,* Standard and Poor's
3. *Annual Statement Studies,* Robert Morris Associates
4. *The Almanac of Business and Industrial Financial Ratios,* Prentice-Hall
5. *Dow Jones-Irwin Business and Investment Almanac,* Dow Jones-Irwin

A number of online sources are useful for competitive information on a company's ratios. Some of these are:

1. http://www.bizstats.com
2. http://www.fidelity.com
3. http://moneycentral.msn.com/investor/invsub/results/compare.asp?
4. http://biz.yahoo.com/r/

Even though the industrial figures provide a useful reference point, they should be used with care. Companies within the same industry may use different accounting methods, which diminishes the validity of the average. Other problems such as small sample sizes for the industrial report, different labor markets, the impact of extreme values, and terms of sale can produce variations among companies within the same industry. The industrial statistics should not be taken as absolute norms but rather as general guidelines for purposes of making comparisons.

Classification of Ratios

Ratios are generally classified into one of three categories: liquidity, borrowing capacity or leverage, and profitability.

- **Liquidity ratios** measure the ability of a company to meet its current obligations.
- **Leverage ratios** measure the ability of a company to meet its long- and short-term obligations. These ratios provide a measure of the degree of protection provided to a company's creditors.
- **Profitability ratios** measure the earning ability of a company. These ratios allow investors, creditors, and managers to evaluate the extent to which invested funds are being used efficiently.

Some of the more common and popular ratios for each category will be defined and illustrated. Exhibits 16-3 and 16-4 provide an income statement, a statement of retained earnings, and comparative balance sheets for Payne Company, a manufacturer of glassware. These financial statements provide the basis for subsequent analyses.

16-3

EXHIBIT

Income Statement and Statement of Retained Earnings for Payne Company for Year 2

Payne Company
Income Statement
For the Year Ended December 31, Year 2
(dollars in thousands)

	Amount	Percent
Net sales	$ 50,000	100.0%
Less: Cost of goods sold	(35,000)	70.0
Gross margin	$ 15,000	30.0
Less: Operating expenses	(10,000)	20.0
Operating income	$ 5,000	10.0
Less: Interest expense	(400)	0.8
Net income before taxes	$ 4,600	9.2
Less: Taxes (50%)*	(2,300)	4.6
Net income	$ 2,300	4.6

Payne Company
Statement of Retained Earnings
For the Year Ended December 31, Year 2

Balance, beginning of period	$ 5,324
Net income	2,300
Total	$ 7,624
Less: Preferred dividends	(224)
Dividends to common stockholders	(1,000)
Balance, end of period	$ 6,400

*Includes both state and federal taxes.

Comparative Balance Sheets for Payne Company for Years 1 and 2

Payne Company
Comparative Balance Sheets
For the Years Ended December 31, Year 1 and Year 2
(dollars in thousands)

Assets	Year 2	Year 1
Current assets:		
Cash	$ 1,600	$ 2,500
Marketable securities	1,600	2,000
Accounts receivable (net)	8,000	10,000
Inventories	10,000	3,000
Other	800	1,500
Total current assets	$22,000	$19,000
Property and equipment:		
Land	$ 4,000	$ 6,000
Building and equipment (net)	6,000	5,000
Total long-term assets	$10,000	$11,000
Total assets	$32,000	$30,000

Liabilities and Stockholders' Equity		
Current liabilities:		
Notes payable, short term	$ 3,200	$ 3,000
Accounts payable	6,400	5,800
Current maturity of long-term debt	400	400
Accrued payables	2,000	1,876
Total current liabilities	$12,000	$11,076
Long-term liabilities:		
Bonds payable, 10%	4,000	4,000
Total liabilities	$16,000	$15,076
Stockholder's equity:		
Preferred stock, $25 par, 7%	$ 3,200	$ 3,200
Common stock, $2 par	1,600	1,600
Additional paid-in capital*	4,800	4,800
Retained earnings	6,400	5,324
Total equity	$16,000	$14,924
Total liabilities and stockholders' equity	$32,000	$30,000

*For common stock only.

LIQUIDITY RATIOS

OBJECTIVE 3

Calculate and use liquidity ratios to assess the ability of a company to meet its current obligations.

Liquidity ratios are used to assess the short-term debt-paying ability of a company. If a company does not have the short-term financial strength to meet its current obligations, it is likely to have difficulty meeting its long-term obligations. Accordingly, evaluation of the short-term financial strength of a company is a good starting point in financial analysis. Although there are numerous liquidity ratios, only the most common ones will be discussed in this section. These liquidity ratios are the current ratio, quick or acid-test ratio, accounts receivable turnover ratio, and inventory turnover ratio.

Current Ratio

The **current ratio** is a measure of the ability of a company to pay its short-term liabilities out of short-term assets. The current ratio is computed by dividing the current assets by the current liabilities:

$$\text{Current ratio} = \text{Current assets/Current liabilities}$$

Since current liabilities must be paid within an operating cycle (usually within a year) and current assets can be converted to cash within an operating cycle, the current ratio provides a direct measure of the ability of a company to meet its short-term obligations. Payne Company's current ratio for year 2 is computed as follows, using data from Exhibit 16-4:

$$\text{Current ratio} = \$22,000,000/\$12,000,000$$
$$= 1.83$$

But what does a current ratio of 1.83 mean? Does the ratio of 1.83 signal good or poor debt-paying ability? Additional information is needed to interpret it. Many creditors use the rule of thumb that a 2.0 ratio is needed to provide good debt-paying ability. Based on this assessment, Payne does not have sufficient liquidity; however, this rule has many exceptions. For example, the industrial norm might be less than 2.0. Information on the ratio's trend is also helpful. Suppose that the upper quartile, median, and lower quartile values of the current ratio for the glassware industry are 2.2, 1.7, and 1.3, respectively. Payne's current ratio of 1.83 is above the median ratio for its industry, suggesting that Payne does not have liquidity problems. More than half of the firms in its industry have lower current ratios. It is possible, however, that Payne's current ratio for year 2 is representative of what usually happens. By comparing this year's ratio with ratios for prior years, some judgment about whether it is representative or not can be made. For example, if the ratio in prior years has been reasonably stable with values in the 1.7 to 1.9 range, this year's ratio is representative. If the ratio has been declining for the past several years, the company's financial position could be deteriorating.

A declining current ratio is not necessarily bad, particularly if it is falling from a high value. A high current ratio may signal excessive investment in current resources. Some of these current resources may be more productively employed by reducing long-term debt, paying dividends, or investing in long-term assets. Thus, a declining current ratio may signal a move toward more efficient utilization of resources. But a declining current ratio coupled with a current ratio lower than that of the other firms in the industry supports the judgment that a company is having liquidity problems.

Quick or Acid-Test Ratio

For many companies, inventory represents 50 percent or more of total current assets. For example, Payne Company's inventory represents 45 percent of its total current assets. The liquidity of inventory is often less than that of receivables, marketable securities, and cash. Inventory may be slow moving, nearly obsolete, or even pledged in part to creditors. Because including inventory may produce a misleading measure of liquidity, it is often excluded in computing liquidity ratios. For similar reasons, other current assets, such as miscellaneous assets, are excluded.

The **quick** or **acid-test ratio** is a measure of liquidity that compares only the most liquid assets to current liabilities. Excluded from the quick or acid-test ratio are nonliquid current assets such as inventories. The numerator of the quick or acid-test ratio includes only the most liquid assets (cash, marketable securities, and receivables).

Quick ratio = (Cash + Marketable securities + Receivables)/Current liabilities

For Payne Company, the quick ratio is calculated as follows (using data from Exhibit 16-4 for year 2):

Quick ratio = ($1,600,000 + $1,600,000 + $8,000,000)/$12,000,000
= $11,200,000/$12,000,000
= 0.93

Payne's quick ratio reveals that it does not have the capability to meet its current obligations with its most liquid assets; a ratio of 1.0 is the usual standard. Payne's quick ratio is not far below the standard level, and perhaps some attention should be paid to raise it somewhat. Cornerstone 16-3 shows how to calculate the current ratio and the quick ratio.

Concept Q & A

This year, Bellows Company had the same level of current assets and current liabilities as last year. However, last year, current assets were 50 percent cash and accounts receivable, while this year, current assets were 75 percent inventories. How would the change in the current asset mix affect this year's current ratio? Quick (acid-test) ratio?

Answer:
The current ratio would be unaffected (i.e., this year's current ratio would equal last year's current ratio). The quick ratio would be lower this year than last year because cash and accounts receivable are lower than last year.

Hint: Sometimes it helps to put numbers into this type of a question. For example, you could choose to let last year's (as well as this year's) current assets equal $2,000 and to let last year's (as well as this year's) current liabilities equal $1,000. Then, the current ratio last year would be $2,000/$1,000 or 2. This year's current ratio is the same. The quick ratio for last year would be 1 ($1,000/$1,000), while this year's quick ratio would be 0.5 ($500/$1,000).

Cornerstone 16-3

HOW TO Calculate the Current Ratio and the Quick (or Acid-Test) Ratio

Information: Bordner Company had current assets equal to $120,000. Of these, $15,000 was cash, $30,000 was accounts receivable, and the remainder was inventories. Current liabilities totaled $50,000.

Required:
1. Calculate the current ratio.
2. Calculate the quick ratio (acid-test ratio).

Calculation:
1. Current ratio = Current assets/Current liabilities
= $120,000/$50,000
= 2.4
2. Quick ratio = (Cash + Marketable securities + Receivables)/Current liabilities
= ($15,000 + 0 + $30,000)/$50,000
= 0.90

Accounts Receivable Turnover Ratio

The extent of Payne's liquidity problem can be further investigated by examining the liquidity of its receivables, or how long it takes the company to turn its receivables into cash. A low liquidity of receivables signals more difficulty since the quick ratio would be overstated. The liquidity of receivables is measured by the **accounts receivable turnover ratio**. This ratio is computed by dividing net sales by average accounts receivable.

Accounts receivable turnover ratio = Net sales/Average accounts receivable

Average accounts receivable is defined as follows:

Average accounts receivable = (Beginning receivables + Ending receivables)/2

The accounts receivable turnover ratio can be taken further to determine the number of days the average balance of accounts receivable is outstanding before being converted into cash. This is found by dividing the days in a year by the receivables turnover ratio:

Turnover in days = 365/Receivables turnover ratio

Payne Company's accounts receivable turnover is computed as follows (using data from Exhibits 16-3 and 16-4):

Accounts receivable turnover = $50,000,000/$9,000,000*
= 5.56 times per year

*Average receivables = ($10,000,000 + $8,000,000)/2

Accounts receivable turnover in days = (365/5.56) = 65.6 days

Payne's receivables are held for almost 66 days before being converted to cash. Whether this is good or bad depends to some extent on what other companies in the industry are experiencing. The low turnover ratio suggests a need for Payne's managers to modify credit and collection policies to speed up the conversion of receivables to cash. This need is particularly acute if a historical analysis shows a persistent problem or a trend downward. Note that net sales were used to compute the turnover ratio. Technically, credit sales should be used; however, external financial reports do not usually break net sales into credit and cash components. Consequently, if a turnover ratio is to be computed by external users, net sales must be used. For many firms, most sales are credit sales, and the computation is a good approximation. If sales are mostly for cash, liquidity is not an issue. In that case, the ratio provides a measure of the company's operating cycle. Cornerstone 16-4 shows how to calculate the average accounts receivable, the accounts receivable turnover ratio, and the accounts receivable turnover in days.

Cornerstone 16-4

HOW TO Calculate the Average Accounts Receivable, the Accounts Receivable Turnover Ratio, and the Accounts Receivable Turnover in Days

Information: Last year, Shuster Company had net sales of $750,000 and cost of goods sold of $400,000. Shuster had the following balances:

	January 1	December 31
Accounts receivable	$ 98,500	$101,500
Inventories	463,000	497,000

Required:
1. Calculate the average accounts receivable.
2. Calculate the accounts receivable turnover ratio.
3. Calculate the accounts receivable in days.

Calculation:
1. Average accounts receivables = (Beginning receivables + Ending receivables)/2
= ($98,500 + $101,500)/2 = $100,000
2. Accounts receivable turnover ratio = Net sales/Average accounts receivable
= $750,000/$100,000 = 7.5
3. Accounts receivable in days = Days in a year/Accounts receivable turnover ratio
= (365/7.5) = 48.7 days

Inventory Turnover Ratio

Inventory turnover is also an important liquidity measure. The **inventory turnover ratio** is computed by dividing the cost of goods sold by the average inventory.

$$\text{Inventory turnover ratio} = \text{Cost of goods sold/Average inventory}$$

Average inventory is found as follows:

$$\text{Average inventory} = (\text{Beginning inventory} + \text{Ending inventory})/2$$

This ratio tells an analyst how many times the average inventory turns over, or is sold, during the year. The number of days inventory is held before being sold can be computed by dividing the number of days in a year by the inventory turnover ratio:

$$\text{Turnover in days} = 365/\text{Inventory turnover ratio}$$

The inventory turnover ratio for Payne Company is computed as follows, using data from Exhibits 16-3 and 16-4:

$$\text{Inventory turnover} = \$35,000,000/\$6,500,000^*$$
$$= 5.38 \text{ times per year, or every } 67.8 \text{ days } (365/5.38)$$

*Average inventory = $3,000,000 + $10,000,000/2

Suppose that the glassware industry revealed the upper quartile, median, and lower quartile turnover figures in days to be 34, 57, and 79, respectively. Payne's turnover ratio is midway between the median and the lower quartile. The evidence seems to indicate that the turnover ratio is lower than it should be. A low turnover ratio may signal the presence of too much inventory or sluggish sales. More attention to inventory policies and marketing activities may be in order. Cornerstone 16-5 shows how to calculate the average inventory, the inventory turnover ratio, and the inventory turnover in days.

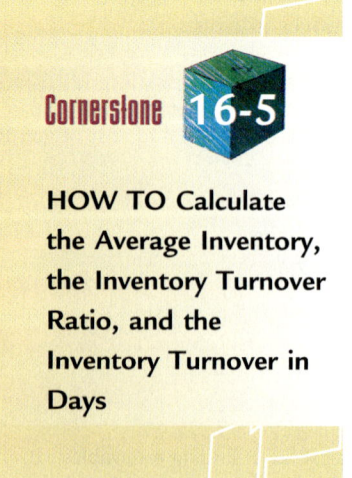

Cornerstone 16-5

HOW TO Calculate the Average Inventory, the Inventory Turnover Ratio, and the Inventory Turnover in Days

Information: Last year, Shuster Company had net sales of $750,000 and cost of goods sold of $400,000. Shuster had the following balances:

	January 1	December 31
Accounts receivable	$98,500	$101,500
Inventories	83,000	87,000

Required:
1. Calculate the average inventory.
2. Calculate the inventory turnover ratio.
3. Calculate the inventory turnover in days.

Calculation:
1. Average inventory = (Beginning inventory + Ending inventory)/2
$$= (\$83,000 + \$87,000)/2$$
$$= \$85,000$$

2. Inventory turnover ratio = Cost of goods sold/Average inventory
$$= \$400,000/\$85,000$$
$$= 4.7$$

3. Inventory turnover in days = Days in a year/Inventory turnover ratio
$$= (365/4.7) = 77.7 \text{ days}$$

LEVERAGE RATIOS

OBJECTIVE 4

Calculate and use leverage ratios to assess the ability of a company to meet its long- and short-term obligations.

When a company incurs debt, it has the obligation to repay the principal and the interest. Holding debt increases the riskiness of a company. Unlike other sources of capital (e.g., retained earnings or proceeds from the sale of capital stock), debt carries with it the threat of default foreclosure and bankruptcy if income does not meet projections. Both potential investors and creditors need to evaluate a company's debt position. A potential creditor may find that the amount of debt and debt-servicing requirements of a company make it too risky to grant further credit. Similarly, the company may be too risky for some potential investors. Leverage ratios can help an individual evaluate a company's debt-carrying ability.

Times-Interest-Earned Ratio

The first leverage ratio uses the income statement to assess a company's ability to service its debt. This ratio, called the **times-interest-earned ratio**, is computed by dividing net income before taxes and interest by interest expense:

Times-interest-earned ratio = (Income before taxes + Interest expense)/Interest expense

Income before taxes must be recurring income; thus, unusual or infrequent items appearing on the income statement should be excluded in order to compute the ratio. Recurring income is used because it is the income that is available each year to cover interest payments. The times-interest-earned ratio for Payne Company is computed as follows, using data from Exhibit 16-3:

Times-interest-earned ratio = ($4,600,000 + $400,000)/$400,000
= $5,000,000/$400,000
= 12.5

Since the assumed upper quartile for the glassware industry is 10.0, Payne's times-interest-earned ratio is among the highest in its industry. Payne does not have a significant interest expense burden. Cornerstone 16-6 shows how to calculate the times-interest-earned ratio.

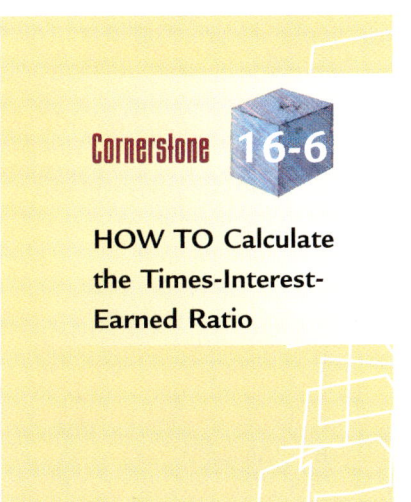

Cornerstone 16-6

HOW TO Calculate the Times-Interest-Earned Ratio

Information: Calvin Company provided the following income statement for last year:

Sales	$900,000
Cost of goods sold	350,000
Gross margin	$550,000
Operating expenses	270,000
Operating income	$280,000
Interest expense	15,000
Net income before taxes	$265,000
Income taxes	80,000
Net income	$185,000

Required: Calculate the times-interest-earned ratio.
Calculation:

Times-interest-earned ratio = (Income before taxes + Interest expense)/Interest expense
= ($265,000 + $15,000)/$15,000
= 18.7

Debt Ratio

Investors and creditors are the two major sources of capital. As the percentage of assets financed by creditors increases, the riskiness of the company increases. The **debt ratio** measures this percentage. It is computed by dividing a company's total liabilities by its total assets:

$$\text{Debt ratio} = \text{Total liabilities/Total assets}$$

Since total liabilities are compared with total assets, the ratio measures the degree of protection afforded creditors in case of insolvency. Creditors often impose restrictions on the percentage of liabilities allowed. If this percentage is exceeded, the company is in default, and foreclosure can take place. The debt ratio for Payne Company is calculated as follows, using data from Exhibit 16-4:

$$\text{Debt ratio} = \$16,000,000/\$32,000,000$$
$$= 0.50$$

Payne's debt ratio indicates that 50 percent of its assets are financed by creditors. Is this good or bad? How much risk will the stockholders allow? Will creditors be willing to provide more capital? For guidance, we again turn to industrial figures. The upper quartile, median, and lower quartile figures are 0.47, 0.55, and 0.69, respectively. With respect to industrial performance, Payne's debt ratio is not out of line. In fact, Payne is close to the upper quartile figure of 0.47. This may indicate that Payne still has the capability to use additional credit.

Another ratio useful in assessing the leverage used by a company is the debt to equity ratio. This ratio compares the amount of debt that is financed by stockholders. For Payne Company, the debt to equity ratio is calculated as follows, using data from Exhibit 16-4:

$$\text{Debt to equity ratio} = \text{Total liabilities/Total stockholders' equity}$$
$$\text{Debt to equity ratio} = \$16,000,000/\$16,000,000$$
$$= 1.00$$

Creditors would like this ratio to be relatively low, indicating that stockholders have financed most of the assets of the firm. Stockholders, on the other hand, may wish this ratio to be higher since that indicates that the company is more highly leveraged and stockholders can reap the return of the creditors' financing. Cornerstone 16-7 shows how to calculate the debt ratio and the debt to equity ratio.

Cornerstone 16-7

HOW TO Calculate the Debt Ratio and the Debt to Equity Ratio

Information: Jemell Company's balance sheet showed total liabilities of $450,000, total stockholders' equity of $300,000, and total assets of $750,000.

Required:
1. Calculate the debt ratio for Jemell Company.
2. Calculate the debt to equity ratio for Jemell Company.

Calculation:
1. Debt ratio = Total liabilities/Total assets
       = $450,000/$750,000
       = 0.6, or 60%
2. Debt to equity ratio = Total liabilities/Total stockholders' equity
       = $450,000/$300,000
       = 1.5

PROFITABILITY RATIOS

Investors earn a return through the receipt of dividends and appreciation of the market value of their stock. Dividends and market price of shares are both related to the profits generated by companies. Since they are the source of debt-servicing payments, profits are also of concern to creditors. Managers also have a vested interest in profits. Bonuses, promotions, and salary increases are often tied to reported profits. Profitability ratios, therefore, are given particular attention by both internal and external users of financial statements.

Return on Sales

Return on sales is the profit margin on sales. It tells what percentage of each sales dollar is earned as net income. **Return on sales** is one measure of the efficiency of a firm; it is computed by dividing net income by sales as follows:

$$\text{Return on sales} = \text{Net income/Sales}$$

Cornerstone 16-8 shows how to calculate the return on sales for Payne Company for year 2.

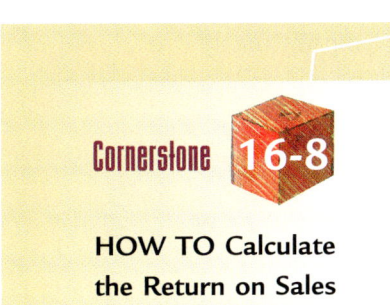

Cornerstone 16-8

HOW TO Calculate the Return on Sales

Information: Refer to Exhibits 16-3 and 16-4 for information on Payne Company.
Required: Calculate the return on sales.
Calculation: Return on sales = $2,300,000/$50,000,000
= 0.046, or 4.6%

Return on Total Assets

Return on assets measures how efficiently assets are used by calculating the return on total assets used to generate profits. **Return on total assets** is computed by dividing net income plus the after-tax cost of interest by the average total assets:

$$\text{Return on total assets} = \frac{\text{Operating income after taxes}}{\text{Average total assets}}$$

$$= \frac{[\text{Net income} + \text{Interest expense } (1 - \text{Tax rate})]}{\text{Average total assets}}$$

Average total assets is found as follows:

$$\text{Average total assets} = (\text{Beginning total assets} + \text{Ending total assets})/2$$

By adding back the after-tax cost of interest, this measure reflects only how the assets were employed; it does not consider the manner in which they were financed (interest expense is a cost of obtaining the assets, not a cost of *using* them). For Payne Company, the return on assets for year 2 is computed in Cornerstone 16-9.

Cornerstone 16-9

HOW TO Calculate the Average Total Assets and the Return on Assets

Information: Refer to Exhibits 16-3 and 16-4 for information on Payne Company.
Required:
1. Calculate the average total assets.
2. Calculate the return on total assets.
Calculation:
1. Average total assets = ($30,000,000 + $32,000,000)/2
2. Return on total assets = [$2,300,000 + (0.5 × $400,000)]/$31,000,000
                     = ($2,300,000 + $200,000)/$31,000,000
                     = $2,500,000/$31,000,000
                     = 0.0806, or 8.06%

Return on Common Stockholders' Equity

Return on total assets is measured without regard to the source of invested funds. For common stockholders, however, the return they receive on their investment is of paramount importance. Of special interest to common stockholders is how they are being treated relative to other suppliers of capital funds. The **return on stockholders' equity** is computed by dividing net income less preferred dividends by the average common stockholders' equity; it provides a measure that can be used to compare against other return measures (e.g., preferred dividend rates and bond rates). The beginning and ending common stockholders' equity require further calculations for Payne Company because the company has preferred stock. The preferred stock must be backed out of the total equity to get the common stockholders' equity. For Payne Company, the beginning and ending common stockholders' equity are calculated as follows:

$$\text{Beginning common stockholders' equity} = \$14,924,000 - \$3,200,000$$
$$= \$11,724,000$$

$$\text{Ending common stockholders' equity} = \$16,000,000 - \$3,200,000$$
$$= \$12,800,000$$

$$\text{Average common stockholders' equity} = (\$12,800,000 + \$11,724,000)/2$$
$$= \$12,262,000$$

Return on stockholders' equity is calculated as follows:

$$\text{Return on stockholders' equity} = (\text{Net income} - \text{Preferred dividends})/$$
$$\text{Average common stockholders' equity}$$

Payne Company's return on stockholders' equity is computed in Cornerstone 16-10.

Cornerstone 16-10

HOW TO Calculate the Average Common Stockholders' Equity and the Return on Stockholders' Equity

Information: Refer to Exhibits 16-3 and 16-4 for information on Payne Company.
Required:
1. Calculate the average common stockholders' equity.
2. Calculate the return on stockholders' equity.
Calculation:
1. Average common stockholders' equity = ($11,724,000 + $12,800,000)/2
                     = $12,262,000
2. Return on stockholders' equity = ($2,300,000 – $224,000)/$12,262,000
                     = $2,076,000/$12,262,000
                     = 0.1693, or 16.93%

As we can see in Cornerstone 16-10, compared with the bond return of 10 percent and the preferred dividend rate of 7 percent, common stockholders are faring quite well. Furthermore, since the industrial average is about 14 percent, the rate of return provided common stockholders is above average.

Earnings per Share

Investors also pay considerable attention to a company's profitability on a per-share basis. **Earnings per share** is computed by dividing net income less preferred dividends by the average number of shares of common stock outstanding during the period.

Earnings per share = (Net income − Preferred dividends)/Average common shares

Average common shares outstanding is computed by taking a weighted average of the common shares for the period under study. For example, assume that a company has 8,000 common shares at the beginning of the year. At the end of the first quarter, 4,000 additional shares are issued. No other transactions take place during the period. The weighted average is computed as follows:

	Outstanding Shares	**Weight**	**Weighted Shares**
First quarter	8,000	3/12	2,000
Last three quarters	12,000	9/12	9,000
Average common shares outstanding			11,000

Cornerstone 16-11 shows how to compute earnings per share for Payne Company.

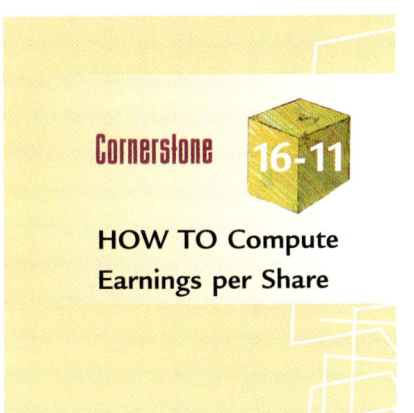

Cornerstone 16-11

HOW TO Compute Earnings per Share

Information: Refer to Exhibits 16-3 and 16-4 for data on Payne Company.
Required:
1. Compute the dollar amount of preferred dividends.
2. Compute the number of common shares.
3. Compute earnings per share for Payne Company.
Calculation:
1. Preferred dividends = $3,200,000 × 0.07 = $224,000

   (Recall that the preferred shares pay a dividend of 7 percent as shown in Exhibit 16-4.)

2. Number of common shares = $1,600,000/$2 = 800,000
3. Earnings per share = ($2,300,000 − $224,000)/800,000
   = $2,076,000/800,000
   = $2.60

Since the median value for the industry is about $3.47 per share, Payne's earnings per share is somewhat low and may signal a need for management to focus on increasing earnings.

Price-Earnings Ratio

The **price-earnings ratio** is found by dividing the market price per share by the earnings per share:

Price-earnings ratio = Market price per share/Earnings per share

Price-earnings ratios are viewed by many investors as important indicators of stock values. If investors believe that a company has good growth prospects, then the price-earnings ratio should be high. If investors believe that the current price-earnings ratio is low based on their view of future growth opportunities, the market price of the stock may be bid up. Cornerstone 16-12 shows how to compute the price-earnings ratio.

Cornerstone 16-12

HOW TO Compute the Price-Earnings Ratio

Information: Assume that the price per common share for Payne Company is $15.
Required: Compute the price-earnings ratio.
Calculation: Price-earnings ratio = $15/$2.60
                    = 5.7692, or 5.8
Note: Price-earnings ratios are typically rounded to one significant digit.

As Cornerstone 16-12 shows, Payne's stock is selling for 5.8 times its current earnings per share. This ratio compares with an industrial median value of 6.3. Thus, Payne's price-earnings ratio is lower than more than half of the firms in the industry.

Dividend Yield and Payout Ratios

The profitability measure called **dividend yield** is computed by dividing the dividends received per unit of common share by the market price per common share.

Dividend yield = Dividends per common share/Market price per common share

By adding the dividend yield to the percentage change in stock price, a reasonable approximation of the total return accruing to an investor can be obtained. For Payne Company, the dividend yield is computed in Cornerstone 16-13.

The **dividend payout ratio** is computed by dividing the total common dividends by the earnings available to common stockholders, as follows:

Dividend payout ratio = Common dividends/(Net income − Preferred dividends)

The payout ratio tells an investor the proportion of earnings that a company pays in dividends. Investors who prefer regular cash payments instead of returns through price appreciation will want to invest in companies with a high payout ratio; investors who prefer gains through appreciation will generally prefer a lower payout ratio. Cornerstone 16-13 shows how to compute the dividend yield and dividend payout ratio.

Cornerstone 16-13

HOW TO Compute the Dividend Yield and the Dividend Payout Ratio

Information: Assume that the market price per common share is $15. Refer to Exhibits 16-3 and 16-4.
Required:
1. Compute the dividends per share.
2. Compute the dividend yield.
3. Compute the dividend payout ratio.
Calculation:
1. Dividends per share = $1,000,000/800,000 = $1.25
2. Dividend yield = $1.25/$15
                 = 0.0833, or 8.33%
3. Dividend payout ratio = $1,000,000/($2,300,000 − $224,000)
                        = $1,000,000/$2,076,000
                        = 0.48

Impact of the JIT Manufacturing Environment

In the new manufacturing environment, reducing inventories and increasing quality are critical activities. Both activities are essential for many companies to retain their competitive ability. Accordingly, users of financial statements should have a special interest in ratios that measure a company's progress in achieving the goals of zero inventories and total quality. As a company reduces its inventory, the inventory turnover ratio should increase dramatically. Traditionally, high inventory turnovers have had a negative connotation. It was argued that a high inventory turnover ratio might signal such problems as stockouts and disgruntled customers. In the new manufacturing environment, however, a high turnover ratio is viewed positively. High turnover is interpreted as a signal of success—of achieving the goal of zero inventories with all of the efficiency associated with that state (see Chapter 13). As inventory levels drop, the current ratio is also affected. Without significant inventories, the current ratio will drop; in fact, it will approach the value of the quick ratio. Since many lenders require a 2.0 current ratio to grant and control a loan, some reevaluation of the use of this ratio is needed for customers with a JIT system. It may be necessary to rely more on the quick ratio or other alternative ratios (such as cash flow divided by current maturities of long-term debt). A ratio that says something about quality is also desirable for JIT firms. The usual approach is to express quality costs as a percentage of sales. External users, however, may not have access to quality costs as a separate category. Warranty costs, returns and allowances, unfavorable materials quantity variances, and other quality costs that are readily identifiable from the financial statement can be added. This sum can then be divided by sales to give the external users some idea of the company's capability in this important area. Tracking this ratio over time will reveal the progress that the company is making. As quality improves, quality costs as a percentage of sales should decline.

APPLICATIONS IN BUSINESS

© BROWNIE HARRIS/CORBIS

Harley-Davidson, Inc., has been working for more than 20 years to improve its productivity and efficiency. One example of that is its emphasis on developing a just-in-time system. The company works together with its suppliers and manufacturing and administrative employees to reduce waste and improve performance. For example, it reduced inventories, increasing its inventory turnover within one 18-month period from 5.9 times to 20 times.

To show employees that inventory reduction (in raw materials, work-in-process, and finished goods inventories) is important, management made it one of 10 criteria for measuring manufacturing efficiency. Quality is also a major initiative to decrease manufacturing and warranty cost. The company's cross-functional teams meet regularly to ensure that their actions are in harmony with the strategic plan. For example, Harley-Davidson employees were able to provide real-time inventory and order information across product lines and dealerships. This improvement in information technology has enabled the company to more quickly understand consumer demand and translate that into production—further enhancing its ability to operate in a JIT environment.

Sources: Gene Schwind, "Man Arrives Just in Time to Save Harley-Davidson," *Material Handling Engineering* (August 1984): 28; Robert D. McIlhattan, "How Cost Management Systems Can Support the JIT Philosophy," *Management Accounting* 69, No. 3, p. 25; Harley-Davidson's Web site at **http://www.harley-davidson.com**.

Six months later, Patricia and Doug met to review the new standards for ratio analysis in the commercial loan department. Patricia updated Doug on the way large commercial loan applicants now provided significantly more financial information, which allowed the loan officers to assess their liquidity and ability to repay the loans. Already, the default rate had decreased, and Patricia was pleased with the way the various ratios helped to guide conversations with loan applicants.

SUMMARY OF LEARNING OBJECTIVES

Financial statement analysis is an important activity for managers, creditors, and investors. Managers can identify both strengths and weaknesses and reveal areas for which particular attention is needed. Creditors need to carefully evaluate the financial statements of a company to make sound loan decisions and control outstanding loans. Investors can assess the risk and profitability associated with investing in a company.

Two types of comparative analysis are horizontal analysis and vertical analysis. Common-size analysis expresses accounts or line items in financial statements as percentages, either horizontally, over time, or vertically, as compared to some other line item. Horizontal analysis allows an analyst to assess trends. Vertical analysis allows an analyst to assess relationships among financial statement items. When using ratios for evaluation, it is important to have a standard against which the ratios can be compared. The most common standards are historical values and industrial values. By comparing ratio values against prior-period values or the values of other companies in the same industry, meaningful analysis becomes possible.

Liquidity ratios are used to assess the short-term debt-paying ability of a company. Frequently used liquidity ratios include the current ratio, the quick or acid-test ratio, accounts receivable turnover, and inventory turnover.

Leverage ratios measure the ability of a company to meet its long-term debt obligations. Frequently used leverage ratios include the times-interest-earned ratio and the debt ratio.

Profitability ratios relate the firm's earnings to the resources used to create those earnings. Profitability ratios include return on sales, return on total assets, earnings per share, price-earnings ratio, dividend yield, and dividend payout.

Exhibit 16-5 summarizes all of the ratios discussed above.

Summary of Ratios

	Formula
Liquidity ratios:	
Current ratio	Current assets/Current liabilities
Quick ratio	(Cash + Marketable securities + Receivables)/Current liabilities
Accounts receivable turnover ratio	Net sales/Average accounts receivable
Inventory turnover ratio	Cost of goods sold/Average inventory
Turnover in days	Days in a year/Receivables turnover ratio
Leverage ratios:	
Times-interest-earned ratio	(Income before taxes + Interest expense)/Interest expense
Debt ratio	Total liabilities/Total assets
Debt to equity ratio	Total liabilities/Total stockholders' equity
Profitability ratios:	
Return on sales	Net income/Sales
Return on total assets	[Net income + Interest expense (1 − Tax rate)]/Average total assets
Return on common stockholders' equity	(Net income − Preferred dividends)/Average common stockholders' equity
Earnings per share	(Net income − Preferred dividends)/Average common shares
Price-earnings ratio	Market price per share/Earnings per share
Dividend yield	Dividends per common share/Market price per common share
Dividend payout ratio	Common dividends/(Net income − Preferred dividends)

Cornerstones for Chapter 16

Cornerstone 16-1 How to prepare common-size income statements using base period horizontal analysis, page 657

Cornerstone 16-2 How to prepare income statements using net sales as the base: vertical analysis, page 658

Cornerstone 16-3 How to calculate the current ratio and the quick (or acid-test) ratio, page 664

Cornerstone 16-4 How to calculate the average accounts receivable, the accounts receivable turnover ratio, and the accounts receivable turnover in days, page 665

KEY TERMS

DISCUSSION QUESTIONS

1. Name the two major types of financial statement analysis discussed in this chapter.
2. What is horizontal analysis? Vertical analysis? Should both horizontal and vertical analyses be done? Why?
3. Explain how creditors, investors, and managers can use common-size analysis as aids in decision making.
4. What are liquidity ratios? Leverage ratios? Profitability ratios?
5. Identify two types of standards used in ratio analysis. Explain why it is desirable to use both types.
6. What information does the quick ratio supply that the current ratio does not?
7. Suppose that the accounts receivable turnover ratio of a company is low when compared to other firms within its industry. How would this information be useful to the managers of this company?
8. A high inventory turnover ratio provides evidence that a company is having problems with stockouts and disgruntled customers. Do you agree? Explain.
9. A loan agreement between a bank and a customer specified that the debt ratio could not exceed 60 percent. Explain the purpose of this restrictive agreement.
10. A manager decided to acquire some expensive equipment through the use of an operating lease even though a capital budgeting analysis showed that it was more profitable to buy than to lease. However, the purchase alternative would have required the issuance of some bonds. Offer some reasons that would explain the manager's choice.
11. Explain why an investor would be interested in a company's debt ratio.

12. Assume that you have been given the responsibility to invest some funds in the stock market to provide an annuity to an individual who has just retired. Explain how you might use the dividend yield and the dividend payout ratio to help you with this investment decision.

13. Explain how an investor might use the price-earnings ratio to value the stock of a company.

14. Why would investors and creditors be interested in knowing the dilutive effects of convertible securities on earnings per share?

15. Explain the significance of the inventory turnover ratio in a JIT manufacturing environment.

16. In a JIT manufacturing environment, the current ratio and the quick ratio are virtually the same. Do you agree? Why?

MULTIPLE-CHOICE EXERCISES

16-1 A company provided income statements for the past five years. In looking at the percentage columns for each year, you notice that sales are 46 percent higher in year 5 than in year 1. The company has most likely provided

a. a horizontal analysis using the prior period as the base year.
b. a vertical analysis using sales as the base.
c. a horizontal analysis using year 1 as the base year.
d. a vertical analysis using net income as the base.
e. none of the above.

16-2 An advantage of common-size analysis is that

a. the size of dollar amounts impact the analysis.
b. larger companies will have higher common-size percentages.
c. the effects of size are eliminated.
d. it focuses only on vertical analysis.
e. it focuses only on horizontal analysis.

16-3 Fractions or percentages computed by dividing one account or line-item amount by another are called

a. ratios.
b. industry averages.
c. common-size statements.
d. dividend yields.
e. returns.

16-4 The measures of the ability of a company to meet its long- and short-term obligations are called

a. ratios.
b. liquidity ratios.
c. leverage ratios.
d. profitability ratios.
e. percentage changes.

16-5 A company's inventory turnover in days is 80 days. Which of the following actions could help to improve that ratio?

a. Increase in sales price
b. Increase in manufacturing costs
c. Reduction in cost of goods sold
d. Reduction in average inventory
e. All of the above

16-6 Company B shows that 46 percent of its assets are financed by creditors. Which of the following shows this result?

a. Current ratio
b. Times-interest-earned
c. Return on sales
d. Inventory turnover in days
e. Debt ratio

16-7 Profitability ratios are used by which of the following groups?

a. Company managers
b. Creditors
c. Lenders
d. Investors
e. All of the above

16-8 Fred and Torrie Jones are a retired couple looking for income. They are currently rebalancing their portfolio of stocks to include more high dividend stocks. Fred and Torrie will be most interested in which of the following?

a. Dividend payout ratio
b. Current ratio
c. Return on assets
d. Price-earnings ratio
e. Dividend yield

16-9 A small pizza restaurant, founded and owned by the Martinelli sisters, would be expected to have which of the following?

a. High price-earnings ratio
b. High inventory turnover and low gross margin
c. Low inventory turnover and high gross margin
d. Low accounts receivable turnover and low gross margin
e. All of the above

16-10 The after-tax cost of interest expense is used in calculating which of the following?

a. Times-interest-earned
b. Return on total assets
c. Debt ratio
d. Inventory turnover ratio
e. All of the above

EXERCISES

Exercise 16-1 *Horizontal Analysis*

Fogel Company's income statements for two years are shown at the top of the following page.

Required:
Prepare a common-size income statement for year 2 by expressing each line item for year 2 as a percentage of that same line item from year 1. (Round percentages to the nearest tenth of a percent.)

Fogel Company
Income Statements
For the Years 1 and 2

	Year 1	Year 2
Sales	$2,000,000	$1,800,000
Less: Cost of goods sold	(1,400,000)	(1,200,000)
Gross margin	$ 600,000	$ 600,000
Less operating expenses:		
Selling expenses	(300,000)	(300,000)
Administrative expenses	(100,000)	(110,000)
Net operating income	$ 200,000	$ 190,000
Less: Interest expense	(50,000)	(40,000)
Income before taxes	$ 150,000	$ 150,000

Exercise 16-2 *Vertical Analysis*

Refer to the income statements in **Exercise 16-1**.

Required:
1. Prepare a common-size income statement for year 1 by expressing each line item as a percentage of sales revenue. (Round percentages to the nearest tenth of a percent.)
2. Prepare a common-size income statement for year 2 by expressing each line item as a percentage of sales revenue. (Round percentages to the nearest tenth of a percent.)

Exercise 16-3 *Horizontal Analysis*

Camellia Company's income statements for the last three years are as follows:

Camellia Company
Income Statements
For the Years 1, 2, and 3

	Year 1	Year 2	Year 3
Sales	$1,000,000	$1,200,000	$1,700,000
Less: Cost of goods sold	(700,000)	(700,000)	(1,000,000)
Gross margin	$ 300,000	$ 500,000	$ 700,000
Less operating expenses:			
Selling expenses	(150,000)	(220,000)	(250,000)
Administrative expenses	(50,000)	(60,000)	(120,000)
Net operating income	$ 100,000	$ 220,000	$ 330,000
Less: Interest expense	(25,000)	(25,000)	(25,000)
Income before taxes	$ 75,000	$ 195,000	$ 305,000

Required:
1. Prepare a common-size income statement for year 2 by expressing each line item for year 2 as a percentage of that same line item from year 1. (Round percentages to the nearest tenth of a percent.)
2. Prepare a common-size income statement for year 3 by expressing each line item for year 3 as a percentage of that same line item from year 1. (Round percentages to the nearest tenth of a percent.)

Exercise 16-4 *Vertical Analysis*

Refer to the income statements in **Exercise 16-3**.

Required:
1. Prepare a common-size income statement for year 1 by expressing each line item as a percentage of sales revenue. (Round percentages to the nearest tenth of a percent.)
2. Prepare a common-size income statement for year 2 by expressing each line item as a percentage of sales revenue. (Round percentages to the nearest tenth of a percent.)
2. Prepare a common-size income statement for year 3 by expressing each line item as a percentage of sales revenue. (Round percentages to the nearest tenth of a percent.)

Exercise 16-5 *Current Ratio and Quick (Acid-Test) Ratio*

Matalin Company provided the following information:

Current assets:	
Cash	$ 50,000
Accounts receivable	100,000
Inventories	138,000
Total current assets	$288,000
Current liabilities	$ 80,000

Required:
1. Compute the current ratio for Matalin Company.
2. Compute the quick (acid-test) ratio for Matalin Company. (Do not round your answer.)

Exercise 16-6 *Current Ratio and Quick (Acid-Test) Ratio*

Nbulio Company had current assets equal to $180,000. Of these, $20,000 was cash, $40,000 was accounts receivable, and the remainder was inventories. Current liabilities totaled $75,000.

Required:
1. Compute the current ratio for Nbulio Company.
2. Compute the quick (acid-test) ratio for Nbulio Company.

Exercise 16-7 *Average Accounts Receivable, Accounts Receivable Turnover Ratio, Accounts Receivable Turnover in Days*

Calista Company had net sales of $400,000. Calista had the following balances:

	January 1	December 31
Accounts receivable	$ 82,400	$ 77,600
Inventories	113,000	107,000

Required:
1. Calculate the average accounts receivable.
2. Calculate the accounts receivable turnover ratio.
3. Calculate the accounts receivable in days.

Exercise 16-8 *Average Accounts Receivable, Accounts Receivable Turnover Ratio, Accounts Receivable Turnover in Days*

Franklin Company had net sales of $593,400. Franklin had the following balances:

	January 1	December 31
Accounts receivable	$ 51,400	$ 77,600
Inventories	113,000	107,000

Required:
1. Calculate the average accounts receivable.
2. Calculate the accounts receivable turnover ratio.
3. Calculate the accounts receivable in days (take your answer out to one decimal place).

Exercise 16-9 *Average Inventory, Inventory Turnover Ratio, Inventory Turnover in Days*

Calista Company had net sales of $400,000 and cost of goods sold of $250,000. Calista had the following balances:

	January 1	December 31
Inventories	$113,000	$107,000

Required:
1. Calculate the average inventory.
2. Calculate the inventory turnover ratio. (Round your answer to one decimal place.)
3. Calculate the inventory turnover in days. (Round your answer to one decimal place.)

Exercise 16-10 *Average Inventory, Inventory Turnover Ratio, Inventory Turnover in Days*

Dejong Company had cost of goods sold of $1,232,000. Dejong had beginning inventory of $45,000 and ending inventory of $43,000.

Required:
1. Calculate the average inventory.
2. Calculate the inventory turnover ratio. (Round your answer to one decimal place.)
3. Calculate the inventory turnover in days. (Round your answer to one decimal place.)

Exercise 16-11 *Times-Interest-Earned*

Bessette Company provided the following income statement for last year:

Sales	$600,000
Cost of goods sold	350,000
Gross margin	$250,000
Operating expenses	160,000
Operating income	$ 90,000
Interest expense	15,000
Net income before taxes	$ 75,000
Income taxes	20,000
Net income	$ 55,000

Required:
Calculate the times-interest-earned ratio.

Exercise 16-12 *Debt Ratio, Debt to Equity Ratio*

Sasquall Company's balance sheet showed total liabilities of $585,000, total equity of $715,000, and total assets of $1,300,000.

Required:
1. Calculate the debt ratio for Sasquall Company.
2. Calculate the debt to equity ratio for Sasquall Company. (Round your answer to two decimal places.)

Exercise 16-13 *Times-Interest-Earned, Debt Ratio, Debt to Equity Ratio,*

Woodall, Inc., provided the following income statement for last year:

Sales	$12,600,000
Cost of goods sold	7,500,000
Gross margin	$ 5,100,000
Operating expenses	2,400,000
Operating income	$ 2,700,000
Interest expense	400,000
Net income before taxes	$ 2,300,000
Income taxes	690,000
Net income	$ 1,610,000

Woodall's balance sheet as of December 31 last year showed total liabilities of $2,500,000, total equity of $9,500,000, and total assets of $12,000,000.

Required:
1. Calculate the times-interest-earned ratio. (Round your answer to two decimal places.)
2. Calculate the debt ratio. (Round your answer to two decimal places.)
3. Calculate the debt to equity ratio. (Round your answer to two decimal places.)

Exercise 16-14 *Return on Sales*

Refer to **Exercise 16-13** for information on Woodall, Inc.

Required:
Calculate the return on sales. (Round your answer to three decimal places.)

Exercise 16-15 *Average Total Assets, Return on Assets*

Refer to **Exercise 16-13** for information on Woodall, Inc. Woodall's total assets at the beginning of last year also equaled $12,000,000. The tax rate applicable to Woodall is 30 percent.

Required:
1. Calculate the average total assets.
2. Calculate the return on assets.

Exercise 16-16 *Average Common Stockholders' Equity, Return on Stockholders' Equity*

Haidary, Inc., showed the following balances for last year:

	January 1	December 31
Stockholder's equity:		
Preferred stock, $100 par, 8%	$ 4,000,000	$ 4,000,000
Common stock, $3 par	3,000,000	3,000,000
Additional paid-in capital*	4,800,000	4,800,000
Retained earnings	4,000,000	4,250,000
Total equity	$15,800,000	$16,050,000

*For common stock only.

Haidary's net income for last year was $3,182,000.

Required:
1. Calculate the average common stockholders' equity.
2. Calculate the return on stockholders' equity.

Exercise 16-17 *Earnings per Share, Price-Earnings Ratio*

Refer to the data in **Exercise 16-16**. The market price per share for Haidary, Inc., is $51.50.

Required:
1. Compute the dollar amount of preferred dividends.
2. Compute the number of common shares.
3. Compute earnings per share.
4. Compute the price-earnings ratio. (Round to the nearest whole number.)

Exercise 16-18 *Dividend Yield Ratio, Dividend Payout Ratio*

Refer to **Exercise 16-16** for data. The dividends paid to common stockholders for last year were $2,600,000. The market price per share of common stock is $51.50.

Required:
1. Compute the dividends per share.
2. Compute the dividend yield. (Round to two decimal places.)
3. Compute the dividend payout ratio. (Round to two decimal places.)

PROBLEMS

(*Note:* Whenever you see a [image] next to a requirement, it signals a "Building on a Cornerstone" requirement. Assigning this requirement will usually entail additional work, such as a group project, analytical reasoning, Internet research, decision making, and the use of written communication skills.)

Problem 16-1 *Liquidity Analysis*

Spreadsheet

The following selected information is taken from the financial statements of Riflen Company for its most recent year of operations:

Beginning balances:	
Inventory	$200,000
Accounts receivable	300,000
Ending balances:	
Inventory	$250,000
Accounts receivable	400,000
Cash	100,000
Marketable securities (short term)	200,000
Prepaid expenses	50,000
Accounts payable	175,000
Taxes payable	85,000
Wages payable	90,000
Short-term loans payable	50,000

During the year, Riflen Company had net sales of $2.45 million. The cost of goods sold was $1.3 million.

Required:
1. Compute the current ratio.
2. Compute the quick or acid-test ratio.
3. Compute the accounts receivable turnover ratio.
4. Compute the accounts receivable turnover in days.
5. Compute the inventory turnover ratio.
6. Compute the inventory turnover ratio in days.

Problem 16-2 *Leverage Ratios*

Spreadsheet

Timmins Company has just completed its third year of operations. The income statement is as follows:

Sales	$2,460,000
Less: Cost of goods sold	(1,410,000)
Gross profit	$1,050,000
Less: Selling and administrative expenses	(710,000)
Operating income	$ 340,000
Less: Interest expense	(140,000)
Income before taxes	$ 200,000
Less: Income taxes	(68,000)
Net income	$ 132,000

Selected information from the balance sheet is as follows:

Current liabilities	$1,000,000
Long-term liabilities	1,500,000
Total liabilities	$2,500,000
Common stock	$4,000,000
Retained earnings	750,000
Total equity	$4,750,000

Required:
1. Compute the times-interest-earned ratio.
2. Compute the debt ratio.
3. Assume that the lower quartile, median, and upper quartile values for debt and times-interest-earned ratios in Timmins's industry are as follows:

Times-interest-earned:	2.3, 5.4, 16.1
Debt:	2.4, 0.8, 0.5

How does Timmins compare to the industrial norms? Does it have too much debt?

Problem 16-3 *Profitability Ratios*

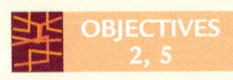

The following information has been gathered for Leatroy Manufacturing:

Net income	$5,000,000
Interest expense	$400,000
Average total assets	$60,000,000
Preferred dividends	$400,000
Common dividends	$1,200,000
Average common shares outstanding	800,000
Average common stockholders' equity	$20,000,000
Market price per common share	$40

Assume that the firm has no common stock equivalents. The tax rate is 34 percent.

Required:
1. Compute the return on total assets.
2. Compute the return on common stockholders' equity.

3. Compute the earnings per share.
4. Compute the price-earnings ratio.
5. Compute the dividend yield.
6. Compute the dividend payout ratio.

Problem 16-4 *Horizontal Analysis*

 **OBJECTIVE 1**

Mike Sanders is considering the purchase of Kepler Company, a firm specializing in the manufacture of office supplies. To be able to assess the financial capabilities of the company, Mike has been given the company's financial statements for the two most recent years.

Kepler Company
Comparative Balance Sheets

Assets

	This Year	Last Year
Current assets:		
Cash	$ 50,000	$100,000
Accounts receivable, net	300,000	150,000
Inventory	600,000	400,000
Prepaid expenses	25,000	30,000
Total current assets	$ 975,000	$680,000
Property and equipment, net	125,000	150,000
Total assets	$1,100,000	$830,000

Liabilities and Stockholders' Equity

	This Year	Last Year
Liabilities:		
Accounts payable	$ 400,000	$290,000
Short-term notes payable	200,000	60,000
Total current liabilities	$ 600,000	$350,000
Long-term bonds payable, 12%	100,000	150,000
Total liabilities	$ 700,000	$500,000
Stockholders' equity:		
Common stock (100,000 shares)	200,000	200,000
Retained earnings	200,000	130,000
Total liabilities and equity	$1,100,000	$830,000

Kepler Company
Comparative Income Statements

	This Year	Last Year
Sales	$ 950,000	$900,000
Less: Cost of goods sold	(500,000)	(490,000)
Gross margin	$ 450,000	$410,000
Less: Selling and administrative expenses	(275,000)	(260,000)
Operating income	$ 175,000	$150,000
Less: Interest expense	(12,000)	(18,000)
Income before taxes	$ 163,000	$132,000
Less: Taxes	(65,200)	(52,800)
Net income	$ 97,800	$ 79,200
Less: Dividends	(27,800)	(19,200)
Net income, retained	$ 70,000	$ 60,000

Required:

1. Compute the percentage change for each item in the balance sheet and income statement.
2. Comment on any significant trends.

Problem 16-5 *Vertical Analysis*

Refer to the financial statements for Kepler Company in **Problem 16-4**. (Round all percentages to three significant digits.)

Required:
1. Express each item in the asset section of the balance sheet as a percentage of total assets for each year.
2. Express each item in the liabilities and equity section as a percentage of total liabilities and equity for each year.
3. Express each item in the income statement as a percentage of sales for each year.

Problem 16-6 *Liquidity Ratios*

Refer to the financial statements for Kepler Company in **Problem 16-4**.

Required:
1. Compute the following ratios for each year:
   a. Current ratio.
   b. Quick ratio.
   c. Receivables turnover (in days).
   d. Inventory turnover (in days).
2. Has the liquidity of Kepler improved over the past year? Explain why industrial liquidity performance would be useful information in assessing Kepler's liquidity performance.

Problem 16-7 *Leverage Ratios*

Refer to the financial statements for Kepler Company in **Problem 16-4**.

Required:
1. Compute the following for each year:
   a. The times-interest-earned ratio.
   b. The debt ratio.
2. Does Kepler have too much debt? What other information would help in answering this question?

Problem 16-8 *Profitability Ratios*

Refer to the financial statements for Kepler Company in **Problem 16-4**. For the current year, the market price per share of common stock is $2.98. For last year, assets and equity were the same at the beginning and end of the year.

Required:
1. Compute the following for each year:
   a. Return on total assets.
   b. Return on stockholders' equity.
   c. Earnings per share.
   d. Price-earnings ratio.
   e. Dividend yield.
   f. Dividend payout.
2. Based on the analysis in Requirement 1, would you invest in the common stock of Kepler Company?

Problem 16-9 *Profitability Analysis*

Albion, Inc., provided the following information for its most recent year of operation. The tax rate is 40 percent.

Sales	$100,000
Cost of goods sold	$45,000
Net income	$10,500
Interest expense	$350
Assets—beginning balance	$120,000
Assets—ending balance	$126,000
Preferred dividends	$300
Common dividends (paid December 31)	$8,000
Common shares outstanding—January 1	30,000
Common shares outstanding—December 31	40,000
Average common stockholders' equity	$55,000
Market price per common share	$12

Required:
1. Compute the following:
   a. Return on sales.
   b. Return on assets.
   c. Return on common stockholders' equity.
   d. Earnings per share.
   e. Price-earnings ratio.
   f. Dividend yield.
   g. Dividend payout ratio.
2. If you were considering purchasing stock in Albion, Inc., which of the above ratios would be of most interest to you? Explain.

Problem 16-10 *Analysis of Accounts Receivable and Credit Policy*

Based on customer feedback, Ted Pendleton, manager of a company that produces photo supplies, decided to grant more liberal credit terms. Ted decided to allow customers to have 60 days before full payment of the account was required. From 2000 through 2002, the company's credit policy for sales on account was 2/10, n/30. In 2003, the policy of 2/10, n/60 became effective. By the end of 2005, Ted's company was beginning to experience cash flow problems. Although sales were strong, collections were sluggish, and the company was having a difficult time meeting its short-term obligations. Ted noted that the cash flow problems materialized after the credit policy was changed and wondered if there was a connection. To help assess the situation, he gathered the following data pertaining to the collection of accounts receivable (balances are end-of-year balances; the 2000 balance was the same as that in 1999):

	2000	2001	2002	2003	2004
Accounts receivable	$100,000	$120,000	$100,000	$150,000	$190,000
Net credit sales	500,000	600,000	510,000	510,000	520,000

Required:
1. Compute the number of times receivables turned over per year for each of the five years. Also express the turnover in days instead of times per year.
2. Based on your computation in Requirement 1, evaluate the effect of the new credit policy. Include in this assessment the impact on the company's cash inflows.
3. Assume that the industry has an average receivables turnover of six times per year. If this knowledge had been available in 2002, along with knowledge of the company's receivable turnover rate, do you think that Ted Pendleton would have liberalized his company's credit policy?

Problem 16-11 *Profitability Analysis for an Investment Decision*

 **OBJECTIVE 5**

Suppose that you are considering investing in one of two companies, each in the same industry. The most recent income statements for each company and other relevant information are as follows:

Income Statements (in thousands)	Company A	Company B
Sales	$50,000	$40,000
Less: Cost of goods sold	(30,000)	(26,000)
Gross margin	$20,000	$14,000
Less: Selling and administrative expenses	(15,000)	(7,000)
Operating income	$ 5,000	$ 7,000
Less: Interest expense	(1,000)	(3,000)
Income before taxes	$ 4,000	$ 4,000
Less: Taxes	(1,360)	(1,360)
Net income	$ 2,640	$ 2,640
Retained earnings	8,000	6,000
	$10,640	$ 8,640
Less: Dividends	(840)	(1,040)
Ending retained earnings	$ 9,800	$ 7,600
Average total assets	$20,000,000	$22,000,000
Average common equity	$10,000,000	$13,000,000
Average common shares	1,000,000	1,200,000
Average preferred shares*	300,000	100,000
Market price per common share	$5.00	$9.80

*For both Company A and Company B, the preferred dividend is $1 per share.

Required:
1. Compute the following for each company:
   a. Earnings per share.
   b. Dividend yield ratio.
   c. Dividend payout ratio.
   d. Price-earnings ratio.
   e. Return on total assets.
   f. Return on common equity.
2. In which of the two companies would you invest? Explain.

Problem 16-12 *Manipulation of Ratios and Ethical Behavior*

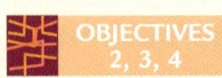 **OBJECTIVES 2, 3, 4**

Pete Donaldson, president and owner of Donaldson Mining Supplies, was concerned about the firm's liquidity. He had an easy time selling supplies to the local coal mines but had a difficult time collecting the receivables. He had even tried offering discounts for prompt payment. The outcome wasn't as expected. The coal mines still took as long to pay as before but took the discount as well. Although he had complained about the practice, he was told that other suppliers would provide the supplies for the same terms. Collections were so slow that he was unable to pay his own payables on time and was receiving considerable pressure from his own creditors.

The solution was a line of credit that could be used to smooth his payment patterns. Getting the line of credit was another matter, however. One bank had turned him down, indicating that he already had too much debt and that his short-term liquidity ratios were marginal. Pete had begun the business with $5,000 of his own capital and a $30,000 loan from his father-in-law. He was making interest payments of $3,000 per year to his father-in-law with a promise to pay the principal back in five years (three years from now).

While mulling over his problem, Pete suddenly saw the solution. By changing accountants, he could tell the next accountant that the $30,000 had been donated to the business and therefore would be reclassified into the equity section. This would dramatically improve the debt ratio. He would simply not disclose the $3,000 annual payment—or he could call it a dividend. Additionally, he would not tell the next accountant about the $6,000 of safety gear that was now obsolete. That gear could be added back, and the current ratio would also improve. With an improved financial statement, the next bank would be more likely to grant the needed line of credit.

Required:

1. Evaluate Pete Donaldson's ethical behavior.
2. Suppose that you have been hired as the chief finance officer for Donaldson Mining Supplies. You have been told that the $30,000 has been donated to the company. During the second week of your employment, the father-in-law drops in unexpectedly and introduces himself. He then asks you how the company is doing and wants to know if his $30,000 loan is still likely to be repaid in three years. Suppose also that same day you overhear an employee mention that the safety equipment is no longer usable because regulations now require a newer and different model.
   a. Assume that you have yet to prepare the financial statements for the loan application. What should you do?
   b. Suppose that the financial statements have been prepared and have been submitted to the bank. In fact, that morning, you received a call from the bank indicating that a decision was imminent and that the line of credit would likely be approved. What should you do under these circumstances?
3. Suppose that Pete invites you in as a consultant. He describes his problem to you. Can you think of a better solution?

GLOSSARY

A

Absorption costing A product-costing method that assigns all manufacturing costs to units of product: direct materials, direct labor, variable overhead, and fixed overhead.

Accounting rate of return The rate of return obtained by dividing the average accounting net income by the original investment (or by average investment).

Accounts receivable turnover ratio A ratio that measures the liquidity of receivables. It is computed by dividing net sales by average accounts receivable.

Accumulating costs The way that costs are measured and recorded.

Activity analysis The process of identifying, describing, and evaluating the activities an organization performs.

Activity attributes Nonfinancial and financial information items that describe individual activities.

Activity dictionary A list of activities described by specific attributes such as name, definition, classification as primary or secondary, and activity driver.

Activity drivers Factors that measure the consumption of activities by products and other cost objects.

Activity elimination The process of eliminating non-value-added activities.

Activity flexible budgeting Predicting what activity costs will be as activity usage changes.

Activity format A format for the statement of cash flows that reports cash flows for three categories: (1) cash flows from operating activities, (2) cash flows from investing activities, and (3) cash flows from financing activities.

Activity inputs The resources consumed by an activity in producing its output (they are the factors that enable the activity to be performed).

Activity output The result or product of an activity.

Activity output measure The number of times an activity is performed. It is the quantifiable measure of the output.

Activity reduction Decreasing the time and resources required by an activity.

Activity selection The process of choosing among sets of activities caused by competing strategies.

Activity sharing Increasing the efficiency of necessary activities by using economies of scale.

Activity-based budget A budget that requires three steps: (1) the activities within an organization must be identified, (2) the demand for each activity's output must be estimated, and (3) the cost of resources required to produce this activity output must be assessed.

Activity-based costing (ABC) system A cost assignment approach that first uses direct and driver tracing to assign costs to activities and then uses drivers to assign costs to cost objects.

Activity-based management A systemwide, integrated approach that focuses management's attention on activities with the objective of improving customer value and the profit achieved by providing this value. It includes driver analysis, activity analysis, and performance evaluation, and draws on activity-based costing as a major source of information.

Actual cost system An approach that assigns actual costs of direct materials, direct labor, and overhead to products.

Adjusted cost of goods sold The cost of goods sold after all adjustments for overhead variances are made.

Administrative costs All costs associated with research, development, and general administration of the organization that cannot reasonably be as-signed to either selling or production.

Allocation When an indirect cost is assigned to a cost object using a reasonable and convenient method.

Annuity A series of future cash flows.

Applied overhead Overhead assigned to production using predetermined rates.

Appraisal costs Cost incurred to determine whether products and services are conforming to requirements.

Assigning costs The way that a cost is linked to some cost object.

B

Balanced Scorecard A strategic management system that defines a strategic-based responsibility accounting system. The Balanced Scorecard translates an organization's mission and strategy into operational objectives and performance measures for four different perspectives: the financial perspective, the customer perspective, the internal business process perspective, and the learning and growth (infrastructure) perspective.

Break-even point The point where total sales revenue equals total cost; at this point, neither profit nor loss is earned.

Budget committee A committee responsible for setting budgetary policies and goals, reviewing and approving the budget, and resolving any differences that may arise in the budgetary process.

Budget director The individual responsible for coordination and directing the overall budgeting process.

Budgetary slack The process of padding the budget by overestimating costs and underestimating revenues.

Budgets Plans of action expressed in financial terms.

C

Capital budgeting The process of making capital investment decisions.

Capital investment decisions The process of planning, setting goals and priorities, arranging financing, and identifying criteria for making long-term investments.

Carrying costs The costs of holding inventory.

Cash budget A detailed plan that outlines all sources and uses of cash.

Cash equivalents Highly liquid investments such as Treasury bills, money market funds, and commercial paper.

Cash inflows Activities that increase cash and are sources of cash.

Cash outflows Activities that decrease cash and are uses of cash.

Causal factors Activities or variables that invoke service costs. Generally, it is desirable to use causal factors as the basis for allocating service costs.

Certified Internal Auditor (CIA) The CIA has passed a comprehensive examination designed to ensure technical competence and has two years' experience.

Certified Management Accountant (CMA) A certified management accountant has passed a rigorous qualifying examination, met an experience requirement, and participates in continuing education.

Certified Public Accountant (CPA) A certified accountant who is permitted (by law) to serve as an external auditor. CPAs must pass a national examination and be licensed by the state in which they practice.

Coefficient of determination (R^2) The percentage of total variability in a dependent variable that is explained by an independent variable. It assumes a value between 0 and 1.

Committed fixed cost A fixed cost that cannot be easily changed.

Common costs The costs of resources used in the output of two or more services or products.

Common fixed expenses Fixed expenses that cannot be directly traced to individual segments and that are unaffected by the elimination of any one segment.

Common-size analysis A type of analysis that expresses line items or accounts in the financial statements as percentages.

Compounding of interest Paying interest on interest.

Constraints Mathematical expressions that express resource limitations.

Consumption ratio The proportion of an overhead activity consumed by a product.

Continuous budget A moving 12-month budget with a future month added as the current month expires.

Continuous improvement Searching for ways to increase the overall efficiency and productivity of activities by reducing waste, increasing quality, and reducing costs.

Contribution margin Sales revenue minus total variable cost or price minus unit variable cost.

Contribution margin income statement The income statement format that is based on the separation of costs into fixed and variable components.

Contribution margin ratio Contribution margin divided by sales revenue. It is the proportion of each sales dollar available to cover fixed costs and provide for profit.

Control The process of setting standards, receiving feedback on actual performance, and taking corrective action whenever actual performance deviates significantly from planned performance.

Control activities Activities performed by an organization to prevent or detect poor quality (because poor quality may exist).

Control costs Costs incurred from performing control activities.

Control limits The maximum allowable deviation from a standard.

Controllable costs Costs that managers have the power to influence.

Controller The chief accounting officer in an organization.

Controlling The managerial activity of monitoring a plan's implementation and taking corrective action as needed.

Conversion cost The sum of direct labor cost and overhead cost.

Core objectives and measures Those objectives and measures common to most organizations.

Cost The amount of cash or cash equivalent sacrificed for goods and/or services that are expected to bring a current or future benefit to the organization.

Cost behavior The way in which a cost changes when the level of output changes.

Cost center A division of a company that is evaluated on the basis of cost.

Cost object Any item such as products, customers, departments, projects, and so on, for which costs are measured and assigned.

Cost of capital The cost of investment funds, usually viewed as a weighted average of the costs of funds from all sources.

Cost of goods manufactured The total product cost of goods completed during the current period.

Cost of goods sold The total product cost of goods sold during the period.

Cost of goods sold budget The estimated costs for the units sold.

Cost reconciliation The final section of the production report that compares the costs to account for with the costs accounted for to ensure that they are equal.

Costs of quality Costs incurred because poor quality may exist or because poor quality does exist.

Cost-volume-profit graph A graph that depicts the relationships among costs, volume, and profits. It consists of a total revenue line and a total cost line.

Current ratio A measure of the ability of a company to pay its short-term liabilities out of short-term assets.

Currently attainable standards Standards that reflect an efficient operating state; they are rigorous but achievable.

Customer perspective A Balanced Scorecard viewpoint that defines the customer and market segments in which the business will compete.

Customer value Realization less sacrifice, where realization is what the customer receives and sacrifice is what is given up.

Cycle time The length of time required to produce one unit of a product.

D

Debt ratio The ratio that measures the percentage of a company's risk as the percentage of its assets financed by creditors increases. It is computed by dividing a company's total liabilities by its total assets.

Decentralization The granting of decision-making freedom to lower operating levels.

Decision making The process of choosing among competing alternatives.

Decision model A specific set of procedures that, when followed, produces a decision.

Defective product A product or service that does not conform to specifications.

Degree of operating leverage (DOL) A measure of the sensitivity of profit changes to changes in sales volume. It measures the percentage change in profits resulting from a percentage change in sales.

Departmental overhead rate Estimated overhead for a single department divided by the estimated activity level for that same department.

Dependent variable A variable whose value depends on the value of another variable.

Differential cost The difference in total cost between the alternatives in a decision.

Direct costs Costs that can be easily and accurately traced to a cost object.

Direct fixed expenses Fixed costs that are directly traceable to a given segment and, consequently, disappear if the segment is eliminated.

Direct labor The labor that can be directly traced to the goods or services being produced.

Direct labor budget A budget showing the total direct labor hours needed and the associated cost for the number of units in the production budget.

Direct materials Materials that are a part of the final product and can be directly traced to the goods or services being produced.

Direct materials purchases budget A budget that outlines the expected usage of materials production and purchases of the direct materials required.

Direct method A method that allocates service costs directly to producing departments. This method ignores any interactions that may exist among support departments.

Discount factor The factor used to convert a future cash flow to its present value.

Discount rate The rate of return used to compute the present value of future cash flows.

Discounted cash flows Future cash flows expressed in present-value terms.

Discounting The act of finding the present value of future cash flows.

Discounting models Capital investment models that explicitly consider the time value of money in identifying criteria for accepting and rejecting proposed projects.

Discretionary fixed costs Fixed costs that can be changed relatively easily at management discretion.

Dividend payout ratio A ratio that is computed by dividing the total common dividends by the earnings available to common stockholders.

Dividend yield A profitability measure that is computed by dividing the dividends received per unit of common share by the market price per common share.

Double-loop feedback Information about both the effectiveness of strategy implementation and the validity of assumptions underlying the strategy.

Driver A factor that causes or leads to a change in a cost or activity; a driver is an output measure.

Driver analysis The effort expended to identify those factors that are the root causes of activity costs.

Dysfunctional behavior Individual behavior that conflicts with the goals of the organization.

E

Earnings per share Earnings per share is computed by dividing net income less preferred dividends by the average number of shares of common stock outstanding during the period.

Ecoefficiency A view of environmental management maintaining that organizations can produce more useful goods and services while simultaneously reducing negative environmental impacts, resource consumption, and costs.

Economic order quantity (EOQ) The amount that should be ordered (or produced) to minimize the total ordering (or setup) and carrying costs.

Economic value added (EVA) A performance measure that is calculated by taking the after-tax operating profit minus the total annual cost of capital.

Ending finished goods inventory budget A budget that describes planned ending inventory of finished goods in units and dollars.

Environmental costs Costs that are incurred because poor environmental quality exists or may exist.

Environmental detection costs Costs incurred to detect poor environmental performance.

Environmental external failure costs Costs incurred after contaminants are introduced into the environment.

Environmental internal failure costs Costs incurred after contaminants are produced but before they are introduced into the environment.

Environmental prevention costs Costs incurred to prevent damage to the environment.

Equivalent units of output Complete units that could have been produced given the total amount of manufacturing effort expended during the period.

Ethical behavior Choosing actions that are right, proper, and just.

Expenses Costs that are used up (expired) in the production of revenue.

External failure costs Costs incurred because products fail to conform to requirements after being sold to outside parties.

F

Failure activities Activities performed by an organization or its customers in response to poor quality (poor quality does exist).

Failure costs The costs incurred by an organization because failure activities are performed.

Favorable (F) variances Variances produced whenever the actual amounts are less than the budgeted or standard allowances.

FIFO costing method A process-costing method that separates units in beginning inventory from those produced during the current period. Unit costs include only current-period costs and production.

Financial accounting A type of accounting that is primarily concerned with producing information for external users.

Financial budgets The portions of the master budget that include the cash budget, the budgeted balance sheet, the budgeted statement of cash flows, and the capital budget.

Financial perspective A Balanced Scorecard viewpoint that describes the financial consequences of actions taken in the other three perspectives.

Financing activities Those activities that raise (provide) cash from (to) creditors and owners.

Fixed costs Costs that, in total, are constant within the relevant range as the level of output increases or decreases.

Fixed overhead spending variance The difference between actual fixed overhead and applied fixed overhead.

Fixed overhead volume variance The difference between budgeted fixed overhead and applied fixed overhead; it is a measure of capacity utilization.

Flexible budget A budget that can specify costs for a range of activity.

Flexible budget variance The sum of price variances and efficiency variances in a performance report comparing actual costs to expected costs predicted by a flexible budget.

Future value The value that will accumulate by the end of an investment's life if the investment earns a specified compounded return.

G

Goal congruence The alignment of a manager's personal goals with those of the organization.

Gross margin The difference between sales revenue and cost of goods sold.

H

High-low method A method for separating mixed costs into fixed and variable components by using just the high and low data points. [Note: The high (low) data point corresponds to the high (low) output level.]

Horizontal analysis Also called trend analysis, this type of analysis expresses a line item as a percentage of some prior-period amount.

I

Ideal standards Standards that reflect perfect operating conditions.

Incentives The positive or negative measures taken by an organization to induce a manager to exert effort toward achieving the organization's goals.

Independent projects Projects that, if accepted or rejected, will not affect the cash flows of another project.

Independent variable A variable whose value does not depend on the value of another variable.

Indirect costs Costs that cannot be easily and accurately traced to a cost object.

Indirect method A method that computes operating cash flows by adjusting net income for items that do not affect cash flows.

Innovation process A process that anticipates the emerging and potential needs of customers and creates new products and services to satisfy those needs.

Intercept The fixed cost, representing the point where the cost formula intercepts the vertical axis.

Internal business process perspective A Balanced Scorecard viewpoint that describes the internal processes needed to provide value for customers and owners.

Internal failure costs Costs incurred because products and services fail to conform to requirements where lack of conformity is discovered prior to external sale.

Internal rate of return The rate of return that equates the present value of a project's cash inflows with the present value of its cash outflows (i.e., it sets the NPV equal to zero). Also, the rate of return being earned on funds that remain internally invested in a project.

Inventory turnover ratio A ratio that is computed by dividing the cost of goods sold by the average inventory.

Investing activities Those activities that involve the acquisition or sale of long-term assets.

Investment center A division of a company that is evaluated on the basis of return on investment.

J

Job One distinct unit or set of units for which the costs of production must be assigned.

Job-order cost sheet A subsidiary account to the work-in-process account on which the total costs of materials, labor, and overhead for a single job are accumulated.

Job-order costing system A costing system in which costs are collected and assigned to units of production for each individual job.

Joint products Products that are inseparable prior to a split-off point. All manufacturing costs up to the split-off point are joint costs.

Just-in-time (JIT) A demand-pull system whose objective is to eliminate waste by producing a product only when it is needed and only in the quantities demanded by customers.

K

Kaizen standard An interim standard that reflects the planned improvement for a coming period.

Keep-or-drop decisions Relevant costing analyses that focus on keeping or dropping a segment of a business.

L

Labor efficiency variance (LEV) The difference between the actual direct labor hours used and the standard direct labor hours allowed multiplied by the standard hourly wage rate.

Labor rate variance (LRV) The difference between the actual hourly rate paid and the standard hourly rate multiplied by the actual hours worked.

Learning and growth (infrastructure) perspective A Balanced Scorecard viewpoint that defines the capabilities that an organization needs to create long-term growth and improvement.

Leverage ratios Ratios that measure the ability of a company to meet its long- and short-term obligations. These ratios provide a measure of the degree of protection provided to a company's creditors.

Line positions Positions that have direct responsibility for the basic objectives of an organization.

Liquidity ratios Ratios that measure the ability of a company to meet its current obligations.

M

Make-or-buy decisions Relevant costing analyses that focus on whether a component should be made internally or purchased externally.

Management accounting The provision of accounting information for a company's internal users.

Manufacturing Cycle Efficiency (MCE) Measured as value-added time divided by total time. The result tells the company what percentage of total time spent is devoted to actual production.

Manufacturing organization An organization that produces tangible products.

Margin The ratio of net operating income to sales.

Margin of safety The units sold, or expected to be sold, or sales revenue earned, or expected to be earned, above the break-even volume.

Markup The percentage applied to a base cost; it includes desired profit and any costs not included in the base cost.

Master budget The collection of all area and activity budgets representing a firm's comprehensive plan of action.

Materials price variance (MPV) The difference between the actual price paid per unit of materials and the standard price allowed per unit multiplied by the actual quantity of materials purchased.

Materials requisition form A source document that records the type, quantity, and unit price of the direct materials issued to each job.

Materials usage variance (MUV) The difference between the direct materials actually used and the direct materials allowed for the actual output multiplied by the standard price.

Method of least squares (regression) A statistical method to find the best-fitting line through a set of data points. It is used to break out the fixed and variable components of a mixed cost.

Mixed costs Costs that have both a fixed and a variable component.

Monetary incentives The use of economic rewards to motivate managers.

Mutually exclusive projects Projects that, if accepted, preclude the acceptance of competing projects.

Myopic behavior Managerial actions that improve budgetary performance in the short run at the expense of the long-run welfare of the organization.

N

Net present value The difference between the present value of a project's cash inflows and the present value of its cash outflows.

Noncash investing and financing activities Investing and financing activities that take place without affecting cash.

Nondiscounting models Capital investment models that identify criteria for accepting or rejecting projects without considering the time value of money.

Nonmonetary incentives The use of psychological and social rewards to motivate managers.

Non-unit-level activity drivers Factors that measure the consumption of non-unit-level activities by products and other cost objects.

Non-value-added activities All activities other than those that are absolutely essential to remain in business.

Non-value-added costs Costs that are caused either by non-value-added activities or by the inefficient performance of value-added activities.

Normal cost of goods sold The cost of goods sold before adjustment for any overhead variance.

Normal cost system An approach that assigns the actual costs of direct materials and direct labor to products but uses a predetermined rate to assign overhead costs.

O

Operating activities The ongoing, day-to-day, revenue-generating activities of an organization.

Operating assets Assets used to generate operating income, consisting usually of cash, inventories, receivables, and property, plant, and equipment. Average operating assets are found by adding together beginning operating assets and ending operating assets, and dividing the result by 2.

Operating budgets Budgets associated with the income-producing activities of an organization.

Operating income Revenues minus operating expenses from the firm's normal operations. Operating income is before-tax income.

Operating leverage The use of fixed costs to extract higher percentage changes in profits as sales activity changes. Leverage is achieved by increasing fixed costs while lowering variable costs.

Operations process A process that produces and delivers existing products and services to customers.

Opportunity cost The benefit given up or sacrificed when one alternative is chosen over another.

Ordering costs The costs of placing and receiving an order.

Overapplied overhead The amount by which applied overhead exceeds actual overhead.

Overhead A category in which all product costs, other than direct materials and direct labor, are placed.

Overhead budget A budget that reveals the planned expenditures for all indirect manufacturing items.

Overhead variance The difference between actual overhead and applied overhead.

P

Parallel processing A processing pattern in which two or more sequential processes are required to produce a finished good.

Participative budgeting An approach to budgeting that allows managers who will be held accountable for budgetary performance to participate in the budget's development.

Payback period The time required for a project to return its investment.

Performance report A report that compares the actual data with planned data.

Period costs Costs that are expensed in the period in which they are incurred; they are not inventoried.

Physical flow schedule A schedule that reconciles units to account for with units accounted for. The physical units are not adjusted for percent of completion.

Planning A management activity that involves the detailed formulation of action to achieve a particular end.

Plantwide overhead rate A single overhead rate calculated using all estimated overhead for a factory divided by the estimated activity level across the entire factory.

Postaudit A follow-up analysis of an investment decision, comparing actual benefits and costs with expected benefits and costs.

Postpurchase costs The costs of using, maintaining, and disposing of the product.

Postsales service process A process that provides critical and responsive service to customers after the product or service has been delivered.

Predetermined overhead rate An overhead rate computed using estimated data.

Present value The current value of a future cash flow. It represents the amount that must be invested now if the future cash flow is to be received assuming compounding at a given rate of interest.

Prevention costs Cost incurred to prevent defects in products or services being produced.

Price The revenue per unit.

Price (rate) variance The difference between standard price and actual price multiplied by the actual quantity of inputs used.

Price standards The price that should be paid per unit of input.

Price-earnings ratio The price-earnings ratio is found by dividing the market price per share by the earnings per share.

Prime cost The sum of direct materials cost and direct labor cost.

Private costs Environmental costs that an organization has to pay.

Process value chain The innovation, operations, and postsales service processes.

Process-costing system A costing system that accumulates production costs by process or by department for a given period of time.

Process-value analysis An approach that focuses on processes and activities and emphasizes systemwide performance instead of individual performance.

Producing departments Units within an organization responsible for producing the products or services that are sold to customers.

Product diversity The situation present when products consume overhead in different proportions.

Product (manufacturing) costs Costs associated with the manufacture of goods or the provision of services. Product costs include: direct materials, direct labor, and overhead.

Production budget A budget that shows how many units must be produced to meet sales needs and satisfy ending inventory requirements.

Production report A document that summarizes the manufacturing activity that takes place in a process department for a given period of time.

Profit center A division of a company that is evaluated on the basis of operating income or profit.

Profitability ratios Ratios that measure the earning ability of a company. These ratios allow investors, creditors, and managers to evaluate the extent to which invested funds are being used efficiently.

Profit-volume graph A graphical portrayal of the relationship between profits and sales activity in units.

Pseudoparticipation A budgetary system in which top management solicits inputs from lower-level managers and then ignores those inputs. Thus, in reality, budgets are dictated from above.

Q

Quality product (service) A product that meets or exceeds customer expectations.

Quantity standards The quantity of input allowed per unit of output.

Quick or acid-test ratio A measure of liquidity that compares only the most liquid assets to current liabilities.

R

Realized external failure costs Environmental costs caused by environmental degradation and paid for by the responsible organization.

Reciprocal method A method that simultaneously allocates service costs to all user departments. It gives full consideration to interactions among support departments.

Relevant costs Future costs that change across alternatives.

Relevant range The range of output over which an assumed cost relationship is valid for the normal operations of a firm.

Required rate of return The minimum rate of return that a project must earn in order to be acceptable. Usually corresponds to the cost of capital.

Residual income The difference between operating income and the minimum dollar return required on a company's operating assets.

Resource drivers Factors that measure the consumption of resources by activities.

Responsibility center A segment of the business whose manager is accountable for specified sets of activities.

Return on investment (ROI) The ratio of operating income to average operating assets.

Return on sales A measure of the efficiency of a firm that is computed by dividing net income by sales.

Return on stockholders' equity A measure that can be used to compare against other return measures (e.g., preferred dividend rates and bond rates). It is computed by dividing net income less preferred dividends by the average common stockholders' equity.

Return on total assets The result of dividing net income plus the after-tax cost of interest by the average total assets.

Revenue center A segment of the business that is evaluated on the basis of sales.

S

Sales budget A budget that describes expected sales in units and dollars for the coming period.

Sales mix The relative combination of products (or services) being sold by an organization.

Scattergraph method A method to fit a line to a set of data using two points that are selected by judgment. It is used to break out the fixed and variable components of a mixed cost.

Segment A subunit of a company of sufficient importance to warrant the production of performance reports.

Segment margin The contribution a segment makes to cover common fixed costs and provide for profit after direct fixed costs and variable costs are deducted from the segment's sales revenue.

Selling and administrative expenses budget A budget that outlines planned expenditures for nonmanufacturing activities.

Selling (marketing) costs Those costs necessary to market, distribute, and service a product or service.

Sell-or-process-further decision Relevant costing analysis that focuses on whether a product should be processed beyond the split-off point.

Sensitivity analysis The "what-if" process of altering certain key variables to assess the effect on the original outcome.

Sequential (or step) method A method that allocates service costs to user departments in a sequential manner. It gives partial consideration to interactions among support departments.

Sequential processing A processing pattern in which units pass from one process to another in a set order.

Service organization An organization that produces intangible products.

Services Tasks or activities performed for a customer or an activity performed by a customer using an organization's products or facilities.

Single-loop feedback Information about the effectiveness of strategy implementation.

Slope The variable cost per unit of activity usage.

Societal costs (See **Unrealized external failure costs**.)

Special-order decisions Relevant costing analyses that focus on whether a specially priced order should be accepted or rejected.

Split-off point The point at which products become distinguishable after passing through a common process.

Staff positions Positions that are supportive in nature and have only indirect responsibility for an organization's basic objectives.

Standard cost per unit The per-unit cost that should be achieved given materials, labor, and overhead standards.

Standard cost sheet A listing of the standard costs and standard quantities of direct materials, direct labor, and overhead that should apply to a single product.

Standard hours allowed The direct labor hours that should have been used to produce the actual output (Unit labor standard × Actual output).

Standard quantity of materials allowed The quantity of materials that should have been used to produce the actual output (Unit materials standard × Actual output).

Statement of cash flows A statement that provides information regarding the sources and uses of a firm's cash.

Static budget A budget for a particular level of activity.

Step cost A cost that displays a constant level of cost for a range of output and then jumps to a higher level of cost at some point, where it remains for a similar range of output.

Stockout costs The costs of insufficient inventory.

Strategic plan The long-term plan for future activities and operations, usually involving at least five years.

Strategy The process of choosing a business's market and customer segments, identifying its critical internal business processes, and selecting the individual and organizational capabilities needed to meet internal, customer, and financial objectives.

Sunk costs Costs for which the outlay has already been made and that cannot be affected by a future decision.

Supplies Those materials necessary for production that do not become part of the finished product or are not used in providing a service.

Support departments Units within an organization that provide essential support services for producing departments.

Sustainable development Development that meets the needs of the present without compromising the ability of future generations to meet their own needs.

T

Tangible products Goods produced by converting raw materials through the use of labor and capital inputs, such as plant, land, and machinery.

Target cost The difference between the sales price needed to achieve a projected market share and the desired per-unit profit.

Target costing A method of determining the cost of a product or service based on the price (target price) that customers are willing to pay.

Testable strategy A set of linked objectives aimed at an overall goal that can be restated into a sequence of cause-and-effect hypotheses.

Time ticket A source document by which direct labor costs are assigned to individual jobs.

Times-interest-earned ratio A leverage ratio that uses the income statement to assess a company's ability to service its debt. It is computed by dividing net income before taxes and interest by interest expense.

Total budget variance The difference between the actual cost of an input and its planned cost.

Total quality management A management philosophy in which manufacturers strive to create an environment that will enable workers to manufacture perfect (zero-defect) products.

Transfer price The price charged for goods transferred from one division to another.

Transferred-in costs Costs transferred from a prior process to a subsequent process.

Treasurer The individual responsible for the finance function; raises capital and manages cash and investments.

Turnover The ratio of sales to average operating assets.

U

Underapplied overhead The amount by which actual overhead exceeds applied overhead.

Unfavorable (U) variances Variances produced whenever the actual input amounts are greater than the budgeted or standard allowances.

Unit-level activities Activities that are performed each time a unit is produced.

Unit-level activity drivers Factors that measure the consumption of unit-level activities by products and other cost objects.

Unrealized external failure costs Environmental costs caused by an organization but paid for by society.

Usage (efficiency) variance The difference between standard quantities and actual quantities multiplied by standard price.

V

Value chain The set of activities required to design, develop, produce, market, and deliver products and services to customers.

Value-added activities Activities that are necessary for a business to achieve corporate objectives and remain in business.

Value-added costs Costs caused by value-added activities.

Variable budgets (See **Flexible budget**.)

Variable cost A cost that increases as output increases and decreases as output decreases.

Variable cost ratio Variable costs divided by sales revenues. It is the proportion of each sales dollar needed to cover variable costs.

Variable costing A product-costing method that assigns only variable manufacturing costs to production: direct materials, direct labor, and variable overhead. Fixed overhead is treated as a period cost.

Variable costs Costs that, in total, vary in direct proportion to changes in output within the relevant range.

Variable overhead efficiency variance The difference between the actual direct labor hours used and the standard hours allowed multiplied by the standard variable overhead rate.

Variable overhead spending variance The difference between the actual variable overhead and the budgeted variable overhead based on actual hours used to produce the actual output.

Velocity The number of units that can be produced in a given period of time (e.g., output per hour).

Vertical analysis A type of analysis that expresses the line item as a percentage of some other line item for the same period.

W

Weighted average costing method A process-costing method that combines beginning inventory costs with current-period costs to compute unit costs. Costs and output from the current period and the previous period are averaged to compute unit costs.

Work in process (WIP) The cost of the partially completed goods that are still being worked on at the end of a time period.

Z

Zero defects A quality performance standard that requires all products and services to be produced and delivered according to specifications.

CHECK FIGURES

Check Figures are given for selected problems

CHAPTER 2

2-1	1. Total direct materials = $7,810
	2. Income = $6,120
2-2	2. Overhead cost per unit = $250
	4. Gross margin = $3,000,000
2-3	1. Total owed by Natalie = $30
	2. Total cost for Mary = $17.50
2-4	2. Cost of goods manufactured = $224,950
	3. Cost of goods sold = $226,050
2-5	1. Total product cost = $9,200,000
	2. Operating income = $2,000,000
	3. Gross margin = $2,860,000
2-6	1. Cost of goods manufactured = $24,725
	2. Cost of goods sold = $27,160
2-7	3. Conversion cost = $173,000
	5. Operating income = $90,950
2-9	1. Cost of services sold = $920,000
2-10	3. Operating income = $412,100
2-13	2. Magazine total prime costs = $4,500
	4. Income before taxes = $2,010
2-14	1. Total direct kitchen costs = $102,350
2-15	2. Tent sale loss = $1,300

CHAPTER 3

3-4	2. Fixed receiving cost = $6,600
	3. Receiving cost for the year = $295,200
3-5	2. Receiving cost = $25,558
3-6	1. 10 months' data intercept = 3,212.121
3-7	2. Variable power cost = $1.125
3-8	2. Supplies variable rate = $6.50
	4. Charge per hour = $75.69
3-9	2. Fixed rate = $1,349
3-10	2. Plan 2 unused minutes = 75
	3. Plan 2 minutes used = 90
3-12	3. Variable rate = $4.50

CHAPTER 4

4-1	1. Break-even units = 8,000
	2. Units for target profit = 11,750
	4. Margin of safety in units = 2,000
4-2	2. Break-even units = 16,500
4-3	1. Break-even sales = $3,333,333
	2. $94,500
	5. Percent increase in operating income = 41.8%
4-4	2. Breakeven circles = 31,310
	3. Increase in total contribution margin = $300,000
4-5	1. Margin of safety in units = 230,000
	2. Operating income = $20,700
	3. Units for target profit = 1,000,000
4-6	2. $277,778
	4. Break-even point = $294,118
4-7	1. Grade I units = 224
	2. Grade II units = 392
	3. Increase in income = $29,602
	4. Revised breakeven Grade II = 374
4-8	1. Revenue = $450,000
	2. Desk lamps = 8,998
	3. Operating leverage = 4.0
4-9	2. Operating income = $34,000
	3. Trim kits = 32,444
4-10	1. Breakeven units = 21,429
	3. Operating income = $119,900
4-11	1. Contribution margin ratio = 0.62
	3. Margin of safety = $430,000
	4. Contribution margin from increased sales = $4,650
4-12	1. Price = $380

CHAPTER 5

5-1	2. Total cost Job 62 = $126,690
	4. Cost of goods sold = $253,265
5-2	1. Total = $6,752
5-3	2. Total cost of Job 37 = $3,680
	4. Gross margin = $2,955
5-4	2. May overhead assigned = $200
	3. Price = $593.75
5-5	1. Overhead rate = $2
	2. Department B overhead rate = $1.375
5-6	2. Department 3 overhead rate = $12.50
	2. Total manufacturing cost Job 2 = $13,003
5-7	2. Ending work in process = $16,726
5-8	2. Total Job 444 = $2,750
5-9	1. Overhead rate = 175%
	3. Cost of goods manufactured = $245,000

5-10   2. Applied overhead = $4,320
            5. Adjusted cost of goods sold =
               $700,200
5-11   2. Total Job 703 = $41,220
            4. Ending balance Work in Process =
               $40,900
5-13   1. Total Ed's Job = $234

CHAPTER 6

6-1   1. Equivalent units = 6,700
            2. Units transferred out = 6,600
            3. Units transferred out = 1,000
6-2   1. Total units to account for = 120,000
            2. Equivalent units, conversion = 104,000
            3. Unit cost = $320
            4. Cost of EWIP = $4,960,000
6-3   1. Unit cost = $320
6-4   1. Total units to account for = 80,000
            2. Equivalent units = 72,000
            3. Unit conversion cost = $1.16
6-5   1. Cost per equivalent unit = $1.16
6-6   1. Units to account for = 20,000
            2. Equivalent units = 18,500
            3. Unit cost = $0.50
            4. Cost of EWIP = $250
            5. Spoilage cost = $500
6-7   1. Unit cost = $6.20
6-8   1. Cost per equivalent unit = $5.3424
6-9   1. Total equivalent units = 521,000
            2. Unit cost = $21.19
            3. Cost of goods transferred out =
               $10,595,000
            5. Unit paraffin cost = $6.10
6-10   1. Unit cost = $5.74
6-11   1. Cost of units transferred out =
               $160,940
6-12   1. Cost of goods transferred out =
               $17,349
            2. Cost of goods transferred out =
               $23,192
6-13   1. Cost of units started and completed =
               $15,573
            2. Cost of units started and completed =
               $22,950

CHAPTER 7

7-1   1. Unit cost = $0.60
            2. Duffel bags = $2.40 per unit
            3. Backpacks = $1.20 per unit
7-2   1. Model B cost per unit = $1.50

2. Model B cost per unit = $1.66
3. Model B cost per unit = $1.86
7-3   1. Total cost = $120,000
            2. Basic unit cost = $87.50
7-4   1. Cost per patient day = $200
            2. Cost per patient day (complications) =
               $500
7-5   1. Average monthly fee = $6.78
            2. Cost per account (low) = $87.37
            3. Profit (high balance) = $112.50
7-6   2. Category 1 unit cost = $0.075
            3. Reduction = $2,450,000
7-7   1. Watson unit cost = $998.30
7-8   2. Potential reduction per unit = $7.10
            4. Total unit reduction potential = $8.35
            5. $12 price
7-9   1. Total non-value cost = $1,204,800
            2. Materials variance = $164,000 U
7-10   1. Cycle time = 8 minutes
            2. Cycle time = 9.6 minutes
            3. Reduction = $16.67 per binocular
7-11   2. Total net gain = $920,000
7-12   1. Total external failure costs =
               $1,370,000
            2. Appraisal = 14.6%
            4. Bonus pool = $638,000
7-14   1. Unit cost (XA2) = $2.11
            2. Unit cost reduction (XA2) = $0.32

CHAPTER 8

8-1   1. Total cash, September = $253,362
8-2   1. i. Budgeted income = $3,823,760
               j. Ending cash balance (March) =
                  $1,642,076
8-3   1. Total assets = $562,750
            2. Ending cash (Sept.) = $12,005
            3. Total assets = $565,605
8-5   1. Ending cash balance = $113,412
8-6   10. Income before taxes = $16,129,000
8-8   1. Cash deficiency = ($2,904)
            2. Excess cash = $217

CHAPTER 9

9-2   1. MUV = $6,000 F
            2. LRV = $4,000 U
            3. LEV = $4,000 F
9-3   2. LEV, Cutting = $300 U
9-4   1. Standard cost per unit = $126.88
            2. LRV = $2,457.60 F
            3. Average time = 0.768 per unit

9-5 1. Standard cost (normal) = $252 per patient day
2. MUV Cesarean = $20,000 U
3. LEV (normal) = $3,200 U
4. LEV = $24,000 U

9-6 1. UCL (labor) = $645,000
2. Total liquid variance = $48,000 U
3. LEV = $21,875 F

9-7 1. June UCL (labor) = $26,400 (quantity standard)
2. May LRV = $6,996 F (2.3%)

9-8 1. MPV = $975 U
2. LEV = $1,000 U
3. LRV = $0

9-10 3. Cost per bag = $0.8002
4. SQ = 9,350,000

9-12 1. MUV = $100,000 U
2. LEV = $24,000 U
3. Net effect = $46,000 U

9-13 2. SQ (materials) = 552,000 pounds
3. Materials variance = $224,000 U

9-14 1. Target cost to expand = $680
2. Unit non-value-added cost = $230

CHAPTER 10

10-1 1. Total direct labor hours = 18,000
2. Total overhead = $43,950

10-2 1. Variable = $685; Fixed = $13,000,000
2. Optimistic income = $5,750,000

10-3 1. Total = $45,613
2. Supplies, variable = $1.40

10-4 1. Total overhead = $2,425
2. Revised overhead = $2,495

10-6 1. Total variance = $100,000 U
2. Total variance = $6,000 F

10-7 1. Total variance = $2,500 F
2. Unit cost = $15.29
3. Total (20,000 moves) = $165,000

10-8 2. Total variance = $184,360 U

10-9 1. SFOR = $3.00; SVOR = $2.00
2. Total Fixed OH variance = $108,000 U
3. Volume variance = $18,000 U
4. VOH efficiency variance = $35,700 U

10-10 1. VOH efficiency = $20,000 U
2. FOH spending = $20,000 F

10-11 2. Little Rock plant, volume variance = $480,000 U
3. Savings = $100,000

10-12 3. VOH spending variance = $7,996 U
4. 0.26667 hours per unit

10-13 1. Total variance = $40,000 U
2. Volume variance = $15,000 U; Efficiency variance = $15,000 U

CHAPTER 11

11-1 2. Gross margin = $686,400
4. Operating income = $575,200
5. Absorption-costing income = $534,100

11-2 2. Ending inventory = $3,750
3. Segment margin beauty shops = $51,000

11-3 1. (b) 0.15
2. (c) $1,470,000

11-4 1. ROI year 3 = 6.30%
3. Turnover = 0.75
4. Turnover = 0.83

11-5 Turbocharger ROI = 15.2%
3. (c) $280,480
4. (d) $1,445,000

11-6 2. ROI = 10.34% (rounded)
4. Margin = 9.13%
5. EVA with investment = $122,500

11-7 2. Minimum price = $53

11-8 1. Model SC67 contribution margin = $760,000
5. Contribution margin = $320,000

11-9 2. Markup percentage = 42.5%

11-10 1. Theoretical conversion cost per unit = $135

11-12 1. Initial ROI = 11.99% (rounded)

11-13 2. MCE = 60%
3. Actual velocity = 1.2

CHAPTER 12

12-1 1. Total net benefit = $100,000

12-2 1. Cost to make = $367,000
4. Cost to make = $514,000

12-3 2. Additional income per pound = $21.025

12-4 1. Operating income = $6,100
2. Operating income = $16,558
3. Total segment margin = $29,620

12-5 1. Increase Pat's income = $18,400
2. Increase Steve's income = $15,200

12-6 2. Markup = $2,646

12-7 1. Standard contribution margin per machine hour = $20

12-8 1. Loss per box = $0.05

12-9 1. Operating profit = $40,000

12-10 3. $7,500
5. Carrying cost at EOQ = $3,000
7. Cost of ordering 1,000 units = $7,200

12-11 1. Total cost = $1,750
3. Reorder point = 200
4. Total cost = $1,458

12-12 1. $300,000

12-13 1. Differential amount to process further = $4,900

12-14 1. Monthly cost for Community Bank = $5,773

CHAPTER 13

13-1 2. NPV = $44,172
13-2 2. NPV = $184,520
13-3 1. IRR = 0.16
2. Cash flow = $15,730
3. Minimum CF = $18,118
13-4 1. NPV = $22,525,500
2. NPV = ($5,291,100)
3. Seating rate = 84%
4. Seat rate = 77%
13-5 1. Payback = 3.13 years
2. ARR = 10.68%
3. IRR = 14% (approximately)
4. NPV = $(21,009)
13-6 1. NPV = $644,470
13-8 1. Payback = 3.89 years
2. NPV = $(89,000)
3. NPV = $421,529
13-9 1. Cost of capital = 0.10
2. NPV = $24,300
13-10 1. NPV (20% rate) = $(25,390,000)
2. NPV (14%) = $4,375,200
3. NPV (14%) = $1,375,200
13-11 1. NPV = $117,400
2. NPV = $(29,480)
3. NPV = $231,160
13-12 1. NPV (standard) = $190,500
2. NPV (CAM) = $762,100
13-13 1. NPV (CAM) = $199,800
2. NPV (Standard) = $95,450

CHAPTER 14

14-1 1. Single-rate assignment (OEM) = $137,500
2. Dual-rate assignment (OEM) = $155,000
14-2 1. Salt Lake flight = $183,000
2. Salt Lake flight = $173,100
14-3 1. Direct (lab) = $664,500
2. Sequential (lab) = $663,825
14-4 1. Drilling rate = $15.30 per machine hour (direct); $16.23 (sequential)
14-5 2. Cooking: fixed overhead rate = $19.60; variable overhead rate = $7.72
14-6 1. Cost = $0.10 per kilowatt hour
2. Cost = $0.125 per kilowatt hour

4. Total savings = $70,000
14-7 1. PD1 allocation = $261,750
2. PD2 allocation = $352,476
14-8 1. Baton Rouge = $24,653
2. Baton Rouge = $37,050 (total)
14-9 1. Dept. A total = $500,000
2. Job SS bid = $14.63
14-11 1. Income = $139,853
2. Total profit = $69,917
3. Loss = $(131,574)
4. Revised price (500D) = $457.72 per hour

CHAPTER 15

15-1 Cash from operations = $3,600
15-3 Cash from operations = $2,000
15-5 1. Cash from operations = $506,250
2. Cash from investing = $(293,750)
15-7 1. Operating cash = $76,400
2. Cash from investing = $6,000; from financing = $(8,000)
15-8 1. Net operating cash = $76,400; from investing = $6,000
15-9 1. Net operating cash = $10,000; investing = $(60,000)
15-11 1. Net operating cash = $95,800
15-12 1. Net operating cash = $30,000,000; investing = $(10,000,000)
15-13 1. Net operating cash = $80,000; investing = $(55,000)

CHAPTER 16

16-1 1. Current ratio = 2.5
3. Average receivables = $350,000
5. Average inventory = $225,000
16-2 2. Total assets = $7,250,000
16-3 1. 0.088
3. $5.75
5. 0.0375
16-4 1. Percent change total assets = 32.5%
16-5 1. This year percent total current assets = 88.6%
2. Last year percent total liabilities = 60.2%
3. This year percent net income = 10.3%
16-6 1. (b) last year = 0.714
1. (d) last year turnover in days = 297.96
16-7 1. (b) last year debt ratio = 0.6024
16-8 1. (a) Last year return on total assets = 0.0853
(f) Last year dividend payout = 0.32

16-9 1. (b) return on assets = 8.7%

16-10 1. 2001 accounts receivables turnover = 5.45
2004 accounts receivables turnover = 3.06

16-11 1. (a) Company A EPS = 2.34
(b) Company B dividends per common share = $0.7833
(e) Company A return on total assets = 0.165

INDEX